The Military Balance (Print ISSN 0459-7222, Online ISSN 1479-9022) is published annually for a total of one issue per year by Taylor & Francis Group, 4 Park Square, Milton Park, Abingdon, Oxon, OX14 4RN, UK.

Send address changes to Taylor & Francis Customer Services, Informa UK Ltd., Sheepen Place, Colchester, Essex CO3 3LP, UK.

Subscription records are maintained at Taylor & Francis Group, 4 Park Square, Milton Park, Abingdon, OX14 4RN, UK.

Subscription information: For more information and subscription rates, please see tandfonline.com/pricing/journal/tmib. Taylor & Francis journals are available in a range of different packages, designed to suit every library's needs and budget. This journal is available for institutional subscriptions with online only or print & online options. This journal may also be available as part of our libraries, subject collections, or archives. For more information on our sales packages, please visit: librarianresources.taylorandfrancis.com.

For support with any institutional subscription, please visit help.tandfonline.com or email our dedicated team at subscriptions@tandf.co.uk.

Subscriptions purchased at the personal rate are strictly for personal, non-commercial use only. The reselling of personal subscriptions is prohibited. Personal subscriptions must be purchased with a personal check, credit card, or BAC/wire transfer. Proof of personal status may be requested.

Back issues: Taylor & Francis Group retains a current and one-year back issue stock of journals. Older volumes are held by our official stockists to whom all orders and enquiries should be addressed: Periodicals Service Company, 351 Fairview Ave., Suite 300, Hudson, NY 12534, USA. Tel: +1 518 537 4700; email: psc@periodicals.com.

Ordering information: To subscribe to the Journal, please contact: T&F Customer Services, Informa UK Ltd, Sheepen Place, Colchester, Essex, CO3 3LP, United Kingdom. Tel: +44 (0) 20 8052 2030; email: subscriptions@tandf.co.uk.

Taylor & Francis journals are priced in USD, GBP and EUR (as well as AUD and CAD for a limited number of journals). All subscriptions are charged depending on where the end customer is based. If you are unsure which rate applies to you, please contact Customer Services. All subscriptions are payable in advance and all rates include postage. We are required to charge applicable VAT/GST on all print and online combination subscriptions, in addition to our online only journals. Subscriptions are entered on an annual basis, i.e., January to December. Payment may be made by sterling check, dollar check, euro check, international money order, National Giro or credit cards (Amex, Visa and Mastercard).

Disclaimer: The International Institute for Strategic Studies and our publisher Taylor & Francis make every effort to ensure the accuracy of all the information (the "Content") contained in our publications. However, The International Institute for Strategic Studies and our publisher Taylor & Francis, our agents (including the editor, any member of the editorial team or editorial board, and any guest editors), and our licensors make no representations or warranties whatsoever as to the accuracy, completeness, or suitability for any purpose of the Content. Any opinions and views expressed in this publication are the opinions and views of the authors, and are not the views of or endorsed by The International Institute for Strategic Studies and our publisher Taylor & Francis. The accuracy of the Content should not be relied upon and should be independently verified with primary sources of information. The International Institute for Strategic Studies and our publisher Taylor & Francis shall not be liable for any losses, actions, claims, proceedings, demands, costs, expenses, damages, and other liabilities whatsoever or howsoever caused arising directly or indirectly in connection with, in relation to, or arising out of the use of the Content. Terms & Conditions of access and use can be found at http://www.tandfonline.com/page/terms-and-conditions.

All Taylor & Francis Group journals are printed on paper from renewable sources by accredited partners.

Contents

Indexes of Tables, Figures and Maps 6
Editor's Introduction 7

Part One **Capabilities, Trends and Economics**

Chapter 1 **Defence and military analysis** 8
Era of insecurity 8
Defence budgets and expenditure 14

Chapter 2 **North America** 16
Regional trends in 2023 16;   Arms procurements and deliveries 32;
United States: defence policy and economics 18;   Armed forces data section 33
Canada: defence policy 29;

Chapter 3 **Europe** 54
Regional trends in 2023 54;   Arms procurements and deliveries 70;
Regional defence policy and economics 56;   Armed forces data section 71

Chapter 4 **Russia and Eurasia** 158
Regional trends in 2023 158;   Russia: defence policy and economics 164;
Regional defence policy and economics 160;   Arms procurements and deliveries 177;
Ukraine: defence policy 161;   Armed forces data section 178

Chapter 5 **Asia** 218
Regional trends in 2023 218;   Arms procurements and deliveries 244;
Regional defence policy and economics 220;   Armed forces data section 245
China: defence policy and economics 233;

Chapter 6 **Middle East and North Africa** 328
Regional trends in 2023 328;   Arms procurements and deliveries 341;
Regional defence policy and economics 330;   Armed forces data section 342

Chapter 7 **Latin America and the Caribbean** 396
Regional trends in 2023 396;   Arms procurements and deliveries 407;
Regional defence policy and economics 398;   Armed forces data section 408

Chapter 8 **Sub-Saharan Africa** 458
Regional trends in 2023 458;   Regional defence economics 465;
West Africa: defence policy 460;   Arms procurements and deliveries 470;
East Africa: defence policy 461;   Armed forces data section 471
Central and Southern Africa: defence policy 462;

Part Two **Reference**

Explanatory notes 532
    Principal land definitions 536; Principal naval definitions 537; Principal aviation definitions 538
List of abbreviations for data sections 540
International comparisons of defence expenditure and military personnel 542
Index of country/territory abbreviations 548
Index of countries and territories 549

Index of **TABLES**

1. Finland: selected procurements since 2010 10
2. United States Army: Future Vertical Lift (FVL) 22
3. The US DoD budget request by appropriation title, USDm 26
4. The US DoD total budget request by military service, USDm 27
5. US National Defense Budget Function and other selected budgets, 2000, 2010–24, USD in billions, current-year dollars 29
6. Royal Canadian Air Force: selected procurements since 2000 30
7. France: Nexter (KNDS) CAESAR 155mm howitzer 69
8. Ukraine: selected contracts by foreign donors, 2022–October 2023 162
9. Russia: defence expenditure, 2015–24 (trillion roubles, current prices) 172
10. Australia: naval shipbuilding since 2010 232
11. China: selected defence exports to North Africa since 2010 334
12. Exchange rate impacts on Iranian defence budget 337
13. Iran: Selected uninhabited aerial vehicle (UAV) and direct attack munition (DAM) exports 339
14. Chile: selected procurements since 2010 401
15. Angola: selected procurements since 2010 469
16. List of abbreviations for data sections 540
17. International comparisons of defence expenditure and military personnel 542
18. Index of country/territory abbreviations 548
19. Index of countries and territories 549

Index of **FIGURES**

Chapter One
1. Breakdown of uninhabited maritime systems by mission, 2023 9
2. Breakdown of uninhabited maritime platforms by mission, 2023 9

North America
3. US defence budget as % of GDP 26

Europe
4. Selected Western countries: new fleet replenishment oilers with replenishment-at-sea capability (AORs) 59
5. Europe: selected countries, inflation (%) 2018–28 62
6. Europe: defence spending by country and sub-region, 2023 64
7. Europe: regional defence spending as % of GDP (average) 65
8. Europe: defence spending year-on-year change (%) 2022–23 65

Russia and Eurasia
9. Russia: defence expenditure as % of GDP 172
10. Russia: new-build Su-30 *Flanker* exports 174

Asia
11. Japan: selected aircraft procurements, 2010–24 222
12. AUKUS partnership: submarine implementation plan 225
13. Asia: defence spending by country and sub-region, 2023 228
14. Asia: regional defence spending as % of GDP (average) 229
15. Asia: sub-regional real-terms defence-spending growth, 2022–23 (USDbn, constant 2015) 231
16. China: defence budget compared with the rest of Asia (total), 2008–23, USDbn, constant 2015 240

Middle East and North Africa
17. Middle East and North Africa: defence spending by country and sub-region, 2023 337
18. Middle East and North Africa: defence spending as % of GDP (average) 338

Latin America and the Caribbean
19. Latin America and the Caribbean: defence spending by country and sub-region, 2023 402
20. Latin America and the Caribbean: regional defence spending as % of GDP (average) 404
21. Latin America: selected countries, inflation (%), 2018–28 404

Sub-Saharan Africa
22. Sub-Saharan Africa: defence spending by country and sub-region, 2023 465
23. Sub-Saharan Africa: regional defence spending as % of GDP (average) 467
24. Sub-Saharan Africa: total defence spending by sub-region, 2008–22 468

Index of **MAPS**

1. Europe: regional defence spending (USDbn, %ch yoy) 63
2. Turkiye: selected armed-UAV exports since 2018 67
3. Russia: operational fleet inventories and selected submarine, surface-combatant and amphibious-ship dispositions, 2007, 2020 and 2023 168
4. Russia and Eurasia: regional defence spending (USDbn, %ch yoy) 173
5. Asia: regional defence spending (USDbn, %ch yoy) 230
6. People's Liberation Army (PLA) incursions into Taiwan's Air Defence Identification Zone (ADIZ) 236
7. Middle East and North Africa: regional defence spending (USDbn, %ch yoy) 336
8. South America: selected helicopter procurements since 2010 399
9. Latin America and the Caribbean: regional defence spending (USDbn, %ch yoy) 403
10. Latin America and the Caribbean: selected naval procurements, 2019–23 406
11. Sub-Saharan Africa: regional defence spending (USDbn, %ch yoy) 466

Editor's Introduction

Threats to the rules-based order have intensified over the past year, prompting governments to reassess security priorities, defence spending and equipment plans. They have also raised concerns about defence-industrial capacities and driven the realisation that modernisation efforts need to balance maintaining traditional capacities, such as artillery, with embracing newer technologies, such as uninhabited systems and high-speed weapons.

The deteriorating security environment is exemplified by mounting conflicts – such as the Hamas–Israel war, Russia's continued aggression against Ukraine, and Azerbaijan's takeover of the Nagorno-Karabakh region; coups in Niger and Gabon; China's more assertive manoeuvres around Taiwan, in the South China Sea and elsewhere; and attacks on critical national infrastructure, including a gas pipeline and data cables in the Baltic Sea. *The Military Balance 2024* captures these developments and how they are influencing defence budgets and equipment inventories.

Russia has lost over 2,900 main battle tanks since launching its full-scale war on Ukraine, about as many as it had in active inventory at the outset of the operation. Moscow has been able to trade quality for quantity though, by pulling thousands of older tanks out of storage at a rate that may, at times, have reached 90 tanks per month. Russia's stored equipment inventories mean Moscow could potentially sustain around three more years of heavy losses and replenish tanks from stocks, even if at lower technical standard, irrespective of its ability to produce new equipment.

Ukraine also has suffered heavy losses, though Western replenishments have allowed the country to broadly sustain its inventory size while upgrading equipment quality. The situation underscored a growing feeling of a stalemate in the fighting that may persist through 2024.

Russia's aggression spurred European countries to boost defence spending and has strengthened NATO, with Finland adding combat power and experience in societal-resilience plans. NATO member states' defence spending, dominated by the United States, has risen to about 50% of the global total. Adding the defence budgets of China, Russia and India brings the collective total to more than 70% of global military spending.

Although several European countries are spending more, the extra money is often going to fix old problems and is somewhat eroded by high inflation. The pace of ammunition expenditure in the war between Russia and Ukraine has also caused a reckoning in the West that production capacities have atrophied, with countries scrambling to rectify shortcomings from years of underinvestment and a misplaced focus on just-in-time rather than just-in-case.

The war in Europe has left its mark in other ways, too. Ukraine's use of inexpensive uninhabited maritime vehicles (UMVs) to target Russia's Black Sea Fleet has given others greater urgency in pursuing such equipment; this year UMVs feature in *The Military Balance* for the first time. And while uninhabited aerial vehicles (UAVs) have been a staple of modern armed forces for some time, recent conflicts have demonstrated the utility of a far greater range of such systems, such as direct-attack munitions, quadcopters, and more traditional medium- and high-altitude platforms. Demand has spurred a wave of export deals, with Turkiye and Iran providing UAVs to various actors.

Elsewhere, China is upgrading its strategic forces. It continues work on the DF-27 (CH-SS-X-24) intermediate-range ballistic missile armed with a hypersonic glide vehicle aimed at overcoming missile defences. Chinese efforts to turn the People's Liberation Army into a power-projection force also advanced. The navy exercised closer to Guam and, with Russian vessels, near the coast of Alaska. The country's third and most capable aircraft carrier, the *Fujian* (Type-003), neared sea trials. Meanwhile, China sent an alleged spy balloon across the US (it was downed by a US Air Force F-22 *Raptor*).

China demonstrates why *The Military Balance*'s focus on forces and equipment in this, its 65th edition, remains a key element of assessing state power. Nevertheless, The International Institute for Strategic Studies continues to expand its research focus to capture developments in areas such as cyber, artificial intelligence and defence-industrial capacity to capture these increasingly important qualitative factors shaping conflict.

Chapter One: Defence and military analysis

Era of insecurity

Renewed fighting between Israel and Hamas, a resurfaced Houthi missile threat, rising tensions in the Indo-Pacific and the Arctic, turmoil in Sub-Saharan Africa, coupled with Russia's war on Ukraine that is grinding towards its third year created a highly volatile security environment in the past year.

The current military-security situation heralds what is likely to be a more dangerous decade, characterised by the brazen application by some of military power to pursue claims – evoking a 'might is right' approach – as well as the desire among like-minded democracies for stronger bilateral and multilateral defence ties in response. At the same time, governments are trying to balance appetite for advanced weapons with the need to rebuild industrial-scale ammunition production capacity. The demise of the Conventional Forces in Europe Treaty highlighted a lack of interest in arms control.

Moscow's military actions have amplified concerns in other parts of the world, particularly the Indo-Pacific, that a militarily powerful neighbour may try to exert its will over others. In Asia, this has driven Japan and South Korea to seek closer defence ties, the Philippines to re-engage with the United States on military cooperation, Taiwan to bolster its defences, and Australia to embark on an unprecedented expansion of its naval capacity, most visibly through the Australia–United Kingdom–US AUKUS partnership with nuclear-powered submarines at its core.

China is becoming more assertive, not just in its immediate vicinity. The country flew a high-altitude surveillance balloon over the US and deployed ships near American shores, while its maritime assets had tense encounters with Canadian and Philippine vessels. Beijing sustained its defence modernisation, while also stepping up diplomatic engagement, brokering an effort at detente between Iran and Saudi Arabia.

Hamas's surprise attack on Israel on 7 October using a combination of ground fighters, rocket fire and other tactics that killed around 1,200 civilians, and Tel Aviv's assault on Gaza in the aftermath that caused mass civilian casualties have further upset the global security landscape. The fighting arrested efforts at improving relations between Israel and several Arab states and caused diplomatic rifts further afield. The fighting also exposed a potential overreliance by Israel on technology to monitor Hamas, which may have contributed to Tel Aviv not anticipating the attack.

Regional instability also affected other parts of the world. Africa suffered coups in Niger and Gabon, and military regimes now control a belt across the Sahel. The United Nations ended its Mali operations because of political pressure from the new regime, though violence in the country persisted.

All that happened as the costs to Russia of its ill-judged war crystallised during a second year of fighting. The Wagner Group's attempted mutiny highlighted the internal fissures within Russia; Ukraine has gradually, even if only slowly, recaptured territory, though not as much as it – and its backers – hoped. At the same time, Russia's Black Sea Fleet has been badly hit, and Moscow has had to adjust equipment plans to focus on the near-term fight.

Russia's territorial ambitions also have spurred several governments in Europe to refresh their security thinking. Germany published a first national security strategy, and the UK issued an update to its Defence Command Paper. All made clear that national security is no longer an afterthought and that looming challenges require serious attention. They also highlighted, to different levels, that China is becoming an ever-greater security concern, matching, at least to some extent, Washington's tone. China's military developments were also a focus of Australia's Defence Strategic Review.

The result has been an uptick in defence outlays. Governments from Canberra to Washington to Oslo have also realised their ammunition stocks have fallen too low and the ability to restock needs fixing. A just-in-time mindset that has persisted for almost three decades is giving way to a just-in-case approach, though delivering on these ambitions is challenging.

Meanwhile, European countries are pursuing air- and missile-defence capabilities with renewed vigour. Uninhabited aerial vehicles (UAVs) are in strong demand, and defence establishments around the globe are trying to harness the speed of development of entrepreneurial start-ups.

Trench warfare

Russia's assault on Ukraine demonstrated that modern war still has echoes of the past. With its offensive stalled, Russia reverted to trench warfare, highlighting the value of capabilities such as mines and fortifications in defensive belts to slow a Ukrainian counter-offensive underpinned by Western-supplied arms. Some Western armed forces have again realised the requirement to focus on clearing complex obstacles, including trenches, as part of their training syllabus.

In parallel, Moscow and Kyiv have been adapting their operations. Ukraine began launching occasional long-range UAV attacks on Moscow using domestic designs to bring the war home to Russia. Moscow demonstrated its own resilience. It adjusted combat air operations to keep aircraft out of range of Ukrainian surface-to-air systems and paired UAVs and missile raids to overwhelm those defences.

Kyiv has retaken more than 50% of the territory Moscow gained in the early days of fighting, with most ground regained in 2022.

Kyiv's 2023 counter-offensive, and at times criticism of its slow progress, also exposed some fallacies that have crept into some Western military thinking. After several wars in which Western countries enjoyed overwhelming equipment overmatch, the notion appears to have set in that the fighting phase of a conflict should be over quickly. Ukraine is a reminder that wars, more typically, are drawn-out affairs.

In Ukraine, both sides continued to expend weapons at a high, though in some cases carefully managed, pace. Moscow tried to balance the use of long-range air-to-ground missiles and attack UAVs with its ability to replenish its stocks. Ukraine adapted its air-defence operations to use high-capability surface-to-air missiles principally against Russia's more sophisticated systems, leaving it largely to anti-aircraft guns and similar systems to take on less sophisticated UAV threats.

Lessons emerging from the fighting are starting to influence the thinking of many armed forces. They include a heightened appreciation for the value of artillery, loitering munitions and counter-UAV systems, and both the value of and the threat from uninhabited maritime vehicles (UMVs). Interest in UMVs, already on the rise before the war, has grown within many armed forces, also propelled by a recognition that those systems can serve to monitor vulnerable critical national infrastructure that passes along the seabed floor that is not well monitored and is sometimes subject to attack.

NATO renewed

Russia's actions have reinvigorated NATO, with Finland completing its rapid Alliance accession process in April 2023 and amplifying how Moscow misjudged the impact its attack on Ukraine would have on the regional security landscape. Russia's border with NATO members is now more than 1,300 kilometres longer. Germany and Canada have made commitments to bolster their presence in the Baltic states, with Berlin pledging to permanently keep a

▲ **Figure 1 Breakdown of uninhabited maritime systems by mission, 2023**

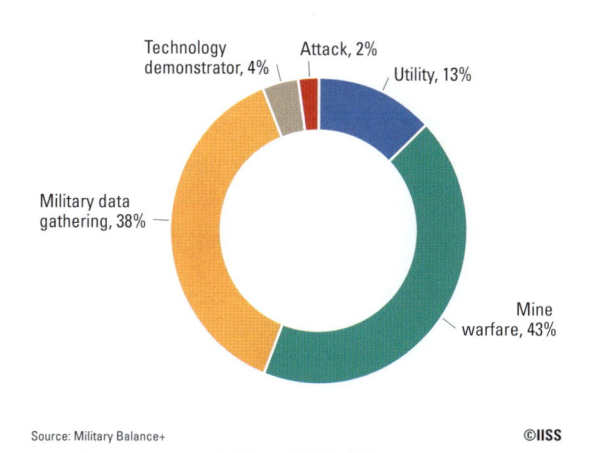

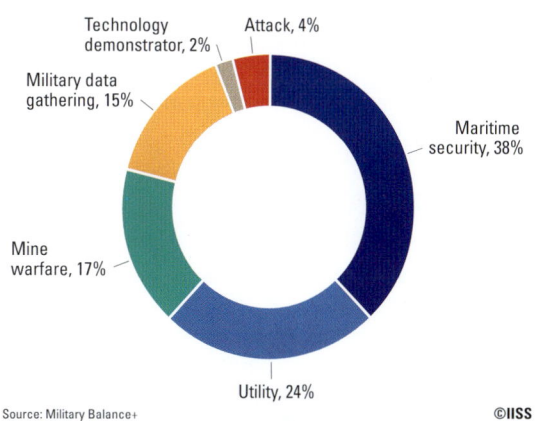

- Technology demonstrator, 4%
- Attack, 2%
- Utility, 13%
- Mine warfare, 43%
- Military data gathering, 38%

Source: Military Balance+ ©IISS

▲ **Figure 2 Breakdown of uninhabited maritime platforms by mission, 2023**

- Technology demonstrator, 2%
- Attack, 4%
- Military data gathering, 15%
- Maritime security, 38%
- Mine warfare, 17%
- Utility, 24%

Source: Military Balance+ ©IISS

Table 1 — Finland: selected procurements since 2010

Finland became the first new NATO member since the end of the Cold War to join the Alliance with an inventory already largely interoperable with the Allies. Helsinki generally relies on local suppliers, as well as vendors from the US and neighbours Norway and Sweden. More recently, Israeli companies have made market inroads. Finland's F-35A buy is by far the most expensive acquisition the country has ever made and will be financed by significant budget increases until 2027. Local company Patria has competencies in armoured vehicle production as well as maintenance and upgrade of platforms across domains. A 6×6 vehicle, called XA-300 in Finnish service, is also being acquired by Germany, Latvia and Sweden through the Helsinki-led Common Armoured Vehicle System. Local shipbuilder Rauma Marine Constructions is teaming with Sweden's Saab to construct four *Pohjanmaa*-class frigates to be delivered by 2028. These will replace the *Rauma*-class missile craft and the *Hameenmaa*-class minelayers. Finland surprised many by selecting the Israel Aerospace Industries *Gabriel* V anti-ship missile for the class. The missiles will also equip *Hamina*-class missile craft and be deployed in a coastal defence version. Similarly, in 2017, Finland became the second export customer for the South Korean K9 *Thunder* 155mm howitzer and in 2023 selected Rafael's *David's Sling* missile system for its long-range air-defence requirement, suggesting a growing diversification of suppliers.

Contract Date	Equipment	Type	Quantity	Value (USD)	Contractor	Deliveries	Service
May 2010	C295M	Electronic-intelligence aircraft	1	148.60m	Airbus (M) / Lockheed Martin	2018	Air Force
Jun 2010	*Rauma*	Missile boat mid-life upgrade	4	92.88m	Patria	2013–14	Navy
May 2011	M270 MLRS	227mm multiple rocket launcher (MRL) upgrade	22	45.30m	Lockheed Martin	n.k.	Army
Dec 2011	*Turva*	Patrol ship	1	128.70m	STX Finland	2014	Border Guard
Mar 2012	AGM-158 JASSM	Air-launched cruise missile	n.k.	229.48m	Lockheed Martin	By 2018	Air Force
Oct 2012	*Jehu*	Fast patrol boat	12	43.71m	Marine Alutech	2015–17	Navy
Dec 2012	H215 (AS332L1) *Super Puma*	Medium transport helicopter	2	79.71m	Airbus (M)	2016	Border Guard
c. 2013	M270 MLRS	227mm MRL	6	n.k.	US government surplus	2014	Army
Dec 2013	XA-180 *Sisu*	Wheeled APC upgrade	275	80.74m	Patria	2014–22	Army
Jan 2014	*Leopard* 2A6	MBT	100	265.64m	Netherlands government surplus	2015–19	Army
May 2015	*Pansio*	Minelayer upgrade	3	23.30m	Atlas Elektronik	2015–17	Navy
Mar 2017	K9 *Thunder*	155mm self-propelled howitzer	58	200.18m	South Korean government surplus	2018–ongoing	Army
Jan 2018	*Hamina*	Missile craft mid-life upgrade	4	262.33m	Patria	2020–25	Navy
Jul 2018	*Gabriel* V	Anti-ship missiles	n.k.	191.40m	IAI	By 2025	Navy
Sep 2019	*Pohjanmaa*	Frigate	4	1.59bn	Rauma Marine / Saab	2025–28*	Navy
Jul 2021	CV9030FIN	IFV upgrade	n.k.	32.00m	BAE Systems Hägglunds	2022–26*	Army
Feb 2022	F-35A *Lightning* II	Fighter ground-attack aircraft	64	8.83bn	Lockheed Martin	2025–30*	Air Force
Jun 2022	*Turva*	Patrol ship	2	505.09m	Meyer Turku	2025–26*	Border Guard
Jun 2023	Patria 6×6 (XA-300)	Wheeled APC	91	221.07m	Patria	2023 onwards*	Army

Planned*

multinational = M

brigade in Lithuania and Ottawa earmarking additional forces to Latvia. On the eve of the Vilnius Summit in July 2023, Türkiye agreed to forward Sweden's accession application to its parliament for approval after months of stonewalling.

That is not to say NATO does not suffer areas of disagreement. Alliance members closest to Ukraine left little doubt going into the Vilnius Summit that they wanted to grant Ukraine membership, but the outcome was merely the promise for a truncated accession process with no clear timeline. NATO and Ukraine also established a joint council to work more closely together. But the summit provided further evidence that the Alliance was looking to strengthen its deterrence and defence posture, with a series of regional defence plans agreed that contain ambitious targets for force size and readiness.

Rethinking plans

Governments and their defence planning staffs have also embarked on adapting tactics and policies to prepare for the new security environment. Australia, Finland, Germany, Norway and the UK are among those to issue new defence-related strategy documents. In 2023, Germany's first-ever national security strategy came after Chancellor Olaf Scholz the year before declared a turning point, a *Zeitenwende*, soon after Russia's invasion of Ukraine. The document calls Russia 'the most significant threat to peace and security in the Euro-Atlantic area'. And while short on detail in many areas, it says the government will 'promote the development and introduction of highly advanced capabilities, such as precision deep-strike weapons'. Britain's Defence Command Paper refresh, an update to a document a mere two years old, similarly puts the emphasis on the Euro-Atlantic.

Although Russia is typically identified as the primary threat in the Western strategy updates, Germany, the UK and others are also signalling a more cautious approach toward China. Berlin described its relationship with Beijing as dealing with a 'partner, competitor and systemic rival'. Canberra was somewhat blunter in the public unveiling of Australia's Defence Strategic Review in April, criticising Beijing for a lack of transparency around its defence plans. New Zealand also, for the first time, produced a National Security Strategy. It emphasised partnerships with others to maintain regional security.

Asian focus

Security tensions in Asia also are rising. North Korea pursued another busy year of missile launches. It unveiled and later tested what appeared to be a road-mobile, solid-fuel intercontinental ballistic missile, the *Hwasong*-18. South Korea's president briefly floated the idea of the country pursuing its own nuclear programme, and China's nuclear arsenal is expanding. Beijing also applied pressure on the Philippines over a territorial dispute in the South China Sea, routinely deploying its maritime militia there and to other areas in the South China Sea that it claims. Japan's defence ministry published a new White Paper that calls for a significant boost in expenditure for the armed forces.

Western states are trying to balance their focus on the war in Ukraine with their largely trade-driven strategic interests in Asia. The UK, for instance, made Europe the centrepiece of its Defence Command Paper, but held firm to its plans to return an aircraft-carrier battlegroup to the Indo-Pacific in 2025. Under the AUKUS partnership, the UK has said it will forward-deploy an attack submarine to Australia. Canada, in 2023, said it intends to boost its naval deployment in the region to three ships from two. Germany's defence minister said the country plans to dispatch two military vessels – a frigate and a supply ship – to the Indo-Pacific in 2024 and boost other activities.

The US also stepped up its efforts to strengthen regional ties and counterbalance a more assertive Chinese foreign policy. Lloyd Austin became the first-ever US secretary of defense to travel to Papua New Guinea to bolster ties. Washington tried to enhance links with India, the Philippines and others. The US also committed to providing Australia with *Virginia*-class attack submarines under AUKUS, in advance of the delivery of the Australian–UK-built SSN-AUKUS boats, and Washington opened foreign-military-financing funding channels to Taiwan to help the island state in its bid to strengthen its defences in the face of increased Chinese military activity.

Various countries in the region are pursuing other partnerships with the clear aim of improving their security situation. Japan and Australia are working together more on defence matters, in parallel with Tokyo's involvement with the UK and Italy in the Global Combat Air Programme, intended to develop a sixth-generation fighter by 2035. South Korea and Japan held talks to mend ties brokered by US President Joe Biden.

Building back

Fighting in Ukraine has exposed how far armed forces and defence industries have fallen in their ability to rapidly replenish munitions stocks. In the aftermath of the Cold War, many Western forces drew down or largely relinquished stockpiles amid pressure from politicians to eliminate inventories that were judged excessive in the absence of a clear threat. Now, military leaders and some politicians acknowledge that was a mistake and are reversing course.

Two years of fighting have strained the West's ability to resupply Ukraine with critical ammunition, including 155mm artillery shells. When Washington, in July, gave the green light to supply cluster munitions to Kyiv, it said the decision was partly driven by the ability to draw on ample stocks of those munitions at a time of artillery-shell shortages. The fighting between Israel and Hamas reinforced concerns about inventory depth and industrial capacity. The United States, as part of its support for Ukraine, had withdrawn some 155mm ammunition from Israel to reinforce stocks in Europe, but replenished those for use by the Israel Defense Forces once fighting there erupted. Washington also rushed *Iron Dome* air-defence equipment to Israel to augment the country's supply.

Western governments have begun to react. The United Kingdom, as part of its updated command paper, said it would invest a further GBP2.5 billion (USD3bn) to make its munitions stockpile more resilient. Australia set up a guided-weapons and explosive-ordnance enterprise to ensure adequate supply. Washington and Canberra also agreed to work together to enable the potential co-production of Guided Multiple Launch Rocket Systems in Australia by 2025 and for the country to be able to produce some 155mm artillery shells. Germany expanded an existing framework agreement to buy 120mm tank ammunition from Rheinmetall, giving the company greater certainty over long-term demand. And at the end of the year Finland announced it would double ammunition production capacity by 2027. But realising some of these ambitions proved problematic. The European Union was on track to miss, by a wide margin, its target of delivering Ukraine 1 million 155mm shells within a year by March 2024.

For many armed forces, the objective is to have stocks to sustain at least 30 days of initial fighting so industry can spool up to sustain war-fighting demand. That has raised another problem: the warehouses to stock those munitions have been drawn down, too, and need to be rebuilt. So too does the workforce. But inflationary pressures are making the challenge of rebuilding supplies harder, with costs for some ammunition up 300% because of economic pressures.

Admiral Robert Bauer, the chair of NATO's Military Committee, said governments may have to make some investments in industry to assure resilience in case of conflict. 'If we want to have the ability to scale up because of a war, then we need to have factories that probably are empty and doing nothing for ten years, but when it is necessary, they need to be up and running within a month', he said at the 2023 IISS Manama Dialogue.

Kyiv has scaled up output of 122mm and 152mm rounds for use with its Soviet-era equipment, in part because global stocks of that ammunition had almost dried up. Plants in Europe that made these rounds also booked orders. The country is also working on longer-range systems. By mid-2023, Ukraine's monthly domestic ammunition production was outpacing the entire output of the year prior. In time, though, these plants will need to transition to Western rounds, to support the artillery pieces donated to Ukraine. US production is expected to surge this year; Europe, but also Russia, are expected to generate meaningfully higher output from 2025 under current plans. The US and Ukraine in December 2023 also said they would explore co-production of critical weapons and other ways to address Kyiv's military equipment needs.

Defence companies are ramping up output. In some cases, weapons are being redesigned to overcome sustained supply-chain bottlenecks and to use more commercial parts to build weapons. General Dynamics, for instance, said in October 2023 that it had brought artillery production up to around 20,000 rounds a month from 14,000 and is eyeing an increase to 85,000 or more.

Tapping Tech

Ukraine's creative use of commercial and defence technologies, often introduced at breakneck pace, has amplified appetite among other armed forces to better harness systems offered by start-ups that have not traditionally been part of the defence-industrial base. Kyiv's ingenuity played out visibly last year, for instance, in Ukrainian uninhabited maritime vehicle attacks on Russian ships, as well as uninhabited aerial vehicle attacks on targets in Russia.

The US Department of Defense, during the past year, stepped up efforts to strengthen its relationships with such smaller, often nimbler suppliers. The Biden administration requested USD115 million for its Office of Strategic Capital. That office, itself only set up a few months earlier, is supposed to find ways to help bring technology from the early research phase to make it to production, overcoming the so-called Valley of Death that has stymied past efforts.

The Pentagon elevated the role of the Defense Innovation Unit and named as its new director former Apple executive Doug Beck, who also serves as an advisor on tech issues to the secretary of defense. As part of Indian Prime Minister Narendra Modi's visit to the United States in June, the countries launched Indus-X, a strategic technology partnership that also aims to work with academia, tech incubators and investors.

NATO took steps to fully establish its investment fund during the Vilnius Summit. The NATO Innovation Fund aims to invest EUR1 billion (USD1.09bn) in early-stage start-ups working on what are viewed as disruptive technologies. The Alliance also set up a defence innovation accelerator to link start-ups with users, scientists and others in areas such as artificial intelligence, high-speed weapons, quantum and biotechnologies. Similarly, Australia launched its Advanced Strategic Capabilities Accelerator, with the government pledging AUD3.4bn (USD2bn) in investments over the coming decade.

Interest in these kinds of arrangements in large part reflects the dual-use nature of many of the technologies military establishments are trying to capture. Quantum sensing, space sensors and artificial intelligence are just some of the areas that offer promising national-security applications, but where the traditional defence sector has not been the pace setter for technology innovation.

The interaction between national-security circles and start-ups is not without its issues, though. Working with the Pentagon or other Western defence establishments can come with limits on access to capital. The US and others have made clear they will not work with start-ups that have funding ties to countries such as China.

AI Anxiety

The release of a chatbot using generative artificial intelligence (AI) that can carry out tasks such as producing passable essays for high-school students has over the past year galvanised the debate over what to do about AI in defence.

The director of the United States' Defense Information Systems Agency, US Air Force Lt. Gen. Robert Skinner, called it 'probably one of the most disruptive technologies and initiatives in a very long, long time'. To punctuate his point, he added during an address at the TechNet Cyber 2023 conference that 'those who harness that and can understand how to best leverage it but also to best protect against it are going to be the ones that have the high ground'. The US requested USD1.8 billion for AI-related capabilities for fiscal year 2024 alone.

Defence organisations, for decades, have grappled with what the advent of AI could mean for armed forces, from improving the management of supplies to generating more autonomous capability in weapons. Those discussions have ebbed and flowed but gained intensity again because of ChatGPT, which was followed in quick succession by numerous other commercial software vendors embracing the technology.

The large language models that underpin generative AI could, for instance, aid intelligence analysts in sifting through often vast amounts of collected but unstructured data. But the advent of generative AI comes with potential risks, too, particularly when it comes to cyber security. Cyber attackers can potentially use generative AI tools to generate more diverse and sophisticated attacks with relative ease and speed.

In August, the Pentagon established a task force to analyse and integrate generative AI tools across the services. The Department of Defense also said it is eager to assess how adversaries may employ the technology to counter US efforts to harness AI. 'We must keep doing more, safely and swiftly, given the nature of strategic competition with the PRC [People's Republic of China]', Deputy Secretary of Defense Kathleen Hicks said.

AI is becoming somewhat of a battleground. The US placed restrictions on some chip exports to China in a bid to slow the country's military AI advances.

Perhaps one of the biggest questions around generative AI, at least for now, is the technology's accuracy. When Microsoft and Google deployed versions of the technology to users, the algorithms famously produced inaccurate or misleading responses. In one case, Microsoft put limits on its chatbot after it said it harboured interest in obtaining nuclear codes. Such so-called hallucinations can be comical or troubling in civil applications. They hold the potential to be devasting in a military setting by misidentifying targets.

Armed forces, just like their civilian counterparts, also need to discern where the bulk of the AI work should be done. Many of the applications being popularised now run on large-scale cloud infrastructure operated by private-sector companies. But there is a view that relying on the cloud to deliver the capability has its downsides and that instead running AI on each device – a laptop or smartphone in the commercial world, but perhaps a tank or an aircraft in the military domain– provides greater data security and system resilience.

The rapid pace of change has fuelled discussions over how to place controls on the technology. But it quickly became clear that establishing any sort of arms-control mechanism to manage the development and deployment of AI would not be easy, in part because the technology is not fully defined and is largely dual use. The questions around setting guardrails for generative AI illustrate what one Asian defence planner argues is the modern world's reality: that control mechanisms simply cannot keep up with the pace of technological change.

Defence budgets and expenditure

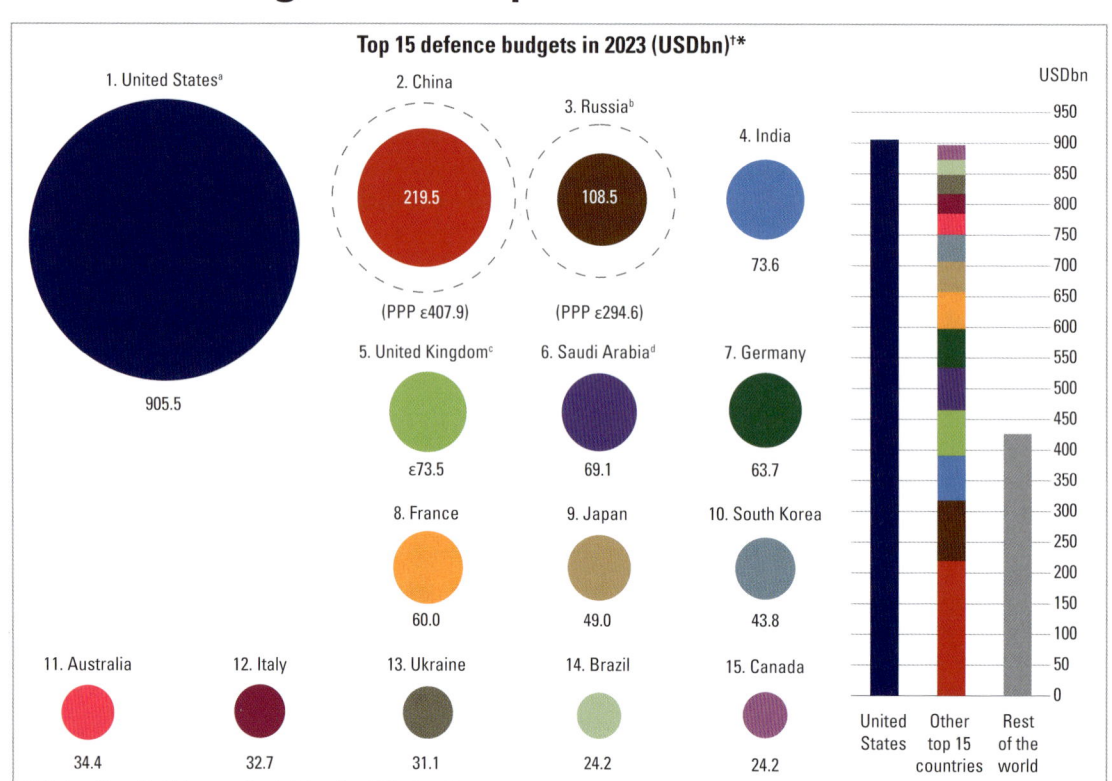

Top 15 defence budgets in 2023 (USDbn)[†]*

1. United States[a] — 905.5
2. China — 219.5 (PPP ɛ407.9)
3. Russia[b] — 108.5 (PPP ɛ294.6)
4. India — 73.6
5. United Kingdom[c] — ɛ73.5
6. Saudi Arabia[d] — 69.1
7. Germany — 63.7
8. France — 60.0
9. Japan — 49.0
10. South Korea — 43.8
11. Australia — 34.4
12. Italy — 32.7
13. Ukraine — 31.1
14. Brazil — 24.2
15. Canada — 24.2

Bar chart (USDbn): United States ~900; Other top 15 countries ~900 (stacked); Rest of the world ~425.

[a] OMB adjusted figure. [b] Total defence expenditure including military R&D funding, military pensions, paramilitary forces' budgets, and other MoD-related expenses such as housing. [c] Includes Armed Forces Pension Scheme and military aid to Ukraine. [d] Excludes security expenditure. Note: Unless otherwise indicated, US dollar totals are calculated using average market exchange rates for 2023, derived using IMF data. The relative position of countries will vary not only as a result of actual adjustments in defence spending levels, but also due to exchange-rate fluctuations between domestic currencies and the US dollar. The use of average exchange rates reduces these fluctuations, but the effects of such movements can be significant in a number of cases. Dashed line reflects an estimate for the value of the Chinese and Russian defence budget in PPP (purchasing power parity) terms to take into account the lower input costs in these countries. These PPP figures are not used in any regional or global totals in this publication and should not be used in comparison with other international data.

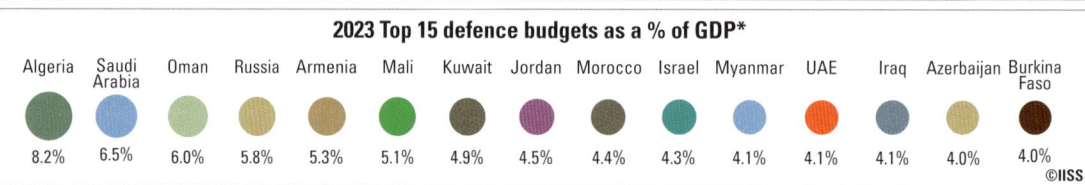

©IISS

2023 Top 15 defence budgets as a % of GDP*

Algeria	Saudi Arabia	Oman	Russia	Armenia	Mali	Kuwait	Jordan	Morocco	Israel	Myanmar	UAE	Iraq	Azerbaijan	Burkina Faso
8.2%	6.5%	6.0%	5.8%	5.3%	5.1%	4.9%	4.5%	4.4%	4.3%	4.1%	4.1%	4.1%	4.0%	4.0%

©IISS

Planned global defence spending by region 2023[†]*

- North America, 41.5%
- Asia, 22.8%
- Europe, 17.3%
- Middle East and North Africa, 8.4%
- Russia and Eurasia, 6.6%
- Latin America and the Caribbean, 2.4%
- Sub-Saharan Africa, 0.9%

Planned defence spending by country 2023[†]*

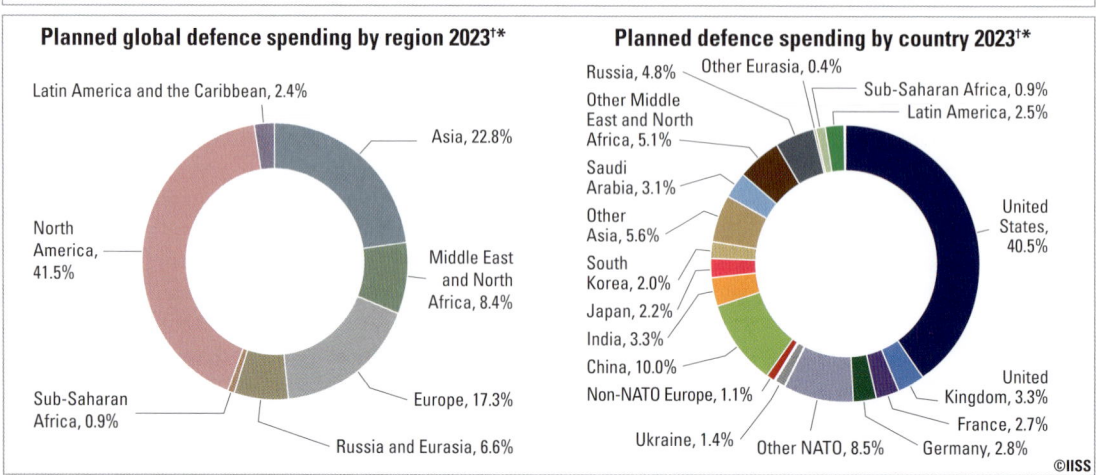

- United States, 40.5%
- China, 10.0%
- Other NATO, 8.5%
- Other Asia, 5.6%
- Other Middle East and North Africa, 5.1%
- Russia, 4.8%
- India, 3.3%
- United Kingdom, 3.3%
- Saudi Arabia, 3.1%
- Germany, 2.8%
- France, 2.7%
- Latin America, 2.5%
- Japan, 2.2%
- South Korea, 2.0%
- Ukraine, 1.4%
- Non-NATO Europe, 1.1%
- Sub-Saharan Africa, 0.9%
- Other Eurasia, 0.4%

©IISS

† At current prices and exchange rates
* Analysis only includes countries for which sufficient comparable data is available. Notable exceptions include Cuba, Eritrea, Libya, North Korea, Syria and Venezuela.

Defence and military analysis: Defence budgets and expenditure 15

Real global defence spending changes by region 2021–23*

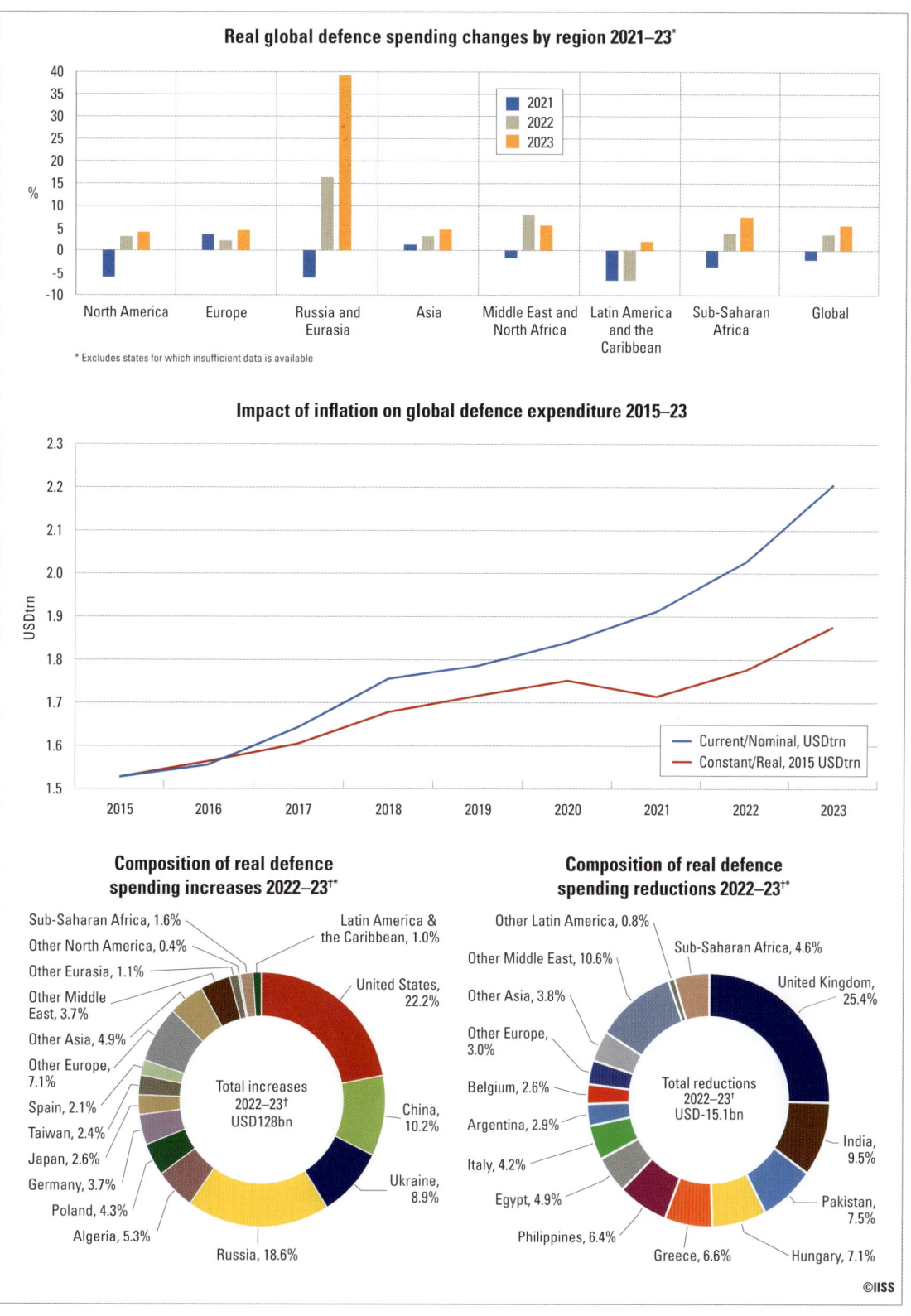

*Excludes states for which insufficient data is available

Impact of inflation on global defence expenditure 2015–23

Composition of real defence spending increases 2022–23[†]

Total increases 2022–23[†] USD128bn

- Sub-Saharan Africa, 1.6%
- Other North America, 0.4%
- Other Eurasia, 1.1%
- Other Middle East, 3.7%
- Other Asia, 4.9%
- Other Europe, 7.1%
- Spain, 2.1%
- Taiwan, 2.4%
- Japan, 2.6%
- Germany, 3.7%
- Poland, 4.3%
- Algeria, 5.3%
- Russia, 18.6%
- Ukraine, 8.9%
- China, 10.2%
- United States, 22.2%
- Latin America & the Caribbean, 1.0%

Composition of real defence spending reductions 2022–23[††]

Total reductions 2022–23[†] USD-15.1bn

- Other Latin America, 0.8%
- Other Middle East, 10.6%
- Other Asia, 3.8%
- Other Europe, 3.0%
- Belgium, 2.6%
- Argentina, 2.9%
- Italy, 4.2%
- Egypt, 4.9%
- Philippines, 6.4%
- Greece, 6.6%
- Hungary, 7.1%
- Pakistan, 7.5%
- India, 9.5%
- United Kingdom, 25.4%
- Sub-Saharan Africa, 4.6%

©IISS

[†] At constant 2015 prices and exchange rates
* Analysis only includes countries for which sufficient comparable data is available. Notable exceptions include Cuba, Eritrea, Libya, North Korea, Syria and Venezuela.

Chapter Two
North America

- The Pentagon says it will pursue a new nuclear bomb, the B61-13. The weapon will have a higher yield than the B61-12 and replace some B61-7s. The US said it would maintain the same-sized nuclear stockpile, making fewer B61-12s to compensate for B61-13s.
- Canadian Prime Minister Justin Trudeau said the country will more than double its military participation in a multinational NATO battlegroup in Latvia. The build-up to a combat-ready brigade, including prepositioned equipment, is due to be completed by 2026.
- A US Air Force F-22 *Raptor* shot down a Chinese reconnaissance balloon that entered Canadian and US airspace. The incident further strained relations between Washington and Beijing. The episode raised concern among some US military officials that China may undertake additional flights of that type and, more generally, about other threats Beijing may pose.
- Canada signed a contract to buy 88 F-35A *Lightning II* combat aircraft to replace the ageing fleet of CF-18 *Hornets*. The Canadian air force should receive the first of the single-engine aircraft in 2026 to phase out the CF-18s early in the next decade.
- The first *Ford*-class aircraft carrier, USS *Gerald R. Ford*, in May embarked on its first operational deployment. In October, it was dispatched to the Eastern Mediterranean in response to Hamas's attack on Israel.
- The US Army is updating its approach to recruitment to address concerns about personnel shortages. The service was on track to miss recruitment targets for new personnel for the second year in a row. The army said it would, among other steps, recruit more widely.

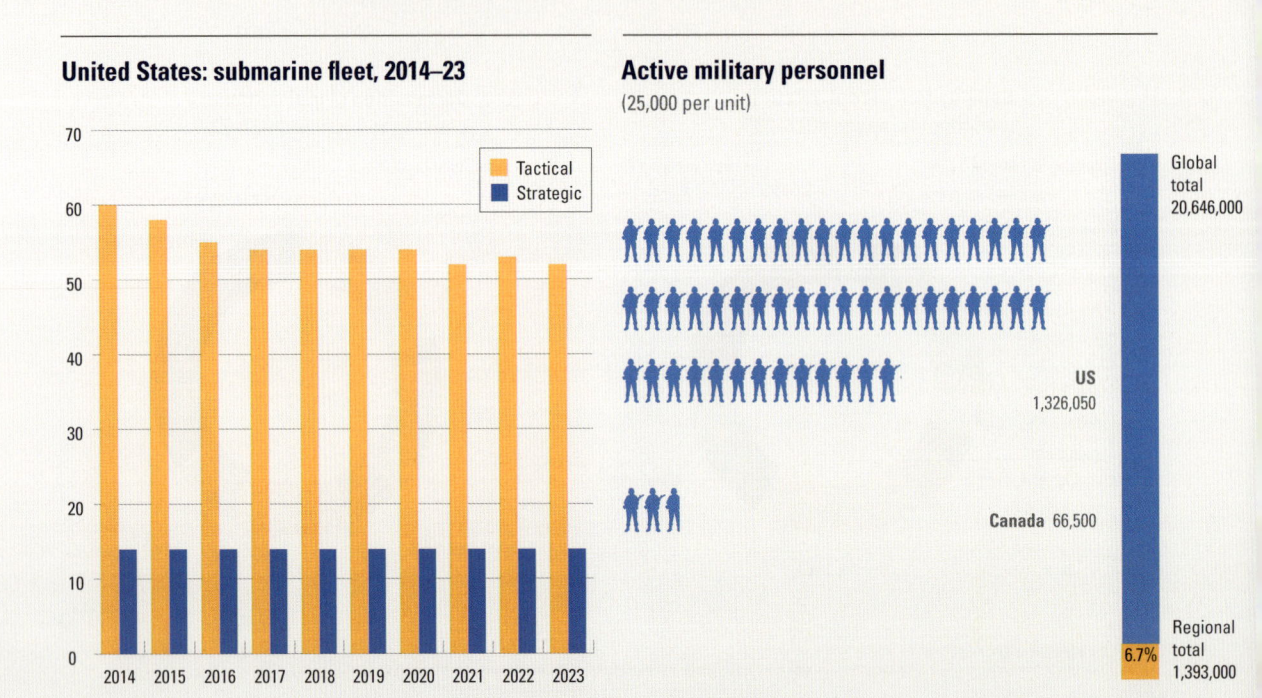

United States: submarine fleet, 2014–23

Active military personnel
(25,000 per unit)

US 1,326,050
Canada 66,500
Global total 20,646,000
Regional total 1,393,000
6.7%

Regional defence policy and economics 18 ▶

Arms procurements and deliveries 32 ▶

Armed forces data section 33 ▶

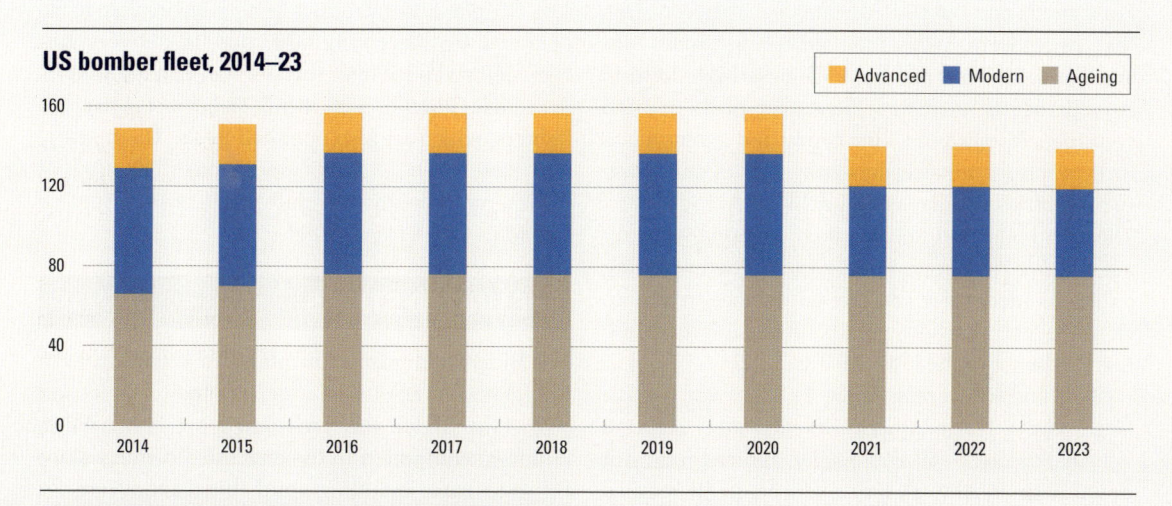

US bomber fleet, 2014–23

Advanced ■ Modern ■ Ageing

Canada: principal surface combatants, 2014–23

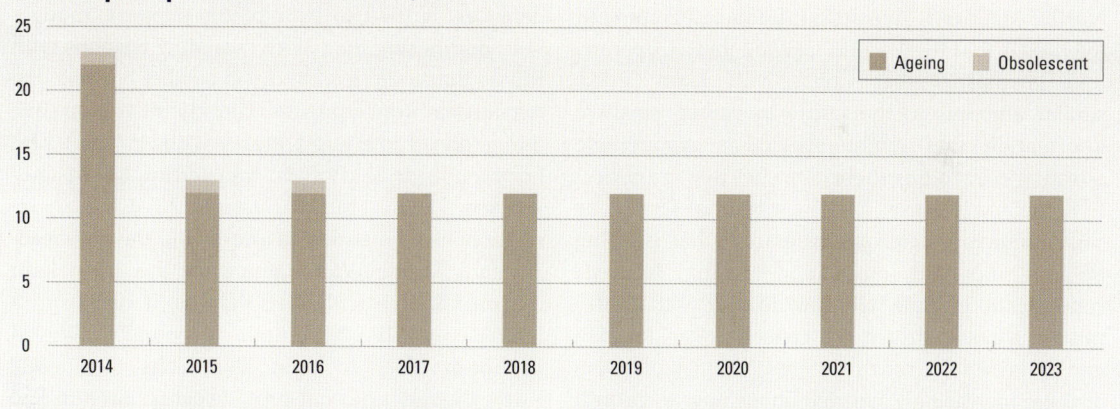

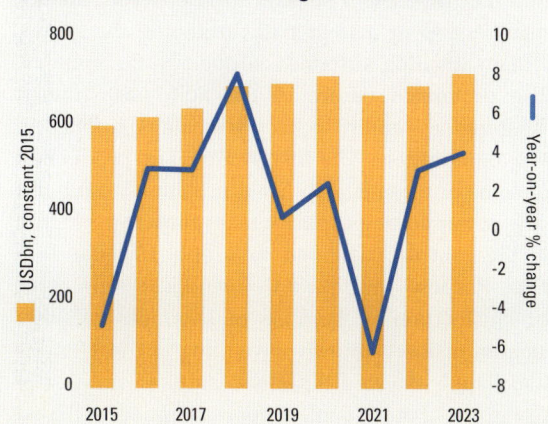

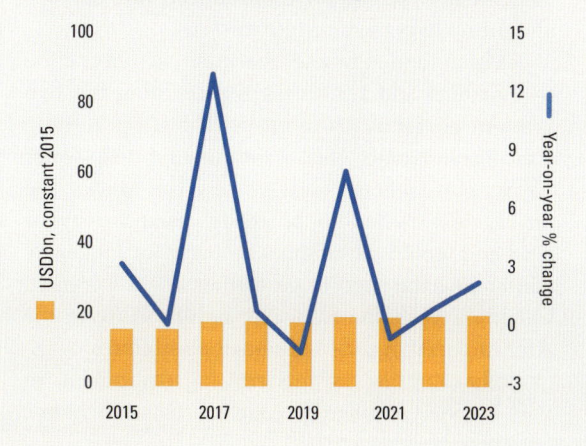

■ Ageing ■ Obsolescent

US real-terms defence budget trend, 2015–23

USDbn, constant 2015 / Year-on-year % change

Canada real-terms defence budget trend, 2015–23

USDbn, constant 2015 / Year-on-year % change

North America

For Canada and the United States, security concerns that once were viewed as emerging issues are starting to become reality. A Chinese high-altitude surveillance balloon flew flew over parts of both countries, Russia and China conducted a joint naval drill in international waters near Alaska and those two countries are increasingly active in Arctic waters. The incidents add to the busy national-security agenda for Washington and Ottawa encompassing efforts to modernise continental defence, maintain close ties with European NATO allies, and boosting their presence in the Indo-Pacific.

A Chinese reconnaissance balloon traversed a large part of North America in early 2023 before a US Air Force (USAF) F-22 *Raptor* fighter brought it down with an AIM-9X *Sidewinder* air-to-air missile. USAF Gen. Gregory Guillot, nominated to run the North American Aerospace Defense Command (NORAD) that the US and Canada jointly operate, told lawmakers that China 'will likely make similar attempts in the future to gather sensitive information that might provide a competitive advantage, including flight over sites that are critical to homeland defense'. Dealing with that reality, he said, requires greater awareness of what is going on and improved information sharing. NORAD continues to grapple with how to deal with cruise-missile threats, driven by concern over Russian and Chinese long-range systems. Military planners also are increasingly worried about how to protect against hypersonic glide vehicles, which both Moscow and Beijing have introduced into service, and future hypersonic cruise missiles.

Russian and Chinese maritime activity close to Canadian and US shores is prompting the two Western governments to adapt. The US is turning a facility in Nome, Alaska, into its first deep-water Arctic port, where naval vessels can dock. The facility is expected to be ready around 2027 or 2028 and would allow ships to linger for longer by eliminating the need to go further afield to refuel. Canada expects the Nanisivik naval facility in the Arctic to open in 2024 as a refuelling station.

Both countries are modernising equipment, in part because of security concerns close to home. The US plans to introduce a new icebreaker to be operated by the coastguard, but its delivery has been delayed until later this decade. Canada said its decision in January 2023 to buy 88 F-35A *Lightning* II fighters, which are also operated by the US military, will strengthen NORAD operations. The first of these aircraft are due for delivery in 2026 to replace Canada's CF-18 *Hornet* fleet.

THE UNITED STATES

The Biden administration played a pivotal role in the international support for Ukraine for a second year. Washington has provided more than USD44 billion in equipment to the embattled country since February 2022, including uninhabited aerial vehicles (UAVs), mine-clearing tools and *Patriot* air and missile defences. It tried to balance the support, though, with minimising the risk of escalating tensions with Russia that could lead to direct conflict between the two nuclear-armed powers. The administration gave the go-ahead to equip Ukraine with *Abrams* tanks. For months, it held off on transferring MGM-140/-168 Army Tactical Missile Systems (ATACMS) short-range ballistic missiles, before giving the go-ahead. Similarly, while Washington gave the green light to arm Ukraine with F-16 fighters, it did so in a limited capacity. Washington eventually allowed European allies to train Ukrainians to operate F-16s, though it did not provide actual aircraft. The Biden administration also resisted efforts going into the July NATO summit to offer Kyiv Alliance membership or a clear path to joining the group, while signalling sustained support to the country. The prolonged nature of the fight has strained Washington's ability to keep Ukraine resupplied in key ammunitions. The US is ramping up production of some of those heavily used munitions to rebuild stocks, but adding capacity takes time. Washington in the past year decided to supply Ukraine with Dual-Purpose Improved Conventional Munitions, or cluster bombs, because of shortages of other 155mm artillery rounds. Providing aid to Ukraine had largely enjoyed bipartisan support, not just in Congress, though some opponents have criticised the aid. The US also worked to support Sweden's push to join NATO in the wake of Russia's aggression, offering Ankara the delivery of F-16s after President Recep Tayyip Erdoğan indicated he would finally get Turkiye's parliament to vote on the Nordic country's accession.

The Ukraine conflict also shaped the Pentagon's new cyber-security strategy. The update of a 2018 document calls China the 'pacing challenge in the cyber domain' for the US armed forces. Russia is designated 'an acute threat', with North Korea, Iran and violent extremist organisations labelled as persistent cyber threats. The document also showed to what extent the cyber realm has become an active area of operations for the US. The Pentagon said that since 2018 'the Department has conducted a number of significant cyberspace operations through its policy of defending forward, actively disrupting malicious cyber activity before it can affect the US Homeland'. The cyber-security strategy is one of several documents the Pentagon released in 2023 to implement the policy objectives spelled out in high-level documents published the year prior, including the National Defense Strategy, Missile Defense Review and Nuclear Posture Review. They already framed China as the 'pacing challenge' and Russia as an 'acute threat'. The US has been adjusting its overseas presence to reflect its new strategic outlook, although its historic footprint is little changed, with epicentres in Europe and Northeast Asia and sizeable numbers retained in the Middle East. The military force structure in Europe increased since the start of 2022, taking US force levels in Europe to around 100,000 troops, above the numbers seen in the recent past. But the total, which was still far below Cold War-era figures, when they exceeded 300,000 troops, has somewhat receded again.

Changes are playing out elsewhere, too, as the US builds ties in Asia with an eye on stemming China's aspirations for greater sway over the region. Washington is deepening ties with the Philippines under President Ferdinand Marcos Jr and has secured access, though not substantial permanent basing, at additional military facilities in the Asian country. The US is also building a new radar installation in Palau. Papua New Guinea granted the US basing access, including for port and airfield facilities. Those steps are part of wider, long-planned force-posture adjustments in the region that also involve 4,000 marines relocating to Guam from Okinawa, Japan. The US had already moved around 2,500 marines to Darwin, Australia, on a rotational basis and has temporarily deployed bombers there. Similarly, the US has tried to strengthen ties with India, even if New Delhi has remained somewhat on the sidelines on the issue of Russia's invasion of Ukraine. Still, the US and India launched a project called Indus-X to cooperate on defence technologies and industrial matters to strengthen bilateral ties.

Even as it tried to contain Beijing, Washington made efforts to revitalise talks with China on various national-security issues. US Secretary of Defens Lloyd Austin tried to arrange a meeting with his Chinese counterpart but was rebuffed. Secretary of State Antony Blinken travelled to China in June 2023, after an earlier planned visit was scrapped over the Chinese balloon incident. Presidents Biden and Xi then met in November in the US. At the same time, the US military and some politicians on both sides of the aisle have been pushing for enhanced American arms exports and weapons delivery to Taiwan, to help bolster the island country's defences amid concern Beijing may aim to take it by force in coming years.

Despite the Pentagon's effort to focus more on the Indo-Pacific, the Middle East once again demonstrated the need for attention. The US deployed forces to the region to deal with security problems there, including Iran seizing commercial ships and Hamas's attack on Israel. The region also remained a source of tension between the US and Russia. The US accused Russian fighter pilots of unsafe operations after they, on several occasions, harassed American UAVs operating over Syria.

The US demonstrated a desire to preserve its lead in critical technology fields. It unveiled a science and technology strategy that calls for closer collaboration with allies – building on and emulating the AUKUS partnership with Australia and the United Kingdom – while avoiding the so-called Valley of Death between prototyping and production of defence equipment, shortening modernisation cycles and enhancing collaboration. The Pentagon is also allocating USD1bn over five years to underpin a new biomanufacturing strategy, while a small-business strategy aims to make it easier for such enterprises to do business with the Department of Defense (DoD). Many of these initiatives evoke past efforts to broaden the military supply base, which failed to generate meaningful impact.

In August, the Pentagon launched what it termed the 'replicator initiative', involving the fielding of thousands of autonomous systems across domains within 18 to 24 months. The project 'is meant to help us overcome the PRC's [People's Republic of China] biggest advantage, which is mass', Deputy Secretary of Defense Kathleen Hicks said.

Artificial intelligence (AI) is becoming another battleground. Washington has pursued efforts to curb China's use of AI technology to enhance its war-fighting potential by placing export limits on some of the advanced semiconductors used in high-intensity computing. The move is one of several examples where the Biden administration has embraced policy tools of the Trump era, which also viewed technology as a front in the arms race with Beijing. The Pentagon's autonomous-weapons report released in January establishes a working group to monitor key developments in the field and intensified oversight in this domain. The guidance also tries to tackle concerns about any unintended consequences of applying the nascent technology in military operations.

To underpin the tech ambition, Congress approved a record USD140bn for research, development, testing and evaluation (RDT&E) in fiscal year 2023, with the procurement budget at almost USD170bn. The RDT&E budget has grown as systems that were in their early stage of development are now reaching advanced prototyping and field-testing phases, such as the B-21 *Raider* bomber, various hypersonic-glide-vehicle and hypersonic-cruise-missile systems and a next-generation, land-based intercontinental ballistic missile, dubbed LGM-35A *Sentinel*. The Pentagon is stepping up investments to counter very-high-speed mission technology and plans to build a missile-defence architecture using *Aegis Ashore* to safeguard Guam.

It continues efforts to bolster its forces with an ever-growing array of uninhabited combat systems. The army in June moved forward with two contracts for the Optionally Manned Fighting Vehicle programme, with teams led by General Dynamics Land Systems and American Rheinmetall Vehicles making the cut ahead of a final selection for the XM30 project around 2027. The air force is working on what it calls a Collaborative Combat Aircraft, an uninhabited platform to partner with its future fighter, the Next Generation Air Dominance (NGAD) system, to give the service more mass. The navy also is working on maritime versions of such systems.

Efforts to modernise the US nuclear-warhead arsenal are progressing, including through the deployment of the upgraded B61-12 nuclear bomb and the Pentagon's announcement in October that it would pursue the B61-13, a new, higher-yield bomb than the -12. The stockpile will remain the same, the DoD said, with B61-13 production offset by making fewer -12s. The US is advancing several other updated warhead designs for new delivery vehicles and is working on the W93, in effect a new warhead for *Ohio*- and *Columbia*-class nuclear-powered ballistic-missile submarines. It is also taking steps to modernise its nuclear-weapons production infrastructure.

The projects are part of the Biden administration's effort to balance strengthening deterrence, as the US prepares to face two major nuclear-power rivals, with trying to reduce the role of nuclear weapons in overall defence policy. The 2022 National Security Strategy delineated the dual ambition, stating that 'by the 2030s, the United States for the first time will need to deter two major nuclear powers, each of whom will field modern and diverse global and regional nuclear forces', while later adding 'we remain equally committed to reducing the risks of nuclear war'.

Some of the fiercest political battles that have embroiled the US military in recent months have played out more at home than abroad. The DoD increasingly has been pulled into domestic political skirmishes. While such issues are not new, the scale of such political fighting appears to be increasing and now ranges from environmental to abortion to recruitment-related policies. The tension slowed progress on defence budgeting and the appointment of some of the senior leaders of the armed forces. The US military also has been caught up in fighting over the US debt ceiling, with a budget agreement limiting spending growth in the coming years.

The Pentagon, at the same time, has been has been confronting a recruitment crisis in some areas. The army, navy and air force all warned they would likely miss recruitment targets in 2023, though the marine corps indicated it would meet its goal. The military faces a variety of headwinds in getting personnel in the door, including the effects of 20 years of fighting in Afghanistan and Iraq, a shrinking pool of viable recruits because of public-health problems, and problems in military housing and healthcare, among many factors.

US Army

The US Army is in rethinking mode, in part to ensure it captures lessons from Russia's war in Ukraine and to better position the service for a potential conflict in the Indo-Pacific. In 2023, the army initiated the development of a new artillery strategy (officially termed a conventional-fires strategy), has been reconsidering its divisional structures and has revised its recruitment approach.

The service is also trying to deliver on earlier commitments, particularly to be able to engage targets at range – a mission set validated by the Ukraine war. The army pronounced fiscal year (FY) 2023 to be a 'year of long-range precision fires', earmarking four key development programmes to reach early operational capability (EOC) or initial fielding by the end of September 2023. However, at least two of these programmes appear to have fallen behind schedule.

Delivery delays for the first prototype battalion set of the XM1299 Extended Range Cannon Artillery (ERCA) 155mm howitzer system emerged early in 2023, due to challenges uncovered in the operational evaluation process. The anticipated operational test period for ERCA now appears to be planned to begin sometime later in FY24. Fielding of the *Dark Eagle* Long-Range Hypersonic Weapon (LRHW) to its first battery also slipped into FY24 after an initial test launch of the system's missile was delayed for a third successive time in early September 2023. The army subsequently revised the planned EOC date to the end of 2023, but a further test launch in late October was also cancelled. In contrast, initial test launches of the *Typhon* Mid-Range Capability (MRC) system, capable of firing SM-6 and RGM/UGM-109E *Tomahawk* missiles, took place successfully in 2023 and the system reached the equivalent of EOC status on 29 September 2023. Lockheed Martin was also due to deliver the first Precision Strike Missile (PrSM) Increment 1 short-range ballistic missiles to units for EOC by the end of September 2023. Deliveries slipped to year-end, with an initial operational capability (IOC) due in fiscal year 2025.

The fighting in Ukraine is also shaping US Army armoured-fighting-vehicle developments. The planned M1A2 SEPv4 *Abrams* tank upgrade was cancelled in favour of a more ambitious programme, designated M1E3. Modifications to the M1 design have led to significant weight gain over the years, so the revised M1E3 will aim at reduced weight and logistical requirements. The M1E3 is expected to reach IOC in the 2030s. In the interim, the army will continue upgrading older models to the current M1A2 SEPv3 standard.

The first Armored Brigade Combat Team to receive the Armored Multi-Purpose Vehicle (AMPV), intended to replace the venerable M113 in a variety of roles, completed deliveries and training on the type in July 2023. The army subsequently signed a full-rate production contract for the AMPV with BAE Systems. Deliveries are scheduled to commence in 2025, following the delivery of the last of the 450 low-rate production vehicles previously ordered.

Following a request for proposals, the army, in September 2023, selected four companies for the prototype phase of the Robotic Combat Vehicle – Light (RCV-L) uninhabited ground vehicle programme. The initial prototype vehicles from this contract are expected to be delivered in 2024, with a further prototype phase anticipated in 2025 ahead of a first production contract in 2027.

Two more army armoured-vehicle programmes received new names in 2023, with the Optionally Manned Fighting Vehicle (OMFV) programme officially redesignated as the XM30 Mechanized Infantry Combat Vehicle. The Mobile Protected Firepower (MPF) light tank became the M10 *Booker* Combat Vehicle. The service picked General Dynamics and Rheinmetall for the detailed design, prototype and testing phase of the XM30 programme.

In February 2023, the US Army Training and Doctrine Command published an updated version of its proposed divisional structure for 'Army 2030' (formerly known as Waypoint 2028). Formation compositions are largely unchanged, but the previous 'Heavy', 'Penetration' and 'Joint Forcible Entry' division designs have been adapted to 'Armored', 'Armored (Reinforced)' and 'Airborne', respectively, more closely aligning them with current names.

Successfully implementing the proposed new formational structures, however, will require the army to generate and sustain sufficient personnel end-strength. In 2023, the army is expected to miss its recruitment target for new personnel for the second year in a row. Although it has continued to meet its retention targets, even among the most stressed parts of the force, end-strength has now been reduced, and officials have raised the prospect of possible force-structure reductions if this trend is not reversed. In October, the army said it would recruit more widely along with other changes in its personnel approach to address shortages, while noting it would meet end-strength goals for its active-duty force.

The service also continues to grapple with changes in its equipment plans. After about a year of delay, the initial launcher prototypes for the Indirect

Table 2 — United States Army: Future Vertical Lift (FVL)

The US Army has been working on a wide-ranging aviation modernisation plan to replace ageing helicopters and uninhabited aerial vehicles (UAVs). The FVL programme began in 2009 and was later augmented by the Joint Multi-Role Technology Demonstrator (JMR-TD) effort to fund development of related prototypes and technologies.

The most advanced FVL effort is the Future Long Range Assault Aircraft (FLRAA) programme that seeks to replace a portion of the UH-60 *Black Hawk* transport helicopter fleet. FLRAA follows the US Department of Defense Middle Tier of Acquisition (MTA) procurement pathway that allows for rapid prototyping before becoming a Major Capability Acquisition (MCA). The army in December 2022 picked Bell's V-280 *Valor* tiltrotor, with a physical prototype expected in 2025. The *Valor*'s tiltrotor design promises better speed, range and agility than the *Black Hawk*. However, the aircraft is also much heavier and has a wider fuselage, which could make deployments more challenging.

The FVL's Future Attack Reconnaissance Aircraft (FARA) began in 2018 to replace the now-retired OH-58 *Kiowa* reconnaissance helicopter and a portion of the AH-64 *Apache* fleet that took over the *Kiowa*'s role. This is the fourth attempt to replace that aircraft, dating back to the Light Helicopter Family (LHX) programme initiated in 1982. Each effort was cancelled because of cost overruns and delays. The army selected Bell's 360 *Invictus* and Sikorsky's *Raider* X designs in 2020, with prototypes due to fly in 2024. Each aircraft will be powered by the army's new T901 Improved Turbine Engine Program turboshaft engine.

The Future Tactical Uncrewed Aircraft System (FTUAS) is intended to replace the RQ-7B *Shadow* intelligence, surveillance and reconnaissance UAV. FTUAS, which is also using the MTA contracting route, will be a vertical take-off and landing UAV allowing runway-independent operations. The army picked Griffon Aerospace and Textron designs in September 2023, with a final system selection due in 2025 ahead of the first unit being equipped in 2026.

Classification	Replacing	Acquisition pathway	Status	Quantity to be acquired	Estimated acquisition cost (USD billions)	Potential contractors	First unit equipped
Programme: FARA							
Attack helicopter	OH-58 *Kiowa*; some AH-64 *Apache*	MCA	Technology Maturation and Risk Reduction phase	300–400	15–20	🇺🇸 Bell 🇺🇸 Sikorsky	By 2030
Notes: Bell and Sikorsky downselected March 2020							
Programme: FLRAA							
Tiltrotor transport	UH-60 *Black Hawk*	MTA	Virtual prototype to be developed before transitioning to MCA pathway	600	25+	🇺🇸 Bell	2030
Notes: Bell V-280 *Valor* selected December 2022; preliminary design review completed Q1 2023; physical prototype expected 2025							
Programme: FTUAS							
Medium ISR UAV	RQ-7B *Shadow*	MTA	Three-year early prototyping	76 'systems'	n.k.	🇺🇸 Griffon Aerospace 🇺🇸 Textron	2026
Notes: Griffon Aerospace and Textron downselected late 2023							

Fires Protection Capability (IFPC) Increment 2 missile-defence system were in production in late 2023. The initial M-SHORAD Increment 2/DE M-SHORAD directed-energy air-defence systems made it to the Yuma proving ground for testing in early 2023, several months later than originally anticipated. The army reportedly shifted planned funding in the FY24 President's Budget request elsewhere since the directed-energy systems were judged to be 'not quite ready'. Still, user assessment work is now likely to go ahead in FY24.

The army also held fire on the competitive-demonstration phase of the Future Attack Reconnaissance Aircraft helicopter programme to replace the OH-58 *Kiowa*. It was delayed by issues with the engine intended for use in both prototypes and is now not expected to take place before mid-2024.

US Navy

The US Navy continues to struggle with juggling its current and planned fleet make-up in the face of operational demands, budgetary and shipbuilding capacity constraints, and political differences about the path forward. In 2016, the navy set an ambition to deliver a battle force of 355 ships. Efforts to update (and raise) this target, reflecting global demands and the aim of producing a more distributed fleet with increased integration of uninhabited platforms, have failed to settle on an agreed and credible plan. The navy's fleet size in late 2023 stood at just under 300 ships by its count.

In May, the first *Ford*-class aircraft carrier, USS *Gerald R. Ford*, which will replace the *Nimitz* class, introduces an electric- rather than steam-powered aircraft launching system. The ship's operational debut took place in European waters as part of the US Navy's revived effort at carrier presence there, initiated in December 2021 in response to growing tensions with Russia and the subsequent conflict in Ukraine. There was a brief gap in presence between the *Ford*'s arrival and the departure of the USS *George H.W. Bush*, signalling how stretched the navy has become. Later in the year, the Pentagon sent the *Ford* to the Eastern Mediterranean after Hamas's attack on Israel.

A drumbeat of commitments throughout the year added to the strain on the operational fleet. Tensions with Iran in and around the Gulf saw the deployment of US naval and other reinforcements in the region, including an Amphibious Ready Group led by the large-deck amphibious assault ship USS *Bataan*. The navy and the US Coast Guard maintained a tempo of transits of the Taiwan Strait amid tensions there, including a reported close encounter with a Chinese destroyer in June. Other activities in the Pacific included ballistic-missile-defence exercises with Japan and South Korea in light of concerns over North Korean missile and nuclear-related developments.

During August, the navy undertook its second multi-theatre large-scale exercise to demonstrate its ability to operate in a synchronised way around the globe. The navy also appeared to be undertaking more overt deployments of *Ohio*-class guided-missile (SSGN) and ballistic-missile submarines (SSBNs) in the Middle East and the Pacific in an apparent attempt to shore up its deterrent posture.

Nevertheless, the operational pace hampered the service's efforts to rebuild overall fleet readiness. Submarine operational availability emerged as a particular concern due to maintenance delays and the capacity of the support infrastructures, with the navy announcing investments to fix the situation. The US has been making *Virginia*-class attack submarines well below the target pace of two per year. The US is making investments in its industrial base to boost output. However, Washington's commitment under the AUKUS programme to provide Australia with *Virginia*-class submarines could hamper efforts to meet domestic demand even though Canberra has pledged to invest in the US submarine-building infrastructure. Another concern is possible delays with the new *Columbia*-class SSBN, long described as the navy's top-priority programme.

Despite ongoing wrangling with Congress, the navy continued decommissioning the elderly *Ticonderoga*-class cruisers to free up funds for newer capabilities. But the cruisers' departure is denting the navy's overall capacity in vertical launch systems that will not be made up quickly. Their role as task group air warfare command ships will eventually pass to the new Flight III *Arleigh Burke*-class destroyers. The navy commissioned the first of these in October, but it will likely not become fully operational for some time. The Littoral Combat Ship programme also saw both arrivals and departures of vessels, some being decommissioned after just a few years of service.

The navy's plans to integrate uninhabited surface vessels (USVs) into its fleet inched forward with further test deployments into the Pacific. These included forward-deploying a number of prototype USVs to Japan for the first time. The navy is also gearing up for the arrival of hypersonic glide vehicle weapons, with the USS *Zumwalt* cruiser taken to a shipyard in August for upgrades to accommodate the high-speed strike system.

Naval aviation is also working on its next-generation equipment with the F/A-XX future fighter or air-combat platform. The navy hopes to begin buying the systems in the late 2020s for service in the 2030s. Boeing, Lockheed Martin, Northrop Grumman, GE and RTX's Pratt & Whitney are competing for key elements of the project. However, IOC for another key element of the navy's future aviation vision, the MQ-25A *Stingray* UAV, has been delayed a year to 2026. *Stingray* is part of the navy's effort to extend the reach, survivability and lethality of its embarked carrier air wings in the face of the increasing challenge posed by Chinese anti-carrier systems.

The US Marine Corps (USMC) continued its controversial transformation plan, Force Design 2030. It aims to deliver a force more capable of operating in a contested maritime space, including island-hopping, with a particular focus on China and the Pacific. The first of the new Marine Littoral Regiments undertook its initial operational exercises in 2023. The service's first MQ-9A *Reaper* squadron also became operational and, to augment its long-range fires capability, the USMC activated its first of three ground-launched *Tomahawk* cruise-missile batteries. The marines and the navy continued to spar over amphibious-shipping requirements, with the USMC identifying a requirement for at least 31 large amphibious vessels and additional medium-sized ships of a new design. The navy meanwhile decided on a 'strategic pause' in procurement while it assessed priorities and options.

For the US Coast Guard, with an increased focus on Arctic security, a major priority is its requirement for new heavy icebreakers. While steel was cut on the first of these Polar Security Cutters, delivery of the first completed ship was put back to 2028. The coast guard aimed to increase its presence in the Western Pacific, but some vessels were deactivated because of personnel shortages.

Air Force

Irrespective of Russia's invasion of Ukraine, the US Air Force (USAF) continues to focus its modernisation on China. The service, in September 2023, launched its latest effort to move on from two decades of counter-insurgency operations in a permissive air environment to preparing for war in contested battlespace.

Air Force Secretary Frank Kendall, in announcing the review in a September 2023 memo, said the service is 'not optimized for great power competition'. Kendall asked for the air force's commands and organisations to provide their input by January 2024. A central aim of the review is to identify ways to accelerate acquisition to counter China. The effort follows the 2020 'Accelerate, Change or Lose' paper published by Gen. Charles Q. Brown when he served as USAF chief of staff.

Recapitalisation is only one of the USAF's challenges. In 2023, the service remained below target strength for pilots by just under 10%. For some time, the USAF has been unable to meet its need for 21,000 pilots, made up of 13,000 in the active force and the remainder in the Air Force Reserve or Air National Guard. The shortfall has largely been caused by problems with pilot training and competition for talent from the airline sector. Low availability rates of the ageing Northrop T-38 *Talon* jet trainer have been part of the problem, while the intended replacement, the Boeing T-7A *Red Hawk*, is around three years behind the original schedule. Kendall has made training part of his review.

Availability rates also continue to hamper the Lockheed Martin F-35 *Lighting* II because of maintenance and logistics problems. The USAF had considered an F-35A engine upgrade to provide more power and range, but the plan has been shelved. Rather than pursue the Adaptive Engine Transition Programme (AETP) for the F-35, the service is embarking on an upgrade to the fighter's RTX F135 power plant. The AETP work will instead support the development of the Next-Generation Adaptive Propulsion programme to provide an engine for future combat aircraft.

The air force's aircraft and weapons acquisition programmes are largely aimed at responding to China's emergence as a credible first-tier air power and Beijing's increasing assertiveness. The Next-Generation Air Dominance (NGAD) system will be central to the service's tactical combat capability from the 2030s, when it should start replacing the Lockheed Martin F-22 *Raptor*. The USAF plans to augment the crewed element of NGAD with a fleet of high-end UAVs, referred to as Collaborative Combat Aircraft (CCA). The service is expected to try and replace the F-22 with the costly, sixth-generation crewed NGAD on a near one-for-one basis. The CCA purchase would be far larger and give the USAF the combat mass it struggled to secure with past equipment programmes.

NGAD has been a highly classified programme that, at the outset of 2023, had three likely potential competitors. The air force issued a request for proposals (RFP) in May 2023; Northrop Grumman in July said it would not compete. Boeing and Lockheed Martin have released concept illustrations of notional next-generation multi-role fighters, and both have almost certainly been working on classified research and technology efforts to support any NGAD bid. One NGAD demonstrator was in flight testing by 2020, according to Will Roper, then the assistant secretary of the Air Force for acquisition, technology and logistics. A winner for the crewed NGAD could emerge in 2024.

The USAF intends to introduce a CCA in advance of the crewed NGAD to operate in support of the F-35A as well as fourth-generation combat aircraft. The service had not issued a CCA RFP by the end of September 2023, though multiple bidders are near-certain to respond once it is released.

Air force efforts to retire 33 F-22 Block 20 aircraft remained in limbo during 2023, with some lawmakers blocking the move. The service uses the Block 20 aircraft only for training and has argued bringing them up to an operationally more relevant Block 35 standard is prohibitively expensive. The retirement of the Fairchild A-10 *Warthog*, which lawmakers previously rejected, began in 2023, with 20 aircraft due to be withdrawn.

Northrop Grumman completed the first flight of the B-21 *Raider* in November. The B-21 will replace the Rockwell B-1B and the Northrop Grumman B-2, which are notionally due for retirement in the early 2030s. The timeline is contingent on progress with fielding and ramping up production of the new bomber in the late 2020s.

The service also is upgrading key elements of its support force. The USAF is planning to acquire additional tanker aircraft, has embarked on getting E-7 *Wedgetail* air surveillance aircraft from Boeing and is introducing the EA-37B *Compass Call* electronic-warfare aircraft into the inventory.

Though the USAF is focusing on China, Russia's invasion of Ukraine has prompted the service to bolster inventory numbers of key weapons after observing the high utilisation rates in the war, combined with the difficulties of rapidly increasing production. Production of the RTX AIM-120D3 Advanced Medium-Range Air-to-Air Missile is being increased over the next few years until the replacement Lockheed Martin AIM-260 missile enters service in adequate numbers. The US has said little about the design or the performance of the weapon.

The service also is pressing ahead with efforts to introduce air-launched Mach 5-plus weapons but shifted gears in 2023. After several test failures, the USAF decided not to proceed with the AGM-183A Air-Launched Rapid Response Weapon, which was intended for the B-52. Work on the Hypersonic Attack Cruise Missile and likely several classified efforts in the very high-speed weapons arena continued. The RTX AGM-181 Long-Range Stand-Off cruise missile is earmarked to replace the ageing Boeing AGM-86B Air Launched Cruise Missile. The nuclear-armed AGM-181 will enter service first on the Boeing B-52J towards the end of this decade and be integrated on the B-21.

DEFENCE ECONOMICS

In March, the Biden administration submitted its FY2024 budget request to Congress and asked for USD886.38 billion for defence-related activities. The record sum in nominal terms continued the trend of higher military spending. Perhaps more importantly, the United States, with the FY24 request, continued the process of aligning its financial focus with the 2022 National Defense Strategy (NDS), which emphasised countering an increasingly assertive China, which Washington regards as its 'pacing challenge'. Although the US regards many others as competitor states, Washington is adjusting its spending power to focus on responding to Beijing's ambition and military modernisation.

The FY24 request included USD842bn for the Department of Defense's (DoD) discretionary base budget and USD44.37bn for non-DoD defence spending, made up of USD32.85bn for the Department of Energy's National Nuclear Security Administration and USD11.52bn for other defence-related activities. NDS priorities shaped the FY24 budget throughout, and key areas in the FY24 budget included funding for munitions and long-range strike; research, development, testing and evaluation (RDT&E); space capabilities; modernisation of the nuclear triad; and personnel. US concerns about China are perhaps most clearly demonstrated in the USD9.1bn funding for the

Figure 3 US defence budget as % of GDP[1]

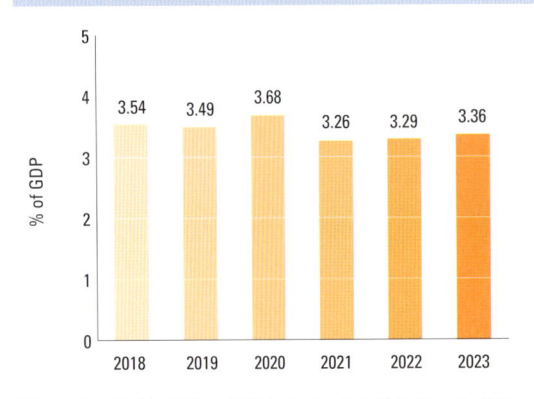

Year	% of GDP
2018	3.54
2019	3.49
2020	3.68
2021	3.26
2022	3.29
2023	3.36

[1] Figures refer to the National Defense (050) Budget Function (Budget Authority) as a % of GDP
Note: GDP data from IMF World Economic Outlook, October 2023

key aspects of America's war-fighting capability. Overall, the FY24 budget request allocates nearly USD30bn for air and missile defence in the Indo-Pacific and elsewhere.

Congressional concern and constraints

The budget contained significant trade-offs. Despite the record top line, some within Congress called the 3.3% nominal increase of USD26bn insufficient to meet the range of threats facing US national security, especially the layered challenges posed by China. Factoring in an assumed inflation rate of 2.4%, the real increase in spending is 0.8%. Given the likelihood that inflation will exceed 2.4%, it is possible that the nominally growing FY24 budget will deliver a year-on-year decline in purchasing power compared to FY23's enacted budget. However, year-on-year comparisons are complicated by the use of emergency supplemental funding to supply Ukraine, worth USD35bn. Including supplementals, actual FY23 total discretionary spending on defence was over USD890bn, topping the president's FY24 request of USD886bn for defence spending.

What's more, the annual budget process in Washington became more difficult with some Republicans in Congress raising concerns about the government's deficit. In past years, Congress had leeway to add tens of billions of dollars to the base budget. For example, in FY23 Congress added nearly USD40bn to the administration's request of USD776bn to address lawmakers' defence-spending priorities. However, Congress also enacted spending limits on the government via the June 2023 Fiscal Responsibility Act, as part of a deal to raise the country's debt ceiling. The Act caps overall spending on defence in FY24 at the president's requested level of USD886bn and prescribes a 1% increase to total defence spending for FY25. It also contains a provision that could take defence spending down to 99% of the FY23 enacted budget, should any of the 12 budget bills that fund the US government not be passed by 1 January 2024. Funding can be restored to agreed FY24 levels once all bills are signed into law. This provision could serve as motivation for Congress to pass these 12 bills – including the National Defense Authorization Act (NDAA) – quickly and, as a result, avoid DoD operating under another damaging continuing resolution that reduces the Pentagon's spending flexibility.

Although Congress can still alter how the FY24 budget is allocated, members seeking to increase defence spending will have to rely on emergency supplemental funding to do so, setting up a likely showdown between budget and defence hawks. Senators from both parties have raised the possibility of using emergency supplementals to get around caps on the base budget. The Senate version of the NDAA asks the Biden administration to initiate an emergency request to augment the capped base budget. Emergency funding for Ukraine is also likely as the FY24 request only includes USD300 million of aid to Kyiv. The question is whether those bills

Table 3 The US DoD budget request by appropriation title, USDm

Requests/Enacted budget by Appropriation Title (USDm)	2023 DoD Requested	2023 Base Enacted	2024 DoD Base Requested	Change between FY2023 Enacted and FY24 Requested
Military Personnel	173,883	172,231	178,874	+6,643
Operations and Maintenance	309,343	319,907	329,749	+9,842
Procurement	145,939	163,736	170,049	+6,313
Research, Development, Testing, and Evaluation	130,097	139,400	144,980	+5,580
Military Construction	10,198	16,673	14,734	-1,939
Family Housing	1,956	2,327	1,941	-386
Revolving Management and Trust Funds	1,583	1,718	1,683	-35
Totals	773,009	815,982	842,000	+26,018

Source: Defense Comptroller, Defense Budget Overview Book FY23 and FY24, Appendix A.

will be packed with other items normally included in the base budget, similar to how the now defunct Overseas Contingency Operations fund was used to navigate around the Budget Control Act in the 2010s.

Munitions

Reflecting the 2022 NDS and global concerns about ammunition sourcing, the FY24 budget boosts production of munitions and long-range strike capabilities. The high rate of munitions expenditure in the Ukraine war, combined with eroded US production capacity, raised concern within the DoD that industry would not be able to quickly reconstitute stocks in the case of a prolonged conflict, especially with China. The FY24 budget allots USD30.6bn for munitions across the services to start fixing the situation, a 12% increase above the FY23 enacted budget. This includes USD11bn for various hypersonic glide vehicles and hypersonic cruise missiles. Crucially, the president requested multi-year procurement authorities for five missile systems that Deputy Secretary of Defense Kathleen Hicks described as 'the most relevant for deterring and, if necessary, prevailing over aggression in the Indo-Pacific'. These include Naval Strike Missile, RIM-174 Standard Extended Range Active Missile (ERAM), Advanced Medium-Range Air-to-Air Missile (AMRAAM), Joint Air-to-Surface Stand-Off Missile-Extended Range (JASSM-ER), and Long-Range Air-to-Surface Missile (LRASM) purchases. The multi-year procurement authority should provide demand stability for suppliers and give companies confidence to invest in additional capacity.

Investment and Divestment

The FY24 budget request includes record amounts for investment accounts, with USD170bn earmarked for procurement and an additional USD145bn for RDT&E. The high procurement budget reflects efforts to modernise all aspects of the nuclear triad to reinforce US deterrence efforts. The LGM-35A *Sentinel* intercontinental ballistic-missile system, the B-21 *Raider* and the long-range stand-off missile are all fully funded in the air force budget. The navy budget includes a commitment to procure one *Columbia*-class ballistic-missile submarine to be delivered in FY28.

The RDT&E budget request is USD5.3bn above FY23 enacted levels and contains USD19.2bn for the space force, a 16% increase from the prior year. This record spending on RDT&E is a positive trend for armed services that are looking to accelerate the development of next-generation capabilities. However, funding these capabilities has created a trade-off in which some observers fear future capabilities are being prioritised over sustaining existing force structures.

Both the navy and air force budget requests rest on 'divest to invest' strategies to save money today that can be invested in creating 'the force of the future'. The air force budget calls for the retiring of 310 aircraft in FY24 – while procuring 95 – to pay for the B-21 *Raider*, Next Generation Air Dominance (NGAD) fighter, Uncrewed Collaborative Combat Aircraft loyal wingman programme and a future tanker programme. The air force's proposed RDT&E budget (USD36.2bn) exceeded its procurement budget (USD35.4bn). The navy request adds nine ships to the fleet but retires 11 ships early to fund its own future air combat programme, known as F/A-XX, as well as other crewed- and uncrewed-system development programmes, leaving fleet-size projections below 300 ships well into the 2030s.

Military Departments

The budget request contained increases for both the navy and air force. The army budget is nominally flat, reflecting a trend of stagnation throughout the 2020s as the force transitions from a focus on Middle East contingencies to supporting Indo-Pacific deterrence.

US Army

The army's requested budget of USD185.5bn is only USD600m more than the FY22 actual budget of USD184.9bn, and USD600m less than FY20's budget of USD186.1bn. Army procurement funding was down to USD23.4bn from USD23.6bn, though the service did not terminate any programmes. Within the procurement budget, the army prioritised investment in long-range fires, air defence and deep sensing as well as training and experimentation with partners.

Table 4 **The US DoD total budget request by military service, USDm**

Service	FY2023 bn (enacted)	FY2024 bn (requested)	Nominal Change bn
Department of the Army	185.2	185.5	+0.3
Department of the Navy	244.8	255.8	+11.0
Department of the Air Force	205.8	215.1	+9.3
	Air Force:	185.1	5.4
	Space Force:	30.0	3.9

Source: Department of the Army, Navy and Air Force Budget Reviews.

Recruitment, retention and readiness also feature prominently in army budget documents as the service copes with recruiting shortfalls. The army's force structure stays at 452,000 active-duty personnel, with a total army size of 951,800, including the national guard and reserve. This figure is below the 980,000 minimum level contained in the 2016 National Commission on the Future of the Army. In response, the service stressed a need to 'transform the way we recruit, train, educate, and prepare America's sons and daughters for an increasingly complex battlefield' and describes plans and programmes to incentivise recruiting efforts and increases in enlistment and recruiting bonuses.

Recruitment and retention issues have been recognised across all parts of the US military, and the FY24 budget also includes a 5.2% increase in pay for service members, though this is a statutory measure to keep their pay increases in line with those in the private sector. The budget also includes USD1.9bn to support family housing and additional funds for reduced childcare and food costs, suicide prevention and implementing recommendations for reducing sexual assault. Each of the services' budget narratives includes references to programmes to improve recruitment, retention and training to ensure the readiness of the force.

US Navy

The Department of the Navy's total request was USD255.8bn, a USD11bn or 4.5% increase from FY23. As part of its USD76.8bn procurement budget, the navy will procure, in addition to the *Columbia*-class nuclear-powered ballistic-missile submarine, two *Virginia*-class nuclear-powered submarines, two *Arleigh Burke*-class destroyers, two *Constellation*-class frigates, one submarine tender and one *John Lewis*-class fleet replenishment ship in FY24. The budget request fully funds private and public shipyards with a focus on 'increasing capacity and retaining highly skilled labour at our public shipyards'. A lack of resilient shipbuilding capacity and requirements for domestic warship production have hamstrung the DoD's ability to make progress on navy fleet-size projections and detracted from the United States' ability to project power in theatres such as the Indo-Pacific. These challenges are amplified by the AUKUS partnership through which the United States and United Kingdom commit to help Australia introduce nuclear-powered submarines.

The navy budget also calls for the procurement of 88 aircraft including 19 F-35Cs, 26 T-54 trainers and two KC-130Js, and 15 CH-53K helicopters. The aircraft procurement also covers two MQ-4C high-altitude long-endurance uninhabited aerial vehicles (UAVs) and three MQ-25 tanker UAVs. The USD26.9bn RDT&E budget represents a USD0.9bn (3.4%) increase over FY23 and will fund development of not just a new fighter for the navy, but also a future attack submarine SSN(X), next-generation destroyer DDG(X), the Large Uncrewed Surface Vehicle (LUSV) and Extra-Large Uncrewed Underwater Vehicle (XLUUV). The budget also provides about USD200m to buy Naval Strike Missiles, Tactical *Tomahawk* cruise missiles and the final five of 18 MQ-9s UAVs, as well as to accelerate the marines' Force Design 2030 restructure and purchases of 16 F-35Bs for the marines.

US Air Force and US Space Force

The Department of the Air Force total request was USD259.4bn, though USD44.4bn of this top line is 'pass through' funding which, after being issued, is then transferred directly to other relevant bodies. The remaining USD215.1bn is a USD9.3bn and 4.5% increase over the FY23 enacted position. The air force request of USD185.1bn represented a USD5.4bn increase over the FY23 enacted budget, while the space force request of USD30bn was the force's highest budget yet, representing a USD3.9bn or 15% year-on-year increase.

Aircraft procurement funding for FY24 declined by USD1.4bn from FY23. Still, the budget called for the purchase of 95 aircraft, including 72 combat aircraft (48 F-35s, 24 F-15EXs). Missile procurement jumped from USD3.0bn to USD7.2bn as the service prioritised the production of JASSM-ER, AMRAAM and LRASM missiles. The space force's record budget – including a 16% increase in RDT&E funding – and end strength to 9,400 personnel (up from around 8,600) reflect the growing importance of space to current and future DoD operations. The service's main procurement priority was to increase the number of annual launches to 15 from ten. The FY24 missions cover ten for the National Security Space Launch programme, placing spacecraft in geostationary and medium orbit, and five launches for the Space Development Agency's Low Earth Orbit constellation. Key RDT&E programmes include resilient missile warning and missile tracking, space-technology development and prototyping, and next-generation overhead persistent infrared satellites.

Table 5 **US National Defense Budget Function and other selected budgets, 2000, 2010–24,** USD in billions, current-year dollars

FY	National Defense Budget Function BA	National Defense Budget Function Outlay	Atomic Energy Defense Activities BA	Other Defense Activities BA	Total National Defense BA	Total National Defense BA**	Total National Defense Outlay	Department of Homeland Security BA	Department of Veterans' Affairs BA	Total Federal Government Outlays	Total Federal Budget Surplus/Deficit
2000	290.3	281.0	12.4	1.3	304.0	300.8	294.4	13.8	45.5	1,789.0	236.2
2010	695.6	666.7	18.2	7.3	721.2	714.1	693.5	45.4	124.3	3,457.1	-1,294.4
2011	691.5	678.1	18.5	7.0	717.0	710.1	705.6	41.6	122.8	3,603.1	-1,299.6
2012	655.4	650.9	18.3	7.7	681.4	669.6	677.9	45.9	124.0	3,526.6	-1,076.6
2013	585.2	607.8	17.5	7.4	610.2	600.4	633.4	61.9	136.0	3,454.9	-679.8
2014	595.7	577.9	18.4	8.2	622.3	606.2	603.5	44.1	165.7	3,506.3	-484.8
2015	570.8	562.5	19.0	8.5	598.4	585.9	589.7	45.3	160.5	3,691.9	-442.0
2016	595.7	565.4	20.1	8.3	624.1	606.8	593.4	46.0	163.3	3,852.6	-584.7
2017	626.2	568.9	21.4	8.7	656.3	634.1	598.7	62.3	178.8	3,981.6	-665.4
2018	694.5	600.7	23.3	9.0	726.8	700.9	631.2	103.0	191.8	4,109.0	-779.1
2019	712.6	654.0	24.0	9.1	745.7	718.8	686.0	61.4	194.2	4,447.0	-983.6
2020	738.8	690.4	26.0	9.7	774.5	756.6	724.6	114.2	233.3	6,553.6	-3,132.4
2021	719.5	717.6	29.4	10.8	759.6	741.7	753.9	123.2	255.4	6,822.5	-2,775.4
2022	795.7	726.6	32.0	11.1	838.8	816.3	765.8	78.0	269.5	6,273.3	-1,375.9
2023*	860.2	771.3	33.7	11.6	905.5	891.4	814.8	85.6	303.2	6,371.8	-1,569.3
2024*	863.5	863.0	35.1	12.1	910.8	886.4	909.4	86.4	320.2	6,882.7	-1,846.4

Notes
FY = Fiscal Year (1 October–30 September)
* (request) ** Discretionary
[1] The National Defense Budget Function subsumes funding for the DoD, the Department of Energy Atomic Energy Defense Activities and some smaller support agencies (including Federal Emergency Management and Selective Service System). It does not include funding for International Security Assistance (under International Affairs), the Veterans Administration, the US Coast Guard (Department of Homeland Security), nor for the National Aeronautics and Space Administration (NASA). Funding for civil projects administered by the DoD is excluded from the figures cited here.
[2] Early in each calendar year, the US government presents its defence budget to Congress for the next fiscal year, which begins on 1 October. Until approved by Congress, the budget is called the Budget Request; after approval, it becomes the Budget Authority (BA).

CANADA

The debate surrounding Canada's defence spending has intensified because of the war in Ukraine. Ottawa is facing increasing criticism for its lowly standing within NATO in terms of defence spending as a proportion of national income. It allocated around 1.38% of GDP to defence in 2023, according to Alliance figures. Prime Minister Justin Trudeau has even reportedly conceded to NATO officials that Canada would never reach the Alliance's 2% target.

However, Canadian officials stress that the country stands seventh in NATO rankings of defence spending in absolute terms, with some modest increases in outlays planned over the coming years and a significant investment in equipment. Canada has also announced that, by 2026, it will more than double the size of its lead component of the NATO Enhanced Presence Battlegroup in Latvia to a brigade strength of up to 2,200 'persistently deployed' personnel.

Through October 2023, Canada had committed more than CAD2.4 billion (USD1.8bn) in military support to Ukraine. It included eight *Leopard* 2A4 main battle tanks and other armoured vehicles, anti-tank weapons, M777 howitzers, air-defence equipment and more. Ottawa has committed to maintain its *Operation Unifier* training and capacity-building for Ukraine until March 2026, with activities chiefly in the United Kingdom but also in Poland and Latvia.

The Canadian armed forces themselves, like multiple other NATO members, face significant challenges in terms of overstretch, a lack of critical mass in key areas, and readiness and recruitment problems. The forces are believed to be facing a shortage of several thousand trained personnel. Recruitment has been dogged by public concern

Table 6 🇨🇦 Royal Canadian Air Force: selected procurements since 2000

Twenty-four years after first joining the Joint Strike Fighter programme, the Royal Canadian Air Force (RCAF) announced in 2022 that it would buy the Lockheed Martin F-35A. The Future Fighter Capability Project contract Canada signed in January 2023 carries a CAD19 billion (USD13.98bn) total price and is the service's largest-ever procurement. Other competitors dropped out, citing onerous security requirements from Canada's involvement in the North American Aerospace Defense Command mission. Canada acquires most of its major air platforms from the US, with more diverse sources of supply in other domains. Not including the F-35A programme, the RCAF has signed USD14.38bn in aircraft acquisition and major upgrade contracts over the last two decades, more than half going to US companies (not counting Canadian subsidiaries of US firms). Delays and cost overruns have dogged several programmes, most notably the CH-148 *Cyclone* anti-submarine-warfare helicopter. In 2023, the RCAF signed a contract with Airbus for A330 MRTT (CC-330 *Husky*) tanker/transport planes after Boeing fell out of favour over a commercial-aircraft trade dispute. However, Canada subsequently selected Boeing's P-8A *Poseidon* to replace the P-3 *Orion* (CP-140M *Aurora*) maritime patrol aircraft fleet, though local champion Bombardier may still try to convince the RCAF to buy a design based on the *Global* 6500 business jet.

Contract Date	Equipment	Type	Quantity	Value	Contractor	Deliveries
Nov 2004	CH-148 *Cyclone*	ASW helicopter	28	CAD3.2bn (USD2.41bn)	Sikorsky	2011–ongoing
Feb 2007	C-17A (CC-177) *Globemaster* III	Heavy transport aircraft	5	CAD1.8bn (USD1.68bn)	Boeing	2007–08, 2015
Dec 2007	C-130J-30 (CC-130) *Hercules*	Medium transport aircraft	17	USD1.4bn	Lockheed Martin	2010–12
Aug 2009	CH-47F (CH-147F) *Chinook*	Heavy transport helicopter	15	USD1.5bn	Boeing	2013–14
Dec 2016	C295W (CC-295 *Kingfisher*)	Search-and-rescue aircraft	16	CAD2.4bn (USD1.82bn)	M Airbus	2019–24
Nov 2018	F/A-18A/B (CF-18AM/BM) *Hornet*	Fighter ground-attack aircraft	18	CAD339.3m (USD258.09m)	Australian government surplus; L3Harris MAS	2019–ongoing
May 2020	F/A-18A/B (CF-18AM/BM) *Hornet*	Fighter ground-attack aircraft upgrade	Up to 94	CAD1.3bn (USD969.32m)	Lockheed Martin; L3Harris MAS; Northrop Grumman; RTX	2023–26
Jun 2020	*Challenger* 650 (CC-144)	Passenger transport aircraft	2	CAD105m (USD79.87m)	Bombardier	2020
May 2022	Bell 412 (CH-146 *Griffon*)	Multi-role helicopter upgrade	85	CAD800m (USD614.65m)	Textron	2023–27
Jun 2022	A330-200	Passenger transport aircraft	2	USD102m	International Airfinance Corporation	2023
Dec 2022	AW101 *Merlin* (CH-149 *Cormorant*)	Search-and-rescue helicopter upgrade	13*	CAD1.17bn (USD897.39m)	Leonardo UK	From 2026
Jan 2023	F-35A *Lightning* II	Fighter ground-attack aircraft	88	CAD19bn (USD13.98bn)	Lockheed Martin	2026–35
Jul 2023	A330 MRTT (CC-330 *Husky*)	Tanker/transport aircraft	9	CAD3.6bn (USD2.65bn)	M Airbus	2027–30
TOTAL				**USD28.36bn**		
Pending	Remotely Piloted Aircraft System	Heavy CISR UAV	n.k.	CAD1–5bn (USD753.37m–3.77bn)	tbd	2025–30
Pending	P-8A *Poseidon*	ASW aircraft	Up to 16	CAD5bn+ (USD3.86bn+)	Boeing	2032–37

*Plus 3 additional helicopters

M = multinational

over military culture and allegations of sexual misconduct within its ranks, including at the highest level. The US Department of Defense has reportedly concluded that enduring defence shortfalls mean that Canada could not undertake a major military operation while simultaneously continuing to support its military commitment in Latvia and provide military aid to Ukraine.

Ottawa is trying to balance a deteriorating security outlook in three key regions of interest – the Euro-Atlantic, the Arctic and the High North, and the Indo-Pacific. The government, in April 2022, embarked on a defence-policy update which is due to report in 2024 at the earliest. In July 2023, the prime minister also announced the creation of a cabinet-level National Security Council.

Several policy documents underscore how Canada is trying to juggle regional interests. The government, in November 2022, issued a new Indo-Pacific strategy calling for greater focus in the region, including through naval presence. Royal Canadian Navy warships have participated in transits through the Taiwan Strait alongside US vessels. In May 2023, the navy unveiled an Arctic and Northern Strategic Framework with a target for enhanced presence, increased situational awareness and strengthened cooperation with domestic and international partners, including local communities and indigenous peoples. In part to support that policy, the navy took delivery in August 2023 of the fourth *Harry DeWolf*-class Arctic Offshore Patrol Ship. Steel-cutting for the first of two similar vessels for the Royal Canadian Coast Guard took place in August 2023.

Canadian modernisation efforts are significant, though many have been slow-going. After a tortuous process, Ottawa finalised the purchase of 88 Lockheed Martin F-35A *Lightning* II aircraft for CAD19bn (USD14bn), the first to be delivered in 2026, to replace its current ageing combat air fleet of CF-18 *Hornet*s. It has also committed to upgrade its North American Aerospace Defense Command capabilities, but that CAD38.6bn (USD29bn) programme stretches over 20 years. Canada, in July 2023, made a big investment in its deployment capacity, signing a contract for four Airbus A330 Multi-Role Tanker Transports in addition to the conversion of five used A330-200s.

The navy's programme for 15 Canadian Surface Combatants, designed to replace the entirety of its main surface fleet, remains dogged by controversy and concern over cost increases and potential delays. The plans to sustain and modernise its ageing and troublesome flotilla of *Victoria*-class conventionally powered attack submarines also remains a challenge. Efforts to replace them under the Patrol Submarine Project remain nebulous even though the requirement is quite urgent. Another much-delayed key programme is the navy's new *Protecteur*-class auxiliaries. The first was structurally completed in September 2023 and a ceremonial keel laying for the second vessel took place the following month. Delivery of the first ship is now planned for 2025, almost two decades after Ottawa initially embarked on an auxiliary replacement programme.

Land-force procurements have been similarly difficult. The service entry of the 66 Light Armoured Vehicle Reconnaissance Surveillance (LRSS) variant has faced delays because of delivery problems with its Reconnaissance Surveillance System. Questions also remain over other elements of the army's vehicle fleet, including readiness and modernisation and ultimate replacement of its *Leopard* 2 main battle tanks.

Significant procurement and delivery events – 2023

JANUARY

CANADA JOINS THE F-35 BUYER CLUB

Canada announced plans to buy 88 Lockheed Martin F-35A *Lightning* II fighters after years of controversy over how to replace the Royal Canadian Air Force (RCAF) fleet of F/A-18s (CF-18) *Hornets*. The government said it expects to spend about CAD19bn (USD13.98bn) on the project, including sustainment and some infrastructure costs. The RCAF plans to take delivery of the first four aircraft in 2026 and reach an initial operational capability for the single-engine fighter fleet around the end of this decade. Ottawa wants to phase out the CF-18 by late 2032. Canada joined the US-run Joint Strike Fighter cooperative development programme in 1998 but had held off on committing to F-35A purchases for several years as it considered its options, including the Boeing F/A-18E/F *Super Hornet*, Saab *Gripen* E and Dassault *Rafale*. Delays in deciding necessitated greater investment in the existing *Hornet* fleet, including acquisition of surplus Australian aircraft.

MARCH

DoD ESTABLISHES JOINT PRODUCTION ACCELERATOR CELL

US Department of Defense (DoD) acquisition chief Bill LaPlante directed the establishment of the Joint Production Accelerator Cell to generate a more resilient production capacity for key weapon systems and supplies. The effort is also designed to create surge capabilities for some systems such as 155mm ammunition. The Pentagon acted after the war in Ukraine highlighted shortfalls in Western industrial capacities to respond quickly to the demands of high-intensity combat. LaPlante suggested the accelerator cell is supposed to institutionalise process changes that the DoD implemented to ramp up production for Ukraine. In August, LaPlante said the US was also planning deals with partners for joint weapons development, production and sustainment.

MAY

USAF ASKS FOR BIDS FOR FUTURE FIGHTER

The US Air Force (USAF) issued a classified request for proposals for the Next Generation Air Dominance (NGAD) fighter programme intended to replace the F-22A *Raptor*. The service said it plans to award one contract in 2024 for the platform's engineering and manufacturing development phase. The USAF has been secretive about who is competing and other details of the project. Northrop Grumman in July said it would not pursue a prime-contractor role on NGAD, with Chief Executive Kathy Warden saying, 'We have other opportunities we are pursuing'. The air force has been coy about exactly how many fighters it wants to acquire, though Air Force Secretary Frank Kendall has suggested a buy of around 200 aircraft. Early development on the project dates to around 2015. The Pentagon has not disclosed a precise schedule for the programme, but the combat aircraft is expected to enter service in the 2030s.

JULY

ROCKET MOTOR M&A

Defence start-up Anduril Industries acquired solid rocket motor maker Adranos for an undisclosed amount, while L3Harris completed the acquisition of Aerojet Rocketdyne for around USD4.7bn in July. Demand for rocket motors has surged largely because of Russia's full-scale invasion of Ukraine. L3Harris's all-cash bid in December 2022 came after US regulators blocked Lockheed Martin's planned purchase of Aerojet on antitrust grounds. Anduril's deal came a few months after it raised USD1.48bn in a Series E funding round that, the company said, valued the business at about USD8.5bn.

AUGUST

BAE SYSTEMS MAKES BALL AEROSPACE BID

BAE Systems offered to buy Ball Aerospace for about USD5.55bn in cash to expand its space business. The deal is expected to close in 2024, when Ball Aerospace would become a stand-alone unit in the Electronic Systems segment of BAE Systems' US operations. BAE said it expects Ball Aerospace business to see about a 10% compound annual growth rate in sales. About 85% of Ball Aerospace's revenue comes from defence customers.

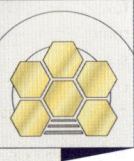

Canada CAN

Canadian Dollar CAD		2022	2023	2024
GDP	CAD	2.78trn	2.84trn	2.97trn
	USD	2.14trn	2.12trn	2.24trn
per capita	USD	55,037	53,247	55,528
Growth	%	3.4	1.3	1.6
Inflation	%	6.8	3.6	2.4
Def exp [a]	CAD	33.9bn	39.3bn	
	USD	26.0bn	29.0bn	
Def bdgt [b]	CAD	31.5bn	32.5bn	
	USD	24.2bn	24.2bn	
USD1= CAD		1.30	1.34	1.33

[a] NATO figure

[b] Department of National Defence and Veterans Affairs

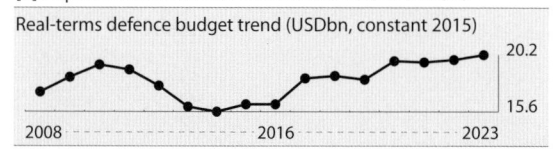

Real-terms defence budget trend (USDbn, constant 2015)

20.2 / 15.6 (2008 – 2016 – 2023)

Population 38,516,736

Age	0–14	15–19	20–24	25–29	30–64	65 plus
Male	8.0%	2.7%	2.8%	3.3%	23.3%	9.4%
Female	7.6%	2.6%	2.6%	3.0%	23.4%	11.1%

Capabilities

Canada's armed forces are focused principally on territorial defence, as well as contributing important capabilities to international missions, chiefly through NATO. The 2017 defence review reaffirmed commitments not only to NATO, but also to modernising capabilities, increasing regular and reserve forces, and enhancements in the areas of cyber power and intelligence. In April 2022, the government announced a boost in defence spending over five years as a result of Russia's invasion of Ukraine and a new policy review, whose outcome was still pending as of late 2023. Canada has faced increased criticism within NATO over its defence provision as a proportion of GDP. It has pledged to more than double its leadership contribution to a NATO battlegroup in Latvia, while also providing military support and training for Ukraine. In November 2022, the government issued a new Indo-Pacific strategy with increased focus and investment there, including naval presence. However, Canadian forces are stretched to maintain commitments in three key arenas – the Indo-Pacific, the Arctic and the Euro-Atlantic. Military procurement efforts continue to suffer delays. Ottawa is recapitalising various parts of it inventory, including with a deal for 88 F-35A *Lightning* II combat aircraft signed in 2023. The armed forces have suffered recruitment and retention problems. Canada maintains a well-developed range of mainly small and medium-sized defence firms. The strongest sector is in combat vehicles and components, though the government is using its latest naval procurements to establish a long-term national shipbuilding strategy.

ACTIVE 62,300 (Army 22,500 Navy 8,400 Air Force 12,100 Other 19,300) Gendarmerie & Paramilitary 5,800

RESERVE 31,600 (Army 24,000 Navy 4,100 Air 2,000 Other 1,500)

ORGANISATIONS BY SERVICE

Space
EQUIPMENT BY TYPE

SATELLITES • SPACE SURVEILLANCE 1 *Sapphire*

Army 22,500
FORCES BY ROLE

MANOEUVRE

Mechanised

1 (1st) mech bde gp (1 armd regt, 2 mech inf bn, 1 lt inf bn, 1 arty regt, 1 cbt engr regt, 1 log bn)

2 (2nd & 5th) mech bde gp (1 armd recce regt, 2 mech inf bn, 1 lt inf bn, 1 arty regt, 1 cbt engr regt, 1 log bn)

COMBAT SUPPORT

1 engr regt

3 MP pl

AIR DEFENCE

1 AD regt

EQUIPMENT BY TYPE

ARMOURED FIGHTING VEHICLES

MBT 74: 34 *Leopard* 2A4 (trg role); 20 *Leopard* 2A4M (upgraded); 20 *Leopard* 2A6M (52 *Leopard* 1C2 in store)

RECCE 125: 5 LAV 6.0 Reconnaissance; ε120 LAV-25 *Coyote*

IFV 550 LAV 6.0

APC 443

APC (T) 268: 235 M113; 33 M577 (CP)

APC (W) 175 LAV *Bison* (incl 10 EW, 32 amb, 32 repair, 64 recovery)

AUV 507: 7 *Cougar*; 500 TAPV

ENGINEERING & MAINTENANCE VEHICLES

AEV 23: 5 *Buffalo*; 18 *Wisent* 2

ARV 12 BPz-3 *Büffel*

ANTI-TANK/ANTI-INFRASTRUCTURE

MSL • MANPATS TOW-2

RCL 84mm *Carl Gustaf*

ARTILLERY 283

TOWED 163 105mm 126: 98 C3 (M101); 28 LG1 MkII; 155mm 33 M777

MOR 124: 81mm 100; SP 81mm 24 LAV *Bison*

UNINHABITED AERIAL VEHICLES

ISR • Light 5 RQ-21A *Blackjack*

Reserve Organisations 24,000

Canadian Rangers 5,000 Reservists
Provide a limited military presence in Canada's northern, coastal and isolated areas. Sovereignty, public-safety and surveillance roles

FORCES BY ROLE
MANOEUVRE
  Other
    5 (patrol) ranger gp (209 patrols)

Army Reserves 19,000 Reservists
Most units have only coy-sized establishments

FORCES BY ROLE
COMMAND
  10 bde gp HQ
MANOEUVRE
  Reconnaissance
    18 recce regt (sqn)
  Light
    51 inf regt (coy)
COMBAT SUPPORT
  16 fd arty regt (bty)
  3 indep fd arty bty
  10 cbt engr regt (coy)
  1 EW regt (sqn)
  4 int coy
  10 sigs regt (coy)
COMBAT SERVICE SUPPORT
  10 log bn (coy)
  3 MP coy

Royal Canadian Navy 8,400

EQUIPMENT BY TYPE
SUBMARINES 4
  SSK 4 *Victoria* (ex-UK *Upholder*) (of which 1 in long-term refit) with 6 single 533mm TT with Mk 48 HWT
PRINCIPAL SURFACE COMBATANTS • FRIGATES 12
  FFGHM 12 *Halifax* with 2 quad lnchr with RGM-84L *Harpoon* Block II AShM, 2 8-cell Mk 48 mod 0 VLS with RIM-162C ESSM SAM, 2 twin 324mm SVTT Mk 32 mod 9 ASTT with Mk 46 LWT, 1 Mk 15 *Phalanx* Block 1B CIWS, 1 57mm gun (capacity 1 CH-148 *Cyclone* hel)
PATROL AND COASTAL COMBATANTS 3
  PSOH 3 *Harry DeWolf* (capacity 1 CH-148 *Cyclone* hel)
MINE WARFARE • MINE COUNTERMEASURES 12
  MCO 12 *Kingston* (also used in patrol role)
LOGISTICS AND SUPPORT 10
  AORH 1 *Asterix* (*Resolve*) (capacity 2 CH-148 *Cyclone* hel)
  AX 9: **AXL** 8 *Orca*; **AXS** 1 *Oriole*
UNINHABITED MARITIME SYSTEMS
  UUV • DATA REMUS 100; *Seabotix*

Reserves 4,100 reservists
24 units tasked with crewing 10 of the 12 MCOs, harbour defence & naval control of shipping

Royal Canadian Air Force (RCAF) 12,100

FORCES BY ROLE
FIGHTER/GROUND ATTACK
  4 sqn with F/A-18A/B *Hornet* (CF-18AM/BM)
ANTI-SUBMARINE WARFARE
  2 sqn with CH-148 *Cyclone*
MARITIME PATROL
  2 sqn with P-3 *Orion* (CP-140M *Aurora*)
SEARCH & RESCUE/TRANSPORT
  3 sqn with AW101 *Merlin* (CH-149 *Cormorant*); C-130H/H-30 (CC-130) *Hercules*
  1 sqn with C295W (CC-295)
TANKER/TRANSPORT
  1 sqn with A310/A310 MRTT (CC-150/CC-150T); A330 (CC-330)
  1 sqn with KC-130H
TRANSPORT
  1 sqn with C-17A (CC-177) *Globemaster*
  1 sqn with CL-600 (CC-144B)
  1 sqn with C-130J-30 (CC-130) *Hercules*
  1 (utl) sqn with DHC-6 (CC-138) *Twin Otter*
TRAINING
  1 OCU sqn with F/A-18A/B *Hornet* (CF-18AM/BM)
  1 OCU sqn with C-130H/H-30/J (CC-130) *Hercules*
  1 OCU sqn with CH-148 *Cyclone*
  1 OCU sqn with Bell 412 (CH-146 *Griffon*)
  1 sqn with P-3 *Orion* (CP-140M *Aurora*)
TRANSPORT HELICOPTER
  5 sqn with Bell 412 (CH-146 *Griffon*)
  3 (cbt spt) sqn with Bell 412 (CH-146 *Griffon*)
  1 (Spec Ops) sqn with Bell 412 (CH-146 *Griffon* – OPCON Canadian Special Operations Command)
  1 sqn with CH-47F (CH-147F) *Chinook*

EQUIPMENT BY TYPE
AIRCRAFT 103 combat capable
  FGA 89 F/A-18A/B (CF-18AM/BM) *Hornet*
  ASW 14 P-3 *Orion* (CP-140M *Aurora*)
  SAR 5 C295W (CC-295)
  TKR/TPT 5: 2 A310 MRTT (CC-150T); 3 KC-130H
    TPT 43: **Heavy** 5 C-17A (CC-177) *Globemaster* III; **Medium** 26: 7 C-130H (CC-130) *Hercules*; 2 C-130H-30 (CC-130) *Hercules*; 17 C-130J-30 (CC-130) *Hercules*; **Light** 4 DHC-6 (CC-138) *Twin Otter*; **PAX** 8: 3 A310 (CC-150 *Polaris*); 1 A330 (CC-330) (VIP); 2 CL-600 (CC-144B/C); 2 CL-650 (CC-144D)
  TRG 4 DHC-8 (CT-142)
HELICOPTERS
  ASW up to 27 CH-148 *Cyclone*
  MRH 68 Bell 412 (CH-146 *Griffon*)

SAR 13 AW101 *Merlin* (CH-149 *Cormorant*)
TPT • **Heavy** 14 CH-47F (CH-147F) *Chinook*
RADAR 53
  AD RADAR • **NORTH WARNING SYSTEM** 47: 11 AN/FPS-117 (range 200nm); 36 AN/FPS-124 (range 80nm)
  STRATEGIC 6: 4 Coastal; 2 Transportable
AIR-LAUNCHED MISSILES
  AAM • **IR** AIM-9L *Sidewinder*
  ARH AIM-120C AMRAAM
BOMBS
  Laser-guided: GBU-10/-12/-16 *Paveway* II; GBU-24 *Paveway* III
  Laser & INS/GPS-guided GBU-49 *Enhanced Paveway* II
  INS/GPS-guided: GBU-31 JDAM; GBU-38 JDAM

NATO Flight Training Canada

EQUIPMENT BY TYPE
AIRCRAFT
  TRG 45: 26 T-6A *Texan* II (CT-156 *Harvard* II); 19 *Hawk* 115 (CT-155) (advanced wpns/tactics trg)

Contracted Flying Services – Southport

EQUIPMENT BY TYPE
AIRCRAFT
  TPT • **Light** 7 Beech C90B *King Air*
  TRG 11 G-120A
HELICOPTERS
  MRH 9 Bell 412 (CH-146)
  TPT • **Light** 7 Bell 206 *Jet Ranger* (CH-139)

Canadian Special Operations Forces Command 1,500

FORCES BY ROLE
SPECIAL FORCES
  1 SF regt (Canadian Special Operations Regiment)
  1 SF unit (JTF 2)
COMBAT SERVICE SUPPORT
  1 CBRN unit (Canadian Joint Incident Response Unit – CJIRU)
TRANSPORT HELICOPTER
  1 (spec ops) sqn, with Bell 412 (CH-146 *Griffon* – from the RCAF)
EQUIPMENT BY TYPE
NBC VEHICLES 4 LAV *Bison* NBC
HELICOPTERS • MRH 10 Bell 412 (CH-146 *Griffon*)

Canadian Forces Joint Operational Support Group

FORCES BY ROLE
COMBAT SUPPORT
  1 engr spt coy
  1 (close protection) MP coy
  1 (joint) sigs regt

COMBAT SERVICE SUPPORT
  1 (spt) log unit
  1 (movement) log unit

Gendarmerie & Paramilitary 5,800

Canadian Coast Guard 5,800

Incl Department of Fisheries and Oceans; all platforms are designated as non-combatant
EQUIPMENT BY TYPE
PATROL AND COASTAL COMBATANTS 79
  PSOH 1 *Leonard J Cowley*
  PSO 1 *Sir Wilfred Grenfell*
  PCO 13: 2 *Cape Roger*; 1 *Gordon Reid*; 9 *Hero*; 1 *Tanu*
  PBF 1 Response Boat-Medium (RB-M)
  PB 63: 14 *Baie de Plaisance* (SAR); 9 Type-300A (SAR); 36 Type-300B (SAR); 3 *S. Dudka*; 1 *Vakta*
AMPHIBIOUS • **LANDING CRAFT** 4
  UCAC 4 Type-400
LOGISTICS AND SUPPORT 44
  ABU 4
  AG 8
  AGB 8
  AGBH 11
  AGOR 9
  AGS 2
  ATF 2
HELICOPTERS
  MRH 7 Bell 412EP
  TPT • **Light** 15 Bell 429

DEPLOYMENT

CYPRUS: UN • UNFICYP (*Operation Snowgoose*) 1
DEMOCRATIC REPUBLIC OF THE CONGO: UN • MONUSCO (*Operation Crocodile*) 8
EGYPT: MFO (*Operation Calumet*) 55; 1 MP team
IRAQ: NATO • NATO Mission Iraq 16
KOSOVO: NATO • KFOR • *Joint Enterprise* (*Operation Kobold*) 5
KUWAIT: *Operation Inherent Resolve* (*Impact*) 200
LATVIA: NATO • Enhanced Forward Presence (*Operation Reassurance*) 1,000; 1 mech inf bn HQ; 1 mech inf BG; 1 tk sqn
MIDDLE EAST: UN • UNTSO (*Operation Jade*) 6
NORTH SEA: NATO • SNMCMG 1: 90; 2 MCO
POLAND: *Operation Unifier* 40 (UKR trg)
SOUTH SUDAN: UN • UNMISS (*Operation Soprano*) 9
UNITED KINGDOM: Air Task Force Prestwick (ATF-P) 55; 3 C-130J-30 *Hercules* (CC-130J); *Operation Unifier* 170 (UKR trg)

FOREIGN FORCES

United Kingdom BATUS 400; 1 trg unit
United States 150

United States US

United States Dollar USD		2022	2023	2024
GDP	USD	25.5trn	26.9trn	28.0trn
per capita	USD	76,343	80,412	83,063
Growth	%	2.1	2.1	1.5
Inflation	%	8.0	4.1	2.8
Def exp [a]	USD	822bn	860bn	
Def bdgt [b]	USD	839bn	905bn	911bn

[a] NATO figure

[b] National Defense Budget Function (50) Budget Authority. Includes DoD funding, as well as funds for nuclear weapons-related activities undertaken by the Department of Energy. Excludes some military retirement and healthcare costs.

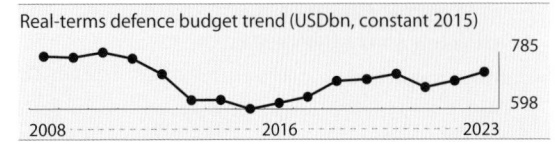

Real-terms defence budget trend (USDbn, constant 2015)

785
598
2008 — 2016 — 2023

Population	339,665,118					
Age	0–14	15–19	20–24	25–29	30–64	65 plus
Male	9.3%	3.2%	3.3%	3.4%	22.0%	8.1%
Female	8.9%	3.1%	3.2%	3.3%	22.3%	10.0%

Capabilities

The US remains the world's most capable military power, with a unique ability to project power on a global basis. The Biden administration issued several national security policy documents in 2023, including on cyber and science and technology, that reflected the National Security Strategy published in 2022. It prioritised China as the 'most consequential geopolitical challenge' facing the US, with Russia an immediate but mainly regional threat. These priorities were echoed the same year in a new National Defense Strategy (NDS) that was accompanied by a new Nuclear Posture Review and a Missile Defense Review. Washington, in 2023, announced it had destroyed the last chemical weapons in its stockpile. The US has sustained its support of Ukraine, providing an increasing array of equipment to help Kyiv in its counteroffensive against Russia. The US also has bolstered its presence in Europe to reassure allies there and strengthened its Indo-Pacific footprint with new basing rights in Papua New Guinea and the Philippines. The Pentagon is continuing with its modernisation efforts, including to its nuclear arsenal and it is aiming to field hypersonic cruise missiles and other such systems. In 2023, the Joint Chiefs of Staff issued a Joint Concept for Competing, aimed at adjusting plans for an era of persistent strategic competition rather than being focused just on warfighting. The US maintains an all-volunteer force, including significant reserves, with high levels of training throughout all commands and services. The Pentagon has struggled, though, to meet recruitment targets and is trying to improve readiness. The country has the world's most capable defence industry, active in all sectors, and with a dominant position in the international defence market. The US also is allocating funds to strengthen areas of its industrial base.

ACTIVE 1,326,050 (Army 452,750 Navy 334,400 Air Force 319,500 Space Force 8,850 US Marine Corps 170,800 US Coast Guard 39,750)

RESERVE 806,700 (Army 501,250 Navy 94,800 Air Force 171,250 Marine Corps Reserve 33,200 US Coast Guard 6,200)

ORGANISATIONS BY SERVICE

US Strategic Command

HQ at Offutt AFB (NE)

US Navy
EQUIPMENT BY TYPE
SUBMARINES • STRATEGIC • SSBN 14 *Ohio* with up to 20 UGM-133A *Trident* D-5/D-5LE nuclear SLBM, 4 single 533mm TT with Mk 48 ADCAP mod 6/7 HWT

US Air Force • Global Strike Command
FORCES BY ROLE
MISSILE
  9 sqn with LGM-30G *Minuteman* III
BOMBER
  5 sqn with B-52H *Stratofortress*
  2 sqn with B-2A *Spirit* (+1 ANG sqn personnel only)
EQUIPMENT BY TYPE
SURFACE-TO-SURFACE MISSILE LAUNCHERS
  ICBM • Nuclear 400 LGM-30G *Minuteman* III (1 Mk12A or Mk21 re-entry veh per missile)
AIRCRAFT
  BBR 66: 20 B-2A *Spirit*; 46 B-52H *Stratofortress*
AIR-LAUNCHED MISSILES
  ALCM • Nuclear AGM-86B

Strategic Defenses – Early Warning
EQUIPMENT BY TYPE
RADAR
  NORTH WARNING SYSTEM 50: 14 AN/FPS-117; 36 AN/FPS-124
  SOLID STATE PHASED ARRAY RADAR SYSTEM (SSPARS) 5 AN/FPS-132 Upgraded Early Warning Radar located at Beale AFB (CA), Cape Cod SFS (MA), Clear SFS (AK), Thule AB (GL) and RAF Fylingdales (UK)
  SPACETRACK SYSTEM 7: 1 AN/FPS-85 Spacetrack Radar at Eglin AFB (FL); 6 contributing radars at Cavalier SFS (ND), Clear SFS (AK), Thule AB (GL), RAF Fylingdales (UK), Beale AFB (CA) and Cape Cod SFS (MA); 3 Spacetrack Optical Trackers located at Socorro (NM), Maui (HI), Diego Garcia (BIOT)
  PERIMETER ACQUISITION RADAR ATTACK CHARACTERISATION SYSTEM (PARCS) 1 AN/FPQ-16 at Cavalier SFS (ND)
  DETECTION AND TRACKING RADARS 5 located at Kwajalein Atoll, Ascension Island, Australia, Kaena

Point (HI), MIT Lincoln Laboratory (MA)
GROUND BASED ELECTRO OPTICAL DEEP SPACE SURVEILLANCE SYSTEM (GEODSS)
Socorro (NM), Maui (HI), Diego Garcia (BIOT)
STRATEGIC DEFENCES – MISSILE DEFENCES
SEA-BASED: *Aegis* engagement cruisers and destroyers
LAND-BASED: 40 ground-based interceptors at Fort Greely (AK); 4 ground-based interceptors at Vandenburg SFB (CA)

Space
EQUIPMENT BY TYPE
SATELLITES 171
  COMMUNICATIONS 66: 6 AEHF; 6 DSCS-III; 2 *Milstar*-I; 3 *Milstar*-II; 5 MUOS; 5 SDS-III; 2 SDS-IV; 1 *TacSat*-4; 1 *TacSat*-6; 19 Transport Layer Tranche 0; 6 UFO; 10 WGS SV2
  POSITIONING, NAVIGATION & TIMING 30: 12 NAVSTAR Block IIF; 7 NAVSTAR Block IIR; 7 NAVSTAR Block IIRM; 4 NAVSTAR Block III
  METEOROLOGY/OCEANOGRAPHY 4 DMSP-5
  ISR 14: 5 FIA *Radar*; 5 *Evolved Enhanced/Improved Crystal* (visible and infrared imagery); 2 NRO L-71; 2 NRO L-76
  ELINT/SIGINT 32: 7 *Mentor* (advanced *Orion*); 2 *Mercury*; 2 *Nemesis*; 1 *Sharp* (NRO L-67); 3 *Trumpet*; 4 Improved *Trumpet*; 12 Naval Ocean Surveillance System (NOSS); 1 NRO L-85
  SPACE SURVEILLANCE 11: 6 GSSAP; 1 ORS-5; 1 SBSS (Space Based Surveillance System); 3 *Silent Barker* (NRO L-107)
  EARLY WARNING 14: 4 DSP; 6 SBIRS *Geo*; 4 Tracking Layer Tranche 0
REUSABLE SPACECRAFT 1 X-37B OTV
COUNTERSPACE • EW Counter Communications System (CCS)

US Army 452,750
FORCES BY ROLE
Sqn are generally bn sized and tp are generally coy sized
COMMAND
  4 (I, III, V & XVIII AB) corps HQ
  1 (2nd) inf div HQ
  1 (56th) arty comd
SPECIAL FORCES
  (see USSOCOM)
MANOEUVRE
  Armoured
  2 (1st Armd & 1st Cav) armd div (3 (1st–3rd ABCT) armd bde (1 armd recce sqn, 2 armd bn, 1 armd inf bn, 1 SP arty bn, 1 cbt engr bn, 1 CSS bn); 1 SP arty bde HQ; 1 log bde; 1 (hy cbt avn) hel bde; 1 SAM bn)
  1 (1st) inf div (2 (1st & 2nd ABCT) armd bde (1 armd recce sqn, 2 armd bn, 1 armd inf bn, 1 SP arty bn, 1 cbt engr bn, 1 CSS bn); 1 SP arty bde HQ; 1 log bde; 1 (cbt avn) hel bde)
  1 (3rd) inf div (2 (1st & 2nd ABCT) armd bde (1 armd recce sqn, 2 armd bn, 1 armd inf bn, 1 SP arty bn, 1 cbt engr bn, 1 CSS bn); 1 lt inf bn; 1 SP arty bde HQ; 1 log bde; 1 (cbt avn) hel bde)
  Mechanised
  1 (4th) inf div (1 (3rd ABCT) armd bde (1 armd recce sqn, 2 armd bn, 1 armd inf bn, 1 SP arty bn, 1 cbt engr bn, 1 CSS bn); 2 (1st & 2nd SBCT) mech bde (1 armd recce sqn, 3 mech inf bn, 1 arty bn, 1 cbt engr bn, 1 CSS bn); 1 SP arty bde HQ; 1 log bde; 1 (hy cbt avn) hel bde)
  1 (7th) inf div (2 (1st & 2nd SBCT, 2nd ID) mech bde (1 armd recce sqn, 3 mech inf bn, 1 arty bn, 1 cbt engr bn, 1 CSS bn))
  2 (2nd & 3rd CR) mech bde (1 armd recce sqn, 3 mech sqn, 1 arty sqn, 1 cbt engr sqn, 1 CSS sqn)
  Light
  1 (10th Mtn) inf div (3 (1st–3rd IBCT) lt inf bde (1 recce sqn, 3 inf bn, 1 arty bn, 1 cbt engr bn, 1 CSS bn); 1 log bde; 1 (cbt avn) hel bde)
  1 (25th) inf div (2 (2 & 3rd IBCT) inf bde (1 recce sqn, 2 inf bn, 1 arty bn, 1 cbt engr bn, 1 CSS bn); 1 log bde; 1 (cbt avn) hel bde)
  5 (Sy Force Assist) inf bde(-)
  Air Manoeuvre
  1 (11th) AB div (1 (1st IBCT) inf bde (1 recce sqn, 3 inf bn, 1 arty bn, 1 cbt engr bn, 1 CSS bn); 1 (2nd AB BCT) AB bde (1 recce bn, 2 para bn, 1 arty bn, 1 cbt engr bn, 1 CSS bn))
  1 (82nd) AB div (1 (1st AB BCT) AB bde (1 recce bn, 1 mech coy; 3 para bn, 1 arty bn, 1 cbt engr bn, 1 CSS bn); 2 (2nd & 3rd AB BCT) AB bde (1 recce bn, 3 para bn, 1 arty bn, 1 cbt engr bn, 1 CSS bn); 1 (cbt avn) hel bde; 1 log bde)
  1 (101st) air aslt div (3 (1st–3rd AB BCT) air aslt bde (1 recce bn, 3 air aslt bn, 1 arty bn, 1 cbt engr bn, 1 CSS bn); 1 (cbt avn) hel bde; 1 log bde)
  1 (173rd AB BCT) AB bde (1 recce bn, 2 para bn, 1 arty bn, 1 cbt engr bn, 1 CSS bn)
  Other
  1 (11th ACR) trg armd cav regt (OPFOR) (2 armd cav sqn, 1 CSS bn)
COMBAT SUPPORT
  3 MRL bde (2 MRL bn)
  1 MRL bde (1 MRL bn; 1 SSM bn (forming))
  1 MRL bde (5 MRL bn)
  4 engr bde
  2 EOD gp (2 EOD bn)
  10 int bde
  2 int gp
  4 MP bde
  1 NBC bde
  3 (strat) sigs bde
  4 (tac) sigs bde
  1 (1st MDTF) cbt spt bde (1 (I2CEWS) cbt spt bn)
  2 (2nd & 3rd MDTF) cbt spt bde(-)

COMBAT SERVICE SUPPORT
2 log bde
3 med bde
1 tpt bde
ISR
1 ISR avn bde
HELICOPTER
2 (cbt avn) hel bde
1 (cbt avn) hel bde HQ
AIR DEFENCE
6 SAM bde

Reserve Organisations

Army National Guard 324,500 reservists

Normally dual-funded by DoD and states. Civil-emergency responses can be mobilised by state governors. Federal government can mobilise ARNG for major domestic emergencies and for overseas operations

FORCES BY ROLE
COMMAND
8 div HQ
SPECIAL FORCES
(see USSOCOM)
MANOEUVRE
Reconnaissance
1 armd recce sqn
Armoured
5 (ABCT) armd bde (1 armd recce sqn, 2 armd bn, 1 armd inf bn, 1 SP arty bn, 1 cbt engr bn, 1 CSS bn)
Mechanised
2 (SBCT) mech bde (1 armd recce sqn, 3 mech inf bn, 1 arty bn, 1 cbt engr bn, 1 CSS bn)
Light
14 (IBCT) inf bde (1 recce sqn, 3 inf bn, 1 arty bn, 1 cbt engr bn, 1 CSS bn)
6 (IBCT) inf bde (1 recce sqn, 2 inf bn, 1 arty bn, 1 cbt engr bn, 1 CSS bn)
1 (Sy Force Assist) inf bde(-)
4 inf bn
Air Manoeuvre
1 AB bn
COMBAT SUPPORT
8 arty bde
1 SP arty bn
8 engr bde
1 EOD regt
3 int bde
3 MP bde
1 NBC bde
2 (tac) sigs bde
17 (Mnv Enh) cbt spt bde
COMBAT SERVICE SUPPORT
10 log bde
17 (regional) log spt gp

HELICOPTER
8 (cbt avn) hel bde
5 (theatre avn) hel bde
AIR DEFENCE
3 SAM bde

Army Reserve 176,750 reservists

Reserve under full command of US Army. Does not have state-emergency liability of Army National Guard

FORCES BY ROLE
SPECIAL FORCES
(see USSOCOM)
COMBAT SUPPORT
4 engr bde
4 MP bde
2 NBC bde
2 sigs bde
3 (Mnv Enh) cbt spt bde
COMBAT SERVICE SUPPORT
9 log bde
11 med bde
HELICOPTER
2 (exp cbt avn) hel bde

Army Stand-by Reserve 700 reservists

Trained individuals for mobilisation

EQUIPMENT BY TYPE
ARMOURED FIGHTING VEHICLES
MBT 2,640: ε540 M1A1 SA *Abrams*; ε1,500 M1A2 SEPv2 *Abrams*; ε600 M1A2 SEPv3 *Abrams*; (ε2,000 more M1A1/A2 *Abrams* in store)
RECCE 1,745: ε1,200 M3A2/A3 *Bradley*; 545 M1127 *Stryker* RV (ε800 more M3 *Bradley* in store)
IFV 2,774: ε14 LAV-25; ε2,100 M2A2/A3 *Bradley*; ε240 M2A4 *Bradley*; ε300 M7A3/SA BFIST (OP); ε30 M7A4 BFIST (OP); 83 M1296 *Stryker Dragoon*; 7 *Stryker* MCWS (in test); (ε2,000 more M2 *Bradley* in store)
APC 10,437
APC (T) 4,980: ε280 AMPV; ε4,700 M113A2/A3 (ε8,000 more in store)
APC (W) 2,523: 1,218 M1126 *Stryker* ICV; 261 M1130 *Stryker* CV (CP); 151 M1131 *Stryker* FSV (OP); 203 M1133 *Stryker* MEV (Amb); 37 M1251A1 *Stryker* FSV (OP); 101 M1254A1 *Stryker* MEV (Amb); 87 M1255A1 *Stryker* CV (CP); 465 M1256A1 *Stryker* ICV
PPV 2,934: 2,633 *MaxxPro Dash*; 301 *MaxxPro* LWB (Amb)
AUV 21,516: ε12,500 JLTV; 2,900 M1117 ASV; 465 M1200 *Armored Knight* (OP); 5,651 M-ATV
ENGINEERING & MAINTENANCE VEHICLES
AEV 567: 149 M1150 ABV; 250 M9 ACE; 136 M1132 *Stryker* ESV; 32 M1257A1 *Stryker* ESV
ARV 1,293+: 360 M88A1; 933 M88A2 (ε1,000 more M88A1 in store); some M578
VLB 394: ε230 M60 AVLB; 104 M1074 Joint Assault

Bridge; 20 REBS; 40 *Wolverine* HAB

MW 3+: *Aardvark* JSFU Mk4; some *Husky* 2G; 3+ *Hydrema* 910 MCV-2; M58/M59 MICLIC; M139; *Rhino*

NBC VEHICLES 234 M1135 *Stryker* NBCRV

ANTI-TANK/ANTI-INFRASTRUCTURE

MSL

SP 1,133: 110 M1134 *Stryker* ATGM; 23 M1253A1 *Stryker* ATGM; ε1,000 M1167 HMMWV TOW

MANPATS FGM-148 *Javelin*

RCL 84mm *Carl Gustaf*

ARTILLERY 4,984

SP 155mm 671: 400 M109A6; 271 M109A7 (ε850 more M109A6 in store)

TOWED 1,212: **105mm** 821 M119A2/3; **155mm** 391 M777A2

MRL 227mm 594: 368 M142 HIMARS; 226+ M270A1/A2 MLRS

MOR 2,507: **81mm** 990 M252; **120mm** 1,076 M120/M1064A3; **SP 120mm** 441; 345 M1129 *Stryker* MC; 96 M1252A1 *Stryker* MC

SURFACE-TO-SURFACE MISSILE LAUNCHERS

SSM • **Conventional** 4 *Typhon*; SM-6 Block IA (launched from *Typhon*)

SRBM • **Conventional** MGM-140A/B ATACMS; MGM-168 ATACMS (All launched from M270A1 MLRS or M142 HIMARS MRLs)

GLCM • **Conventional** RGM-109E *Tomahawk* Block V (launched from *Typhon*)

AMPHIBIOUS

PRINCIPAL AMPHIBIOUS SHIPS 8

LST 8 *Frank Besson* (capacity 24 *Abrams* MBT)

LANDING CRAFT 48

LCT 21 LCU 2000 (capacity 5 M1 *Abrams* MBT)

LCM 27 LCM 8 (capacity either 1 M1 *Abrams* MBT or 200 troops)

LOGISTICS AND SUPPORT • **ATF** 4 LT-800

AIRCRAFT

ISR 38: 8 EMARSS-G; 4 EMARSS-V; 7 EMARSS-M; 19 RC-12X *Guardrail* (5 trg)

SIGINT 3: 2 CL-600 *Artemis* (in test); 1 Global-6500 *Ares* (in test)

ELINT 9: 4 EMARSS-S; 4 EO-5C ARL-M (COMINT/ELINT); 1 TO-5C (trg)

TPT 161: **Light** 157: 116 Beech A200 *King Air* (C-12 *Huron*); 30 Cessna 560 *Citation* (UC-35A/B); 11 SA-227 *Metro* (C-26E); **PAX** 4: 1 Gulfstream IV (C-20F); 2 Gulfstream V (C-37A); 1 Gulfstream G550 (C-37B)

TRG 4 T-6D *Texan* II

HELICOPTERS

ATK 750: ε250 AH-64D *Apache*; ε500 AH-64E *Apache*

SAR 337: 19 HH-60L *Black Hawk*; 318 HH-60M *Black Hawk* (medevac)

TPT 2,818: **Heavy** 450 CH-47F *Chinook*; **Medium** 1,828: ε20 UH-60A *Black Hawk*; ε850 UH-60L *Black Hawk*; 918 UH-60M *Black Hawk*; ε40 UH-60V *Black Hawk*; **Light** 540: 457 UH-72A *Lakota*; 18 UH-72B *Lakota*; 65 UH-1H/V *Iroquois*

UNINHABITED AERIAL VEHICLES 416

CISR • **Heavy** ε180 MQ-1C *Gray Eagle*

ISR • **Medium** 236 RQ-7B *Shadow*

AIR DEFENCE

SAM 1,187+

Long-range 480 M902/M903 *Patriot* PAC-3/PAC-3 MSE

Short-range NASAMS

Point-defence 533+: FIM-92 *Stinger*; ε80 M-SHORAD; 453 M1097 *Avenger*

GUNS • **Towed** • **20mm** *Phalanx* (LPWS)

MISSILE DEFENCE • **Long-range** 42 THAAD

AIR-LAUNCHED MISSILES

ASM AGM-114K/L/M/N/R *Hellfire* II; AGM-179A JAGM; AGR-20A APKWS

US Navy 334,400

Comprises 2 Fleet Areas, Atlantic and Pacific. 6 Fleets: 2nd – Atlantic; 3rd – Pacific; 4th – Caribbean, Central and South America; 5th – Arabian Sea, Persian Gulf, Red Sea; 6th – Mediterranean; 7th – Indian Ocean, East Asia, W. Pacific; plus Military Sealift Command (MSC); Naval Reserve Force (NRF). For Naval Special Warfare Command, see US Special Operations Command

EQUIPMENT BY TYPE

SUBMARINES 66

STRATEGIC • **SSBN** 14 *Ohio* (opcon US STRATCOM) with up to 20 UGM-133A *Trident* D-5/D-5LE nuclear SLBM, 4 single 533mm TT with Mk 48 ADCAP mod 6/7 HWT

TACTICAL 52

SSGN 50:

4 *Ohio* (mod) with 22 7-cell MAC VLS with UGM-109E *Tomahawk* Block IV LACM, 4 single 533mm TT with Mk 48 ADCAP mod 6/7 HWT

2 *Los Angeles* Flight II with 1 12-cell VLS with UGM-109E *Tomahawk* Block IV LACM, 4 single 533mm TT with Mk 48 ADCAP mod 6/7 HWT

22 *Los Angeles* Flight III with 1 12-cell VLS with UGM-109E *Tomahawk* Block IV LACM, 4 single 533mm TT with Mk 48 ADCAP mod 6/7 HWT

10 *Virginia* Flight I/II with 1 12-cell VLS with UGM-109E *Tomahawk* Block IV LACM, 4 single 533mm TT with Mk 48 ADCAP mod 6/7 HWT

8 *Virginia* Flight III with 2 6-cell VPT VLS with UGM-109E *Tomahawk* Block IV LACM, 4 single 533mm TT with Mk 48 ADCAP mod 6/7 HWT

4 *Virginia* Flight IV with 2 6-cell VPT VLS with UGM-109E *Tomahawk* Block IV LACM, 4 single 533mm TT with Mk 48 ADCAP mod 6/7 HWT

SSN 2 *Seawolf* (one other damaged in collision in 2021, repair began in 2023) with 8 single 660mm TT with UGM-109E *Tomahawk* Block IV LACM/Mk 48 ADCAP mod 6/7 HWT

PRINCIPAL SURFACE COMBATANTS 122
  AIRCRAFT CARRIERS • CVN 11:
    1 *Gerald R. Ford* with 2 octuple Mk 29 mod 5 GMLS with RIM-162D ESSM SAM, 2 Mk 49 mod 3 GMLS with RIM-116C RAM Block 2 SAM, 3 Mk 15 *Phalanx* Block 1B CIWS (typical capacity 75+ F/A-18E/F *Super Hornet* FGA ac; F-35C *Lightning* II FGA ac; E-2D *Hawkeye* AEW&C ac; EA-18G *Growler* EW ac; MH-60R *Seahawk* ASW hel; MH-60S *Knight Hawk* MRH hel)
    10 *Nimitz* with 2 8-cell Mk29 GMLS with RIM-162 ESSM SAM, 2 21-cell Mk 49 GMLS with RIM-116 RAM Block 2 SAM, 3 Mk 15 *Phalanx* Block 1B CIWS (typical capacity 55 F/A-18E/F *Super Hornet* FGA ac; F-35C *Lightning* II FGA ac; 4 EA-18G *Growler* EW ac; 4 E-2C/D *Hawkeye* AEW ac; 6 MH-60R/S *Seahawk/Knight Hawk* hel)
  CRUISERS • CGHM 15:
    13 *Ticonderoga* with *Aegis* Baseline 5/6/8/9 C2, 2 quad lnchr with RGM-84D *Harpoon* Block 1C AShM, 16 8-cell Mk 41 VLS (of which 2 only 5-cell and fitted with reload crane) with RGM-109E *Tomahawk* Block IV LACM/SM-2 Block III/IIIA/IIIB/IV SAM/SM-3 Block IA/B SAM/SM-6 Block I/IA SAM, 2 triple 324mm SVTT Mk 32 ASTT with Mk 54 LWT, 2 Mk 15 *Phalanx* Block 1B CIWS, 2 127mm guns (capacity 2 MH-60R *Seahawk*/MH-60S *Knight Hawk* hels)
    2 *Zumwalt* with 20 4-cell Mk 57 VLS with RGM-109E *Tomahawk* Block IV LACM/RIM-162 ESSM SAM/SM-2 Block IIIA SAM/ASROC A/S msl, 2 155mm guns (capacity 2 MH-60R *Seahawk* ASW hel or 1 MH-60R *Seahawk* ASW hel and 3 *Fire Scout* UAV)
  DESTROYERS 73:
    DDGHM 45:
      5 *Arleigh Burke* Flight IIA with *Aegis* Baseline 5/9 C2, 12 8-cell Mk 41 VLS with RGM-109E *Tomahawk* Block IV LACM/RIM-162A ESSM SAM/SM-2 Block III/IIIA/IIIB/IV SAM/SM-3 Block IA/B SAM/SM-6 Block I/IA SAM/ASROC A/S msl, 2 triple 324mm SVTT Mk 32 ASTT with Mk 54 LWT, 2 Mk 15 *Phalanx* Block 1B CIWS, 1 127mm gun (capacity 2 MH-60R *Seahawk*/MH-60S *Knight Hawk* hels)
      39 *Arleigh Burke* Flight IIA with *Aegis* Baseline 6/7/9 C2, 12 8-cell Mk 41 VLS with RGM-109E *Tomahawk* Block IV LACM/RIM-162A ESSM SAM/SM-2 Block III/IIIA/IIIB/IV SAM/SM-3 Block IA/B SAM/SM-6 Block I/IA SAM/ASROC A/S msl, 2 triple 324mm SVTT Mk 32 ASTT with Mk 54 LWT, 1 Mk 15 *Phalanx* Block 1B CIWS, 1 127mm gun (capacity 2 MH-60R *Seahawk*/MH-60S *Knight Hawk* hels) (of which 3 vessels also with 1 Mk 15 SeaRAM with RIM-116C RAM Block 2 and 5 vessels also with 1 Optical Dazzling Interdictor, Navy (ODIN) LWS)
      1 *Arleigh Burke* Flight III with *Aegis* Baseline 10 C2, 12 8-cell Mk 41 VLS with RGM-109E *Tomahawk* Block IV LACM/RIM-162A ESSM SAM/SM-2 Block III/IIIA/IIIB/IV SAM/SM-3 Block IA/B SAM/SM-6 Block I/IA SAM/ASROC A/S msl, 2 triple 324mm SVTT Mk 32 ASTT with Mk 54 LWT, 1 Mk 15 *Phalanx* Block 1B CIWS, 1 127mm gun (capacity 2 MH-60R *Seahawk*/MH-60S *Knight Hawk* hels)
    DDGM 28 *Arleigh Burke* Flight I/II with *Aegis* Baseline 5/9 C2, 2 quad lnchr with RGM-84D *Harpoon* Block 1C AShM, 12 8-cell Mk 41 VLS (of which 2 only 5-cell and fitted with reload crane) with RGM-109E *Tomahawk* Block IV LACM/RIM-162A ESSM SAM/SM-2 Block III/IIIA/IIIB/IV SAM/SM-3 Block IA/B SAM/SM-6 Block I SAM/ASROC A/S msl, 2 triple 324mm SVTT Mk 32 ASTT with Mk 54 LWT, 2 Mk 15 *Phalanx* Block 1B CIWS (of which 5 vessels with 1 Mk 15 SeaRAM with RIM-116C RAM Block 2, 1 Mk 15 *Phalanx* Block 1B instead of 2 *Phalanx*), 1 127mm gun, 1 hel landing platform
  FRIGATES 23:
    FFGHM 6 *Independence* with 2 quad lnchr with NSM (RGM-184A) AShM, 1 11-cell SeaRAM lnchr with RIM-116C Block 2 SAM, 1 57mm gun (capacity 2 MH-60R/S *Seahawk/Knight Hawk* hel and 3 MQ-8 *Fire Scout* UAV)
    FFHM 17:
      8 *Freedom* with 1 21-cell Mk 49 lnchr with RIM-116C RAM Block 2 SAM, 1 57mm gun (capacity 2 MH-60R/S *Seahawk/Knight Hawk* hel or 1 MH-60 with 3 MQ-8 *Fire Scout* UAV)
      9 *Independence* with 1 11-cell SeaRAM lnchr with RIM-116C Block 2 SAM, 1 57mm gun (capacity 2 MH-60R/S *Seahawk/Knight Hawk* hel and 3 MQ-8 *Fire Scout* UAV)
PATROL AND COASTAL COMBATANTS 85
  PBF 85: 32 Combatant Craft Assault; 3 Combatant Craft Heavy; 30 Combatant Craft Medium Mk 1; 20 Defiant 40 (40PB)
MINE WARFARE
  MINE COUNTERMEASURES • MCO 8 *Avenger*
COMMAND SHIPS
  LCC 2 *Blue Ridge* with 2 Mk 15 *Phalanx* Block 1B CIWS (capacity 3 LCPL; 2 LCVP; 700 troops; 1 med hel) (of which 1 vessel partially crewed by Military Sealift Command personnel)
AMPHIBIOUS
  PRINCIPAL AMPHIBIOUS SHIPS 31:
    LHA 2 *America* with 2 8-cell Mk 29 GMLS with RIM-162D ESSM SAM, 2 Mk 49 GMLS with RIM-116C RAM Block 2 SAM, 2 Mk 15 *Phalanx* Block 1B CIWS (capacity up to 29 ac/hel incl: 6-13 F-35B *Lightning* II FGA ac (possible 20 as full '*Lightning*' carrier'); 4 AH-1Z *Viper* atk hel; up to 12 MV-22B *Osprey* tpt ac; 2 MH-60S *Knight Hawk* MRH; 4 CH-53E *Sea Stallion* tpt hel; 2 UH-1Y *Iroquois* tpt hel; up to 1,800 troops)
    LHD 7 *Wasp* with 2 8-cell Mk 29 GMLS with RIM-7M/P *Sea Sparrow* SAM, 2 Mk 49 GMLS with RIM-116C RAM Block 2 SAM, 2 Mk 15 *Phalanx* Block 1B CIWS (capacity up to 23 ac/hel incl: 6 AV-8B *Harrier* II FGA or F-35B *Lightning* II FGA ac (possible 20 F-35B

as full '*Lightning* carrier'); 4 AH-1Z *Viper* atk hel; 4 CH-53E *Sea Stallion* hel; up to 6 MV-22B *Osprey* tpt ac; 3 UH-1Y *Iroquois* tpt hel; 3 LCAC(L); 60 tanks; 1,687 troops)

LPD 12 *San Antonio* with 2 21-cell Mk 49 GMLS with RIM-116C RAM Block 2 SAM (1 vessel also fitted with 1 Solid-State Laser Technology Maturation (SSL-TM) LWS) (capacity 2 CH-53E *Sea Stallion* hel or 2 MV-22 *Osprey*; 2 LCAC(L); 14 AAV; 720 troops)

LSD 10:
  4 *Harpers Ferry* with 2 Mk 49 GMLS with RIM-116C RAM Block 2 SAM, 2 Mk 15 *Phalanx* Block 1B CIWS (capacity 2 CH-53E *Sea Stallion* hel; 2 LCAC(L); 40 tanks; 500 troops)
  6 *Whidbey Island* with 2 Mk 49 GMLS with RIM-116C RAM Block 2 SAM, 2 Mk 15 *Phalanx* Block 1B CIWS (capacity 2 CH-53E *Sea Stallion* hel; 4 LCAC(L); 40 tanks; 500 troops)

LANDING CRAFT 141:
  LCU 25 LCU 1610 (capacity either 1 M1 *Abrams* MBT or 350 troops)
  LCM 7 LCM 8
  LCP 33 Maritime Positioning Force Utility Boat (MPF-UB)
  LCAC 76: 68 LCAC(L) (MLU ongoing) (capacity either 1 MBT or 60 troops); 8 *Ship to Shore Connector* (SSC) (capacity 1 MBT or 145 troops)

LOGISTICS AND SUPPORT 16
  AFD 2
  AFDL 1 *Dynamic*
  AGOR 6 (all leased out): 2 *Neil Armstrong*; 3 *Thomas G. Thompson*; 1 *Kilo Moana*
  AX 1 *Prevail*
  ESB 4 *Lewis B. Puller* (MSC) (capacity 4 MH-53/MH-60 hel)
  SSA 2 *Dry Combat Submersible*

UNINHABITED MARITIME PLATFORMS
  USV 11
    DATA • Medium 1 *Arabian Fox* (MAST-13)
    MW • Medium 3 UISS
    UTL 7: **Large** 4: 3 *Ranger*; 1 *Vanguard*; **Medium** 2 *Sea Hunter*; **Small** 1 *Devil Ray* T38
  UUV • UTL • Extra-large 2: 1 *Orca*; 1 *Proteus*

UNINHABITED MARITIME SYSTEMS
  USV • DATA *Adaro*; *Saildrone Explorer*; *Wave Glider*
  UUV
    DATA *Iver-3*; *Kingfish* Mk 18 mod 2; *Knifefish*; LBS-AUV (REMUS 600); LBS-G *Razorback*; *Lionfish* (REMUS 300); *Marlin*; *Riptide Micro*; *Sealion* (*Bluefin-9*); *Submaran*; *Swordfish* Mk 18 mod 1 (REMUS 100); *Viperfish* Mk 18 mod 3 (*Iver-4* 900)
    MW *Archerfish*; EX-116; *Seafox* (AN/SLQ-60); SLQ-48; SRS *Fusion*
    UTL *Bluefin*-12D; CURV 21; *Deep Drone* 8000; HUGIN; *Iver*-4 580; MR2 *Hydros*

MISSILE DEFENCE • Long-range 3 8-cell Mk 41 VLS with SM-3

Naval Reserve Forces 94,800

Selected Reserve 55,000

Individual Ready Reserve 39,800

Naval Inactive Fleet

Notice for reactivation: 60–90 days minimum (still on naval-vessel register)

EQUIPMENT BY TYPE
PRINCIPAL SURFACE COMBATANTS
  FRIGATES • FFH 1 *Independence* with 1 57mm gun
AMPHIBIOUS 3
  LHA 2 *Tarawa*
  LSD 1 *Whidbey Island*
LOGISTICS AND SUPPORT 7
  AOR 1 *Henry J. Kaiser* with 1 hel landing platform
  ARS 2 *Safeguard*
  EPF 2 *Spearhead*
  ESD 2 *Montford Point*

Military Sealift Command (MSC)

Fleet Oiler (PM1)

EQUIPMENT BY TYPE
LOGISTICS AND SUPPORT 16
  AOR 16: 2 *John Lewis* with 1 hel landing platform; 14 *Henry J. Kaiser* with 1 hel landing platform

Special Mission (PM2)

EQUIPMENT BY TYPE
LOGISTICS AND SUPPORT 22
  AGM 2: 1 *Howard O. Lorenzen*; 1 Sea-based X-band radar
  AGOR 6 *Pathfinder*
  AGOS 5: 1 *Impeccable*; 4 *Victorious*
  AGE 1 *Waters*
  ARC 2: 1 *Global Sentinel* (long-term chartered); 1 *Zeus*
  AS 4 *Arrowhead*
  ATF 2: 1 HOS *Red Rock* (leased, surv role); 1 *Hercules*

Prepositioning (PM3)

EQUIPMENT BY TYPE
LOGISTICS AND SUPPORT 24
  AG 2: 1 *V Adm K.R. Wheeler*; 1 *Fast Tempo*
  AK 4: 2 *LTC John U.D. Page* (long-term chartered); 1 *Maj. Bernard F. Fisher* (long-term chartered); 1 *Cpt David I. Lyon* (long-term chartered)
  AKR 11: 2 *Bob Hope*; 1 *Stockham*; 8 *Watson*
  AKRH 5 *2nd Lt John P. Bobo*

Service Support (PM4)

EQUIPMENT BY TYPE
LOGISTICS AND SUPPORT 13
  AGE 1 HOS *Resolution* (long-term chartered)

AH 2 *Mercy* with 1 hel landing platform
ARS 2 *Safeguard*
AS 5: 1 *Dominator* (long-term chartered); 2 *Emory S. Land*; 1 *Kellie Chouest* (long-term chartered); 1 *Malama* (long-term chartered)
ATF 3: 1 *Gary Chouest* (long-term chartered); 1 *Ocean Valor* (long-term chartered, used as AGE); 1 *Powhata*n

Fleet Ordnance and Dry Cargo (PM6)
EQUIPMENT BY TYPE
LOGISTICS AND SUPPORT 16
AOE 2 *Supply*
AFS 14 *Lewis and Clark*

Expeditionary Fast Transport (PM8)
EQUIPMENT BY TYPE
LOGISTICS AND SUPPORT 13
EPF 13: 2 *Guam*; 11 *Spearhead*

Dry Cargo and Tankers
EQUIPMENT BY TYPE
LOGISTICS AND SUPPORT 6
AK 1 SLNC *Corsica* (long-term chartered)
AO 5: 2 *Empire State*; 1 SLNC *Pax*; 1 SLNC *Goodwill*; 1 *Stena Polaris* (all long-term chartered)

US Maritime Administration (MARAD)

National Defense Reserve Fleet
EQUIPMENT BY TYPE
LOGISTICS AND SUPPORT 18
AGOS 2 *General Rudder* (trg role)
AGM 2: 1 *Pacific Collector*; 1 *Pacific Tracker*
AK 7: 2 *Cape Ann* (breakbulk); 1 *Cape Chalmers* (breakbulk); 2 *Cape May*; 1 *Del Monte* (breakbulk); 1 *Savannah*
AP 3: 1 *Golden Bear* (trg role); 1 *Kennedy* (trg role); 1 *State of Maine* (trg role)
AX 4: 1 *Freedom Star*; 1 *Invincible*; 1 *Kings Pointer*; 1 *Empire State*

Ready Reserve Force
Ships at readiness up to a maximum of 30 days
EQUIPMENT BY TYPE
LOGISTICS AND SUPPORT 52
AK 4: 2 *Gopher State*; 2 *Keystone State*
AKR 48: 1 *Adm W.M. Callaghan*; 8 *Algol*; 5 *Bob Hope*; 2 *Cape Arundel*; 5 *Cape Ducato*; 1 *Cape Edmont*; 3 *Cape Hudson*; 2 *Cape Knox*; 4 *Cape Island*; 1 *Cape Orlando*; 3 *Cape Race*; 3 *Cape Sable*; 3 *Cape Texas*; 2 *Cape Victory*; 2 *Cape Washington*; 2 *Gordon*; 2 *Wright* (breakbulk)

Naval Aviation 98,600

10 air wg. Average air wing comprises 8 sqns: 4 with F/A-18; 1 with MH-60R; 1 with EA-18G; 1 with E-2C/D; 1 with MH-60S
FORCES BY ROLE
FIGHTER/GROUND ATTACK
22 sqn with F/A-18E *Super Hornet*
10 sqn with F/A-18F *Super Hornet*
2 sqn with F-35C *Lightning* II
ANTI-SUBMARINE WARFARE
12 sqn with P-8A *Poseidon*
1 (special projects) sqn with P-8A *Poseidon*
12 sqn with MH-60R *Seahawk*
3 ASW/ISR sqn with MH-60R *Seahawk*; MQ-8B *Fire Scout*
ELINT
1 sqn with EP-3E *Aries* II
ELINT/ELECTRONIC WARFARE
14 sqn with EA-18G *Growler*
AIRBORNE EARLY WARNING & CONTROL
2 sqn with E-2C *Hawkeye*
7 sqn with E-2D *Hawkeye*
COMMAND & CONTROL
2 sqn with E-6B *Mercury*
MINE COUNTERMEASURES
2 sqn with MH-53E *Sea Dragon*
TRANSPORT
2 sqn with CMV-22B *Osprey*
1 sqn with C-2A *Greyhound*
TRAINING
1 (FRS) sqn with EA-18G *Growler*
1 (FRS) sqn with C-2A *Greyhound*; E-2C/D *Hawkeye*; TE-2C *Hawkeye*
1 sqn with E-6B *Mercury*
2 (FRS) sqn with F/A-18E/F *Super Hornet*
1 (FRS) sqn with F-35C *Lightning* II
1 (FRS) sqn with MH-53 *Sea Dragon*
2 (FRS) sqn with MH-60S *Knight Hawk*; HH-60H *Seahawk*
2 (FRS) sqn with MH-60R *Seahawk*
1 (FRS) sqn with MQ-4C *Triton*; P-8A *Poseidon*
6 sqn with T-6A/B *Texan* II
2 sqn with T-44C *Pegasus*
5 sqn with T-45C *Goshawk*
2 hel sqn with TH-57B/C *Sea Ranger*
1 hel sqn with TH-73A
1 (FRS) UAV sqn with MQ-8B *Fire Scout*; MQ-8C *Fire Scout*
TRANSPORT HELICOPTER
13 sqn with MH-60S *Knight Hawk*
1 tpt hel/ISR sqn with MH-60S *Knight Hawk*; MQ-8B *Fire Scout*; MQ-8C *Fire Scout*
ISR UAV
1 sqn with MQ-4C *Triton*
EQUIPMENT BY TYPE
AIRCRAFT 970 combat capable
FGA 679: 10 F-16A *Fighting Falcon*; 4 F-16B *Fighting Falcon*; 8 F-16C *Fighting Falcon*; 6 F-16D *Fighting Falcon*; 68 F-35C *Lightning* II; 8 F/A-18C *Hornet*; 2 F/A-18D *Hornet*; 323 F/A-18E *Super Hornet*; 250 F/A-18F *Super Hornet*
ATK 2 AT-6E *Wolverine*

ASW 133: 10 P-3C *Orion*; 123 P-8A *Poseidon*
EW 156 EA-18G *Growler**
ELINT 6 EP-3E *Aries* II
AEW&C 78: 19 E-2C *Hawkeye*; 59 E-2D *Hawkeye*
C2 16 E-6B *Mercury*
TKR/TPT 6: 5 KC-130T *Hercules*; 1 KC-130J *Hercules*
TPT • **Light** 44: 3 Beech A200 *King Air* (C-12C *Huron*); 6 Beech A200 *King Air* (UC-12F *Huron*); 7 Beech A200 *King Air* (UC-12M *Huron*); 19 C-2A *Greyhound*; 2 DHC-2 *Beaver* (U-6A); 7 SA-227-BC *Metro* III (C-26D)
TRG 409: 43 T-6A *Texan* II; 174 T-6B *Texan* II; 13 T-34C *Turbo Mentor*; 10 T-38C *Talon*; 32 T-44C *Pegasus*; 134 T-45C *Goshawk*; 2 TE-2C *Hawkeye*; 1 TE-6B
TILTROTOR • **TPT** 34 CMV-22B *Osprey*
HELICOPTERS
ASW 252 MH-60R *Seahawk*
MRH 235 MH-60S *Knight Hawk* (Multi Mission Support)
MCM 22 MH-53E *Sea Dragon*
ISR 6 OH-58C *Kiowa*
TPT 14: **Heavy** 1 CH-53E *Sea Stallion*; **Medium** 3 UH-60L *Black Hawk*; **Light** 10: 5 UH-72A *Lakota*; 2 UH-1N *Iroquois*; 3 UH-1Y *Venom*
TRG 103: 25 TH-57B *Sea Ranger*; 37 TH-57C *Sea Ranger*; 41 TH-73A
UNINHABITED AERIAL VEHICLES
ISR 69: **Heavy** 57: 8 MQ-4C *Triton*; 13 MQ-8B *Fire Scout*; 36 MQ-8C *Fire Scout*; **Light** 12 RQ-21A *Blackjack*
AIR-LAUNCHED MISSILES
AAM • **IR** AIM-9M *Sidewinder*; **IIR** AIM-9X *Sidewinder* II; **SARH** AIM-7 *Sparrow* (being withdrawn); **ARH** AIM-120C-5/C-7/D AMRAAM
ASM AGM-65F *Maverick*; AGM-114B/K/M *Hellfire*; APKWS
AShM AGM-84D *Harpoon*; AGM-119A *Penguin* 3; AGM-158C LRASM
ARM AGM-88B/C/E HARM/AARGM
LACM • **Conventional** AGM-84E/H/K SLAM/SLAM-ER
BOMBS
Laser-guided: GBU-10/-12/-16 *Paveway* II; GBU-24 *Paveway* III; GBU-51 LCDB
Laser & INS/GPS-guided: EGBU-12 *Paveway* II; EGBU-24 *Paveway* III; GBU-52 LCDB; GBU-54 Laser JDAM
INS/GPS-guided: GBU-31/-32/-38 JDAM; AGM-154A/C/C-1 JSOW
Multi-mode guided GBU-53/B *Stormbreaker*

Naval Aviation Reserve
FORCES BY ROLE
FIGHTER/GROUND ATTACK
1 sqn with F/A-18E/F *Super Hornet*
ANTI-SUBMARINE WARFARE
2 sqn with P-8A *Poseidon* (forming)
1 sqn with MH-60R *Seahawk*
ELECTRONIC WARFARE
1 sqn with EA-18G *Growler*
TRANSPORT
6 log spt sqn with B-737-700 (C-40A *Clipper*)
1 log spt sqn with Gulfstream V/G550 (C-37A/B)
5 sqn with C-130T/KC-130T *Hercules*
TRAINING
2 (aggressor) sqn with F-5F/N *Tiger* II
1 (aggressor) sqn with F-16C *Fighting Falcon*
EQUIPMENT BY TYPE
AIRCRAFT 70 combat capable
FTR 39: 8 F-5F *Tiger* II; 31 F-5N *Tiger* II
FGA 24: 12 F-16C *Fighting Falcon*; 9 F/A-18E *Super Hornet*; 3 F/A-18F *Super Hornet*
ASW 2 P-8A *Poseidon*
EW 5 EA-18G *Growler**
TKR/TPT 11 KC-130T *Hercules*
TPT 37: **Medium** 16 C-130T *Hercules*; **PAX** 21: 17 B-737-700 (C-40A *Clipper*); 1 Gulfstream V (C-37A); 3 Gulfstream G550 (C-37B)
TRG 152: 76 T-6B *Texan* II; 22 T-44C *Pegasus*; 54 T-45C *Goshawk*
HELICOPTERS
ASW 7 MH-60R *Seahawk*
MCM 7 MH-53E *Sea Dragon*

US Marine Corps 170,800

3 Marine Expeditionary Forces (MEF), 3 Marine Expeditionary Brigades (MEB), 7 Marine Expeditionary Units (MEU) drawn from 3 div. An MEU usually consists of a battalion landing team (1 SF coy, 1 lt armd recce coy, 1 recce pl, 1 armd pl, 1 amph aslt pl, 1 inf bn, 1 arty bty, 1 cbt engr pl), an aviation combat element (1 medium-lift sqn with attached atk hel, FGA ac and AD assets) and a composite log bn, with a combined total of about 2,200 personnel. Composition varies with mission requirements
FORCES BY ROLE
SPECIAL FORCES
(see USSOCOM)
MANOEUVRE
Reconnaissance
3 (MEF) recce coy
Amphibious
1 (1st) mne div (2 armd recce bn, 1 recce bn, 3 mne regt (4 mne bn), 1 amph aslt bn, 1 arty regt (3 arty bn, 1 MRL bn, 1 GLCM bty), 1 cbt engr bn, 1 EW bn, 1 int bn, 1 sigs bn)
1 (2nd) mne div (1 armd recce bn, 1 recce bn, 3 mne regt (3 mne bn), 1 amph aslt bn, 1 arty regt (2 arty bn), 1 cbt engr bn, 1 EW bn, 1 int bn, 1 sigs bn)
1 (3rd) mne div (1 recce bn, 1 mne regt (1 mne bn, 1 AD bn, 1 log bn), 1 arty regt HQ, 1 cbt spt bn (1 armd recce coy, 1 amph aslt coy, 1 cbt engr coy), 1 EW bn, 1 int bn, 1 sigs bn)

COMBAT SERVICE SUPPORT
 3 log gp

EQUIPMENT BY TYPE

ARMOURED FIGHTING VEHICLES
 IFV 488 LAV-25
 APC • APC (W) 207 LAV variants (66 CP; 127 log; 14 EW)
 AAV 1,401: 1,200 AAV-7A1 (all roles); 201 ACV
 AUV 6,929: 1,725 *Cougar*; ε4,500 JLTV; 704 M-ATV

ENGINEERING & MAINTENANCE VEHICLES
 AEV 42 M1 ABV
 ARV 105: 60 AAVRA1; 45 LAV-R
 MW 38 *Buffalo*; some *Husky* 2G
 VLB ε30 M60 AVLB

ANTI-TANK/ANTI-INFRASTRUCTURE
 MSL
  SP 106 LAV-AT
  MANPATS FGM-148 *Javelin*; FGM-172B SRAW-MPV; TOW

ARTILLERY 1,459
 TOWED 812: **105mm:** 331 M101A1; **155mm** 481 M777A2
 MRL 227mm 47 M142 HIMARS
 MOR 600: **81mm** 535 M252; **SP 81mm** 65 LAV-M; **120mm** (49 EFSS in store for trg)

UNINHABITED MARITIME PLATFORMS
 USV • Data 5 LRUSV

UNINHABITED AERIAL VEHICLES
 ISR • Light 100 BQM-147 *Exdrone*
 TPT 6 TRV-150C

AIR DEFENCE • SAM • Point-defence FIM-92 *Stinger*

Marine Corps Aviation 34,700

3 active Marine Aircraft Wings (MAW) and 1 MCR MAW

FORCES BY ROLE

FIGHTER/GROUND ATTACK
 2 sqn with AV-8B *Harrier* II
 1 sqn with F/A-18C *Hornet*
 4 sqn with F/A-18C/D *Hornet*
 7 sqn with F-35B *Lightning* II
 1 sqn with F-35C *Lightning* II
 1 sqn with F-35C *Lightning* II (forming)

COMBAT SEARCH & RESCUE/TRANSPORT
 1 sqn with Beech A200/B200 *King Air* (UC-12F/M *Huron*); Beech 350 *King Air* (UC-12W *Huron*); Cessna 560 *Citation Ultra/Encore* (UC-35C/D); Gulfstream IV (C-20G)

TANKER
 4 sqn with KC-130J *Hercules*

TRANSPORT
 15 sqn with MV-22B *Osprey*

TRAINING
 2 sqn with F-35B *Lightning* II

 1 sqn with MV-22B *Osprey*
 1 hel sqn with AH-1Z *Viper*; UH-1Y *Venom*
 1 hel sqn with CH-53E *Sea Stallion*

ATTACK HELICOPTER
 5 sqn with AH-1Z *Viper*; UH-1Y *Venom*

TRANSPORT HELICOPTER
 5 sqn with CH-53E *Sea Stallion*
 1 sqn with CH-53K *King Stallion* (forming)
 1 (VIP) sqn with MV-22B *Osprey*; VH-3D *Sea King*; VH-60N *White Hawk*

CISR UAV
 2 sqn with MQ-9A *Reaper*

ISR UAV
 1 sqn with RQ-21A *Blackjack*

AIR DEFENCE
 2 bn with M1097 *Avenger*; FIM-92 *Stinger*

EQUIPMENT BY TYPE

AIRCRAFT 381 combat capable
 FGA 381: 148 F-35B *Lightning* II; 15 F-35C *Lightning* II; 98 F/A-18C *Hornet*; 71 F/A-18D *Hornet*; 43 AV-8B *Harrier* II; 6 TAV-8B *Harrier*
 TKR/TPT 55 KC-130J *Hercules*
 TPT 20: **Light** 18: 2 Beech B200 *King Air* (UC-12F *Huron*); 2 Beech B200 *King Air* (UC-12M *Huron*); 7 Beech 350 *King Air* (C-12W *Huron*); 7 Cessna 560 *Citation Encore* (UC-35D); **PAX** 2 Gulfstream IV (C-20G)
 TRG 3 T-34C *Turbo Mentor*

TILTROTOR • TPT 291 MV-22B *Osprey*

HELICOPTERS
 ATK 130 AH-1Z *Viper*
 TPT 285: **Heavy** 140: 123 CH-53E *Sea Stallion*; 17 CH-53K *King Stallion* (in test); **Medium** 36: 10 VH-3D *Sea King* (VIP tpt); 5 VH-60N *White Hawk* (VIP tpt); 21 VH-92A; **Light** 109 UH-1Y *Venom*
 TRG 47: 10 TH-57B *Sea Ranger*; 14 TH-57C *Sea Ranger*; 23 TH-73A

UNINHABITED AERIAL VEHICLES
 CISR • Heavy 7 MQ-9A *Reaper*
 ISR • Light 40 RQ-21A *Blackjack*

AIR DEFENCE
 SAM • Point-defence FIM-92 *Stinger*; M1097 *Avenger*

AIR-LAUNCHED MISSILES
 AAM • IR AIM-9M *Sidewinder*; **IIR** AIM-9X *Sidewinder* II; **SARH** AIM-7P *Sparrow*; **ARH** AIM-120C AMRAAM
 ASM AGM-65E/F IR *Maverick*; AGM-114 *Hellfire*; AGM-176 *Griffin*; AGM-179A JAGM; AGR-20A APKWS
 AShM AGM-84D *Harpoon*
 ARM AGM-88 HARM
 LACM AGM-84E/H/K SLAM/SLAM-ER

BOMBS
 Laser-guided GBU-10/-12/-16 *Paveway* II

Laser & INS/GPS-guided: EGBU-12 *Paveway* II; GBU-49 Enhanced *Paveway* II; GBU-54 Laser JDAM
INS/GPS guided GBU-31/-32/-38 JDAM; AGM-154A/C/C-1 JSOW

Reserve Organisations

Marine Corps Reserve 33,200
FORCES BY ROLE
MANOEUVRE
Reconnaissance
2 MEF recce coy
Amphibious
1 (4th) mne div (1 armd recce bn, 1 recce bn, 2 mne regt (3 mne bn), 1 amph aslt bn, 1 arty regt (2 arty bn, 1 MRL bn), 1 cbt engr bn, 1 int bn, 1 sigs bn)
COMBAT SERVICE SUPPORT
1 log gp

Marine Corps Aviation Reserve 12,000 reservists
FORCES BY ROLE
FIGHTER/GROUND ATTACK
1 sqn with F/A-18C/C+ *Hornet*
TANKER
2 sqn with KC-130J *Hercules*
TRANSPORT
2 sqn with MV-22B *Osprey*
TRAINING
1 sqn with F-5F/N *Tiger* II
ATTACK HELICOPTER
2 sqn with AH-1Z *Viper*; UH-1Y *Venom*
TRANSPORT HELICOPTER
1 sqn with CH-53E *Sea Stallion*
EQUIPMENT BY TYPE
AIRCRAFT 26 combat capable
   FTR 14: 1 F-5F *Tiger* II; 13 F-5N *Tiger* II
   FGA 12: 5 F/A-18C *Hornet*; 7 F/A-18C+ *Hornet*
   TKR/TPT 12 KC-130J *Hercules*
   TPT 9: **Light** 7: 2 Beech A200 *King Air* (UC-12F); 2 Beech 350 *King Air* (UC-12W *Huron*); 3 Cessna 560 *Citation Encore* (UC-35D); **PAX** 2 B-737-700 (C-40A *Clipper*)
TILTROTOR • TPT 24 MV-22B *Osprey*
HELICOPTERS
   ATK 25 AH-1Z *Viper*
   TPT 28: **Heavy** 8 CH-53E *Sea Stallion*; **Light** 20 UH-1Y *Venom*

Marine Stand-by Reserve 700 reservists
Trained individuals available for mobilisation

US Coast Guard 39,750
9 districts (4 Pacific, 5 Atlantic)
EQUIPMENT BY TYPE
PATROL AND COASTAL COMBATANTS 330
   PSOH 23: 1 *Alex Haley*; 13 *Famous* with 1 76mm gun; 9 *Legend* with 1 Mk 15 *Phalanx* Block 1B CIWS, 1 57mm gun (capacity 2 MH-65 hel)
   PCO 65: 13 *Reliance* (with 1 hel landing platform); 52 *Sentinel* (Damen 4708)
   PCC 9 *Island*
   PBF 173 *Response Boat-Medium* (RB-M)
   PBI 60 *Marine Protector*
LOGISTICS AND SUPPORT 182
   AAR 117 47-foot *Motor Life Boat*
   ABU 52: 16 *Juniper*; 4 WLI; 14 *Keeper*; 18 WLR
   AGB 12: 9 *Bay*; 1 *Mackinaw*; 1 *Healy*; 1 *Polar* (1 additional *Polar* in reserve)
   AXS 1 *Eagle* (ex-GER *Gorch Fock*)
UNINHABITED MARITIME SYSTEMS
   UUV • MW SRS *Fusion*

US Coast Guard Aviation
EQUIPMENT BY TYPE
AIRCRAFT
   SAR 44: 11 HC-130H *Hercules*; 15 HC-130J *Hercules*; 5 HC-144A; 13 HC-144B
   TPT 16: **Medium** 14 C-27J *Spartan*; **PAX** 2 Gulfstream V (C-37A)
HELICOPTERS
   SAR 142: 44 MH-60T *Jayhawk*; 49 AS366G1 (MH-65D) *Dauphin* II; 49 AS366G1 (MH-65E) *Dauphin* II

US Air Force (USAF) 319,500

Almost the entire USAF (plus active-force ANG and AFR) is divided into 10 Aerospace Expeditionary Forces (AEF), each on call for 120 days every 20 months. At least 2 of the 10 AEFs are on call at any one time, each with 10,000–15,000 personnel, 90 multi-role ftr and bbr ac, 31 intra-theatre refuelling aircraft and 13 aircraft for ISR and EW missions

Global Strike Command (GSC)
2 active air forces (8th & 20th); 8 wg
FORCES BY ROLE
SURFACE-TO-SURFACE MISSILE
   9 ICBM sqn with LGM-30G *Minuteman* III
BOMBER
   4 sqn with B-1B *Lancer*
   2 sqn with B-2A *Spirit*
   5 sqn (incl 1 trg) with B-52H *Stratofortress*
COMMAND & CONTROL
   1 sqn with E-4B
TRANSPORT HELICOPTER
   3 sqn with UH-1N *Iroquois*

Air Combat Command (ACC)
2 active air forces (9th & 12th); 12 wg. ACC numbered air forces provide the air component to CENTCOM, SOUTHCOM and NORTHCOM

FORCES BY ROLE
FIGHTER
  2 sqn with F-22A *Raptor*
FIGHTER/GROUND ATTACK
  4 sqn with F-15E *Strike Eagle*
  3 sqn with F-16C/D *Fighting Falcon* (+4 sqn personnel only)
  4 sqn with F-35A *Lightning* II (+2 sqn personnel only)
GROUND ATTACK
  3 sqn with A-10C *Thunderbolt* II (+1 sqn personnel only)
ELECTRONIC WARFARE
  1 sqn with EA-18G *Growler* (personnel only – USN aircraft)
  2 sqn with EC-130H *Compass Call*
ISR
  1 sqn with E-11A
  5 sqn with RC-135/WC-135
  2 sqn with U-2S
AIRBORNE EARLY WARNING & CONTROL
  5 sqn with E-3 *Sentry*
COMBAT SEARCH & RESCUE
  2 sqn with HC-130J *Combat King* II
  3 sqn with HH-60W *Jolly Green* II
TRAINING
  1 (aggressor) sqn with F-16C *Fighting Falcon*
  1 (aggressor) sqn with F-35A *Lightning* II
  1 sqn with A-10C *Thunderbolt* II
  1 sqn with E-3 *Sentry*
  2 sqn with F-15E *Strike Eagle*
  1 sqn with F-22A *Raptor*
  1 sqn with RQ-4A *Global Hawk*; TU-2S
  1 UAV sqn with MQ-9A *Reaper*
COMBAT/ISR UAV
  9 sqn with MQ-9A *Reaper*
ISR UAV
  2 sqn with RQ-4B *Global Hawk*
  2 sqn with RQ-170 *Sentinel*
  1 sqn with RQ-180

Pacific Air Forces (PACAF)
Provides the air component of INDOPACOM, and commands air units based in Alaska, Hawaii, Japan and South Korea. 3 active air forces (5th, 7th, & 11th); 8 wg

FORCES BY ROLE
FIGHTER
  2 sqn with F-15C/D *Eagle*
  2 sqn with F-22A *Raptor* (+1 sqn personnel only)
FIGHTER/GROUND ATTACK
  5 sqn with F-16C/D *Fighting Falcon*
  2 sqn with F-35A *Lightning* II
GROUND ATTACK
  1 sqn with A-10C *Thunderbolt* II
AIRBORNE EARLY WARNING & CONTROL
  2 sqn with E-3 *Sentry*
COMBAT SEARCH & RESCUE
  1 sqn with HH-60G *Pave Hawk*
TANKER
  1 sqn with KC-135R (+1 sqn personnel only)
TRANSPORT
  1 sqn with B-737-200 (C-40B); Gulfstream V (C-37A)
  1 sqn with C-17A *Globemaster* (+1 sqn personnel only)
  1 sqn with C-130J-30 *Hercules*
  1 sqn with Beech 1900C (C-12J); UH-1N *Huey*
TRAINING
  1 (aggressor) sqn with F-16C/D *Fighting Falcon*

United States Air Forces in Europe - Air Forces Africa (USAFE-AFAFRICA)
Provides the air component to both EUCOM and AFRICOM. 1 active air force (3rd); 5 wg

FORCES BY ROLE
FIGHTER/GROUND ATTACK
  2 sqn with F-15E *Strike Eagle*
  3 sqn with F-16C/D *Fighting Falcon*
  2 sqn with F-35A *Lightning* II
COMBAT SEARCH & RESCUE
  1 sqn with HH-60G *Pave Hawk*
TANKER
  1 sqn with KC-135R *Stratotanker*
TRANSPORT
  1 sqn with C-130J-30 *Hercules*
  2 sqn with Gulfstream V (C-37A); Learjet 35A (C-21A); B-737-700 (C-40B)

Air Mobility Command (AMC)
Provides strategic and tactical airlift, air-to-air refuelling and aeromedical evacuation. 1 active air force (18th); 12 wg and 1 gp

FORCES BY ROLE
TANKER
  1 sqn with KC-10A *Extender*
  4 sqn with KC-46A *Pegasus*
  8 sqn with KC-135R/T *Stratotanker* (+2 sqn with personnel only)
TRANSPORT
  1 VIP sqn with B-737-200 (C-40B); B-757-200 (C-32A)
  1 VIP sqn with Gulfstream V (C-37A); Gulfstream 550 (C-37B)
  1 VIP sqn with VC-25 *Air Force One*
  2 sqn with C-5M *Super Galaxy*
  8 sqn with C-17A *Globemaster* III (+1 sqn personnel only)
  5 sqn with C-130J-30 *Hercules* (+1 sqn personnel only)
  1 sqn with Learjet 35A (C-21A)

Air Education and Training Command
1 active air force (2nd), 10 active air wg and 1 gp
FORCES BY ROLE
TRAINING
1 sqn with C-17A *Globemaster* III
1 sqn with C-130J-30 *Hercules*
3 sqn with F-16C/D *Fighting Falcon*
6 sqn with F-35A *Lightning* II
1 sqn with KC-46A *Pegasus*
1 sqn with KC-135R *Stratotanker*
5 (flying trg) sqn with T-1A *Jayhawk*
10 (flying trg) sqn with T-6A *Texan* II
10 (flying trg) sqn with T-38C *Talon*
5 UAV sqn with MQ-9A *Reaper*
EQUIPMENT BY TYPE
SURFACE-TO-SURFACE MISSILE LAUNCHERS
ICBM • Nuclear 400 LGM-30G *Minuteman* III (1 Mk12A or Mk21 re-entry veh per missile)
AIRCRAFT 1,511 combat capable
BBR 122: 44 B-1B *Lancer*; 20 B-2A *Spirit*; 58 B-52H *Stratofortress* (46 nuclear capable)
FTR 185: 20 F-15C/D *Eagle*; 165 F-22A *Raptor*
FGA 1,075: 218 F-15E *Strike Eagle*; 2 F-15EX *Eagle* II; 390 F-16C *Fighting Falcon*; 90 F-16D *Fighting Falcon*; 375 F-35A *Lightning* II
ATK 129 A-10C *Thunderbolt* II
CSAR 17 HC-130J *Combat King* II
EW 7: 1 EA-37B *Compass Call* (in test); 6 EC-130H *Compass Call*
ISR 42: 2 E-9A; 7 E-11A; 27 U-2S; 4 TU-2S; 2 WC-135R *Constant Phoenix*
ELINT 22: 8 RC-135V *Rivet Joint*; 9 RC-135W *Rivet Joint*; 3 RC-135S *Cobra Ball*; 2 RC-135U *Combat Sent*
AEW&C 20: 2 E-3B *Sentry*; 1 E-3C *Sentry*; 17 E-3G *Sentry*
C2 4 E-4B
TKR 153: 124 KC-135R *Stratotanker*; 29 KC-135T *Stratotanker*
TKR/TPT 68: 19 KC-10A *Extender*; 49 KC-46A *Pegasus*
TPT 336: **Heavy** 182: 36 C-5M *Super Galaxy*; 146 C-17A *Globemaster* III; **Medium** 105: 10 C-130J *Hercules*; 95 C-130J-30 *Hercules*; **Light** 23: 4 Beech 1900C (C-12J); 19 Learjet 35A (C-21A); **PAX** 26: 4 B-737-700 (C-40B); 4 B-757-200 (C-32A); 9 Gulfstream V (C-37A); 7 Gulfstream 550 (C-37B); 2 VC-25A *Air Force One*
TRG 1,074: 127 T-1A *Jayhawk*; 443 T-6A *Texan* II; 504 T-38A/C *Talon*
HELICOPTERS
MRH 4 MH-139A *Grey Wolf* (in test)
CSAR 64: 42 HH-60G *Pave Hawk*; 22 HH-60W *Jolly Green* II
TPT • Light 61 UH-1N *Huey*
UNINHABITED AERIAL VEHICLES 197
CISR • Heavy 170 MQ-9A *Reaper*
ISR • Heavy 27: 10 RQ-4B *Global Hawk*; ε10 RQ-170 *Sentinel*; ε7 RQ-180

AIR DEFENCE
SAM • Point-defence FIM-92 *Stinger*
AIR-LAUNCHED MISSILES
AAM • IR AIM-9M *Sidewinder*; **IIR** AIM-9X *Sidewinder* II; **SARH** AIM-7M *Sparrow*; **ARH** AIM-120C/D AMRAAM
ASM AGM-65D/G *Maverick*; AGM-114K/M/N/R *Hellfire* II; AGM-130A; AGM-176 *Griffin*; AGR-20A APKWS
AShM AGM-158C LRASM
LACM
  Nuclear AGM-86B (ALCM)
  Conventional AGM-158A JASSM; AGM-158B JASSM-ER
ARM AGM-88B/C HARM
EW MALD/MALD-J
BOMBS
Laser-guided GBU-10/-12/-16 *Paveway* II, GBU-24 *Paveway* III; GBU-28
Laser & INS/GPS-guided EGBU-24 *Paveway* III; EGBU-28; GBU-49 Enhanced *Paveway* II; GBU-54 Laser JDAM
INS/GPS-guided GBU-15 (with BLU-109 penetrating warhead or Mk84); GBU-31/-32/-38 JDAM; GBU-39B Small Diameter Bomb (250lb); GBU-43B MOAB; GBU-57A/B MOP
Multi-mode guided GBU-53/B *Stormbreaker*

Reserve Organisations
Air National Guard 104,850 reservists
FORCES BY ROLE
BOMBER
1 sqn with B-2A *Spirit* (personnel only)
FIGHTER
5 sqn with F-15C/D *Eagle*
1 sqn with F-22A *Raptor* (+1 sqn personnel only)
FIGHTER/GROUND ATTACK
8 sqn with F-16C/D *Fighting Falcon*
1 sqn with F-16C/D *Fighting Falcon* (forming)
3 sqn with F-35A *Lightning* II
GROUND ATTACK
3 sqn with A-10C *Thunderbolt* II
COMBAT SEARCH & RESCUE
3 sqn with HC-130J *Combat King* II
3 sqn with HH-60G *Pave Hawk*
TANKER
1 sqn with KC-46A *Pegasus*
16 sqn with KC-135R *Stratotanker* (+1 sqn personnel only)
3 sqn with KC-135T *Stratotanker*
TRANSPORT
1 sqn with B-737-700 (C-40C)
6 sqn with C-17A *Globemaster* (+2 sqn personnel only)
8 sqn with C-130H *Hercules*
1 sqn with C-130H/LC-130H *Hercules*
6 sqn with C-130J-30 *Hercules*

TRAINING
1 sqn with C-130H *Hercules*
1 sqn with F-15C/D *Eagle*
4 sqn with F-16C/D *Fighting Falcon*
1 sqn with MQ-9A *Reaper*
COMBAT/ISR UAV
10 sqn with MQ-9A *Reaper*
EQUIPMENT BY TYPE
AIRCRAFT 561 combat capable
FTR 157: 123 F-15C *Eagle*; 14 F-15D *Eagle*; 20 F-22A *Raptor*
FGA 332: 261 F-16C *Fighting Falcon*; 46 F-16D *Fighting Falcon*; 25 F-35A *Lightning* II
ATK 72 A-10C *Thunderbolt* II
CSAR 12 HC-130J *Combat King* II
TKR 159: 136 KC-135R *Stratotanker*; 23 KC-135T *Stratotanker*
TKR/TPT 12 KC-46A *Pegasus*
TPT 188: **Heavy** 50 C-17A *Globemaster* III; **Medium** 135: 83 C-130H *Hercules*; 42 C-130J-30 *Hercules*; 10 LC-130H *Hercules*; **PAX** 3 B-737-700 (C-40C)
HELICOPTERS • CSAR 16 HH-60G *Pave Hawk*
UNINHABITED AERIAL VEHICLES
CISR • Heavy 24 MQ-9A *Reaper*

Air Force Reserve Command 66,400 reservists
FORCES BY ROLE
BOMBER
1 sqn with B-52H *Stratofortress* (personnel only)
FIGHTER
2 sqn with F-22A *Raptor* (personnel only)
FIGHTER/GROUND ATTACK
2 sqn with F-16C/D *Fighting Falcon* (+1 sqn personnel only)
1 sqn with F-35A *Lightning* II (personnel only)
GROUND ATTACK
1 sqn with A-10C *Thunderbolt* II (+2 sqn personnel only)
ISR
1 (Weather Recce) sqn with WC-130J *Hercules*
AIRBORNE EARLY WARNING & CONTROL
1 sqn with E-3 *Sentry* (personnel only)
COMBAT SEARCH & RESCUE
1 sqn with HC-130J *Combat King* II
2 sqn with HH-60G *Pave Hawk*
TANKER
1 sqn with KC-10A *Extender* (personnel only)
1 sqn with KC-46A *Pegasus*
4 sqn with KC-46A *Pegasus* (personnel only)
6 sqn with KC-135R *Stratotanker* (+2 sqn personnel only)
TRANSPORT
1 (VIP) sqn with B-737-700 (C-40C)
2 sqn with C-5M *Super Galaxy* (+2 sqn personnel only)
3 sqn with C-17A *Globemaster* (+9 sqn personnel only)
6 sqn with C-130H *Hercules*
1 sqn with C-130J-30 *Hercules*
TRAINING
1 (aggressor) sqn with A-10C *Thunderbolt* II; F-15C/E *Eagle*; F-16 *Fighting Falcon*; F-22A *Raptor* (personnel only)
1 sqn with A-10C *Thunderbolt* II
1 sqn with B-52H *Stratofortress*
1 sqn with C-5M *Super Galaxy*
1 sqn with F-16C/D *Fighting Falcon*
5 (flying training) sqn with T-1A *Jayhawk*; T-6A *Texan* II; T-38C *Talon* (personnel only)
COMBAT/ISR UAV
2 sqn with MQ-9A *Reaper* (personnel only)
ISR UAV
1 sqn with RQ-4B *Global Hawk* (personnel only)
EQUIPMENT BY TYPE
AIRCRAFT 130 combat capable
BBR 18 B-52H *Stratofortress*
FGA 53: 51 F-16C *Fighting Falcon*; 2 F-16D *Fighting Falcon*
ATK 59 A-10C *Thunderbolt* II
CSAR 6 HC-130J *Combat King* II
ISR 10 WC-130J *Hercules* (Weather Recce)
TKR 59 KC-135R *Stratotanker*
TKR/TPT 12 KC-46A *Pegasus*
TPT 90: **Heavy** 42: 16 C-5M *Super Galaxy*; 26 C-17A *Globemaster* III; **Medium** 44: 34 C-130H *Hercules*; 10 C-130J-30 *Hercules*; **PAX** 4 B-737-700 (C-40C)
HELICOPTERS • CSAR 16 HH-60G *Pave Hawk*

Civil Reserve Air Fleet
Commercial ac numbers fluctuate
AIRCRAFT • TPT 517 international (391 long-range and 126 short-range); 36 national

Air Force Stand-by Reserve 16,850 reservists
Trained individuals for mobilisation

US Space Force 8,850
New service established December 2019, currently in the process of being stood up. Tasked with organising, training and equipping forces to protect US and allied space interests and to provide space capabilities to the joint Combatant Commands
EQUIPMENT BY TYPE
SATELLITES see Space
COUNTERSPACE see Space
RADAR see Strategic Defenses – Early Warning

US Special Operations Command (USSOCOM) 67,500
Commands all active, reserve and National Guard Special Operations Forces (SOF) of all services based in CONUS

Joint Special Operations Command

Reported to comprise elite US SOF, including Special Forces Operations Detachment Delta ('Delta Force'), SEAL Team 6 and integral USAF support

US Army Special Operations Command 36,000

FORCES BY ROLE
SPECIAL FORCES
  5 SF gp (4 SF bn, 1 spt bn)
  1 ranger regt (3 ranger bn; 1 cbt spt bn)
COMBAT SUPPORT
  1 civil affairs bde (5 civil affairs bn)
  1 psyops gp (3 psyops bn)
  1 psyops gp (4 psyops bn)
COMBAT SERVICE SUPPORT
  1 (sustainment) log bde (1 sigs bn)
HELICOPTER
  1 (160th SOAR) hel regt (4 hel bn)
EQUIPMENT BY TYPE
ARMOURED FIGHTING VEHICLES
  APC • **APC (W)** 28: 16 M1126 *Stryker* ICV; 12 *Pandur*
  AUV 640 M-ATV
ARTILLERY 20
  MOR • **120mm** 20 XM905 AMPS
AIRCRAFT
  TPT 12: **Medium** 7 C-27J *Spartan* (parachute training); **Light** 5 C-212 (parachute training)
HELICOPTERS
  MRH 51 AH-6M/MH-6M *Little Bird*
  TPT 139: **Heavy** 68 MH-47G *Chinook*; **Medium** 71 MH-60M *Black Hawk*
UNINHABITED AERIAL VEHICLES
  CISR • **Heavy** 24 MQ-1C *Gray Eagle*
  ISR • **Light** 29: 15 XPV-1 *Tern*; 14 XPV-2 *Mako*
  TPT • **Heavy** 28 CQ-10 *Snowgoose*

Reserve Organisations

Army National Guard
FORCES BY ROLE
SPECIAL FORCES
  2 SF gp (3 SF bn)

Army Reserve
FORCES BY ROLE
COMBAT SUPPORT
  2 psyops gp
  4 civil affairs comd HQ
  8 civil affairs bde HQ
  32 civil affairs bn (coy)

US Navy Special Warfare Command 11,000

FORCES BY ROLE
SPECIAL FORCES
  8 SEAL team (total: 48 SF pl)
  2 SEAL Delivery Vehicle team

Reserve Organisations

Naval Reserve Force
FORCES BY ROLE
SPECIAL FORCES
  8 SEAL det
  10 Naval Special Warfare det
  2 Special Boat sqn
  2 Special Boat unit
  1 SEAL Delivery Vehicle det

US Marine Special Operations Command (MARSOC) 3,500

FORCES BY ROLE
SPECIAL FORCES
  1 SF regt (3 SF bn)
COMBAT SUPPORT
  1 int bn
COMBAT SERVICE SUPPORT
  1 spt gp

Air Force Special Operations Command (AFSOC) 17,000

FORCES BY ROLE
GROUND ATTACK
  4 sqn with AC-130J *Ghostrider*
TRANSPORT
  4 sqn with CV-22B *Osprey*
  1 sqn with Do-328 (C-146A)
  5 sqn with MC-130J *Commando* II
  4 sqn with PC-12 (U-28A)
TRAINING
  1 sqn with CV-22A/B *Osprey*
  1 sqn with HC-130J *Combat King* II; MC-130J *Commando* II
  1 sqn with Bell 205 (TH-1H *Iroquois*)
  1 sqn with HH-60W *Jolly Green* II; UH-1N *Huey*
COMBAT/ISR UAV
  3 sqn with MQ-9 *Reaper*
EQUIPMENT BY TYPE
AIRCRAFT 31 combat capable
  ATK 31 AC-130J *Ghostrider*
  ISR 21 MC-12 *Javaman*
  CSAR 3 HC-130J *Combat King* II
  TPT 109: **Medium** 54 MC-130J *Commando* II; **Light** 55: 20 Do-328 (C-146A); 35 PC-12 (U-28A)
TILT-ROTOR 52 CV-22A/B *Osprey*
HELICOPTERS
  CSAR 7 HH-60W *Jolly Green* II
  TPT • **Light** 34: 28 Bell 205 (TH-1H *Iroquois*); 6 UH-1N *Huey*
UNINHABITED AERIAL VEHICLES • **CISR** • **Heavy** 50 MQ-9 *Reaper*

Reserve Organisations

Air National Guard
FORCES BY ROLE
ELECTRONIC WARFARE
1 sqn with EC-130J *Commando Solo*; MC-130J *Commando* II
ISR
1 sqn with MC-12W *Liberty*
TRANSPORT
1 flt with B-737-200 (C-32B)
EQUIPMENT BY TYPE
AIRCRAFT
EW 4 EC-130J *Commando Solo*
ISR 13 MC-12W *Liberty*
TPT 7: **Medium** 5: 3 C-130J *Hercules*; 2 MC-130J *Commando* II; **PAX** 2 B-757-200 (C-32B)

Air Force Reserve
FORCES BY ROLE
TRAINING
1 sqn with AC-130J *Ghostrider* (personnel only)
COMBAT/ISR UAV
1 sqn with MQ-9 *Reaper* (personnel only)

DEPLOYMENT

ARABIAN SEA: US Central Command • US Navy • 5th Fleet 400: 2 SSGN; **Combined Maritime Forces** • TF 53: 3 AKEH; 1 AOR

ARUBA: US Southern Command • 1 Cooperative Security Location at Reina Beatrix Airport

ASCENSION ISLAND: US Strategic Command • 1 detection and tracking radar at Ascension Auxiliary Air Field

AUSTRALIA: US Indo-Pacific Command • 1,700; 1 SEWS at Pine Gap; 1 comms facility at Pine Gap; 1 SIGINT stn at Pine Gap; **US Strategic Command** • 1 detection and tracking radar at Naval Communication Station Harold E. Holt

BAHRAIN: US Central Command • 4,500; 1 HQ (5th Fleet); 4 MCO; 1 ESB; 1 ASW flt with 3 P-8A *Poseidon*; 1 EP-3E *Aries* II; 2 SAM bty with M902/M903 *Patriot* PAC-3/PAC-3 MSE

BELGIUM: US European Command • 1,150

BRITISH INDIAN OCEAN TERRITORY: US Strategic Command • 300; 1 Spacetrack Optical Tracker at Diego Garcia; 1 ground-based electro-optical deep space surveillance system (GEODSS) at Diego Garcia **US Indo-Pacific Command** • 1 MPS sqn (MPS-2 with equipment for one MEB) at Diego Garcia with 2 AKRH; 3 AKR; 1 AKEH; 1 ESD; 1 naval air base at Diego Garcia, 1 support facility at Diego Garcia

BULGARIA: NATO • Enhanced Vigilance Activities 150; 1 armd inf coy with M2A3 *Bradley*

CANADA: US Northern Command • 150

CENTRAL AFRICAN REPUBLIC: UN • MINUSCA 9

COLOMBIA: US Southern Command • 70

CUBA: US Southern Command • 650 (JTF-GTMO) at Guantanamo Bay

CURACAO: US Southern Command • 1 Cooperative Security Location at Hato Airport

DEMOCRATIC REPUBLIC OF THE CONGO: UN • MONUSCO 3

DJIBOUTI: US Africa Command • 4,000; 1 tpt sqn with C-130H/J-30 *Hercules*; 1 tpt sqn with 12 MV-22B *Osprey*; 2 KC-130J *Hercules*; 1 spec ops sqn with MC-130J; PC-12 (U-28A); 1 CSAR sqn with HH-60G *Pave Hawk*; 1 CISR UAV sqn with MQ-9A *Reaper*; 1 naval air base

EGYPT: MFO 465; elm 1 ARNG inf bn; 1 ARNG spt bn

EL SALVADOR: US Southern Command • 1 Cooperative Security Location at Comalapa Airport

GERMANY: US Africa Command • 1 HQ at Stuttgart **US European Command** • 39,050; 1 Combined Service HQ (EUCOM) at Stuttgart–Vaihingen
US Army 24,700
FORCES BY ROLE
1 HQ (US Army Europe & Africa (USAREUR-AF)) at Wiesbaden; 1 arty comd; 1 spec ops gp; 1 recce bn; 1 mech bde(-); 1 MRL bde (3 MRL bn); 1 fd arty bn; 1 (cbt avn) hel bde; 1 (cbt avn) hel bde HQ; 2 int bde; 1 MP bde; 1 sigs bde; 1 (MDTF) cbt spt bde(-); 1 spt bde; 1 SAM bde; 1 (APS) armd bde eqpt set
EQUIPMENT BY TYPE
M1A2 SEPv2/v3 *Abrams*; M2A3/M3A3 *Bradley*; M1296 *Stryker Dragoon*, M109A6; M119A3; M777A2; M270A1; M142 HIMARS; AH-64E *Apache*; CH-47F *Chinook*; UH-60L/M *Black Hawk*; HH-60M *Black Hawk*; M902 *Patriot* PAC-3; M1097 *Avenger*; M-SHORAD
US Navy 400
USAF 13,400
FORCES BY ROLE
1 HQ (US Air Forces in Europe and Africa) at Ramstein AB; 1 HQ (3rd Air Force) at Ramstein AB; 1 FGA wg at Spangdahlem AB with (1 FGA sqn with 24 F-16C/D *Fighting Falcon*); 1 tpt wg at Ramstein AB with 14 C-130J-30 *Hercules*; 2 Gulfstream V (C-37A); 5 Learjet 35A (C-21A); 1 B-737-700 (C-40B)
USMC 550

GREECE: US European Command • 600; 1 hel bn with UH-60M/HH-60M *Black Hawk*; 1 ELINT flt with 1 EP-3E *Aries* II; 1 naval base at Makri; 1 naval base at Souda Bay; 1 air base at Iraklion

GREENLAND (DNK): US Strategic Command • 100; 1 AN/FPS-132 Upgraded Early Warning Radar and 1 Spacetrack Radar at Thule

GUAM: US Indo-Pacific Command • 9,000; 4 SSGN; 1 MPS sqn (MPS-3 with equipment for one MEB) with 2 AKRH; 4 AKR; 1 ESD; 1 AKEH; 1 tkr sqn with 12 KC-135R *Stratotanker*; 1 tpt hel sqn with MH-60S; 1 ISR UAV unit with 2 MQ-4C *Triton*; 1 SAM bty with THAAD; 1 air base; 1 naval base

HONDURAS: US Southern Command • 400; 1 avn bn with 4 CH-47F *Chinook*; 12 UH-60L/HH-60L *Black Hawk*

HUNGARY: NATO • Enhanced Vigilance Activities 150; 1 armd inf coy with M2A3 *Bradley*

IRAQ: US Central Command • *Operation Inherent Resolve* 2,000; 1 inf bde(-); 1 atk hel bn with AH-64E *Apache*; MQ-1C *Gray Eagle*; 1 spec ops hel bn with MH-47G *Chinook*; MH-60M *Black Hawk*; 1 CISR UAV sqn with MQ-9A *Reaper*; 2 SAM bty with M902/M903 *Patriot* PAC-3/PAC-3 MSE; **NATO** • NATO Mission Iraq 12

ISRAEL: US Strategic Command • 100; 1 AN/TPY-2 X-band radar at Mount Keren

ITALY: US European Command • 13,050
US Army 4,250; 1 AB bde(-)
US Navy 3,600; 1 HQ (US Naval Forces Europe-Africa (NAVEUR-NAVAF/6th Fleet) at Naples; 1 LCC; 1 ASW sqn with 5 P-8A *Poseidon* at Sigonella
USAF 4,800; 1 FGA wg with (2 FGA sqn with 21 F-16C/D *Fighting Falcon* at Aviano; 1 CSAR sqn with 8 HH-60G *Pave Hawk* at Aviano); 1 CISR UAV sqn with MQ-9A *Reaper* at Sigonella; 1 ISR UAV flt with RQ-4B *Global Hawk* at Sigonella
USMC 400; 1 tpt sqn with 6 MV-22B *Osprey*; 2 KC-130J *Hercules*

JAPAN: US Indo-Pacific Command • 55,600
US Army 2,600; 1 corps HQ (fwd); 1 SF gp; 1 avn bn; 1 SAM bn with M903 *Patriot* PAC-3 MSE
US Navy 20,000; 1 HQ (7th Fleet) at Yokosuka; 1 base at Sasebo; 1 base at Yokosuka

FORCES BY ROLE

3 FGA sqn at Iwakuni with 10 F/A-18E *Super Hornet*; 1 FGA sqn at Iwakuni with 10 F/A-18F *Super Hornet*; 2 ASW sqn at Misawa/Kadena AB with 5 P-8A *Poseidon*; 2 EW sqn at Iwakuni/Misawa with 5 EA-18G *Growler*; 1 ELINT flt at Kadena AB with 2 EP-3E *Aries* II; 1 AEW&C sqn at Iwakuni with 5 E-2D *Hawkeye*; 2 ASW hel sqn at Atsugi with 12 MH-60R;1 tpt hel sqn at Atsugi with 12 MH-60S

EQUIPMENT BY TYPE

1 CVN; 3 CGHM; 6 DDGHM; 3 DDGM; 1 LCC; 4 MCO; 1 LHA; 2 LPD; 1 LSD
USAF 13,000

FORCES BY ROLE

1 HQ (5th Air Force) at Kadena AB; 1 ftr wg at Misawa AB with (2 FGA sqn with 22 F-16C/D *Fighting Falcon*); 1 wg at Kadena AB with (2 ftr sqn with 10 F-15C/D *Eagle*; 1 ftr sqn with 12 F-15C *Eagle*; 2 FGA sqn with 14 F-15E *Strike Eagle*; 1 FGA sqn with 12 F-35A *Lightning* II; 1 tkr sqn with 15 KC-135R *Stratotanker*; 1 AEW&C sqn with 2 E-3G *Sentry*; 1 CSAR sqn with 10 HH-60G *Pave Hawk*; 1 CISR UAV sqn with 4 MQ-9A *Reaper*); 1 tpt wg at Yokota AB with 10 C-130J-30 *Hercules*; 3 Beech 1900C (C-12J); 1 Spec Ops gp at Kadena AB with (1 sqn with 5 MC-130J *Commando* II; 1 sqn with 5 CV-22B *Osprey*); 1 ISR sqn with RC-135 *Rivet Joint*; 1 ISR UAV flt with 5 RQ-4A *Global Hawk*
USMC 20,000

FORCES BY ROLE

1 mne div; 1 mne regt HQ; 1 arty regt HQ; 1 recce bn; 1 mne bn; 1 amph aslt bn; 1 arty bn; 1 FGA sqn with 12 F/A-18C/D *Hornet*; 2 FGA sqn with 10 F-35B *Lightning* II; 1 tkr sqn with 12 KC-130J *Hercules*; 2 tpt sqn with 12 MV-22B *Osprey*

US Strategic Command • 1 AN/TPY-2 X-band radar at Shariki; 1 AN/TPY-2 X-band radar at Kyogamisaki

JORDAN: US Central Command • *Operation Inherent Resolve* 3,000: 1 FGA sqn with 18 F-15E *Strike Eagle*; 1 FGA sqn with 12 F-16C *Fighting Falcon*; 1 CISR UAV sqn with 12 MQ-9A *Reaper*; 2 SAM bty with M902/M903 *Patriot* PAC-3/PAC-3 MSE

KOREA, REPUBLIC OF: US Indo-Pacific Command • 30,400
US Army 21,500

FORCES BY ROLE

1 HQ (8th Army) at Pyeongtaek; 1 div HQ (2nd Inf) located at Pyeongtaek; 1 mech bde; 1 (cbt avn) hel bde; 1 MRL bde; 1 AD bde; 1 SAM bty with THAAD

EQUIPMENT BY TYPE

M1A2 SEPv2 *Abrams*; M2A3/M3A3 *Bradley*; M109A6; M270A1 MLRS; AH-64D/E *Apache*; CH-47F *Chinook*; UH-60L/M *Black Hawk*; M902 *Patriot* PAC-3; THAAD; FIM-92A *Avenger*; 1 (APS) armd bde eqpt set
US Navy 350
USAF 8,350

FORCES BY ROLE

1 (AF) HQ (7th Air Force) at Osan AB; 1 ftr wg at Osan AB with (1 ftr sqn with 20 F-16C/D *Fighting Falcon*; 1 atk sqn with 24 A-10C *Thunderbolt* II); 1 ftr wg at Kunsan AB with (2 ftr sqn with 20 F-16C/D *Fighting Falcon*); 1 ISR sqn at Osan AB with U-2S
USMC 200

KOSOVO: NATO • KFOR • *Joint Enterprise* 593; elm 1 ARNG inf bde HQ; 1 ARNG AB bn HQ; 1 ARNG inf coy; 1 hel flt with UH-60

KUWAIT: US Central Command • 10,000; 1 ARNG armd bn; 1 ARNG (cbt avn) hel bde; 1 spt bde; 1 CISR UAV sqn with MQ-9A *Reaper*; 1 (APS) armd bde set; 1 (APS) inf bde set; 2 SAM bty with M902/M903 *Patriot* PAC-3/PAC-3 MSE

LIBYA: UN • UNSMIL 1

LITHUANIA: US European Command • 250; 1 radar unit

MARSHALL ISLANDS: US Strategic Command • 20; 1 detection and tracking radar at Kwajalein Atoll

MEDITERRANEAN SEA: US European Command • 6th Fleet 12,500; 2 SSGN; 2 CVN; 2 CGHM; 3 DDGHM; 1 LPD

MIDDLE EAST: UN • UNTSO 3

NETHERLANDS: US European Command • 450

NIGER: US Africa Command • 1,100; 1 CISR sqn with MQ-9A *Reaper*

NORWAY: US European Command • 1,100; 1 (USMC) MEU eqpt set; 1 (APS) SP 155mm arty bn set

PERSIAN GULF: US Central Command • US Navy • 5th Fleet 800: 2 DDGHM; 6 (Coast Guard) PCC

PHILIPPINES: US Indo-Pacific Command • *Operation Pacific Eagle – Philippines* 200

POLAND: NATO • Enhanced Forward Presence 1,000; 1 armd bn with M1A2 SEPv3 *Abrams*; M2A3 *Bradley*; 1 arty bty with M109A6 **US European Command** • 15,000; 1 corps HQ; 2 div HQ; 2 armd bde with M1A2 SEPv2 *Abrams*; M3A3 *Bradley*; M2A3 *Bradley*; M109A6/A7; 2 SAM bty with M902 *Patriot* PAC-3; 1 FGA flt with 4 F-16C *Fighting Falcon*; 1 CISR UAV sqn with MQ-9A *Reaper*

PORTUGAL: US European Command • 250; 1 spt facility at Lajes

QATAR: US Central Command • 10,000: 1 ISR sqn with 4 RC-135 *Rivet Joint*; 2 tkr sqn with 12 KC-135R/T *Stratotanker*; 1 tpt sqn with 4 C-17A *Globemaster*; 4 C-130H/J-30 *Hercules*; 2 SAM bty with M902/M903 *Patriot* PAC-3/PAC-3 MSE **US Strategic Command** • 1 AN/TPY-2 X-band radar

RED SEA: US Central Command • 5th Fleet 4,500; 3 DDGHM; 1 LHD; 1 LSD

ROMANIA: NATO • Enhanced Air Policing 100; 4 F-16C *Fighting Falcon*; **US European Command** • 4,000; 1 air aslt bde with M119A3; M777A3; 1 *Aegis Ashore* BMD unit with three 8-cell Mk 41 VLS launchers with SM-3

SAUDI ARABIA: US Central Command • 2,500; 2 FGA sqn with 12 F-16C *Fighting Falcon*; 1 tkr sqn with 12 KC-135R *Stratotanker*; 1 AEW&C sqn with 4 E-3B/G *Sentry*; 1 SAM bty with M902/M903 *Patriot* PAC-3/PAC-3 MSE; 1 SAM bty with THAAD

SINGAPORE: US Indo-Pacific Command • 200; 1 log spt sqn; 1 spt facility

SLOVAKIA: NATO • Enhanced Vigilance Activities 160; 1 recce tp (coy)

SOMALIA: US Africa Command • 100

SOUTH SUDAN: UN • UNMISS 6

SPAIN: US European Command • 3,250; 4 DDGM; 1 air base at Morón; 1 naval base at Rota

SYRIA: US Central Command • *Operation Inherent Resolve* 900; 1 armd inf coy; 1 spec ops bn(-)

THAILAND: US Indo-Pacific Command • 100

TURKIYE: US European Command • 1,700; 1 air base at Incirlik **US Strategic Command** • 1 AN/TPY-2 X-band radar at Kürecik

UNITED ARAB EMIRATES: US Central Command • 5,000: 2 atk sqn with 12 A-10C *Thunderbolt* II; 1 ISR sqn with 4 U-2S; 1 ISR UAV sqn with RQ-4 *Global Hawk*; 2 SAM bty with M902/M903 *Patriot* PAC-3/PAC-3 MSE

UNITED KINGDOM: US European Command • 10,000

FORCES BY ROLE

1 bbr flt at RAF Fairford with 4 B-1B *Lancer*; 1 ftr wg at RAF Lakenheath with (2 FGA sqn with 27 F-15E *Strike Eagle*, 1 FGA sqn with 27 F-35A *Lightning* II; 1 FGA sqn with 14 F-35A *Lightning* II); 1 ISR sqn at RAF Mildenhall with RC-135; 1 tkr wg at RAF Mildenhall with 15 KC-135R/T *Stratotanker*; 1 spec ops gp at RAF Mildenhall with (1 sqn with 8 CV-22B *Osprey*; 1 sqn with 8 MC-130J *Commando* II)

US Strategic Command • 1 AN/FPS-132 Upgraded Early Warning Radar and 1 Spacetrack Radar at Fylingdales Moor

WESTERN SAHARA: UN • MINURSO 1

FOREIGN FORCES

Germany Air Force: trg units with 40 T-38 *Talon*; 69 T-6A *Texan* II; • Missile trg at Fort Bliss (TX)

Netherlands 1 hel trg sqn with AH-64D *Apache*; CH-47D *Chinook*

Singapore Air Force: trg units with F-16C/D; 12 F-15SG; AH-64D *Apache*; 6+ CH-47D *Chinook* hel

Chapter Three
Europe

- Finland became the 31st NATO member, adding considerable military capability to the Alliance. The country joined less than a year after formally applying for membership. Sweden was still awaiting Turkiye and Hungary to sign off on its application as of December.
- The European Sky Shield Initiative promoted by Germany to create greater capacity and cohesion in the region around air- and missile-defence gained steam. More than a dozen countries signed on, although France, along with Italy, remained outside.
- NATO's European members have increased military spending, with more reaching the Alliance's target of spending 2% of GDP on defence. *Military Balance* data shows that in 2023, ten European NATO allies reached the agreed objective, up from eight countries in 2022 and just two in 2014. Efforts at the NATO summit in Vilnius last year to turn the 2% target into a minimum commitment failed to win sufficient backing, though.
- Europe's defence industry has been ramping up output of ammunition, missiles and other equipment to satisfy demand from Ukraine and local needs after several countries transferred military equipment to Kyiv. Germany's Rheinmetall acquired Spanish ammunition maker Expal to boost production capacity, Nexter increased the production rate and cut lead-times for CAESAR artillery systems, and MBDA began making more *Mistral* air-defence missiles.
- The European Union, in March, proposed an ammunition initiative to provide Ukraine with one million rounds of artillery ammunition within a year, replenish European stockpiles and boost production capacities. But the effort was on pace to miss the commitment to get Kyiv the shells by March 2024, highlighting the scale of the ramp-up challenge.
- Concerns over critical infrastructure vulnerabilities grew in Europe in 2023. Little more than a year after the deliberate rupture of the Nord Stream gas pipelines in September 2022, Finland and Estonia said an undersea gas pipeline and telecommunications cable linking the two countries were damaged in a deliberate act. Sweden reported a similar event. The precise actor behind each attack was not immediately identified.

Europe defence spending, 2023 – top 5

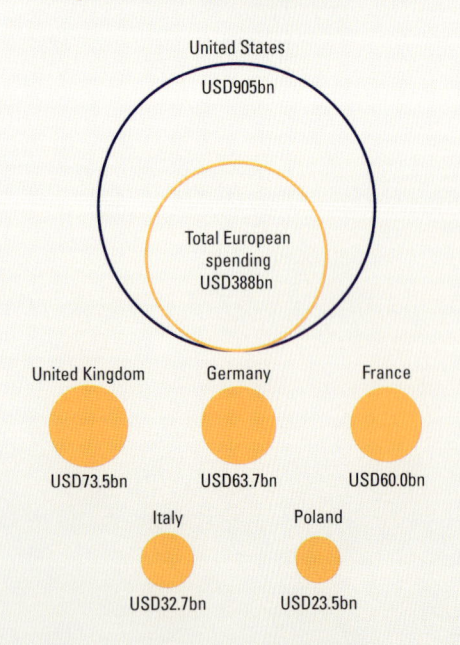

- United States USD905bn
- Total European spending USD388bn
- United Kingdom USD73.5bn
- Germany USD63.7bn
- France USD60.0bn
- Italy USD32.7bn
- Poland USD23.5bn

Active military personnel – top 10
(15,000 per unit)

- Turkiye 355,200
- France 203,850
- Germany 181,000
- Italy 160,900
- United Kingdom 144,400
- Greece 132,200
- Spain 124,150
- Poland 100,450
- Romania 69,900
- Bulgaria 36,950

Global total 20,646,000

Regional total 1,933,000 (9.4%)

Regional defence policy and economics   56 ▶

Arms procurements and deliveries   70 ▶

Armed forces data section   71 ▶

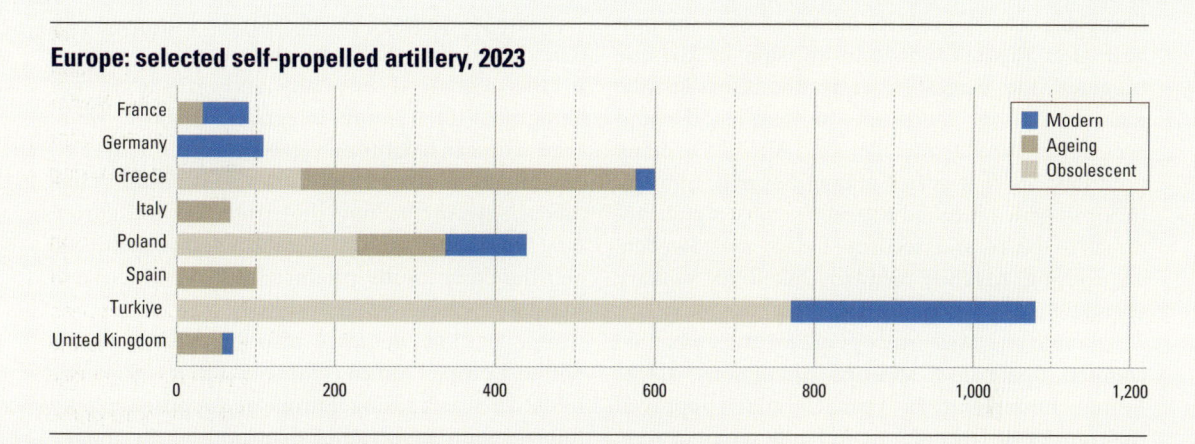

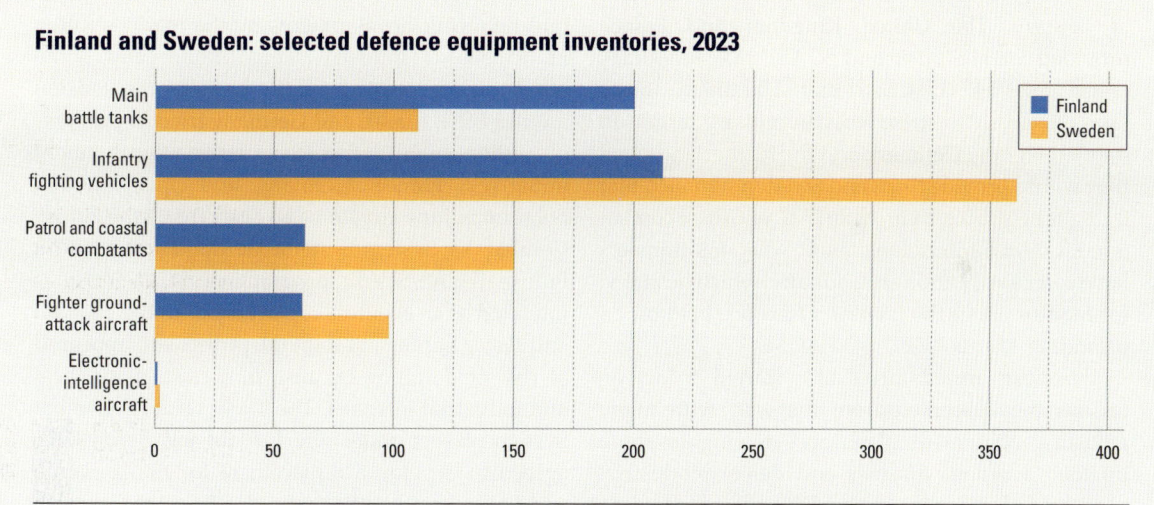

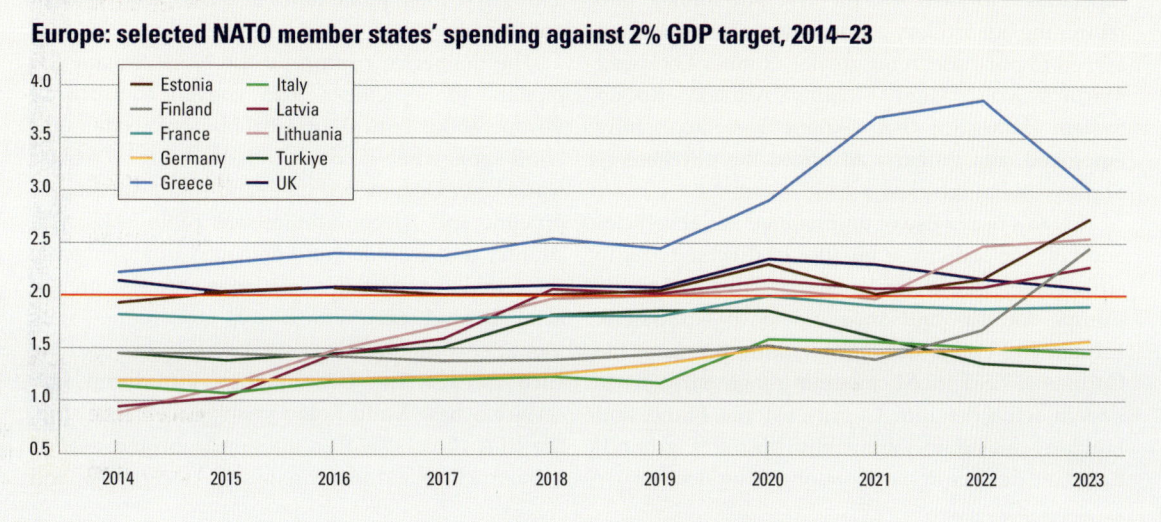

Europe: selected self-propelled artillery, 2023

Legend: Modern, Ageing, Obsolescent

Countries: France, Germany, Greece, Italy, Poland, Spain, Turkiye, United Kingdom

X-axis: 0 to 1,200

Finland and Sweden: selected defence equipment inventories, 2023

Legend: Finland, Sweden

Categories: Main battle tanks, Infantry fighting vehicles, Patrol and coastal combatants, Fighter ground-attack aircraft, Electronic-intelligence aircraft

X-axis: 0 to 400

Europe: selected NATO member states' spending against 2% GDP target, 2014–23

Legend: Estonia, Finland, France, Germany, Greece, Italy, Latvia, Lithuania, Turkiye, UK

Y-axis: 0.5 to 4.0

X-axis: 2014 to 2023

Europe

European defence postures hardened over the past year after Russia's full-scale invasion of Ukraine triggered the biggest reset in the Euro-Atlantic region's security landscape in decades. Finland became a NATO member in April; Germany published its first-ever National Security Strategy (NSS) in which it called Russia the most significant threat to peace and security today; and Sweden, an aspiring Alliance member, hiked its military spending plan by around 28%.

Ukraine and Western support for the embattled country dominated security discussions across Europe throughout the year. Germany approved the transfer of *Leopard* 2 main battle tanks to Kyiv in January. The United Kingdom and France provided *Storm Shadow* and SCALP EG land-attack cruise missiles (LACMs) that Ukrainian forces used effectively to strike Russian military targets in depth. Belgium, Denmark and the Netherlands said they would provide F-16s and Sweden signalled that it might be willing to provide JAS-39 *Gripen* combat aircraft. Not all decisions about weapons transfers have come easily, though. Germany, which hesitated for months about the *Leopard* 2 transfer, held off on providing Taurus KEPD 350 LACMs.

European armed forces also started to act on lessons they observed from the war, with many adjusting equipment plans and moving to shore up their weapons arsenals and defence-industrial capacities. For instance, the UK put money into rebuilding its artillery-ammunition stocks, Poland agreed to purchase in far greater number Lockheed Martin's M142 High Mobility Artillery Rocket System (HIMARS) that Ukraine has successfully employed, and Bulgaria advanced the purchase of *Stryker* combat vehicles.

Russia's heavy use of uninhabited aerial vehicles and ballistic and cruise missiles of diverse types to strike targets in Ukraine has spurred demand across Europe for air- and missile-defence equipment. Estonia and Latvia decided to jointly purchase the German IRIS-T SLM medium-range air-defence system, while Belgium, Cyprus, Estonia, France and Hungary intend to jointly buy *Mistral* 3 ground-based air-defence systems, among other deals.

Germany pressed ahead with the European Sky Shield Initiative (ESSI) to prevail upon countries in the region to buy air- and missile-defence equipment in a more integrated manner. More than a dozen countries signed on. Germany also committed to investment in its own capacity in this arena, agreeing to buy the *Arrow* 3 system from Israel to defend against intermediate-range threats, and the domestically produced IRIS-T SLM system to counter shorter-range systems.

But Berlin's initiative also exposed divisions within Europe. France complained that Germany's initiative was causing European countries to buy foreign equipment rather than putting the money into financing developments by the region's (often France-based) industry. Paris, Rome and some others stayed outside ESSI. Despite the tension around ESSI, France and Germany tried to progress on other high-profile cooperative development initiatives. France, Germany and Spain invited Belgium in June 2023 to be an observer on the Future Combat Air System/Systeme de Combat Aerien du Future (FCAS/SCAF) programme. FCAS/SCAF is intended as an eventual replacement for the *Typhoon* and *Rafale* fighters, though the project still appeared at risk of derailing because of a clash of political and industrial interests. The Major Ground Combat System project under which Paris and Berlin have agreed to develop a replacement for the *Leopard* 2 and *Leclerc* main battle tanks also advanced, though only slowly.

The deliberate rupture of the Nord Stream gas pipeline in September 2022 revived concerns in Europe about critical-infrastructure protection and blind spots when it comes to issues such as seabed warfare. In October 2023, Finland said a subsea gas pipeline and telecommunications cable linking its country and Estonia were damaged in a deliberate act. Sweden reported a similar event. The precise actor behind each attack was not immediately identified, highlighting weaknesses in tracking such threats. The UK, in 2023, introduced into service a new Multi-Role Ocean Surveillance ship, the RFA *Proteus*, with a mission to protect seabed infrastructure and to mitigate such uncertainty, and established a strategic partnership with Norway to counter undersea threats. Germany reflected similar concerns in its Fleet and Force Structure 2035+ vision for the country's navy, which called for greater use of uninhabited maritime systems. The European Union, in May 2023, launched an Italian-led cooperative programme to improve operational efficiency to protect critical maritime infrastructure.

While Ukraine was the driver of defence-policy developments, European security planners kept an eye on the economically vital Indo-Pacific region. The UK committed to play a role in Asia and stuck with plans for a Carrier Strike Group deployment in 2025. German Defence Minister Boris Pistorius, at the IISS Shangri-La Dialogue in June, said the country's navy would send two warships to the region in 2024, and Berlin later issued its first China strategy that aimed to balance economic interests with differences over security issues. The German army, for the first time, participated in the *Talisman Sabre* exercise in Australia in 2023 to underline Berlin's interest in the Indo-Pacific. Following on from its deployment of six *Typhoons*, and some A400Ms and A330 MRTTs to Australia's Exercise *Pitch Black* in 2022, the German air force announced a greater ambition for its 2024 participation. Alongside aircraft from France and Spain, the air force plans to send more *Typhoons* and over ten *Tornados*. Italy conducted a bilateral air-force training drill with Japan in August 2023, deployed an offshore patrol ship to the region last year and planned to deploy the *Cavour* aircraft carrier to the region.

European efforts to help bring about greater stability in Africa, however, suffered setbacks in 2023. A coup in Niger that inflamed sentiment against former colonial power France caused Paris to withdraw its forces. It also resulted in the suspension of two EU security-assistance missions to the country. Germany redeployed troops from Mali after the military rulers that had taken power in a coup in 2021 called for an end to the UN operation there, which Berlin had supported. France drew down in Mali and Burkina Faso, and others, including the Czech Republic, Italy, and Sweden, adjusted their footprint in the region.

Despite much common ground in the European security-policy debate in 2023, there were also sharp differences. Turkiye and Hungary, as of December, had not ratified Sweden's application for NATO membership. A Russia-leaning politician won parliamentary elections in Slovakia, potentially weakening the European consensus on supporting Ukraine. Tensions also flared in the Balkans, with Serbia becoming more aggressive towards Kosovo and marshalling troops along the shared border, drawing strong rebukes and the deployment of additional forces from Western countries that had backed Kosovo's move towards independence.

Ukraine and other security challenges kept European defence budgets on an upward trajectory, bringing more of the region's NATO members in line with the Alliance's target of each partner spending 2% of GDP on defence. Latvia planned to spend 3% of GDP on defence by 2027, matching Estonia's ambition. But policy debates in 2023 also demonstrated that meeting and sustaining the headline figure is not a given in many European capitals.

Germany, the region's biggest economy, is meeting the 2% target largely because of a EUR100 billion (USD105bn) special defence fund agreed in 2022 in response to Russia's invasion of Ukraine. Berlin, in the discussion around its new NSS, passed on making a clear commitment to the NATO goal, saying merely that the country aimed to meet the objective as an average on a multi-year period. The NSS reflected an outcome of months of wrangling among the coalition government. Berlin held back on creating a national security council, which was under consideration, and tried to strike a balance between more hawkish and dovish elements when it comes to China. Germany in November issued its first defence policy guidelines since 2011 to translate the country's NSS into a framework underpinning the Bundeswehr's military strategy, culture and planning. The guidelines signal a greater interest in Indo-Pacific defence engagement and argue that Beijing is 'trying to reshape the international order as it sees fit'. The document also aimed to reassure allies, especially those on NATO's eastern flank, about Germany's willingness to play a central role in collective defence. The document also stressed the country's desire to move with pace on equipment modernisation, with Berlin planning to prioritise availability in making procurement decisions. The UK also revisited security-policy documents in 2023 with refreshed editions of its Integrated Review and its Defence Command Paper. The documents, even more than the earlier iterations two years prior, put the defence of the Euro-Atlantic region at the centre of the country's national-security thinking, though they kept alive the ambition to be active elsewhere. In addition to its carrier-deployment commitment to Asia, London said it would forward-deploy an attack submarine to Western Australia from 2027 as part of the AUKUS agreement with the United States and Australia.

Poland sustained the momentum behind its extensive force-modernisation drive. The country cut steel on its first *Miecznik*-class frigate and on a new signals-intelligence vessel. It began taking delivery of FA-50 light attack aircraft and received its first battery of *Patriot* air-defence systems, among other programmes. Poland remained one of the main hubs for Western countries to resupply Ukraine, though a spat with Kyiv over wheat exports briefly threatened to derail the close partnership between the countries amid election politics in Warsaw. Poland also was on alert for hybrid-warfare-type activities from Belarus, a close ally of Moscow.

France laid out a road map for higher defence outlays as part of its multi-year Loi de Programmation Militaire (LPM) defence-spending plan. The financial commitment would see France spend EUR60.0bn (USD64.0bn) on defence by 2030, a hike of more than 36% from the 2023 figure. Advancing towards the next LPM, France is expected to define a midterm national strategic review and agree on a new defence white paper to underpin a future LPM. French defence-modernisation efforts include a desire to develop a new aircraft carrier and hypersonic cruise missile. In June, Paris conducted the first launch of a hypersonic glide vehicle, the V-MaX, spotlighting its interest in high-speed-weapons technology.

Other European countries also committed to big-ticket equipment plans that will shape the nature of their armed forces for decades to come. Romania and the Czech Republic said they would acquire F-35A *Lightning* II combat aircraft to recapitalise their air forces, while Denmark took delivery of its first F-35s. The UK and Italy advanced work on the low-observable Global Combat Air Programme (GCAP), in which Japan is an equal partner. The project aims to deliver a new combat aircraft for service entry in 2035. GCAP entered the concept and assessment phase and is due to begin its detailed design and development phase in 2025, by which time the partners will need to resolve critical and often fraught questions about workshare allocation and other issues. European armed forces are also looking to upgrade other domains. The Netherlands plans to pick a supplier for a new class of submarines in 2024 and Norway is eyeing the acquisition of new and larger frigates. Hungary, meanwhile, is upgrading its inventory of main battle tanks to *Leopard* 2s, phasing out the T-72, while Sweden decided to upgrade a first batch of 44 *Leopard* 2A5 (Strv 122) tanks.

Defence-industrial developments in Europe also illustrated the breadth of the security challenges facing countries in the region. Companies in Germany, the UK and elsewhere were busy ramping up ammunition production to meet Ukraine's needs and replenish their nations' inventories and those of others. Germany's Rheinmetall, which in August 2023 opened a new factory in Hungary to produce *Lynx* armoured vehicles, earlier in the year committed to set up shop in Ukraine, first to repair and maintain combat vehicles and later to produce armoured vehicles in the country. Finland's Patria, among others, considered similar moves. Saab made investments in emerging-technology fields, highlighting how companies are trying to keep pace with the evolution of advanced capabilities. The Swedish arms maker agreed to buy CrowdAI and the UK's BlueBear Systems Group in a bet that artificial-intelligence (AI) software will play an ever-more central role in future weapons systems. Saab also made a strategic investment in German AI company Helsing, taking a 5% stake. Britain's BAE Systems in August proposed the acquisition of Ball Aerospace in a deal valued at around USD5.6bn, highlighting the growing importance of the space domain in military planning.

Meanwhile, European companies deepened their integration with Ukraine's defence industry. For example, in May 2023, Rheinmetall announced a strategic cooperation agreement with UkrOboronProm (renamed Ukraine Defence Industry in June). The partnership will initially focus on repair and maintenance of combat vehicles and could evolve into production of armoured vehicles, including main battle tanks. Similarly, in August 2023, the UK's BAE Systems said it had established a local entity in Ukraine that could produce 105mm howitzers among other things. The Czech Republic also agreed to strengthen industrial links with Ukraine, including around the maintenance of armoured vehicles and ammunition production. Slovakia agreed to work with Kyiv on the joint development of 155mm self-propelled howitzers, while Sweden said it would seek to jointly produce and service CV90 infantry fighting vehicles with Ukraine.

▼ Figure 4 **Selected Western countries: new fleet replenishment oilers with replenishment-at-sea capability (AORs)**

Auxiliaries with the capability to conduct replenishment at sea (RAS) have been a staple of the large Western fleets with ambitions to deploy at range and undertake sustained operations since the Second World War. Much of the recent stock of auxiliaries in Western inventories dated from the 1970s and 1980s and has been overdue for replacement. This has led to a new surge of Western procurement. The United States, the United Kingdom, Germany, France, Italy, Norway, the Netherlands, Canada and Turkiye have recently commissioned or laid down new replenishment ships. Portugal and Poland are planning to do so. Australia and New Zealand, too, have recently commissioned new oilers. Compared to their predecessors, the new replenishment oilers boast significant increases in displacement and therefore logistic capacity, and also include important additional features such as medical facilities, command-and-control spaces and systems as well as larger aviation facilities, increasingly used for vertical replenishment via helicopter or in the future uninhabited aerial systems with payload capacity. This all significantly expands the utility and flexibility of these vessels. Generally, these vessels are also being procured as one-for-one replacements for their immediate predecessors, leading to an overall boost in Western afloat support and RAS capacity.

Large, capable replenishment ships are an important prerequisite for operating task groups on sustained missions. For that reason, the aspiring navies of Asia are also currently in the process of acquiring or expanding their capabilities in this area. A notable feature of China's naval expansion has been Beijing's investment in modern and capable auxiliaries. India, Pakistan and Indonesia are also currently engaged or have completed procurements of similar capabilities. In all cases, there is a major challenge in that new improved capabilities of these more modern auxiliaries do not come cheap. European navies have in some cases tried to cut costs by adopting similar base designs (the UK and Norway and France and Italy being cases in point – while Australia adopted a Spanish design and Canada a German one for speed of procurement, although in the latter case there have been significant subsequent delays). But there have also been conflicting issues over seeking cost-effective procurements while also sustaining national industrial bases. There has been some standardisation in RAS equipment fits to facilitate common support of NATO naval forces. But, in general, navies still pursue national building programmes. The lessons of Ukraine on high-intensity warfare, plus increasing Western naval focus on enhanced forward presence, will likely see a continuing appetite for such shipping.

Logistic Support Ship (Italy/France)
Italian variant illustrated

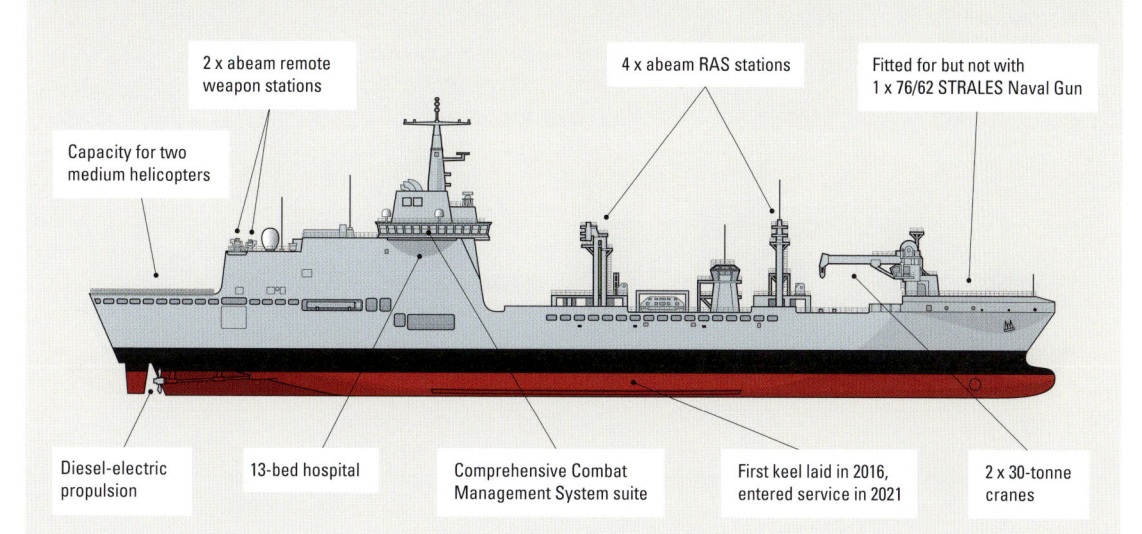

- 2 x abeam remote weapon stations
- 4 x abeam RAS stations
- Fitted for but not with 1 x 76/62 STRALES Naval Gun
- Capacity for two medium helicopters
- Diesel-electric propulsion
- 13-bed hospital
- Comprehensive Combat Management System suite
- First keel laid in 2016, entered service in 2021
- 2 x 30-tonne cranes

Selected features (Italian variant)
- 193m x 27.2m; 27,200 tonnes full-load displacement
- Crew complement: 130 + up to 60 non-crew
- Speed: 20 knots

Cargo capacity
- 13,500 cubic metres of fuels
- 850 cubic metres of fresh water
- 1,000 square meters of dry cargo and eight standard shipping containers (1,500 tonnes)

Users
- Italy: 1 active (1 under construction)
- France: 1 active (1 under construction, 2 ordered) (lengthened variant)

60 THE MILITARY BALANCE 2024

John Lewis (US)

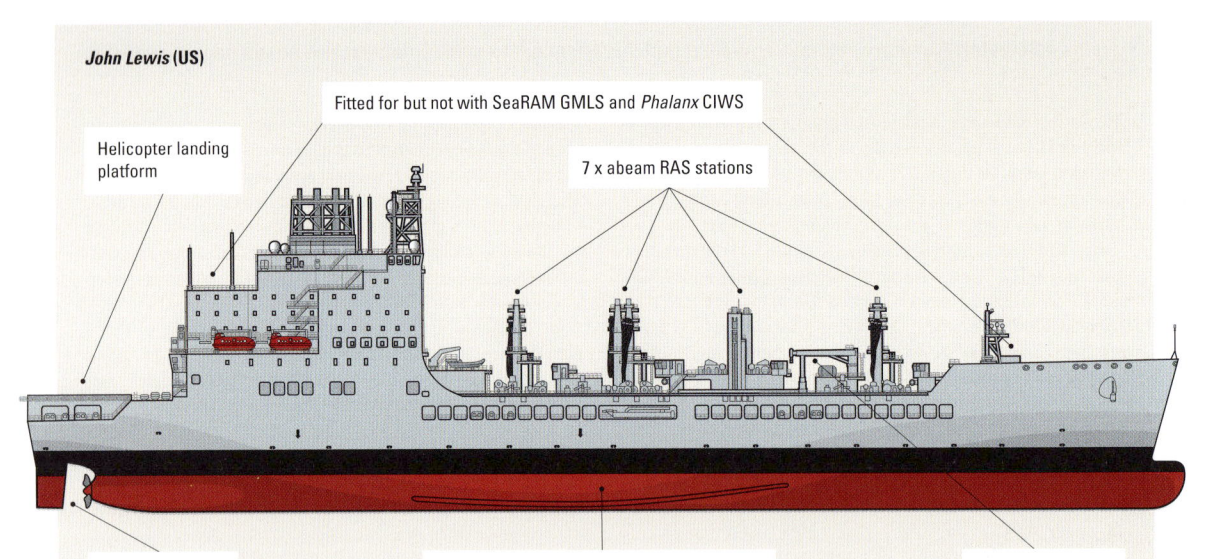

- Helicopter landing platform
- Fitted for but not with SeaRAM GMLS and *Phalanx* CIWS
- 7 x abeam RAS stations
- Diesel propulsion
- First keel laid in 2019, entered service in 2022
- 2 x 5-tonne cranes

Selected features
- 227.3m x 32.2m; 49,850 tonnes full-load displacement
- Crew complement: 95 + up to 30 non-crew
- Speed: 20 knots

Cargo capacity
- 25,780 cubic metres of fuels
- 200 cubic metres of fresh water
- 850 square metres of dry cargo

Users
- US: 2 active (3 under construction, 4 ordered)

Tide (UK/Norway)
UK variant illustrated

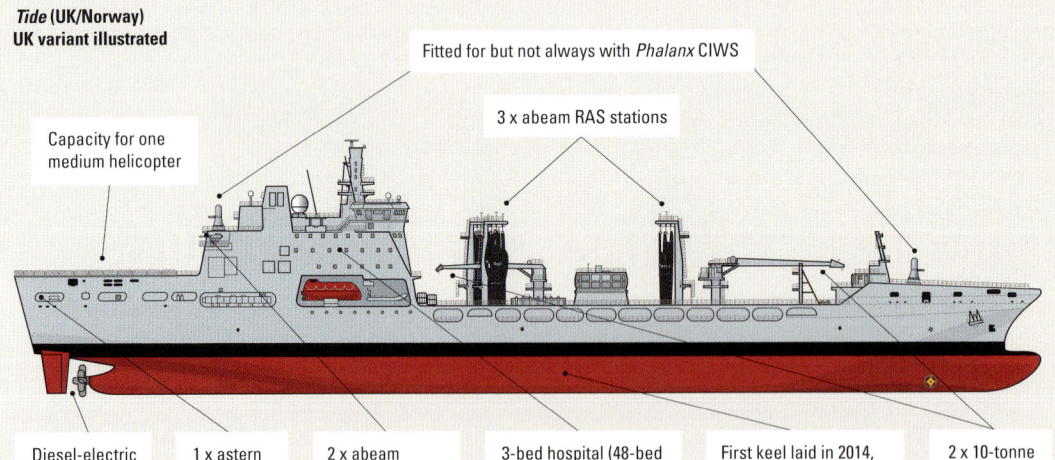

- Capacity for one medium helicopter
- Fitted for but not always with *Phalanx* CIWS
- 3 x abeam RAS stations
- Diesel-electric propulsion
- 1 x astern RAS station
- 2 x abeam weapon stations
- 3-bed hospital (48-bed in Norwegian service)
- First keel laid in 2014, entered service in 2017
- 2 x 10-tonne cranes

Selected features (UK variant)
- 200.9m x 28.6m; 39,000 tonnes full-load displacement
- Crew complement: 63 + up to 46 non-crew
- Speed: 20 knots

Cargo capacity
- 19,000 cubic metres of fuels
- 1,400 cubic metres of fresh water
- Eight standard shipping containers

Users
- UK: 4 active
- Norway: 1 active (shortened variant)

GMLS = Guided missile launching system **CIWS** = Close-in weapon system

Sources: IISS, Fincantieri, Naval Group, seaforces.org, navalanalyses.com, Congressional Research Service

©IISS

NATO strengthens deterrence and operational capability

Russia's war against Ukraine ensured that the NATO Alliance persisted with efforts – generally agreed at its summit in June 2022 – to strengthen deterrence and enhance operational readiness, effectiveness and resilience. It also pursued ways to shore up support for Ukraine and sought to more substantively address China's growing global reach.

The annual NATO summit, held in Vilnius from 11–12 July 2023, included Finland for the first time as the Alliance's 31st member. On the eve of the summit, Turkiye unexpectedly dropped its objections to Sweden's accession, with Secretary General Jens Stoltenberg announcing that Turkish President Recep Tayyip Erdoğan had agreed to 'work closely' with his country's legislature 'to ensure ratification'. Hungary also signalled it would not block Sweden's full membership. Bilateral relations between Sweden and Turkiye remained fraught, though. Ankara has disagreements with Sweden over terrorism and organised-crime issues that have prevented speedy ratification. Regardless, NATO's posture increasingly focuses on an integrated Baltic–Nordic strategic space.

In this context, the Vilnius Summit communiqué announced 'significant measures to further enhance NATO's deterrence and defence posture in all domains'. Among those steps was the adoption of three regional plans to account for Finnish and (potentially) Swedish (given hard to judge what Ankara and Budapest will do next) membership and to enable more geographically focused defence planning. Joint Force Command Norfolk will lead NATO operations in the High North and the Atlantic; Joint Force Command Brunssum assumes responsibility for regional plan Central, which stretches from the Baltic region to the Alps; while Joint Force Command Naples looks after the Mediterranean and the Black Sea.

Moreover, a new 'Allied Reaction Force' was established. It remained unclear, though, whether allies would meet the required force levels to implement the new NATO Force Model principally agreed upon at the Madrid Summit a year earlier that calls for the Alliance to be able to deploy at least 300,000 high-readiness troops within the first 30 days of a crisis. Shortly before the Vilnius gathering, Canada offered to double its contingent in Latvia, adding some 1,200 troops, while German Defence Minister Boris Pistorius announced plans to 'permanently station a robust brigade in Lithuania'. Additionally, allies decided to strengthen NATO's Integrated Air and Missile Defence posture, including through rotating modern air-defence systems across the eastern flank and by increasing readiness. NATO also backed a raft of measures designed to deter hybrid threats, including through a Maritime Centre for the Security of Critical Undersea Infrastructure; a Virtual Cyber Incident Support Capability, a new cyber-defence concept; and a NATO Space Centre of Excellence (CoE) in France. It also opened in Canada a new CoE for Climate Change and Security.

However, significant challenges remained for NATO to provide a credible and robust answer to Russia's threat to Alliance security and to peace and stability in the Euro-Atlantic area. Despite widespread budget increases among NATO members, funding remains a point of disagreement. Some in the Alliance were aiming for the members to enshrine NATO's long-held target of members spending 2% of GDP on defence as a 'floor, not the ceiling', but Vilnius only resulted in a recommitment to spend 2%. That all but assures the 'burden-sharing' debate will feature prominently at NATO's 2024 summit in Washington, taking place during the US presidential election campaign.

How to assist Ukraine also remained a sticking point at the Vilnius gathering. Several member states supported Ukrainian President Volodymyr Zelenskyy's plea for a membership invitation. However, concerned about potential conflict escalation, Germany, the United States and others limited the summit declaration to a promise of membership 'when allies agree, and conditions are met'. However, allies removed the requirement for Ukraine to go through a Membership Action Plan before joining, created a new NATO–Ukraine Council and upgraded NATO's Comprehensive Assistance Package to a multi-year military-assistance programme to support the country for 'as long as it takes'. In the absence of a major breakthrough in Ukraine's counteroffensive, maintaining Alliance cohesion and support remained paramount.

Although NATO's main effort focused on rebuilding deterrence and combat capability for the Euro-Atlantic area, it also attempted to pay closer attention to global security challenges. Most prominently, the communiqué declared that China's stated ambitions and coercive policies 'challenge our interests, security and values'. Tellingly, the leaders of Australia, Japan, New Zealand and South Korea attended the summit, confirming the NATO Asia-Pacific-partners format. In July, Japan and NATO also signed an 'Individually Tailored Partnership Programme'. However, allies could not agree on a proposed NATO liaison office in Japan flagged prior to the summit, with France apparently voicing opposition.

NATO exited Vilnius on a trajectory to become more operationally resilient and with much higher readiness. Those efforts were underpinned by several military exercises. In June, Germany hosted *Air Defender* 23, the largest air-force deployment exercise in NATO's history, comprising some 250 aircraft from 25 nations and approximately 10,000 personnel. In 2024, the exercise *Steadfast Defender* is slated to be NATO's largest military drill since the end of the Cold War, bringing together over 40,000 troops for an exercise stretching from the Baltic states to Poland and Germany. The exercise *Nordic Response* will also unfold as the largest exercise yet seen in the Nordic countries, with all five Nordic countries hosting multiple Alliance members with a view to integrating them into NATO's revised defence plans.

DEFENCE ECONOMICS

In 2023, Europe faced another year of economic disruption after Russia's full-scale invasion of Ukraine derailed the region's recovery. Prior to the start of fighting in February 2022, European economies were recovering from the upheaval related to COVID-19, with increasing GDP growth rates beginning to put national economies back on trend. The war cut short the recovery. Prior to the conflict, Russia was a key supplier of gas and oil to Europe, and both Russia and Ukraine were principal sources of food and fertilisers to the continent. The subsequent shocks to energy and food supplies spurred higher prices, driving up inflation rates across Europe. In addition to the direct effect on household consumption and business investments, efforts to reduce high inflation led central banks to tighten monetary policies. This, in turn, slowed European economies.

Headline inflation in advanced and emerging European economies in 2023 was 6.28% and 9.8% respectively (excluding Turkiye's 51.2% inflation). The high levels represented an improvement, though, from 2022, when those rates were 9.9% and 12.8%, respectively. Energy prices in the past year also declined and businesses adapted to supply-chain disruption. However, the impact on GDP growth was felt more acutely in 2023 than in the previous year. In almost all European countries, growth was slower than the year prior. According to the IMF, economies contracted in Estonia, Finland, Germany, Lithuania, Luxembourg and Sweden, while the euro area only eked out 1.05% growth.

High energy prices, inflation and the subsequent hike in interest rates triggered government actions that weighed on European states' public finances. Most governments implemented support for households and companies to alleviate the rise in energy prices, via direct subsidies (Belgium, Germany, Greece and Norway, for example); tax cuts or credits (Austria, Latvia, Luxembourg and the Netherlands); or price caps (Malta and Romania). Such steps followed the fiscal measures to help businesses weather the COVID-19 lockdowns, resulting in public spending in Europe remaining high at a time when soaring interest rates made borrowing more expensive.

As a result, in most European countries the gross-debt-to-GDP ratio remained higher in 2023 than their pre-COVID levels in 2019. In the United Kingdom, the ratio was 20 percentage points higher, while the Czech Republic, Estonia, France, Malta and Romania all averaged increases of between 12 and 15 percentage points. Fiscal deficits, measured by the government structural balance, were also higher for many countries on the continent in 2023 than in the pre-COVID era. That said, ten European economies countries (Croatia, Cyprus, Denmark, Greece, Iceland, Ireland, Norway, Portugal, Sweden and Switzerland) improved their fiscal position over the four-year period.

Nonetheless, slowing growth and persistent inflation were driving pressure to cut spending. This was the case in Germany, where the 2024 draft budget proposed cuts on social benefits. France also expects to reduce public spending by at least EUR4.80 billion (USD5.25bn).

Europe's continued support for Ukraine, and concerns about its own military strength, suggest that defence spending will be shielded from tightening budgets. Nonetheless, defence issues still compete

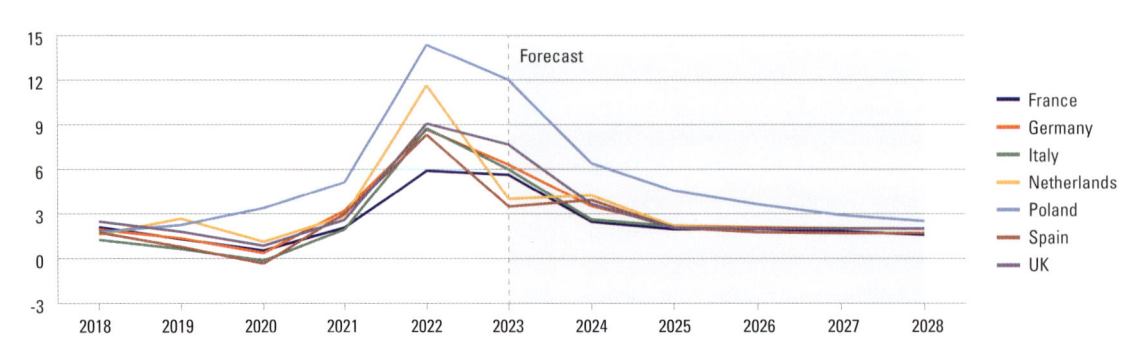

▲ Figure 5 **Europe: selected countries, inflation (%) 2018–28**

Source: IMF World Economic Outlook, October 2023

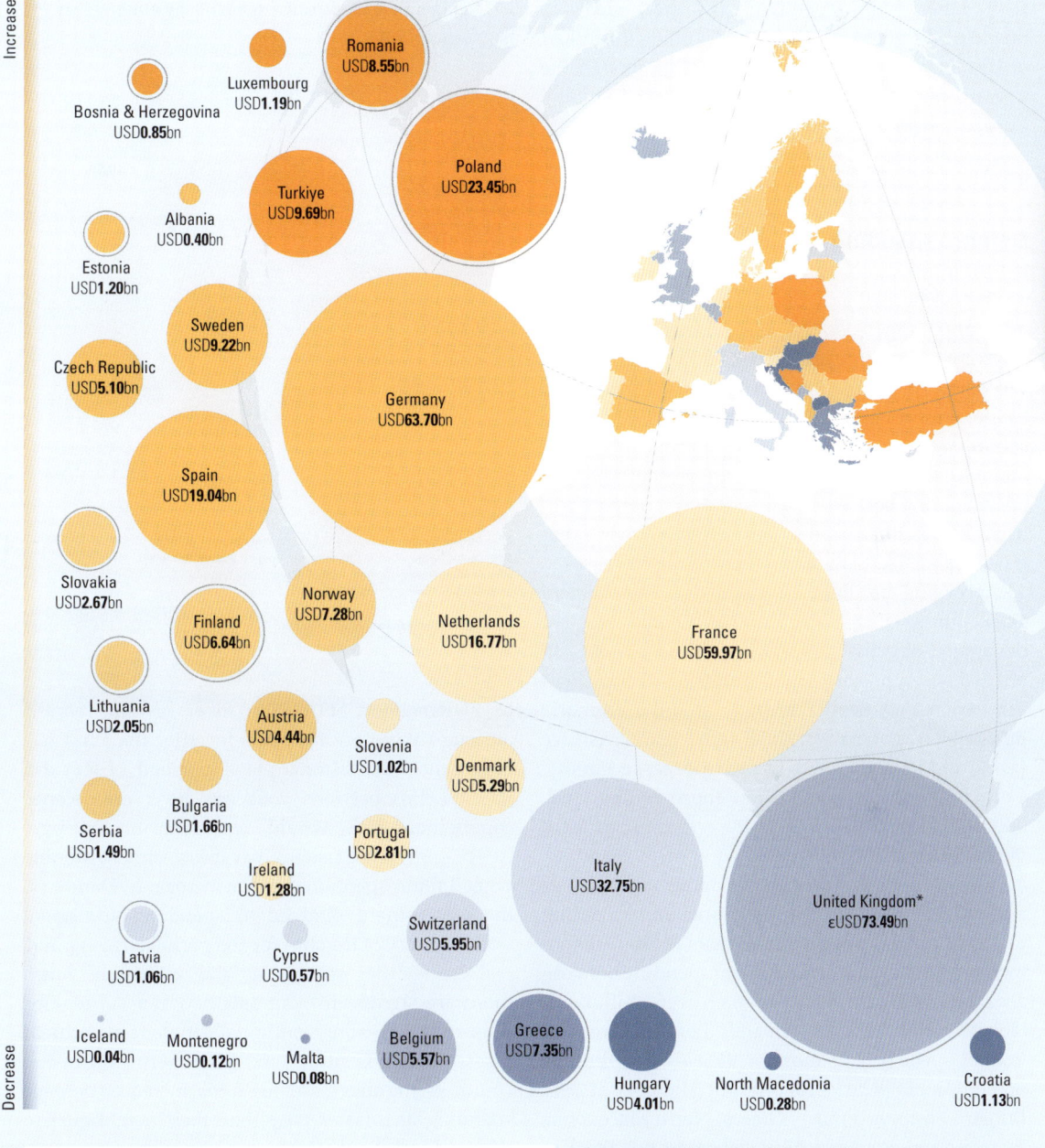

Map 1 Europe: regional defence spending (USDbn, %ch yoy)[1]

Increase

- Bosnia & Herzegovina USD**0.85**bn
- Luxembourg USD**1.19**bn
- Romania USD**8.55**bn
- Albania USD**0.40**bn
- Turkiye USD**9.69**bn
- Poland USD**23.45**bn
- Estonia USD**1.20**bn
- Sweden USD**9.22**bn
- Czech Republic USD**5.10**bn
- Germany USD**63.70**bn
- Spain USD**19.04**bn
- Slovakia USD**2.67**bn
- Finland USD**6.64**bn
- Norway USD**7.28**bn
- Netherlands USD**16.77**bn
- France USD**59.97**bn
- Lithuania USD**2.05**bn
- Austria USD**4.44**bn
- Slovenia USD**1.02**bn
- Denmark USD**5.29**bn
- Serbia USD**1.49**bn
- Bulgaria USD**1.66**bn
- Portugal USD**2.81**bn
- Ireland USD**1.28**bn
- Switzerland USD**5.95**bn
- Italy USD**32.75**bn
- United Kingdom* εUSD**73.49**bn
- Latvia USD**1.06**bn
- Cyprus USD**0.57**bn
- Iceland USD**0.04**bn
- Montenegro USD**0.12**bn
- Malta USD**0.08**bn
- Belgium USD**5.57**bn
- Greece USD**7.35**bn
- Hungary USD**4.01**bn
- North Macedonia USD**0.28**bn
- Croatia USD**1.13**bn

Decrease

Real % Change (2022–23)

- More than 20% increase
- Between 10% and 20% increase
- Between 3% and 10% increase
- Between 0% and 3% increase
- ◯ Spending 2% of GDP or above
- Between 0% and 3% decrease
- Between 3% and 10% decrease
- Between 10% and 20% decrease
- More than 20% decrease
- ε Estimate

*includes Armed Forces Pension Service and military aid to Ukraine

[1] Map illustrating 2023 planned defence-spending levels (in USDbn at market exchange rates) as well as the annual real percentage change in planned defence spending between 2022 and 2023 (at constant 2015 prices and exchange rates). Percentage changes in defence spending can vary considerably from year to year, as states revise the level of funding allocated to defence. Changes indicated here highlight the short-term trend in planned defence spending between 2022 and 2023. Actual spending changes prior to 2022, and projected spending levels post-2023, are not reflected.

©IISS

Sub-regional groupings referred to in defence economics text: Central Europe (Austria, Czech Republic, Germany, Hungary, Poland, Slovakia and Switzerland), Northern Europe (Denmark, Estonia, Finland, Latvia, Lithuania, Norway and Sweden), Southern Europe (Cyprus, Greece, Italy, Malta, Portugal and Spain), Southeastern Europe (Bulgaria, Romania and Turkiye), the Balkans (Albania, Bosnia-Herzegovina, Croatia, Montenegro, North Macedonia, Serbia and Slovenia) and Western Europe (Belgium, France, Iceland, Ireland, Luxembourg, the Netherlands and the United Kingdom).

with other public-spending priorities, such as financing the green transition or absorbing the inflow of Ukrainian refugees. As a result, even though the upward trend in defence outlays continued in 2023, Europe's economic situation and fiscal uncertainty cast doubt over long-term government commitments to increase defence spending.

Defence spending

In real terms, European defence spending grew by 4% between 2022 and 2023, picking up pace after a 2% annual increase the year prior. The continent registered the same defence-spending increase as that of Europe's NATO members, who were expected to spend more aggressively. By comparison, defence spending grew faster across European Union member states. Across the EU, aggregate spending advanced 6% between 2022 and 2023, compared to a 4% annual increase the year before, showing that it is not just NATO membership driving increases.

According to data captured by *The Military Balance*, in 2023, ten European NATO allies reached the agreed objective of spending at least 2% of GDP on defence, up from eight countries in 2022 and just two in 2014. Several are near or at the 3% mark: Bosnia-Herzegovina (3.2%), Estonia (2.9%), Greece (3.0%) and Poland (2.8%). Europe's largest economy, Germany, remained well below the spending level, allocating only 1.4% of GDP to the armed forces. Most of these increases target higher equipment spending, a category which includes weapons acquisitions and defence research and development. According to NATO, most European members of the Alliance increased their share of equipment spending between 2022 and 2023, except for Croatia, Greece, Lithuania, Slovakia and Turkiye. Finland, Luxembourg and Poland spent half or more of their defence budget on equipment in 2023, followed by Hungary at 48%. Bulgaria, Estonia, France, Greece, North Macedonia, Norway and Romania allocated around a third of total spending to equipment. All European allies exceeded the NATO benchmark of spending 20% of defence expenditures on equipment.

Europe also demonstrated a willingness to spend more over the long term. France's defence-spending plan for the period 2024–30, the Loi de Programmation Militaire, foresees defence-budget growth (in current terms, excluding pensions) from EUR47.4bn (USD51.6bn) in 2024 to EUR69.0bn (USD75.1bn) in 2030. Germany set up a special fund for the armed forces that amounts to EUR100bn (USD108.8bn) over several years – although there are no plans for after the fund has been exhausted. Estonia plans to spend EUR13.4bn (USD14.6bn) between 2022 and 2031 on defence capabilities. This would represent ,on average, EUR1.34bn (USD1.50bn) per year, almost double what Tallinn spent on defence in 2022. In Denmark, the government pledged to spend an additional DKK143bn (USD20.9bn) for the period 2024–33.

Despite the growth at the aggregate level, there are significant contrasts between subregions (Figure 8), revealing continued differences in threat assessments. Central and Northern European countries, the ones closer to Russia, increased defence spending at a faster pace than their neighbours in Western and Southern Europe.

A decline in the UK's real defence expenditure swung the Western Europe subregion to a decline. Although London increased defence spending nominally by GBP100m (USD126m) in 2023 from 2022, in real terms that represented a 1% decline. That said, the UK's Integrated Review Refresh outlined the government's long-term aspiration to invest up to 2.5% of GDP in defence, albeit 'as the fiscal and economic circumstances allow'. Towards this, the UK's Spring Budget, released in March 2023, earmarked an additional GBP5bn (USD6.29bn) for

▼ Figure 6 **Europe: defence spending by country and sub-region, 2023**

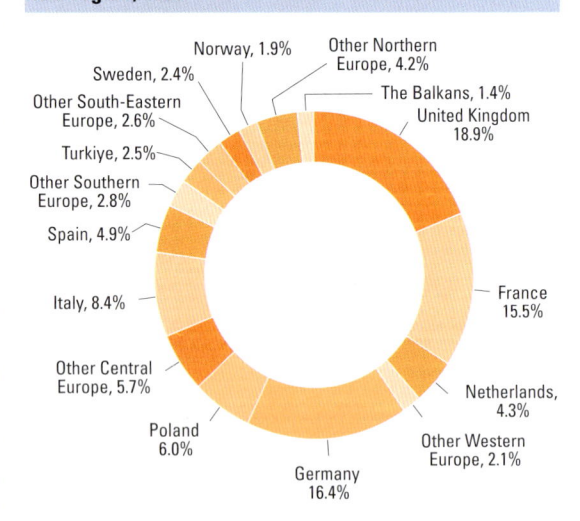

- United Kingdom 18.9%
- France 15.5%
- Germany 16.4%
- Italy 8.4%
- Poland 6.0%
- Other Central Europe 5.7%
- Spain 4.9%
- Netherlands 4.3%
- Other Northern Europe 4.2%
- Other Southern Europe 2.8%
- Other South-Eastern Europe 2.6%
- Turkiye 2.5%
- Sweden 2.4%
- Other Western Europe 2.1%
- Norway 1.9%
- The Balkans 1.4%

Other Western Europe – Belgium, Iceland, Ireland, Luxembourg
Other Central Europe – Austria, Czech Republic, Hungary, Slovakia, Switzerland
Other Northern Europe – Denmark, Estonia, Finland, Latvia, Lithuania
Other Southern Europe – Cyprus, Greece, Malta, Portugal
The Balkans – Albania, Bosnia-Herzegovina, Croatia, Montenegro, North Macedonia, Serbia, Slovenia
Other South-Eastern Europe – Bulgaria, Romania

©IISS

▼ Figure 7 **Europe: regional defence spending** as % of GDP (average)

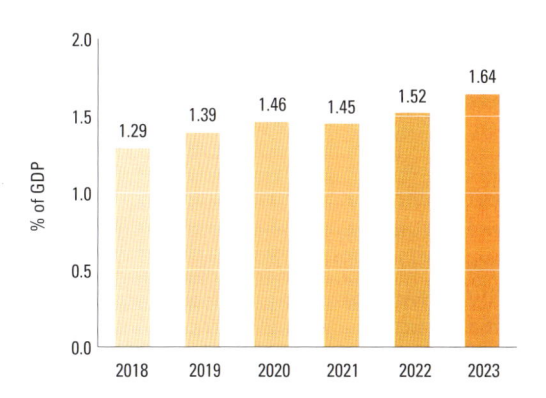

Year	% of GDP
2018	1.29
2019	1.39
2020	1.46
2021	1.45
2022	1.52
2023	1.64

Source: GDP data from IMF World Economic Outlook, October 2023

defence and national-security priorities over the next two years, and an additional GBP2bn (USD2.51bn) each year for the next two years. In Southern Europe, only Spain substantially lifted defence expenditure, with real-term growth of 20%, to reach EUR17.5bn (USD18.6bn) in 2023. Portugal allocated a more modest 1% increase in real terms. All other countries in the subregion reduced their military outlays. Greece's 13% decline in real terms reflects the fact that several large procurement expenses are spread out over years, with significant ongoing purchases including three frigates and 24 *Rafale* fighter ground-attack aircraft. Greek procurement spending remained at a high EUR3.1bn (USD3.33bn) in 2023, though short of the EUR3.41bn (USD3.59bn) of the previous year.

Poland principally caused the increase in Central Europe. Warsaw's defence budget grew in real terms by 46% between 2022 and 2023. Poland aims to spend at least 4% of GDP on defence from 2023 onwards. Part of this increase is funded through an off-budget mechanism, the Armed Forces Support Fund, financed by additional debt. In addition to this specific funding instrument, Poland heavily leaned on loans from the Export–Import Bank of Korea to finance its contracts for arms deliveries from South Korea. Korean media reports have suggested that loans cover up to 70% of the costs of the 2022 contracts for K2 *Black Panther* main battle tanks, K9 *Thunder* 155mm self-propelled artillery systems, FA-50 fighter ground-attack aircraft and *Chunmoo* multiple-rocket launchers. Moreover, in September 2023, Polish Defence Minister Mariusz Blaszczak signed additional contracts at a local defence exhibition worth PLN100bn (USD23.8bn), including six additional *Patriot* batteries (each comprised of two 'fire units'), as well as equipment for 23 batteries of the CAMM-ER (*Narew*) medium-range air-defence system, four more Naval Strike Missile coastal-defence squadrons and some 1,700 *FlyEye* surveillance UAVs. Poland's spending spree sparked concerns about the affordability of such procurements, and the extent to which the domestic arms industry is benefiting.

All three countries in Southeastern Europe increased their defence spending in 2023 compared to 2022, with 6% growth in Bulgaria and 32% in Romania. In Turkiye, allocations in local-currency terms doubled between 2022 and 2023, which translated into 39% real-terms growth. The real-term spending jump is even more noteworthy given the country's staggering inflation rate of over 50% in 2023. In the Balkans, total defence spending rose by 7%, although this was driven by a large swing in Bosnia-Herzegovina's defence budget. According to its 2023–25 budget framework document, defence

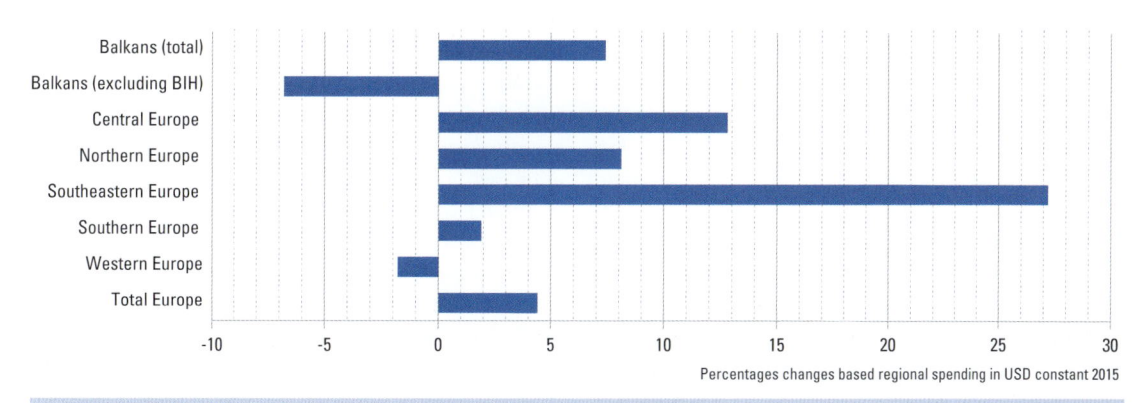

Percentages changes based regional spending in USD constant 2015

▲ Figure 8 **Europe: defence spending year-on-year change (%) 2022–23**

spending for 2023 will increase to BAM1.53bn (USD849m), up from BAM306m (USD165m) in 2022. This near fivefold increase is likely driven by rising insecurity in the region, although the 2023–25 budget framework suggests that funding will later ease to BAM576m (USD320m) and BAM704m (USD391m) in 2024 and 2025, respectively. Excluding Bosnia-Herzegovina, defence spending in the Balkans fell in real terms by 6.8%.

European defence-spending increases in 2022 and 2023 included part of the funds disbursed to cover military assistance to Ukraine. EU member states contribute to the European Peace Facility (EPF). Within this framework, the Council of the European Union adopted several assistance measures to refund a portion of the military equipment that EU member states have transferred to Ukraine. The EPF's total budgetary ceiling for the period 2021–27 was raised from an initial envelope of EUR5.7bn (USD6.2bn) to EUR12bn (USD13bn). EU member states contribute to the fund from their national budgets, from ministries of foreign affairs, ministries of defence or separate budgetary lines. Similarly, part of the UK's financial military assistance was funded from a Treasury Special Reserve in 2022.

Defence industry

European defence companies enjoyed an uptick in demand, in part from governments providing military support to Ukraine and having to backfill their inventory. But the spike in demand exposed the reality that European arms production was not geared for wartime. In the post-Cold War period, European defence companies implemented lean management and just-in-time production flows, encouraged by governments looking to cut costs. Stockpiling was discouraged as a drag on the books. As a result, Europe's defence-industrial capacity has not been sufficient to meet Ukraine's needs, as the European Commission acknowledged.

In response, governments and industry implemented measures to ramp up production. For instance, Nexter, the French arm of Franco-German KNDS, produced two to four CAESAR 155mm self-propelled artillery systems per month before the war. It increased production to six units per month in 2023 and aims to reach eight in 2024. The supplier also aims to cut delivery times to 17 months from 30. MBDA's production rate of the *Mistral* man-portable air-defence system, which was 20 units per month in 2022, rose to 30 in 2023, and it aims to scale up to 40 units per month by 2025. Meanwhile, MBDA aims to cut production times to ten months from 40. The increase in pace has benefited industry. For example, in its 2023 half-year financial statement, Rheinmetall stated that investments in its vehicle-systems division increased by EUR66.0m (USD71.8m) in the first six months of 2023, compared to the year-earlier period, to expand capacity. Meanwhile, Swedish defence contractor Saab reported a 39% jump in order bookings in the first nine months of 2023 compared to the year-earlier period.

Munitions have been a particular focus for boosting output given the rate of expenditures in Ukraine. In late 2022, Germany's Rheinmetall acquired the Spanish ammunition maker EXPAL in response to increased demand. Simmel Difesa, an Italian subsidiary of KNDS, wants to produce 4,000 artillery shells per month by March 2024, up from 2,000 previously. Similarly, in 2022, the Norwegian–Finnish ammunition maker Nammo reported that the company had 'invested heavily in new buildings, machinery, raw materials, and storage facilities'. Poland's Polska Grupa Zbrojeniowa (PGZ) signed a deal with RTX and Lockheed Martin to produce the *Javelin* anti-tank weapons system in Poland. In addition to ramping up production, states have looked to increase cooperation in procuring supplies, with media reports indicating that Germany was in talks with Denmark and the Netherlands on the joint procurement of ammunition.

In general, defence companies across Europe have faced considerable uncertainty about long-term demand and remained reticent to significantly increase their production capacities. Governments have sought to address those concerns, as has the EU, which developed new initiatives to provide financial incentives for companies to ramp up production. The EU also announced a plan to increase ammunition and missile deliveries to Ukraine. This plan has three tracks. The first allocates EUR1bn (USD1.09bn) to pay member states for their ammunition donations to Ukraine, while the second allocates another EUR1bn for ammunition jointly procured and provided to Kyiv. The third track earmarks an additional EUR500m (USD544m) to boost Europe's manufacturing capacity for artillery rounds and missiles. To support this expansion of production capacity, the EU's 'Act in Support of Ammunition Production' allocates EUR50.0m (USD5.44m) of the total to assist with access to private and public financing.

Map 2 🇹🇷 Turkiye: selected armed-UAV exports since 2018

Turkiye has evolved into a major exporter of uninhabited aerial vehicles (UAVs). Growing sales have helped the country more than double its defence and aerospace exports from USD1.82 billion in 2017 to USD4.4bn in 2022. This trend started in 2018 with a deal with Qatar for delivery of *Bayraktar* TB2s. Other than TB2-maker Baykar, the main UAV manufacturer is Turkish Aerospace Industries (TAI), while Roketsan and ASELSAN make the weapons systems, with the latter producing sensors as well. The ease of use of the UAVs, their employment in conflicts (Libya, Syria, Nagorno-Karabakh and Ukraine), the low political cost of procuring from Turkiye and the relatively loose constraints placed by the country offered an attractive alternative to the Chinese, Israeli and US competitors. Turkiye signed contracts to deliver armed UAVs and laser-guided bombs to roughly 30 countries between 2018 and 2023. These included projects on the local manufacturing of the *Bayraktar* TB2 in Ukraine, the joint production of *Anka* in Kazakhstan and its local assembly in Indonesia. On 18 July 2023, Turkiye and Saudi Arabia announced plans to co-produce *Akinci* in what is Ankara's biggest arms-export deal so far.

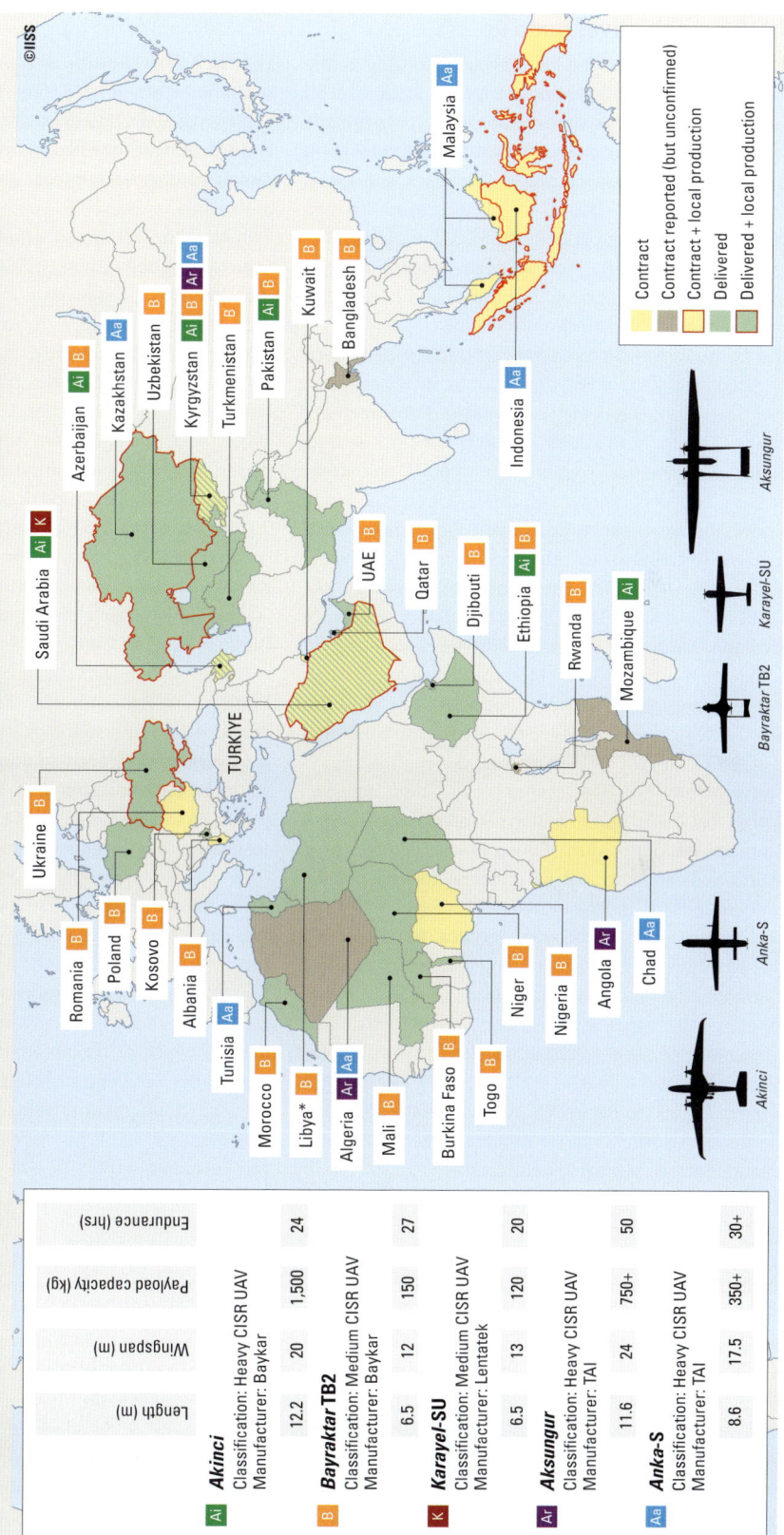

Akinci (Ai)
Classification: Heavy CISR UAV
Manufacturer: Baykar

Length (m)	Wingspan (m)	Payload capacity (kg)	Endurance (hrs)
12.2	20	1,500	24

Bayraktar TB2 (B)
Classification: Medium CISR UAV
Manufacturer: Baykar

Length (m)	Wingspan (m)	Payload capacity (kg)	Endurance (hrs)
6.5	12	150	27

Karayel-SU (K)
Classification: Medium CISR UAV
Manufacturer: Lentatek

| 6.5 | 13 | 120 | 20 |

Aksungur (Ar)
Classification: Heavy CISR UAV
Manufacturer: TAI

| 11.6 | 24 | 750+ | 50 |

Anka-S (Aa)
Classification: Heavy CISR UAV
Manufacturer: TAI

| 8.6 | 17.5 | 350+ | 30+ |

Legend:
- Contract
- Contract reported (but unconfirmed)
- Contract + local production
- Delivered
- Delivered + local production

Countries labelled: Ukraine B; Romania B; Poland B; Kosovo B; Albania B; Tunisia Aa; Morocco B; Libya* B; Algeria Ar Aa; Mali B; Burkina Faso B; Togo B; Niger B; Nigeria B; Angola Ar; Chad Aa; Saudi Arabia Ai K; UAE B; Qatar B; Djibouti B; Ethiopia Ai B; Rwanda B; Mozambique Ai; Azerbaijan Ai B; Kazakhstan B; Uzbekistan B; Kyrgyzstan Ai B Aa; Turkmenistan B; Pakistan Ai; Kuwait B; Bangladesh B; Indonesia Aa; Malaysia Aa.

*Turkiye delivered the TB2 to the Tripoli-based government between May and June 2019 to help it repel an offensive launched in April by Khalifa Haftar's Libyan Arab Armed Forces.

EU defence initiatives ramp up

European Union defence policy evolved further in the shadow of the war in Ukraine. In March 2023, the EU Commission proposed an Ammunition Initiative to provide Ukraine with one million rounds of artillery ammunition within a year, replenish European stockpiles and boost production capacities. The EU in July approved steps to clear hurdles to ramping up joint ammunition production. To underpin the effort, the European Defence Agency signed framework contracts with European industry for the joint procurement of 155mm ammunition.

The EU budget effort to address critical capability gaps and incentivise joint procurement from member states under the European Defence Industry Reinforcement Through Common Procurement Act remains limited, though, in comparison to national and NATO initiatives. Moreover, the uncertainty over the budget and scope of the European Defence Investment Programme raises doubt over its ability to facilitate more meaningful defence-industry cooperation. The EU Council has provided more than EUR31.0 billion (USD32.0bn) in military assistance under the European Peace Facility (EPF) to support the Ukrainian armed forces. Moreover, in July, EU High Representative Josep Borrell proposed a EUR20.0bn (USD21.3bn) fund under the EPF for weapons, ammunition and other military aid for Ukraine over four years, although EU governments still had to endorse the idea. However, ensuring that the EU's ammunition plans fully bear fruit has not proven straightforward: reports in late year indicated that it was falling short of its ambition for one million artillery rounds for Ukraine by March 2024.

The lack of pace in boosting output has frustrated some, particularly with Russia turning to allies to augment its ammunition supplies. Lithuanian foreign minister Gabrielius Landsbergis late last year lamented that 'The EU promised Ukraine 1,000,000 artillery rounds. So far, we have delivered only 300,000. Meanwhile, North Korea delivered 350,000 to Russia. We surely have the resources to outperform North Korea. We should stop being frozen in the headlights while brave Ukrainians die.'

In March 2023, the EU also published an updated maritime-security strategy to provide a framework to respond to evolving and growing threats in the maritime domain. A changing security environment, including the war in Ukraine, required the strategy to place greater emphasis on the harder-edged aspects of maritime defence and security, areas where the EU has traditionally struggled to establish a role and identity. The strategy stated that the EU would consider new maritime areas of interest and also called for EU member states to expand their presence and action in the Indo-Pacific. Moreover, it called for greater capacity to ensure EU 'surface superiority, to project power at sea, to enable underwater control, and to contribute to air defence', a clear reference to changing threat environments in Europe's northern and southern waters. However, whether EU naval-rearmament ambitions will translate into major new capabilities remained unclear, not least given NATO's renewed focus in this area.

In May 2023, Denmark officially joined the Permanent Structured Cooperation (PESCO) on defence between EU member states, following a referendum in June 2022 to allow the country to participate in defence-related EU cooperation. Concurrently, the EU Council launched a fifth round of PESCO projects, adding 11 new initiatives in the areas of training; land, maritime and air systems; cyber; and enabling joint services. In another sign of closer defence cooperation among European nations following Russia's invasion of Ukraine, the EU in November 2022 invited the United Kingdom to join the military-mobility PESCO project, the first such move since it exited the EU. Similarly, Norway, an EU-aligned state, assumed leadership in at least three projects of the EU's European Defence Fund scheme.

The EU also moved ahead on standing up a new Rapid Deployment Capacity (RDC) by 2025. The modular force of about 5,000 personnel is slated to consist of modified EU battlegroups and additional forces from member states to rapidly respond to international crises outside the EU. In October 2023, the RDC held its first live exercise. Member states also continued to explore the option of a more flexible interpretation of Article 44 of the EU treaty, which allows 'coalitions of the willing' to conduct missions and operations on behalf of the bloc but still requires a unanimous Council decision. In a progress report on the RDC, the EU said its conceptual development was advancing, though more work lay ahead, including to identify which of the member states' military forces and capabilities would be available.

Even so, uncertainty remained over whether the EU was prepared to play a more active defence role outside the European continent. For instance, French President Emmanuel Macron caused consternation in Brussels and many European capitals during a visit to China in April 2023 when he suggested that in a potential war between China and Taiwan, Europeans should not automatically side with Washington in allying with Taipei. His remarks drew a strong rebuke from senior EU officials, including High Representative Borrell, who called for 'European navies to patrol the Taiwan Strait to signify Europe's commitment to freedom of navigation'. Individual EU members continued to conduct naval operations in the region, though strictly under national flags, and the EU as an institution struggled to develop a clearer security and defence profile in the region.

Table 7 — France: Nexter (KNDS) CAESAR 155mm howitzer

France's CAESAR is the West's best-selling wheeled howitzer. Development began in the early 1990s as a self-funded effort by designer GIAT Industries, now known as Nexter and merged into KNDS. The first series-production units were delivered to the French Army in 2008 and deployed to Afghanistan the year after. CAESAR has achieved significant export success. The manufacturer says CAESAR's longer barrel and enhanced metallurgy allow the system to strike targets up to 55 km away depending on ammunition type. This compares with 30 km for the legacy TRF1. In mid-2022, France contracted Nexter to develop a Mk II standard over four years, followed either by production of 33 new systems and upgrade of the Mk I systems or manufacture of 109 brand new CAESARs. The upgrade mostly focuses on the vehicle (extra protection, new engine), indicating that the French Army is satisfied with the CAESAR's shooting performance. The war in Ukraine has given a new profile to artillery systems, including CAESAR, spurring demand for such equipment. CAESAR is competing in a busy market against Israeli and Swedish designs, with German, South Korean and other systems set to join. To meet growing demand, Nexter has spent its own funds to increase production from two to four systems a month in 2022 to six in 2023.

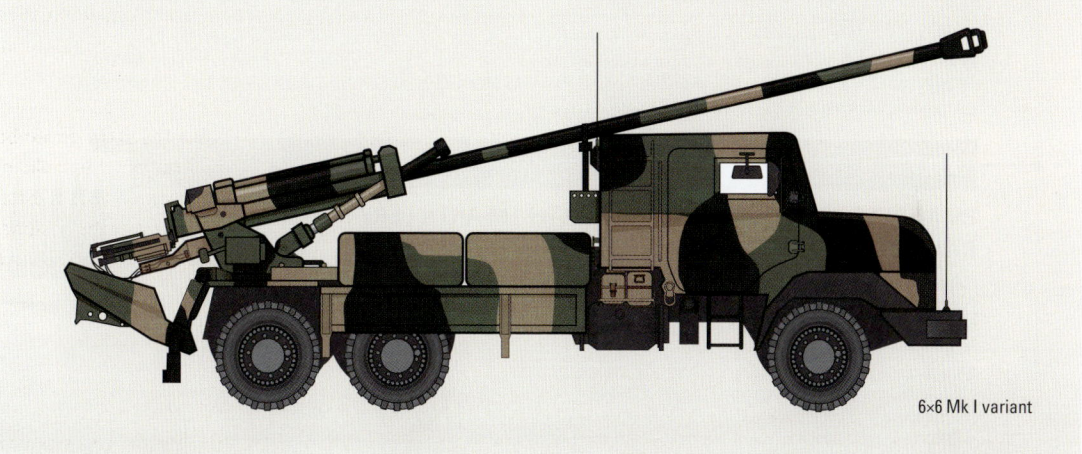

6×6 Mk I variant

Contract Date	Recipient	Variant	Quantity	Value	Deliveries
Sep 2000	France	6×6 Mk I	5	EUR19.31m (USD21.8m)	2003
Dec 2004	France	6×6 Mk I	72*	EUR339m (USD471.36m)	2008–11
Apr 2006	Thailand	6×6 Mk I	6	n.k.	2009
Jul 2006	Saudi Arabia	6×6 Mk I	132	n.k.	2010–16
Nov 2012	Indonesia	6×6 Mk I	37	EUR115m (USD147.84m)	2014–16
Feb 2017	Indonesia	6×6 Mk I	18	EUR60m (USD67.76m)	2020
May 2017	Denmark	8×8 Mk I	19	DKK458.7m (USD69.31m)	2019–23
2020	Morocco	6×6 Mk I	36	EUR200m (USD227.93m)	2022–ongoing
Sep 2021	Czech Republic	8×8 Mk I	62	CZK10.27bn (USD467.88m)	2024–26**
2022	Ukraine	6×6 Mk I	18†	Donation (France)	2022
Feb 2022	France	6×6 Mk II	33‡	Up to EUR600m (USD632.33m)	2026–31**
May 2022	Belgium	6×6 Mk II	9	EUR62m (USD65.34m)	2027**
Jul 2022	France	6×6 Mk I	18	EUR85m (USD89.58m)	2023–ongoing
Dec 2022	Lithuania	6×6 Mk II	18	EUR130m (USD137m)	By 2027**
2023	Ukraine	8×8 Mk I	19†	Donation (Denmark)	2023**
2023	Ukraine	6×6 Mk I	18	Donation (France)	2023–24**
TOTAL (minus donations from stocks)			**483**		

*Plus upgrades to five prototypes. **Planned. †Donated from stocks. ‡Plus upgrades to Mk I CAESARs.

Significant procurement and delivery events - 2023

JANUARY

FRANCE ISSUES NEW MILITARY PLANNING LAW (LPM)

France issued a new LPM covering 2024–30 worth EUR413bn (USD449.8bn) and representing a 40% increase over the previous law, which was valued at EUR295bn (USD321.05bn) for 2019–25. This extra money will be used to invest in ammunition stocks, air defence and uninhabited systems such as additional SAMP/T NG SAM batteries and more *Patroller* UAVs, but also in intelligence and cyber capabilities. Greater digitalisation of the armed forces, instead of more costly investment in mass, is expected to increase capability. Despite this extra funding, difficult decisions have still had to be made, with some programmes extended beyond 2030 rather than cut. This mostly affects the army's *Scorpion* modernisation effort, which encompasses several armoured vehicle types. The navy and air force seem to have protected their most important programmes, though some deliveries of *Rafale* fighters, A400M transport aircraft and frigates will now stretch beyond the LPM's 2030 planning horizon. France is likely taking a gamble that exports will help industry manage this change in plans.

JULY

EU AGREES TO PROVIDE UKRAINE WITH 1M ARTILLERY ROUNDS AND RAMP UP PRODUCTION

Following a Ukrainian request for the provision of 155mm artillery ammunition in March, the Council of the European Union agreed to donate 1m rounds to Ukraine within 12 months. A three-track approach would consist of donations from existing stocks, joint procurement of ammunition and the ramp-up of production capacity. In April, the EU dedicated EUR1bn (USD1.09bn) of its European Peace Facility fund to partially reimburse EU nations donating ammunition to Ukraine from existing stocks or orders. This was followed in May by EUR1bn (USD1.09bn) to procure ammunition, through the European Defence Agency, in the EU and Norway. Finally, in July, the council and the European Parliament ratified the Act in Support of Ammunition Production (ASAP). Worth EUR500m (USD544.16m) and coming partly from existing budgets, ASAP makes grant funding available to industry to allow for the ramp-up of production of ammunition and missiles, although proposed regulatory changes were cut from the final draft after pushback from member states. Internal Market Commissioner Thierry Breton has spoken about the need for a 'war economy' after years of relatively low production and a resulting reduction in capacity to match. But the EU, in late 2023, was on a pace to miss the ammunition delivery commitment to Ukraine.

SEPTEMBER

PARTNERS SIGN NEW GCAP AGREEMENT

Defence companies from the UK, Italy and Japan signed a collaboration agreement for the Global Combat Air Programme, a project to develop a next-generation fighter for entry into service by 2035. The industrial partners BAE Systems, Leonardo and Mitsubishi Heavy Industries, along with their government counterparts, now aim to complete preparatory work in order for the detailed design and development phase to begin in 2025. It is slated to involve a flying demonstrator. Government and industry stakeholders still need to resolve questions concerning workshare allocation and the management structure for the programme that are supposed to be wrapped up before the start of the development phase. The companies are building on technology developments undertaken in efforts such as the UK's Team Tempest development programme launched in 2018 and Japan's X-2 project launched in 2009.

OCTOBER

EUROPEAN COUNTRIES SEEK TO JOINTLY PROCURE AIR-DEFENCE SYSTEMS

Belgium, Cyprus, Estonia, France and Hungary signed a letter of intent to jointly purchase the *Mistral* 3 ground-based SAM system in large numbers through the French defence procurement agency. The signing took place at a conference of defence ministers that was organised by Paris to discuss air defence. The conference was likely in part a response to the German-led European Sky Shield Initiative (ESSI), which includes the use of non-European systems. Launched in 2022, ESSI brings together 19 countries, with ten of those signing a memorandum of understanding in October, and envisages joint procurement of off-the-shelf systems. One of these is Diehl Defence's IRIS-T series of SAM systems, which Germany is purchasing. Estonia and Latvia announced in June 2022 that they would purchase the medium-range version, which was followed by a framework agreement in September. That month, Austria suggested that it would acquire a combination of short- and medium-range batteries jointly with Germany. Poland's acquisition of large numbers of MBDA CAMM-based systems, including the CAMM-ER developed originally for Italy, has been accompanied by agreements with the UK to cooperate closely on air-defence weapons.

Albania ALB

Albanian Lek ALL		2022	2023	2024
GDP	ALL	2.14trn	2.31trn	2.48trn
	USD	19.1bn	23.0bn	25.3bn
per capita	USD	6,658	8,057	8,877
Growth	%	4.8	3.6	3.3
Inflation	%	6.7	4.8	4.0
Def exp [a]	ALL	25.8bn	40.3bn	
	USD	231m	401m	
Def bdgt [b]	ALL	32.2bn	40.3bn	45.8bn
	USD	288m	401m	468m
FMA (US)	USD	15m	0m	0m
USD1=ALL		112.05	100.40	97.90

[a] NATO figure

[b] Excludes military pensions

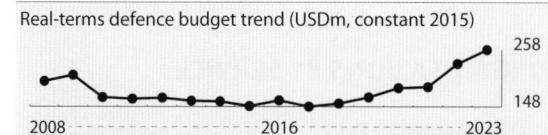

Real-terms defence budget trend (USDm, constant 2015)
258
148
2008 — 2016 — 2023

Population 3,101,621

Age	0–14	15–19	20–24	25–29	30–64	65 plus
Male	9.4%	2.9%	3.8%	4.5%	21.9%	6.7%
Female	8.5%	2.6%	3.5%	4.3%	24.0%	7.9%

Capabilities

The government's 2023 defence directive emphasises improved conditions and training for personnel, equipment modernisation, institutional reform, strengthening civil defence capabilities, better cyber security, and greater contributions to regional operations and engagements. Albania's military is likely to see force structure changes emerge from the Long-Term Development Plan for the Armed Forces (AF) 2023–2031. The application of the Integrity Plan 2022–2025 is expected to be extended to the General Staff of the armed forces. Tirana is working to improve readiness and capability of its infantry battalion. It addressed similar issues with the command and control of the multinational brigade Task Force South that was used during the *Defender Europe* 2023 drill hosted by the country. Tirana is trying to improve recruitment and retention with enhanced benefits and educational and training opportunities. Salary increases continued in 2023. Modernisation is underway, including the acquisition of UH-60 *Black Hawk* helicopters, *Bayraktar* TB2 UAVs, and the renewal of the Integrated Maritime Surveillance System. The Cyber Defence Military Unit worked with international partners to enhance its skills. Albania contributes to NATO – including battlegroups in Bulgaria and Latvia – UN and EU missions but does not possess an independent expeditionary capability. In 2022, US Special Operations Command Europe established a forward-deployed headquarters in Albania. The country deepened cooperation with Washington, signing of a framework focused on strengthening the Light Infantry Group, cyber defence air force training and modernisation, among others. NATO allies Greece and Italy police Albania's airspace. Albania has little in the way of a domestic defence industry, with no ability to design and manufacture modern military platforms. Nevertheless, the country has some publicly owned defence companies that are capable of producing small arms, explosives and ammunition.

ACTIVE 7,500 (Land Force 2,350 Naval Force 700 Air Force 650 Support Command 1,650 Other 2,150)

ORGANISATIONS BY SERVICE

Land Force 2,350

FORCES BY ROLE

SPECIAL FORCES

1 spec ops regt (1 SF bn, 1 cdo bn)

MANOEUVRE

Light

3 lt inf bn

COMBAT SUPPORT

1 mor bty

1 NBC coy

EQUIPMENT BY TYPE

ARMOURED FIGHTING VEHICLES

APC • **PPV** 40 *MaxxPro Plus*

ARTILLERY • **MOR** 32: **82mm** 20; **120mm** 12

Naval Force 700

EQUIPMENT BY TYPE

All operational patrol vessels under 10t FLD

Coast Guard

EQUIPMENT BY TYPE

PATROL AND COASTAL COMBATANTS 19

PBF 5 *Drini* (US *Archangel*)

PBR 5: 2 Type-227; 1 Type-246; 2 Type-2010

PB 9: 4 *Iliria* (Damen Stan Patrol 4207); 3 Mk3 *Sea Spectre*; 2 *Shqypnia*

LOGISTICS AND SUPPORT • **AG** 1

Air Force 650

EQUIPMENT BY TYPE

HELICOPTERS

TPT 16: **Medium** 4 AS532AL *Cougar*†; **Light** 12: 1 AW109; 3 Bell 205 (AB-205); 2 Bell 206C (AB-206C); 4 Bo-105; 2 H145

Military Police

FORCES BY ROLE

COMBAT SUPPORT

1 MP bn

EQUIPMENT BY TYPE

ARMOURED FIGHTING VEHICLES

AUV 8 IVECO LMV

Support Command 1,650

FORCES BY ROLE

COMBAT SUPPORT

1 engr bn

1 cbt spt bn

COMBAT SERVICE SUPPORT

1 log bde (1 tpt bn, 1 log bn)

1 maint unit

DEPLOYMENT

BOSNIA-HERZEGOVINA: EU • EUFOR (*Operation Althea*) 1

BULGARIA: NATO • Enhanced Vigilance Activites 30; 1 inf pl

IRAQ: NATO • NATO Mission Iraq 1

KOSOVO: NATO • KFOR 89

LATVIA: NATO • Enhanced Forward Presence 21; 1 EOD pl

SOUTH SUDAN: UN • UNMISS 2

Austria AUT

Euro EUR		2022	2023	2024
GDP	EUR	447bn	483bn	505bn
	USD	471bn	526bn	552bn
per capita	USD	52,192	58,013	60,594
Growth	%	4.8	0.1	0.8
Inflation	%	8.6	7.8	3.7
Def bdgt [a]	EUR	3.45bn	4.08bn	4.49bn
	USD	3.63bn	4.44bn	4.91bn
USD1=EUR		0.95	0.92	0.91

[a] Includes military pensions

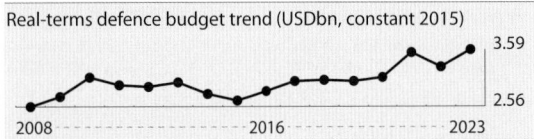

Real-terms defence budget trend (USDbn, constant 2015)

Population	8,940,860					
Age	0–14	15–19	20–24	25–29	30–64	65 plus
Male	7.2%	2.4%	2.6%	3.1%	24.5%	9.2%
Female	6.9%	2.3%	2.5%	3.0%	24.6%	11.6%

Capabilities

Austria is constitutionally non-aligned but is an EU member and actively engaged in the bloc's Common Security and Defence Policy. Vienna bases its defence-policy objectives on the 2013 National Security Strategy, the 2014 Defence Strategy and the 2017 Military Strategy. They direct that military capabilities maintain sovereignty and territorial integrity, enable military assistance to civil authorities and participate in crisis-management missions. Authorities are shifting emphasis from international operations to homeland defence, and capabilities needed to counter hybrid threats at home. Austrian assets for international deployments may eventually be embedded in the EUFOR Crisis Response Operation Core. Vienna aims to be able to deploy and sustain a minimum (on average) of 1,100 troops. The military plans to group cyber, CIS and EW capabilities in one directorate. While not a NATO member, Austria joined the Alliance's Partnership for Peace framework in 1995. In early 2023, a defence report highlighted the need to strengthen the armed forces to adapt to a changed security environment, and an investment plan has been drawn up to 2032. To address shortfalls, Vienna announced plans to upgrade *Leopard* 2 MBTs and *Pandur* wheeled APCs and the purchase of additional IFVs is being considered. The country, in September, said it plans to modernise its airlift capacity with the acquisition of KC-390 transports, possibly in conjunction with the Netherlands. The country's defence-industrial base comprises some 100 companies with niche capabilities and international ties in the areas of weapons and ammunition, communications equipment and vehicles.

ACTIVE 22,200 (Land Forces 12,500 Air 3,200 Support 6,500)

Conscript liability 6 months recruit trg, 30 days reservist refresher trg for volunteers; 120–150 days additional for officers, NCOs and specialists. Authorised maximum wartime strength of 55,000

RESERVE 109,200 (Joint structured 35,200 Joint unstructured 74,000)

Some 8,600 reservists a year undergo refresher trg in tranches

ORGANISATIONS BY SERVICE

Land Forces 12,500
FORCES BY ROLE
MANOEUVRE
  Armoured
  1 (4th) armd inf bde (1 recce/SP arty bn, 1 tk bn, 2 armd inf bn, 1 spt bn)
  Mechanised
  1 (3rd) mech inf bde (1 recce/SP arty bn, 3 mech inf bn, 1 cbt engr bn, 1 spt bn)
  Light
  1 (7th) lt inf bde (1 recce bn, 3 inf bn, 1 cbt engr bn, 1 spt bn)
  1 (6th) mtn inf bde (3 mtn inf bn, 1 cbt engr bn, 1 spt bn)
EQUIPMENT BY TYPE
ARMOURED FIGHTING VEHICLES
  MBT 56 *Leopard* 2A4
  IFV 112 *Ulan*
  APC 163
    APC (T) 32 BvS-10
    APC (W) 131: 71 *Pandur*; 60 *Pandur* EVO
  AUV 216: 66 *Dingo* 2; 150 IVECO LMV
ENGINEERING & MAINTENANCE VEHICLES
  ARV 65: 27 4KH7FA-SB *Greif* (11 more in store); 28 *Dingo* 2 ARV; 10 M88A1
NBC VEHICLES 12 *Dingo* 2 AC NBC
ANTI-TANK/ANTI-INFRASTRUCTURE
  MSL • MANPATS *Bill* 2 (PAL 2000)
  RCL 84mm *Carl Gustaf*
ARTILLERY 119
  SP 155mm 48 M109A5ÖE
  MOR 71+: **81mm** L16; **120mm** 71 sGrW 86 (22 more in store)

Reserve

FORCES BY ROLE

MANOEUVRE

Light

10 inf bn

Air Force 3,200

The Air Force is part of Joint Forces Comd and consists of 2 bde; Air Support Comd and Airspace Surveillance Comd

FORCES BY ROLE

FIGHTER

2 sqn with Eurofighter *Typhoon*

ISR

1 sqn with PC-6B *Turbo Porter*

TRANSPORT

1 sqn with C-130K *Hercules*

TRAINING

1 trg sqn with PC-7 *Turbo Trainer*

TRANSPORT HELICOPTER

2 sqn with Bell 212 (AB-212)

1 sqn with OH-58B *Kiowa*

1 sqn with S-70A *Black Hawk*

2 sqn with SA316/SA319 *Alouette* III

AIR DEFENCE

2 bn

1 radar bn

EQUIPMENT BY TYPE

AIRCRAFT 13 combat capable

FTR 13 Eurofighter *Typhoon* (Tranche 1)

TPT 11: **Medium** 3 C-130K *Hercules*; **Light** 8 PC-6B *Turbo Porter*

TRG 16: 12 PC-7 *Turbo Trainer*; 4 DA40NG

HELICOPTERS

MRH 18 SA316/SA319 *Alouette* III

ISR 10 OH-58B *Kiowa*

TPT 36: **Medium** 9 S-70A-42 *Black Hawk*; **Light** 27: 5 AW169M LUH; 22 Bell 212 (AB-212)

AIR DEFENCE

SAM • **Point-defence** *Mistral*

GUNS **35mm** 24 GDF-005 (6 more in store)

AIR-LAUNCHED MISSILES • AAM • IIR IRIS-T

Special Operations Forces

FORCES BY ROLE

SPECIAL FORCES

2 SF gp

1 SF gp (reserve)

Support 6,500

Support forces comprise Joint Services Support Command and several agencies, academies and schools

DEPLOYMENT

BOSNIA-HERZEGOVINA: EU • EUFOR (*Operation Althea*) 47; 1 inf bn HQ; 1 hel unit

CYPRUS: UN • UNFICYP 3

KOSOVO: NATO • KFOR 271; 1 recce coy; 1 mech inf coy; 1 log coy; **UN** • UNMIK 1

LEBANON: UN • UNIFIL 152; 1 log coy

MALI: EU • EUTM Mali 4

MIDDLE EAST: UN • UNTSO 6

WESTERN SAHARA: UN • MINURSO 4

Belgium BEL

Euro EUR		2022	2023	2024
GDP	EUR	549bn	577bn	602bn
	USD	579bn	628bn	658bn
per capita	USD	49,843	53,657	56,085
Growth	%	3.2	1.0	0.9
Inflation	%	10.3	2.5	4.3
Def exp [a]	EUR	6.53bn	6.66bn	
	USD	6.88bn	7.25bn	
Def bdgt [b]	EUR	5.36bn	5.11bn	5.09bn
	USD	5.65bn	5.57bn	5.57bn
USD1=EUR		0.95	0.92	0.91

[a] NATO figure

[b] Includes military pensions

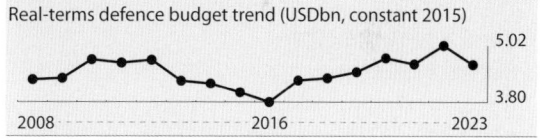

Real-terms defence budget trend (USDbn, constant 2015)

5.02 / 3.80 (2008 – 2016 – 2023)

Population	11,913,633					
Age	0–14	15–19	20–24	25–29	30–64	65 plus
Male	8.7%	2.9%	2.9%	3.1%	22.9%	8.8%
Female	8.3%	2.8%	2.8%	3.0%	22.7%	11.1%

Capabilities

Brussels, in June 2022, updated a six-year-old strategic defence vision with a Security/Service, Technology, Ambition, Resilience (STAR) plan. Soon after, it approved a new military programming law, which heralded increased defence budgets out to 2030. The funds are intended to address three key areas: increasing personnel numbers, strengthening the defence technological and industrial base, and delivering major equipment investments. Recruitment and retention criteria are under scrutiny following retirements and establishment reductions in recent decades. The motorised brigade, medical support and mobility are supposed to secure investments, with over half of the STAR plan's investments slated for the land domain. Investments with 'dual capability' to be used in contingencies at home as well as for military operations are being prioritised. Belgium inaugurated a cyber command in October 2022 that falls under the military intelligence service. NATO, EU and UN membership are central to defence policy.

Belgium often cooperates with neighbours and has committed with Denmark and the Netherlands to form a composite combined special-operations command. It is modernising across the force, including purchases of fighter aircraft, frigates, and armoured vehicles. Belgium has an advanced, export-focused defence industry, focusing on components and subcontracting, though in FN Herstal it has one of the world's largest manufacturers of small arms.

ACTIVE 22,900 (Army 8,500 Navy 1,400 Air 4,600 Medical Service 1,450 Joint Service 6,950)

RESERVE 5,900

ORGANISATIONS BY SERVICE

Land Component 8,500
FORCES BY ROLE
SPECIAL FORCES
  1 spec ops regt (1 SF gp, 1 cdo bn, 1 para bn, 1 sigs gp)
MANOEUVRE
  Mechanised
  1 mech bde (1 ISR bn; 3 mech bn; 2 lt inf bn; 1 arty bn; 2 engr bn; 2 sigs gp; 2 log bn)
COMBAT SUPPORT
  1 CIMIC gp
  1 EOD unit
  1 MP coy
COMBAT SERVICE SUPPORT
  1 log bn
EQUIPMENT BY TYPE
ARMOURED FIGHTING VEHICLES
  ASLT 18 *Piranha* III-C DF90
  RECCE 30 *Pandur Recce*
  IFV 16 *Piranha* III-C DF30
  APC • APC (W) 78: 64 *Piranha* III-C; 14 *Piranha* III-PC (CP)
  AUV 575: 219 *Dingo* 2 (inc 52 CP); 356 IVECO LMV
ENGINEERING & MAINTENANCE VEHICLES
  AEV 14: 6 Pionierpanzer 2 *Dachs*; 8 *Piranha* III-C
  ARV 13: 4 *Pandur*; 9 *Piranha* III-C
ANTI-TANK/ANTI-INFRASTRUCTURE
  MSL • MANPATS *Spike*-MR
ARTILLERY 60
  TOWED 105mm 14 LG1 MkII
  MOR 46: **81mm** 14 Expal; **120mm** 32 RT-61

Naval Component 1,400
EQUIPMENT BY TYPE
PRINCIPAL SURFACE COMBATANTS • FRIGATES 2
  FFGHM 2 *Leopold* I (ex-NLD *Karel Doorman*) with 2 quad lnchr with RGM-84 *Harpoon* AShM, 1 16-cell Mk 48 mod 1 VLS with RIM-7P *Sea Sparrow* SAM, 2 twin 324mm SVTT Mk 32 ASTT with Mk 46 LWT, 1 *Goalkeeper* CIWS, 1 76mm gun (capacity 1 med hel)
PATROL AND COASTAL COMBATANTS

  PCC 2 *Castor* (FRA *Kermorvan* mod)
MINE WARFARE • MINE COUNTERMEASURES
  MHC 5 *Flower* (*Tripartite*)
LOGISTICS AND SUPPORT 2
  AGOR 1 *Belgica*
  AXS 1 *Zenobe Gramme*
UNINHABITED MARITIME SYSTEMS • UUV
  DATA REMUS 100; *Seascan*
  MW A18-M; *Double Eagle* Mk III; *K-Ster* C/I; *Seafox* C/I

Air Component 4,600
FORCES BY ROLE
FIGHTER/GROUND ATTACK/ISR
  4 sqn with F-16AM/BM *Fighting Falcon*
SEARCH & RESCUE
  1 sqn with NH90 NFH
TRANSPORT
  1 sqn with *Falcon* 7X (VIP)
  1 sqn (BEL/LUX) with A400M
TRAINING
  1 OCU sqn with F-16AM/BM *Fighting Falcon*
  1 sqn with SF-260D/M
  1 OCU unit with AW109
TRANSPORT HELICOPTER
  2 sqn with AW109 (ISR)
EQUIPMENT BY TYPE
AIRCRAFT 53 combat capable
  FTR 53: 44 F-16AM *Fighting Falcon*; 9 F-16BM *Fighting Falcon*
  TPT 8: **Heavy** 6 A400M; **PAX** 2 *Falcon* 7X (VIP, leased)
  TRG 32: 9 SF-260D; 23 SF-260M
HELICOPTERS
  ASW 4 NH90 NFH (opcon Navy)
  TPT 11: **Medium** 4 NH90 TTH; **Light** 7 AW109 (ISR) (7 more in store)
AIR-LAUNCHED MISSILES
  AAM • IR AIM-9M *Sidewinder*; **IIR** AIM-9X *Sidewinder* II; **ARH** AIM-120B AMRAAM
BOMBS
  Laser-guided: GBU-10/-12 *Paveway* II; GBU-24 *Paveway* III
  Laser & INS/GPS-guided: GBU-54 Laser JDAM (dual-mode)
  INS/GPS guided: GBU-31 JDAM; GBU-38 JDAM; GBU-39 Small Diameter Bomb

Medical Service 1,450
FORCES BY ROLE
COMBAT SERVICE SUPPORT
  4 med unit
  1 fd hospital
EQUIPMENT BY TYPE
ARMOURED FIGHTING VEHICLES

APC • **APC (W)** 10: 4 *Pandur* (amb); 6 *Piranha* III-C (amb)
AUV 10 *Dingo* 2 (amb)

DEPLOYMENT

BOSNIA-HERZEGOVINA: EU • EUFOR (*Operation Althea*) 5
DEMOCRATIC REPUBLIC OF THE CONGO: UN • MONUSCO 1
LITHUANIA: NATO • Enhanced Forward Presence 250; 1 mech inf coy with *Piranha* DF30/DF90
MALI: EU • EUTM Mali 5
MIDDLE EAST: UN • UNTSO 2
MOZAMBIQUE: EU • EUTM Mozambique 2
NORTH SEA: NATO • SNMCMG 1: 50; 1 MHC
ROMANIA: NATO • Enhanced Vigilance Activities 250; 1 mech inf coy with *Piranha* IIIC

FOREIGN FORCES

United States US European Command: 1,150

Bosnia-Herzegovina BIH

Convertible Mark BAM		2022	2023	2024
GDP	BAM	45.5bn	48.4bn	51.4bn
	USD	24.5bn	26.9bn	28.7bn
per capita	USD	7,060	7,778	8,317
Growth	%	4.1	2.0	3.0
Inflation	%	14.0	5.5	3.0
Def bdgt	BAM	307m	1.53bn	
	USD	165m	849m	
USD1=BAM		1.86	1.80	1.79

Real-terms defence budget trend (USDm, constant 2015)
651
136
2008 – 2016 – 2023

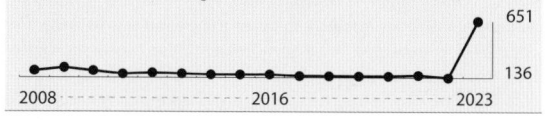

Population 3,807,764

Age	0–14	15–19	20–24	25–29	30–64	65 plus
Male	6.8%	2.3%	2.7%	3.2%	26.5%	7.3%
Female	6.3%	2.1%	2.5%	3.0%	26.7%	10.6%

Capabilities

Bosnia-Herzegovina's armed forces' primary objectives are to defend territorial integrity and contribute to peacekeeping missions, and potential tasks to aid civil authorities. The armed forces are professional and represent all three ethnic groups. However, low salaries may negatively affect recruitment and retention. In 2023, the country signed agreements with Germany and the US to assist and support the infrastructure of its armed forces and to support the Ministry of Defence with planning, programming and budgeting. The country is reforming its armed forces and modernising its equipment in accordance with a Defence Review, Development and Modernisation Plan for 2017–27 and its NATO aspirations. Bosnia-Herzegovina joined NATO's Partnership for Peace in 2006 and presented a Membership Action Plan in 2010, though progress has been slow. Ethnic tensions persist, with the Serb community threatening to withdraw from national structures, including the armed forces. Bosnia-Herzegovina contributes to EU, NATO and UN missions, but the armed forces have no capacity to deploy independently and self-sustain beyond national borders. The inventory comprises mainly ageing Soviet-era equipment, though some new helicopters have been procured from the US. Bosnia-Herzegovina has little in the way of a domestic defence industry, with only the capability to produce small arms, ammunition and explosives.

ACTIVE 10,500 (Armed Forces 10,500)
RESERVE 6,000 (Armed Forces 6,000)

ORGANISATIONS BY SERVICE

Armed Forces 10,500

1 ops comd; 1 spt comd
FORCES BY ROLE
MANOEUVRE
  Light
  3 inf bde (1 recce coy, 3 inf bn, 1 arty bn)
COMBAT SUPPORT
  1 cbt spt bde (1 tk bn, 1 engr bn, 1 EOD bn, 1 int bn, 1 MP bn, 1 CBRN coy, 1 sigs bn)
COMBAT SERVICE SUPPORT
  1 log comd (5 log bn)
EQUIPMENT BY TYPE
ARMOURED FIGHTING VEHICLES
  MBT 45 M60A3
  APC • **APC (T)** 20 M113A2
ENGINEERING & MAINTENANCE VEHICLES
  VLB MTU
  MW *Bozena*
ANTI-TANK/ANTI-INFRASTRUCTURE • MSL
  SP 60: 8 9P122 *Malyutka*; 9 9P133 *Malyutka*; 32 BOV-1; 11 M-92
  MANPATS 9K11 *Malyutka* (RS-AT-3 *Sagger*); 9K111 *Fagot* (RS-AT-4 *Spigot*); 9K115 *Metis* (RS-AT-7 *Saxhorn*); HJ-8; *Milan*
ARTILLERY 224
  TOWED 122mm 100 D-30
  MRL 122mm 24 APRA-40
  MOR 120mm 100 M-75

Air Force and Air Defence Brigade 800

FORCES BY ROLE
HELICOPTER
  1 sqn with Bell 205 (UH-1H *Iroquois*); Mi-8MTV *Hip*; Mi-17 *Hip* H
  1 sqn with Bell 205 (UH-1H *Huey* II); Mi-8 *Hip*; SA-341H/SA-342L *Gazelle* (HN-42/45M)
AIR DEFENCE
  1 AD bn

EQUIPMENT BY TYPE

AIRCRAFT
- **FGA** (7 J-22 *Orao* in store)
- **ATK** (6 J-1 (J-21) *Jastreb*; 3 TJ-1(NJ-21) *Jastreb* all in store)
- **ISR** (2 RJ-1 (IJ-21) *Jastreb** in store)
- **TRG** (1 G-4 *Super Galeb* (N-62)* in store)

HELICOPTERS
- **MRH** 9: 4 Mi-8MTV *Hip*; 1 Mi-17 *Hip* H; 1 SA-341H *Gazelle* (HN-42); up to 3 SA-342L *Gazelle* (HN-45M)
- **TPT** 17: **Medium** 8 Mi-8 *Hip* **Light** 9: 6 Bell 205 (UH-1H *Iroquois*) (of which 2 MEDEVAC); 3 Bell 205 (UH-1H *Huey* II) (1 UH-1H *Huey* II in store)

AIR DEFENCE
- **SAM**
  - **Short-range** 20 2K12 *Kub* (RS-SA-6 *Gainful*)
  - **Point-defence** 9K34 *Strela*-3 (RS-SA-14 *Gremlin*); 9K310 *Igla*-1 (RS-SA-16 *Gimlet*)
- **GUNS • TOWED 40mm** 47: 31 L/60, 16 L/70

DEPLOYMENT

CENTRAL AFRICAN REPUBLIC: EU • EUTM RCA 3
DEMOCRATIC REPUBLIC OF THE CONGO: UN • MONUSCO 2

FOREIGN FORCES

Part of EUFOR – *Operation Althea* unless otherwise stated
Albania 1
Austria 47; 1 inf bn HQ; 1 hel unit
Belgium 5
Bulgaria 116; 1 inf coy
Chile 7
Czech Republic 2
Denmark 2
France 5
Germany 31
Greece 7
Hungary 192; 1 inf coy
Ireland 4
Italy 195; 1 ISR coy
Macedonia, North 32
Netherlands 160; 1 mne coy
Poland 49
Romania 270; 1 inf coy
Slovakia 54
Slovenia 20
Spain 2
Switzerland 20
Turkiye 238; 1 inf coy

Bulgaria BLG

Bulgarian Lev BGN		2022	2023	2024
GDP	BGN	165bn	185bn	197bn
	USD	89.1bn	103bn	110bn
per capita	USD	13,821	16,087	17,320
Growth	%	3.4	1.7	3.2
Inflation	%	13.0	8.5	3.0
Def exp [a]	BGN	2.67bn	3.41bn	
	USD	1.44bn	1.90bn	
Def bdgt [b]	BGN	2.48bn	2.97bn	3.95bn
	USD	1.34bn	1.66bn	2.21bn
FMA (US)	USD	25m	0m	0m
USD1=BGN		1.86	1.80	1.79

[a] NATO figure
[b] Excludes military pensions

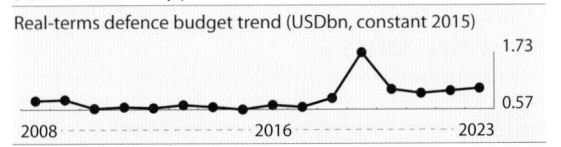

Real-terms defence budget trend (USDbn, constant 2015)
1.73 / 0.57
2008 — 2016 — 2023

Population	6,827,736					
Age	0–14	15–19	20–24	25–29	30–64	65 plus
Male	7.2%	2.7%	2.5%	2.5%	25.4%	8.4%
Female	6.8%	2.5%	2.3%	2.3%	24.9%	12.5%

Capabilities

The armed forces' main priority is defending state sovereignty and territorial integrity. A long-term development plan was adopted in 2021, involving significant re-equipment and modernisation and a focus on artificial intelligence and cyber capabilities. The country plans to reach the NATO goal of spending 2% of GDP on defence by 2024 and remain at or above that level. Bulgaria is updating its national defence strategy to cover the period out to 2033. The document is expected to review and optimise processes, better focus on the inclusion of technology and higher levels of interoperability. A new Investment Expenditure Programme was expected by the end of 2023. There are several bilateral defence cooperation agreements with regional states, including Ukraine and the US. Bulgaria has a strategic partnership with Romania. Bulgaria's airspace is protected by NATO's Air Policing Mission due to the country's limited combat aircraft fleet. Bulgaria expects to receive new F-16 Block 70s in 2025 and ordered a second batch in 2022. As a gap filler, Bulgaria has upgraded some MiG-29s to extend their service life. In December 2022, the NATO multinational battle group established in Bulgaria reached full operational capability. To cope with staffing problems, the government has increased the military retirement age and salaries, but the armed forces still suffer from a shortage of personnel. Units intended for international operations and those with certain readiness levels declared to NATO and the EU get higher priority in training. Bulgaria regularly trains and exercises with NATO partners and regional allies. Work towards the formation of battalion battlegroups within its mechanised brigades is ongoing. The navy is awaiting two multipurpose modular patrol vessels to be used for NATO and EU naval missions. Bulgaria's defence industry exports small arms but has limited capacity to design and manufacture platforms.

ACTIVE 36,950 (Army 17,000 Navy 4,450 Air 8,500 Central Staff 7,000)

RESERVE 3,000 (Joint 3,000)

ORGANISATIONS BY SERVICE

Army 17,000
FORCES BY ROLE
MANOEUVRE
Reconnaissance
 1 recce bn
Mechanised
 2 mech bde (4 mech inf bn, 1 SP arty bn, 1 cbt engr bn, 1 log bn, 1 SAM bn)
Light
 1 mtn inf regt
COMBAT SUPPORT
 1 arty regt (1 fd arty bn, 1 MRL bn)
 1 engr regt (1 cbt engr bn, 1 ptn br bn, 1 engr spt bn)
 1 NBC bn
COMBAT SERVICE SUPPORT
 1 log regt
EQUIPMENT BY TYPE
ARMOURED FIGHTING VEHICLES
 MBT 90 T-72M1/M2†
 IFV 160: 90 BMP-1; 70 BMP-23
 APC 120
  APC (T) 100 MT-LB
  APC (W) 20 BTR-60
 AUV 44: 17 M1117 ASV; 27 Plasan *SandCat*
ENGINEERING & MAINTENANCE VEHICLES
 AEV MT-LB
 ARV T-54/T-55; MTP-1; MT-LB
 VLB BLG67; TMM
ANTI-TANK/ANTI-INFRASTRUCTURE
 MSL
  SP 24 9P148 *Konkurs* (RS-AT-5 *Spandrel*)
  MANPATS 9K111 *Fagot* (RS-AT-4 *Spigot*); 9K111-1 *Konkurs* (RS-AT-5 *Spandrel*); (9K11 *Malyutka* (RS-AT-3 *Sagger*) in store)
 GUNS 126: **85mm** (150 D-44 in store); **100mm** 126 MT-12
ARTILLERY 176
 SP 122mm 48 2S1
 TOWED 152mm 24 D-20
 MRL 122mm 24 BM-21
 MOR 120mm ε80 *Tundza/Tundza Sani*
SURFACE-TO-SURFACE MISSILE LAUNCHERS
 SRBM • Conventional 9K79 *Tochka* (RS-SS-21 *Scarab*)
AIR DEFENCE
 SAM • Point-defence 9K32 *Strela* (RS-SA-7 *Grail*)‡; 24 9K33 *Osa* (RS-SA-8 *Gecko*)
 GUNS 400
 SP 23mm ZSU-23-4
 TOWED 23mm ZU-23-2; **57mm** S-60

Navy 4,450
EQUIPMENT BY TYPE
PRINCIPAL SURFACE COMBATANTS • FRIGATES 3
 FFM 3 *Drazki* (ex-BEL *Wielingen*) (of which 1†) with 1 octuple Mk 29 GMLS with RIM-7P *Sea Sparrow* SAM, 2 single 533mm ASTT with L5 mod 4 HWT, 1 sextuple Bofors ASW Rocket Launcher System 375mm A/S mor, 1 100mm gun (Fitted for but not with 2 twin lnchr with MM38 *Exocet* AShM)
PATROL AND COASTAL COMBATANTS 4
 CORVETTES • FS 1 *Smeli* (ex-FSU *Koni*) with 2 RBU 6000 *Smerch* 2 A/S mor, 2 twin 76mm guns
 PCF 1 *Molnya*† (ex-FSU *Tarantul* II) with 2 AK630M CIWS, 1 76mm gun
 PCT 2 *Reshitelni* (ex-FSU *Pauk* I) with 4 single 406mm TT, 2 RBU 1200 *Uragan* A/S mor, 1 76mm gun
MINE COUNTERMEASURES 10
 MHC 3: 2 *Mesta* (ex-NLD *Alkmaar*); 1 *Tsibar* (ex-BEL *Flower*)
 MSC 3 *Briz* (ex-FSU *Sonya*) (of which 1†)
 MSI 4 *Olya* (ex-FSU)
AMPHIBIOUS • LANDING CRAFT
 LCM 2 *Vydra* (capacity either 3 MBT or 200 troops)
LOGISTICS AND SUPPORT 10
 AG 1
 AGS 2
 AGOR 1
 AOL 2
 ARS 1
 ATF 2
 AX 1
UNINHABITED MARITIME SYSTEMS
 UUV • MW *Double Eagle* Mk III

Naval Aviation
EQUIPMENT BY TYPE
HELICOPTERS
 ASW 2 AS565MB *Panther*
 MRH 1 AS365N3+ *Dauphin* 2

Air Force 8,500
FORCES BY ROLE
FIGHTER/ISR
 1 sqn with MiG-29/MiG-29UB *Fulcrum*
TRANSPORT
 1 sqn with An-30 *Clank*; C-27J *Spartan*; L-410UVP-E; PC-12M
TRAINING
 1 sqn with L-39ZA *Albatros**
 1 sqn with PC-9M

ATTACK HELICOPTER
  1 sqn with Mi-24D/V *Hind* D/E
TRANSPORT HELICOPTER
  1 sqn with AS532AL *Cougar*; Bell 206 *Jet Ranger*; Mi-17 *Hip* H
EQUIPMENT BY TYPE
AIRCRAFT 26 combat capable
  FTR 14: 11 MiG-29 *Fulcrum*; 3 MiG-29UB *Fulcrum*†
  FGA (Some MiG-21bis *Fishbed*/MiG-21UM *Mongol* B in store)
  ATK 6: 5 Su-25K *Frogfoot* K; 1 Su-25UBK *Frogfoot* B
  ISR 1 An-30 *Clank*
  TPT 7: **Medium** 3 C-27J *Spartan*; **Light** 4: 1 An-2T *Colt*; 2 L-410UVP-E; 1 PC-12M
  TRG 12: 6 L-39ZA *Albatros**; 6 PC-9M (basic)
HELICOPTERS
  ATK 6 Mi-24V *Hind* E (6 Mi-24D *Hind* D in store)
  MRH 5 Mi-17 *Hip* H
  TPT 18: **Medium** 12 AS532AL *Cougar*; **Light** 6 Bell 206 *Jet Ranger*
UNINHABITED AERIAL VEHICLES • **EW** *Yastreb*-2S
AIR DEFENCE
  SAM 20
    Long-range 20: 12 S-200 (RS-SA-5 *Gammon*); 8 S-300PMU (RS-SA-10 *Grumble*)
    Short-range S-125M *Neva*-M (RS-SA-3 *Goa*); 2K12 *Kub* (RS-SA-6 *Gainful*)
AIR-LAUNCHED MISSILES
  AAM • **IR** R-3 (RS-AA-2 *Atoll*)‡; R-73 (RS-AA-11A *Archer*); **SARH** R-27R (RS-AA-10 *Alamo* A)
  ASM Kh-29 (RS-AS-14 *Kedge*); Kh-25 (RS-AS-10 *Karen*)

Special Forces
FORCES BY ROLE
SPECIAL FORCES
  1 spec ops bde (1 SF bn, 1 para bn)

DEPLOYMENT
BOSNIA-HERZEGOVINA: EU • EUFOR (*Operation Althea*) 116; 1 inf coy
IRAQ: NATO • NATO Mission Iraq 2
KOSOVO: NATO • KFOR 142; 1 inf coy
MALI: EU • EUTM Mali 4

FOREIGN FORCES
Albania NATO Enhanced Vigilance Activities: 30; 1 inf pl
Greece Enhanced Vigilance Activities: 30; 1 AT pl
Italy NATO Enhanced Vigilance Activities: 750; 1 mech inf BG
United States NATO Enhanced Vigilance Activities: 150; 1 armd inf coy

Croatia CRO

Euro EUR		2022	2023	2024
GDP	EUR	66.9bn	73.7bn	78.9bn
	USD	70.5bn	80.2bn	86.3bn
per capita	USD	18,305	20,876	22,520
Growth	%	6.2	2.7	2.6
Inflation	%	10.7	8.6	4.2
Def exp [a]	EUR	1.22bn	1.31bn	
	USD	1.29bn	1.39bn	
Def bdgt [b]	EUR	1.24bn	1.03bn	1.10bn
	USD	1.30bn	1.13bn	1.20bn
FMA (US)	USD	25m	0m	0m
USD1=EUR		0.95	0.92	0.91

[a] NATO figure
[b] Includes military pensions

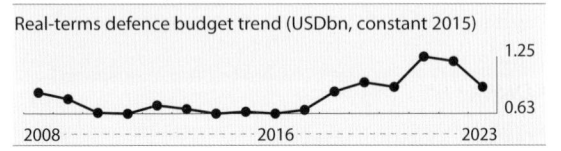

Real-terms defence budget trend (USDbn, constant 2015)

Population	4,169,239					
Age	0–14	15–19	20–24	25–29	30–64	65 plus
Male	7.2%	2.5%	2.6%	3.1%	23.4%	9.4%
Female	6.8%	2.4%	2.5%	3.0%	23.9%	13.2%

Capabilities

The principal tasks for the armed forces include defending national sovereignty and territorial integrity, as well as tackling terrorism and contributing to international peacekeeping missions. The defence ministry is working on a new long-term development plan and defence strategy. Croatia reformed its armed forces to create a small professional force prior to joining NATO in 2009. The government has tried to improve conditions of service and to increase the proportion of the budget focused on equipment investment. In 2023, Zagreb deepened defence and security cooperation with the UK. It established a new cooperative framework with India and signed a 2023–2028 US-Croatia Framework for Defence Cooperation on cyber security, combatting disinformation and improving personnel training in October 2023. Croatia hosts the NATO Multinational Special Aviation Programme and training centre and participates in EU and NATO missions, including NATO's Enhanced Forward Presence in Hungary, Lithuania, and Poland. The country committed to improve its modernisation efforts to provide a mechanised infantry brigade in the NATO framework. The inventory is mainly composed of ageing Soviet-era equipment but being updated. For instance, in October 2023, Croatia received the first of 12 second-hand *Rafale* F3-R fighters from France. Croatia has a limited defence industry, focused on small arms, ammunition, explosives and naval systems.

ACTIVE 16,800 (Army 7,800 Navy 1,650 Air 1,600 Joint 5,750)

Conscript liability Voluntary conscription, 8 weeks

RESERVE 21,000 (Army 21,000)

ORGANISATIONS BY SERVICE

Army 7,800
FORCES BY ROLE
MANOEUVRE
  Armoured
    1 armd bde (1 tk bn, 2 armd inf bn, 1 SP arty bn, 1 ADA bn, 1 cbt engr bn)
  Mechanised
    1 mech bde (3 mech inf bn, 1 lt mech inf bn, 1 fd arty bn, 1 ADA bn, 1 cbt engr bn)
  Other
    1 inf trg regt
COMBAT SUPPORT
  1 arty/MRL regt
  1 engr regt
  1 MP regt
  1 NBC bn
  1 sigs bn
COMBAT SERVICE SUPPORT
  1 log regt
AIR DEFENCE
  1 ADA regt
EQUIPMENT BY TYPE
ARMOURED FIGHTING VEHICLES
  MBT 74 M-84
  IFV 100 M-80
  APC 178
    APC (T) 11: 7 BTR-50; 4 OT M-60
    APC (W) 126 Patria AMV (incl variants)
    PPV 41: 21 Maxxpro Plus; 20 RG-33 HAGA (amb)
    AUV 63: 10 IVECO LMV; 53 M-ATV
ENGINEERING & MAINTENANCE VEHICLES
  ARV 22: 12 JVBT-55A; 2 M-84AI; 1 WZT-2; 2 WZT-3; 5 Maxxpro Recovery
  VLB 6 MT-55A
  MW 4 MV-4
ANTI-TANK/ANTI-INFRASTRUCTURE • MSL
  SP 20 BOV-1
  MANPATS 9K11 Malyutka (RS-AT-3 Sagger); 9K111 Fagot (RS-AT-4 Spigot); 9K111-1 Konkurs (RS-AT-5 Spandrel); 9K115 Metis (RS-AT-7 Saxhorn)
ARTILLERY 176
  SP 21: **122mm** 8 2S1 Gvozdika; **155mm** 13 PzH 2000
  TOWED **122mm** 27 D-30
  MRL **122mm** 27: 6 M91 Vulkan; 21 BM-21 Grad
  MOR 101: **82mm** 55 LMB M96; **120mm** 46 M-75/UBM 52
PATROL AND COASTAL COMBATANTS • PBR 5
AIR DEFENCE
  SAM • Point-defence 9+: 3 9K35 Strela-10M3 (RS-SA-13 Gopher); 6 9K35 Strela-10CRO; 9K310 Igla-1 (RS-SA-16 Gimlet); 9K32M Strela-2M (RS-SA-7B Grail)‡
  GUNS SP **20mm** 10 BOV-3 SP

Reserve
FORCES BY ROLE
MANOEUVRE
  Light
    6 inf regt
COMBAT SUPPORT
  2 arty regt

Navy 1,650
Navy HQ at Split
EQUIPMENT BY TYPE
PATROL AND COASTAL COMBATANTS 5
  PCFG 1 Končar with 2 twin lnchr with RBS15B Mk I AShM, 1 AK630 CIWS, 1 57mm gun
  PCG 4:
    2 Kralj with 4 twin lnchr with RBS15B Mk I AShM, 1 AK630 CIWS, 1 57mm gun (with minelaying capability)
    2 Vukovar (ex-FIN Helsinki) with 4 single lnchr with RBS15B Mk I AShM, 1 57mm gun
MINE WARFARE • MINE COUNTERMEASURES 1
  MHI 1 Korcula
AMPHIBIOUS • LANDING CRAFT 5:
  LCT 2 Cetina (with minelaying capability)
  LCVP 3: 2 Type-21; 1 Type-22
UNINHABITED MARITIME SYSTEMS
  UUV • DATA REMUS 100
COASTAL DEFENCE • AShM 3 RBS15K

Marines
FORCES BY ROLE
MANOEUVRE
  Amphibious
    1 mne coy

Coast Guard 270
FORCES BY ROLE
Two divisions, headquartered in Split (1st div) and Pula (2nd div)
EQUIPMENT BY TYPE
PATROL AND COASTAL COMBATANTS 5
  PB 5: 4 Mirna; 1 Omiš
LOGISTICS AND SUPPORT 7
  AAR 5: 1 Faust Vrancic (YUG Spasilac); 4 Other
  AKL 1 PDS 713
  AXL 1 Andrija Mohorovicic (POL Project 861)

Air Force and Air Defence 1,600
FORCES BY ROLE
FIGHTER/GROUND ATTACK
  1 (mixed) sqn with MiG-21bis/UMD Fishbed; Rafale B
TRAINING
  1 sqn with PC-9M; Z-242L

ISR HELICOPTER
1 hel sqn with Bell 206B *Jet Ranger* II; OH-58D *Kiowa Warrior*

TRANSPORT HELICOPTER
2 sqn with Mi-171Sh

EQUIPMENT BY TYPE

AIRCRAFT 8 combat capable
  FGA 8: 4 MiG-21bis *Fishbed*; 3 MiG-21UMD *Fishbed*; 1 *Rafale* B
  TPT • Light (2 An-32 *Cline* in store)
  TRG 21: 17 PC-9M; 4 Z-242L

HELICOPTERS
  MRH 15 OH-58D *Kiowa Warrior*
  TPT 22: **Medium** 14: 10 Mi-171Sh; 4 UH-60M *Black Hawk*; **Light** 8 Bell 206B *Jet Ranger* II

AIR DEFENCE • SAM
  Point-defence 9K31 *Strela*-1 (RS-SA-9 *Gaskin*); 9K34 *Strela*-3 (RS-SA-14 *Gremlin*); 9K310 Igla-1 (RS-SA-16 *Gimlet*)

AIR-LAUNCHED MISSILES
  AAM • IR R-60; R-60MK (RS-AA-8 *Aphid*)
  ASM AGM-114R *Hellfire*

Special Forces Command
FORCES BY ROLE
SPECIAL FORCES
  5 SF gp

DEPLOYMENT

HUNGARY: NATO • Enhanced Vigilance Activities 70
INDIA/PAKISTAN: UN • UNMOGIP 9
IRAQ: *Operation Inherent Resolve* 2; **NATO** • NATO Mission Iraq 10
KOSOVO: NATO • KFOR 151; 1 inf coy; 1 hel unit with Mi-171Sh
LEBANON: UN • UNIFIL 1
LITHUANIA: NATO • Enhanced Forward Presence ε200; 1 mech inf coy
POLAND: NATO • Enhanced Forward Presence 69; 1 SP arty bty
WESTERN SAHARA: UN • MINURSO 5

Cyprus CYP

Euro EUR		2022	2023	2024
GDP	EUR	27.0bn	29.4bn	31.1bn
	USD	28.5bn	32.0bn	34.1bn
per capita	USD	31,459	34,791	36,976
Growth	%	5.6	2.2	2.7
Inflation	%	8.1	3.5	2.4
Def bdgt	EUR	506m	525m	535m
	USD	533m	571m	585m
USD1=EUR		0.95	0.92	0.91

Real-terms defence budget trend (USDm, constant 2015)
512 / 328 / 2008–2016–2023

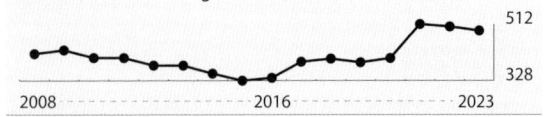

Population	1,308,120					
Age	0–14	15–19	20–24	25–29	30–64	65 plus
Male	8.0%	2.8%	3.4%	4.3%	26.6%	6.1%
Female	7.6%	2.4%	2.8%	3.5%	24.7%	7.9%

Capabilities

The National Guard is focused on protecting the island's territorial integrity and sovereignty, and safeguarding Cyprus's EEZ. The guard's main objective is to deter any Turkish incursion and to provide enough opposition until military support can be provided by Greece, its primary ally. Greece is a long-time defence cooperation partner for Cyprus, working together also on cyber defence. Nicosia has pledged to develop deeper military ties with Israel, while France has renewed and enhanced its defence-cooperation agreement with Cyprus. In 2018, Cyprus signed a memorandum of understanding on enhancing defence and security cooperation with the UK. Significantly, the US lifted an arms embargo on Cyprus in 2022 and the first of the planned annual *Silver Falcon* bilateral exercises was conducted in early 2023. Having reduced conscript liability in 2016, Nicosia began recruiting additional contract-service personnel as part of the effort to modernise and professionalise its forces. Cyprus exercises with several international partners, most notably France, Greece and Israel. External deployments have been limited to some officers joining EU and UN missions. Cyprus has little logistics capability to support operations abroad. Equipment comprises a mix of Soviet-era and modern European systems. A new government, in early 2023, pledged to increase defence spending to reach 2% of GDP, which should aid equipment recapitalisation. Cyprus has little in the way of a domestic defence industry, with no ability to design and manufacture modern equipment.

ACTIVE 12,000 (National Guard 12,000)
Gendarmerie & Paramilitary 250

Conscript liability 15 months

RESERVE 50,000 (National Guard 50,000)

Reserve service to age 50 (officers dependent on rank; military doctors to age 60)

ORGANISATIONS BY SERVICE

National Guard 12,000 (incl conscripts)
FORCES BY ROLE
SPECIAL FORCES
  1 comd (regt) (1 SF bn)
MANOEUVRE
  Armoured
  1 armd bde (2 armd bn, 1 armd inf bn)
  Mechanised
  4 (1st, 2nd, 6th & 7th) mech bde
  Light
  1 (4th) lt inf bde
  2 (2nd & 8th) lt inf regt
COMBAT SUPPORT
  1 arty comd (8 arty bn)
COMBAT SERVICE SUPPORT
  1 (3rd) spt bde
ISR UAV
  1 sqn with *Aerostar*
EQUIPMENT BY TYPE
ARMOURED FIGHTING VEHICLES
  MBT 134: 82 T-80U; 52 AMX-30B2
  RECCE 79 EE-9 *Cascavel*
  IFV 43 BMP-3
  APC 294
    APC (T) 168 *Leonidas*
    APC (W) 126 VAB (incl variants)
  AUV 8 BOV M16 *Milos*
ENGINEERING & MAINTENANCE VEHICLES
  ARV 10: 2 AMX-30D; 8 BREM-80U
ANTI-TANK/ANTI-INFRASTRUCTURE
  MSL
    SP 33: 15 EE-3 *Jararaca* with *Milan*; 18 VAB with HOT
  RCL 106mm 144 M40A1
  GUNS • TOWED 100mm 6 M-1944
ARTILLERY 412
  SP 155mm 48: 24 NORA B-52; 12 Mk F3; 12 *Zuzana*
  TOWED 60: **105mm** 48 M-56; **155mm** 12 TR-F-1
  MRL 22: **122mm** 4 BM-21; **128mm** 18 M-63 *Plamen*
  MOR 282: **81mm** 170 E-44 (70+ M1/M9 in store); **120mm** 112 RT61
UNINHABITED AERIAL VEHICLES
  ISR • Medium 4 *Aerostar*
AIR DEFENCE
  SAM 22+
    Medium-range 4 9K37M1 *Buk* M1-2 (RS-SA-11 *Gadfly*)
    Short-range 18: 12 *Aspide*; 6 9K331 *Tor*-M1 (RS-SA-15 *Gauntlet*)
    Point-defence *Mistral*
  GUNS • TOWED 60: **20mm** 36 M-55; **35mm** 24 GDF-003 (with *Skyguard*)

Maritime Wing
FORCES BY ROLE
COMBAT SUPPORT
  1 (coastal defence) AShM bty with MM40 *Exocet* AShM
EQUIPMENT BY TYPE
PATROL AND COASTAL COMBATANTS 7
  PCM 1 OPV 62 (ISR *Sa'ar* 4.5 derivative) with 1 twin *Simbad* lnchr with *Mistral* SAM
  PCC 1 *Alasia* (ex-OMN *Al Mabrukha*) with 1 hel landing platform;
  PBF 4: 2 Rodman 55; 2 *Vittoria*
  PB 1 *Ammachostos* (FIN)
COASTAL DEFENCE • AShM 3 MM40 *Exocet*

Air Wing
EQUIPMENT BY TYPE
HELICOPTERS
  ATK 4 Mi-35P *Hind* E (offered for sale)
  MRH 7: 3 AW139 (SAR); 4 SA342L1 *Gazelle* (with HOT for anti-armour role)

Paramilitary 250

Maritime Police 250
EQUIPMENT BY TYPE
PATROL AND COASTAL COMBATANTS 13
  PBF 5: 1 *Odysseus* (ISR *Shaldag* II); 2 *Poseidon*; 2 *Vittoria*
  PB 3 *Kyrenia* (CRO Tehnomont 16m)
  PBI 5 SAB-12

DEPLOYMENT
LEBANON: UN • UNIFIL 2

FOREIGN FORCES
Argentina UNFICYP 248; 2 inf coy; 1 hel flt
Austria UNFICYP 3
Brazil UNFICYP 2
Canada UNFICYP 1
Chile UNFICYP 6
Ghana UNFICYP 1
Greece Army: 950
Hungary UNFICYP 11
India UNFICYP 1
Pakistan UNFICYP 3
Paraguay UNFICYP 12
Russia UNFICYP 4
Serbia UNFICYP 8
Slovakia UNFICYP 238; 2 inf coy; 1 engr pl
United Kingdom 2,260; 2 inf bn; 1 hel sqn with 3 SA330 *Puma* HC2 • Operation Inherent Resolve (*Shader*) 500: 1 FGA sqn with 10 *Typhoon* FGR4; 1 A330 MRTT *Voyager* KC3; 2 C-130J-30 *Hercules* • UNFICYP (*Operation Tosca*) 257: 2 inf coy

NORTHERN CYPRUS

Data here represents the de facto situation on the northern section of the island. This does not imply international recognition as a sovereign state.

Capabilities

ACTIVE 3,000 (Army 3,000) Gendarmerie & Paramilitary 150

Conscript liability 15 months

RESERVE 15,000

Reserve liability to age 50

ORGANISATIONS BY SERVICE

Army ε3,000
FORCES BY ROLE
MANOEUVRE
  Light
    5 inf bn
    7 inf bn (reserve)
EQUIPMENT BY TYPE
ANTI-TANK/ANTI-INFRASTRUCTURE
  MSL • MANPATS *Milan*
  RCL • 106mm 36
ARTILLERY • MOR • 120mm 73

Gendarmerie & Paramilitary

Armed Police ε150
FORCES BY ROLE
SPECIAL FORCES
  1 (police) SF unit

Coast Guard
EQUIPMENT BY TYPE
PATROL AND COASTAL COMBATANTS 6
  PCC 5: 2 SG45/SG46; 1 *Rauf Denktash*; 2 US Mk 5
  PB 1

FOREIGN FORCES

TURKIYE

Army ε33,800
FORCES BY ROLE
1 corps HQ; 1 SF regt; 1 armd bde; 2 mech inf div; 1 mech inf regt; 1 arty regt; 1 avn comd
EQUIPMENT BY TYPE
ARMOURED FIGHTING VEHICLES
  MBT 287 M48A5T1
  IFV 145 ACV AIFV
  APC • APC (T) 488: 70 ACV AAPC (incl variants); 418 M113 (incl variants)
ANTI-TANK/ANTI-INFRASTRUCTURE
  MSL
    SP 66 ACV TOW
    MANPATS *Milan*
  RCL 106mm 219 M40A1
ARTILLERY 656
  SP 155mm 178: 30 M44T; 144 M52T1; 4 T-155 *Firtina*
  TOWED 84: 105mm 36 M101A1; 155mm 36 M114A2; 203mm 12 M115
  MRL 122mm 18 T-122
  MOR 376: 81mm 171; 107mm 70 M30; 120mm 135 HY-12
PATROL AND COASTAL COMBATANTS • PB 1
AIRCRAFT • TPT • Light 3 Cessna 185 (U-17)
HELICOPTERS • TPT 3: Medium 2 AS532UL *Cougar*
Light 1 Bell 205 (UH-1H *Iroquois*)
AIR DEFENCE
  SAM Point-defence FIM-92 *Stinger*
  GUNS • TOWED 150: 20mm 122: 44 Rh 202; 78 GAI-D01; 35mm 28 GDF-003

Czech Republic CZE

Czech Koruna CZK		2022	2023	2024
GDP	CZK	6.79trn	7.36trn	7.92trn
	USD	291bn	335bn	359bn
per capita	USD	26,832	30,475	32,391
Growth	%	2.3	0.2	2.3
Inflation	%	15.1	10.9	4.6
Def exp [a]	CZK	91.0bn	112bn	
	USD	3.90bn	5.11bn	
Def bdgt [b]	CZK	89.1bn	112bn	151bn
	USD	3.82bn	5.10bn	6.86bn
FMA (US)	USD	100m	0m	0m
USD1=CZK		23.36	21.94	22.05

[a] NATO figure
[b] Includes military pensions

Real-terms defence budget trend (USDbn, constant 2015)
3.29
1.73
2008 — 2016 — 2023

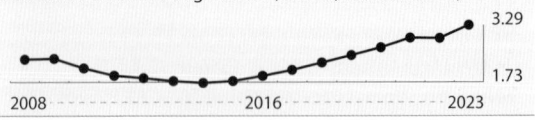

Population	10,830,412					
Age	0–14	15–19	20–24	25–29	30–64	65 plus
Male	8.1%	2.6%	2.4%	2.7%	25.0%	8.5%
Female	7.7%	2.5%	2.3%	2.5%	23.8%	12.0%

Capabilities

In 2023, the Czech Republic published its latest security strategy. It identifies NATO and EU membership as of critical importance to its security and points to Russia and deteriorating international security as key threats to the country. It also raised issues around cyber and information operations, along with China's questioning of the international order. Military modernisation priorities include infantry fighting vehicles, self-propelled howitzers, multi-role helicopters, transport aircraft, short-range air-defence systems and UAVs. Prague, in 2023, said it would buy F-35 *Lightning* IIs to replace the leased *Gripen* fleet. The Czech Republic has signed a letter of intent with Germany to affiliate the 4th Czech Rapid Reaction Brigade with the 10th German Armoured Division under NATO's Framework Nations Concept. Recruitment and retention are a challenge, with shortfalls in specialised trades such as engineers and pilots. The armed forces are capable of deploying on international crisis-management operations, including NATO's Enhanced Forward Presence and Baltic Air Policing, as well as contribute to NATO's Very High Readiness Joint Task Force. There are plans to upgrade military training and simulation facilities by 2025. The defence-industrial base includes development and manufacturing capability, in particular small arms, vehicles, and training and light attack aircraft. The holding company Czechoslovak Group brings together several companies across the munitions, vehicles, and aerospace sectors. The government has set up an agency to support the defence industry in government-to-government procurement activities.

ACTIVE 26,600 (Army 14,700 Air 5,850 Other 6,050)

ORGANISATIONS BY SERVICE

Army 14,700
FORCES BY ROLE
MANOEUVRE
  Reconnaissance
  1 ISR/EW regt (1 recce bn, 1 EW bn, 1 ISR UAV bn)
  Armoured
  1 (7th) mech bde (1 tk bn, 2 armd inf bn, 1 mot inf bn)
  Mechanised
  1 (4th) rapid reaction bde (2 mech inf bn, 1 mot inf bn)
  Airborne
  1 AB regt
COMBAT SUPPORT
  1 (13th) arty regt (2 arty bn)
  1 engr regt (2 engr bn, 1 EOD bn)
  1 CBRN regt (2 CBRN bn)
COMBAT SERVICE SUPPORT
  1 log regt (2 log bn, 1 maint bn)

Active Reserve
FORCES BY ROLE
COMMAND
  14 (territorial defence) comd
MANOEUVRE
  Armoured
  1 armd coy
  Light
  14 inf coy (1 per territorial comd) (3 inf pl, 1 cbt spt pl, 1 log pl)
EQUIPMENT BY TYPE
ARMOURED FIGHTING VEHICLES
  MBT 33: 3 *Leopard* 2A4; 30 T-72M4CZ
  RECCE 50: 34 BPzV *Svatava*; 8 *Pandur* II (KBV-PZ); 8 *Pandur* II (KBV-PZLOK)
  IFV 227: 120 BMP-2; 107 *Pandur* II (incl 17 CP, 14 comms, 4 amb)
  APC • PPV 26 *Titus*
  AUV 141: 21 *Dingo* 2; 120 IVECO LMV
ENGINEERING & MAINTENANCE VEHICLES
  AEV 4 *Pandur* II (KOT-Z)
  ARV 13+: 10 VPV-ARV (12 more in store); VT-55A; 3 VT-72M4
  VLB 6 MT-55A (3 more in store)
  MW *Bozena* 5; UOS-155 *Belarty*
NBC VEHICLES BRDM-2RCH
ANTI-TANK/ANTI-INFRASTRUCTURE
  MSL • MANPATS 9K111-1 *Konkurs* (RS-AT-5 *Spandrel*); FGM-148 *Javelin*; Spike-LR
  RCL 84mm *Carl Gustaf*
ARTILLERY 96
  SP 152mm 48 M-77 *Dana* (up to 38 more in store)
  MOR 48: **81mm** *Expal*; **120mm** 40 M-1982; (45 more in store); **SP 120mm** 8 SPM-85

Air Force 5,850
Principal task is to secure Czech airspace. This mission is fulfilled within NATO Integrated Extended Air Defence System (NATINADS) and, if necessary, by means of the Czech national reinforced air-defence system. The air force also provides CAS for army SAR, and performs a tpt role

FORCES BY ROLE
FIGHTER/GROUND ATTACK
  1 sqn with *Gripen* C/D
  1 sqn with L-159 ALCA; L-159T1*
TRANSPORT
  2 sqn with A319CJ; C295M/MW; L-410FG/UVP-E *Turbolet*
TRAINING
  1 sqn with L-159 ALCA; L-159T1*; L-159T2*
ATTACK HELICOPTER
  1 sqn with AH-1Z *Viper*; Mi-35 *Hind* E
TRANSPORT HELICOPTER
  1 sqn with Mi-17 *Hip* H; Mi-171Sh; UH-1Y *Venom*
  1 sqn with Mi-17 *Hip* H; PZL W-3A *Sokol*
AIR DEFENCE
  1 (25th) SAM regt (2 AD gp)
EQUIPMENT BY TYPE
AIRCRAFT 38 combat capable
  FGA 14: 12 *Gripen* C; 2 *Gripen* D
  ATK 16 L-159 ALCA
  TPT 14: **Light** 12: 4 C295M; 2 C295MW; 2 L-410FG *Turbolet*; 4 L-410UVP-E *Turbolet*; **PAX** 2 A319CJ
  TRG 8: 5 L-159T1*; 3 L-159T2*
HELICOPTERS
  ATK 13: 3 AH-1Z *Viper*; 10 Mi-35 *Hind* E

MRH 5 Mi-17 *Hip H*
TPT 26: **Medium** 25: 15 Mi-171Sh; 10 PZL W3A *Sokol*; **Light** 1 UH-1Y *Venom*

AIR DEFENCE • SAM
Short-range 8 2K12M2 *Kub*-M2 (RS-SA-6B *Gainful*)
Point-defence 9K35 *Strela*-10 (RS-SA-13 *Gopher*); 9K32 *Strela*-2‡ (RS-SA-7 *Grail*) (available for trg RBS-70 gunners); RBS-70; RBS-70NG

AIR-LAUNCHED MISSILES
AAM • IR AIM-9M *Sidewinder*; **ARH** AIM-120C-5/C-7 AMRAAM

BOMBS
Laser-guided: GBU-12/-16 *Paveway* II

Other Forces 6,050

FORCES BY ROLE
SPECIAL FORCES
  1 SF gp
MANOEUVRE
  Other
    1 (presidential) gd bde (2 bn)
    1 (honour guard) gd bn (2 coy)
COMBAT SUPPORT
  1 int gp
  1 (central) MP comd
  3 (regional) MP comd
  1 (protection service) MP comd

DEPLOYMENT

BOSNIA-HERZEGOVINA: EU • EUFOR (*Operation Althea*) 2
CENTRAL AFRICAN REPUBLIC: UN • MINUSCA 3
DEMOCRATIC REPUBLIC OF THE CONGO: UN • MONUSCO 2
EGYPT: MFO 18; 1 C295M
IRAQ: *Operation Inherent Resolve* 60; **NATO** • NATO Mission Iraq 3
KOSOVO: NATO • KFOR 36; UN • UNMIK 1
LATVIA: NATO • Enhanced Forward Presence ε 70; 1 engr pl
LITHUANIA: NATO • Enhanced Forward Presence 135; 1 AD unit; 1 CBRN unit
SLOVAKIA: NATO • Enhanced Vigilance Activities 400; 1 mech inf bn HQ; 1 mech inf coy
SYRIA/ISRAEL: UN • UNDOF 4

Denmark DNK

Danish Krone DKK		2022	2023	2024
GDP	DKK	2.84trn	2.88trn	2.97trn
	USD	401bn	421bn	431bn
per capita	USD	68,295	71,402	72,940
Growth	%	2.7	1.7	1.4
Inflation	%	8.5	4.2	2.8
Def exp [a]	DKK	38.7bn	47.2bn	
	USD	5.47bn	6.89bn	
Def bdgt [b]	DKK	35.7bn	36.2bn	
	USD	5.04bn	5.29bn	
USD1=DKK		7.08	6.85	6.88

[a] NATO figure
[b] Includes military pensions

Real-terms defence budget trend (USDbn, constant 2015)
4.59
3.36
2008 — 2016 — 2023

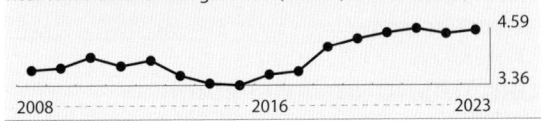

Population	5,946,984				
Age	0–14	15–19	20–24	25–29	30–64	65 plus
Male	8.3%	3.0%	3.1%	3.5%	22.4%	9.5%
Female	7.9%	2.8%	3.0%	3.3%	22.0%	11.1%

Capabilities

Denmark maintains a compact but effective force focused on contributing to NATO operations. Ties to NATO, Nordic Defence Cooperation (NORDEFCO) and regional neighbours have increased. Russia's invasion of Ukraine in February 2022 was a key factor in Denmark's June 2022 referendum to end the opt-out on Danish participation in European Union defence cooperation under the Common Security and Defence Policy. The next defence agreement (2024–28) is being planned and will be influenced by the changing threat environment. Copenhagen has prioritised the Baltic and the Arctic regions as well as efforts to receive and host allies that deploy to the country as reinforcements. In 2023, Denmark more closely integrated its air force with those of Finland, Norway, and Sweden, 'aiming for the ability to operate seamlessly together as one force'. The Danish government has pledged to increase defence spending to 2% of GDP. Current defence modernisation priorities include the acquisition of the F-35A *Lightning* II combat aircraft to replace the air force's F-16 fleet, and the upgrade of armoured vehicles within the mechanised brigades. Challenges, including understaffing, are reportedly affecting the operational capability of Denmark's mechanised brigades. The Danish armed forces consist primarily of professional personnel, supplemented by a substantial number of conscripts. The Danish armed forces have little ability to deploy independently but have contributed to a number of larger multinational deployments. Denmark is reliant on imported equipment for defence but maintains a small defence industry focused on exports to Europe and North America. The government in 2023 pushed for a restart of ammunition production, with Sweden, Denmark, Finland and Norway signing an agreement on joint procurement. The Danish defence industry is mainly active in defence electronics and the design and manufacture of components and subsystems. Under NATO's DIANA initiative, Denmark hosts a quantum technology centre.

ACTIVE 15,400 (Army 8,000 Navy 2,250 Air 3,000 Joint 2,150)

Conscript liability 4–12 months, most voluntary

RESERVES 44,200 (Army 34,400 Navy 5,300 Air Force 4,500)

ORGANISATIONS BY SERVICE

Army 8,000

Div and a bde HQ transforming into operational formations

FORCES BY ROLE

COMMAND
  1 (MND-N) div HQ
MANOEUVRE
  Mechanised
  1 (1st) mech bde (1 ISR bn, 3 mech inf bn, 1 SP arty bn, 1 cbt engr bn, 1 sigs bn, 1 log bn)
  1 (2nd) mech bde (1 recce bn, 1 tk bn, 1 lt inf bn)
COMBAT SUPPORT
  1 CBRN/construction bn
  1 EOD bn
  1 int bn
  1 MP bn
  2 sigs bn
COMBAT SERVICE SUPPORT
  1 log bn
  1 maint bn
  1 spt bn

EQUIPMENT BY TYPE

ARMOURED FIGHTING VEHICLES
  MBT 44: 15 *Leopard* 2A5 (to be upgraded to 2A7V); 29 *Leopard* 2A7V
  IFV 44 CV9035 MkIII
  APC 390
    APC (W) 390: 81 *Piranha* III (incl variants); 309 *Piranha* V
  AUV 158: 84 *Eagle* IV; 59 *Eagle* V; 15 HMT-400
ENGINEERING & MAINTENANCE VEHICLES
  ARV *Wisent*
  VLB BRP-1 *Biber*
ANTI-TANK/ANTI-INFRASTRUCTURE
  MSL • MANPATS *Spike*-LR2
  RCL 84mm *Carl Gustaf*
ARTILLERY 16
  SP 155mm 1 ATMOS 2000
  MOR 15: **81mm** M252; **SP 120mm** 15 *Piranha* V with Cardom-10; (**120mm** 20 Soltam K6B1 in store)
AIR DEFENCE • SAM • Point-defence FIM-92 *Stinger*

Navy 2,250

Three naval squadrons, headquartered at naval bases in Frederikshavn and Korsør

EQUIPMENT BY TYPE

PRINCIPAL SURFACE COMBATANTS 5
  DESTROYERS • DDGHM 3 *Iver Huitfeldt* with 4 quad lnchr with RGM-84L *Harpoon* Block II AShM, 4 8-cell Mk 41 VLS (to be fitted with SM-2 SAM), 2 12-cell Mk 56 VLS with RIM-162B ESSM SAM, 2 twin 324mm TT with MU90 LWT, 1 *Millennium* CIWS, 2 76mm guns (capacity 1 AW101 *Merlin*/MH-60R *Seahawk* hel)
  FRIGATES • FFGHM 2 *Absalon* (flexible support ships) with 4 quad lnchr with RGM-84L *Harpoon* Block II AShM, 3 12-cell Mk 56 VLS with RIM-162B ESSM SAM, 2 twin 324mm TT with MU90 LWT, 2 *Millennium* CIWS, 1 127mm gun (capacity 2 AW101 *Merlin*/MH-60R *Seahawk* hel; 2 LCP, 7 MBT or 40 vehicles; 130 troops)
PATROL AND COASTAL COMBATANTS 12
  PSOH 4 *Thetis* 1 76mm gun (capacity 1 MH-60R *Seahawk*)
  PSO 3 *Knud Rasmussen* with 1 76mm gun, 1 hel landing platform (ice-strengthened hull)
  PCC 5 *Diana* (1 other non-operational)
MINE WARFARE • MINE COUNTERMEASURES 6
  MCI 4 MSF Mk I
LOGISTICS AND SUPPORT 12
  ABU 2 *Gunnar Thorson* (primarily used for marine pollution duties)
  AGS 2 *Holm*
  AKL 3: 1 *Sleipner* 2 *Seatruck*
  AXL 3: 2 *Holm*; 1 *Søløven* (DNK *Flyvefisken*)
  AXS 2 *Svanen*
UNINHABITED MARITIME PLATFORMS
  USV • MW • Medium 2 *Holm*
UNINHABITED MARITIME SYSTEMS
  UUV • MW *Double Eagle* Mk II/SAROV
UNINHABITED AERIAL VEHICLES
  ISR • Light S-100 *Camcopter* (owned by European Maritime Safety Agency)

Air Force 3,000

Tactical Air Command

FORCES BY ROLE

FIGHTER/GROUND ATTACK
  1 sqn with F-16AM/BM *Fighting Falcon*; F-35A *Lightning* II
  1 sqn with F-16AM/BM *Fighting Falcon*
ANTI-SUBMARINE WARFARE
  1 sqn with MH-60R *Seahawk*
SEARCH & RESCUE/TRANSPORT HELICOPTER
  1 sqn with AW101 *Merlin*
  1 sqn with AS550 *Fennec* (ISR)
TRANSPORT
  1 sqn with C-130J-30 *Hercules*; CL-604 *Challenger* (MP/VIP)
TRAINING
  1 unit with MFI-17 *Supporter* (T-17)

EQUIPMENT BY TYPE
AIRCRAFT 54 combat capable
 FTR 44: 34 F-16AM *Fighting Falcon*; 10 F-16BM *Fighting Falcon* (30 operational)
 FGA 10 F-35A *Lightning* II
 TPT 8: **Medium** 4 C-130J-30 *Hercules*; **PAX** 4 CL-604 *Challenger* (MP/VIP)
 TRG 27 MFI-17 *Supporter* (T-17)
HELICOPTERS
 ASW 9 MH-60R *Seahawk*
 SAR 8 AW101 *Merlin*
 MRH 8 AS550 *Fennec* (ISR) (4 more non-operational)
 TPT • **Medium** 6 AW101 *Merlin*
AIR-LAUNCHED MISSILES
 AAM • **IR** AIM-9L *Sidewinder*; **IIR** AIM-9X *Sidewinder* II; **ARH** AIM-120B/C-7 AMRAAM
BOMBS
 Laser-guided GBU-24 *Paveway* III
 Laser & INS/GPS-guided EGBU-12 *Paveway* II
 INS/GPS guided GBU-31 JDAM

Control and Air Defence Group
1 Control and Reporting Centre, 1 Mobile Control and Reporting Centre. 4 Radar sites

Special Operations Command
FORCES BY ROLE
SPECIAL FORCES
 1 SF unit
 1 diving unit

Reserves

Home Guard (Army) 34,400 reservists (to age 50)
2 (local) def region

Home Guard (Navy) 5,300 reservists (to age 50)
EQUIPMENT BY TYPE
PATROL AND COASTAL COMBATANTS 30
 PB 30: 18 MHV800; 12 MHV900

Home Guard (Air Force) 4,500 reservists (to age 50)
EQUIPMENT BY TYPE
AIRCRAFT • **TPT** • **Light** 2 BN-2A *Islander*

DEPLOYMENT

BALTIC SEA: NATO • SNMG 1; 170; 1 FFGHM
BOSNIA-HERZEGOVINA: EU • EUFOR (*Operation Althea*) 2
IRAQ: *Operation Inherent Resolve* 39; **NATO** • NATO Mission Iraq 125; 1 SF gp; 1 trg team
KOSOVO: NATO • KFOR 35
MIDDLE EAST: UN • UNTSO 12
UNITED KINGDOM: *Operation Interflex* 130 (UKR trg)

Estonia EST

Euro EUR		2022	2023	2024
GDP	EUR	36.0bn	38.4bn	40.7bn
	USD	38.0bn	41.8bn	44.5bn
per capita	USD	28,136	30,998	33,018
Growth	%	-0.5	-2.3	2.4
Inflation	%	19.4	10.0	3.8
Def exp [a]	EUR	779m	1.10bn	
	USD	821m	1.20bn	
Def bdgt [b]	EUR	771m	1.10bn	1.36bn
	USD	812m	1.20bn	1.48bn
FMA (US)	USD	75.0m	9.80m	9.80m
USD1=EUR		0.95	0.92	0.91

[a] NATO figure
[b] Includes military pensions

Real-terms defence budget trend (USDm, constant 2015)
807
328
2008 — 2016 — 2023

Population	1,202,762					
Age	0–14	15–19	20–24	25–29	30–64	65 plus
Male	8.0%	2.8%	2.2%	2.3%	24.0%	7.8%
Female	7.6%	2.6%	2.1%	2.1%	24.3%	14.3%

Capabilities

Estonia has small active armed forces and relies on NATO membership as a security guarantor. Tallinn's principal security concern is Russia. In the wake of Russia's February 2022 full-scale invasion of Ukraine, Estonia boosted defence spending and transferred military equipment to Ukraine, including ammunition, anti-armour systems and artillery. The defence ministry publishes medium-term development plans annually covering a four-year period. They are designed to assure the goals of a long-term National Defence Development Plan (NDPP) will be achieved within the planned timeframe. The NDPP for 2031, adopted in December 2021, focuses on improving territorial defence and indirect fire and anti-tank capabilities, as well as boosting maritime and surveillance systems. Estonia is procuring rocket artillery systems from the US, medium-range air defence systems are being jointly with Latvia and point-range air-defences with Poland. Estonia has joined the German-led European Sky Shield Initiative, to boost air defence capability across the region. Modernisation spending is also intended to improve infrastructure and readiness. A reserve component supplements the active armed forces. Force development plans include the creation of a supplementary reserve and additional active and conscript personnel. NATO in 2022 bolstered its battlegroup based in Estonia, present since mid-2017 as part of the Alliance's Enhanced Forward Presence. The Amari air base hosts a NATO Air Policing detachment. Estonia is a member of the UK-led Joint Expeditionary Force. Tallinn also hosts NATO's Cybersecurity Centre of Excellence. The country has limited capability to deploy abroad, though Estonian forces take part in EU, NATO and UN missions on a small scale. The country has a small defence industry with some niche capabilities, including in robotics, ship repair and digital systems.

ACTIVE 7,100 (Army 3,750 Navy 450 Air 400 Other 2,500)

Conscript liability 8 or 11 months (depending on specialisation; conscripts cannot be deployed)

RESERVE 41,200 (Defence League 21,200; Joint 20,000)

ORGANISATIONS BY SERVICE

Army 1,300; 2,450 conscript (total 3,750)

4 def region. All units except one inf bn are reserve based

FORCES BY ROLE
COMMAND
  1 div HQ
MANOEUVRE
  Mechanised
  1 (1st) mech bde (1 recce coy, 1 armd inf bn; 2 mech inf bn, 1 SP arty bn, 1 AT coy, 1 cbt engr bn, 1 spt bn, 1 AD bn)
  Light
  1 (2nd) inf bde (1 inf bn, 1 spt bn)
EQUIPMENT BY TYPE
ARMOURED FIGHTING VEHICLES
  IFV 44 CV9035EE (incl 2 CP)
  APC • APC (W) 136: 56 XA-180 *Sisu*; 80 XA-188 *Sisu*
ENGINEERING & MAINTENANCE VEHICLES
  AEV 2 Pionierpanzer 2 *Dachs*
  ARV 2 BPz-2
  VLB 2 *Biber*
ANTI-TANK/ANTI-INFRASTRUCTURE
  MSL • MANPATS FGM-148 *Javelin*; *Spike*-SR/-LR
  RCL 84mm *Carl Gustaf*; **90mm** PV-1110
ARTILLERY 180
  SP 155mm 18 K9 *Thunder*
  TOWED 122mm 36 D-30 (H 63)
  MOR 126: **81mm** 60 B455/NM 95/M252; **120mm** 66 2B11/M/41D
AIR DEFENCE
  SAM • Point-defence *Mistral*
  GUNS • TOWED 23mm ZU-23-2

Reserve

Reserve units subordinate to 2nd inf bde and territorial defence

FORCES BY ROLE
MANOEUVRE
  Reconnaissance
  1 recce coy
  Light
  3 inf bn
  4 (territorial) inf bn
COMBAT SUPPORT
  1 arty bn

  1 AT coy
  1 cbt engr bn
AIR DEFENCE
  1 AD bn

Navy 300; 150 conscript (total 450)

EQUIPMENT BY TYPE
PATROL AND COASTAL COMBATANTS 6
  PCO 1 *Kindral Kurvits* (FIN *Tursas* derivative)
  PB 5: 1 *Pikker*; 1 *Raju* (Baltic 4500WP); 2 *Roland*; 1 *Valve*
MINE WARFARE • MINE COUNTERMEASURES 4:
  MCCS 1 *Tasuja* (ex-DNK *Lindormen*)
  MHC 3 *Admiral Cowan* (ex-UK *Sandown*)
UNINHABITED MARITIME SYSTEMS • UUV
  DATA REMUS 100
  MW A9-M; *Seafox*

Air Force 400

FORCES BY ROLE
TRANSPORT
  1 sqn with M-28 *Skytruck*
TRANSPORT HELICOPTER
  1 sqn with R-44 *Raven* II
EQUIPMENT BY TYPE
AIRCRAFT
  TPT • Light 2 M-28 *Skytruck*
  TRG 1+ L-39C *Albatros* (leased)
HELICOPTERS • TPT • Light 2 R-44 *Raven* II

Other 1,600; 900 conscript (total 2,500)

Includes Cyber Command, Support Command and Special Operations Forces

FORCES BY ROLE
SPECIAL FORCES
  1 spec ops bn
COMBAT SUPPORT
  2 MP coy
  1 sigs bn
COMBAT SERVICE SUPPORT
  1 log bn

Defence League 21,200 reservists

Subordinate to the Ministry of the Defence. Totals include affiliated Women's Voluntary Defence Organization.

DEPLOYMENT

IRAQ: *Operation Inherent Resolve* 88 • NATO Mission Iraq 1
LEBANON: UN • UNIFIL 1
MIDDLE EAST: UN • UNTSO 5
MOZAMBIQUE: EU • EUTM Mozambique 1

FOREIGN FORCES

All NATO Enhanced Forward Presence unless stated
France 350; 1 mech inf coy
Spain NATO Baltic Air Policing: 280; 8 Eurofighter *Typhoon*
United Kingdom 1,000; 1 armd BG; 1 SP arty bty; 1 MRL bty; 1 cbt engr coy

Finland FIN

Euro EUR		2022	2023	2024
GDP	EUR	269bn	281bn	289bn
	USD	283bn	306bn	316bn
per capita	USD	51,030	54,507	56,157
Growth	%	1.6	-0.1	1.0
Inflation	%	7.2	4.5	1.9
Def exp [a]	EUR	n.a.	6.90bn	
	USD	n.a.	7.50bn	
Def bdgt [b]	EUR	5.51bn	6.10bn	6.19bn
	USD	5.80bn	6.64bn	6.77bn
USD1=EUR		0.95	0.92	0.91

[a] NATO figure
[b] Includes military pensions

Real-terms defence budget trend (USDbn, constant 2015)
5.66
3.07
2008   2016   2023

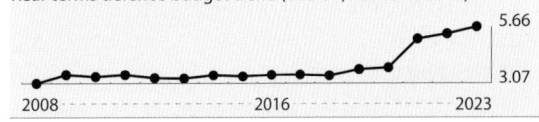

Population	5,614,571				
Age	0–14	15–19	20–24	25–29	30–64	65 plus
Male	8.3%	2.8%	2.8%	3.1%	22.1%	10.2%
Female	7.9%	2.7%	2.6%	2.9%	21.5%	13.0%

Capabilities

Finland's armed forces are primarily focused on defence against Russia. Finland's national security posture has significantly evolved in recent years, spurred on by comments made in late 2021 by Russian President Vladimir Putin about regional security and followed by Moscow's full-scale invasion of Ukraine in February 2022. Finland's security policy changes culminated in the European Union member formally becoming a NATO member in April 2023. The government that took office in Finland this past year reinforced the view on Moscow, stating in a policy document that 'Russia's foreign and security policy is irreconcilable with European stability and security.' Helsinki said it would pursue greater cooperation regionally and with like-minded countries further afield, including Australia, Japan and Canada. The government added that 'Finland wants to see a stronger European Union and stronger European defence within the framework of NATO'. Finland has been a participant in key multilateral defence relationships, including NORDEFCO, the Northern Group and the Joint Expeditionary Force. In 2022, Finland signed a mutual-security agreement with the UK and is looking to deepen defence ties with the US by negotiating a Defence Cooperation Agreement. The country contributes to UN peacekeeping missions and to NATO operations. Finland maintains a well-trained military, supported by reserves.

The country has emphasised security resilience, including maintaining adequate stockpiles of ammunition. It is modernising core equipment, including combat aircraft and naval vessels. Finland's defence industry consists largely of privately owned SMEs, concentrating on niche products for international markets, but it also features some internationally competitive larger companies.

ACTIVE 23,850 (Army 17,400 Navy 3,150 Air 3,300)
Gendarmerie & Paramilitary 2,900

Conscript liability 165, 255 or 347 days (latter for NCOs, officers or those on 'especially demanding' duties)

RESERVE 233,000 (Army 180,000 Navy 24,000 Air 29,000) Gendarmerie & Paramilitary 12,000

18,000 reservists a year conduct refresher training: total obligation 80 days (150 for NCOs, 200 for officers) between conscript service and age 50 (NCOs and officers to age 60)

ORGANISATIONS BY SERVICE

Army 4,400; 13,000 conscript (total 17,400)
FORCES BY ROLE
Finland's army maintains a mobilisation strength of about 285,000. In support of this requirement, two conscription cycles, each for about 9,000 conscripts, take place each year. After conscript training, reservist commitment is to the age of 60. Reservists are usually assigned to units within their local geographical area. All service appointments or deployments outside Finnish borders are voluntary for all members of the armed services. All brigades are reserve based

Reserve Organisations 180,000
FORCES BY ROLE
SPECIAL FORCES
  1 SF regt (1 SF bn, 1 tpt hel bn, 1 spt coy)
MANOEUVRE
  Armoured
  2 armd BG (regt)
  Mechanised
  2 (Karelia & Pori Jaeger) mech bde
  Light
  3 (Jaeger) bde
  6 lt inf bde
COMBAT SUPPORT
  1 arty bde
  1 AD regt
  7 engr regt
  3 sigs bn
COMBAT SERVICE SUPPORT
  3 log regt
EQUIPMENT BY TYPE
ARMOURED FIGHTING VEHICLES
  MBT 200: 100 *Leopard* 2A4; 100 *Leopard* 2A6
  IFV 212: 110 BMP-2MD; 102 CV9030FIN
  APC 995

APC (T) 320 MT-LBu/MT-LBV
APC (W) 675: 464 XA-180/185 Sisu; 101 XA-202 Sisu (CP); 48 XA-203 Sisu; 62 AMV (XA-360)
AUV 6 SISU GTP (in test)

ENGINEERING & MAINTENANCE VEHICLES
AEV 5 Dachs
ARV 36: 9 BPz-2; 15 MTP-LB; 12 VT-55A
VLB 32: 12 BLG-60M2; 10 Leopard 2L AVLB; 10 SISU Leguan
MW 3+: Aardvark Mk 2; KMT T-55; 3 Leopard 2R CEV; RA-140 DS

ANTI-TANK/ANTI-INFRASTRUCTURE
MSL • MANPATS NLAW; Spike-MR; Spike-LR

ARTILLERY 1,518
SP 97: **122mm** 74 2S1 Gvozdika (PsH 74); **155mm** 23 K9 Thunder
TOWED 630: **122mm** 474 D-30 (H 63); **152mm** 24 2A36 Giatsint-B (K 89); **155mm** 132 K 83/GH-52 (K 98)
MRL 75: **122mm** 34 RM-70; **227mm** 41 M270 MLRS
MOR 716+: **81mm** Krh/71; **120mm** 698 Krh/92; **SP 120mm** 18 XA-361 AMOS

HELICOPTERS
MRH 7: 5 Hughes 500D; 2 Hughes 500E
TPT • **Medium** 20 NH90 TTH

UNINHABITED AERIAL VEHICLES
ISR
  Medium 11 ADS-95 Ranger

AIR DEFENCE
SAM 60+
  Short-range 44: 20 Crotale NG (ITO 90); 24 NASAMS II FIN (ITO 12)
  Point-defence 16+: 16 ASRAD (ITO 05); FIM-92 Stinger (ITO 15); RBS 70 (ITO 05/05M)
GUNS 407+: **23mm** ItK 95/ZU-23-2 (ItK 61); **35mm** GDF-005 (ItK 88); **SP 35mm** 7 Leopard 2 ITK Marksman

Navy 1,400; 1,750 conscript (total 3,150)
FORCES BY ROLE
Naval Command HQ located at Turku
EQUIPMENT BY TYPE
PATROL AND COASTAL COMBATANTS 20
  PCGM 4 Hamina with 2 twin lnchr with Gabriel V (PTO2020) AShM, 1 8-cell VLS with Umkhonto-IR (ITO2004) SAM; 1 single 400mm ASTT with Torped 45/47 LWT
  PBG 4 Rauma with 6 single lnchr with RBS15 Mk3 (MTO-85M) AShM
  PBF 12 Jehu (U-700) (capacity 24 troops)
MINE WARFARE 8
  MINE COUNTERMEASURES 3
    MCC 3 Katanpää (ITA Gaeta mod)
  MINELAYERS • ML 5:
    2 Hameenmaa with 1 8-cell VLS with Umkhonto-IR (ITO2004) SAM, 2 RBU 1200 Uragan A/S mor, 1 57mm gun (can carry up to 120 mines)
    3 Pansio with 50 mines
AMPHIBIOUS • LANDING CRAFT 51
  LCVP 1+ Utö
  LCP ε50
LOGISTICS AND SUPPORT 6
  AG 3: 1 Louhi; 2 Hylje
  AXL 3 Fabian Wrede
UNINHABITED MARITIME SYSTEMS • UUV
  DATA REMUS 100
  MW Double Eagle Mk II; Seafox I
  UTL HUGIN 1000

Coastal Defence
FORCES BY ROLE
MANOEUVRE
  Amphibious
  1 mne bde
COMBAT SUPPORT
  1 cbt spt bde (1 AShM bty)
EQUIPMENT BY TYPE
COASTAL DEFENCE
  AShM 4 RBS15K
  ARTY • **130mm** 30 K-53tk (static)
ANTI-TANK/ANTI-INFRASTRUCTURE
  MSL • MANPATS Spike (used in AShM role)

Air Force 2,000; 1,300 conscript (total 3,300)
3 Air Comds: Satakunta (West), Karelia (East), Lapland (North)
FORCES BY ROLE
FIGHTER/GROUND ATTACK
  2 sqn with F/A-18C/D Hornet
ISR
  1 (survey) sqn with Learjet 35A
TRANSPORT
  1 flt with C295M
  1 (liaison) flt with PC-12NG
TRAINING
  1 sqn with Hawk Mk50/51A/66* (air-defence and ground-attack trg)
  1 unit with G-115EA
EQUIPMENT BY TYPE
AIRCRAFT 89 combat capable
  FGA 62: 55 F/A-18C Hornet; 7 F/A-18D Hornet
  ELINT 1 C295M
  TPT • **Light** 11: 2 C295M; 3 Learjet 35A (survey; ECM trg; tgt-tow); 6 PC-12NG
  TRG 55: 28 G-115EA; 11 Hawk Mk50/51A*; 16 Hawk Mk66*
AIR-LAUNCHED MISSILES
  AAM • **IR** AIM-9 Sidewinder; **IIR** AIM-9X Sidewinder
  ARH AIM-120C AMRAAM
  ALCM • **Conventional** AGM-158 JASSM

BOMBS
INS/GPS-guided GBU-31 JDAM; AGM-154C JSOW

Gendarmerie & Paramilitary

Border Guard 2,900
Ministry of Interior. 4 Border Guard Districts and 2 Coast Guard Districts

FORCES BY ROLE
MARITIME PATROL
 1 sqn with Do-228 (maritime surv); AS332 *Super Puma*; Bell 412EP (AB-412EP) *Twin Huey*; AW119KE *Koala*
EQUIPMENT BY TYPE
PATROL AND COASTAL COMBATANTS 58
 PSO 1 *Turva* with 1 hel landing platform
 PCC 2 *Tursas*
 PB 55
AMPHIBIOUS • LANDING CRAFT 4
 UCAC 4
AIRCRAFT • TPT • Light 2 Do-228
HELICOPTERS
 MRH 2 Bell 412EP (AB-412EP) *Twin Huey*
 TPT 9: **Medium** 5 AS332 *Super Puma*; **Light** 4 AW119KE *Koala*

Reserve 12,000 reservists on mobilisation

DEPLOYMENT

IRAQ: *Operation Inherent Resolve* 75; 1 trg team; **NATO** • NATO Mission Iraq 5
KOSOVO: NATO • KFOR 70
LEBANON: UN • UNIFIL 157; 1 inf coy
MALI: EU • EUTM Mali 12
MIDDLE EAST: UN • UNTSO 16
MOZAMBIQUE: EU • EUTM Mozambique 5
SOMALIA: EU • EUTM Somalia 12
UNITED KINGDOM: *Operation Interflex* 20 (UKR trg)

France FRA

Euro EUR		2022	2023	2024
GDP	EUR	2.64trn	2.80trn	2.91trn
	USD	2.78trn	3.05trn	3.18trn
per capita	USD	42,350	46,315	48,223
Growth	%	2.5	1.0	1.3
Inflation	%	5.9	5.6	2.5
Def exp [a]	EUR	49.6bn	53.3bn	
	USD	52.3bn	58.0bn	
Def bdgt [b]	EUR	51.5bn	55.1bn	58.8bn
	USD	54.3bn	60.0bn	64.3bn
USD1=EUR		0.95	0.92	0.91

[a] NATO figure
[b] Includes pensions

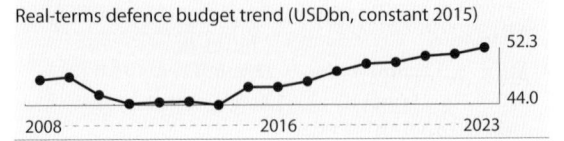

Real-terms defence budget trend (USDbn, constant 2015)
52.3
44.0
2008 — 2016 — 2023

Population	68,235,759				
Age	0–14	15–19	20–24	25–29	30–64	65 plus
Male	8.9%	3.1%	3.0%	2.9%	21.5%	9.5%
Female	8.6%	3.0%	2.9%	2.8%	21.5%	12.1%

Capabilities

In November 2022, France published a new National Strategic Review, which highlighted the deteriorating security environment, the need to strengthen resilience and the importance of the NATO Alliance and European strategic autonomy. France plays a leading military role in the EU, NATO and the UN, and maintains globally deployed forces. France is also expanding its capabilities in non-traditional domains, having set up a space command, developed a space strategy, formalised an offensive cyber doctrine and adopted a seabed warfare strategy. In 2023, Paris issued a new Military Programming Law (LPM) with a significant increase in defence spending. The LPM reflects Russia's 2022 invasion of Ukraine and greater doctrinal emphasis on high-intensity warfare. It increases investment in combat-support capabilities, maintenance, combat training and readiness. Weapons stocks, security of supply and industrial capacity are set to be improved. The size of the operational reserve should double and have higher combat readiness. At the same time, armoured and mechanised brigades will be partially reorganised to increase their combat support element and to become more deployable. A new army command will be created to organise combat support in-depth, with the creation of an artillery brigade. France, before the end of this decade, wants to be able to deploy a complete division to NATO's eastern frontier within less than a month. France has a demonstrated ability to support expeditionary forces, although some strategic and intra-theatre military air-transport requirements rely on allies and external contractors. Coups caused France to reorganise its presence in the Sahel, with the country effectively withdrawing troops from Mali, Burkina Faso, and Niger. France has a sophisticated multi-domain defence industry, exemplified by companies such as Dassault, Naval Group, and Nexter, with most procurements undertaken domestically.

ACTIVE 203,850 (Army 113,800 Navy 34,650 Air 40,200, Other Staffs 15,200) Gendarmerie & Paramilitary 95,100

RESERVE 37,300 (Army 22,550 Navy 4,900 Air 5,000 Other Staffs 4,850) Gendarmerie & Paramilitary 31,500

ORGANISATIONS BY SERVICE

Strategic Nuclear Forces

Navy 2,200
EQUIPMENT BY TYPE
SUBMARINES • STRATEGIC 4
  SSBN 4 *Le Triomphant* with 16 M51 SLBM with 6 TN-75 nuclear warheads, 4 single 533mm TT with SM39 *Exocet* AShM/F17 mod 2 HWT
AIRCRAFT • FGA 20 *Rafale* M F3 with ASMPA msl

Air Force 1,800

Air Strategic Forces Command
FORCES BY ROLE
STRIKE
  2 sqn with *Rafale* B with ASMPA msl
TANKER
  2 sqn with A330 MRTT; C-135FR; KC-135 *Stratotanker*
EQUIPMENT BY TYPE
AIRCRAFT 20 combat capable
  FGA 20 *Rafale* B
  TKR/TPT 15: 12 A330 MRTT; 3 C-135FR
  TKR 3 KC-135 *Stratotanker*

Paramilitary

Gendarmerie 40

Space
EQUIPMENT BY TYPE
SATELLITES 14
  COMMUNICATIONS 5: 2 *Syracuse*-3 (designed to integrate with UK *Skynet* & ITA *Sicral*); 2 *Syracuse*-4; 1 *Athena-Fidus* (also used by ITA)
  ISR 6: 1 CSO-1; 1 CSO-2; 1 *Helios* 2A; 1 *Helios* 2B; 2 *Pleiades*
  ELINT/SIGINT 3 CERES

Army 113,800
Regt and BG normally bn size
FORCES BY ROLE
COMMAND
  1 corps HQ (CRR-FR)
  2 div HQ
MANOEUVRE
Reconnaissance
  1 recce regt

Armoured
  1 (2nd) armd bde (2 tk regt, 3 armd inf regt, 1 SP arty regt, 1 engr regt)
  1 (7th) armd bde (1 tk regt, 1 armd BG, 3 armd inf regt, 1 SP arty regt, 1 engr regt)
  1 armd BG HQ (UAE)
Mechanised
  1 (6th) lt armd bde (2 armd cav regt, 1 armd inf regt, 1 mech inf regt, 1 mech inf regt, 1 SP arty regt, 1 engr regt)
  1 (FRA/GER) mech bde (1 armd cav regt, 1 mech inf regt)
  1 mech regt HQ (Djibouti)
Light
  1 (27th) mtn bde (1 armd cav regt, 3 mtn inf regt, 1 arty regt, 1 engr regt)
  3 inf regt (French Guiana & French West Indies)
  1 inf regt HQ (New Caledonia)
  2 inf bn HQ (Côte d'Ivoire & Gabon)
Air Manoeuvre
  1 (11th) AB bde (1 armd cav regt, 4 para regt, 1 arty regt, 1 engr regt, 1 spt regt)
  1 AB regt (La Réunion)
Amphibious
  1 (9th) amph bde (2 armd cav regt, 1 armd inf regt, 2 mech inf regt, 1 SP arty regt, 1 engr regt)
Other
  4 SMA regt (French Guiana, French West Indies & Indian Ocean)
  3 SMA coy (French Polynesia, Indian Ocean & New Caledonia)
COMBAT SUPPORT
  1 MRL regt
  2 engr regt
  2 EW regt
  1 int bn
  1 CBRN regt
  5 sigs regt
COMBAT SERVICE SUPPORT
  5 tpt regt
  1 log regt
  1 med regt
  3 trg regt
HELICOPTER
  1 (4th) hel bde (3 hel regt, 1 maint regt)
ISR UAV
  1 UAV regt
AIR DEFENCE
  1 SAM regt

Special Operation Forces 2,200
FORCES BY ROLE
SPECIAL FORCES
  2 SF regt

HELICOPTER
1 hel regt

Reserves 22,550 reservists

Reservists form 79 UIR (Reserve Intervention Units) of about 75 to 152 troops, for 'Proterre' – combined land projection forces bn, and 23 USR (Reserve Specialised Units) of about 160 troops, in specialised regt

EQUIPMENT BY TYPE
ARMOURED FIGHTING VEHICLES
  MBT 215 Leclerc
  ASLT 210 AMX-10RC
  RECCE 102: 62 EBRC *Jaguar*; 40 ERC-90D *Sagaie*
  IFV 622: 515 VBCI VCI; 107 VBCI VPC (CP)
  APC 2,507
    APC (T) 49 BvS-10
    APC (W) 2,438: 587 VBMR *Griffon*; 11 *Griffon* VOA; ε1,800 VAB; 40 VAB VOA (OP)
    PPV 20 *Aravis*
  AUV 1,569: 1,134 VBL/VB2L; 246 VBL Ultima; 189 VBMR-L *Serval*
ENGINEERING & MAINTENANCE VEHICLES
  AEV 110: 38 AMX-30EBG; 72 VAB GE
  ARV 44: 27 AMX-30D; 17 *Leclerc* DNG; VAB-EHC
  VLB 48: 20 EFA; 18 PTA; 10 SPRAT
  MW 16+: AMX-30B/B2; 4 *Buffalo*; 12 *Minotaur*
NBC VEHICLES 26 VAB NRBC
ANTI-TANK/ANTI-INFRASTRUCTURE • MSL
  SP 177: 64 VAB *Milan*; 113 VAB with *Akeron*
  MANPATS *Akeron*; *Eryx*; FGM-148 *Javelin*; *Milan*
ARTILLERY 245+
  SP 155mm 92: 32 AU-F-1; 60 CAESAR
  TOWED 155mm 12 TR-F-1
  MRL 227mm 9 M270 MLRS
  MOR 132+: **81mm** LLR 81mm; **120mm** 132 RT-F-1
AIRCRAFT • TPT • Light 13: 5 PC-6B *Turbo Porter*; 5 TBM-700; 3 TBM-700B
HELICOPTERS
  ATK 67: 17 *Tiger* HAP (to be upgraded to HAD); 50 *Tiger* HAD
  MRH 104: 18 AS555UN *Fennec*; 86 SA341F/342M *Gazelle* (all variants)
  TPT 172: **Heavy** 8 H225M *Caracal* (CSAR); **Medium** 129: 24 AS532UL *Cougar*; 2 EC225LP *Super Puma*; 57 NH90 TTH; 46 SA330 *Puma*; **Light** 35 H120 *Colibri* (leased)
AIR DEFENCE • SAM • Point-defence *Mistral*
AIR-LAUNCHED MISSILES
  ASM AGM-114 *Hellfire* II; HOT

Navy 34,650

EQUIPMENT BY TYPE
SUBMARINES 9
  STRATEGIC • SSBN 4 *Le Triomphant* opcon Strategic Nuclear Forces with 16 M51 SLBM with 6 TN-75 nuclear warheads, 4 single 533mm TT with SM39 *Exocet* AShM/F17 mod 2 HWT
  TACTICAL • SSN 5
    2 *Rubis* with 4 single 533mm TT with SM39 *Exocet* AShM/F17 mod 2 HWT
    1 *Rubis* with 4 single 533mm TT with SM39 *Exocet* AShM/F17 mod 2 HWT/*Artémis* (F-21) HWT
    2 *Suffren* with 4 single 533mm TT with MdCN (SCALP Naval) LACM/SM39 *Exocet* AShM/*Artémis* (F-21) HWT
PRINCIPAL SURFACE COMBATANTS 22
  AIRCRAFT CARRIERS • CVN 1 *Charles de Gaulle* with 4 8-cell *Sylver* A43 VLS with *Aster* 15 SAM, 2 sextuple *Sadral* lnchr with *Mistral* SAM (capacity 30 *Rafale* M FGA ac, 2 E-2C *Hawkeye* AEW&C ac, 8 AS365 *Dauphin*/NH90 NFH hel)
  DESTROYERS • DDGHM 4:
    2 *Aquitaine* (FREMM FREDA) with 2 quad lnchr with MM40 *Exocet* Block 3 AShM, 4 8-cell *Sylver* A50 VLS with *Aster* 15 SAM/*Aster* 30 SAM, 2 twin 324mm B-515 ASTT with MU90 LWT, 1 76mm gun (capacity 1 NH90 NFH hel)
    2 *Forbin* with 2 quad lnchr with MM40 *Exocet* Block 3 AShM, 4 8-cell *Sylver* A50 VLS with *Aster* 30 SAM, 2 8-cell *Sylver* A50 VLS with *Aster* 15 SAM, 2 twin 324mm ASTT with MU90 LWT, 2 76mm gun (capacity 1 NH90 NFH hel)
  FRIGATES 17
  FFGHM 11:
    4 *Aquitaine* (FREMM ASM) with 2 8-cell *Sylver* A70 VLS with MdCN (SCALP Naval) LACM, 2 quad lnchr with MM40 *Exocet* Block 3 AShM, 2 8-cell *Sylver* A43 VLS with *Aster* 15 SAM, 2 twin 324mm B-515 ASTT with MU90 LWT, 1 76mm gun (capacity 1 NH90 NFH hel)
    2 *Aquitaine* (FREMM ASM) with 2 8-cell *Sylver* A70 VLS with MdCN (SCALP Naval) LACM, 2 quad lnchr with MM40 *Exocet* Block 3 AShM, 2 8-cell *Sylver* A50 VLS with *Aster* 15 SAM/*Aster* 30 SAM, 2 twin 324mm B-515 ASTT with MU90 LWT, 1 76mm gun (capacity 1 NH90 NFH hel)
    2 *La Fayette* with 2 quad lnchr with MM40 *Exocet* Block 3 AShM, 2 twin *Simbad* lnchr with *Mistral* SAM, 1 octuple lnchr with *Crotale* SAM, 1 100mm gun (capacity 1 AS565SA *Panther* hel)
    3 *La Fayette* with 2 quad lnchr with MM40 *Exocet* Block 3 AShM, 2 sextuple *Sadral* lnchr with *Mistral* 3 SAM, 1 100mm gun (capacity 1 AS565SA *Panther* hel)
  FFH 6 *Floreal* with 1 100mm gun (fitted for but not with 1 twin *Simbad* lnchr with *Mistral* SAM) (capacity 1 AS565SA *Panther* hel)
PATROL AND COASTAL COMBATANTS 21
  FSM 6 *D'Estienne d'Orves* with 1 twin *Simbad* lnchr with *Mistral* SAM, 1 100mm gun
  PSO 4 *d'Entrecasteaux* (BSAOM) with 1 hel landing platform
  PCO 7: 1 *Auguste Benebig* (POM); 3 *La Confiance*, 1 *Lapérouse*; 1 *Le Malin*; 1 *Fulmar*

PCC 3 *Flamant*
PBF 1 *Bir Hakeim* (VFM)
MINE WARFARE • MINE COUNTERMEASURES 16
  MCD 5: 1 *Ophrys* (VSP); 4 *Vulcain*
  MHC 3 *Antarès*
  MHO 8 *Éridan*
AMPHIBIOUS
  PRINCIPAL AMPHIBIOUS SHIPS 3
    LHD 3 *Mistral* with 2 twin *Simbad* lnchr with *Mistral* SAM (capacity up to 16 NH90/SA330 *Puma*/AS532 *Cougar*/*Tiger* hel; 2 LCT or 4 LCM/LCU; 13 MBTs; 50 AFVs; 450 troops)
  LANDING CRAFT 25
    LCU 2 *Arbalète* (EDA-S) (capacity 1 *Leclerc* MBT or 2 *Griffon*/*Jaguar*)
    LCT 4 EDA-R (capacity 1 *Leclerc* MBT or 6 VAB)
    LCM 9 CTM
    LCVP 10
LOGISTICS AND SUPPORT 37
  ABU 1 *Telenn Mor*
  AFD 1
  AG 3: 1 *Alize* (BSP) with 1 hel landing platform; 1 Caouanne (ERF); 1 *Chamois*
  AGB 1 *Astrolabe* with 1 hel landing platform
  AGE 1 *Thetis* (*Lapérouse* mod) (used as trials ships for mines and divers)
  AGI 1 *Dupuy de Lome* with 1 hel landing platform
  AGM 1 *Monge* (capacity 2 med hels)
  AGOR 2: 1 *Pourquoi pas?* (used 150 days per year by Ministry of Defence; operated by Ministry of Research and Education otherwise); 1 *Beautemps-Beaupre*
  AGS 3 *Lapérouse*
  AORH 3: 2 *Durance* with 3 twin *Simbad* lnchr with *Mistral* SAM (capacity 1 SA319 *Alouette* III/AS365 *Dauphin*/*Lynx*); 1 *Jacques Chevallier* (BRF) with 2 twin *Simbad* lnchr with *Mistral* SAM (capacity 1 AS365 *Dauphin*/H160)
  ARS 4 *Loire* (BSAM)
  AXL 12: 2 *Glycine*; 1 *Jules* with 1 hel landing platform; 8 *Léopard*; 1 *Palyvestre* (VSMP mod)
  AXS 4: 2 *La Belle Poule*; 1 *La Grand Hermine*; 1 *Mutin*
UNINHABITED MARITIME PLATFORMS
  USV • MW • **Medium** 1 *Artemis*
UNINHABITED MARITIME SYSTEMS • UUV
  DATA A18D; *Victor* 6000
  MW A9-M; *Double Eagle* Mk II; PAP

Naval Aviation 6,500

FORCES BY ROLE
STRIKE/FIGHTER/GROUND ATTACK
  2 sqn with *Rafale* M F3
  1 sqn with *Rafale* M F3/F3-R
ANTI-SURFACE WARFARE
  1 sqn with AS565SA *Panther*
ANTI-SUBMARINE WARFARE
  2 sqn with NH90 NFH

MARITIME PATROL
  2 sqn with *Atlantique* 2
  1 sqn with *Falcon* 20H *Gardian*
  1 sqn with *Falcon* 50MI
AIRBORNE EARLY WARNING & CONTROL
  1 sqn with E-2C *Hawkeye*
SEARCH & RESCUE
  1 sqn with AS365N/F *Dauphin* 2
TRAINING
  1 sqn with AS365F/N *Dauphin* 2
  1 sqn with EMB 121 *Xingu*
  1 unit with *Falcon* 10MER
  1 unit with CAP 10M
  1 unit with H160B
EQUIPMENT BY TYPE
AIRCRAFT 60 combat capable
  FGA 42 *Rafale* M F3-R
  ASW 18: 11 *Atlantique*-2 (standard 6); 7 *Atlantique*-2 (being upgraded to standard 6)
  AEW&C 3 E-2C *Hawkeye*
  SAR 4 *Falcon* 50MS
  TPT 25: **Light** 10 EMB-121 *Xingu*; **PAX** 15: 6 *Falcon* 10MER; 5 *Falcon* 20H *Gardian*; 4 *Falcon* 50MI
  TRG 5 CAP 10M
HELICOPTERS
  ASW 27 NH90 NFH
  MRH 29: 3 AS365F *Dauphin* 2; 6 AS365N *Dauphin* 2; 2 AS365N3; 16 AS565SA *Panther*; 4 H160B (leased)
UNINHABITED AERIAL VEHICLES
  ISR • **Light** 4 S-100 *Camcopter*
AIR-LAUNCHED MISSILES
  AAM • **IIR** *Mica* IR; **ARH** *Mica* RF
  ASM AASM
  AShM AM39 *Exocet*
  LACM Nuclear ASMPA
BOMBS
  Laser-guided: GBU-12/16 *Paveway* II

Marines 2,400

Commando Units 700
FORCES BY ROLE
MANOEUVRE
  Reconnaissance
  1 recce gp
  Amphibious
  2 aslt gp
  1 atk swimmer gp
  1 raiding gp
COMBAT SUPPORT
  1 cbt spt gp
COMBAT SERVICE SUPPORT
  1 spt gp

Fusiliers-Marin 1,700
FORCES BY ROLE
MANOEUVRE
  Other

2 sy gp
7 sy coy

Reserves 4,900 reservists

Air and Space Force 40,200
FORCES BY ROLE
STRIKE
2 sqn with *Rafale* B with ASMPA msl
SPACE
1 (satellite obs) sqn
FIGHTER
1 sqn with *Mirage* 2000-5
1 sqn with *Mirage* 2000B
FIGHTER/GROUND ATTACK
3 sqn with *Mirage* 2000D
1 (composite) sqn with *Mirage* 2000-5/D (Djibouti)
2 sqn with *Rafale* B/C
1 sqn with *Rafale* B/C (UAE)
ISR
1 sqn with Beech 350ER *King Air*
AIRBORNE EARLY WARNING & CONTROL
1 (Surveillance & Control) sqn with E-3F *Sentry*
SEARCH & RESCUE/TRANSPORT
5 sqn with CN235M; SA330 *Puma*; AS555 *Fennec* (Djibouti, French Guiana, French Polynesia, Indian Ocean & New Caledonia)
TANKER
1 sqn with A330 MRTT
TANKER/TRANSPORT
1 sqn with C-135FR; KC-135 *Stratotanker*
TRANSPORT
1 VIP sqn with A330
2 sqn with A400M
1 sqn with C-130H/H-30 *Hercules*
1 sqn with C-130H/H-30/J-30 *Hercules*; KC-130J *Hercules*
1 sqn (joint FRA-GER) with C-130J-30 *Hercules*; KC-130J *Hercules*
2 sqn with CN235M
1 sqn with *Falcon* 7X (VIP); *Falcon* 900 (VIP); *Falcon* 2000
3 flt with TBM-700A
1 gp with DHC-6-300 *Twin Otter*
TRAINING
1 OCU sqn with *Mirage* 2000D
1 OCU sqn with *Rafale* B/C
1 OCU sqn with SA330 *Puma*; AS555 *Fennec*
2 (aggressor) sqn with *Alpha Jet**
1 sqn with G 120AF
2 sqn with G 120AF; PC-21
1 sqn with EMB-121
TRANSPORT HELICOPTER
2 sqn with AS555 *Fennec*
2 sqn with AS332C/L *Super Puma*; SA330 *Puma*; H225M

ISR UAV
1 sqn with MQ-9A *Reaper*
AIR DEFENCE
3 sqn with *Crotale* NG; SAMP/T
1 sqn with SAMP/T

EQUIPMENT BY TYPE
SATELLITES see Space
AIRCRAFT 234 combat capable
  FTR 34: 27 *Mirage* 2000-5; 7 *Mirage* 2000B
  FGA 155: 60 *Mirage* 2000D (55 being upgraded to *Mirage* 2000D RMV); 54 *Rafale* B; 41 *Rafale* C (*Rafale* being upgraded to F3-R standard)
  ISR 2 Beech 350ER *King Air*
  AEW&C 4 E-3F *Sentry*
  TKR 3 KC-135 *Stratotanker*
  TKR/TPT 17: 12 A330 MRTT; 3 C-135FR (7 more in store); 2 KC-130J *Hercules*
  TPT 114: **Heavy** 21 A400M; **Medium** 16: 5 C-130H *Hercules*; 9 C-130H-30 *Hercules*; 2 C-130J-30 *Hercules*; **Light** 69: 19 CN235M-100; 8 CN235M-300; 5 DHC-6-300 *Twin Otter*; 22 EMB-121 *Xingu*; 15 TBM-700; **PAX** 8: 1 A330 (VIP); 2 *Falcon* 7X; 3 *Falcon* 900 (VIP); 2 *Falcon* 2000
  TRG 124: 45 *Alpha Jet**; 17 D140 Jodel; 3 Extra 300/330;17 G 120AF (leased); 17 PC-21; 5 *Super Dimona* HK36; 13 SR20 (leased); 7 SR22 (leased)
HELICOPTERS
  MRH 37 AS555 *Fennec*
  TPT 38: **Heavy** 11 H225M *Caracal*; **Medium** 27: 1 AS332C *Super Puma*; 4 AS332L *Super Puma*; 2 H225; 20 SA330B *Puma*
UNINHABITED AERIAL VEHICLES
  CISR • Heavy 12 MQ-9A *Reaper*
AIR DEFENCE • SAM 60: **Long-range** 40 SAMP/T; **Short-range** 20 *Crotale* NG
AIR-LAUNCHED MISSILES
  AAM • IR R-550 *Magic* 2; **IIR** *Mica* IR; **ARH** *Meteor*; *Mica* RF
  ASM AASM; *Apache*
  LACM
    Nuclear ASMPA
    Conventional SCALP EG
BOMBS
  Laser-guided: GBU-12/-16 *Paveway* II
  Laser & INS/GPS-guided GBU-49 Enhanced *Paveway* II

Security and Intervention Brigade
FORCES BY ROLE
SPECIAL FORCES
  3 SF gp
MANOEUVRE
  Other
  24 protection units
  30 (fire fighting and rescue) unit

Reserves 5,000 reservists

Gendarmerie & Paramilitary 95,100

Gendarmerie 95,100; 31,500 reservists
EQUIPMENT BY TYPE
ARMOURED FIGHTING VEHICLES
  APC 112:
    APC (W) 80: 60 VXB-170 (VBRG-170); 20 VAB
    PPV 32 *Centaure*
ARTILLERY • MOR 81mm some
PATROL AND COASTAL COMBATANTS 41
  PB 41: 1 *Armoise*; 4 *Géranium*; 3 *Maroni* (VCSM NG); 24 VCSM; 9 VSMP
HELICOPTERS • TPT • Light 60: 25 AS350BA *Ecureuil*; 20 H135; 15 H145

DEPLOYMENT

BOSNIA-HERZEGOVINA: EU • EUFOR (*Operation Althea*) 5

CENTRAL AFRICAN REPUBLIC: EU • EUTM RCA 1; UN • MINUSCA 4

CHAD: 1,500; 1 mech inf BG; 1 FGA det with 3 *Mirage 2000D*; 1 tkr/tpt det with 1 A330 MRTT; 1 C-130H; 2 CN235M

CÔTE D'IVOIRE: 900; 1 inf bn; 1 (army) hel unit with 2 SA330 *Puma*; 2 SA342 *Gazelle*; 1 (air force) hel unit with 1 AS555 *Fennec*

CYPRUS: *Operation Inherent Resolve* 30: 1 Atlantique-2

DEMOCRATIC REPUBLIC OF THE CONGO: UN • MONUSCO 4

DJIBOUTI: 1,500; 1 combined arms regt with (2 recce sqn, 2 inf coy, 1 arty bty, 1 engr coy); 1 hel det with 4 SA330 *Puma*; 3 SA342 *Gazelle*; 1 LCM; 1 FGA sqn with 4 *Mirage 2000-5*; 1 SAR/tpt sqn with 1 CN235M; 3 SA330 *Puma*

EGYPT: MFO 1

ESTONIA: NATO • Enhanced Forward Presence (*Operation Lynx*) 350; 1 mech inf coy

FRENCH GUIANA: 2,100: 2 inf regt; 1 SMA regt; 2 PCO; 1 tpt sqn with 3 CN235M; 5 SA330 *Puma*; 4 AS555 *Fennec*; 3 gendarmerie coy; 1 AS350BA *Ecureuil*; 1 H145

FRENCH POLYNESIA: 950: 1 inf bn; 1 SMA coy; 1 naval HQ at Papeete; 1 FFH; 1 PSO; 1 PCO; 1 AFS; 3 *Falcon 200 Gardian*; 1 SAR/tpt sqn with 2 CN235M; 3 SA330 *Puma*

FRENCH WEST INDIES: 1,000; 1 inf regt; 2 SMA regt; 2 FFH; 1 AS565SA *Panther*; 1 SA319 *Alouette* III; 1 naval base at Fort de France (Martinique); 4 gendarmerie coy; 1 PCO; 1 PB; 2 AS350BA *Ecureuil*

GABON: 350; 1 inf bn

GERMANY: 2,000 (incl elm Eurocorps and FRA/GER bde); 1 (FRA/GER) mech bde (1 armd cav regt, 1 mech inf regt)

GULF OF GUINEA: *Operation Corymbe* 1 LHD

IRAQ: *Operation Inherent Resolve* 6; **NATO** • NATO Mission Iraq 3

JORDAN: *Operation Inherent Resolve* (*Chammal*) 300: 4 *Rafale* F3

LA REUNION/MAYOTTE: 1,750; 1 para regt; 1 inf coy; 1 SMA regt; 1 SMA coy; 2 FFH; 1 PCO; 1 LCM; 1 naval HQ at Port-des-Galets (La Réunion); 1 naval base at Dzaoudzi (Mayotte); 1 Falcon 50M; 1 SAR/tpt sqn with 2 CN235M; 5 gendarmerie coy; 1 SA319 *Alouette* III

LEBANON: UN • UNIFIL 554; 1 bn HQ; 1 recce coy, 1 log coy, 1 maint coy, 1 tpt coy, VBCI; VAB; VBL; *Mistral*

MALI: EU • EUTM Mali 7

MEDITERRANEAN SEA: Navy 500; 1 DDGHM; 1 LHD **NATO** • SNMG 2: 150; 1 FFGHM; **EU** • EUNAVFOR MED • *Operation Irini*: 90; 1 FSM

MOZAMBIQUE: EU • EUTM Mozambique 6

NEW CALEDONIA: 1,450; 1 mech inf regt; 1 SMA coy; 6 ERC-90F1 *Lynx*; 1 FFH; 1 PSO; 1 PCO; 1 base with 2 *Falcon 200 Gardian* at Nouméa; 1 tpt unit with 2 CN235 MPA; 3 SA330 *Puma*; 4 gendarmerie coy; 2 AS350BA *Ecureuil*

QATAR: *Operation Inherent Resolve* (*Chammal*) 70; 1 E-3F *Sentry*

ROMANIA: NATO • Enhanced Vigilance Activities 750; 1 armd BG with *Leclerc*; VBCI; 1 SP arty bty with CAESAR 1 SAM bty with SAMP/T

SAUDI ARABIA: 50 (radar det)

SENEGAL: 400; 1 *Falcon* 50MI

UNITED ARAB EMIRATES: 700: 1 armd BG (1 tk coy, 1 arty bty); *Leclerc*; CAESAR; • *Operation Inherent Resolve* (*Chammal*); 1 FGA sqn with 7 *Rafale* F3

WESTERN SAHARA: UN • MINURSO 2

FOREIGN FORCES
Germany 400 (GER elm Eurocorps)
Singapore 200; 1 trg sqn with 12 M-346 *Master*

Germany GER

Euro EUR		2022	2023	2024
GDP	EUR	3.88trn	4.07trn	4.30trn
	USD	4.09trn	4.43trn	4.70trn
per capita	USD	48,756	52,824	56,037
Growth	%	1.8	-0.5	0.9
Inflation	%	8.7	6.3	3.5
Def exp [a]	EUR	57.7bn	64.1bn	
	USD	60.8bn	69.7bn	
Def bdgt [b]	EUR	50.4bn	58.5bn	71.0bn
	USD	53.1bn	63.7bn	77.6bn
USD1=EUR		0.95	0.92	0.91

[a] NATO figure
[b] Includes military pensions

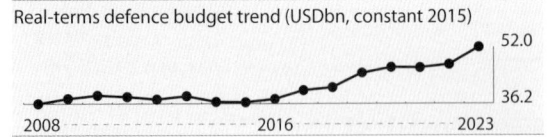

Real-terms defence budget trend (USDbn, constant 2015)

Population 84,220,184

Age	0–14	15–19	20–24	25–29	30–64	65 plus
Male	7.0%	2.3%	2.6%	2.8%	24.3%	10.4%
Female	6.7%	2.3%	2.5%	2.7%	23.5%	12.9%

Capabilities

Germany released its first National Security Strategy in June, laying out a cross-government approach to address challenges ranging from military threats to the climate crisis. The NSS was spurred by Russia's full-scale invasion of Ukraine, which prompted Chancellor Olaf Scholz to invoke a turning point, or *Zeitenwende*, in German security policy. It included setting up a EUR100 billion (USD109bn) special fund for the German armed forces. The NSS calls out Russia as 'for now the most significant threat to peace and security in the Euro-Atlantic area' and sets other important markers. Germany pledged to 'contribute more to security on the European continent' and the government said it would 'promote the development and introduction of highly advanced capabilities, such as precision deep-strike weapons'. Germany also committed to bolster NATO's eastern flank and subsequently signalled its intent to deploy 4,000 troops to Lithuania. Berlin also issued a China strategy. In November 2023, Berlin issued its first defence policy guidelines since 2011 to translate the country's NSS into a framework underpinning the Bundeswehr´s military strategy, culture and planning. The guidelines signal a greater interest in Indo-Pacific defence engagement and argues that Beijing is ´trying to reshape the international order as it sees fit´. The document also aimed to reassure allies, especially those on NATO´s eastern flank, about Germany´s willingness to play a central role in collective defence. The German government said that it would meet NATO's long-standing target of spending at least 2% of GDP on defence in 2024. The NSS indicates, though, that the financial commitment may fluctuate, with Berlin saying it would meet the 2% commitment on average over a multi-year basis. Germany is becoming more militarily present in the Indo-Pacific and, in 2024, plans to dispatch a frigate and a supply ship to the area, following a one-ship deployment to the region in 2021. Germany has established close military cooperation with the Czech Republic, France, the Netherlands and Romania, including the affiliation of units. The defence ministry has announced its objective to increase authorised active personnel numbers. The voluntary conscript model involves between seven and 23 months of military service. In September 2022, Germany set up a Territorial Operations Command to strengthen the armed forces' homeland security functions and to take on command-and-control functions for forces deployed in Germany. The armed forces are struggling to improve readiness levels due to increasing demands on NATO's eastern flank. Germany has indicated that it intends to provide, from 2025, around 30,000 personnel and some 85 vessels and aircraft at 30 days' notice for NATO's New Force Model, agreed at the Alliance's 2022 Madrid summit. Shortages of spare parts and maintenance problems are reported in all three services. Germany's defence-industrial base can design and manufacture equipment to meet requirements across all military domains, with strengths in land and naval systems. The government is pursuing a policy of closer defence-industrial cooperation in Europe.

ACTIVE 181,000 (Army 61,900 Navy 15,550 Air 26,650 Joint Support Service 22,450 Joint Medical Service 20,050 Cyber 13,950 Other 20,450)

Conscript liability Voluntary conscription only. Voluntary conscripts can serve up to 23 months

RESERVE 34,750 (Army 7,600 Navy 1,800 Air 4,150 Joint Support Service 13,700 Joint Medical Service 4,450 Cyber 1,650 Other 1,400)

ORGANISATIONS BY SERVICE

Space
EQUIPMENT BY TYPE
SATELLITES 8
  COMMUNICATIONS 2 COMSATBw (1 & 2)
  ISR 6: 1 SARah; 5 SAR-*Lupe*

Army 61,900
FORCES BY ROLE
COMMAND
  elm 2 (1 GNC & MNC NE) corps HQ
MANOEUVRE
  Armoured
  1 (1st) armd div (1 (9th) armd bde (1 armd recce bn, 1 tk bn, 2 armd inf bn, 1 mech inf bn, 1 cbt engr bn, 1 spt bn); 1 (21st) armd bde (1 armd recce bn, 1 tk bn, 1 armd inf bn, 1 mech inf bn, 1 cbt engr bn, 1 spt bn); 1 (41st) mech inf bde (1 armd recce bn, 2 armd inf bn, 1 mech inf bn, 1 cbt engr bn, 1 sigs coy, 1 spt bn); 1 tk bn (for NLD 43rd Bde); 1 SP arty bn; 1 sigs coy)
  1 (10th) armd div (1 (12th) armd bde (1 armd recce bn, 1 tk bn, 2 armd inf bn, 1 cbt engr bn, 1 sigs coy, 1 spt bn); 1 (37th) mech inf bde (1 armd recce bn, 2 tk bn, 2 armd inf bn, 1 SP arty bn (forming), 1 engr bn, 1 sigs coy, 1 spt bn); 1 (23rd) mtn inf bde (1 recce bn, 3 mtn inf bn, 1 cbt engr bn, 1 spt bn); 1 SP arty bn; 1 SP arty trg bn; 2 mech inf bn (GER/FRA bde); 1 arty bn (GER/FRA bde); 1 cbt engr coy (GER/FRA bde); 1 spt bn (GER/FRA bde))
  Air Manoeuvre
  1 (rapid reaction) AB div (1 SOF bde (3 SOF bn); 1 AB

bde (2 recce coy, 2 para regt, 2 cbt engr coy); 1 atk hel regt; 2 tpt hel regt; 1 sigs coy)

COMBAT SUPPORT
1 engr bn(-) (Joint GER-UK unit)

EQUIPMENT BY TYPE

ARMOURED FIGHTING VEHICLES
MBT 313: 209 *Leopard* 2A5/A6; 104 *Leopard* 2A7V
RECCE 220 *Fennek* (incl 24 engr recce, 50 fires spt)
IFV 680: 258 *Marder* 1A3/A4; 72 *Marder* 1A5; 350 *Puma*
APC 876
 APC (T) 112: 75 Bv-206S; 37 M113 (inc variants)
 APC (W) 764: 405 *Boxer* (inc variants); 359 TPz-1 *Fuchs* (inc variants)
AUV 683: 247 *Dingo* 2; 363 *Eagle* IV/V; 73 *Wiesel* 1 Mk20 (with 20mm gun)

ENGINEERING & MAINTENANCE VEHICLES
AEV 51 *Dachs*
ARV 170: 95 BPz-2 1; 75 BPz-3 *Büffel*
VLB 43: 6 *Biber*; 7 *Leopard* 2 with *Leguan*; 30 M3
MW 30: 6 *Fuchs* KAI; 24 *Keiler*

NBC VEHICLES 44 TPz-1 *Fuchs* NBC

ANTI-TANK/ANTI-INFRASTRUCTURE • MSL
SP 107 *Wiesel* ATGM with TOW or MELLS
MANPATS *Milan*; *Spike*-LR (MELLS)

ARTILLERY 245
SP 155mm 109 PzH 2000
MRL 227mm 38 M270 MLRS
MOR 98: 120mm 58 Tampella; SP 120mm 40 M113 with Tampella

HELICOPTERS
ATK 51 *Tiger*
TPT 108: **Medium** 82 NH90; **Light** 26: 6 Bell 206B3 *Jet Ranger* III (leased); 13 H135; 7 H145 (SAR)

UNINHABITED AERIAL VEHICLES
ISR 123: **Medium** 35 KZO; **Light** 87 LUNA

AIR-LAUNCHED MISSILES • ASM HOT; PARS 3 LR

Navy 15,550

EQUIPMENT BY TYPE

SUBMARINES 6
SSK 6 Type-212A (fitted with AIP) with 6 single 533mm TT with DM2A4 HWT

PRINCIPAL SURFACE COMBATANTS 11
DESTROYERS • DDGHM 3 *Sachsen* (F124) with 2 quad lnchr with RGM-84C *Harpoon* Block 1B AShM, 4 8-cell Mk 41 VLS with SM-2 Block IIIA SAM/RIM-162B ESSM SAM, 2 21-cell Mk 49 GMLS with RIM-116 RAM SAM, 2 triple 324mm SVTT Mk 32 ASTT with MU90 LWT, 1 76mm gun (capacity 2 *Sea Lynx* Mk88A hel)
FRIGATES • FFGHM 8:
 4 *Baden-Württemberg* (F125) with 2 quad lnchr with RGM-84C *Harpoon* Block 1B AShM, 2 21-cell Mk 49 GMLS with RIM-116C RAM Block 2 SAM, 1 127mm gun (capacity 2 NH90 hel)
 4 *Brandenburg* (F123) with 2 twin lnchr with RGM-84C *Harpoon* Block 1B AShM, 2 8-cell Mk 41 VLS with RIM-7P *Sea Sparrow* SAM/RIM-162B ESSM SAM, 2 Mk 49 GMLS with RIM-116 RAM SAM, 2 twin 324mm SVTT Mk 32 ASTT with Mk 46 LWT, 1 76mm gun (capacity 2 *Sea Lynx* Mk88A hel)

PATROL AND COASTAL COMBATANTS 5
CORVETTES • FSGM 5 *Braunschweig* (K130) with 2 twin lnchr with RBS15 Mk3 AShM, 2 21-cell Mk 49 GMLS with RIM-116 RAM SAM, 1 76mm gun, 1 hel landing platform

MINE WARFARE • MINE COUNTERMEASURES 12
MHO 10: 7 *Frankenthal* (2 used as diving support); 3 *Frankenthal* (mod. MJ332CL)
MSO 2 *Ensdorf*

AMPHIBIOUS • LANDING CRAFT 1
LCU 1 Type-520

LOGISTICS AND SUPPORT 26
AFD 1
AG 6: 2 *Kalkgrund*; 2 *Schwedeneck* (Type-748); 2 *Stollergrund* (Type-745)
AGE 1 *Wilhelm Pullwer* (Type-741)
AGI 3 *Oste* (Type-423)
AGOR 1 *Planet* (Type-751)
AOR 8: 2 *Rhön* (Type-704); 6 *Elbe* (Type-404) with 1 hel landing platform (2 specified for PFM support; 1 specified for SSK support; 3 specified for MHO/MSO support)
AORH 3 *Berlin* (Type-702) (fitted for but not with RIM-116 RAM SAM) (capacity 2 *Sea King* Mk41/NH90 hel)
ATF 2: 1 *Helgoland*; 1 *Rügen*
AXS 1 *Gorch Fock*

UNINHABITED MARITIME PLATFORMS
USV • MW • **Medium** 12 *Seehund*

UNINHABITED MARITIME SYSTEMS • UUV
DATA REMUS 1000
MW *Seafox*

Naval Aviation 2,100

FORCES BY ROLE

MARITIME PATROL
1 sqn with Do-228; AP-3C *Orion*

ANTI-SUBMARINE WARFARE/SEARCH & RESCUE
1 sqn *Lynx* Mk88A; NH90 NFH (*Sea Lion*); *Sea King* Mk41

EQUIPMENT BY TYPE

AIRCRAFT 4 combat capable
ASW 4 AP-3C *Orion*
TPT • **Light** 2 Do-228 (pollution control)

HELICOPTERS
ASW 22 *Lynx* Mk88A
SAR 29: 11 *Sea King* Mk41; 18 NH90 NFH (*Sea Lion*)

UNINHABITED AERIAL VEHICLES • ISR • Light 2 *Skeldar* V-200 (*Sea Falcon*)

Naval Special Forces Command
FORCES BY ROLE
SPECIAL FORCES
  1 SF coy

Sea Battalion
FORCES BY ROLE
MANOEUVRE
  Amphibious
  1 mne bn

Air Force 26,650
FORCES BY ROLE
FIGHTER
  3 wg (2 sqn with Eurofighter *Typhoon*)
FIGHTER/GROUND ATTACK
  1 wg (2 sqn with *Tornado* IDS)
  1 wg (2 sqn with Eurofighter *Typhoon* (multi-role))
ISR
  1 wg (1 ISR sqn with *Tornado* ECR/IDS; 2 UAV sqn with *Heron*)
TANKER/TRANSPORT
  1 (special air mission) wg (3 sqn with A319; A321; A321LR; A350; AS532U2 *Cougar* II; *Global* 5000; *Global* 6000)
TRANSPORT
  1 wg (3 sqn (forming) with A400M *Atlas*)
  1 sqn (joint FRA-GER) with C-130J-30 *Hercules*; KC-130J *Hercules*
TRAINING
  1 sqn located at Holloman AFB (US) with *Tornado* IDS
  1 unit (ENJJPT) located at Sheppard AFB (US) with T-6A *Texan* II; T-38C *Talon*
  1 hel unit located at Fassberg
TRANSPORT HELICOPTER
  1 tpt hel wg (3 sqn with CH-53G/GA/GE/GS *Stallion*; 1 sqn with H145M)
AIR DEFENCE
  1 wg (3 SAM gp) with M902 *Patriot* PAC-3
  1 AD gp with ASRAD *Ozelot*; C-RAM Mantis and trg unit
  1 AD trg unit located at Fort Bliss (US) with MIM-104C/F *Patriot* PAC-2/3
  3 (tac air ctrl) radar gp

Air Force Regiment
FORCES BY ROLE
MANOEUVRE
  Other
  1 sy regt
EQUIPMENT BY TYPE
AIRCRAFT 226 combat capable
  FTR 138 Eurofighter *Typhoon*
  ATK 68 *Tornado* IDS (8 in store)
  ATK/EW 20 *Tornado* ECR*
  ISR 1 A319CJ (Open Skies)
  TPT 61: **Heavy** 43 A400M (several fitted with aerial refuelling kit); **Medium** 3 C-130J-30 *Hercules* **PAX** 15: 1 A321; 2 A321LR; 3 A350 (VIP); 2 A319; 4 *Global* 5000; 3 *Global* 6000
  TRG 109: 69 T-6A *Texan* II, 40 T-38C *Talon*
HELICOPTERS
  MRH 16 H145M
  TPT 63: **Heavy** 60 CH-53G/GA/GS/GE *Stallion*; **Medium** 3 AS532U2 *Cougar* II (VIP)
UNINHABITED AERIAL VEHICLES
  ISR • Heavy 6 *Heron* 1 (leased)
AIR DEFENCE
  SAM 50
    Long-range 30 M902 *Patriot* PAC-3
    Point-defence 20 ASRAD *Ozelot* (with FIM-92 *Stinger*)
AIR-LAUNCHED MISSILES
  AAM • IR AIM-9L/Li *Sidewinder*; **IIR** IRIS-T; **ARH** AIM-120B AMRAAM
  LACM Taurus KEPD 350
  ARM AGM-88B HARM
BOMBS
  Laser-guided GBU-24 *Paveway* III; GBU-48 Enhanced *Paveway* II
  Laser & INS/GPS-guided GBU-54 Laser JDAM

Joint Support Service 22,450
FORCES BY ROLE
COMBAT SUPPORT
  3 MP regt
  2 NBC bn
COMBAT SERVICE SUPPORT
  1 log regt (4 log bn)
  1 log regt (3 log bn)
  1 spt regt
EQUIPMENT BY TYPE
ARMOURED FIGHTING VEHICLES
  AUV 451: 206 *Dingo* 2; 245 *Eagle* IV/V
ENGINEERING & MAINTENANCE VEHICLES
  ARV 35: 23 BPz-2; 12 BPz-3 *Büffel*
NBC VEHICLES 35 TPz-1 *Fuchs* A6/A7/A8 NBC

Joint Medical Services 19,850
FORCES BY ROLE
COMBAT SERVICE SUPPORT
  4 med regt
EQUIPMENT BY TYPE
ARMOURED FIGHTING VEHICLES
  APC • APC (W) 109: 72 *Boxer* (amb); 37 TPz-1 *Fuchs* (amb)
  AUV 42 *Eagle* IV/V (amb)

Cyber & Information Command 13,950

FORCES BY ROLE

COMBAT SUPPORT

4 EW bn

6 sigs bn

DEPLOYMENT

BALTIC SEA: NATO • SNMG 1: 280; 1 DDGHM; 1 AOR

BOSNIA-HERZEGOVINA: EU • EUFOR • *Operation Althea* 31

FRANCE: 400 (incl GER elm Eurocorps)

IRAQ: *Operation Inherent Resolve* 100; **NATO** • NATO Mission Iraq 30

JORDAN: *Operation Inherent Resolve* 150; 1 A400M

KOSOVO: NATO • KFOR 70

LEBANON: UN • UNIFIL 130; 2 FSGM

LITHUANIA: NATO • Enhanced Forward Presence 1,000; 1 mech inf bde HQ; 1 armd inf BG with *Leopard* 2A6; *Fennek*; *Marder* 1A3; *Boxer*

NORTH SEA: NATO • SNMG 1: 40; 1 MHC

POLAND: 95 (GER elm MNC-NE)

SLOVAKIA: NATO • Enhanced Vigilance Activities 160; 1 tk coy

SOUTH SUDAN: UN • UNMISS 14

UNITED STATES: Trg units with 40 T-38 *Talon*; 69 T-6A *Texan* II at Goodyear AFB (AZ)/Sheppard AFB (TX); NAS Pensacola (FL); Fort Rucker (AL); Missile trg at Fort Bliss (TX)

WESTERN SAHARA: UN • MINURSO 3

FOREIGN FORCES

France 2,000; 1 (FRA/GER) mech bde (1 armd cav regt, 1 mech inf regt)

United Kingdom 185

United States

US Africa Command: Army; 1 HQ at Stuttgart

US European Command: 39,050; 1 combined service HQ (EUCOM) at Stuttgart-Vaihingen

Army 24,700; 1 HQ (US Army Europe & Africa (USAREUR-AF) at Wiesbaden; 1 arty comd; 1 SF gp; 1 recce bn; 1 mech bde(-); 1 fd arty bn; 1 MRL bde (3 MRL bn); 1 (cbt avn) hel bde; 1 (cbt avn) hel bde HQ; 2 int bde; 1 MP bde; 1 sigs bde; 1 spt bde; 1 (MDTF) cbt spt bde(-); 1 SAM bde; 2 (APS) armd bde eqpt set; M1A2 SEPv2/v3 *Abrams*; M3A3 *Bradley*; M2A3 *Bradley*; M1296 *Stryker Dragoon*; M109A6; M119A3; M777A2; M270A1; M142 HIMARS; AH-64E *Apache*; CH-47F *Chinook*; UH-60L/M *Black Hawk*; HH-60M *Black Hawk*; M902 *Patriot* PAC-3; M1097 *Avenger*; M-SHORAD

Navy 400

USAF 13,400; 1 HQ (US Air Forces Europe & Africa) at Ramstein AB; 1 HQ (3rd Air Force) at Ramstein AB; 1 FGA wg at Spangdahlem AB with (1 FGA sqn with 24 F-16C *Fighting Falcon*); 1 tpt wg at Ramstein AB with 14 C-130J-30 *Hercules*; 2 Gulfstream V (C-37A); 5 Learjet 35A (C-21A); 1 B-737-700 (C-40B)

USMC 550

Greece GRC

Euro EUR		2022	2023	2024
GDP	EUR	208bn	223bn	234bn
	USD	219bn	242bn	256bn
per capita	USD	20,960	23,173	24,513
Growth	%	5.9	2.5	2.0
Inflation	%	9.3	4.1	2.8
Def exp [a]	EUR	8.05bn	6.70bn	
	USD	8.49bn	7.30bn	
Def bdgt [b]	EUR	7.44bn	6.76bn	
	USD	7.85bn	7.35bn	
FMA (US)	USD	30m	0m	0m
USD1=EUR		0.95	0.92	0.91

[a] NATO figure

[b] Includes military pensions

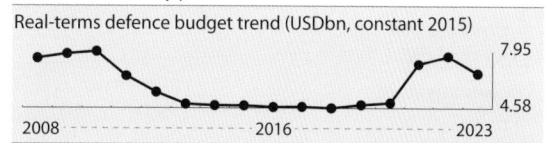

Real-terms defence budget trend (USDbn, constant 2015)
2008 – 2016 – 2023; 7.95; 4.58

Population	10,497,595					
Age	0–14	15–19	20–24	25–29	30–64	65 plus
Male	7.2%	2.9%	2.9%	2.8%	22.7%	10.3%
Female	6.8%	2.5%	2.5%	2.5%	23.9%	13.0%

Capabilities

Greece's National Military Strategy identifies safeguarding sovereignty and territorial integrity as principal defence objectives. The country also expects to employ the armed forces to support Cyprus in the event of a conflict there. Athens, in the Force Structure 2020–34 document, established a US-style Special Warfare Command with the ambition to create new units with a higher level of readiness. Greece is a NATO member and has led the EU's Balkan Battlegroup. In recent years, it signed defence-cooperation agreements with Cyprus, Egypt and Israel, and it is developing ties with the UAE and Saudi Arabia. The Mutual Defense Cooperation Agreement is the cornerstone of the close US–Greek defence relationship and provides for a naval-support facility and an airfield at Souda Bay in Crete. More recently, it grants the US access to northern Greek ports to reinforce NATO's eastern flank. The armed forces still contain conscripts, but most personnel are regulars and Athens is looking to move to a fully professional force. Training levels are good and focus on joint operations. Greek troop deployments generally involve limited numbers of personnel and focus on the near abroad, although the country contributes to EU, NATO and UN missions. Athens is acquiring *Rafale* combat aircraft and frigates from France as part of a new strategic partnership that includes a mutual-assistance clause. Defence spending cuts from 2010 to 2020 resulted in numerous modernisation efforts being cut or postponed, with the army the most affected and now requiring substantial investment. Greece's defence industry has suffered from a lack of investment, with several state-owned firms struggling to achieve profitability. A defence industrial strategy published in 2017 described a need to increase R&D spending and participate more in European programmes.

ACTIVE 132,200 (Army 93,500 Navy 16,700 Air 22,000) Gendarmerie & Paramilitary 7,400

Conscript liability 9 to 12 months

RESERVE 289,000 (Army 248,900 Navy 6,100 Air 34,000)

ORGANISATIONS BY SERVICE

Army 48,500; 45,000 conscripts (total 93,500)

FORCES BY ROLE

COMMAND
  2 corps HQ (incl NRDC-GR)
  1 armd div HQ
  3 mech inf div HQ
  1 inf div HQ

SPECIAL FORCES
  1 SF comd
  1 cdo/para bde

MANOEUVRE
  Reconnaissance
  4 recce bn
  Armoured
  4 armd bde (2 armd bn, 1 mech inf bn, 1 SP arty bn)
  Mechanised
  10 mech inf bde (1 armd bn, 2 mech bn, 1 SP arty bn)
  Light
  2 inf regt
  Air Manoeuvre
  1 air mob bde
  1 air aslt bde
  Amphibious
  1 mne bde

COMBAT SUPPORT
  2 MRL bn
  3 AD bn (2 with I-*Hawk*, 1 with *Tor* M1)
  3 engr regt
  2 engr bn
  1 EW regt
  10 sigs bn

COMBAT SERVICE SUPPORT
  1 log corps HQ
  1 log div (3 log bde)

HELICOPTER
  1 hel bde (1 hel regt with (2 atk hel bn), 2 tpt hel bn, 4 hel bn)

EQUIPMENT BY TYPE

ARMOURED FIGHTING VEHICLES
  MBT 1,228: 170 *Leopard* 2A6HEL; 183 *Leopard* 2A4; 500 *Leopard* 1A4/5; 375 M48A5

  IFV 169: 129 BMP-1; 40 *Marder* 1A3
  APC • APC (T) 2,107: 74 *Leonidas* Mk1/2; 1,846 M113A1/A2; 187 M577 (CP)
  AUV 686: 444 M1117 *Guardian*; 242 VBL

ENGINEERING & MAINTENANCE VEHICLES
  ARV 262: 12 *Büffel*; 43 BPz-2; 94 M88A1; 113 M578
  VLB 52: 34 M48/M60 AVLB; 10 *Biber*; 8 *Leopard* 1 with *Leguan*
  MW *Giant Viper*

ANTI-TANK/ANTI-INFRASTRUCTURE
  MSL
    SP 556: 195 HMMWV with 9K135 *Kornet*-E (RS-AT-14 *Spriggan*); 361 M901
    MANPATS 9K111 *Fagot* (RS-AT-4 *Spigot*); *Milan*; TOW
  RCL 687+: **84mm** *Carl Gustaf*; **90mm** EM-67; **SP 106mm** 687 M40A1

ARTILLERY 3,526
  SP 599: **155mm** 442: 418 M109A1B/A2/A3GEA1/A5; 24 PzH 2000; **175mm** 12 M107; **203mm** 145 M110A2
  TOWED 463: **105mm** 233: 214 M101; 19 M-56; **155mm** 230 M114
  MRL 144: **122mm** 108 RM-70; **227mm** 36 M270 MLRS
  MOR 2,320: **81mm** 1,700; **107mm** 620 M30 (incl 231 SP)

SURFACE-TO-SURFACE MISSILE LAUNCHERS
  SRBM • Conventional MGM-140A ATACMS (launched from M270 MLRS)

AIRCRAFT • TPT • Light 12: 1 Beech 200 *King Air* (C-12C) 2 Beech 200 *King Air* (C-12R/AP *Huron*); 9 Cessna 185 (U-17A/B) (liaison)

HELICOPTERS
  ATK 28: 19 AH-64A *Apache*; 9 AH-64D *Apache*
  MRH 60 OH-58D *Kiowa Warrior*
  TPT 128: **Heavy** 25: 19 CH-47D *Chinook*; 6 CH-47SD *Chinook*; **Medium** 14 NH90 TTH; **Light** 89: 74 Bell 205 (UH-1H *Iroquois*); 14 Bell 206 (AB-206) *Jet Ranger*; 1 Bell 212 (VIP)
  TRG 15 NH-300C

UNINHABITED AERIAL VEHICLES
  ISR • Medium 4 *Sperwer*

AIR-LAUNCHED MISSILES
  ASM AGM-114K/M *Hellfire* II

AIR DEFENCE
  SAM 155+
    Medium-range 42 MIM-23B I-*Hawk*
    Short-range 21 9K331 *Tor*-M1 (RS-SA-15 *Gauntlet*)
    Point-range 92+: 38 9K33 *Osa*-M (RS-SA-8B *Gecko*); 54 ASRAD HMMWV; FIM-92 *Stinger*
  GUNS • TOWED 727: **20mm** 204 Rh 202; **23mm** 523 ZU-23-2

National Guard 38,000 reservists

Internal security role

FORCES BY ROLE
MANOEUVRE

Light
1 inf div
Air Manoeuvre
1 para regt
COMBAT SUPPORT
8 arty bn
4 AD bn
HELICOPTER
1 hel bn

Navy 14,300; 2,400 conscript (total 16,700)
EQUIPMENT BY TYPE
SUBMARINES • SSK 10:
 3 *Poseidon* (GER Type-209/1200) with 8 single 533mm TT with SUT HWT
 1 *Poseidon* (GER Type-209/1200) (fitted with AIP technology) with 8 single 533mm TT with UGM-84C *Harpoon* Block 1B AShM/SUT HWT
 2 *Glavkos* (GER Type-209/1100) with 8 single 533mm TT with UGM-84C *Harpoon* Block 1B AShM/SUT HWT
 4 *Papanikolis* (GER Type-214) (fitted with AIP) with 8 single 533mm TT with UGM-84C *Harpoon* Block 1B AShM/SUT HWT
PRINCIPAL SURFACE COMBATANTS 13
 FRIGATES • FFGHM 13:
  2 *Elli* Batch I (NLD *Kortenaer* mod) with 2 quad lnchr with RGM-84C/G *Harpoon* Block 1B/G AShM, 1 octuple Mk 29 GMLS with RIM-7P *Sea Sparrow* SAM, 2 twin 324mm SVTT Mk 32 mod 9 ASTT with Mk 46 mod 5 LWT, 1 Mk 15 *Phalanx* CIWS, 1 76mm gun (capacity 2 Bell 212 (AB-212) hel or 1 S-70B *Seahawk* hel)
  7 *Elli* Batch II (ex-NLD *Kortenaer*) with 2 quad lnchr with RGM-84C/G *Harpoon* Block 1B/G AShM, 1 octuple Mk 29 GMLS with RIM-7P *Sea Sparrow* SAM, 2 twin 324mm SVTT Mk 32 mod 9 ASTT with Mk 46 mod 5 LWT, 1 Mk 15 *Phalanx* CIWS, 2 76mm gun (capacity 2 Bell 212 (AB-212) hel or 1 S-70B *Seahawk* hel)
  4 *Hydra* (GER MEKO 200) with 2 quad lnchr with RGM-84G *Harpoon* Block 1G AShM, 1 16-cell Mk 48 mod 2 VLS with RIM-162C ESSM SAM, 2 triple 324mm SVTT Mk 32 mod 5 ASTT with Mk 46 LWT, 2 Mk 15 *Phalanx* CIWS, 1 127mm gun (capacity 1 S-70B *Seahawk* ASW hel/*Alpha* 900 UAV)
PATROL AND COASTAL COMBATANTS 40
 PCGM 7 *Roussen* (*Super Vita*) with 2 quad lnchr with MM40 *Exocet* Block 3 AShM (of which 2 still fitted with Block 2), 1 21-cell Mk 49 GMLS with RIM-116 RAM SAM, 1 76mm gun
 PCFG 10:
  5 *Kavaloudis* (FRA *La Combattante* IIIB) with 2 twin lnchr with RGM-84C *Harpoon* Block 1B AShM, 2 single 533mm TT with SST-4 HWT, 2 76mm gun
  4 *Laskos* (FRA *La Combattante* III) with 2 twin lnchr with RGM-84C *Harpoon* Block 1B AShM, 2 single 533mm TT with SST-4 HWT, 2 76mm gun
  1 *Votsis* (ex-GER *Tiger*) with 2 twin lnchr with RGM-84C *Harpoon* AShM, 1 76mm gun
 PCF 1 *Votsis* (ex-GER *Tiger*) with 1 76mm gun
 PCO 8:
  2 *Armatolos* (DNK *Osprey*) with 1 76mm gun
  2 *Kasos* (DNK *Osprey* derivative) with 1 76mm gun
  4 *Machitis* with 1 76mm gun
 PBF 8: 4 *Aeolos* (ex-US Mk V FPB); 1 *Agenor*; 1 *Okyalos*; 2 ST60
 PB 6: 3 *Andromeda* (ex-NOR *Nasty*); 2 *Stamou*; 1 *Tolmi*
MINE WARFARE • MINE COUNTERMEASURES 3
 MHO 3: 1 *Evropi* (ex-UK *Hunt*); 2 *Evniki* (ex-US *Osprey*)
AMPHIBIOUS
 LANDING SHIPS • LST 5 *Chios* (capacity 4 LCVP; 300 troops) with 1 76mm gun, 1 hel landing platform
 LANDING CRAFT 13
  LCU 2
  LCA 7
  LCAC 4 *Kefallinia* (*Zubr*) with 2 AK630 CIWS (capacity either 3 MBT or 10 APC (T); 230 troops)
LOGISTICS AND SUPPORT 42
 ABU 1 *Thetis*
 AFD 4
 AFS 4 *Atlas* I
 AG 4: 2 *Pandora*; 2 *Karavogiannos*
 AGOR 1 *Naftilos*
 AGS 2: 1 *Stravon*; 1 *Pytheas*
 AOL 5: 1 *Ilissos*; 4 *Ouranos*
 AORH 1 *Prometheus* (ITA *Etna*) with 1 Mk 15 *Phalanx* CIWS
 AOR 1 *Axios* (ex-GER *Luneburg*)
 AP 6: 2 Type-520; 4 Other
 AWT 7: 2 *Kerkini*; 2 *Ouranos*; 3 *Prespa*
 AXL 1 *Kyknos*
 AXS 5
UNINHABITED MARITIME SYSTEMS
 UUV • MW *Pluto* Plus

Coastal Defence
EQUIPMENT BY TYPE
COASTAL DEFENCE • AShM 2 MM40 *Exocet*

Naval Aviation
FORCES BY ROLE
ANTI-SUBMARINE WARFARE
 1 div with S-70B *Seahawk*; Bell 212 (AB-212) ASW
EQUIPMENT BY TYPE
AIRCRAFT 1 combat capable
 ASW 1 P-3B *Orion* (4 P-3B *Orion* in store undergoing modernisation)
HELICOPTERS
 ASW 14: 3 Bell 212 (AB-212) ASW; 11 S-70B *Seahawk*
AIR-LAUNCHED MISSILES
 ASM AGM-114 *Hellfire*
 AShM AGM-119 *Penguin*

Air Force 18,800; 3,000 conscripts (total 21,800)

Tactical Air Force
FORCES BY ROLE
FIGHTER/GROUND ATTACK
1 sqn with F-4E *Phantom* II
3 sqn with F-16CG/DG Block 30/50 *Fighting Falcon*
2 sqn with F-16CG/DG Block 52+ *Fighting Falcon*
1 sqn with F-16CG/DG Block 52+ *Fighting Falcon*; F-16V(C/D) *Viper*
2 sqn with F-16C/D Block 52+ ADV *Fighting Falcon*
1 sqn with *Mirage* 2000-5EG/BG Mk2
1 sqn with *Rafale* B/C F-3R
AIRBORNE EARLY WARNING
1 sqn with EMB-145H *Erieye*
ISR UAV
1 sqn with *Heron* 1; *Pegasus* II
EQUIPMENT BY TYPE
AIRCRAFT 229 combat capable
FGA 229: 33 F-4E *Phantom* II; 69 F-16CG/DG Block 30/50 *Fighting Falcon*; 55 F-16CG/DG Block 52+; 20 F-16C/D Block 52+ ADV *Fighting Falcon*; 10 F-16V(C/D) *Viper*; 19 *Mirage* 2000-5EG Mk2; 5 *Mirage* 2000-5BG Mk2; 14 *Rafale* C F3-R; 4 *Rafale* B F3-R; (10 *Mirage* 2000EG in store)
AEW 4 EMB-145AEW (EMB-145H) *Erieye*
UNINHABITED AERIAL VEHICLES
ISR 4: **Heavy** 2 *Heron* 1 (leased); **Medium** 2 *Pegasus* II (up to 4 in store)
AIR-LAUNCHED MISSILES
AAM • IR AIM-9L/P *Sidewinder*; R-550 *Magic* 2; **IIR** IRIS-T; *Mica* IR; **ARH** AIM-120B/C AMRAAM; *Meteor*; *Mica* RF
ASM AGM-65A/B/G *Maverick*
LACM SCALP EG
AShM AM39 *Exocet*
ARM AGM-88 HARM
BOMBS
Electro-optical guided: GBU-8B HOBOS
Laser-guided: GBU-10/12/16 *Paveway* II; GBU-24 *Paveway* III; GBU-50 Enhanced *Paveway* II
INS/GPS-guided GBU-31 JDAM; AGM-154C JSOW

Air Defence
FORCES BY ROLE
AIR DEFENCE
6 sqn/bty with M901 *Patriot* PAC-2
2 sqn/bty with S-300PMU1 (RS-SA-20 *Gargoyle*)
12 bty with *Skyguard*/RIM-7 *Sparrow*/guns; *Crotale* NG/GR; *Tor-M1* (RS-SA-15 *Gauntlet*)
EQUIPMENT BY TYPE
AIR DEFENCE
SAM 81
Long-range 48: 36 M901 *Patriot* PAC-2; 12 S-300PMU1 (RS-SA-20 *Gargoyle*)
Short-range 33: 9 *Crotale* NG/GR; 4 9K331 *Tor*-M1 (RS-SA-15 *Gauntlet*); 20 RIM-7M *Sparrow* with *Skyguard*
GUNS 59: **20mm** some Rh-202; **30mm** 35+ Artemis-30; **35mm** 24 GDF-005 with *Skyguard*

Air Support Command
FORCES BY ROLE
SEARCH & RESCUE/TRANSPORT HELICOPTER
1 sqn with AS332C *Super Puma* (SAR/CSAR)
1 sqn with AW109; Bell 205A (AB-205A) (SAR); Bell 212 (AB-212 - VIP, tpt)
TRANSPORT
1 sqn with C-27J *Spartan*
1 sqn with C-130B/H *Hercules*
1 sqn with EMB-135BJ *Legacy*; ERJ-135LR; *Falcon* 7X; *Gulfstream* V
EQUIPMENT BY TYPE
AIRCRAFT
TPT 27: **Medium** 23: 8 C-27J *Spartan*; 5 C-130B *Hercules*; 10 C-130H *Hercules*; **Light** 2: 1 EMB-135BJ *Legacy*; 1 ERJ-135LR; **PAX** 2: 1 *Falcon* 7X (VIP); 1 *Gulfstream* V
HELICOPTERS
TPT 31: **Medium** 12 AS332C *Super Puma*; **Light** 19: 12 Bell 205A (AB-205A) (SAR); 4 Bell 212 (AB-212) (VIP, Tpt); 3 AW109

Air Training Command
FORCES BY ROLE
TRAINING
2 sqn with M-346; T-2C/E *Buckeye*
2 sqn with T-6A/B *Texan* II
1 sqn with P2002JF
EQUIPMENT BY TYPE
AIRCRAFT • TRG 70: 2 M-346; 12 P2002JF; 28 T-2C/E *Buckeye*; ε13 T-6A *Texan* II; ε15 T-6B *Texan* II

Gendarmerie & Paramilitary
Coast Guard and Customs 7,400
EQUIPMENT BY TYPE
PATROL AND COASTAL COMBATANTS 84
PCO 1 *Gavdos* (Damen 5009)
PCC 3 *Fournoi* (ISR *Sa'ar* 4.5 mod)
PBF 48: 1 *Arkoi* (UK Vosper Europatrol 250); 3 CB90; 4 *Marinos Zampatis* (ITA CNV P355); 40 Other
PB 32: 2 *Faiakas* (CRO POB 24); 30 Other
LOGISTICS AND SUPPORT • AG 4
AIRCRAFT • TPT • Light 7: 2 Cessna 172RG *Cutlass*; 3 F406 *Caravan* II; 2 TB-20 *Trinidad*
HELICOPTERS • MRH 6 AS365N3 (SAR role)
UNINHABITED AERIAL VEHICLES
ISR • Heavy 1 *Heron* 1 (leased)

DEPLOYMENT
BOSNIA-HERZEGOVINA: EU • EUFOR (Operation Althea) 7
BULGARIA: NATO • Enhanced Vigilance Activities 30; 1 AT pl with M901

CYPRUS: Army 950; 1 mech bde (1 armd bn, 2 mech inf bn, 1 arty bn); 61 M48A5 MOLF MBT; 80 *Leonidas* APC; 12 M114 arty; 6 M110A2 arty

IRAQ: NATO • NATO Mission Iraq 2

KOSOVO: NATO • KFOR 260; 1 inf bn HQ; 2 inf coy

LEBANON: UN • UNIFIL 110; 1 FFGHM

MALI: EU • EUTM Mali 2

MEDITERRANEAN SEA: EU • EUNAVFOR MED • *Operation Irini*; 190; 1 FFGHM

MOZAMBIQUE: EU • EUTM Mozambique 8

SAUDI ARABIA: Air Force 100; 1 SAM bty with M901 *Patriot* PAC-2

FOREIGN FORCES

United States US European Command: 600; 1 nhel bn with UH-60M/HH-60M *Black Hawk*; 1 ELINT flt with 1 EP-3E *Aries* II; 1 naval base at Makri; 1 naval base at Souda Bay; 1 air base at Iraklion

Hungary HUN

Hungarian Forint HUF		2022	2023	2024
GDP	HUF	66.6trn	72.3trn	78.4trn
	USD	180bn	204bn	222bn
per capita	USD	18,579	21,076	23,008
Growth	%	4.6	-0.3	3.1
Inflation	%	14.5	17.7	6.6
Def exp [a]	HUF	1.21trn	1.81trn	
	USD	3.28bn	5.11bn	
Def bdgt [b]	HUF	1.77trn	1.42trn	1.30trn
	USD	4.79bn	4.01bn	3.68bn
USD1=HUF		370.06	354.77	352.96

[a] NATO figure
[b] Includes military pensions

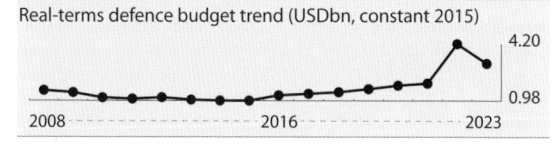

Real-terms defence budget trend (USDbn, constant 2015)
4.20
0.98
2008 – – – – – – – – – – – 2016 – – – – – – – – – – – 2023

Population 9,885,834

Age	0–14	15–19	20–24	25–29	30–64	65 plus
Male	7.7%	2.9%	2.8%	2.9%	23.9%	8.7%
Female	6.9%	2.5%	2.5%	2.7%	23.9%	12.7%

Capabilities

Hungary published a National Security Strategy in April 2020 and a National Military Strategy in June 2021. The documents reflect a deteriorating security environment, marked by great-power competition. The security strategy also characterises mass migration as a key concern for Hungary. Budapest is implementing the Zrinyi 2026 national-defence and armed-forces modernisation plan. A large majority of its units were renamed in 2023. Similar to other countries in the region, Hungary is establishing new territorial defence units. The country, in 2022, set up a Cyber- and Information Operations Centre and published a Military Cyberspace Operations Doctrine. Hungary coordinates policy, including on defence, with other member states of the Visegrád Group, and hosts the NATO Centre of Excellence for Military Medicine. The armed forces participate in international crisis-management missions, notably in the Balkans and Iraq, but have limited organic capacity to deploy forces beyond national borders. In 2023, the government announced its intention to deploy forces to Chad to help the government there deal with security challenges. Hungary's defence forces are modernising, with purchases such as NASAMS air defence systems and PzH 2000 artillery equipment. Hungary's defence-industrial base is limited but developing. In 2023, Rheinmetall opened a factory to build *Lynx* IFVs, for example. The defence ministry has set up an inter-ministerial working group to boost domestic capacity in the small-arms sector and ammunition.

ACTIVE 32,150 (Army 10,450 Air 5,750 Joint 15,950)

RESERVE 20,000

ORGANISATIONS BY SERVICE

Hungary's armed forces have reorganised into a joint force

Land Component 10,450 (incl riverine element)

FORCES BY ROLE
SPECIAL FORCES
  1 SF bde (4 spec ops bn)
MANOEUVRE
  Reconnaissance
    1 ISR regt
  Armoured
    1 (1st) armd inf bde (1 tk bn; 1 armd inf bn, 1 SP arty bn, 1 AT bn, 1 log bn)
  Mechanised
    1 (11th) mech inf bde (3 mech inf bn, 1 cbt engr coy, 1 sigs coy, 1 log bn)
COMBAT SUPPORT
  1 engr regt
  1 EOD/rvn regt
  1 CBRN bn
  1 sigs regt
COMBAT SERVICE SUPPORT
  1 log regt
EQUIPMENT BY TYPE
ARMOURED FIGHTING VEHICLES
  MBT 57: 12 *Leopard* 2A4HU; 1 *Leopard* 2A7HU; 44 T-72M1
  IFV 128: 120 BTR-80A/AM; 8+ KF41 *Lynx* (in test)
  APC 322
    APC (W) 260 BTR-80
    PPV 62: 50 *Ejder Yalcin* 4×4 (*Gidran*); 12 *MaxxPro Plus*
ENGINEERING & MAINTENANCE VEHICLES
  AEV 5 BAT-2
  ARV 10: 1 BPz-3 *Buffel*; 8 VT-55A; 1 *Wisent* 2

VLB 8 BLG-60; MTU; TMM
NBC VEHICLES 14 BTR-80M-NBC
ANTI-TANK/ANTI-INFRASTRUCTURE
  MSL • MANPATS 9K111 *Fagot* (RS-AT-4 *Spigot*); 9K111-1 *Konkurs* (RS-AT-5 *Spandrel*)
ARTILLERY 71
  SP 155mm 21+ PzH 2000
  MOR 82mm 50 M-37
PATROL AND COASTAL COMBATANTS • PBR 2
MINE COUNTERMEASURES • MSR 3 *Nestin*

Air Component 5,750

FORCES BY ROLE
FIGHTER/GROUND ATTACK
  1 sqn with *Gripen* C/D
TRANSPORT
  1 sqn with A319; *Falcon* 7X
TRAINING
  1 sqn with Z-143LSi; Z-242L; AS350 *Ecureuil*
ATTACK HELICOPTER
  1 sqn with Mi-24V/P *Hind* E/F
TRANSPORT HELICOPTER
  1 sqn with H145M; H225M
AIR DEFENCE
  1 SAM regt (9 bty with *Mistral*; 1 bty with 2K12 *Kub* (RS-SA-6 *Gainful*); 2 bty with NASAMS III)
  1 radar regt
EQUIPMENT BY TYPE
AIRCRAFT 14 combat capable
  FGA 14: 12 *Gripen* C; 2 *Gripen* D
  TPT • PAX 4: 2 A319; 2 *Falcon* 7X
  TRG 8: 2 Z-143LSi; 6 Z-242L
HELICOPTERS
  ATK 8: 6 Mi-24V *Hind* E; 2 Mi-24P *Hind* F
  MRH 20 H145M (incl 2 SAR)
  TPT 4: **Heavy** 2 H225M; **Light** 2 AS350 *Ecureuil*
AIR DEFENCE • SAM
  Medium-range 8 NASAMS III
  Short-range 16 2K12 *Kub* (RS-SA-6 *Gainful*)
  Point-defence *Mistral*
AIR-LAUNCHED MISSILES
  AAM • IR AIM-9 *Sidewinder*; **ARH** AIM-120C AMRAAM
  ASM AGM-65 *Maverick*; 3M11 *Falanga* (RS-AT-2 *Swatter*); 9K114 *Shturm*-V (RS-AT-6 *Spiral*)
BOMBS • Laser-guided *Paveway* II

DEPLOYMENT

BOSNIA-HERZEGOVINA: EU • *Operation Althea* 192; 1 inf coy
CYPRUS: UN • UNFICYP 11
IRAQ: *Operation Inherent Resolve* 133; **NATO •** NATO Mission Iraq 3
KOSOVO: NATO • KFOR 433; 1 inf bn HQ; 2 inf coy; **UN •** UNMIK 1
LEBANON: UN • UNIFIL 14
MALI: EU • EUTM Mali 20
WESTERN SAHARA: UN • MINURSO 7

FOREIGN FORCES

Croatia NATO Enhanced Vigilance Activities: 70
United States NATO Enhanced Vigilance Activities: 150; 1 armd inf coy

Iceland ISL

Icelandic Krona ISK		2022	2023	2024
GDP	ISK	3.80trn	4.15trn	4.39trn
	USD	28.1bn	30.6bn	34.1bn
per capita	USD	74,591	78,837	87,865
Growth	%	7.2	3.3	1.7
Inflation	%	8.3	8.6	4.5
Sy Bdgt [a]	ISK	5.56bn	5.58bn	6.70bn
	USD	41.1m	41.2m	52.2m
USD1=ISK		135.28	135.62	128.55

[a] Coast guard budget

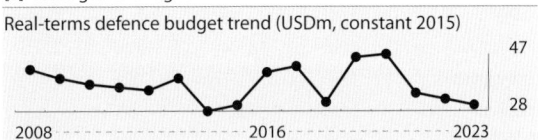

Real-terms defence budget trend (USDm, constant 2015)

Population	360,872					
Age	0–14	15–19	20–24	25–29	30–64	65 plus
Male	10.2%	3.2%	3.1%	3.4%	22.3%	7.9%
Female	9.8%	3.1%	3.1%	3.3%	21.8%	8.8%

Capabilities

Iceland is a NATO member but maintains only a coast guard service. In 2016, the country established a National Security Council to implement and monitor security policy. The coast guard controls the NATO Iceland Air Defence System, as well as a NATO Control and Reporting Centre that feeds into NATO air- and missile-defence and air-operations centres. Helsinki has raised concerns over increased Russian air and naval activities in the Atlantic and close to NATO airspace. Geographically, Iceland plays an important role in connecting Europe and North America with communication links via subsea cables. In 2022, Iceland published its National Cybersecurity Strategy, which outlines a five-year plan to strengthen and increase cooperation with private and public actors, locally and internationally. Iceland considers its bilateral defence agreement with the US to be an important pillar of its security policy and also participates in the security-policy dialogue of NORDEFCO. Iceland joined the UK-led Joint Expeditionary Force in 2021. Iceland hosts NATO and regional partners for exercises, transits and naval task groups, as well as a NATO Icelandic Air Policing mission. Despite there being no standing armed forces, Iceland makes financial contributions and, on occasion, deploys civilian personnel to NATO missions. Iceland hosts US Navy P-8A *Poseidon* maritime-patrol aircraft in a rotational deployment based at Keflavik air base.

ACTIVE NIL Gendarmerie & Paramilitary 250

ORGANISATIONS BY SERVICE

Gendarmerie & Paramilitary

Iceland Coast Guard 250
EQUIPMENT BY TYPE
PATROL AND COASTAL COMBATANTS 2
  PSO 2: 1 *Freyja*; 1 *Thor*
LOGISTICS AND SUPPORT • AGS 1 *Baldur*
AIRCRAFT • TPT • **Light** 1 DHC-8-300 (MP)
HELICOPTERS • TPT • **Medium** 3 H225 (leased)

FOREIGN FORCES

Icelandic Air Policing: Aircraft and personnel from various NATO members on a rotating basis

Ireland IRL

Euro EUR		2022	2023	2024
GDP	EUR	506bn	542bn	576bn
	USD	534bn	590bn	630bn
per capita	USD	103,311	112,248	117,979
Growth	%	9.4	2.0	3.3
Inflation	%	8.1	5.2	3.0
Def bdgt [a]	EUR	1.11bn	1.17bn	1.23bn
	USD	1.17bn	1.28bn	1.35bn
USD1=EUR		0.95	0.92	0.91

[a] Includes military pensions and capital expenditure

Real-terms defence budget trend (USDbn, constant 2015)
1.22
0.99
2008 — 2016 — 2023

Population   5,180,761

Age	0–14	15–19	20–24	25–29	30–64	65 plus
Male	9.7%	3.3%	3.0%	3.0%	23.2%	7.3%
Female	9.3%	3.2%	2.9%	2.9%	23.9%	8.2%

Capabilities

The core mission of Ireland's armed forces is to defend the state against armed aggression. Over recent years, Ireland has begun to take a more all-encompassing approach towards the national security risks its armed forces should be prepared to tackle, including cyberattacks, national disasters and terrorism. Ireland is active in EU defence cooperation and contributes to multinational operations. The country has begun a Strategic Defence Review to assess the threat landscape. It follows a series of changes sparked by a February 2022 report issued by a Commission on the Defence Forces that called for immediate enhancements to the armed forces and recommended a long-term vision beyond 2030. The government, in response, acted on some of the recommendations, particularly to address defence shortcomings and bolster the ability of the armed forces to participate in higher intensity peace support operations. The government pledged to increase defence spending and boost ranks by around 2,000 personnel. Dublin plans to create a Chief of Defence post and elevate the air corps and naval service to branches on par with the army. Ireland has also created an Office of Reserve Affairs intended to develop a regeneration plan for the Reserve Defence Force. It is pursuing limited capability upgrades. The country has a small defence industry specialising in areas such as drivetrain technologies for land systems.

ACTIVE 7,700 (Army 6,250 Navy 700 Air 750)

RESERVE 1,600 (Army 1,500 Navy 100)

ORGANISATIONS BY SERVICE

Army 6,250
FORCES BY ROLE
SPECIAL FORCES
  1 ranger coy
MANOEUVRE
  Reconnaissance
  1 armd recce sqn
  Mechanised
  1 mech inf coy
  Light
  1 inf bde (1 cav recce sqn, 4 inf bn, 1 arty regt (3 fd arty bty, 1 AD bty), 1 fd engr coy, 1 sigs coy, 1 MP coy, 1 tpt coy)
  1 inf bde (1 cav recce sqn, 3 inf bn, 1 arty regt (3 fd arty bty, 1 AD bty), 1 fd engr coy, 1 sigs coy, 1 MP coy, 1 tpt coy)
EQUIPMENT BY TYPE
ARMOURED FIGHTING VEHICLES
  RECCE 6 *Piranha* IIIH 30mm
  APC 101
    APC (W) 74: 56 *Piranha* III; 18 *Piranha* IIIH
    PPV 27 RG-32M
ANTI-TANK/ANTI-INFRASTURCTURE
  MSL • MANPATS FGM-148 *Javelin*
  RCL 84mm *Carl Gustaf*
ARTILLERY 131
  TOWED • **105mm** 23: 17 L118 Light Gun; 6 L119 Light Gun
  MOR 108: **81mm** 84 Brandt; **120mm** 24 Ruag M87
AIR DEFENCE
  SAM • **Point-defence** RBS-70

Reserves 1,500 reservists
FORCES BY ROLE
MANOEUVRE
  Reconnaissance
  1 (integrated) armd recce sqn
  2 (integrated) cav sqn
  Mechanised
  1 (integrated) mech inf coy

Light
  14 (integrated) inf coy
COMBAT SUPPORT
  4 (integrated) arty bty
  2 engr gp
  2 MP coy
  3 sigs coy
COMBAT SERVICE SUPPORT
  2 med det
  2 tpt coy

Naval Service 700
EQUIPMENT BY TYPE
PATROL AND COASTAL COMBATANTS 2
  PSO 2 *Samuel Beckett* (2 more in reserve) with 1 76mm gun (2 *Roisin* with 1 76mm gun in reserve of which 1 in refit)
LOGISTICS AND SUPPORT • **AXS** 2

Air Corps 750
2 ops wg; 2 spt wg; 1 trg wg; 1 comms and info sqn
FORCES BY ROLE
MARITIME PATROL
  1 sqn with C295 MPA
TRANSPORT
  1 sqn with Learjet 45; PC-12NG
TRAINING
  1 sqn with PC-9M
HELICOPTER
  1 sqn with AW139; H135
EQUIPMENT BY TYPE
AIRCRAFT
  MP 2 C295 MPA
  TPT • Light 5: 1 Learjet 45 (VIP); 4 PC-12NG
  TRG 8 PC-9M
HELICOPTERS:
  MRH 6 AW139
  TPT • Light 2 H135 (incl trg/medevac)

DEPLOYMENT
BOSNIA-HERZEGOVINA: EU • EUFOR (*Operation Althea*) 4
KOSOVO: NATO • KFOR 13
LEBANON: UN • UNIFIL 335; 1 mech inf bn(-)
MALI: EU • EUTM Mali 7
MIDDLE EAST: UN • UNTSO 13
SYRIA/ISRAEL: UN • UNDOF 135; 1 inf coy

Italy ITA

Euro EUR		2022	2023	2024
GDP	EUR	1.91trn	2.01trn	2.09trn
	USD	2.01trn	2.19trn	2.28trn
per capita	USD	34,085	37,146	38,926
Growth	%	3.7	0.7	0.7
Inflation	%	8.7	6.0	2.6
Def exp [a]	EUR	28.8bn	29.7bn	
	USD	30.3bn	32.3bn	
Def bdgt [b]	EUR	29.4bn	30.1bn	30.3bn
	USD	31.0bn	32.7bn	33.1bn
USD1=EUR		0.95	0.92	0.91

[a] NATO figure
[b] Includes military pensions

Real-terms defence budget trend (USDbn, constant 2015)
29.9
24.9
2008 — 2016 — 2023

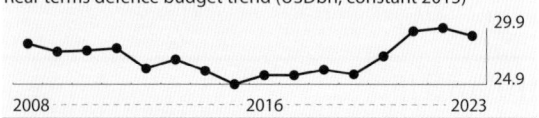

Population	61,021,855				
Age	0–14	15–19	20–24	25–29	30–64	65 plus
Male	6.2%	2.5%	2.4%	2.5%	24.4%	10.2%
Female	5.9%	2.4%	2.4%	2.6%	25.3%	13.1%

Capabilities

Italy is concerned by security challenges in the Euro-Atlantic area and those on Europe's southern borders. A defence plan for 2023–25 outlined modernisation goals. The Ministry of Defence is revising its organisational structure to improve functionality, developing a three-year investment law, and updating plans for personnel al numbers. It set up a new cadre of voluntary personnel with an initial three-year duty period and a new auxiliary reserve force. Italy adopted a defence space strategy, a new cyber strategy for the Ministry of Defence and a plan to address artificial intelligence threats. Italy has taken part in NATO's air-policing missions in the Baltic states, Iceland, Romania, Albania and Montenegro, is deployed to Latvia and Hungary as part of the Enhanced Forward Presence and is the framework nation for the battlegroup in Bulgaria. It has deployed the SAMP/T air defence system to Slovakia under the Enhanced Vigilance Activity framework. The EUNAVFOR-MED force is headquartered in Rome, while the US Navy's 6th Fleet is based in Naples. The country takes part in and hosts NATO and other multinational exercises and continues to support NATO, EU and UN operations abroad and is planning to increasingly focus on Europe's southern flank. By 2026, Rome intends to restructure the national intervention force and be able to deploy an autonomous limited joint force for high-intensity operations for six to eight months on a sub-regional scale. Italy has a fleet of medium transport aircraft and tankers to support overseas deployments, and it plans to procure fixed-wing aircraft to support special forces. The country is modernising military missions across domains. Rome is a partner with Japan and the UK on the Global Combat Air Programme to develop a next-generation fighter. The country takes part in European defence-industrial cooperation activities, including PESCO projects. Italy has an advanced defence industry capable of producing equipment across all domains, with particular strengths in ship, aircraft, and helicopter production.

ACTIVE 160,900 (Army 94,300 Navy 27,900 Air 38,700) Gendarmerie & Paramilitary 178,600

RESERVES 14,500

ORGANISATIONS BY SERVICE

Space
EQUIPMENT BY TYPE
SATELLITES 10
  COMMUNICATIONS 3: 1 *Athena-Fidus* (also used by FRA); 2 *Sicral*
  ISR 7: 4 *Cosmo* (*Skymed*); 2 *Cosmo* SG; 1 OPTSAT-3000

Army 94,300
Regt are bn sized
FORCES BY ROLE
COMMAND
  1 (NRDC-ITA) corps HQ (1 spt bde, 1 sigs regt, 1 spt regt)
  3 div HQ
MANOEUVRE
  Armoured
  1 (*Ariete*) armd bde (1 cav regt, 2 tk regt, 1 armd inf regt, 1 SP arty regt, 1 cbt engr regt, 1 log regt)
  1 (*Garibaldi Bersaglieri*) armd inf bde (1 cav regt, 1 tk regt, 2 armd inf regt, 1 SP arty regt, 1 cbt engr regt, 1 log regt)
  Mechanised
  1 (*Aosta*) mech bde (1 cav regt, 1 armd inf regt, 2 mech inf regt, 1 fd arty regt, 1 cbt engr regt, 1 log regt)
  1 (*Granatieri*) mech bde (1 cav regt, 2 mech inf regt)
  1 (*Pinerolo*) mech bde (1 cav regt, 3 armd inf regt, 1 fd arty regt, 1 cbt engr regt, 1 log regt)
  1 (*Sassari*) lt mech bde (1 armd inf regt, 2 mech inf regt, 1 cbt engr regt, 1 log regt)
  Mountain
  2 mtn bde (1 cav regt, 3 mtn inf regt, 1 arty regt, 1 mtn cbt engr regt, 1 spt bn, 1 log regt)
  Air Manoeuvre
  1 (*Folgore*) AB bde (1 cav regt, 3 para regt, 1 arty regt, 1 cbt engr regt, 1 log regt)
  1 (*Friuli*) air mob bde (1 air mob regt, 2 atk hel regt)
  Amphibious
  1 (*Pozzuolo del Friuli*) amph bde (1 cav regt, 1 amph regt, 1 arty regt, 1 cbt engr regt, 1 log regt);
COMBAT SUPPORT
  1 arty comd (1 arty regt, 1 MRL regt, 1 NBC regt)
  1 AD comd (3 SAM regt)
  1 engr comd (2 engr regt, 1 ptn br regt)
  1 EW/sigs comd (1 EW/ISR bde (1 CIMIC regt, 1 EW regt, 1 int regt, 1 STA regt); 1 sigs bde with (7 sigs regt))
COMBAT SERVICE SUPPORT
  1 log comd (3 log regt, 4 med unit)
HELICOPTER
  1 hel bde (3 hel regt)
EQUIPMENT BY TYPE
ARMOURED FIGHTING VEHICLES
  MBT 150: 147 C1 *Ariete*; 3 C2 *Ariete* AMV (in test)
  ASLT 263: 255 B1 *Centauro*; 8 *Centauro* II
  IFV 449: 165 VCC-80 *Dardo*; 284 VBM 8×8 *Freccia* (incl 20 CP and 60 with *Spike*-LR)
  APC 370
    APC (T) 138 Bv-206S
    APC (W) 199 *Puma* 6×6
    PPV 33 VTMM *Orso* (incl 16 amb)
  AUV 1,842: 10 *Cougar*; 1,798 IVECO LMV (incl 82 amb); 34 IVECO LMV 2
  AAV 15: 14 AAVP-7; 1 AAVC-7
ENGINEERING & MAINTENANCE VEHICLES
  AEV 25: 25 *Dachs*; M113
  ARV 74: 73 BPz-2; 1 AAVR-7
  VLB 30 *Biber*
  MW 43: 15 *Buffalo*; 3 *Miniflail*; 25 VTMM *Orso*
  NBC VEHICLES 14: 5 VBR NBC; 9 VBR NBC Plus
ANTI-TANK/ANTI-INFRASTRUCTURE
  MSL • MANPATS *Spike*
ARTILLERY 763
  SP 155mm 67 PzH 2000
  TOWED 167: **105mm** 25 Oto Melara Mod 56; **155mm** 142 FH-70
  MRL 227mm 21 M270 MLRS
  MOR 508: **81mm** 283 Expal; **120mm** 204: 62 Brandt; 142 RT-61 (RT-F1) **SP 120mm** 21 VBM 8×8 *Freccia*
AIRCRAFT • TPT • Light 6: 3 Do-228 (ACTL-1); 3 P.180 *Avanti*
HELICOPTERS
  ATK 33 AW129CBT *Mangusta*
  MRH 13 Bell 412 (AB-412) *Twin Huey*
  TPT 148: **Heavy** 16 CH-47F *Chinook*; **Medium** 60 NH90 TTH (UH-90A); **Light** 72: 2 AW169LUH (UH-169B); 29 Bell 205 (AB-205); 28 Bell 206 *Jet Ranger* (AB-206); 13 Bell 212 (AB-212)
AIR DEFENCE • SAM 16+
  Long-range 16 SAMP/T
  Point-defence FIM-92 *Stinger*
AIR-LAUNCHED MISSILES
  ASM *Spike*-ER

Navy 27,900
EQUIPMENT BY TYPE
SUBMARINES • SSK 8:
  4 *Pelosi* (imp *Sauro*, 3rd and 4th series) with 6 single 533mm TT with A184 mod 3 HWT
  4 *Salvatore Todaro* (Type-212A) (fitted with AIP) with 6 single 533mm TT with *Black Shark* HWT
PRINCIPAL SURFACE COMBATANTS 19
  AIRCRAFT CARRIERS • CVS 2:
    1 *Cavour* with 4 8-cell *Sylver* A43 VLS with *Aster* 15

SAM, 2 76mm guns (capacity mixed air group of 20 AV-8B *Harrier* II; F-35B *Lightning* II; AW101 *Merlin*; NH90; Bell 212)

1 *G. Garibaldi* with 2 octuple *Albatros* lnchr with *Aspide* SAM, 2 triple 324mm ASTT with Mk 46 LWT (capacity mixed air group of 18 AV-8B *Harrier* II; AW129CBT *Mangusta*; AW101 *Merlin*; NH90; Bell 212)

DESTROYERS • DDGHM 4:

2 *Andrea Doria* with 2 quad lnchr with *Otomat* (*Teseo*) Mk2A AShM, 6 8-cell *Sylver* A50 VLS with *Aster* 15/*Aster* 30 SAM, 2 single 324mm B-515 ASTT with MU90 LWT, 3 76mm guns (capacity 1 AW101 *Merlin*/NH90 hel)

2 *Luigi Durand de la Penne* (ex-*Animoso*) with 2 quad lnchr with *Otomat* (*Teseo*) Mk2A AShM/*Milas* A/S msl, 1 Mk 13 mod 4 GMLS with SM-1MR Block VI SAM, 1 octuple *Albatros* lnchr with *Aspide* SAM, 2 triple 324mm B-515 ASTT with Mk 46 LWT, 1 127mm gun, 3 76mm guns (capacity 1 NH90 or 2 Bell 212 (AB-212) hel)

FRIGATES 13

FFGHM 10:

4 *Bergamini* (GP) with 2 quad lnchr with *Otomat* (*Teseo*) Mk2A AShM, 2 8-cell *Sylver* A50 VLS with *Aster* 15/*Aster* 30 SAM, 2 triple 324mm B-515 ASTT with MU90 LWT, 1 127mm gun, 1 76mm gun (capacity 2 AW101/NH90 hel)

4 *Bergamini* (ASW) with 2 twin lnchr with *Otomat* (*Teseo*) Mk2A AShM, 2 twin lnchr with MILAS A/S msl, 2 8-cell *Sylver* A50 VLS with *Aster* 15/*Aster* 30 SAM, 2 triple 324mm B-515 ASTT with MU90 LWT, 2 76mm gun (capacity 2 AW101/NH90 hel)

2 *Maestrale* with 4 single lnchr with *Otomat* (*Teseo*) Mk2 AShM, 1 octuple *Albatros* lnchr with *Aspide* SAM, 2 triple 324mm SVTT Mk 32 ASTT with Mk 46 LWT, 1 127mm gun (capacity 1 NH90 or 2 Bell 212 (AB-212) hel)

FFHM 1 *Paolo Thaon di Revel* (PPA Light+) with 2 8-cell *Sylver* A50 VLS with *Aster* 30 SAM, 1 127mm gun, 1 76mm gun (capacity 2 NH90 or 1 AW101)

FFH 2 *Paolo Thaon di Revel* (PPA Light) with 1 127mm gun, 1 76mm gun (capacity 2 NH90 or 1 AW101)

PATROL AND COASTAL COMBATANTS 16

PSOH 10:

4 *Cassiopea* with 1 76mm gun (capacity 1 Bell 212 (AB-212) hel)

4 *Comandante Cigala Fuligosi* with 1 76mm gun (capacity 1 Bell 212 (AB-212)/NH90 hel)

2 *Sirio* (capacity 1 Bell 212 (AB-212) or NH90 hel)

PB 6: 2 *Angelo Cabrini*; 4 *Esploratore*

MINE WARFARE • MINE COUNTERMEASURES 10

MHO 10: 8 *Gaeta*; 2 *Lerici*

AMPHIBIOUS

PRINCIPAL AMPHIBIOUS SHIPS • LHD 3:

2 *San Giorgio* (capacity 3-4 AW101/NH90/Bell 212; 3 LCM; 2 LCVP; 30 trucks; 36 APC (T); 350 troops)

1 *San Giusto* with 1 76mm gun (capacity 2 AW101 *Merlin*/NH90/Bell 212/S-100; 3 LCM; 2 LCVP; 30 trucks; 36 APC (T); 350 troops)

LANDING CRAFT 28: 15 **LCVP**; 13 **LCM**

LOGISTICS AND SUPPORT 61

ABU 5 *Ponza*
AFD 7
AFDL 11
AGE 3: 1 *Leonardo* (coastal); 1 *Raffaele Rosseti*; 1 *Vincenzo Martellota*
AGI 1 *Elettra*
AGOR 1 *Alliance*
AGS 3: 1 *Ammiraglio Magnaghi* with 1 hel landing platform; 2 *Aretusa* (coastal)
AKL 6 *Gorgona*
AORH 2: 1 *Etna* with 1 76mm gun (capacity 1 AW101/NH90/Bell 212 hel); 1 *Vulcano* (capacity 2 AW101/NH90/Bell 212)
AOR 1 *Stromboli* with 1 76mm gun (capacity 1 AW101/NH90 hel)
AOL 4 *Panarea*
ARSH 1 *Anteo* (capacity 1 Bell 212 (AB-212) hel)
ATF 6 *Ciclope*
AWT 2 *Simeto*
AXS 8: 1 *Amerigo Vespucci*; 5 *Caroly*; 1 *Italia*; 1 *Palinuro*

UNINHABITED MARITIME SYSTEMS • UUV

DATA REMUS 1000
MW *Pluto* Gigas; *Pluto* Plus
UTL HUGIN 1000

Naval Aviation 2,000

FORCES BY ROLE

FIGHTER/GROUND ATTACK
1 sqn with AV-8B *Harrier* II; TAV-8B *Harrier* II; F-35B *Lightning* II

ANTI-SUBMARINE WARFARE/TRANSPORT
5 sqn with AW101 ASW *Merlin*; Bell 212 ASW (AB-212AS); Bell 212 (AB-212); NH90 NFH; S-100 *Camcopter*

MARITIME PATROL
1 flt with P-180

AIRBORNE EARLY WANRING & CONTROL
1 flt with AW101 AEW *Merlin*

EQUIPMENT BY TYPE

AIRCRAFT 14 combat capable
FGA 14: 9 AV-8B *Harrier* II; 1 TAV-8B *Harrier* II; 4 F-35B *Lightning* II
MP 3 P.180 *Avanti*

HELICOPTERS
ASW 62: 10 AW101 ASW *Merlin*; 6 Bell 212 ASW; 46 NH90 NFH (SH-90)
AEW 4 AW101 AEW *Merlin*
TPT • Medium 20: 10 AW101 *Merlin*; 10 NH90 MITT (MH-90)

UNINHABITED AERHIAL VEHICLES

ISR • Light 1 S-100 *Camcopter*

AIR-LAUNCHED MISSILES
AAM • **IR** AIM-9L *Sidewinder*; **ARH** AIM-120 AMRAAM
ASM AGM-65 *Maverick*
AShM Marte Mk 2/S

Marines 3,000
FORCES BY ROLE
MANOEUVRE
Amphibious
1 mne regt (1 recce coy, 2 mne bn, 1 log bn)
1 (boarding) mne regt (2 mne bn)
1 landing craft gp
Other
1 sy regt (3 sy bn)
EQUIPMENT BY TYPE
ARMOURED FIGHTING VEHICLES
AAV 17: 15 AAVP-7; 2 AAVC-7
AUV 70 IVECO LMV
ENGINEERING & MAINTENANCE VEHICLES
ARV 1 AAVR-7
ANTI-TANK/ANTI-INFRASTRUCTURE
MSL • **MANPATS** Spike
ARTILLERY
MOR 22: **81mm** 16 Expal; **120mm** 6 RT-61 (RT-F1)
AIR DEFENCE • **SAM** • **Point-defence** FIM-92 *Stinger*

Air Force 38,700
FORCES BY ROLE
FIGHTER
5 sqn with Eurofighter *Typhoon*
FIGHTER/GROUND ATTACK
1 sqn with F-35A *Lightning* II
1 sqn with F-35A/B *Lightning* II
GROUND ATTACK
1 sqn with *Tornado* IDS
1 (SEAD/EW) sqn with *Tornado* ECR
MARITIME PATROL
1 sqn (opcon Navy) with ATR-72MP (P-72A)
TANKER/TRANSPORT
1 sqn with KC-767A
COMBAT SEARCH & RESCUE
1 sqn with AB-212 ICO; AW101 SAR (HH-101A)
SEARCH & RESCUE
1 wg with AW139 (HH-139A)
TRANSPORT
2 (VIP) sqn with A319CJ; AW139 (VH-139A); *Falcon* 50; *Falcon* 900 *Easy*; *Falcon* 900EX
2 sqn with C-130J/C-130J-30/KC-130J *Hercules*
1 sqn with C-27J *Spartan*
1 (calibration) sqn with P-180 *Avanti*/Gulfstream G550 CAEW
TRAINING
1 OCU sqn with Eurofighter *Typhoon*
1 sqn with MB-339PAN (aerobatic team)
1 sqn with MD-500D/E (NH-500D/E)
1 sqn with MB-339A
1 sqn with M-346
1 sqn with SF-260EA; 3 P2006T (T-2006A)
1 hel sqn with AW101 SAR (HH-101A)
ISR UAV
1 sqn with MQ-9A *Reaper*
AIR DEFENCE
2 bty with *Spada*
EQUIPMENT BY TYPE
AIRCRAFT 192 combat capable
FTR 93 Eurofighter *Typhoon*
FGA 22: 20 F-35A *Lightning* II; 2 F-35B *Lightning* II
ATK 34 *Tornado* IDS
ATK/EW 15 *Tornado* ECR*
MP 4 ATR-72MP (P-72A)
SIGINT 1 Beech 350 *King Air*
AEW&C 3 Gulfstream G550 CAEW
TKR/TPT 4 KC-767A
TPT 76: **Medium** 33: 11 C-130J *Hercules* (5+ KC-130J tanker pods); 10 C-130J-30 *Hercules*; 12 C-27J *Spartan*; **Light** 35: 17 P-180 *Avanti*; 18 S-208 (liaison); **PAX** 8: 3 A319CJ; 2 *Falcon* 50 (VIP); 2 *Falcon* 900 *Easy*; 1 *Falcon* 900EX (VIP)
TRG 114: 21 MB-339A; 28 MB-339CD*; 15 MB-339PAN (aerobatics); 2+ M-345; 22 M-346; 26 SF-260EA
HELICOPTERS
MRH 54: 13 AW139 (HH-139A/VH-139A); 2 MD-500D (NH-500D); 39 MD-500E (NH-500E)
CSAR 12 AW101 (HH-101A)
SAR 17 AW139 (HH-139B)
UNINHABITED AERIAL VEHICLES 6
CISR • **Heavy** 6 MQ-9A *Reaper* (unarmed)
AIR DEFENCE • **SAM** • **Short-range** SPADA
AIR-LAUNCHED MISSILES
AAM • **IR** AIM-9L *Sidewinder*; **IIR** IRIS-T; **ARH** AIM-120C AMRAAM; *Meteor*
ARM AGM-88C HARM; AGM-88E AARGM
LACM SCALP EG/*Storm Shadow*
BOMBS
Laser-guided GBU-16 *Paveway* II; *Lizard* 2
Laser & INS/GPS-guided GBU-48 Enhanced *Paveway* II; GBU-54 Laser JDAM
INS/GPS-guided GBU-31/-32/-38 JDAM; GBU-39 Small Diameter Bomb

Joint Special Forces Command (COFS)
Army
FORCES BY ROLE
SPECIAL FORCES
1 SF regt (9th *Assalto paracadutisti*)
1 STA regt

1 ranger regt (4th *Alpini paracadutisti*)
COMBAT SUPPORT
  1 psyops regt
TRANSPORT HELICOPTER
  1 spec ops hel regt

Navy (COMSUBIN)
FORCES BY ROLE
SPECIAL FORCES
  1 SF gp (GOI)
  1 diving gp (GOS)

Air Force
FORCES BY ROLE
SPECIAL FORCES
  1 wg (sqn) (17th *Stormo Incursori*)

Paramilitary

Carabinieri
FORCES BY ROLE
SPECIAL FORCES
  1 spec ops gp (GIS)

Gendarmerie & Paramilitary 178,600

Carabinieri 110,500
The Carabinieri are organisationally under the MoD. They are a separate service in the Italian Armed Forces as well as a police force with judicial competence

Mobile and Specialised Branch
FORCES BY ROLE
MANOEUVRE
  Other
    1 (mobile) paramilitary div (1 bde (1st) with (1 horsed cav regt, 11 mobile bn); 1 bde (2nd) with (1 (1st) AB regt, 2 (7th & 13th) mobile regt))
HELICOPTER
  1 hel gp
EQUIPMENT BY TYPE
ARMOURED FIGHTING VEHICLES
  APC • **APC (T)** 3 VCC-2
  AUV 30 IVECO LMV
AIRCRAFT • **TPT** • **Light:** 2 P.180 *Avanti*
HELICOPTERS
  MRH 15 Bell 412 (AB-412)
  TPT • **Light** 31: 19 AW109; 2 AW109E; 2 AW139; 8 MD-500D (NH-500D)

Customs 68,100
(Servizio Navale Guardia Di Finanza)
EQUIPMENT BY TYPE
PATROL AND COASTAL COMBATANTS 207
  PCO 3: 1 *Bandiera* (Damen Stan Patrol 5509 mod); 2 *Monti* (Damen Stan Patrol 5509)
  PCF 1 *Antonio Zara*
  PBF 178: 19 *Bigliani*; 3 *Corrubia*; 9 *Mazzei*; 1 *Tenente Petrucci*; 29 V-800; 5 V-1600; 77 V-2000; 8 V-3000; 11 V-5000; 4 V-6000; 12 V-7000
  PB 25: 23 *Buratti*; 2 GL1400
LOGISTICS AND SUPPORT 2
  AX 1 *Giorgio Cini*
  AXS 1 *Grifone*
AIRCRAFT
  MP 8: 4 ATR-42-500MP; 4 ATR-72-600 (P-72B)
  TPT • **Light** 2 P.180 *Avanti*
HELICOPTERS
  TPT • **Light** 54: 10 AW109N; 17 AW139; 7 AW169M; 8 Bell 412HP *Twin Huey*; 4 MD-500MC (NH-500MC); 8 MD-500MD (NH-500MD)

DEPLOYMENT

BALTIC SEA: NATO • SNMG 2: 200; 1 FFGHM

BOSNIA-HERZEGOVINA: EU • EUFOR (*Operation Althea*) 195; 1 ISR coy

BULGARIA: NATO • Enhanced Vigilance Activities 750; 1 mech inf BG with *Centauro* B1; VBM *Freccia* 8×8; IVECO LMV; PzH 2000

DJIBOUTI: 92

EGYPT: MFO 75; 3 PB

GULF OF ADEN & INDIAN OCEAN: EU • *Operation Atalanta* 380; 1 DDGHM

GULF OF GUINEA: Navy 190; 1 FFGHM

INDIA/PAKISTAN: UN • UNMOGIP 2

IRAQ: *Operation Inherent Resolve* (*Prima Parthica*) 900; 1 inf regt; 1 trg unit; 1 hel sqn with 3 NH90; **NATO** • NATO Mission Iraq 60

KOSOVO: NATO • KFOR 873; 1 armd inf BG HQ; 1 inf coy; 1 ISR bn HQ; 1 Carabinieri unit

KUWAIT: *Operation Inherent Resolve* (*Prima Parthica*) 417; 4 Eurofighter *Typhoon*; 2 MQ-9A *Reaper*; 1 C-27J *Spartan*; 1 KC-767A; 1 SAM bty with SAMP/T

LATVIA: NATO • Enhanced Forward Presence (*Baltic Guardian*) 370; 1 armd inf coy with C1 *Ariete*; VCC-80 *Dardo*

LEBANON: MIBIL 22; **UN** • UNIFIL 961; 1 mech bde HQ; 1 mech inf bn; 1 MP coy; 1 sigs coy; 1 hel sqn

LIBYA: MIASIT 160; 1 inf coy; 1 CRBN unit; 1 trg unit

LITHUANIA: NATO • Baltic Air Policing: 200; 4 Eurofighter *Typhoon*

MEDITERRANEAN SEA: EU • EUNAVFOR MED • *Operation Irini*; 220; 1 FFGHM; **NATO** • SNMG 2: 200; 1 FFGHM; **NATO** • SNMCMG 2: 180; 1 MHO; 1 AORL

MOZAMBIQUE: EU • EUTM Mozambique 7

PERSIAN GULF: EMASOH 150; 1 FFGHM

POLAND: NATO • Baltic Air Policing: 200; 4 F-35A *Lightning* II

SLOVAKIA: NATO • 1 SAM bty with SAMP/T

SOMALIA: EU • EUTM Somalia 169

WESTERN SAHARA: UN • MINURSO 2

FOREIGN FORCES

United States US European Command: 13,050
Army 4,250; 1 AB bde(-)
Navy 3,600; 1 HQ (US Naval Forces Europe-Africa (NAVEUR-NAVAF)/6th Fleet) at Naples; 1 ASW Sqn with 5 P-8A *Poseidon* at Sigonella
USAF 4,800; 1 FGA wg with (2 FGA sqn with 21 F-16C/D *Fighting Falcon* at Aviano; 1 CSAR sqn with 8 HH-60G *Pave Hawk*); 1 CISR UAV sqn with MQ-9A *Reaper* at Sigonella; 1 ISR UAV flt with RQ-4B *Global Hawk* at Sigonella
USMC 400; 1 tpt sqn with 6 MV-22B *Osprey*; 2 KC-130J *Hercules*

Latvia LVA

Euro EUR		2022	2023	2024
GDP	EUR	39.1bn	42.9bn	46.0bn
	USD	41.2bn	46.7bn	50.4bn
per capita	USD	21,947	24,929	26,952
Growth	%	2.8	0.5	2.6
Inflation	%	17.2	9.9	4.2
Def exp [a]	EUR	813m	967m	
	USD	857m	1.10bn	
Def bdgt [b]	EUR	813m	967m	1.11bn
	USD	857m	1.05bn	1.21bn
FMA (US)	USD	75.0m	9.80m	9.80m
USD1=EUR		0.95	0.92	0.91

[a] NATO figure
[b] Includes military pensions

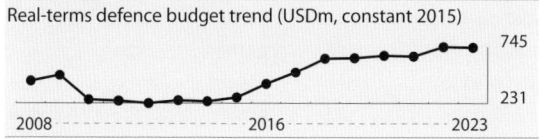

Real-terms defence budget trend (USDm, constant 2015)
745
231
2008 — 2016 — 2023

Population	1,821,750				
Age	0–14	15–19	20–24	25–29	30–64	65 plus
Male	7.7%	2.7%	2.3%	2.4%	24.0%	7.4%
Female	7.2%	2.5%	2.2%	2.2%	25.1%	14.3%

Capabilities

Latvia has small armed forces focused on maintaining national sovereignty and territorial integrity. The Baltic state relies on NATO membership for security guarantees. Russia is Latvia's overriding security concern. In the wake of the February 2022 invasion of Ukraine, Latvia boosted defence spending and transferred military equipment to Ukraine. A State Defence Service law took effect in April 2023, with two intakes of conscripts planned annually. Under the law, males between 18–27 are obligated to serve, with women serving voluntarily. Conscripts must serve either 11 months in the military, five years of National Guard or complete a reserve officer programme. The September 2023 National Security Concept emphasised societal resilience and comprehensive defence as well as the importance of border protection. Latvia plans to increase the size of the armed forces significantly. NATO has a battlegroup based in Latvia, present since 2017, as part of the Alliance's Enhanced Forward Presence that was bolstered in 2022. Latvia is also a member of the UK-led Joint Expeditionary Force. There is no capacity to independently deploy and sustain forces beyond national boundaries, although the armed forces have taken part in NATO and EU missions. Improvements are being made to logistics and procurement systems. A National Cyber Security Centre was set up under the Ministry of Defence and the country published a cybersecurity strategy in 2023. Latvia has recently recapitalised its artillery capability with second-hand howitzers from Austria and is acquiring medium-range air defences jointly with Estonia. Other procurements are also underway. Latvia has only a niche defence-industrial capability, with cyber security a focus.

ACTIVE 6,600 (Army 1,500 Navy 500 Air 500 Joint Staff 2,400 National Guard 1,400 Other 300)

Conscript liability 11 months, 18–27 years

RESERVE 16,000 (National Guard 10,000 Other 6,000)

ORGANISATIONS BY SERVICE

Joint 2,400
FORCES BY ROLE
SPECIAL FORCES
  1 SF unit
COMBAT SUPPORT
  1 MP bn

Army 1,500
FORCES BY ROLE
MANOEUVRE
  Mechanised
  1 mech inf bde (2 mech inf bn, 1 SP arty bn, 1 cbt spt bn (1 recce coy, 1 engr coy, 1 AD coy), 1 CSS bn HQ)

National Guard 1,400; 10,000 part-time (11,400 total)
FORCES BY ROLE
MANOEUVRE
  Light
  1 (2nd) inf bde (3 inf bn; 3 spt bn, 1 engr coy, 1 med coy)
  3 (1st, 3rd & 4th) inf bde (3 inf bn; 2 spt bn, 1 engr coy, 1 med coy)
COMBAT SUPPORT
  1 cyber unit
  1 NBC coy
  1 psyops pl
EQUIPMENT BY TYPE
ARMOURED FIGHTING VEHICLES
  RECCE 170 FV107 *Scimitar* (incl variants)
  APC • APC(W) 34 XA-300
ANTI-TANK/ANTI-INFRASTRUCTURE
  MANPATS *Spike*-LR
  RCL 84mm *Carl Gustaf*; **90mm** Pvpj 1110
ARTILLERY 112

SP 155mm 59 M109A5ÖE
TOWED 100mm (23 K-53 in store)
MOR 53: 81mm 28 L16; **120mm** 25 M120

Navy 500 (incl Coast Guard)

Naval Forces Flotilla separated into an MCM squadron and a patrol-boat squadron. LVA, EST and LTU have set up a joint naval unit, BALTRON, with bases at Liepaja, Riga, Ventspils (LVA), Tallinn (EST), Klaipeda (LTU). Each nation contributes 1–2 MCMVs

EQUIPMENT BY TYPE
PATROL AND COASTAL COMBATANTS 5
  PB 5 *Skrunda* (GER *Swath*)
MINE WARFARE • MINE COUNTERMEASURES 4
  MCCS 1 *Vidar* (ex-NOR)
  MHO 3 *Imanta* (ex-NLD *Alkmaar/Tripartite*)
LOGISTICS AND SUPPORT • AXL 1 *Varonis* (comd and spt ship, ex-NLD)
UNINHABITED MARITIME SYSTEMS
  UUV • MW A18-M

Coast Guard
Under command of the Latvian Naval Forces
EQUIPMENT BY TYPE
PATROL AND COASTAL COMBATANTS 6
  PB 6: 1 *Astra*; 5 KBV 236 (ex-SWE)

Air Force 500

Main tasks are airspace control and defence, maritime and land SAR and air transportation

FORCES BY ROLE
TRANSPORT
  1 (mixed) tpt sqn with An-2 *Colt*; UH-60M *Black Hawk*
AIR DEFENCE
  1 AD bn
  1 radar sqn (radar/air ctrl)
AIRCRAFT
  TPT • Light 4 An-2 *Colt*
  TRG 2 *Tarragon*
HELICOPTERS
  TPT • Medium 2 UH-60M *Black Hawk*
AIR DEFENCE
  SAM • Point-defence RBS-70
  GUNS • TOWED 40mm 24 L/70

Gendarmerie & Paramilitary

State Border Guard
EQUIPMENT BY TYPE
PATROL AND COASTAL COMBATANTS 3
  PB 3: 1 *Valpas* (ex-FIN); 1 *Tiira* (ex-FIN); 1 *Randa*
HELICOPTERS
  TPT • Light 6: 2 AW109E *Power*; 2 AW119Kx; 2 Bell 206B (AB-206B) *Jet Ranger* II

DEPLOYMENT

IRAQ: *Operation Inherent Resolve* 1; **NATO** • NATO Mission Iraq 2
KOSOVO: NATO • KFOR 136; 1 inf coy
MIDDLE EAST: UN • UNTSO 1

FOREIGN FORCES

All NATO Enhanced Forward Presence/Enhanced Vigilance Activities unless stated
Albania 21; 1 EOD pl
Canada 1,000; 1 mech inf bn HQ; 1 mech inf BG, 1 tk sqn
Czech Republic 70; 1 engr plt
Italy 370; 1 armd inf coy
Macedonia, North 9
Montenegro 11
Poland 200; 1 tk coy
Slovakia 130; 1 arty bty
Slovenia 42; 1 arty bty
Spain 600; 1 armd inf coy(+); 1 arty bty; 1 cbt engr coy; 1 SAM bty

Lithuania LTU

Euro EUR		2022	2023	2024
GDP	EUR	66.8bn	73.0bn	78.6bn
	USD	70.4bn	79.4bn	86.0bn
per capita	USD	24,989	28,482	31,119
Growth	%	1.9	-0.2	2.7
Inflation	%	18.9	9.3	3.9
Def exp [a]	EUR	1.60bn	1.87bn	
	USD	1.74bn	2.04bn	
Def bdgt [b]	EUR	1.50bn	1.87bn	1.96bn
	USD	1.58bn	2.04bn	2.14bn
FMA (US)	USD	75.0m	9.75m	9.75m
USD1=EUR		0.95	0.92	0.91

[a] NATO figure
[b] Includes military pensions

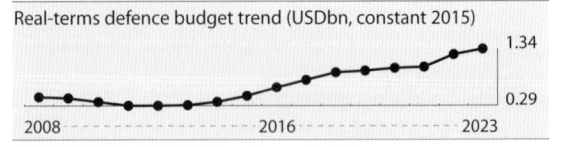

Real-terms defence budget trend (USDbn, constant 2015)
1.34 / 0.29 / 2008 — 2016 — 2023

Population 2,655,755

Age	0–14	15–19	20–24	25–29	30–64	65 plus
Male	7.9%	2.5%	2.6%	2.9%	22.9%	7.4%
Female	7.4%	2.4%	2.4%	2.6%	24.8%	14.2%

Capabilities

Lithuania's armed forces are focused on maintaining sovereignty and territorial integrity, though the country relies on its NATO membership for its security. Like the other Baltic states, it benefits from NATO's air policing deployment for a combat-aircraft capacity. The country adopted a new National Security Strategy in December 2021, which reflected the worsening regional security environment. Russia is the country's predominant security concern, a focus sharpened by Russia's 2022 invasion of Ukraine. Lithuanian authorities have signalled they will increase defence spending and are reviewing the 10-year National Defence System Development Programme, first adopted by parliament in 2018. Lithuania has transferred some military equipment to Ukraine and has also repaired combat-damaged equipment. Vilnius wants to improve readiness and the mobilisation system is being reformed. In mid-2022, the government raised the upper limit for conscript numbers. The number of reservists called to annual exercises is also going up. Lithuania has a limited medium-airlift capability for use in supporting its forces on multinational deployed operations. It takes part in NATO and EU operations. The government plans widespread improvements to its defence infrastructure. The country joined the German-led European Sky Shield initiative to boost air defence capability. Vilnius is upgrading other parts of its defensive capacity, including the purchase of CAESAR artillery systems. In early 2023, the head of the armed forces announced plans to transform a mechanised infantry battalion into a tank battalion. NATO, in 2022, bolstered the battlegroup based in Lithuania, which has been present since 2017 as part of the Alliance's Enhanced Forward Presence. Lithuania is a member of the UK-led Joint Expeditionary Force. Germany announced that it would permanently deploy a brigade in the country. A Regional Cyber Defence Centre was set up in 2021 and a cyber range opened in 2022, both coming under the National Cyber Security Centre, itself under the defence ministry. The Roadmap for the Development of Lithuania's Defence and Security Industry 2023–2027 seeks to help the country's small defence industry access new sources of funding.

ACTIVE 25,300 (Army 16,100 Navy 800 Air 1,700 Other 6,700) Gendarmerie & Paramilitary 18,400

Conscript liability 9 months, 18–23 years

RESERVE 7,100 (Army 7,100)

ORGANISATIONS BY SERVICE

Army 10,250; 5,850 active reserves (total 16,100)
FORCES BY ROLE
MANOEUVRE
 Mechanised
  1 (1st) mech bde (4 mech inf bn, 1 arty bn, 1 log bn)
 Light
  1 (2nd) mot inf bde (3 mot inf bn, 1 arty bn)
COMBAT SUPPORT
 1 engr bn
COMBAT SERVICE SUPPORT
 1 trg regt
EQUIPMENT BY TYPE
ARMOURED FIGHTING VEHICLES
 IFV 89 *Boxer* (*Vilkas*) (incl 2 trg)
 APC • APC (T) 236: 214 M113A1; 22 M577 (CP)
 AUV 200 JLTV
ENGINEERING & MAINTENANCE VEHICLES
 AEV 8 MT-LB AEV
 ARV 6: 2 BPz-2; 4 M113
ANTI-TANK/ANTI-INFRASTRUCTURE
 MSL
  SP 10 M1025A2 HMMWV with FGM-148 *Javelin*
  MANPATS FGM-148 *Javelin*
 RCL 84mm *Carl Gustaf*
ARTILLERY 108
 SP 16 PzH 2000
 TOWED 105mm 18 M101
 MOR 74: **120mm** 42: 20 2B11; 22 M/41D; **SP 120mm** 32 M113 with Tampella
AIR DEFENCE • SAM • Point-defence *Grom*

Reserves

National Defence Voluntary Forces 5,850 active reservists
FORCES BY ROLE
MANOEUVRE
 Other
  6 (territorial) def unit

Navy 800
LVA, EST and LTU established a joint naval unit, BALTRON, with bases at Liepaja, Riga, Ventpils (LVA), Tallinn (EST), Klaipeda (LTU).
EQUIPMENT BY TYPE
PATROL AND COASTAL COMBATANTS 4
 PCC 4 *Zemaitis* (ex-DNK *Flyvefisken*) with 1 76mm gun
MINE WARFARE • MINE COUNTERMEASURES 3
 MHC 2 *Skalvis* (ex-UK *Hunt*)
 MCCS 1 *Jotvingis* (ex-NOR *Vidar*)
LOGISTICS AND SUPPORT • AAR 1 *Šakiai*
UNINHABITED MARITIME SYSTEMS
 UUV • MW *K-Ster* C/I; PAP Mk6

Air Force 1,700
FORCES BY ROLE
AIR DEFENCE
 1 AD bn
EQUIPMENT BY TYPE
AIRCRAFT
 TPT 6: **Medium** 3 C-27J *Spartan*; **Light** 3: 1 Cessna 172RG; 2 L-410 *Turbolet*
HELICOPTERS
 MRH 3 AS365M3 *Dauphin* (SAR)
 TPT • Medium 3 Mi-8 *Hip* (tpt/SAR)
AIR DEFENCE • SAM 6+
 Medium-range 6 NASAMS III
 Point-defence FIM-92 *Stinger*; RBS-70

Special Operation Force

FORCES BY ROLE
SPECIAL FORCES
1 SF gp (1 CT unit; 1 Jaeger bn, 1 cbt diver unit)

Logistics Support Command 1,800

FORCES BY ROLE
COMBAT SERVICE SUPPORT
1 log bn

Training and Doctrine Command 1,800

FORCES BY ROLE
COMBAT SERVICE SUPPORT
1 trg regt

Other Units 3,100

FORCES BY ROLE
COMBAT SUPPORT
1 MP bn

Gendarmerie & Paramilitary 18,400

Riflemen Union 14,250

State Border Guard Service 4,150
Ministry of Interior
EQUIPMENT BY TYPE
PATROL AND COASTAL COMBATANTS • PB 3: 1 *Gintaras Zagunis*; 1 KBV 041 (ex-SWE); 1 *Barauskas* (Baltic Patrol 2700)
AMPHIBIOUS • LANDING CRAFT • UCAC 2 *Christina* (*Griffon* 2000)
HELICOPTERS • TPT • Light 5: 1 BK-117 (SAR); 2 H120 *Colibri*; 2 H135

DEPLOYMENT

CENTRAL AFRICAN REPUBLIC: EU • EUTM RCA 1
IRAQ: NATO • NATO Mission Iraq 30
KOSOVO: NATO • KFOR 1
MALI: EU • EUTM Mali 1
MOZAMBIQUE: EU • EUTM Mozambique 2
UNITED KINGDOM: Operation Interflex 15 (UKR trg)

FOREIGN FORCES

All NATO Enhanced Forward Presence unless stated
Belgium 250; 1 mech inf coy
Croatia 200; 1 mech inf coy
Czech Republic 135; 1 AD unit; 1 CBRN unit
Germany 1,000; 1 mech inf bde HQ; 1 armd inf bn(+)
Italy NATO Baltic Air Policing: 200; 4 Eurofighter *Typhoon*
Luxembourg 6
Netherlands 250; 1 armd inf coy
Norway 150; 1 armd inf coy(+)
United States US European Command: 250; 1 radar unit

Luxembourg LUX

Euro EUR		2022	2023	2024
GDP	EUR	77.5bn	81.9bn	86.0bn
	USD	81.7bn	89.1bn	94.0bn
per capita	USD	126,598	135,605	140,308
Growth	%	1.4	-0.4	1.5
Inflation	%	8.1	3.2	3.3
Def exp [a]	EUR	485m	573m	
	USD	511m	624bn	
Def bdgt	EUR	420m	1.09bn	
	USD	443m	1.19bn	
USD1=EUR		0.95	0.92	0.91

[a] NATO figure

Real-terms defence budget trend (USDm, constant 2015)
954
154
2008 — 2016 — 2023

Population	660,924					
Age	0–14	15–19	20–24	25–29	30–64	65 plus
Male	8.6%	2.8%	3.0%	3.6%	25.2%	7.3%
Female	8.1%	2.6%	2.9%	3.4%	23.8%	8.6%

Capabilities

Luxembourg maintains a limited military capability to participate in European collective security and crisis management, primarily focused on providing reconnaissance capability to NATO. The 'Defence Guidelines for 2035 and Beyond,' published in 2023, identify the creation of a joint medium combat reconnaissance battalion with Belgium by 2030 as the centre of this plan. Defence spending is to rise to 1% of GDP by 2028, and acquisition priorities in this timeframe include ISR, air transport and surveillance, cyber defence and uninhabited capabilities. There are plans to improve space situational awareness, SATCOM and Earth observation capabilities. In 2022, Luxembourg joined the NATO Cooperative Cyber Defence Centre of Excellence. Luxembourg has contributed troops to NATO's Enhanced Forward Presence. It is part of the European Multi-Role Tanker Transport Fleet programme, in which it partially funds one A330 MRTT. It has contributed its A400M to an airlift squadron formed jointly with Belgium. The Belgian and Dutch air forces are responsible for policing Luxembourg's airspace. Sustaining the army's personnel strength depends on better recruiting and retention. The country has a small but advanced space industry, but the country is largely reliant on imports. The defence guidelines call for the development of a defence industry, innovation and research strategy.

ACTIVE 900 (Army 900) **Gendarmerie & Paramilitary 600**

ORGANISATIONS BY SERVICE

Space
EQUIPMENT BY TYPE

SATELLITES • COMMUNICATIONS 1 *Govsat-1*

Army 900
FORCES BY ROLE
MANOEUVRE
  Reconnaissance
  2 recce coy (1 to Eurocorps/BEL div, 1 to NATO pool of deployable forces)
EQUIPMENT BY TYPE
ARMOURED FIGHTING VEHICLES
  AUV 48 *Dingo 2*
ANTI-TANK/ANTI-INFRASTRUCTURE
  MSL • MANPATS NLAW; TOW
ARTILLERY • MOR 81mm 6+
AIRCRAFT • TPT • **Heavy** 1 A400M
HELICOPTERS • MRH 2 H145M (jointly operated with Police)

Gendarmerie & Paramilitary 600
  Gendarmerie 600

DEPLOYMENT

LITHUANIA: NATO • *Enhanced Forward Presence* 6
ROMANIA: NATO • *Enhanced Vigilance Activity* 26; 1 recce pl
MEDITERRANEAN SEA: EU • EUNAVFOR MED 2 *Merlin IIIC* (leased)

Macedonia, North MKD

Macedonian Denar MKD		2022	2023	2024
GDP	MKD	795bn	895bn	982bn
	USD	13.6bn	15.8bn	17.4bn
per capita	USD	6,600	7,672	8,463
Growth	%	2.1	2.5	3.2
Inflation	%	14.2	10.0	4.3
Def exp [a]	MKD	12.9bn	17.0bn	
	USD	221m	301m	
Def bdgt	MKD	13.3bn	15.6bn	
	USD	228m	275m	
FMA (US)	USD	64m	0m	0m
USD1=MKD		58.47	56.62	56.33

[a] NATO figure

Real-terms defence budget trend (USDm, constant 2015)

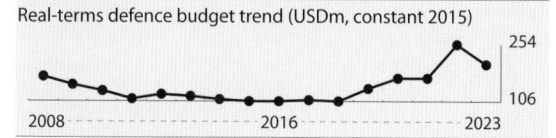

Population	2,133,410				
Age	0–14	15–19	20–24	25–29	30–64	65 plus
Male	8.3%	2.7%	3.2%	3.7%	25.2%	6.7%
Female	7.8%	2.6%	3.0%	3.4%	24.8%	8.5%

Capabilities

The armed forces' primary goals are safeguarding the state's territorial integrity and sovereignty, as well as contributing to operations under the EU, NATO and UN umbrellas. North Macedonia formally became NATO's 30th member in 2020 and is working towards increasing its defence budget to the 2% GDP target. It also enacted a new defence strategy with a focus on capability development and improved planning based on NATO and EU standards, among other areas. A 2019–2028 Defence Capability Development Plan (DCDP) consolidated long-term goals aimed at collective defence, cooperative security and crisis-management capabilities. Modernisation and equipment investments represent about a third of the annual defence budget. The country has decided to reduce its military fleet of helicopters through donations to Ukraine, opting for future acquisition of multirole helicopters to support military and civilian tasks. Work on defence ministry restructuring is underway. Skopje maintains a professional armed forces it aims to bring to NATO standards. A number of units are earmarked for participation in EU and NATO-led operations. North Macedonia has established and strengthened cooperation with international partners. It has defined a 10-year cooperation roadmap with the US, put defence cooperation agreements in place with Portugal and continued cooperation with France, Slovenia and the UK. There is little in the way of a domestic defence industry, with no ability to design and manufacture modern equipment.

ACTIVE 8,000 (Army 8,000) Gendarmerie & Paramilitary 7,600

RESERVE 4,850

ORGANISATIONS BY SERVICE

Army 8,000
FORCES BY ROLE
SPECIAL FORCES
  1 SF regt (1 SF bn, 1 ranger bn)
MANOEUVRE
  Mechanised
  1 mech inf bde (3 mech inf bn, 1 arty bn, 1 engr bn, 1 int coy, 1 NBC coy, 1 sigs coy)
COMBAT SUPPORT
  1 MP bn
  1 sigs bn
COMBAT SERVICE SUPPORT
  1 log bde (3 log bn)

Reserves
FORCES BY ROLE
  MANOEUVRE Light
  1 inf bde
EQUIPMENT BY TYPE
ARMOURED FIGHTING VEHICLES
  IFV 11: 10 BMP-2; 1 BMP-2K (CP)
  APC 198
    APC (T) 46: 9 *Leonidas*; 27 M113; 10 MT-LB
    APC (W) 152: 56 BTR-70; 12 BTR-80; 84 TM-170 *Hermelin*
  AUV 34: 2 *Cobra*; 32 JLTV

ANTI-TANK/ANTI-INFRASTRUCTURE
MSL • MANPATS Milan
RCL 82mm M60A
ARTILLERY 131
TOWED 70: 105mm 14 M-56; 122mm 56 M-30 M-1938
MRL 17: 122mm 6 BM-21; 128mm 11
MOR • 120mm 44

Marine Wing
EQUIPMENT BY TYPE
PATROL AND COASTAL COMBATANTS 2
PB 2 Botica†

Aviation Brigade
FORCES BY ROLE
TRAINING
1 flt with Z-242; Bell 205 (UH-1H *Iroquois*); Bell 206B
ATTACK HELICOPTER
1 sqn with Mi-24V *Hind* E
TRANSPORT HELICOPTER
1 sqn with Mi-8MTV *Hip*; Mi-17 *Hip* H
AIR DEFENCE
1 AD bn
EQUIPMENT BY TYPE
AIRCRAFT
TPT • Light 1 An-2 *Colt*
TRG 5 Z-242
HELICOPTERS
ATK 2 Mi-24V *Hind* E (8: 2 Mi-24K *Hind* G2; 6 Mi-24V *Hind* E in store)
MRH 6: 4 Mi-8MTV *Hip*; 2 Mi-17 *Hip* H
TPT • Light 6: 2 Bell 205 (UH-1H *Iroquois*); 4 Bell 206B *Jet Ranger*
AIR DEFENCE
SAM • Point-defence 8+: 8 9K35 *Strela*-10 (RS-SA-13 *Gopher*); 9K310 Igla-1 (RS-SA-16 *Gimlet*)
GUNS 40mm 36 L/60

Gendarmerie & Paramilitary 7,600

Police 7,600 (some 5,000 armed)
incl 2 SF units
EQUIPMENT BY TYPE
ARMOURED FIGHTING VEHICLES
APC • APC (T) M113; APC (W) BTR-80; TM-170 *Heimlin*
AUV Ze'ev
HELICOPTERS
MRH 1 Bell 412EP *Twin Huey*
TPT 3: **Medium** 1 Mi-171; **Light** 2: 1 Bell 206B (AB-206B) *Jet Ranger* II; 1 Bell 212 (AB-212)

DEPLOYMENT
BOSNIA-HERZEGOVINA: EU • EUFOR (*Operation Althea*) 32
IRAQ: NATO • NATO Mission Iraq 4
KOSOVO: NATO • KFOR 60
LATVIA: NATO • Enhanced Forward Presence 9
LEBANON: UN • UNIFIL 3

Malta MLT

Euro EUR		2022	2023	2024
GDP	EUR	17.2bn	18.7bn	19.8bn
	USD	18.1bn	20.3bn	21.7bn
per capita	USD	34,819	38,715	41,124
Growth	%	6.9	3.8	3.3
Inflation	%	6.1	5.8	3.1
Def bdgt [a]	EUR	82.7m	73.9m	
	USD	87.2m	80.5m	
USD1=EUR		0.95	0.92	0.91

[a] Excludes military pensions

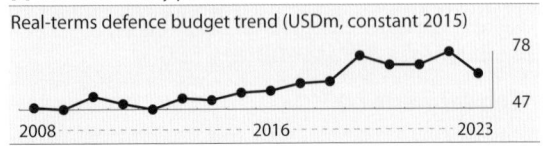

Real-terms defence budget trend (USDm, constant 2015)

Population	467,138					
Age	0–14	15–19	20–24	25–29	30–64	65 plus
Male	7.5%	2.3%	2.6%	3.4%	24.2%	10.5%
Female	7.1%	2.2%	2.4%	3.0%	22.7%	12.2%

Capabilities

The principal roles of the armed forces are external security and support for civil emergencies and the police. They also focus on maritime security in the Mediterranean. Malta is neutral but is a member of NATO's Partnership for Peace programme. The Armed Forces of Malta Strategy Paper 2016–2026 laid out defence-policy objectives, including operational and organisational reforms. A new Joint Military Operations Centre for the Armed Forces of Malta is nearly completion. The country issued a National Cybersecurity Strategy 2023–2026 that, for the defence sector, focuses on resilience, monitoring capacity and required technology. Malta cooperates with the UK on active cyber defence. The country also participates in bilateral and multilateral exercises. Although its deployment capacity is limited, Malta has contributed to European and UN missions. The armed forces have a personnel retention problem, keeping force levels below authorised levels. Italy has assisted Malta in meeting some security requirements, including air surveillance. The European Internal Security Fund is funding some modernisation, such as offshore patrol ships that entered service in 2023. Malta has some shipbuilding and ship-repair activity and a small aviation-maintenance industry but no dedicated defence industry. The country relies on imports to equip its armed forces.

ACTIVE 1,700 (Armed Forces 1,700)

RESERVE 260 (Volunteer Reserve Force 110 Individual Reserve 150)

ORGANISATIONS BY SERVICE

Armed Forces of Malta 1,700

FORCES BY ROLE

SPECIAL FORCES

1 SF unit

MANOEUVRE

Light

1 (1st) inf regt (3 inf coy, 1 cbt spt coy)

COMBAT SUPPORT

1 (3rd) cbt spt regt (1 cbt engr sqn, 1 EOD sqn, 1 maint sqn)

COMBAT SERVICE SUPPORT

1 (4th) CSS regt (1 CIS coy, 1 sy coy)

EQUIPMENT BY TYPE

ARTILLERY • MOR 81mm L16

AIR DEFENCE • GUNS 14.5mm 1 ZPU-4

Maritime Squadron 500

Organised into 5 divisions: offshore patrol; inshore patrol; rapid deployment and training; marine engineering; and logistics

EQUIPMENT BY TYPE

PATROL AND COASTAL COMBATANTS 9

PSO 1 P71 (ITA OPV 748) with 1 hel landing platform

PCO 1 P62 (ex-IRL *Emer*)

PCC 1 P61 (ITA *Saettia* mod) with 1 hel landing platform

PB 6: 4 Austal 21m; 2 *Marine Protector*

LOGISTICS AND SUPPORT • AAR 2 *Vittoria*

Air Wing

1 base party. 1 flt ops div; 1 maint div; 1 integrated log div; 1 rescue section

EQUIPMENT BY TYPE

AIRCRAFT

TPT • Light 5: 3 Beech 200 *King Air* (maritime patrol); 2 BN-2B *Islander*

TRG 3 *Bulldog* T MK1

HELICOPTERS MRH 6: 3 AW139 (SAR); 3 SA316B *Alouette* III

DEPLOYMENT

LEBANON: UN • UNIFIL 9

Montenegro MNE

Euro EUR		2022	2023	2024
GDP	EUR	5.80bn	6.49bn	7.00bn
	USD	6.11bn	7.06bn	7.66bn
per capita	USD	9,820	11,339	12,297
Growth	%	6.1	4.5	3.7
Inflation	%	13.1	8.3	4.3
Def exp [a]	EUR	81.6m	124m	
	USD	86.0m	134m	
Def bdgt [b]	EUR	94.7m	113m	
	USD	99.8m	123m	
FMA (US)	USD	16m	0m	0m
USD1=EUR		0.95	0.92	0.91

[a] NATO figure
[b] Includes military pensions

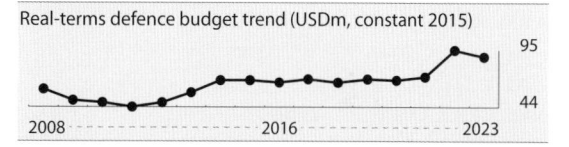

Real-terms defence budget trend (USDm, constant 2015)

Population	602,445					
Age	0–14	15–19	20–24	25–29	30–64	65 plus
Male	9.2%	3.1%	3.3%	3.1%	22.8%	7.6%
Female	8.7%	2.8%	3.1%	3.0%	23.5%	9.8%

Capabilities

Montenegro intends to develop an integrated defence system capable of defending and preserving independence, sovereignty and national territory. In 2023, the country developed its Action Plan for the Implementation of the Defence Strategy, which focuses on strengthening the country's resilience and cyber structures as well as integration of Montenegro into relevant NATO and EU structures. Since becoming a NATO member in 2017, Montenegro has accepted Alliance capability targets and has been aligning its defence-planning process to its standards. The army doctrine is due to be updated before the end of 2024. In 2023, the government agreed a Handbook on the *Standardization of Gender Equality Training for Military Personnel*. The armed forces are not designed to have an expeditionary capability, and, as such, have little to support deployments beyond national borders. Personnel have deployed to EU-, UN- and NATO-led operations, although with small contributions. Podgorica intends to replace ageing Soviet-era equipment. The Action Plan 2023–2026 dedicates EUR195 million in the modernisation of equipment. Patrol ships and airspace surveillance radars are among procurement priorities that include light and medium helicopters and light armoured vehicles, as well as improved communications capacities in accordance with NATO standards. Montenegro is procuring UAVs together with Slovenia with the aim of increasing bilateral cooperation in airborne ISR. The country's defence industry is capable of producing small arms and ammunition.

ACTIVE 2,885 (Army 1,850 Navy 310 Air Force 225 Other 500) Gendarmerie & Paramilitary 4,100

RESERVE 2,800

ORGANISATIONS BY SERVICE

Army 1,850
FORCES BY ROLE
MANOEUVRE
  Reconnaissance
    1 recce coy
  Light
    1 mot inf bn
COMBAT SUPPORT
  1 cbt spt bn
  1 sigs coy
COMBAT SERVICE SUPPORT
  1 med bn
  1 spt bn
EQUIPMENT BY TYPE
ARMOURED FIGHTING VEHICLES
  APC • **APC (W)** 6 BOV-VP M-86
  AUV 32 JLTV
NBC VEHICLES 1 *Cobra* CBRN
ANTI-TANK/ANTI-INFRASTRUCTURE
  SP 9 BOV-1
  MSL • **MANPATS** 9K111 *Fagot* (RS-AT-4 *Spigot*); 9K111-1 *Konkurs* (RS-AT-5 *Spandrel*)
ARTILLERY 135
  TOWED 122mm 12 D-30
  MRL 128mm 18 M-63/M-94 *Plamen*
  MOR 105: **82mm** 73; **120mm** 32

Reserve
FORCES BY ROLE
MANOEUVRE
  Light
    2 inf bn
  COMBAT SUPPORT
    1 arty bn

Navy 310
1 Naval Cmd HQ with 4 operational naval units (patrol boat; coastal surveillance; maritime detachment; and SAR) with additional sigs, log and trg units with a separate coastguard element.
EQUIPMENT BY TYPE
PATROL AND COASTAL COMBATANTS • **PCC** 1 *Rade Končar* with 2 57mm guns (1 more in reserve)
LOGISTICS AND SUPPORT • **AXS** 1 *Jadran*

Air Force 225
Golubovci (Podgorica) air base under army command
FORCES BY ROLE
TRAINING
  1 (mixed) sqn with G-4 *Super Galeb*; Utva-75 (none operational)
TRANSPORT HELICOPTER
  1 sqn with SA341/SA342L *Gazelle*
EQUIPMENT BY TYPE
AIRCRAFT • **TRG** (4 G-4 *Super Galeb* non-operational; 4 Utva-75 non-operational)
HELICOPTERS
  MRH 16: 1 Bell 412EP *Twin Huey*; 2 Bell 412EPI *Twin Huey*; 13 SA341/SA342L (HN-45M) *Gazelle*
  TPT • **Light** 2 Bell 505 *Jet Ranger* X

Gendarmerie & Paramilitary ε4,100
  Special Police Units ε4,100

DEPLOYMENT
IRAQ: NATO • NATO Mission Iraq 1
KOSOVO: NATO • KFOR 2
LATVIA: NATO • Enhanced Forward Presence 11
WESTERN SAHARA: UN • MINURSO 1

Multinational Organisations

Capabilities
The following represent shared capabilities held by contributors collectively rather than as part of national inventories

ORGANISATIONS BY SERVICE

NATO AEW&C Force
Based at Geilenkirchen (GER). Original participating countries (BEL, CAN, DNK, GER, GRC, ITA, NLD, NOR, PRT, TUR, US) have been subsequently joined by five more (CZE, ESP, HUN, POL, ROM).
FORCES BY ROLE
AIRBORNE EARLY WARNING & CONTROL
  1 sqn with B-757 (trg); E-3A *Sentry* (NATO standard)
EQUIPMENT BY TYPE
AIRCRAFT
  AEW&C 16 E-3A *Sentry* (NATO standard)
  TPT • **PAX** 1 B-757 (trg)

NATO Alliance Ground Surveillance
Based at Sigonella (ITA)
EQUIPMENT BY TYPE
UNINHABITED AERIAL VEHICLES
  ISR • **Heavy** 5 RQ-4D *Phoenix*

NATO Multinational Multi-Role Tanker Transport Fleet (MMF)
Based at Eindhoven (NLD). Six participating countries

(BEL, CZE, GER, NLD, NOR & LUX)
EQUIPMENT BY TYPE
AIRCRAFT • TKR/TPT 7 A330 MRTT

Strategic Airlift Capability

Heavy Airlift Wing based at Papa air base (HUN). 12 participating countries (BLG, EST, FIN, HUN, LTU, NLD, NOR, POL, ROM, SVN, SWE, US)
EQUIPMENT BY TYPE
AIRCRAFT • TPT • Heavy 3 C-17A *Globemaster* III

Strategic Airlift International Solution

Intended to provide strategic-airlift capacity pending the delivery of A400M aircraft by leasing An-124s. 11 participating countries (BEL, CZE, FIN, FRA, GER, HUN, NOR, POL, SVK, SVN, SWE)
EQUIPMENT BY TYPE
AIRCRAFT • TPT • Heavy 2 An-124-100 (3 more available on 6–9 days' notice)

Netherlands NLD

Euro EUR		2022	2023	2024
GDP	EUR	959bn	1.00trn	1.06trn
	USD	1.01trn	1.09trn	1.16trn
per capita	USD	57,428	61,770	65,195
Growth	%	4.3	0.6	1.2
Inflation	%	11.6	4.0	4.2
Def exp [a]	EUR	14.8bn	15.8bn	
	USD	15.6bn	17.1bn	
Def bdgt [b]	EUR	14.4bn	15.4bn	
	USD	15.2bn	16.8bn	
USD1=EUR		0.95	0.92	0.91

[a] NATO figure
[b] Includes military pensions

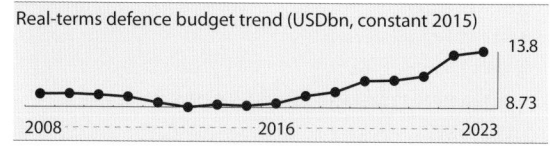

Real-terms defence budget trend (USDbn, constant 2015)
13.8
8.73
2008 — 2016 — 2023

Population	17,694,798					
Age	0–14	15–19	20–24	25–29	30–64	65 plus
Male	7.8%	2.9%	3.4%	3.5%	22.7%	9.5%
Female	7.4%	2.7%	3.2%	3.4%	22.5%	11.0%

Capabilities

The armed forces are responsible for territorial defence, supporting national civil authorities, and contributing to NATO. The government issued a security strategy in April 2023 that called for cooperation within Europe, with NATO and others, and strengthening of the armed forces. It echoed a White Paper issued in June 2022 that urged the military to address shortfalls in areas such as operational readiness, combat power and agility. The armed forces also are to address recruitment shortfalls. A National Cyber Security Strategy 2022-2028 was published in September 2022. Dutch forces have increasingly integrated with NATO allies, particularly Germany. The army contributes to a Dutch–German tank battalion. The Dutch armed forces have air-policing agreements with France, Belgium and Luxembourg and the country is a member of the Joint Expeditionary Force and the European Intervention Initiative. The Netherlands, Belgium and Denmark have committed to forming a composite special-operations command. Dutch forces are fully professional and well-trained, and the Netherlands can deploy and sustain a medium-scale force for a single operation or a small-scale joint force for an extended period. The Netherlands makes significant contributions to NATO and EU military operations. An agreement is in place with Belgium on the joint acquisition of new frigates and minehunters. The Netherlands, working with Denmark and the US, is in charge of training Ukrainian pilots to fly F-16s, and in November, stationed F-16s in Romania to train them and their Romanian counterparts. The Netherlands and Denmark also are jointly buying *Leopard* 2A4 MBTs for delivery to Ukraine in 2024. The country is upgrading all aspects of its forces and is expected to make a decision in 2024 on its *Walrus*-class submarine replacement. There are plans to boost defence innovation and research and to expand the Defence Space Security Centre. The country has an advanced domestic defence industry in areas such as ships and air-defence systems.

ACTIVE 33,600 (Army 15,350 Navy 7,350 Air 6,400 Other 4,500) **Military Constabulary 6,500**

RESERVE 6,000 (Army 3,900 Navy 1,100 Air 800 Other 200) **Military Constabulary 300**

Reserve liability to age 35 for soldiers/sailors, 40 for NCOs, 45 for officers

ORGANISATIONS BY SERVICE

Army 15,350
FORCES BY ROLE
COMMAND
  elm 1 (1 GNC) corps HQ
SPECIAL FORCES
  4 SF coy
MANOEUVRE
  Reconnaissance
  1 ISR bn (2 armd recce sqn, 1 EW coy, 2 int sqn, 1 UAV bty)
  Mechanised
  1 (13th) mech bde (1 recce sqn, 2 mech inf bn, 1 engr bn, 1 maint coy, 1 med coy)
  1 (43rd) mech bde (1 armd recce sqn, 2 armd inf bn, 1 engr bn, 1 maint coy, 1 med coy)
  Air Manoeuvre
  1 (11th) air mob bde (3 air mob inf bn, 1 engr coy, 1 med coy, 1 supply coy, 1 maint coy)
COMBAT SUPPORT
  1 SP arty bn (3 SP arty bty)
  1 CIMIC bn
  1 engr bn
  2 EOD coy 1 (CIS) sigs bn 1 CBRN coy

COMBAT SERVICE SUPPORT
1 med bn
5 fd hospital
3 maint coy
2 tpt bn
AIR DEFENCE
1 SAM comd (1 SAM sqn; 2 SAM bty)

Reserves 3,900 reservists

National Command
Cadre bde and corps tps completed by call-up of reservists (incl Territorial Comd)
FORCES BY ROLE
MANOEUVRE
  Light
  3 inf bn (could be mobilised for territorial def)
EQUIPMENT BY TYPE
ARMOURED FIGHTING VEHICLES
  RECCE 185 *Fennek* (incl 47 OP)
  IFV 117 CV9035NL (being upgraded; 32 more in store)
  APC • APC (W) 200 *Boxer* (8 driver trg; 52 amb; 36 CP; 92 engr; 12 log)
  AUV 242: 92 *Bushmaster* IMV; 140 *Fennek* (incl 4 CP; 10 trg)
ENGINEERING & MAINTENANCE VEHICLES
  AEV 10+: *Dachs*; 10 *Kodiak*
  ARV 25+: BPz-2; 25 BPz-3 *Büffel*
  VLB 28: 16 *Leopard* 1 with *Legaun*; 8 *Leopard* 2 with *Leguan*; 4 MLC70 with *Leguan*
  MW *Bozena*
NBC VEHICLES 6 TPz-1 *Fuchs* NBC
ANTI-TANK/ANTI-INFRASTRUCTURE
  MSL • MANPATS *Spike*-MR
ARTILLERY 122
  SP 155mm 21 PzH 2000 (27 more in store)
  MOR 101: **81mm** 83 L16/M1; **120mm** 18 Brandt
AIR DEFENCE • SAM 42+
  Long-range 18 M902 *Patriot* PAC-3
  Short-range 6 NASAMS II
  Point-defence 18+: FIM-92 *Stinger*; 18 *Fennek* with FIM-92 *Stinger*

Navy 7,350 (incl Marines)

EQUIPMENT BY TYPE
SUBMARINES 3
  SSK 3 *Walrus* with 4 single 533mm TT with Mk 48 ADCAP mod 7 HWT
PRINCIPAL SURFACE COMBATANTS 6
  DESTROYERS • DDGHM 4:
    3 *De Zeven Provinciën* with 2 quad lnchr with RGM-84C *Harpoon* Block 1B AShM, 5 8-cell Mk 41 VLS with SM-2 Block IIIA/RIM-162B ESSM SAM, 2 twin 324mm SVTT Mk 32 ASTT with Mk 46 LWT, 1 *Goalkeeper* CIWS, 1 127mm gun (capacity 1 NH90 hel)
    1 *De Zeven Provinciën* with 2 quad lnchr with RGM-84C *Harpoon* Block 1B AShM, 5 8-cell Mk 41 VLS with SM-2 Block IIIA/RIM-162B ESSM SAM, 2 twin 324mm SVTT Mk 32 ASTT with Mk 46 LWT, 2 *Goalkeeper* CIWS, 1 127mm gun (capacity 1 NH90 hel)
  FRIGATES • FFGHM 2 *Karel Doorman* with 2 quad lnchr with RGM-84C *Harpoon* Block 1B AShM, 1 16-cell Mk 48 mod 1 VLS with RIM-7P *Sea Sparrow* SAM, 2 twin 324mm SVTT Mk 32 ASTT with Mk 46 LWT, 1 *Goalkeeper* CIWS, 1 76mm gun (capacity 1 NH90 hel)
PATROL AND COASTAL COMBATANTS 4
  PSOH 4 *Holland* with 1 76mm gun (capacity 1 NH90 hel)
MINE WARFARE • MINE COUNTERMEASURES 5
  MHO 5 *Alkmaar* (*Tripartite*)
AMPHIBIOUS
  PRINCIPAL AMPHIBIOUS SHIPS • LPD 2:
    1 *Rotterdam* with 2 *Goalkeeper* CIWS (capacity 6 NH90/AS532 *Cougar* hel; either 6 LCVP or 2 LCM and 3 LCVP; either 170 APC or 33 MBT; 538 troops)
    1 *Johan de Witt* with 2 *Goalkeeper* CIWS (capacity 6 NH90 hel or 4 AS532 *Cougar* hel; either 6 LCVP or 2 LCM and 3 LCVP; either 170 APC or 33 MBT; 700 troops)
  LANDING CRAFT 17
    LCU 5 LCU Mk II
    LCVP 12 Mk5
LOGISTICS AND SUPPORT 9
  AGS 3: 1 *Hydrograaf*; 2 *Snellius*
  AKL 1 *Pelikaan*
  AKR 1 *New Amsterdam* (capacity 200 containers and 300 vehs) (leased)
  AORH 1 *Karel Doorman* with 2 *Goalkeeper* CIWS (capacity 6 NH90/AS532 *Cougar* or 2 CH-47F *Chinook* hel; 2 LCVP)
  AS 1 *Mercuur*
  AXL 1 *Van Kingsbergen*
  AXS 1 *Urania*
UNINHABITED MARITIME SYSTEMS
  UUV • MW A18-M; *Double Eagle* Mk III; *K-Ster* C/I; *Seafox*; *Seascan*

Marines 2,650

FORCES BY ROLE
SPECIAL FORCES
  1 SF gp (1 SF sqn, 1 CT sqn)
MANOEUVRE
  Amphibious
  2 mne bn
  1 amph aslt gp
COMBAT SERVICE SUPPORT
  1 spt gp (coy)
EQUIPMENT BY TYPE
ARMOURED FIGHTING VEHICLES

APC • **APC (T)** 64 BvS-10 *Viking* (incl 20 CP)
ENGINEERING & MAINTENANCE VEHICLES
ARV 8: 4 BvS-10; 4 BPz-2
MED 4 BvS-10
ANTI-TANK/ANTI-INFRASTRUCTURE
MSL • **MANPATS** *Spike*-MR
ARTILLERY • **MOR 81mm** 12 L16/M1
AIR DEFENCE • **SAM** • **Point-defence** FIM-92 *Stinger*

Air Force 6,400
FORCES BY ROLE
FIGHTER/GROUND ATTACK
1 sqn with F-16AM/BM *Fighting Falcon*
2 sqn with F-35A *Lightning* II
ANTI-SUBMARINE WARFARE/SEARCH & RESCUE
1 sqn with NH90 NFH
TANKER/TRANSPORT
1 sqn with C-130H/H-30 *Hercules*
1 sqn with Gulfstream G650ER
TRAINING
1 OEU sqn with F-35A *Lightning* II
1 sqn with PC-7 *Turbo Trainer*
1 hel sqn with AH-64D/E *Apache*; CH-47F *Chinook* (based at Fort Cavazos, TX)
ATTACK HELICOPTER
1 sqn with AH-64D/E *Apache*
TRANSPORT HELICOPTER
1 sqn with AS532U2 *Cougar* II; NH90 NFH
1 sqn with CH-47F *Chinook*
ISR UAV
1 sqn with MQ-9A *Reaper*
EQUIPMENT BY TYPE
AIRCRAFT 78 combat capable
FTR 42 F-16AM/BM *Fighting Falcon*
FGA 36 F-35A *Lightning* II
TPT 5: **Medium** 4: 2 C-130H *Hercules*; 2 C-130H-30 *Hercules*; **PAX** 1 Gulfstream G650ER
TRG 13 PC-7 *Turbo Trainer*
HELICOPTERS
ATK 28: 24 AH-64D *Apache*; 4 AH-64E *Apache*
ASW 19 NH90 NFH (of which 8 not fitted with sonar)
TPT 32: **Heavy** 20 CH-47F *Chinook*; **Medium** 12 AS532U2 *Cougar* II
UNINHABITED AERIAL VEHICLES
CISR • **Heavy** 4 MQ-9 *Reaper* (unarmed)
AIR-LAUNCHED MISSILES
AAM • **IR** AIM-9L/M *Sidewinder*; **IIR** AIM-9X *Sidewinder* II; **ARH** AIM-120B/C-7 AMRAAM
ASM AGM-114K *Hellfire* II
BOMBS
Laser-guided GBU-10/GBU-12 *Paveway* II; GBU-24 *Paveway* III (all supported by LANTIRN)
INS/GPS guided GBU-39 Small Diameter Bomb

Gendarmerie & Paramilitary 6,500
Royal Military Constabulary 6,500
Subordinate to the Ministry of Defence, but performs most of its work under the authority of other ministries
FORCES BY ROLE
MANOEUVRE
Other
1 paramilitary comd (total: 28 paramilitary unit)
EQUIPMENT BY TYPE
ARMOURED FIGHTING VEHICLES
APC • **APC (W)** 24 YPR-KMar

DEPLOYMENT
BALTIC SEA: NATO • SNMG 1: 230; 1 DDGHM
BOSNIA-HERZEGOVINA: EU • EUFOR (*Operation Althea*) 160; 1 mne coy
IRAQ: *Operation Inherent Resolve* 4; **NATO** • NATO Mission Iraq 2
LEBANON: UN • UNIFIL 1
LITHUANIA: NATO • Enhanced Forward Presence 250; 1 armd inf coy
MALI: EU • EUTM Mali 4
MIDDLE EAST: UN • UNTSO 12
NORTH SEA: NATO • SNMCMG 1: 100; 2 MHO
SYRIA/ISRAEL: UN • UNDOF 1
UNITED KINGDOM: *Operation Interflex* 90 (UKR trg)
UNITED STATES: 1 hel trg sqn with AH-64D/E *Apache*; CH-47F *Chinook* based at Fort Cavazos (TX)

FOREIGN FORCES
United States US European Command: 450

Norway NOR

Norwegian Kroner NOK		2022	2023	2024
GDP	NOK	5.57trn	5.70trn	5.92trn
	USD	579bn	547bn	568bn
per capita	USD	105,826	99,266	102,459
Growth	%	3.3	2.3	1.5
Inflation	%	5.8	5.8	3.7
Def exp [a]	NOK	83.9bn	89.7bn	
	USD	8.72bn	8.60bn	
Def bdgt [b]	NOK	71.3bn	75.8bn	
	USD	7.42bn	7.28bn	
USD1=NOK		9.61	10.42	10.43

[a] NATO figure
[b] Includes military pensions

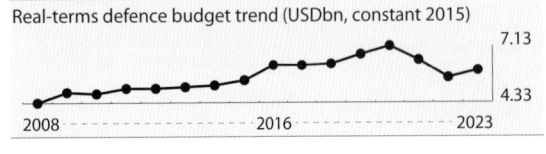

Real-terms defence budget trend (USDbn, constant 2015)

Population	5,597,924				
Age	0–14	15–19	20–24	25–29	30–64	65 plus
Male	8.5%	3.0%	3.1%	3.4%	23.4%	8.9%
Female	8.1%	2.9%	3.0%	3.2%	22.5%	10.0%

Capabilities

Norway sustains small but well-equipped and well-trained armed forces. Territorial defence is at the heart of security policy. Oslo published a long-term defence plan in 2020, arguing that the security environment had deteriorated faster than expected. It envisages a gradual increase in personnel numbers and further measures to strengthen readiness and capability in the High North. Following Russia's further invasion of Ukraine in February 2022, Norway announced that it would allocate additional funds to strengthen its defence in the North. The government has pledged to spend at least 2% of GDP on defence by 2026. A US Marine Corps contingent has deployed to Vaernes on a rotational basis since January 2017 and a second location was added at Setermoen a year later. In April 2021, Norway and Washington signed a Supplementary Defense Cooperation Agreement, which, among other things, provides authorities for US forces to access specific Norwegian facilities and conduct mutual defence activities. Four locations were mentioned as 'focal points' for increased cooperation: Evenes, Rygge and Sola air stations and Ramsund naval station. At any one time, around one-third of troops are conscripts. Senior officers reportedly expressed concerns in 2019 that Norway's force structure was too small for defence requirements, and plans are underway to expand the army with additional support units out to 2030. Norway maintains a small presence in a range of international crisis-management missions. Equipment recapitalisation is ongoing, but large procurements will stretch budgets. In 2023, Norway, along with Denmark, Finland, and Sweden, further integrated their air forces, 'aiming for the ability to operate seamlessly together as one force'. The country's ability to monitor its maritime environment will improve with the introduction of P-8s to replace its P-3s. New submarines are being procured as part of a strategic partnership with Germany. There are plans to strengthen Brigade North with new equipment and manoeuvre and support units. In June 2023, Oslo announced that the country's MBT fleet would be upgraded to *Leopard* 2A7s. Norway has an advanced and diverse defence-industrial base, such as Kongsberg, with a high percentage of SMEs and a mix of private and state-owned companies.

ACTIVE 25,400 (Army 8,300 Navy 4,600 Air 4,300 Central Support 7,400 Home Guard 800)

Conscript liability 19 months maximum. Conscripts first serve 12 months from 19–28, and then up to 4–5 refresher training periods until age 35, 44, 55 or 60 depending on rank and function. Conscription was extended to women in 2015

RESERVE 40,000 (Home Guard 40,000)

Readiness varies from a few hours to several days

ORGANISATIONS BY SERVICE

Army 3,900; 4,400 conscript (total 8,300)

The armoured infantry brigade – Brigade North – trains new personnel of all categories and provides units for international operations. At any time around one-third of the brigade will be trained and ready to conduct operations. The brigade includes one high-readiness armoured battalion (Telemark Battalion) with combat-support and combat-service-support units on high readiness

FORCES BY ROLE

MANOEUVRE

  Reconnaissance

  1 armd recce bn (forming)

  1 ISR bn

  1 (GSV) bn (1 (border) recce coy, 1 ranger coy, 1 spt coy, 1 trg coy)

  Armoured

  1 armd inf bde (2 armd bn, 1 lt inf bn, 1 arty bn, 1 engr bn, 1 MP coy, 1 CIS bn, 1 spt bn, 1 med bn)

  Light

  1 lt inf bn (His Majesty The King's Guards)

EQUIPMENT BY TYPE

ARMOURED FIGHTING VEHICLES

  MBT 36 *Leopard* 2A4 (8 more in store)

  RECCE 21 CV9030N MkIIIB

  IFV 91: 76 CV9030N; 15 CV9030N (CP)

  APC 390

    APC (T) 315 M113 (incl variants)

    APC (W) 75 XA-186 *Sisu*/XA-200 *Sisu*/XA-203 (amb)

  AUV 165: 20 *Dingo* 2; 25 HMT *Extenda*; 120 IVECO LMV (22 more in store)

ENGINEERING & MAINTENANCE VEHICLES

  AEV 34+: 20 CV90 STING; 8 M113 AEV; NM109; 6 *Wisent*-2

  ARV 12: 6 BPz-2; 6 *Wisent*-2

  VLB 37: 26 *Leguan*; 2 *Leopard* 2 with *Leguan*; 9 *Leopard* 1

  MW 9 910 MCV-2

NBC VEHICLES 6 TPz-1 *Fuchs* NBC

ANTI-TANK/ANTI-INFRASTRUCTURE
MANPATS FGM-148 *Javelin*
RCL **84mm** *Carl Gustaf*
ARTILLERY 167
SP 155mm 24 K9 *Thunder*
MOR 143: **81mm** 115 L16; **SP 81mm** 28: 16 CV9030; 12 M125A2
AIR DEFENCE
SAM • **Medium-range** NASAMS III

Navy 2,350; 2,250 conscripts (total 4,600)
Joint Command – Norwegian National Joint Headquarters. The Royal Norwegian Navy is organised into five elements under the command of the Chief of the Navy: the fleet (*Marinen*), the Coast Guard (*Kystvakten*), the recruit training school (KNM *Harald Haarfagre*), the naval medical branch and the naval bases (*Haakonsvern* and *Ramsund*)
FORCES BY ROLE
MANOEUVRE
Reconnaissance
1 ISR coy (Coastal Rangers)
COMBAT SUPPORT
1 EOD pl
EQUIPMENT BY TYPE
SUBMARINES 6
SSK 6 *Ula* with 8 single 533mm TT with *SeaHake* (DM2A3) HWT
PRINCIPAL SURFACE COMBATANTS • FRIGATES 4
FFGHM 4 *Fridtjof Nansen* with *Aegis* C2 (mod), 2 quad lnchr with NSM AShM, 1 8-cell Mk 41 VLS with RIM-162A ESSM SAM, 2 twin 324mm ASTT with *Sting Ray* mod 1 LWT, 1 76mm gun (capacity 1 med hel)
PATROL AND COASTAL COMBATANTS 13
PSOH 1 *Nordkapp* with 1 57mm gun (capacity 1 med tpt hel)
PCFG 6 *Skjold* with 8 single lnchr with NSM AShM, 1 76mm gun
PBF 6 CB90N (capacity 20 troops)
MINE WARFARE • MINE COUNTERMEASURES 4
MSC 2 *Alta* with 1 twin *Simbad* lnchr with *Mistral* SAM
MHC 2 *Oksoy* with 1 twin *Simbad* lnchr with *Mistral* SAM
LOGISTICS AND SUPPORT 6
AGI 1 *Marjata* IV
AGS 2: 1 *HU Sverdrup* II; 1 *Eger* (*Marjata* III) with 1 hel landing platform
AORH 1 *Maud* (BMT *Aegir*) (capacity 2 med hel)
AXL 2 *Reine*
UNINHABITED MARITIME SYSTEMS • UUV
DATA REMUS 100
MW *Minesniper* Mk III
UTL HUGIN 1000

Coast Guard
EQUIPMENT BY TYPE
PATROL AND COASTAL COMBATANTS 12
PSOH 2 *Jan Mayen* (capacity 2 med hel)
PSO 5: 3 *Barentshav*; 1 *Harstad*; 1 *Svalbard* with 1 57mm gun, 1 hel landing platform
PCC 5 *Nornen*

Air Force 2,900; 1,400 conscript (total 4,300)
Joint Command – Norwegian National HQ
FORCES BY ROLE
FIGHTER/GROUND ATTACK
2 sqn with F-35A *Lightning* II
MARITIME PATROL
1 sqn with P-8A *Poseidon*
SEARCH & RESCUE
1 sqn with *Sea King* Mk43B; AW101
TRANSPORT
1 sqn with C-130J-30 *Hercules*
TRAINING
1 sqn with MFI-15 *Safari*
TRANSPORT HELICOPTER
2 sqn with Bell 412SP *Twin Huey*
AIR DEFENCE
2 bn with NASAMS III
EQUIPMENT BY TYPE
AIRCRAFT 45 combat capable
FGA 40 F-35A *Lightning* II
ASW 5 P-8A *Poseidon*
TPT • **Medium** 4 C-130J-30 *Hercules*
TRG 16 MFI-15 *Safari*
HELICOPTERS
ASW (13 NH90 NFH in store)
SAR 23: 13 AW101; 10 *Sea King* Mk43B
MRH 18: 6 Bell 412HP; 12 Bell 412SP
AIR DEFENCE
SAM • **Medium-range** 6 NASAMS III
AIR-LAUNCHED MISSILES
AAM • **IR** AIM-9L *Sidewinder*; **IIR** AIM-9X *Sidewinder* II; IRIS-T; **ARH** AIM-120B/C-7 AMRAAM
BOMBS
Laser-guided EGBU-12 *Paveway* II
INS/GPS guided JDAM

Special Operations Command (NORSOCOM)
FORCES BY ROLE
SPECIAL FORCES
1 (armed forces) SF comd (2 SF gp)
1 (navy) SF comd (1 SF gp)
EQUIPMENT BY TYPE
PATROL AND COASTAL COMBATANTS • PBF 2 IC20M

Central Support, Administration and Command 5,850; 1,550 conscripts (total 7,400)

Central Support, Administration and Command includes military personnel in all joint elements and they are responsible for logistics and CIS in support of all forces in Norway and abroad

Home Guard 400; 400 conscripts (40,000 reserves)

The Home Guard is a separate organisation, but closely cooperates with all services. The Home Guard is organised in 11 Districts with mobile Rapid Reaction Forces (3,000 troops in total) as well as reinforcements and follow-on forces (37,000 troops in total)

EQUIPMENT BY TYPE
PATROL AND COASTAL COMBATANTS • PB 11: 4 *Harek*; 2 *Gyda*; 5 *Alusafe* 1290

DEPLOYMENT

EGYPT: MFO 3

IRAQ: *Operation Inherent Resolve* 30; 1 trg unit; **NATO** • NATO Mission Iraq 2

JORDAN: *Operation Inherent Resolve* 20

LITHUANIA: NATO • Enhanced Forward Presence 150; 1 armd inf coy(+); CV9030

MIDDLE EAST: UN • UNTSO 14

SOUTH SUDAN: UN • UNMISS 15

UNITED KINGDOM: *Operation Interflex* 150 (UKR trg)

FOREIGN FORCES

United States US European Command: 1,100; 1 (USMC) MEU eqpt set; 1 (APS) 155mm SP Arty bn eqpt set

Poland POL

Polish Zloty PLN		2022	2023	2024
GDP	PLN	3.08trn	3.50trn	3.80trn
	USD	691bn	842bn	880bn
per capita	USD	18,343	22,393	23,434
Growth	%	5.1	0.6	2.3
Inflation	%	14.4	12.0	6.4
Def exp [a]	PLN	73.9bn	134bn	
	USD	16.6bn	32.2bn	
Def bdgt [b]	PLN	57.8bn	97.4bn	158bn
	USD	13.0bn	23.5bn	36.6bn
FMA (US)	USD	275m	0m	0m
USD1=PLN		4.46	4.15	4.32

[a] NATO figure
[b] Includes military pensions

Real-terms defence budget trend (USDbn, constant 2015)
17.6
6.79
2008 — 2016 — 2023

Population		39,142,267				
Age	0–14	15–19	20–24	25–29	30–64	65 plus
Male	7.4%	2.5%	2.5%	2.9%	24.5%	7.8%
Female	7.0%	2.4%	2.4%	3.0%	26.1%	11.5%

Capabilities

Territorial defence and NATO membership are central pillars of Poland's defence policy. The primary focus of the 2017–32 defence concept is to prepare the armed forces to deter Russian aggression. Russia is characterised as a direct threat to Poland and to a stable international order, a view sharpened by Russia's February 2022 invasion of Ukraine. The protection of the border with Belarus has become an important mission of the Polish armed forces. Poland is one of the main European contributors to efforts to support Ukraine and has delivered a variety of defence equipment, including armour and anti-armour systems. Warsaw has increased defence outlays to support modernisation projects. The exiting government continued to pursue the goal of permanently stationing US troops in the country. The US Army's V Corps Headquarters (Forward) was established in Poznań at the end of 2020. A new coalition government may review ambitious plans to boost personnel numbers to 300,000 by 2035, as well as the establishment of new divisions. A technical-modernisation plan, covering the period 2021–35, was released in October 2019, which extended the planning horizon from ten to 15 years. Modernisation efforts include the F-35A combat aircraft, due for arrival in Poland in 2024, and land forces capabilities, among other efforts. Warsaw continues work on strengthening its defence-industrial base, much of which is now consolidated in the state-owned holding company PGZ, using technology transfers and international partnering agreements.

ACTIVE 100,400 (Army 71,350 Navy 6,150 Air Force 15,000 Special Forces 3,250 Territorial 4,650) **Gendarmerie & Paramilitary 14,300**

RESERVE 32,450 (Territorial 32,450)

ORGANISATIONS BY SERVICE

Army 71,350
FORCES BY ROLE
COMMAND
  elm 1 (MNC NE) corps HQ
MANOEUVRE
  Reconnaissance
  3 recce regt
  Armoured
  1 (11th) armd cav div (1 armd bde (1 recce coy, 2 tk bn, 1 armd inf bn, 1 SP arty bn, 1 cbt engr coy, 1 log bn, 1 AD bn), 1 armd bde (1 recce coy, 2 tk bn, 1 armd inf bn, 1 SP arty bn, 1 cbt engr coy, 1 log bn), 1 mech bde (1 recce coy, 1 armd inf bn, 2 mech inf bn, 1 SP arty bn, 1 engr bn, 1 log bn, 1 AD bn), 1 arty regt, 1 AD regt)
  1 (16th) mech div (1 armd bde (1 recce coy, 2 tk bn, 1 armd inf bn, 1 SP arty bn, 1 cbt engr coy, 1 log bn), 2 armd inf bde (1 recce coy, 1 tk bn, 2 armd inf bn, 1 SP arty bn, 1 cbt engr coy, 1 log bn), 1 arty bde, 1 AT regt, 1 log regt, 1 AD regt)
  1 (18th) mech div (1 armd bde (1 recce coy, 2 tk bn, 1 armd inf bn, 1 SP arty bn, 1 cbt engr coy, 1 log bn), 1 armd inf bde (1 tk bn, 2 armd inf bn, 1 SP arty bn, 1 AD bn), 1 mech bde (1 tk bn, 3 mech inf bn, 1 SP arty bn, 1 cbt engr bn, 1 log bn, 1 AD bn), 1 mech bde (forming), 1 log regt, 1 AD regt)
  Mechanised
  1 (12th) mech div (1 armd inf bde (1 recce coy, 1 tk bn, 2 armd inf bn, 1 SP arty bn, 1 cbt engr coy, 1 log bn), 1 mech bde (1 recce coy, 3 mech inf bn, 1 SP arty bn, 1 cbt engr bn, 1 log bn, 1 AD bn), 1 (coastal) mech bde (1 recce coy, 3 armd inf bn, 1 SP arty bn, 1 cbt engr coy, 1 log bn), 1 arty regt, 1 maint bn, 1 AD regt)
  Air Manoeuvre
  1 (6th) AB bde (3 para bn, 1 log bn)
  1 (25th) air cav bde (2 air cav bn, 2 tpt hel bn, 1 log bn)
COMBAT SUPPORT
  2 engr regt
  2 ptn br regt
  2 chem def regt
COMBAT SERVICE SUPPORT
  1 log bde (3 log bn, 2 maint bn, 1 supply bn, 1 spt bn)
  1 log bde (3 log bn, 1 maint bn, 1 med bn, 1 supply bn, 1 spt bn)
  1 log bde
HELICOPTER
  1 (1st) hel bde (2 atk hel sqn with Mi-24D/V *Hind* D/E, 1 CSAR sqn with Mi-24V *Hind* E; PZL W-3PL *Gluszec*; 2 ISR hel sqn with Mi-2URP; 2 tpt hel sqn with Mi-2)
EQUIPMENT BY TYPE
ARMOURED FIGHTING VEHICLES
  MBT 476: 28 K2; 71 *Leopard* 2A4 (being upgraded to 2PL); 105 *Leopard* 2A5; 57 *Leopard* 2PL; 14 M1A1 *Abrams*; 201 PT-91 *Twardy*

  RECCE 396: 265 BRDM-2; 44 BWR-1 (being upgraded); 87 BRDM-2 R5
  IFV 1,271: 916 BMP-1; 4 *Borsuk* (in test); 351 *Rosomak* IFV
  APC 444
    APC (W) 344: 300 *Rosomak* APC (incl variants); 44 AWD RAK (arty CP)
    PPV 100 *Maxxpro*
    AUV 255: 210 *Cougar*; 45 M-ATV
ENGINEERING & MAINTENANCE VEHICLES
  AEV 97+: IWT; 58 MT-LB AEV; 31 *Rosomak* WRT; 8 MID *Bizon*
  ARV 59: 31 BPz-2; 3 M88A2 *Hercules*; 25 WZT-3M
  VLB 122: 4 *Biber*; 107 BLG67M2; 11 MS-20 *Daglezja*
  MW 27: 17 *Bozena* 4; 6 ISM *Kroton*; 4 *Kalina* SUM
ANTI-TANK/ANTI-INFRASTRUCTURE
  MSL • MANPATS 9K11 *Malyutka* (RS-AT-3 *Sagger*); 9K111 *Fagot* (RS-AT-4 *Spigot*); *Spike*-LR
ARTILLERY 664
  SP 391: **122mm** 206 2S1 *Gvozdika*; **152mm** 111: 108 M-77 *Dana*; 3 *Dana*-M; **155mm** 74: 48 K9A1; 26 *Krab*
  MRL 140: **122mm** 131: 27 BM-21; 29 RM-70; 75 WR-40 *Langusta*; **227mm** 7 M142 HIMARS; **239mm** 2 K239 *Chunmoo* (*Homar*-K)
  MOR 133: **120mm** 35 M120; **SP 120mm** 98 SMK120 RAK
HELICOPTERS
  ATK 16 Mi-24D/V *Hind* D/E
  MRH 66: 2 AW149; 7 Mi-8MT *Hip*; 3 Mi-17 *Hip* H; 1 Mi-17AE *Hip* (aeromedical); 5 Mi-17-1V *Hip*; 16 PZL Mi-2URP *Hoplite*; 24 PZL W-3W/WA *Sokol*; 8 PZL W-3PL *Gluszec* (CSAR)
  TPT 37: **Medium** 12: 6 Mi-8T *Hip*; 2 PZL W-3AE *Sokol* (aeromedical); 4 S-70i *Black Hawk*; **Light** 25 PZL Mi-2 *Hoplite*
UNINHABITED AERIAL VEHICLES
  ISR • Light F-T5
AIR DEFENCE
  SAM 169
    Short-range 26: 6 CAMM (*Narew*); 20 2K12 *Kub* (RS-SA-6 *Gainful*)
    Point-defence 143+: 64 9K33 *Osa*-AK (RS-SA-8 *Gecko*); GROM; *Piorun*; 79 *Poprad*
  SPAAGM 23mm 20 ZSU-23-4MP *Biala*
  GUNS 345
    SP 23mm 2 ZSU-23-4
    TOWED 23mm 343: 268 ZU-23-2; 75 ZUR-23-2KG *Jodek*-G (with GROM msl)
BOMBS • Laser-guided MAM-C/L

Navy 6,150
EQUIPMENT BY TYPE
SUBMARINES • SSK 1 *Orzel* (ex-FSU *Kilo*)† with 6 single 533mm TT with 53-65KE/TEST-71ME HWT
PRINCIPAL SURFACE COMBATANTS • FRIGATES 2
  FFH 2 *Pułaski* (ex-US *Oliver Hazard Perry*) (of which 1

used as training ship) with 2 triple 324mm SVTT Mk 32 ASTT with MU90 LWT, 1 Mk 15 *Phalanx* CIWS, 1 76mm gun (capacity 2 SH-2G *Super Seasprite* ASW hel)

PATROL AND COASTAL COMBATANTS 5

CORVETTES • FSM 1 *Kaszub* with 2 quad lnchr with 9K32 *Strela*-2 (RS-SA-N-5 *Grail*) SAM, 2 twin 533mm ASTT with SET-53 HWT, 2 RBU 6000 *Smerch* 2 A/S mor, 1 76mm gun

PSO 1 *Ślązak* (MEKO A-100) with 1 76mm gun, 1 hel landing platform

PCFGM 3 *Orkan* (ex-GDR *Sassnitz*) with 1 quad lnchr with RBS15 Mk3 AShM, 1 quad lnchr (manual aiming) with 9K32 *Strela*-2M (RS-SA-N-5 *Grail*) SAM, 1 AK630 CIWS, 1 76mm gun

MINE WARFARE • MINE COUNTERMEASURES 21

MCCS 1 *Kontradmiral Xawery Czernicki*
MCO 3 *Kormoran* II
MSI 17: 1 *Gopło*; 12 *Gardno*; 4 *Mamry*

AMPHIBIOUS 8

LANDING SHIPS • LSM 5 *Lublin* (capacity 9 tanks; 135 troops)

LANDING CRAFT • LCU 3 *Deba* (capacity 50 troops)

LOGISTICS AND SUPPORT 26

AGI 2 *Moma*
AGS 8: 2 *Heweliusz*; 4 *Wildcat* 40; 2 (coastal)
AOR 1 *Bałtyk*
AOL 1 *Moskit*
ARS 4: 2 *Piast*; 2 *Zbyszko*
ATF 8: 6 *Bolko* (B860); 2 H960
AXL 1 *Wodnik* with 1 twin AK230 CIWS
AXS 1 *Iskra*

UNINHABITED MARITIME SYSTEMS • UUV

DATA *Gavia*
MW *Double Eagle* Mk III/SAROV

COASTAL DEFENCE • AShM 12 NSM

Naval Aviation 1,300

FORCES BY ROLE

ANTI SUBMARINE WARFARE/SEARCH & RESCUE
1 sqn with Mi-14PL *Haze* A; Mi-14PL/R *Haze* C
1 sqn with PZL W-3WA RM *Anakonda*; SH-2G *Super Seasprite*

MARITIME PATROL
1 sqn with An-28E/RM *Bryza*

TRANSPORT
1 sqn with An-28TD; M-28B TD *Bryza*
1 sqn with An-28TD; M-28B; PZL Mi-2 *Hoplite*

EQUIPMENT BY TYPE

AIRCRAFT
MP 10: 8 An-28RM *Bryza*; 2 An-28E *Bryza*
TPT • Light 4: 2 An-28TD *Bryza*; 2 M-28B TD *Bryza*

HELICOPTERS
ASW 5: 1 AW101 ASW Merlin HM2; 3 Mi-14PL *Haze*; 1 SH-2G *Super Seasprite*
SAR 10: 2 Mi-14PL/R *Haze* C; 8 PZL W-3WA RM *Anakonda*
TPT • Light 4 PZL Mi-2 *Hoplite*

Air Force 15,000

FORCES BY ROLE

FIGHTER
1 sqn with MiG-29A/UB *Fulcrum*

FIGHTER/GROUND ATTACK
3 sqn with F-16C/D Block 52+ *Fighting Falcon*
1 sqn with FA-50 *Fighting Eagle*

FIGHTER/GROUND ATTACK/ISR
2 sqn with Su-22M-4 *Fitter*

SEARCH AND RESCUE
1 sqn with Mi-2; PZL W-3 *Sokol*

TRANSPORT
1 sqn with C-130H/E; M-28 *Bryza*
1 sqn with C295M; M-28 *Bryza*

TRAINING
1 sqn with PZL-130 *Orlik*
1 sqn with M-346
1 hel sqn with SW-4 *Puszczyk*

TRANSPORT HELICOPTER
1 (Spec Ops) sqn with Mi-17 *Hip* H
1 (VIP) sqn with Mi-8 *Hip*; W-3WA *Sokol*

ISR UAV
1 sqn with Bayraktar TB2; MQ-9A *Reaper*

AIR DEFENCE
1 bde with M903 *Patriot* PAC-3 MSE; S-125 *Newa* SC

EQUIPMENT BY TYPE

AIRCRAFT 83 combat capable
FTR 14: 11 MiG-29A *Fulcrum*; 3 MiG-29UB *Fulcrum*
FGA 69: 36 F-16C Block 52+ *Fighting Falcon*; 12 F-16D Block 52+ *Fighting Falcon*; 10 FA-50 *Fighting Eagle*; 8 Su-22M4 *Fitter*; 3 Su-22UM3K *Fitter*
TPT 51: **Medium** 7: 2 C-130H *Hercules*; 5 C-130E *Hercules*; **Light** 39: 16 C295M; 10 M-28 *Bryza* TD; 13 M-28 *Bryza* PT; **PAX** 5: 2 Gulfstream G550; 3 B-737-800 (VIP)
TRG 40: 12 M-346; 28 PZL-130 *Orlik*

UNIHABITED AERIAL VEHICLES
CISR 22: **Heavy** 4 MQ-9A *Reaper* (leased; unarmed); **Medium** 18 Bayraktar TB2

HELICOPTERS
MRH 8 Mi-17 *Hip* H
TPT 65: **Medium** 29: 9 Mi-8 *Hip*; 10 PZL W-3 *Sokol*; 10 PZL W-3WA *Sokol* (VIP); **Light** 36: 14 PZL Mi-2 *Hoplite*; 22 SW-4 *Puszczyk* (trg)

AIR DEFENCE
SAM 16
  Long-range 2 M903 *Patriot* PAC-3 MSE
  Short-range 14 S-125 *Newa* SC
SPAAGM 23mm 12 *Pilica* (with *Piorun* msl)

AIR-LAUNCHED MISSILES

AAM • IR AIM-9 *Sidewinder*; R-60 (RS-AA-8 *Aphid*); R-73 (RS-AA-11A *Archer*); R-27T (RS-AA-10B *Alamo*); **IIR** AIM-9X *Sidwinder* II; **ARH** AIM-120C AMRAAM
ASM AGM-65J/G *Maverick*; Kh-25 (RS-AS-10 *Karen*); Kh-29 (RS-AS-14 *Kedge*)
ALCM • Conventional AGM-158 JASSM
BOMBS
Laser-guided MAM-C/L

Special Forces 3,250
FORCES BY ROLE
SPECIAL FORCES
3 SF units (GROM, FORMOZA & cdo)
COMBAT SUPPORT/
1 cbt spt unit (AGAT)
COMBAT SERVICE SUPPORT
1 spt unit (NIL)

Territorial Defence Forces 4,650 (plus 32,450 reservists)
FORCES BY ROLE
MANOEUVRE
Other
15 sy bde
2 sy bde (forming)

Gendarmerie & Paramilitary 14,300

Border Guards 14,300
Ministry of Interior

Maritime Border Guard 2,000
EQUIPMENT BY TYPE
PATROL AND COASTAL COMBATANTS 14
  PCO 1 *Jozef Haller* (FRA Socarenam 70m OPV)
  PCC 2 *Kaper*
  PBF 6: 2 *Strażnik*; 4 IC16M
  PB 5: 2 *Wisłoka*; 2 *Baltic* 24; 1 Project MI-6
AMPHIBIOUS
  LANDING CRAFT • UCAC 2 *Griffon* 2000TDX

DEPLOYMENT
BOSNIA-HERZEGOVINA: EU • EUFOR (*Operation Althea*) 49
CENTRAL AFRICAN REPUBLIC: EU • EUTM RCA 2
DEMOCRATIC REPUBLIC OF THE CONGO: UN • MONUSCO 2
IRAQ: *Operation Inherent Resolve* 208; **NATO • NATO Mission Iraq** 51
KOSOVO: NATO • KFOR 245; 1 inf coy; **UN • UNMIK** 2
LATVIA: NATO • Enhanced Forward Presence up to 200; 1 tk coy
LEBANON: UN • UNIFIL 193; 1 mech inf coy
MIDDLE EAST: UN • UNTSO 4
NORTH SEA: NATO • SNMCMG 1: 75; 1 MCCS; 1 MSI
ROMANIA: NATO • MNB-SE 220; 1 mech inf coy; *Rosomak*
SOUTH SUDAN: UN • UNMISS 1
WESTERN SAHARA: UN • MINURSO 1

FOREIGN FORCES
All NATO Enhanced Forward Presence unless stated
Canada *Operation Unifier* 40 (UKR trg)
Croatia 69; 1 SP arty bty
Germany MNC-NE corps HQ: 95
Romania 100; 1 sp ADA bty
Italy NATO Baltic Air Policing: 200; 4 F-35A *Lightning* II
United Kingdom 140; 1 recce sqn; 1 SAM bty with CAMM (*Land Ceptor*)
United States: 1,000; 1 armd bn with M1A2 SEPv2 *Abarms*; M2A3 *Bradley*; 1 SP arty bty with M109A6 • *Operation Atlantic Resolve* 15,000; 1 corps HQ; 2 div HQ; 2 armd bde with M1A2 SEPv2 *Abrams*; M3A3 *Bradley*; M2A3 *Bradley*; M109A6/A7; 2 SAM bty with M902 *Patriot* PAC3; 1 FGA flt with 4 F-16C *Fighting Falcon*; 1 CISR UAV sqn with MQ-9A *Reaper*

Portugal PRT

Euro EUR		2022	2023	2024
GDP	EUR	239bn	254bn	265bn
	USD	252bn	276bn	290bn
per capita	USD	24,540	26,879	28,123
Growth	%	6.7	2.3	1.5
Inflation	%	8.1	5.3	3.4
Def exp [a]	EUR	3.39bn	3.92bn	
	USD	3.57bn	4.27bn	
Def bdgt	EUR	2.45bn	2.58bn	
	USD	2.58bn	2.81bn	
USD1=EUR		0.95	0.92	0.91

[a] NATO figure

Real-terms defence budget trend (USDbn, constant 2015)
2.84
2.30
2008 — 2016 — 2023

Population	10,223,150					
Age	0–14	15–19	20–24	25–29	30–64	65 plus
Male	6.6%	2.7%	2.9%	2.8%	23.7%	8.8%
Female	6.3%	2.5%	2.8%	2.7%	25.2%	13.2%

Capabilities

Principal tasks for Portugal's all-volunteer armed forces are homeland defence, maritime security, multinational operations and responding to humanitarian disasters. Investment plans support Portugal's ambition to field rapid-reaction and maritime-surveillance capabilities for territorial defence and multinational operations. A new military programme law for 2019–30 was approved by parliament, modernising the country's force projection capacity through the purchase of five KC-390 aircraft. The naval inventory also is being upgraded. Lisbon in 2022 approved a modest increase in defence spending and suggested further hikes could happen. Portugal hosts NATO's cyber-security academy and the country also contributes to EU military structures. The country has a close relationship with former dependencies and with the US, which operates out of Lajes air base. All three services have programmes to modernise and sustain existing equipment. The country has an active defence industry, though principally in relation to shipbuilding, broader maintenance tasks and the manufacture of components, small arms and light weapons.

ACTIVE 26,050 (Army 13,350 Navy 6,750 Air 5,950) Gendarmerie & Paramilitary 22,600

RESERVE 23,500 (Army 10,000 Navy 9,000, Air Force 4,500) Gendarmerie & Paramilitary 220

Reserve obligation to age 35

ORGANISATIONS BY SERVICE

Army 13,350

5 territorial comd (2 mil region, 1 mil district, 2 mil zone)

FORCES BY ROLE

SPECIAL FORCES
1 SF bn

MANOEUVRE

Mechanised
1 mech bde (1 recce sqn, 1 tk regt, 1 mech inf bn, 1 arty bn, 1 AD bty, 1 engr coy, 1 sigs coy, 1 spt bn)
1 (intervention) mech bde (1 recce regt, 2 mech inf bn, 1 arty bn, 1 AD bty, 1 engr coy, 1 sigs coy, 1 spt bn)

Air Manoeuvre
1 (rapid reaction) bde (1 cdo bn, 1 ISR bn, 2 para bn, 1 arty bn, 1 AD bty, 1 engr coy, 1 sigs coy, 1 spt bn)

Other
1 (Azores) inf gp (2 inf bn, 1 AD bty)
1 (Madeira) inf gp (1 inf bn, 1 AD bty)

COMBAT SUPPORT
1 STA bty
1 engr bn (1 construction coy; 1 EOD unit; 1 ptn br coy; 1 CBRN coy)
1 EW coy
1 MP bn
1 psyops unit
1 CIMIC coy (joint)
1 sigs bn

COMBAT SERVICE SUPPORT
1 maint coy
1 log coy
1 tpt coy
1 med unit

AIR DEFENCE
1 AD bn

Reserves 210,000

FORCES BY ROLE
MANOEUVRE

Light
3 (territorial) def bde (on mobilisation)

EQUIPMENT BY TYPE

ARMOURED FIGHTING VEHICLES
MBT 34 *Leopard* 2A6
IFV 30 *Pandur* II MK 30mm
APC 405
  APC (T) 238: 189 M113A1/M113A2; 49 M577A2 (CP)
  APC (W) 167: 9 V-150 *Commando*; 12 V-200 *Chaimite*; 146 *Pandur* II (incl variants)
AUV 16 VBL

ENGINEERING & MAINTENANCE VEHICLES
AEV M728
ARV 13: 6 M88A1, 7 *Pandur* II ARV
VLB M48

ANTI-TANK/ANTI-INFRASTRUCTURE
MSL
  SP 26: 17 M113 with TOW; 4 M901 with TOW; 5 *Pandur* II with TOW
  MANPATS *Milan*
RCL • 84mm *Carl Gustaf*; 106mm M40A1

ARTILLERY 293
SP 155mm 18 M109A5; (6 M109A2 in store)
TOWED 41: 105mm 17 L119 Light Gun; (21 M101A1 in store); 155mm 24 M114A1
MOR 234: 81mm 143; SP 81mm 12: 2 M125A1; 10 M125A2; 107mm 11 M30; SP 107mm 18: 3 M106A1; 15 M106A2; 120mm 50 Tampella

AIR DEFENCE
SAM • Point-defence FIM-92 *Stinger*
GUNS • TOWED 20mm 20 Rh 202

Navy 6,750 (incl 950 Marines)

EQUIPMENT BY TYPE

SUBMARINES 2
SSK 2 *Tridente* (GER Type-214) (fitted with AIP) with 8 533mm TT with UGM-84L *Harpoon* Block II AShM/*Black Shark* HWT

PRINCIPAL SURFACE COMBATANTS • FRIGATES 4
FFGHM 4:
  2 *Bartolomeu Dias* (ex-NLD *Karel Doorman*) with 2 quad lnchr with RGM-84L *Harpoon* Block II AShM, 1 16-cell Mk 48 mod 1 VLS with RIM-162 ESSM SAM, 2 twin 324mm SVTT Mk 32 ASTT with Mk 46 LWT, 1 *Goalkeeper* CIWS, 1 76mm gun (capacity 1 *Lynx* Mk95 (*Super Lynx*) hel)
  2 *Vasco Da Gama* (1 other non operational) with 2 quad lnchr with RGM-84C *Harpoon* Block 1B AShM, 1 octuple Mk 29 GMLS with RIM-7M *Sea Sparrow* SAM, 2 triple 324mm SVTT Mk 32 ASTT with Mk 46 LWT, 1 Mk 15 *Phalanx* Block 1B CIWS, 1 100mm gun (capacity 2 *Lynx* Mk95 (*Super Lynx*) hel)

PATROL AND COASTAL COMBATANTS 21
CORVETTES • FS 2:
  1 *Baptista de Andrade* with 1 100mm gun, 1 hel landing

platform
1 *Joao Coutinho* with 1 twin 76mm gun, 1 hel landing platform
PSO 4 *Viana do Castelo* with 1 hel landing platform
PCC 5: 1 *Cacine*; 4 *Tejo* (ex-DNK *Flyvisken*)
PBR 10: 5 *Argos*; 4 *Centauro*; 1 *Rio Minho*
LOGISTICS AND SUPPORT 20
  AAR 12: 8 *Amelia* (ESP Rodman 46); 4 *Vigilante*
  AGS 4: 2 *D Carlos* I (ex-US *Stalwart*); 2 *Andromeda*
  AXS 4: 1 *Sagres* (ex-GER *Gorch Fock*); 1 *Creoula*; 1 *Polar*; 1 *Zarco*
UNINHABITED MARITIME SYSTEMS
  USV • DATA X-2601
  UUV • UTL *Falcon*; *Navajo*

Marines 950
FORCES BY ROLE
SPECIAL FORCES
  1 SF det
MANOEUVRE
  Light
  1 lt inf bn
COMBAT SUPPORT
  1 mor coy
  1 MP coy
EQUIPMENT BY TYPE
ANTI-TANK/ANTI-INFRASTRUCTURE
  MSL • MANPATS *Milan*; TOW
  RCL • 84mm *Carl Gustaf*
ARTILLERY • MOR 30+: **81mm** some; **120mm** 30

Naval Aviation
EQUIPMENT BY TYPE
HELICOPTERS • ASW 5: 4 *Lynx* Mk95 (*Super Lynx*); 1 *Lynx* Mk95A (*Super Lynx*)

Air Force 5,950
FORCES BY ROLE
FIGHTER/GROUND ATTACK
  2 sqn with F-16AM/BM *Fighting Falcon*
MARITIME PATROL
  1 sqn with P-3C *Orion*
ISR/TRANSPORT
  1 sqn with C295M
COMBAT SEARCH & RESCUE
  1 sqn with with AW101 *Merlin*
TRANSPORT
  1 sqn with C-130H/C-130H-30 *Hercules*
  1 sqn with KC-390 *Millenium*
  1 sqn with *Falcon* 50/900B
TRAINING
  1 sqn with AW119 *Koala*
  1 sqn with TB-30 *Epsilon*
EQUIPMENT BY TYPE
AIRCRAFT 33 combat capable
  FTR 28: 24 F-16AM *Fighting Falcon*; 4 F-16BM *Fighting Falcon*
  ASW 5 P-3C *Orion*
  ISR: 7: 5 C295M (maritime surveillance), 2 C295M (photo recce)
  TPT 15: **Medium** 6: 2 C-130H *Hercules*; 3 C-130H-30 *Hercules* (tpt/SAR); 1 KC-390 *Millenium*; **Light** 5 C295M;
  PAX 4: 3 *Falcon* 50 (tpt/VIP); 1 Falcon 900B (tpt/VIP)
  TRG 16 TB-30 *Epsilon*
HELICOPTERS
  TPT 17: **Medium** 12 AW101 *Merlin* (6 SAR, 4 CSAR, 2 fishery protection); **Light** 5 AW119 *Koala*
AIR-LAUNCHED MISSILES
  AAM • IR AIM-9L/I *Sidewinder*; **ARH** AIM-120C AMRAAM
  ASM AGM-65A *Maverick*
  AShM AGM-84A *Harpoon*
BOMBS
  Laser & INS/GPS-guided GBU-49 Enhanced *Paveway* II
  INS/GPS guided GBU-31 JDAM

Gendarmerie & Paramilitary 22,600
National Republican Guard 22,600
EQUIPMENT BY TYPE
PATROL AND COASTAL COMBATANTS 46
  PBF 15 *Ribamar*
  PBI 30
  PB 1 *Bojador* (Damen FCS 3307)
HELICOPTERS • MRH 7 SA315 *Lama*

DEPLOYMENT
CENTRAL AFRICAN REPUBLIC: EU • EUTM RCA 12; **UN** • MINUSCA 219; 1 AB coy
IRAQ: NATO • NATO Mission Iraq 1
MALI: EU • EUTM Mali 4
MOZAMBIQUE: EU • EUTM Mozambique 61
ROMANIA: NATO • *Enhanced Vigilance Activity* 235; 1 injf coy(+)
SOMALIA: EU • EUTM Somalia 2

FOREIGN FORCES
United States US European Command: 250; 1 spt facility at Lajes

Romania ROM

Romanian Leu RON		2022	2023	2024
GDP	RON	1.41trn	1.59trn	1.74trn
	USD	301bn	350bn	383bn
per capita	USD	15,821	18,413	20,214
Growth	%	4.7	2.2	3.8
Inflation	%	13.8	10.7	5.8
Def exp [a]	RON	24.3bn	39.3bn	
	USD	5.20bn	8.66bn	
Def bdgt [b]	RON	25.9bn	38.8bn	
	USD	5.54bn	8.55bn	
FMA (US)	USD	75m	0m	0m
USD1=RON		4.68	4.54	4.54

[a] NATO figure
[b] Includes military pensions

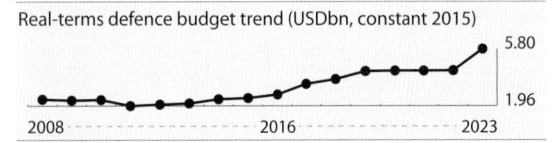

Real-terms defence budget trend (USDbn, constant 2015)
5.80
1.96
2008 — 2016 — 2023

Population	18,326,327					
Age	0–14	15–19	20–24	25–29	30–64	65 plus
Male	8.0%	2.8%	2.5%	2.3%	23.5%	9.2%
Female	7.6%	2.6%	2.4%	2.3%	23.7%	13.1%

Capabilities

Romania's armed forces are structured around territorial defence, support to NATO and EU missions, and contributing to regional and global stability and security. According to the National Defence Strategy 2020–2024, principal security threats include Russia's increased presence in the Black Sea, hybrid warfare, cyber-attacks, and terrorism. Under the armed forces transformation programme, updated in 2022, authorities are looking to modernise and upgrade the military to NATO standards. Bucharest, in February 2023, said it was increasing defence spending to 2.5% of GDP. The country has defence cooperation agreements with regional allies and, in the aftermath of Russia's 2022 full-scale invasion of Ukraine, reviewed the Roadmap for Defence Cooperation 2020–2030 with the US and bolstered other ties. The country has strategic partnerships with the US, France, the UK and, since October 2023, with Ukraine. Romania hosts the *Aegis Ashore* ballistic-missile-defence system at Deveselu. In May 2022, NATO's multinational Battle Group Forward Presence achieved initial operational capability. The country contributes to EU and NATO missions and has increased the national contingent to Kosovo KFOR. The military inventory largely comprises Soviet-era equipment, limiting its capability. Romanian airspace benefits from NATO's Enhanced Air Policing mission. The country retired the last MiG-21 *Lancer* fighters in May 2023, which are being replaced by the F-16. In 2023, Romania agreed to buy F-35 *Lightning* IIs and *Bayraktar* TB2 UAVs from Turkiye, among other modernisation efforts. The country's defence industry has struggled since 1989. Current production focuses on small arms and ammunition. However, Bucharest plans to revitalise its industry through license production efforts, such as one with General Dynamics to locally produce a new batch of *Piranha* V armoured vehicles.

ACTIVE 69,900 (Army 35,500 Navy 5,200 Air 11,700 Joint 17,500) **Gendarmerie & Paramilitary 57,000**

RESERVE 55,000 (Joint 55,000)

ORGANISATIONS BY SERVICE

Army 35,500

Readiness is reported as 70–90% for NATO-designated forces (1 div HQ, 1 mech bde, 1 inf bde & 1 mtn inf bde) and 40–70% for other forces

FORCES BY ROLE
COMMAND
  2 div HQ (2nd & 4th)
  elm 1 div HQ (MND-SE)
SPECIAL FORCES
  1 SF bde (2 SF bn, 1 para bn, 1 log bn)
MANOEUVRE
  Reconnaissance
  1 recce bde (3 recce bn, 1 AD bn, 1 log bn)
  2 recce regt
  Mechanised
  1 mech bde (2 tk bn, 2 mech inf bn, 1 arty bn, 1 AD bn, 1 log bn)
  1 mech bde (1 tk bn, 3 mech inf bn, 1 arty bn, 1 AD bn, 1 log bn)
  2 mech bde (1 tk bn, 2 mech inf bn, 1 arty bn, 1 AD bn, 1 log bn)
  1 mech bde (4 mech inf bn, 1 arty bn, 1 AD bn, 1 log bn)
  1 (MNB-SE) mech inf bde (2 armd inf bn, 1 inf bn, 1 arty bn, 1 AD bn, 1 log bn)
  Light
  2 mtn inf bde (3 mtn inf bn, 1 arty bn, 1 AD bn, 1 log bn)
COMBAT SUPPORT
  1 cbt spt bde (1 AB bn, 1 arty bn, 1 CBRN bn, 1 log bn, 1 AD bn)
  1 MRL bde (3 MRL bn, 1 STA bn, 1 log bn)
  2 arty regt
  1 engr bde (1 engr bn, 4 ptn br bn, 1 log bn)
  2 engr bn
  3 sigs bn
  1 CIMIC bn
  1 MP bn
  2 CBRN bn
COMBAT SERVICE SUPPORT
  3 spt bn
AIR DEFENCE
  3 AD regt
EQUIPMENT BY TYPE
ARMOURED FIGHTING VEHICLES
  MBT 377: 220 T-55AM; 103 TR-85; 54 TR-85 M1
  IFV 241: 41 MLI-84 (incl CP); 101 MLI-84M *Jderul*; 99 *Piranha* V
  APC 743
    APC (T) 76 MLVM
    APC (W) 607: 69 B33 TAB *Zimbru*; 31 *Piranha* IIIC; 354

TAB-71 (incl variants); 153 TAB-77 (incl variants)
PPV 60 *Maxxpro*
AUV 513: 33 JLTV; 480 TABC-79 (incl variants)
ENGINEERING & MAINTENANCE VEHICLES
ARV 55: 3 MLI-84M TEHEVAC; 8 TERA-71L; 44 TERA-77L
VLB 43 BLG-67
NBC VEHICLES 109 RCH-84
ANTI-TANK/ANTI-INFRASTRUCTURE
MSL
SP 158: 12 9P122 *Malyutka* (RS-AT-3 *Sagger*); 98 9P133 *Malyutka* (RS-AT-3 *Sagger*); 48 9P148 *Konkurs* (RS-AT-5 *Spandrel*)
MANPATS *Spike*-LR
GUNS
SP 100mm (23 SU-100 in store)
TOWED 100mm 218 M-1977
ARTILLERY 1,142
SP 122mm 40: 6 2S1 *Gvozdika*; 34 Model 89
TOWED 447: **122mm** 96 (M-30) M-1938 (A-19); **152mm** 351: 247 M-1981; 104 M-1985
MRL 206: **122mm** 170: 134 APR-40; 36 LAROM; **227mm** 36 M142 HIMARS (ATACMS-capable)
MOR 449: **SP 82mm** 177: 92 TAB-71AR; 85 TABC-79AR; **120mm** 272: 266 M-1982; 6 Piranha IIIC with *Cardom*
SURFACE-TO-SURFACE MISSILE LAUNCHERS
SRBM • Conventional MGM-168 ATACMS (Launched from M142 HIMARS MRLS)
AIR DEFENCE
SAM 96
Short-range 48: 32 2K12 *Kub* (RS-SA-6 *Gainful*); 16 9K33 *Osa* (RS-SA-8 *Gecko*)
Point-defence 48 CA-95
GUNS 65+
SP 35mm 41 *Gepard*
TOWED 24+: **14.5mm** ZPU-2; **35mm** 24 GDF-003; **57mm** S-60

Navy 5,200
EQUIPMENT BY TYPE
PRINCIPAL SURFACE COMBATANTS • FRIGATES 3
FFGH 1 *Marasesti* with 4 twin lnchr with P-22 (RS-SS-N-2C *Styx*) AShM, 2 triple 533mm ASTT with 53–65 HWT, 2 RBU 6000 *Smerch* 2 A/S mor, 4 AK630M CIWS, 2 twin 76mm guns (capacity 2 SA-316 (IAR-316) *Alouette* III hel)
FFH 2 *Regele Ferdinand* (ex-UK Type-22), with 2 triple STWS Mk.2 324mm TT, 1 76mm gun (capacity 1 SA330 (IAR-330) *Puma*)
PATROL AND COASTAL COMBATANTS 22
CORVETTES 4
FSH 2 *Tetal* II with 2 twin 533mm ASTT with SET-53M HWT, 2 RBU 6000 *Smerch* 2 A/S mor, 2 AK630 CIWS, 1 76mm gun (capacity 1 SA316 (IAR-316) *Alouette* III hel)
FS 2 *Tetal* I with 2 twin 533mm ASTT with SET-53M HWT, 2 RBU 2500 *Smerch* 1 A/S mor, 2 AK230 CIWS, 2 twin 76mm guns
PCFG 3 *Zborul* with 2 twin lnchr with P-22 (RS-SS-N-2C *Styx*) AShM, 2 AK630 CIWS, 1 76mm gun
PCR 8: 5 *Brutar* II with 2 BM-21 122mm MRL, 1 100mm gun; 3 *Kogalniceanu* with 2 BM-21 122mm MRL, 2 100mm guns
PBR 7: 1 ESM12; 6 VD141 (ex-MSR now used for river patrol)
MINE WARFARE 11
MINE COUNTERMEASURES 10
MHC 1 *Ghiculescu* (ex-UK *Sandown*)
MSO 3 *Musca* with 2 RBU 1200 *Uragan* A/S mor, 2 AK230 CIWS
MSR 6 VD141
MINELAYERS • ML 1 *Corsar* with up to 120 mines, 2 RBU 1200 *Uragan* A/S mor, 2 AK230 CIWS
LOGISTICS AND SUPPORT 8
AE 2 *Constanta* with 2 RBU 1200 *Uragan* A/S mor, 2 AK230 CIWS, 2 twin 57mm guns
AGOR 1 *Corsar*
AGS 1 *Catuneanu*
AOL 2: 1 *Tulcea*; 1 Other
ATF 1 *Grozavul*
AXS 1 *Mircea* (GER *Gorch Fock*)

Naval Infantry
FORCES BY ROLE
MANOEUVRE
Light
1 naval inf regt
EQUIPMENT BY TYPE
ARMOURED FIGHTING VEHICLES
AUV 14: 11 ABC-79M; 3 TABC-79M

Air Force 11,700
FORCES BY ROLE
FIGHTER/GROUND ATTACK
2 sqn with with F-16AM/BM *Fighting Falcon*
GROUND ATTACK
1 sqn with IAR-99 *Soim**
TRANSPORT
1 sqn with An-26 *Curl*; An-30 *Clank*; C-27J *Spartan*
1 sqn with C-130B/H *Hercules*
TRAINING
1 sqn with IAR-99 *Soim**
1 sqn with SA316B *Alouette* III (IAR-316B); Yak-52 (Iak-52)
TRANSPORT HELICOPTER
2 (multi-role) sqn with IAR-330 SOCAT *Puma*
3 sqn with SA330L/M *Puma* (IAR-330L/M)
AIR DEFENCE
1 AD bde
1 AD regt
COMBAT SERVICE SUPPORT
1 engr spt regt

EQUIPMENT BY TYPE

AIRCRAFT 41 combat capable
FTR 17: 14 F-16AM *Fighting Falcon*; 3 F-16BM *Fighting Falcon*
ISR 2 An-30 *Clank*
TPT 16: **Medium** 14: 7 C-27J *Spartan*; 4 C-130B *Hercules*; 3 C-130H *Hercules*; **Light** 2 An-26 *Curl*
TRG 36: 12 IAR-99*; 12 IAR-99C *Soim*; 12 Yak-52 (Iak-52)
HELICOPTERS
MRH 31: 23 IAR-330 SOCAT *Puma*; 8 SA316B *Alouette III* (IAR-316B)
TPT • Medium 36: 6 IAR-330L-RM; 14 SA330L *Puma* (IAR-330L); 16 SA330M *Puma* (IAR-330M)
AIR DEFENCE • SAM 8
Long-range 4 M903 *Patriot* PAC-3 MSE
Medium-range 4 MIM-23 *Hawk* PIP III
AIR-LAUNCHED MISSILES
AAM • IR AIM-9M *Sidewinder*; **IIR** AIM-9X *Sidewinder II*; **ARH** AIM-120C AMRAAM
ASM *Spike*-ER
BOMBS
Laser-guided GBU-12 *Paveway*
Laser & INS/GPS-guided GBU-54 Laser JDAM
INS/GPS guided GBU-38 JDAM

Gendarmerie & Paramilitary ε57,000

Gendarmerie ε57,000
Ministry of Interior

DEPLOYMENT

BOSNIA-HERZEGOVINA: EU • EUFOR (*Operation Althea*) 270; 1 inf coy
CENTRAL AFRICAN REPUBLIC: EU • EUTM RCA 15
DEMOCRATIC REPUBLIC OF THE CONGO: UN • MONUSCO 7
INDIA/PAKISTAN: UN • UNMOGIP 2
IRAQ: *Operation Inherent Resolve* 30; **NATO •** NATO Mission Iraq 5
KOSOVO: NATO • KFOR 214; 1 inf coy; **UN •** UNMIK 1
MALI: EU • EUTM Mali 40
MOZAMBIQUE: EU • EUTM Mozambique 12
POLAND: NATO • Enhnaced Forward Presence ε100; 1 SP ADA bty
SOMALIA: EU • EUTM Somalia 5
SOUTH SUDAN: UN • UNMISS 6

FOREIGN FORCES

Belgium NATO Enhanced Vigilance Activities: 250; 1 mech inf coy
France NATO Enhanced Vigilance Activities: 750; 1 armd BG; 1 SP arty bty with CAESAR; 1 SAM bty with SAMP/T
Luxembourg NATO Enhanced Vigilance Activities: 26; 1 recce pl
Poland NATO MNB-SE 220; 1 mech inf coy; *Rosomak*
Portugal NATO Enhanced Vigilance Activities: 235; 1 inf coy(+)
United States US European Command: 4,000; 1 air aslt bde with M119A3; M777A2; 1 *Aegis Ashore* BMD unit with 3 8-cell Mk 41 VLS with SM-3; **NATO** Air Policing: 100; 4 F-16C *Fighting Falcon*

Serbia SER

Serbian Dinar RSD		2022	2023	2024
GDP	RSD	7.09trn	8.10trn	8.77trn
	USD	63.5bn	75.0bn	81.7bn
per capita	USD	9,528	11,301	12,357
Growth	%	2.3	2.0	3.0
Inflation	%	12.0	12.4	5.3
Def bdgt	RSD	136bn	161bn	
	USD	1.22bn	1.49bn	
USD1=RSD		111.66	108.02	107.40

Real-terms defence budget trend (USDbn, constant 2015)
1.01 / 0.51 (2008 – 2016 – 2023)

Population		6,693,375				
Age	0–14	15–19	20–24	25–29	30–64	65 plus
Male	7.4%	2.8%	2.8%	3.0%	24.6%	8.2%
Female	7.0%	2.6%	2.7%	2.9%	24.5%	11.6%

Capabilities

Serbia's government adopted a Total Defence Concept in September 2023, reflected also in a defence white paper. The concept focuses on military neutrality, protection of its sovereignty and citizens, cooperation and partnership, and improvement of national security. Belgrade views separatism, ethnic and religious extremism, climate change and further international recognition of Kosovo as key threats. The Serbian armed forces are modernising to address long-term capability shortfalls and personnel shortages. Priorities include improving capabilities for combat support, bolstering air-defence, cyber and electronic warfare capacities. Serbia is pursuing air force modernisation across most capabilities sets. Belgrade has continued cooperation and dialogue with NATO through the Individual Partnership Action Plan. The country aspires to join the EU but not NATO. Serbia maintains a close relationship with Russia, which has provided military equipment. However, the country has also intensified its security relations with China, purchasing Chinese military equipment, including air defence systems. Serbia mostly trains with its Balkan neighbours, Russia and NATO countries. It contributes to EU, OSCE and UN peacekeeping missions, while firmly expressing its military neutrality. Serbia's defence industry focuses on missile and artillery systems, and small arms and ammunition, with a plan to enhance its capabilities. However, the country is reliant on external suppliers for major platforms.

ACTIVE 28,150 (Army 13,250 Air Force and Air

Defence 5,100 Training Command 3,000 Guards 1,600 Other MoD 5,200) Gendarmerie & Paramilitary 3,700

Conscript liability 6 months (voluntary)

RESERVE 50,150

ORGANISATIONS BY SERVICE

Army 13,250
FORCES BY ROLE
SPECIAL FORCES
1 spec ops bde (3 spec ops bn, 1 log coy)
MANOEUVRE
Mechanised
1 (1st) bde (1 tk bn, 2 mech inf bn, 1 inf bn, 1 SP arty bn, 1 MRL bn, 1 AD bn, 1 engr bn, 1 log bn)
3 (2nd, 3rd & 4th) bde (1 tk bn, 2 mech inf bn, 2 inf bn, 1 SP arty bn, 1 MRL bn, 1 AD bn, 1 engr bn, 1 log bn)
Air Manoeuvre
1 para bde
COMBAT SUPPORT
1 (mixed) arty bde (4 arty bn, 1 MRL bn, 1 spt bn)
2 ptn bridging bn
1 NBC bn
1 sigs bn
2 MP bn

Reserve Organisations
FORCES BY ROLE
MANOEUVRE
Light
8 (territorial) inf bde
EQUIPMENT BY TYPE
ARMOURED FIGHTING VEHICLES
  MBT 229: 195 M-84; 4+ M-84AS1 (in test); 30 T-72MS
  RECCE 76: 46 BRDM-2; 30 BRDM-2M
  IFV 326: 320 M-80; 3 M-80AB1
  APC 160
    APC(T) 44: 12 BTR-50 (CP); 32 MT-LB (CP)
    APC (W) 106: 20 BOV-KIV (CP); 9 BOV-OT M-21; 39 BOV-VP M-86; 38+ *Lazar*-3 APC
    PPV 10 M-20 MRAP
  AUV 40+ BOV M-16 *Milos*
ENGINEERING & MAINTENANCE VEHICLES
  AEV IWT
  ARV M-84A1; T-54/T-55
  VLB MT-55; TMM
ANTI-TANK/ANTI-INFRASTRUCTURE
  MSL
    SP 48 BOV-1 (M-83) with 9K11 *Malyutka* (RS-AT-3 *Sagger*)
    MANPATS 9K11 *Malyutka* (RS-AT-3 *Sagger*); 9K111 *Fagot* (RS-AT-4 *Spigot*); *Kornet*-EM
  RCL 90mm M-79

ARTILLERY 461
  SP 85: **122mm** 67 2S1 *Gvozdika*; **155mm** 18 B-52 NORA
  TOWED 132: **122mm** 78 D-30; **130mm** 18 M-46; **152mm** 36 M-84 NORA-A
  MRL 81: **128mm** 78: 18 M-63 *Plamen*; 60 M-77 *Organj*; **262mm** 3 M-87 *Orkan*
  MOR 163: **82mm** 106 M-69; **120mm** 57 M-74/M-75
AIR DEFENCE
  SAM 94+
    Short-range 77 2K12 *Kub* (RS-SA-6 *Gainful*);
    Point-defence 17+: 12 9K31M *Strela*-1M (RS-SA-9 *Gaskin*); 5 9K35M *Strela*-10M; 9K32M *Strela*-2M (RS-SA-7B *Grail*)‡; *Šilo* (RS-SA-16 *Gimlet*)
  GUNS
    SP 40mm 26+ *Pasars*-16
    TOWED 40mm 36 Bofors L/70
UNINHABITED AERIAL VEHICLES
  CISR • Medium 6 CH-92A
AIR-LAUNCHED MISSILES
  ASM FT-8C

River Flotilla
The Serbian–Montenegrin navy was transferred to Montenegro upon independence in 2006, but the Danube flotilla remained in Serbian control. The flotilla is subordinate to the Land Forces
EQUIPMENT BY TYPE
PATROL AND COASTAL COMBATANTS 4
  PBR 4: 3 Type-20; 1 *Jadar*
MINE WARFARE • MINE COUNTERMEASURES 4
  MSI 4 *Nestin* with 1 quad lnchr with 9K32 *Strela*-2M (RS-SA-N-5 *Grail*) SAM
AMPHIBIOUS • LANDING CRAFT
  LCVP 4 Type-22 (1 more non-operational)
LOGISTICS AND SUPPORT 4
  AFDL 1 RDOK-15
  AG 1 *Šabac* (deguassing vessel also used for patrol and troop transport) (capacity 80 troops)
  AGF 1 *Kozara*
  AOL 1 RPN-43

Air Force and Air Defence 5,100
FORCES BY ROLE
FIGHTER
1 sqn with MiG-29 *Fulcrum*; MiG-29UB *Fulcrum* B; MiG-29SE *Fulcrum* C
FIGHTER/GROUND ATTACK
1 sqn with J-22/NJ-22 *Orao* 1
TRANSPORT
1 sqn with An-2; An-26; Yak-40 (Jak-40); 1 PA-34 *Seneca* V
TRAINING
1 sqn with G-4 *Super Galeb** (adv trg/light atk); SA341/342 *Gazelle*; *Lasta* 95; Utva-75 (basic trg)
ATTACK HELICOPTER
1 sqn with SA341H/342L *Gazelle*; (HN-42/45); Mi-24

Hind; Mi-35M *Hind*

TRANSPORT HELICOPTER
 2 sqn with H145M; Mi-8 *Hip*; Mi-17 *Hip* H; Mi-17V-5 *Hip*

AIR DEFENCE
 1 bde (5 bn (2 msl, 3 SP msl) with S-125M *Neva*-M (RS-SA-3 *Goa*); 2K12 *Kub* (RS-SA-6 *Gainful*); 9K32 *Strela*-2 (RS-SA-7 *Grail*); 9K310 *Igla*-1 (RS-SA-16 *Gimlet*))
 2 radar bn (for early warning and reporting)

COMBAT SUPPORT
 1 sigs bn

COMBAT SERVICE SUPPORT
 1 maint bn

EQUIPMENT BY TYPE
 AIRCRAFT 51 combat capable
  FTR 14: 3 MiG-29 *Fulcrum*; 3 MiG-29UB *Fulcrum* B; 8 MiG-29SE *Fulcrum* C
  FGA up to 18 J-22/NJ-22 *Orao* 1
  ISR (10 IJ-22R *Orao* 1* in store)
  TPT • Light 9: 1 An-2 *Colt*; 4 An-26 *Curl*; 1 C295W; 2 Yak-40 (Jak-40); 1 PA-34 *Seneca* V
  TRG 44: 19 G-4 *Super Galeb**; 11 Utva-75; 14 *Lasta* 95
 HELICOPTERS
  ATK 6: 2 Mi-24 *Hind*†; 4 Mi-35M *Hind*
  MRH 52: 5 H145M; 1 Mi-17 *Hip* H; 5 Mi-17V-5 *Hip*; 2 SA341H *Gazelle* (HI-42); 26 SA341H *Gazelle* (HN-42)/SA342L *Gazelle* (HN-45); 13 SA341H *Gazelle* (HO-42)/SA342L1 *Gazelle* (HO-45)
  TPT • Medium 8 Mi-8T *Hip* (HT-40)
 AIR DEFENCE
  SAM 19+
   Long-range 4 FK-3 (HQ-22)
   Short-range 15: 6 S-125M *Neva*-M (RS-SA-3 *Goa*); 9 2K12 *Kub* (RS-SA-6 *Gainful*)
   Point-defence 9K32 *Strela*-2 (RS-SA-7 *Grail*)‡; 9K310 *Igla*-1 (RS-SA-16 *Gimlet*)
  SPAAGM 30mm 6 96K6 *Pantsir*-S1 (RS-SA-22 *Greyhound*)
  GUNS • TOWED 40mm 24 Bofors L/70
 AIR-LAUNCHED MISSILES
  AAM • IR R-60 (RS-AA-8 *Aphid*); R-73 (RS-AA-11A *Archer*); **SARH** R-27ER (RS-AA-10C *Alamo*); **ARH** R-77 (RS-AA-12 *Adder*)
  ASM AGM-65 *Maverick*; A-77 *Thunder*; Kh-29T (RS-AS-14B *Kedge*)

Guards 1,600
FORCES BY ROLE
MANOEUVRE
 Other
  1 (ceremonial) gd bde (1 gd bn, 1 MP bn, 1 spt bn)

Gendarmerie & Paramilitary 3,700

Gendarmerie 3,700

EQUIPMENT BY TYPE
ARMOURED FIGHTING VEHICLES
 APC • APC (W) 24: 12 *Lazar*-3; 12 BOV-VP M-86
 AUV BOV M16 *Milos*

DEPLOYMENT

CENTRAL AFRICAN REPUBLIC: EU • EUTM RCA 7; **UN •** MINUSCA 74; 1 med coy
CYPRUS: UN • UNFICYP 8
LEBANON: UN • UNIFIL 182; 1 mech inf coy
MIDDLE EAST: UN • UNTSO 1
SOMALIA: EU • EUTM Somalia 6

KOSOVO

In February 2008, Kosovo declared itself independent. Serbia remains opposed to this, and while Kosovo has not been admitted to the United Nations, a number of states have recognised Kosovo's self-declared status. Data here represents the de facto situation in Kosovo. This does not imply international recognition as a sovereign state.

Kosovo Security Force 3,000

The Kosovo Security Force (KSF), formed in January 2009, is tasked with defence of the country, support to civil authorities in case of national emergencies and participation in international operations. A series of legislative changes passed by the Kosovo Assembly in 2018 redefined it as a regular military organisation as part of a transformation process intended to be complete by 2028.

FORCES BY ROLE
SPECIAL FORCES
 1 spec ops unit
MANOEUVRE
 Light
  3 inf bn
COMBAT/ISR UAV
 1 sqn with *Bayraktar* TB2
EQUIPMENT BY TYPE
ARMOURED FIGHTING VEHICLES
 AUV 71: 55 M1117 *Guardian*; 16+ *Cobra*
ANTI-TANK/ANTI-INFRASTRUCTURE
 MANPATS OMTAS
ARTILLERY
 MOR 2+: **81mm** some; **120mm** some; **SP 120mm** 2 *Vuran* with *Alkar*
UNIHABITED AERIAL VEHICLES
 CISR • Medium 5 *Bayraktar* TB2

FOREIGN FORCES

All under Kosovo Force (KFOR) command unless otherwise specified

Albania 89

Armenia 57

Austria 271; 1 recce coy; 1 mech inf coy; 1 log coy • UNMIK 1

Bulgaria 142; 1 inf coy

Canada 5

Croatia 151; 1 inf coy; 1 hel flt with Mi-8

Czech Republic 36 • UNMIK 1

Denmark 35

Finland 70

Germany 70

Greece 260; 1 inf bn HQ; 2 inf coy

Hungary 433; 1 inf bn HQ; 2 inf coy • UNMIK 1

Ireland 13

Italy 873; 1 armd inf regt BG HQ; 1 ISR bn; 1 Carabinieri unit

Latvia 136; 1 inf coy

Lithuania 1

Macedonia, North 60

Moldova 41 • UNMIK 1

Montenegro 2

Poland 245; 1 inf coy • UNMIK 2

Romania 214; 1 inf coy • UNMIK 1

Slovenia 129; 1 mot inf coy; 1 MP unit; 1 hel unit • UNMIK 1

Sweden 3

Switzerland 190; 1 engr pl; 1 hel flt with AS332

Turkiye 369; 1 inf coy • UNMIK 1

Ukraine 40

United Kingdom 600; 1 inf bn

United States 593; elm 1 ARNG inf bde HQ; 1 ARNG AB bn HQ; 1 ARNG inf coy; 1 hel flt with UH-60

Slovakia SVK

Euro EUR		2022	2023	2024
GDP	EUR	110bn	122bn	133bn
	USD	116bn	133bn	145bn
per capita	USD	21,263	24,471	26,714
Growth	%	1.7	1.3	2.5
Inflation	%	12.1	10.9	4.8
Def exp [a]	EUR	1.98bn	2.46bn	
	USD	2.09bn	2.68bn	
Def bdgt	EUR	1.90bn	2.46bn	
	USD	2.00bn	2.67bn	
FMA (US)	USD	200m	0m	0m
USD1=EUR		0.95	0.92	0.91

[a] NATO figure

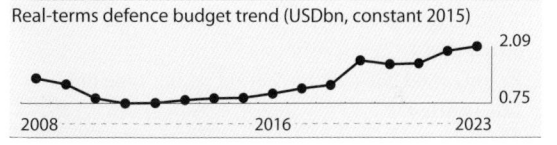

Real-terms defence budget trend (USDbn, constant 2015)
2.09
0.75
2008 — 2016 — 2023

Population	5,569,395					
Age	0–14	15–19	20–24	25–29	30–64	65 plus
Male	8.0%	2.5%	2.5%	2.7%	25.5%	7.1%
Female	7.4%	2.5%	2.4%	2.9%	25.9%	10.7%

Capabilities

Slovakia is looking to modernise its armed forces and replace obsolete equipment while contributing to international crisis management missions. A defence white paper in September 2016 set out security priorities and a plan to increase defence capabilities. In 2017, the government approved a Long-Term Defence Development Plan. A new national-security strategy and a new defence strategy were drafted in 2020 and adopted by parliament in January 2021. A NATO and EU member state, Slovakia cooperates closely with the Visegrád Group. Bratislava has signed an agreement to enable air policing and closer integration of air-defence capabilities. A Defence Cooperation Agreement was signed with the US in 2022 and funds were allocated to Slovakia under the Foreign Military Financing Programme to help the country replace part of the military equipment sent to Ukraine since the Russian invasion. In 2022, Germany began delivering *Leopard* 2A4 MBTs to Slovakia to replenish infantry fighting vehicles that Bratislava sent to Ukraine. The country also is modernising its air force and ground forces. Slovakia has deployed a company-sized unit to NATO's Enhanced Forward Presence in Latvia and stood up the EFP Battlegroup Slovakia to assist in defending NATO's eastern flank. Part of Slovakia's defence-industrial base is organised within the state-controlled holding company DMD Group, including KONSTRUKTA Defence, which produces land systems. Other companies focus on maintenance, repair and overhaul services.

ACTIVE 17,850 (Army 10,450 Air 4,400 Special Forces 1,200 Central Staff 1,800)

ORGANISATIONS BY SERVICE

Special Forces 1,200
FORCES BY ROLE
SPECIAL FORCES
  1 (5th) spec ops bn
MANOEUVRE
  Air Manoeuvre
  1 AB bn
COMBAT SUPPORT
  1 psyops unit

Army 10,450
FORCES BY ROLE
MANOEUVRE
  Reconnaissance
  1 recce bn
  Armoured
  1 (2nd) armd bde (1 tk bn, 2 armd inf bn, 1 log bn)
  Mechanised
  1 (1st) mech bde (3 armd inf bn, 1 engr bn, 1 log bn)
COMBAT SUPPORT
  1 arty regt (1 mixed SP arty bn, 1 MRL bn)
  1 MP bn
  1 NBC bn
COMBAT SERVICE SUPPORT
  1 spt bde (1 maint bn, 1 spt bn)
EQUIPMENT BY TYPE
ARMOURED FIGHTING VEHICLES
  MBT 36: 6 *Leopard* 2A4; 30 T-72M
  RECCE 18 BPsVI
  IFV 213: 105 BMP-1; 91 BMP-2; 17 BVP-M
  APC 101+
    APC (T) 72 OT-90
    APC (W) 22: 7 OT-64; 15 *Tatrapan* (6×6)
    PPV 7+ RG-32M
  AUV IVECO LMV
ENGINEERING & MAINTENANCE VEHICLES
  ARV MT-55; VT-55A; VT-72B; WPT-TOPAS
  VLB AM-50; MT-55A
  MW *Bozena*; UOS-155 *Belarty*
ANTI-TANK/ANTI-INFRASTRUCTURE
  SP 9S428 with *Malyutka* (RS-AT-3 *Sagger*) on BMP-1; 9P135 *Fagot* (RS-AT-4 *Spigot*) on BMP-2; 9P148 *Konkurs* (RS-AT-5 *Spandrel*) on BRDM-2
  MANPATS 9K11 *Malyutka* (RS-AT-3 *Sagger*); 9K111-1 *Konkurs* (RS-AT-5 *Spandrel*)
  RCL 84mm *Carl Gustaf*
ARTILLERY 60
  SP 30: **152mm** 3 M-77 *Dana*; **155mm** 27: 16 M-2000 *Zuzana*; 11 *Zuzana*-2
  MRL 30: **122mm** 4 RM-70; **122/227mm** 26 RM-70/85 MODULAR

AIR DEFENCE
  SAM • **Point-defence** 9K310 *Igla*-1 (RS-SA-16 *Gimlet*)

Air Force 4,400
FORCES BY ROLE
TRANSPORT
  1 flt with C-27J *Spartan*
  1 flt with L-410FG/T *Turbolet*
TRANSPORT HELICOPTER
  1 sqn with Mi-17 *Hip* H
  1 sqn with UH-60M *Black Hawk*
TRAINING
  1 sqn with L-39CM/ZAM *Albatros**
AIR DEFENCE
  1 bde with 2K12 *Kub* (RS-SA-6 *Gainful*)
EQUIPMENT BY TYPE
AIRCRAFT 8 combat capable
  TPT 5: **Medium** 2 C-27J *Spartan*; **Light** 3: 1 L-410FG *Turbolet*; 2 L-410T *Turbolet*; (4 L-410UVP *Turbolet* in store)
  TRG 8: 6 L-39CM *Albatros**; 2 L-39ZAM *Albatros** (1 more in store)
HELICOPTERS
  ATK (15: 5 Mi-24D *Hind* D; 10 Mi-24V *Hind* E all in store)
  MRH 13 Mi-17 *Hip* H (incl 4 SAR)
  TPT • **Medium** 9 UH-60M *Black Hawk*
AIR DEFENCE • SAM
  Short-range 2K12 *Kub* (RS-SA-6 *Gainful*)

DEPLOYMENT

BOSNIA-HERZEGOVINA: EU • EUFOR (*Operation Althea*) 54
CYPRUS: UN • UNFICYP 238; 2 inf coy; 1 engr pl
IRAQ: *Operation Inherent Resolve* 1; **NATO** • NATO Mission Iraq 7
LATVIA: NATO • Enhanced Forward Presence 130; 1 arty bty with M-2000 *Zuzana*
MALI: EU • EUTM Mali 5
MIDDLE EAST: UN • UNTSO 2

FOREIGN FORCES

All under NATO Enhanced Vigilance Activities
Czech Republic 400; 1 mech inf bn HQ; 1 mech inf coy
Germany 160; 1 tk coy
Italy 1 SAM bty with SAMP/T
Slovenia 100; 1 mot inf coy
United States 160; 1 recce tp (coy)

Slovenia SVN

Euro EUR		2022	2023	2024
GDP	EUR	57.0bn	62.8bn	67.5bn
	USD	60.1bn	68.4bn	73.9bn
per capita	USD	28,527	32,350	34,914
Growth	%	2.5	2.0	2.2
Inflation	%	8.8	7.4	4.2
Def exp [a]	EUR	737m	873m	
	USD	777m	950m	
Def bdgt [b]	EUR		835m	939m
	USD		880m	1.02bn
FMA (US)	USD	13m	0m	0m
USD1=EUR		0.95	0.92	0.91

[a] NATO figure
[b] Includes military pensions

Real-terms defence budget trend (USDm, constant 2015)
816
396
2008　2016　2023

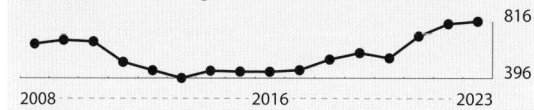

Population	2,099,790					
Age	0–14	15–19	20–24	25–29	30–64	65 plus
Male	7.5%	2.4%	2.4%	2.5%	25.3%	9.9%
Female	7.1%	2.3%	2.2%	2.3%	23.3%	12.8%

Capabilities

Since joining NATO and the EU in 2004, territorial defence and the ability to take part in peace-support operations have been central to Slovenia's defence strategy. The government in 2020 published a white paper and in 2022 authorised the Long-Term Development Programme for the Slovenian Armed Forces 2022-35. Subsequently, the government adopted a Medium-Term Development Programme to serve as the guiding document for defence programming and planning. Defence spending is increasing. Short term plans are focused on developing a medium-weight infantry battalion and an armoured reconnaissance battalion, both to be equipped with new wheeled armoured vehicles. Fixed-wing and rotary-wing transport capabilities are modestly improving with new acquisitions and upgrades. The country plans to establish a cyber reserve force. Slovenia acts as the framework nation for the NATO Mountain Warfare Centre of Excellence. Italy and Hungary provide air policing capability under NATO arrangements. The country has contributed to EU, NATO and UN operations. Slovenia participates in NATO's Enhanced Forward Presence, where it contributes to the Canadian-led battlegroup in Latvia and to the newly formed battlegroup in Slovakia. Its defence industry relies heavily on exports for its revenue and focuses on personal equipment, small arms and ammunition, and CBRN protection and detection.

ACTIVE 6,400 (Army 6,400)

RESERVE 750 (Army 750)

ORGANISATIONS BY SERVICE

Army 6,400
FORCES BY ROLE
Regt are bn sized
SPECIAL FORCES
1 SF unit (1 spec ops coy, 1 CSS coy)
MANOEUVRE
  Mechanised
1 (1st) mech inf bde (1 mech inf regt, 1 mtn inf regt, 1 cbt spt bn (1 ISR coy, 1 arty bty, 1 engr coy, 1 MP coy, 1 CBRN coy, 1 sigs coy, 1 SAM bty))
1 (72nd) mech inf bde (2 mech inf regt, 1 cbt spt bn (1 ISR coy, 1 arty bty, 1 engr coy, 1 MP coy, 1 CBRN coy, 1 sigs coy, 1 SAM bty))
COMBAT SUPPORT
1 EW coy
COMBAT SERVICE SUPPORT
1 log bde (1 log regt, 1 maint regt (1 tk coy), 1 med regt)

Reserves
FORCES BY ROLE
MANOEUVRE
  Mountain
2 inf regt (territorial – 1 allocated to each inf bde)
EQUIPMENT BY TYPE
ARMOURED FIGHTING VEHICLES
  MBT 14 M-84 (trg role) (32 more in store)
  APC 95+:
    APC (W) 95: 65 *Pandur* 6×6 (*Valuk*); 30 Patria 8×8 (*Svarun*)
    PPV *Cougar* 6×6 JERRV
  AUV 38 JLTV
ENGINEERING & MAINTENANCE VEHICLES
  ARV VT-55A
  VLB MT-55A
NBC VEHICLES 10 *Cobra* CBRN
ANTI-TANK/ANTI-INFRASTRUCTURE
  MSL • MANPATS *Spike* MR/LR
ARTILLERY 68
  TOWED • 155mm 18 TN-90
  MOR 50+: 82mm M-69; 120mm 50 MN-9/M-74
AIR DEFENCE • SAM • Point-defence 9K338 *Igla*-S (RS-SA-24 *Grinch*)

Army Maritime Element 130
FORCES BY ROLE
SPECIAL FORCES
1 SF unit
EQUIPMENT BY TYPE
PATROL AND COASTAL COMBATANTS 2
  PCC 1 *Triglav* III (RUS *Svetlyak*) with 1 AK630 CIWS
  PBF 1 *Super Dvora* MkII

UNINHABITED MARITIME SYSTEMS
UUV • MW *Comet*-MCM

Air Element 600
FORCES BY ROLE
TRANSPORT
1 sqn with *Falcon* 2000EX; L-410 *Turbolet*; PC-6B *Turbo Porter*
TRAINING
1 unit with Bell 206 *Jet Ranger* (AB-206); PC-9M*; Z-143L; Z-242L
TRANSPORT HELICOPTER
1 sqn with AS532AL *Cougar*; Bell 412 *Twin Huey*
COMBAT SERVICE SUPPORT
1 maint sqn
EQUIPMENT BY TYPE
AIRCRAFT 9 combat capable
TPT 4: **Light** 3: 1 L-410 *Turbolet*; 2 PC-6B *Turbo Porter*
PAX 1 *Falcon* 2000EX
TRG 19: 9 PC-9M*; 2 Z-143L; 8 Z-242L
HELICOPTERS
MRH 8: 5 Bell 412EP *Twin Huey*; 2 Bell 412HP *Twin Huey*; 1 Bell 412SP *Twin Huey*
TPT 8: **Medium** 4 AS532AL *Cougar*; **Light** 4 Bell 206 *Jet Ranger* (AB-206)

DEPLOYMENT
BOSNIA-HERZEGOVINA: EU • EUFOR (*Operation Althea*) 20
IRAQ: *Operation Inherent Resolve* 3
KOSOVO: NATO • KFOR 129; 1 mot inf coy; 1 MP unit; 1 hel unit; UN • UNMIK 1
LATVIA: NATO • Enhanced Forward Presence 42; 1 arty bty
LEBANON: UN • UNIFIL 1
MIDDLE EAST: UN • UNTSO 4
SLOVAKIA: NATO • Enhanced Vigilance Activities 100; 1 mot inf coy

Spain ESP

Euro EUR		2022	2023	2024
GDP	EUR	1.35trn	1.45trn	1.53trn
	USD	1.42trn	1.58trn	1.68trn
per capita	USD	29,800	33,090	34,933
Growth	%	5.8	2.5	1.7
Inflation	%	8.3	3.5	3.9
Def exp [a]	EUR	14.1bn	18.0bn	
	USD	14.9bn	19.6bn	
Def bdgt [b]	EUR	13.9bn	17.5bn	
	USD	14.6bn	19.0bn	
USD1=EUR		0.95	0.92	0.91

[a] NATO figure
[b] Includes military pensions

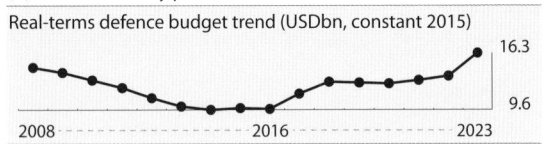

Real-terms defence budget trend (USDbn, constant 2015): 16.3 (2023), 9.6 (low, ~2016), from 2008 to 2023.

Population 47,222,613

Age	0–14	15–19	20–24	25–29	30–64	65 plus
Male	6.8%	2.7%	2.6%	2.4%	25.4%	8.8%
Female	6.5%	2.6%	2.5%	2.4%	25.5%	11.7%

Capabilities

The 2021 National Security Strategy put an increased emphasis on strengthening capacity against hybrid threats. Following Russia's full-scale invasion of Ukraine in February 2022, the government unveiled plans to increase defence spending with the eventual goal of reaching the NATO goal of spending 2% of GDP on defence by 2029. The National Defence Directive, issued in June 2020, updated defence policy guidelines and indicated a desire to foster an integrated approach to security alongside a drive to strengthen the national defence industry. Spain continues to support NATO, EU and UN operations abroad, and hosts one of NATO's two Combined Air Operations Centres. The armed forces are well trained and routinely participate in domestic and multinational exercises. The country's equipment and logistics-support capability appears to be sufficient to meet its national commitments and contribution to NATO operations and exercises. Madrid has significant equipment modernisation plans. Spain participates in the Future Combat Air System project with France and Germany. Spain's defence industry manufactures across all domains and exports globally, with major firms including state-owned shipbuilder Navantia, Airbus, and Santa Barbara Sistemas, part of General Dynamics.

ACTIVE 124,150 (Army 71,900 Navy 20,500 Air 20,350 Joint 11,400) Gendarmerie & Paramilitary 80,000

RESERVE 14,500 (Army 8,550 Navy 2,900 Air 2,550 Other 500) Gendarmerie & Paramilitary 6,950

ORGANISATIONS BY SERVICE

Space
EQUIPMENT BY TYPE
SATELLITES 3
  COMMUNICATIONS 2: 1 *Spainsat*; 1 *Xtar-Eur*
  ISR 1 *Paz*

Army 71,900
The Land Forces High Readiness HQ Spain provides one NATO Rapid Deployment Corps HQ (NRDC-ESP)
FORCES BY ROLE
COMMAND
  1 corps HQ (CGTAD/NRDC-ESP) (1 int regt, 1 MP bn)
  2 div HQ
SPECIAL FORCES
  1 comd (3 spec ops bn, 1 int coy, 1 sigs coy, 1 log bn)
MANOEUVRE
  Reconnaissance
  1 armd cav regt (2 armd recce bn)
  Mechanised
  2 (10th & 11th) mech bde (1 armd regt (1 armd recce bn, 1 tk bn), 1 mech inf regt (1 armd inf bn, 1 mech inf bn), 1 lt inf bn, 1 SP arty bn, 1 AT coy, 1 AD coy, 1 engr bn, 1 int coy, 1 NBC coy, 1 sigs coy, 1 log bn)
  1 (12th) mech bde (1 armd regt (1 armd recce bn, 1 tk bn), 1 mech inf regt (1 armd inf bn, 1 mech inf bn), 1 SP arty bn, 1 AT coy, 1 AD coy, 1 engr bn, 1 int coy, 1 NBC coy, 1 sigs coy, 1 log bn)
  1 (1st) mech bde (1 armd regt (1 armd recce bn, 1 tk bn), 1 armd inf regt (1 armd inf bn), 1 mot inf bn, 1 SP arty bn, 1 AT coy, 1 AD coy, 1 engr bn, 1 int coy, 1 NBC coy, 1 sigs coy, 1 log bn)
  2 (2nd/La Legion & 7th) lt mech bde (1 armd recce bn, 1 mech inf regt (2 mech inf bn), 1 lt inf bn, 1 fd arty bn, 1 AT coy, 1 AD coy, 1 engr bn, 1 int coy, 1 NBC coy, 1 sigs coy, 1 log bn)
  Mountain
  1 mtn comd (1 mtn inf regt (1 mtn inf bn, 1 mtn inf coy); 1 mtn inf bn)
  Air Manoeuvre
  1 (6th) bde (1 recce bn, 2 para bn, 1 lt inf bn, 1 fd arty bn, 1 AT coy, 1 AD coy, 1 engr bn, 1 int coy, 1 NBC coy, 1 sigs coy, 1 log bn)
  Other
  1 (Canary Islands) comd (1 lt inf bde (2 mech inf regt (1 mech inf bn), 1 lt inf regt (1 lt inf bn), 1 fd arty regt,1 AT coy, 1 engr bn, 1 int coy, 1 NBC coy, 1 sigs coy, 1 log bn); 1 EW regt; 1 spt hel bn; 1 AD regt)
  1 (Balearic Islands) comd (1 inf regt (1 lt inf bn))
  2 (Ceuta and Melilla) comd (1 recce regt, 1 mech inf bn, 1 inf bn, 1 arty regt (1 fd arty bn, 1 ADA bn), 1 engr bn, 1 sigs coy, 1 log bn)
COMBAT SUPPORT
  1 arty comd (2 arty regt; 1 coastal arty regt)
  1 engr comd (2 engr regt, 1 bridging regt)
  1 EW/sigs bde (2 EW regt, 3 sigs regt)
  1 NBC regt
  1 info ops regt (1 CIMIC bn; 1 Psyops bn)
  1 int regt
COMBAT SERVICE SUPPORT
  1 log bde (5 log regt; 1 tpt regt; 1 med regt (1 log bn, 2 med bn, 1 fd hospital bn))
HELICOPTER
  1 hel comd (1 atk hel bn, 2 spt hel bn, 1 tpt hel bn, 1 sigs bn, 1 log unit (1 spt coy, 1 supply coy))
AIR DEFENCE
  1 AD comd (3 SAM regt, 1 sigs unit)
EQUIPMENT BY TYPE
ARMOURED FIGHTING VEHICLES
  MBT 219 *Leopard* 2E; (98 *Leopard* 2A4 in store)
  ASLT 84 B1 *Centauro*
  RECCE 187 VEC-M1
  IFV 225: 204 *Pizarro*; 21 *Pizarro* (CP)
  APC 890
    APC (T) 453: 20 Bv-206S; 433 M113 (incl variants)
    APC (W) 327: 320 BMR-600/BMR-600M1; 7 VCR 8x8 *Dragon* (in test)
  PPV 110 RG-31
  AUV 258 IVECO LMV
ENGINEERING & MAINTENANCE VEHICLES
  AEV 27: 26 CZ-10/25E; 1 *Pizarro* CEV (*Castor*) (in test)
  ARV 51: 16 *Leopard* REC; 5 BMR REC; 4 *Centauro* REC; 14 *Maxxpro* MRV; 12 M113
  VLB 15 M60 AVLB
  MW 6 *Husky* 2G
ANTI-TANK/ANTI-INFRASTRUCTURE
  MSL • MANPATS *Spike*-LR; TOW
ARTILLERY 1,552
  SP 155mm 95 M109A5
  TOWED 268: **105mm** 204: 56 L118 Light Gun; 148 Model 56 pack howitzer; **155mm** 64 SBT 155/52 SIAC
  MOR 1,189: **81mm** 777; **SP 81mm** 10 VAMTAC with *Cardom* 81mm; **120mm** 402
COASTAL DEFENCE • ARTY 155mm 19 SBT 155/52 APU SBT V07
HELICOPTERS
  ATK 18 *Tiger* HAD-E
  TPT 85: **Heavy** 17: 13 CH-47D *Chinook* (HT-17D); 4 CH-47F *Chinook*; **Medium** 49: 16 AS332B *Super Puma* (HU-21); 12 AS532UL *Cougar*; 6 AS532AL *Cougar*; 15 NH90 TTH; **Light** 19: 3 Bell 212 (HU.18); 16 H135 (HE.26/HU.26)
UAV • ISR • Medium 6: 2 *Searcher* MkII-J (PASI); 4 *Searcher* MkIII (PASI)
AIR DEFENCE
  SAM 75+
    Long-range 18 M901 *Patriot* PAC-2
    Medium-range 36 MIM-23B I-*Hawk* Phase III
    Short-range 21: 8 NASAMS; 13 *Skyguard/Aspide*

Point-defence Mistral
GUNS • TOWED 35mm 67: 19 GDF-005; 48 GDF-007
AIR-LAUNCHED MISSILES • ASM Spike-ER

Navy 20,500 (incl Naval Aviation and Marines)
EQUIPMENT BY TYPE
SUBMARINES • SSK 2:
  1 *Isaac Peral* (S-80 plus) with 6 single 533mm TT with UGM-84L *Harpoon* Block II AShM/DM2A4 HWT
  1 *Galerna* with 4 single 533mm TT with F17 mod 2 HWT
PRINCIPAL SURFACE COMBATANTS 11
  DESTROYERS • DDGHM 5 *Alvaro de Bazan* with *Aegis* Baseline 5 C2, 2 quad lnchr with RGM-84F *Harpoon* Block 1D AShM, 6 8-cell Mk 41 VLS with SM-2 Block IIIA/RIM-162B ESSM SAM, 2 twin 324mm SVTT Mk 32 mod 9 ASTT with Mk 46 mod 5 LWT, 1 127mm gun (capacity 1 SH-60B *Seahawk* ASW hel)
  FRIGATES • FFGH 6 *Santa Maria* with 1 Mk 13 GMLS with RGM-84C *Harpoon* Block 1B AShM, 2 triple 324mm SVTT Mk 32 ASTT with Mk 46 mod 5 LWT, 1 *Meroka* mod 2B CIWS, 1 76mm gun (capacity 2 SH-60B *Seahawk* ASW hel)
PATROL AND COASTAL COMBATANTS 23
  PSOH 6 *Meteoro* (*Buques de Accion Maritima*) with 1 76mm gun
  PSO 4: 3 *Alboran* each with 1 hel landing platform; 1 *Descubierta* with 1 76mm gun
  PCO 4 *Serviola* with 1 76mm gun
  PCC 3 *Anaga* with 1 76mm gun
  PB 5: 1 *Isla Pinto* (Rodman 66); 1 Rodman 101; 2 *Toralla*
  PBR 2: 1 *Cabo Fradera*; 1 P-101
MINE WARFARE • MINE COUNTERMEASURES 6
  MHO 6 *Segura*
AMPHIBIOUS
  PRINCIPAL AMPHIBIOUS SHIPS 3:
    LHD 1 *Juan Carlos* I (capacity 18 hel or 10 AV-8B FGA ac; 4 LCM-1E; 42 APC; 46 MBT; 900 troops)
    LPD 2 *Galicia* (capacity 6 Bell 212 hel; 4 LCM or 2 LCM & 8 AAV; 130 APC or 33 MBT; 540 troops)
  LANDING CRAFT • LCM 12 LCM 1E
LOGISTICS AND SUPPORT 31
  AGI 1 *Alerta*
  AGOR 2: 1 *Hesperides* with 1 hel landing platform; 1 *Las Palmas*
  AGS 3: 2 *Malaspina*; 1 *Castor*
  AKR 1 *Ysabel*
  AORH 2: 1 *Patino* (capacity 3 Bell 212 hel); 1 *Cantabria* (capacity 3 Bell 212 hel)
  AP 1 *Contramaestre Casado* with 1 hel landing platform
  ASR 1 *Neptuno*
  ATF 3: 1 *Mar Caribe*; 1 *Mahon*; 1 *La Grana*
  AX 1 *Intermares*
  AXL 6: 2 *Maestre de Marinería*; 4 *Guardiamarina*
  AXS 10

UNINHABITED MARITIME SYSTEMS
USV • DATA *Mariner*; *Otter*
UUV
  DATA *Sparus* II
  MW *Pluto* Plus

Naval Aviation 850
FORCES BY ROLE
FIGHTER/GROUND ATTACK
  1 sqn with AV-8B *Harrier* II Plus
ANTI-SUBMARINE WARFARE
  2 sqn with SH-60B/F *Seahawk*
TRANSPORT
  1 (liaison) sqn with Cessna 550 *Citation* II; Cessna 650 *Citation* VII
TRAINING
  1 flt with TAV-8B *Harrier*
TRANSPORT HELICOPTER
  1 sqn with Bell 212 (HU-18)
  1 sqn with H135
EQUIPMENT BY TYPE
AIRCRAFT 13 combat capable
  FGA 13: 12 AV-8B *Harrier* II Plus; 1 TAV-8B *Harrier* (on lease from USMC)
  TPT • Light 3: 2 Cessna 550 *Citation* II; 1 Cessna 650 *Citation* VII
HELICOPTERS
  ASW 18: 12 SH-60B *Seahawk*; 6 SH-60F *Seahawk*
  TPT • Light 8: 7 Bell 212 (HA-18); 1 H135
AIR-LAUNCHED MISSILES
  AAM • IR AIM-9L *Sidewinder*; **ARH** AIM-120 AMRAAM
  ASM AGM-65G *Maverick*; AGM-114K/R *Hellfire* II
  AShM AGM-119 *Penguin*

Marines 5,350
FORCES BY ROLE
SPECIAL FORCES
  1 spec ops bn
MANOEUVRE
  Amphibious
  1 mne bde (1 recce unit, 1 mech inf bn, 2 inf bn, 1 arty bn, 1 log bn)
  Other
  1 sy bde (5 mne garrison gp)
EQUIPMENT BY TYPE
ARMOURED FIGHTING VEHICLES
  APC • APC (W) 34: 32 *Piranha* IIIC; 1 *Piranha* IIIC (amb); 1 *Piranha* IIIC EW (EW)
  AAV 18: 16 AAV-7A1/AAVP-7A1; 2 AAVC-7A1 (CP)
ENGINEERING & MAINTENANCE VEHICLES
  AEV 4 *Piranha* IIIC
  ARV 3: 1 AAVR-7A1; 1 M88; 1 *Piranha* IIIC
ARTILLERY 30
  SP 155mm 6 M109A2
  TOWED 105mm 24 Model 56 pack howitzer

ANTI-TANK/ANTI-INFRASTRUCTURE
MSL • MANPATS Spike-LR; TOW-2
AIR DEFENCE • SAM • Point-defence Mistral

Air Force 20,350

The Spanish Air Force is organised in 3 commands – General Air Command, Combat Air Command and Canary Islands Air Command

FORCES BY ROLE
FIGHTER
2 sqn with Eurofighter *Typhoon*
FIGHTER/GROUND ATTACK
5 sqn with F/A-18A/B MLU *Hornet* (EF-18A/B MLU)
ISR
1 sqn with Beech C90 *King Air*
1 sqn with Cessna 550 *Citation* V; CN235 (TR-19A)
SEARCH & RESCUE
1 sqn with AS332B/B1 *Super Puma*; CN235 VIGMA
1 sqn with AS332B *Super Puma*; CN235 VIGMA; H215 (AS332C1) *Super Puma*
1 sqn with C-212 *Aviocar*; CN235 VIGMA
TANKER/TRANSPORT
1 sqn with A400M
TRANSPORT
1 VIP sqn with A310; *Falcon* 900
1 sqn with A400M
1 sqn with C-212 *Aviocar*
2 sqn with C295
1 sqn with CN235
TRAINING
1 OCU sqn with Eurofighter *Typhoon*
1 OCU sqn with F/A-18A/B (EF-18A/B MLU) *Hornet*
1 sqn with Beech F33C *Bonanza*
1 sqn with C-212 *Aviocar*
1 sqn with PC-21
2 (LIFT) sqn with F-5B *Freedom Fighter*
1 hel sqn with H120 *Colibri*
1 hel sqn with H135; S-76C
TRANSPORT HELICOPTER
1 sqn with AS332M1 *Super Puma*; AS532UL *Cougar* (VIP)
ISR UAV
1 sqn with MQ-9A *Reaper* (forming)
EQUIPMENT BY TYPE
AIRCRAFT 174 combat capable
  FTR 88: 69 Eurofighter *Typhoon*; 19 F-5B *Freedom Fighter*
  FGA 83: 20 F/A-18A *Hornet* (EF-18A); 51 EF-18A MLU; 12 EF-18B MLU
  MP 8 CN235 VIGMA
  ISR 2 CN235 (TR-19A)
  EW 1 C-212 *Aviocar* (TM.12D)
  TPT 73: **Heavy** 13 A400M; **Light** 51: 3 Beech C90 *King Air*; 15 Beech F33C *Bonanza*; 10 C-212 *Aviocar* (incl 9 trg); 12 C295; 8 CN235; 3 Cessna 560 *Citation* V (ISR);

PAX 9: 2 A310; 2 A330 (to be converted to MRTT tkt/tpt configuration); 5 *Falcon* 900 (VIP)
  TRG 24 PC-21
HELICOPTERS
  TPT 44: **Medium** 21: 5 AS332B/B1 *Super Puma*; 4 AS332M1 *Super Puma*; 4 H215 (AS332C1) *Super Puma*; 2 AS532UL *Cougar* (VIP); 6 NH90 TTH; **Light** 23: 14 H120 *Colibri*; 1 H135; 8 S-76C
UNINHABITED AERIAL VEHICLES
  CISR • **Heavy** 4 MQ-9A *Reaper* (unarmed)
AIR DEFENCE • SAM
  Short-range *Skyguard/Aspide*
  Point-defence *Mistral*
AIR-LAUNCHED MISSILES
  AAM • **IR** AIM-9L/JULI *Sidewinder*; **IIR** IRIS-T; **SARH** AIM-7P *Sparrow*; **ARH** AIM-120B/C AMRAAM; *Meteor*
  ARM AGM-88B HARM
  ASM AGM-65G *Maverick*
  AShM AGM-84D *Harpoon*
  LACM Taurus KEPD 350
BOMBS
  Laser-guided: GBU-10/-12/-16 *Paveway* II; GBU-24 *Paveway* III; BPG-2000
  Laser & INS/GPS-guided EGBU-16 *Paveway* II
  INS/GPS guided: GBU-38 JDAM

Emergencies Military Unit (UME) 3,500

FORCES BY ROLE
COMMAND
  1 div HQ
MANOEUVRE
  Other
  5 Emergency Intervention bn
  1 Emergency Support and Intervention regt
COMBAT SUPPORT
  1 sigs bn
HELICOPTER
  1 hel bn (opcon Army)

Gendarmerie & Paramilitary 80,000

Guardia Civil 80,000

17 regions, 54 Rural Comds
FORCES BY ROLE
SPECIAL FORCES
  8 (rural) gp
MANOEUVRE
  Other
  15 (traffic) sy gp
  1 (Special) sy bn
EQUIPMENT BY TYPE
PATROL AND COASTAL COMBATANTS 75
  PSO 1 *Rio Segura* with 1 hel landing platform
  PCO 2: 1 *Rio Mino*; 1 *Rio Tajo*
  PBF 41: 1 *Aister* HS60; 12 *Alusafe* 2100; 5 *Gondan* 21; 22

Rodman 55; 1 Rodman 46

PB 31: 5 *Rio Arlanza* (SAR); 1 *Rio Segre*; 1 Rodman 58; 12 Rodman 66; 1 Rodman 82; 11 Rodman 101

AIRCRAFT • TPT • Light 3: 2 CN235-300; 1 Beech 350i *King Air*

HELICOPTERS

MRH 20: 4 AS653N3 *Dauphin*; 16 Bo-105ATH

TPT • Light 21: 8 BK-117; 13 H135

DEPLOYMENT

BOSNIA-HERZEGOVINA: EU • EUFOR (*Operation Althea*) 2

CENTRAL AFRICAN REPUBLIC: EU • EUTM RCA 8

DJIBOUTI: EU • *Operation Atalanta* 60; 1 CN235 VIGMA

ESTONIA: NATO • Baltic Air Policing: 280; 8 Eurofighter *Typhoon*

GULF OF ADEN & INDIAN OCEAN: EU • *Operation Atalanta* 220; 1 FFGHM

GULF OF GUINEA: Navy 50; 1 PCO

IRAQ: *Operation Inherent Resolve* 170; 1 trg unit; 1 hel unit with 3 NH90 TTH; **NATO** • NATO Mission Iraq 120; 1 inf coy

LATVIA: NATO • Enhanced Forward Presence 600; 1 armd inf coy(+); 1 arty bty; 1 cbt engr coy; 1 SAM bty with NASAMS

LEBANON: UN • UNIFIL 667; 1 mech bde HQ; 1 mech inf bn(-); 1 engr coy; 1 sigs coy; 1 log coy

MALI: EU • EUTM Mali 140; 1 hel unit with 3 NH90 TTH

MEDITERRANEAN SEA: NATO • SNMG 2: 400; 1 DDGHM; 1 AORH; **NATO** • SNMCMG 2: 40; 1 MHO

MOZAMBIQUE: EU • EUTM Mozambique 2

SENEGAL: 65; 2 C295M

SOMALIA: EU • EUTM Somalia 20

TURKIYE: NATO • *Operation Active Fence* 150; 1 SAM bty with M901 *Patriot* PAC-2

FOREIGN FORCES

United States US European Command: 3,550; 4 DDGM; 1 air base at Morón; 1 naval base at Rota

Sweden SWE

Swedish Krona SEK		2022	2023	2024
GDP	SEK	5.98trn	6.33trn	6.62trn
	USD	591bn	597bn	621bn
per capita	USD	56,188	55,216	56,894
Growth	%	2.8	-0.7	0.6
Inflation	%	8.1	6.9	3.6
Def bdgt	SEK	79.9bn	97.6bn	126bn
	USD	7.90bn	9.22bn	11.8bn
USD1=SEK		10.11	10.59	10.66

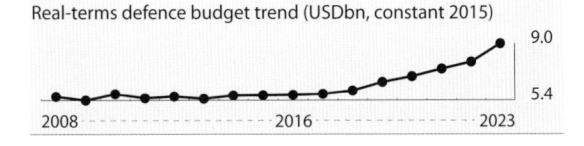

Real-terms defence budget trend (USDbn, constant 2015): 9.0 (2023), 5.4 (2008–2016)

Population	10,536,338					
Age	0–14	15–19	20–24	25–29	30–64	65 plus
Male	8.9%	2.9%	2.9%	3.2%	22.8%	9.7%
Female	8.4%	2.8%	2.6%	3.0%	22.0%	11.0%

Capabilities

Sweden's armed forces remain configured for territorial defence, with growing concern over Russia's military activity in the Baltic area. Sweden, which was already increasing cooperation with NATO in recent years, applied for Alliance membership in May 2022, three months after Russia's full-scale invasion of Ukraine. Turkiye and Hungary, as of late 2023, still had to ratify the application. Sweden plans to increase its defence budget to 2% of GDP. Under the 2021–25 defence bill, which was presented in October 2020, Sweden had already envisaged increased spending. The country is also working on an updated, long-term defence plan, expected to be published in April 2024. Stockholm has also announced measures to enhance societal resilience and the ability to deal with civil emergencies. Concerns over readiness levels have led to greater cooperation with NORDEFCO. In May 2018, Sweden, Finland and the US said they would work together on exercises and interoperability. In 2023, Sweden, along with Denmark, Norway, and Finland, further integrated their air forces, 'aiming for the ability to operate seamlessly together as one force'. Sweden is transforming its two mechanised brigades, while two new additional brigades will be created. These four brigades, including the battlegroup on Gotland, will be under divisional command by 2030. The country is buying additional artillery systems and armoured fighting vehicles and modernising its tank fleet. Readiness challenges in the air force triggered a discussion about extending the service life of the JAS-39C *Gripen* combat aircraft beyond their intended 2026 retirement date, not least since the air force was slated to receive a lower number of JAS-39Es than requested. The country's export-oriented defence industry is privately owned and capable of meeting most of the armed forces' equipment needs, including for advanced combat aircraft, conventional submarines and EW equipment.

ACTIVE 14,850 (Army 6,850 Navy 2,350 Air 2,700 Other 2,950) **Voluntary Auxiliary Organisations 21,500**

Conscript liability 4–11 months, depending on branch (selective conscription; 4,000 in total, gender neutral)

RESERVE 11,450

ORGANISATIONS BY SERVICE

Army 6,850

The army has been transformed to provide brigade-sized task forces depending on the operational requirement

FORCES BY ROLE

COMMAND
 1 div HQ
 4 bde HQ

MANOEUVRE
 Reconnaissance
 1 recce bn
 Armoured
 5 armd bn
 1 armd BG
 Mechanised
 1 mech bn
 Light
 1 mot inf bn
 1 lt inf bn
 Air Manoeuvre
 1 AB bn
 Other
 1 sy bn

COMBAT SUPPORT
 2 arty bn
 2 engr bn
 2 MP coy
 1 CBRN coy

COMBAT SERVICE SUPPORT
 1 tpt coy

AIR DEFENCE
 2 AD bn

Reserves

FORCES BY ROLE

MANOEUVRE
 Other
 40 Home Guard bn

EQUIPMENT BY TYPE

ARMOURED FIGHTING VEHICLES
 MBT 110 *Leopard* 2A5 (Strv 122)
 IFV 361: 319 CV9040 (Strf 9040; incl CP); 42 Epbv 90 (OP)
 APC 1,017
  APC (T) 322: 172 Pbv 302 (incl variants); 150 BvS-10 MkII
  APC (W) 335+: some *Bastion* APC; 34 XA-180 *Sisu* (Patgb 180); 20 XA-202 *Sisu* (Patgb 202); 148 XA-203 *Sisu* (Patgb 203); 20 XA-300 (Patgb 300); 113 Patria AMV (XA-360/Patgb 360)
 PPV 360 RG-32M

ENGINEERING & MAINTENANCE VEHICLES
 AEV 6 Pionierpanzer-3 *Kodiak* (Ingbv 120)
 ARV 39: 14 Bgbv 120; 25 Bgbv 90
 VLB 6 Brobv 120
 MW 33+: *Aardvark* Mk2; 33 Area Clearing System

ANTI-TANK/ANTI-INFRASTRUCTURE
 MSL • MANPATS NLAW; RBS-55
 RCL 84mm *Carl Gustaf*

ARTILLERY 254
 SP 155mm 26 *Archer*
 MOR 228: **81mm** 108 M/86; **120mm** 80 M/41D **SP 120mm** 40 CV90 *Mjolner* (Gkpbv 90)

AIR DEFENCE
 SAM 20+
  Long-range 12 M903 *Patriot* PAC-3 MSE
  Medium-range MIM-23B *Hawk* (RBS-97)
  Short-range 8+: 8 IRIS-T SLS (RBS-98); RBS-23 BAMSE
  Point-defence RBS-70
 GUNS • SP 40mm 30 Lvkv 90

Navy 1,250; 1,100 Amphibious (total 2,350)

EQUIPMENT BY TYPE

SUBMARINE • SSK 4:
 1 *Gotland* (fitted with AIP) with 2 single 400mm TT with Torped 431 LWT/Torped 451 LWT, 4 single 533mm TT with Torped 613 HWT/Torped 62 HWT
 2 *Gotland* mod (fitted with AIP) with 2 single 400mm TT with Torped 431 LWT/Torped 451 LWT, 4 single 533mm TT with Torped 613 HWT/Torped 62 HWT
 1 *Södermanland* (fitted with AIP; 1 more non-operational) with 3 single 400mm TT with Torped 431 LWT/Torped 451 LWT, 6 single 533mm TT with Torped 613 HWT/Torped 62 HWT

PATROL AND COASTAL COMBATANTS 150
 CORVETTES • FSG 5 *Visby* with 2 quad lnchr with RBS15 Mk2 AShM, 4 single 400mm ASTT with Torped 45 LWT, 1 57mm gun, 1 hel landing platform
 PCGT 4:
  2 *Göteborg* with 4 twin lnchr with RBS15 Mk2 AShM, 4 single 400mm ASTT with Torped 431 LWT, 1 57mm gun
  2 *Stockholm* with 4 twin lnchr with RBS15 Mk2 AShM, 4 single 400mm ASTT with Torped 431 LWT, 1 57mm gun
 PBF 133: 100+ Combat Boat 90H (capacity 18 troops); 27 Combat Boat HS (capacity 18 troops); 6 Combat Boat 90HSM (capacity 18 troops)
 PB 8: 3 *Tapper* (Type 80); 5 *Tapper* mod (Type 88)

MINE WARFARE • MINE COUNTERMEASURES 7
 MCC 5 *Koster* (SWE *Landsort* mod)
 MCD 2 *Spårö* (*Styrsö* mod)

AMPHIBIOUS • LANDING CRAFT 6
 LCVP 3 *Trossbat*
 LCAC 3 *Griffon* 8100TD

LOGISTICS AND SUPPORT 15

AG 2: 1 *Carlskrona* with 1 hel landing platform (former ML); 1 *Trosso* (spt ship for corvettes and patrol vessels but can also be used as HQ ship)
AGF 2 *Ledningsbåt* 2000
AGI 1 *Artemis*
AKL 1 *Loke*
ARS 2: 1 *Belos* III; 1 *Furusund* (former ML)
AXL 5 *Altair*
AXS 2: 1 *Falken*; 1 *Gladan*

UNINHABITED MARITIME SYSTEMS • UUV
MW AUV62-MR; *Double Eagle* Mk II/III; *Seafox*
UTL AUV62-AT

Amphibious 1,100
FORCES BY ROLE
MANOEUVRE
  Amphibious
  2 amph bn
EQUIPMENT BY TYPE
ARTILLERY • MOR 81mm 12 M/86
COASTAL DEFENCE • AShM 8 RBS-17 *Hellfire*

Coastal Defence
FORCES BY ROLE
COASTAL DEFENCE
  1 AShM bty with RBS-15
EQUIPMENT BY TYPE
COASTAL DEFENCE • AShM RBS-15

Air Force 2,700
FORCES BY ROLE
FIGHTER/GROUND ATTACK/ISR
  6 sqn with JAS 39C/D *Gripen*
TRANSPORT/ISR/AEW&C
  1 sqn with C-130H *Hercules* (Tp-84); KC-130H *Hercules* (Tp-84); Gulfstream IV SRA-4 (S-102B); S-100B/D *Argus*
TRAINING
  1 unit with G 120TP (Sk-40); Sk-60
AIR DEFENCE
  1 (fighter control and air surv) bn
EQUIPMENT BY TYPE
AIRCRAFT 99 combat capable
  FGA 99: 96 JAS 39C/D *Gripen*; 3 JAS 39E *Gripen* (in test)
  ELINT 2 Gulfstream IV SRA-4 (S-102B)
  AEW&C 3: 1 S-100B *Argus*; 2 S-100D *Argus*
  TKR/TPT 1 KC-130H *Hercules* (Tp-84)
  TPT 8: **Medium** 5 C-130H *Hercules* (Tp-84); **Light** 2 Saab 340 (OS-100A/Tp-100C); **PAX** 1 Gulfstream 550 (Tp-102D)
  TRG 70: 3 G 120TP (Sk-40); 67 Sk-60W
UNINHABITED AERIAL VEHICLES
  ISR • Medium 8 RQ-7 *Shadow* (AUV 3 *Örnen*)

AIR-LAUNCHED MISSILES
ASM AGM-65 *Maverick* (RB-75)
AShM RB-15F
AAM • IR AIM-9L *Sidewinder* (RB-74); **IIR** IRIS-T (RB-98); **ARH** AIM-120B AMRAAM (RB-99); *Meteor*
BOMBS
Laser-Guided GBU-12 *Paveway* II
INS/GPS guided GBU-39 Small Diameter Bomb

Armed Forces Hel Wing
FORCES BY ROLE
TRANSPORT HELICOPTER
  3 sqn with AW109 (Hkp 15A); AW109M (Hkp-15B); NH90 TTH (Hkp-14) (SAR/ASW); UH-60M *Black Hawk* (Hkp-16)
EQUIPMENT BY TYPE
HELICOPTERS
  TPT 53: **Medium** 33: 15 UH-60M *Black Hawk* (Hkp-16); 18 NH90 TTH (Hkp-14) (of which 9 configured for ASW); **Light** 20: 12 AW109 (Hkp-15A); 8 AW109M (Hkp-15B)

Special Forces
FORCES BY ROLE
SPECIAL FORCES
  1 spec ops gp
COMBAT SUPPORT
  1 cbt spt gp

Other 2,950
Includes staff, logistics and intelligence personnel
FORCES BY ROLE
COMBAT SUPPORT
  1 EW bn
  1 psyops unit
COMBAT SERVICE SUPPORT
  2 log bn
  1 maint bn
  4 med coy
  1 tpt coy

DEPLOYMENT
INDIA/PAKISTAN: UN • UNMOGIP 3
IRAQ: *Operation Inherent Resolve* 2; **NATO** • NATO Mission Iraq 1
KOREA, REPUBLIC OF: NNSC • 5
KOSOVO: NATO • KFOR 3
MIDDLE EAST: UN • UNTSO 6
SOMALIA: EU • EUTM Somalia 6
UNITED KINGDOM: *Operation Interflex* 50 (UKR trg)

Switzerland CHE

Swiss Franc CHF		2022	2023	2024
GDP	CHF	782bn	808bn	836bn
	USD	818bn	906bn	978bn
per capita	USD	93,657	102,866	110,246
Growth	%	2.7	0.9	1.8
Inflation	%	2.8	2.2	2.0
Def bdgt [a]	CHF	5.27bn	5.30bn	
	USD	5.52bn	5.95bn	
USD1=CHF		0.95	0.89	0.85

[a] Includes military pensions

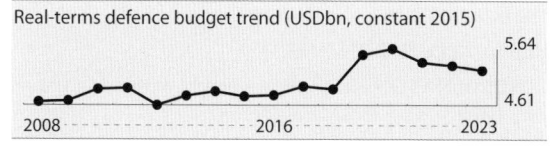

Real-terms defence budget trend (USDbn, constant 2015)

5.64
4.61
2008 — 2016 — 2023

Population		8,793,404				
Age	0–14	15–19	20–24	25–29	30–64	65 plus
Male	7.7%	2.4%	2.6%	2.9%	24.9%	9.2%
Female	7.3%	2.3%	2.5%	2.9%	24.5%	10.8%

Capabilities

The conscript-based armed forces are postured for territorial defence and limited participation in international peace-support operations. The government has begun to reduce its armed forces, reflecting an assessment that in the militia-based system not all personnel would realistically be available for active service. With permanent neutrality a core feature of foreign and security policy, Switzerland is not a member of any alliances, although it joined NATO's Partnership for Peace programme in 1996 and on occasion contributes to NATO- and EU-led operations alongside its engagement in UN or OSCE missions. In light of the full-scale invasion of Ukraine in 2022, Switzerland is adjusting and reworking its foreign and defence strategies. The Swiss government intends to increase ways to contribute to European security while remaining neutral. Bern invoked its neutrality in blocking some arms transfers to Ukraine. In 2023, Switzerland created a state secretariat for security, reflecting the deteriorating security environment. Its mission is to coordinate national security policy starting in 2024. Switzerland does not participate in combat operations for peace-enforcement purposes and its deployments are limited in size. In 2022, the defence ministry published a paper on the future of the armed forces out to the 2030s, summarising its approach to modernisation requirements for air defence and ground forces and for stronger cyber capabilities. The country's approach to readiness is changing to a flexible model in which different units are gradually called up for active service and on different timelines. Switzerland is modernising its air defences through the purchase of the F-35A *Lightning* II combat aircraft and *Patriot* surface-to-air missile system. Switzerland's defence industry has capacity in the land-vehicles sector, which has links to North American firms, and trainers.

ACTIVE 21,300 (Armed Forces 21,300)

Conscript liability 260–600 compulsory service days depending on rank. 18 or 23 weeks' training (depending on branch) generally at age 20, followed by 6 refresher trg courses (3 weeks each). Alternative service available

RESERVE 123,450

Civil Defence 73,000 (51,000 Reserve)

ORGANISATIONS BY SERVICE

Armed Forces 3,100 active; 18,200 conscript (21,300 total)

Operations Command 72,600 on mobilisation

4 Territorial Regions. With the exception of military police all units are non-active

FORCES BY ROLE
COMMAND
  4 regional comd
SPECIAL FORCES
  2 SF bn
MANOEUVRE
  Armoured
  2 (1st & 11th) bde (1 recce bn, 1 tk bn, 2 armd inf bn, 1 SP arty bn, 1 engr bn, 1 sigs bn)
  Mechanised
  1 (4th) bde (2 recce bn, 2 SP arty bn, 1 ptn br bn)
  Light
  10 inf bn
  7 mtn inf bn
  1 mtn inf unit
COMBAT SUPPORT
  4 engr bn
  4 MP bn
  1 NBC bn
  1 int unit
COMBAT SUPPORT
  4 engr rescue bn
EQUIPMENT BY TYPE
ARMOURED FIGHTING VEHICLES
  MBT 134 *Leopard* 2 (Pz-87 *Leo*)
  IFV 186: 154 CV9030CH; 32 CV9030 (CP)
  APC 1,113
    APC (T) 309 M113A2 (incl variants)
    APC (W) 804 *Piranha* I/II/IIIC
  AUV 292: 173 *Eagle* II; 119 *Eagle* III (CP)
ENGINEERING & MAINTENANCE VEHICLES
  AEV 12 *Kodiak*
  ARV 25 *Büffel*
  VLB 9 *Leopard* 2 with *Leguan*
  MW 46: 26 Area Clearing System; 20 M113A2
NBC VEHICLES 12 *Piranha* IIIC CBRN
ANTI-TANK/ANTI-INFRASTRUCTURE
  MSL • MANPATS NLAW
ARTILLERY 349
  SP 155mm 133 M109 KAWEST
  MOR • 81mm 216 Mw-72
PATROL AND COASTAL COMBATANTS 14

PB 14 *Watercat* 1250
AIR DEFENCE • SAM • Point-defence FIM-92 *Stinger*

Air Force 18,900 on mobilisation
FORCES BY ROLE
FIGHTER
 2 sqn with F-5E/F *Tiger* II
 3 sqn with F/A-18C/D *Hornet*
TRANSPORT
 1 sqn with Beech 350 *King Air*; DHC-6 *Twin Otter*;
  PC-6 *Turbo Porter*; PC-12
 1 VIP Flt with Cessna 560XL *Citation*; CL-604
  Challenger; Falcon 900EX
TRAINING
 1 sqn with PC-7CH *Turbo Trainer*; PC-21
 1 OCU Sqn with F-5E/F *Tiger* II
TRANSPORT HELICOPTER
 6 sqn with AS332M *Super Puma*; AS532UL *Cougar*;
  H135M
ISR UAV
 1 sqn with *Hermes* 900
EQUIPMENT BY TYPE
AIRCRAFT 55 combat capable
 FTR 25: 20 F-5E *Tiger* II; 5 F-5F *Tiger* II
 FGA 30: 25 F/A-18C *Hornet*; 5 F/A-18D *Hornet*
 TPT 23: **Light** 19: 1 Beech 350 *King Air*; 1 Cessna
  560XL *Citation*; 1 DHC-6 *Twin Otter*; 14 PC-6
  Turbo Porter; 1 PC-6 (owned by armasuisse, civil
  registration); 1 PC-12 (owned by armasuisse, civil
  registration); **PAX** 4: 2 CL-604 *Challenger*; 1 Falcon
  900EX
 TRG 35: 27 PC-7CH *Turbo Trainer*; 8 PC-21
HELICOPTERS
 MRH 20 H135M
 TPT • **Medium** 24: 15 AS332M *Super Puma*; 9
  AS532UL *Cougar*
UNINHABITED AERIAL VEHICLES
 ISR • **Medium** 2 *Hermes* 900
AIR-LAUNCHED MISSILES • **AAM** • **IIR** AIM-9X
Sidewinder II; **ARH** AIM-120B/C-7 AMRAAM

Ground Based Air Defence (GBAD)
GBAD assets can be used to form AD clusters to be deployed independently as task forces within Swiss territory
EQUIPMENT BY TYPE
AIR DEFENCE
 SAM • **Point-defence** 56+: 56 *Rapier*; FIM-92 *Stinger*
 GUNS 35mm 27 GDF-003/-005 with *Skyguard*

Armed Forces Logistic Organisation 14,500 on mobilisation
FORCES BY ROLE
COMBAT SERVICE SUPPORT
 1 log bde (6 log bn; 1 tpt bn; 6 med bn)

Command Support Organisation 15,300 on mobilisation

FORCES BY ROLE
COMBAT SERVICE SUPPORT
 1 spt bde

Training Command 25,100 on mobilisation
COMBAT SERVICE SUPPORT
 5 trg unit

Civil Defence 73,000 (51,000 Reserve)
(not part of armed forces)

DEPLOYMENT
BOSNIA-HERZEGOVINA: EU • EUFOR (*Operation Althea*) 20
INDIA/PAKISTAN: UN • UNMOGIP 3
KOREA, REPUBLIC OF: NNSC • 5
KOSOVO: NATO • KFOR 190 (military volunteers); 1 engr pl; 1 hel flt with AS332M *Super Puma*
MIDDLE EAST: UN • UNTSO 13
SOUTH SUDAN: UN • UNMISS 1
WESTERN SAHARA: UN • MINURSO 1

Turkiye TUR

New Turkish Lira TRY		2022	2023	2024
GDP	TRY	15.0trn	24.6trn	40.1trn
	USD	906bn	1.15trn	1.34trn
per capita	USD	10,622	13,384	15,368
Growth	%	5.5	4.0	3.0
Inflation	%	72.3	51.2	62.5
Def exp [a]	TRY	204bn	340bn	
	USD	12.3bn	16.0bn	
Def bdgt [b]	TRY	104bn	206bn	
	USD	6.25bn	9.69bn	
USD1=TRY		16.57	21.27	29.92

[a] NATO figure

[b] Includes funding for Undersecretariat of Defence Industries; Defence Industry Support Fund; TUBITAK Defense Industries R&D Institute (SAGE); and military pensions.

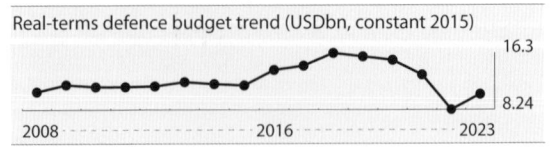

Real-terms defence budget trend (USDbn, constant 2015)

Population	83,593,483					
Age	0–14	15–19	20–24	25–29	30–64	65 plus
Male	11.3%	4.0%	3.9%	3.7%	23.2%	4.2%
Female	10.8%	3.8%	3.7%	3.6%	22.8%	5.1%

Capabilities
Turkiye has large, generally well-equipped armed forces that are primarily structured for national defence, with a six-month-minimum compulsory military service for men. The Turkish

Armed Forces (TSK) have conducted ground operations in Syria since 2016 and resumed missions in Iraq in 2019. Turkiye has also deployed forces to assist the UN-recognised government in Libya since 2020. The conflict with various Kurdish armed groups, both in and outside of Turkiye, continues, with Ankara treating the different groups as parts of a whole. The government's large increases in defence spending are dampened by rampant inflation. Ankara spends increasing amounts of the budget locally. Turkiye is a NATO member, though relationships with the Alliance allies have come under strain after a series of disagreements, including Ankara's delay in ratifying Sweden's NATO membership. Turkiye maintains close relationships with Azerbaijan, Libya and Qatar, which has included training, deployments, arms sales and, in the case of Libya, direct military support. Turkiye has permanent bases in Qatar and Somalia. Following an attempted coup in July 2016, Ankara passed legislation directing the three service commands to report to the president, through the defence minister, instead of to the general staff and then prime minister. The chief of the general staff is now the operational commander of the TSK during wartime but not peacetime. Large numbers of officers were also dismissed from the armed forces, which likely had a negative impact on capability and may have resulted in a politicisation of appointments since. The TSK trains regularly, including with NATO allies, but also increasingly with countries such as Azerbaijan and Pakistan. Turkiye is investing substantially in its naval capability. The amphibious assault ship *Anadolu* was commissioned in 2023. Ankara controversially agreed to buy Russia's S-400 air-defence system, with deliveries starting in 2019. In response, the US government terminated Turkiye's participation in the F-35 *Lightning* II programme. Efforts to upgrade and expand the large F-16 fleet have been stymied by tensions with Washington over Sweden's NATO membership and other issues. Many of Turkiye's largest defence companies (such as ASELSAN, Roketsan and TAI) are either entirely or majority-owned by the armed forces. The country also has important privately-owned enterprises in land systems, shipbuilding and UAV production. Turkish defence exports have grown substantially.

ACTIVE 355,200 (Army 260,200 Navy 45,000 Air 50,000) Gendarmerie & Paramilitary 156,800

Conscript liability 12 months (5.5 months for university graduates; 21 days for graduates with exemption) (reducing to 6 months)

RESERVE 378,700 (Army 258,700 Navy 55,000 Air 65,000)

Reserve service to age 41 for all services

ORGANISATIONS BY SERVICE

Space
EQUIPMENT BY TYPE
SATELLITES • ISR 2 *Gokturk*

Army ε260,200 (incl conscripts)
FORCES BY ROLE
COMMAND
 4 army HQ
 9 corps HQ
SPECIAL FORCES
 15 cdo bde
 1 cdo regt

MANOEUVRE
 Armoured
 8 armd bde
 Mechanised
 2 (28th & 29th) mech div
 14 mech inf bde
 Light
 1 (52nd) mot inf div (2 cdo bde)
 1 (3rd) inf div (1 mtn cdo bde, 1 mot inf bde, 1 sy bde, 1 arty regt)
 1 (23rd) inf div (1 cdo bde, 1 armd bde, 1 sy bde)
 1 mot inf bde
 Other
 2 (border) sy bde
COMBAT SUPPORT
 2 arty bde
 1 trg arty bde
 6 arty regt
 2 engr regt
HELICOPTER
 4 hel regt
 4 hel bn
COMBAT/ISR UAV
 3 bn with *Akinci*; *Bayraktar* TB2
EQUIPMENT BY TYPE
ARMOURED FIGHTING VEHICLES
 MBT 2,378: 316 *Leopard* 2A4 (being upgraded); 170 *Leopard* 1A4; 227 *Leopard* 1A3; 100 M60A1; 650 M60A3 TTS; 165 M60TM *Firat*; 750 M48A5 T2 *Patton*
 IFV 645 ACV AIFV
 APC 6,403
  APC (T) 3,636: 823 ACV AAPC; 2,813 M113/M113A1/M113A2
  APC (W) 57 *Pars* 6×6 (incl variants)
  PPV 2,710: 360 *Edjer Yalcin* 4×4; ε2,000 *Kirpi/Kirpi*-II; ε350 *Vuran*
 AUV 1,450: ε250 *Akrep*; 800+ *Cobra*; ε400 *Cobra* II
ENGINEERING & MAINTENANCE VEHICLES
 AEV 12+: AZMIM; 12 M48 AEV; M113A2T2
 ARV 150: 12 BPz-2; 105 M48T5; 33 M88A1
 VLB 88: 36 *Leguan*; 52 Mobile Floating Assault Bridge
 MW 14+: 4 *Husky* 2G; 10 *Meti*; *Tamkar*; *Bozena*
ANTI-TANK/ANTI-INFRASTRUCTURE
 MSL
  SP 665: 365 ACV TOW; ε200 *Kaplan* STA; ε100 *Pars* STA 4×4
  MANPATS 9K135 *Kornet*-E (RS-AT-14 *Spriggan*); *Eryx*; FGM-148 *Javelin*; *Milan*; OMTAS; *Sungur*
 RCL 106mm M40A1
ARTILLERY 2,762
 SP 1,061: **155mm** 806: ε150 M44T1; 365 M52T (mod); ε280 T-155 *Firtina*; 11 T-155 *Firtina* II; **175mm** 36 M107; **203mm** 219 M110A2
 TOWED 675+: **105mm** 82: 7 *Boran* (in test); 75+ M101A1;

155mm 557: 517 M114A1/M114A2; 40 *Panter*; **203mm** 36+ M115
MRL 98+: **122mm** ε36 T-122; **227mm** 12 M270 MLRS; **302mm** 50+ TR-300 *Kasirga* (WS-1)
MOR 928+:
  SP 350+: **81mm** some; **107mm** ε150 M106; **120mm** ε200
  TOWED 578+: **81mm** some; **120mm** 578 HY12

SURFACE-TO-SURFACE MISSILE LAUNCHERS
  SRBM • Conventional *Bora*; MGM-140A ATACMS (launched from M270 MLRS); J-600T *Yildrim* (B-611/CH-SS-9 mod 1)

AIRCRAFT
  ISR 5 Beech 350 *King Air*
  TPT • Light 8: 5 Beech 200 *King Air*; 3 Cessna 421
  TRG 49: 45 Cessna T182; 4 T-42A *Cochise*

HELICOPTERS
  ATK 91: 18 AH-1P *Cobra*; 12 AH-1S *Cobra*; 4 TAH-1P *Cobra*; 9 T129A; 48 T129B
  MRH 28 Hughes 300C
  TPT 214+: **Heavy** 6 CH-47F *Chinook*; **Medium** 69+: 28 AS532UL *Cougar*; 40+ S-70A *Black Hawk*; 1 T-70 *Black Hawk* **Light** 139: 12 Bell 204B (AB-204B); ε43 Bell 205 (UH-1H *Iroquois*); 64 Bell 205A (AB-205A); 20 Bell 206 *Jet Ranger*

UNINHABITED AERIAL VEHICLES
  CISR 73: **Heavy** 3 *Akinci*; **Medium** ε70 *Bayraktar* TB2
  ISR • Heavy *Falcon* 600/*Firebee*; **Medium** CL-89; *Gnat*

LOITERING & DIRECT ATTACK MUNITIONS
  Harpy

AIR-LAUNCHED MISSILES • ASM *Mizrak*-U (UMTAS)

BOMBS • Laser-guided MAM-C/L

AIR DEFENCE
  SAM
    Short-range HISAR-A/A+; HISAR-O
    Point-defence 148+: 70 *Atilgan* PMADS octuple *Stinger* lnchr, 78 *Zipkin* PMADS quad *Stinger* lnchr; FIM-92 *Stinger*
  GUNS 1,404
    SP 35mm 42 *Korkut*
    TOWED 1,362: **20mm** 439 GAI-D01/Rh-202; **35mm** 120 GDF-001/-003; **40mm** 803 L/60/L/70

Navy ε45,000 (incl conscripts)

EQUIPMENT BY TYPE

SUBMARINES • SSK 12
  4 *Atilay* (GER Type-209/1200) with 8 single 533mm TT with SST-4 HWT
  4 *Gür* (GER Type-209/1400) with 8 single 533mm TT with UGM-84 *Harpoon* AShM/Mk 24 *Tigerfish* mod 2 HWT/*SeaHake* mod 4 (DM2A4) HWT
  4 *Preveze* (GER Type-209/1400) (MLU ongoing) with 8 single 533mm TT with UGM-84 *Harpoon* AShM/Mk 24 *Tigerfish* mod 2 HWT/*SeaHake* mod 4 (DM2A4) HWT

PRINCIPAL SURFACE COMBATANTS • FRIGATES 16

  FFGHM 16:
    4 *Barbaros* (GER MEKO 200 mod) with 2 quad lnchr with RGM-84C *Harpoon* Block 1B AShM, 2 8-cell Mk 41 VLS with RIM-162B ESSM SAM, 2 triple 324mm SVTT Mk 32 ASTT with Mk 46 LWT, 3 *Sea Zenith* CIWS, 1 127mm gun (capacity 1 Bell 212 (AB-212) hel)
    4 *Gabya* (ex-US *Oliver Hazard Perry*) with 1 Mk 13 GMLS with RGM-84C *Harpoon* Block 1B AShM/SM-1MR Block VI SAM, 1 8-cell Mk 41 VLS with RIM-162B ESSM SAM, 2 triple 324mm SVTT Mk 32 ASTT with Mk 46 LWT, 1 Mk 15 *Phalanx* Block 1B CIWS, 1 76mm gun (capacity 1 S-70B *Seahawk*/AB-212 ASW hel)
    4 *Gabya* (ex-US *Oliver Hazard Perry*) with 1 Mk 13 GMLS with RGM-84C *Harpoon* Block 1B AShM/SM-1MR Block VI SAM, 2 triple 324mm SVTT Mk 32 ASTT with Mk 46 LWT, 1 Mk 15 *Phalanx* Block 1B CIWS, 1 76mm gun (capacity 1 S-70B *Seahawk*/AB-212 ASW hel)
    4 *Yavuz* (GER MEKO 200TN) with 2 quad lnchr with RGM-84C *Harpoon* Block 1B AShM, 1 octuple Mk 29 GMLS with RIM-7M *Sea Sparrow* SAM, 2 triple 324mm SVTT Mk 32 ASTT with Mk 46 LWT, 3 *Sea Zenith* CIWS, 1 127mm gun (capacity 1 Bell 212 (AB-212) hel)

PATROL AND COASTAL COMBATANTS 50
  CORVETTES 9:
    FSGHM 4 *Ada* with 2 quad lnchr with ATMACA AShM/RGM-84C *Harpoon* Block 1B AShM, 1 Mk 49 21-cell lnchr with RIM-116 SAM, 2 twin 324mm SVTT Mk 32 ASTT with Mk 46 LWT, 1 76mm gun (capacity 1 S-70B *Seahawk* hel)
    FSG 5 *Burak* (ex-FRA *d'Estienne d'Orves*) with 2 single lnchr with MM38 *Exocet* AShM, 4 single 324mm ASTT with Mk 46 LWT, 1 Creusot-Loire Mk 54 A/S mor, 1 100mm gun (1 vessel with 1 76mm gun instead)
  PCFG 18:
    3 *Dogan* (GER Lurssen-57) with 2 quad lnchr with RGM-84C *Harpoon* Block 1B AShM, 1 76mm gun
    9 *Kilic* (GER Lurssen-62) with 2 quad lnchr with RGM-84C *Harpoon* Block 1B AShM, 1 76mm gun
    4 *Rüzgar* (GER Lurssen-57) with 2 quad lnchr with RGM-84C *Harpoon* Block 1B AShM, 1 76mm gun
    2 *Yildiz* with 2 quad lnchr with RGM-84C *Harpoon* Block 1B AShM, 1 76mm gun
  PCC 16 *Tuzla*
  PBF 7: 2 *Kaan* 20 (MRTP 20); 3 MRTP 22; 2 MRTP 24/U

MINE WARFARE • MINE COUNTERMEASURES 11
  MHO 11: 5 *Engin* (ex-FRA *Circe*); 6 *Aydin*

AMPHIBIOUS
  PRINCIPAL AMPHIBIOUS SHIPS • LHD 1 *Anadolu* (ESP *Juan Carlos* I mod) with 2 Mk 15 *Phalanx* CIWS (capacity 21 hel; 4 LCM or 2 LCAC; up to 80 vehicles; 900 troops)
  LANDING SHIPS • LST 5:
    2 *Bayraktar* with 2 Mk 15 *Phalanx* Block 1B CIWS, 1 hel landing platform (capacity 20 MBT; 250 troops)

1 *Osmangazi* with 1 Mk 15 *Phalanx* CIWS (capacity 4 LCVP; 17 tanks; 980 troops; 1 hel landing platform)
2 *Sarucabey* with 1 Mk 15 *Phalanx* CIWS (capacity 11 tanks; 600 troops; 1 hel landing platform)
LANDING CRAFT 41
  LCT 21: 2 C-120/130; 11 C-140; 8 C-151
  LCM 12: 4 LCM-1E; 8 LCM 8
  LCVP 8 Anadolu 16m
LOGISTICS AND SUPPORT 42
  ABU 2: 1 AG5; 1 AG6 with 1 76mm gun
  AFD 8
  AG 2 *Dalgic*
  AGI 1 *Ufuk* (MILGEM) (capacity 1 S-70B *Seahawk* hel)
  AGS 2: 1 *Cesme* (ex-US *Silas Bent*); 1 *Cubuklu*
  AOR 2 *Akar* with 1 Mk 15 *Phalanx* CIWS, 1 hel landing platform
  AO 3: 2 *Burak*; 1 *Yuzbasi Gungor Durmus* with 1 hel landing platform
  AP 1 *Iskenderun*
  ASR 3: 1 *Alemdar* with 1 hel landing platform; 2 *Isin* II
  ATF 5: 1 *Akbas*; 1 *Darica*; 1 *Inebolu*; 2 *Kizilirmak*
  AWT 3 *Sogut*
  AXL 8
  AX 2 *Pasa* (ex-GER *Rhein*)
UNINHABITED MARITIME PLATFORMS
  USV • MARSEC 14: **Medium** 6: 1 *Marlin*; 2 *Mir*; 1 *Salvo*; 1 *Sancar*; 1 *ULAQ*; **Small** 8 *Albatros* S
UNINHABITED MARITIME SYSTEMS
  UUV • MW PAP

Marines 3,000
FORCES BY ROLE
MANOEUVRE
  Amphibious
    1 mne bde (3 mne bn; 1 arty bn)
ARMOURED FIGHTING VEHICLES
  AAV 9 MAV *Zaha*

Naval Aviation
FORCES BY ROLE
ANTI-SUBMARINE WARFARE
  2 sqn with Bell 212 ASW (AB-212 ASW); S-70B *Seahawk*
  1 sqn with ATR-72-600; CN235M-100; TB-20 *Trinidad*
ATTACK HELICOPTER
  1 sqn with AH-1W *Cobra*
EQUIPMENT BY TYPE
AIRCRAFT 6 combat capable
  ASW 6 ATR-72-600
  MP 6 CN235M-100
  TPT • Light 7: 3 ATR-72-600; 4 TB-20 *Trinidad*
HELICOPTERS
  ATK 10 AH-1W *Cobra*
  ASW 33: 9 Bell 212 ASW (AB-212 ASW); 24 S-70B *Seahawk*
UNINHABITED AERIAL VEHICLES 20

CISR 22: **Heavy** 13: 5 *Aksungur*; 8 *Anka-S*; **Medium** 9 *Bayraktar* TB2
AIR-LAUNCHED MISSILES
  ASM AGM-114M *Hellfire* II
  BOMBS • Laser-guided MAM-C/L

Air Force ε50,000
2 tac air forces (divided between east and west)
FORCES BY ROLE
FIGHTER/GROUND ATTACK
  1 sqn with F-4E *Phantom* 2020
  8 sqn with F-16C/D *Fighting Falcon*
ISR
  1 sqn with F-16C/D *Fighting Falcon*
  1 unit with King Air 350
AIRBORNE EARLY WARNING & CONTROL
  1 sqn (forming) with B-737 AEW&C
EW
  1 unit with CN235M EW
SEARCH & RESCUE
  1 sqn with AS532AL/UL *Cougar*; T-70 *Black Hawk*
TANKER
  1 sqn with KC-135R *Stratotanker*
TRANSPORT
  1 sqn with A400M; C-160D *Transall*
  1 sqn with C-130B/E *Hercules*
  1 (VIP) sqn with Cessna 550 *Citation* II (UC-35); Cessna 650 *Citation* VII; CN235M; Gulfstream 550
  3 sqn with CN235M
  10 (liaison) flt with Bell 205 (UH-1H *Iroquois*); CN235M
TRAINING
  1 sqn with F-16C/D *Fighting Falcon*
  1 sqn (display team) with NF-5A-2000/NF-5B-2000 *Freedom Fighter*
  1 sqn with MFI-395 *Super Mushshak*; SF-260D
  1 sqn with *Hurkus*-B; KT-IT
  1 sqn with T-38A/M *Talon*
  1 sqn with T-41D *Mescalero*
COMBAT/ISR UAV
  1 sqn with *Akinci*
AIR DEFENCE
  4 bn with S-400 (RS-SA-21 *Growler*)
  4 sqn with MIM-14 *Nike Hercules*
  2 sqn with *Rapier*
  8 (firing) unit with MIM-23 *Hawk*
MANOEUVRE
  Air Manoeuvre
  1 AB bde
EQUIPMENT BY TYPE
AIRCRAFT 294 combat capable
  FTR 15: 9 NF-5A-2000 *Freedom Fighter* (display team); 6 NF-5B-2000 *Freedom Fighter* (display team)
  FGA 279: 19 F-4E *Phantom* 2020; 27 F-16C *Fighting Falcon*

Block 30; 162 F-16C *Fighting Falcon* Block 50; 14 F-16C *Fighting Falcon* Block 50+; 8 F-16D Block 30 *Fighting Falcon*; 33 F-16D *Fighting Falcon* Block 50; 16 F-16D *Fighting Falcon* Block 50+

ISR 9: 5 Beech 350 *King Air*; 3 C-160D *Transall*; 1 CN235M (Open Skies)

EW 2 C-160D *Transall*

SIGINT 3 CN235M

AEW&C 4 B-737 AEW&C

TKR 7 KC-135R *Stratotanker*

TPT 84: **Heavy** 10 A400M; **Medium** 24: 6 C-130B *Hercules*; 13 C-130E *Hercules*; 5 C-160D *Transall*; **Light** 49: 2 Cessna 550 *Citation* II (UC-35 - VIP); 2 Cessna 650 *Citation* VII; 45 CN235M; **PAX** 1 Gulfstream 550

TRG 174: 4 *Hurkus*-B; 39 KT-IT; 3 MFI-395 *Super Mushshak*; 33 SF-260D; 70 T-38A/M *Talon*; 25 T-41D *Mescalero*

HELICOPTERS
TPT 36: **Medium** 21: 6 AS532AL *Cougar* (CSAR); 14 AS532UL *Cougar* (SAR); 1 T-70 *Black Hawk*; **Light** 15 Bell 205 (UH-1H *Iroquois*)

UNINHABITED AERIAL VEHICLES
CISR • **Heavy** 31: 12 *Akinci*; 19 *Anka*-S

ISR 27: **Heavy** 9: 9 *Heron*; **Medium** 18 *Gnat* 750

AIR DEFENCE • SAM 32+
Long-range 32+: MIM-14 *Nike Hercules*; 32 S-400 (RS-SA-21 *Growler*)

Medium-range MIM-23 *Hawk*

Point-defence *Rapier*

AIR-LAUNCHED MISSILES
AAM • **IR** AIM-9S *Sidewinder*; *Shafrir* 2‡; **IIR** AIM-9X *Sidewinder* II; **SARH** AIM-7E *Sparrow*; **ARH** AIM-120A/B AMRAAM

ARM AGM-88A HARM

ASM AGM-65A/G *Maverick*; *Popeye* I

LACM Conventional AGM-84K SLAM-ER

BOMBS
Electro-optical guided GBU-8B HOBOS (GBU-15)

Laser-guided MAM-C/-L; *Paveway* I/II

INS/GPS guided AGM-154A JSOW; AGM-154C JSOW

Special Forces Command
FORCES BY ROLE
SPECIAL FORCES
4 spec ops bde

1 spec ops regt

EQUIPMENT BY TYPE
HELICOPTERS
TPT 14: **Heavy** 5 CH-47F *Chinook*; **Medium** 9: 8 S-70A *Black Hawk*; 1 T-70 *Black Hawk*

Gendarmerie & Paramilitary 156,800

Gendarmerie 152,100

Ministry of Interior; Ministry of Defence in war

FORCES BY ROLE
SPECIAL FORCES
1 cdo bde

MANOEUVRE
Other

1 (border) paramilitary div

2 paramilitary bde

EQUIPMENT BY TYPE
ARMOURED FIGHTING VEHICLES
RECCE 57+: *Akrep*; 57 *Ates*

APC 760+
  APC (W) 560: 535 BTR-60/BTR-80; 25 *Condor*
  PPV 200+: *Edjer Yaclin* 4×4; *Kirpi*; 200 *Kirpi* II; *Vuran*
  AUV *Cobra*; *Cobra* II; Otokar *Ural*

ARTILLERY • MOR • SP 120mm *Vuran* with *Alkar*

AIRCRAFT
ISR Some O-1E *Bird Dog*

TPT • **Light** 2 Do-28D

HELICOPTERS
ATK 13 T129B

MRH 19 Mi-17 *Hip* H

TPT 35: **Medium** 12 S-70A *Black Hawk*; **Light** 23: 8 Bell 204B (AB-204B); 6 Bell 205A (AB-205A); 8 Bell 206A (AB-206A) *Jet Ranger*; 1 Bell 212 (AB-212)

UNINHABITED AERIAL VEHICLES
CISR 42: **Heavy** 6 *Anka*-S; **Medium** ε36 *Bayraktar* TB2

BOMBS
Laser-guided MAM-C/L

Coast Guard 4,700

EQUIPMENT BY TYPE
PATROL AND COASTAL COMBATANTS 125
PSOH 4 *Dost*

PBF 76: 6+ *Ares* 35; 13 *Ares* 42; 18 *Kaan* 15; 17 *Kaan* 19; 9 *Kaan* 29; 13 *Kaan* 33

PB 45: 15 Damen SAR 1906; 8 *Saar* 33 (1 more non-operational); 4 *Saar* 35; 18 Type-80

AIRCRAFT • MP 3 CN235 MPA

HELICOPTERS • MRH 8 Bell 412EP (AB-412EP – SAR)

UNINHABITED AERIAL VEHICLES 6
CISR • **Medium** 6 *Bayraktar* TB2

DEPLOYMENT

AZERBAIJAN: Army 170; 1 EOD unit

BOSNIA-HERZEGOVINA: EU • EUFOR • *Operation Althea* 238; 1 inf coy

CYPRUS (NORTHERN): ε33,800; 1 army corps HQ; 1 SF regt; 1 armd bde; 2 mech inf div; 1 mech inf regt; 1 arty regt; 1 avn comd; 287 M48A5T2; 145 ACV AIFV; 70 ACV AAPC (incl variants); 418 M113 (incl variants); 36 M101A1; 36 M114A2; 12 M115; 30 M44T; 144 M52T1; 4 T-155; 18 T-122; 171 81mm mor; 70 M30; 135 HY-12; *Milan*; 66 ACV TOW; 219 M40A1; FIM-92 *Stinger*; 44 Rh 202; 78 GAI-D01; 16 GDF-003; 3 Cessna 185 (U-17); 2 AS532UL *Cougar*; 1 Bell 205 (UH-1H *Iroquois*); 1 PB

IRAQ: Army: 4,000; **NATO** • NATO Mission Iraq 86
KOSOVO: NATO • KFOR 369; 1 inf coy; **UN** • UNMIK 1
LEBANON: UN • UNIFIL 100; 1 FSGHM
LIBYA: ε500; ACV-AAPC; *Kirpi*; 1 arty unit with T-155 *Firtina*; 1 AD unit with MIM-23B *Hawk*; *Korkut*; GDF-003; 1 CISR UAV unit with *Bayraktar* TB2
QATAR: Army: 300 (trg team); 1 mech inf coy; 1 arty unit; 12+ ACV AIFV/AAPC; 2 T-155 *Firtina*
SOMALIA: 200 (trg team); **UN** • UNSOM 1
SYRIA: ε3,000; some cdo units; 3 armd BG; 1 SAM unit; 1 gendarmerie unit

FOREIGN FORCES

Spain *Active Fence*: 150; 1 SAM bty with M901 *Patriot* PAC-2
United States US European Command: 1,700; 1 spt facility at Izmir; 1 spt facility at Ankara; 1 air base at Incirlik • **US Strategic Command**: 1 AN/TPY-2 X-band radar at Kürecik

United Kingdom UK

British Pound GBP		2022	2023	2024
GDP	GBP	2.49trn	2.65trn	2.76trn
	USD	3.08trn	3.33trn	3.59trn
per capita	USD	45,461	48,913	52,426
Growth	%	4.1	0.5	0.6
Inflation	%	9.1	7.7	3.7
Def exp [a]	GBP	53.9bn	54.1bn	
	USD	66.7bn	68.1bn	
Def bdgt [b]	GBP	ε58.4bn	ε58.5bn	
	USD	ε72.2bn	ε73.5bn	
USD1=GBP		0.81	0.80	0.77

[a] NATO figure

[b] Includes total departmental expenditure limits; costs of military operations; Armed Forces Pension Service; military aid to Ukraine; and external income earned by the MoD

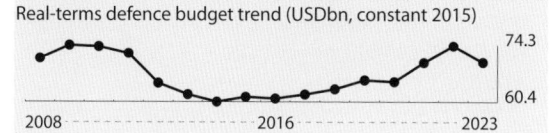

Real-terms defence budget trend (USDbn, constant 2015)
74.3
60.4
2008   2016   2023

Population   68,138,484

Age	0–14	15–19	20–24	25–29	30–64	65 plus
Male	8.7%	2.9%	3.0%	3.3%	23.1%	8.7%
Female	8.2%	2.8%	3.0%	3.4%	22.5%	10.3%

Capabilities

The UK armed forces provide nuclear and conventional deterrence, with a broad range of conventional capabilities. They also support counterterrorism and management of civil emergencies. They are relatively well trained. A March 2023 'refresh' of the 2021 Integrated Review of Security, Defence, Development and Foreign Policy assessed that UK security has deteriorated more quickly than anticipated. A following Defence Command Paper prioritised the military contribution to NATO with armed forces 'optimised' to fight in the Euro-Atlantic and in defence of the homeland. The army plans to strengthen its partnership with Estonia to be able to rapidly reinforce there to brigade strength. Existing reaction forces are set to be assigned to reinforce NATO and to a new national Global Response Force. The modest military 'tilt' to the Indo-Pacific is being sustained. In 2023 the UK continued its support Ukraine, including donating land and air weapons. Those contributions, along with the army's large-scale training programme for Ukrainian troops, reduced readiness of British forces. Weapons transfers have shown weaknesses in UK stockpiles and defence industrial capacity that London is trying to address. The Ukraine war exposed that the Army was the least modernised of the UK services. In 2024–25 it should receive a range of new and modernised equipment including *Challenger* 3 tanks, *Archer* guns and AH-64E *Apache* helicopters. The Royal Navy inducted a new seabed operations ship into service and demonstrated a ballistic missile defence capability. Other plans to transform and grow naval capabilities have been slow to materialise. The UK is partnering with Italy and Japan in the Global Combat Air Programme to field a next-generation fighter in 2035, and with Australia and the US in the AUKUS partnership to collaboratively develop nuclear-powered submarines and other advanced military technology. Efforts to improve cross-domain capability centre on Strategic Command, comprising key joint force elements, such as special forces, defence intelligence and the military component of the National Cyber Force. The government has pledged to increase defence spending to 2.5% of GDP, subject to affordability. The independent National Audit Office in late 2023 assessed that costs of the future equipment plan exceeded funding by up to GBP16.9 billion (USD21.2bn) and forecast that funding for other military capability was insufficient. Nuclear programmes absorb a significant and increasing proportion of defence funding. Weaknesses in defence procurement persist, not least those identified by a critical, independent report into the *Ajax* vehicle procurement, and by a House of Commons defence committee report that judged defence procurement to be 'broken'. The UK's defence industry is globally competitive in some capability areas, particularly aerospace, but cannot meet the full spectrum of UK military requirements, particularly for land equipment.

ACTIVE 144,400 (Army 80,350 Navy 32,350 Air 31,700)

RESERVE 70,650 (Regular Reserve 35,550 (Army 22,650, Navy 6,200, Air 6,700); Volunteer Reserve 35,100 (Army 26,750, Navy 3,350, Air 3,050); Sponsored Reserve 1,950)

Includes both trained and those currently under training within the Regular Forces, excluding university cadet units

ORGANISATIONS BY SERVICE

Strategic Forces 1,000

Royal Navy
EQUIPMENT BY TYPE
SUBMARINES • STRATEGIC
 SSBN 4 *Vanguard* with 16 UGM-133A *Trident* II D-5/D-5LE nuclear SLBM, 4 533mm TT with *Spearfish* HWT (recent deployment practice of no more than 8 missiles/40 warheads per boat; each missile could carry up to 12 MIRV; some *Trident* D-5 capable of

being configured for sub-strategic role)

MSL • SLBM • Nuclear 48 UGM-133A *Trident* II D-5

Royal Air Force
EQUIPMENT BY TYPE
RADAR • STRATEGIC 1 Ballistic Missile Early Warning System (BMEWS) at Fylingdales Moor

Space
EQUIPMENT BY TYPE
SATELLITES • COMMUNICATIONS 6: 2 *Skynet*-4; 4 *Skynet*-5

Army 76,200; 4,150 Gurkhas (total 80,350)
Regt normally bn size. Many cbt spt and CSS regt and bn have reservist sub-units

FORCES BY ROLE
COMMAND
  1 (ARRC) corps HQ
MANOEUVRE
  Armoured
  1 (3rd) armd inf div (1 armd recce/arty bde (2 armd recce regt, 1 recce regt, 2 SP arty regt, 2 MRL regt, 1 STA regt, 1 maint bn); 1 (12th) armd inf bde (2 tk regt, 2 armd inf bn, 1 inf bn, 1 log regt, 1 maint regt, 1 med regt); 1 (20th) armd inf bde (1 armd recce regt, 1 tk regt, 2 armd inf bn, 1 log regt, 1 maint regt, 1 med regt); 1 cbt engr gp (3 cbt engr regt); 1 int bn; 1 sigs gp (3 sigs regt); 1 log bde (2 log regt); 1 AD gp (2 SAM regt))
  Light
  1 (1st) inf div (1 (4th) inf bde (1 recce regt, 6 inf bn); 1 (7th) lt mech inf bde (1 recce regt, 3 lt mech inf bn, 3 inf bn; 1 fd arty regt; 1 cbt engr regt, 1 log regt, 1 maint bn, 1 med regt); 1 (11th) inf bde (3 inf bn); 1 engr bde (1 CBRN regt, 3 EOD regt, 1 (MWD) EOD search regt, 1 engr regt, 1 (air spt) engr regt); 1 int bn; 1 sigs regt; 1 log bde (1 log regt; 1 maint bn); 1 med bde (2 fd hospital))
  1 inf bn (London)
  Air Manoeuvre
  1 (16th) air aslt bde (1 recce pl, 2 para bn, 1 air aslt bn, 1 inf bn, 1 fd arty regt, 1 cbt engr regt, 1 log regt, 1 med regt)
  Other
  1 inf bn (trials gp)
COMBAT SUPPORT
  1 (6th) cbt spt div (1 ranger bde (4 ranger bn); 1 (77th) info ops bde (3 info ops gp, 1 spt gp, 1 engr spt/log gp); 1 int bn)
  1 (geographic) engr regt
  1 ISR gp (1 EW regt, 1 int bn, 2 ISR UAV regt)
  1 MP bde (2 MP regt)
  1 sigs bde (1 EW regt, 4 sigs regt)
COMBAT SERVICE SUPPORT
  1 log bde (3 log regt; 1 maint regt)
  1 maint bn

  1 (ARRC) spt bn

Reserves
Army Reserve 28,350 reservists
The Army Reserve (AR) generates individuals, sub-units and some full units. The majority of units are subordinate to regular-formation headquarters and paired with one or more regular units

FORCES BY ROLE
MANOEUVRE
  Reconnaissance
  1 recce regt
  Armoured
  1 armd regt
  Light
  1 inf bde (2 recce regt, 8 inf bn)
  7 inf bn
  Air Manoeuvre
  1 para bn
COMBAT SUPPORT
  3 arty regt
  1 STA regt
  1 MRL regt
  3 engr regt
  1 EOD regt
  3 int bn
  4 sigs regt
COMBAT SERVICE SUPPORT
  11 log regt
  3 maint regt
  5 med regt
  9 fd hospital
AIR DEFENCE
  1 AD regt
EQUIPMENT BY TYPE
ARMOURED FIGHTING VEHICLES
  MBT 213 *Challenger* 2
  RECCE 59 *Ajax* (in test)
  IFV 388+: 388 FV510 *Warrior*; FV511 *Warrior* (CP); FV514 *Warrior* (OP); FV515 *Warrior* (CP)
  APC 806
    APC (T) 476: 41 *Ares* (in test); 26 *Ares* (in test); 409 FV430 *Bulldog* (incl variants)
    PPV 330 *Mastiff* (6×6)
  AUV 1,587: 398 *Foxhound*; 138 FV103 *Spartan*; 63 FV105 *Sultan* (CP); 17 *Spartan* Mk2; 4 *Sultan* Mk2 (CP); 197 *Jackal*; 110 *Jackal* 2; 130 *Jackal* 2A; 380 *Panther* CLV; 150 *Ridgback*
ENGINEERING & MAINTENANCE VEHICLES
  AEV 104: 16 *Argus* (in test); 56 *Terrier*; 32 *Trojan*
  ARV 283: 21 *Apollo* (in test); 19 *Atlas* (in test); 80 *Challenger* ARRV; 12 FV106 *Samson*; 5 *Samson* Mk2; 105 FV512 *Warrior*; 41 FV513 *Warrior*
  MW 64 *Aardvark*
  VLB 60: 27 M3; 33 *Titan*

NBC VEHICLES 8 TPz-1 *Fuchs* NBC
ANTI-TANK/ANTI-INFRASTRUCTURE • MSL
   SP *Exactor*-2 (*Spike* NLOS)
   MANPATS FGM-148 *Javelin*; NLAW
ARTILLERY 574
   SP 155mm 71: 14 *Archer*; 57 AS90
   TOWED 105mm 114 L118 Light Gun
   MRL 227mm 29 M270B1 MLRS
   MOR 81mm 360 L16A1
AMPHIBIOUS • LCM 3 Ramped Craft Logistic
AIR DEFENCE • SAM 60+
   Short-range CAMM (*Land Ceptor*)
   Point-defence 60 FV4333 *Stormer* with *Starstreak*; *Starstreak* (LML)
UNINHABITED AERIAL VEHICLES • ISR • Medium 12 *Watchkeeper* (33 more in store)

Joint Helicopter Command

Tri-service joint organisation including Royal Navy, Army and RAF units

Army
FORCES BY ROLE
HELICOPTER
   1 bde (1 atk hel regt (2 sqn with AH-64E *Apache*; 1 trg sqn with AH-64D/E *Apache*); 1 atk hel regt (1 sqn with AH-64E *Apache*; 1 sqn with AH-64D *Apache*); 1 regt (2 sqn with AW159 *Wildcat* AH1; 1 trg sqn with AW159 *Wildcat* AH1); 1 (spec ops) sqn with AS365N3; 1 maint regt)
TRAINING
   1 hel regt (1 sqn with AH-64E *Apache*; 1 sqn with AS350B *Ecureuil*)

Army Reserve
FORCES BY ROLE
HELICOPTER
   1 hel regt (4 sqn personnel only)

Royal Navy
FORCES BY ROLE
ATTACK HELICOPTER
   1 lt sqn with AW159 *Wildcat* AH1
TRANSPORT HELICOPTER
   2 sqn with AW101 *Merlin* HC4/4A

Royal Air Force
FORCES BY ROLE
TRANSPORT HELICOPTER
   3 sqn with CH-47D/F/SD *Chinook* HC6A/6/5
   2 sqn with SA330 *Puma* HC2
TRAINING
   1 OCU sqn with CH-47D/SD/F *Chinook* HC3/4/4A/6; SA330 *Puma* HC2
EQUIPMENT BY TYPE
HELICOPTERS
   ATK 50: 12 AH-64D *Apache*; 38 AH-64E *Apache*
   MRH 39: 5 AS365N3; 34 AW159 *Wildcat* AH1
   TPT 111: Heavy 60: 38 CH-47D *Chinook* HC6A; 14 CH-47F *Chinook* HC6; 8 CH-47SD *Chinook* HC5; Medium 42: 25 AW101 *Merlin* HC4/4A; 14 SA330 *Puma* HC2; (6 SA330 *Puma* HC2 in store); Light 9 AS350B *Ecureuil*; (5 H135 in store)

Royal Navy 32,350
EQUIPMENT BY TYPE
SUBMARINES 10
   STRATEGIC • SSBN 4 *Vanguard*, opcon Strategic Forces with 16 UGM-133A *Trident* II D-5/D-5LE nuclear SLBM, 4 single 533mm TT with *Spearfish* HWT (recent deployment practice of no more than 8 missiles/40 warheads per boat; each missile could carry up to 12 MIRV; some *Trident* D-5 capable of being configured for sub-strategic role)
   TACTICAL • SSN 6
      1 *Trafalgar* with 5 single 533mm TT with UGM-109E *Tomahawk* Block IV LACM/*Spearfish* HWT
      5 *Astute* with 6 single 533mm TT with UGM-109E *Tomahawk* Block IV LACM/*Spearfish* HWT
PRINCIPAL SURFACE COMBATANTS 19
   AIRCRAFT CARRIERS 2:
      CV 2 *Queen Elizabeth* with up to 3 Mk 15 *Phalanx* Block 1B CIWS (capacity 40 ac/hel, incl 24+ F-35B *Lightning* II, 14+ *Merlin* HM2/*Wildcat* HMA2/CH-47 *Chinook* hel)
   DESTROYERS 6:
      DDGHM 3 *Daring* (Type-45) with 2 quad lnchr with RGM-84D *Harpoon* Block 1C AShM, 6 8-cell *Sylver* A50 VLS with *Aster* 15/30 (*Sea Viper*) SAM, 2 Mk 15 *Phalanx* Block 1B CIWS, 1 114mm gun (capacity 1 AW159 *Wildcat*/AW101 *Merlin* hel)
      DDHM 3 *Daring* (Type-45) with 6 8-cell *Sylver* A50 VLS with *Aster* 15/30 (*Sea Viper*) SAM, 2 Mk 15 *Phalanx* Block 1B CIWS, 1 114mm gun (capacity 1 AW159 *Wildcat*/AW101 *Merlin* hel)
   FRIGATES • FFGHM 11:
      10 *Duke* (Type-23) with 2 quad lnchr with RGM-84D *Harpoon* Block 1C AShM, 1 32-cell VLS with *Sea Ceptor* SAM, 2 twin 324mm ASTT with *Sting Ray* LWT, 1 114mm gun (capacity either 2 AW159 *Wildcat* or 1 AW101 *Merlin* hel)
      1 *Duke* (Type-23) with 2 quad lnchr with NSM AShM, 1 32-cell VLS with *Sea Ceptor* SAM, 2 twin 324mm ASTT with *Sting Ray* LWT, 1 114mm gun (capacity either 2 AW159 *Wildcat* or 1 AW101 *Merlin* hel)
PATROL AND COASTAL COMBATANTS 26
   PSO 8: 3 *River* Batch 1; 5 *River* Batch 2 with 1 hel landing platform
   PBF 2 *Cutlass*
   PBI 16 *Archer* (14 in trg role, 2 deployed to Gibraltar sqn)
MINE WARFARE • MINE COUNTERMEASURES 8
   MCO 6 *Hunt* (incl 4 mod *Hunt*)

MHC 2 Sandown
AMPHIBIOUS
  PRINCIPAL AMPHIBIOUS SHIPS 2
    LPD 2 *Albion* with 2 Mk 15 *Phalanx* Block 1B CIWS (capacity 2 med hel; 4 LCU or 2 LCAC; 4 LCVP; 6 MBT; 300 troops) (of which 1 at extended readiness)
  LOGISTICS AND SUPPORT 5
    AGB 1 *Protector* with 1 hel landing platform
    AGE 2: 1 XV *Patrick Blackett* (Damen Fast Crew Supplier 4008); 1 *Proteus*
    AGS 2: 1 *Scott* with 1 hel landing platform; 1 *Magpie*
  UNINHABITED MARITIME PLATFORMS
    USV • **MW** 8: **Medium** 1 *Hebe* (*Hussar* mod); **Small** 7: 2 *Apollo*; 5 *Hussar*
  UNINHABITED MARITIME SYSTEMS • **UUV**
    DATA *Gavia*; *Iver*-4 580; REMUS 100/600; *Slocum* G3 Glider
    MW *Seafox* C/I
    UTL AUV62-AT

Royal Fleet Auxiliary

Support and miscellaneous vessels are mostly crewed and maintained by the Royal Fleet Auxiliary (RFA), a civilian fleet owned by the UK MoD, which has approximately 1,900 personnel with type comd under Fleet Commander
  AMPHIBIOUS • **PRINCIPAL AMPHIBIOUS SHIPS** 3:
    LSD 3 *Bay* (capacity 4 LCU; 2 LCVP; 24 *Challenger* 2 MBT; 350 troops)
  LOGISTICS AND SUPPORT 12
    AORH 7: 4 *Tide* (capacity 1 AW159 *Wildcat*/AW101 *Merlin* hel); 2 *Wave* (extended readiness); 1 *Fort Victoria* with 2 Mk 15 *Phalanx* Block 1B CIWS
    AG 1 *Argus* with 1 Mk 15 *Phalanx* Block 1B CIWS (primary casualty-receiving ship with secondary aviation trg ship role)
    AKR 4 *Point* (not RFA manned)

Naval Aviation (Fleet Air Arm) 4,900
FORCES BY ROLE
ANTI-SUBMARINE WARFARE
  3 sqn with AW101 ASW *Merlin* HM2
  2 sqn with AW159 *Wildcat* HMA2
TRAINING
  1 sqn with Beech 350ER *King Air*
  1 sqn with G-115
EQUIPMENT BY TYPE
AIRCRAFT
  TPT • **Light** 4 Beech 350ER *King Air* (*Avenger*)
  TRG 5 G-115
HELICOPTERS
  ASW 58: 28 AW159 *Wildcat* HMA2; 30 AW101 ASW *Merlin* HM2
AIR-LAUNCHED MISSILES • **ASM** *Martlet*

Royal Marines 6,600

FORCES BY ROLE
MANOEUVRE
  Amphibious
  1 (3rd Cdo) mne bde (2 mne bn; 2 sy bn; 1 amph gp; 1 amph aslt sqn; 1 (army) arty regt; 1 (army) engr regt; 1 ISR gp (1 EW sqn; 1 cbt spt sqn; 1 sigs sqn; 1 log sqn), 1 log regt)
  2 amph sqn
EQUIPMENT BY TYPE
ARMOURED FIGHTING VEHICLES
  APC (T) 99 BvS-10 Mk2 *Viking* (incl 19 cabs with 81mm mor)
ANTI-TANK/ANTI-INFRASTUCTURE
  MSL • **MANPATS** FGM-148 *Javelin*
ARTILLERY 39
  TOWED 105mm 12 L118 Light Gun
  MOR 81mm 27 L16A1
PATROL AND COASTAL COMBATANTS • **PB** 2 *Island*
AMPHIBIOUS • **LANDING CRAFT** 26
  LCU 10 LCU Mk10 (capacity 4 *Viking* APC or 120 troops)
  LCVP 16 LCVP Mk5B (capacity 35 troops)
AIR DEFENCE • **SAM** • **Point-defence** *Starstreak*

Royal Air Force 31,700
FORCES BY ROLE
FIGHTER
  2 sqn with *Typhoon* FGR4/T3
FIGHTER/GROUND ATTACK
  4 sqn with *Typhoon* FGR4/T3 (including one joint QTR-UK sqn)
  1 sqn with *Typhoon* FGR4/T3 (aggressor)
  1 sqn with F-35B *Lightning* II
ANTI-SUBMARINE WARFARE
  2 sqn with P-8A *Poseidon* (MRA Mk1)
ISR
  1 sqn with *Shadow* R1
ELINT
  1 sqn with RC-135W *Rivet Joint*
SEARCH & RESCUE
  1 sqn with SA330 *Puma* HC2
TANKER/TRANSPORT
  2 sqn with A330 MRTT *Voyager* KC2/3
TRANSPORT
  1 (VIP) sqn with *Falcon* 900LX (*Envoy* IV CC Mk1)
  2 sqn with A400M *Atlas*
  1 sqn with C-17A *Globemaster*
TRAINING
  1 OCU sqn with A400M *Atlas*; C-17A *Globemaster*
  1 OCU sqn with F-35B *Lightning* II
  1 OCU sqn with *Typhoon* FGR4/T3
  1 OCU sqn with RC-135W *Rivet Joint*
  1 sqn with EMB-500 *Phenom* 100

2 sqn with *Hawk* T2
1 sqn with T-6C *Texan* II
2 sqn with G-115E *Tutor*

COMBAT/ISR UAV
1 sqn with MQ-9A *Reaper*

EQUIPMENT BY TYPE
AIRCRAFT 201 combat capable
FGA 159: 32 F-35B *Lightning* II; 121 *Typhoon* FGR4; 6 *Typhoon* T3; (10 *Typhoon* FGR4 in store)
ASW 9 P-8A *Poseidon* (MRA Mk1)
ISR 8 *Shadow* R1
ELINT 3 RC-135W *Rivet Joint*
AEW&C 3 E-3D *Sentry*
TKR/TPT 10: 3 A330 MRTT *Voyager* KC2 (of which 1 equipped for VIP tpt); 7 A330 MRTT Voyager KC3
TPT 32: **Heavy** 30: 22 A400M *Atlas*; 8 C-17A *Globemaster*; **PAX** 2 *Falcon* 900LX (*Envoy* IV CC Mk1)
TRG 144: 5 EMB-500 *Phenom* 100; 86 G-115E *Tutor*; 28 *Hawk* T2*; 11 *Hawk* T1* (Red Arrows) (ε60 more in store); 14 T-6C *Texan* II
HELICOPTERS
TPT • **Medium** 3 SA330 *Puma* HC2
UNINHABITED AERIAL VEHICLES
CISR • **Heavy** 11: 10 MQ-9A *Reaper*; 1 MQ-9B *Sky Guardian* (*Protector* RG Mk1)
AIR-LAUNCHED MISSILES
AAM • **IR** AIM-9L/L(I) *Sidewinder*; **IIR** ASRAAM; **ARH** AIM-120C-5 AMRAAM; *Meteor*
ASM AGM-114 *Hellfire*; *Brimstone*; *Dual-Mode Brimstone*; *Brimstone* II
LACM *Storm Shadow*
BOMBS
Laser-guided GBU-10 *Paveway* II; GBU-24 *Paveway* III
Laser & INS/GPS-guided Enhanced *Paveway* II/III; *Paveway* IV

Royal Air Force Regiment
FORCES BY ROLE
MANOEUVRE
Other
6 sy sqn

No. 1 Flying Training School (Tri-Service Helicopter Training)
FORCES BY ROLE
TRAINING
1 hel sqn with H135 (*Juno* HT1); H145 (*Jupiter*)
3 hel sqn with H135 (*Juno* HT1)
EQUIPMENT BY TYPE
HELICOPTERS
MRH 7 H145 (*Jupiter*)
TPT • **Light** 31: 2 AW109E; 29 H135 (*Juno* HT1)

Volunteer Reserve Air Forces
(Royal Auxiliary Air Force/RAF Reserve)

MANOEUVRE
Other
5 sy sqn
COMBAT SUPPORT
2 int sqn
COMBAT SERVICE SUPPORT
1 med sqn
1 (air movements) sqn
1 (HQ augmentation) sqn
1 (C-130 Reserve Aircrew) flt

UK Special Forces
Includes Royal Navy, Army and RAF units
FORCES BY ROLE
SPECIAL FORCES
1 (SAS) SF regt
1 (SBS) SF regt
1 (Special Reconnaissance) SF regt
1 SF BG (based on 1 para bn)
AVIATION
1 wg (includes assets drawn from 3 Army hel sqn, 1 RAF tpt sqn and 1 RAF hel sqn)
COMBAT SUPPORT
1 sigs regt

Reserve
FORCES BY ROLE
SPECIAL FORCES
2 (SAS) SF regt
EQUIPMENT BY TYPE
ARMOURED FIGHTING VEHICLES
AUV 24 *Bushmaster* IMV
ANTI-TANK/ANTI-INFRASTRUCTURE • **MSL**
MANPATS FGM-148 *Javelin*; NLAW

DEPLOYMENT
ASCENSION ISLAND: 20
ATLANTIC (NORTH)/CARIBBEAN: 140; 1 PSO; 1 AOEH
ATLANTIC (SOUTH): 40; 1 PSO
BAHRAIN: *Operation Kipion* 1,000; 1 FFGHM; 2 MCO; 2 MHC; 1 LSD; 1 naval facility
BELIZE: BATSUB 12
BRITISH INDIAN OCEAN TERRITORY: 40; 1 navy/marine det
BRUNEI: 2,000; 1 (Gurkha) lt inf bn; 1 jungle trg centre; 1 hel sqn with 3 SA330 *Puma* HC2
CANADA: BATUS 400; 1 trg unit
CYPRUS: 2,260; 2 inf bn; 1 SAR sqn with 3 SA330 *Puma* HC2; 1 radar (on det); *Operation Shader* 450: 1 FGA sqn with 10 *Typhoon* FGR4; 1 A330 MRTT *Voyager*; 2 C-130J-30 *Hercules*; **UN** • UNFICYP (*Operation Tosca*) 257; 2 inf coy
DEMOCRATIC REPUBLIC OF THE CONGO: UN • MONUSCO 3
EGYPT: MFO 2

ESTONIA: NATO • Enhanced Forward Presence (*Operation Cabrit*) 1,000; 1 armd BG; 1 SP arty bty; 1 MRL bty; 1 cbt engr coy

FALKLAND ISLANDS: 1,200: 1 inf coy(+); 1 sigs unit; 1 AD det with CAMM (*Land Ceptor*); 1 PSO; 1 ftr flt with 4 *Typhoon* FGR4; 1 tkr/tpt flt with 1 A330 MRTT *Voyager*; 1 A400M; 1 hel flt with 2 *Chinook*

GERMANY: 185

GIBRALTAR: 600 (including Royal Gibraltar regt); 1 PSO; 2 PBI

IRAQ: *Operation Shader* 100; **NATO •** NATO Mission Iraq 12

KENYA: BATUK 350; 1 trg unit

KOSOVO: NATO • KFOR 600; 1 inf bn

KUWAIT: *Operation Shader* 50; 1 CISR UAV sqn with 8 MQ-9A *Reaper*

LEBANON: UN • UNIFIL 1

MEDITERRANEAN SEA: NATO • SNMG 2: 200; 1 DDGHM

NEPAL: 60 (Gurkha trg org)

NIGERIA: 80 (trg team)

OMAN: 90

PACIFIC OCEAN: 60; 2 PSO

POLAND: Army; 1 SAM bty with CAMM (*Land Ceptor*); **NATO •** Enhanced Forward Presence 140; 1 recce sqn

SAUDI ARABIA: *Operation Crossways* 100; 1 SAM bty with FV4333 *Stormer* with *Starstreak*

SOMALIA: 65 (trg team); **UN •** UNSOM (*Operation Praiser*) 2; **UN •** UNSOS (*Operation Catan*) 10

SOUTH SUDAN: UN • UNMISS (*Operation Vogul*) 5

UNITED ARAB EMIRATES: 100

FOREIGN FORCES

Australia *Operation Kudu* (*Interflex*) 70 (UKR trg)
Canada Air Task Force Prestwick (ATF-P) 55; 3 C-130J-30 *Hercules* (CC-130J); *Operation Unifier* 170 (UKR trg)
Denmark *Operation Interflex* 120 (UKR trg)
Finland *Operation Interflex* 20 (UKR trg)
Lithuania *Operation Interflex* 15 (UKR trg)
Netherlands *Operation Interflex* 90 (UKR trg)
New Zealand *Operation Tieke* (*Interflex*) 71 (UKR trg)
Norway *Operation Interflex* 150 (UKR trg)
Sweden *Operation Interflex* 50 (UKR trg)
United States US European Command: 10,000; 1 bbr flt at RAF Fairford with 4 B-1B *Lancer*; 1 FGA wg at RAF Lakenheath (2 FGA sqn with 27 F-15E *Strike Eagle*, 1 FGA sqn with 27 F-35A *Lightning* II; 1 FGA sqn with 14 F-35 *Lightning* II); 1 ISR sqn at RAF Mildenhall with RC-135; 1 tkr wg at RAF Mildenhall with 15 KC-135R/T *Stratotanker*; 1 spec ops gp at RAF Mildenhall (1 sqn with 8 CV-22B *Osprey*; 1 sqn with 8 MC-130J *Commando* II) • **US Strategic Command**: 1 AN/FPS-132 Upgraded Early Warning Radar and 1 *Spacetrack* radar at Fylingdales Moor

Chapter Four
Russia and Eurasia

- Ukraine recaptured some of the territory Russia took in the opening days of the full-scale invasion of its neighbour that began in February 2022. Kyiv's troops failed in their efforts, though, to achieve an all-out breakthrough against Russia's heavily entrenched defensive lines in 2023. Russia attempted counterattacks, suffering heavy losses. Ukraine also conducted numerous deep strikes using UAVs, including on Moscow and logistics targets.
- The Wagner Group mutiny in June became one of the biggest threats to Russian President Vladimir Putin's rule since taking office. During the uprising, Wagner troops advanced rapidly toward Moscow and shot down a Russian command-and-control aircraft before a deal involving Belarus defused the situation. Weeks later, Wagner's leadership team, including Yevgeny Prigozhin, were killed when their business jet was downed while flying in Russia.
- Azerbaijan took control of the remainder of the Nagorno-Karabakh region principally inhabited by Armenians, spurring a wave of refugees fleeing the territory. Russian peacekeepers were killed during the operation, but Moscow did not intervene.
- Kyrgyzstan and Tajikistan have been investing heavily in UAV acquisitions amid border tensions between the two countries. The dispute turned violent in 2022 and continued to cause friction throughout 2023.
- Russia's Black Sea fleet suffered big setbacks in the country's war with Ukraine. The fleet was put on the defensive by several events, including a Ukrainian attack using uninhabited surface vessels that badly damaged a Project 775-class (*Ropucha*) landing ship off Novorossiysk and a cruise-missile strike in September that left another Project 775-class vessel and the *Varshavyanka*-class (Improved *Kilo*) submarine *Rostov-on-Don* crippled, perhaps irreparably.
- Moscow turned to Iran and North Korea to augment domestic production of weapons in support of its war on Ukraine. Iran supplied various UAVs and direct-attack munitions to Russia, while North Korea, following a meeting between Putin and Kim Jong-un, provided at least a month's worth of artillery ammunition.

Russia real-terms total military expenditure, 2015–23 (USDbn, constant 2015)

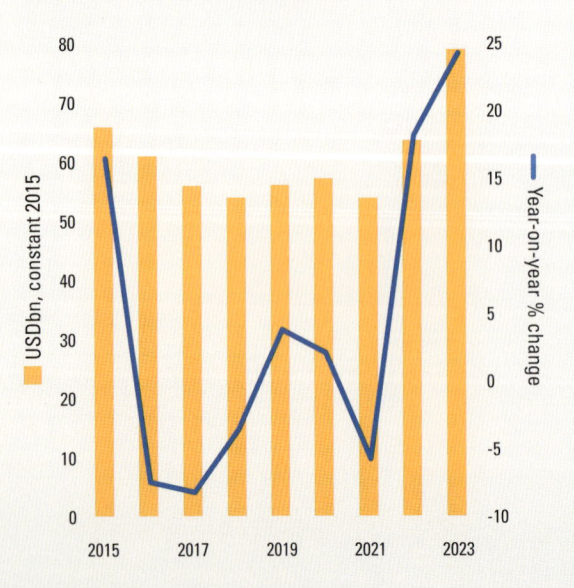

Active military personnel – top 10
(25,000 per unit)

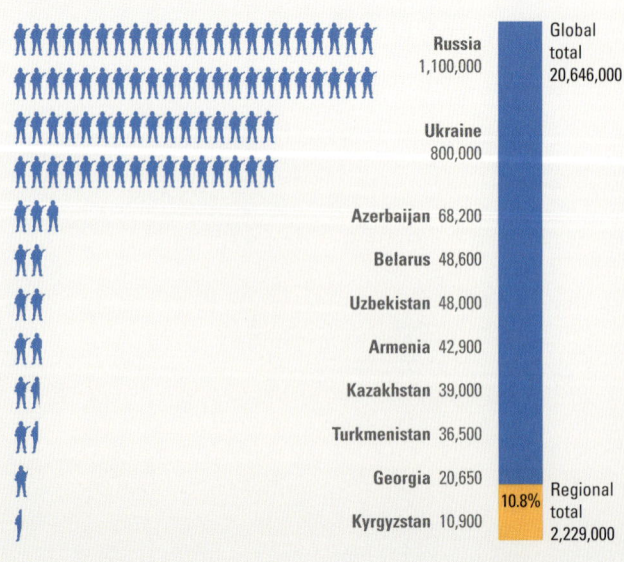

Russia	1,100,000
Ukraine	800,000
Azerbaijan	68,200
Belarus	48,600
Uzbekistan	48,000
Armenia	42,900
Kazakhstan	39,000
Turkmenistan	36,500
Georgia	20,650
Kyrgyzstan	10,900

Global total 20,646,000

Regional total 2,229,000 (10.8%)

Regional defence policy and economics   160 ▶
Arms procurements and deliveries   177 ▶
Armed forces data section   178 ▶

Russia: combat aircraft, 2014–23*

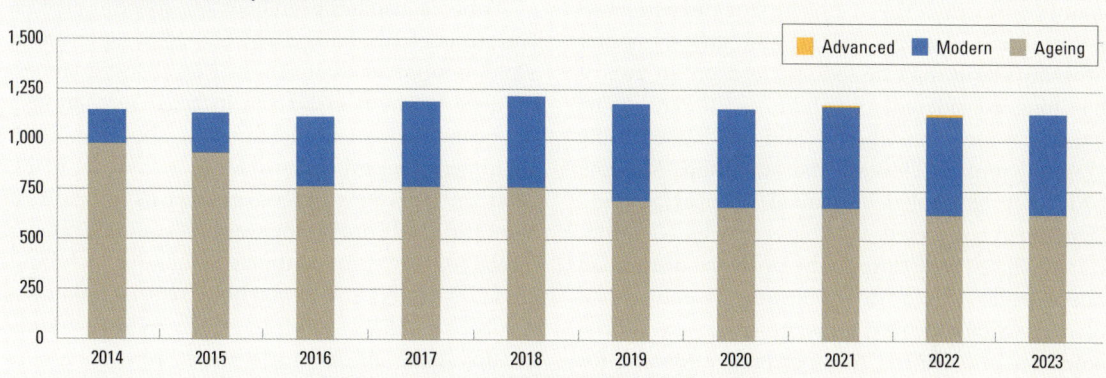

Legend: Advanced, Modern, Ageing

*Active inventory of fighters, fighter ground-attack, ground attack and bomber aircraft

Russia: modern rotary-wing aircraft, 2014–23

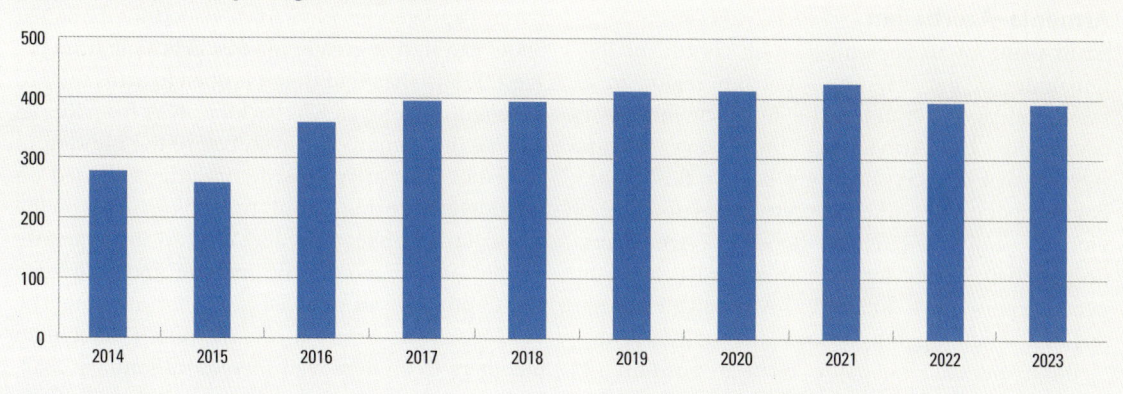

Ukraine: artillery inventory, 2021–23

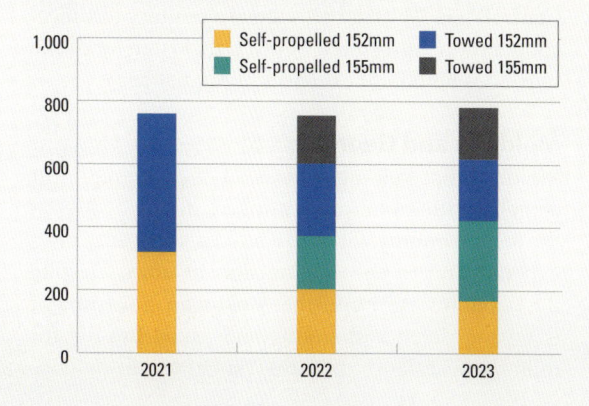

Legend: Self-propelled 152mm, Towed 152mm, Self-propelled 155mm, Towed 155mm

Ukraine: main-battle-tank inventory, 2021–23*

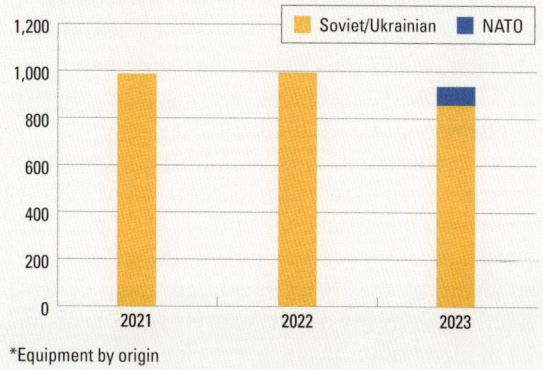

Legend: Soviet/Ukrainian, NATO

*Equipment by origin

Russia and Eurasia

Moscow's full-scale invasion of Ukraine caused upheaval in Russia, but also had ripple effects in the countries nearby. The region in 2023 experienced political and economic fallout and saw signs that Moscow's grip may be less assured on an area it has long considered its sphere of influence. The Kremlin's focus on Ukraine and dealing with the Wagner mutiny limited the attention Moscow could pay to what it has called its 'near abroad'. Azerbaijan completed its takeover of the Nagorno-Karabakh territory despite the presence of Russian peacekeepers, Moldova is boosting its defences in case it becomes the next target of Russia's territorial ambition, and Central Asian states are looking for non-Russian weapons suppliers. The Russian-led post-Soviet Collective Security Treaty Organization (CSTO) appears moribund.

Armenia–Azerbaijan

Azerbaijan, on 19 September, took control of the remainder of the Nagorno-Karabakh region in a rapid military operation. The territory inhabited principally by Armenians, but lying within Azerbaijan's borders, has long been a flashpoint. Baku's operation sparked concern about spreading violence and triggered a flood of Armenians fleeing their homes for fear of reprisals. Russian peacekeepers were killed by Azerbaijani forces during the fighting, but Moscow did not intervene.

Baku entered the battle from a position of economic strength, benefitting in part from the economic effects of the war in Ukraine that have made Azerbaijan's natural-gas exports to European Union countries more lucrative. Azerbaijan, in recent years, has parlayed its economic wealth into stronger armed forces, sourcing equipment from Turkiye and Israel. Baku, for instance, selected Turkish Aerospace Industries to upgrade its Su-25 combat aircraft. Israel Aerospace Industries agreed to sell Azerbaijan a 0.5-metre-resolution remote-sensing satellite and sold *Barak*-Long Range Air Defence equipment to the country, augmenting the *Barak* medium-range systems Azerbaijan already has in its inventory. To support its modernisation push, Azerbaijan plans to hike military spending in 2024 by around 6% to about USD3.8 billion.

Armenia also has been boosting spending levels. The 2023 defence budget of USD1.28bn represented a 46% jump over the prior-year level and is due to advance to about USD1.4bn in 2024. Yerevan also has been looking beyond Russia to source military equipment, in part because Moscow has not made good on deliveries agreed in 2021 as a result of domestic needs due to the war in Ukraine. Armenia signed several major contracts with India, including for 90 155mm ATAGS towed howitzers, an unknown number of *Pinaka* multiple-launch rocket systems and for *Akash* air-defence systems. Yerevan is also moving closer to the West, gradually transitioning to NATO-standard artillery and embracing Western military-education systems and command-and control-approaches. Armenia's Minister of Defence Suren Papikyan, in June 2023, visited the Paris Air Show in a sign of greater interest in buying from the West. France has said that it is open to arms sales to the country. Yerevan was backing away from Russia as a security guarantor even before the fighting in 2023, not least after Moscow in 2022 remained on the sidelines during an outbreak of hostilities on the Armenia–Azerbaijan border. Yerevan subsequently invited an EU monitoring mission and refused a CSTO proposal to establish a similar mission. The EU Mission in Armenia consists of 103 all-civilian members to be deployed there until January 2025, with an option for renewal. Armenia has de facto frozen its participation in CSTO activities.

Baku, meanwhile, also expanded links into Central Asia. The country signed a military technical cooperation agreement with Uzbekistan and the two sides held joint exercises in August 2023.

Moldova and Georgia

Moldova has felt the effects of the Ukraine war acutely, with an influx of refugees and pressure on the local economy. GDP advanced 2.5% in 2023 after experiencing a 5.9% contraction in 2022. Despite the economic turmoil, the Moldovan government is raising defence spending and asked the EU for military assistance in areas such as air-defence equipment. Moscow, which already occupies the country's Transnistria region, expressed misgivings over Moldavian President Maia Sandu pro-Western policies that included a turn towards NATO, fuelling concern in Chisinau that Russia may make the country its next target after Ukraine. The EU responded to Moldova's request by allocating funding to buy a long-range air-surveillance radar, as well as high-mobility light tactical vehicles, buses, trucks and communication equipment, as well cyber-security hardware and software. The EU also has provided support through the European Peace Facility, including armoured personnel carriers and small arms.

Georgia, where Russian troops supporting the breakaway regions of Abkhazia and South Ossetia, raised its defence budget by 22.5% in 2023, partly on the strength of economic growth. The money is being used to establish a cyber-security department in the Georgian defence ministry and to buy equipment. Georgia is establishing a licence-production deal for Polish *Warmate* loitering munitions and *FlyEye* UAVs. Georgia is also continuing its overhaul of its Su-25 combat aircraft fleet, Mi-24 helicopters and L-39 jet trainers. Russia appeared to be hardening its grip on the occupied regions, including plans to potentially create a naval base in Abkhazia, though some troops were redeployed because of the war against Ukraine.

Central Asia

Countries in Central Asia have been trying to avoid being drawn into the geopolitical battle between Moscow and the West over Ukraine, retaining ties to Russia, though largely without providing overt support. Border concerns and regional security challenges including from Afghanistan were predominant. China, meanwhile, is becoming increasingly active in the region, potentially threatening Moscow's role as the dominant power in Central Asia. Beijing signalled its willingness to step up security cooperation at the May 2023 China–Central Asia summit in Xi'an, particularly in the fields of military education and arms sales. Kazakhstan, the regional state perhaps moving most evidently from Moscow's orbit, still nominally participated in the annual CSTO *Combat Brotherhood* 2023 exercise held in Belarus but did not send equipment.

The region is also contending with a territorial dispute between Kyrgyzstan and Tajikistan that turned violent in 2022 and continued to cause friction between the countries throughout 2023. Both sides are strengthening their military capabilities through domestic manufacturing and foreign purchases, with a particular emphasis on UAV acquisitions. In 2022, Kyrgyzstan's defence budget reportedly rose significantly, and the country struck supplier agreements with entities in Turkiye and Belarus. Kyrgyzstan used Turkish *Bayraktar* TB2 UAVs procured in 2021 in its conflict with Tajikistan, and in 2023 it acquired *Aksungur* and *Anka* models from Turkiye. Tajikistan turned to Iran to aid with local production of *Ababil* 2 UAVs that reportedly commenced in 2022. Meanwhile, Kyrgyzstan returned to participating in CSTO military exercises after it cancelled exercises that it had been due to host in late 2022.

UKRAINE

A second year of fighting following Russia's February 2022 full-scale invasion showed the continued ability of Ukraine's armed forces to take the war to the aggressor in the land, maritime and air domains. But after Ukraine's forces made rapid gains in regaining ground in the north and south in 2022, the past year also highlighted the challenge for a counter-offensive against a foe that spent months digging in.

Throughout 2023, Ukraine was able to place the Russian Black Sea Fleet on the back foot, strike key targets even in Russia, including some in the Moscow area, and limit Russian air-force operations to a stand-off role. Kyiv was unable, though, to match those successes with significant progress in a highly anticipated 2023 counter-offensive that boasted modern Western equipment and troops that had received specialised training in the West.

Kyiv launched its 2023 counter-offensive in June to retake Russian occupied territory in eastern and southern Ukraine, including Crimea. But Russia's series of defensive belts combining linear trench systems and extensive minefields slowed Ukrainian forces, exposing those troops to attrition by direct fire, artillery and airstrikes. Ukraine, which reportedly had plans for rapid combined arms offensives, switched to more limited dismounted attacks by infantry and combat engineers. Ukrainian forces were able to push back Russian troops in some sectors, but only by a few kilometres.

Russia selectively tried counter-attacks of its own. In the autumn, it committed eight brigades

Table 8 — Ukraine: selected contracts by foreign donors, 2022–October 2023

Russia's full-scale invasion of Ukraine in February 2022 met with a level of US and European support for Kyiv that the Kremlin had not anticipated. Western governments have supplied Ukraine with large amounts of munitions and other military equipment. Most donations in 2022 came from existing equipment inventories and exposed the relative shallowness of many NATO countries' munitions stocks. Since mid-2022, several states have funded equipment acquisitions from their local industries, either as new-build systems or overhauled equipment in industrial inventories. Air-defence equipment has featured heavily in the transfers. The strong performance of these systems in Ukraine is likely to drive demand elsewhere. Most countries have preferred to finance equipment produced by their own industry, but some have funded systems made elsewhere. Denmark, Germany and Norway have paid for the delivery of *Zuzana*-2 howitzers from Slovakia. France, by contrast, established a special fund, starting at EUR200m (USD221m), that Ukraine can use to buy equipment from French industry. Kyiv used the funds to buy CAESAR howitzers among other items. In some cases, countries have financed the acquisition of systems not yet in service anywhere. The US, for instance, funded loitering munitions and air-defence systems, the latter based on the Advanced Precision Kill Weapons System (APKWS) laser-guided rocket, while the UK financed a 35mm air-defence artillery system from MSI-Defence. The German army's development of the LUNA NG has been dogged by delays, but the UAV is now scheduled to enter service with Ukraine before the Bundeswehr.

Contract Date	Equipment	Type	Qty	Value (USD)	Contractor	Funded by	Deliveries
Spring 2022	*Marder* 1A3*	IFV	20	n.k.	Rheinmetall (Germany)	Germany	2023
Apr 2022	*Phoenix Ghost*	Loitering munition	n.k.	95m	Aevex (US)	US	n.k.
Apr 2022	*Senator*	AUV	8	1.54m	Roshel (Canada)	Canada	2022
May 2022	*Switchblade* 300	Loitering munition	n.k.	22m	AeroVironment (US)	US	n.k.
May 2022	APKWS	Laser-guided rocket	n.k.	64m	BAE Systems (UK)	US	n.k.
Jun 2022	IRIS-T SLM	Medium-range SAM	12	n.k.	Diehl (Germany)	Germany	2022–ongoing
Jun 2022	LAV 6.0 Armoured Combat Support Vehicle	Wheeled APC	39	188.24m	GDLS-C (Canada)	Canada	2022
Aug 2022	NASAMS	Medium-range SAM	8 bty	1.40bn	RTX (US)	US	2023–ongoing
Sep 2022	*Switchblade* 600	Loitering munition	n.k.	3m	AeroVironment (US)	US	n.k.
Oct 2022	*Zuzana*-2	155mm self-propelled howitzer	16	96.96m	KONŠTRUKTA-Defence (Slovakia)	Denmark, Germany, Norway	2023–ongoing
Nov 2022	T-72EA*	MBT	90	90m	Excalibur Army (Czech Republic)	Netherlands, US	2022–ongoing
Dec 2022	*Skynex*	35mm self-propelled air defence artillery	8	n.k.	Rheinmetall (Germany)	Germany	2024
Jan 2023	CAESAR	155mm self-propelled howitzer	6	n.k.	Nexter (France)	France	2023–24
Jan 2023	MR-2 *Viktor*	14.5mm self-propelled air defence artillery	100	n.k.	Excalibur Army (Czech Republic)	Netherlands	2023
Jan 2023	*Senator*	AUV	200	52.15m	Roshel (Canada)	Canada	2023–ongoing
Jan 2023	TRML-3D	Air-surveillance radar	2	n.k.	Hensoldt (Germany)	Germany	2023
Jan 2023	*Vampire*	Point-defence SAM	14	40m	L3Harris (US)	US	n.k.
Feb 2023	*Leopard* 1A5*	MBT	100+	n.k.	Flensburger Fahrzeugbau Gesellschaft (FFG), Rheinmetall (Germany)	Denmark, Germany, Netherlands	2023–24

May 2023	TRML-3D	Air surveillance radar	6	n.k.	Germany	Hensoldt	Germany	2023–ongoing
May 2023	*Marder* 1A3*	IFV	20	n.k.	Germany	Rheinmetall	Germany	2023
Jun 2023	Bv-206*	Tracked APC	64	n.k.	Sweden	BAE Systems Hägglunds	Germany	2023–ongoing
Jun 2023	*Leopard* 2A4*	MBT	14	177.03m	Germany	Rheinmetall	Denmark Netherlands	2024
Jun 2023	NASAMS	Medium-range SAM	2 lnchr	10.51m	Norway	Kongsberg	Lithuania	2023
Jul 2023	NASAMS	Medium-range SAM	4 bty	n.k.	US	RTX	US	n.k.
Aug 2023	LUNA NG	Light ISR UAV	n.k.	n.k.	Germany	Rheinmetall	Germany	2023
Aug 2023	*Marder* 1A3*	IFV	40	n.k.	Germany	Rheinmetall	Germany	2023
Sep 2023	CAESAR	155mm self-propelled howitzer	6	n.k.	France	Nexter	France	2024
Oct 2023	*Terrahawk Paladin*	35mm self-propelled air defence artillery	n.k.	88m	UK	MSI-Defence	UK	n.k.

*Second-hand equipment overhauled by industry

bty = batteries. lnchr= launchers.

to assault Avdiivka, where tenacious Ukrainian defences inflicted heavy casualties, highlighting a common problem: defensive operations are much easier than attacks.

Ukraine's conduct of the operation and the limited progress drew criticism from some Western military backers and somewhat overshadowed the successes Kyiv achieved in the deep battle. That unfolded through diverse means, including Ukrainian partisans and special forces conducting bombings and assassinations of pro-Russian officials; strikes using United Kingdom and French-supplied cruise missiles on targets such as Russian headquarters, ammunition dumps, naval bases and bridges; the employment of United States-provided Army Tactical Missile System short-range ballistic missiles to strike Russian airfields and other sites; and uninhabited aerial vehicle (UAV) raids deep into Russia proper. Those operations, coupled with attacks along the lengthy front line, tried to stretch Russian forces committed to Ukraine operations and bring them to a point where their combat power and morale may begin to break.

In the maritime domain, Ukraine repeatedly struck Russia's Black Sea Fleet employing a combination of missiles and the innovative use of uninhabited maritime vehicles (UMVs). Amid those losses, Russian ships largely withdrew to the perceived safety of Novorossiysk, though even there Ukraine almost managed to sink a Russian amphibious landing ship using an uninhabited surface vessel. Ukraine's successes stifled Russia's attempt to impose a complete maritime blockade on the country and opened the door for some grain exports by ship.

Ukrainian air defences, bolstered by the inflow of Western equipment, were able to limit Russian combat-aircraft operations over the front line, but struggled to keep pace with the barrage of cruise missiles, UAVs, direct-attack munitions and high-speed weapons launched by Russia. Moscow, at times, had to reduce the pace of its attacks to restock, but has been able to replenish.

To gain an edge, Kyiv continued to try to innovate weapons technology. Ukrainian S200 *Gammon* air-defence missiles were reconfigured as land-attack missiles, for example, and locally made UMVs were used in many of the counter-Black Sea Fleet operations. Still, Ukraine urged backers to provide more assistance, including in areas such as electronic warfare, air power, counter-battery fire and minefield breaching.

Armed forces not directly involved in the fighting, meanwhile, have been trying to determine what lessons to learn and which to ignore from the fighting. The war has rekindled an appreciation for artillery, but also the need for mobility of such systems to evade counter-battery fire. Direct-attack munitions, UMVs and air defences all have gained prominence in modernisation plans. And Western countries are trying to rebuild their defence-industrial base after the heavy-weapons consumption rates seen in the fighting in Ukraine demonstrated a lack of surge capacity.

As a second wartime winter approached, Kyiv was bracing for an onslaught of Russian long-range strikes on civilian infrastructure intended to break the population's will. While Ukraine has more formidable defences this winter, Moscow was seemingly building up its inventory to attempt to overwhelm Ukraine's air defences.

RUSSIA

Russia's full-scale invasion of Ukraine in February 2022 demonstrated how war is a test not only of military force in the field, but also of the domestic systems, societies and leaders. It has exposed cracks in the system and incompetence that have generated unease, criticism and division within the country. Rivalries over influence and access to resources within the elite have intensified and sparked one of the biggest crises in contemporary Russian politics with the revolt of the Wagner Group.

The Kremlin has become even more repressive since the war began, though it has not suppressed all criticism. It has allowed a degree of public debate within two limits: no direct criticism of President Vladimir Putin and no public opposition to the war. Transgressors must flee the country or risk arrest and a prison sentence of up to five years for discrediting the armed forces. In April, the anti-war opposition leader Vladimir Kara-Murza was handed a 25-year prison sentence. Some prominent opposition figures have been prosecuted for 'extremism' and even 'treason'. The Soviet-era practice of denunciation has returned, with cases of students reporting their teachers and teachers reporting the parents of their students.

In the limited space for public debate, an online group of commentators and journalists is reporting on the war as 'milbloggers'. Some have millions of followers and have become trusted sources of information in Russia. Graphic and detailed in their reporting, they are mostly Russian nationalists who consider it their patriotic duty to expose the failures and mistakes of the military. Putin occasionally meets with them. Elite figures commanding significant forces were also vocal, most notably Yevgeny Prigozhin, head of the Wagner Group, and Ramzan Kadyrov, the head of the Chechen Republic.

Such sanctioned criticism is a striking exception to the growing Sovietisation of many institutions and practices in Russia. In Soviet times, unity and conformity were imposed on public discussion of all important policy issues, and especially on matters of war and peace, on which cautious and coded differences, at most, were permitted. There is no precedent for shrill, public criticism of a fundamental policy, let alone for it to be amplified by heads of force structures.

These voices have criticised the methods of what Russia has termed a 'special military operation' against Ukraine. They have drawn attention to inadequate equipment and poor decision-making, including by senior officers. Many demand the commitment of more resources to the war. For all the brutality of Russia's campaign, President Putin has so far balanced its conduct against the need to avoid imposing strains on public support. As a result, Russia has devoted far less of its human and material capacity to the war than is potentially available. When Russia announced a partial mobilisation in September 2022, which for the first time compelled large numbers to fight, it was late and limited (though the authorising decree remains in place). As the Kremlin feared, the move led to a sharp increase in public anxiety and a decline in support for the war. In his state of the nation address in March 2023, Putin sought to reassure the country that the demands of war would not lead to material privation, insisting there would be no 'guns or butter' trade-off. Many milbloggers and their followers continued to demand an escalation of resources for the war.

Putin responded to military setbacks with changes of commanders and other senior officers. In September 2022, he dismissed Dmitry Bulgakov, deputy minister of defence responsible for logistics, due to failures in this area. Putin's most notable appointment was of Sergei Surovikin as overall commander of the war in Ukraine in October 2022. Surovikin's nickname, 'General Armageddon', reflects his particularly ruthless reputation. In August 1991, he commanded the unit responsible for the only civilian deaths during the coup against Mikhail Gorbachev. His appointment to lead the war effort was publicly welcomed by Prigozhin and Kadyrov.

Early in 2023, the Russian General Staff undertook moves to reinforce their control of operations in Ukraine. Those included the elevation of General of the Army Valery Gerasimov to overall military commander of Russia's 'special military operation', with Surovikin demoted to his deputy, as well as the formal transfer of the nominally independent 1st and 2nd Army Corps (formerly the forces of the so-called Donetsk and Luhansk People's Republics) to the Russian Armed Forces and the signing of a Presidential decree that required members of the numerous private military companies (PMCs) operating in Ukraine to sign contracts with the Russian Ministry of Defence.

Wagner mutiny

Putin remained loyal to Gerasimov and Defence Minister Sergei Shoigu, who have held their roles since 2012, despite Russia's disastrous military performance. That loyalty helped fuel the most serious threat Putin has faced to his rule. In early 2023, Prigozhin escalated his public criticism of Gerasimov and Shoigu, intensifying a simmering feud between them. As the Wagner Group suffered huge losses in trying to take the city of Bakhmut, Prigozhin issued a series of extraordinary videos, one of which showed him in front of rows of freshly killed Wagner troops, in which he accused Shoigu and Gerasimov of failing to provide promised ammunition, and even of carrying out an attack on Wagner forces. He also referred derisively to a 'happy grandad who thinks everything is fine', a phrase widely interpreted as a thinly veiled reference to Putin himself.

Putin had given Prigozhin, a loyal servant since the 1990s, a long leash. But in early June, Putin intervened on the side of Shoigu and Gerasimov, announcing that all Wagner forces would have to sign contracts with the Ministry of Defence by the end of the month. That would have meant the end of Wagner as a separate entity. The directive triggered one of the most dramatic moments in recent Russian domestic history. On 23 June, Prigozhin responded by leading part of the Wagner forces in revolt, first rapidly occupying Rostov-on-Don – the location of the Southern Military District headquarters and a key planning centre for the war – and then marching on Moscow. While his ostensible demands were the removal of Shoigu and Gerasimov, there was no guarantee that the volatile mix of anger, ego and desperation that drove him would not escalate into a full-scale threat to the Kremlin.

At the height of the affair, Putin warned about the possibility of state collapse in a national television broadcast, invoking the 1917 revolution, and referring to the *smuta*, the early seventeenth-century Time of Troubles that gripped Russia in instability. Putin and others, including Surovikin, appealed to Wagner troops and to wider loyalties across the military, suggesting that they feared the revolt might attract backing among non-Wagner forces. As Wagner's forces turned largely unhindered towards Moscow while shooting down six military aircraft, the authorities prepared for a defence of the capital. Only a deal brokered by Belarus's leader, Alyaksandr Lukashenka, defused the crisis. Prigozhin apparently agreed to end his revolt in return for being allowed to move, with Wagner troops, to Belarus in safety.

The revolt revealed Putin's misreading of domestic politics, exposed the brittleness of the Russian state, and deeply alarmed Russia's elites. It also woke the Kremlin up to the threat from hardline opinion that it had tolerated. An investigation into the revolt led to a number of officers, notably Surovikin, being detained or demoted. On 21 July, Igor Girkin, a hardline critic of Putin and of his conduct of the war, was arrested on charges of 'extremism'. He was a key commander in Russia's first invasion of Ukraine in 2014 and was implicated in the downing of Malaysia Airlines Flight MH17. Two months after the revolt, Prigozhin and other senior Wagner figures were killed when their private plane exploded in flight over Russia. The event is widely assumed to be Putin's belated retribution.

Since the Wagner revolt, the bounds of criticism have narrowed. Hardline dissent about the conduct of the war is now subject to growing repression, though still far less severe than dissent against the war itself. But Putin appears to have tacitly responded to such criticism as well as suppressing it by moving to prosecute the war more ruthlessly. In July, he ended Russia's participation in the Black Sea Grain Initiative, which, over the previous year, had allowed some Ukrainian foodstuffs to be shipped to world markets. The 2024 budget drawn up over the summer nearly doubles defence expenditure. Even Finance Minister Anton Siluanov, a cautious technocrat, has used the Stalin-era slogan 'everything for the front'.

Russia has shown no interest in negotiation and has rejected Chinese and African peace plans. Moscow remains committed to victory, not compromise, even if achieved over years rather than days, through a steady mobilisation of resources that it hopes will enable it to outlast the West in a contest of resolve.

The most acute dilemma for the Kremlin, as it tries to balance the demands of war with domestic cohesion, is whether to order a second 'partial mobilisation'. This would be unpopular and as the March 2024 presidential election approaches, the Kremlin will become more sensitive to public opinion. Even though the election will be neither free nor fair, the experience of other authoritarian states shows elections can be flashpoints of popular discontent.

However, the fate of the war and of Putin's regime hinges largely on the view of elites. Except for the hardline *siloviki* (security and military officials), most elites wish that the war had not begun, but nor do they want Russia to lose. If a critical mass concludes that the war is becoming so disastrous for the country and for their own future that they must try to end it without victory, then a new and broader challenge to Putin's rule could emerge. The Kremlin, sensitive to this danger and ever-more authoritarian, is not behaving like a secure and confident regime. But the domestic politics of his war will loom larger in his conduct of it.

Ground Forces, Airborne Forces and Naval Infantry

Almost all of Russia's deployable ground-combat power remained committed to operations in Ukraine in late 2023. Persistently high casualty rates have kept most units below establishment strength. Shortages of replacement officers and the limited training time allotted to newly mobilised personnel significantly hampered the combat effectiveness of many units. Bullish statements by government and industry officials about recruitment and equipment production to support forces deployed in Ukraine in 2023 appeared to belie reality and presumably were intended primarily as propaganda for Russia's domestic audience.

Nonetheless, personnel numbers of existing formations and units were partially replenished, and a number of new wartime regiments were established through limited mobilisation efforts conducted in late 2022, coupled with a variety of ongoing recruitment efforts. In addition, the armed forces established additional higher-level formation headquarters in 2023 to help command the expanded force structure.

Since the 1990s, Russia's military planning has faced a tension between focusing limited resources on a legacy Soviet, mobilisation-based model – one anticipating large-scale attritional conflict with NATO or possibly China – or optimising for smaller, higher-readiness forces for operations in post-Soviet states on Russia's periphery. The failure of Moscow's February 2022 plan for Ukraine operations, coupled with the attritional nature of subsequent fighting, has likely damaged confidence in the hybrid, mostly higher-readiness force design put in place between 2012 and 2022 and revived interest in a mobilisation-based approach.

The formations added in 2023, along with announced plans to expand Russia's Ground Forces (SV), Airborne Forces (VDV) and Naval Infantry, suggest that Moscow has identified a lack of overall mass as a key issue for Russia's ground forces. Indeed, plans to revive large-scale formations predate the 2022 war. However, the Kremlin's ability to resource that expansion remains questionable, however, raising the prospect of a return to the 'hollow force' of the 1990s.

Without significant and likely costly changes to the recruitment, training and long-term retention of professional personnel, any expanded future force would be dependent on low-quality conscript and mobilised personnel to an even greater extent than before 2022. This would probably inhibit such a force's ability to sustain and deploy combat power at high readiness for operations.

Equipping an expanded force structure would also further strain Russia's domestic defence industry and remaining stockpiles of Cold War-era armour and artillery. Although the inventory of that equipment is nominally still sizeable, many of the remaining platforms are probably either in poor condition or have been stripped of parts to sustain the current fleet. The actual number of platforms available for reactivation is, therefore, likely to be significantly lower than headline totals suggest. Depending on when they begin, and unless suitable platforms are left in store, future re-equipment plans would require a large-scale expansion of the domestic industry's capacity to produce new-build platforms or become dependent on widespread imports, both of which would likely prove expensive.

For now, Moscow continues to make significant use of PMCs to generate combat power in Ukraine and overseas, most notably the Redut group, which has very close links to Russian military intelligence and the Ministry of Defence. This likely reflects the ability of these PMCs to bolster recruitment efforts for operations in Ukraine as well as to offer Moscow geopolitical proxies for operations outside of Russia's 'near abroad'.

Naval Forces

The Russian navy in the past year suffered some of its biggest setbacks in decades, principally because of reverses experienced by the Black Sea Fleet in the war with Ukraine. The events have added to doubts about the service's combat effectiveness. A combination of audacious and unconventional Ukrainian tactics at sea has forced the Black Sea Fleet to be largely on the defensive. The increased reach of some of the Ukrainian strikes limited Russia's room for safe manoeuvre.

In August, a Ukrainian attack using uninhabited surface vessels (USVs) badly damaged a Project 775-class (*Ropucha*) landing ship off Novorossiysk. In a cruise-missile strike on 13 September, another Project 775-class vessel and the *Varshanyanka*-class (Improved *Kilo*) submarine *Rostov-on-Don* were crippled, perhaps irreparably, in dry-dock at the Sevastopol naval base in Russian-occupied Crimea. A subsequent strike on the headquarters building in Sevastopol underscored the vulnerability of the base, further questioning its viability as a safe operating hub, and potentially forcing Russian naval commanders to concentrate operations on the more distant Novorossiysk base.

Despite the setbacks, the Black Sea Fleet still appeared able to impose a partial blockade on Ukraine. The war has also seemed to validate, in operational terms, the increased focus of the Russian navy on its ability to undertake stand-off land-attack cruise-missile strikes, which the Black Sea Fleet continued to deliver against Ukrainian targets using surface and sub-surface platforms. However, its material losses and Russia's inability to provide naval reinforcements due to the strictures imposed by Turkiye on access into and out of the Black Sea under the Montreux Convention cast doubt on the extent to which Moscow could sustain its operations.

Map 3 — Russia: operational fleet inventories and selected submarine, surface-combatant and amphibious-ship dispositions, 2007, 2020 and 2023

Overall, fleet numbers have not altered significantly since 2007, except for a notable boost for the Black Sea Fleet and some bolstering of the Pacific Fleet. However, the offensive missile capability particularly of submarines and small surface combatants has increased considerably under modernisation programmes. The Black Sea Fleet has suffered reverses and been constrained in its operations since the start of the Ukraine war, due to both Ukrainian actions and the strictures of warship access through the Turkish straits as imposed by Turkiye under the Montreux Convention. The Northern and Baltic Fleets' amphibious capacity was depleted by the deployments of tank landing ships (LSTs) to the Black Sea Fleet prior to the start of hostilities. Otherwise, Russian naval capacity has been little affected by the war, and the Northern and Pacific Fleets have been notably active in deployments and exercises. Long term, war in Ukraine and sanctions on the Russian naval industrial base could affect maintenance and new commissionings.

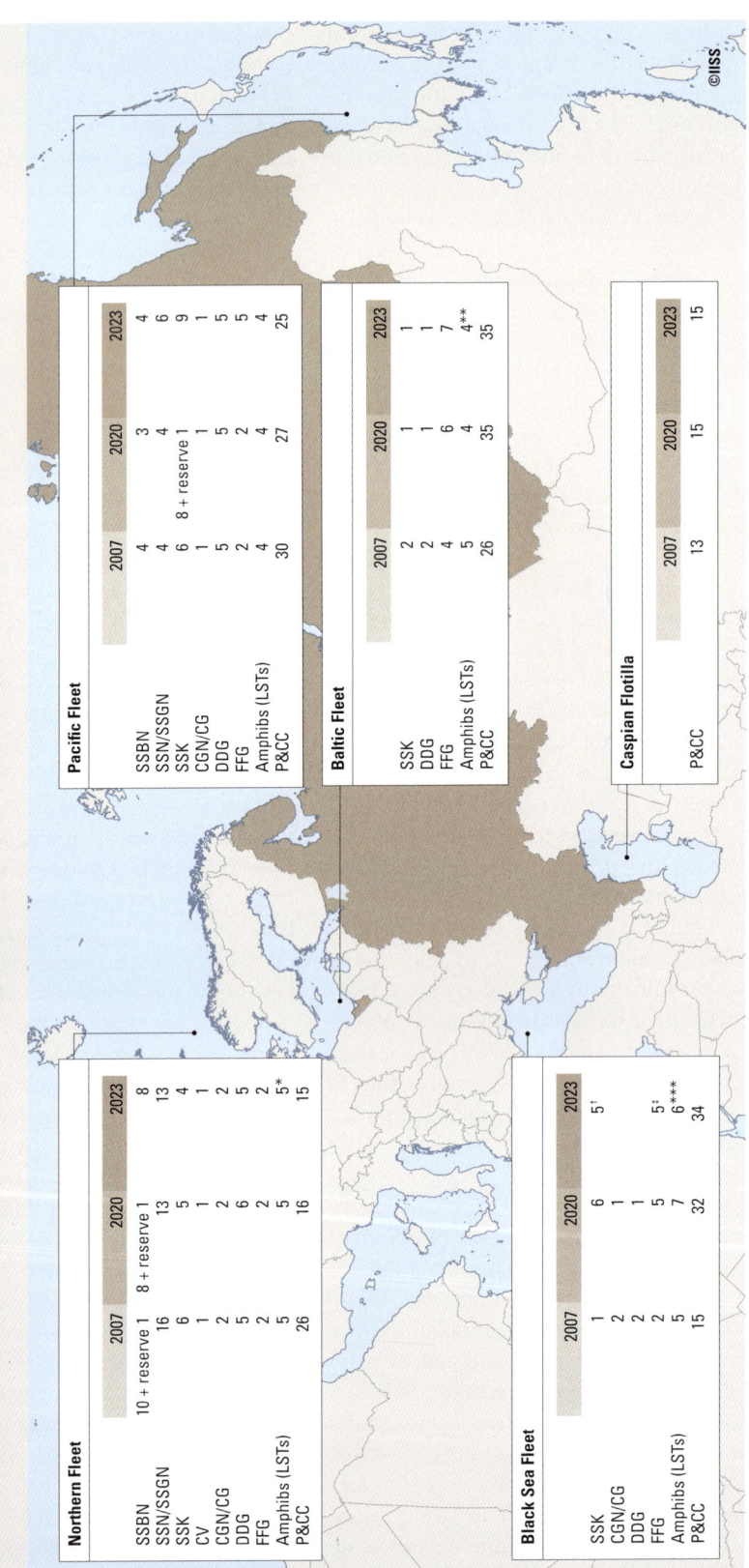

Northern Fleet

	2007	2020	2023
SSBN	10 + reserve 1	8 + reserve 1	8
SSN/SSGN	16	13	13
SSK	6	5	4
CV	1	1	1
CGN/CG	2	2	2
DDG	5	6	5
FFG	2	2	5
Amphibs (LSTs)	5	5	5*
P&CC	26	16	15

Pacific Fleet

	2007	2020	2023
SSBN	4	3	4
SSN/SSGN	4	4	6
SSK	6	8 + reserve 1	9
CGN/CG	1	1	1
DDG	5	5	5
FFG	2	2	5
Amphibs (LSTs)	4	4	4
P&CC	30	27	25

Baltic Fleet

	2007	2020	2023
SSK	2	1	1
DDG	2	1	1
FFG	4	6	7
Amphibs (LSTs)	5	4	4**
P&CC	26	35	35

Black Sea Fleet

	2007	2020	2023
SSK	1	6	5†
CGN/CG	2	1	
DDG	2		
FFG	2	5	5‡
Amphibs (LSTs)	5	7	6***
P&CC	15	32	34

Caspian Flotilla

	2007	2020	2023
P&CC	13	15	15

Notes: Correct as of 1 December 2023. P&CC = Patrol and coastal combatants. *Including vessels deployed to Black Sea Fleet. **Including vessels deployed to Black Sea Fleet. One additional vessel deployed, non-operational, damaged in combat, possibly beyond repair. ***Not including Northern Fleet and Baltic Fleet reinforcements. †One submarine redeployed to Baltic; one further submarine non-operational, damaged in combat possibly beyond repair. ‡One vessel deployed outside Black Sea.
Sources: *The Military Balance 2008*; Military Balance+

Russia's naval modernisation also appeared to be hobbled by the effects of Moscow's decision to launch the full-scale invasion of Ukraine in February 2022. The navy's inventory saw few notable additions, adding to the challenges faced by an already frail and poorly performing shipbuilding industrial base because of international sanctions imposed in response to the war. Russia introduced a *Borey*-A ballistic-missile submarine, a *Buyan*-M missile corvette and an *Alexandrit*-class mine-countermeasures vessel in December 2022. Two new Project 20380-class (*Steregushchiy* II) frigates, *Merkurii* and *Rezkiy*, were commissioned in May and September 2023. Several other significant vessels were either in trials or appeared near completion, but the timing of their introduction into service was uncertain.

The pace of the fleet additions means the navy's legacy blue-water surface capabilities are likely to atrophy further, potentially at an accelerating rate. That could include its aircraft-carrier capability. The navy's sole carrier, *Admiral Kuznetsov*, has been in refit for more than six years. Russia scrapped the modernisation of the *Orlan*-class (*Kirov* I) nuclear-powered battlecruiser *Pyotr Velikiy*, according to reports, which may be an indicator of a shift in focus away from sustaining that type of capability (although sister ship *Admiral Nakhimov* may still emerge from its protracted modernisation in 2024–25). Several new, more elaborate design projects, including for a class of large destroyers and a new stealth-frigate programme, also appear to have been abandoned.

The changes in Russian fleet plans suggest a new focus for Moscow on delivering the smaller but still oceangoing principal surface combatants currently in production, such as the Project 22350 (*Gorshkov*) and Project 20380 (*Steregushchiy* II) frigates. The name-ship of the *Gorshkov* class, also the lead ship equipped with the *Zircon* scramjet-powered hypersonic anti-ship cruise missile, undertook an extended global deployment from January to September 2023, while two of the *Steregushchiys*, assigned to the Pacific Fleet performed high-profile Pacific deployments. The increased deployments of these more modern units may, in some respects, benefit the Russian navy's global profile even if its blue-water capacity is dwindling.

Development of the potentially nuclear-powered and nuclear-armed *Poseidon* torpedo, or extra-large uninhabited underwater vehicle, seemed to continue. Trials of *Belgorod*, the first submarine designed to carry the nuclear weapon, have taken place and it was potentially ready to become operational by the end of 2023. *Belgorod* also has a special-mission capability. A successor class of *Poseidon*-carrying submarines is planned, with the first, *Khabarovsk*, now reportedly in advanced stages of construction. Russia appears intent on fielding four *Poseidon*-equipped submarines distributed equally between the Northern and Pacific fleets.

Amid the Black Sea Fleet's troubles, the rest of the Russian navy appeared to go out of its way to portray an image of business as usual. That included relatively high levels of activity and exercises by the Northern and Baltic fleets as a challenge to NATO, and Russian naval exercises with Chinese naval units. A joint 11-ship China–Russia flotilla made a high-profile foray close to Alaska and the Aleutian Islands. And China and Russia undertook small-scale joint naval manoeuvres with both Iran and South Africa. While these exercises appear designed to underline a Russian narrative that it remains a major global power, the extent to which such activities provide real operational benefits and display genuine power projection, rather than merely the image of power, is open to debate.

Aerospace Forces

Russia's Aerospace Forces (VKS) has shown clear limitations with a lacklustre performance in the war in Ukraine. It failed to gain air superiority, was unable to sufficiently degrade Ukrainian ground-based air defences, did not carry out deep interdiction attacks against Ukrainian military targets, and was unable to provide adequate fire support to front-line ground forces. The service, of course, has also faced determined resistance from Ukrainian ground-based air defences, bolstered by Europe and the United States.

As with the other Russian services, the VKS appeared to expect Ukrainian opposition to be limited and the invasion rapidly concluded. The air force's inability to gain an upper hand was not for lack of effort, though, as combat losses have shown. The VKS lost nearly 20% of the initial strength of the Sukhoi Su-34 *Fullback* fighter ground-attack fleet – the highest attrition rate across all aircraft types – with Su-25 *Frogfoot* ground-attack losses also meaningful. Russia also suffered heavy rotor-wing losses, particularly among Ka-52 *Hokum* B attack helicopters. Wagner forces, during their mutiny in

June 2023, also downed an Il-22M *Coot B* command-and-control aircraft.

The attrition among fighter aircraft caused Russia to rely more heavily on long-range aviation that operated further from Ukrainian air defences and land-attack cruise-missiles launches. The sporadic nature of the attacks reflected supply constraints on the Raduga Kh-101 (RS-AS-23A *Kodiak*) as well as Russia's desire to conserve its precision-strike resources for a potential Winter campaign against Ukrainian critical infrastructure. The VKS also employed some tactical weapons long in development, including at least one variant of the Kh-38M, the replacement for the Kh-25/Kh-27 (RS-AS-10 *Karen*/RS-AS-12 *Kegler*), as well as the *Grom* glide bomb.

The VKS also had to contend with leadership turmoil in 2023. The Kremlin removed service chief General Sergei Surovikin, who was associated closely with Wagner chief Yevgeny Prigozhin, shortly after the group's rebellion in June. Moscow did not name his acting replacement, Col. General Viktor Afzalov, until late August. He was confirmed permanently in post towards the end of October 2023.

Combat-aircraft deliveries through 2023, including Su-34s, helped replenish some battlefield losses. The *Fullback* deliveries could represent the culmination of a 2020 order for 24 Su-34NVO. Sometimes described as the Su-34M, the Su-34NVO, capable of using a broader suite of weapons, is more likely an interim standard aircraft rather than the complete Su-34M upgrade, deliveries of which have yet to begin. Small numbers of the Su-35S *Flanker* M and Su-57 *Felon* fighters also continued be handed over. Russia remains reliant on the Beriev A-50U *Mainstay* airborne early-warning and control aircraft, delivering an additional unit in 2023. A follow-on programme, the A-100 *Premier*, was launched in 2006, but only one full prototype has been built.

State trials of the Tupolev Tu-160M upgrade of the *Blackjack* long-range bomber began in 2023, with new *Blackjack*s also being built. Russia is upgrading the Tu-95MS *Bear* H and Tu-22M3 *Backfire* C bombers, but the PAK DA low-observable bomber programme may be suffering further delays because of the cost of the war and pressure on industry. With a focus on near-term needs, Moscow appears to be prioritising procurement of existing platforms and weapons over development projects. For instance, work on the *Zmeyevik* anti-ship ballistic missile was reportedly suspended.

The VKS's underperformance in Ukraine has also illustrated its gap in special-mission aircraft. A dearth of intelligence, surveillance and reconnaissance aircraft, as well as electronic-warfare and jamming aircraft, have limited the service's ability to play a more meaningful role in the war.

Strategic Rocket Forces

Russia's decade-long modernisation of its Strategic Rocket Forces is nearing completion. Defence Minister Shoigu said Russia planned to deploy 22 new intercontinental ballistic missiles (ICBMs) during the past year. Most of them were road-mobile RS-24 *Yars* (RS-SS-27 Mod 2) to replace the Strategic Rocket Forces' remaining Soviet-era road-mobile RS-12M *Topol* (RS-SS-25 *Sickle*) ICBMs. Russian defence officials have suggested that once the replacement of the RS-12M is completed, the Strategic Rocket Forces' limited number of single-warhead silo-based and road-mobile RS-12M2 *Topol*-Ms (RS-SS-27 Mod 1s) may also be replaced by the *Yars* variant.

Russia is also deploying a very small number (two per year) of the *Avangard* (RS-SS-19 Mod 4 *Stiletto*) hypersonic glide vehicle (HGV). *Avangard* was first deployed in 2019. Eight HGVs are now assessed to be in service on adapted silo-based RS-18 (RS-SS-19 Mod 4 *Stiletto*) ICBMs. Although the RS-18 is being retired, a limited number have had service-life extensions and will continue to be deployed for some time due to delays to *Avangard*'s intended delivery vehicle, the *Sarmat* (RS-SS-X-29) ICBM.

Sarmat is intended to replace Russia's remaining Soviet silo-based ICBMs including the RS-18 and the RS-20V (RS-SS-18 Mod 6 *Satan*). The RS-20V constitutes a large proportion of the Strategic Rocket Forces' capability because each missile may carry up to ten multiple independently targetable re-entry vehicles. In late 2023, Defence Minister Shoigu announced that *Sarmat* would be placed on combat duty soon, though similar deadlines have been missed. Nonetheless, the Strategic Rocket Forces have partially completed construction and renovation of multiple silos that are connected to the *Sarmat* programme. The missile was successfully tested in April 2022, although it appears that at least one other test since then failed. Wide-scale deployment of *Sarmat* in 2024 is unlikely given remaining testing requirements, putting pressure on operating the remaining RS-20Vs beyond their planned lifespans.

Russia Adapts Its Ukraine Cyber Campaign

Russia's cyber and information-warfare units have adapted their approach to fighting Ukraine, echoing changes undertaken by other elements of the country's armed forces to deal with battlefield realities and their lack of success in the opening days of the conflict in 2022.

While the setbacks Russia has suffered on the ground, at sea and elsewhere are more evident, Moscow's inability to press its advantage in cyberspace is particularly stark. Russia's cyber and information-warfare units appeared far better prepared for the start of the full-scale invasion in February 2022 than their counterparts in the ground forces. Cyber operations at the start of the invasion were expected to suppress Ukrainian government and military communications and showed evidence of long planning and preparation. But just like the ground campaign, Ukrainian resistance, along with a healthy amount of outside support, derailed Moscow's pre-war digital plans. Russia's information and cyber operations had to shift once it became clear the war was morphing into an extended conflict and would not play out as a swift decapitation operation.

While Moscow was expected to unleash large-scale and successful destructive cyber attacks on Ukrainian critical infrastructure, Russia's expectation that Kyiv would fall without a prolonged fight and that infrastructure would therefore be taken over intact limited those efforts. Early attacks were also thwarted by Ukraine's defensive preparations, carried out with long-term and extensive support from foreign states and private industry. Cloud-service providers, for instance, helped Ukraine secure troves of data to keep it out of Moscow's reach. Russia also suffered because many cyber professionals left the country before the full-scale invasion took place.

As the conflict developed, Russian cyber forces transitioned from long-planned, long-duration operations, which combined destructive potential with long dwell time on Ukrainian networks exploiting their access, to tactics that required less forward planning and were swifter and more straightforward to implement. These included distributed denial of service attacks and the deployment of a new generation of less sophisticated and modular 'wiper' malware. As with munitions in conventional operations, Russia, during 2022 and 2023, used cyber weapons at a higher rate than anticipated, rapidly burning and cycling through exploit variants as they were expended and detected.

The apparent objectives of these attacks have been consistent with Russia's doctrinal approach of treating cyber and information warfare as integrated and indistinguishable. Cyber and kinetic attacks on telecommunications infrastructure in particular were limited in scope and scale, except in areas where Russia could achieve information isolation of the civilian population to support its long-term propaganda and indoctrination objectives. There is limited evidence of ongoing coordination between cyber and conventional operations, and the destructive impact of cyber-attacks has been of limited significance in the context of full-scale warfare. Still, Russia has continued to exploit cyber power for intelligence gathering and psychological warfare.

Russia's information and influence operations directed abroad have also evolved under wartime conditions. Media sanctions in the European Union, United Kingdom and United States have forced the adoption of new channels for delivering disinformation, including existing assets like embassies and individual diplomats, and an extensive network of mirrored websites and fake news outlets. But Moscow's network of covert and overt influencers in the West, and campaigns directed at the so-called Global South, remain largely unaffected. Meanwhile, Russia has appeared careful to avoid unintended escalation through directly targeting Ukraine's NATO backers with cyber effects. Western governments have not reported a substantial increase in hostile cyber activity from Russia, and Russian attacks on the logistics chains and organisations delivering aid to Ukraine through Poland display greater efforts at obfuscation and deniability than in attacks within Ukraine itself. This suggests that concern over NATO responses remains a key constraint on Russian willingness to escalate the conflict.

DEFENCE ECONOMICS

Russia

Despite international sanctions and other trade restrictions, Russia's economy proved resilient throughout 2023, with state revenues buoyed by high oil and gas prices. The country's economy outperformed expectations, contracting less than expected in 2022 and returning to growth in the second quarter of 2023. It was expected to expand by 3.5% for all of 2023, according to remarks made by Vladimir Putin in December.

Increased military and social spending have impacted the Russian balance sheet, though. The country registered a federal budget deficit of 2.2% of GDP in 2022. Similarly, rising inflation, a devalued rouble and increasing currency controls point to economic stresses caused by the international response to the February 2022 attack. Nonetheless, available data suggests that the Russian economy can support the country's military campaign for the foreseeable future. Moscow also appears to be digging in for the long term, with defence spending remaining a priority, the defence industry undergoing increased political attention and social spending being sustained to insulate the population from the effects of war.

Defence spending

Accurately estimating Russian defence spending became increasingly difficult after February 2022. Moscow began censoring information related to military expenditure and other war costs, classifying detailed budget reports and only referring to top-level revenues and total spending. However, in October 2023, the Russian Finance Ministry announced the Ministry of Defence's draft 2024 budget. As expected, the figures show increased spending although, as a share of GDP, spending levels remain somewhat modest and less than in previous years when Russia sharply increased spending to modernise its armed forces and equipment.

Russia has been working to modernise its armed forces since the 1990s, with the 2008 New Look programme providing the basis for much of Russia's pre-invasion strength. During the past decade, Russia's nominal spending on national defence has increased near constantly. However, in real terms, allocations have been somewhat volatile. For example, in 2022, spending on the 'national defence' budget, which mainly outlines Ministry of Defence spending, hit RUB5.11 trillion (USD74.7 billion). This represented a nominal increase of more than 40% from the previous year and an increase of more than 0.6% of GDP. Accordingly, for 2022 total military spending, which includes some other accounts, is estimated to have risen to RUB6.65trn (USD97.2bn) – 4.3% of GDP and an 18% increase in real terms.

However, Russia's failure to achieve a decisive victory in the early stages of the war has led to a prolonged and costly conflict, with original budgets revised. According to the 2023 budget law, despite the ongoing conflict, military spending was planned to be largely flat in nominal terms, partly because the budget was based on a forecast that GDP would see a near 1% decline during the year. This was later revised sharply upwards, with the initial allocation rising to RUB6.41trn (USD74.8bn) from RUB4.9trn (USD57.2bn).

Reflecting Moscow's increasing economic confidence – and Russia's need to replace battlefield losses – the approved 2024 budget raised defence spending for fiscal year 2024 even further, proposing that the country spend RUB10.4trn (USD117bn) on 'national defence' in 2024, or about 6.2% of GDP. In turn, this suggests that total military spending could reach at least 7.54% of GDP once all other elements are considered. However, with inflationary pressures in the economy and uncertainties about future budget revenues, the outcome remains difficult to predict.

Table 9 **Russia: defence expenditure, 2015–24** (trillion roubles, current prices)

Year	'National Defence' ('ND') RUB (trn)	'National Defence' ('ND') % of GDP	Total military expenditure[1] RUB (trn)	Total military expenditure[1] % of GDP	Total military expenditure[1] % change real terms
2024[B]	10.370	6.12	ε12.765	7.54	+29.5
2023[R]	6.407	4.01	ε9.300	5.83	+23.5
2023[B]	4.973	3.32	6.925	4.34	+2.4
2022	5.110	3.33	6.648	4.33	+27.1
2021	3.573	2.64	4.859	3.59	-6.4
2020	3.169	2.94	4.335	4.03	+2.1
2019	2.997	2.73	4.209	3.84	+4.1
2018	2.827	2.72	3.911	3.78	-4.0
2017	2.666[2]	2.90	3.704	4.03	-8.2
2016	2.982[2]	3.48	3.831	4.47	-7.5
2015	3.181	3.83	4.026	4.85	+16.5

B = Budget. REV = Revised Budget. 1. According to NATO definition. GDP figures from IMF World Economic Outlook, October 2023. 2. Excluding a one-off payment to reduce accumulated debts of defence industry enterprises under the scheme of state guaranteed credits. If this debt payment is included the total GDP share in 2016 rises to 5.4%, and 4.2% in 2017.

Figure 9 **Russia: defence expenditure** as % of GDP

Year	% of GDP
2018	3.78
2019	3.84
2020	4.03
2021	3.59
2022	4.33
2023	5.83

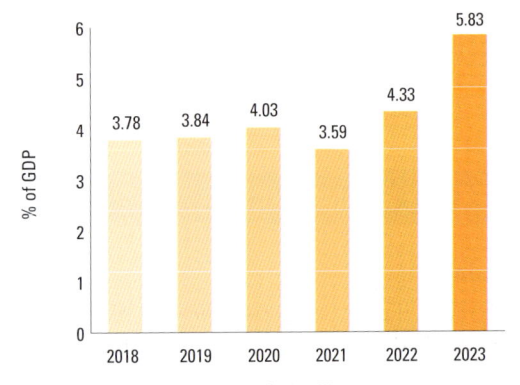

Note: GDP data from IMF World Economic Outlook, October 2023

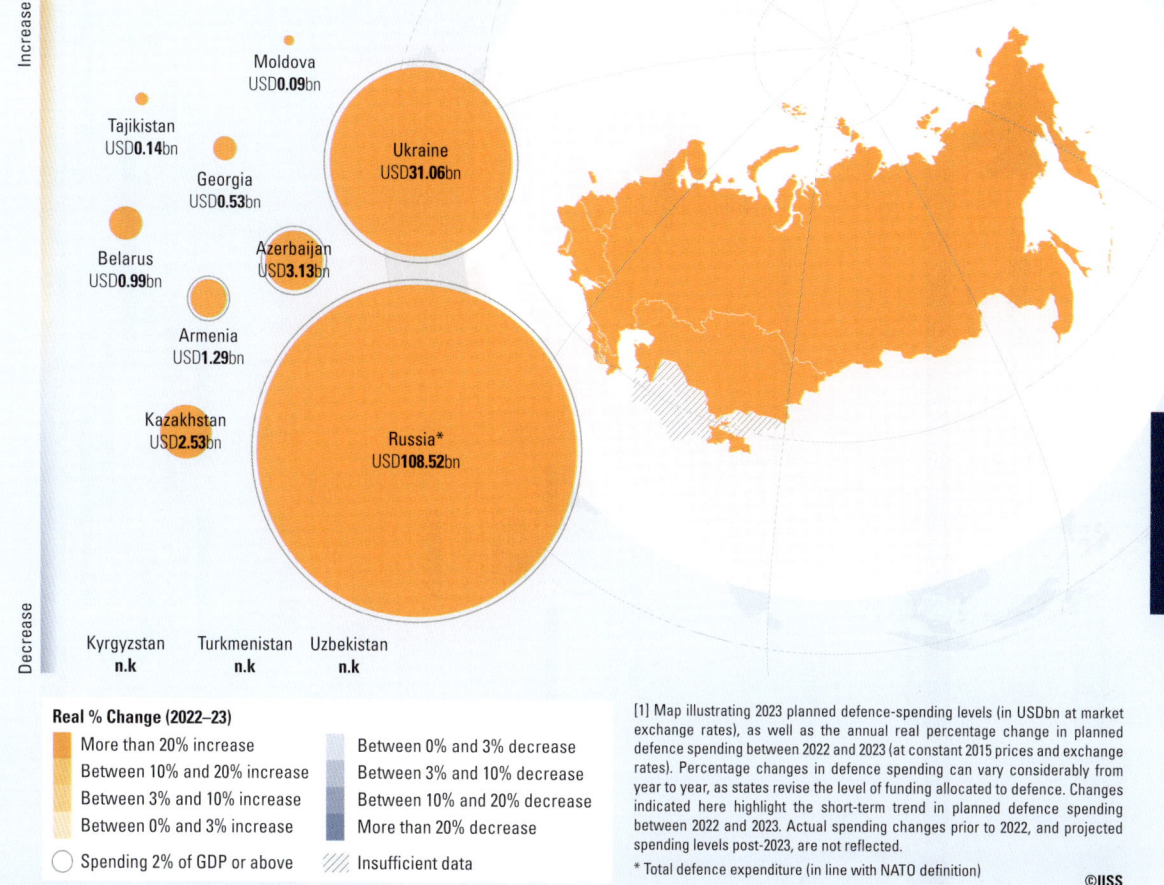

Map 4 Russia and Eurasia: regional defence spending (USDbn, %ch yoy)[1]

Increase
- Moldova USD**0.09**bn
- Tajikistan USD**0.14**bn
- Georgia USD**0.53**bn
- Ukraine USD**31.06**bn
- Belarus USD**0.99**bn
- Azerbaijan USD**3.13**bn
- Armenia USD**1.29**bn
- Kazakhstan USD**2.53**bn
- Russia* USD**108.52**bn

Decrease
- Kyrgyzstan n.k
- Turkmenistan n.k
- Uzbekistan n.k

Real % Change (2022–23)
- More than 20% increase
- Between 10% and 20% increase
- Between 3% and 10% increase
- Between 0% and 3% increase
- Spending 2% of GDP or above
- Between 0% and 3% decrease
- Between 3% and 10% decrease
- Between 10% and 20% decrease
- More than 20% decrease
- Insufficient data

[1] Map illustrating 2023 planned defence-spending levels (in USDbn at market exchange rates), as well as the annual real percentage change in planned defence spending between 2022 and 2023 (at constant 2015 prices and exchange rates). Percentage changes in defence spending can vary considerably from year to year, as states revise the level of funding allocated to defence. Changes indicated here highlight the short-term trend in planned defence spending between 2022 and 2023. Actual spending changes prior to 2022, and projected spending levels post-2023, are not reflected.
* Total defence expenditure (in line with NATO definition)

©IISS

Defence industry

Russia's defence industry was not prepared for the implications of the decision to invade Ukraine. As the war dragged on, the arms industry began to retool in late 2022 and Moscow sought to boost output and meet critical needs via changes in leadership, organisational structure and production procedures. Although Russia has been able to sustain arms supplies in key areas, including guided weapons, the pace of operations has at times lessened to give industry time to restock. The Russian government also has turned abroad to meet equipment needs. Iran is providing Moscow with some uninhabited aerial vehicle types and direct attack munitions and in October, the United States said that North Korea had supplied up to 1,000 containers of equipment and munitions to Russia.

Moscow also overhauled the leadership of its arms-production sector. In October 2022, Russian President Vladimir Putin created a special council to meet the military's needs in Ukraine. It appears to have focused on overcoming logistical issues, overseeing the delivery and repair of armaments and munitions, uniforms and other supplies. Chaired by Premier Mikhail Mishustin, the council meets regularly. Its 19 members include ministers of all the main 'power' ministries, including defence, internal affairs, national guard, FSB and SVR (the foreign intelligence service), and the ministers of industry, finance, economic development and the tax service.

The council appears to have largely supplanted the Military-Industrial Commission (VPK), which is chaired by the president. However, Putin did not preside over the meetings of the group in 2023 until September, suggesting it had a somewhat diminished role as the VPK's staff now largely monitors a detailed schedule of deliveries to the armed forces and other agencies.

Figure 10 Russia: new-build Su-30 *Flanker* exports

Komsomolsk-on-Amur Aviation Plant (KnAAZ)
Coloured horizontal bars show years of deliveries; years indicated next to flags are contract dates.

■ Deliveries for export customer   ■ Deliveries to VKS

China
- 1999: 38 x Su-30MKK (USD3bn)
- 2001: 38 x Su-30MKK (USD3bn)
- 2003: 24 x Su-30MK2 (USD1bn)
- 2015: Su-30MKK *Flanker* G
- 2016: 24 x Su-35 (USD2bn)

Egypt
- 2018: 24 x Su-35 (USD2bn) — Order cancelled

Indonesia
- 2003: 2 x Su-30MK et al. (USD0.19bn)
- 2007: 3 x Su-30MK2 et al. (USD0.3bn)
- 2011: 6 x Su-30MK2 (USD0.47bn)

Uganda
- 2009: 6 x Su-30MK2 (USD0.33bn)

Venezuela
- 2006: 24 x Su-30MKV (USD1.5bn)

Vietnam
- 2003: 4 x Su-30MK2 (USD0.1bn)
- 2004 & 2010: 8 x & 12 x Su-30MK2 (USD1.1bn)
- 2009: 4 x Su-30M2 (n.k.)
- 2012: 16 x Su-30M2 (n.k.)
- 2013: 12 x Su-30MK2 (USD0.6bn)

Russia
- 2009: 48 x Su-35S (n.k.)
- 2015: 50 x Su-35S (USD0.98bn)
- 2020: 30 x Su-35S (USD1.01bn)

1997 1998 1999 2000 2001 2002 2003 2004 2005 2006 2007 2008 2009 2010 2011 2012 2013 2014 2015 2016 2017 2018 2019 2020 2021 2022 2023

The Su-30 *Flanker* family of aircraft is one of Russia's most successful recent combat-aircraft exports, with over 600 sold. Versions have also been developed for the Russian Aerospace Forces (VKS). Based on the Su-27UB – a twin-seat variant of the Su-27 – the Su-30 first flew in December 1989. A collapse in procurement funding in the 1990s meant that only a handful of the original Su-30s were bought in that decade. Su-27UBs had been made in Irkutsk since 1986, and a two-seat combat aircraft based on the UB airframe was later developed at Komsomolsk-on-Amur.

The Su-30MKI *Flanker* H was developed after mid-1990s negotiations between Irkutsk and India. This design was also the baseline for sales to Algeria (the Su-30MKA), and Malaysia (the Su-30MKM). Irkutsk-manufactured Su-30 developments were more advanced than the Su-30s from Komsomolsk-on-Amur which lacked many Su-30MKI features, including canards and thrust-vectoring engines, and could carry Russian weapons only.

In 1999 Komsomolsk-on-Amur secured a deal with China to produce the Su-30MKK *Flanker* G for the People's Liberation Army Air Force (PLAAF), based on the same airframe as the Su-27UB. The site had been producing single- and twin-

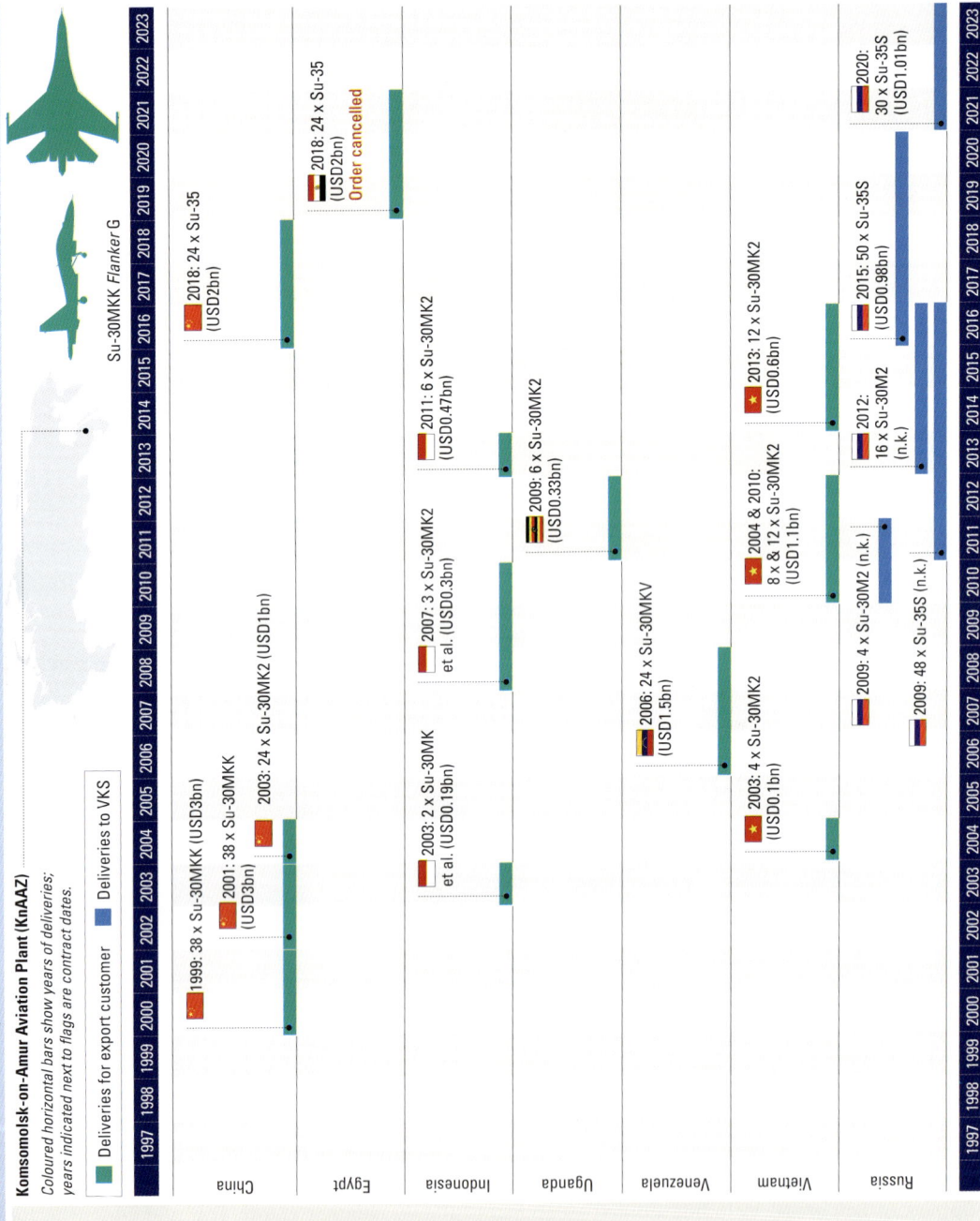

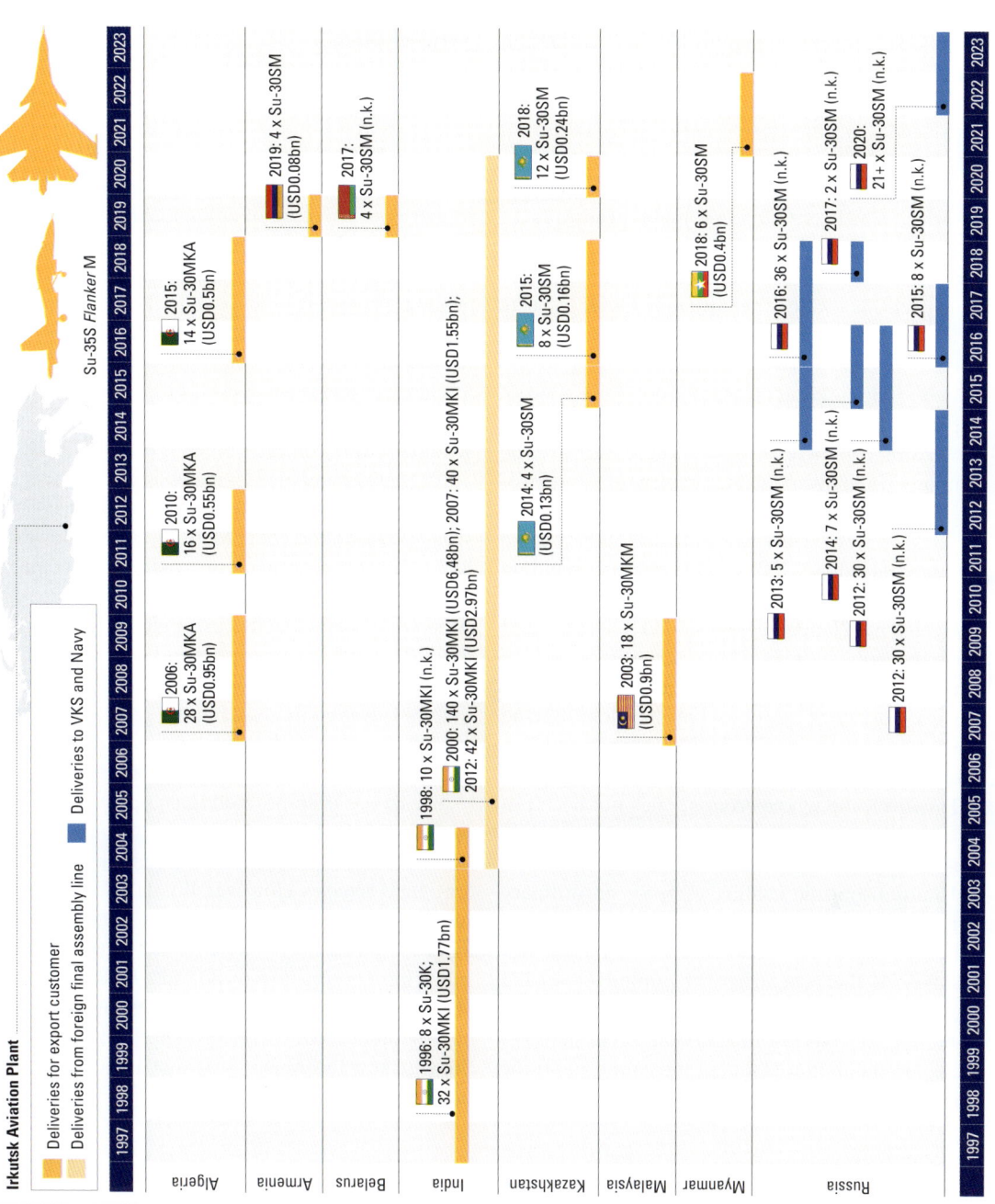

Irkutsk Aviation Plant

Legend:
- Deliveries for export customer
- Deliveries from foreign final assembly line
- Deliveries to VKS and Navy

Su-35S *Flanker M*

Algeria
- 2006: 28 x Su-30MKA (USD0.95bn)
- 2010: 16 x Su-30MKA (USD0.55bn)
- 2015: 14 x Su-30MKA (USD0.5bn)
- 2019: 4 x Su-30SM (USD0.08bn)

Armenia
- 2017: 4 x Su-30SM

Belarus
- 2018: 12 x Su-30SM (USD0.24bn)

India
- 1996: 8 x Su-30K; 32 x Su-30MKI (USD1.77bn)
- 1998: 10 x Su-30MKI (n.k.)
- 2000: 140 x Su-30MKI (USD6.48bn); 2007: 40 x Su-30MKI (USD1.55bn); 2012: 42 x Su-30MKI (USD2.97bn)

Kazakhstan
- 2014: 4 x Su-30SM (USD0.13bn)
- 2015: 8 x Su-30SM (USD0.16bn)

Malaysia
- 2003: 18 x Su-30MKM (USD0.9bn)

Myanmar
- 2018: 6 x Su-30SM (USD0.4bn)

Russia
- 2012: 30 x Su-30SM (n.k.)
- 2013: 5 x Su-30SM (n.k.)
- 2014: 7 x Su-30SM (n.k.)
- 2012: 30 x Su-30SM (n.k.)
- 2015: 8 x Su-30SM (n.k.)
- 2016: 36 x Su-30SM (n.k.)
- 2017: 2 x Su-30SM (n.k.)
- 2020: 21+ x Su-30SM (n.k.)

---

seat Su-27s for the PLAAF since the early 1990s, and in the early 2000s helped China with licensed final assembly and eventually production of a domestic version of the single-seat Su-27: the J-11. In 2003, China agreed with Komsomolsk-on-Amur to produce for the PLA Navy the Su-30MK2 (with a radar upgrade enabling maritime strike), derived from the Su-30MKK. Further Su-30MK2 sales went to Indonesia, Uganda, Venezuela and Vietnam.

The Su-30M2 – an Su-30MK2 for the VKS – was developed at Komsomolsk-on-Amur, but the VKS only ordered 20. It ordered more of Irkutsk's Su-30SM, a domestic version of the Su-30MKI. A follow-on version, the Su-30SM2, is now in production at Irkutsk.

Komsomolsk-on-Amur has had more success with the Su-35. This is another development of the Su-27, intended mainly for export. It is a single-seat aircraft without canards and with thrust-vectoring engines. After Irkutsk won most Su-30 production - and possibly in order to maintain workflow at Komsomolsk-on-Amur – the VKS ordered the Su-35S, a domestic version of the Su-35BM that had failed to find an export customer. In 2015, China ordered 24 of the export version and in 2018 Egypt also ordered 24, though the latter have not been delivered.

Moscow also streamlined its industrial organisation in a bid to boost output. Fourteen leading enterprises and research centres were transferred to the Rostec state corporation in January 2023 to drive their modernisation. The shift included the Kazan, Perm and Tambov factories, which are Russia's main producers of explosives. Rostec later added artillery and tank main-gun factories, establishing a single body for all aspects of artillery equipment. Other aspects of Russia's arms industry got similar treatment. In October 2023, 10% of shares belonging to the United Shipbuilding Corporation (USC) were instructed to be transferred for a five-year period to the leading commercial bank, VTB, to improve the company's management and finances after years of large losses.

To keep pace with wartime demands, Russia increased its military-industrial footprint, expanding facilities from aviation plants to missile factories. Many defence companies also added personnel and moved to multi-shift operations, some working with no downtime, even on weekends and holidays. This drove a shortage of labour in some locations, forcing many companies to hike wages and benefits, adding to inflationary pressures.

However, the whole economy has not been put on a war footing, as Putin has sought to maintain pre-war pledges of improving living standards and minimising the conflict's impact on ordinary Russians. Speaking in late 2022, Putin told defence-industry executives that 'We will not repeat mistakes of the past, when in pursuit of raising defence capabilities, when we needed to and when not, we wrecked our economy. We shall not engage in the militarisation of the country and the militarisation of the economy.'

Arms exports

Since the start of the war and the imposition of sanctions, Russian authorities have said little about arms exports. Limited evidence indicates exports contracted. In November 2022, Russia indicated annual arms exports would reach around USD10bn in that year, a decline of at least USD3bn compared with 2021, although even this may understate the scale of the decline. In August 2023, the director general of export organisation Rosoboronexport, Aleksandr Mikheev, said that it had a USD50bn backlog of orders, 75% of which represented deals for aircraft and air-defence equipment. However, there were signs some customers have or will withdraw from contracts because of US sanctions.

The implementation of some large contracts has continued, including the sale of S-400 air-defence systems to India concluded in 2018. However, with Russia prioritising its own armed forces, final deliveries appeared delayed. Russia also has suffered customer setbacks. India is starting to diversify its sources of supply and, in 2022, abruptly ended negotiations to buy ten Ka-31 helicopters. Indonesia was becoming a regular partner for Russia but is buying Dassault *Rafale* fighters and has agreed to buy Boeing F-15 aircraft instead of Russia's Su-35.

Russia has been promoting equipment as battle-proven in Ukraine, including the *Orlan* UAV and *Lancet* direct-attack munition, T-72 tanks and *Titan* armoured vehicles. However, Russia's need for those weapons trumps exports. Even if contracts were agreed, sanctions on Russia could cause payment problems. These factors could cause Russia to lose its status as one of the world's top arms exporters, and analysts at the Moscow-based Centre for Analysis of Strategy and Technology said that arms exports are unlikely to recover before 2027–28.

Significant procurement and delivery events - 2023

MAY

TAJIKISTAN DEVELOPS DEFENCE INDUSTRY

President Emomali Rahmon established Tajikistan's first armoured-vehicle production company. Sipar Group has around 100 employees at a new facility in Tursunzoda which is run in partnership with UAE-based STREIT Group. The company claims to be able to assemble 17 variants of wheeled armoured vehicles, with parts supplied by STREIT. The company seeks to satisfy domestic demand first and then explore exports. The Tursunzoda site is expected to produce around 120 vehicles annually at the outset. A year earlier, Tajikistan inaugurated a factory in capital Dushanbe to manufacture an unarmed version of Iran's *Ababil* 2 UAV under licence and with a training package deal included. The status of that production is unclear. Tajikistan's agreements with Iran and STREIT signal Dushanbe's ambition to generate a more substantial defence industry.

MAY

RUSSIA SHIPBUILDING OUTPUT

The Russian Navy announced that it had accepted six vessels of various classes in January–May, with 30 more warships, boats and support vessels scheduled to be delivered during the rest of the year. The figure represents a step up from earlier plans for 2023, when the navy said it aimed to introduce five submarines, including the fourth Project 955A *Borey*-A SSBN (launched in December 2022), and 12 surface ships. Russia has been trying to keep its shipbuilding rate steady despite the fallout from its invasion of Ukraine. It said it took delivery of 46 vessels in 2022, 40 in 2021 and 40 in 2020. Vessels commissioned in 2023 include two Project 20380 (*Steregushchiy* II) frigates and a Project 22800 (*Uragan*) *Karakurt*-class corvette. A Ukrainian cruise missile attack on Zaliv Shipyard in Crimea in November caused significant damage to a *Karakurt*-class vessel that was close to delivery. Russia will either need to divert air-defence assets to protect shipyards now within Ukrainian strike range or relocate activity elsewhere. This will put far greater pressure on Russia's ability to reinforce the Black Sea Fleet with new vessels.

SEPTEMBER

UKRAINE SIGNS DEALS WITH EUROPEAN ENTITIES

The German Federal Cartel Office approved the creation of a joint venture between Rheinmetall and UkrOboronProm (now Ukrainian Defense Industry (UDI)) four months after the two companies signed a strategic partnership, with the German company holding a 51% share. UDI is hoping to domestically repair and maintain armoured vehicles with Rheinmetall's assistance and later to manufacture vehicles in Ukraine via technology transfers. During the Rheinmetall half-year earnings call in August, Rheinmetall CEO Armin Papperger laid out plans to establish medium- and large-calibre ammunition and air-defence systems production in the country. Ukraine pledged to simplify procurement and to spend up to UAH55.8bn (USD1.49bn) to ramp up defence production in the draft budget for 2024. Ukraine is prioritising localising procurement, tackling internal corruption and establishing mutually beneficial international partnerships. Construction of a UAV factory with Turkiye's Baykar is planned to be completed in 2024. Ukraine has also signed multiple agreements with other European entities, including the Norwegian Defence Materiel Agency (to build transparency in defence procurement), a German–Polish–Ukrainian trilateral coalition (to set up an MRO centre in Poland for the *Leopard* 2 MBT), the Ministry of Defence of the Czech Republic (to repair and modernise vehicles and develop weapons and ammunition) and the UK's BAE Systems (to explore potential partnership options including in artillery production).

OCTOBER

RUSSIAN DEFENCE PRODUCTION SURGES

Russia's defence industry continued to expand production of a number of systems, with one industry executive boasting output has grown two to ten times. Western countries placed extensive sanctions on Russian companies after the start of the Ukraine war in February 2022. These slowed Russian defence production for most of the year before a combination of massive increases in defence spending; sanctions evasion, often through third countries; import substitution; and government prioritisation of the war economy spurred higher output. This was particularly true of munitions output, which surged beyond pre-war levels. Russian officials have announced plans to resume production of platforms such as the T-80 MBT. Russia should be able to sustain this level of production and spending into the near future as gas and oil prices remain healthy, but its focus on domestic requirements is denting its ability to support export customers.

Armenia ARM

Armenian Dram AMD		2022	2023	2024
GDP	AMD	8.50trn	9.55trn	10.5trn
	USD	19.5bn	24.5bn	26.9bn
per capita	USD	6,587	8,283	9,091
Growth	%	12.6	7.0	5.0
Inflation	%	8.6	3.5	4.0
Def bdgt [a]	AMD	340bn	501bn	550bn
	USD	781m	1.29bn	1.41bn
USD1=AMD		435.66	389.13	388.85

[a] Includes imported military equipment, excludes military pensions

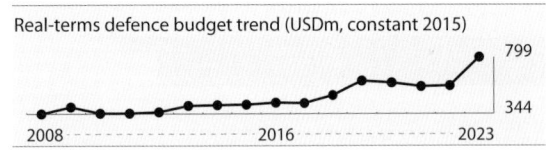

Real-terms defence budget trend (USDm, constant 2015)

799
344
2008 — 2016 — 2023

Population 2,989,091

Age	0–14	15–19	20–24	25–29	30–64	65 plus
Male	9.4%	2.9%	2.9%	3.3%	24.3%	6.0%
Female	8.5%	2.7%	2.6%	3.2%	25.6%	8.5%

Capabilities

The focus of the armed forces is the defence and maintenance of the territorial integrity of the state. In September 2023, Azerbaijani forces seized the disputed territory of Nagorno-Karabakh, with almost all Armenians fleeing the territory. The Armenian armed forces did not react effectively. The goal of moving the armed forces from a conscript to a contract-based force remains an ambition, though with no clear timetable. In late 2022, the Defence Ministry introduced the 'Motherland Defender' initiative with a financial incentive to encourage enlistment on a contract basis. The 2020 National Security Strategy identified Azerbaijan as Armenia's primary security concern, while also highlighting the role it claims Turkiye plays in supporting Azerbaijan's policy aims. Relations with Russia, Armenia's strategic partner, have been strained by the loss of Nagorno-Karabakh, Moscow's lack of intervention and steps Yerevan has taken to improve relations with the West. Armenia remains a member of the CSTO but did not participate in the October 2023 *Indestructible Brotherhood* exercise. Armenia held a joint exercise with the US, dubbed *Eagle Partner*, in September 2023, to the apparent consternation of Moscow. Armenia is engaged in a NATO Individual Partnership Action Plan. Yerevan has also distanced itself from Russia's war on Ukraine.

ACTIVE 42,900 (Army 40,000 Air/AD Aviation Forces (Joint) 1,100 other Air Defence Forces 1,800) **Paramilitary 4,300**

Conscript liability 24 months

RESERVE

Some mobilisation reported, possibly 210,000 with military service within 15 years

ORGANISATIONS BY SERVICE

Army ε40,000
FORCES BY ROLE
SPECIAL FORCES
  1 SF bde
MANOEUVRE
  Mechanised
  1 (Special) corps (1 recce bn, 1 tk bn(-), 5 MR regt, 1 sigs bn, 1 maint bn)
  1 (2nd) corps (1 recce bn, 1 tk bn, 2 MR regt, 1 lt inf regt, 1 arty bn)
  1 (3rd) corps (1 recce bn, 1 tk bn, 5 MR regt, 1 arty bn, 1 MRL bn, 1 sigs bn, 1 maint bn)
  1 (5th) corps (2 MR regt)
  Other
  1 indep MR trg bde
COMBAT SUPPORT
  1 arty bde
  1 MRL bde
  1 AT regt
  1 AD bde
  2 AD regt
  2 (radiotech) AD regt
  1 engr regt
SURFACE-TO-SURFACE MISSILE
  1 SRBM regt
EQUIPMENT BY TYPE
Available estimates should be treated with caution following losses suffered in the fighting since late 2020 in Nagorno-Karabakh
ARMOURED FIGHTING VEHICLES
  MBT 109: 3 T-54; 5 T-55; ε100 T-72A/B; 1 T-90A
  RECCE 12 BRM-1K (CP)
  IFV 140: 100 BMP-1; 25 BMP-1K (CP); 15 BMP-2
  APC 171
    APC (T) 20 MT-LB
    APC (W) 151: 21+ *Bastion* APC; 108 BTR-60 (incl variants); 18 BTR-70; 4 BTR-80
  AUV *Tigr*
ENGINEERING & MAINTENANCE VEHICLES
  AEV MT-LB
  ARV BREhM-D; BREM-1
ANTI-TANK/ANTI-INFRASTRUCTURE
  MSL • SP 22+: 9 9P148 *Konkurs* (RS-AT-5 *Spandrel*); 13 9P149 *Shturm* (RS-AT-6 *Spiral*); 9K129 *Kornet*-E (RS-AT-14 *Spriggan*)
ARTILLERY 225
  SP 37: **122mm** 9 2S1 *Gvozdika*; **152mm** 28 2S3 *Akatsiya*
  TOWED 122: **122mm** 60 D-30; **152mm** 62: 26 2A36 *Giatsint*-B; 2 D-1; 34 D-20
  MRL 54: **122mm** up to 50 BM-21 *Grad*; **273mm** 2 WM-80; **300mm** 2 9A52 *Smerch*

MOR 120mm 12 M120
SURFACE-TO-SURFACE MISSILE LAUNCHERS
SRBM • **Conventional** 14: 7+ 9K72 *Elbrus* (RS-SS-1C *Scud* B); 3+ 9K79 *Tochka* (RS-SS-21 *Scarab*); 4 9K720 *Iskander*-E
UNINHABITED AERIAL VEHICLES
ISR • **Light** *Krunk*
AIR DEFENCE
SAM
Medium-range 2K11 *Krug* (RS-SA-4 *Ganef*); S-75 *Dvina* (RS-SA-2 *Guideline*); 9K37M *Buk*-M1 (RS-SA-11 *Gadfly*)
Short-range 2K12 *Kub* (RS-SA-6 *Gainful*); S-125 *Pechora* (RS-SA-3 *Goa*); 9K331MKM *Tor*-M2KM
Point-defence 9K33 *Osa* (RS-SA-8 *Gecko*); 9K35M *Strela*-10 (RS-SA-13 *Gopher*); 9K310 *Igla*-1 (RS-SA-16 *Gimlet*); 9K38 *Igla* (RS-SA-18 *Grouse*); 9K333 *Verba* (RS-SA-29 *Gizmo*); 9K338 *Igla*-S (RS-SA-24 *Grinch*)
GUNS
SP 23mm ZSU-23-4 *Shilka*
TOWED 23mm ZU-23-2

Air and Air Defence Aviation Forces 1,100

1 Air & AD Joint Command
FORCES BY ROLE
GROUND ATTACK
1 sqn with Su-25/Su-25UBK *Frogfoot*
EQUIPMENT BY TYPE
AIRCRAFT 17 combat capable
FGA 4 Su-30SM *Flanker* H
ATK 13: up to 12 Su-25 *Frogfoot*; 1 Su-25UBK *Frogfoot*
TPT 4: **Heavy** 3 Il-76 *Candid*; **PAX** 1 A319CJ
TRG 14: 4 L-39 *Albatros*; 10 Yak-52
HELICOPTERS
ATK 7 Mi-24P *Hind*
ISR 4: 2 Mi-24K *Hind*; 2 Mi-24R *Hind* (cbt spt)
MRH 14: 10 Mi-8MT (cbt spt); 4 Mi-8MTV-5 *Hip*
C2 2 Mi-9 *Hip* G (cbt spt)
TPT • **Light** 7 PZL Mi-2 *Hoplite*
AIR DEFENCE • SAM • **Long-range** S-300PT (RS-SA-10 *Grumble*); S-300PS (RS-SA-10B *Grumble*)
AIR-LAUNCHED MISSILES
AAM • **IR** R-73 (RS-AA-11A *Archer*); **SARH** R-27R (RS-AA-10A *Alamo*)

Gendarmerie & Paramilitary 4,300

Police
FORCES BY ROLE
MANOEUVRE
Other
4 paramilitary bn
EQUIPMENT BY TYPE
ARMOURED FIGHTING VEHICLES
RECCE 5 BRM-1K (CP)
IFV 45: 44 BMP-1; 1 BMP-1K (CP)
APC • **APC (W)** 24 BTR-60/BTR-70/BTR-152
ABCV 5 BMD-1

Border Troops
Ministry of National Security
EQUIPMENT BY TYPE
ARMOURED FIGHTING VEHICLES
RECCE 3 BRM-1K (CP)
IFV 35 BMP-1
APC • **APC (W)** 23: 5 BTR-60; 18 BTR-70
ABCV 5 BMD-1

DEPLOYMENT
KOSOVO: NATO • KFOR 40
LEBANON: UN • UNIFIL 1

FOREIGN FORCES
Russia 3,000: 1 mil base with (1 MR bde; 74 T-72; 80 BMP-1; 80 BMP-2; 12 2S1; 12 BM-21); 1 ftr sqn with 18 MiG-29 *Fulcrum*; 1 hel sqn with 4 Ka-52 *Hokum* B; 8 Mi-24P *Hind*; 4 Mi-8AMTSh *Hip*; 4 Mi-8MT *Hip*; 2 SAM bty with S-300V (RS-SA-12 *Gladiator/Giant*); 1 SAM bty with *Buk*-M1-2 (RS-SA-11 *Gadfly*)

Azerbaijan AZE

Azerbaijani New Manat AZN		2022	2023	2024
GDP	AZN	134bn	132bn	138bn
	USD	78.7bn	77.4bn	81.0bn
per capita	USD	7,751	7,530	7,786
Growth	%	4.6	2.5	2.5
Inflation	%	13.9	10.3	5.7
Def bdgt [a]	AZN	4.49bn	5.32bn	
	USD	2.64bn	3.13bn	
USD1=AZN		1.70	1.70	1.70

[a] Official defence budget. Excludes a significant proportion of procurement outlays.

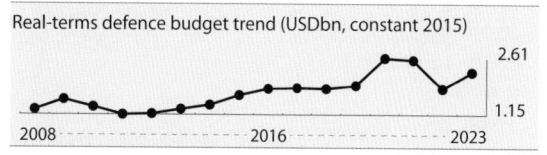

Real-terms defence budget trend (USDbn, constant 2015)
2.61
1.15
2008 2016 2023

Population 10,604,731

Age	0–14	15–19	20–24	25–29	30–64	65 plus
Male	12.2%	3.8%	3.2%	3.8%	23.6%	3.5%
Female	10.6%	3.3%	2.8%	3.5%	24.9%	4.9%

Capabilities

The armed forces' principal focus is territorial defence. Following intermittent fighting in recent years, Azerbaijan in September

2023 seized the territory of Nagorno-Karabakh from Armenia. Russia has been the traditional defence partner for Azerbaijan, but more recently, it has bought weapons from Israel and forged a strategic relationship with Turkiye. In June 2021, Baku and Ankara signed the 'Shusha Declaration', which included cooperation if either nation is threatened by a third state. Pakistan has also begun to emerge as a defence-industrial partner. Azerbaijan maintains a defence relationship with NATO. Readiness within Azerbaijan's conscript-based armed services varies between units. Azerbaijan has taken part in multilateral exercises and its forces also train bilaterally with Turkiye. In October 2023, the two countries held the *Mustafa Kemal Ataturk*-2023 joint exercise in Azerbaijan. The armed forces have little expeditionary capability. Defence modernisation and procurement have been a focus in the past decade, intended to replace the ageing inventory of mainly Soviet-era equipment. Recent orders include air-defence and artillery systems and wheeled and tracked armoured vehicles, predominantly of Russian origin. In 2023, Azerbaijan agreed bilateral defence cooperation deals with Uzbekistan and Kazakhstan. Azerbaijan's limited but growing defence-industrial capabilities are centred on the Ministry of Defence Industry, which manages and oversees the production of small arms and light weapons. While the country is reliant on external suppliers for major defence equipment, some local defence companies have started to export.

ACTIVE 64,050 (Army 57,800 Navy 1,750 Air 8,650) Gendarmerie & Paramilitary 15,000

Conscript liability 18 months (12 for graduates)

RESERVE 300,000

Some mobilisation reported; 300,000 with military service within 15 years

ORGANISATIONS BY SERVICE

Army 57,800

FORCES BY ROLE

COMMAND
  5 corps HQ

SPECIAL FORCES
  9 cdo bde

MANOEUVRE
  Mechanised
  4 MR bde
  Light
  13 MR bde

COMBAT SUPPORT
  2 arty bde
  1 MRL bde
  1 engr bde
  1 sigs bde

COMBAT SERVICE SUPPORT
  1 log bde

SURFACE TO SURFACE MISSILE
  1 SRBM bde

EQUIPMENT BY TYPE

ARMOURED FIGHTING VEHICLES

MBT 497: 404 T-72A/AV/B/SIM2; 93 T-90S

RECCE 7 BRM-1K

IFV 311: 60 BMP-1; 91 BMP-2; 46 BMP-3; 7 BTR-80A; 107 BTR-82A

APC 506
  APC (T) 336 MT-LB
  APC (W) 142: 10 BTR-60; 132 BTR-70
  PPV 28: 14 *Marauder*; 14 *Matador*
  AUV 141: 35 *Cobra*; 106 *SandCat*
ABCV 20 BMD-1

ENGINEERING & MAINTENANCE VEHICLES

AEV 10+: 1 IMR-2; 9 IMR-3M; MT-LB
ARV BREM-L *Brelianka*
MW 4+: *Bozena*; GW-3 (minelayer); 3 UR-67; 1 UR-77
VLB 12: 1 MTU-20; 11 MTU-90M

ANTI-TANK/ANTI-INFRASTRUCTURE

MSL
  SP 53+: 18 9P157-2 *Khrizantema*-S (RS-AT-15 *Springer*); *Cobra* with *Skif*; 26 *SandCat* with *Spike*-ER; 9 *SandCat* with *Spike*-LR
  MANPATS 9K11 *Malyutka* (RS-AT-3 *Sagger*); 9K111 *Fagot* (RS-AT-4 *Spigot*); 9K111-1 *Konkurs* (RS-AT-5 *Spandrel*); 9K115 *Metis* (RS-AT-7 *Saxhorn*); 9K135 *Kornet* (RS-AT-14 *Spriggan*) (reported); *Spike*-LR
GUNS • TOWED 85mm some D-44

ARTILLERY 1,232

SP 153: **122mm** 68 2S1 *Gvozdika*; **152mm** 68: 14 2S3 *Akatsiya*; 18 2S19 *Msta*-S; 36 *Dana*-M1M; **155mm** 5 ATMOS 2000; **203mm** 12 2S7 *Pion*

TOWED 550: **122mm** 423 D-30; **130mm** 35 M-46; **152mm** 92: 49 2A36 *Giatsint*-B; 43 D-20

GUN/MOR **120mm** 17 2S31 *Vena*

MRL 282: **107mm** 71 T-107; **122mm** 130: 54 BM-21 *Grad*; 24 BM-21V; 16 IMI *Lynx*; 18 RM-70 *Vampir*; 18 T-122; **128mm** 10 RAK-12; **220mm** 17 TOS-1A; **300mm** 36: 30 9A52 *Smerch*; 6 *Polonez*; **302mm** 18 T-300 *Kasirga*

MOR 230: **120mm** 212: 5 *Cardom*; 27 M-1938 (PM-38); 180 2S12; SP **120mm** 18 *SandCat* with *Spear*

SURFACE-TO-SURFACE MISSILE LAUNCHERS

SRBM • **Conventional** 7: 4 IAI LORA; 3 9K79-1 *Tochka*-U (RS-SS-21B *Scarab*)

AIR DEFENCE

SAM
  Short-range 9K33-1T *Osa*-1T (RS-SA-8 *Gecko*)
  Point-defence 9K35 *Strela*-10 (RS-SA-13 *Gopher*); 9K32 *Strela* (RS-SA-7 *Grail*)‡; 9K34 *Strela*-3 (RS-SA-14 *Gremlin*); 9K310 *Igla*-1 (RS-SA-16 *Gimlet*); 9K338 *Igla*-S (RS-SA-24 *Grinch*)
GUNS
  SP **23mm** ZSU-23-4
  TOWED **23mm** ZU-23-2

Navy 1,750

EQUIPMENT BY TYPE

PATROL AND COASTAL COMBATANTS 11

CORVETTES • FS 1 *Kusar* (ex-FSU *Petya* II) with 2 RBU 6000 *Smerch* 2 A/S mor, 2 twin 76mm gun

PSO 1 *Luga* (*Wodnik* 2) (FSU Project 888; additional trg role)

PCC 3: 2 *Petrushka* (FSU UK-3; additional trg role); 1 *Shelon* (ex-FSU Project 1388M)

PB 3: 1 *Araz* (ex-TUR AB 25); 1 *Bryza* (ex-FSU Project 722); 1 *Poluchat* (ex-FSU Project 368)

PBF 3 *Stenka*

MINE WARFARE • MINE COUNTERMEASURES 4

MHC 4: 2 *Korund* (Project 1258 (*Yevgenya*)); 2 *Yakhont* (FSU *Sonya*)

AMPHIBIOUS 5

LSM 2: 1 Project 770 (FSU *Polnochny* A) (capacity 6 MBT; 180 troops); 1 Project 771 (*Polnochny* B) (capacity 6 MBT; 180 troops)

LCM 3: 2 T-4 (FSU); 1 *Vydra*† (FSU) (capacity either 3 MBT or 200 troops)

LOGISTICS AND SUPPORT • ATF 2 *Neftegaz* (Project B-92) (ex-Coast Guard)

Marines
FORCES BY ROLE
MANOEUVRE
  Amphibious
  1 mne bn

Air Force and Air Defence 8,650
FORCES BY ROLE
FIGHTER
1 sqn with MiG-29 *Fulcrum* A; MiG-29UB *Fulcrum* B
GROUND ATTACK
1 regt with Su-25 *Frogfoot*; Su-25UB *Frogfoot* B
TRANSPORT
1 sqn with Il-76TD *Candid*
TRAINING
1 sqn with L-39 *Albatros*
ATTACK/TRANSPORT HELICOPTER
1 regt with Bell 407; Bell 412; Ka-32 *Helix* C; MD-530; Mi-8 *Hip*; Mi-17-1V *Hip*; Mi-24 *Hind*; Mi-35M *Hind*

EQUIPMENT BY TYPE
AIRCRAFT 52 combat capable
  FTR 14: 11 MiG-29 *Fulcrum* A; 3 MiG-29UB *Fulcrum* B
  ATK 38: 33 Su-25 *Frogfoot*; 5 Su-25UB *Frogfoot* B
  TPT • Heavy 2 Il-76TD *Candid*
  TRG 24: 14 L-39 *Albatros*; 10 *Super Mushshak*
HELICOPTERS
  ATK 47: 23 Mi-24 *Hind*; 24 Mi-35M *Hind*
  MRH 38: 1 Bell 407; 3 Bell 412; 1 MD-530; 33 Mi-17-1V *Hip*
  TPT 11: Medium 11: 3 Ka-32 *Helix* C; 8 Mi-8 *Hip*
UNINHABITED AERIAL VEHICLES
  CISR • Medium *Bayraktar* TB2

ISR 7+: Heavy 3+ *Heron*; Medium 4+ *Aerostar*

AIR DEFENCE • SAM
  Long-range S-200 *Vega* (RS-SA-5 *Gammon*); S-300PMU2 (RS-SA-20 *Gargoyle*)
  Medium-range 24+: *Barak*-LRAD; *Barak*-MRAD; Buk-MB; S-75 *Dvina* (RS-SA-2 *Guideline*); ε24 S-125-2TM *Pechora*-2TM; 9K37M *Buk*-M1 (RS-SA-11 *Gadfly*)

AIR-LAUNCHED MISSILES
  AAM • IR R-27T (RS-AA-10B *Alamo*); R-60 (RS-AA-8 *Aphid*); R-73 (RS-AA-11A *Archer*); SARH R-27R (RS-AA-10A *Alamo*)
  ASM *Barrier*-V

BOMBS
  Laser-guided MAM-L
  INS/GPS-guided KGK-82; KGK-83

Gendarmerie & Paramilitary ε15,000

State Border Service ε5,000
Ministry of Internal Affairs
EQUIPMENT BY TYPE
ARMOURED FIGHTING VEHICLES
  IFV 168 BMP-1/BMP-2
  APC • APC (W) 19 BTR-60/70/80
AIRCRAFT • TPT • Light 40 An-2 *Colt* (modified for use as decoys)
UNINHABITED AERIAL VEHICLES
  ISR • Medium 7+: 4+ *Hermes* 450; 3+ *Hermes* 900
LOITERING & DIRECT ATTACK MUNITIONS
  Harop; *Skystriker* (two variants)

Coast Guard
The Coast Guard was established in 2005 as part of the State Border Service
EQUIPMENT BY TYPE
PATROL AND COASTAL COMBATANTS 19
  PCG 6 *Sa'ar* 62 with 1 8-cell *Typhoon* MLS-NLOS lnchr with *Spike* NLOS SSM, 1 hel landing platform
  PBF 9: 1 Project 205 (FSU *Osa* II); 6 *Shaldag* V; 2 Silver Ships 48ft
  PB 4: 2 Baltic 150; 1 *Point* (US); 1 *Grif* (FSU *Zhuk*)
LOGISTICS AND SUPPORT 3
  ATF 3 *Neftegaz* (Project B-92) (also used for patrol duties)

Internal Troops 10,000+
Ministry of Internal Affairs
EQUIPMENT BY TYPE
ARMOURED FIGHTING VEHICLES
  APC • APC (W) 7 BTR-60/BTR-70/BTR-80

DEPLOYMENT
SOUTH SUDAN: UN • UNMISS 2

FOREIGN FORCES

Russia 1,960; 1 MR bde(-) (peacekeeping)
Turkiye 170; 1 EOD unit

Belarus BLR

Belarusian Ruble BYN		2022	2023	2024
GDP	BYN	191bn	208bn	226bn
	USD	72.8bn	68.9bn	66.3bn
per capita	USD	7,869	7,477	7,238
Growth	%	-3.7	1.6	1.3
Inflation	%	15.2	4.7	5.7
Def bdgt	BYN	2.00bn	3.00bn	
	USD	761m	994m	
USD1=BYN		2.63	3.02	3.41

Real-terms defence budget trend (USDm, constant 2015)
846
383
2008 — 2016 — 2023

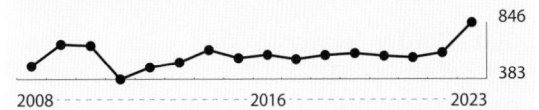

Population	9,539,576				
Age	0–14	15–19	20–24	25–29	30–64	65 plus
Male	8.4%	2.6%	2.5%	2.7%	24.7%	5.8%
Female	7.9%	2.4%	2.3%	2.6%	26.6%	11.5%

Capabilities

The main task of Belarus's armed forces is maintaining territorial integrity, though the army has also been used for internal security tasks. A draft of an updated national state security concept reportedly will be submitted to the Belarus All-People's Congress in April 2024. The revisions are meant to address what the regime views as changes in the security environment over the last decade, and particularly recent events. The current national military doctrine was approved in July 2016 and identified as security challenges 'hybrid methods' and 'colour revolutions'. Minsk agreed on a revised joint military doctrine with Russia, the Military Doctrine of the Union State, in November 2021, superseding a 2001 agreement. In late 2019, the government finalised a plan for the development of the armed forces until 2030. Belarus is a member of the CSTO and aims to become a member of the Shanghai Cooperation Organisation at the 2024 summit. Russia remains the country's principal defence partner, with Belarus vocal in support of Moscow's war in Ukraine. Russian forces used Belarussian territory to launch attacks on Ukraine. Belarus also 'hosted' some Wagner forces following the private military company's short-lived rebellion in June 2023. Moscow and Minsk have repeatedly discussed the prospect of nuclear weapons being stationed in Belarus, and in April 2023, the Russian defence ministry said Belarusian troops were being trained in the use of the 9M723 (RS-SS-26 *Stone*) short-range ballistic missile, including the use of special warheads, with 'special warheads' in this context understood to refer to tactical nuclear payloads. Russia has reportedly begun sending nuclear capability to Belarus; Russia is near-certain to retain control of the weapons. Despite Moscow's invasion of Ukraine, joint training continued with Russian forces during 2023, including air defence exercises. Russian forces also continue to train in Belarus prior to deployment in Ukraine. Minsk's forces remain conscript-based and train regularly with other CSTO partners. Belarus has emphasised the training of territorial-defence troops to allow them to operate more effectively with the regular forces. The country has a small heavy-airlift fleet that could be supplemented by civil transport aircraft, and Minsk has a special-forces brigade trained for the air-assault role. The country has no requirement to independently deploy and sustain the armed forces, though force elements assigned to CSTO may have capability in that area. Russia is Minsk's main defence-equipment supplier. The local defence industry manufactures vehicles, guided weapons and electronic-warfare systems, among other equipment. However, there is no capacity to design or manufacture modern combat aircraft.

ACTIVE 48,600 (Army 13,100 Air 10,700 Special Operations Forces 6,300 Joint 18,500) **Gendarmerie & Paramilitary 110,000**

Conscript liability 18 months; 12 months for graduates (alternative service option)

RESERVE 289,500

(Joint 289,500 with mil service within last 5 years)

ORGANISATIONS BY SERVICE

Army 13,100

FORCES BY ROLE

COMMAND
  2 comd HQ (West & North West)

MANOEUVRE
  Mechanised
  4 mech bde

COMBAT SUPPORT
  2 arty bde
  1 engr bde
  1 engr regt
  2 EW bn
  2 sigs regt

COMBAT SERVICE SUPPORT
  2 log regt
  1 tpt bde

EQUIPMENT BY TYPE

ARMOURED FIGHTING VEHICLES
  MBT 497: 477 T-72B; 20 T-72B3 mod
  RECCE 132 BRM-1
  IFV 976: 906 BMP-2; 70 BTR-82A
  APC • APC (T) 58 MT-LB
  AUV *Tigr*; *Volat* V1

ENGINEERING & MAINTENANCE VEHICLES
  AEV BAT-2; IMR-2; MT-LB
  ARV 2 BREM-K; BREM-1
  VLB 24: 20 MTU-20; 4 MT-55A
  MW UR-77

NBC VEHICLES BRDM-2RKhB; *Cayman* NRBC *Chimera*; RKhM-4; RKhM-K

ANTI-TANK/ANTI-INFRASTRUCTURE • MSL
  SP 160: 75 9P148 *Konkurs* (RS-AT-5 *Spandrel*); 85 9P149 *Shturm* (RS-AT-6 *Spiral*)

MANPATS 9K111 *Fagot* (RS-AT-4 *Spigot*); 9K111-1 *Konkurs* (RS-AT-5 *Spandrel*); 9K115 *Metis* (RS-AT-7 *Saxhorn*)

ARTILLERY 571
SP 321: **122mm** 125 2S1 *Gvozdika*; **152mm** 196: 125 2S3 *Akatsiya*; 71 2S5 *Giatsint*-S
TOWED **152mm** 72 2A65 *Msta*-B
MRL 164: **122mm** 128 BM-21 *Grad*; **220mm** 36 9P140 *Uragan*
MOR **120mm** 14 2S12

AIR DEFENCE
SAM Point-defence 2K22 *Tunguska* (RS-SA-19 *Grison*)
GUNS • SP **23mm** ZU-23-2 (tch)

Air Force and Air Defence Forces 10,700
FORCES BY ROLE
FIGHTER
2 sqn with MiG-29/S/UB *Fulcrum* A/C/B
1 sqn with Su-30SM *Flanker* H

GROUND ATTACK
2 sqn with L-39 *Albatros**; Su-25K/UBK *Frogfoot* A/B; Yak-130 *Mitten**

TRANSPORT
1 base with An-26 *Curl*; Il-76 *Candid*; Tu-134 *Crusty*

TRAINING
Some sqn with L-39 *Albatros*

ATTACK HELICOPTER
Some sqn with Mi-24 *Hind*; Mi-24K *Hind*; Mi-35M *Hind*

TRANSPORT HELICOPTER
Some (cbt spt) sqn with Mi-8 *Hip*; Mi-8MTV-5 *Hip*

EQUIPMENT BY TYPE
AIRCRAFT 63 combat capable
FTR 18 MiG-29/UB/S *Fulcrum* A/B/C (16 more in store); (21 Su-27/Su-27UB *Flanker* B/C in store)
FGA 4 Su-30SM *Flanker* H
ATK 21 Su-25K/UBK *Frogfoot* A/B
TPT 5: **Heavy** 2 Il-76 *Candid* (+9 civ Il-76 available for mil use); **Light** 3: 2 An-26 *Curl*; 1 Tu-134 *Crusty*
TRG 20: 9 L-39 *Albatros**; 11 Yak-130 *Mitten**

HELICOPTERS
ATK 11: 7 Mi-24 *Hind*; 4 Mi-35M *Hind*
ISR 5 Mi-24K *Hind*
TPT • **Medium** 20: 8 Mi-8 *Hip*; 12 Mi-8MTV-5 *Hip*

AIR-LAUNCHED MISSILES
AAM • **IR** R-60 (RS-AA-8 *Aphid*); R-73 (RS-AA-11A *Archer*) **SARH** R-27R (RS-AA-10 *Alamo* A); R-27ER (RS-AA-10C *Alamo*)
ASM Kh-25 (RS-AS-10 *Karen*); Kh-29 (RS-AS-14 *Kedge*)
ARM Kh-58 (RS-AS-11 *Kilter*) (likely WFU)

Air Defence
AD data from Uzal Baranovichi EW radar
FORCES BY ROLE

AIR DEFENCE
1 bde with S-300PT (RS-SA-10A *Grumble*); S-400 (RS-SA-21 *Growler*); 9K331MK *Tor*-M2K
4 regt with S-300PS (RS-SA-10B *Grumble*)
1 bde with 9K37 *Buk* (RS-SA-11 *Gadfly*); 9K331ME *Tor*-M2E (RS-SA-15 *Gauntlet*)
1 regt with 9K331ME *Tor*-M2E (RS-SA-15 *Gauntlet*)
2 regt with 9K33 *Osa* (RS-SA-8 *Gecko*)

EQUIPMENT BY TYPE
AIR DEFENCE • SAM
Long-range 124: 60 S-300PT (RS-SA-10 Grumble); 48 S-300PS (RS-SA-10B *Grumble*); 16 S-400 (RS-SA-21 *Growler*)
Medium-range 9K37 *Buk* (RS-SA-11 *Gadfly*)
Short-range 25: 21 9K331ME *Tor*-M2E (RS-SA-15 *Gauntlet*); 4 9K331MK *Tor*-M2K
Point-defence 9K33 *Osa* (RS-SA-8 *Gecko*); 9K35 *Strela*-10 (RS-SA-13 *Gopher*)

Special Operations Command 6,300
FORCES BY ROLE
SPECIAL FORCES
1 SF bde

MANOEUVRE
Mechanised
2 mech bde

EQUIPMENT BY TYPE
ARMOURED FIGHTING VEHICLES
RECCE 13+ *Cayman* BRDM
IFV 30+ BTR-82A
APC • **APC (W)** 217: ε64 BTR-70M1; 153 BTR-80
AUV 12 CS/VN3B mod

ARTILLERY 114
TOWED **122mm** 24 D-30
GUN/MOR • TOWED **120mm** 18 2B23 NONA-M1

ANTI-TANK/ANTI-INFRASTRUCTURE • MSL
MANPATS 9K111 *Fagot* (RS-AT-4 *Spigot*); 9K111-1 *Konkurs* (RS-AT-5 *Spandrel*); 9K115 *Metis* (RS-AT-7 *Saxhorn*)

Joint 18,500 (Centrally controlled units and MoD staff)
FORCES BY ROLE
SURFACE-TO-SURFACE MISSILE
1 SRBM bde with 9K720 *Iskander*-M (RS-SS-26 *Stone*)

COMBAT SUPPORT
1 arty bde
1 MRL bde
2 engr bde
1 EW regt
1 NBC bde
3 sigs bde

COMBAT SUPPORT
2 tpt bde

EQUIPMENT BY TYPE
ARMOURED FIGHTING VEHICLES
  APC • **APC (T)** 20 MT-LB
  AUV Volat V1
NBC VEHICLES BRDM-2RKhB; RKhM-4; RKhM-K
ARTILLERY 118
  SP 152mm 36 2S5 Giatsint-S
  TOWED 152mm 36 2A65 Msta-B
  MRL 300mm 46: 36 9A52 Smerch; 6 Polonez; 4 Polonez-M
SURFACE-TO-SURFACE MISSILE LAUNCHERS
  SRBM • Dual-capable 8 9K720 Iskander-M (RS-SS-26 Stone)

Gendarmerie & Paramilitary 110,000

State Border Troops 12,000
Ministry of Interior

Militia 87,000
Ministry of Interior

Internal Troops 11,000

FOREIGN FORCES
Russia 2,000; 2 SAM bn with S-400; 1 radar station at Baranovichi (Volga system; leased); 1 naval comms site

Georgia GEO

Georgian Lari GEL		2022	2023	2024
GDP	GEL	71.8bn	78.6bn	84.8bn
	USD	24.6bn	30.0bn	31.4bn
per capita	USD	6,671	8,165	8,573
Growth	%	10.1	6.2	4.8
Inflation	%	11.9	2.4	2.7
Def bdgt	GEL	918m	1.26bn	1.37bn
	USD	315m	481m	507m
FMA (US)	USD	25m	25m	25m
USD1=GEL		2.92	2.62	2.70

Real-terms defence budget trend (USDm, constant 2015)
914 (2008) – 283 (2023)

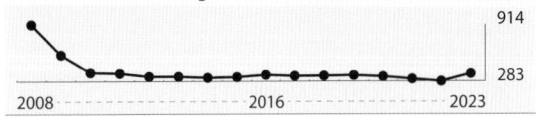

Population	4,927,228				
Age	0–14	15–19	20–24	25–29	30–64	65 plus
Male	10.7%	2.8%	2.8%	3.2%	22.0%	6.5%
Female	10.0%	2.5%	2.4%	2.9%	24.3%	9.9%

Capabilities
Georgia's security concerns principally focus on Russian military deployments and the breakaway regions of Abkhazia and South Ossetia, which were heightened by Moscow's February 2022 invasion of Ukraine. The country wants to join NATO but has made little progress beyond a package of 'tailored support measures' agreed at the alliance's 2022 Madrid Summit. The NATO communique from the July 2023 Vilnius Summit only echoed the language of the 2008 summit. Bilateral security cooperation with the US continued with the Georgia Defense Readiness Program, succeeded by the Georgia Defense and Deterrence Enhancement Initiative, signed in October 2021. The GDRP is intended to bring nine Georgian infantry battalions up to NATO standards. Georgia's armed forces take part in several NATO multinational exercises but have limited expeditionary logistic capability. A revised Defense Code was approved in September 2023, which will come into force in 2025, aimed at closing loopholes in conscription. The backbone of the armed forces' military equipment remains legacy Soviet-era systems, though the country is aiming to replace them. The Major Systems Acquisitions Strategy 2019–25 outlines efforts to procure new equipment, though funding availability will be key to meeting aspirations. The military aims to boost special-forces capacity, anti-armour and air-defence capability. The country has begun to develop a defence-industrial base. The State Military Scientific-Technical Center has demonstrated some maintenance, repair, overhaul and design capabilities to produce light armoured vehicles. A combat training centre is being developed under the NATO–Georgia Joint Training and Evaluation Centre. Conscription was reinstated with revised terms and increased pay in early 2017.

ACTIVE 20,650 (Army 19,050 National Guard 1,600) Gendarmerie & Paramilitary 5,400

Conscript liability 12 months

ORGANISATIONS BY SERVICE

Army 15,000; 4,050 conscript (total 19,050)
FORCES BY ROLE
SPECIAL FORCES
  1 SF bde
MANOEUVRE
  Mechanised
  1 (4th) mech inf bde (1 armd bn, 2 mech inf bn, 1 SP arty bn)
  Light
  1 (1st) inf bde (1 mech inf bn, 3 inf bn)
  1 (2nd) inf bde (3 inf bn, 1 fd arty bn)
  1 (3rd) inf bde (3 inf bn, 1 SP arty bn)
  Amphibious
  2 mne bn (1 cadre)
COMBAT SUPPORT
  1 (5th) arty bde (1 fd arty bn; 1 MRL bn)
  1 (6th) arty bde (1 SP arty bn; 1 MRL bn)
  1 engr bde
  1 engr bn
  1 sigs bn
  1 SIGINT bn
  1 MP bn
COMBAT SERVICE SUPPORT
  1 med bn
EQUIPMENT BY TYPE
ARMOURED FIGHTING VEHICLES

MBT 123: 23 T-55AM2; 100 T-72B/SIM1
RECCE 41: 1 BRM-1K; 40+ *Didgori*-2
IFV 71: 25 BMP-1; 46 BMP-2
APC 221
  APC (T) 69+: 3+ *Lazika*; 66 MT-LB
  APC (W) 152+: 25 BTR-70; 19 BTR-80; 40+ *Didgori*-1; 3+ *Didgori*-3; 65 *Ejder*
  AUV 10+: ATF *Dingo*; *Cobra*; 10 *Cougar*
ENGINEERING & MAINTENANCE VEHICLES
  ARV IMR-2
ANTI-TANK/ANTI-INFRASTRUCTURE
  MSL • MANPATS 9K111 *Fagot* (RS-AT-4 *Spigot*); 9K111-1 *Konkurs* (RS-AT-5 *Spandrel*); FGM-148 *Javelin*
  GUNS • TOWED ε40: 85mm D-44; 100mm T-12
ARTILLERY 240
  SP 67: 122mm 20 2S1 *Gvozdika*; 152mm 46: 32 M-77 *Dana*; 13 2S3 *Akatsiya*; 1 2S19 *Msta*-S; 203mm 1 2S7 *Pion*
  TOWED 71: 122mm 58 D-30; 152mm 13: 3 2A36 *Giatsint*-B; 10 2A65 *Msta*-B
  MRL 122mm 37: 13 BM-21 *Grad*; 6 GradLAR; 18 RM-70
  MOR 120mm 65: 14 2S12 *Sani*; 33 M-75; 18 M120
AIR DEFENCE • SAM
  Short-range *Spyder*-SR
  Point-defence *Grom*; *Mistral*-2; 9K32 *Strela*-2 (RS-SA-7 *Grail*)‡; 9K35 *Strela*-10 (RS-SA-13 *Gopher*); 9K36 *Strela*-3 (RS-SA-14 *Gremlin*); 9K310 *Igla*-1 (RS-SA-16 *Gimlet*)

Aviation and Air Defence Command 1,300 (incl 300 conscript)

1 avn base, 1 hel air base
EQUIPMENT BY TYPE
AIRCRAFT 5 combat capable
  ATK 5: 3 Su-25KM *Frogfoot*; 2 Su-25UB *Frogfoot* B (2 Su-25 *Frogfoot* in store)
  TPT • Light 9: 6 An-2 *Colt*; 2 Yak-40 *Codling*
HELICOPTERS
  ATK 6 Mi-24 *Hind*
  TPT 18: Medium 17 Mi-8T *Hip*; Light 1+ Bell 205 (UH-1H *Iroquois*) (up to 8 more in store)
UNINHABITED AERIAL VEHICLES
  ISR • Medium 1+ *Hermes* 450
AIR DEFENCE • SAM
  Medium-range 9K37 *Buk*-M1 (RS-SA-11 *Gadfly*) (1–2 bn)
  Point-defence 8 9K33 *Osa*-AK (RS-SA-8B *Gecko*) (two bty); 9K33 *Osa*-AKM (6–10 updated SAM systems)

National Guard 1,600 active reservists opcon Army

FORCES BY ROLE
MANOEUVRE
  Light
  2 inf bde

Gendarmerie & Paramilitary 5,400

Border Police 5,400
EQUIPMENT BY TYPE
HELICOPTERS
  TPT • Medium 3 Mi-8MTV-1 *Hip*

Coast Guard
HQ at Poti. The Navy was merged with the Coast Guard in 2009 under the auspices of the Georgian Border Police, within the Ministry of the Interior
EQUIPMENT BY TYPE
PATROL AND COASTAL COMBATANTS 10
  PCC 2 *Ochamchira* (ex-US *Island*)
  PBF 2+: some *Ares* 43m; 1 *Kaan* 33; 1 *Kaan* 20
  PB 6: 2 *Dauntless*; 2 *Dilos* (ex-GRC); 1 *Kutaisi* (ex-TUR AB 25); 2 *Point*; some *Zhuk* (3 ex-UKR)

DEPLOYMENT

CENTRAL AFRICAN REPUBLIC: EU • EUTM RCA 35
MALI: EU • EUTM Mali 1

TERRITORY WHERE THE GOVERNMENT DOES NOT EXERCISE EFFECTIVE CONTROL

Following the August 2008 war between Russia and Georgia, the areas of Abkhazia and South Ossetia declared themselves independent. Data presented here represents the de facto situation and does not imply international recognition as sovereign states.

FOREIGN FORCES

Russia ε4,000; 1 mil base at Gudauta (Abkhazia) with 1 MR bde(-); 1 SAM regt with S-300PS; 1 mil base at Djava/Tskhinvali (S. Ossetia) with 1 MR bde(-)

Kazakhstan KAZ

Kazakhstani Tenge KZT		2022	2023	2024
GDP	KZT	104trn	118trn	136trn
	USD	226bn	259bn	291bn
per capita	USD	11,409	12,968	14,396
Growth	%	3.3	4.6	4.2
Inflation	%	15.0	15.0	9.0
Def bdgt	KZT	859bn	1.15tr	
	USD	1.87bn	2.53bn	
USD1=KZT		460.10	453.31	468.04

Real-terms defence budget trend (USDbn, constant 2015)

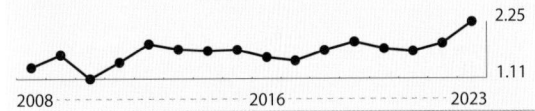

2.25 — 1.11 (2008 – 2016 – 2023)

Population 20,082,154

Age	0–14	15–19	20–24	25–29	30–64	65 plus
Male	14.4%	3.7%	2.9%	3.4%	20.8%	3.3%
Female	13.5%	3.5%	2.8%	3.2%	22.6%	5.9%

Capabilities

Kazakhstan's 2017 military doctrine indicates a change in focus from countering violent extremism to addressing concerns over border security and hybrid threats. In 2022, the doctrine was updated by consolidating the authority of the president's office, enhancing the capabilities of the national guard to respond to domestic disorder, strengthening cyber and information capabilities across all security agencies, and creating a new military territorial directorate. Kazakhstan has a military agreement with Uzbekistan to cooperate on training and education, countering violent extremism and reducing militant movements in their region. In 2023, Kazakhstan and Turkiye signed a military cooperation plan for 2024. The country has a close, traditional defence relationship with Russia, reinforced by CSTO and SCO membership. Moscow operates a radar station at Balkash. In January 2022, Russian troops led a brief CSTO mission to the country following anti-government protests. Kazakhstan takes part in regional and CSTO exercises, including anti-terror drills. However, Kazakhstan in 2022 also sent humanitarian aid to Ukraine and did not recognise the independence of the Luhansk and Donetsk territories backed by Moscow. The armed forces are reportedly integrating lessons from the war in Ukraine, including a desire to improve artillery, reconnaissance and UAV capabilities. Salary increases were announced in 2023, particularly for specialist trades, including pilots. By regional standards, the armed forces are sizeable and well equipped, following the acquisition of significant amounts of new and upgraded materiel in recent years, primarily from Russia. Turkish Aerospace Industries announced in 2023 that its *Anka* UAVs will be assembled in Kazakhstan, which is expanding its indigenous defence industry.

ACTIVE 39,000 (Army 20,000 Navy 3,000 Air 12,000 MoD 4,000) **Gendarmerie & Paramilitary 31,500**

Conscript liability 12 months (due to be abolished)

ORGANISATIONS BY SERVICE

Army 20,000

4 regional comd: Astana, East, West and Southern

FORCES BY ROLE

MANOEUVRE

Armoured
2 tk bde
2 mech bde
1 aslt bde

Mechanised
1 naval inf bde
1 (peacekeeping) inf regt

Air Manoeuvre
4 air aslt bde

COMBAT SUPPORT

3 arty bde
1 SRBM unit
3 cbt engr regt

EQUIPMENT BY TYPE

ARMOURED FIGHTING VEHICLES
MBT 350 T-72BA
TSV 3 BMPT
RECCE 100: 40 BRDM-2; 60 BRM-1
IFV 413: 280 BMP-2; 70 BTR-80A; 63 BTR-82A
APC 340
  APC (T) 50 MT-LB
  APC (W) 152: 2 BTR-3E; 150 BTR-80
  PPV 138: 138 *Arlan*
  AUV 17+: 17 *Cobra*; Roshel *Senator*; *SandCat*

ENGINEERING & MAINTENANCE VEHICLES
AEV MT-LB

ANTI-TANK/ANTI-INFRASTRUCTURE
MSL
  SP 6+: HMMWV with 9K111-1 *Konkurs* (RS-AT-5 *Spandrel*); 6 9P149 *Shturm* (MT-LB with RS-AT-6 *Spiral*)
  MANPATS 9K111 *Fagot* (RS-AT-4 *Spigot*); 9K111-1 *Konkurs* (RS-AT-5 *Spandrel*); 9K115 *Metis* (RS-AT-7 *Saxhorn*)
GUNS 100mm 20 MT-12

ARTILLERY 490
SP 126: **122mm** 66: 60 2S1 *Gvozdika*; 6 *Semser*; **152mm** 60 2S3M *Akatsiya*
TOWED 194: **122mm** 100 D-30; **152mm** 94: 70 2A65 *Msta-B*; 24 D-20
MRL 107: **122mm** 80 BM-21 *Grad*; **220mm** 3 TOS-1A; **300mm** 24: 6 BM-30 *Smerch*; 18 IMI *Lynx* (with 50 msl)
MOR 63+: **82mm** some; SP **120mm** 18 *Cardom*; **120mm** 45 2B11 *Sani*/M120

SURFACE-TO-SURFACE MISSILE LAUNCHERS
SRBM • Conventional 12 9K79 *Tochka* (RS-SS-21 *Scarab*)

Navy 3,000
EQUIPMENT BY TYPE
PATROL AND COASTAL COMBATANTS 14
  PCGM 3 *Kazakhstan* with 1 4-cell lnchr with 4 *Barrier-VK* SSM, 1 *Arbalet-K* lnchr with 4 9K38 *Igla* (RS-SA-18 *Grouse*), 1 AK630 CIWS
  PCC 1 *Kazakhstan* with 1 122mm MRL
  PBF 3 *Sea Dolphin*
  PB 7: 3 *Archangel*; 1 *Dauntless*; 1 *Lashyn*; 1 *Turk* (AB 25); 1 Other
MINE WARFARE • MINE COUNTERMEASURES 1
  MCC 1 *Alatau* (Project 10750E)
LOGISTICS AND SUPPORT • AGS 1 *Zhaik*
UNINHABITED MARITIME SYSTEMS • UUV
  DATA *Alister 9* (A9-E)
  MW K-Ster I/C

Air Force 12,000 (incl Air Defence)
FORCES BY ROLE
FIGHTER/GROUND ATTACK
  1 sqn with Su-27/Su-27UB *Flanker* B/C
  1 sqn with Su-27/Su-30SM *Flanker* B/H
GROUND ATTACK
  1 sqn with Su-25 *Frogfoot*
TRANSPORT
  1 unit with Tu-134 *Crusty*; Tu-154 *Careless*
  1 sqn with An-12 *Cub*, An-26 *Curl*, An-30 *Clank*, An-72 *Coaler*, C295M
TRAINING
  1 sqn with L-39 *Albatros*
ATTACK HELICOPTER
  5 sqn with Mi-24V *Hind*
TRANSPORT HELICOPTER
  Some sqn with Bell 205 (UH-1H *Iroquois*); H145; Mi-8 *Hip*; Mi-17V-5 *Hip*; Mi-171Sh *Hip*; Mi-26 *Halo*
COMBAT/ISR UAV
  1 sqn with *Anka*-S (forming)
AIR DEFENCE
  1 bty with 9K317M2 *Buk*-M2E (RS-SA-17 *Grizzly*)
  2 bty with S-75M *Volkhov* (RS-SA-2 *Guideline*)
  1 bty with S-125-1T
  1 bty with S-200 *Angara* (RS-SA-5 *Gammon*)
  10 bty with S-300PS (RS-SA-10 *Grumble*)
  Some regt with 2K12 *Kub* (RS-SA-6 *Gainful*)
EQUIPMENT BY TYPE
AIRCRAFT 61 combat capable
  FTR (12 MiG-29 *Fulcrum* A; 2 MiG-29UB *Fulcrum* B; 31 MiG-31/MiG-31BM *Foxhound* all stored for sale)
  FGA 47: 20 Su-27 *Flanker*; 4 Su-27UB *Flanker*; 23 Su-30SM *Flanker* H (12 MiG-27 *Flogger* D; 2 MiG-23UB *Flogger* C stored for sale)
  ATK 14: 12 Su-25 *Frogfoot*; 2 Su-25UB *Frogfoot*
  ISR 1 An-30 *Clank*

TPT 20: **Medium** 2 An-12 *Cub*; **Light** 17: 6 An-26 *Curl*; 2 An-72 *Coaler*; 8 C295; 1 C295W; **PAX** 1 Tu-154 *Careless*
TRG 19: 17 L-39 *Albatros*; 2 Z-242L
HELICOPTERS
  ATK 32: 20 Mi-24V *Hind* (some upgraded); 12 Mi-35M *Hind*
  MRH 26: 20 Mi-17V-5 *Hip*; 6 Mi-171Sh *Hip*
  TPT 16: **Heavy** 4 Mi-26 *Halo*; **Light** 12: 4 Bell 205 (UH-1H *Iroquois*); 8 H145
UNINHABITED AERIAL VEHICLES
  CISR • Heavy 5: 3 *Anka*-S (in test); 2 *Wing Loong* (GJ-1)
AIR DEFENCE • SAM
  Long-range 43+: 3 S-200 *Angara* (RS-SA-5 *Gammon*); 40+ S-300PS (RS-SA-10B *Grumble*)
  Medium-range 15: 3 9K317M2 *Buk*-M2E (RS-SA-17 *Grizzly*); 12 S-75M *Volkhov* (RS-SA-2 *Guideline*)
  Short-range 3+: some 2K12 *Kub* (RS-SA-6 *Gainful*); 3 S-125-1T
  Point-defence 9K35 *Strela*-10 (RS-SA-13 *Gopher*)
AIR-LAUNCHED MISSILES
  AAM • IR R-27T (RS-AA-10B *Alamo*); R-60 (RS-AA-8 *Aphid*); R-73 (RS-AA-11A *Archer*); **SARH** R-27ER (RS-AA-10C *Alamo*); R-27R (RS-AA-10A *Alamo*); **ARH** R-77 (RS-AA-12A *Adder*)
  ASM Kh-25 (RS-AS-10 *Karen*); Kh-29 (RS-AS-14 *Kedge*)
  ARM Kh-27 (RS-AS-12 *Kegler*); Kh-58 (RS-AS-11 *Kilter*)

Gendarmerie & Paramilitary 31,500
National Guard ε20,000
Ministry of Interior
EQUIPMENT BY TYPE
ARMOURED FIGHTING VEHICLE
  APC
    APC (W) Kamaz-43629 *Vystrel*
    PPV *Ural*-VV
AIRCRAFT
  TPT • Medium 1 Y-8F-200WA

State Security Service 2,500

Border Service ε9,000
Ministry of Interior
EQUIPMENT BY TYPE
AIRCRAFT 7: **Light** 6: 3 An-26 *Curl*; 1 An-74T; 1 An-74TK; 1 C295W; **PAX** 1 SSJ-100
HELICOPTERS • TPT • Medium 15: 1 Mi-171; 14 Mi-171Sh

Coast Guard
EQUIPMENT BY TYPE
PATROL AND COASTAL COMBATANTS 25
  PBF 12: 2 *Aibar* (Project 0210); 8 FC-19; 2 *Saygak*
  PB 13: 7 *Almaty*; 6 *Sardar*

DEPLOYMENT

CENTRAL AFRICAN REPUBLIC: UN • MINUSCA 1
LEBANON: UN • UNIFIL 9
WESTERN SAHARA: UN • MINURSO 6

Kyrgyzstan KGZ

Kyrgyzstani Som KGS		2022	2023	2024
GDP	KGS	971bn	1.13trn	1.27trn
	USD	11.7bn	12.7bn	13.7bn
per capita	USD	1,718	1,830	1,930
Growth	%	6.3	3.4	4.3
Inflation	%	13.9	11.7	8.6
Def bdgt	KGS	n.k.	n.k.	n.k.
	USD	n.k.	n.k.	n.k.
USD1=KGS		83.19	88.76	93.28
Population	6,122,781			

Age	0–14	15–19	20–24	25–29	30–64	65 plus
Male	15.2%	4.3%	3.7%	3.9%	19.3%	2.5%
Female	14.4%	4.2%	3.6%	3.8%	21.1%	4.1%

Capabilities

Kyrgyzstan has started expanding ties with its neighbours on issues such as defence-industrial cooperation, though it remains generally dependent on Russian assistance for its defence requirements. Kyrgyzstan is a member of both the CSTO and the SCO. The country hosted a CSTO peacekeeping drill in 2023 after cancelling its participation in a command staff exercise in 2022 because of border tensions with Tajikistan. Moscow has a military presence in the country, including a squadron of Su-25SM ground-attack aircraft at Kant air base, which it has leased since 2003. In 2020, Kyrgyzstan increased its annual fees, reportedly because Russian forces are using more land than outlined in the 2003 agreement. Talks are ongoing over a possible second Russian base. In 2023, Russia said it would 'develop' its facilities in Kyrgyzstan, following a meeting between the countries' leaders. Russia's government has approved plans to set up a common air defence system, which were endorsed by Kyrgyzstan's parliament in 2023. The military conducts joint training with regional countries, including anti-terror drills, but combat readiness remains an issue. In 2021, Indian and Kyrgyz special forces held the eighth iteration of bilateral exercises that focus on high-altitude and mountain operations in the broader context of counterterrorism missions. Kyrgyzstan has a limited capability to deploy externally, though personnel have been deployed to OSCE and UN missions. The armed forces possess ageing land equipment and limited air capabilities, relying instead on Russian support, training and deployments. The country acquired additional air-defence equipment from Belarus that arrived in 2023 alongside upgraded helicopters. UAV capabilities have improved with the addition of Turkish-origin equipment. There is little local defence industry, although, in 2018, Kazakhstan and Kyrgyzstan discussed defence-industrial cooperation. Defence ties with India have increased and a joint working group on defence cooperation has been formed.

ACTIVE 10,900 (Army 8,500 Air 2,400) **Gendarmerie & Paramilitary 9,500**

Conscript liability 18 months

ORGANISATIONS BY SERVICE

Army 8,500
FORCES BY ROLE
SPECIAL FORCES
 1 SF bde
MANOEUVRE
 Mechanised
 2 MR bde
 1 (mtn) MR bde
COMBAT SUPPORT
 1 arty bde
 1 AD bde
EQUIPMENT BY TYPE
ARMOURED FIGHTING VEHICLES
 MBT 150 T-72
 RECCE 39: 30 BRDM-2; 9 BRDM-2M
 IFV 320: 230 BMP-1; 90 BMP-2
 APC • APC (W) 55: 25 BTR-70; 20 BTR-70M; 10 BTR-80
ANTI-TANK/ANTI-INFRASTRUCTURE
 MSL • MANPATS 9K11 *Malyutka* (RS-AT-3 *Sagger*); 9K111 *Fagot* (RS-AT-4 *Spigot*); 9K111-1 *Konkurs* (RS-AT-5 *Spandrel*)
 RCL 73mm SPG-9
 GUNS 100mm 36: 18 MT-12/T-12; 18 M-1944
ARTILLERY 228
 SP 122mm 18 2S1 *Gvozdika*
 TOWED 123: **122mm** 107: 72 D-30; 35 M-30 (M-1938); **152mm** 16 D-1
 GUN/MOR 120mm 12 2S9 NONA-S
 MRL 21: **122mm** 15 BM-21; **220mm** 6 9P140 *Uragan*
 MOR 120mm 54: 6 2S12; 48 M-120
AIR DEFENCE
 SAM • Point-defence 9K32 *Strela*-2 (RS-SA-7 *Grail*)‡; 9K35 *Strela*-10 (RS-SA-13 *Gopher*)
 GUNS 48
  SP 23mm 24 ZSU-23-4
  TOWED 57mm 24 S-60

Air Force 2,400
FORCES BY ROLE
FIGHTER
 1 regt with L-39 *Albatros**
TRANSPORT
 1 regt with An-2 *Colt*; An-26 *Curl*
ATTACK/TRANSPORT HELICOPTER
 1 regt with Mi-24 *Hind*; Mi-8/-8MT/-17V-5 *Hip*
AIR DEFENCE
 2 bty with S-125 *Neva*-M1 (RS-SA-3 *Goa*)
 1 bty with S-75M3 *Dvina* (RS-SA-2 *Guideline*)

EQUIPMENT BY TYPE
AIRCRAFT 4 combat capable
　TPT • **Light** 6: 4 An-2 *Colt*; 2 An-26 *Curl*
　TRG 4 L-39 *Albatros**
HELICOPTERS
　ATK 2 Mi-24 *Hind*
　MRH 6: 2 Mi-17V-5 *Hip* H; 4 Mi-8MT *Hip*
　TPT • **Medium** 8 Mi-8 *Hip*
AIR DEFENCE • SAM
　Medium-range 6 S-75M3 *Dvina* (RS-SA-2 *Guideline*)
　Short-range 8 S-125M1 *Neva*-M1 (RS-SA-3 *Goa*)

Gendarmerie & Paramilitary 9,500

Border Guards 5,000 (KGZ conscript, RUS officers)
FORCES BY ROLE
　ISR UAV 1 sqn with *Akinci*; *Aksungur*; *Bayraktar* TB2
EQUIPMENT BY TYPE
ARMOURED FIGHTING VEHICLES
　AUV 54 *Tigr*
UNINHABITED AERIAL VEHICLES
　CISR 6: **Heavy** 3: 2 *Akinci*; 1 *Aksungur*; **Medium** 3 *Bayraktar* TB2
BOMBS • **Laser-guided** MAM-L/T

Internal Troops 3,500

National Guard 1,000

DEPLOYMENT
SOUTH SUDAN: UN • UNMISS 2
SUDAN: UN • UNISFA 2

FOREIGN FORCES
Russia ε500 Military Air Forces: 13 Su-25SM *Frogfoot*; 2 Mi-8 *Hip*

Moldova MDA

Moldovan Leu MDL		2022	2023	2024
GDP	MDL	276bn	312bn	343bn
	USD	14.6bn	16.0bn	17.2bn
per capita	USD	5,726	6,411	7,002
Growth	%	-5.0	2.0	4.3
Inflation	%	28.6	13.3	5.0
Def bdgt	MDL	902m	1.70bn	
	USD	47.6m	87.0m	
USD1=MDL		18.94	19.50	20.00

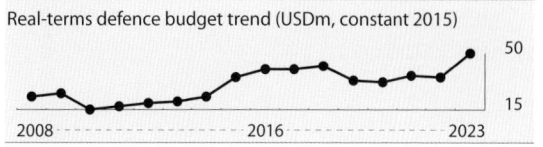

Real-terms defence budget trend (USDm, constant 2015)

Population　　3,620,399

Age	0–14	15–19	20–24	25–29	30–64	65 plus
Male	7.5%	2.9%	2.7%	3.2%	25.4%	5.5%
Female	7.5%	2.8%	2.7%	3.3%	27.5%	9.0%

Capabilities

The primary role of Moldova's armed forces is to maintain territorial integrity, though their size means they would be unable to offer more than very limited resistance to a determined adversary. The country is constitutionally neutral. Tensions with Russia over the breakaway region of Transnistria, which Moscow supports, worsened following Russia's February 2022 invasion of Ukraine. Russian 'peacekeeping' forces in Transnistria remain a source of concern for Moldova. The Moldovan government during 2023 continued to warn of Russian attempts to destabilise the country. A state of emergency was declared after Russia's 2022 invasion of Ukraine and was extended throughout 2023. Moldova is building relations with European states and NATO. The 2022 NATO Summit in Madrid agreed measures to support Moldova's 'national resilience and civil preparedness', with NATO defence ministers approving an Enhanced Defence Capacity Building package in February 2023. In late 2023, the EU said it was opening accession talks with Moldova. A Long-Term Military Capabilities Development Plan was approved in March 2020, covering the period to 2030. The country plans to improve land forces mobility, develop more capable ground-based air defences, and replace Soviet-era equipment. The services exercise regularly with NATO states. Moldova has no requirement or capability to independently deploy and support its forces overseas, though personnel were again deployed to the NATO-led KFOR mission to Kosovo in 2023. Moldova has no defence-industrial capabilities beyond the basic maintenance of front-line equipment. The country retains the goal of fielding a fully professional military, though as of 2023, conscription remained.

ACTIVE 5,150 (Army 3,250 Air 600 Logistic Support 1,300) **Gendarmerie & Paramilitary 900**

Conscript liability 12 months (3 months for university graduates)

RESERVE 58,000 (Joint 58,000)

ORGANISATIONS BY SERVICE

Army 1,300; 1,950 conscript (total 3,250)

FORCES BY ROLE
SPECIAL FORCES
1 SF bn
MANOEUVRE
Light
3 mot inf bde
1 lt inf bn
Other
1 gd bn
COMBAT SUPPORT
1 arty bn
1 engr bn
1 NBC coy
1 sigs bn

EQUIPMENT BY TYPE
ARMOURED FIGHTING VEHICLES
APC 158
APC (T) 61: 9 BTR-D; 52 MT-LB (variants)
APC (W) 97: 12 BTR-80; 5 *Piranha*-IIIH; 80 TAB-71
ABCV 44 BMD-1
ANTI-TANK/ANTI-INFRASTRUCTURE
MSL • MANPATS 9K111 *Fagot* (RS-AT-4 *Spigot*); 9K111-1 *Konkurs* (RS-AT-5 *Spandrel*)
RCL 73mm SPG-9
GUNS 100mm 31 MT-12
ARTILLERY 219
TOWED 67: 122mm 16 M-30 (M-1938); 152mm 51: 20 2A36 *Giatsint*-B; 31 D-20
GUN/MOR • SP 120mm 9 2S9 NONA-S
MRL 220mm 11 9P140 *Uragan*
MOR 132: 82mm 75 BM-37; 120mm 57: 50 M-1989; 7 PM-38
AIR DEFENCE • GUNS • TOWED 39: 23mm 28 ZU-23; 57mm 11 S-60

Air Force 600 (incl 250 conscripts)

FORCES BY ROLE
TRANSPORT
1 sqn with An-2 *Colt*; Mi-8MTV-1/PS *Hip*; Yak-18
AIR DEFENCE
1 regt with S-125M1 *Neva*-M1 (RS-SA-3 *Goa*)
EQUIPMENT BY TYPE
AIRCRAFT
TPT • Light 3: 2 An-2 *Colt*; 1 Yak-18 *Max*
HELICOPTERS
TPT • Medium 6: 2 Mi-8PS *Hip*; 4 Mi-8MTV-1 *Hip*
AIR DEFENCE • SAM • Short-range 3 S-125M1 *Neva*-M1 (RS-SA-3 *Goa*)

Gendarmerie & Paramilitary 900

Special Police Brigade 900
Ministry of Interior

DEPLOYMENT

CENTRAL AFRICAN REPUBLIC: UN • MINUSCA 4
KOSOVO: NATO • KFOR 41; UN • UNMIK 1
LEBANON: UN • UNIFIL 32
MALI: EU • EUTM Mali 1
SOUTH SUDAN: UN • UNMISS 5

TRANSNISTRIA

Data presented here represents the de facto situation in the territory of Transnistria and does not imply international recognition.

FOREIGN FORCES

Russia ε1,500 (including 400 peacekeepers); 7 Mi-24 *Hind*/Mi-8 *Hip*

Russia RUS

Russian Rouble RUB		2022	2023	2024
GDP	RUB	153trn	160trn	169trn
	USD	2.24trn	1.86trn	1.90trn
per capita	USD	15,646	13,006	13,324
Growth	%	-2.1	2.2	1.1
Inflation	%	13.8	5.3	6.3
Def exp [a]	RUB	ε6.65trn	ε9.3trn	ε12.8trn
	USD	ε97.2bn	ε108bn	ε143bn
Def bdgt	RUB	5.11trn	6.41trn	10.4trn
	USD	74.7bn	74.8bn	117bn
USD1=RUB		68.37	85.70	88.95

[a] Calculated to be comparable with NATO definition of defence expenditure

Real-terms defence budget trend (USDbn, constant 2015)
(chart: 2008 – 2016 – 2023; range 30.5 to 60.1)

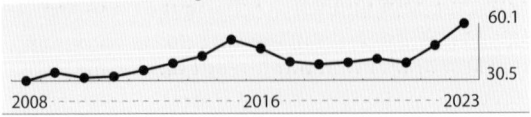

Population 141,505,279

Age	0–14	15–19	20–24	25–29	30–64	65 plus
Male	8.6%	2.8%	2.4%	2.5%	24.4%	5.8%
Female	8.2%	2.6%	2.3%	2.4%	26.6%	11.4%

Capabilities

Russia supports large conventional military forces and retains the world's second-largest nuclear arsenal. However, its ground forces have suffered extensive losses in personnel and equipment from its 2022 full-scale invasion of Ukraine. The attack exposed weaknesses in leadership, planning, personnel, and equipment, particularly within the ground and airborne forces, in the face of a committed opponent. A lack of airborne intelligence, surveillance and reconnaissance systems was evident in Moscow's poor performance. Western estimates of personnel losses vary widely, but as of late 2023, tens of thousands of Russian ground forces had been killed, yet more injured, and many ground units rendered combat ineffective at times. The ground forces have lost large numbers of its most modern main battle tanks and armoured fighting vehicles, while the conflict also exposed the relative vulnerability of airborne units and their armour when faced with an opponent well-equipped with heavier assets. The navy and air force have also suffered reverses, with Ukraine destroying or damaging several Black Sea Fleet vessels and inflicting losses of modern combat aircraft and helicopters. The Ukraine operation reflects the Russian military's role in increasing the country's sphere of influence in its periphery and abroad, in addition to guaranteeing sovereignty and territorial integrity. An updated National Security Policy was adopted in June 2021, extending beyond core military concerns to include countering the influence of the US and its allies. The 2021–2025 Defence Plan was also agreed, though it remains classified. The 2027 State Armament Programme (SAP) and the follow-on SAP 2033 have been affected by Russia's war and are having to be modified; the details remain unclear. Substantial recapitalisation of ground forces equipment will be required. Russia is the leading member of both the CSTO and the SCO. An updated CSTO security strategy was planned to cover 2026–2030, and work was due to begin in 2023, but the CSTO's status was somewhat in question. Prior to the February 2022 invasion of Ukraine, volunteers outweighed conscripts in the armed forces. Defence reforms launched in 2008 had emphasised the shift from a conscript-based mass-mobilisation army to smaller, more professional ground forces. However, the limits of Russia's professionalisation process have become evident in Ukraine. Setbacks and losses in Ukraine led President Vladimir Putin to introduce a partial mobilisation in September 2022. Russia's Wagner Group, an ostensibly private military company, was a pillar of the country's Ukraine fighting until its June 2023 rebellion. Its forces in Ukraine then relocated to Belarus, with their involvement diminished greatly. Prior to the invasion, the armed forces could independently deploy and sustain forces on a global scale, although likely only in modest size at extended distances. Ground force losses in Ukraine, however, further limit the size and the competency of the units Moscow is able to deploy. Russia continues to modernise its nuclear and conventional weapons. Russia can design, develop, and manufacture advanced nuclear and conventional weaponry. However, Western sanctions aimed at curtailing access to key components are forcing import substitution and likely hampering the production of some weapons.

ACTIVE 1,100,000 (Army 500,000 Navy 140,000 Air 165,000 Strategic Rocket Force 50,000 Airborne 35,000 Special Operations Forces 1,000 Railway Forces 29,000 Command and Support 180,000) Gendarmerie & Paramilitary 559,000

Conscript liability 12 months (conscripts now can opt for contract service immediately, which entails a 24-month contract)

RESERVE 1,500,000 (all arms)

Some 1,500,000 with service within last 5 years; reserve obligation to age 50

ORGANISATIONS BY SERVICE

Strategic Deterrent Forces ε80,000 (incl personnel assigned from the Navy and Aerospace Forces)

Navy
EQUIPMENT BY TYPE
SUBMARINES • STRATEGIC • SSBN 12:
  6 *Delfin* (Project 667BDRM (*Delta* IV)) with 16 R-29RMU2 *Sineva*/R-29RMU2.1 *Layner* (RS-SS-N-23 *Skiff*) nuclear SLBM, 4 single 533mm TT with 53-65K HWT/SET-65K HWT/USET-80K *Keramika* HWT
  3 *Borey* (Project 955 (*Dolgorukiy*)) with 16 *Bulava* (RS-SS-N-32) nuclear SLBM, 6 single 533mm TT with USET-80K *Keramika* HWT/UGST *Fizik* HWT
  3 *Borey*-A (Project 955A) with 16 *Bulava* (RS-SS-N-32) nuclear SLBM, 6 single 533mm TT with USET-80K *Keramika* HWT/UGST *Fizik* HWT

UNINHABITED MARITIME PLATFORMS • UUV
  ATK • Nuclear • Extra-Large *Poseidon* (*Status*-6) (nuclear powered) (in test)

Strategic Rocket Forces 50,000

3 Rocket Armies operating silo and mobile launchers organised in 12 divs. Regt normally with 6 to 10 silos or 9 mobile launchers, and one control centre

FORCES BY ROLE
SURFACE-TO-SURFACE MISSILE
  1 ICBM regt with RS-12M *Topol* (RS-SS-25 *Sickle*) (to convert to RS-24 *Yars* by 2024)
  8 ICBM regt with RS-12M2 *Topol*-M (RS-SS-27 mod 1)
  2 ICBM regt with RS-18 with Avangard HGV (RS-SS-19 mod 4 *Stiletto*)
  6 ICBM regt with RS-20 (RS-SS-18 *Satan*)
  14 ICBM regt with RS-24 *Yars* (RS-SS-27 mod 2)
  7 ICBM regt with *Yars*-S

EQUIPMENT BY TYPE
SURFACE-TO-SURFACE MISSILE LAUNCHERS
  ICBM • Nuclear 328: 9 RS-12M *Topol* (RS-SS-25 *Sickle*) (mobile single warhead) (to be withdrawn by 2024); 60 RS-12M2 *Topol*-M (RS-SS-27 mod 1) silo-based (single warhead); 18 RS-12M2 *Topol*-M (RS-SS-27 mod 1) road mobile (single warhead); ε8 RS-18 with *Avangard* HGV (RS-SS-19 mod 4 *Stiletto*); 40 RS-20 (RS-SS-18 *Satan*) (mostly mod 5, 10 MIRV per msl); ε99 RS-24 *Yars* (RS-SS-27 mod 2; ε3 MIRV per msl) road mobile; ε22 RS-24 *Yars* (RS-SS-27 mod 2; ε3 MIRV per msl) silo-based; ε72 *Yars*-S (ε3 MIRV per msl) road mobile

COUNTERSPACE • DE • Laser *Peresvet*

Long-Range Aviation Command
FORCES BY ROLE
BOMBER
  1 sqn with Tu-160/Tu-160 mod *Blackjack*
  3 sqn with Tu-95MS/MS mod *Bear*

EQUIPMENT BY TYPE
AIRCRAFT
  BBR 71: 6 Tu-160 *Blackjack* with Kh-55SM (RS-AS-15B

Kent) nuclear LACM; 7 Tu-160 mod *Blackjack* with Kh-55SM (RS-AS-15B *Kent*)/Kh-102 (RS-AS-23B *Kodiak*) nuclear LACM; 31 Tu-95MS *Bear* H with Kh-55SM (RS-AS-15B *Kent*) nuclear LACM; 27 Tu-95MS mod *Bear* H with Kh-55SM (RS-AS-15B *Kent*)/Kh-102 (RS-AS-23B *Kodiak*) nuclear LACM; (3 Tu-160M in test)

Space Command
EQUIPMENT BY TYPE
SATELLITES 93
  COMMUNICATIONS 32: 4 *Blagovest*; 1 *Garpun*; 3 *Globus*-M (*Raduga*-1M); 6 *Meridian*; 3 *Meridian*-M; 15 *Rodnik*-S (*Strela*-3M)
  POSITIONING, NAVIGATION & TIMING 26: 4 GLONASS-K1; 1 GLONASS-K2; 21 GLONASS-M
  ISR 13: 4 *Bars*-M; 1 EMKA; 2 GEO-IK-2; 1 *Kondor*-FKA; 1 *Neitron*; 2 *Persona*; 2 *Resurs*-P
  ELINT/SIGINT 8: 6 *Lotos*-S; 1 *Pion*-NKS; 1 *Tselina*-2
  EARLY WARNING 6 *Tundra* (EKS)
  RENDEZVOUS & PROXIMITY OPERATIONS 8: 6 *Nivelir*; 2 *Olymp*-K (*Luch*)
MISSILE DEFENCE some S-500 (entering service)
RADAR 12; Russia leases ground-based radar stations in Baranovichi (Belarus) and Balkhash (Kazakhstan). It also has radars on its own territory at Lekhtusi (St Petersburg); Armavir (Krasnodar); Olenegorsk (Murmansk); Mishelevka (Irkutsk); Kaliningrad; Pechora (Komi); Yeniseysk (Krasnoyarsk); Baranul (Altayskiy); Orsk (Orenburg); and Gorodets/Kovylkino (OTH)

Aerospace Defence Command
FORCES BY ROLE
AIR DEFENCE
2 AD div HQ
4 SAM regt with S-300PM1/PM2 (RS-SA-20 *Gargoyle*)
5 SAM regt with S-400 (RS-SA-21 *Growler*); 96K6 *Pantsir*-S1 (RS-SA-22 *Greyhound*)
EQUIPMENT BY TYPE
AIR DEFENCE
  SAM • Long-range 186: 90 S-300PM1/PM2 (RS-SA-20 *Gargoyle*); 96 S-400 (RS-SA-21 *Growler*)
  SPAAGM 30mm 36 96K6 *Pantsir*-S1 (RS-SA-22 *Greyhound*)
MISSILE DEFENCE 68 53T6 (RS-AB-4A *Gazelle*)
RADAR 1 BMD engagement system located at Sofrino (Moscow)

Army ε500,000 (incl ε100,000 conscripts)
FORCES BY ROLE
As a result of sustained heavy losses suffered during the invasion of Ukraine, almost all of the manoeuvre formations listed are currently understrength.
COMMAND
14 army HQ
4 corps HQ

SPECIAL FORCES
8 (Spetsnaz) SF bde
1 (Spetsnaz) SF regt
MANOEUVRE
  Reconnaissance
  2 recce bde
  Armoured
  1 (4th) tk div (1 armd recce bn, 2 tk regt, 1 MR regt, 1 arty regt, 1 AD regt)
  1 (47th) tk div (1 tk regt, 2 MR regt)
  1 (90th) tk div (1 armd recce bn, 2 tk regt, 1 MR regt, 1 arty regt)
  1 tk bde (1 armd recce bn, 3 tk bn, 1 MR bn, 1 arty bn, 1 MRL bn, 2 AD bn, 1 engr bn, 1 EW coy, 1 NBC coy)
  2 tk regt (mobilised)
  1 (3rd) MR corps (1 MR div, 1 MR bde, 1 SP arty bde, 1 fd arty regt, 1 AD bn)
  2 (3rd & 144th) MR div (1 armd recce bn, 1 tk regt, 2 MR regt, 1 arty regt)
  1 (19th) MR div (2 MR regt, 1 arty regt)
  1 (20th) MR div (2 MR regt, 1 arty regt)
  1 (67th MR div) (1 tk regt, 3 MR regt)
  1 (70th) MR div (1 tk regt, 2 MR regt, 1 arty regt)
  1 (127th) MR div (1 tk regt, 3 MR regt, 1 arty regt, 1 AD regt)
  1 (150th) MR div (1 armd recce bn, 2 tk regt, 2 MR regt; 1 arty regt, 1 AD regt)
  12 (BMP) MR bde (1 armd recce bn, 1 tk bn, 3 armd inf bn, 2 arty bn, 1 MRL bn, 1 AT bn, 2 AD bn, 1 engr bn, 1 EW coy, 1 NBC coy)
  Mechanised
  1 (2nd) MR div (1 armd recce bn, 1 tk regt, 2 MR regt, 1 arty regt, 1 AD regt)
  1 (42nd) MR div (1 armd recce bn, 4 MR regt, 1 arty regt)
  1 (47th) MR div (reported) (forming)
  8 (BTR/MT-LB) MR bde (1 recce bn, 1 tk bn, 3 mech inf bn, 2 arty bn, 1 MRL bn, 1 AT bn, 2 AD bn, 1 engr bn,1 EW coy, 1 NBC coy)
  2 MR bde (4–5 mech inf bn, 1 arty bn, 1 AD bn, 1 engr bn)
  10 MR bde (1st & 2nd Army Corps)
  14 MR regt (1st & 2nd Army Corps)
  3 (lt/mtn) MR bde (1 recce bn, 2 mech inf bn, 1 arty bn)
  1 (18th) MGA div (1 tk bn, 2 MGA regt, 1 arty regt, 2 AD bn)
  Light
  ε65 MR regt (mobilised)
SURFACE-TO-SURFACE MISSILE
12 SRBM/GLCM bde with 9K720 *Iskander*-M (RS-SS-26 *Stone*/RS-SSC-7 *Southpaw*) (3+ brigades also with 9M729 (RS-SSC-8 *Screwdriver*))
COMBAT SUPPORT
9 arty bde
1 hy arty bde
1 arty regt (mobilised)
1 arty bn (mobilised)
4 MRL bde

4 engr bde
7 engr regt
1 ptn br bde
5 EW bde
5 NBC bde
10 NBC regt

COMBAT SERVICE SUPPORT
11 log bde

AIR DEFENCE
16 AD bde

EQUIPMENT BY TYPE(ε)
Surface-to-surface missile systems may have very limited numbers of available missiles remaining.

ARMOURED FIGHTING VEHICLES
MBT 1,750: 30 T-55A; 200 T-62M/MV; 100 T-64A/BV; 300 T-72A/AV/B/BA; 650 T-72B3/B3M; 150 T-80BV/U; 100 T-80BVM; 100 T-90A; 120 T-90M; (up to 4,000 T-55A/T-62M/T-62MV/T-72/T-72A/T-72B/T-80B/T-80BV/T-80U/T-90/T-90A in store)
TSV ε8 BMPT
RECCE 200 BRM-1K (CP); (up to 100 BRDM-2/-2A in store)
IFV 4,050: 800 BMP-1/-1AM; 2,100 BMP-2/-2M; 350 BMP-3/-3M; 100 BTR-80A; 700 BTR-82A/AM; (2,800 BMP-1/-2 in store)
APC 4,700+
  APC (T) 2,500+: some BMO-T; 2,500 MT-LB/MT-LB VM1K; (1,000 MT-LB in store)
  APC (W) 2,200: 800 BTR-60 (all variants); 200 BTR-70 (all variants); 1,200 BTR-80; (1,300 BTR-60/-70 in store)
  PPV Typhoon-K 4×4; Typhoon-K 6×6
AUV IVECO LMV; *Linza*; *Tigr*; *Tigr*-M; *Tigr*-M SpN; *Vystrel*

ENGINEERING & MAINTENANCE VEHICLES
AEV BAT-2; IMR; IMR-2; IMR-3; IRM; MT-LB
ARV BMP-1; BREM-1/64/K/L; BTR-50PK(B); M1977; MTP-LB; RM-G; T-54/55; VT-72A
VLB KMM; MT-55A; MTU; MTU-20; MTU-72; PMM-2
MW BMR-3M; GMX-3; MCV-2 (reported); MTK; MTK-2; UR-77

NTI-TANK/ANTI-INFRASTRUCTURE
  MSL
    SP 9P149 with 9K114 *Shturm* (RS-AT-6 *Spiral*); 9P149M with 9K132 *Shturm*-SM (RS-AT-9 *Spiral*-2); 9P157-2 with 9K123 *Khrizantema* (RS-AT-15 *Springer*); 9P163-3 with 9M133 *Kornet* (RS-AT-14 *Spriggan*); 9K128-1 *Kornet*-T (RS-AT-14 *Spriggan*)
    MANPATS 9K111M *Fagot* (RS-AT-4 *Spigot*); 9K111-1 *Konkurs* (RS-AT-5 *Spandrel*); 9K115 *Metis* (RS-AT-7 *Saxhorn*); 9K115-1 *Metis*-M (RS-AT-13); 9K115-2 *Metis*-M1 (RS-AT-13); 9K135 *Kornet* (RS-AT-14 *Spriggan*)
  RCL 73mm SPG-9
  GUNS • TOWED 100mm 500 MT-12 (**100mm** 800 T-12/MT-12 in store)

ARTILLERY 4,397
  SP 1,583: **122mm** 130 2S1 *Gvozdika*; **152mm** 1,328+: 600 2S3/2S3M *Akatsiya*; 120 2S5 *Giatsint*-S; 300 2S19/2S19M1 *Msta*-S; 300 2S19M2/2S33 *Msta*-SM; 8 2S35 *Koalitsiya*-SV (in test); some 2S43 *Malva*; **203mm** 125: 50 2S7M *Malka*; 75 2S7 *Pion*; (3,610 in store: **122mm** 1,800 2S1 *Gvozdika*; **152mm** 1,650: 750 2S3 *Akatsiya*; 750 2S5 *Giatsint*-S; 150 2S19 *Msta*-S; **203mm** 160 2S7 *Pion*)
  TOWED 220: **152mm** 220: 20+ D-1 (M-1943); 100 D-20; 100 2A65 *Msta*-B (6,890 in store: **122mm** 4,400: 2,400 D-30; 2,000 M-30 (M-1938); **130mm** 350 M-46; **152mm** 2,100: 550 2A36 *Giatsint*-B; 250 2A65 *Msta*-B; 500 D-1 (M-1943); 700 D-20; 100 M-1937 (ML-20); **203mm** 40 B-4M)
  GUN/MOR 139
    SP 120mm 64+: 24 2S23 NONA-SVK; 40 2S34; some 2S40 *Phlox*
    TOWED 120mm 75 2B16 NONA-K
  MRL 941: **122mm** 560: 400 BM-21 *Grad*; 160 9K51M *Tornado*-G; **220mm** 261+: 200 9P140 *Uragan*; 6 9K512 *Uragan*-1M; 55 TOS-1A; **300mm** 120: 100 9A52 *Smerch*; 20 9K515 *Tornado*-S; (2,350 in store: **122mm** 1,700: 1,500 BM-21 *Grad*; 200 9P138; **132mm** 100 BM-13; **220mm** 550 9P140 *Uragan*)
  MOR 1,514: **82mm** 800+ 2B14; **120mm** 675 2S12 *Sani*; **240mm** 39 2S4 *Tulpan* (1,260 in store: **120mm** 950: 500 2S12 *Sani*; 450 M-1938 (PM-38); **160mm** 150 M-160; **SP 240mm** 160 2S4 *Tulpan*)

SURFACE-TO-SURFACE MISSILE LAUNCHERS
  SRBM • Dual-capable 200: 50 9K79-1 *Tochka*-U (RS-SS-21B *Scarab*); 150 9K720 *Iskander*-M (RS-SS-26 *Stone*)
  GLCM • Dual-capable Some 9M728 (RS-SSC-7 *Southpaw*); some 9M729 (RS-SSC-8 *Screwdriver*)

UNINHABITED AERIAL VEHICLES
  ISR • Light BLA-07; *Granat*-4; *Orlan*-30;

LOITERING & DIRECT ATTACK MUNITIONS
Geran 1 (*Shahed* 131); *Geran* 2 (*Shahed* 136); KUB-BLA; *Lancet*-1; *Lancet*-3; (multiple systems below 20kg in weight)

AIR DEFENCE
  SAM 1,520+
    Long-range S-300V (RS-SA-12A/B *Gladiator/Giant*); S-300V4 (RS-SA-23)
    Medium-range 350: ε200 9K37M1-2 *Buk*-M1-2 (RS-SA-11 *Gadfly*); ε90 9K317 *Buk*-M2 (RS-SA-17 *Grizzly*); ε60 9K317M *Buk*-M3 (RS-SA-27)
    Short-range 120+ 9K331/9K331M/9K331MU *Tor*-M1/M2/M2U (RS-SA-15 *Gauntlet*) (9M338 msl entering service)
    Point-defence 780+: 390 9K33M3 *Osa*-AKM (RS-SA-8B *Gecko*); 390 9K35M3 *Strela*-10 (RS-SA-13 *Gopher*); 9K310 *Igla*-1 (RS-SA-16 *Gimlet*); 9K34 *Strela*-3 (RS-SA-14 *Gremlin*); 9K38 *Igla* (RS-SA-18 *Grouse*); 9K333 *Verba* (RS-SA-29 *Gizmo*); 9K338 *Igla*-S (RS-SA-24 *Grinch*)

SPAAGM 30mm 240+ 2K22M *Tunguska* (RS-SA-19 *Grison*)
GUNS
SP 23mm ZSU-23-4
TOWED 23mm ZU-23-2; **57mm** S-60

Navy ε140,000 (incl conscripts)

4 major fleet organisations (Northern Fleet, Pacific Fleet, Baltic Fleet, Black Sea Fleet) and Caspian Sea Flotilla

EQUIPMENT BY TYPE
SUBMARINES 50
  STRATEGIC • SSBN 12:
    6 *Delfin* (Project 667BDRM (*Delta* IV)) with 16 R-29RMU2 *Sineva*/R-29RMU2.1 *Layner* (RS-SS-N-23 *Skiff*) nuclear SLBM, 4 single 533mm TT with 53-65K HWT/SET-65K HWT/USET-80K *Keramika* HWT
    3 *Borey* (Project 955 (*Dolgorukiy*)) with 16 *Bulava* (RS-SS-N-32) nuclear SLBM, 6 single 533mm TT with USET-80K *Keramika* HWT/UGST *Fizik* HWT
    3 *Borey*-A (Project 955A) with 16 *Bulava* (RS-SS-N-32) nuclear SLBM, 6 single 533mm TT with USET-80K *Keramika* HWT/UGST *Fizik* HWT
  TACTICAL 38
    SSGN 9:
      6 *Antey* (Project 949A (*Oscar* II)) (1 more non-operational, in long-term refit) with 24 single SM-225A lnchr with 3M45 *Granit* (RS-SS-N-19 *Shipwreck*) dual-capable AShM, 2 single 650mm TT each with T-65 HWT/RPK-7 (RS-SS-N-16 *Stallion*) ASW msl, 4 single 553mm TT with 53-65K HWT/SET-65K HWT/USET-80K *Keramika* HWT
      1 *Yasen* (Project 885 (*Severodvinsk* I)) with 8 4-cell SM-346 VLS with 3M14K (RS-SS-N-30A *Sagaris*) dual-capable LACM/3M54K1 (RS-SS-N-27) AShM/3M54K (RS-SS-N-27B *Sizzler*) AShM/3M55 *Oniks* (RS-SS-N-26 *Strobile*) AShM (3M54K/K1 operational status unclear); 10 single 533mm TT with USET-80K *Keramika* HWT/UGST *Fizik* HWT
      2 *Yasen*-M (Project 08851 (*Severodvinsk* II)) with 8 4-cell SM-346 VLS with 3M14K (RS-SS-N-30A *Sagaris*) dual-capable LACM/3M54K1 (RS-SS-N-27) AShM/3M54K (RS-SS-N-27B *Sizzler*) AShM/3M55 *Oniks* (RS-SS-N-26 *Strobile*) AShM (3M54K/K1 operational status unclear); up to 10 single 533mm TT with UGST *Fizik* HWT
    SSN 10:
      1 *Kalmar* (Project 667BDR (*Delta* III)) with 2 single 400mm TT with SET-72 LWT, 4 single 533mm TT with 53-65K HWT/SET-65K HWT/USET-80K *Keramika* HWT (re-roled SSBN)
      2 *Kondor* (Project 945A (*Sierra* II)) with 4 single 533mm TT with TEST-71M HWT/USET-80K *Keramika* HWT (unclear if dual-capable 3M14 (RS-SS-N-30A *Sagaris*) has replaced 3M10 *Granat* (RS-SS-N-21 *Sampson*) nuclear LACM which is possibly withdrawn; AShM capability unconfirmed), 4 single 650mm TT with 65-73 HWT
      2 *Schuka* (Project 671RTMK (*Victor* III)) with 4 single 533mm TT with 53-65K HWT/SET-65K HWT/USET-80K *Keramika* HWT (unclear if dual-capable 3M14 (RS-SS-N-30A *Sagaris*) has replaced 3M10 *Granat* (RS-SS-N-21 *Sampson*) nuclear LACM which is possibly withdrawn; AShM capability unconfirmed), 2 single 650mm TT with 65-73 HWT
      3 *Schuka*-B (Project 971 (*Akula* I)) (5 more non-operational, return to service significantly delayed) with 4 single 533mm TT with 53-65K HWT/TEST-71M HWT/USET-80K *Keramika* HWT (unclear if dual-capable 3M14 (RS-SS-N-30A *Sagaris*) has replaced 3M10 *Granat* (RS-SS-N-21 *Sampson*) nuclear LACM which is possibly withdrawn; AShM capability unconfirmed), 4 single 650mm TT with 65-73 HWT/RPK-7 (RS-SS-N-16 *Stallion*) ASW msl
      2 *Schuka*-B (Project 971/09711 (*Akula* II)) with 4 single 533mm TT with 53-65K HWT/TEST-71M HWT/USET-80K *Keramika* HWT (unclear if dual-capable 3M14 (RS-SS-N-30A *Sagaris*) has replaced 3M10 *Granat* (RS-SS-N-21 *Sampson*) nuclear LACM which is possibly withdrawn; AShM capability unconfirmed), 4 single 650mm TT with 65-73 HWT/RPK-7 (RS-SS-N-16 *Stallion*) ASW msl
    SSK 19:
      9 *Paltus* (Project 877 (*Kilo*)) (1 more non-operational, in long-term refit) with 6 single 533mm TT with 53-65K HWT/TEST-71M HWT/USET-80K *Keramika* HWT
      10 *Varshavyanka* (Project 06363 (*Improved Kilo*)) (1 more non-operational) with 6 single 533mm TT with 3M14K *Kalibr*-PL (RS-SS-N-30A *Sagaris*) dual-capable LACM/3M54K (RS-SS-N-27B *Sizzler*) AShM/3M54K1 (RS-SS-N-27) AShM/53-65K HWT/TEST-71M HWT/USET-80K *Keramika* HWT (3M54K/K1 operational status unclear)
      (1 *Lada* (Project 677 (*Petersburg*)) with 6 single 533mm TT with 3M14K *Kalibr*-PL (RS-SS-N-30A *Sagaris*) dual-capable LACM/3M54K (RS-SS-N-27B *Sizzler*) AShM/3M54K1 (RS-SS-N-27) AShM/USET-80K *Keramika* HWT (3M54K/K1 operational status unclear) non-operational)
PRINCIPAL SURFACE COMBATANTS 33
  AIRCRAFT CARRIERS • CV 1 *Admiral Kuznetsov* (in extended refit) with 12 single SM-233A lnchr with 3M45 *Granit* (RS-SS-N-19 *Shipwreck*) AShM, 24 8-cell 3S95 VLS with 3K95 *Kinzhal* (RS-SA-N-9 *Gauntlet*) SAM, 2 RBU 12000 *Udav* 1 A/S mor, 8 3M87 *Kortik* CIWS with 9M311 SAM (RS-CADS-N-1), 6 AK630M CIWS (capacity 18–24 Su-33 *Flanker* D/MiG-29KR/KUBR Ftr/FGA ac; 15 Ka-27 *Helix* ASW hel, 2 Ka-31R *Helix* AEW hel)
  CRUISERS 3:
    CGHMN 1 *Orlan* (Project 11442 (*Kirov* I)) (1 other non-operational; undergoing extensive refit and planned to return to service in 2024) with 20 single SM-233 lnchr with 3M45 *Granit* (RS-SS-N-19 *Shipwreck*) AShM, 6 8-cell B-203A VLS with S-300F

Fort (RS-SA-N-6 *Grumble*) SAM, 6 8-cell B-203A VLS with S-300FM *Fort*-M (RS-SA-N-20 *Gargoyle*) SAM, 16 8-cell 3S95 VLS with 3K95 *Kinzhal* (RS-SA-N-9 *Gauntlet*) SAM, 2 quintuple 533mm TT with RPK-6M *Vodopad*-NK (RS-SS-N-16 *Stallion*) A/S msl, 1 RBU 6000 *Smerch* 2 A/S mor, 2 RBU 1000 *Smerch* 3 A/S mor, 6 3M87 *Kortik* CIWS with 9M311 SAM (RS-CADS-N-1), 1 twin 130mm gun (capacity 3 Ka-27 *Helix* ASW hel)

CGHM 2 *Atlant* (Project 1164 (*Slava*)) with 8 twin SM-248 lnchr with 3M70 *Vulkan* (RS-SS-N-12 mod 2 *Sandbox*) AShM, 8 octuple VLS with S-300F *Fort* (RS-SA-N-6 *Grumble*) SAM/S-300FM *Fort* M (RS-SA-N-20 *Gargoyle*) SAM, 2 twin ZIF-122 lnchr with 4K33 *Osa*-M (RS-SA-N-4 *Gecko*) SAM, 2 quintuple 533mm PTA-53-1164 ASTT with SET-65K HWT, 2 RBU 6000 *Smerch* 2 A/S mor, 6 AK630 CIWS, 1 twin 130mm gun (capacity 1 Ka-27 *Helix* ASW hel)

DESTROYERS • DDGHM 11:

3 *Sarych* (Project 956 (*Sovremenny* I)) with 2 quad lnchr with 3M80 *Moskit* (RS-SS-N-22 *Sunburn*) AShM, 2 twin 3S90 lnchr with 9M317 *Yezh* (RS-SA-N-7B) SAM, 2 twin DTA-53-956 533mm TT with 53-65K HWT/SET-65K HWT, 2 RBU 1000 *Smerch* 3 A/S mor, 4 AK630 CIWS, 2 twin 130mm guns (capacity 1 Ka-27 *Helix* ASW hel)

6 *Fregat* (Project 1155 (*Udaloy* I)) with 2 quad lnchr with URK-5 *Rastrub*-B (RS-SS-N-14 *Silex*) AShM/ASW, 8 8-cell 3S95 VLS with 3K95 *Kinzhal* (RS-SA-N-9 *Gauntlet*) SAM, 2 quad 533mm ChTA-53-1155 ASTT with 53-65K HWT/SET-65K HWT, 2 RBU 6000 *Smerch* 2 A/S mor, 4 AK630 CIWS, 2 100mm guns (capacity 2 Ka-27 *Helix* ASW hel)

1 *Fregat* (Project 1155 (*Udaloy* I)) with 2 8-cell 3S14 UKSK VLS with with 3M14T *Kalibr*-NK (RS-SS-N-30A *Sagaris*) dual-capable LACM/3M54T (RS-SS-N-27B *Sizzler*) AShM/3M54T1 (RS-SS-N-27) AShM/3M55 *Oniks* (RS-SS-N-26 *Strobile*) AShM (3M54T/T1 operational status unclear), 2 quad lnchr with 3M24 *Uran* (RS-SS-N-25 *Switchblade*) AShM, 2 quad 533mm ChTA-53-1155 ASTT with 53-65K HWT/SET-65K HWT, 2 RBU 6000 *Smerch* 2 A/S mor, 4 AK630 CIWS, 1 100mm gun (capacity 2 Ka-27 *Helix* ASW hel)

1 *Fregat* (Project 11551 (*Udaloy* II)) (in refit) with 2 quad lnchr with 3M80 *Moskit* (RS-SS-N-22 *Sunburn*) AShM, 8 8-cell 3S95 VLS with 3K95 *Kinzhal* (RS-SA-N-9 *Gauntlet*) SAM, 2 3M87 *Kortik* CIWS with 9M311 SAM (RS-CADS-N-1), 2 RBU 6000 *Smerch* 2 A/S mor, 1 twin 130mm gun (capacity 2 Ka-27 *Helix* ASW hel)

FRIGATES 18

FFGHM 16:

3 Project 11356 (*Grigorovich*) with 1 8-cell 3S14 UKSK VLS with 3M14T *Kalibr*-NK (RS-SS-N-30A *Sagaris*) dual-capable LACM/3M54T (RS-SS-N-27B *Sizzler*) AShM/3M54T1 (RS-SS-N-27) AShM/3M55 *Oniks* (RS-SS-N-26 *Strobile*) AShM/91RT2 A/S msl (3M54T/T1 operational status unclear), 2 12-cell 3S90.1 VLS with 9M317 *Yezh* (RS-SA-N-7B) SAM/9M317M *Yezh* (RS-SA-N-7C) SAM, 2 twin DTA-53-11356 533mm TT with 53-65K HWT/SET-65K HWT, 1 RBU 6000 A/S mor, 2 AK630 CIWS, 1 100mm gun (capacity 1 Ka-27 *Helix* ASW hel)

2 *Jastreb* (Project 11540 (*Neustrashimyy*)) with 2 quad lnchr with 3M24 *Uran* (RS-SS-N-25 *Switchblade*) AShM, 4 8-cell 3S95 VLS with 3K95 *Kinzhal* (RS-SA-N-9 *Gauntlet*), 6 single 533mm ASTT with RPK-6M *Vodopad*-NK (RS-SS-N-16 *Stallion*) A/S msl, 1 RBU 6000 *Smerch* 2 A/S mor, 2 3M87 *Kortik* CIWS with 9M311 SAM (RS-CADS-N-1), 1 100mm gun (capacity 1 Ka-27 *Helix* ASW hel)

1 Project 20380 (*Steregushchiy* I) with 2 quad lnchr with 3M24 *Uran* (RS-SS-N-25 *Switchblade*) AShM, 2 quad 324mm SM-588 ASTT with MTT LWT, 1 3M87 *Kortik*-M CIWS with 9M311 SAM (RS-CADS-N-1), 2 AK630 CIWS, 1 100mm gun (capacity 1 Ka-27 *Helix* ASW hel)

7 Project 20380 (*Steregushchiy* II) with 2 quad lnchr with 3M24 *Uran* (RS-SS-N-25 *Switchblade*) AShM, 3 4-cell 3S97 VLS with 3K96-3 *Redut* (RS-SA-N-28) SAM, 2 quad 324mm SM-588 ASTT with MTT LWT, 2 AK630 CIWS, 1 100mm gun (capacity 1 Ka-27 *Helix* ASW hel)

1 Project 20385 (*Gremyashchiy*) with 1 8-cell 3S14 UKSK VLS with 3M14T *Kalibr*-NK (RS-SS-N-30A *Sagaris*) dual-capable LACM/3M54T (RS-SS-N-27B *Sizzler*) AShM/3M54T1 (RS-SS-N-27) AShM/3M55 *Oniks* (RS-SS-N-26 *Strobile*) AShM (3M54T/T1 operational status unclear), 4 4-cell 3S97 VLS with 3K96-2 *Poliment-Redut* (RS-SA-N-28) SAM, 2 quad 324mm TT with MTT LWT, 2 AK630 CIWS, 1 100mm gun (capacity 1 Ka-27 *Helix* ASW hel)

2 Project 22350 (*Gorshkov*) with 2 8-cell 3S14 UKSK VLS with 3M14T *Kalibr*-NK (RS-SS-N-30A *Sagaris*) dual-capable LACM/3M54T (RS-SS-N-27B *Sizzler*) AShM/3M54T1 (RS-SS-N-27) AShM/3M55 *Oniks* (RS-SS-N-26 *Strobile*) AShM (3M54T/T1 operational status unclear), 4 8-cell 3S97 VLS with 3K96-2 *Poliment-Redut* (RS-SA-N-28) SAM, 2 quad 324mm TT with MTT LWT, 2 3M89 *Palash* CIWS (RS-CADS-N-2), 1 130mm gun (capacity 1 Ka-27 *Helix* ASW hel)

FFGM 2:

1 *Burevestnik* (Project 1135 (*Krivak* I))† with 1 quad lnchr with URK-5 *Rastrub*-B (RS-SS-N-14 *Silex*) AShM/ASW, 1 twin ZIF-122 lnchr with *Osa*-M (RS-SA-N-4 *Gecko*) SAM, 2 quad 533mm ChTA-53-1135 ASTT with 53-65K HWT/SET-65K HWT, 2 RBU 6000 *Smerch* 2 A/S mor, 2 twin 76mm guns

1 *Burevestnik* M (Project 1135M (*Krivak* II)) with 1 quad lnchr with URK-5 *Rastrub*-B (RS-SS-N-14 *Silex*) AShM/ASW, 2 twin ZIF-122 lnchr with 4K33 *Osa*-M (RS-SA-N-4 *Gecko* SAM), 2 quad 533mm ChTA-53-1135 ASTT with 53-65K HWT/SET-65K HWT, 2 RBU 6000 *Smerch* 2 A/S mor, 2 100mm guns

PATROL AND COASTAL COMBATANTS 124

CORVETTES 44
  FSGM 16
   10 *Buyan*-M (Project 21631 (*Sviyazhsk*)) with 1 8-cell 3S14 UKSK VLS with 3M14T *Kalibr*-NK (RS-SS-N-30A *Sagaris*) dual-capable LACM/3M54T (RS-SS-N-27B *Sizzler*) AShM/3M54T1 (RS-SS-N-27) AShM/3M55 *Oniks* (RS-SS-N-26 *Strobile*) AShM (3M54T/T1 operational status unclear), 2 sextuple 3M47 *Gibka* lnchr with Igla-1M (RS-SA-N-10 *Grouse*) SAM, 1 AK630M-2 CIWS, 1 100mm gun
   2 *Karakurt* (Project 22800 (*Uragan*)) with 1 8-cell 3S14 UKSK VLS with 3M14T *Kalibr*-NK (RS-SS-N-30A *Sagaris*) dual-capable LACM/3M54T (RS-SS-N-27B *Sizzler*) AShM/3M54T1 (RS-SS-N-27) AShM/3M55 *Oniks* (RS-SS-N-26 *Strobile*) AShM (3M54T/T1 operational status unclear), 2 *Pantsir*-M with 57E6 SAM, 1 76mm gun
   1 Project 11661K (*Gepard* I) with 2 quad lnchr with 3M24 *Uran* (RS-SS-N-25 *Switchblade*) AShM, 1 twin ZIF-122 lnchr with 4K33 *Osa*-M (RS-SA-N-4 *Gecko*) SAM, 2 AK630 CIWS, 1 76mm gun
   1 Project 11661K (*Gepard* II) with 1 8-cell VLS with 3M14T *Kalibr*-NK (RS-SS-N-30A *Sagaris*) dual-capable LACM/3M54T (RS-SS-N-27B *Sizzler*) AShM/3M54T1 (RS-SS-N-27) AShM/3M55 *Oniks* (RS-SS-N-26 *Strobile*) AShM (3M54T/T1 operational status unclear), 1 3M89 *Palash* CIWS with 9M337 *Sosna*-R SAM (RS-CADS-N-2), 1 76mm gun
   2 *Sivuch* (Project 1239 (*Dergach*)) with 2 quad lnchr with 3M80 *Moskit* (RS-SS-N-22 *Sunburn*) AShM, 1 twin ZIF-122 lnchr with 4K33AM *Osa*-MA2 (RS-SA-N-4 *Gecko*) SAM, 2 AK630M CIWS, 1 76mm gun
  FSG 2 *Karakurt* (Project 22800 (*Uragan*)) with 1 8-cell 3S14 VLS with 3M14T *Kalibr*-NK (RS-SS-N-30A *Sagaris*) dual-capable LACM/3M54T (RS-SS-N-27B *Sizzler*) AShM/3M54T1 (RS-SS-N-27) AShM/3M55 *Oniks* (RS-SS-N-26 *Strobile*) AShM (3M54T/T1 operational status unclear), 2 AK630M CIWS, 1 76mm gun
  FSM 26:
   2 *Albatros* (Project 1124 (*Grisha* III)) with 1 twin ZIF-122 lnchr with 4K33 *Osa*-M (RS-SA-N-4 *Gecko*) SAM, 2 twin 533mm DTA-53-1124 ASTT, 2 RBU 6000 *Smerch* 2 A/S mor, 1 twin 57mm gun
   18 *Albatros* (Project 1124M (*Grisha* V)) with 1 twin ZIF-122 lnchr with 4K33 *Osa*-M (RS-SA-N-4 *Gecko*) SAM, 2 twin 533mm DTA-53-1124 ASTT, 1 RBU 6000 *Smerch* 2 A/S mor, 1 AK630 CIWS, 1 76mm gun
   6 Project 1331M (*Parchim* II) with 2 quad lnchr with 9K32 *Strela*-2 (RS-SA-N-5 *Grail*) SAM, 2 twin 533mm ASTT, 2 RBU 6000 *Smerch* 2 A/S mor, 1 AK630 CIWS, 1 76mm gun
  PSOH 4 Project 22160 (*Bykov*) with 1 76mm gun (capacity 1 Ka-27 *Helix* ASW hel)
  PCGM 7:
   6 *Ovod*-1 (Project 1234.1 (*Nanuchka* III)) (1 more in reserve) with 2 triple lnchr with P-120 *Malakhit* (RS-SS-N-9 *Siren*) AShM, 1 twin ZIF-122 lnchr with 4K33 *Osa*-M (RS-SA-N-4 *Gecko*) SAM, 1 AK630 CIWS, 1 76mm gun
   1 *Ovod*-1 (Project 1234.1 (*Nanuchka* III)) with 4 quad lnchr with 3M24 *Uran* (RS-SS-N-25 *Switchblade*) AShM, 1 twin lnchr with 4K33 *Osa*-M (RS-SA-N-4 *Gecko*) SAM, 1 AK630 CIWS, 1 76mm gun
  PCFG 20:
   4 *Molnya* (*Tarantul* II) with 2 twin lnchr with P-22 *Termit*-R (RS-SS-N-2D *Styx*) AShM, 2 AK630M CIWS, 1 76mm gun
   15 *Molnya* (*Tarantul* III) with 2 twin lnchr with 3M80 *Moskit* (RS-SS-N-22 *Sunburn*) AShM, 2 AK630M CIWS, 1 76mm gun
   1 *Molnya* (*Tarantul* III) with 2 twin lnchr with 3M80 *Moskit* (RS-SS-N-22 *Sunburn*) AShM, 1 3K89 *Palash* (RS-CADS-N-2) CIWS, 1 76mm gun
  PCM 3 *Buyan* (Project 21630 (*Astrakhan*)) with 1 sextuple lnchr with 3M47 *Gibka* lnchr with Igla-1M (RS-SA-N-10 *Grouse*) SAM, 1 A-215 *Grad*-M 122mm MRL, 1 100mm gun
  PCF 1 *Molnya* (*Tarantul* III) with 2 AK630M CIWS, 1 76mm gun
  PBF 14: 12+ *Raptor* (capacity 20 troops); 2 *Mangust*
  PBR 4 *Shmel* with 1 17-cell BM-14 MRL, 1 76mm gun
  PB 27 *Grachonok*

MINE WARFARE • MINE COUNTERMEASURES 43
  MCC 7 *Alexandrit* (Project 12700)
  MHI 7 *Sapfir* (Project 10750 (*Lida*)) with 1 AK630 CIWS
  MHO 2 *Rubin* (Project 12660 (*Gorya*)) with 2 quad lnchr with 9K32 *Strela*-2 (RS-SA-N-5 *Grail*) SAM, 1 AK630 CIWS, 1 76mm gun
  MSC 20: 19 *Yakhont* (Project 1265 (*Sonya*)) with 4 AK630 CIWS (some with 2 quad lnchr with 9K32 *Strela*-2 (RS-SA-N-5 *Grail*) SAM); 1 *Korund*-E (Project 1258E (*Yevgenya*))
  MSO 7: 6 *Akvamaren*-M (Project 266M (*Natya*)); 1 *Agat* (Project 02668 (*Natya* II)) (all with 2 quad lnchr (manual aiming) with 9K32 *Strela*-2 (RS-SA-N-5 *Grail*) SAM, 2 RBU 1200 *Uragan* A/S mor, 2 twin AK230 CIWS

AMPHIBIOUS
  LANDING SHIPS • LST 19:
   11 Project 775 (*Ropucha* I/II) (1 more non-operational) with 2 twin 57mm guns (capacity either 10 MBT and 190 troops or 24 APC (T) and 170 troops)
   3 Project 775M (*Ropucha* III) with 2 AK630 CIWS, 1 76mm gun (capacity either 10 MBT and 190 troops or 24 APC (T) and 170 troops)
   3 *Tapir* (Project 1171 (*Alligator*)) with at least 2 twin lnchr with 9K32 *Strela*-2 (RS-SA-N-5 *Grail*) SAM, 2 twin 57mm guns (capacity 20 tanks; 300 troops)
   2 Project 11711 (*Gren*) with 1 AK630M-2 CIWS, 2 AK630M CIWS (capacity 1 Ka-29 *Helix* B hel; 13 MBT/36 AFV; 300 troops)
  LANDING CRAFT 26
   LCM 24: 8 *Akula* (Project 1176 (*Ondatra*)) (capacity 1 MBT); 5 *Dyugon* (Project 21820) (capacity 5 APC or

100 troops); 11 *Serna* (Project 11770) (capacity 2 APC or 100 troops)

LCAC 2 *Zubr* (Project 12322 (*Pomornik*)) with 2 22-cell 140mm MS-227 *Ogon* MRL, 2 AK630 CIWS (capacity 230 troops; either 3 MBT or 10 APC(T))

LOGISTICS AND SUPPORT 284

SSAN 9:
  1 *Belgorod* (Project 22870 (*Oscar* II mod))
  2 *Halibut* (Project 18511 (*Paltus*))
  3 *Kashalot* (Project 1910 (*Uniform*))
  1 *Nelma* (Project 1851 (*X-Ray*))
  1 *Orenburg* (*Delta* III Stretch)
  1 *Podmoskovye* (Project 09787)
  (1 non-operational *Losharik* (Project 10831 (*Norsub*-5)) reportedly damaged by fire in 2019)

SSA 1 *Sarov* (Project 20120)

ABU 12: 8 *Kashtan*; 4 Project 419 (*Sura*)

AE 9: 6 *Muna*; 1 *Dubnyak*; 2 *Akademik Kovalev* (Project 20181) with 1 hel landing platform

AEM 2: 1 *Kalma-3* (Project 1791R); 1 *Lama*

AFS 2 *Longvinik* (Project 23120)

AGB 6: 1 *Dobrynya Mikitich*; 1 *Ilya Muromets*; 1 *Ilya Muromets* (Project 21180); 2 *Ivan Susanin*; 1 *Vladimir Kavraisky*

AGE 2: 1 *Potok*; 1 *Tchusovoy*

AGI 14: 2 *Alpinist*; 2 *Dubridium* (Project 1826); 1 *Moma*; 7 *Vishnya*; 2 *Yuri Ivanov*

AGM 1 *Marshal Nedelin*

AGOR 6: 1 *Akademik Alexandrov* (Project 20183); 1 *Akademik Krylov*; 2 *Seliger*; 2 *Vinograd*

AGOS 1 *Yantar*

AGS 77: 7 *Baklan* (Project 19920); 5 *Baklan* (Project 19920B); 8 *Biya*; 16+ *Finik*; 7 *Kamenka*; 5 *Moma*; 8+ *Onega*; 6 Project 23040G; 2 *Sibiriyakov*; 4 *Vaygach*; 9+ *Yug*

AGSH 1 *Samara*

AH 3 *Ob†*

AK 1 *Pevek*

AKL 2 *Irgiz*

AO 9: 3+ *Altay* (mod); 2+ *Dubna*; 3 *Uda*; 1 *Platforma-Arktika* (Project 03182) with 1 hel landing plaftorm

AOL 1 *Luza*

AOR 6: 1 *Akademik Pashin* (Project 23130); 3 *Boris Chilikin*; 1+ *Kaliningradneft*; 1 *Olekma*

AR ε7 *Amur*

ARC 5: 4 *Emba*; 1 Improved *Klasma*

ARS 38: 1 *Kommuna*; 5 *Goryn*; 4 *Mikhail Rudnitsky*; 5 Project 22870; 22 Project 23040; 1 *Zvezdochka* (Project 20180)

AS 3 Project 2020 (*Malina*)

ASR 2: 1 *Elbrus*; 1 *Igor Belousov*

ATF 54: 1 *Okhotsk*; 1 *Baklan*; ε3 *Katun*; 3 *Ingul*; 1 *Neftegaz*; 10 *Okhtensky*; 13 *Prometey*; 3 Project 23470 with 1 hel landing platform; 1 *Prut*; 4 *Sliva*; 14 *Sorum*

AWT 1 *Manych*

AX 2 *Smolny* with 2 RBU 2500 *Smerch* 1 A/S mor, 2 twin 76mm guns

AXL 7 *Petrushka*

UNINHABITED MARITIME PLATFORMS

USV • MW • Small 3 *Inspektor* Mk2

UUV
  ATK • Nuclear • Extra-Large *Poseidon* (*Status*-6) (nuclear powered) (in test)
  DATA • Extra-Large *Klavesin*-1R (*Harpsichord*); *Klavesin*-2R-PM (*Harpsichord*); *Vityaz*-D
  UTL • Extra-Large *Sarma*; *Sarma*-D (*Sarma* mod)

UNINHABITED MARITIME SYSTEMS • USV
  DATA *Alister* 9 (A9-E); *Galtel*
  MW K-Ster C/I; SEASCAN

Naval Aviation ε31,000

FORCES BY ROLE

FIGHTER
  1 regt with MiG-31B/BS/BM *Foxhound*
  1 regt with Su-27/Su-27UB *Flanker*
  1 regt with Su-33 *Flanker* D; Su-25UTG *Frogfoot*

FIGHTER/GROUND ATTACK
  1 regt with MiG-29KR/KUBR *Fulcrum*
  1 regt with MiG-31BM *Foxhound*; Su-24M/M2/MR *Fencer*

ANTI-SURFACE WARFARE/ISR
  2 regt with Su-24M/MR *Fencer*; Su-30SM

ANTI-SUBMARINE WARFARE
  1 regt with Il-38/Il-38N *May**; Il-18D; Il-20RT *Coot* A; Il-22 *Coot* B
  2 sqn with Il-38/Il-38N *May**; Il-18D; Il-20RT *Coot* A; Il-22 *Coot* B
  1 regt with Ka-27/Ka-29 *Helix*
  1 sqn with Ka-27/Ka-29 *Helix*
  2 sqn with Tu-142MK/MZ/MR *Bear* F/J*
  1 unit with Ka-31R *Helix*

MARITIME PATROL/TRANSPORT
  1 regt with An-26 *Curl*; Be-12 *Mail**; Ka-27 *Helix*; Mi-8 *Hip*

SEARCH & RESCUE/TRANSPORT
  1 sqn with An-12PS *Cub*; An-26 *Curl*; Tu-134

TRANSPORT
  1 sqn with An-12BK *Cub*; An-24RV *Coke*; An-26 *Curl*; An-72 *Coaler*; An-140
  2 sqn with An-26 *Curl*; Tu-134

TRAINING
  1 sqn with L-39 *Albatros*; Su-25UTG *Frogfoot*
  1 sqn with An-140; Tu-134; Tu-154, Il-38 *May*

ATTACK/TRANSPORT HELICOPTER
  1 sqn with Mi-24P *Hind*; Mi-8 *Hip*

TRANSPORT HELICOPTER
  1 sqn with Mi-8 *Hip*

COMBAT/ISR UAV
  1 regt with *Forpost* (*Searcher* II); *Inokhodets*

AIR DEFENCE
4 AD div HQ
1 SAM regt with S-300PM1 (RS-SA-20 *Gargoyle*); S-300PS (RS-SA-10B *Grumble*)
1 SAM regt with S-300PM1 (RS-SA-20 *Gargoyle*); S-400 (RS-SA-21 *Growler*); 96K6 *Pantsir*-S1 (RS-SA-22 *Greyhound*)
1 SAM regt with S-300PS (RS-SA-10B *Grumble*)
1 SAM regt with S-300PS (RS-SA-10B *Grumble*); S-400 (RS-SA-21 *Growler*); 96K6 *Pantsir*-S1 (RS-SA-22 *Greyhound*)
4 SAM regt with S-400 (RS-SA-21 *Growler*); 96K6 *Pantsir*-S1 (RS-SA-22 *Greyhound*)

EQUIPMENT BY TYPE
AIRCRAFT 208 combat capable
FTR 65: 9 MiG-31B/BS *Foxhound*; 21 MiG-31BM *Foxhound* C; 17 Su-33 *Flanker* D; 18 Su-27/Su-27UB *Flanker*
FGA 48: 19 MiG-29KR *Fulcrum*; 3 MiG-29KUBR *Fulcrum*; up to 18 Su-30SM *Flanker* H; 8+ Su-30SM2 *Flanker* H
ATK 35: up to 30 Su-24M *Fencer*; 5 Su-25UTG *Frogfoot* (trg role)
ASW 44: 12 Tu-142MK/MZ *Bear* F; 10 Tu-142MR *Bear* J (comms); 15 Il-38 *May*; 7 Il-38N *May*
MP 7: 6 Be-12PS *Mail**; 1 Il-18D
ISR 10 Su-24MR *Fencer* E*
SAR 4: 3 An-12PS *Cub*; 1 Be-200ES
ELINT 4: 2 Il-20RT *Coot* A; 2 Il-22 *Coot* B
TPT 49: **Medium** 2 An-12BK *Cub*; **Light** 45: 1 An-24RV *Coke*; 24 An-26 *Curl*; 6 An-72 *Coaler*; 4 An-140; 9 Tu-134; 1 Tu-134UBL; **PAX** 2 Tu-154M *Careless*
TRG 4 L-39 *Albatros*
HELICOPTERS
ATK 8 Mi-24P *Hind*
ASW 67: ε45 Ka-27PL *Helix*; 22 Ka-27M *Helix*
EW 8 Mi-8 *Hip* J
AEW 2 Ka-31R *Helix*
SAR 16 Ka-27PS *Helix* D
TPT 41: **Medium** 35: 27 Ka-29 *Helix*; 4 Mi-8T *Hip*; 4 Mi-8MT *Hip*; **Light** 6 Ka-226T
AIR DEFENCE
SAM • Long-range 200: 56 S-300PM1 (RS-SA-20 *Gargoyle*); 40 S-300PS (RS-SA-10B *Grumble*); 104 S-400 (RS-SA-21 *Growler*)
SPAAGM 30mm 30 96K6 *Pantsir*-S1 (RS-SA-22 *Greyhound*)
UNINHABITED AERIAL VEHICLES
CISR• Heavy *Inokhodets*
ISR• Medium *Forpost* (*Searcher* II)
AIR-LAUNCHED MISSILES
AAM • IR R-27T/ET (RS-AA-10B/D *Alamo*); R-60 (RS-AA-8 *Aphid*); R-73 (RS-AA-11A *Archer*); R-74M (RS-AA-11B *Archer*); **ARH** R-37M (RS-AA-13A *Axehead*); R-77-1 (RS-AA-12B *Adder*); **SARH** R-27R/ER (RS-AA-10A/C *Alamo*); R-33 (RS-AA-9A *Amos*)
ARM Kh-25MP (RS-AS-12A *Kegler*); Kh-31P (RS-AS-17A *Krypton*); Kh-58 (RS-AS-11 *Kilter*)
ASM Kh-59 (RS-AS-13 *Kingbolt*); Kh-59M (RS-AS-18 *Kazoo*); Kh-29T (RS-AS-14 *Kedge*)
AShM Kh-31A/AM (RS-AS-17B/D *Krypton*)

Naval Infantry (Marines) ε25,000
FORCES BY ROLE
As a result of sustained heavy losses suffered during the invasion of Ukraine, almost all of the manoeuvre formations listed are currently understrength.
COMMAND
3 corps HQ
SPECIAL FORCES
4 (OMRP) SF unit
11 (PDSS) cbt diver unit
MANOEUVRE
Reconnaissance
1 recce bde
Mechanised
1 MR div (1 tk regt, 2 MR regt; 1 SAM regt)
2 MR bde
1 MR regt
6 naval inf bde
1 naval inf regt
SURFACE-TO-SURFACE MISSILE
1 SRBM/GLCM bde with 9K720 *Iskander*-M (RS-SS-26 *Stone*/RS-SSC-7 *Southpaw*)
COMBAT SUPPORT
2 arty bde
2 engr regt
AIR DEFENCE
1 SAM regt with 9K33 *Osa* (RS-SA-8 *Gecko*); *Strela*-1/*Strela*-10 (RS-SA-9 *Gaskin*/RS-SA-13 *Gopher*)
EQUIPMENT BY TYPE(ε)
ARMOURED FIGHTING VEHICLES
MBT 200: 100 T-72B3/B3M; 100 T-80BV/BVM
IFV 1,010: 300 BMP-2; 70 BMP-3; 40 BMP-3F; 600 BTR-82A
APC 300
APC (T) 250 MT-LB
APC (W) 50 BTR-80
AUV *Vystrel*
ANTI-TANK/ANTI-INFRASTRUCTURE
MSL
SP 60+: 60 9P148 with 9K111-1 *Konkurs* (RS-AT-5 *Spandrel*); 9P149 with 9K114 *Shturm* (RS-AT-6 *Spiral*); 9P157-2 with 9K123 *Khrisantema* (RS-AT-15 *Springer*)
MANPATS 9K111-1 *Konkurs* (RS-AT-5 *Spandrel*); 9K135 *Kornet* (RS-AT-14 *Spriggan*)
GUNS 100mm T-12
ARTILLERY 395
SP 171: **122mm** 85 2S1 *Gvozdika*; **152mm** 86: 50 2S3

Akatsiya; 36 2S19M1 *Msta-S*

TOWED 152mm 100: 50 2A36 *Giatsint*-B; 50 2A65 *Msta*-B

GUN/MOR 66

    SP 120mm 42: 12 2S23 NONA-SVK; 30 2S9 NONA-S

    TOWED 120mm 24 2B16 NONA-K

MRL 58: **122mm** 36 BM-21 *Grad*/*Tornado*-G; **220mm** 18 9P140 *Uragan*; **300mm** 4+ 9A52 *Smerch*

SURFACE-TO-SURFACE MISSILE LAUNCHER

    SRBM • Dual-capable 12 9K720 *Iskander*-M (RS-SS-26 *Stone*)

    GLCM • Dual-capable Some 9M728 (RS-SSC-7 *Southpaw*)

AIR DEFENCE

    SAM

        Short-range 9 *Tor*-M2DT

        Point-defence 70+: 20 9K33 *Osa* (RS-SA-8 *Gecko*); 40 9K31 *Strela*-1/9K35 *Strela*-10 (RS-SA-9 *Gaskin*/RS-SA-13 *Gopher*); 9K338 *Igla*-S (RS-SA-24 *Grinch*)

    GUNS • SP 23mm 60 ZSU-23-4

Coastal Missile and Artillery Forces 2,000

FORCES BY ROLE

COASTAL DEFENCE

5 AShM bde

1 AShM regt

EQUIPMENT BY TYPE

COASTAL DEFENCE

    ARTY • SP 130mm 36 A-222 *Bereg*

    AShM 96+: 40 3K60 *Bal* (RS-SSC-6 *Sennight*); 56 3K55 *Bastion* (RS-SSC-5 *Stooge*); some 4K44 *Redut* (RS-SSC-1 *Sepal*); some 4K51 *Rubezh* (RS-SSC-3 *Styx*)

UNINHABITED AERIAL VEHICLES

    ISR • Light *Granat*-4

Aerospace Forces ε165,000 (incl conscripts)

A joint CIS Unified Air Defence System covers RUS, ARM, BLR, KAZ, KGZ, TJK, TKM and UZB

FORCES BY ROLE

BOMBER

3 regt with Tu-22M3 *Backfire* C

3 sqn with Tu-95MS/MS mod *Bear*

1 sqn with Tu-160/Tu-160 mod *Blackjack*

FIGHTER

1 sqn with MiG-29/MiG-29UB *Fulcrum* (Armenia)

2 regt with MiG-31BM *Foxhound* C

1 regt with MiG-31BM *Foxhound* C; Su-35S *Flanker* M

1 regt with Su-27/Su-27SM/Su-27UB *Flanker* B/J/C; Su-30M2 *Flanker* G

2 regt with Su-30SM *Flanker* H

FIGHTER/GROUND ATTACK

1 regt with MiG-31BM *Foxhound* C; Su-27SM *Flanker* J; Su-30M2 *Flanker* G; Su-30SM *Flanker* H; Su-35S *Flanker* M

1 regt with Su-27SM *Flanker* J; Su-35S *Flanker* M

1 regt with Su-35S *Flanker* M; Su-30SM *Flanker* H

1 regt with Su-27SM3 *Flanker*; Su-30M2 *Flanker* G

1 regt with Su-25 *Frogfoot*; Su-30SM *Flanker* H

GROUND ATTACK

1 regt with MiG-31K

1 regt with Su-24M/M2 *Fencer*; Su-34 *Fullback*

1 regt with Su-24M *Fencer*; Su-25SM *Frogfoot*

3 regt with Su-25SM/SM3 *Frogfoot*

1 sqn with Su-25SM *Frogfoot* (Kyrgyzstan)

3 regt with Su-34 *Fullback*

GROUND ATTACK/ISR

1 regt with Su-24M/MR *Fencer*

ISR

3 sqn with Su-24MR *Fencer*

1 flt with An-30 *Clank*

AIRBORNE EARLY WARNING & CONTROL

1 sqn with A-50/A-50U *Mainstay*

TANKER

1 sqn with Il-78/Il-78M *Midas*

TRANSPORT

6 regt/sqn with An-12BK *Cub*; An-148-100E; An-26 *Curl*; Tu-134 *Crusty*; Tu-154 *Careless*; Mi-8 *Hip*

1 regt with An-124 *Condor*; Il-76MD *Candid*

1 regt with An-124 *Condor*; Il-76MD/MD-90A *Candid*

1 regt with An-12BK *Cub*; Il-76MD *Candid*

1 sqn with An-22 *Cock*

3 regt with Il-76MD *Candid*

ATTACK/TRANSPORT HELICOPTER

1 bde with Ka-52A *Hokum* B; Mi-28N *Havoc* B; Mi-35 *Hind*; Mi-26 *Halo*; Mi-8MTV-5 *Hip*

1 bde with Ka-52A *Hokum* B; Mi-26 *Halo*; Mi-8 *Hip*

1 bde with Mi-28N *Havoc* B; Mi-35 *Hind*; Mi-26 *Halo*; Mi-8 *Hip*

2 regt with Ka-52A *Hokum* B; Mi-28N *Havoc* B; Mi-35 *Hind*; Mi-8 *Hip*

1 regt with Ka-52A *Hokum* B; Mi-24P *Hind*; Mi-8MTPR-1 *Hip*; Mi-8 *Hip*

1 regt with Ka-52A *Hokum* B; Mi-8 *Hip*

1 regt with Mi-28N *Havoc* B; Mi-35 *Hind*; Mi-8 *Hip*

1 regt with Mi-28N *Havoc* B; Mi-24P *Hind*; Mi-35 *Hind*; Mi-8 *Hip*

2 regt with Mi-24P *Hind*; Mi-8 *Hip*

2 sqn with Mi-24P *Hind*; Mi-8 *Hip*

AIR DEFENCE

9 AD div HQ

4 regt with 9K37M1-2 *Buk*-M1-2 (RS-SA-11 *Gadfly*); 9K317 *Buk*-M2 (RS-SA-17 *Grizzly*); S-300V (RS-SA-12 *Gladiator*/*Giant*)

1 bde with S-300PS (RS-SA-10B *Grumble*)

2 regt with S-300PS (RS-SA-10B *Grumble*)

6 regt with S-300PM1/PM2 (RS-SA-20 *Gargoyle*)

12 regt with S-400 (RS-SA-21 *Growler*); 96K6 *Pantsir*-S1 (RS-SA-22 *Greyhound*)

EQUIPMENT BY TYPE

AIRCRAFT 1,169 combat capable

BBR 129: 57 Tu-22M3 *Backfire* C; 1 Tu-22MR *Backfire*† (1 in overhaul); 31 Tu-95MS *Bear*; 27 Tu-95MS mod *Bear*; 6 Tu-160 *Blackjack*; 7 Tu-160 mod *Blackjack*; (3 Tu-160M *Blackjack* in test)

FTR 188: 70 MiG-29/MiG-29UB *Fulcrum*; 88 MiG-31BM *Foxhound* C; 12 Su-27 *Flanker* B; 18 Su-27UB *Flanker* C

FGA 433+: 14 MiG-29SMT *Fulcrum*; 2 MiG-29UBT *Fulcrum*; 47 Su-27SM *Flanker* J; 24 Su-27SM3 *Flanker*; 19 Su-30M2 *Flanker* G; ε80 Su-30SM *Flanker* H; 102 Su-34 *Fullback*; ε22 Su-34 mod *Fullback*; 111 Su-35S *Flanker* M; 12+ Su-57 *Felon*; (4 MiG-35S *Fulcrum*; 2 MiG-35UB *Fulcrum* in test)

ATK 257: ε24 MiG-31K; 68 Su-24M/M2 *Fencer*; 40 Su-25 *Frogfoot*; ε110 Su-25SM/SM3 *Frogfoot*; 15 Su-25UB *Frogfoot*

ISR 58: 4 An-30 *Clank*; up to 50 Su-24MR *Fencer**; 2 Tu-214ON; 2 Tu-214R

EW 3 Il-22PP *Mute*

ELINT 14 Il-20M *Coot* A

AEW&C 10: 2 A-50 *Mainstay*; 8 A-50U *Mainstay*

C2 24: 5 Il-22 *Coot* B; 11 Il-22M *Coot* B; 2 Il-80 *Maxdome*; 1 Il-82; 4 Tu-214SR; 1 Tu-214PU-SBUS

TKR 15: 5 Il-78 *Midas*; 10 Il-78M *Midas*

TPT 427: **Heavy** 126: 10 An-124 *Condor*; 4 An-22 *Cock*; 94 Il-76MD *Candid*; 3 Il-76MD-M *Candid*; 15 Il-76MD-90A *Candid*; **Medium** 45 An-12BK *Cub*; **Light** 224: ε113 An-26 *Curl*; 25 An-72 *Coaler*; 5 An-140; 27 L-410; 54 Tu-134 *Crusty*; **PAX** 32: 15 An-148-100E; 17 Tu-154 *Careless*

TRG 234: 35 DA42T; 87 L-39 *Albatros*; 112 Yak-130 *Mitten**

HELICOPTERS

ATK 340: ε65 Ka-52A *Hokum* B; ε20 Ka-52M *Hokum*; ε96 Mi-24D/V/P *Hind*; ε70 Mi-28N *Havoc* B; ε9 Mi-28NM *Havoc*; 24 Mi-28UB *Havoc*; ε56 Mi-35 *Hind*

EW ε16 Mi-8MTPR-1 *Hip*

TPT 307: **Heavy** 33 Mi-26/Mi-26T *Halo*; **Medium** 274 Mi-8/AMTSh/AMTSh-VA/MT/MTV-5/MTV-5-1 *Hip*

TRG 36: 19 Ka-226U; 17 Ansat-U

UNINHABITED AERIAL VEHICLES

CISR • **Heavy** some *Inokhodets*; **Medium** *Forpost* R; *Mohajer* 6

ISR • **Medium** *Forpost* (*Searcher* II); *Korsar*; **Light** *Eleron* T-16

AIR DEFENCE

SAM 714:

Long-range 584: 160 S-300PS (RS-SA-10B *Grumble*); 150 S-300PM1/PM2 (RS-SA-20 *Gargoyle*); 20 S-300V (RS-SA-12 *Gladiator/Giant*); 6 S-350 *Vityaz* (RS-SA-28); 248 S-400 (RS-SA-21 *Growler*)

Medium-range 80 9K37M1-2 *Buk*-M1-2/9K317 *Buk*-M2 (RS-SA-11 *Gadfly*/RS-SA-17 *Grizzly*)

SPAAGM 30mm 50 96K6 *Pantsir*-S1/S2 (RS-SA-22 *Greyhound*)

AIR-LAUNCHED MISSILES

AAM • **IR** *Igla*-V; R-27T/ET (RS-AA-10B/D *Alamo*); R-73 (RS-AA-11A *Archer*); R-74M (RS-AA-11B *Archer*); R-60T (RS-AA-8 *Aphid*); **SARH** R-27R/ER (RS-AA-10A/C *Alamo*); R-33 (RS-AA-9A *Amos*); **ARH** R-77-1 (RS-AA-12B *Adder*); R-37M (RS-AA-13A *Axehead*); **PRH** R-27P/EP (RS-AA-10E/F *Alamo*)

ARM Kh-25MP (RS-AS-12A *Kegler*); Kh-31P/PM (RS-AS-17A/C *Krypton*); Kh-58 (RS-AS-11 *Kilter*)

ASM 9M133; Item 305/LMUR; Kh-25ML (RS-AS-12B *Kegler*); Kh-29 (RS-AS-14 *Kedge*); Kh-38; Kh-59 (RS-AS-13 *Kingbolt*) Kh-59M (RS-AS-18 *Kazoo*); *Kinzhal* (RS-AS-24 *Killjoy*); 9M114 *Kokon* (RS-AT-6 *Spiral*); 9M120 *Ataka* (RS-AT-9 *Spiral* 2); 9M120-1 *Vikhr* (RS-AT-16 *Scallion*)

AShM Kh-22 (RS-AS-4 *Kitchen*); Kh-31A/AM (RS-AS-17B/D *Krypton*); Kh-32 (RS-AS-4A mod); Kh-35U (RS-AS-20 *Kayak*)

LACM

Nuclear Kh-55SM (RS-AS-15B *Kent*); Kh-102 (RS-AS-23B *Kodiak*)

Conventional Kh-101 (RS-AS-23A *Kodiak*); Kh-555 (RS-AS-22 *Kluge*)

BOMBS

INS/SAT-guided FAB-250 UMPK; FAB-500 UMPK; *Grom*-2; KAB-20S (reported); KAB-500S

Laser-guided KAB-20L (reported); KAB-50L (reported); KAB-250LG-E; KAB-500L; KAB-1500L

TV-guided *Ghaem*-5; KAB-500KR; KAB-1500KR; KAB-500OD; UPAB 1500

Airborne Forces ε35,000

FORCES BY ROLE

As a result of sustained heavy losses suffered during the invasion of Ukraine, almost all of the manoeuvre formations listed are currently understrength.

SPECIAL FORCES

1 (AB Recce) SF bde

MANOEUVRE

Air Manoeuvre

2 AB div (1 tk bn, 3 air aslt regt, 1 arty regt, 1 AD regt)

2 AB div (2 para regt, 1 inf regt, 1 arty regt, 1 AD regt)

1 AB div (2 para regt)

2 air aslt bde

COMBAT SUPPORT

1 arty bde

EQUIPMENT BY TYPE

ARMOURED FIGHTING VEHICLES(ε)

MBT 50 T-72B3/B3M

IFV 120 BTR-82AM

APC 640+

APC (T) 640: 550 BTR-D; 90 BTR-MDM

PPV *Typhoon*-VDV

ABCV 700: 500 BMD-2; 200 BMD-4M

AUV GAZ *Tigr*; UAMZ *Toros*

ENGINEERING & MAINTENANCE VEHICLES
 ARV BREM-D; BREhM-D
ANTI-TANK/ANTI-INFRASTRUCTURE
 MSL
  SP 100 BTR-RD
  MANPATS 9K111 *Fagot* (RS-AT-4 *Spigot*); 9K113 *Konkurs* (RS-AT-5 *Spandrel*); 9K115 *Metis* (RS-AT-7 *Saxhorn*); 9K115-1 *Metis*-M (RS-AT-13); 9K135 *Kornet* (RS-AT-14 *Spriggan*)
 RCL 73mm SPG-9
 GUNS • **SP 125mm** 36+ 2S25 *Sprut*-SD
ARTILLERY 568+
 SP • **122mm** 2S1 *Gvozdika*; **152mm** 2S5 *Giatsint*-S
 TOWED 140+: **122mm** 140 D-30; **152mm** 2A36 *Giatsint*-B
 GUN/MOR • **SP 120mm** 210+: 180 2S9 NONA-S; 30 2S9 NONA-SM; some 2S31 *Vena*; (350 2S9 NONA-S in store)
 MRL 21: **122mm** 18 BM-21 *Grad*; **220mm** 3 TOS-1A
 MOR • **TOWED** 200+ **82mm** 150 2B14; **120mm** 50+ 2B23 NONA-M1
AIR DEFENCE
 SAM • **Point-defence** 30+: 30 *Strela*-10MN (RS-SA-13 *Gopher*); 9K310 *Igla*-1 (RS-SA-16 *Gimlet*); 9K38 *Igla* (RS-SA-18 *Grouse*); 9K333 *Verba* (RS-SA-29 *Gizmo*); 9K338 *Igla*-S (RS-SA-24 *Grinch*); 9K34 *Strela*-3 (RS-SA-14 *Gremlin*)
 GUNS • **SP 23mm** 150 BTR-ZD
UNINHABITED AERIAL VEHICLES
 ISR • **Light** *Granat*-4

Special Operations Forces ε1,000
FORCES BY ROLE
SPECIAL FORCES
 3 SF unit

Railway Forces ε29,000
4 regional commands
FORCES BY ROLE
COMBAT SERVICE SUPPORT
 10 (railway) tpt bde

Russian Military Districts
5 military districts each with a unified Joint Strategic Command. Organisational data presented here represents peacetime assignments rather than operational deployments resulting from Russia's full-scale invasion of Ukraine and does not include mobilised units whose peacetime assignment is unclear.

Western Military District
HQ at St Petersburg

Army
FORCES BY ROLE
COMMAND
 3 army HQ
 1 corps HQ
SPECIAL FORCES
 2 (Spetsnaz) SF bde
MANOEUVRE
 Reconnaissance
 1 recce bde
 Armoured
 2 tk div
 3 MR div
 1 MR bde
 Mechanised
 1 MR div
 3 MR bde
SURFACE-TO-SURFACE MISSILE
 3 SRBM/GLCM bde with *Iskander*-M
COMBAT SUPPORT
 2 arty bde
 1 (hy) arty bde
 1 MRL bde
 1 engr bde
 3 engr regt
 1 ptn br bde
 1 EW bde
 1 NBC bde
 2 NBC regt
COMBAT SERVICE SUPPORT
 3 log bde
AIR DEFENCE
 4 AD bde

Baltic Fleet
EQUIPMENT BY TYPE
SUBMARINES • **TACTICAL** • **SSK** 1
PRINCIPAL SURFACE COMBATANTS 8: 1 **DDGHM**; 7 **FFGHM**
PATROL AND COASTAL COMBATANTS 35: 4 **FSGM**; 2 **FSG**; 6 **FSM**; 4 **PCGM**; 7 **PCFG**; 12 **PBF**; 1 **PB**
MINE WARFARE • **MINE COUNTERMEASURES** 12: 2 **MCC**; 4 **MSC**; 6 **MHI**
AMPHIBIOUS 13: 3 **LST**; 7 **LCM**; 2 **LCAC**

Naval Aviation
FORCES BY ROLE
FIGHTER
 1 regt with Su-27 *Flanker* B
ANTI-SURFACE WARFARE/ISR
 1 regt with Su-24M/MR *Fencer*; Su-30SM *Flanker* H
TRANSPORT
 1 sqn with An-26 *Curl*; Tu-134 *Crusty*
ATTACK/TRANSPORT HELICOPTER
 1 regt with Ka-27/Ka-29 *Helix*; Mi-24P *Hind*; Mi-8 *Hip*
AIR DEFENCE

2 SAM regt with S-400 (RS-SA-21 *Growler*); 96K6 *Pantsir*-S1 (RS-SA-22 *Greyhound*)

Naval Infantry
FORCES BY ROLE
COMMAND
  1 corps HQ
MANOEUVRE
  Mechanised
  1 MR div
  1 MR regt
  1 naval inf bde
SURFACE-TO-SURFACE MISSILE
  1 SRBM/GLCM bde with *Iskander*-M
COMBAT SUPPORT
  1 arty bde

Coastal Artillery and Missile Forces
FORCES BY ROLE
COASTAL DEFENCE
  1 AShM regt

Military Air Force
6th Air Force & Air Defence Army
FORCES BY ROLE
FIGHTER
  1 regt with Su-30SM *Flanker* H
  1 regt with MiG-31BM *Foxhound* C; Su-35S *Flanker* M
  1 regt with Su-27SM *Flanker* J; Su-35S *Flanker* M
GROUND ATTACK
  1 regt with Su-34 *Fullback*
ISR
  1 sqn with Su-24MR *Fencer* E; An-30 *Clank*
TRANSPORT
  1 regt with An-12 *Cub*; An-26 *Curl*; Tu-134 *Crusty*
ATTACK HELICOPTER
  1 bde with Ka-52A *Hokum* B; Mi-28N *Havoc* B; Mi-35 *Hind*; Mi-26 *Halo*; Mi-8MTV-5 *Hip*
  1 regt with Mi-24P/Mi-35 *Hind*; Mi-28N *Havoc* B; Mi-8 *Hip*
  1 regt with Mi-24P *Hind*; Ka-52A *Hokum* B; Mi-8 *Hip*; Mi-8PPA *Hip*
AIR DEFENCE
  3 SAM regt with S-300PM1/PM2 (RS-SA-20 *Gargoyle*)
  4 SAM regt with S-400 (RS-SA-21 *Growler*); 96K6 *Pantsir*-S1 (RS-SA-22 *Greyhound*)

Airborne Forces
FORCES BY ROLE
SPECIAL FORCES
  1 (AB Recce) SF bde
MANOEUVRE
  Air Manoeuvre
  3 AB div

Northern Fleet Military District
HQ at Severomorsk

Northern Fleet
EQUIPMENT BY TYPE
SUBMARINES 25
  STRATEGIC 8 **SSBN** (of which 2 in refit)
  TACTICAL 17: 5 **SSGN**; 8 **SSN**; 4 **SSK**
PRINCIPAL SURFACE COMBATANTS 9: 1 **CV** (in refit); 1 **CGHMN**; 1 **CGHM**; 5 **DDGHM** (1 more in reserve); 2 **FFGHM**
PATROL AND COASTAL COMBATANTS 15: 6 **FSM**; 1 **PCGM**; 8 **PB**
MINE WARFARE • MINE COUNTERMEASURES 7: 1 **MHO**; 6 **MSC**
AMPHIBIOUS 7: 5 **LST**; 2 **LCM**

Naval Aviation
FORCES BY ROLE
FIGHTER
  1 regt with Su-33 *Flanker* D; Su-25UTG *Frogfoot*
FIGHTER/GROUND ATTACK
  1 regt with MiG-29KR/KUBR *Fulcrum*
FIGHTER/GROUND ATTACK/ISR
  1 regt with MiG-31BM *Foxhound* C; Su-24M/M2/MR *Fencer*
ANTI-SUBMARINE WARFARE
  1 regt with Il-38/Il-38N *May*; Il-20RT *Coot* A; Tu-134
  1 regt with Ka-27/Ka-29 *Helix*
  1 sqn with Tu-142MK/MZ/MR *Bear* F/J
AIR DEFENCE
  5 SAM regt with S-300PS (RS-SA-10B *Grumble*); S-300PM1 (RS-SA-20 *Gargoyle*); S-400 (RS-SA-21 *Growler*); 96K6 *Pantsir*-S1 (RS-SA-22 *Greyhound*)

Naval Infantry
FORCES BY ROLE
COMMAND
  1 corps HQ
MANOEUVRE
  Mechanised
  2 MR bde
  1 naval inf bde
COMMAND
  1 engr regt

Coastal Artillery and Missile Forces
FORCES BY ROLE
COASTAL DEFENCE
  1 AShM bde

Central Military District
HQ at Yekaterinburg

Army
FORCES BY ROLE
COMMAND
  3 army HQ
SPECIAL FORCES
  2 (Spetsnaz) SF bde
MANOEUVRE
  Armoured
  1 tk div
  1 MR div
  4 MR bde
  Mechanised
  3 (lt/mtn) MR bde
SURFACE-TO-SURFACE MISSILE
  2 SRBM/GLCM bde with *Iskander*-M
COMBAT SUPPORT
  2 arty bde
  1 MRL bde
  1 engr bde
  3 engr regt
  1 EW bde
  2 NBC bde
  2 NBC regt
COMBAT SERVICE SUPPORT
  2 log bde
AIR DEFENCE
  3 AD bde

Military Air Force

14th Air Force & Air Defence Army
FORCES BY ROLE
FIGHTER
  2 regt with MiG-31BM *Foxhound* C
GROUND ATTACK
  1 regt with Su-34 *Fullback*
  1 sqn with Su-25SM *Frogfoot* (Kyrgyzstan)
ISR
  1 sqn with Su-24MR *Fencer* E
TRANSPORT
  1 regt with An-12 *Cub*; An-26 *Curl*; Tu-134 *Crusty*; Tu-154; Mi-8 *Hip*
ATTACK/TRANSPORT HELICOPTER
  1 bde with Mi-24P *Hind*; Mi-8 *Hip*
  1 regt with Mi-24P *Hind*; Mi-8 *Hip*
  1 sqn with Mi-24P *Hind*; Mi-8 *Hip* (Tajikistan)
AIR DEFENCE
  1 regt with S-300PS (RS-SA-10B *Grumble*)
  1 bde with S-300PS (RS-SA-10B *Grumble*)
  1 regt with S-300PM2 (RS-SA-20 *Gargoyle*)
  4 regt with S-400 (RS-SA-21 *Growler*); 96K6 *Pantsir*-S1 (RS-SA-22 *Greyhound*)

Airborne Troops
FORCES BY ROLE
MANOEUVRE
  Air Manoeuvre
  1 AB div

Southern Military District
HQ at Rostov-on-Don

Army
FORCES BY ROLE
COMMAND
  4 army HQ
  3 corps HQ
SPECIAL FORCES
  3 (Spetsnaz) SF bde
  1 (Spetsnaz) SF regt
MANOEUVRE
  Reconnaissance
  1 recce bde
  Armoured
  3 MR div
  1 MR bde
  1 MR bde (Armenia)
  1 MR bde (South Ossetia)
  Mechanised
  3 MR div
  1 MR bde
  1 MR bde (Abkhazia)
  1 (lt/mtn) MR bde
SURFACE-TO-SURFACE MISSILE
  3 SRBM/GLCM bde with *Iskander*-M
COMBAT SUPPORT
  3 arty bde
  1 MRL bde
  1 engr bde
  1 EW bde
  1 NBC bde
  2 NBC regt
COMBAT SERVICE SUPPORT
  2 log bde
AIR DEFENCE
  3 AD bde

Black Sea Fleet
The Black Sea Fleet is primarily based in Crimea, at Sevastopol, Karantinnaya Bay and Streletskaya Bay
EQUIPMENT BY TYPE
SUBMARINES • TACTICAL 5 SSK
PRINCIPAL SURFACE COMBATANTS 5: 3 FFGHM; 2 FFGM
PATROL AND COASTAL COMBATANTS 34: 9 FSGM; 6 FSM; 4 PSOH; 5 PCFG; 6 PB; 4 PBF
MINE WARFARE • MINE COUNTERMEASURES 10: 3 MCC; 1 MHO; 5 MSO; 1 MSC

AMPHIBIOUS 8: 6 LST; 2 LCM

Naval Aviation
FORCES BY ROLE
FIGHTER
ANTI-SURFACE WARFARE/ISR
  1 regt with Su-24M/MR *Fencer*; Su-30SM *Flanker* H
MARITIME PATROL/TRANSPORT
  1 regt with Ka-27 *Helix*; An-26 *Curl*; Be-12PS *Mail*; Mi-8 *Hip*
  TPT • Medium Mi-8 *Hip*

Naval Infantry
FORCES BY ROLE
COMMAND
  1 corps HQ
MANOEUVRE
  Mechanised
  2 naval inf bde
COMBAT SUPPORT
  1 arty regt
  1 engr regt
AIR DEFENCE
  1 SAM regt

Coastal Artillery and Missile Forces
FORCES BY ROLE
COASTAL DEFENCE
  2 AShM bde

Caspian Sea Flotilla
EQUIPMENT BY TYPE
PATROL AND COASTAL COMBATANTS 15: 3 FSGM; 1 PCFG; 3 PCM; 3 PB; 1 PBF; 4 PBR
MINE WARFARE • MINE COUNTERMEASURES 3: 2 MSC; 1 MHI
AMPHIBIOUS 9 LCM

Naval Infantry
FORCES BY ROLE
MANOEUVRE
  Mechanised
  1 naval inf regt

Military Air Force

4th Air Force & Air Defence Army
FORCES BY ROLE
FIGHTER
  1 regt with Su-30SM *Flanker* H
  1 sqn with MiG-29 *Fulcrum*; Su-30SM *Flanker* H (Armenia)
FIGHTER/GROUND ATTACK
  1 regt with Su-27/Su-27SM *Flanker* B/J; Su-30M2 *Flanker* G
  1 regt with Su-27SM3 *Flanker*; Su-30M2 *Flanker* G

GROUND ATTACK
  1 regt with Su-24M *Fencer*; Su-25SM *Frogfoot*
  2 regt with Su-25SM/SM3 *Frogfoot*
  1 regt with Su-34 *Fullback*
GROUND ATTACK/ISR
  1 regt with Su-24M/MR *Fencer* D/E
TRANSPORT
  1 regt with An-12 *Cub*/Mi-8 *Hip*
ATTACK/TRANSPORT HELICOPTER
  1 bde with Mi-28N *Havoc* B; Mi-35 *Hind*; Mi-8 *Hip*; Mi-26 *Halo*
  1 regt with Mi-28N *Havoc* B; Mi-35 *Hind*; Mi-8 *Hip*
  2 regt with Ka-52A *Hokum* B; Mi-28N *Havoc* B; Mi-35 *Hind*; Mi-8AMTSh *Hip*
  1 sqn with Mi-24P *Hind*; Mi-8 *Hip* (Armenia)
AIR DEFENCE
  1 SAM regt with 9K317 *Buk*-M2 (RS-SA-17 *Grizzly*)
  1 SAM regt with S-300PM1 (RS-SA-20 *Gargoyle*)
  3 SAM regt with S-400 (RS-SA-21 *Growler*); 96K6 *Pantsir*-S1 (RS-SA-22 *Greyhound*)

Airborne Forces
FORCES BY ROLE
MANOEUVRE
  Air Manoeuvre
  1 AB div

Eastern Military District
HQ at Khabarovsk

Army
FORCES BY ROLE
COMMAND
  4 army HQ
SPECIAL FORCES
  1 (Spetsnaz) SF bde
MANOEUVRE
  Armoured
  1 tk bde
  1 MR div
  6 MR bde
  Mechanised
  2 MR bde
  1 MGA div
SURFACE-TO-SURFACE MISSILE
  4 SRBM/GLCM bde with *Iskander*-M
COMBAT SUPPORT
  4 arty bde
  1 MRL bde
  1 engr bde
  1 EW bde
  1 NBC bde
  4 NBC regt
COMBAT SERVICE SUPPORT

4 log bde
AIR DEFENCE
5 AD bde

Pacific Fleet

EQUIPMENT BY TYPE
SUBMARINES 19
  STRATEGIC 4 **SSBN**
  TACTICAL 15: 4 **SSGN** (2 more non-operational in long-term refit); 2 **SSN** (3 more non-operational in long-term refit; 9 **SSK**
PRINCIPAL SURFACE COMBATANTS 11: 1 **CGHM**; 5 **DDGHM**; 5 **FFGHM**
PATROL AND COASTAL COMBATANTS 25: 8 **FSM**; 2 **PCGM**; 9 **PCFG**; 6 **PB**
MINE WARFARE 11: 2 **MCC**; 2 **MSO**; 7 **MSC**
AMPHIBIOUS 9: 4 **LST**; 5 **LCM**

Naval Aviation

FORCES BY ROLE
FIGHTER
  1 sqn with MiG-31BS/BM *Foxhound* A/C
ANTI-SUBMARINE WARFARE
  1 sqn with Ka-27/Ka-29 *Helix*
  2 sqn with Il-38/Il-38N *May*; Il-18D; Il-22 *Coot* B
  1 sqn with Tu-142MK/MZ/MR *Bear* F/J
TRANSPORT
  1 sqn with An-12BK *Cub*; An-26 *Curl*; Tu-134
AIR DEFENCE
  1 SAM regt with S-400 (RS-SA-21 *Growler*); 96K6 *Pantsir*-S1 (RS-SA-22 *Greyhound*)

Naval Infantry

FORCES BY ROLE
MANOEUVRE
  Mechanised
  2 naval inf bde

Coastal Artillery and Missile Forces

FORCES BY ROLE
COASTAL DEFENCE
  2 AShM bde

Military Air Force

11th Air Force & Air Defence Army

FORCES BY ROLE
FIGHTER/GROUND ATTACK
  1 regt with MiG-31BM *Foxhound* C; Su-27SM *Flanker* J; Su-30M2 *Flanker* G; Su-30SM *Flanker* H; Su-35S *Flanker* M
  1 regt with Su-35S *Flanker* M; Su-30SM *Flanker* H
  1 regt with Su-25 *Frogfoot*; Su-30SM *Flanker* H
GROUND ATTACK
  1 regt with Su-24M/M2 *Fencer* D/D mod; Su-34 *Fullback*
  1 regt with Su-25SM *Frogfoot*
ISR
  1 sqn with Su-24MR *Fencer* E
TRANSPORT
  1 regt with An-12 *Cub*; An-26 *Curl*; Tu-134 *Crusty*/Tu-154 *Careless*
ATTACK/TRANSPORT HELICOPTER
  1 bde with Ka-52A *Hokum* B; Mi-8 *Hip*; Mi-26 *Halo*
  1 regt with Ka-52A *Hokum* B; Mi-8 *Hip*; Mi-26 *Halo*
  1 regt with Mi-24P *Hind*; Mi-8 *Hip*
AIR DEFENCE
  1 regt with 9K37M *Buk*-M1-2 (RS-SA-11 *Gadfly*);
  1 regt with S-300V (RS-SA-12 *Gladiator/Giant*); S-400 (RS-SA-21 *Growler*)
  4 regt with S-300PS (RS-SA-10B *Grumble*); S-400 (RS-SA-21 *Growler*); 96K6 *Pantsir*-S1 (RS-SA-22 *Greyhound*)

Airborne Forces

FORCES BY ROLE
MANOEUVRE
  Air Manoeuvre
  2 air aslt bde

Gendarmerie & Paramilitary 559,000

Border Guard Service ε160,000

Subordinate to Federal Security Service
FORCES BY ROLE
10 regional directorates
MANOEUVRE
  Other
  7 frontier gp
EQUIPMENT BY TYPE
ARMOURED FIGHTING VEHICLES
  IFV/APC (W) 1,000 BMP/BTR
  AUV BPM-97
ARTILLERY 90
  SP 122mm 2S1 *Gvozdika*
  GUN/MOR • SP 120mm 2S9 NONA-S
  MOR 120mm 2S12 *Sani*
PATROL AND COASTAL COMBATANTS 204
  PSO 7: 4 *Komandor*; 3 *Okean* (Project 22100) with 1 76mm gun, 1 hel landing platform
  PCM 1 *Okhotnik* (Project 22460) with 1 sextuple GMLS with *Igla*-1M (RS-SA-N-10 *Grouse*) SAM, 1 AK630 CIWS
  PCO 29: 8 *Alpinist* (Project 503); 1 *Sprut*; 13 *Okhotnik* (Project 22460) with 1 AK630M CIWS, 1 hel landing platform; 8 *Purga* with 1 hel landing platform
  PCC 33: 4 *Molnya* II (*Pauk* II); 6 *Svetlyak* (Project 10410); 13 *Svetlyak* (Project 10410) with 1 AK630M CIWS, 1 76mm gun; 8 *Svetlyak* (Project 10410) with 2 AK630M CIWS; 1 *Svetlyak* (Project 10410) with 1 AK630M CIWS; 1 *Yakhont*
  PCR 1 *Slepen* (*Yaz*) with 1 AK630 CIWS, 2 100mm guns

PBF 87: 57 *Mangust*; 3 *Mirazh* (Project 14310); 4 *Mustang*-2 (Project 18623); 21 *Sobol*; 2 *Sokzhoi*
PBR 27: 4 *Ogonek*; 8 *Piyavka* with 1 AK630 CIWS; 15 *Moskit* (*Vosh*) with 1 AK630 CIWS, 1 100mm gun
PB 18: 6 *Gyuys* (Project 03050); 2 *Morzh* (Project 1496M); 10 *Lamantin* (Project 1496M1)
LOGISTICS AND SUPPORT 30
 AE 1 *Muna*
 AGB 2 *Ivan Susanin* (primarily used as patrol ships) with 2 AK630 CIWS, 1 76mm gun, 1 hel landing platform
 AK 4 *Pevek*
 AKL 5 *Kanin*
 AO 3: 1 *Ishim* (Project 15010); 2 *Evoron*
 ATF 15: 14 *Sorum* (primarily used as patrol ships) with 2 AK230M CIWS; 1 *Sorum* (primarily used as patrol ship)
AIRCRAFT • TPT ε86: 70 An-24 *Coke*/An-26 *Curl*/An-72 *Coaler*/Il-76 *Candid*/Tu-134 *Crusty*/Yak-40 *Codling*; 16 SM-92
HELICOPTERS: ε200 Ka-27PS *Helix*/Mi-24 *Hind*/Mi-26 *Halo*/Mi-8 *Hip*

Federal Guard Service ε40,000–50,000

Org include elm of ground forces (mech inf bde and AB regt)

FORCES BY ROLE
MANOEUVRE
 Mechanised
  1 mech inf regt
 Air Manoeuvre
  1 AB regt
 Other
  1 (Presidential) gd regt

Federal Security Service Special Purpose Centre ε4,000

FORCES BY ROLE
SPECIAL FORCES
 2 SF unit (Alfa and Vympel units)

National Guard ε335,000

FORCES BY ROLE
MANOEUVRE
 Other
  10 paramilitary div (2–5 paramilitary regt)
  17 paramilitary bde (3 mech bn, 1 mor bn)
  36 indep paramilitary rgt
  90 paramilitary bn (incl special motorised units)
COMBAT SUPPORT
 1 arty regt
TRANSPORT
 8 sqn
EQUIPMENT BY TYPE
ARMOURED FIGHTING VEHICLES
 RECCE some BRDM-2A
 IFV/APC (W) 1,600 BMP-1/BMP-2/BTR-70M/BTR-80/BTR-82A/BTR-82AM
 PPV Ural-VV
 AUV *Patrol*-A; *Tiger* 4×4; *Tigr*
ARTILLERY 35
 TOWED 122mm 20 D-30
 MOR 120mm 15 M-1938 (PM-38); 2S12 *Sani*
PATROL AND COASTAL COMBATANTS 5
 PBF 3 BK-16 (Project 02510)
 PB 2+ *Grachonok*
AIRCRAFT
 TPT 29: **Heavy** 9 Il-76 *Candid*; **Medium** 2 An-12 *Cub*; **Light** 18: 12 An-26 *Curl*; 6 An-72 *Coaler*
HELICOPTERS
 TPT 71: **Heavy** 10 Mi-26 *Halo*; **Medium** 60+: 60 Mi-8 *Hip*; some Mi-8AMTSh *Hip*; **Light** 1 Ka-226T
UNINHABITED AERIAL VEHICLES
 ISR • Light ZALA 421-16E5

Private Military Companies ε10,000

Elements of Russian private military companies integrated into the Russian command structure within Ukraine.

DEPLOYMENT

ARMENIA: 3,000: 1 mil base with (1 MR bde; 74 T-72; 80 BMP-1; 80 BMP-2; 12 2S1; 12 BM-21); 1 ftr sqn with 18 MiG-29 *Fulcrum*; 1 hel sqn with 4 Ka-52 *Hokum* B; 8 Mi-24P *Hind*; 4 Mi-8AMTSh *Hip*; 4 Mi-8MT *Hip*; 2 AD bty with S-300V; 1 AD bty with *Buk*-M1-2)

AZERBAIJAN: 1,960; 1 MR bde(-) (peacekeeping)

BELARUS: 2,000; 2 SAM bn with S-400; 1 radar station at Baranovichi (*Volga* system; leased); 1 naval comms site

CENTRAL AFRICAN REPUBLIC: UN • MINUSCA 13

CYPRUS: UN • UNFICYP 4

DEMOCRATIC REPUBLIC OF THE CONGO: UN • MONUSCO 10

GEORGIA: ε4,000; Abkhazia: 1 mil base with 1 MR bde(-); 1 SAM regt with S-300PS; South Ossetia: 1 mil base with 1 MR bde(-)

KAZAKHSTAN: 1 radar station at Balkash (*Dnepr* system; leased)

KYRGYZSTAN: ε500; 13 Su-25SM *Frogfoot*; 2 Mi-8 *Hip*

MEDITERRANEAN SEA: 2 SSK; 1 FFGHM; 1 FFGM; 1 AGI

MIDDLE EAST: UN • UNTSO 4

MOLDOVA: Transnistria ε1,500 (including 400 peacekeepers): 2 MR bn; 7 Mi-24 *Hind*; some Mi-8 *Hip*

SOUTH SUDAN: UN • UNMISS 2

SYRIA: 4,000; 1 inf BG; 3 MP bn; 1 engr unit; ε10 T-72B3; ε20 BTR-82A; BPM-97; *Typhoon*-K; *Tigr*; 12 2A65; 4 9A52 *Smerch*; 10 Su-24M *Fencer* D; 6 Su-34; 6 Su-35S *Flanker* M; 1 A-50U *Mainstay*; 1 Il-20M; 12 Mi-24P/Mi-35M *Hind*; 4

Mi-8AMTSh *Hip*; 1 AShM bty with 3K55 *Bastion*; 1 SAM bty with S-400; 1 SAM bty with *Pantsir*-S1/S2; air base at Latakia; naval facility at Tartus

TAJIKISTAN: ε3,000; 1 (201st) mil base with 1 MR bde(-); 1 hel sqn with 4 Mi-24P *Hind*; 4 Mi-8MTV *Hip*; 2 Mi-8MTV-5-1 *Hip*; 1 SAM bn with 8 S-300PS

UKRAINE: Donetsk, Kharkiv, Kherson, Luhansk & Zaporizhzhia: ε200,000; Crimea: ε25,000; 1 recce bde, 2 naval inf bde(-); 1 air aslt regt(-); 1 arty bde; 1 NBC regt; 1 AShM bde with 3K60 *Bal*; 3K55 *Bastion*; 1 FGA regt with Su-24M/MR; Su-30SM; 1 FGA regt with Su-27SM/SM3; Su-30M2; 1 atk regt with Su-24M/Su-25SM; 1 atk/tpt hel regt; 1 ASW hel regt; 2 AD regt with S-400; *Pantsir*-S1; 1 Fleet HQ located at Sevastopol

WESTERN SAHARA: UN • MINURSO 11

Tajikistan TJK

Tajikistani Somoni TJS		2022	2023	2024
GDP	TJS	116bn	128bn	143bn
	USD	10.5bn	11.8bn	12.9bn
per capita	USD	1,067	1,180	1,268
Growth	%	8.0	6.5	5.0
Inflation	%	6.6	4.6	5.8
Def bdgt [a]	TJS	1.19bn	1.53bn	
	USD	108m	141m	
USD1=TJS		11.03	10.85	11.09

[a] Excludes budget for law enforcement

Real-terms defence budget trend (USDm, constant 2015)

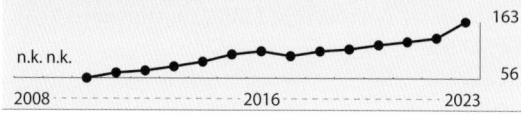

n.k. n.k. ... 163 ... 56
2008 — 2016 — 2023

Population 10,195,445

Age	0–14	15–19	20–24	25–29	30–64	65 plus
Male	18.9%	4.4%	3.9%	3.6%	17.8%	1.7%
Female	18.2%	4.2%	3.8%	3.5%	18.0%	2.1%

Capabilities

The Tajikistan's armed forces are largely focused on addressing regional security and terrorism concerns, especially given the border with Afghanistan. Border deployments have been stepped up recently in response to security concerns. The force have little capacity to deploy other than in token numbers. Most equipment is of Soviet-era origin. In late 2022, the president indicated that a national defence concept was under development. Tajikistan has been building its military capability by hosting CSTO counterterrorism exercises and participating in exercises organised by US CENTCOM. Tajikistan is a member of the CSTO and the SCO, and the armed forces also conduct exercises with Russian troops based at Russia's 201st military base. Reports in early 2019 indicated that there may be a Chinese military facility in eastern Tajikistan, though this remains unconfirmed by either Beijing or Dushanbe. India and Tajikistan have agreed to strengthen defence cooperation, in particular on counterterrorism, and there were reports in 2021 of agreements on security cooperation with Iran. In 2023, Tajikistan signed military cooperation agreements with Turkiye and explored a similar arrangement with Azerbaijan. Moscow is the historic arms provider to the country, though the US has made some equipment donations. Tajikistan has only minimal defence-industrial capacity, though, in 2022, Iran reportedly opened a UAV production facility in the country. A military vehicle assembly facility was opened in 2023 by Tajikistan's Shield Group, with parts reportedly produced by the UAE's Streit Group.

ACTIVE 8,800 (Army 7,300 Air Force/Air Defence 1,500) **Gendarmerie & Paramilitary 7,500**

Conscript liability 24 months

RESERVE 20,000 (Army 20,000)

ORGANISATIONS BY SERVICE

Army 7,300
FORCES BY ROLE
MANOEUVRE
  Mechanised
  3 MR bde
  Air Manoeuvre
  1 air aslt bde
COMBAT SUPPORT
  1 arty bde
AIR DEFENCE
  1 SAM regt
EQUIPMENT BY TYPE
ARMOURED FIGHTING VEHICLES
  MBT 38: 28 T-72 Ural/T-72A/T-72AV/T-72B; 3 T-72B1; 7 T-62/T-62AV/T-62AM
  RECCE 31: 9 BRDM-2; 22 BRDM-2M
  IFV 23: 8 BMP-1; 15 BMP-2
  APC 36
    APC (W) 23 BTR-60/BTR-70/BTR-80
    PPV 13 VP11
  AUV 24 CS/VN3B mod; *Tigr*
ARTILLERY 40
  SP 122mm 3 2S1 *Gvozdika*
  TOWED 122mm 13 D-30
  MRL 14+: 122mm 14 BM-21 *Grad*; **220mm** some TOS-1A
  MOR 10+: SP 82mm CS/SS4; **120mm** 10
AIR DEFENCE
  SAM
    Medium-range 3 S-125 *Pechora*-2M (RS-SA-26)
    Short-range 5 S-125M1 *Neva*-M1 (RS-SA-3 *Goa*)
    Point-defence 9K32 *Strela*-2 (RS-SA-7 *Grail*)‡
  GUNS
    SP 23mm 8 BTR-ZD
    TOWED 23mm ZU-23M1

Air Force/Air Defence 1,500
FORCES BY ROLE
TRANSPORT

1 sqn with Tu-134A *Crusty*

ATTACK/TRANSPORT HELICOPTER
1 sqn with Mi-24 *Hind*; Mi-8 *Hip*; Mi-17TM *Hip* H

EQUIPMENT BY TYPE
AIRCRAFT
TPT • **Light** 1 Tu-134A *Crusty*
TRG 4+: 4 L-39 *Albatros*; some Yak-52
HELICOPTERS
ATK 4 Mi-24 *Hind*
TPT • **Medium** 11 Mi-8 *Hip*/Mi-17TM *Hip* H

Gendarmerie & Paramilitary 7,500

Internal Troops 3,800

National Guard 1,200

Emergencies Ministry 2,500

Border Guards

FOREIGN FORCES
China ε300 (trg)
Russia ε3,000; 1 (201st) mil base with 1 MR bde(-); 1 hel sqn with 4 Mi-24P *Hind*; 4 Mi-8MTV *Hip*; 2 Mi-8MTV-5-1 *Hip*; 1 SAM bn with 8 S-300PS

Turkmenistan TKM

Turkmen New Manat TMT		2022	2023	2024
GDP	TMT	270bn	286bn	318bn
	USD	77.3bn	81.8bn	90.9bn
per capita	USD	12,380	12,934	14,184
Growth	%	1.6	2.5	2.1
Inflation	%	11.2	5.9	10.5
Def bdgt	TMT	n.k.	n.k.	n.k.
	USD	n.k.	n.k.	n.k.
USD1=TMT		3.50	3.50	3.50
Population	5,690,818			

Age	0–14	15–19	20–24	25–29	30–64	65 plus
Male	12.5%	3.8%	3.9%	4.4%	22.1%	2.9%
Female	12.2%	3.7%	3.8%	4.4%	22.7%	3.7%

Capabilities

Turkmenistan has concerns over potential spillover from security challenges in Afghanistan, but its armed forces lack significant capabilities and equipment. Ashgabat has maintained a policy of neutrality since 1995. It confirmed that stance in its 2016 military doctrine that aimed to increase the armed forces' defensive capability to safeguard national interests and territorial integrity. Turkmenistan is not a member of the CSTO or the SCO. In 2022, Turkmenistan participated in the Organization of Turkic States as an observer with plans for further cooperation. While the ground forces are shifting from a Soviet-era divisional structure to a brigade system, progress is slow. The armed forces are largely conscript-based and reliant on Soviet-era equipment and doctrine. The government wants to improve service conditions. Turkmenistan has participated in multinational exercises and is reported to have restarted joint exercises with Russia and Uzbekistan. The country has limited capacity to deploy abroad. Turkmenistan and four other Caspian littoral states signed an agreement in 2019 on military cooperation, including on maritime security. The country has plans to strengthen the border guard with new equipment and facilities. Turkmenistan has enhanced its naval presence in the Caspian Sea through limited procurements. The country has also purchased UAVs, including from China and Turkiye. Apart from maintenance facilities, Turkmenistan has little domestic defence industry, although it is building, under license, patrol vessels of Turkish design.

ACTIVE 36,500 (Army 33,000 Navy 500 Air 3,000)
Gendarmerie & Paramilitary 20,000

Conscript liability 24 months

ORGANISATIONS BY SERVICE

Army 33,000
5 Mil Districts
FORCES BY ROLE
SPECIAL FORCES
1 spec ops regt
MANOEUVRE
Armoured
1 tk bde
Mechanised
1 (3rd) MR div (1 tk regt; 3 MR regt, 1 arty regt)
1 (22nd) MR div (1 tk regt; 1 MR regt, 1 arty regt)
4 MR bde
1 naval inf bde
Other
1 MR trg div
SURFACE-TO-SURFACE MISSILE
1 SRBM bde with 9K72 *Elbrus* (RS-SS-1C *Scud* B)
COMBAT SUPPORT
1 arty bde
1 (mixed) arty/AT regt
1 MRL bde
1 AT regt
1 engr regt
AIR DEFENCE
2 SAM bde
EQUIPMENT BY TYPE†
ARMOURED FIGHTING VEHICLES
MBT 654: 4 T-90S; 650 T-72/T-72UMG
RECCE 260+: 200 BRDM-2; 60 BRM-1; Nimr *Ajban*
IFV 1,050: 600 BMP-1/BMP-1M; 4 BMP-1UM; 430 BMP-2; 4 BMP-2D; 4 BMP-3; 4 BTR-80A; 4 BTR-80 *Grom*
APC 907+
   APC (W) 870+: 120 BTR-60 (all variants); 300 BTR-70; 450 BTR-80

PPV 37+: 28+ *Kirpi*; 9+ Titan-DS; some *Typhoon*-K
AUV 12+: 8 Nimr *Ajban* 440A; 4+ *Cobra*
ABCV 8 BMD-1

ANTI-TANK/ANTI-INFRASTRUCTURE
MSL
SP 58+: 8 9P122 *Malyutka*-M (RS-AT-3 *Sagger* on BRDM-2); 8 9P133 *Malyutka*-P (RS-AT-3 *Sagger* on BRDM-2); 2 9P148 *Konkurs* (RS-AT-5 *Spandrel* on BRDM-2); 36 9P149 *Shturm* (RS-AT-6 *Spiral* on MT-LB); 4+ *Baryer* (on *Karakal*)
MANPATS 9K11 *Malyutka* (RS-AT-3 *Sagger*); 9K111 *Fagot* (RS-AT-4 *Spigot*); 9K111-1 *Konkurs* (RS-AT-5 *Spandrel*); 9K115 *Metis* (RS-AT-7 *Saxhorn*)
GUNS 100mm 60 MT-12/T-12

ARTILLERY 769
SP 122mm 40 2S1
TOWED 457: 122mm 350 D-30; 130mm 6 M-46; 152mm 101: 17 D-1; 72 D-20; 6 2A36 *Giatsint*-B; 6 2A65 *Msta*-B
GUN/MOR 120mm 17 2S9 NONA-S
MRL 158: 122mm 92: 18 9P138; 70 BM-21 *Grad*; 4 BM-21A; RM-70; 220mm 60 9P140 *Uragan*; 300mm 6 9A52 *Smerch*
MOR 97: 82mm 31; 120mm 66 M-1938 (PM-38)

SURFACE-TO-SURFACE MISSILE LAUNCHERS
SRBM • Conventional 16 9K72 *Elbrus* (RS-SS-1C *Scud* B)

AIR DEFENCE
SAM
Short-range: FM-90 (CH-SA-4); 2K12 *Kub* (RS-SA-6 *Gainful*)
Point-defence 53+: 40 9K33 *Osa* (RS-SA-8 *Gecko*); 13 9K35 *Strela*-10 mod (RS-SA-13 *Gopher*); 9K38 *Igla* (RS-SA-18 *Grouse*); 9K32M *Strela*-2M (RS-SA-7 *Grail*)‡; 9K34 *Strela*-3 (RS-SA-14 *Gremlin*); *Mistral* (reported); QW-2 (CH-SA-8)
GUNS 70
SP 23mm 48 ZSU-23-4
TOWED 22+: 23mm ZU-23-2; 57mm 22 S-60

AIR-LAUNCHED MISSILES
ASM CM-502KG; AR-1

Navy 500
EQUIPMENT BY TYPE
PATROL AND COASTAL COMBATANTS 5
CORVETTES • FSGM 1 *Deñiz Han* with 4 twin lnchr with *Otomat* AShM, 1 16-cell CLA VLS with VL MICA, 1 Roketsan ASW Rocket Launcher System A/S mor, 1 *Gokdeniz* CIWS, 1 76mm gun, 1 hel landing platform
PCFG 2 *Edermen* (RUS *Molnya*) with 4 quad lnchr with 3M24E *Uran*-E (RS-SS-N-25 *Switchblade*) AShM, 2 AK630 CIWS, 1 76mm gun
PCGM 2 *Arkadag* (TUR *Tuzla*) with 2 twin lnchr with *Otomat* AShM, 2 twin *Simbad*-RC lnchr with *Mistral* SAM, 1 Roketsan ASW Rocket Launcher System A/S mor

AMPHIBIOUS • LANDING CRAFT • UCAC 1 *Berdaşly*
LOGISTICS AND SUPPORT • AGS 1 (Dearsan 41m)

Air Force 3,000
FORCES BY ROLE
FIGHTER
2 sqn with MiG-29A/S/UB *Fulcrum*
GROUND ATTACK
1 sqn with Su-25 *Frogfoot*
1 sqn with Su-25MK *Frogfoot*
1 sqn with M-346FA*
TRANSPORT
1 sqn with An-26 *Curl*; Mi-8 *Hip*; Mi-24 *Hind*
TRAINING
1 unit with EMB-314 *Super Tucano**
1 unit with L-39 *Albatros*
AIR DEFENCE
1 bty with FD-2000 (CH-SA-9)
1 bty with KS-1C (CH-SA-12)
3 bty with S-125 *Neva*-M1 (RS-SA-3 *Goa*)
1 bty with S-125 *Pechora*-2M (RS-SA-26)
2 bty with S-200 *Angara* (RS-SA-5 *Gammon*)

EQUIPMENT BY TYPE
AIRCRAFT 65 combat capable
FTR 24: 22 MiG-29A/S *Fulcrum*; 2 MiG-29UB *Fulcrum*
ATK 31: 19 Su-25 *Frogfoot*; 12 Su-25MK *Frogfoot*
TPT 5: Medium 2 C-27J *Spartan*; Light 3: 1 An-26 *Curl*; 2 An-74TK *Coaler*
TRG 12: 5 EMB-314 *Super Tucano**; 5 M-346FA*; 2 L-39 *Albatros*
HELICOPTERS
ATK 10 Mi-24P *Hind* F
MRH 2+ AW139
TPT 11+: Medium 8: 6 Mi-8 *Hip*; 2 Mi-17V-V *Hip*; Light 3+ AW109
UNINHABITED AERIAL VEHICLES
CISR 3+: Heavy CH-3A; WJ-600; Medium 3+ *Bayraktar* TB2
ISR 3+: Medium 3+ *Falco* Light *Orbiter*-2
LOITERING & DIRECT ATTACK MUNITIONS
Skystriker
AIR DEFENCE • SAM
Long-range 18: 2 2K11 *Krug* (RS-SA-4 *Ganef*); 4 FD-2000 (CH-SA-9); 12 S-200 *Angara* (RS-SA-5 *Gammon*);
Medium-range 8: 4 S-125 *Pechora*-2M (RS-SA-26); 4 KS-1A (CH-SA-12)
Short-range 12: 12 S-125M1 *Neva*-M1 (RS-SA-3 *Goa*); some S-125-2BM *Pechora*
AIR-LAUNCHED MISSILES
AAM • IR R-60 (RS-AA-8 *Aphid*); R-73 (RS-AA-11A *Archer*)
BOMBS
Laser-guided MAM-C; MAM-L

Gendarmerie & Paramilitary 20,000

Internal Troops ε15,000
EQUIPMENT BY TYPE
ARMOURED FIGHTING VEHICLES
IFV 2+ *Lazar*-3
APC • PPV 9: 4+ *Survivor* II; 5 *Titan*-DS
AUV 4+ Plasan *Stormrider*

Federal Border Guard Service ε5,000
EQUIPMENT BY TYPE
ARMOURED FIGHTING VEHICLES
APC • PPV 8: 4+ *Kirpi*; 4+ *Survivor* II
AUV 6+ *Cobra*
ARTILLERY • MRL 122mm 4 BM-21A
AIR DEFENCE
GUNS • TOWED • 23mm ZU-23-2
PATROL AND COASTAL COMBATANTS 33
PCGM 8 *Arkadag* (TUR *Tuzla*) with 2 twin lnchr with *Otomat* AShM, 2 twin *Simbad*-RC lnchr with *Mistral* SAM, 1 Roketsan ASW Rocket Launcher System A/S mor
PBFG 6 *Nazya* (Dearsan 33) with 2 single lnchr with *Marte* Mk2/N AShM
PBF 18: 10 *Bars*-12; 5 *Grif*-T; 3 *Sobol*
PB 1 *Point*
AMPHIBIOUS • LCM 1 Dearsan LCM-1
HELICOPTERS
MRH 2 AW139
TPT 3+: **Medium** some Mi-8 *Hip*; **Light** 3 AW109

Ukraine UKR

Ukrainian Hryvnia UAH		2022	2023	2024
GDP	UAH	5.19trn	6.50trn	7.71trn
	USD	161bn	173bn	186bn
per capita	USD	4,607	5,225	5,531
Growth	%	-29.1	2.0	3.2
Inflation	%	20.2	17.7	13.0
Def bdgt	UAH	131bn	1.14trn	
	USD	3.55bn	30.9bn	
FMA (US)	USD	1.32bn	165m	165m
USD1=UAH		36.93	36.93	37.93

Real-terms defence budget trend (USDbn, constant 2015)
14.7
0.94
2008 — 2016 — 2023

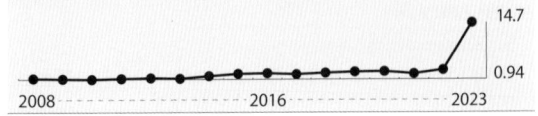

Population 34,831,102

Age	0–14	15–19	20–24	25–29	30–64	65 plus
Male	6.2%	2.4%	2.5%	3.3%	28.6%	6.9%
Female	5.7%	2.0%	1.8%	2.3%	25.2%	13.1%

Capabilities

After absorbing the initial assault of Russia's February 2022 invasion, Ukrainian forces halted Russia's attempt to seize Kyiv. Ukrainian counter-offensives in 2022 recovered much of the territory initially lost, including in the Donetsk region and also around Kherson in the south and to the east of Kharkiv further north. Counter-offensives in 2023, however, faced prepared Russian defence in depth, regained far less territory, and suffered considerable personnel and equipment costs. Nevertheless, the Ukrainian military inflicted heavy losses on Russian forces. Ukraine continued to receive support from Western states in the form of military materiel. This support has included intelligence support and the supply of main battle tanks, artillery, anti-armour and anti-air weapons. Ukraine received air-launched cruise missiles and short-range ballistic missile in 2023. Kyiv remains intent on securing membership of the European Union and NATO. President Volodymyr Zelenskyy announced Ukraine's application to join NATO in response to Russia's September 2022 annexation of several regions, but the Alliance has merely said it would consider such a step in the future. General mobilisation was declared on 24 February 2022 and remained in place throughout 2023: 18–60-year-old men were not allowed to leave the country, while women between 18–60 in certain professions also had to register for military service. After the invasion, substantial numbers of civilians volunteered for defence duties. At the outset of the war, Ukraine's equipment inventory consisted predominantly of Soviet-era weaponry, though more modern ground equipment from Western sources has increasingly supplemented and replaced Russian systems. A number of Western states provide training assistance to Ukrainian troops in their own nations, ranging from basic training to instruction on new equipment, including the F-16. Foreign partners also provide maintenance support. Since 2014, Western-delivered training support developed combat and command skills. Ukraine's development of an NCO cadre after 2014 under Western guidance proved valuable. In 2021, Ukraine replaced its Military Doctrine with a new Military Security Strategy, which built on the 2020

National Security Strategy. Part of the reform programme included the establishment of several new commands, including a Joint Forces Command. The war is spurring Kyiv's ambition to replace its Soviet-era equipment, though the country will need considerable financial support to meet this goal and to fund reconstruction efforts. Ukraine has a broad defence-industrial base, operating in all sectors, though its capability remains shaped and limited by its Soviet heritage. The condition of its defence-industrial facilities is unclear; many have been attacked by Russia, though Western companies have pledged to help rebuild key industrial capacities. Ongoing combat and Ukraine's mobilisation mean that accurate equipment, forces and personnel assessments are difficult.

ACTIVE 500,000–800,000 (Army 200,000–350,000 Navy 20,000 Air Force 37,000 Airborne 40,000 Special Operations Forces 3,000 Territorial Defence 200,000–350,000) Gendarmerie & Paramilitary 250,000

Conscript liability Army, Air Force 18 months, Navy 2 years. Minimum age for conscription raised from 18 to 20 in 2015. The Armed Forces of Ukraine had an officially stated strength of 800,000 personnel by late 2023; it is unclear if this figure represented a mandated total or an actual headcount.

RESERVE 300,000–400,000 (Joint 300,000–400,000)

Military service within 5 years

ORGANISATIONS BY SERVICE

Army 200,000–350,000

4 regional HQ

FORCES BY ROLE
COMMAND
2 corps HQ
MANOEUVRE
Reconnaissance
5 recce bn
Armoured
2 tk bde
Mechanised
3 (aslt) mech bde
28 mech bde
1 mech bde (forming)
2 mtn bde
Light
4 mot inf bde
1 (volunteer) lt inf regt
SURFACE-TO-SURFACE MISSILES
1 SRBM bde
COMBAT SUPPORT
7 arty bde
2 MRL bde
1 STA regt
1 engr bde
1 engr regt
1 ptn br regt
1 EW regt
1 EW bn
2 EW coy
1 CBRN regt
4 sigs regt
COMBAT SERVICE SUPPORT
1 engr spt bde
3 maint regt
1 maint coy
HELICOPTERS
4 avn bde
AIR DEFENCE
4 AD regt

Reserves
FORCES BY ROLE
MANOEUVRE
Armoured
3 tk bde
Mechanised
5 mech bde
Light
1 inf bde
4 inf bde (forming)
COMBAT SUPPORT
2 arty bde

EQUIPMENT BY TYPE (ε)
ARMOURED FIGHTING VEHICLES
MBT 937: 20 *Leopard* 1A5/1A5BE; 60 *Leopard* 2A4/2A5 (Strv 122)/2A6; 26 M-55S; 26 PT-91 *Twardy*; some T-62M/MV; 200 T-64BM/BV/BV mod 2017; 520 T-72AMT/AV/AV mod 2021/B1/B3/EA/M1/M1R; 80 T-80BV/BVM/U/UK; some T-90A; 5 T-84 *Oplot*

RECCE 170: 120 BRDM-2/-2L1/-2T; 50 BRM-1K (CP)

IFV 1,020: 400 BMP-1/-1AK/-2; 40 BMP-3; some BTR-3DA/-3E1/-4E/-4MV1; 75 BTR-82A; 28 BVP M-80A; 140 M2A2 *Bradley*/M7SA BFIST; 48 CV9040; 98 Rosomak IFV (including variants); 54 PbV-501; 137 YPR-765

APC 1,274
  APC (T) 635: 510 M113A1/AS4/G3DK/G4DK; 125 MT-LB
  APC (W) 199: 39 ACSV; 130 BTR-60/-70/-80; 20 *Pandur* 6×6 (*Valuk*); 10 XA-180 *Sisu*
  PPV 440+: *Kozak*-2/-2M/-5/-7; 440 *Maxxpro*; *Varta*
AUV 73+: 43 *Dingo* 2; 30 FV103 *Spartan*; IVECO LMV; *Novator*; *Panthera* T6; Roshel *Senator*

ENGINEERING & MAINTENANCE VEHICLES
AEV 49+: 40 BAT-2; M1150 ABV; MT-LB; 5 Pionierpanzer 2 *Dachs*; 10 *Wisent*

ARV 15+: 15 BPz-2; BPz-3 *Buffel*; BREM-1; BREM-M; BREM-2; BREM-64; BTS-4; IMR-2; VT-72M4CZ

MW *Bozena*

VLB 17+: 17 *Biber*; MTU-20

ANTI-TANK/ANTI-INFRASTRUCTURE
MSL
SP 9P148 *Konkurs* (RS-AT-5 *Spandrel*); 9P148 with *Stugna*-P; 9P149 with 9K114 *Shturm* (RS-AT-6 *Spiral*); M1064A1 HMMWV with TOW; *Brimstone; Brimstone* II
MANPATS 9K111 *Fagot* (RS-AT-4 *Spigot*); 9K113 *Konkurs* (RS-AT-5 *Spandrel*); *Corsar*; FGM-148 *Javelin*; NLAW; *Stugna*-P
GUNS 100mm ε200 MT-12/T-12

ARTILLERY 1,639
SP 566: **122mm** 125 2S1 *Gvozdika*; **152mm** 167+: 120 2S3 *Akatsiya*; some 2S5 *Giatsint*-S; 35 2S19 *Msta*-S; some *Dana*-M2; 12 M-77 *Dana*; **155mm** 254: 4 2S22 *Bohdana*; 8 *Archer*; 20 AS90; 26 CAESAR 6×6; 17 CAESAR 8×8; 53 *Krab*; 90 M109A3GN/A4/A5Oe/A6/L; 28 PzH 2000; 8 *Zuzana*-2; **203mm** 20 2S7 *Pion*
TOWED 537: **105mm** 103: 100 L119 Light Gun/M119A3; 3+ M101; **122mm** 60 D-30; **130mm** 15 M-46; **152mm** 195: 75 2A36 *Giatsint*-B; 70 2A65 *Msta*-B; 50 D-20; **155mm** 164: 20 FH 70; 130 M777A2; 14 TR-F1
GUN/MOR • 120mm • TOWED 2B16 NONA-K
MRL 248: **122mm** 112: 100 9K51M *Tornado*-G/BM-21 *Grad*; 4 APR-40; 8 RM-70 *Vampir*; **220mm** 35 *Bureivy*/9P140 *Uragan*; **227mm** 61: 38 M142 HIMARS; 23 M270A1/B1 MLRS; **300mm** 40+: some *Vilkha/Vilkha*-M; 40 9A52 *Smerch*†
MOR 300+: **SP 107mm** M106; **120mm** 300: 100 2S12 *Sani*; 140 EM-120; some Krh/92; 60 M120-15; **SP 120mm** BTR-3M2

SURFACE-TO-SURFACE MISSILE LAUNCHERS
SRBM • Conventional 9K79 *Tochka* (RS-SS-21 *Scarab*)†
COASTAL • DEFENCE AShM RBS-17 *Hellfire*

HELICOPTERS
ATK ε45 Mi-24/Mi-35 *Hind*
TPT • Medium ε15 Mi-8 *Hip*

UNINHABITED AERIAL VEHICLES
ISR • Medium *Primoco UAV One* 150

LOITERING & DIRECT ATTACK MUNITIONS
(Multiple systems below 20kg in weight)

AIR DEFENCE
SAM 81+
Long-range Some S-300V (RS-SA-12A *Gladiator*)
Short-range 10: 4 *Crotale* NG; 6 9K330 *Tor*-M (RS-SA-15 *Gauntlet*)
Point-defence ε65 9K33 *Osa*-AKM (RS-SA-8 *Gecko*); 9K35 *Strela*-10 (RS-SA-13 *Gopher*); 9K38 *Igla* (RS-SA-18 *Grouse*); 6 FV4333 *Stormer* with *Starstreak*; 6 M1097 *Avenger*; *Martlet; Mistral; Piorun; Starstreak*
SPAAGM 30mm 75 2K22 *Tunguska* (RS-SA-19 *Grison*)
GUNS
SP 23mm ZSU-23-4 *Shilka*; **35mm** 46 *Gepard*
TOWED 23mm ZU-23-2; **40mm** 36 L/70; **57mm** S-60
AIR-LAUNCHED MISSILES • ASM *Barrier*-V

Navy ε20,000
After Russia's annexation of Crimea, HQ shifted to Odessa. Several additional vessels remain in Russian possession in Crimea

EQUIPMENT BY TYPE
PATROL AND COASTAL COMBATANTS 13
PCC 3 *Slavyansk* (ex-US *Island*)
PBG 3 *Gyurza*-M (Project 51855) with 2 *Katran*-M RWS with *Barrier* SSM
PBF 7: 6 *Defiant* 40; 1 *Kentavr*-LK†

MINE WARFARE • MINE COUNTERMEASURES 2
MHC 2 *Chernihiv* (ex-UK *Sandown*)

LOGISTICS AND SUPPORT 8
ABU 1 Project 419 (*Sura*)
AG 1 *Bereza*
AGI 1 *Muna*
AKL 1
AWT 1 *Sudak*
AXL 3 *Petrushka*

UNINHABITED MARITIME PLATFORMS • USV
ATK *Kherson; Magura* V5

UNINHABITED MARITIME SYSTEMS • UUV
ATK *Toloka*

Naval Aviation ε1,000
EQUIPMENT BY TYPE
FIXED-WING AIRCRAFT
ASW (2 Be-12 *Mail* non-operational)
TPT • Light (2 An-26 *Curl* in store)
HELICOPTERS
ASW 2+: some Ka-27 *Helix* A; 1 Mi-14PS *Haze* A; 1 Mi-14PL *Haze* C
TPT • Medium 3 *Sea King* HU5
TRG 1 Ka-226
UNINHABITED AERIAL VEHICLES
CISR • Medium *Bayraktar* TB2
BOMBS • Laser-guided MAM-C/-L

Naval Infantry ε11,000
FORCES BY ROLE
MANOEUVRE
Reconnaissance
1 recce bn
Light
4 nav inf bde
EQUIPMENT BY TYPE
ARMOURED FIGHTING VEHICLES
MBT T-64BV
ASLT 35 AMX-10RC
IFV BMP-1; BMP-3
APC
APC (T) MT-LB
APC (W) 26+: BTR-60; BTR-80; 26 XA-185 *Sisu*

PPV 17+: *Kirpi*; 17 *Mastiff*; *Varta*
AUV M-ATV
ANTI-TANK/ANTI-INFRASTRUCTURE
GUNS 100mm MT-12
ARTILLERY
SP 122mm 2S1 *Gvozdika*
TOWED 152mm 2A36 *Giatsint*-B
AIR DEFENCE
GUNS • SP 23mm ZSU-23-4

Coastal Defence ε1,500
FORCES BY ROLE
COASTAL DEFENCE
1 arty bde
1 MRL regt
EQUIPMENT BY TYPE
ARTILLERY
TOWED 152mm D-20
MRL 220mm 9P140 *Uragan*
COASTAL DEFENCE
AShM *Maritime Brimstone*; RGM-84 *Harpoon*; RK-360MC *Neptun*

Air Forces 37,000
4 Regional HQ
FORCES BY ROLE
FIGHTER
4 bde with MiG-29 *Fulcrum*; Su-27 *Flanker* B; L-39 *Albatros*
FIGHTER/GROUND ATTACK
2 bde with Su-24M *Fencer*; Su-25 *Frogfoot*
ISR
1 sqn with Su-24MR *Fencer* E*
TRANSPORT
3 bde with An-24 *Curl*; An-26 *Coke*; An-30 *Clank*; Il-76 *Candid*; Tu-134 *Crusty*
TRAINING
Some sqn with L-39 *Albatros*
TRANSPORT HELICOPTER
Some sqn with Mi-8 *Hip*; Mi-9 *Hip*; PZL Mi-2 *Hoplite*
AIR DEFENCE
6 bde with S-300PS/PT (RS-SA-10 *Grumble*)
3 regt with S-300PS/PT (RS-SA-10 *Grumble*)
3 regt with 9K37M *Buk*-M1 (RS-SA-11 *Gadfly*)
EQUIPMENT BY TYPE
AIRCRAFT 78 combat capable
FTR 49: ε24 MiG-29 *Fulcrum*; ε25 Su-27 *Flanker* B
ATK 21: ε5 Su-24M *Fencer* D; ε16 Su-25 *Frogfoot*
ISR 11: 3 An-30 *Clank*; ε8 Su-24MR *Fencer* E*
TPT 22: **Heavy** (7 Il-76 *Candid* non-operational); **Medium** 1 An-70; **Light** ε21: 3 An-24 *Coke*; ε17 An-26 *Curl*; 1 Tu-134 *Crusty*
TRG ε29 L-39 *Albatros*

HELICOPTERS
C2 2+ Mi-9 *Hip*
MRH 32: 10 Mi-8MTV *Hip* H; ε22 Mi-17/-17V-5 *Hip*
TPT 25: **Medium** ε18 Mi-8 *Hip*; **Light** 7: ε5 PZL Mi-2 *Hoplite*; 2 Mi-2MSB
UNINHABITED AERIAL VEHICLES
CISR • **Medium** *Bayraktar* TB2
ISR • **Heavy** some Tu-141 *Strizh*; **Light** UJ-22
AIR DEFENCE
SAM 289:
Long-range 220: 200 S-300PS/PT (RS-SA-10 *Grumble*); 8 S-300PMU (RS-SA-10 *Grumble*); 12 M902 *Patriot* PAC-3
Medium-range 60: ε50 9K37M *Buk*-M1 (RS-SA-11 *Gadfly*) (some systems converted to AIM-7); 6 IRIS-T SLM; 4 MIM-23B I-*Hawk*
Short-range 9 NASAMS
GUNS • **TOWED 23mm** some ZU-23-2
AIR-LAUNCHED MISSILES
AAM • **IR** R-27ET (RS-AA-10D *Alamo*); R-60 (RS-AA-8 *Aphid*); R-73 (RS-AA-11A *Archer*); **SARH** R-27R (RS-AA-10A *Alamo*); R-27ER (RS-AA-10C *Alamo*)
ASM Kh-25 (RS-AS-10 *Karen*); Kh-29 (RS-AS-14 *Kedge*)
ARM AGM-88 HARM; Kh-25MP (RS-AS-12A *Kegler*); Kh-58 (RS-AS-11 *Kilter*)
EW MALD
LACM SCALP EG; *Storm Shadow*
BOMBS
INS/GPS-guided JDAM-ER
Laser-guided MAM-C/-L

Airborne Assault Troops ε40,000
FORCES BY ROLE
MANOEUVRE
Reconnaissance
1 recce bn
Mechanised
4 air aslt bde
1 air aslt regt
4 air mob bde
Air Manoeuvre
1 AB bde
COMBAT SUPPORT
1 SP arty bde
EQUIPMENT BY TYPE
ARMOURED FIGHTING VEHICLES
MBT 13+ 13 *Challenger* 2; T-80BV mod
IFV BTR-3E1; BTR-4 *Bucephalus*; 55 *Marder* 1A3
APC 466
APC (T) 30 BTR-D
APC (W) 266+: BTR-80; *Dozor*-B; 180 M1126 *Stryker* ICV; *Oncilla*; 86+ VAB
PPV 170 *Kirpi*

ABCV BMD-2
AUV 75+: 75 *Bushmaster*; IVECO LMV; KrAZ *Spartan*; MLS *Shield*; *Novator*
ANTI-TANK/ANTI-INFRASTRUCTURE
MSL • MANPATS 9K111 *Fagot* (RS-AT-4 *Spigot*); 9K111-1 *Konkurs* (RS-AT-5 *Spandrel*); NLAW
ARTILLERY
SP 122mm 2S1 *Gvozdika*; 152mm 2S3 *Akatsiya*
TOWED • 122mm D-30; 155mm M777A2
MRL 122mm BM-21 *Grad*
GUN/MOR • SP • 120mm 20 2S9 NONA-S; 2S17-2 NONA-SV; 2S23 NONA-SVK
MOR 120mm 2S12 *Sani*
AIR DEFENCE
SAM • Point-defence 9K35M *Strela*-10M; LMM; *Piorun*
GUNS • SP 23mm some ZU-23-2 (truck mounted)

Special Operations Forces ε3,000
FORCES BY ROLE
SPECIAL FORCES
1 SF bn
2 spec ops regt
2 (volunteer) spec ops regt
1 spec ops bn

Territorial Defence Force 200,000–350,000
FORCES BY ROLE
MANOEUVRE
Light
31 (territorial def) inf bde

Gendarmerie & Paramilitary 250,000
National Guard ε90,000
Ministry of Internal Affairs; 5 territorial comd
FORCES BY ROLE
MANOEUVRE
Mechanised
5 (aslt) mech inf bde
Light
1 mot inf bde
Other
3 sy bde
1 sy regt
EQUIPMENT BY TYPE
ARMOURED FIGHTING VEHICLES
MBT T-64; T-64BV; T-64BM; T-72; T-90M
IFV BMP-2; BTR-3; BTR-3E1; BTR-4 *Bucephalus*; BTR-4E; YPR-765
APC
APC (W) BTR-70; BTR-80
PPV Streit *Cougar*; Streit *Spartan*; Kozak-2; *Varta*
AUV *Novator*
ANTI-TANK/ANTI-INFRASTRUCTURE
MSL • MANPATS NLAW
RCL 73mm SPG-9
ARTILLERY
TOWED 122mm D-30
MOR 120mm some
AIRCRAFT
TPT • Light 24: 20 An-26 *Curl*; 2 An-72 *Coaler*; 2 Tu-134 *Crusty*
HELICOPTERS • TPT 14: Medium 11: 4 H225; 7 Mi-8 *Hip*; Light 3: 2 H125; 1 Mi-2MSB
AIR DEFENCE
SAM • Point-defence 9K38 *Igla* (RS-SA-18 *Grouse*); *Piorun*
GUNS • SP 23mm some ZU-23-2 (tch)

Border Guard ε60,000
FORCES BY ROLE
MANOEUVRE
Mechanised
1 (mobile) lt mech bn
Light
1 (mobile) inf bn
Other
19 sy bn
EQUIPMENT BY TYPE
ARMOURED FIGHTING VEHICLES
APC • PPV Kozak-2; *Mamba* (Alvis 4)
AUV Triton-01

Maritime Border Guard
The Maritime Border Guard is an independent subdivision of the State Commission for Border Guards and is not part of the navy
EQUIPMENT BY TYPE
PATROL AND COASTAL COMBATANTS 21
PCT 1 *Molnya* (*Pauk* I) with 4 single 406mm TT, 2 RBU 1200 *Uragan* A/S mor, 1 76mm gun
PCC 4 *Tarantul* (*Stenka*)
PB 12: 11 *Zhuk*; 1 *Orlan*
PBR 4 *Shmel* with 1 76mm gun
LOGISTICS AND SUPPORT • AGF 1
AIRCRAFT • TPT Medium An-8 *Camp*; Light An-24 *Coke*; An-26 *Curl*; An-72 *Coaler*
HELICOPTERS • ASW: Ka-27 *Helix* A

National Police ε100,000
Ministry of Internal Affairs

DEPLOYMENT
KOSOVO: NATO • KFOR 40

SOUTHERN AND EASTERN UKRAINE
Russia annexed the Ukrainian region of Crimea in March 2014, having occupied the territory the previous month.

It has been used by Russia as a basing area since the start of its full-scale invasion of Ukraine in February 2022. Data presented here represents the de facto situation and does not imply international recognition.

FOREIGN FORCES

Russia Donetsk, Kharkiv, Kherson, Luhansk & Zaporizhzhia, ε200,000; Crimea: ε25,000; 1 recce bde(-), 2 naval inf bde(-); 1 air aslt regt; 1 arty bde; 1 NBC bde; 1 AShM bde with 3K60 *Bal*; 3K55 *Bastion*; 1 FGA regt with Su-24M/MR; Su-30SM; 1 FGA regt with Su-27SM/SM3; Su-30M2; 1 atk regt with Su-24M/Su-25SM; 1 atk sqn(-) with Su-34; 1 atk/tpt hel regt; 1 ASW hel regt; 1 AD regt with S-300PM; 1 AD regt with S-400; 1 Fleet HQ located at Sevastopol

Uzbekistan UZB

Uzbekistani Som UZS		2022	2023	2024
GDP	UZS	888trn	1,048trn	1,222trn
	USD	80.4bn	90.4bn	99.6bn
per capita	USD	2,280	2,509	2,710
Growth	%	5.7	5.5	5.5
Inflation	%	11.4	10.2	10.0
Def exp	UZS	n.k.	n.k.	n.k.
	USD	n.k.	n.k.	n.k.
US$1=UZS		11,047	11,593	12,274
Population	35,971,103			

Age	0–14	15–19	20–24	25–29	30–64	65 plus
Male	15.4%	3.8%	3.6%	4.1%	20.5%	2.8%
Female	14.3%	3.6%	3.4%	4.1%	21.0%	3.6%

Capabilities

Uzbekistan introduced a new military doctrine in early 2018, which highlighted increased concern over terrorism and the potential impact of conflicts, including in Afghanistan. It emphasised border security and hybrid-warfare concerns while spelling out a requirement for military modernisation and defence industrial improvements. Uzbekistan is a member of the SCO but suspended its CSTO membership in 2012. The country is a member of the Organization of Turkic States. It maintains bilateral defence ties with Moscow. However, in 2022, Uzbekistan sent humanitarian aid to Ukraine and did not recognise the independence of the Luhansk and Donetsk 'people's republics'. Uzbekistan and Turkiye held bilateral exercises in 2021 and signed an agreement on military cooperation in 2022. Uzbekistan, in 2023, signed a military cooperation plan with Azerbaijan and participated in joint military exercises in Kazakhstan. The armed forces are army-dominated and conscript-based. Uzbekistan has no foreign deployments and limited capacity for such operations. It inherited a sizeable air fleet from the Soviet Union, but the active inventory has shrunk in the absence of recapitalisation efforts. Logistical and maintenance shortcomings hinder aircraft availability. Uzbekistan relies on foreign suppliers for advanced military equipment and procured equipment, including military helicopters and armoured personnel carriers, from Russia in 2019. It held meetings with India in 2020 to advance defence cooperation and, in 2021, the leaders of Pakistan and Uzbekistan signed a defence cooperation pact. A State Committee for the Defence Industry was established in late 2017 to organise domestic industry and defence orders. In recent years, Uzbekistan's defence industry has showcased domestically produced light-armoured vehicles. In 2023, Russian FlySeeagro signed a deal to manufacture agricultural drones in Uzbekistan, raising concerns about the potential for their eventual military use and Russian sanctions evasion.

ACTIVE 48,000 (Army 24,500 Air 7,500 Joint 16,000) **Gendarmerie & Paramilitary 20,000**

Conscript liability 12 months

ORGANISATIONS BY SERVICE

Army 24,500

4 Mil Districts; 2 op comd; 1 Tashkent Comd

FORCES BY ROLE
SPECIAL FORCES
  1 SF bde
MANOEUVRE
  Armoured
  1 tk bde
  Mechanised
  11 MR bde
  Air Manoeuvre
  1 air aslt bde
  1 AB bde
  Mountain
  1 lt mtn inf bde
COMBAT SUPPORT
  3 arty bde
  1 MRL bde

EQUIPMENT BY TYPE
ARMOURED FIGHTING VEHICLES
  MBT 340: 70 T-72; 100 T-64B/MV; 170 T-62
  RECCE 19: 13 BRDM-2; 6 BRM-1
  IFV 370: 270 BMP-2; ε100 BTR-82A
  APC 388
    APC (T) 50 BTR-D
    APC (W) 259: 24 BTR-60; 25 BTR-70; 210 BTR-80
    PPV 79: 24 *Ejder Yalcin*; 50 *Maxxpro+*; 5 *Typhoon*-K 4×4
  ABCV 129: 120 BMD-1; 9 BMD-2
  AUV 11+: 7 *Cougar*; 4+ M-ATV; some *Tigr*-M
ENGINEERING & MAINTENANCE VEHICLES
  ARV 20 *Maxxpro* ARV
ANTI-TANK/ANTI-INFRASTRUCTURE
  MSL • MANPATS 9K11 *Malyutka* (RS-AT-3 *Sagger*); 9K111 *Fagot* (RS-AT-4 *Spigot*)
  GUNS 100mm 36 MT-12/T-12
ARTILLERY 487+
  SP 83+: **122mm** 18 2S1 *Gvozdika*; **152mm** 17+: 17 2S3 *Akatsiya*; 2S5 *Giatsint*-S (reported); **203mm** 48 2S7 *Pion*
  TOWED 200: **122mm** 60 D-30; **152mm** 140 2A36

Giatsint-B
GUN/MOR 120mm 54 2S9 NONA-S
MRL 108: **122mm** 60: 36 BM-21 *Grad*; 24 9P138; **220mm** 48 9P140 *Uragan*
MOR 120mm 42: 5 2B11 *Sani*; 19 2S12 *Sani*; 18 M-120
AIR DEFENCE • SAM
 Point-defence QW-18 (CH-SA-11)

Air Force 7,500
FORCES BY ROLE
FIGHTER
 1 sqn with MiG-29/MiG-29UB *Fulcrum* A/B
GROUND ATTACK
 1 sqn with Su-25/Su-25BM *Frogfoot*
TRANSPORT
 1 regt with Il-76 *Candid*; An-12 *Cub*; An-26 *Curl*; C295W; Tu-134 *Crusty*
TRAINING
 1 sqn with L-39 *Albatros*
ATTACK/TRANSPORT HELICOPTER
 1 regt with Mi-24 *Hind*; Mi-26 *Halo*; Mi-35M *Hind*; Mi-8 *Hip*
AIR DEFENCE
 1 bty with FD-2000 (CH-SA-9)
 1 bty with S-125-2M *Pechora*-2M (RS-SA-26)
 2 bty with S-125M1 *Neva*-M1 (RA-SA-3 *Goa*)
EQUIPMENT BY TYPE
AIRCRAFT 24 combat capable
 FTR 12 MiG-29/MiG-29UB *Fulcrum* A/B; (18 more in store); (26 Su-27/Su-27UB *Flanker* B/C in store)
 ATK 12: 12 Su-25/Su-25BM *Frogfoot*; (15 Su-24 *Fencer* in store)
 TPT 11: **Heavy** 2 Il-76 *Candid*; **Medium** 2 An-12 *Cub*; **Light** 7: 2 An-26 *Curl*; 4 C295W; 1 Tu-134 *Crusty*
 TRG 6 L-39 *Albatros*
HELICOPTERS
 ATK 41: 29 Mi-24 *Hind*; 12 Mi-35M *Hind*
 TPT 32: **Heavy** 9: 8 H225M *Caracal*; 1 Mi-26 *Halo*; **Medium** ε15 Mi-8 *Hip*; **Light** 8 AS350 *Ecureuil*
UNINHABITED AERIAL VEHICLES
 CISR 4+: **Heavy** *Wing Loong*; **Medium** 4+ *Bayraktar* TB2
AIR DEFENCE • SAM 18
 Long-range 4 FD-2000 (CH-SA-9)
 Medium-range 4 S-125-2M *Pechora*-2M (RS-SA-26)
 Short-range 10 S-125M1 *Neva*-M1 (RS-SA-3 *Goa*)
AIR-LAUNCHED MISSILES
 AAM • IR R-60 (RS-AA-8 *Aphid*); R-73 (RS-AA-11A *Archer*); **IR/SARH** R-27 (RS-AA-10 *Alamo*)
 ASM Kh-25 (RS-AS-10 *Karen*)
 ARM Kh-25MP (RS-AS-12A *Kegler*); Kh-28 (RS-AS-9 *Kyle*); Kh-58 (RS-AS-11 *Kilter*)
BOMBS • Laser-guided MAM-L

Gendarmerie & Paramilitary up to 20,000

Internal Security Troops up to 19,000
Ministry of Interior

National Guard 1,000
Ministry of Defence

Chapter Five
Asia

- China has reshuffled some of its senior military personnel amid an anti-corruption investigation and other probes. Beijing replaced defence minister Li Shangfu. Other departures included senior officials in the rocket forces.
- Australia in March committed to its biggest single defence investment, agreeing to buy nuclear-powered, conventionally armed attack submarines. Canberra plans to first introduce US-made *Virginia*-class SSNs before fielding the SSN-AUKUS boats the country plans to co-develop with the UK.
- Taiwan proposed its largest-ever defence budget in the face of heightened tensions with China. The spending plan represents a 21% increase over the prior year and a 2.6% share of GDP. Taiwan has been upgrading its military across domains. In 2023, the country unveiled its first domestically built submarine but was still awaiting delayed delivery of F-16Vs from the US.
- China logged progress on its newest aircraft carrier, the *Fujian* (Type-003). The larger design will feature catapults, allowing for more potent and comprehensive air operations and making it more capable than the PLAN's two current operational units, the *Liaoning* (Type-001) and the *Shandong* (Type-002).
- India's government focused military spending more on fostering its domestic industry. New Delhi earmarked a record 75% of procurement spending to local sources. The move was partly driven by Russia's full-scale invasion of Ukraine, which has prompted Moscow to prioritise its domestic needs.
- North Korea tested a solid-fuel ICBM in April 2023 and another in July, demonstrating the country's sustained commitment to expanding its ability to deliver nuclear weapons. Pyongyang later in the year also unveiled a submarine that may be capable of firing nuclear-armed missiles.

Asia defence spending, 2023 – top 5

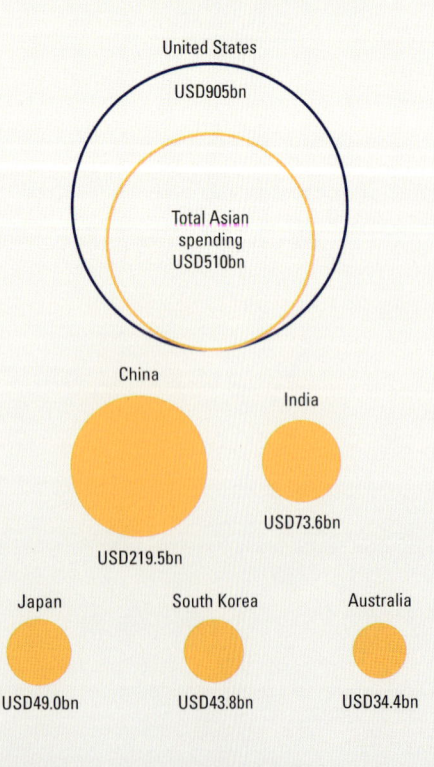

- United States USD905bn
- Total Asian spending USD510bn
- China USD219.5bn
- India USD73.6bn
- Japan USD49.0bn
- South Korea USD43.8bn
- Australia USD34.4bn

Active military personnel – top 10
(25,000 per unit)

Country	Personnel
China	2,035,000
India	1,475,750
North Korea	1,280,000
Pakistan	660,000
South Korea	500,000
Vietnam	450,000
Indonesia	404,500
Thailand	360,850
Sri Lanka	265,900
Japan	247,200

Global total 20,646,000

Regional total 9,029,000 (43.7%)

Regional defence policy and economics 220
Arms procurements and deliveries 244
Armed forces data section 245

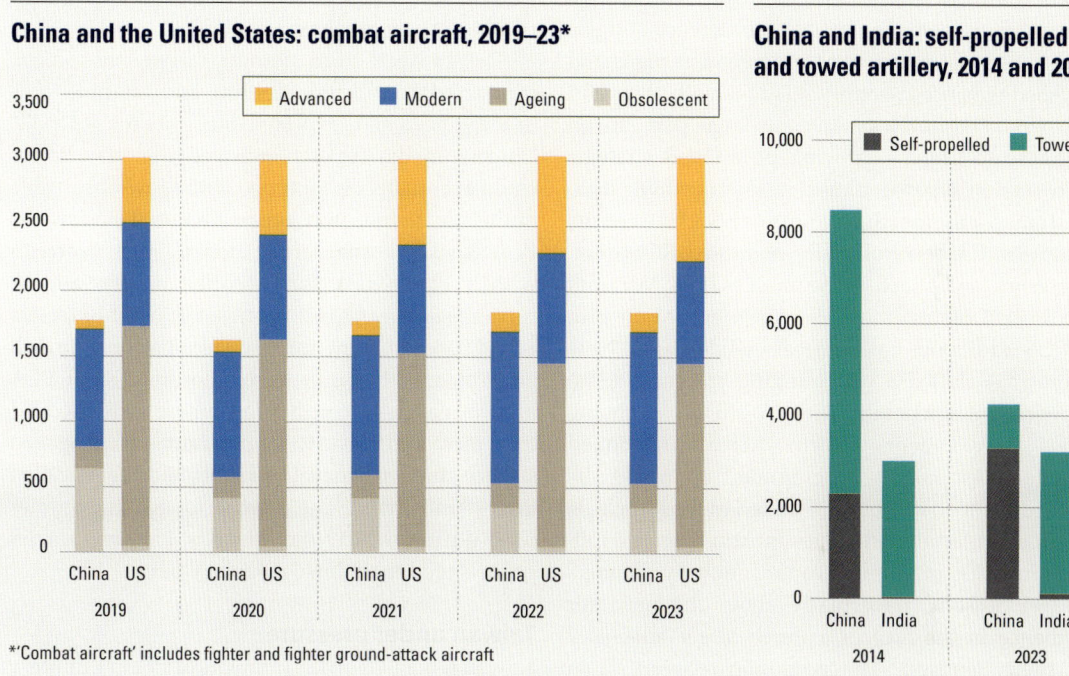

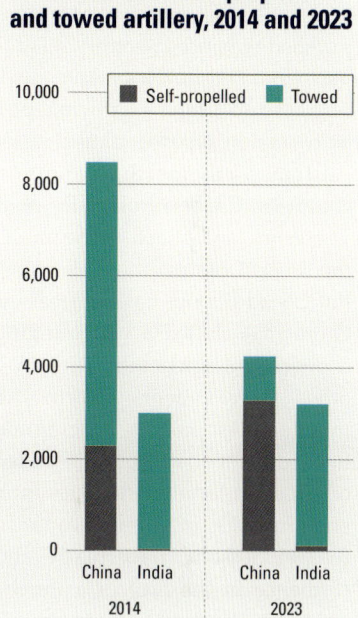

China and the United States: combat aircraft, 2019–23*

Legend: Advanced, Modern, Ageing, Obsolescent

*'Combat aircraft' includes fighter and fighter ground-attack aircraft

China and India: self-propelled and towed artillery, 2014 and 2023

Legend: Self-propelled, Towed

China: real-terms defence budget trend, 2008–23 (USDbn, constant 2015)

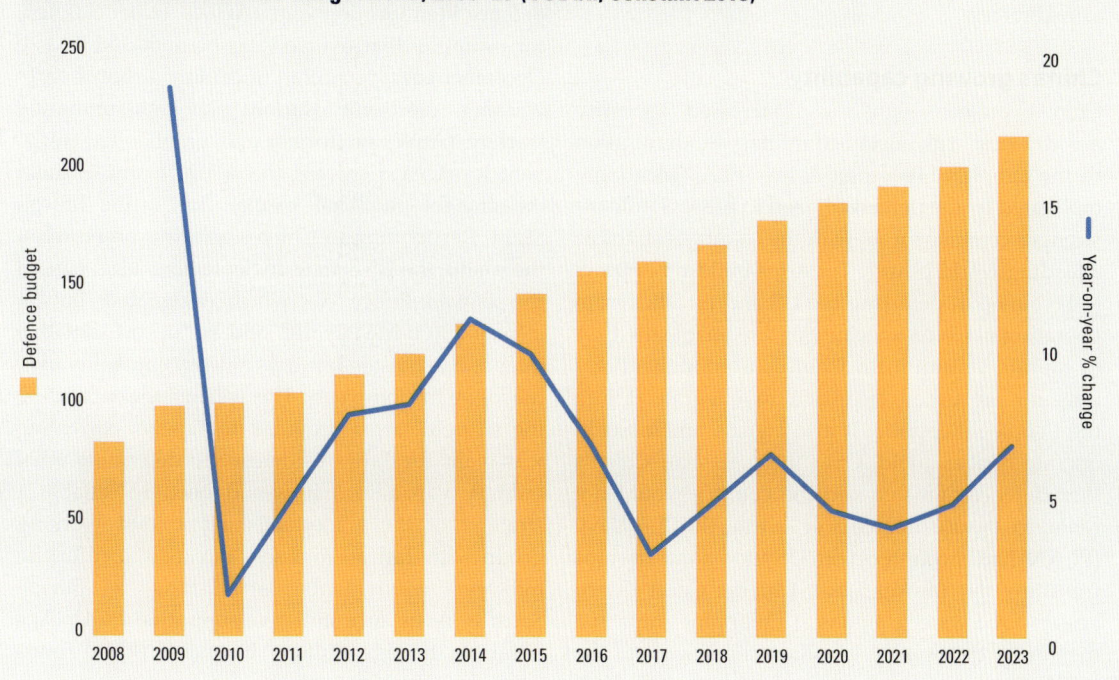

Left axis: Defence budget
Right axis: Year-on-year % change

Asia

Asian countries have intensified their defence focus. Many governments increased their defence budgets in 2023, set out major arms procurement plans and pursued enhanced security relations with allies and partners. The developments, in large part, are in response to China's growing power and strategic extroversion. Japan deployed its F-35 *Lightning* IIs to Australia for the first time to improve ties between the countries, Canberra officially requested RGM-109E *Tomahawk* land-attack cruise missiles (LACMs) from the United States, the Philippines agreed to give the US additional basing access while Papua New Guinea concluded a wide-ranging 15-year defence cooperation agreement with Washington, among other developments. North Korea's continued missile-development programme, alongside its nuclear-weapons ambitions, added to the high level of attention to military issues in Asia. Russia's full-scale invasion of Ukraine caused military planners to seek lessons, particularly about the need for resilience in the face of a much larger adversary on their doorstep. The economic recovery from the COVID-19 pandemic helped governments financially underpin their increased attention on the armed forces.

China's growing capability

China paired signs of increased security assertiveness with sustained military modernisation of the People's Liberation Army (PLA), seemingly motivated by the perceived need to possess military strength commensurate with the country's status as a leading world power. The arms build-up appears to be aimed at deterring the US and its allies from operating in China's vicinity and to enable the PLA to capture Taiwan if the Chinese Communist Party opts for an armed approach to integrate it into the People's Republic. It also signals ambitions to operate further afield. Over the past year, China's then-defence minister said the country would not renounce the use of force over Taiwan, the PLA Navy (PLAN) had encounters with US and Canadian ships transiting the Taiwan Strait, Chinese Coast Guard vessels fired water cannons at Philippine ships in a dispute in the Spratly Islands archipelago and the Chinese and Russian navies exercised jointly near Alaska, among other activities.

The PLAN's third aircraft carrier, the *Fujian*, conducted propulsion, mooring and catapult trials in 2023 ahead of its expected departure for sea trials. Chinese media reports indicated that the carrier could eventually be equipped with a low-observable multi-role fighter and other aircraft. In 2023, the PLA Rocket Force participated in joint exercises with a PLAN task force centred on the aircraft carrier *Shandong* 740 kilometres northwest of the US island base of Guam in the western Pacific. The drill illustrated both the growing coordination of PLA branches and – according to Chinese state media – their increased capacity for precision strikes against surface ships and naval bases beyond the so-called 'first island chain'. The exercise followed an earlier one, during which the PLAN's *Liaoning* carrier group sailed to within 670 km of Guam.

Taiwan under pressure

Taiwan remained on the front line of China's military activity, with record numbers of PLA aircraft making incursions into the island's self-declared air defence identification zone (ADIZ). Taipei claimed, for example, that over one 24-hour period in late December 2022, 71 aircraft (including airborne early warning, electronic warfare and anti-submarine warfare (ASW) platforms) and uninhabited aerial vehicles (UAVs) entered the ADIZ, many of them crossing the unofficial 'median line' in the Taiwan Strait. Responding to China's growing pressure on the island, the US Senate, in September 2022, passed the Taiwan Policy Act which designated Taiwan a 'major non-NATO ally' and set up an initiative intended to bolster Taiwan's military capability over the following four years. This will include expanding the scope of arms provided to Taiwan; reviewing war plans for Taiwan's defence to determine what military capabilities it would need to 'enable a strategy of denial'; establishing a joint working group with Taiwan to assess threats and prioritise military requirements; establishing a Taiwan Security Assistance Initiative supported by USD4.5 billion in Foreign Military Financing (FMF) funds (with the provision that Taiwan must increase its defence spending); agreeing with Taiwan the scope of the 'asymmetric capabilities' that it needs; and establishing a 'comprehensive training program' with Taiwan to improve its military capabilities and to increase 'armed forces interoperability'. In August 2023, the Biden administration followed by approving the first-ever assistance to Taiwan using the FMF mechanism, angering Beijing.

Taiwan has meanwhile tried to bolster its defences, in part with the realisation it would be hard for the US to quickly supply the island with military equipment in a conflict. Taipei over the past year acquired more M142 High Mobility Artillery Rocket Systems, General Atomics MQ-9B *Sea Guardian* UAVs and other items. In December 2022, a US senator complained about an alleged USD18.7bn backlog in arms supplies for Taiwan, blaming it on equipment transfers to Ukraine following the Russian invasion of February 2022. Among the delayed items were 66 new F-16V fighters ordered in 2019. In May 2023, Taiwan's defence ministry said that delivery of the first of these aircraft would be postponed from the end of 2023 to the third quarter of 2024 due to supply-chain disruptions related to the COVID-19 pandemic.

Japan's major capability development efforts

In December 2022, Japan's government published its first National Security Strategy (NSS) since 2013, accompanied by a National Defense Strategy (NDS) and a Defense Buildup Program. The government also set a target of spending 2% of GDP on defence. In a significant departure from earlier pronouncements, these three documents emphasised the need for Japan to strengthen its capabilities to defend its home territory against direct attack, particularly by missiles. The NSS asserted that Japan faced the 'most severe and complex security environment' since 1945 and pointed to China as the 'greatest strategic challenge' and North Korea as an 'even more grave and imminent threat'. It also expressed strong concern over Sino-Russian strategic cooperation. The strategy emphasised the importance of economic security and an overall approach exploiting all elements of national power, but the need for comprehensive improvements to Japan's defence capabilities loomed large.

The accompanying NDS identified several areas for the Japan Self Defense Force (JSDF) to focus on and signalled concern in Tokyo that Japan's missile-defence network could be overwhelmed in the event of conflict with North Korea or China. It asserted that the JSDF needed capabilities that would allow it to defend Japan by responding to a first wave of enemy missile attacks on its territory with 'effective counterstrikes against the opponent to prevent further attacks'. Tokyo is investing in missiles with increasingly long ranges to enhance the JSDF's capacity to attack vessels and landing forces invading Japan and, in the longer term, to introduce a counterstrike capability. In May 2023, Japan's defence ministry signed a series of contracts with Mitsubishi Heavy Industries covering mass production of the Type 12 anti-ship missile, with work also going into developing a longer-range version, according to reports, while production of the Hyper Velocity Gliding Projectile (HVGP) and development of a submarine-launched missile based on the Type 12 are also under way. The HVGP is reported to have an initial range of 500–900 km, but versions to be developed later this decade are expected to reach 3,000 km or more. The NDS also emphasised Japan's capability development efforts in other areas, including uninhabited platforms, enhanced space capabilities, intelligence and electronic warfare, and it called for the country to have adequate supplies of ammunition, fuel and equipment spares, and other items to prevail in a conflict. In July 2023, Tokyo's annual Defense of Japan White Paper reiterated these ambitions.

That document stressed the importance of bolstering the 'deterrence and response capabilities of the Japan–US Alliance' and reinforcing 'collaboration with likeminded countries' as vital for realising the country's defence objectives.

In a joint statement following a meeting of the Japanese and US defence ministers in June 2023, the two principals affirmed the 'significant role' of US Air Force MQ-9A medium-altitude, long-endurance UAVs temporarily deployed to Japan's Kanoya air base, and an associated Bilateral Information Analysis Cell, in boosting intelligence, surveillance and reconnaissance capabilities, and the document called for maintaining and strengthening such capabilities. Japan and the US deepened their missile-defence ties with an agreement in August to jointly work on an interceptor to defeat hypersonic weapons. Tokyo also agreed to buy *Tomahawk* LACMs from the US. In January 2023, Japanese Prime Minister Kishida Fumio and his British counterpart, Rishi Sunak, signed a Reciprocal Access Agreement

Figure 11 — Japan: selected aircraft procurements, 2010–24

Successive Japanese governments have prioritised domestic production or assembly of aircraft for the Japan Self-Defense Forces (JSDF), even if this has meant higher unit costs. Almost all foreign aircraft designs since 2010, either imported directly or produced under licence in Japan, have been of US origin due to several factors including a desire to be interoperable with Japan's main ally. Acquisition of the F-35 multi-role fighter aircraft represents by far the biggest outlay over this period. Mitsubishi Heavy Industries (MHI) maintains one of three global F-35 'final assembly and check-out' sites. Since the 1980s, Japan has bought several variants of the Sikorsky *Black Hawk*, licence-built by MHI in Nagoya; it is the only aircraft design in service with all three JSDF branches. In the 1980s, Japan resumed production of locally designed military aircraft. About 28% of JSDF aircraft spending since 2010 has gone to indigenous designs, including Kawasaki's C-2 medium transport and P-1 ASW aircraft. Tokyo has continued to import aircraft when Japanese industry does not have the capability to make them or setting up an assembly line would be cost-prohibitive. Despite this long relationship with the US, Japan is participating in the Global Combat Aircraft Programme with Italy and the UK – a significant diversification of procurement signalling a desire to take the country's defence aerospace sector to another level of sophistication with a new set of partners.

Budgeted value (USDbn) and quantity, FY2010–24

Aircraft	Quantity	Force
F-35A *Lightning II**	71	Air Self-Defense Force
P-1	41	Maritime Self-Defense Force
E-2D *Hawkeye*	17	Air Self-Defense Force
F-35B *Lightning II*	27	Air Self-Defense Force
C-2	16	Air Self-Defense Force
SH-60K *Seahawk**	43	Maritime Self-Defense Force
CH-47JA *Chinook**	26	Ground Self-Defense Force
KC-46A *Pegasus*	6	Air Self-Defense Force
MV-22B *Osprey*	17	Ground Self-Defense Force
UH-60J *Black Hawk**	25	Air Self-Defense Force
Bell 412EPX (UH-2)*	48	Ground Self-Defense Force
SH-60L *Seahawk** ‡	12	Maritime Self-Defense Force
CH-47J *Chinook**	6	Ground Self-Defense Force
MCH-101*	8	Maritime Self-Defense Force
RQ-4B *Global Hawk*	3	Air Self-Defense Force
RC-2	1	Air Self-Defense Force
UH-60JA *Black Hawk**	8	Ground Self-Defense Force
US-2	2	Maritime Self-Defense Force
AH-64D *Apache Longbow**	3	Ground Self-Defense Force
OH-1	4	Ground Self-Defense Force
Enstrom 480B (TH-480B)	29	Ground Self-Defense Force
H135 (TH-135)	10	Joint Force

Future combat-aircraft development programmes investment, FY2010–24** (USDm)

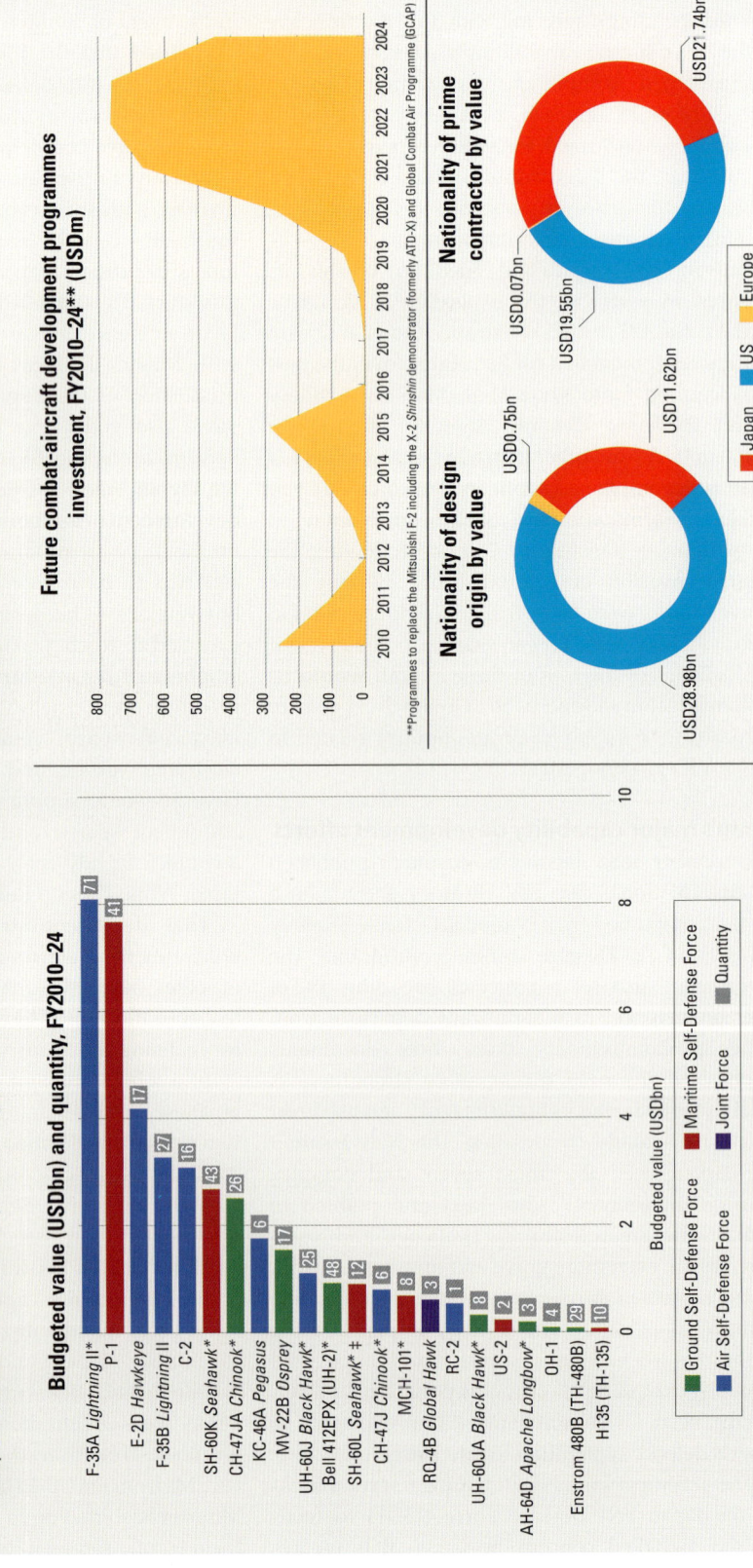

Nationality of design origin by value
- Japan: USD0.75bn
- US: USD28.98bn
- Europe: USD11.62bn

Nationality of prime contractor by value
- Japan: USD0.07bn
- US: USD19.55bn
- Europe: USD21.74bn

*Licensed production or final assembly in Japan; ‡ A tentative name; currently in development
**Programmes to replace the Mitsubishi F-2 including the X-2 *Shinshin* demonstrator (formerly ATD-X) and Global Combat Air Programme (GCAP)

intended to facilitate bilateral military cooperation; this followed a similar agreement with Australia, signed a year earlier. Another important element of Japan's defence collaboration with the United Kingdom is the Global Combat Air Programme, a trilateral project also involving Italy. In 2022, the three countries signed a partnership agreement, with the goal of developing a next-generation combat aircraft to be ready for operational service around 2035. Japan also deepened its relations with NATO. Following a meeting with NATO Secretary General Jens Stoltenberg in Tokyo in January 2023, Kishida participated for the second year running in the annual NATO leaders' summit. At the summit, Kishida and Stoltenberg announced that NATO and Tokyo had concluded negotiations for an Individually Tailored Partnership Program (ITPP) for Japan. The ITPP involves 16 areas of cooperation aimed at strengthening dialogue, enhancing military interoperability and bolstering resilience during the period from 2023–26. However, a plan that Kishida and Stoltenberg had discussed in January for establishing a NATO liaison office in Tokyo proved controversial among some NATO members and was not mentioned in the summit's communiqué.

South Korea reacts to Pyongyang's tests

North Korea intensified its missile testing during 2022, launching approximately 90 cruise and ballistic missiles, more than in any previous year. These tests continued in 2023, with the first trial of a submarine-launched cruise missile in March. Pyongyang tested a solid-fuelled intercontinental ballistic missile in April and another in July. It did not conduct a widely expected seventh nuclear test, however, and it was unclear if it had succeeded in miniaturising nuclear devices to enable their use as deliverable warheads. In September, North Korea unveiled a submarine that may be capable of firing ballistic missiles. Pyongyang's threatening behaviour and widening array of potential delivery systems for nuclear weapons remained by far the most important concerns for defence policymakers in Seoul.

Those developments are driving an array of defence-modernisation efforts in South Korea. In January 2023, President Yoon Suk-yeol surprised observers by saying that South Korea – already protected by US extended nuclear deterrence – might consider developing its own nuclear weapons if the North Korean threat 'continued intensifying'. This may have reflected a widely held view among conservative politicians in Seoul that, as the North's nuclear forces became more sophisticated, a US president might lack the resolve to make US nuclear retaliation against North Korea a credible threat. However, an official subsequently said that Yoon was talking about a 'worst-case scenario' and that South Korea continued to abide by the Non-Proliferation Treaty. Nevertheless, the US made moves to reassure Seoul of its commitment to extended nuclear deterrence in support of South Korea's security. When President Yoon visited Washington in April, he and President Joe Biden issued the Washington Declaration, a joint statement in which the US confirmed that 'any nuclear attack by the DPRK against the ROK will be met with a swift, overwhelming and decisive response'. South Korea, for its part, said it has 'full confidence in US extended deterrence commitments and recognizes the importance, necessity, and benefit of its enduring reliance on the US nuclear deterrent'.

Moreover, the US and South Korea committed to 'deeper, cooperative decision-making on nuclear deterrence' and announced that they were setting up a Nuclear Consultative Group (NCG) 'to strengthen extended deterrence, discuss nuclear and strategic planning and manage the threat to the non-proliferation regime [from North Korea]'. The NCG, comprising senior defence and foreign-affairs officials from South Korea and the US, met for the first time in Seoul in July. Relations between Seoul and Tokyo have also improved since Yoon came to power in 2022. Following a three-way meeting on the sidelines of the IISS Shangri-La Dialogue in early June, Japan, South Korea and the US announced that they had agreed to set up a mechanism for sharing real-time data on North Korean missile launches before the end of 2023. In August, the Camp David summit meeting between the US and South Korean presidents and Japan's prime minister resulted in an agreement to intensify trilateral defence cooperation to 'unprecedented levels', including through annual multi-domain military exercises.

India boosts domestic procurement

In 2023, New Delhi faced continuing challenges from the PLA on the Himalayan border and the PLAN's growing presence in the Indian Ocean, along with sustained concerns over Pakistani support for anti-Indian terrorist groups. The government of Prime Minister Narendra Modi took steps to boost India's domestic defence industry, an initiative that gained momentum from Russia's full-scale invasion of Ukraine. Russia is a major supplier of arms to India, and Western sanctions on Moscow in the wake of the invasion and Russia's own military needs hampered New Delhi's military-equipment supply chain. However, India's military inventory still heavily features Russian-supplied equipment. Despite New Delhi's efforts to reduce that dependence, keeping alive a defence-procurement relationship with Moscow is vital to maintain the Indian armed forces' capabilities. In May 2023, the Indian and Russian defence ministers agreed a way for India to pay Moscow for military equipment despite sanctions, along with a plan for India to produce additional Russian equipment and spares locally. Meanwhile, procurement of Western-produced defence systems also continued. India moved forward with buying MQ-9B UAVs, for instance, and agreed to purchase further submarines from France.

Australia steps up its defence efforts

Australia moved on multiple fronts to shore up its defence posture to deal with what Canberra has framed as its biggest threat, China. In March 2023, Australia committed to its biggest single defence investment, agreeing to buy nuclear-powered, conventionally armed attack submarines under the AUKUS security partnership with the UK and US. The multi-decade effort involves increased US and UK submarine visits to Australia, which the US began last year, with the UK joining from 2026. From around 2032, Australia should receive two used US Navy *Virginia*-class submarines and one newly built one. These might be followed by two more boats of the same class, replacing the *Collins*-class conventionally powered attack submarines due for retirement before the first SSN-AUKUS boats are ready. Canberra also published the Defence Strategic Review in April 2023, which provided a strategic framework for its defence plan and called for faster force generation. The review called for applying several 'critical capabilities', including enhanced long-range strike systems in all domains as well as crewed and uninhabited undersea-warfare capabilities.

New Zealand, whose defence effort remained relatively small, signalled a new resolve to improve its defences, and it published its first National Security Strategy in August 2023. The wide-ranging document, which touches on issues as varied as climate change and Russia's invasion of Ukraine, also called out China's more assertive foreign policy as a driver of strategic competition. New Zealand, meanwhile, has continued force-modernisation efforts, including through the introduction of P-8A maritime patrol aircraft and Australian-made *Bushmaster* 5.5 armoured utility vehicles. Five C-130J-30 transport aircraft are due to enter service in 2024–25.

Asia focuses on subsurface warfare

Asia is becoming a hotbed for undersea-warfare developments. China, Australia and the two antagonistic neighbours on the Korean Peninsula are pursuing major upgrades of their submarine capacities. Indonesia is expanding its fleet of such vessels, and Singapore is introducing new submarines to replace older models it will phase out. Other countries in the region are planning to break into the field. The modernisation drive reflects long-standing interest by several Asian navies to improve their existing capacities and, by others, to create an undersea arm to their naval inventories to provide insurance against political uncertainties.

China, with the region's biggest submarine fleet by displacement, is arguably focusing even more on the underwater domain as it continues its naval-modernisation plans. It is planning additional construction of both nuclear- and conventionally powered fleets. Satellite imagery of the submarine yard in Bohai published in early 2021 indicated that the first hull of either the anticipated Type-093B design for a nuclear-powered attack submarine (SSN) or guided-missile submarine (SSGN) or the expected Type-096 nuclear-powered ballistic-missile submarine (SSBN) is under construction. Meanwhile, Beijing is advancing its conventional-submarine programme – an official navy social-media account revealed an image in July 2022 of the latest *Yuan*-class Type-039A/B variant sporting a sail that may herald new stealth capabilities. The Pentagon expects China to begin fielding land-attack cruise missiles on its submarines, particularly on the projected *Shang*-class Type-093Bs.

Australia, in partnership with the United Kingdom and the United States, is aiming to field conventionally armed, nuclear-powered attack submarines. The US will initially provide *Virginia*-class boats from the early 2030s that are due to be augmented later by the SSN-AUKUS, a new design set to arrive in the 2040s.

Figure 12 AUKUS partnership: submarine implementation plan

After an 18-month study, the leaders of Australia, the United Kingdom and the United States unveiled a phased plan in March 2023 under the AUKUS initiative to deliver a fleet of at least eight Australian nuclear-powered submarines by the 2050s. The plan promises incremental increases in capability over two and a half decades. However, the complexity of the effort underscores the challenge for all three partners to deliver on their commitment. This includes Australia purchasing US submarines in the 2030s. Ultimately, the Royal Australian Navy and the Royal Navy will be equipped with the SSN-AUKUS, based on the UK next-generation submarine design (previously dubbed SSN(R)). It will be constructed in UK and Australian shipyards. All the nuclear-reactor sections will be UK-built, while the boats will incorporate enhanced US technology including a vertical-launch missile system. The design is expected to supplement and eventually replace the *Virginia*-class submarines in Australian service. Canberra has pledged to help fund the US and UK submarine-building industries to undertake the project. While the programme promises to enhance the collective capabilities of the three partners, it also carries considerable risks in terms of political support, funding and industrial capacity over its duration.

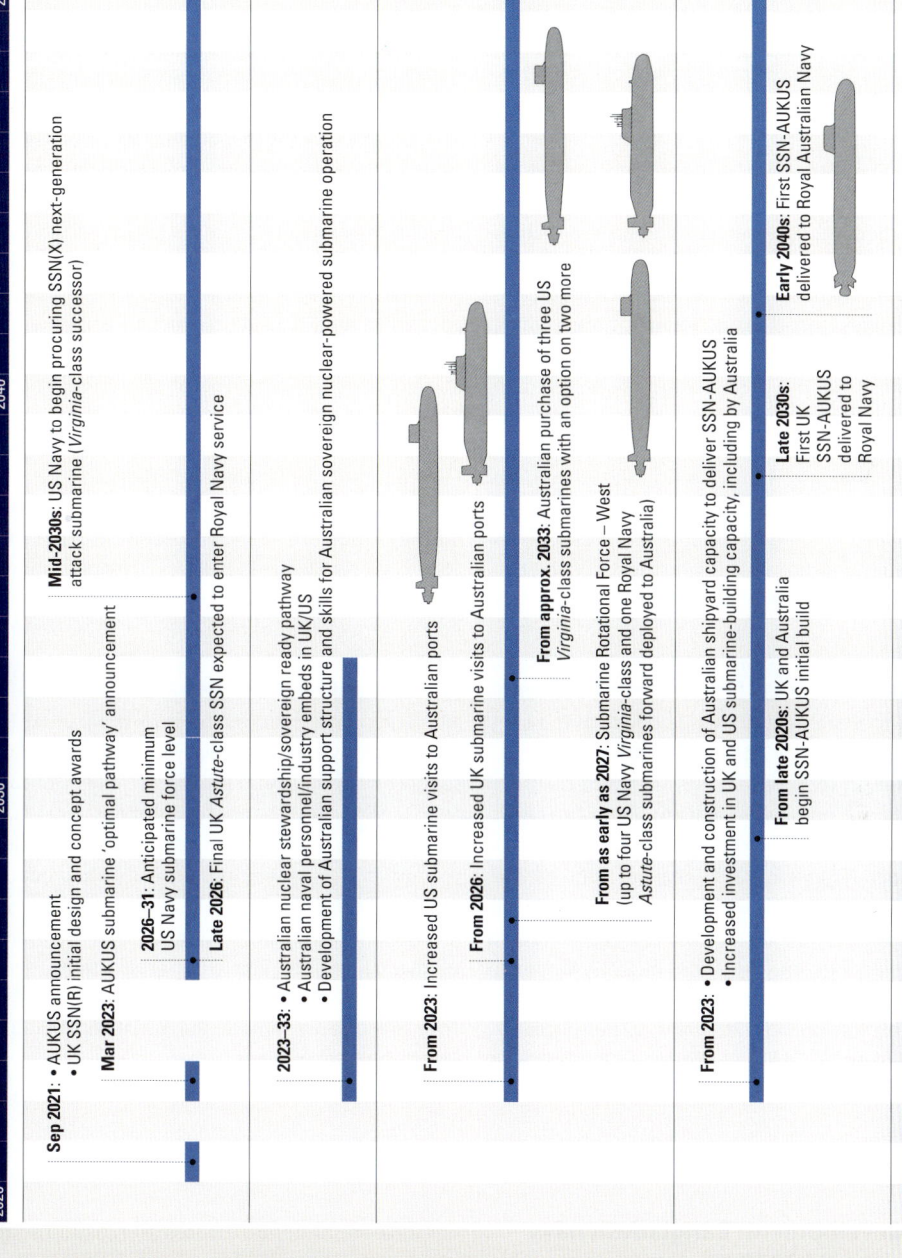

Sep 2021:
- AUKUS announcement
- UK SSN(R) initial design and concept awards

Mar 2023: AUKUS submarine 'optimal pathway' announcement

2026–31: Anticipated minimum US Navy submarine force level

Mid-2030s: US Navy to begin procuring SSN(X) next-generation attack submarine (*Virginia*-class successor)

Late 2026: Final UK *Astute*-class SSN expected to enter Royal Navy service

2023–33:
- Australian nuclear stewardship/sovereign ready pathway
- Australian naval personnel/industry embeds in UK/US
- Development of Australian support structure and skills for Australian sovereign nuclear-powered submarine operation

From 2023: Increased US submarine visits to Australian ports

From 2026: Increased UK submarine visits to Australian ports

From as early as 2027: Submarine Rotational Force – West (up to four US Navy *Virginia*-class and one Royal Navy *Astute*-class submarines forward deployed to Australia)

From approx. 2033: Australian purchase of three US *Virginia*-class submarines with an option on two more

From 2023:
- Development and construction of Australian shipyard capacity to deliver SSN-AUKUS
- Increased investment in UK and US submarine-building capacity, including by Australia

From late 2020s: UK and Australia begin SSN-AUKUS initial build

Late 2030s: First UK SSN-AUKUS delivered to Royal Navy

Early 2040s: First SSN-AUKUS delivered to Royal Australian Navy

2020–42: Sustainment, capability upgrades and Life of Type Extension programme for Australia's existing *Collins*-class conventionally powered submarines

Meanwhile, Japan commissioned its first *Taigei*-class submarine in March 2022 and the second in March 2023. They augment Tokyo's existing *Oyashio*-class and *Soryu*-class boats. The older *Oyashio* boats are scheduled to continue being phased out of service as more *Taigei* boats are commissioned.

The Korean Peninsula also is busy with submarine activity. North Korea, whose submarine fleet dates to the Cold War, launched in 2023 what it described as a 'tactical nuclear attack submarine'. It carried the hull number 841 and the name *Hero Kim Kun-Ok*. Imagery suggested the vessel features ten vertical launch tubes which might accommodate either ballistic or cruise missiles. The real capability of the vessel, which is believed to be a heavily reworked Soviet-vintage *Romeo*-class, is uncertain, however. South Korea's first KSS-III submarine, the *Dosan Ahn Changho*, with a vertical launch system installation for conventionally armed ballistic missiles, was commissioned in August 2021 and embarked on its maiden patrol a year later. Given fiscal constraints, Seoul appears to have put its CVX light aircraft-carrier programme on the back burner in pursuit of more advanced submarines. After three initial KSS-III boats, the navy is switching to a KSS-III Batch-II design, which is stretched and sports a greater missile payload. The keel for the first of these was laid in March 2023.

Southeast Asia, in recent years, has seen an expansion of submarine fleets. Indonesia maintains a four-boat fleet based on the German Type 209 design – one *Cakra*-class and three newer *Nagapasa*-class – having suffered the devastating loss of one *Cakra*-class submarine with all hands in 2021. The country has long-standing ambitions to expand its inventory to ten submarines by 2029. Myanmar first acquired a *Kilo*-class boat from India, followed by a *Ming*-class vessel from China, in 2020 and 2021 respectively. Malaysia maintains a pair of French-built *Scorpène* submarines (*Tunku Abdul Rahman*-class in Malaysian service) and, as part of its long-term fleet-modernisation plan, eyes another pair. Singapore is progressively retiring the *Challenger*-class boats while maintaining the pair of newer *Archer*-class – all second-hand Swedish vessels – and is in the process of inducting the latest German-built Type-218SG *Invincible*-class into service. Vietnam does not appear to have a further submarine expansion programme beyond the existing fleet of six Improved *Kilo*-class boats. The Philippines and Thailand are regional submarine aspirants, but turning their ambitions into reality may be another matter. Manila's submarine plan has long been beset by financial constraints but may finally be close to making some headway. Thailand's current programme to build three S26T submarines in China has been mired in uncertainty over diesel-engine supply.

In South Asia, India and Pakistan are the main submarine-operating navies, although Bangladesh has recently acquired a nascent capability with two ex-Chinese *Ming*-class boats. The Indian Navy commissioned the fifth *Kalvari*-class conventional submarine in 2023. The final boat is expected to enter service in 2024, along with the *Arighat*, the second *Arihant*-class SSBN. In total, New Delhi envisages a fleet of at least 18 conventional submarines although progress on its Project 75I programme is unclear, with Germany now potentially among the contenders to support it. Delhi is also aiming for a fleet of four SSBNs and six SSNs. Besides new acquisitions, India is planning to retrofit its first locally developed air-independent propulsion (AIP) system on the lead *Kalvari* boat, possibly during refit in 2024. The Pakistan Navy in early 2023 said it was making steady progress with its *Hangor*-class submarine project. The eight-vessel-strong fleet, which will feature AIP technology, is based on China's Type-039A. They are due to replace the country's ageing force of French-built submarines.

Capability development: Bangladesh navy and the forces goal 2030

The opening of BNS Sheikh Hasina and BNS Sher-e-Bangla naval bases in Bangladesh in March and July 2023 heralded a new phase in the modernisation and expansion of the country's navy. Except for some legacy units of limited capability, Bangladesh historically geared its naval focus primarily toward low-level protection of its exclusive economic zone from poachers, pirates and smugglers. However, a 2008 naval confrontation with Myanmar over disputed territory and its natural resources in the Bay of Bengal demonstrated to Dhaka the need for a more capable naval force equipped to undertake more challenging combat missions. Bangladesh's government, in 2009, formulated a plan called Forces Goal 2030 to transform the navy from a brown-water force to a competent and independent green-water navy capable of operating farther from shore and in all three dimensions (surface, sub-surface and air). It reflected Dhaka's concerns about Myanmar, but also growing volatility in the wider region. The plan also marked a turning point for a navy that had been overshadowed by the other services considered more important in the face of border tensions with India. That secondary status was reflected in the navy's capabilities.

Before embarking on its modernisation, the core of the fleet consisted of several patrol craft and boats, bolstered by three 1950s-vintage former Royal Navy frigates. Already in 2001, the country had added a more capable showpiece, the South Korean-built frigate *Bangabandhu*. The fleet at the time the modernisation began in 2009 also included the smaller frigate *Osman* and nine fast missile boats, all acquired from China, as well as a landing flotilla of ten craft, most of which were over 20 years old and in poor condition. But the country had notable weaknesses, particularly in anti-submarine warfare, undersea capability and anti-air warfare (AAW). It also lacked any meaningful shipbuilding capacity.

Today's navy has been transformed in relative terms. Spending on the service has increased by 50% since 2009; the fleet now numbers 82 combat ships of mixed size and capability and further capacity enhancements are planned.

The purchase of two submarines from China reflected Bangladesh's intent to upgrade its navy, realising a capability ambition that had existed since its independence in 1971. The events in 2008 finally prompted the government in Dhaka to spend USD203 million on the purchase. Although the Type-035G (*Ming*) is based on 1950s technology, it provides the navy with potentially valuable experience in operating such a capability. Bangladesh began operating the submarines in 2017 and has an ambition to field eight boats. Surface-fleet upgrades included the purchase of multi-purpose combatants from China, giving it's the navy anti-surface warfare (ASuW) and some AAW capabilities that, even if not world-class, represent a critical step up in enhancing the country's naval combat capacity. The fleet also sports two ex-US Coast Guard *Hamilton*-class high-endurance cutters, added in May 2013 and May 2015, and two refitted ex-British *Castle*-class corvettes. Bangladesh also brought second-hand Chinese Type-053H2 (*Jianghu* III) frigates into its inventory in 2014. Two years later, Dhaka commissioned two new *Shadhinota*-class corvettes, based on the Chinese Type-056 (*Jiangdao*), followed by two sister ships in 2020. The same year, the country acquired two further second-hand frigates from China, which it renamed *Umar Farooq* and *Abu Ubaidah*. These additions have increased the number of anti-ship missile launchers in the navy to 84 from 34. In addition to its seafaring ambitions, the navy has been building a small aviation capacity since 2011, now boasting four Do-228NG maritime-patrol aircraft and shipborne helicopters for surveillance and reconnaissance tasks.

Dhaka has spent more than USD1 billion in its naval shopping spree since 2008, though the exact value of the deals with China has been opaque. Bangladesh has further spent hundreds of millions of dollars on naval infrastructure, expanding indigenous facilities such as the large naval dockyards in Chittagong and Khulna. The infrastructure upgrades have enabled the navy to field two indigenously produced anti-submarine warfare-focused patrol craft and nine *Padma*-class patrol vessels. Similar vessels have also been built for the Bangladesh Coast Guard. The country also has had success in building landing craft, more than doubling the number of those vessels, seen as key to patrolling the delta of the country's coastline.

Despite all the high-level political commitment and money spent so far, Bangladesh still lacks experience in constructing larger ships. An indigenous frigate project started in 2017 with the aim to build six multi-role vessels has been hobbled by high cost and lack of progress and is now at least eight years behind schedule. It is doubtful that indigenously built frigates will join the fleet before 2030. In any case, the shipyards remain largely reliant on Chinese assistance in ship design and construction. Deficiencies also hamper the country's ability to conduct mine warfare tasks. Dhaka continues to rely on four fairly rudimentary ex-British *River*-class minesweepers acquired in the mid-1990s, with aspirations to replace those and remaining older patrol vessels.

Bangladesh is now well past the halfway point of Forces Goal 2030. With steady and systematic investments, the country has transformed its littoral force into a navy with greater utility across a wider range of missions. However, the project has highlighted the challenge that a country of Bangladesh's size faces in achieving a significant capability improvement in a 20-year period. The problems of scaling up indigenous warship construction and the dependence on China illustrates those issues. Moreover, both the air and underwater components only exist still with token platforms. Expanding those will crucially depend on the lessons and experience gained to date.

DEFENCE ECONOMICS

Macroeconomics

2023 represented another year of post-pandemic recovery, with growth gradually returning the region to pre-pandemic trajectories. According to the IMF, East Asia and the Pacific (excluding China) grew by an average of 2.9% in 2023 from the year earlier. This was less, though, than the fund's mid-year projections of a rise of 3.3%. The region still exceeded the global average and, according to the IMF, remains a key driver of global growth 'despite facing headwinds from changing global demand from goods to services and tighter monetary policies'.

Economic growth enabled regional governments to sustain the process of fiscal consolidation made necessary by the exceptional spending of the pandemic years. While raised debt levels limited the scope for expansionary spending in countries such as India, Indonesia and Malaysia, in general, faster growth in government revenues served to limit the need for widespread cuts. This fiscal breathing space facilitated a modest uptick in defence spending in a region that traditionally cuts back during times of fiscal consolidation. Nevertheless, the region encountered challenges related to the lingering impact of the global pandemic and the war in Ukraine. Although energy prices moderated after surging in 2022 and supply-chain pressures eased, inflation remained stubbornly high and well above target rates set by the region's central banks. The resulting tightening of monetary conditions served to discourage investment and temper growth rates, with fiscal conservatism expected to prevail for the foreseeable future.

Asia's aggregated growth rate masks marked variations across the region. While internal demand within Asia remained strong, short-term prospects for the region's export-led economies, those most exposed to headwinds from the wider global economy, were blunted. Despite lower commodity prices benefitting headline inflation rates, lower prices for crude, coal, palm oil and nickel produced by the emerging economies of Southeast Asia negatively impacted government revenues. Regional economies are expected to grow in 2024, in part due to prudent financial planning, even if at different rates. For example, the IMF expects growth in Asia's advanced economies to slow from 5.2% in 2023 to 4.8%, while growth in emerging markets and developing economies will increase to 3.8% in 2024, up from 3.2% in 2023.

Defence spending

Despite underlying economic and fiscal constraints, military spending in Asia accelerated in 2023, largely reflecting moves by the region's more mature, lower-growth economies to address strategic challenges. States such as Australia, Japan, South Korea and Taiwan pursued increases in defence spending both in dollar terms and in relation to GDP to counter perceived threats within the region, principally from China and North Korea.

Australia was arguably the first country within the region to pursue such a path, outlining ambitious spending plans as far back as 2016. Despite raising core defence expenditure from AUD38.7 billion (USD28.8bn) to AUD51.7bn (USD34.4bn) – an increase of more than 33% over seven years – the country's 2023 Defence Strategic Review outlined budgetary challenges. For example, according to the review, AUD42bn (USD28bn) of new spending outlined since a 2020 Defence Strategic Update remains unfunded, necessitating difficult choices over the coming years. While spending will continue to grow – projections within the 2023–24 budget show Australia's budget expanding by 14% over the next three years to reach AUD58.4bn (USD39bn) by 2026–27 – this will not be sufficient to fill the gap. Simultaneously, the review outlined plans that emphasised undersea warfare (including

Note: Analysis excludes Afghanistan, North Korea and Laos ©IISS

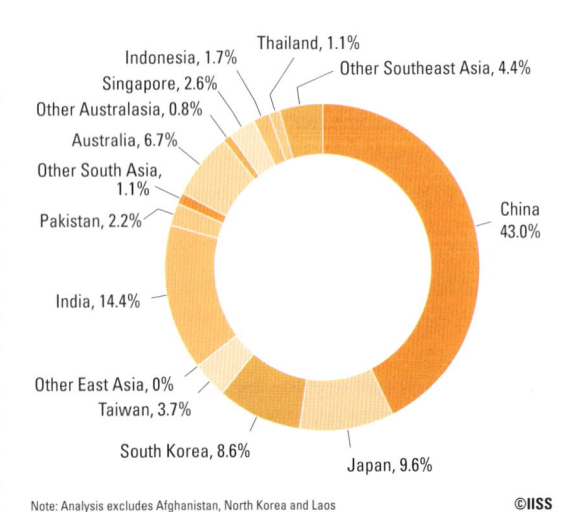

▲ Figure 13 **Asia: defence spending by country and sub-region, 2023**

- China, 43.0%
- India, 14.4%
- Japan, 9.6%
- South Korea, 8.6%
- Australia, 6.7%
- Other Southeast Asia, 4.4%
- Taiwan, 3.7%
- Singapore, 2.6%
- Pakistan, 2.2%
- Indonesia, 1.7%
- Thailand, 1.1%
- Other South Asia, 1.1%
- Other Australasia, 0.8%
- Other East Asia, 0%

conventionally armed, nuclear-powered submarines through the AUKUS partnership with the United Kingdom and the United States), long-range fires, and integrated air and missile defence, which will require existing funding to be reprogrammed. In the short term, the acquisition of new infantry fighting vehicles has been scaled back from 450 to 129 vehicles, with a follow-on order for the K9 *Thunder* (AS9 *Huntsman* in Australian service) 155mm self-propelled artillery piece cancelled. Given the scale of overcommitment on spending and the reorientation of capability priorities within the new defence review, cuts to existing procurement projects seem likely to persist.

Japan's efforts to raise defence spending are in their relative infancy but are on an ambitious scale. In November 2022, Prime Minister Kishida Fumio's government announced plans to raise defence and related security spending to 2% of GDP by 2027. Given that Japan's defence spending represented 1.16% of GDP in 2023, this would almost double military expenditure. It is unclear, though, how the country would finance the expenditure given Japan's large national debt and widespread opposition to tax increases. Nonetheless, these ambitions were formalised in the December 2022 National Security Strategy and the accompanying National Defense Strategy. As a result, Japan's 2023 defence budget increased sharply, with core spending rising from JPY5.18 trillion to JPY6.60trn (USD37.2–47.4bn) in the first year of the Defense Buildup Program (DBP). The subsequent 2023 defence White Paper outlined plans to spend JPY43trn (USD309bn) reinforcing capabilities over the next five years, providing the Japan Self Defense Force (JSDF) with resourcing 'which is on a completely different level from the past'. While the DBP will ostensibly enhance the full scope of the JSDF's capabilities, the programme will focus on air and missile defence and long-range strike, echoing Australian priorities. Japan intends to invest JPY5trn (USD35.9bn) in stand-off systems, including the Joint Strike Missile and Joint Air-to-Surface Stand-off Missile and a range of high-speed weapons over the next five years. In April–June, the country signed eight contracts for the development and production of indigenous new long-range anti-ship and Mach 5+ weapons.

South Korea's defence budget for fiscal year 2024 will increase military spending by approximately 4.5%. According to its 2023–27 mid-term plan, announced in December 2022, a substantial proportion of the spending is earmarked for capability improvement and Seoul's 'three-axis' deterrent. The 'three-axis' concept was enhanced in February 2023 and is based on the capacity for pre-emptive strikes against North Korean military targets, detection and elimination of incoming missiles through air and missile defences, and massive punishment and retaliation against North Korea, preparing for a potential attack by Pyongyang. The mid-term plan calls for the procurement of tactical surface-to-surface missiles, additional submarines armed with ballistic missiles, the *Cheongung*-II surface-to-air missile system with new long-range interceptors, and additional F-35A *Lightning* II combat aircraft. It also spells out the need for the long-range artillery rocket and missile defence system by 2026.

Taiwan proposed its largest-ever defence budget, allocating TWD606.8bn (USD19.1bn) — or 2.6% of GDP — to defence spending in 2024, in the face of heightened tensions with China. In real terms, this represents a 21% increase on the previous year. Increased spending will support ongoing Taiwanese defence-modernisation programmes. For example, in 2021, Taiwan passed its Sea–Air Combat Power Improvement Plan Purchase Special Regulation. This requires the rapid acquisition of precision missiles for land-attack and coastal defence, naval fast attack vessels, the arming of coast guard vessels and other defensive means. Pursuant to the Sea–Air Combat Power Improvement Plan, new weapons, including anti-ship and air-to-ground missiles, are

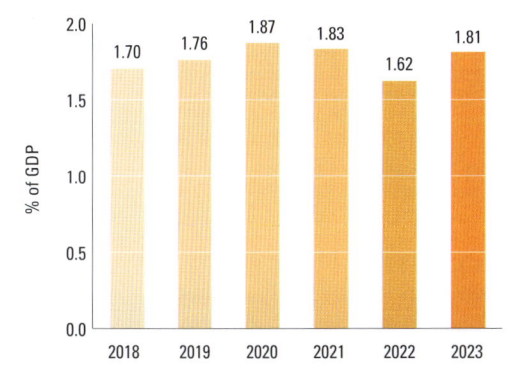

Note: GDP data from IMF World Economic Outlook, October 2023. Analysis excludes Afghanistan, North Korea and Laos

▲ Figure 14 **Asia: regional defence spending** as % of GDP (average)

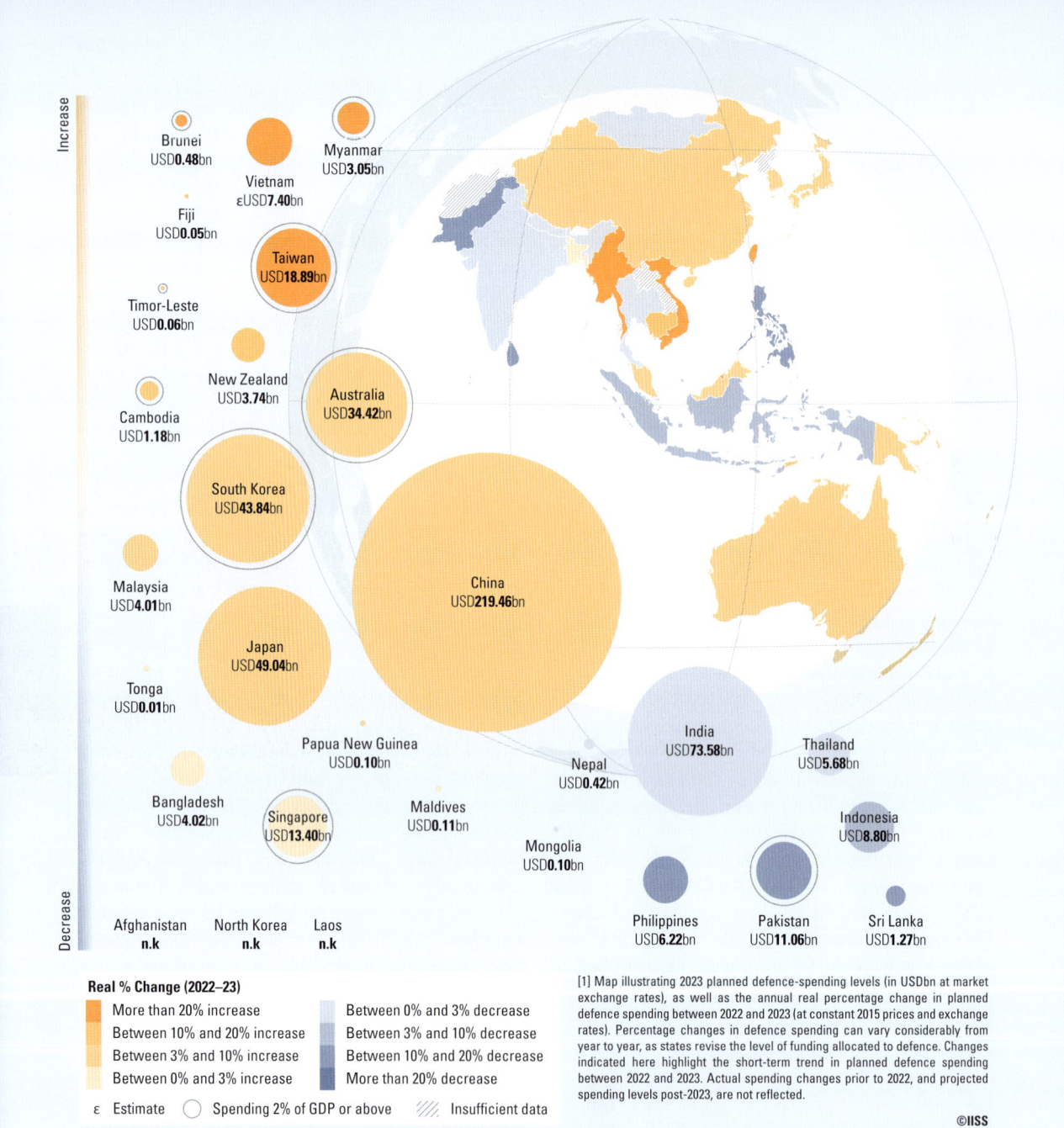

▲ Map 5 **Asia: regional defence spending** (USDbn, %ch yoy)[1]

[1] Map illustrating 2023 planned defence-spending levels (in USDbn at market exchange rates), as well as the annual real percentage change in planned defence spending between 2022 and 2023 (at constant 2015 prices and exchange rates). Percentage changes in defence spending can vary considerably from year to year, as states revise the level of funding allocated to defence. Changes indicated here highlight the short-term trend in planned defence spending between 2022 and 2023. Actual spending changes prior to 2022, and projected spending levels post-2023, are not reflected.

©IISS

to be produced locally by the end of 2026. In March 2023, the US approved the potential sale of USD619 million in new weapons to Taiwan. These included missiles for Taiwan's F-16s, as well as spare parts, consumables and logistics support services to bolster the readiness of Taiwanese forces. That followed the February 2022 approval of up to USD100m in potential military sales of air- and missile-defence equipment, including *Patriot* Advanced Capability-3 (PAC-3) missiles. In September, Taiwan unveiled its first domestically built submarine, the *Narwhal*. Completing the vessel, one of eight planned, reportedly cost TWD49.4bn (USD1.59bn).

The impact of economic and fiscal pressures on defence budgets was felt most keenly in the region's high-growth, emerging economies. For example, in India, defence spending for 2023–24 increased by just 1.5% over the previous year's revised budget.

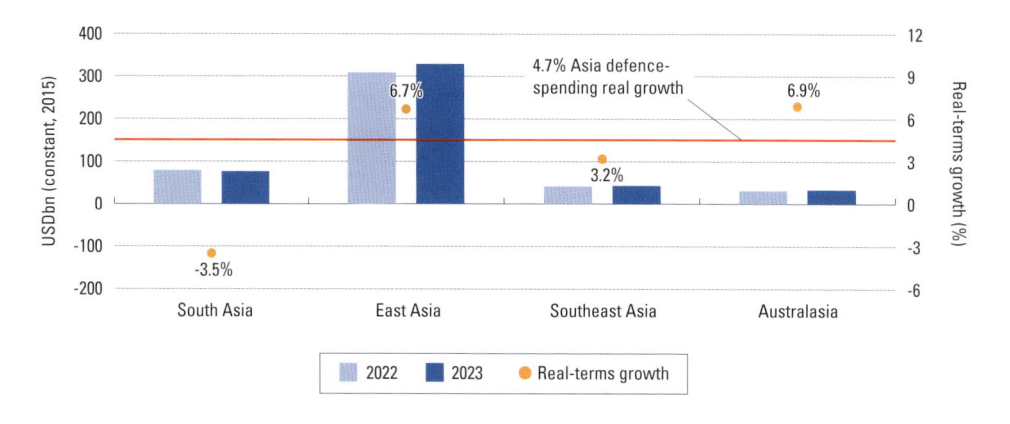

▲ Figure 15 **Asia: sub-regional real-terms defence-spending growth, 2022–23** (USDbn, constant 2015)

This represented a spending reduction in real terms, given the country's inflation rate of over 5%. Budgetary documentation indicates that the small headline increase was primarily the result of a large in-year upward revision to the Ministry of Defence's budget during the previous fiscal year. Government figures show that this change was motivated primarily by military pensions obligations, rather than the modernisation of the Indian armed forces.

Budgetary restraints also affected several Southeast Asian states where, despite ongoing tensions related to Beijing's claims within the South China Sea, fiscal conditions continued to be the primary influence on defence-budget trends. For example, **Indonesia** and **Thailand** cut their defence budgets to IDR132trn (USD8.78bn) and THB195bn (USD5.67bn), respectively. Thailand has now reduced spending in three of the last four years. Despite budgetary challenges, Indonesia maintained the fast-paced international defence procurement programme that began after Prabowo Subianto became defence minister in 2019. After raising USD3.9bn in foreign loans, in June 2023 Jakarta's defence ministry confirmed the purchase of 12 second-hand *Mirage* 2000 fighters from Qatar. Further increases in airpower are expected. In August, Indonesia finalised a contract for a second tranche of 18 *Rafale* fighters, confirming deals for 24 aircraft out of 42 agreed in 2022. Soon after, the government signed a memorandum of understanding with Boeing for the acquisition of 24 F-15IDN combat aircraft (a version of the F-15EX). Indonesia also ordered 13 Thales *Ground Master* 403 radars to reinforce its nationwide airspace surveillance.

Malaysia's defence budget received a timely 15.4% increase, jumping from MYR16.1bn (USD3.67bn) to MYR17.7bn (USD4.01bn) in 2023. However, as a share of GDP, defence spending has fallen consistently since 2016 and now forms less than 1% of GDP. This may soon change as Malaysia's new government, led by Prime Minister Anwar Ibrahim, prioritised an anti-corruption agenda including reforms to defence procurement. Nevertheless, the 2023 budget included a 26% increase for maintenance and procurement, allowing for the purchase of new aircraft, including 18 South Korean FA-50 Block 20 fighter ground-attack aircraft (14 of them to be assembled in Malaysia), two of Italy's ATR-72 maritime patrol aircraft and three Turkish *Anka*-S heavy combat intelligence, surveillance and reconnaissance uninhabited aerial vehicles.

At a time when the war in Ukraine has raised questions about the reliability of supply and effectiveness of Russian weapons, **Vietnam** held its first international defence exhibition in December 2022. While Russian weapons remain the backbone of Hanoi's armed forces, the event provided foreign arms manufacturers an opportunity to market their products to the Vietnam People's Army (VPA). Budgetary constraints and conservatism on the part of the VPA's senior officers meant that there was no rush by Hanoi to order non-Russian equipment, though. In mid-2023, India announced it would donate a 32-year-old decommissioned *Khukri*-class corvette to the Vietnamese navy. Integrating this elderly vessel, which is equipped with Russian weapons systems, into Vietnamese service should not prove a major challenge but it was not part of a long-term response to the challenge of modernising the VPA.

Table 10 — Australia: naval shipbuilding since 2010

Australia in 2017 issued a Naval Shipbuilding Plan calling for continuous, in-country naval shipbuilding, and reaffirmed the objective in the 2023 Defence Strategic Review (DSR). The DSR recommended shifting funding from existing projects, particularly in the land domain, to achieve the naval construction goal. The most important contracted element of the effort currently is the *Hunter*-class frigate programme. Australia is buying nine of those vessels, based on BAE Systems' Type-26, which are primarily being built at the multi-user Osborne Naval Shipyard. Originally established in 1987 to build *Collins*-class submarines, the facility is being operated by BAE Systems through its temporary subsidiary ASC Shipbuilding for the duration of the *Hunter*-class programme. On the same site, Australia intends to build nuclear-powered submarines emerging from the AUKUS partnership, with the first to be delivered in the early 2040s. Both programmes will require substantial investment at Osborne Naval Shipyard, which could see the facility become one of the most capable in the world. Even so, delivering sufficient capacity to satisfy domestic demand will be a challenge, making it likely that naval exports will have to be generated by other shipyards. To date, the export charge has largely been led by Austal. Headquartered in Western Australia, the company has subsidiaries in the Philippines and Vietnam, as well as its biggest revenue generator, Austal USA in Alabama. Austal is building 22 *Guardian*-class patrol craft for 12 Pacific Island states and Timor-Leste under the Australian government-funded Pacific Patrol Boat Replacement (SEA 3036 Phase 1) programme initiated in 2016. Other exports have included expeditionary fast transport vessels for Oman as well as patrol craft for Trinidad and Tobago.

Selected shipyards
- Austal
- Civmec
- Forgacs
- Osborne Naval Shipyard (ONS)
- Submarine Construction Yard (SCY)

Contract Date	Recipient(s)	Equipment	Type	Quantity	Value (USD)	Deliveries	Shipyard(s)	Designer	Programme
Mar 2014	Oman	*Al Mubshir*	EPF	2	124.9m	2016	Austal	Austal	
May 2014	Tonga	VOEA *Late*	LCVP	1	4.51m	2015	Forgacs	Incat Crowther	
Dec 2015	Australia	*Cape*	PCO	2	47.4m	2017	Austal	Austal	Cape Class Patrol Boat
May 2016	12 Pacific Island states and Timor-Leste	*Guardian* (*Bay* mod)	PCO	22	258.99m	2018–24*	Austal	Austal	SEA 3036 Phase 1
Jan 2018	Australia	*Arafura* (OPV 80)	PSO	12**	2.77bn	2023–30*	ONS Civmec	Naval Vessels Lürssen	SEA 1180 Phase 1
Dec 2018	Australia	*Hunter* (Type-26 mod)	Frigate	9	33.1bn+	From 2031*	ONS	BAE Systems	SEA 5000 Phase 1
Aug 2019	Trinidad and Tobago	*Port of Spain* (*Cape*)	PCO	2	Approx. 87.62m	2021	Austal	Austal	
Apr 2020	Australia	*Cape*	PCO	8	322.78m	2021–24*	Austal	Austal	SEA 1445 Phase 1
Pending	Australia	SSN-AUKUS	SSGN	5+	178–245bn***	From early 2040s*	SCY	BAE Systems	AUKUS

*Planned.
**Two to be built by ASC in Osborne; ten to be built by Civmec in Henderson. ***Estimated Australian share of entire AUKUS project.

Defence industry

Many countries in the region have sought foreign collaboration to enhance their domestic production capabilities as part of their modernisation drive. Both Australia and Japan typify the move. The partnerships allow access to new technologies, while ensuring that local companies and their technical capabilities benefit from increased levels of investment. These efforts come with something of a trade-off, though, as seen by Australia's Defence Strategic Review, which noted that the preference for local content must be balanced against timely capability acquisition. The document placed the domestic industry at the centre of its development of advanced and asymmetric capabilities. In addition to the acquisition of nuclear-powered submarines under the AUKUS programme, Australia will use the second pillar of the partnership with the UK and US to enhance its own domestic defence capabilities in areas such as cyber, artificial intelligence and high-speed weapons.

Japan's programme goes further, describing its industrial base as 'integral' to its defence, requiring the ability to develop, manufacture and support the capabilities of the JSDF. Tokyo joined London and Rome in the Global Combat Air Programme (GCAP) to develop a next-generation fighter, reflecting its wider ambition to bolster technological capabilities and supply-chain resilience. The GCAP and AUKUS partnerships are a clear example of closer industrial cooperation between states within the Asia-Pacific region and their allies in Europe and North America. Such agreements cover a vast number of areas, from fighter aircraft and nuclear-powered submarines to Mach 5+ weapons, autonomy and uninhabited combat aircraft.

AUKUS and GCAP are ambitious from an industrial and capability perspective. GCAP aims to complete the development of a next-generation combat aircraft by 2035, leveraging earlier work by the UK and Italy on the *Tempest* project and Japan's F-X programme. Development and production costs have been a key motivation for cooperation between the GCAP nations, with the UK alone expected to invest GBP10bn (USD12.6bn) in the programme over the next ten years, almost exclusively in the development phase. The resultant aircraft is slated to become an integral part of each country's air combat fleet, but retaining and enhancing technical and industrial capabilities remains a central motivation from Tokyo's perspective, as it does for London and Rome.

The Asia-Pacific's growing footprint within the global fighter-aircraft market is arguably one of the most pertinent examples of expanding defence-industrial capabilities within the region. Poland's USD3bn contract for 48 Korea Aerospace Industries (KAI) FA-50 fighter ground-attack aircraft in September 2022 was followed by news in May 2023 that Polish manufacturer Polska Grupa Zbrojeniowa (PGZ) is eager to participate in South Korea's KF-21 fighter development programme, alongside Indonesia, which is a developmental partner. In May, South Korea's Defense Acquisition Program Administration (DAPA) approved the KF-21's provisional combat suitability, which means KAI is able to start low-rate production next year ahead of the KF-21's planned delivery in 2026.

Similarly, in February 2023, officials from India's Defence Research Development Organisation announced the finalisation of the Advanced Medium Combat Aircraft (AMCA) design. Development work on the *Tejas* Mk 2 and low-rate production of the *Tejas* Mk 1A fighter ground-attack aircraft also is continuing. Against this backdrop, the Indian Ministry of Defence said that the value of defence goods produced domestically in 2022–23 hit a record high of INR1.07trn (USD13.2bn), demonstrating the growing capacity of the local defence sector and the increased focus on indigenous suppliers. In August, neighbouring Pakistan said it would soon begin talks with Turkish officials on joining the *Kaan* next-generation combat-aircraft programme, indicating ambitions in this critical area beyond the indigenous JF-17 *Thunder* programme being pursued in conjunction with China. Islamabad and Ankara have also demonstrated growing ties relating to uninhabited aircraft, signalling an interest by Pakistan to be less reliant on China.

CHINA

China's national-security environment became more challenging in 2023, with a purge among parts of the People's Liberation Army (PLA), further deterioration in relations with the United States and rising tensions over Taiwan.

The PLA Central Military Commission (CMC) underwent a reshuffle in 2022 following the 20th National Party Congress, and a new cabinet and defence minister were appointed in early 2023 at the 14th National People's Congress in Beijing. A number of these officials, hand-picked by President

Xi Jinping for their positions in the CMC, have since been implicated in an anti-corruption investigation in China, according to reports that remain unconfirmed by Beijing.

The PLA Rocket Force (PLARF), which oversees China's land-based nuclear missiles, and the Equipment Development Department are at the centre of the reported investigation. Xi abruptly replaced the PLARF's commander and its political commissar in August 2023 without public explanation. PLA Navy (PLAN) former Vice Admiral Wang Houbin replaced the PLARF commander. Former deputy political commissar of the Southern Theatre Command General Xu Xisheng replaced the PLARF political commissar. Both replacements were drawn from outside the PLARF. Additionally, defence minister Li Shangfu was ousted from his role and former defence minister Wei Fenghe disappeared from public view, also reportedly under investigation. General Wei formerly commanded the PLARF, while General Li previously served as the head of the PLA's Equipment Development Department. The Equipment Development Department stated on its social-media account that it was investigating corruption allegations related to procurement bids and the formation of private cliques within the armed forces at high levels that resulted in cronyism and a lack of focus on the core task of building combat readiness. Corruption alone is an unlikely explanation for the removal by Xi of top military officials that he had appointed just months earlier, raising the possibility that intelligence leaks may have triggered the action.

The leadership changes suggest that despite Xi's calls for absolute loyalty and a zero-tolerance approach to corruption, problems within the PLA persist.

Tension with Washington

US–China tensions rose at the start of 2023 after an alleged Chinese surveillance balloon crossed over the US and was shot down by an American combat aircraft. The Chinese government claimed the balloon was for weather surveillance and called the US response disproportionate. Though the two sides did communicate during the incident, it highlighted the lack of effective crisis communication mechanisms between Washington and Beijing or their respective armed forces. The US has urged China to create more crisis communication channels (or hotlines) between the countries' armed forces, but Beijing has not been receptive. Both sides are approaching the issue from fundamentally opposing starting points. China refuses to establish crisis communication mechanisms when there is a lack of trust between the countries, while the US argues such links are a logical step towards preventing relations from further deteriorating. The lack of such hotlines has raised concern among regional states that a potential accident or crisis could easily escalate into conflict.

By contrast, China agreed to several such mechanisms in 2023 with US allies and partners in the region. In March, China and Japan established a bilateral defence hotline as a 'maritime and aerial communication mechanism' to build trust and avoid contingencies. China and Singapore agreed on a 'secure defence telephone link'. South Korea and China expanded bilateral military communications channels. The US has criticised Beijing for failing to use hotlines where they exist.

Relations between Washington and Beijing have been further strained by China's deepened relationship with Russia. Since the start of the Kremlin's full-scale war against Ukraine in 2022, China has exported dual-use technology to Russia's defence industry, even if it held back on providing weapons. China also has permitted the export of civilian uninhabited aerial vehicles (UAVs) that Russia has used for military purposes. The two countries signed an agreement to cooperate on military law-enforcement issues in the Arctic, coordinated air and maritime patrols in East Asia, and participated in trilateral military exercises with South Africa.

Taiwanese election

Tensions around Taiwan are rising ahead of the country's presidential election in 2024. President Tsai Ing-wen has reached her final term and will be replaced, raising the electoral stakes also for Beijing, which views the island as part of China. The People's Republic of China's Taiwan White Paper, published in 2022, stated that 'resolving the Taiwan question' and achieving China's complete reunification is a 'historic mission' of the Chinese Communist Party. The Paper reinforced the point that the use of force remains on the table against what China considers 'separatists' as well as any external forces that may try to intervene in any conflict across the Taiwan Strait.

PLA modernisation reflects preparation for a potential war over Taiwan. PLA drills also suggest the armed forces are trying to learn lessons from

Russia's full-scale invasion of Ukraine. For example, the PLA's 82nd Army Group in Hebei province conducted an exercise in June 2023 that used reconnaissance UAVs and radars to counter portable anti-aircraft and anti-tank missiles. In addition to preparing for conflict, the PLA maintained sustained pressure on Taiwan's armed forces through aerial incursions into the island's air defence identification zone with greater intensity.

PLA Army

PLA Army studies of emerging military lessons from the Ukraine war are likely informing its own modernisation efforts. Although public discussion of these lessons is tightly restricted and censored, some initial output of this work is evidenced by changes in emphasis in official PLA writing and training.

The heavy use of UAVs by both Russia and Ukraine, for example, is likely behind the higher prominence accorded to the discussion of the concept of 'low altitude dominance' in relation to the PLA Army's own UAV, surveillance and air-defence capabilities. Meanwhile, the protracted nature of the fighting in Ukraine is likely to have driven the PLA Army leadership to re-examine operational plans for long-term industrial and logistic sustainment, as well as for casualty evacuation and treatment.

Given the scale of a 2017 army reorganisation, a new round of major force-structure changes within the regular service is unlikely in the short term, even if Russian concerns about a lack of mass may resonate with some Chinese officers. Instead, it is possible that the PLA Reserve Force, which had been largely overlooked in favour of modernising the active services up until 2022, may attract greater attention. There is little open-source indication that intended changes to the army elements of the reserves as part of the 2017 reorganisation made significant progress. The nominal size and depth of the current reserve force is severely limited by low levels of personnel training and mostly obsolescent equipment inventories. The enactment of a new law on PLA reserve service in March 2023 aimed to both clarify the status and improve the benefits enjoyed by those personnel and may be the first part of an attempt to remedy defects.

In 2023, the PLA also began implementing revisions to its existing regulations covering the recruitment of civilian and military personnel, including conscripts. Official coverage of these measures highlighted the goal of enlisting and retaining greater numbers of high-quality recruits, particularly college graduates and those with key scientific and engineering skill sets. That may be a tacit admission of the challenge the PLA continues to face in meeting its targets in these areas despite years of effort. The revised military recruitment regulations also contain specific text on the CMC's ability to conduct wartime mobilisation, possibly influenced by Russia's struggles to mobilise personnel for service in Ukraine. In wartime, the document empowers the State Council and CMC to change the terms and conditions of military recruitment as well as to recall former military personnel to service in their old units.

Significant changes to the army's re-equipment plan are unlikely before the start of the next five-year plan in 2026. In 2023, the army continued to roll out new armour, artillery and air-defence platforms to its combined arms units, and the re-equipment of combined arms regiments in Xinjiang Military District now appears to be nearing completion. The re-equipment of aviation brigades with the Z-20 medium helicopter has also continued. The effort has focused on the PLA Army's air-assault formations, the group armies assigned to the Eastern and Western theatre commands, as well as the Xinjiang and Tibet military districts.

PLA Navy

Amid heightened tensions at sea in Asia, China's naval and maritime security arms became increasingly assertive in their activities. The PLAN also seemed to embark on a new phase of force development and deployment.

Beijing's publication of an updated 'standard map' that highlighted its territorial claims on maritime zones of countries such as the Philippines and Vietnam illustrated its heightened assertiveness. China's navy increased operations in the waters around Taiwan, while the Chinese coast guard undertook activities that bordered on aggressiveness. Beijing's maritime-militia assets, which purport to be part of its fishing fleet, conducted operations in the waters disputed with the Philippines around the Spratly Islands and in Vietnam's exclusive economic zone.

China also logged progress on its newest aircraft carrier, the *Fujian* (Type-003). The larger design will feature catapults, allowing for more potent and comprehensive air operations, and making it more capable than the PLAN's two current operational units, the *Liaoning* (Type-001) and the *Shandong* (Type-002). The new carrier, as of late 2023, was

Map 6 People's Liberation Army (PLA) incursions into Taiwan's Air Defence Identification Zone (ADIZ)

China's PLA has sustained a significantly elevated level of activity in the airspace around Taiwan following the August 2022 visit to Taipei of then-speaker of the US House of Representatives Nancy Pelosi.

According to data published by Taiwan's Ministry of National Defense (MND), the number of PLA aircraft tracked crossing the median line in the Taiwan Strait or flying into the southwestern and eastern portions of Taiwan's ADIZ was around 50% higher year-on-year from January to July 2023.

Higher numbers of multi-role tactical-combat aircraft missions accounted for the bulk of this increase, while the rate of flights of bombers, helicopters and special-mission aircraft appears to have remained relatively steady. The aircraft types and flight paths recorded suggest that locally based PLA brigades are still flying most if not all of these tactical-combat aircraft missions, suggesting an increase in individual units' operational tempo rather than a wider number of participants.

A small number of missions in Taiwan's eastern ADIZ were flown from one of China's new aircraft carriers as part of the *Shandong* carrier group's deployment in the Western Pacific in April 2023. There has also been an increase in the number of ship-based helicopter operations tracked by the MND, particularly off the island's east coast.

PLA incursions into Taiwan's ADIZ: January 2022–September 2023

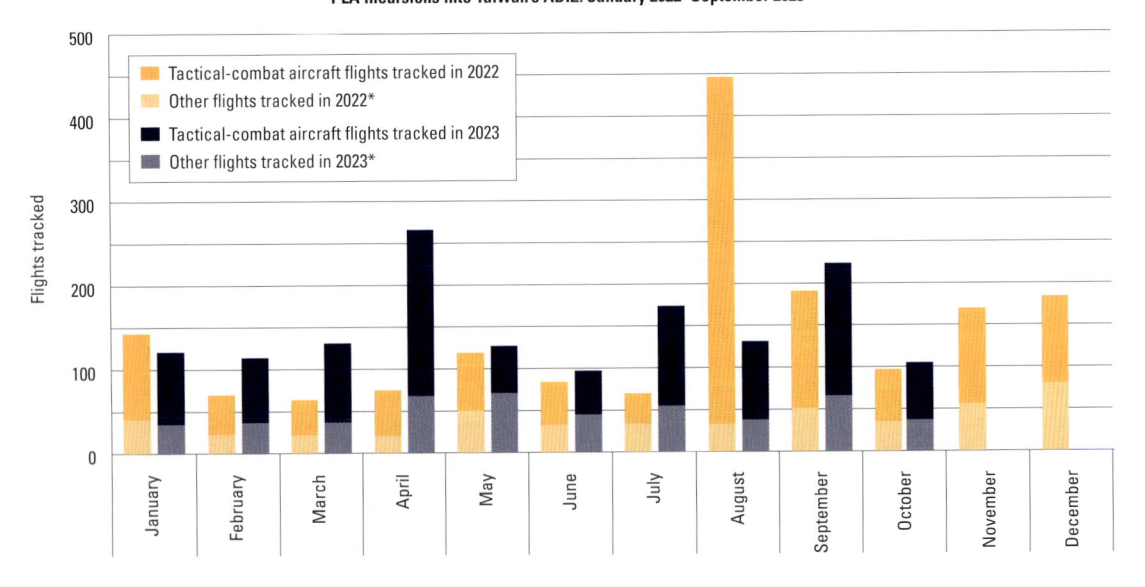

*'Other flights' include flights by bombers, tankers, special-mission aircraft, helicopters and uninhabited aerial vehicles.

Sources: IISS; Taiwan Ministry of National Defense

potentially close to sea trials and is expected to be commissioned in 2025.

The PLAN in 2023 added the eighth Type-055 (*Renhai*) cruiser to its operational fleet along with additional Type-054A frigates. Potentially more meaningful, though, was the much-anticipated launch in August of the new Type-054B frigate, which appears to be larger and considerably more capable. The new frigate promises to be a major addition to the PLAN's blue-water fleet as a component of future task-group deployments, depending on the scale and pace of series production.

The navy also continued to develop its blue-water deployment capabilities, including with more significant formations. Units led by Type-075 (*Yushen*) amphibious assault ships (LHDs) made two forays into the Western Pacific, including waters near Japan. The service has also gradually pushed carrier operations further out. The *Liaoning* and *Shandong* undertook sorties out towards Guam. They also carried out more intense air operations, even if still not on a par with those of US carriers. The PLAN, in September 2023, carried out a further large-scale carrier exercise in the Western Pacific.

The service also appears to be strengthening its LHD forces. It launched the fourth Type-075 *Yushen*-class LHD in December. The navy has also added at least two new *Zubr*-class air-cushion landing craft to its inventory, as well as other landing craft.

China's pace of adding surface ships to the fleet appears to have slowed, though, which may signal the PLAN's increased focus on developing sub-surface forces. Those efforts include the development of the new-generation Type-095 nuclear-powered attack submarine and Type-096 nuclear-powered ballistic-missile submarine. The US assesses that the PLAN has equipped its Type-094 ballistic-missile boats with a longer-range submarine-launched ballistic missile, the JL-3 (CH-SS-N-20). That would represent a significant step up in capability, potentially enabling the PLAN to threaten the continental US from the relative safety of China's littoral waters.

The PLAN maintained its drumbeat of deployments into the northwestern Indian Ocean, established as a counter-piracy mission back in 2008. It carried out exercises with Russia and Iran and with Russia and South Africa, port visits in the United Arab Emirates and Pakistan, and a rare foray to Africa's Atlantic coast with a port visit to Nigeria. Another set of manoeuvres with Russia off Alaska in August 2023 further underscored that the PLAN is expanding its pattern of long-range deployments.

The PLAN is now regularly and widely touted as 'the world's largest navy', including by the Pentagon, which is angling for its own fleet increases. However, while the PLAN's fleet has evolved to be more modern, it still lags the US Navy in terms of total tonnage and capability, though the gaps are narrowing. Moreover, the US Navy is widely dispersed as a genuinely globally deployed fleet, whereas the PLAN, despite its increasing emergence onto the world's oceans, is still significantly concentrated in waters closer to home, with inevitable implications in terms of the balance of naval power in those waters.

PLA Air Force

The PLA Air Force (PLAAF) received considerable numbers of combat aircraft in 2023, in part from an unexpected source. Along with the new-build Chengdu J-10C *Firebird*, Shenyang J-16 *Flanker* N and Chengdu J-20 multi-role fighter aircraft, the service received upward of 200 tactical combat aircraft from the PLAN. The PLAN appears to be divesting itself of almost all its land-based multi-role fighters, ground-attack aircraft, bomber aircraft and numerous air bases. Many of the transferred aircraft are unlikely to be retained in the medium term. The initial version of the Xi'an JH-7, the JH-7 *Flounder* A, as well as the even older Shenyang J-8 *Finback*, may be retired.

The PLAAF also appears to be taking on the roles of the transferred formations. The air force would, therefore, be responsible for land-based maritime strike tasks, requiring considerable coordination with the PLAN.

The addition of the PLAN aircraft will bolster the PLAAF's inventory of modern aircraft types, which is already increasing because of the service's own modernisation efforts. The number of J-20 fighters, for instance, continues to grow. The J-20 heavy multi-role fighter is the premier combat aircraft in PLAAF service and remains the focus of incremental upgrades. The PLAAF, which introduced the J-20 in 2017–18, operated at least six operational brigades equipped with the type by late 2023. China had built around 200 J-20s by the fourth quarter of the year.

An upgraded J-20 continued flight testing during 2023. The aircraft's forward fuselage has been modified with a revised cockpit profile and a raised fuselage section to the rear of the cockpit. The aircraft, as of mid-2023, may have been fitted with the Shenyang WS-15 afterburning turbofan. The WS-15 offers more power than the previously used Shenyang WS-10. Two prototypes of a twin-seat J-20 also remained in flight test.

The PLAAF continued to receive Shenyang J-16 *Flankers*. The two-seat J-16 remains an important type for the air force. It provides a long-range surface-attack capability and serves as an air-to-air platform, in which it will carry the PL-17 (CH-AA-X-12) very long-range air-to-air missile that is likely in development.

While the US first flew its B-21 *Raider* bomber aircraft at the end of 2023, Beijing had, as of the fourth quarter of 2023, yet to show its low-observable bomber design, the Xi'an H-20. Uncertainty also continued around the possible development of a new fighter-bomber design.

The roles of the PLAAF bomber force continued to expand. The Xi'an H-6 carries the air-launched Mach 3+ WZ-8 reconnaissance UAV that, post-release, climbs to an altitude of up to 100,000 feet to fly its mission profile. The WZ-8 has now entered service and may have been used for reconnaissance missions against South Korea and Taiwan.

PLA Rocket Force

The PLA Rocket Force (PLARF) has enhanced and expanded its capabilities across all range thresholds in the past year, although at varying qualitative and quantitative pace. The PLARF's capabilities are evolving most rapidly through the introduction of intermediate-range ballistic missiles (IRBMs) to replace some medium-range ballistic missiles (MRBMs) that are being retired.

Variants of the DF-21 (CH-SS-5) MRBM, including the nuclear-armed DF-21A (CH-SS-5 Mod 2) and conventional DF-21C (CH-SS-5 Mod 4), are being swiftly replaced by the longer-range DF-26 (CH-SS-18) IRBM. The DF-26 is designed to allow crews to rapidly swap conventional and nuclear warheads and to conduct precision strikes against land and maritime targets up to the second island chain, providing the PLARF with greater reach and accuracy. The DF-26's so-called hot-swappable warhead introduces a potential escalation dilemma for both China and its adversaries: adversaries targeted with the weapon may be unsure if they are under nuclear or conventional attack prior to the warhead detonating. The PLARF is also developing an IRBM armed with a hypersonic glide vehicle (HGV) that appears to be similar to the DF-26 and is known as the DF-27 (CH-SS-X-24). The missile is entering service.

The PLARF is introducing more capable equipment to either augment or replace older and shorter-range systems. Some brigades are being re-equipped with the DF-17 (CH-SS-22) medium-range missile carrying an HGV. The units operated DF-11A (CH-SS-7 Mod 2), DF-15 (CH-SS-6) and DF-16 (CH-SS-11) short-range ballistic missiles. The PLARF appears to be in the process of upgrading three brigades to the DF-17, which are based in eastern China. The DF-17's HGV is more manoeuvrable and therefore more capable of evading adversary missile defences than traditional ballistic missiles of similar ranges. Its features suggest the weapon was developed to strike high-value targets such as air and missile defences at the outset of a conflict, opening the way for less manoeuvrable systems to reach their objective with a lower probability of being intercepted. The PLARF will likely continue to retain some types of older equipment, given recent periodic upgrades to these systems and its requirement to strike multiple targets within short time frames.

China continues to modernise its intercontinental ballistic missile (ICBM) forces, although generally more slowly than other areas of the PLARF's inventory. The DF-41 (CH-SS-20) is the PLARF's newest ICBM and is equipped with multiple independently targetable re-entry vehicles (MIRVs), thereby providing China with a higher number of warheads with a smaller force. This is likely why DF-41 brigades are equipped with fewer launchers than those still equipped with the DF-31. Even with the introduction of the DF-41, the service appears to be focused first on enhancing the survivability and responsiveness of its inventory by upgrading the DF-31A (CH-SS-10 Mod 2) to the more mobile and responsive DF-31AG configuration with an integrated transport erector launcher that is off-road capable.

The PLARF is also expanding a small number of silos for the older DF-5 (CH-SS-4) ICBM at several locations. More ambitiously, reports in 2021 revealed China was building three large ICBM silo fields in the western part of the country. The US assesses that the PLARF has begun loading some of these silos. Some analysts have suggested that China will only fill a small proportion of the roughly 330 silos to complicate an adversary's targeting plans. However, the quantitative expansion of the PLARF's nuclear capabilities and of China's strategic forces in other services has raised concerns that China may be moving from a stated policy of nuclear no-first-use and a minimum credible deterrent to a launch-on-warning posture.

The PLAN's aircraft-carrier voyage of discovery

Over the next couple of years, the People's Liberation Army Navy (PLAN) will undertake intensive trials of its newest aircraft carrier, the *Fujian* (Type-003), to bring it into service. The ship represents a significant advance on the navy's first two carriers, the *Liaoning* and *Shandong*. The indigenous design is larger than its predecessors and equipped with an electromagnetic catapult launch system rather than a 'ski ramp' for aircraft launches, enabling a larger and more capable air group. While that requires a step change in the PLAN's capacity to support the operation of such a vessel, it will bring the PLAN closer to its ambition for a fully capable carrier force.

China has been intent on building its carrier capacity since the 1970s. The effort accelerated in the 1980s under Liu Huaqing, commander-in-chief of the navy for much of that decade, who subsequently served on the Central Military Commission. He is widely credited as the father of the modern Chinese navy and its carrier capability.

The journey has been a voyage of discovery and determination for a country with no previous carrier experience and little assistance in its endeavour. Beijing's early moves were surreptitious and creative. China closely studied the decommissioned Australian aircraft carrier HMAS *Melbourne*, sold for scrap to a Chinese company in 1985 with a surprising amount of its aircraft-operating equipment – catapults, arresting gear, mirror landing sights and flight-deck arrangements – left intact. The ship was not dismantled for many years after it arrived in China.

In the 1990s, China gambled on the purchased ex-Soviet hybrid carriers *Kiev* and *Minsk* and the incomplete hull of the larger *Varyag* (which would have been a sister ship to the Soviet and then Russian navy's *Admiral Kuznetsov*), supposedly to turn them into floating hotels or casinos. While two of them, after extensive evaluation, took on their civilian role, the ex-*Varyag* was completed in China as the PLAN's prototype carrier *Liaoning*. China reportedly bought eight truckloads of detailed design drawings of the ship.

The effort allowed the PLAN to gain rapid early experience at sea of at least rudimentary carrier operations. That experience proved invaluable since China lacked the opportunity to embed personnel with seasoned carrier operators to learn complex ship handling and maintenance skills, let alone the know-how about how to run high-performance carrier air operations or how to integrate them into a task-group formation.

It is clear that Chinese planners carefully studied others' practices, particularly those of the US Navy. Two months after the PLAN commissioned the *Liaoning*, it carried out the first landing and take-off of a J-15 fighter at sea. Footage of the occasion included a flight-deck launch officer, or 'shooter', in the classic pose popularised by the movie *Top Gun*. The PLAN also adapted US flight-deck procedures and organisations, including colour-coding uniforms to denote the role of personnel.

Beijing declared the *Liaoning* 'combat ready' in November 2016 and an initial operating capability for the carrier and its task group in May 2018. China's second carrier, the *Shandong*, a domestically built improved version, was commissioned in December 2019 and supposedly achieved initial operating capability the following year.

Given its challenges, the PLAN's development of carrier capabilities was relatively cautious, and the operational capability remains limited. The carriers only recently have embarked on more extended deployments further from Chinese home waters. More complex operational flying at sea, including night-time operations, remains a work in progress, hobbled also by a shortage of qualified pilots.

Carrier-capable fighters are in relatively short supply and barely sufficient for two carrier air groups. The PLAN's current carrier fighter, the J-15, an unlicensed development of the Russian Su-33, has shortcomings due to its size, weight and operational characteristics. The size and design of the existing carriers, especially the lack of a catapult launching system, significantly constrain aircraft range and payload.

The arrival of the *Fujian* addresses some of these issues given its greater capability, coupled with an upgraded version of the J-15 or, in time, a carrier-compatible variant of the J-35, a development from variant of the J-31 low-observable technology demonstrator. That evolution will pose its own challenges, including having to handle higher-intensity and more complex operations. What's more, the vessel is expected to introduce electromagnetic catapult system technology, which adds complexity. At least three prototypes of the twin-engine J-35 are undergoing flight testing. Along with the J-35, the PLAN is supporting the development of the KJ-600 airborne early warning platform for carrier operations, with several airframes in flight testing.

The PLAN's experience fielding the *Fujian* will no doubt influence the further development of its carrier force and whether additional ships of this design will follow, or whether the service will place another gamble on an even larger vessel, perhaps with nuclear propulsion as used by the US Navy's carriers. For now, the PLAN appears intent on having a force of at least six carriers sometime in the 2030s.

While a fully-fledged carrier force may still be some way off, with a decade of experience in carrier operations the PLAN appears to have mastered a limited degree of power-projection capability. The next near-term evolution may be more long-range deployments by the current force, perhaps into the Indian Ocean as a logical next step.

DEFENCE ECONOMICS

In 2023, China's economy grew by over 5%. The results were better than expected, met government growth targets and indicated strong post-pandemic recovery. Nonetheless, in the long run, Chinese growth will continue to be hampered by structural imbalances in the economy, such as the over-reliance on debt-fuelled investments and low consumer demand.

In recent years, Chinese authorities have sought to address these imbalances by cracking down on property speculation and placing a renewed emphasis on domestic markets under the new economic model of 'dual circulation'. Long-term concerns notwithstanding, China's fiscal balance remains healthy and capable of supporting Beijing's aim to achieve military modernisation by 2035 and 'world-class' armed forces no later than 2049.

China's ambitions to modernise its armed forces are underpinned by long-standing efforts to foster industrial innovation. Beijing's pursuit of military–civil fusion (MCF) is the most prominent example, as authorities have sought to improve coordination and remove institutional barriers between the country's defence and civilian research sectors. MCF is driven by Chinese President Xi Jinping's vision of 'integrated national strategic systems and capabilities'. This seems focused on ensuring the government's oversight and direction of research efforts – civilian and military – across sectors identified as 'strategic' by the government.

Challenges ahead

Despite largely recovering from the pandemic-related slowdown, the pace of China's longer-term growth remains uncertain. A combination of mainly export-led manufacturing, supported by large investments in national infrastructure, facilitated by high rates of household savings, drove China's remarkable economic growth and raised national living standards. However, it also led to structural imbalances. Awareness of these imbalances has been growing since the early 2000s, and in 2003, China's central bank cautioned against four major imbalances, namely 'between investment and consumption; urban and rural development; regional development; and development of different industrial lines'.

In the post-pandemic era, China's exports have plateaued as demand from key trading partners lagged because of a global economic slowdown and rising costs of living worldwide. Previously, local governments may have sought to compensate via additional spending, such as on infrastructure projects. However, many local governments now have considerable debt levels and have limited options for large-scale investments. Thus, it is household consumption that is expected to be the driver of future economic growth. But, as a proportion of GDP, Chinese household consumption remains among the lowest in the world. The government, in the 14th five-year plan (FYP 2021–25), articulated measures emphasising domestic consumption under the 'dual circulation' paradigm. This envisions the

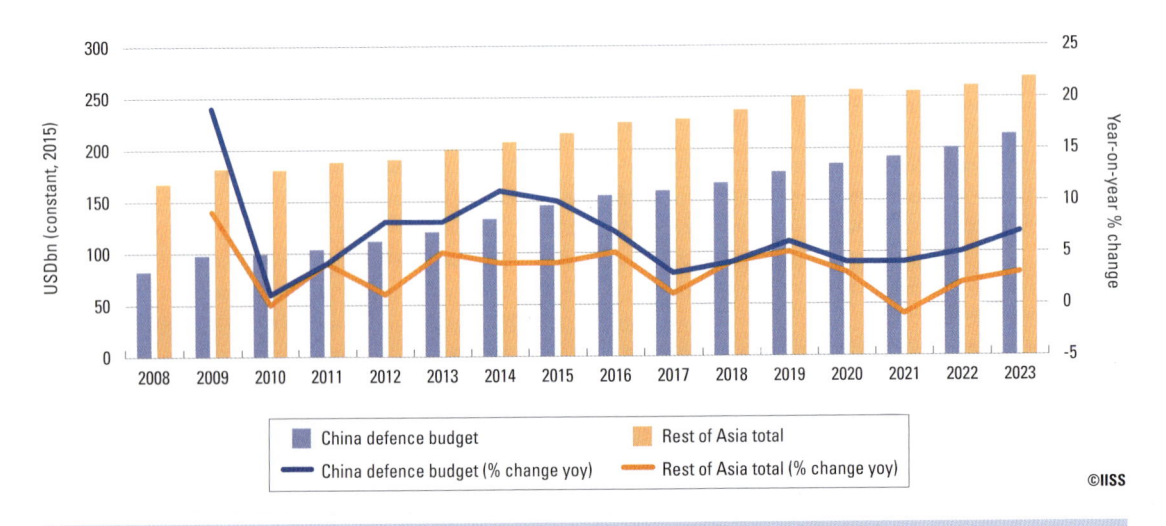

▲ Figure 16 **China: defence budget compared with the rest of Asia (total), 2008–23**, USDbn, constant 2015

domestic and international markets reinforcing each other, with the domestic market being the mainstay of economic growth. This should rebalance the economy in the longer term. Beginning in mid-2023, Beijing also announced measures to shore up household spending and boost housing demand, which include tax-relief measures, easing borrowing for home buyers and lending-rate cuts. Although the success of these initiatives will depend on consumer confidence and local government implementation, metrics across tourist revenues, box-office collections and catering revenues all suggest improved contact-related consumption as the country emerges from COVID-19.

However, the Chinese economy faces additional risks. For example, real estate has traditionally been seen as a safe investment by many households, such that China's real-estate sector now holds upwards of 70% of all household investment. However, the sector continues to face problems that stem from overinvestment. In 2020, Chinese authorities tightened control over the country's property sector. However, measures failed to address the full scope of the problem and in December 2021, the Evergrande Group, China's largest property developer, defaulted on USD300 billion of debt. Up to a third of China's over-stretched property developers could face liquidity problems. In October 2023, property developer Country Garden also defaulted on its debt, while in the same month Chinese officials urged calm after fears about the property market sparked a run on local banks. Although the risks of wider financial contagion are low, especially since the central government maintains tight control over credit instruments, the continuing problems in the sector only compound issues of consumer confidence. Beijing is navigating economic problems with targeted government incentives rather than a wide-ranging stimulus package.

Defence spending

China's improving economic outlook helped underpin sustained defence spending and modernisation efforts in 2023. In March 2023, Beijing announced a 2023 defence budget of CNY1.58 trillion (USD223bn) to support its modernisation programme and desire to create a 'world-class' military by the middle of the century. This represents a nominal increase of 7.2% over the previous year and marked the 29th consecutive year of increasing Chinese defence expenditure.

Despite increasing top lines, from Beijing's perspective military spending remains restrained, with its defence budgets consistently below 2% of GDP. Official defence budgets have fallen as a percentage of GDP to an average of 1.23% between 2019 and 2023, from 1.28% between 2014 and 2018. The small increase in national-defence burden in 2023 to 1.24% of GDP mainly stems from the relative slowdown in economic growth.

Reflecting the goal of military modernisation by 2035, equipment forms the largest proportion of defence-budget spending and has done since at least 2016. This is likely to continue as Xi called for the acquisition of new equipment and the acceleration of new combat capabilities in the August 2023 lead-up to the People's Liberation Army's (PLA) 96th founding anniversary. Outlays on training and maintenance are also increasing, while direct expenditure on personnel now forms the smallest proportion of defence expenditure. This reflects Chinese efforts to rationalise personnel numbers since 2015 and vastly increase its air and naval fleets with an emphasis on the procurement of fighters, air tankers and new naval combatants to form carrier battle groups. Increased spending on training is also consistent with the PLA's emphasis on preparing for combat and is evident in the heightened pace of military exercises. These include not only exercises to enhance joint operations across services but also those reinforcing China's claims in disputed regions such as the South and East China seas, around Taiwan and the Himalayan border.

China's modernisation of its national infrastructure, which is not part of the defence budget, also has implications for the armed forces. The 14th FYP includes infrastructure-development plans that will enhance the PLA's ability to mobilise and project power. For example, work is under way to extend the Chengdu–Lhasa railway from Ya'an to Linzhi (Nyingchi) close to the disputed eastern border with India. Construction of the Shigatse–Gyirong rail link, announced in early 2023, will provide a connection close to the border with Nepal. The FYP also provides for completing China's National Highway 291 that traverses its western and southern borders, including the region of Aksai Chin contested with India.

Defence industry: from imitation to innovation

As China's defence industry becomes increasingly capable of indigenous production, upgrades and maintenance, the country is seeking to steadily reduce its reliance on foreign technology. This includes domestic production of defence materiel such as advanced aircraft engines and radars, traditionally sourced from Russia. Chinese industry is also making strides in embracing advanced dual-use technology areas such as in artificial intelligence (AI) and semiconductor manufacturing.

China's advances build on multiple efforts to tap the country's science and technology sector to improve defence-industrial capabilities and drive innovation – having long relied on copying others. Xi's vision of 'integrated national strategic systems and capabilities' represents an evolution of the MCF framework. The term was first used in 2017, though without detail. It re-emerged at the 14th National People's Congress in March 2023 in the context of fostering collaborative innovation between the civil and military spheres around original innovation and national self-reliance in high-end technologies. China's interest in emerging technology is wide-ranging, with the 14th FYP listing seven areas of 'cutting-edge science and technology' for special development that range from deep-sea and polar exploration to next-generation AI and quantum information.

To achieve this, China is looking to enact even greater government oversight over developments in 'strategic' sectors, as prioritised by the Party Central Committee's 2023 call for 'the consolidation and improvement of the integrated national strategic system and capabilities'. This also ties in with the March 2023 reorganisation of government institutions overseeing science and technology (S&T). Here, Beijing established the Central Science and Technology Commission (CSTC) to coordinate the construction of the national innovation system and deliberate on major strategies, plans and policies for S&T development. These include determining major scientific research projects and coordinating the layout of strategic S&T forces such as national laboratories. The CSTC is also responsible for coordinating the integration of military and civilian S&T and serves as a decision-making and coordinating body of the Party Central Committee. As such, the central government has further increased its hold over the direction of S&T innovation within China. This builds on previous policies, such as the Made in China 2025 programme, which was launched in 2015 to increase China's competitiveness across high-tech industries, and the 2017 New Generation Artificial Intelligence Development Plan.

In practice, state involvement to foster collaboration will likely see the increased use of research hubs to co-locate facilities. Authorities are also likely to increase efforts to link research and industry to bridge the gaps between knowledge discovery and product development. Known as the 'valley of death' in the innovation cycle, bridging the gap between original research and adoption by businesses remains problematic across all innovation ecosystems. This coincides with China's plan to develop the country's top 98 universities into world-class institutions by 2050 and accelerate core research at important universities. These include public universities with historic ties to the defence industry. Known as the 'seven sons of national defence', these universities produce three-quarters of all new recruits into China's defence state-owned enterprises. Should these efforts to shorten the timeline between scientific discovery and product development succeed, the acceleration of novel innovation could feed directly into military applications across a range of technologies.

China's interest in ensuring that technological advances assist the armed forces is well illustrated by developments in the AI field, which have sparked concern in Washington and efforts there to slow Beijing's progress. In August, the White House signed an executive order restricting US private-equity and venture-capital investments in Chinese technology firms. AI is of particular concern to the United States, which asserts that China's investment in high technology stems from a belief that AI 'will drive the next revolution in military affairs, and that the first country to apply AI to next generation warfare will achieve military dominance'. China has made multi-year funding available to foster 25–30 projects on next-generation AI-related methods. Additionally, state-backed funds aim to raise capital for the development of key technologies, illustrated by plans for the China Integrated Circuit Industry Investment Fund. It aims to raise around USD40bn for the semiconductor sector, focusing on equipment for chip-making.

Yet China treads a fine line as it seeks to balance increasing state intervention and the Chinese Communist Party's desire for control with market forces, as illustrated by the crackdown on its tech sector. This began in November 2020, after the sector grew in size but also in influence. High-profile players were deemed to have become too influential politically. Though there are signs that this crackdown is ending, the state may seek to gain greater control over the sector through 'guidance funds' that encourage private–public investment in industries or technologies in its 'strategic' industries. Guidance funds are investment vehicles that use public–private partnerships to further national industrial policy goals. In general, they are good indicators of government priorities within given sectors as there is less emphasis on securing returns and more on the development of technologies and capabilities in identified sectors. These government-guided funds have met with mixed success, often investing only part of the capital raised – in part due to their rapid proliferation, and in part due to the trouble in identifying endeavours worthy of investment. In addition to guidance funds, priority sectors may also receive capital from commercial entities that mimic the direction of government investment – either to ingratiate themselves with state authorities or in the hopes of securing higher returns. As such, there has been a proliferation of investment funds for the development and production of new technologies with military applications.

Beyond individual cases, however, assessing China's research and development (R&D) expenditure levels on defence is difficult. Spending on priority areas falls outside of the national-defence budget, in part because of the dual-use nature of the work. Nonetheless, the share of R&D in government spending has clearly been increasing. In 2022, China's spending on R&D surpassed CNY3trn (USD423.7bn) for the first time, accounting for more than 2.55% of national GDP. This represented a 10.4% increase on the previous year, with growth rates exceeding 10% for seven consecutive years.

Such rates look set to continue as technological advances remain a key pillar of Xi's growth strategy. China looks set to continue its major investments in R&D, investing USD1.4trn as it seems poised to overtake the West in critical technologies by 2025. But growth may slow here too as innovation becomes more expensive. Part of this will happen naturally as original innovation is, by its nature, more expensive than re-innovation, where much of the original research has been done previously. Yet it will also become more expensive as Western export controls and China's desire for self-sufficiency restrict the ease of technology transfer. Nonetheless, for the foreseeable future growth in national R&D spending will be yet another area of strategic competition between US and China.

Significant procurement and delivery events – 2023

MARCH
INDIA BOOSTS BUDGET TO ACCELERATE MODERNISATION EFFORT

India approved a INR1.63 trillion (USD20.16bn) spending boost for its armed forces to acquire weapons and equipment, with an additional INR22.9bn (USD283.90m) for repairs and refits for the navy (mostly for its attack submarines) in FY2023–24, which started 1 April. The details were provided in its INR5.94trn (USD73.58bn) defence budget proposal for FY2023–24, which represents a 13% increase over the previous year. Funding for modernisation also covers outstanding liabilities from existing contracts. In March alone, the last month of FY2022, India committed over INR518.83bn (USD6.43bn) by awarding more than 14 contracts to local companies in line with the government's ambition to foster its local industry. New Delhi spent the last part of the FY2022–23 budget on 11 Next Generation Offshore Patrol Vessels (NGOPV), at INR97.81bn (USD1.21bn); six Next Generation Missile Vessels, at INR98.05bn (USD1.22bn); and long-range Next Generation Maritime Mobile Coastal Batteries and *BrahMos* missiles, at INR17bn (USD210.75m) for the navy.

MARCH
AUKUS SELECTS A DESIGN

The trilateral AUKUS security partnership announced plans to develop Australian submarine capability. In the early 2030s, Australia will acquire three *Virginia*-class submarines from the US with an option for two more. Then, Australia will acquire a design based on the UK Royal Navy's Submersible Ship Nuclear Replacement project incorporating US submarine technology. The first UK-built SSN-AUKUS is expected to be delivered in the late 2030s and the first Australia-built boat is to be delivered in the early 2040s from the new Submarine Construction Yard in Osborne. BAE Systems will lead that project and Rolls-Royce will supply the nuclear reactors. Australia's six *Collins*-class attack submarines are expected to be retired in the 2030s and will require additional modernisation to keep them going until then. Australia estimates that its share of the SSN-AUKUS programme will cost AUD268bn–368bn (USD178.42bn–244.99bn). Ultimately, Australia plans to operate a fleet of at least eight nuclear-powered submarines by the mid-2050s, which includes both SSN-AUKUS and the *Virginia*-class. There are growing concerns in the US regarding attack submarine numbers for the US Navy if Australia must also be supplied from the two yards which are struggling to meet existing demand.

MAY
HANWHA RESTRUCTURING

Daewoo Shipbuilding & Marine Engineering (DSME) renamed itself Hanwha Ocean following the completion of its acquisition by Hanwha Group. The takeover enables Hanwha Group to offer a portfolio of products across domains, including guided weapons, armoured vehicles, aircraft parts, space launch vehicles, satellites, sensors and now shipbuilding – led by Hanwha Aerospace. In April, Hanwha Corp.'s defence business (munitions) merged with Hanwha Aerospace. In November 2022, Hanwha Defense (formerly Hanwha Land Systems) was integrated into Hanwha Aerospace's land division. Hanwha Group's ambition to expand its business to the space sector was boosted in 2020–21 when Hanwha Systems (formerly Hanwha Thales), a subsidiary of Hanwha Aerospace, acquired an 8.8% stake in the UK's OneWeb for USD300m in August 2021 and bought the UK's Phasor Solutions (now Hanwha Phasor, specialising in satellite antenna technology) in June 2020. A local shipbuilding competitor of Hanwha Ocean, HD Hyundai Heavy Industries (HD HHI, renamed in March from HHI), sought to acquire DSME in 2019, but the deal was blocked by the European Commission in January 2022 on antitrust grounds.

JULY
JAPAN OUTLINES PROCUREMENT PRIORITIES IN NEW WHITE PAPER

Japan's 2023 Defence White Paper (WP) detailed procurement priorities for a 'fundamental reinforcement' of the Japan Self-Defense Forces (JSDF) which was originally proposed in Japan's first National Defense Strategy adopted in December 2022. JSDF's capability requirements are set out in pillars including: stand-off defence capabilities, at JPY5trn (USD35.94bn); integrated air and missile defence capabilities, at JPY3trn (USD21.57bn); uninhabited defence capabilities, at JPY1trn (USD7.19bn); cross-domain operation capabilities, at JPY8trn (USD57.51bn); and command and control and intelligence-related functions, at JPY1trn (USD7.19bn). For cross-domain operations, Japan plans to acquire 12 destroyers, five submarines, ten patrol vessels, 19 P-1 ASW aircraft, and 40 F-35A and 25 F-35B multirole fighter aircraft. According to Japan's FY2023 defence budget published earlier in 2023, most of the acquisition processes (including the acquisition of the *Tomahawk* for JPY211.3bn (USD1.52bn)) had already been initiated prior to the WP.

Afghanistan AFG

New Afghan Afghani AFN		2022	2023	2024
GDP	AFN			
	USD			
per capita	USD			
Growth	%			
Inflation	%			
Def bdgt	AFN			
	USD			
USD1=AFN				

Definitive economic data not available

Real-terms defence budget trend (USDbn, constant 2015)

3.60
n.k. n.k. n.k.
1.41
2008 ---- 2016 ---- 2023

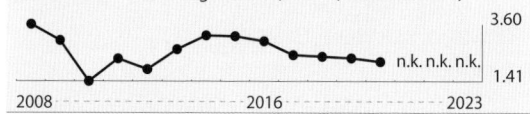

Population	39,232,003					
Age	0–14	15–19	20–24	25–29	30–64	65 plus
Male	20.2%	5.3%	5.0%	4.6%	14.2%	1.3%
Female	19.6%	5.1%	4.9%	4.5%	13.8%	1.5%

Capabilities

Over two years after the collapse of the former Afghan National Security and Defence Forces (ANSDF), the strength and capability of the Afghan Taliban's armed forces and the extent to which they have been able to use the foreign-supplied equipment seized from former government forces remains difficult to assess. Governance between the capital, Kabul, and Kandahar, where the Taliban leader Mullah Haibatullah Akhundzada resides, were divergent. Mullah Haibatullah reportedly raised a force of 30,000 fighters around Kandahar. The Taliban claim they will increase force size by 50,000 troops. US authorities indicated that the Taliban administration is reorganising its defence ministry and retained some formation structures used by the ANSDF. The Taliban have employed armoured vehicles and a small number of Soviet-era helicopters for troop movements, including equipment the West provided the ANSDF. The Taliban will likely struggle to maintain Western equipment because of sanctions and limited supplies of spares. They said they would prioritise procurement of anti-aircraft missiles to defend against UAVs. Efforts to recruit former ANSDF personnel, including pilots and maintainers, have been hampered by continued attacks on some of those personnel. Although the government's priority for its forces is internal and border security, its General Directorate of Intelligence also has an outward-facing mandate. It has prioritised operations against the National Resistance Front in the mountainous east of the country, as well as intelligence-led operations against Islamic State terrorist cells, reducing terrorist attacks. Efforts to modernise the security forces are limited by the Taliban's lack of international recognition.

ACTIVE 150,000 (Taliban 150,000)

ORGANISATIONS BY SERVICE

Taliban ε150,000

The Taliban has announced plans to expand their regular armed forces to 200,000 personnel

FORCES BY ROLE
SPECIAL FORCES
  3 spec ops bn
MANOEUVRE
  Light
  8 inf corps
EQUIPMENT BY TYPE
ARMOURED FIGHTING VEHICLES
  MBT T-62M†
  APC • PPV *Maxxpro*
  AUV MSFV
ARTILLERY
  TOWED 122mm D-30
  MRL 122mm BM-21
  MOR 82mm 2B14
AIRCRAFT • TPT • Light 3: 1 An-26 *Curl*; 1 An-32 *Cline*; 1 Cessna 208B *Grand Caravan*
HELICOPTERS
  ATK 5; 1 Mi-25 *Hind*: 4 Mi-35 *Hind*
  MRH 14: 8 MD-530F; 6 Mi-17 *Hip* H
  TPT • Medium 4 UH-60A *Black Hawk*

Australia AUS

Australian Dollar AUD		2022	2023	2024
GDP	AUD	2.45trn	2.54trn	2.59trn
	USD	1.70trn	1.69trn	1.69trn
per capita	USD	64,814	63,487	62,596
Growth	%	3.7	1.8	1.2
Inflation	%	6.6	5.8	4.0
Def bdgt [a]	AUD	47.8bn	51.7bn	55.0bn
	USD	33.2bn	34.4bn	35.9bn
USD1=AUD		1.44	1.50	1.53

[a] Includes pensions

Real-terms defence budget trend (USDbn, constant 2015)

30.8
20.1
2008 ---- 2016 ---- 2023

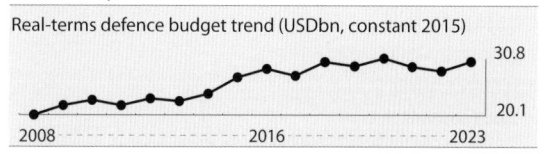

Population	26,461,166					
Age	0–14	15–19	20–24	25–29	30–64	65 plus
Male	9.5%	3.2%	3.5%	3.8%	22.1%	7.7%
Female	8.9%	2.9%	3.1%	3.5%	22.8%	9.0%

Capabilities

The Australian Defence Force (ADF) is capable, well-trained and well-equipped. It has considerable recent operational experience. The ADF has capabilities across domains, with an ability to support deployments abroad. In 2023, Canberra published a Defence Strategic Review to address what it views as a deteriorating security situation in its region. The document called for strengthening the armed forces to address 'the significant military challenge posed by China'. It also committed Australia to close security ties with the US. The review said that the ADF needed to move from a balanced force structure to one capable of delivering a strategy of denial. It reflected the judgement of the 2020 Strategic Update that assumptions around a ten-year 'strategic warning time' no longer held. Australia will improve the ADF's force projection and positioning, notably in the country's north, as well as its anti-access/area denial capabilities. In addition to its links with Washington, Australia is forging closer defence ties with India, Japan, South Korea and the UK, while remaining committed to the Five Power Defence Arrangements and its close defence relations with New Zealand. In March 2023, Canberra, Washington and London announced a plan to provide the Royal Australian Navy nuclear-powered submarines, first through the acquisition of US *Virginia*-class boats, followed by the development and production of SSN-AUKUS, a new conventionally armed nuclear-powered submarine. A second pillar of the AUKUS partnership centres on advanced capability developments. In advance of the arrival of new Australian submarines, the UK and US have pledged to increase submarine visits to Australia and update other elements of its force, including through the acquisition of *Tomahawk* land-attack cruise missiles. Canberra was working on a first National Defence Strategy due for release in 2024. Australia imports most of its defence equipment but possesses an increasingly capable defence industry.

ACTIVE 58,450 (Army 28,400 Navy 15,250 Air 14,800)

RESERVE 21,450 (Army 15,600 Navy 1,900 Air 3,950)

Integrated units are formed from a mix of reserve and regular personnel.

ORGANISATIONS BY SERVICE

Space
EQUIPMENT BY TYPE
SATELLITES • COMMUNICATIONS 1 *Optus* C1 (dual use for civil/mil comms)

Army 28,400
FORCES BY ROLE
COMMAND
　1 (1st) div HQ (1 sigs regt)
MANOEUVRE
　Mechanised
　2 (3rd & 7th) mech inf bde (1 armd cav regt, 1 mech inf bn, 1 lt mech inf bn, 1 arty regt, 1 cbt engr regt, 1 sigs regt, 1 spt bn)
　1 (1st) mech inf bde (1 lt mech inf bn, 1 arty regt, 1 cbt engr regt, 1 sigs regt, 1 spt bn)
　1 (9th) mech inf bde (integrated) (1 armd cav regt, 1 mech inf bn)
　Amphibious
　1 (2nd RAR) amph bn
　Aviation
　1 (16th) avn bde (1 regt (2 ISR hel sqn), 1 regt (3 tpt hel sqn), 1 regt (2 spec ops hel sqn, 1 avn sqn))
COMBAT SUPPORT
　1 (6th) cbt spt bde (1 STA regt (1 STA bty, 2 UAV bty, 1 spt bty), 1 AD/FAC regt (integrated), 1 engr regt (2 construction sqn, 1 EOD sqn), 1 EW regt, 1 int bn, 1 MP bn)
COMBAT SERVICE SUPPORT
　1 (17th) log bde (3 log bn)
　1 (2nd) med bde (4 med bn)

Special Operations Command
FORCES BY ROLE
SPECIAL FORCES
　1 (SAS) SF regt
　1 (SF Engr) SF regt
　2 cdo regt
COMBAT SUPPORT
　3 sigs sqn (incl 1 reserve sqn)
COMBAT SERVICE SUPPORT
　1 CSS sqn

Reserve Organisations 15,600 reservists
FORCES BY ROLE
COMMAND
　1 (2nd) div HQ
MANOEUVRE
　Reconnaissance
　1 recce sqn (assigned to 9th Bde)
　3 (regional force) surv unit (integrated)
　Light
　1 (4th) inf bde (1 recce regt, 3 inf bn, 1 engr regt, 1 spt bn)
　1 (5th) inf bde (1 recce regt, 4 inf bn, 1 engr regt, 2 spt bn)
　1 (11th) inf bde (1 recce regt, 3 inf bn, 1 engr regt, 1 spt bn)
　1 (13th) inf bde (1 recce sqn, 2 inf bn, 1 spt bn)
　1 inf bn (assigned to 9th Bde)
COMBAT SUPPORT
　1 arty regt
　1 sigs regt
COMBAT SERVICE SUPPORT
　1 trg bde
EQUIPMENT BY TYPE
ARMOURED FIGHTING VEHICLES
　MBT 59 M1A1 *Abrams*
　RECCE ε50 *Boxer* CRV (incl variants)
　IFV 221 ASLAV-25 (incl 100 Type II vehicles)
　APC • APC (T) 416 M113AS4
　AUV 1,950: ε950 *Bushmaster* IMV; 1,000 *Hawkei*
ENGINEERING & MAINTENANCE VEHICLES
　ARV 45: 15 ASLAV-F; 17 ASLAV-R; 13 M88A2
　VLB 5 *Biber*
　MW 20: 12 *Husky*; 8 MV-10
ANTI-TANK/ANTI-INFRASTRUCTURE
　MSL • MANPATS FGM-148 *Javelin*
　RCL • 84mm *Carl Gustaf*
ARTILLERY 264
　TOWED 155mm 48 M777A2
　MOR 81mm 216: 40 L16; 176 M252A1

AIR DEFENCE • SAM • Point-defence RBS-70
AMPHIBIOUS 15 LCM 8 (capacity either 1 MBT or 200 troops)
HELICOPTERS
ATK 22 *Tiger*
MRH 2 AW139 (leased)
TPT 17: **Heavy** 14 CH-47F *Chinook*; **Medium** 3 UH-60M *Black Hawk*; (40 NH90 TTH (MRH90) in store)
UNINHABITED AERIAL VEHICLES
ISR • **Medium** 15 RQ-7B *Shadow* 200
AIR-LAUNCHED MISSILES
ASM AGM-114M *Hellfire* II

Navy 15,250
EQUIPMENT BY TYPE
SUBMARINES 6
SSK 6 *Collins* with 6 single 533mm TT with UGM-84C *Harpoon* Block 1B AShM/Mk 48 ADCAP mod 7 HWT
PRINCIPAL SURFACE COMBATANTS 11
DESTROYERS • DDGHM 3 *Hobart* with *Aegis* Baseline 8.1 C2, 2 quad lnchr with RGM-84L *Harpoon* Block II AShM, 6 8-cell Mk 41 VLS with SM-2 Block IIIB SAM/RIM-162A ESSM SAM, 2 twin 324mm SVTT Mk 32 mod 9 ASTT with MU90 LWT/Mk 54 LWT, 1 MK 15 *Phalanx* Block 1B CIWS, 1 127mm gun (capacity 1 MH-60R *Seahawk*)
FRIGATES • FFGHM 8 *Anzac* (GER MEKO 200) with 2 quad lnchr with RGM-84L *Harpoon* Block II AShM, 1 8-cell Mk 41 VLS with RIM-162B ESSM SAM, 2 triple 324mm SVTT Mk 32 mod 5 ASTT with MU90 LWT, 1 127mm gun (capacity 1 MH-60R *Seahawk* hel)
PATROL AND COASTAL COMBATANTS 12
PCO 12: 4 *Armidale* (*Bay* mod); 8 *Cape* (of which 2 leased)
MINE WARFARE • MINE COUNTERMEASURES 4
MHC 4 *Huon*
AMPHIBIOUS
PRINCIPAL AMPHIBIOUS SHIPS 3
LHD 2 *Canberra* (capacity 18 hel; 4 LCM-1E; 110 veh; 12 M1 *Abrams* MBT; 1,000 troops)
LSD 1 *Choules* (ex-UK *Bay*) (capacity 2 med hel; 32 MBT; 350 troops)
LANDING CRAFT • LCM 12 LCM-1E
LOGISTICS AND SUPPORT 11
AGS 2 *Leeuwin* with 1 hel landing platform
AORH 2 *Supply* (ESP *Cantabria*) (capacity 1 MH-60R *Seahawk* hel)
AXS 1 *Young Endeavour*
The following vessels are operated by a private company:
AFS 2: 1 *Ocean Protector* with 1 hel landing platform; 1 *Reliant* with 1 hel landing platform
ASR 2: 1 *Besant*; 1 *Stoker*
AX 1 *Sycamore* (capacity 1 med hel)
AXL 1 *Mercator* (*Pacific* mod)

UNINHABITED MARITIME PLATFORMS • USV 9
DATA • **Small** 5 *Bluebottle*
MW • **Small** 3 SEA 1778
UTL • **Small** 1 *Devil Ray* T38
UNINHABITED MARITIME SYSTEMS • UUV
DATA *Bluefin*-9/12
MW *Double Eagle* Mk II; *SeaFox*

Naval Aviation 1,450
FORCES BY ROLE
ANTI SUBMARINE WARFARE
2 sqn with MH-60R *Seahawk*
TRAINING
1 OCU sqn with MH-60R *Seahawk*
1 sqn with H135
EQUIPMENT BY TYPE
HELICOPTERS
ASW 23 MH-60R *Seahawk*
TPT 15: **Medium** (6 NH90 TTH (MRH90) in store); **Light** 15 H135
UNINHABITED AERIAL VEHICLES
ISR • **Light** ε6 S-100 *Camcopter*
AIR-LAUNCHED MISSILES
ASM AGM-114N *Hellfire* II

Clearance Diving Branch
FORCES BY ROLE
SPECIAL FORCES
2 diving unit

Air Force 14,800
FORCES BY ROLE
FIGHTER/GROUND ATTACK
1 sqn with F/A-18F *Super Hornet*
3 sqn with F-35A *Lightning* II
ANTI SUBMARINE WARFARE
1 sqn with P-8A *Poseidon*
ELECTRONIC WARFARE
1 sqn with EA-18G *Growler*
ISR
1 (FAC) sqn with PC-21
AIRBORNE EARLY WARNING & CONTROL
1 sqn with E-7A *Wedgetail*
TANKER/TRANSPORT
1 sqn with A330 MRTT (KC-30A)
TRANSPORT
1 VIP sqn with B-737BBJ; *Falcon* 7X
1 sqn with C-17A *Globemaster* III
1 sqn with C-27J *Spartan*
1 sqn with C-130J-30 *Hercules*
TRAINING
1 OCU sqn with F-35A *Lightning* II
1 sqn with Beech 350 *King Air*

2 sqn with PC-21
2 (LIFT) sqn with *Hawk MK127**

ISR UAV
1 sqn (forming)

EQUIPMENT BY TYPE

AIRCRAFT 143 combat capable
FGA 87: 24 F/A-18F *Super Hornet*; 63 F-35A *Lightning* II
ASW 12 P-8A *Poseidon*
EW 11 EA-18G *Growler**
AEW&C 6 E-7A *Wedgetail*
TKR/TPT 7 A330 MRTT (KC-30A)
TPT 47: **Heavy** 8 C-17A *Globemaster* III; **Medium** 22: 10 C-27J *Spartan*; 12 C-130J-30 *Hercules*; **Light** 12 Beech 350 *King Air*; **PAX** 5: 2 B-737BBJ (VIP); 3 *Falcon* 7X (VIP)
TRG 82: 33 *Hawk* Mk127*; 49 PC-21

AIR-LAUNCHED MISSILES
AAM • IIR AIM-9X *Sidewinder* II; ASRAAM; **ARH** AIM-120B/C-5/C-7 AMRAAM
ARM AGM-88B HARM; AGM-88E AARGM
AShM AGM-84A *Harpoon*
ALCM • Conventional AGM-158A JASSM

BOMBS
Laser-guided *Paveway* II
Laser & INS/GPS-guided GBU-54 Laser JDAM; *Paveway* IV
INS/GPS-guided AGM-154C JSOW; JDAM; JDAM-ER

DEPLOYMENT

EGYPT: MFO (*Operation Mazurka*) 27
IRAQ: *Operation Inherent Resolve* (*Okra*) 110; 1 SF gp; NATO • NATO Mission Iraq 2
MALAYSIA: 120; 1 inf coy (on 3-month rotational tours); 1 P-8A *Poseidon* (on rotation)
MIDDLE EAST: UN • UNTSO (*Operation Paladin*) 11
PHILIPPINES: *Operation Augury* 100 (trg team)
SOUTH SUDAN: UN • UNMISS (*Operation Aslan*) 14
SYRIA/ISRAEL: UN • UNDOF 1
UNITED ARAB EMIRATES: *Operation Accordion* 400: 1 tpt det with 2 C-130J-30 *Hercules*
UNITED KINGDOM: *Operation Interflex* (*Kudu*) 70 (UKR trg)

FOREIGN FORCES

Singapore 230: 1 trg sqn at Pearce with PC-21 trg ac; 1 trg sqn at Oakey with 12 AS332 *Super Puma*; AS532 *Cougar*
United States US Indo-Pacific Command: 1,700; 1 SEWS at Pine Gap; 1 comms facility at NW Cape; 1 SIGINT stn at Pine Gap • US Strategic Command: 1 detection and tracking radar at Naval Communication Station Harold E. Holt

Bangladesh BGD

Bangladeshi Taka BDT		2022	2023	2024
GDP	BDT	39.7trn	44.4trn	50.1trn
	USD	460bn	446bn	455bn
per capita	USD	2,731	2,621	2,646
Growth	%	7.1	6.0	6.0
Inflation	%	6.2	9.0	7.9
Def bdgt	BDT	373bn	400bn	417bn
	USD	4.32bn	4.02bn	3.79bn
USD1=BDT		86.30	99.46	110.00

Real-terms defence budget trend (USDbn, constant 2015): 3.50 / 1.23 (2008–2023)

Population	167,184,465					
Age	0–14	15–19	20–24	25–29	30–64	65 plus
Male	12.9%	4.3%	4.4%	4.2%	19.6%	3.5%
Female	12.5%	4.2%	4.4%	4.4%	21.4%	4.0%

Capabilities

Bangladesh's limited military capability is optimised for border and domestic security, including disaster relief. The country has embarked on a defence-modernisation plan called Forces 2030, although acquisitions have been limited. Bangladesh has relied on Chinese and Russian aid and credit to augment limited procurement funding. It procured several former Chinese naval vessels, including submarines. In March 2023, Bangladesh operationalised its first submarine base. The country has increased defence collaboration with India and France. Tensions on the border with Myanmar have been rising and may drive Bangladesh to boost border security. The country has a long record of UN peacekeeping deployments. Dhaka is pursing naval-recapitalisation and expansion, including through local manufacture of patrol boats, to better protect the country's large EEZ. The country plans to recapitalise its combat air fleet and has invested in its fixed-wing training inventory. Bangladesh's airlift capability has improved with the addition of C295s and ex-UK C-130Js. The armed forces reportedly retain extensive commercial interests, including in real estate, banks and other businesses.

ACTIVE 171,250 (Army 132,150 Navy 25,100 Air 14,000) Gendarmerie & Paramilitary 63,900

ORGANISATIONS BY SERVICE

Army 132,150
FORCES BY ROLE
COMMAND
10 inf div HQ
SPECIAL FORCES
1 cdo bde (2 cdo bn)
MANOEUVRE
Armoured

1 armd bde
2 armd regt
1 lt armd regt
Light
25 inf bde
2 (composite) bde
COMBAT SUPPORT
10 arty bde
1 engr bde
1 sigs bde
AVIATION
1 avn regt (1 avn sqn; 1 hel sqn)
AIR DEFENCE
1 AD bde
EQUIPMENT BY TYPE
ARMOURED FIGHTING VEHICLES
MBT 276: 174 Type-59/-59G(BD); 58 Type-69/-69G; 44 Type-90-II (MBT-2000)
LT TK 52: 8 Type-62; 44 VT-5
RECCE 8+ BOV M11
APC 545
  APC (T) 134 MT-LB
  APC (W) 330 BTR-80
  PPV 81+ Maxxpro
AUV 188: 36 Cobra; 152 Cobra II
ENGINEERING & MAINTENANCE VEHICLES
AEV MT-LB
ARV 3+: T-54/T-55; Type-84; 3 Type-654
VLB MTU
ANTI-TANK/ANTI-INFRASTRUCTURE
MSL • MANPATS 9K115-2 Metis M1 (RS-AT-13)
RCL 106mm 238 M40A1
ARTILLERY 907+
SP 155mm 18 NORA B-52
TOWED 363+: **105mm** 170 Model 56 pack howitzer; **122mm** 131: 57 Type-54/54-1 (M-30); 20 Type-83; 54 Type-96 (D-30), **130mm** 62 Type-59-1 (M-46)
MRL 54: **122mm** 36+ WS-22; **302mm** 18 T-300
MOR 472: **81mm** 11 M29A1; **82mm** 366 Type-53/type-87/M-31 (M-1937); **120mm** 95 AM-50/UBM 52
AMPHIBIOUS • LANDING CRAFT 3: 1 LCT; 2 LCVP
AIRCRAFT • TPT • Light 8: 1 C295; 5 Cessna 152; 1 Cessna 208B; 1 PA-31T Cheyenne
HELICOPTERS
MRH 2 AS365N3 Dauphin
TPT 10: **Medium** 6 Mi-171Sh **Light** 4: 2 Bell 206L-4 Long Ranger IV; 2 Bell 407GXi
AIR DEFENCE
SAM
  Short-range FM-90 (CH-SA-4)
  Point-defence FN-16 (CH-SA-14); QW-2 (CH-SA-8)
GUNS • TOWED 174: **35mm** 8 GDF-009 (with Skyguard-3);

37mm 132 Type-65/74; **57mm** 34 Type-59 (S-60)

Navy 25,100
EQUIPMENT BY TYPE
SUBMARINES 2
  SSK 2 Nabajatra (ex-PRC Type-035G (Ming)) with 8 single 533mm TT with Yu-3/Yu-4 HWT
PRINCIPAL SURFACE COMBATANTS • FRIGATES 5
  FFGHM 3:
    1 Bangabandhu (ROK modified Ulsan) with 2 twin lnchr with Otomat Mk2 AShM, 1 octuple FM-90N (CH-SA-N-4) SAM, 2 triple ILAS-3 (B-515) 324mm TT with A244/S LWT, 1 76mm gun (capacity 1 AW109E hel)
    2 Umar Farooq (ex-PRC Type-053H3 (Jiangwei II)) with 2 quad lnchr with C-802A AShM, 1 octuple GMLS with HHQ-7 (CH-SA-N-4) SAM, 2 FQF 3200 A/S mor, 1 twin 100mm gun (capacity 1 hel)
  FFG 2 Abu Bakr (ex-PRC Type-053H2 (Jianghu III)) with 2 quad lnchr with C-802A AShM, 2 RBU 1200 Uragan A/S mor, 2 twin 100mm gun
PATROL AND COASTAL COMBATANTS 47
  CORVETTES 6
    FSGM 4 Shadhinota (PRC C13B) with 2 twin lnchr with C-802 (CH-SS-N-6) AShM, 1 octuple lnchr with FL-3000N (HHQ-10) (CH-SA-N-17) SAM, 1 76mm gun, 1 hel landing platform
    FSG 2 Bijoy (ex-UK Castle) with 2 twin lnchr with C-704 AShM, 1 76mm gun, 1 hel landing platform
  PSOH 2 Somudra Joy (ex-US Hero) with 1 76mm gun, hel landing platform (1 used for trg)
  PCFG 4 Durdarsha (ex-PRC Huangfeng) with 4 single lnchr with C-704 AShM
  PCG 2 Durjoy with 2 twin lnchr with C-704 AShM, 1 76mm gun
  PCO 8: 1 Madhumati (ROK Sea Dragon) with 1 57mm gun; 5 Kapatakhaya (ex-UK Island); 2 Durjoy with 2 triple 324mm ASTT, 1 76mm gun
  PCC 11: 2 Meghna with 1 57mm gun (fishery protection); 9 Padma
  PBF 12: 8 X12 Combat Craft; 4 Titas (ROK Sea Dolphin) (1 used for trg)
  PB 2: 1 Barkat (ex-PRC Shanghai III); 1 Salam (ex-PRC Huangfen)
MINE WARFARE • MINE COUNTERMEASURES 5
  MSO 5: 1 Sagar; 4 Shapla (ex-UK River)
AMPHIBIOUS
  LANDING SHIPS • LSL 1
  LANDING CRAFT 20
    LCU 12: 4 Dolphin; 8 Other (of which 2†)
    LCT 2
    LCM 3 Darshak (PRC Yuchin)
    LCVP 3†
LOGISTICS AND SUPPORT 10
  AFD 1 Sundarban

AGS 5: 1 *Anushandhan* (ex-UK *Roebuck*); 2 *Darshak*; 2 *Jarip*
AOR 1 *Khan Jahan Ali*
AR 1†
ATF 1 *Khadem* (ex-PRC *Hujiu*)†

Naval Aviation
EQUIPMENT BY TYPE
AIRCRAFT • MP 4 Do-228NG
HELICOPTERS • TPT • Light 2 AW109E *Power*

Special Warfare and Diving Command 300

Air Force 14,000
FORCES BY ROLE
FIGHTER
1 sqn with MiG-29/MiG-29UB *Fulcrum*
FIGHTER/GROUND ATTACK
1 sqn with F-7MB/FT-7B *Airguard*
1 sqn with F-7BG/FT-7BG *Airguard*
1 sqn with F-7BGI/FT-7BGI *Airguard*
GROUND ATTACK
1 sqn with Yak-130 *Mitten**
TRANSPORT
1 sqn with An-32 *Cline*
1 sqn with C-130B/J *Hercules*
1 sqn with L-410UVP
TRAINING
1 sqn with K-8W *Karakorum**; L-39ZA *Albatros**
1 sqn with PT-6
TRANSPORT HELICOPTER
1 sqn with AW139; Mi-17 *Hip* H; Mi-17-1V *Hip* H; Mi-171Sh
1 sqn with Mi-17 *Hip* H; Mi-17-1V *Hip* H; Mi-171Sh
1 sqn with Bell 212
1 trg sqn with Bell 206L *Long Ranger*; AW119 *Koala*
EQUIPMENT BY TYPE
AIRCRAFT 88 combat capable
FTR 53: 9 F-7MB *Airguard*; 11 F-7BG *Airguard*; 12 F-7BGI *Airguard*; 5 FT-7B *Airguard*; 4 FT-7BG *Airguard*; 4 FT-7BGI *Airguard*; 6 MiG-29 *Fulcrum*; 2 MiG-29UB *Fulcrum* B
TPT 16: **Medium** 8: 4 C-130B *Hercules*; 4 C-130J *Hercules*; **Light** 8: 3 An-32 *Cline*†; 2 C295W; 3 L-410UVP
TRG 64: 4 DA40NG; 12 G 120TP; 15 K-8W *Karakorum**; 7 L-39ZA *Albatros**; 13+ PT-6; 13 Yak-130 *Mitten**
HELICOPTERS
MRH 18: 4 AW139 (SAR); 12 Mi-17 *Hip* H; 2 Mi-17-1V *Hip* H (VIP)
TPT 25: **Medium** 11 Mi-171Sh; **Light** 14: 2 Bell 206L *Long Ranger*; 10+ Bell 212; 2 AW119 *Koala*
AIR-LAUNCHED MISSILES
AAM • IR R-73 (RS-AA-11A *Archer*); PL-5; PL-7; **SARH** R-27R (RS-AA-10A *Alamo*)

Gendarmerie & Paramilitary 63,900
Ansars 20,000+
Security Guards
Rapid Action Battalions 5,000
Ministry of Home Affairs
FORCES BY ROLE
MANOEUVRE
Other
14 paramilitary bn

Border Guard Bangladesh 38,000
FORCES BY ROLE
MANOEUVRE
Amphibious
1 rvn coy
Other
54 paramilitary bn

Coast Guard 900
EQUIPMENT BY TYPE
PATROL AND COASTAL COMBATANTS 54
PSO 4 *Syed Nazrul* (ex-ITA *Minerva*) with 1 hel landing platform
PCC 7 *Sobuj Bangla* (*Padma* mod)
PB 25: 1 *Ruposhi Bangla*; 2 *Shetgang*; 2 *Sonadia*; 4 *Tawfiq* (ex-PRC Type-062 *Shanghai* II)); 16 Other
PBF 13: 3 *Hurricane*; 10 X12 *Combat Craft*
PBR 5 *Pabna*
LOGISTICS AND SUPPORT • AAR 5

DEPLOYMENT

CENTRAL AFRICAN REPUBLIC: UN • MINUSCA 1,419; 1 cdo coy; 1 inf bn; 2 med coy; 1 hel coy

DEMOCRATIC REPUBLIC OF THE CONGO: UN • MONUSCO 1,679; 1 inf bn; 1 engr coy; 1 MP coy; 1 tpt flt with 1 C-130B *Hercules*; 1 hel coy with 6 Mi-17/Mi-171Sh

LEBANON: UN • UNIFIL 118; 1 FSGM

LIBYA: UN • UNSMIL 1

SOUTH SUDAN: UN • UNMISS 1,630; 1 inf bn; 2 rvn coy; 2 engr coy

SUDAN: UN • UNISFA 513; 1 inf bn(-)

WESTERN SAHARA: UN • MINURSO 30; 1 fd hospital

Brunei BRN

Brunei Dollar BND		2022	2023	2024
GDP	BND	23.0bn	20.3bn	21.5bn
	USD	16.7bn	15.2bn	15.8bn
per capita	USD	37,851	34,384	35,813
Growth	%	-1.6	-0.8	3.5
Inflation	%	3.7	1.7	1.5
Def bdgt	BND	598m	ε650m	
	USD	433m	ε485m	
USD1=BND		1.38	1.34	1.36

Real-terms defence budget trend (USDm, constant 2015)

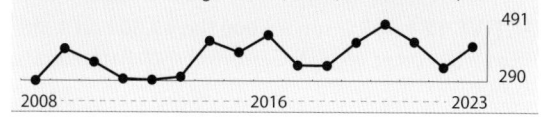

Population	484,991					
Age	0–14	15–19	20–24	25–29	30–64	65 plus
Male	11.2%	3.5%	4.1%	4.5%	22.0%	3.5%
Female	10.6%	3.4%	4.2%	4.8%	24.7%	3.7%

Capabilities

The Royal Brunei Armed Forces are professional and well-trained. Its core missions are ensuring territorial integrity, counterterrorism and counter-insurgency operations, and assisting civil authorities. In May 2021, the government published Brunei's fourth defence white paper in 17 years within the context of the Vision Brunei 2035 framework. C4ISR capabilities are being improved to offset the forces' relatively small size, and the white paper advocates procurements to strengthen airspace control and harden C4 systems. Under a long-standing bilateral arrangement, which currently extends to 2025, Brunei hosts a British military presence including a Gurkha infantry battalion, a helicopter-flight and a jungle-warfare school. Brunei has a close defence relationship with Singapore and hosts a permanent Singapore Armed Forces training facility. It participates in regular bilateral exercises with Singapore and other Southeast Asian countries. The armed forces also take part in multinational exercises organised by ASEAN and the ADMM–Plus. Brunei has limited capacity to deploy forces abroad without assistance but has nevertheless maintained a small deployment to UNIFIL in Lebanon since 2008. Brunei has no domestic defence industry and imports all its military equipment.

ACTIVE 7,200 (Army 4,400 Navy 1,200 Air 1,100 Special Forces 500) Gendarmerie & Paramilitary 400–500

RESERVE 700 (Army 700)

ORGANISATIONS BY SERVICE

Army 4,400
FORCES BY ROLE
MANOEUVRE
　Light
　　3 inf bn
COMBAT SUPPORT
　1 cbt spt bn (1 armd recce sqn, 1 engr sqn)

Reserves 700
FORCES BY ROLE
MANOEUVRE
　Light
　　1 inf bn

EQUIPMENT BY TYPE
ARMOURED FIGHTING VEHICLES
　LT TK 20 FV101 *Scorpion* (incl FV105 *Sultan* CP)
　APC • APC (W) 45 VAB
ENGINEERING & MAINTENANCE VEHICLES
　ARV 2 *Samson*
ARTILLERY • MOR 81mm 24

Navy 1,200
FORCES BY ROLE
SPECIAL FORCES
　1 SF sqn
EQUIPMENT BY TYPE
PATROL AND COASTAL COMBATANTS 11
　CORVETTES • FSG 4 *Darussalam* with 2 twin lnchr with MM40 *Exocet* Block 2 AShM, 1 57mm gun, 1 hel landing platform
　PCO 2 *As-Siddiq* (ex-SGP *Fearless*)
　PCC 4 *Ijtihad*
　PBF 1 *Mustaed*
AMPHIBIOUS • LANDING CRAFT • LCM 4: 2 *Damuan* (*Cheverton Loadmaster*); 2 *Teraban*;

Air Force 1,100
FORCES BY ROLE
MARITIME PATROL
　1 sqn with CN235M
TRAINING
　1 sqn with Bell 206B *Jet Ranger* II
TRANSPORT HELICOPTER
　1 sqn with Bell 214 (SAR)
　1 sqn with S-70i *Black Hawk*
AIR DEFENCE
　1 sqn with *Mistral*
　1 sqn with *Rapier*
EQUIPMENT BY TYPE
AIRCRAFT
　TPT • Light 1 CN235M
　TRG 4 PC-7
HELICOPTERS
　TPT 15: **Medium** 13: 1 Bell 214 (SAR); 12 S-70i *Black Hawk*; **Light** 2 Bell 206B *Jet Ranger* II
AIR DEFENCE • SAM • Point-defence *Mistral*; *Rapier*

Special Forces Regiment ε500
FORCES BY ROLE

SPECIAL FORCES
1 SF regt

Gendarmerie & Paramilitary 400–500

Gurkha Reserve Unit 400–500
FORCES BY ROLE
MANOEUVRE
  Light
    2 inf bn(-)

DEPLOYMENT
LEBANON: UN • UNIFIL 30

FOREIGN FORCES
Singapore 1 trg camp with infantry units on rotation; 1 trg school; 1 hel det with AS332 *Super Puma*
United Kingdom 2,000; 1 (Gurkha) inf bn; 1 jungle trg centre; 1 hel sqn with 3 SA330 *Puma* HC2

Cambodia CAM

Cambodian Riel KHR		2022	2023	2024
GDP	KHR	121trn	131trn	143trn
	USD	28.8bn	30.9bn	33.2bn
per capita	USD	1,802	1,916	2,037
Growth	%	5.2	5.6	6.1
Inflation	%	5.3	2.0	3.0
Def bdgt [a]	KHR	4.21trn	5.02trn	
	USD	1.00bn	1.18bn	
USD1=KHR		4,199.80	4,246.10	4,292.73

[a] Defence and security budget

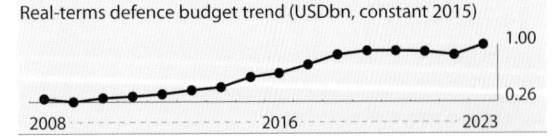

Real-terms defence budget trend (USDbn, constant 2015)
1.00
0.26
2008   2016   2023

Population	16,891,245					
Age	0–14	15–19	20–24	25–29	30–64	65 plus
Male	14.9%	4.4%	3.8%	3.9%	19.7%	1.8%
Female	14.6%	4.4%	3.9%	4.1%	21.1%	3.3%

Capabilities

The Royal Cambodian Armed Forces (RCAF) were established in 1993 after the merger of the Communist government's Cambodian People's Armed Forces (formerly the Kampuchean People's Revolutionary Armed Forces: KPRAF) and two non-communist resistance armies. The country does not face any direct external military threats, although Cambodia continues to emphasise its border security with Laos, Thailand and Vietnam. Cambodia and Thailand clashed in 2011 over disputed land surrounding the Preah Vihear temple, though relations have warmed since the International Court of Justice in 2013 ruled in Cambodia's favour. Internally, security concerns include civil unrest and transnational threats, such as drug trafficking. Cambodia's most important international defence links are with China and Vietnam. Despite a traditional reliance on Russia for defence equipment, China has emerged as another key supplier. Beijing also is funding upgrades at the Ream naval base located on the Gulf of Thailand. This raised concerns that Beijing could use the facility as an overseas military base – a first in the Indo-Pacific region. Such uses have been consistently denied by Cambodian authorities. The US imposed a largely symbolic arms embargo on Cambodia in December 2021 over the country's military links to China. Phnom Penh's equipment funding is limited, although the 2022 National Defence White Paper stated that modernisation of the RCAF is the top priority. The document also encouraged the development of a domestic defence industry; Cambodia currently lacks the ability to design and manufacture modern equipment for its armed forces.

ACTIVE 124,300 (Army 75,000 Navy 2,800 Air 1,500 Provincial Forces 45,000) Gendarmerie & Paramilitary 67,000

Conscript liability 18 months service authorised but not implemented since 1993

ORGANISATIONS BY SERVICE

Army ε75,000

6 Military Regions (incl 1 special zone for capital)
FORCES BY ROLE
SPECIAL FORCES
  1 (Spec Ops Comd) AB/SF Bde
MANOEUVRE
  Light
    2 (2nd & 3rd Intervention) inf div (3 inf bde)
    5 (Intervention) indep inf bde
    8 indep inf bde
  Other
    1 (70th) sy bde (4 sy bn)
    17 (border) sy bn
COMBAT SUPPORT
  2 arty bn
  4 fd engr regt
COMBAT SERVICE SUPPORT
  1 (construction) engr regt
  2 tpt bde
AIR DEFENCE
  1 AD bn
EQUIPMENT BY TYPE
ARMOURED FIGHTING VEHICLES
  MBT 200+: 50 Type-59; 150+ T-54/T-55
  LT TK 20+: Type-62; 20 Type-63
  RECCE 20+ BRDM-2
  IFV 70 BMP-1
  APC 230+
    APC (T) M113
    APC (W) 230: 200 BTR-60/BTR-152; 30 OT-64
  AUV 27: 12 Dongfeng *Mengshi*; 15 *Tiger* 4×4

ENGINEERING & MAINTENANCE VEHICLES
ARV T-54/T-55
MW *Bozena*; RA-140 DS

ANTI-TANK/ANTI-INFRASTRUCTURE
RCL 82mm B-10; **107mm** B-11

ARTILLERY 486+
SP 155mm 12 SH-1
TOWED 400+: **76mm** ZIS-3 (M-1942)/**122mm** D-30/**122mm** M-30 (M-1938)/**130mm** Type-59-I
MRL 74+: **107mm** Type-63; **122mm** 48+: 8 BM-21; ε20 PHL-81; some PHL-90B; 20 RM-70; **132mm** BM-13-16 (BM-13); **140mm** 20 BM-14-16 (BM-14); **300mm** 6 PHL-03
MOR 82mm M-37; **120mm** M-43; **160mm** M-160

AIR DEFENCE
SAM • Point-defence FN-6 (CH-SA-10); FN-16 (CH-SA-14) (reported)
GUNS • TOWED 14.5mm ZPU-1/ZPU-2/ZPU-4; **37mm** M-1939; **57mm** S-60

Navy ε2,800 (incl 1,500 Naval Infantry)
EQUIPMENT BY TYPE
PATROL AND COASTAL COMBATANTS 13
PBF 4 Project 205P (ex-FSU *Stenka*)
PB 7: 3 (PRC 20m); 4 (PRC 46m)
PBR 2 *Kaoh Chhlam*
AMPHIBIOUS • LANDING CRAFT 1
LCU 1 Type-067 (*Yunnan*)
LOGISTICS AND SUPPORT • AFDL 1

Naval Infantry 1,500
FORCES BY ROLE
MANOEUVRE
Light
1 (31st) nav inf bde
COMBAT SUPPORT
1 arty bn

Air Force 1,500
FORCES BY ROLE
ISR/TRAINING
1 sqn with P-92 *Echo*
TRANSPORT
1 VIP sqn (reporting to Council of Ministers) with A320; AS350 *Ecureuil*; AS355F2 *Ecureuil* II
1 sqn with MA60; Y-12 (II)
TRANSPORT HELICOPTER
1 sqn with Mi-17 *Hip* H; Mi-8 *Hip*; Z-9
EQUIPMENT BY TYPE
AIRCRAFT
TPT 10: **Light** 9: 2 MA60; 5 P-92 *Echo* (pilot trg/recce); 2 Y-12 (II) (2 An-24RV *Coke*; 1 BN-2 *Islander* in store); **PAX** 1 A320 (VIP)
TRG (5 L-39C *Albatros** in store)

HELICOPTERS
MRH 17: 6 Mi-17 *Hip* H; 11 Z-9
TPT 6+: **Heavy** (2 Mi-26 *Halo* in store); **Medium** some Mi-8 *Hip*; **Light** 6: 2 AW109 (reported); 2 AS350 *Ecureuil*; 2 AS355F2 *Ecureuil* II

Provincial Forces 45,000+
Reports of at least 1 inf regt per province, with varying numbers of inf bn (with lt wpn)

Gendarmerie & Paramilitary 67,000
Police 67,000 (including gendarmerie)

DEPLOYMENT
CENTRAL AFRICAN REPUBLIC: UN • MINUSCA 345; 1 engr coy
LEBANON: UN • UNIFIL 181; 1 EOD coy
SOUTH SUDAN: UN • UNMISS 85; 1 MP coy
SUDAN: UN • UNISFA 1

China, People's Republic of PRC

Chinese Yuan Renminbi CNY		2022	2023	2024
GDP	CNY	120.5trn	125.3trn	132.9trn
	USD	17.9trn	17.7trn	18.6trn
per capita	USD	12,670	12,541	13,156
Growth	%	3.0	5.0	4.2
Inflation	%	1.9	0.7	1.7
Def exp	CNY	ε1.95trn	ε1.95trn	
	USD	ε319bn	ε319bn	
Def bdgt [a]	CNY	1.47trn	1.55trn	
	USD	218.6bn	219.5bn	
USD1=CNY		6.74	7.08	7.16

[a] Central Expenditure budget including local militia funding

Real-terms defence budget trend (USDbn, constant 2015)
213
82.4
2008 — 2016 — 2023

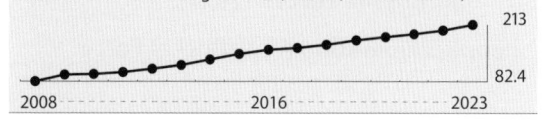

Population 1,421,070,984

Age	0–14	15–19	20–24	25–29	30–64	65 plus
Male	8.8%	2.9%	2.9%	3.5%	26.3%	6.6%
Female	7.7%	2.5%	2.5%	3.1%	25.6%	7.6%

Capabilities
The People's Liberation Army (PLA) is the world's largest armed force, with an increasingly advanced equipment inventory. Its operational effectiveness, however, remains hampered by training and doctrine issues. China's 2019 defence White Paper did not significantly alter the strategic direction laid out in the 2015 edition

and was focused more on updating the progress of PLA modernisation efforts. In 2021, amendments to the National Defense Law were enacted, which handed responsibility for defence mobilisation fully to the Central Military Commission and removed the role of the State Council. The Strategic Support Force continues to develop China's cyber, space and information-dominance capabilities. China does not maintain any formal alliances but has several defence relationships with regional states and through its membership of the SCO. It has also worked to develop defence ties with African and Middle Eastern states. In February 2022, China and Russia announced a friendship with 'no limits', though Beijing has been reluctant to assist Moscow militarily in its war on Ukraine. The PLA lacks any significant recent combat experience, and its training has traditionally suffered from over-scripted and unrealistic exercises. Though these weaknesses are acknowledged, it is unclear how effective the newly established structures will be at generating and controlling high-intensity combined-arms capabilities. PLA conscripts twice a year with the aim of improving readiness. Recruitment focuses largely on college graduates and those skilled in science and engineering, particularly with specialisms in cyber and space. In 2023, China adopted the Reserve Personnel Law, which instituted a system for military personnel replenishment. A requirement for out-of-area operations is relatively new for the PLA; the navy is the only service to have experience in extended deployments, assisted by its support base in Djibouti. Major platform inventories in all the services comprise a mix of modern, older and obsolescent designs as modernisation efforts continue. China has an extensive defence-industrial base, capable of producing advanced equipment across all domains, although questions persist over quality and reliability. In 2023, the PLA underwent an anti-corruption investigation that saw the removal of the PLA Rocket Force Commander and Political Commissar, as well as China's Defence Minister.

ACTIVE 2,035,000 (Ground Forces 965,000 Navy 252,000 Air Force 403,000 Strategic Missile Forces 120,000 Strategic Support Force 145,000 Other 150,000) Gendarmerie & Paramilitary 500,000

Conscript liability Selective conscription; all services 24 months

RESERVE ε510,000

ORGANISATIONS BY SERVICE

Strategic Missile Forces 120,000+

People's Liberation Army Rocket Force

The People's Liberation Army Rocket Force organises and commands its own troops to launch nuclear counter-attacks with strategic missiles and to conduct operations with conventional missiles. Organised as launch brigades subordinate to 6 army-level missile bases.

FORCES BY ROLE
SURFACE-TO-SURFACE MISSILE
  5 ICBM bde with DF-5A/B/C
  2 ICBM bde with DF-31A
  5 ICBM bde with DF-31A(G)
  1 ICBM bde with DF-31 (silo) (forming)
  4 ICBM bde with DF-41
  6 IRBM bde with DF-26
  4 MRBM bde with DF-17 with HGV
  2 MRBM bde with DF-21A/E
  2 MRBM bde with DF-21C/D
  2 SRBM bde with DF-11A/DF-15B
  2 SRBM bde with DF-16
  3 GLCM bde with CJ-10/CJ-10A/CJ-100
  4 SSM bde (forming)

EQUIPMENT BY TYPE
SURFACE-TO-SURFACE MISSILE LAUNCHERS
  ICBM • Nuclear 140: 18+ DF-5A/B/C (CH-SS-4 Mod 2/3/4); ε6 DF-31 (silo); ε24 DF-31A (CH-SS-10 Mod 2); ε56 DF-31A(G); ε36 DF-41 (CH-SS-20)
  IRBM • Dual-capable 140+: 140+ DF-26 (CH-SS-18); DF-27 with HGV (CH-SS-X-24) (entering service)
  MRBM 102: **Nuclear** ε24 DF-21A/E (CH-SS-5 Mod 2/6); **Conventional** 78: ε48 DF-17 with HGV (CH-SS-22); ε30 DF-21C/D (CH-SS-5 Mod 4/5)
  SRBM • Conventional 225: ε108 DF-11A (CH-SS-7 Mod 2); ε81 DF-15B (CH-SS-6 Mod 3); ε36 DF-16 (CH-SS-11 Mod 1/2)
  GLCM • Conventional 126: ε72 CJ-10/CJ-10A (CH-SSC-9 Mod 1/2); ε54 CJ-100 (CH-SSC-13 *Splinter*)

Navy
EQUIPMENT BY TYPE
SUBMARINES • STRATEGIC 6
  SSBN 6 Type-094 (*Jin*) with up to 12 JL-2 (CH-SS-N-14)/JL-3 (CH-SS-N-20) nuclear SLBMs, 6 single 533mm TT with Yu-6 HWT

Defensive
EQUIPMENT BY TYPE
RADAR • STRATEGIC: 4+ large phased array radars; some detection and tracking radars

Space
EQUIPMENT BY TYPE
SATELLITES 245
  COMMUNICATIONS 11: 2 *Shen Tong*-1; 4 *Shen Tong*-2; 2 *Feng Huo*-1; 3 *Feng Huo*-2
  POSITIONING, NAVIGATION & TIMING 45: 3 *Beidou*-2(M); 5 *Beidou*-2(G); 7 *Beidou*-2(IGSO); 24 *Beidou*-3(M); 3 *Beidou*-3(G); 3 *Beidou*-3(ISGO)
  METEOROLOGY/OCEANOGRAPHY 8: 2 *Yunhai*-1; 6 *Yunhai*-2
  ISR 92: 2 *Jianbing*-5; 4 *Jianbing*-6; 4 *Jianbing*-7; 5 *Jianbing*-9; 3 *Jianbing*-10; 3 *Jianbing*-11/-12; 3 *Jianbing*-16; 4 LKW; 10 *Tianhui*; 5 *Yaogan*-29; 4 *Yaogan*-34; 15 *Yaogan*-35; 15 *Yaogan*-36; 12 *Yaogan*-39; 3 *Yaogan*-40
  ELINT/SIGINT 81: 30 *Chuangxin*-5 (*Yaogan*-30); 15 *Jianbing*-8; 3 *Qianshao*-3; 10 *Shijian*-6 (5 pairs – reported ELINT/SIGINT role); 7 *Shijian*-11 (reported ELINT/SIGINT role); 12 *Yaogan*-31; 4 *Yaogan*-32
  EARLY WARNING 5 *Huoyan*-1
  RENDEZVOUS & PROXIMITY OPERATIONS 3: 1 *Shijian*-17; 1 *Shijian*-21; 1 *Shijian*-23

REUSABLE SPACECRAFT 1 CSSHQ
COUNTERSPACE • MSL SC-19 (reported)

Army ε965,000
FORCES BY ROLE
COMMAND
13 (Group) army HQ
SPECIAL FORCES
15 spec ops bde
MANOEUVRE
Armoured
33 (cbd arms) armd bde
Mechanised
1 (high alt) mech inf div (1 (cbd arms) armd regt, 2 (cbd arms) mech regt, 1 arty /AD regt)
18 (cbd arms) mech inf bde
2 indep mech inf regt
Light
3 (high alt) inf div (1 (cbd arms) armd regt, 2 (cbd arms) inf regt, 1 arty/AD regt)
24 (cbd arms) inf bde
Air Manoeuvre
2 air aslt bde
Amphibious
6 amph aslt bde
Other
1 (OPFOR) armd bde
1 mech gd div (1 armd regt, 2 mech inf regt, 1 arty regt, 1 AD regt)
1 sy gd div (4 sy regt)
16 (border) sy bde
15 (border) sy regt
1 (border) sy gp
COMBAT SUPPORT
15 arty bde
9 engr/NBC bde
5 engr bde
5 NBC bde
1 engr regt
COMBAT SERVICE SUPPORT
13 spt bde
COASTAL DEFENCE
19 coastal arty/AShM bde
AVIATION
1 mixed avn bde
HELICOPTER
12 hel bde
TRAINING
4 hel trg bde
AIR DEFENCE
15 AD bde

Reserves
The People's Liberation Army Reserve Force is being restructured, and the army component reduced. As a result some of the units below may have been re-roled or disbanded
FORCES BY ROLE
MANOEUVRE
Armoured
2 armd regt
Light
18 inf div
4 inf bde
3 indep inf regt
COMBAT SUPPORT
3 arty div
7 arty bde
15 engr regt
1 ptn br bde
3 ptn br regt
10 chem regt
10 sigs regt
COMBAT SERVICE SUPPORT
9 log bde
1 log regt
AIR DEFENCE
17 AD div
8 AD bde
8 AD regt
EQUIPMENT BY TYPE
ARMOURED FIGHTING VEHICLES
MBT 4,700: 400 ZTZ-59/-59-II/-59D; 200 ZTZ-79; 300 ZTZ-88A/B; 1,000 ZTZ-96; 1,500 ZTZ-96A; 600 ZTZ-99; 700 ZTZ-99A
LT TK 1,250: 750 ZTD-05; 500 ZTQ-15
ASLT 1,200 ZTL-11
IFV 8,050: 400 ZBD-04; 2,000 ZBD-04A; 3,250 ZBL-08; 600 ZBD-86; 650 ZBD-86A; 550 ZSL-92; 600 ZSL-92B
APC 3,600
  APC (T) 1,950: 200 ZSD-63; 1,750 ZSD-89/-89A
  APC (W) 1,650: 700 ZSL-92A; 900 ZSL-10; 50 ZSL-93
AAV 750 ZBD-05
AUV Dongfeng Mengshi; *Tiger* 4×4
ENGINEERING & MAINTENANCE VEHICLES
ARV Type-73; Type-84; Type-85; Type-97; Type-654
VLB MTU; TMM; GQL-110A (Type-84A); GQL-111 (HZQL75); GQL-321 (HZQL22); GQL-410; High Altitude VLB; HZQL-18; ZGQ-84
MW Type-74; Type-79; Type-81-II; Type-84
ANTI-TANK/ANTI-INFRASTRUCTURE
MSL
  SP 1,125: 450 HJ-8 (veh mounted); 200 HJ-10; 25 HJ-10A; 450 ZSL-02B
  MANPATS HJ-73D; HJ-8A/C/E; HJ-11; HJ-12

RCL 3,966: **75mm** PF-56; **82mm** PF-65 (B-10); PF-78; **105mm** PF-75; **120mm** PF-98
GUNS 1,788
  SP 480: **100mm** 250 PTL-02; **120mm** 230 PTZ-89
  TOWED • 100mm 1,308 PT-73 (T-12)/PT-86
ARTILLERY 9,520
  SP 3,240: **122mm** 2,170: 300 PLZ-89; 550 PLZ-07A; 150 PLZ-07B; 300 PCL-09; 600 PLL-09; 120 PCL-161; 120 PCL-171; 30 PCL-181 **152mm** 150 PLZ-83A/B; **155mm** 920: 320 PLZ-05; 600 PCL-181; (600 in store: **122mm** 400 PLZ-89; **152mm** 200 PLZ-83A)
  TOWED 900: **122mm** 300 PL-96 (D-30); **130mm** 100 PL-59 (M-46)/PL-59-I; **152mm** 500 PL-66 (D-20); (4,700 in store: **122mm** 3,000 PL-54-1 (M-1938)/PL-83/PL-60 (D-74)/PL-96 (D-30); **152mm** 1,700 PL-54 (D-1)/PL-66 (D-20))
  GUN/MOR 120mm 1,250: 450 PLL-05; 800 PPZ-10
  MRL 1,330+ **107mm** PH-63; **122mm** 1,095: 200 PHL-81/PHL-90; 350 PHL-11; 375 PHZ-89; 120 PHZ-11; 30 PHL-20; 10+ PHL-21; 10 PHL-161; **300mm** 175 PHL-03; **370mm** 60+ PCH-191; (1,000 in store: **122mm** 1,000 PHL-81)
  MOR 2,800: **82mm** PP-53 (M-37)/PP-67/PP-82/PP-87; **SP 82mm** PCP-001; **100mm** PP-89
COASTAL DEFENCE
  AShM HY-1 (CH-SSC-2 *Silkworm*); HY-2 (CH-SSC-3 *Seersucker*); HY-4 (CH-SSC-7 *Sadsack*); YJ-62
PATROL AND COASTAL COMBATANTS 26
  PB 26: 10 *Huzong*; 16 *Shenyang*
AMPHIBIOUS
  LANDING SHIPS • LSM 2 *Yujiu*
  LANDING CRAFT • LCM 234: 3+ *Yugong*; 40+ *Yunnan II*; 100+ *Yupen*; 16+ *Yutu*; 75+ *Yuwei*
LOGISTICS AND SUPPORT 22
  AK 6+ *Leizhuang*
  AKR 2 *Yunsong* (capacity 1 MBT; 1 med hel)
  ARC 1
  AO 11: 1 *Fuzhong*; 8 *Fubing*; 2 *Fulei*
  ATF 2 *Huntao*
  AX 1 *Haixun* III
AIRCRAFT • TPT 6: **Medium** 4: 2 Y-8; 2 Y-9; **Light** 2 Y-7
HELICOPTERS
  ATK 320+: 200 WZ-10; 120+ WZ-19
  MRH 208: 22 Mi-17 *Hip* H; 3 Mi-17-1V *Hip* H; 38 Mi-17V-5 *Hip* H; 25 Mi-17V-7 *Hip* H; ε120 Z-9WZ
  TPT 512: **Heavy** 135: 9 Z-8A; 96 Z-8B; ε30 Z-8L; **Medium** 309: 140 Mi-171; 19 S-70C2 (S-70C) *Black Hawk*; ε150 Z-20; **Light** 68: 15 H120 *Colibri*; 53 Z-11
UNINHABITED AERIAL VEHICLES
  CISR • Heavy 5+ CH-4B
  ISR • Heavy BZK-005; BZK-009 (reported); **Medium** BZK-006 (incl variants); BZK-007; BZK-008
LOITERING & DIRECT ATTACK MUNITIONS
  Harpy

AIR DEFENCE
  SAM 754+
    Medium-range 250 HQ-16A/B (CH-SA-16)
    Short-range 504: 24 9K331 *Tor-M1* (RS-SA-15 *Gauntlet*); 30 HQ-6D (CH-SA-6); 200 HQ-7A/B (CH-SA-4); 200 HQ-17 (CH-SA-15); 50 HQ-17A (CH-SA-15)
    Point-defence HN-5A/B (CH-SA-3); FN-6 (CH-SA-10); QW-1 (CH-SA-7); QW-2 (CH-SA-8)
  SPAAGM 25mm 270 PGZ-04A
  GUNS 7,126+
    SP 126: **30mm** some PGL-19; **35mm** 120 PGZ-07; **37mm** 6 PGZ-88
    TOWED 7,000+: **25mm** PG-87; **35mm** PG-99 (GDF-002); **37mm** PG-55 (M-1939)/PG-65/PG-74; **57mm** PG-59 (S-60); **100mm** PG-59 (KS-19)
AIR-LAUNCHED MISSILES
  AAM • IR TY-90
  ASM AKD-8; AKD-9; AKD-10

Navy ε252,000

The PLA Navy is organised into five service arms: submarine, surface, naval aviation, coastal defence and marine corps, as well as other specialised units. There are three fleets, one each in the Eastern, Southern and Northern theatre commands

EQUIPMENT BY TYPE
SUBMARINES 59
  STRATEGIC • SSBN 6 Type-094 (*Jin*) with up to 12 JL-2 (CH-SS-N-14)/JL-3 (CH-SS-N-20) nuclear SLBMs, 6 single 533mm TT with Yu-6 HWT
  TACTICAL 53
    SSN 6:
      2 Type-093 (*Shang* I) with 6 single 533mm TT with YJ-82 (CH-SS-N-7) AShM or YJ-18 (CH-SS-N-13) AShM/Yu-3 HWT/Yu-6 HWT
      4 Type-093A (*Shang* II) with 6 single 533mm TT with YJ-82 (CH-SS-N-7) AShM or YJ-18 (CH-SS-N-13) AShM/Yu-3 HWT/Yu-6 HWT
      (3 Type-091 (*Han*) in reserve with 6 single 533mm TT with YJ-82 (CH-SS-N-7) AShM/Yu-3 HWT)
    SSK 46:
      2 Project 636 (Improved *Kilo*) with 6 single 533mm TT with TEST-71ME HWT/53-65KE HWT
      8 Project 636M (Improved *Kilo*) with 6 single 533mm TT with TEST-71ME HWT/53-65KE HWT/3M54E *Klub*-S (RS-SS-N-27B *Sizzler*) AShM
      4 Type-035B (*Ming*) with 8 single 533mm TT with Yu-3 HWT/Yu-4 HWT
      12 Type-039(G) (*Song*) with 6 single 533mm TT with YJ-82 (CH-SS-N-7) AShM or YJ-18 (CH-SS-N-13) AShM/Yu-3 HWT/Yu-6 HWT
      4 Type-039A (*Yuan*) (fitted with AIP) with 6 533mm TT with YJ-82 (CH-SS-N-7) AShM or YJ-18 (CH-SS-N-13) AShM/Yu-3 HWT/Yu-6 HWT
      14 Type-039B (*Yuan*) (fitted with AIP) with 6 533mm TT with YJ-82 (CH-SS-N-7) AShM or YJ-18 (CH-SS-N-13) AShM/Yu-3 HWT/Yu-6 HWT

2 Type-039B mod (*Yuan*) (fitted with AIP) with 6 533mm TT with YJ-82 (CH-SS-N-7) AShM or YJ-18 (CH-SS-N-13) AShM/Yu-3 HWT/Yu-6 HWT (up to 10 Type-035(G) (*Ming*) in reserve with 8 single 533mm TT with Yu-3 HWT/Yu-4 HWT)

SSB 1 Type-032 (*Qing*) (SLBM trials)

PRINCIPAL SURFACE COMBATANTS 101

AIRCRAFT CARRIERS • CV 2:

1 Type-001 (*Kuznetsov*) with 3 18-cell GMLS with HHQ-10 (CH-SA-N-17) SAM, 2 RBU 6000 *Smerch* 2 A/S mor, 3 H/PJ-11 CIWS (capacity 18–24 J-15 ac; 17 Ka-28/Ka-31/Z-8S/Z-8JH/Z-8AEW hel)

1 Type-002 (*Kuznetsov* mod) with 3 18-cell GMLS with HHQ-10 (CH-SA-N-17) SAM, 2 RBU 6000 *Smerch* 2 A/S mor, 3 H/PJ-11 CIWS (capacity 32 J-15 ac; 12 Ka-28/Ka-31/Z-8S/Z-8JH/Z-8AEW hel)

CRUISERS • CGHM 8 Type-055 (*Renhai*) with 14 8-cell VLS (8 fore, 6 aft) with YJ-18A (CH-SS-N-13) AShM/HHQ-9B (CH-SA-N-21) SAM/Yu-8 A/S msl, 1 24-cell GMLS with HHQ-10 (CH-SA-N-17) SAM, 2 triple 324mm ASTT with Yu-7 LWT, 1 H/PJ-11 CIWS, 1 130mm gun (capacity 2 med hel)

DESTROYERS 42

DDGHM 40:

2 *Hangzhou* (Project 956EM (*Sovremenny* II)) with 2 quad lnchr with 3M80MVE *Moskit-E* (RS-SS-N-22B *Sunburn*) AShM, 2 single 3S90E lnchr with 9M38E M-22E *Shtil* (RS-SA-N-7 *Gadfly*) SAM, 2 twin 533mm DTA-53-956 ASTT with SET-65KE HWT/53-65KE HWT, 2 RBU 1000 *Smerch* 3 A/S mor, 2 *Kashtan* (RS-CADS-N-1) CIWS, 1 twin 130mm gun (capacity 1 Z-9C/Ka-28 *Helix* A hel)

2 *Hangzhou* (Project 956E (*Sovremenny* III)) with 2 quad lnchr with YJ-12A AShM, 4 8-cell H/AJK-16 VLS with HHQ-16 (CH-SA-N-16) SAM/Yu-8 A/S msl, 2 triple 324mm ASTT with Yu-7 LWT, 4 AK630M CIWS, 2 twin 130mm gun (capacity 1 Z-9C/Ka-28 *Helix* A hel)

1 Type-051B (*Luhai*) with 4 quad lnchr with YJ-12A AShM, 4 8-cell H/AJK-16 VLS with HHQ-16 (CH-SA-N-16) SAM/Yu-8 A/S msl, 2 triple 324mm ASTT with Yu-7 LWT, 2 H/PJ-11 CIWS, 1 twin 100mm gun (capacity 2 Z-9C/Ka-28 *Helix* A hel)

2 Type-052 (*Luhu*) with 4 quad lnchr with YJ-83 AShM, 1 octuple lnchr with HHQ-7 (CH-SA-N-4) SAM, 2 triple 324mm ASTT with Yu-7 LWT, 2 FQF 2500 A/S mor, 2 H/PJ-12 CIWS, 1 twin 100mm gun (capacity 2 Z-9C hel)

2 Type-052B (*Luyang* I) (in refit) with 4 quad lnchr with YJ-83 AShM, 2 single 3S90E lnchr with 9M317E *Shtil-1* (RS-SA-N-7B) SAM, 2 triple 324mm ASTT with Yu-7 LWT, 2 H/PJ-12 CIWS, 1 100mm gun (capacity 1 Ka-28 *Helix* A hel)

6 Type-052C (*Luyang* II) (of which 1 in refit) with 2 quad lnchr with YJ-62 AShM, 8 8-cell VLS with HHQ-9 (CH-SA-N-9) SAM (CH-SA-N-9), 2 triple 324mm ASTT with Yu-7 LWT, 2 H/PJ-12 CIWS, 1 100mm gun (capacity 2 Ka-28 *Helix* A hel)

10 Type-052D (*Luyang* III) with 8 8-cell VLS with YJ-18A (CH-SS-N-13) AShM/HHQ-9B (CH-SA-N-21) SAM/Yu-8 A/S msl, 1 24-cell GMLS with HHQ-10 (CH-SA-N-17) SAM, 2 triple 324mm ASTT with Yu-7 LWT, 1 H/PJ-12 CIWS, 1 130mm gun (capacity 2 Ka-28 *Helix* A hel)

3 Type-052D (*Luyang* III) with 8 octuple VLS with YJ-18A (CH-SS-N-13) AShM/HHQ-9B (CH-SA-N-21) SAM/Yu-8 A/S msl, 1 24-cell GMLS with HHQ-10 (CH-SA-N-17) SAM, 2 triple 324mm ASTT with Yu-7 LWT, 1 H/PJ-11 CIWS, 1 130mm gun (capacity 2 Ka-28 *Helix* A hel)

12 Type-052D mod (*Luyang* III mod) with 8 octuple VLS with YJ-18A (CH-SS-N-13) AShM/HHQ-9B (CH-SA-N-21) SAM/Yu-8 A/S msl, 1 24-cell GMLS with HHQ-10 (CH-SA-N-17) SAM, 2 triple 324mm ASTT with Yu-7 LWT, 1 H/PJ-11 CIWS, 1 130mm gun (capacity 2 Z-9/Z-20 hel)

DDGM 2 Type-051C (*Luzhou*) with 2 quad lnchr with YJ-83 AShM; 6 6-cell B-204 VLS with S-300FM *Rif-M* (RS-SA-N-20 *Gargoyle*) SAM, 2 H/PJ-12 CIWS, 1 100mm gun, 1 hel landing platform

FRIGATES • FFGHM 49

2 Type-053H3 (*Jiangwei* II) with 2 quad lnchr with YJ-83 AShM, 1 octuple lnchr with HHQ-7 (CH-SA-N-4) SAM, 2 RBU 1200 A/S mor, 1 twin 100mm gun (capacity 1 Z-9C hel)

6 Type-053H3 (*Jiangwei* II Upgrade) with 2 quad lnchr with YJ-83 AShM, 1 8-cell GMLS with HHQ-10 (CH-SA-N-17) SAM, 2 RBU 1200 A/S mor, 1 twin 100mm gun (capacity 1 Z-9C hel)

2 Type-054 (*Jiangkai*) with 2 quad lnchr with YJ-83 AShM, 1 24-cell GMLS with HHQ-10 (CH-SA-N-17) SAM, 2 triple 324mm ASTT with Yu-7 LWT, 2 RBU 1200 A/S mor, 4 AK630 CIWS, 1 100mm gun (capacity 1 Ka-28 *Helix* A/Z-9C hel)

39 Type-054A (*Jiangkai* II) with 2 quad lnchr with YJ-83 AShM, 4 8-cell VLS with Yu-8 A/S msl/HHQ-16 (CH-SA-N-16) SAM, 2 triple 324mm ASTT with Yu-7 LWT, 2 FQF 3200 A/S mor, 2 H/PJ-11/12 CIWS, 1 76mm gun (capacity 1 Ka-28 *Helix* A/Z-9C hel)

PATROL AND COASTAL COMBATANTS 142+

CORVETTES • FSGM 50 Type-056A (*Jiangdao*) with 2 twin lnchr with YJ-83 AShM, 1 8-cell GMLS with HHQ-10 (CH-SA-N-17) SAM, 2 triple 324mm ASTT with Yu-7 LWT, 1 76mm gun, 1 hel landing platform

PCFG ε60 Type-022 (*Houbei*) with 2 quad lnchr with YJ-83 AShM, 1 H/PJ-13 CIWS

PCG 22: 4 Type-037-II (*Houjian*) with 2 triple lnchr with YJ-8 (CH-SS-N-4) AShM; 18 Type-037-IG (*Houxin*) with 2 twin lnchr with YJ-8 (CH-SS-N-4) AShM

PCC some Type-037-IS (*Haiqing*) with 2 FQF-3200 A/S mor

PB up to 10 Type-062-1 (*Shanghai* III)

MINE WARFARE • MINE COUNTERMEASURES 40:

MCO 24: 4 Type-081 (*Wochi*); 10+ Type-081A (*Wochi* mod); 10+ Type-082II (*Wozang*)

MSC 16: 4 Type-082 (*Wosao* I); 12 Type-082-II (*Wosao* II)

AMPHIBIOUS
PRINCIPAL AMPHIBIOUS SHIPS 11:
LHD 3 Type-075 (*Yushen*) with 2 24-cell GMLS with HHQ-10 (CH-SA-N-17) SAM, 2 H/PJ-11 CIWS (capacity 3 *Yuyi* LCAC; 800 troops; at least 60 AFVs; 28 hel)
LPD 8 Type-071 (*Yuzhao*) with 4 AK630 CIWS, 1 76mm gun (capacity 4 *Yuyi* LCAC plus supporting vehicles; 800 troops; 60 armoured vehs; 4 hel)
LANDING SHIPS 50
LST 28:
  4 Type-072-IIG (*Yukan*) (capacity 2 LCVP; 10 tk; 200 troops)
  9 Type-072-II/III (*Yuting* I) (capacity 10 tk; 250 troops; 2 hel)
  9 Type-072A (*Yuting* II) (capacity 4 LCVP; 10 tk; 250 troops)
  6 Type-072B (*Yuting* II) (capacity 4 LCVP; 10 tk; 250 troops)
LSM 22:
  1 Type-073-II (*Yudeng*) with 1 twin 57mm gun (capacity 5 tk or 500 troops)
  10 Type-073A (*Yunshu*) (capacity 6 tk)
  8 Type-074 (*Yuhai*) (capacity 2 tk; 250 troops)
  3 Type-074 (mod)
LANDING CRAFT 78
LCU 11 Type-074A (*Yubei*) (capacity 10 tanks or 150 troops)
LCM 21: 1+ *Yubu*; up to 20 Type-067A (*Yunnan*)
LCAC 46: 40+ Type-726 (*Yuyi*); 6 *Zubr*
LOGISTICS AND SUPPORT 167
ABU 1 Type-744A
AFS 1 Type-904A (*Danyao* I)
AFSH 2 Type-904B (*Danyao* II)
AG 7: 6 *Kanhai*; 1 *Kanwu*
AGB 2 Type-272 (*Yanrao*) with 1 hel landing platform
AGE 11: 2 Type-909 (*Dahua*) with 1 hel landing platform (weapons test platform); 3+ *Dubei*; 1 *Kantan*; 4 Type-636 (*Shupang*); 1 *Yuting* I (naval rail gun test ship)
AGI 18: 1 Type-815 (*Dongdiao*) with 1 hel landing platform; 9 Type-815A (*Dongdiao*) with 1 hel landing platform; 8 FT-14
AGOR 2 *Dahua*
AGOS 4 *Dongjian*
AGS 9 Type-636A (*Shupang*) with 1 hel landing platform
AH 8: 5 *Ankang*; 1 Type-920 (*Anwei*); 2 *Anshen*
AOEH 2 Type-901 (*Fuyu*) with 2 H/PJ-13 CIWS
AORH 10: 2 Type-903 (*Fuchi*); 7 Type-903A (*Fuchi* II); 1 *Fusu*
AO 22: 4 *Fubai*; 16 Type-632 (*Fujian*); 2 *Fuxiao*
AOL 6 *Fuchang*
AP 4: 2 *Daguan*; 2 *Darong*
ARC 3 *Youlan*
ARS 21: 1 *Dadao*; 1 *Dadong*; 1 Type-922III (*Dalang* II); 3 Type-922IIIA (*Dalang* III); 3 *Dasan*; 4 *Datuo*; 2 *Dazhou*; 6 *Hai Jiu* 101 with 1 hel landing platform
ASR 7: 1 *Dalao* mod; 3 Type-926 (*Dalao*); 3 Type-925 (*Dajiang*) (capacity 2 Z-8)
ATF 14: ε11 *Hujiu*; 3 *Tuqiang*
AWT 8: 4 *Fujian*; 3 *Fushi*; 1 *Jinyou*
AX 3:
  1 Type-0891A (*Dashi*) with 2 hel landing platforms
  1 *Daxin* with 2 FQF 1200 A/S mor, 1 57mm gun, 1 hel landing platform
  1 Type-927 (*Qi Ji Guang*) with 1 76mm gun, 1 hel landing platform
AXS 1 *Polang*
ESD 1 *Donghaidao*
UNINHABITED MARITIME PLATFORMS
USV 32+
  MARSEC 2+: 1 JARI; 1 JARI mod; Others
  MW 30+ Type-529 (*Wonang*) (operated by *Wozang* MCO)
UUV • UTL • Extra-Large 2 HSU001
UNINHABITED MARITIME SYSTEMS
UUV • DATA *Haiyi* 300; *Haiyi* 1000-I/II
COASTAL DEFENCE • AShM 72 YJ-12/YJ-62 (3 regt)

Naval Aviation 18,000
FORCES BY ROLE
FIGHTER/GROUND ATTACK
  1 bde with J-11B/BS *Flanker* L
  2 bde with J-15 *Flanker*
ANTI-SUBMARINE WARFARE
  2 regt with Y-9 ASW
ELINT/ISR/ASW
  1 regt with Y-8JB/X; Y-9JZ; Y-9 ASW
AIRBORNE EARLY WARNING & CONTROL
  3 regt with Y-8J; KJ-200; KJ-500
TRANSPORT
  1 regt with Y-7H; Y-8C; CRJ-200/700
TRAINING
  1 regt with CJ-6A
  1 regt with HY-7
  2 regt with JL-8
  1 regt with JL-9G
  1 regt with JL-9
  1 regt with JL-10
  1 regt with Z-9C
HELICOPTER
  1 regt with Ka-27PS; Ka-28; Ka-31
  1 regt with AS365N; Z-9C/D; Z-8J/JH
  1 regt with Y-7G; Z-8; Z-8J; Z-8S; Z-9C/D
EQUIPMENT BY TYPE
AIRCRAFT 198 combat capable
  FGA 110: 50 J-11B/BS *Flanker* L; ε60 J-15 *Flanker*
  ASW 20+ Y-9 ASW
  ELINT 13: 4 Y-8JB *High New* 2; 3 Y-8X; 6 Y-9JZ

AEW&C 24: 6 KJ-200 *Moth*; 14+ KJ-500; 4 Y-8J *Mask*
TPT 38: **Medium** 6 Y-8C; **Light** 28: 20 Y-5; 2 Y-7G; 6 Y-7H; **PAX** 4: 2 CRJ-200; 2 CRJ-700
TRG 118: 38 CJ-6; 12 HY-7; 16 JL-8*; 28 JL-9*; 12 JL-9G*; 12 JL-10*

HELICOPTERS
ASW 33: 14 Ka-28 *Helix* A; 14 Z-9C; 5 Z-18F
AEW 13+: 9 Ka-31; 4+ Z-18 AEW
MRH 18: 7 AS365N; 11 Z-9D
SAR 11: 3 Ka-27PS; 4 Z-8JH; 2 Z-8S; 2 Z-9S
TPT 42: **Heavy** 34: 8 SA321 *Super Frelon*; 9 Z-8; 13 Z-8J; 4 Z-18; **Medium** 8 Mi-8 *Hip*

UNINHABITED AERIAL VEHICLES
ISR • **Heavy** BZK-005; WZ-7; **Medium** BZK-007

AIR-LAUNCHED MISSILES
AAM • **IR** PL-5; PL-8; PL-9; R-73 (RS-AA-11A *Archer*); **IR/SARH** R-27 (RS-AA-10 *Alamo*); **SARH** PL-11; **ARH** R-77 (RS-AA-12A *Adder*); PL-12 (CH-AA-7A *Adze*)
ASM KD-88
AShM Kh-31A (RS-AS-17B *Krypton*); YJ-61; YJ-8K; YJ-83K; YJ-9
ARM Kh-31P (RS-AS-17A *Krypton*); YJ-91

BOMBS
Laser-guided: LS-500J
TV-guided: KAB-500KR; KAB-1500KR

Marines ε35,000
FORCES BY ROLE
SPECIAL FORCES
 1 spec ops bde
MANOEUVRE
 Mechanised
 3 mne bde
 Amphibious
 3 mne bde
HELICOPTER
 1 bde with Z-8C
EQUIPMENT BY TYPE
ARMOURED FIGHTING VEHICLES
 LT TK 80+: ε80 ZTD-05; some ZTQ-15
 ASLT ε50 ZTL-11
 IFV ε150 ZBL-08
 AAV ε240 ZBD-05
ANTI-TANK/ANTI-INFRASTRUCTURE
 MSL • **MANPATS** HJ-73; HJ-8
 RCL 120mm Type-98
ARTILLERY 40+
 SP 122mm 40+: 20+ PLZ-07; 20+ PLZ-89
 MRL 107mm PH-63
 MOR 82mmε
HELICOPTERS
 TPT • **Heavy** 28 Z-8C
AIR DEFENCE • SAM • **Point-defence** HN-5 (CH-SA-3); FN-6 (CH-SA-10); QW-2 (CH-SA-8)

Air Force 403,000
FORCES BY ROLE
BOMBER
 2 regt with H-6DU/G/J
 2 regt with H-6H
 4 regt with H-6K
 1 regt with H-6M; WZ-8
 1 bde with H-6N (forming)
FIGHTER
 1 bde with J-7 *Fishcan*
 7 bde with J-7E *Fishcan*
 4 bde with J-7G *Fishcan*
 1 bde with J-8F/H *Finback*
 1 bde with J-11A/Su-27UBK *Flanker*
 4 bde with J-11A/J-11B/Su-27UBK *Flanker*
 2 bde with J-11B/BS *Flanker* L
FIGHTER/GROUND ATTACK
 1 bde with J-8F *Finback*; JH-7A *Flounder*
 5 bde with J-10A/S *Firebird*
 1 bde with J-10A/S *Firebird*; Su-30MK2 *Flanker* G
 1 bde with J-10B/S *Firebird*
 6 bde with J-10C/S *Firebird*
 1 bde with J-11B/BS *Flanker* L; JH-7A *Flounder*
 7 bde with J-16 *Flanker* N
 1 bde with J-16 *Flanker* N; Su-30MKK *Flanker* G; Su-35 *Flanker* M
 5 bde with J-20A
 2 bde with Su-30MKK *Flanker* G
GROUND ATTACK
 5 bde with JH-7A *Flounder*
ELECTRONIC WARFARE
 4 regt with Y-8CB/DZ/G/XZ; Y-9G/XZ
ISR
 1 regt with JZ-8F *Finback**
 1 bde with JZ-8F *Finback**
AIRBORNE EARLY WARNING & CONTROL
 2 bde with KJ-500
 1 regt with KJ-500
 1 regt with KJ-200 *Moth*; KJ-2000; Y-8T
SEARCH & RESCUE
 3 bde with Mi-171E; Z-8
 1 bde with Y-5; Y-7; Y-8
 1 regt with Mi-171E; Z-8
TANKER
 1 bde with H-6U
TRANSPORT
 1 (VIP) regt with A319; B-737; CRJ-200/-700
 1 (VIP) regt with Tu-154M; Tu-154M/D
 1 regt with Il-76MD/TD *Candid*; Il-78 *Midas*
 1 regt with Y-7

2 regt with Y-9 *Claw*
3 regt with Y-20/YY-20A
TRAINING
5 bde with CJ-6/6A/6B; Y-5
3 bde with J-7; JJ-7A
14 bde with JJ-7A; JL-8; JL-9; JL-10; J-10A/S
1 trg bde with Y-7; Y-8C
TRANSPORT HELICOPTER
1 (VIP) regt with AS332 *Super Puma*; H225
ISR UAV
2 bde with GJ-1; GJ-2
1 regt with WZ-7; WZ-10
AIR DEFENCE
1 SAM div (3 SAM regt)
26 SAM bde
EQUIPMENT BY TYPE
AIRCRAFT 2,919 combat capable
  BBR 209: ε12 H-6A (trg role); 27 H-6G/G mod; 18 H-6J ε40 H-6H/M; ε100 H-6K; 12+ H-6N
  FTR 466: 50 J-7 *Fishcan*; 119 J-7E *Fishcan*; 120 J-7G *Fishcan*; 50 J-8F/H *Finback*; 95 J-11; 32 Su-27UBK *Flanker*
  FGA 1,339+: 236 J-10A *Firebird* A; 55 J-10B *Firebird*; 220 J-10C *Firebird* C; 77 J-10S *Firebird*; 150 J-11B/BS *Flanker* L; ε280 J-16 *Flanker* N; 200+ J-20A; 24 Su-30MK2 *Flanker* G; 73 Su-30MKK *Flanker* G; 24 Su-35 *Flanker* M
  ATK 200 JH-7A *Flounder*
  EW 31: ε12 J-16D *Flanker**; 4 Y-8CB *High New* 1; 2 Y-8DZ; 6 Y-8G *High New* 3; 2 Y-8XZ *High New* 7; 3 Y-9G; 2 Y-9XZ
  ELINT 4 Tu-154M/D *Careless*
  ISR 48: 24 JZ-8 *Finback**; 24 JZ-8F *Finback**
  AEW&C 28: 4 KJ-200 *Moth*; 20 KJ-500; 4 KJ-2000
  C2 5: 2 B-737; 3 Y-8T *High New* 4
  TKR 18: 10 H-6U; 5 H-6DU; 3 Il-78 *Midas*
  TKR/TPT 8 YY-20A
  TPT 275: **Heavy** 70: 20 Il-76MD/TD *Candid*; 50 Y-20; **Medium** 60: 30 Y-8C; 30 Y-9 *Claw*; **Light** 114: 3 Learjet 35A; 70 Y-5; 41 Y-7/Y-7H; **PAX** 31: 3 A319; 10 B-737 (VIP); 5 CRJ-200; 5 CRJ-700; 8 Tu-154M *Careless*
  TRG 1,027+: 400 CJ-6/-6A/-6B; 12+ HY-7; 50 JJ-7*; 150 JJ-7A*; 350 JL-8*; 45 JL-9*; 50+ JL-10*
HELICOPTERS
  SAR 15+ Z-20S
  MRH 22: 20 Z-9; 2 Mi-17V-5 *Hip* H
  TPT 31+: **Heavy** 18+ Z-8; **Medium** 13+: 6+ AS332 *Super Puma* (VIP); 3 H225 (VIP); 4+ Mi-171
UNINHABITED AERIAL VEHICLES
  CISR • Heavy 12+: 12+ GJ-1; some GJ-2; GJ-11 (in test)
  ISR • Heavy 14+: some TB-001; 12+ WZ-7; 2+ WZ-8; some WZ-10 (ELINT/ISR)
AIR DEFENCE
  SAM 894+
    Long-range 670+: 196 HQ-9 (CH-SA-9); 96 HQ-9B (CH-SA-21); 130+ HQ-22; 32 S-300PMU (RS-SA-10 *Grumble*); 64 S-300PMU1 (RS-SA-20 *Gargoyle*); 120 S-300PMU2 (RS-SA-20 *Gargoyle*); 32 S-400 (RS-SA-21B *Growler*)
    Medium-range 150 HQ-12 (CH-SA-12)
    Short-range 74+: 50+ HQ-6A (CH-SA-6); 24 HQ-6D (CH-SA-6)
  GUNS • TOWED • 57mm PG-59 (S-60)
AIR-LAUNCHED MISSILES
  AAM • IR PL-5B/C; PL-8; R-73 (RS-AA-11A *Archer*); **IIR** PL-10 (CH-AA-9); **IR/SARH** R-27 (RS-AA-10 *Alamo*); **SARH** PL-11; **ARH** PL-12 (CH-AA-7A *Adze*); PL-12A (CH-AA-7B *Adze*); PL-15 (CH-AA-10 *Abaddon*); PL-17 (CH-AA-X-12) (entering service); R-77 (RS-AA-12A *Adder*); R-77-1 (RVV-SD) (RS-AA-12B *Adder*)
  ASM AKD-9; AKD-10; AKK-90; BA-21; CM-501GA; KD-88; Kh-29 (RS-AS-14 *Kedge*); Kh-31A (RS-AS-17B *Krypton*); Kh-59M (RS-AS-18 *Kazoo*)
  AShM YJ-12; YJ-83K; YJ-83KH
  ARM Kh-31P (RS-AS-17A *Krypton*); YJ-91 (Domestically produced Kh-31P variant)
  ALCM • Conventional CJ-20; YJ(KD)-63
BOMBS
  Laser-guided: LS-500J; LT-2
  TV-guided: KAB-500KR; KAB-1500KR

Airborne Corps
FORCES BY ROLE
SPECIAL FORCES
  1 spec ops bde
MANOEUVRE
  Air Manoeuvre
  5 AB bde
  1 air aslt bde
COMBAT SERVICE SUPPORT
  1 spt bde
TRANSPORT
  1 bde with Y-5; Y-7; Y-8; Y-12
HELICOPTER
  1 regt with WZ-10K; Z-8KA; Z-9WZ; Z-20K
EQUIPMENT BY TYPE
ARMOURED FIGHTING VEHICLES
  ABCV 180 ZBD-03
  APC • APC (T) 4 ZZZ-03 (CP)
  AUV CS/VN3 mod
ANTI-TANK/ANTI-INFRASTRUCTURE
  SP some HJ-9
ARTILLERY 162+
  TOWED 122mm ε54 PL-96 (D-30)
  MRL 107mm ε54 PH-63
  MOR 54+: **82mm** some; **100mm** 54
AIRCRAFT • TPT 40: **Medium** 6 Y-8; **Light** 34: 20 Y-5; 2 Y-7; 12 Y-12D
HELICOPTERS

ATK 8 WZ-10K
CSAR 8 Z-8KA
MRH 12 Z-9WZ
TPT • Medium 6 Z-20K
AIR DEFENCE
SAM • Point-defence QW-1 (CH-SA-7)
GUNS • TOWED 25mm 54 PG-87
AIR-LAUNCHED MISSILES
ASM AKD-8; AKD-9; AKD-10; BA-21; CM-501GA; CM-502; PL-90/KK-90

Strategic Support Force ε175,000

The Strategic Support Force reports to the Central Military Commission and is responsible for the PLA's space and cyber capabilities

EQUIPMENT BY TYPE
SATELLITES see Space
REUSABLE SPACECRAFT see Space
COUNTERSPACE see Space
LOGISTICS AND SUPPORT • AGM 4 Type-718 (*Yuan Wang*) (space and missile tracking)

Theatre Commands

Eastern Theatre Command

Eastern Theatre Ground Forces

71st Group Army
(1 spec ops bde, 4 armd bde, 1 mech inf bde, 1 inf bde, 1 arty bde, 1 engr/NBC bde bde, 1 spt bde, 1 hel bde, 1 AD bde)

72nd Group Army
(1 spec ops bde, 1 armd bde, 2 mech inf bde, 1 inf bde, 2 amph bde, 1 arty bde, 1 engr bde, 1 NBC bde, 1 spt bde, 1 hel bde, 1 AD bde)

73rd Group Army
(1 spec ops bde, 1 armd bde, 1 mech inf bde, 2 inf bde, 2 amph bde, 1 arty bde, 1 engr/NBC bde, 1 spt bde, 1 hel bde, 1 AD bde)

Eastern Theatre Navy

Coastal defence from south of Lianyungang to Dongshan (approx. 35°10′N to 23°30′N), and to seaward; HQ at Ningbo; support bases at Fujian, Zhoushan, Ningbo
16 **SSK**; 16 **DDGHM**; 19 **FFGHM**; 19 **FSGM**; ε30 **PCFG/PCG**; 9 **MCMV**; 1 **LHD**; 3 **LPD**; ε22 **LST/M**

Eastern Theatre Navy Aviation

1st Naval Aviation Division
(1 AEW&C regt with KJ-500; 1 ASW regt with Y-9 ASW)

Other Forces
(1 hel regt with Ka-27PS; Ka-28; Ka-31)

Eastern Theatre Air Force

10th Bomber Division
(2 bbr regt with H-6K; 1 bbr regt with H-6M/WZ-8)

26th Special Mission Division
(1 AEW&C regt with KJ-500; 1 AEW&C regt with KJ-200/KJ-2000/Y-8T)

Fuzhou Base
(1 ftr bde with J-7E; 1 FGA bde with J-10C; 1 ftr bde with J-11A/B; 1 FGA bde with J-16; 1 FGA bde with Su-30MKK; 2 SAM bde)

Shanghai Base
(1 ftr bde with J-11B; 1 FGA bde with J-10A; Su-30MK2; 2 FGA bde with J-16; 2 FGA bde with J-20A; 2 atk bde with JH-7A; 1 trg bde with J-10/JL-10; Su-27UBK; 2 SAM bde)

Other Forces
(1 bbr regt with H-6DU/G/J; 1 ISR bde with JZ-8F; 1 SAR bde; 1 Flight Instructor Training Base with CJ-6/JL-8/JL-9/JL-10)

Other Forces

Marines
(2 mne bde)

Southern Theatre Command

Southern Theatre Ground Forces

74th Group Army
(1 spec ops bde, 1 armd bde, 1 mech inf bde, 2 inf bde, 2 amph bde, 1 arty bde, 1 engr bde, 1 NBC bde, 1 spt bde, 1 hel bde, 1 AD bde)

75th Group Army
(1 spec ops bde, 2 armd bde, 1 mech inf bde, 3 inf bde, 1 air aslt bde, 1 arty bde, 1 engr/NBC bde, 1 spt bde, 1 AD bde)

Other Forces
(1 (composite) inf bde (Hong Kong); 1 hel sqn (Hong Kong), 1 AD bn (Hong Kong))

Southern Theatre Navy

Coastal defence from Dongshan (approx. 23°30′N) to VNM border, and to seaward (including Paracel and Spratly islands); HQ at Zhanjiang; support bases at Yulin, Guangzhou
6 **SSBN**; 2 **SSN**; 15 **SSK**; 1 **CV**; 4 **CGHM**; 14 **DDGHM**; 15 **FFGHM**; 21 **FSGM**; ε30 **PCFG/PCG**; 13 **MCMV**; 1 **LHD**; 5 **LPD**; ε21 **LST/M**

Southern Theatre Navy Aviation

3rd Naval Aviation Division
(1 ASW regt with Y-9 ASW; 1 AEW&C regt with KJ-500)

Other Forces
(1 FGA bde with J-11B; 1 FGA bde with J-15; 1 tpt/hel regt with Y-7G; Z-8; Z-8J; Z-8S; Z-9C/D)

Southern Theatre Air Force

8th Bomber Division

(2 bbr regt with H-6K)

20th Special Mission Division
(3 EW regt with Y-8CB/DZ/G/XZ; Y-9G/XZ)

Kunming Base
(1 FGA bde with J-10A; 1 FGA bde with J-10C; 1 trg bde with JJ-7A; 1 SAM bde)

Nanning Base
(1 ftr bde with J-11A; 1 FGA bde with J-11B; JH-7A; 1 FGA bde with J-10A; 1 FGA bde with J-16; 1 FGA bde with J-20A; 1 FGA bde with J-16; Su-30MKK; Su-35; 1 FGA bde with Su-30MKK; 1 atk bde with JH-7A; 4 SAM bde)

Other Forces
(1 bbr regt with H-6DU/G/J; 1 tkr bde with H-6U; 1 SAR bde; 1 UAV bde)

Other Forces

Marines
(1 spec ops bde; 2 mne bde)

Western Theatre Command

Western Theatre Ground Forces

76th Group Army
(1 spec ops bde, 4 armd bde, 2 inf bde, 1 arty bde, 1 engr/NBC bde, 1 spt bde, 1 hel bde, 1 AD bde)

77th Group Army
(1 spec ops bde, 2 armd bde, 1 mech inf bde; 3 inf bde, 1 arty bde, 1 engr bde, 1 NBC bde, 1 spt bde, 1 hel bde, 1 AD bde)

Xinjiang Military District
(1 spec ops bde, 1 (high alt) mech div, 3 (high alt) inf div, 2 mech inf regt, 1 arty bde, 1 AD bde, 1 engr regt, 1 hel bde)

Xizang Military District
(1 spec ops bde; 1 mech inf bde; 2 inf bde; 1 arty bde, 1 AD bde, 1 engr/NBC bde, 1 hel bde)

Western Theatre Air Force

4th Transport Division
(2 tpt regt with Y-9; 1 tpt regt with Y-20A)

Lanzhou Base
(1 ftr bde with J-11A/B; 1 ftr bde with J-7E; 1 FGA bde with J-10C; 1 FGA bde with J-16; 1 SAM bde)

Urumqi Base
(1 ftr bde with J-8F/H; 1 FGA bde with J-16; 1 FGA bde with J-20A; 1 atk bde with JH-7A; 2 SAM bde)

Lhasa Base
(1 SAM bde)

Xi'an Flying Academy
(1 trg bde with JJ-7A; 1 trg bde with JL-9A; 2 trg bde with JL-8; 1 trg bde with Y-7; Y-8)

Other Forces
(1 AEW&C bde with KJ-500; 1 SAR regt)

Northern Theatre Command

Northern Theatre Ground Forces

78th Group Army
(1 spec ops bde, 4 armd bde, 1 mech inf bde, 1 inf bde, 1 arty bde, 1 engr/NBC bde, 1 spt bde, 1 hel bde, 1 AD bde)

79th Group Army
(1 spec ops bde, 4 armd bde, 1 mech inf bde, 1 inf bde, 1 arty bde, 1 engr bde, 1 NBC bde, 1 spt bde, 1 hel bde, 1 AD bde)

80th Group Army
(1 spec ops bde, 1 armd bde; 2 mech inf bde, 3 inf bde, 1 arty bde, 1 engr/NBC bde, 1 spt bde, 1 hel bde, 1 AD bde)

Northern Theatre Navy

Coastal defence from the DPRK border (Yalu River) to south of Lianyungang (approx 35°10′N), and to seaward; HQ at Qingdao; support bases at Lushun, Qingdao.

4 **SSN**; 15 **SSK**; 1 **CV**; 4 **CGHM**; 10 **DDGHM**; 2 **DDGM**; 11 **FFGHM**; 10 **FSGM**; ε18 **PCFG/PCG**; 9 **MCMV**; ε7 **LST/M**

Northern Theatre Navy Aviation

2nd Naval Air Division
(1 EW/ISR/ASW regt with Y-8JB/X; Y-9JZ; Y-9 ASW; 1 AEW&C regt with Y-8J; KJ-200; KJ-500)

Other Forces
(1 FGA bde with J-15; 1 hel regt with AS365N; Z-8J/JH; Z-9C/D; 1 tpt regt with Y-7H/Y-8C/CRJ-200/CRJ-700; 1 trg regt with CJ-6A; 2 trg regt with JL-8; 1 trg regt with HY-7; 1 trg regt with JL-9G; 1 trg regt with JL-9; 1 trg regt with JL-10)

Northern Theatre Air Force

16th Special Mission Division
(1 EW regt with Y-8CB/G; 1 ISR regt with JZ-8F; 1 UAV regt with WZ-7/WZ-10)

Dalian Base
(1 ftr bde with J-7; 2 ftr bde with J-7E; 1 ftr bde with J-11B; 1 FGA bde with J-10C; 1 FGA bde with J-10B; 1 FGA bde with J-16; 1 FGA bde with J-20A; 1 atk bde with JH-7A; 3 SAM bde)

Jinan Base
(1 ftr bde with J-7G; 1 FGA bde with J-8F; JH-7A; 1 FGA bde with J-10C; 1 atk bde with JH-7A; 2 SAM bde)

Harbin Flying Academy
(1 trg bde with CJ-6/J-11B/JL-9; Y-5; 1 trg bde with H-6; HY-7; 2 trg bde with JL-8; 1 trg bde with JL-9)

Other Forces
(1 SAR bde with Y-5; Y-7; Y-8)

Other Forces

Marines
(2 mne bde; 1 hel bde)

Central Theatre Command

Central Theatre Ground Forces
81st Group Army
(1 spec ops bde, 2 armd bde, 1 (OPFOR) armd bde, 2 mech inf bde, 1 inf bde, 1 arty bde, 1 engr/NBC bde, 1 spt bde, 1 avn bde, 1 AD bde)

82nd Group Army
(1 spec ops bde, 4 armd bde, 1 mech bde, 2 inf bde, 1 arty bde, 1 engr bde, 1 NBC bde, 1 spt bde, 1 hel bde, 1 AD bde)

83rd Group Army
(1 spec ops bde, 2 armd bde, 4 mech inf bde, 1 air aslt bde, 1 arty bde, 1 engr/NBC bde, 1 spt bde, 1 AD bde)

Other Forces
(2 (Beijing) gd div)

Central Theatre Air Force
13th Transport Division
(1 tpt regt with Y-20A; 1 tpt regt with Il-76MD/TD; 1 tpt regt with Il-76MD; Il-78)

34th VIP Transport Division
(1 tpt regt with A319; B-737; CRJ200/700; 1 tpt regt with Tu-154M; Tu-154M/D; 1 tpt regt with Y-7; 1 hel regt with AS332; H225)

36th Bomber Division
(1 bbr regt with H-6K; 1 bbr regt with H-6H)

Datong Base
(3 ftr bde with J-7E/G; 1 ftr bde with J-11A/B; 2 FGA bde with J-10A; 1 FGA bde with J-10C; 1 SAM div; 4 SAM bde)

Wuhan Base
(2 ftr bde with J-7E/G; 1 ftr bde with J-11A/B; Su-27UBK; 1 FGA bde with J-20A; 1 trg bde with J-7/JJ-7A; 3 SAM bde)

Shijiazhuang Flying Academy
(3 trg bde with JL-8; 1 trg bde with JL-8; JL-10)

Airborne Corps
(5 AB bde; 1 air aslt bde; 1 tpt bde; 1 hel regt)

Other Forces
(1 bbr bde with H-6N; 1 AEW&C bde with KJ-500; 1 SAR bde)

Gendarmerie & Paramilitary 500,000+ active

People's Armed Police ε500,000
In 2018 the People's Armed Police (PAP) divested its border-defence, firefighting, gold, forest, hydropower and security-guard units. In addition to the forces listed below, PAP also has 32 regional commands, each with one or more mobile units

FORCES BY ROLE
MANOEUVRE
  Other
  1 (1st Mobile) paramilitary corps (3 SF regt; 9 (mobile) paramilitary units; 1 engr/CBRN unit; 1 hel unit)
  1 (2nd Mobile) paramilitary corps (2 SF unit; 9 (mobile) paramilitary units; 1 engr/CBRN unit; 1 hel unit)

China Coast Guard (CCG)
In 2018 the CCG was moved from the authority of the State Oceanic Administration to that of the People's Armed Police. The CCG is currently reorganising its pennant-number system, making it problematic to assess the number of vessels that entered service since 2019.

EQUIPMENT BY TYPE
PATROL AND COASTAL COMBATANTS 545
  PSOH 40:
    2 *Zhaotou* with 1 76mm gun (capacity 2 med hel)
    3 Type-053H2G (*Jiangwei* I) (capacity 1 med hel) (ex-PLAN)
    7 Type-054 mod (*Zhaoduan*) with 1 76mm gun (capacity 1 med hel)
    4 *Shuoshi* II (capacity 1 med hel)
    10 *Shucha* II (capacity 1 med hel)
    12 *Zhaoyu* (capacity 1 med hel)
    1 *Zhaochang* (capacity 1 med hel)
    1 *Zhongyang* (capacity 1 med hel)
  PSO 49:
    9 Type-718B (*Zhaojun*) with 1 76mm gun, 1 hel landing platform
    1 Type-922 (*Dalang* I) (ex-PLAN)
    1 Type-625C (*Hai Yang*) (ex-PLAN)
    1 *Haixun*
    1 Type-053H (*Jianghu* I) (ex-PLAN)
    1 Type-636A (*Kanjie*) with 1 hel landing platform (ex-PLAN)
    6 *Shusheng* with 1 hel landing platform
    3 *Shuwu*
    3 *Tuzhong* (ex-PLAN)
    1 Type-918 (*Wolei*) (ex-PLAN)
    1 *Xiang Yang Hong* 9 (ex-PLAN)
    3 *Zhaogao* with 1 hel landing platform
    4 *Zhaolai* with 1 hel landing platform
    14 *Zhaotim*
  PCOH 22 Type-056 (*Jiangdao*) (ex-PLAN) with 1 76mm gun
  PCO 30: 1 *Shuke* I; 4 *Shuke* II; 15 *Shuke* III; 3 *Shuyou*; 4 *Zhaodai*; 3 *Zhaoming*
  PCC 104: 25+ Type-618B-II; 45 *Hailin* I/II; 1 *Shuzao* II; 14 *Shuzao* III; 10 *Zhongeng*; 2 *Zhongmei*; 7 *Zhongsui*
  PB/PBF 300+
AMPHIBIOUS • LANDING SHIPS 2
  LST 2 Type-072-II (*Yuting* I) (ex-PLAN; used as hospital vessels and island supply)
LOGISTICS AND SUPPORT 27
  AG 6: 5+ *Kaobo*; 1 *Shutu*
  AGB 1 Type-210 (*Yanbing*) (ex-PLAN)
  AGOR 8: 3 *Haijian*; 3 *Shuguang* 04 (ex-PLAN); 2

Xiang Yang Hong 9
AKR 1 *Yunsong*
ATF 11
AIRCRAFT
  MP 1+ MA60H
  TPT • Light Y-12 (MP role)
HELICOPTERS
  TPT • Light Z-9

Maritime Militia

Composed of full- and part-time personnel. Reports to PLA command and trains to assist PLAN and CCG in a variety of military roles. These include ISR, maritime law enforcement, island supply, troop transport and supporting sovereignty claims. The Maritime Militia operates a variety of civilian vessels including fishing boats and oil tankers.

DEPLOYMENT

DEMOCRATIC REPUBLIC OF THE CONGO: UN • MONUSCO 231; 1 engr coy; 1 fd hospital

DJIBOUTI: 400; 1 spec ops coy; 1 mne coy; 1 med unit; 2 ZTL-11; 8 ZBL-08

GULF OF ADEN: 1 DDGHM; 1 FFGHM; 1 AORH

LEBANON: UN • UNIFIL 418; 2 engr coy; 1 med coy

MIDDLE EAST: UN • UNTSO 5

SOUTH SUDAN: UN • UNMISS 1,050; 1 inf bn; 1 engr coy; 1 fd hospital

SUDAN: UN • UNISFA 152; 1 inf coy; 1 hel flt with 2 Mi-171

TAJIKISTAN: ε300 (trg)

WESTERN SAHARA: UN • MINURSO 11

Fiji FJI

Fijian Dollar FJD		2022	2023	2024
GDP	FJD	11.0bn	12.3bn	13.4bn
	USD	4.98bn	5.51bn	5.97bn
per capita	USD	5,474	6,025	6,490
Growth	%	20.0	7.5	3.9
Inflation	%	4.3	3.0	3.5
Def bdgt	FJD	94.2m	109m	
	USD	42.8m	48.8m	
USD1=FJD		2.20	2.23	2.25

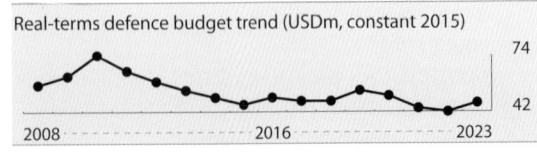

Real-terms defence budget trend (USDm, constant 2015)

Population	947,760					
Age	0–14	15–19	20–24	25–29	30–64	65 plus
Male	12.9%	4.2%	3.6%	3.9%	22.2%	3.9%
Female	12.3%	4.1%	3.5%	3.7%	21.1%	4.6%

Capabilities

The Republic of Fiji Military Forces (RFMF) are infantry-dominated, with a small naval element. The RFMF has intervened heavily in Fiji's domestic politics, and after a third coup in 2006, democracy was effectively suspended until 2014. Guidelines issued in 2018 emphasised the need to confront non-traditional threats such as climate change, terrorism and transnational crime. The government embarked on a defence review in 2023. The RFMF is developing a deployable-force headquarters, funded by Australia, which will also administer and train personnel for peacekeeping and HA/DR roles. It issued a Security Framework in 2023, addressing information security concerns. Engagement in international peacekeeping operations is an important source of revenue for the government. Fiji's principal defence relationships are with Australia and New Zealand, with whom the RFMF regularly conducts training and maritime patrols. A status of forces agreement was signed with Australia in October 2022, while one with New Zealand was approved by the cabinet in early 2023. Defence relations with China, South Korea and the US are growing, with all three countries providing training or donating equipment. The RFMF is attempting to improve the quality of senior NCOs and to raise standards across the rest of the force. Fiji has no significant defence industry and is only able to carry out basic equipment maintenance. Significant upgrade and maintenance work is usually conducted in Australia.

ACTIVE 4,040 (Army 3,700 Navy 340)

RESERVE ε6,000

(to age 45)

ORGANISATIONS BY SERVICE

Army 3,700 (incl 300 recalled reserves)
FORCES BY ROLE
SPECIAL FORCES
  1 spec ops coy
MANOEUVRE
  Light
  3 inf bn
COMBAT SUPPORT
  1 arty bty
  1 engr bn
COMBAT SUPPORT
  1 log bn

Reserves 6,000
FORCES BY ROLE
MANOEUVRE
  Light
  5 inf bn
EQUIPMENT BY TYPE
ARMOURED FIGHTING VEHICLES
  AUV 10 *Bushmaster* IMV
ARTILLERY • MOR 81mm 24 L16

Navy 340
EQUIPMENT BY TYPE

PATROL AND COASTAL COMBATANTS 4:
  PCO 1 *Guardian* (AUS *Bay* mod)
  PB 3: 1 *Kula* (AUS *Pacific*); 2 *Levuka*
LOGISTICS AND SUPPORT 2
  AGS 2: 1 *Kacau*; 1 *Volasiga*

DEPLOYMENT

EGYPT: MFO 170; elm 1 inf bn
IRAQ: UN • UNAMI 156; 2 sy unit
MIDDLE EAST: UN • UNTSO 1
SOUTH SUDAN: UN • UNMISS 2
SYRIA/ISRAEL: UN • UNDOF 147; 1 inf coy

India IND

Indian Rupee INR		2022	2023	2024
GDP	INR	272trn	301trn	333trn
	USD	3.39trn	3.73trn	4.11trn
per capita	USD	2,392	2,612	2,848
Growth	%	7.2	6.3	6.3
Inflation	%	6.7	5.5	4.6
Def bdgt [a]	INR	5.85trn	5.94trn	
	USD	72.8bn	73.6bn	
USD1=INR		80.36	80.66	81.17

[a] Includes defence civil estimates, which include military pensions

Real-terms defence budget trend (USDbn, constant 2015)
63.6 (2023), 27.8 (2008)

Population	1,399,179,585					
Age	0–14	15–19	20–24	25–29	30–64	65 plus
Male	13.0%	4.6%	4.6%	4.6%	21.6%	3.1%
Female	11.8%	4.1%	4.1%	4.1%	20.7%	3.7%

Capabilities

India's armed forces are mainly orientated toward addressing security concerns and territorial disputes with Pakistan and China, though large numbers of paramilitary forces remain employed in internal security. India is looking to improve military infrastructure on its northern border. Mutual reaffirmation of the 2003 ceasefire agreement between India and Pakistan reduced conflict across the Line of Control in the disputed region of Kashmir. The government is increasingly focused on Indian Ocean security, which includes upgrading naval capability. Indian forces participate in numerous bilateral and multilateral exercises, and the country is one of the main troop contributors to UN peacekeeping operations. India, in 2022, agreed to join the Combined Maritime Forces multinational maritime partnership as an associate member. A Joint Armed Forces Doctrine was issued in 2017 that envisaged an 'emerging triad' of space, cyber and special-operations capabilities to complement conventional land, sea and air capabilities. India continues to develop its nuclear capabilities. Army doctrine issued in late 2018 identified requirements including for 'integrated battle groups'

and improved cyber, information-warfare and electronic-warfare capabilities. In 2022, it began setting up integrated battle groups in the border area with China and Pakistan. India operates significant quantities of equipment of Soviet and Russian origin and the two countries cooperate on missile developments. But New Delhi has been looking to diversify suppliers, especially with Moscow focused more on equipping its force than exports because of its war in Ukraine. Recent Indian imports of foreign equipment have primarily been from the US and France. India and the US signed a defence and technology cooperation agreement in 2023 as part of wider efforts to strengthen security ties. The overall capability of India's large conventional forces is limited by inadequate logistics and maintenance, and shortages of ammunition, spare parts and maintenance personnel. Modernisation projects have seen delays and cost overruns. The government's 'Make in India' policy aims to strengthen the defence-industrial base, making slow progress.

ACTIVE 1,475,750 (Army 1,237,000 Navy 75,500 Air 149,900 Coast Guard 13,350) Gendarmerie & Paramilitary 1,616,050

RESERVE 1,155,000 (Army 960,000 Navy 55,000 Air 140,000) Gendarmerie & Paramilitary 941,000

Army first-line reserves (300,000) within 5 years of full-time service, further 500,000 have commitment to age 50

ORGANISATIONS BY SERVICE

Strategic Forces Command

Strategic Forces Command (SFC) is a tri-service command established in 2003. The commander-in-chief of SFC, a senior three-star military officer, manages and administers all strategic forces through army, navy and air-force chains of command

FORCES BY ROLE

SURFACE-TO-SURFACE MISSILE
  1 SRBM bde with *Agni* I
  1 IRBM bde with *Agni* II/III
  2 SRBM bde with SS-250 *Prithvi* II

EQUIPMENT BY TYPE

SURFACE-TO-SURFACE MISSILE LAUNCHERS 66
  ICBM • **Nuclear** *Agni* V (in test)
  IRBM • **Nuclear** 4+: ε4 *Agni* III; *Agni* IV (entering service)
  MRBM • **Nuclear** ε8 *Agni* II
  SRBM • **Nuclear** 54: ε12 *Agni* I; ε42 SS-250 *Prithvi* II; some SS-350 *Dhanush* (naval testbed)
SUBMARINES • **STRATEGIC** • **SSBN** 1 *Arihant* with 4 1-cell VLS with K-15 *Sagarika* SLBM, 6 533mm TT
AIR-LAUNCHED MISSILES • **ALCM** • **Nuclear** *Nirbhay* (likely nuclear capable; in development)

Some Indian Air Force assets (such as *Mirage* 2000H, *Rafale* or Su-30MKI) may be tasked with a strategic role

Space

EQUIPMENT BY TYPE
SATELLITES 26
  NAVIGATION, POSITIONING, TIMING: 8 IRNSS
  COMMUNICATIONS: 2 GSAT-7/-7A

ISR 15: 9 *Cartosat*; 6 RISAT
ELINT/SIGINT 1 EMISAT

Army 1,237,000

6 Regional Comd HQ (Northern, Western, Central, Southern, Eastern, Southwestern), 1 Training Comd (ARTRAC)

FORCES BY ROLE
COMMAND
  4 (strike) corps HQ
  10 (holding) corps HQ
SPECIAL FORCES
  8 SF bn
MANOEUVRE
  Armoured
  2 armd div (3 armd bde, 1 arty bde (2 arty regt))
  1 armd div (3 armd bde, 1 SP arty bde (2 SP arty regt))
  8 indep armd bde
  Mechanised
  6 (RAPID) mech inf div (1 armd bde, 2 mech inf bde, 1 arty bde)
  2 indep mech bde
  Light
  15 inf div (2–5 inf bde, 1 arty bde)
  1 inf div (forming)
  7 indep inf bde
  12 mtn div (3-4 mtn inf bde, 1 arty bde)
  2 indep mtn bde
  Air Manoeuvre
  1 para bde
SURFACE-TO-SURFACE MISSILE
  1 IRBM bde with *Agni* II/III
  1 SRBM bde with *Agni* I
  2 SRBM bde with SS-250 *Prithvi* II
  3 GLCM regt with PJ-10 *Brahmos*
COMBAT SUPPORT
  3 arty div (2 arty bde, 1 MRL bde)
  2 indep arty bde
  4 engr bde
ATTACK HELICOPTER
  1 atk hel sqn
HELICOPTER
  25 hel sqn
AIR DEFENCE
  8 AD bde

Reserve Organisations

Reserves 300,000 reservists (first-line reserve within 5 years full-time service); 500,000 reservists (commitment until age 50) (total 800,000)

Territorial Army 160,000 reservists (only 40,000 regular establishment)

FORCES BY ROLE
MANOEUVRE
  Light
  42 inf bn
COMBAT SUPPORT
  6 (Railway) engr regt
  2 engr regt
  1 sigs regt
COMBAT SERVICE SUPPORT
  6 ecological bn
EQUIPMENT BY TYPE
ARMOURED FIGHTING VEHICLES
  MBT 3,740: 122 *Arjun*; 2,418 T-72M1; ε1,200 T-90S (ε1,100 various models in store)
  RECCE *Ferret* (used for internal-security duties along with some indigenously built armd cars)
  IFV 3,100: 700 BMP-1; 2,400 BMP-2 *Sarath* (incl some BMP-2K CP)
  APC 369+
    APC (W) 163: 157+ OT-64; 6 TASL IPMV
    PPV 206+: 165 *Casspir*; 27 *Kalyani* M4; some TASL QRFV; 14+ *Yukthirath* MPV
ENGINEERING & MAINTENANCE VEHICLES
  AEV BMP-2; FV180
  ARV 730+: T-54/T-55; 156 VT-72B; 222 WZT-2; 352 WZT-3
  VLB AM-50; BLG-60; BLG T-72; *Kartik*; MTU-20; MT-55; *Sarvatra*
  MW 24 910 MCV-2
ANTI-TANK/ANTI-INFRASTRUCTURE
  MSL
    SP 110 9P148 *Konkurs* (RS-AT-5 *Spandrel*)
    MANPATS 9K113 *Konkurs* (RS-AT-5 *Spandrel*); *Milan* 2
  RCL 3,000+: 84mm *Carl Gustaf*; 106mm 3,000+ M40A1 (10 per inf bn)
ARTILLERY 9,743+
  SP 155mm 100 K9 *Vajra*-T
  TOWED 3,095+: 105mm 1,350+: 600+ IFG Mk1/Mk2/Mk3; up to 700 LFG; 50 M-56; 122mm 520 D-30; 130mm ε600 M-46 (500 in store) 155mm 625: ε300 FH-77B; ε200 M-46 (mod); 125 M777A2
  MRL 228: 122mm ε150 BM-21/LRAR 214mm 36 *Pinaka*; 300mm 42 9A52 *Smerch*
  MOR 6,320+: 81mm 5,000+ E1; 120mm ε1,500 AM-50/E1; SP 120mm E1
SURFACE-TO-SURFACE MISSILE LAUNCHERS
  IRBM • Nuclear some *Agni*-III (entering service)
  MRBM • Nuclear ε12 *Agni*-II
  SRBM • Nuclear 42: ε12 *Agni*-I; ε30 250 *Prithvi* II
  GLCM • Conventional 15 PJ-10 *Brahmos*
HELICOPTERS
  ATK 5 LCH *Prachand*
  MRH 339: 78 *Dhruv*; 12 *Lancer*; 74 *Rudra*; 115 SA315B

Lama (*Cheetah*); 60 SA316B *Alouette* III (*Chetak*)
UNINHABITED AERIAL VEHICLES
  ISR • Heavy 4 *Heron* (leased); **Medium** 25: 13 *Nishant*; 12 *Searcher* Mk I/II
AIR DEFENCE
  SAM 748+
    Medium-range ε48 *Akash*
    Short-range 180 2K12 *Kub* (RS-SA-6 *Gainful*)
    Point-defence 500+: 50+ 9K33AKM *Osa*-AKM (RS-SA-8 *Gecko*); 200 9K31 *Strela*-1 (RS-SA-9 *Gaskin*); 250 9K35 *Strela*-10 (RS-SA-13 *Gopher*); 9K310 *Igla*-1 (RS-SA-16 *Gimlet*); 9K38 *Igla* (RS-SA-18 *Grouse*)
  SPAAGM 30mm up to 80 2K22 *Tunguska* (RS-SA-19 *Grison*)
  GUNS 2,315+
    SP 23mm 75 ZSU-23-4; ZU-23-2 (truck-mounted);
    TOWED 2,240+: **20mm** Oerlikon (reported); **23mm** 320 ZU-23-2; **40mm** 1,920 L40/70

Navy 75,500 (incl 7,000 Naval Avn and 1,200 Marines)

Fleet HQ New Delhi. Commands located at Mumbai, Vishakhapatnam, Kochi and Port Blair
EQUIPMENT BY TYPE
SUBMARINES 16
  STRATEGIC • SSBN 1 *Arihant* with 4 1-cell VLS with K-15 *Sagarika* SLBM, 6 533mm TT
  TACTICAL 16
    SSK 16:
      5 *Kalvari* (FRA *Scorpène*) with 6 533mm TT with SM39 *Exocet* Block 2 AShM/SUT HWT
      3 *Shishumar* (GER Type-209/1500) with 8 single 533mm TT with SUT mod 1 HWT
      1 *Shishumar* (GER Type-209/1500) with 8 single 533mm TT with UGM-84L *Harpoon* II AShM/SUT mod 1 HWT
      7 *Sindhughosh* (FSU *Kilo*) with 6 single 533mm TT with 3M54E1/E *Klub*-S (RS-SS-N-27A/B) (*Klub*-S AShM variant unclear) AShM/53-65KE HWT/TEST-71ME HWT/SET-65E HWT
PRINCIPAL SURFACE COMBATANTS 29
  AIRCRAFT CARRIERS • CV 2
    1 *Vikramaditya* (ex-FSU *Kiev* mod) with 3 8-cell VLS with *Barak*-1 SAM, 4 AK630M CIWS (capacity 12 MiG-29K/KUB *Fulcrum* FGA ac; 6 Ka-28 *Helix* A ASW hel/Ka-31 *Helix* B AEW hel)
    1 *Vikrant* with 3 AK630M CIWS (to be fitted with *Barak* 8 SAM) (capacity 30 aircraft including MiG-29K/KUB *Fulcrum*, Ka-31 *Helix* B, MH-60R *Seahawk*, *Dhruv*)
  DESTROYERS 11
    DDGHM 8:
      3 *Delhi* (Project 15) with 2 quad lnchr with *Brahmos* AShM, 2 single 3S90E lnchr with 9M38E M-22E *Shtil* (RS-SA-N-7 *Gadfly*) SAM, 4 8-cell VLS with *Barak*-1 SAM, 5 single 533mm ASTT with SET-65E HWT/*Varunastra* HWT, 2 RBU 6000 *Smerch* 2 A/S mor; 2 AK630 CIWS, 1 76mm gun (capacity either 2 *Dhruv* hel/*Sea King* Mk42A ASW hel)
      3 *Kolkata* (Project 15A) with 2 8-cell UVLM VLS with *Brahmos* AShM, 4 8-cell VLS with *Barak*-8 SAM; 2 twin 533mm TT with SET-65E HWT/*Varunastra* HWT, 2 RBU 6000 *Smerch* 2 A/S mor, 4 AK630M CIWS, 1 76mm gun (capacity 2 *Dhruv*/*Sea King* Mk42B hel)
      2 *Visakhapatnam* (Project 15B) with 2 8-cell UVLM VLS with *Brahmos* AShM, 4 8-cell VLS with *Barak*-8 SAM; 2 twin 533mm TT with *Varunastra* HWT, 2 RBU 6000 *Smerch* 2 A/S mor, 4 AK630M CIWS, 1 76mm gun (capacity 2 *Dhruv*/*Sea King* Mk42B hel)
    DDGM 3:
      1 *Rajput* (FSU *Kashin*) with 2 twin lnchr with P-27 *Termit*-R (RS-SS-N-2D *Styx*) AShM, 2 8-cell VLS with VL-SRSAM SAM, 1 twin ZIF-101 lnchr with 4K91 M-1 *Volnya* (RS-SA-N-1 *Goa*) SAM, 5 single 533mm PTA-51-61ME ASTT with SET-65E HWT/*Varunastra* HWT, 2 RBU 6000 *Smerch* 2 A/S mor, 4 AK630M CIWS, 1 76mm gun (capacity Ka-28 *Helix* A hel)
      2 *Rajput* (FSU *Kashin*) with 1 8-cell UVLM VLS with *Brahmos* AShM, 2 twin lnchr with P-27 *Termit*-R (RS-SS-N-2D *Styx*) AShM, 2 8-cell VLS with *Barak*-1 SAM, 1 twin ZIF-101 lnchr with 4K91 M-1 *Volnya* (RS-SA-N-1 *Goa*) SAM, 5 single 533mm ASTT with SET-65E HWT/*Varunastra* HWT, 2 RBU 6000 *Smerch* 2 A/S mor, 2 AK630M CIWS, 1 76mm gun (capacity 1 Ka-28 *Helix* A hel)
FRIGATES 16
  FFGHM 12:
    3 *Brahmaputra* (Project 16A) with 4 quad lnchr with 3M24E *Uran*-E (RS-SS-N-25 *Switchblade*) AShM, 3 8-cell VLS with *Barak*-1 SAM, 2 triple ILAS-3 (B-515) 324mm ASTT with A244 LWT, 4 AK630M CIWS, 1 76mm gun (capacity 2 SA316B *Alouette* III (*Chetak*)/*Sea King* Mk42 ASW hel)
    3 *Shivalik* (Project 17) with 1 8-cell 3S14E VLS with 3M54TE *Klub*-N (RS-SS-N-27B *Sizzler*) AShM/*Brahmos* AShM, 4 8-cell VLS with *Barak*-1 SAM, 1 single 3S90E lnchr with 9M317E *Shtil*-1 (RS-SA-N-7B) SAM, 2 triple 324mm ILAS-3 (B-515) ASTT, 2 RBU 6000 *Smerch* 2 A/S mor, 2 AK630M CIWS, 1 76mm gun (capacity 1 *Sea King* Mk42B ASW hel)
    3 *Talwar* I with 1 8-cell 3S14E VLS with 3M54TE *Klub*-N (RS-SS-N-27B *Sizzler*) AShM, 1 single 3S90E lnchr with 9M317E *Shtil*-1 (RS-SA-N-7B) SAM, 2 twin 533mm DTA-53-11356 ASTT with SET-65E HWT/*Varunastra* HWT, 2 RBU 6000 *Smerch* 2 A/S mor, 2 *Kashtan* (RS-CADS-N-1) CIWS, 1 100mm gun (capacity 1 *Dhruv*/Ka-28 *Helix* A ASW hel)
    3 *Talwar* II with 1 8-cell UVLM VLS with *Brahmos* AShM, 1 single 3S90E lnchr with 9M317E *Shtil*-1 (RS-SA-N-7B) SAM, 2 twin 533mm DTA-53-11356 ASTT with SET-65E HWT/*Varunastra* HWT, 2 RBU 6000 *Smerch* 2 A/S mor, 2 AK630M CIWS, 1 100mm gun (capacity 1 *Dhruv*/Ka-28 *Helix* A ASW hel)

FFH 4 *Kamorta* (Project 28) with 2 twin 533mm ITTL ASTT with *Varunastra* HWT, 2 RBU 6000 *Smerch* 2 A/S mor, 2 AK630 CIWS, 1 76mm gun (capacity 1 *Dhruv*/Ka-28 *Helix* A ASW hel)

PATROL AND COASTAL COMBATANTS 160
  CORVETTES • FSGM 6:
    2 *Khukri* (Project 25) with 2 twin lnchr with P-27 *Termit*-R (RS-SS-N-2D *Styx*) AShM, 2 twin lnchr (manual aiming) with 9K32M *Strela*-2M (RS-SA-N-5 *Grail*) SAM, 2 AK630M CIWS, 1 76mm gun, 1 hel landing platform (for *Dhruv*/SA316 *Alouette* III (*Chetak*)
    4 *Kora* (Project 25A) with 4 quad lnchr with 3M24E *Uran*-E (RS-SS-N-25 *Switchblade*) AShM, 1 quad lnchr (manual aiming) with 9K32M *Strela*-2M (RS-SA-N-5 *Grail*) SAM, 2 AK630M CIWS, 1 76mm gun, 1 hel landing platform (for *Dhruv*/SA316 *Alouette* III (*Chetak*))
  PSOH 10: 4 *Saryu* with 2 AK630M CIWS, 1 76mm gun (capacity 1 *Dhruv*); 6 *Sukanya* with 4 RBU 2500 A/S mor (capacity 1 SA316 *Alouette* III (*Chetak*))
  PCFGM 7:
    5 *Veer* (FSU *Tarantul*) with 4 single lnchr with P-27 *Termit*-R (RS-SS-N-2D *Styx*) AShM, 2 quad lnchr (manual aiming) with 9K32M *Strela*-2M (RS-SA-N-5 *Grail*), 2 AK630M CIWS, 1 76mm gun
    2 *Prabal* (mod *Veer*) with 4 quad lnchr with 3M24E *Uran*-E (RS-SS-N-25 *Switchblade*) AShM, 1 quad lnchr (manual aiming) with 9K32M *Strela*-2M (RS-SA-N-5 *Grail*) SAM, 2 AK630M CIWS, 1 76mm gun
  PCMT 1 *Abhay* (FSU *Pauk* II) with 1 quad lnchr (manual aiming) with 9K32M *Strela*-2M (RS-SA-N-5 *Grail*) SAM, 2 twin 533mm DTA-53 ASTT with SET-65E, 2 RBU 1200 *Uragan* A/S mor, 1 AK630M CIWS, 1 76mm gun
  PCC 15: 10 *Car Nicobar*; 5 *Trinkat* (*Bangaram* SDB Mk5)
  PCF 3 *Tarmugli* (*Car Nicobar* mod)
  PBF 118: 9 Immediate Support Vessel (Rodman 78); 14 Immediate Support Vessel (Craftway); 15 Plascoa 1300 (SPB); 3 *Super Dvora*; 77 Solas Marine Interceptor

AMPHIBIOUS
  PRINCIPAL AMPHIBIOUS VESSELS • LPD 1 *Jalashwa* (ex-US *Austin*) with 1 Mk 15 *Phalanx* CIWS (capacity up to 6 med spt hel; either 9 LCM or 4 LCM and 2 LCAC; 4 LCVP; 930 troops)
  LANDING SHIPS 7
    LSM 3 *Kumbhir* (FSU *Polnochny* C) with 2 MS-227 *Ogon'* MRL, 2 AK230 CIWS with 1 hel landing platform (capacity 5 MBT or 5 APC; 160 troops)
    LST 4: 1 *Magar* with 2 MS-227 *Ogon'* MRL with 1 hel landing platform (capacity 15 MBT or 8 APC or 10 trucks; 500 troops); 3 *Magar* mod with 2 MS-227 *Ogon'* MRL with 1 hel landing platform (capacity 11 MBT or 8 APC or 10 trucks; 500 troops)
  LANDING CRAFT 12
    LCT 8 LCU Mk-IV (capacity 1 *Arjun* MBT/2 T-90 MBT/4 IFV/160 troops)
    LCM 4 LCM 8 (for use in *Jalashwa*)

LOGISTICS AND SUPPORT 42
  AFD 2: 1 FDN-1; 1 FDN-2
  AGOR 1 *Sagardhwani* with 1 hel landing platform
  AGS 7: 1 *Makar*; 6 *Sandhayak* with 1 hel landing platform
  AGM 2: 1 *Anvesh*; 1 *Dhruv*
  AOL 10: 1 *Ambika*; 4 GSL 1,000T Fuel Barge; 2 *Poshak*; 7 *Purak*
  AOR 1 *Jyoti* with 1 hel landing platform
  AORH 3: 1 *Aditya* (based on *Deepak* (1967) Bremer Vulkan design) (capacity 1 med hel); 2 *Deepak* with 4 AK630 CIWS (capacity 1 *Sea King* Mk42B)
  AP 2 *Nicobar* with 1 hel landing platform
  ASR 1
  ATF 1 *Gaj*
  AWT 3 *Ambuda*
  AX 1 *Tir* with 1 hel landing platform
  AXS 4: 2 *Mhadei*; 2 *Tarangini*

UNINHABITED MARITIME PLATFORMS • USV 3
  DATA • Small 3 SSO

UNINHABITED MARITIME SYSTEMS • UUV
  UTL *Atom* Mk 1; HUGIN

Naval Aviation 7,000
FORCES BY ROLE
FIGHTER/GROUND ATTACK
  2 sqn with MiG-29K/KUB *Fulcrum*
ANTI-SUBMARINE WARFARE
  1 sqn with Ka-28 *Helix* A
  1 sqn with *Sea King* Mk42B
MARITIME PATROL
  5 sqn with Do-228; Do-228-101
  3 sqn with P-8I *Neptune*
AIRBORNE EARLY WARNING & CONTROL
  1 sqn with Ka-31 *Helix* B
SEARCH & RESCUE
  1 sqn with SA316B *Alouette* III (*Chetak*); *Sea King* Mk42C
  4 sqn with *Dhruv* MkI/MkIII
TRANSPORT
  1 sqn with Do-228; HS-748M (HAL-748M)
TRAINING
  1 sqn with Do-228; Do-228-101; *Virus* SW-80
  1 sqn with HJT-16 *Kiran* MkI/II; *Hawk* Mk132*
  1 hel sqn with *Sea King* Mk42B
TRANSPORT HELICOPTER
  1 sqn with UH-3H *Sea King*
ISR UAV
  3 sqn with *Heron*; *Searcher* MkII
EQUIPMENT BY TYPE
AIRCRAFT 71 combat capable
  FTR 42 MiG-29K/KUB *Fulcrum*
  ASW 12 P-8I *Neptune*
  MP 12+ Do-228-101
  TPT 20: **Light** 10 Do-228; (17 BN-2 *Islander* in store);

PAX 10 HS-748M (HAL-748M)

TRG 41: 6 HJT-16 *Kiran* MkI; 6 HJT-16 *Kiran* MkII; 17 *Hawk* Mk132*; 12 *Virus* SW-80

HELICOPTERS

ASW 36: 12 Ka-28 *Helix* A; 6 MH-60R *Seahawk*; 18 *Sea King* Mk42B

MRH 73: 10 *Dhruv* MkI; 16 *Dhruv* MkIII; 24 SA316B *Alouette* III (*Chetak*); 23 SA319 *Alouette* III

AEW 11 Ka-31 *Helix* B

TPT • **Medium** 11: 5 *Sea King* Mk42C; up to 6 UH-3H *Sea King*

UNINHABITED AERIAL VEHICLES 12

CISR • **Heavy** 2 MQ-9A *Reaper* (leased)

ISR 10: **Heavy** 4 *Heron*; **Medium** 6 *Searcher* Mk II

AIR-LAUNCHED MISSILES

AAM • **IR** R-550 *Magic*/*Magic* 2; R-73 (RS-AA-11A *Archer*); **IR/SARH** R-27 (RS-AA-10 *Alamo*); **ARH**: R-77 (RS-AA-12A *Adder*)

AShM AGM-84 *Harpoon* (on P-8I ac); Kh-35 (RS-AS-20 *Kayak*)

BOMBS • **TV-guided** KAB-500KR/OD

Marines ε1,200 (Additional 1,000 for SPB duties)

After the Mumbai attacks, the Sagar Prahari Bal (SPB), with 80 PBF, was established to protect critical maritime infrastructure

FORCES BY ROLE

SPECIAL FORCES

1 (marine) cdo force

MANOEUVRE

Amphibious

1 amph bde

Air Force 149,900

5 regional air comds: Western (New Delhi), Southwestern (Gandhinagar), Eastern (Shillong), Central (Allahabad), Southern (Trivandrum). 2 support comds: Maintenance (Nagpur) and Training (Bangalore)

FORCES BY ROLE

FIGHTER

3 sqn with MiG-29 *Fulcrum*; MiG-29UB *Fulcrum*

FIGHTER/GROUND ATTACK

5 sqn with *Jaguar* IB/IS

2 sqn with MiG-21 *Bison*

3 sqn with *Mirage* 2000E/ED/I/IT (2000H/TH – secondary ECM role)

2 sqn with *Rafale* DH/EH

12 sqn with Su-30MKI *Flanker*

2 sqn with *Tejas*

ANTI SURFACE WARFARE

1 sqn with *Jaguar* IM

ISR

1 unit with Global 5000 ISR

AIRBORNE EARLY WARNING & CONTROL

1 sqn with EMB-145AEW *Netra*

1 sqn with Il-76TD *Phalcon*

TANKER

1 sqn with Il-78 *Midas*

TRANSPORT

1 (VIP) sqn with B-737; B-737BBJ; B-777-300ER; EMB-135BJ

2 sqn with C-130J-30 *Hercules*

1 sqn with C-17A *Globemaster* III

6 sqn with An-32/An-32RE *Cline*

3 sqn with Do-228; HS-748

1 sqn with Il-76MD *Candid*

1 sqn with C295MW; HS-748

TRAINING

1 OCU sqn with Su-30MKI *Flanker*

ATTACK HELICOPTER

1 sqn with AH-64E *Apache Guardian*

1 sqn with LCH *Prachand*

2 sqn with Mi-25 *Hind*; Mi-35 *Hind*

TRANSPORT HELICOPTER

5 sqn with *Dhruv*

7 sqn with Mi-17/Mi-17-1V *Hip* H

12 sqn with Mi-17V-5 *Hip* H

2 sqn with SA316B *Alouette* III (*Chetak*)

1 flt with CH-47F *Chinook*; Mi-26 *Halo*

2 flt with SA315B *Lama* (*Cheetah*)

2 flt with SA316B *Alouette* III (*Chetak*)

ISR UAV

5 sqn with *Heron*; *Searcher* MkII

SURFACE-TO-SURFACE MISSILE

2 GLCM sqn with PJ-10 *Brahmos*

AIR DEFENCE

6 sqn with 9K33M3 *Osa*-AKM (RS-SA-8B *Gecko*)

8 sqn with *Akash*

2 sqn with Barak-8 MR-SAM

25 sqn with S-125M *Pechora*-M (RS-SA-3B *Goa*)

3 sqn with S-400 (RS-SA-21 *Growler*)

10 flt with 9K38 *Igla*-1 (RS-SA-18 *Grouse*)

EQUIPMENT BY TYPE

AIRCRAFT 730 combat capable

FTR 61: 54 MiG-29 *Fulcrum* (incl 12+ MiG-29UPG); 7 MiG-29UB *Fulcrum* B

FGA 455: ε40 MiG-21 *Bison*; 37 MiG-21U/UM *Mongol*; 37 *Mirage* 2000E/I (2000H); 10 *Mirage* 2000ED/IT (2000TH); 8 *Rafale* DH; 28 *Rafale* EH; 262 Su-30MKI *Flanker* H; 33 *Tejas*

ATK 115: 28 *Jaguar* IB; 79 *Jaguar* IS; 8 *Jaguar* IM

ISR 2 Global 5000 ISR

AEW&C 5: 2 EMB-145AEW *Netra* (1 more in test); 3 Il-76TD *Phalcon*

TKR 6 Il-78 *Midas*

TPT 246: **Heavy** 28: 11 C-17A *Globemaster* III; 17 Il-76MD

Candid; **Medium** 10 C-130J-30 *Hercules*; **Light** 142: 47 An-32; 55 An-32RE *Cline*; 1 C295W; 35 Do-228; 4 EMB-135BJ; **PAX** 66: 1 B-707; 4 B-737; 3 B-737BBJ; 2 B-777-300ER; 56 HS-748

TRG 372: 99 *Hawk* Mk132*; 86 HJT-16 *Kiran* MkI/IA; 41 HJT-16 *Kiran* MkII; 75 PC-7 *Turbo Trainer* MkII; 71 *Virus* SW-80

HELICOPTERS

ATK 43: 22 AH-64E *Apache Guardian*; 4 LCH *Prachand*; 17 Mi-25/Mi-35 *Hind*

MRH 402: 60 *Dhruv*; 35 Mi-17 *Hip H*; 45 Mi-17-1V *Hip H*; 148 Mi-17V-5 *Hip H*; 59 SA315B *Lama* (*Cheetah*); 39 SA316B *Alouette* III (*Chetak*); 16 *Rudra*

TPT • Heavy 16: 15 CH-47F *Chinook*; 1 Mi-26 *Halo*

UNINHABITED AERIAL VEHICLES

ISR • Heavy 9 *Heron*; **Medium** some *Searcher* MkII

LOITERING & DIRECT ATTACK MUNITIONS

Harop

AIR DEFENCE • SAM

Long-range 24 S-400 (RS-SA-21 *Growler*)

Medium-range 72: ε64 *Akash*; 8 Barak-8 (MRSAM)

Short-range S-125M *Pechora*-M (RS-SA-3B *Goa*); *Spyder*-SR

Point-defence 9K33M3 *Osa*-AKM (RS-SA-8 *Gecko*); 9K38 *Igla* (RS-SA-18 *Grouse*)

AIR-LAUNCHED MISSILES

AAM • IR R-60 (RS-AA-8 *Aphid*); R-73 (RS-AA-11A *Archer*) R-550 *Magic*; **IIR** *Mica* IR; **IR/SARH** R-27 (RS-AA-10 *Alamo*); **SARH** Super 530D **ARH** R-77 (RS-AA-12A *Adder*); *Meteor*; *Mica* RF

AShM AGM-84 *Harpoon*; AM39 *Exocet*; Kh-31A (RS-AS-17B *Krypton*)

ASM AASM; AGM-114L/R *Hellfire*; Kh-29 (RS-AS-14 *Kedge*); Kh-59 (RS-AS-13 *Kingbolt*); Kh-59M (RS-AS-18 *Kazoo*); AS-30; *Popeye* II (*Crystal Maze*)

ARM Kh-25MP (RS-AS-12A *Kegler*); Kh-31P (RS-AS-17A *Krypton*)

LACM • Conventional *Brahmos*; SCALP-EG

BOMBS

INS/SAT guided *Spice*; *Spice* 2000

Laser-guided *Griffin*; KAB-500L; *Paveway* II

TV-guided KAB-500KR

SURFACE-TO-SURFACE MISSILE LAUNCHERS

GLCM • Conventional PJ-10 *Brahmos*

Coast Guard 13,350

EQUIPMENT BY TYPE

PATROL AND COASTAL COMBATANTS 143

PSOH 27: 2 *Sankalp* (capacity 1 *Chetak/Dhruv* hel); 4 *Samar* with 1 76mm gun (capacity 1 *Chetak/Dhruv* hel); 11 *Samarth* (capacity 1 *Chetak/Dhruv* hel); 7 *Vikram* (capacity 1 *Dhruv* hel); 3 *Vishwast* (capacity 1 *Chetak/Dhruv* hel)

PSO 3 *Samudra Prahari* with 1 hel landing platform

PCC 44: 20 *Aadesh*; 8 *Rajshree* (Flight I); 5 *Rajshree* (Flight II) 5 *Rani Abbakka*; 6 *Sarojini Naidu*

PBF 69: 6 C-154; 2 C-141; 11 C-143; 50 C-401

AMPHIBIOUS • UCAC 17: 5 H-181 (*Griffon* 8000TD); 12 H-187 (*Griffon* 8000TD)

AIRCRAFT • MP 39 Do-228-101

HELICOPTERS • MRH 39: 4 *Dhruv* MkI; 16 *Dhruv* MkIII; 19 SA316B *Alouette* III (*Chetak*)

Gendarmerie & Paramilitary 1,616,050

Rashtriya Rifles 65,000

Ministry of Defence. 15 sector HQ

FORCES BY ROLE

MANOEUVRE

Other

65 paramilitary bn

Assam Rifles 65,150

Ministry of Home Affairs. Security within northeastern states, mainly army-officered; better trained than BSF

FORCES BY ROLE

Equipped to roughly same standard as an army inf bn

COMMAND

7 HQ

MANOEUVRE

Other

47 paramilitary bn

EQUIPMENT BY TYPE

ARTILLERY • MOR 81mm 252

Border Security Force 263,900

Ministry of Home Affairs

FORCES BY ROLE

MANOEUVRE

Other

193 paramilitary bn

EQUIPMENT BY TYPE

Small arms, lt arty, some anti-tank weapons

ARTILLERY • MOR 81mm 942+

AIRCRAFT • TPT • Light 1 ERJ-135BJ

HELICOPTERS • MRH 21: 6 *Dhruv*; 6 Mi-17-1V *Hip*; 8 Mi-17V-5 *Hip*; 1 SA315B *Lama* (*Cheetah*)

Central Industrial Security Force 144,400 (lightly armed security guards)

Ministry of Home Affairs. Guards public-sector locations

Central Reserve Police Force 324,600

Ministry of Home Affairs. Internal-security duties, only lightly armed, deployable throughout the country

FORCES BY ROLE

MANOEUVRE

Other

208 paramilitary bn
15 (rapid action force) paramilitary bn
10 (CoBRA) paramilitary bn
6 (Mahila) paramilitary bn (female)
2 sy gp
COMBAT SUPPORT
5 sigs bn

Defence Security Corps 31,000
Provides security at Defence Ministry sites

Indo-Tibetan Border Police 89,400
Ministry of Home Affairs. Tibetan border security SF/guerrilla-warfare and high-altitude-warfare specialists
FORCES BY ROLE
MANOEUVRE
Other
56 paramilitary bn

National Security Guards 12,000
Anti-terrorism contingency deployment force, comprising elements of the armed forces, CRPF and Border Security Force

Railway Protection Forces 70,000

Sashastra Seema Bal 87,600
Guards the borders with Nepal and Bhutan
FORCES BY ROLE
MANOEUVRE
Other
73 paramilitary bn

Special Frontier Force 10,000
Mainly ethnic Tibetans

Special Protection Group 3,000
Protection of ministers and senior officials

State Armed Police 450,000
For duty primarily in home state only, but can be moved to other states. Some bn with GPMG and army-standard infantry weapons and equipment
FORCES BY ROLE
MANOEUVRE
Other
144 (India Reserve Police) paramilitary bn

Reserve Organisations

Civil Defence 500,000 reservists
Operate in 225 categorised towns in 32 states. Some units for NBC defence

Home Guard 441,000 reservists (547,000 authorised str)
In all states except Arunachal Pradesh and Kerala; men on reserve lists, no trg. Not armed in peacetime. Used for civil defence, rescue and firefighting provision in wartime; 6 bn (created to protect tea plantations in Assam)

DEPLOYMENT

CENTRAL AFRICAN REPUBLIC: UN • MINUSCA 2
CYPRUS: UN • UNFICYP 1
DEMOCRATIC REPUBLIC OF THE CONGO: UN • MONUSCO 1,821; 2 inf bn; 1 med coy
LEBANON: UN • UNIFIL 893; 1 mech inf bn; 1 log coy; 1 med coy
MIDDLE EAST: UN • UNTSO 3
SOMALIA: UN • UNSOM 1
SOUTH SUDAN: UN • UNMISS 2,404; 2 inf bn; 1 engr coy; 1 sigs coy; 2 fd hospital
SUDAN: UN • UNISFA 576; 1 mech inf bn(-)
SYRIA/ISRAEL: UN • UNDOF 222; 1 inf pl, 1 MP pl, 1 log coy(-)
WESTERN SAHARA: UN • MINURSO 3

FOREIGN FORCES

Total numbers for UNMOGIP mission in India and Pakistan
Argentina 4
Croatia 8
Italy 2
Korea, Republic of 6
Philippines 4
Romania 2
Sweden 3
Switzerland 3
Thailand 5
Uruguay 2

Indonesia IDN

Indonesian Rupiah IDR		2022	2023	2024
GDP	IDR	19,588trn	21,293trn	22,906trn
	USD	1.32trn	1.42trn	1.54trn
per capita	USD	4,798	5,109	5,509
Growth	%	5.3	5.0	5.0
Inflation	%	4.2	3.6	2.5
Def bdgt	IDR	133trn	132trn	
	USD	8.98bn	8.78bn	
FMA (US)	USD	14m	14m	14m
USD1=IDR		14,853.17	15,022.52	14,850.96

Real-terms defence budget trend (USDbn, constant 2015)

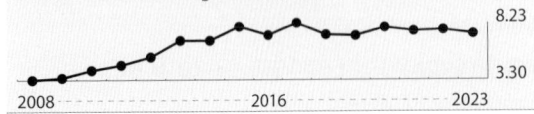

Population 279,476,346

Age	0–14	15–19	20–24	25–29	30–64	65 plus
Male	12.4%	4.3%	4.1%	3.9%	21.8%	3.5%
Female	11.8%	4.1%	3.9%	3.7%	22.3%	4.1%

Capabilities

The Indonesian National Armed Forces are the largest in Southeast Asia. They have traditionally been concerned with internal security, counter-insurgency and counterterrorism. The army, which deployed operationally for a counter-insurgency task in West Papua and in a counterterrorist role in central Sulawesi, remains the dominant service, with limited joint service operational capacity. However, the creation of three new tri-service theatre commands and a tri-service counterterrorism command in 2019 reflects greater emphasis on integration. In 2018, a third regional naval fleet command, a third air-force regional command, a third Army strategic-reserve division and a third Marine group were established in the East. A part-time reserve component was set up in 2021, while air-defence was transferred to air-force command in 2022. The 2015 Defence White Paper outlined a 'Global Maritime Fulcrum' policy and advocated building maritime, satellite, and UAV capabilities. A new modernisation plan is being drafted, likely spanning 25 years, and emphasising development of space, air, and maritime capabilities, as well as the protection of sea lanes. The government has sweeping interests, including ISR, multi-role combat aircraft, submarines, and ballistic missile and air defence systems. Indonesia's defence industry has jointly produced fixed-wing and rotary-wing aircraft, landing platform docks an frigates. Indonesia has no formal defence alliances but has a number of defence cooperation agreements with regional and extra-regional partners. The country hosts multilateral military exercises and frequently participates in UN peacekeeping.

ACTIVE 404,500 (Army 300,400 Navy 74,000 Air 30,100) Gendarmerie & Paramilitary 290,200

Conscription liability 24 months selective conscription authorised (not required by law)

RESERVE 400,000

Army cadre units; numerical str n.k., obligation to age 45 for officers

ORGANISATIONS BY SERVICE

Army ε300,400

Mil Area Commands (KODAM)
15 comd (I, II, III, IV, V, VI, IX, XII, XIII, XIV, XVI, XVII, XVIII, Jaya & Iskandar Muda)

FORCES BY ROLE
MANOEUVRE
  Mechanised
  3 armd cav bn
  8 cav bn
  1 mech inf bde (1 cav bn, 3 mech inf bn)
  1 mech inf bde (3 mech inf bn)
  3 indep mech inf bn
  Light
  1 inf bde (3 cdo bn)
  1 inf bde (2 cdo bn, 1 inf bn)
  1 inf bde (1 cdo bn, 2 inf bn)
  2 inf bde (3 inf bn)
  3 inf bde (1 cdo bn, 1 inf bn)
  3 inf bde (2 inf bn)
  24 indep inf bn
  20 indep cdo bn
COMBAT SUPPORT
  1 SP arty bn
  11 fd arty bn
  11 cbt engr bn
COMBAT SERVICE SUPPORT
  4 construction bn
AVIATION
  1 composite avn sqn
HELICOPTER
  1 hel sqn with Bo-105; Bell 205A; Bell 412; Bell 412EPI *Twin Huey*; AH-64E *Apache Guardian*
  1 hel sqn Mi-35P *Hind*; Mi-17V-5 *Hip H*
AIR DEFENCE
  1 AD regt (2 ADA bn, 1 SAM unit)
  9 ADA bn
  3 SAM unit

Special Forces Command (KOPASSUS)
FORCES BY ROLE
SPECIAL FORCES
  3 SF gp (total: 2 cdo/para unit, 1 CT unit, 1 int unit)

Strategic Reserve Command (KOSTRAD)
FORCES BY ROLE
COMMAND
  3 div HQ
MANOEUVRE
  Armoured
  2 tk bn
  Mechanised

1 mech inf bde (3 mech inf bn)
Light
2 inf bde (3 cdo bn)
1 inf bde (2 inf bn)
Air Manoeuvre
3 AB bde (3 AB bn)
COMBAT SUPPORT
2 arty regt (1 SP arty bn; 1 MRL bn; 1 fd arty bn)
1 fd arty bn
2 cbt engr bn
AIR DEFENCE
3 AD bn

EQUIPMENT BY TYPE
ARMOURED FIGHTING VEHICLES
MBT 103: 42 *Leopard* 2A4; 61 *Leopard* 2RI
LT TK 350: 275 AMX-13 (partially upgraded); 15 PT-76; 60 FV101 *Scorpion*-90
ASLT 7 *Babak*
RECCE 142: 55 *Ferret* (13 upgraded); 69 *Saladin* (16 upgraded); 18 VBL
IFV 64: 22 *Black Fox*; 42 *Marder* 1A3
APC 860+
  APC (T) 267: 75 AMX-VCI; 34 BTR-50PK; 15 FV4333 *Stormer*; 143 M113A1-B
  APC (W) 593+: 376 *Anoa*; some *Barracuda*; 40 BTR-40; 45 FV603 *Saracen* (14 upgraded); 100 LAV-150 *Commando*; 32 VAB-VTT
  PPV some *Casspir*
AUV 54: 14 APR-1; 18 *Bushmaster*; 22 *Commando Ranger*; *Komodo* 4×4

ENGINEERING & MAINTENANCE VEHICLES
AEV 4: 3 PiPz-2RI *Dachs*; 1 M113A1-B-GN
ARV 15+: 2 AMX-13; 6 AMX-VCI; 3 BREM-2; 4 BPz-3 *Buffel*; *Stormer*; T-54/T-55
VLB 19: 10 AMX-13; 3 BPR *Biber*-1; 4 M3; 2 *Stormer*

ANTI-TANK/ANTI-INFRASTRUCTURE
MSL • MANPATS FGM-148 *Javelin*; SS.11; *Milan*; 9K11 *Malyutka* (RS-AT-3 *Sagger*)
RCL 90mm M67; **106mm** M40A1
RL 89mm LRAC

ARTILLERY 1,243+
SP 92: **105mm** 20 AMX Mk61; **155mm** 72: 54 CAESAR; 18 M109A4
TOWED 133+: **105mm** 110+: some KH-178; 60 M101; 50 M-56; **155mm** 23: 5 FH-88; 18 KH-179
MRL 127mm 63 ASTROS II Mk6
MOR 955: **81mm** 800; **120mm** 155: 75 Brandt; 80 UBM 52

PATROL AND COASTAL COMBATANTS 4
PBF 4 Combat Boat 18M (used as fast transports)

AMPHIBIOUS
LANDING SHIPS • LST 2 ADRI LI with 1 hel landing platform (capacity 8 MBT; 500 troops)
LANDING CRAFT • LCU 17: 1 ADRI XXXII; 4 ADRI XXXIII; 1 ADRI XXXIX; 1 ADRI XL; 3 ADRI XLI; 2 ADRI XLIV; 2 ADRI XLVI; 2 ADRI XLVIII; 1 ADRI L

AIRCRAFT • TPT • Light 9: 1 BN-2A *Islander*; 6 C-212 *Aviocar* (NC-212); 2 *Turbo Commander* 680

HELICOPTERS
ATK 14: 8 AH-64E *Apache Guardian*; 6 Mi-35P *Hind*
MRH 50: 12 H125M *Fennec*; 17 Bell 412 *Twin Huey* (NB-412); 5 Bell 412EPI *Twin Huey*; 16 Mi-17V-5 *Hip* H
TPT • Light 29: 7 Bell 205A; 20 Bo-105 (NBo-105); 2 H120 *Colibri*
TRG up to 19 Hughes 300C

AIR DEFENCE
SAM • Point-defence 95+: 2 *Kobra* (with 125 GROM-2 msl); *Starstreak*; TD-2000B (*Giant Bow* II); 51 *Rapier*; 42 RBS-70; QW-3
GUNS • TOWED 411: **20mm** 121 Rh 202; **23mm** *Giant Bow*; **40mm** 90 L/70; **57mm** 200 S-60

AIR-LAUNCHED MISSILES
ASM AGM-114 *Hellfire*

Navy ε74,000 (including Marines and Aviation)

Three fleets: East (Sorong), Central (Surabaya) and West (Jakarta). Two Forward Operating Bases at Kupang (West Timor) and Tahuna (North Sulawesi)

EQUIPMENT BY TYPE
SUBMARINES • SSK 4:
  1 *Cakra* (GER Type-209/1300) with 8 single 533mm TT with SUT HWT
  3 *Nagapasa* (GER Type-209/1400) with 8 single 533mm TT with *Black Shark* HWT

PRINCIPAL SURFACE COMBATANTS 7
FRIGATES 7:
  FFGHM 5:
    1 *Ahmad Yani* (ex-NLD *Van Speijk*) with 2 2-cell VLS with 3M55E *Yakhont* (RS-SS-N-26 *Strobile*) AShM; 2 twin *Simbad* lnchr (manual) with *Mistral* SAM, 2 triple 324mm SVTT Mk 32 ASTT with Mk 46 LWT, 1 76mm gun (capacity 1 Bo-105 (NBo-105) hel)
    2 *Ahmad Yani* (ex-NLD *Van Speijk*) with 2 twin lnchr with C-802 (CH-SS-N-6) AShM, 2 twin *Simbad* lnchr (manual) with *Mistral* SAM, 2 triple 324mm SVTT Mk 32 ASTT with Mk 46 LWT, 1 76mm gun (capacity 1 Bo-105 (NBo-105) hel)
    2 *R.E. Martadinata* (SIGMA 10514) with 2 quad lnchr with MM40 *Exocet* Block 3 AShM, 2 6-cell CLA VLS with VL MICA SAM, 2 triple 324mm ILAS-3 (B-515) ASTT with A244/S LWT, 1 *Millennium* CIWS, 1 76mm gun (capacity 1 med hel)
  FFHM 2 *Ahmad Yani* (ex-NLD *Van Speijk*) with 2 twin *Simbad* lnchr (manual) with *Mistral* SAM, 2 triple 324mm ASTT with Mk 46 LWT, 1 76mm gun (capacity 1 Bo-105 (NBo-105) hel)

PATROL AND COASTAL COMBATANTS 159
CORVETTES 24
  FSGM 7:
    3 *Bung Tomo* with 2 quad lnchr with MM40 *Exocet*

Block 2 AShM, 1 16-cell VLS with *Sea Wolf* SAM, 2 triple 324mm ASTT, 1 76mm gun (capacity: 1 Bo-105 hel)

4 *Diponegoro* (SIGMA 9113) with 2 twin lnchr with MM40 *Exocet* Block 2 AShM, 2 quad *Tetral* lnchr with *Mistral* SAM, 2 triple 324mm ILAS-3 (B-515) ASTT with MU90 LWT, 1 76mm gun, 1 hel landing platform

FSGH 1 *Nala* with 2 twin lnchr with MM38 *Exocet* AShM, 1 twin Bofors ASW Rocket Launcher System 375mm A/S mor, 1 120mm gun (capacity 1 lt hel)

FS 16:

2 *Fatahillah* with 2 triple 324mm SVTT Mk 32 ASTT with Mk 46 LWT, 1 twin 375mm A/S mor, 1 120mm gun

14 *Kapitan Pattimura* (ex-GDR *Parchim* I) with 4 single 400mm ASTT, 2 RBU 6000 *Smerch* 2 A/S mor, 1 AK230 CIWS, 1 twin 57mm gun

PCFG 3 *Mandau* with 4 single lnchr with MM38 *Exocet* AShM, 1 57mm gun

PCG 4:

2 *Sampari* (KCR-60M) with 2 twin lnchr for C-705 AShM, 1 57mm gun

2 *Todak* with 2 single lnchr with C-802 (CH-SS-N-6), 1 57mm gun

PCT 2 *Andau* with 2 single 533mm TT with SUT, 1 57mm gun

PCO 1 *Bung Karno* (capacity: 1 AS565MBe *Panther* hel)

PCC 35: 4 *Dorang*; 4 *Kakap* with 1 hel landing platform; 2 *Pandrong*; 4 *Pari*; 2 *Pulau Rote*; 4 *Sampari* (KCR-60M) with 1 NG-18 CIWS, 1 57 mm gun; 13 *Tatihu* (PC-40); 2 *Todak* with 1 57mm gun

PBG 8: 2 *Clurit* with 2 single lnchr with C-705 AShM, 1 AK630 CIWS; 6 *Clurit* with 2 single lnchr with C-705 AShM

PBF 13 Combat Boat 18M

PB 69: 2 *Badau* (ex-BRN *Waspada*); 1 *Bawean*; 1 *Cucut* (ex-SGP *Jupiter*); 1 *Klewang*; 13 *Kobra*; 1 *Krait*; 1 *Kudungga*; 1 *Mumuja*; 8 *Sibarau*; up to 32 *Sinabang* (KAL-28); 8 *Viper*

MINE WARFARE • MINE COUNTERMEASURES 8

MCO 4: 2 *Pulau Fani* (GER *Frankenthal* (Type-332)); 2 *Pulau Rengat*

MSC 4 *Pulau Rote* (ex-GDR *Wolgast*)

AMPHIBIOUS

PRINCIPAL AMPHIBIOUS VESSELS • LPD 4:

4 *Makassar* (capacity 2 LCU or 4 LCVP; 13 tanks; 500 troops; 2 AS332L *Super Puma*)

LANDING SHIPS • LST 23

1 *Teluk Amboina* (capacity 16 tanks; 800 troops)

4 *Teluk Bintuni* (capacity 4 LCVP; 470 troops; 15 APC or 10 MBT)

2 *Teluk Cirebon* (ex-GDR *Frosch* II) (capacity 11 APC; 80 troops)

9 *Teluk Gilimanuk* (ex-GDR *Frosch*) (capacity 11 APC; 80 troops)

5 *Teluk Lada* with 1 hel landing platform (capacity 4 LCVP; 470 troops; 15 APC; 10 MBT)

2 *Teluk Semangka* (capacity 17 tanks; 200 troops)

LANDING CRAFT 52

LCM 20

LCU 2

LCVP 30

LOGISTICS AND SUPPORT 23

AGF 1 *Multatuli* with 1 hel landing platform

AGOR 3: 1 *Pollux*; 2 *Rigel* (FRA OSV 190)

AGSH 1 *Dewa Kembar* (ex-UK *Hecla*) with 1 hel landing platform

AGS 2: 1 *Leuser* (IDN *Soputan* mod); 1 *Pulau Rote* (ex-GDR *Kondor*)

AH 4:

1 *Dr Soeharso* (ex-*Tanjung Dalpele*) (capacity 2 LCU/LCVP; 500 troops; 2 AS332L *Super Puma*)

2 *Dr Sudirohusodo* (*Semarang* mod) (capacity 2 med hel)

1 *Semarang* (IDN *Makassar* mod) (capacity 2 LCM; 3 hels; 28 vehs; 650 troops)

AK 1 *Mentawai* (HUN *Telaud*)

AOR 3: 1 *Arun* (ex-UK *Rover*); 1 *Bontang* with 1 hel landing platform; 1 *Tarakan* with 1 hel landing platform

AP 2: 1 *Tanjung Kambani* with 1 hel landing platform; 1 *Karang Pilang*

ATF 1 *Soputan*

AXL 2 *Kadet*

AXS 3: 1 *Arung Samudera*; 1 *Bima Suci*; 1 *Dewaruci*

UNINHABITED MARITIME SYSTEMS • UUV

MW PAP

UTL HUGIN 1000

Naval Aviation ε1,000

EQUIPMENT BY TYPE

AIRCRAFT

MP 30: 3 C212-200; 7 CN235-220 (MPA); 14 N-22B *Searchmaster* B; 6 N-22SL *Searchmaster* L

TPT • Light 40: 1 Beech 350i *King Air* (VIP); 7 Beech G36 *Bonanza*; 2 Beech G38 *Baron*; 17 C-212-200 *Aviocar*; 8 PA-28 *Archer* III (trg); 3 TB-9 *Tampico*; 2 TB-10

HELICOPTERS

ASW 11 AS565MBe *Panther*

MRH 4 Bell 412 (NB-412) *Twin Huey*

CSAR 4 H225M *Caracal*

TPT 16: **Medium** 3 AS332L *Super Puma* (NAS322L); **Light** 13: 3 H120 *Colibri*; 1 Bell 505 *Jet Ranger X*; 9 Bo-105 (NBo-105)

UNINHABITED AERIAL VEHICLES

ISR • Light 1 S-100 *Camcopter*

Marines ε20,000

FORCES BY ROLE

SPECIAL FORCES

1 SF bn

MANOEUVRE

Amphibious

2 mne gp (1 cav regt, 3 mne bn, 1 arty regt, 1 cbt spt regt, 1 CSS regt)

1 mne gp (forming)

1 mne bde (3 mne bn)

EQUIPMENT BY TYPE

ARMOURED FIGHTING VEHICLES

LT TK 65: 10 AMX-10 PAC 90; 55 PT-76†

RECCE 21 BRDM-2

IFV 114: 24 AMX-10P; 22 BMP-2; 54 BMP-3F; 2 BTR-4; 12 BTR-80A

APC 103: **APC (T)** 100 BTR-50P; **APC (W)** 3 BTR-4M

AAV 15: 10 LVTP-7A1; 5 M113 *Arisgator*

ARTILLERY 71+

TOWED 50: **105mm** 22 LG1 MK II; **122mm** 28 M-38

MRL 122mm 21: 4 PHL-90B; 9 RM-70; 8 RM-70 *Vampir*

MOR 81mm some

AIR DEFENCE • GUNS • 40mm 5 L/60/L/70; **57mm** S-60

Air Force 30,100

3 operational comd (East, Central and West) plus trg comd

FORCES BY ROLE

FIGHTER

1 sqn with F-16A/B/C/D *Fighting Falcon*

FIGHTER/GROUND ATTACK

1 sqn with F-16C/D *Fighting Falcon*

1 sqn with Su-27SK *Flanker*; Su-30MK *Flanker*

1 sqn with Su-27SKM *Flanker*; Su-30MK2 *Flanker*

2 sqn with *Hawk* Mk109*/Mk209*

1 sqn with T-50i *Golden Eagle**

GROUND ATTACK

1 sqn with EMB-314 (A-29) *Super Tucano**

MARITIME PATROL

1 sqn with B-737-200

1 sqn with CN235M-220 MPA; CN235M-110

TANKER/TRANSPORT

1 sqn with C-130B/KC-130B *Hercules*

TRANSPORT

1 (VIP) sqn with B-737-200; B-737-800; C-130H/H-30 *Hercules*; L-100-30; F-27-400M *Troopship*; F-28-1000/3000; *Falcon* 7X/8X

1 sqn with C-130H/H-30/J-30 *Hercules*; L-100-30

1 sqn with C-130H *Hercules*

1 sqn with C-212 *Aviocar* (NC-212/NC-212i)

1 sqn with C295M

TRAINING

1 sqn with G 120TP

1 sqn with KT-1B

1 UAV sqn (forming) with LH-D

TRANSPORT HELICOPTER

2 sqn with H225M; AS332L *Super Puma* (NAS332L); NAS332 C1+ *Super Puma*; SA330J/L *Puma* (NAS330J/L)

1 sqn (forming) with H225M

1 VIP sqn with AS332L *Super Puma* (NAS332L); SA330SM *Puma* (NAS300SM)

1 sqn with H120 *Colibri*

COMBAT/ISR UAV

1 sqn with CH-4B

ISR UAV

1 sqn with *Aerostar*

AIR DEFENCE

1 SAM unit with NASAMS II

EQUIPMENT BY TYPE

AIRCRAFT 104 combat capable

FTR 9: 7 F-16A *Fighting Falcon*; 2 F-16B *Fighting Falcon* (8 F-5E *Tiger* II; 4 F-5F *Tiger* II non-operational)

FGA 40: 19 F-16C *Fighting Falcon*; 5 F-16D *Fighting Falcon*; 2 Su-27SK *Flanker*; 3 Su-27SKM *Flanker*; 2 Su-30MK *Flanker* F; 9 Su-30MK2 *Flanker* G

MP 7: 3 B-737-200; 2 B-737-800; 2 CN235M-220 MPA

ISR 1 C295M

TKR/TPT 1 KC-130B *Hercules*

TPT 59: **Medium** 21: 3 C-130B *Hercules*; 7 C-130H *Hercules*; 6 C-130H-30 *Hercules*; 3 C-130J-30 *Hercules*; 2 L-100-30; **Light** 26: 9 C295; 9 C-212 *Aviocar* (NC-212); 3 C-212 *Aviocar* (NC-212i); 5 CN235M-110; **PAX** 12: 1 B-737-200; 3 B-737-400; 1 B-737-500; 1 B-737-800BBJ; 1 F-28-1000; 2 F-28-3000; 1 *Falcon* 7X, 2 *Falcon* 8X

TRG 101: 13 EMB-314 (A-29) *Super Tucano**; 30 G 120TP; 7 *Hawk* Mk109*; 22 *Hawk* Mk209*; 16 KT-1B; 13 T-50i *Golden Eagle**

HELICOPTERS

TPT 40: **Heavy** 9 H225M (CSAR); **Medium** 19: 9 AS332 *Super Puma* (NAS332L) (VIP/CSAR); 1 NAS332 C1+ *Super Puma*; 1 SA330SM *Puma* (NAS330SM) (VIP); 4 SA330J *Puma* (NAS330J); 4 SA330L *Puma* (NAS330L); **Light** 12 H120 *Colibri*

UNINHABITED AERIAL VEHICLES

CISR • Heavy CH-4B (in test)

ISR • Medium *Aerostar*; LH-D

AIR-LAUNCHED MISSILES

AAM • IR AIM-9P *Sidewinder*; R-73 (RS-AA-11A *Archer*); **IIR** AIM-9X *Sidewinder* II; **IR/SARH** R-27 (RS-AA-10 *Alamo*)

ARH AIM-120C-7 AMRAAM; R-77 (RS-AA-12A *Adder*)

ASM AGM-65G *Maverick*; AR-2; Kh-59M (RS-AS-18 *Kazoo*); Kh-59T (RS-AS-14B *Kedge*)

ARM Kh-31P (RS-AS-17A *Krypton*)

BOMBS

INS/SAT guided GBU-38 JDAM

Laser-guided GBU-54 Laser JDAM

AIR DEFENCE

SAM • Medium-range NASAMS II

Special Forces (Paskhasau)

FORCES BY ROLE

SPECIAL FORCES

3 (PASKHASAU) SF wg (total: 6 spec ops sqn)

4 indep SF coy

EQUIPMENT BY TYPE

AIR DEFENCE

SAM • Point-defence *Chiron*; QW-3

GUNS • TOWED 35mm 6 Oerlikon *Skyshield*

Gendarmerie & Paramilitary 281,200+

Police ε280,000 (including 14,000 police 'mobile bde' (BRIMOB) org in 56 coy, incl CT unit (Gegana))

EQUIPMENT BY TYPE

ARMOURED FIGHTING VEHICLES

APC (W) 34 *Tactica*

AIRCRAFT • TPT 9: **Light** 7: 2 Beech 18; 1 Beech 1900D; 2 C-212 *Aviocar* (NC-212); 1 C295; 1 *Turbo Commander* 680; **PAX** 3: 1 B-737-800; 1 Hawker 400XP; 1 F-50

HELICOPTERS

MRH 5: 3 AS365N3 *Dauphin*; 2 AW189

TPT • **Light** 34: 9 AW169; 3 Bell 206 *Jet Ranger*; 3 Bell 429; 19 Bo-105 (NBo-105)

KPLP (Coast and Seaward Defence Command) ε9,000

Responsible to Military Sea Communications Agency

EQUIPMENT BY TYPE

PATROL AND COASTAL COMBATANTS 76

PCO 7: 1 *Arda Dedali*; 3 *Chundamani*; 1 *Kalimasada*; 2 *Trisula*

PB 69: 4 *Golok* (SAR); 5 *Kujang*; 6 *Rantos*; 54 (various)

LOGISTICS AND SUPPORT • ABU 5

Bakamla (Maritime Security Agency) 1,200

EQUIPMENT BY TYPE

PATROL AND COASTAL COMBATANTS 10

PSO 4: 3 *Pulau Nipah* with 1 hel landing platform; 1 *Tanjung Datu* with 1 hel landing platform

PB 6 *Bintang Laut* (KCR-40 mod)

Reserve Organisations

Kamra People's Security ε40,000

Report for 3 weeks' basic training each year; part-time police auxiliary

DEPLOYMENT

CENTRAL AFRICAN REPUBLIC: UN • MINUSCA 229; 1 engr coy

DEMOCRATIC REPUBLIC OF THE CONGO: UN • MONUSCO 1,035; 1 inf bn; 1 engr coy

LEBANON: UN • UNIFIL 1,230; 1 mech inf bn; 1 log coy; 1 FSGM

SOUTH SUDAN: UN • UNMISS 4

SUDAN: UN • UNISFA 2

WESTERN SAHARA: UN • MINURSO 3

Japan JPN

Japanese Yen JPY		2022	2023	2024
GDP	JPY	557trn	589trn	613trn
	USD	4.24trn	4.23trn	4.29trn
per capita	USD	33,854	33,950	34,555
Growth	%	1.0	2.0	1.0
Inflation	%	2.5	3.2	2.9
Def bdgt	JPY	6.17trn	6.82trn	7.71trn
	USD	47.0bn	49.0bn	53.9bn
USD1=JPY		131.50	139.11	143.07

Real-terms defence budget trend (USDbn, constant 2015)

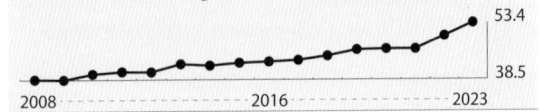

53.4
38.5
2008 ········· 2016 ········· 2023

Population	123,719,238					
Age	0–14	15–19	20–24	25–29	30–64	65 plus
Male	6.3%	2.3%	2.5%	2.6%	21.9%	12.9%
Female	6.0%	2.2%	2.3%	2.4%	22.3%	16.4%

Capabilities

Japan's growing concern over its regional security environment was reflected in the 2023 Defense White Paper. It followed Japan's second National Security Strategy, first National Defense Strategy and the Defense Buildup Program, all issued in late 2022. Tokyo's principal security challenges are a more assertive China and developments in North Korea and Russia. Japan is increasing defence spending and plans to boost outlays to 2% of GDP by 2027. It is pursuing defence-policy and legislative reforms to enable the country to play a more active international security role and to strengthen the Japan Self-Defense Forces (JSDF). The new strategic documents outline major changes to Japan's post-war approach to security, heralding greater coordination across defence and civilian agencies for defence planning and a desire for enhanced military capabilities, including counter-strike systems. The JSDF is set to establish a Permanent Joint Headquarters to achieve unified command and control across three branches by the end of FY2024. Due to their defensive mandate, JSDF deployments are mostly for diplomatic and peacekeeping purposes. While the JSDF's offensive capacity is limited, the navy has strengths in anti-submarine warfare and air-defence. The country has established an Amphibious Rapid Deployment Brigade focused on the defence of remote islands. The *Izumo* helicopter carrier has completed the first stage of modifications to operate fixed-wing aircraft. Japan is developing capabilities in space, cyberspace and the electromagnetic spectrum to develop a 'multi-domain defence force'. In 2020, a Space Operations Squadron was set up with the aim of enhancing space situational-awareness capabilities. The Cyber Defense Group is being expanded. Enhancing integrated air and missile defence is a key priority. Japan's alliance with the US is central to its defence policy, reflected by continued US basing, the widespread use of US equipment across all three services and regular training with US forces. However, its defence and security ties have expanded. In late 2022, Japan, Italy and the UK announced the joint development of a new generation of combat aircraft under the Global Combat Air Programme banner, due to enter service by 2035. In 2022, Japan signed a Reciprocal Access Agreement (RAA) with Australia and one with the UK in 2023. India and Japan concluded an Acquisition and Cross-Servicing Agreement in September 2020. Japan has an advanced defence-industrial base. Defence exports have mainly consisted of components, though there are ambitions to secure more significant export deals.

ACTIVE 247,000 (Ground Self-Defense Force 150,500 Maritime Self-Defense Force 45,300 Air Self-Defense Force 47,000 Central Staff 4,200) Gendarmerie & Paramilitary 14,700

RESERVE 55,900 (General Reserve Army (GSDF) 46,000 Ready Reserve Army (GSDF) 8,000 Navy 1,100 Air 800)

ORGANISATIONS BY SERVICE

Space
EQUIPMENT BY TYPE
SATELLITES 11
  COMMUNICATIONS 2: 1 *Kirameki*-1; 1 *Kirameki*-2
  ISR 9 IGS

Ground Self-Defense Force 150,500
FORCES BY ROLE
COMMAND
  5 army HQ (regional comd)
SPECIAL FORCES
  1 spec ops unit (bn)
MANOEUVRE
  Armoured
  1 (7th) armd div (1 armd recce sqn, 3 tk regt, 1 armd inf regt, 1 hel sqn, 1 SP arty regt, 1 AD regt, 1 cbt engr bn, 1 sigs bn, 1 NBC bn, 1 log regt)
  1 indep tk bn
  Mechanised
  1 (2nd) inf div (1 armd recce sqn, 1 tk regt, 1 mech inf regt, 2 inf regt, 1 hel sqn, 1 SP arty regt, 1 AT coy, 1 ADA bn, 1 cbt engr bn, 1 sigs bn, 1 NBC bn, 1 log regt)
  1 (4th) inf div (1 armd recce bn, 3 inf regt, 1 inf coy, 1 hel sqn, 1 AT coy, 1 SAM bn, 1 cbt engr bn, 1 sigs bn, 1 NBC bn, 1 log regt)
  1 (6th) inf div (1 recce sqn, 1 mech inf regt; 3 inf regt, 1 hel sqn, 1 SAM bn, 1 cbt engr bn, 1 sigs bn, 1 NBC bn, 1 log regt)
  1 (9th) inf div (1 armd recce sqn, 1 tk bn, 3 inf regt, 1 hel sqn, 1 SAM bn, 1 cbt engr bn, 1 sigs bn, 1 NBC bn, 1 log regt)
  1 (5th) inf bde (1 armd recce sqn, 1 tk bn, 1 mech inf regt, 2 inf regt, 1 hel sqn, 1 SP arty bn, 1 SAM coy, 1 cbt engr coy, 1 sigs coy, 1 NBC coy, 1 log bn)
  1 (11th) inf bde (1 armd recce sqn, 1 tk sqn, 3 inf regt, 1 hel sqn, 1 SP arty bn, 1 SAM coy, 1 cbt engr coy, 1 sigs coy, 1 NBC coy, 1 log bn)

  Light
  1 (1st) inf div (1 armd recce bn, 3 inf regt, 1 hel sqn, 1 SAM bn, 1 cbt engr bn, 1 sigs bn, 1 NBC bn, 1 log regt)
  1 (3rd) inf div (1 armd recce bn, 3 inf regt, 1 hel sqn, 1 fd arty bn, 1 SAM bn, 1 cbt engr bn, 1 sigs bn, 1 NBC bn, 1 log regt)
  1 (10th) inf div (1 recce sqn, 1 tk bn, 3 inf regt, 1 hel sqn, 1 fd arty regt, 1 SAM bn, 1 cbt engr bn, 1 sigs bn, 1 NBC bn, 1 log regt)
  1 (8th) inf div (1 recce sqn, 3 inf regt, 1 hel sqn, 1 SAM bn, 1 cbt engr bn, 1 sigs bn, 1 NBC bn, 1 log regt)
  1 (13th) inf bde (1 recce sqn, 1 tk coy, 3 inf regt, 1 hel sqn, 1 fd arty bn, 1 SAM coy, 1 cbt engr coy, 1 NBC coy, 1 sigs coy, 1 log bn)
  1 (14th) inf bde (1 recce sqn, 2 inf regt, 1 hel sqn, 1 SAM coy, 1 cbt engr coy, 1 NBC coy, 1 sigs coy, 1 log bn)
  1 (15th) inf bde (1 recce sqn, 1 inf regt, 1 avn sqn, 1 AD regt, 1 cbt engr coy, 1 NBC coy, 1 sigs coy, 1 log bn)
  Air Manoeuvre
  1 (1st) AB bde (3 AB bn, 1 fd arty bn, 1 cbt engr coy, 1 sigs coy, 1 log bn)
  1 (12th) air mob inf bde (1 armd recce bn, 3 inf regt, 1 avn sqn, 1 SAM coy, 1 cbt engr coy, 1 NBC coy, 1 sigs coy, 1 log bn)
  Amphibious
  1 amph bde (1 recce coy, 2 amph regt, 1 amph aslt bn, 1 log bn)
COMBAT SUPPORT
  1 (1st) arty bde (1 MRL regt (1 MRL bn); 1 SP arty regt (1 SP arty bn, 1 MRL bn); 3 AShM regt)
  1 (Northwestern Army) arty bde (1 fd arty regt (4 fd arty bn); 1 AShM regt)
  1 (Western Army) arty bde (1 fd arty regt (4 fd arty bn); 1 MRL bn; 1 AShM regt)
  1 (Eastern Army) arty bde (1 fd arty regt (2 fd arty bn)
  1 (Central Army) fd arty bn
  4 engr bde
  1 engr unit
  1 EW bn
  5 int bn
  1 MP bde
  1 sigs bde
COMBAT SERVICE SUPPORT
  5 log unit (bde)
  5 trg bde
TILTROTOR
  2 sqn with MV-22B *Osprey* (forming)
HELICOPTER
  1 hel bde (6 tpt hel sqn; 1 VIP tpt hel bn)
  5 hel gp (1 atk hel bn, 1 hel bn)
AIR DEFENCE
  2 SAM bde (2 SAM gp)
  2 SAM gp
EQUIPMENT BY TYPE
ARMOURED FIGHTING VEHICLES
  MBT 449: 106 Type-10; 85 Type-74; 258 Type-90

ASLT 156 Type-16 MCV
RECCE 110 Type-87
IFV 68 Type-89
APC 794
 APC (T) 226 Type-73
 APC (W) 568: 187 Type-82 (CP); 381 Type-96
AAV 52 AAV-7
AUV 8 *Bushmaster*
ENGINEERING & MAINTENANCE VEHICLES
 ARV 55: 5 Type-11; 20 Type-78; 30 Type-90
 VLB 22 Type-91
NBC VEHICLES 55: 34 Chemical Reconnaissance Vehicle; 21 NBC Reconnaissance Vehicle
ANTI-TANK/ANTI-INFRASTRUCTURE
 MSL
  SP 37 Type-96 MPMS
  MANPATS Type-79 *Jyu*-MAT; Type-87 *Chu*-MAT; Type-01 LMAT
 RCL • 84mm *Carl Gustaf*
ARTILLERY 1,584
 SP 152: **155mm** 143; 7 Type-19; 136 Type-99; **203mm** 9 M110A2
 TOWED **155mm** 220 FH-70
 MRL **227mm** 39 M270 MLRS
 MOR 1,173: **81mm** 656 L16 **120mm** 493 RT-61; SP **120mm** 24 Type-96
COASTAL DEFENCE • AShM 94: 32 Type-12; 62 Type-88
AIRCRAFT • TPT • Light 8 Beech 350 *King Air* (LR-2)
TILTROTOR • TPT 12 MV-22B *Osprey*
HELICOPTERS
 ATK 93: 44 AH-1S *Cobra*; 12 AH-64D *Apache*; 37 OH-1
 MRH 7 Bell 412EPX (UH-2)
 TPT 234: **Heavy** 50: 9 CH-47D *Chinook* (CH-47J); 41 CH-47JA *Chinook*; **Medium** 42: 3 H225 *Super Puma* MkII+ (VIP); 39 UH-60L *Black Hawk* (UH-60JA); **Light** 142: 112 Bell 205 (UH-1J); 30 Enstrom 480B (TH-480B)
AIR DEFENCE
 SAM 300+
  Medium-range 119: 41 Type-03 *Chu*-SAM; 12 Type-03 *Chu*-SAM Kai; 66 MIM-23B I-*Hawk*
  Short-range ε44 Type-11 *Tan*-SAM
  Point-defence 137+: 46 Type-81 *Tan*-SAM; 91 Type-93 *Kin*-SAM; Type-91 *Kei*-SAM
 GUNS • SP **35mm** 52 Type-87

Maritime Self-Defense Force 45,300

Surface units organised into 4 Escort Flotillas with a mix of 8 warships each. Bases at Yokosuka, Kure, Sasebo, Maizuru, Ominato. SSK organised into two flotillas with bases at Kure and Yokosuka

EQUIPMENT BY TYPE

SUBMARINES • SSK 24:
 10 *Oyashio* (of which 1 in trg role) with 6 single 533mm TT with UGM-84C *Harpoon* Block 1B AShM/Type-89 HWT
 12 *Soryu* (of which 9 fitted with AIP and 2 fitted with lithium-ion fuel battery) with 6 single 533mm TT with UGM-84C *Harpoon* Block 1B AShM/Type-89 HWT
 2 *Taigei* with (fitted with lithium-ion fuel battery) with 6 single 533mm TT with UGM-84C *Harpoon* Block 1B AShM/Type-89 HWT/Type-18 HWT
PRINCIPAL SURFACE COMBATANTS 52
AIRCRAFT CARRIERS • CVH 4:
 2 *Hyuga* with 2 8-cell Mk 41 VLS with ASROC/RIM-162B ESSM SAM, 2 triple 324mm HOS-303 ASTT with Mk 46/Type-97 LWT, 2 Mk 15 *Phalanx* Block 1B CIWS (normal ac capacity 3 SH-60 *Seahawk* ASW hel; plus additional ac embarkation up to 7 SH-60 *Seahawk* or 7 MCH-101)
 2 *Izumo* (being converted to CVS) with 2 11-cell Mk 15 SeaRAM lnchr with RIM-116 SAM, 2 Mk 15 *Phalanx* Block 1B CIWS (normal ac capacity 7 SH-60 *Seahawk* ASW hel; plus additional ac embarkation up to 5 SH-60 *Seahawk*/MCH-101 hel)
CRUISERS • CGHM 4:
 2 *Atago* with *Aegis* Baseline 9 C2, 2 quad lnchr with SSM-1B (Type-90) AShM, 12 8-cell Mk 41 VLS (8 fore, 4 aft) with SM-2 Block IIIA/B SAM/SM-3 Block IA/IB SAM/ASROC A/S msl, 2 triple 324mm HOS-302 ASTT with Mk 46 LWT, 2 Mk 15 *Phalanx* Block 1B CIWS, 1 127mm gun (capacity 1 SH-60 *Seahawk* ASW hel)
 2 *Maya* (*Atago* mod) with *Aegis* Baseline 9 C2, w quad lnchr with SSM-1B (Type-90) AShM/SSM-2 (Type-17) AShM, 12 8-cell Mk 41 VLS (8 fore, 4 aft) with SM-2 Block IIIA/B SAM/SM-3 Block IA/IB SAM/Type-07 A/S msl, 2 triple 324mm HOS-303 ASTT with Mk 46 LWT, 2 Mk 15 *Phalanx* Block 1B CIWS, 1 127mm gun (capacity 1 SH-60 *Seahawk* ASW hel)
DESTROYERS 34
 DDGHM 28:
 8 *Asagiri* with 2 quad lnchr with RGM-84C *Harpoon* Block 1B AShM, 1 octuple Mk 29 lnchr with RIM-7M *Sea Sparrow* SAM, 2 triple 324mm HOS-302 ASTT with Mk 46 LWT, 1 octuple Mk 112 lnchr with ASROC, 2 Mk 15 *Phalanx* CIWS, 1 76mm gun (capacity 1 SH-60 *Seahawk* ASW hel)
 4 *Akizuki* with 2 quad lnchr with SSM-1B (Type-90) AShM, 4 8-cell Mk 41 VLS with ASROC/RIM-162B ESSM SAM, 2 triple 324mm HOS-303 ASTT with Type-97 LWT, 2 Mk 15 *Phalanx* Block 1B CIWS, 1 127mm gun (capacity 1 SH-60 *Seahawk* ASW hel)
 2 *Asahi* (*Akizuki* mod) with 2 quad lnchr with SSM-1B (Type-90) AShM, 4 8-cell Mk 41 VLS with RIM-162B ESSM SAM/Type-07 A/S msl, 2 triple 324mm HOS-303 ASTT with Type-12 LWT, 2 Mk 15 *Phalanx* Block 1B CIWS, 1 127mm gun (capacity 1 SH-60 *Seahawk* ASW hel)
 9 *Murasame* with 2 quad lnchr with SSM-1B (Type-90) AShM, 1 16-cell Mk 48 mod 0 VLS with RIM-162C ESSM SAM, 2 triple 324mm HOS-302 ASTT with Mk 46 LWT, 2 8-cell Mk 41 VLS with ASROC, 2 Mk 15 *Phalanx* CIWS, 2 76mm gun

(capacity 1 SH-60 *Seahawk* ASW hel)
5 *Takanami* (improved *Murasame*) with 2 quad lnchr with SSM-1B (Type-90) AShM, 4 8-cell Mk 41 VLS with RIM-162B ESSM SAM/ASROC A/S msl, 2 triple 324mm HOS-302 ASTT with Mk 46 LWT, 2 Mk 15 *Phalanx* Block 1B CIWS, 1 127mm gun (capacity 1 SH-60 *Seahawk* ASW hel)

DDGM 6:
2 *Hatakaze* (trg role) with 2 quad lnchr with RGM-84C *Harpoon* Block 1B AShM, 1 Mk 13 GMLS with SM-1MR Block VI SAM, 2 triple 324mm HOS-301 ASTT with Mk 46 LWT, 1 octuple Mk 112 lnchr with ASROC, 2 Mk 15 *Phalanx* CIWS, 2 127mm gun, 1 hel landing platform
4 *Kongou* with *Aegis* Baseline 5 C2, 2 quad lnchr with RGM-84C *Harpoon* Block 1B AShM, 12 8-cell Mk 41 VLS (of which 2 only 5-cell and fitted with reload crane) with SM-2 Block IIIA/B SAM/SM-3 Block IA SAM/ASROC A/S msl, 2 triple 324mm HOS-302 ASTT with Mk 46 LWT, 2 Mk 15 *Phalanx* Block 1B CIWS, 1 127mm gun

FRIGATES 10
FFGHM 4 *Mogami* with 2 quad lnchr with SSM-2 (Type-17) AShM, 1 11-cell Mk 15 SeaRAM GMLS with RIM-116 RAM SAM, 2 triple 324mm HOS-303 ASTT with Mk 46 LWT, 1 127mm gun (capacity 1 SH-60 *Seahawk* hel) (to be fitted with Mk 41 VLS)
FFG 6 *Abukuma* with 2 quad lnchr with RGM-84C *Harpoon* Block 1B AShM, 2 triple 324mm HOS-301 ASTT with Mk 46 LWT, 1 octuple Mk 112 lnchr with ASROC A/S msl, 1 Mk 15 *Phalanx* CIWS, 1 76mm gun

PATROL AND COASTAL COMBATANTS 6
PBFG 6 *Hayabusa* with 4 SSM-1B (Type-90) AShM, 1 76mm gun

MINE WARFARE • MINE COUNTERMEASURES 21
MCCS 2:
1 *Uraga* with 1 76mm gun, 1 hel landing platform (for MCH-101 hel)
1 *Uraga* with 1 hel landing platform (for MCH-101)
MSC 16: 3 *Hirashima*; 10 *Sugashima*; 3 *Enoshima*
MSO 3 *Awaji*

AMPHIBIOUS
PRINCIPAL AMPHIBIOUS SHIPS • LHD 3 *Osumi* with 2 Mk 15 *Phalanx* CIWS (capacity for 2 CH-47 hel) (capacity 10 Type-90 MBT; 2 LCAC(L) ACV; 330 troops)
LANDING CRAFT 7
LCM 1 LCU-2001
LCAC 6 LCAC(L) (capacity either 1 MBT or 60 troops)

LOGISTICS AND SUPPORT 24
AGBH 1 *Shirase* (capacity 2 AW101 *Merlin* hel)
AGEH 1 *Asuka* (wpn trials) with 1 8-cell Mk 41 VLS (capacity 1 SH-60 *Seahawk* hel)
AGOS 3 *Hibiki* with 1 hel landing platform
AGS 3: 1 *Futami*; 1 *Nichinan*; 1 *Shonan*
AOE 5: 2 *Mashu* (capacity 1 med hel); 3 *Towada* with 1 hel landing platform

ARC 1 *Muroto*
ASR 2: 1 *Chihaya* with 1 hel landing platform; 1 Chiyoda with 1 hel landing platform
ATF 5 *Hiuchi*
AX 3:
1 *Kashima* with 2 triple 324mm HOS-301 ASTT, 1 76mm gun, 1 hel landing platform
1 *Kurobe* with 1 76mm gun (trg spt ship)
1 *Tenryu* (trg spt ship); with 1 76mm gun (capacity: 1 med hel)

UNINHABITED MARITIME PLATFORMS • USV
MW • Medium *Mogami* USV

UNINHABITED MARITIME SYSTEMS • UUV
DATA REMUS 100
MW OZZ-5; *SeaFox*

Naval Aviation ε9,800
7 Air Groups
FORCES BY ROLE
ANTI SUBMARINE/SURFACE WARFARE
3 sqn with SH-60B (SH-60J)/SH-60K *Seahawk*
2 sqn with SH-60K *Seahawk*
MARITIME PATROL
2 sqn with P-1
2 sqn with P-3C *Orion*
ELECTRONIC WARFARE
1 sqn with EP-3C *Orion*; Learjet 36A
MINE COUNTERMEASURES
1 sqn with MCH-101
SEARCH & RESCUE
1 sqn with *Shin Meiwa* US-2
1 flt with UH-60J *Black Hawk*
TRANSPORT
1 sqn with Beech 90 *King Air* (LC-90); KC-130R *Hercules*
TRAINING
1 sqn with Beech 90 *King Air* (TC-90)
1 sqn with P-3C *Orion*
1 sqn with T-5J
1 hel sqn with H135 (TH-135); SH-60K *Seahawk*
EQUIPMENT BY TYPE
AIRCRAFT 69 combat capable
ASW 69: 34 P-1; 35 P-3C *Orion*
ELINT 5 EP-3C *Orion*
ISR 4 Learjet 36A
SAR 7 *Shin Meiwa* US-2
TPT 24: **Medium** 6 C-130R *Hercules*; **Light** 18: 5 Beech 90 *King Air* (LC-90); 13 Beech 90 *King Air* (TC-90) (trg)
TRG 30 T-5J
HELICOPTERS
ASW 83: 10 SH-60B *Seahawk* (SH-60J); 73 SH-60K *Seahawk*
MCM 10 MCH-101
SAR 3 UH-60J *Black Hawk*

TPT 18: **Medium** 3 AW101 *Merlin* (CH-101); **Light** 15 H135 (TH-135) (trg)

AIR-LAUNCHED MISSILES
AShM ASM-1C (Type-90)

Air Self-Defense Force 47,000

7 cbt wg

FORCES BY ROLE

FIGHTER
7 sqn with F-15J *Eagle*
3 sqn with Mitsubishi F-2
2 sqn with F-35A *Lightning* II

ELECTRONIC WARFARE
1 sqn with Kawasaki EC-1; YS-11EA

ELINT
1 sqn with RC-2; YS-11EB

AIRBORNE EARLY WARNING & CONTROL
2 sqn with E-2C/D *Hawkeye*
1 sqn with E-767

SEARCH & RESCUE
1 wg with U-125A *Peace Krypton*; UH-60J *Black Hawk*

TANKER
1 sqn with KC-46A *Pegasus* (forming)
1 sqn with KC-767J

TRANSPORT
1 (VIP) sqn with B-777-300ER
1 sqn with C-1; C-2; Gulfstream IV (U-4)
1 sqn with C-2
1 sqn with C-130H *Hercules*; KC-130H *Hercules*
Some (liaison) sqn with Gulfstream IV (U-4); T-4*

TRAINING
1 (aggressor) sqn with F-15J *Eagle*

TEST
1 wg with F-15J *Eagle*; T-4*

TRANSPORT HELICOPTER
4 flt with CH-47J *Chinook*

ISR UAV
1 sqn (forming) with RQ-4B *Global Hawk*

EQUIPMENT BY TYPE

AIRCRAFT 525 combat capable
FTR 200: 156 F-15J *Eagle*; 44 F-15DJ *Eagle*
FGA 128: 64 F-2A; 27 F-2B; 37 F-35A *Lightning* II
EW 3: 1 Kawasaki EC-1; 2 YS-11EA
SIGINT 4: 1 RC-2; 3 YS-11EB
AEW&C 17: 10 E-2C *Hawkeye*; 3 E-2D *Hawkeye*; 4 E-767
SAR 26 U-125A *Peace Krypton*
TKR/TPT 9: 2 KC-46A *Pegasus*; 3 KC-130H *Hercules*; 4 KC-767J
TPT 55: **Medium** 35: 13 C-130H *Hercules*; 6 C-1; 16 C-2; **PAX** 20: 2 B-777-300ER (VIP); 13 Beech T-400; 5 Gulfstream IV (U-4)
TRG 246: 197 T-4*; 49 T-7

HELICOPTERS
SAR 37 UH-60J *Black Hawk*
TPT • **Heavy** 15 CH-47J *Chinook*

UNINHABITED AERIAL VEHICLES 3
ISR • **Heavy** 3 RQ-4B *Global Hawk*

AIR-LAUNCHED MISSILES
AAM • **IR** AAM-3 (Type-90); **IIR** AAM-5 (Type-04); **SARH** AIM-7 *Sparrow*; **ARH** AAM-4 (Type-99); AIM-120C5/C7 AMRAAM
AShM ASM-1 (Type-80); ASM-2 (Type-93)

BOMBS
Laser & INS/SAT-guided GBU-54 Laser JDAM
INS/SAT-guided GBU-38 JDAM

Air Defence

Ac control and warning. 4 wg; 28 radar sites

FORCES BY ROLE

AIR DEFENCE
4 SAM gp (total: 24 SAM bty with M902 *Patriot* PAC-3)
1 AD gp with Type-81 *Tan-SAM*

EQUIPMENT BY TYPE

AIR DEFENCE
SAM 146+
Long-range 120 M902 *Patriot* PAC-3
Short-range ε26 Air Base Defense SAM
Point-defence Type-81 *Tan-SAM*

Gendarmerie & Paramilitary 14,550

Coast Guard 14,700

Ministry of Land, Transport, Infrastructure and Tourism (no cbt role)

EQUIPMENT BY TYPE

PATROL AND COASTAL COMBATANTS 378
PSOH 19: 2 *Mizuho* (capacity 2 hels); 1 *Mizuho* II (capacity 2 hels); 5 *Shikishima* (capacity 2 hels); 1 *Shunko* (capacity 2 hels); 1 *Soya* (capacity 1 hel) (icebreaking capability); 9 *Tsugaru* (*Soya* mod) (capacity 1 hel)
PSO 48: 9 *Hateruma* with 1 hel landing platform; 3 *Hida* with 1 hel landing platform; 6 *Iwami*, 1 *Izu* with 1 hel landing platform; 1 *Kojima* (trg) with 1 hel landing platform; 1 *Miura* with 1 hel landing platform (trg role); 2 *Miyako* with 1 hel landing platform; 5 *Ojika* with 1 hel landing platform; 20 *Taketomi* with 1 hel landing platform
PCO 13: 3 *Aso*; 9 *Katori*; 1 *Teshio*
PCC 24: 4 *Amami*; 20 *Tokara*
PBF 49: 24 *Hayagumo*; 2 *Mihashi*; 15 *Raizan*; 2 *Takatsuki*; 6 *Tsuruugi*
PB 55: 4 *Asogiri*; 4 *Hamagumo*; 11 *Hayanami*; 15 *Katonami*; 1 *Matsunami*; 10 *Shimoji*; 10 *Yodo*
PBI 170: 2 *Hakubai*; 1 *Hayagiku*; 167 *Himegiku*

LOGISTICS AND SUPPORT 18
ABU 1 *Teshio*

AGS 14: 6 *Hamashio*; 1 *Jinbei*; 2 *Meiyo*; 2 *Peiyo*; 1 *Shoyo*; 1 *Takuyo*; 1 *Tenyo*
AX 3
UNINHABITED MARITIME SYSTEMS • UUV
DATA *Naminow*
AIRCRAFT
MP 6 *Falcon* 2000MSA
SAR 4 Saab 340B
TPT 26: **Light** 25: 5 Cessna 172; 10 Beech 350 *King Air* (LR-2); 9 DHC-8-300 (MP); **PAX** 2 Gulfstream V (MP)
HELICOPTERS
MRH 4 Bell 412 *Twin Huey*
SAR 12 S-76D
TPT 39: **Medium** 13: 2 AS332 *Super Puma*; 11 H225 *Super Puma*; **Light** 26: 19 AW139; 4 Bell 505 *Jet Ranger X*; 3 S-76C
UNINHABITED AERIAL VEHICLES 1
CISR • **Heavy** 1 MQ-9B *Sea Guardian* (unarmed) (leased)

DEPLOYMENT

ARABIAN SEA & GULF OF ADEN: 200; 1 DDGHM
DJIBOUTI: 180; 2 P-3C *Orion*
SOUTH SUDAN: UN • UNMISS 4

FOREIGN FORCES

United States
US Indo-Pacific Command: 55,600
Army 2,600; 1 corps HQ (fwd); 1 SF gp; 1 avn bn; 1 SAM bn with M903 *Patriot* PAC MSE
Navy 20,000; 1 CVN; 3 CGHM; 6 DDGHM; 3 DDGM; 1 LCC; 4 MCO; 1 LHA; 2 LPD; 1 LSD; 3 FGA sqn with 10 F/A-18E *Super Hornet*; 1 FGA sqn with 10 F/A-18F *Super Hornet*; 2 ASW sqn with 5 P-8A *Poseidon*; 1 ELINT flt with 2 EP-3E *Aries* II; 2 EW sqn with 5 EA-18G *Growler*; 1 AEW&C sqn with 5 E-2D *Hawkeye*; 2 ASW hel sqn with 12 MH-60R *Seahawk*; 1 tpt hel sqn with MH-60S *Knight Hawk*; 1 base at Sasebo; 1 base at Yokosuka
USAF: 13,000; 1 HQ (5th Air Force) at Okinawa–Kadena AB; 1 ftr wg at Misawa AB (2 ftr sqn with 22 F-16C/D *Fighting Falcon*); 1 ftr wg at Okinawa–Kadena AB (2 ftr sqn with 10 F-15C/D *Eagle*; 1 ftr sqn with 12 F-15C *Eagle*; 2 FGA sqn with 14 F-15E *Strike Eagle*; 1 FGA sqn with 12 F-35A *Lightning* II; 1 tkr sqn with 15 KC-135R *Stratotanker*; 1 AEW sqn with 2 E-3G *Sentry*; 1 CSAR sqn with 10 HH-60G *Pave Hawk*; 1 CISR UAV sqn with 4 MQ-9A *Reaper*); 1 tpt wg at Yokota AB with 10 C-130J-30 *Hercules*; 3 Beech 1900C (C-12J); 1 spec ops gp at Okinawa–Kadena AB with (1 sqn with 5 MC-130J *Commando* II; 1 sqn with 5 CV-22B *Osprey*); 1 ISR sqn with RC-135 *Rivet Joint*; 1 ISR UAV flt with 5 RQ-4A *Global Hawk*
USMC 20,000; 1 mne div; 1 mne regt HQ; 1 arty regt HQ; 1 recce bn; 1 mne bn; 1 amph aslt bn; 1 arty bn; 1 FGA sqn at Iwakuni with 12 F/A-18C/D *Hornet*; 2 FGA sqn at Iwakuni with 12 F-35B *Lightning* II; 1 tkr sqn at Iwakuni with 15 KC-130J *Hercules*; 2 tpt sqn at Futenma with 12 MV-22B *Osprey*
US Strategic Command: 1 AN/TPY-2 X-band radar at Shariki; 1 AN/TPY-2 X-band radar at Kyogamisaki

Korea, Democratic People's Republic of DPRK

North Korean Won KPW		2022	2023	2024
GDP	USD			
per capita	USD			
Def exp	KPW			
	USD			
USD1=KPW				

Definitive economic data not available

Population	26,194,769					
Age	0–14	15–19	20–24	25–29	30–64	65 plus
Male	10.2%	3.4%	3.6%	3.8%	23.6%	4.1%
Female	9.7%	3.3%	3.6%	3.8%	23.9%	6.9%

Capabilities

North Korea continues to signal its interest in building out its nuclear weapons capacity. The country showcased a new tactical warhead design in May 2023 and conducted several claimed simulated nuclear strike drills. The international community has become increasingly concerned that the country may renew nuclear testing. North Korea's continued investment in asymmetric capabilities, particularly the development of nuclear weapons and ballistic-missile delivery systems, reflects an awareness of the qualitative inferiority of its conventional forces. In April 2023, North Korea conducted its first successful test of a solid-fuel ICBM. Pyongyang's ambitions to further diversify shorter-range delivery systems continue. These include quasi-ballistic missiles, claimed hypersonic glide vehicles and apparent land-attack cruise missiles. North Korea is also exploring new, potentially less vulnerable basing options, such as a rail-based system and additional submarine-launched designs. In September, a new ballistic missile submarine was launched that may have cruise missile capability; it is based on a converted and obsolete conventional attack submarine. North Korea remains diplomatically isolated. While foreign defence cooperation is restricted by international pressure and sanctions, Pyongyang has found ways to develop military ties, including with Moscow. Western countries believe North Korea has delivered large quantities of artillery rounds to Moscow to aid Russia in its war on Ukraine. Official conscription for both men and women is often extended, sometimes indefinitely. Training is focused on fighting a short, intensive war on the peninsula, but the armed forces' overall effectiveness in a modern conflict against technologically superior opposition is unclear. The forces regularly conduct exercises, but those publicised are staged and not necessarily representative of wider operational capability. North Korea's conventional forces remain reliant on increasingly obsolete equipment, with older Soviet-era and Chinese-origin equipment supplemented by a growing number of indigenous designs and upgrades. The precise capability of the locally-made equipment is unclear. Pyongyang has maintenance, repair and overhaul capacity and the ability to manufacture light arms, armoured vehicles, artillery and missile systems.

ACTIVE 1,280,000 (Army 1,100,000 Navy 60,000 Air 110,000 Strategic Forces 10,000) Gendarmerie & Paramilitary 189,000

Conscript liability Army 5–12 years, Navy 5–10 years, Air Force 3–4 years, followed by compulsory part-time service to age 40. Thereafter service in the Worker/Peasant Red Guard to age 60

RESERVE ε600,000 (Armed Forces ε600,000), Gendarmerie & Paramilitary 5,700,000

Reservists are assigned to units (see also Paramilitary)

ORGANISATIONS BY SERVICE

Strategic Forces ε10,000

North Korea describes its ballistic missile force as nuclear capable, although there is no conclusive evidence to verify the successful integration of a warhead with any of these systems

EQUIPMENT BY TYPE (ε)
SURFACE-TO-SURFACE MISSILE LAUNCHERS
  ICBM 17+: 6+ *Hwasong*-14/-15/-15 mod 1/-18 (all in test); 11+ *Hwasong*-17 mod 1 (in test); (Earlier *Hwasong*-13/-13 mod designs untested and presumed cancelled)
  IRBM 10+ *Hwasong*-12/-12 mod 1 (in test)
  MRBM 17+: ε10 *Hwasong*-7 (*Nodong* mod 1/mod 2); 7+ *Pukgusong*-2 (in test); some *Scud*-ER
  SBRM 69+: 30+ *Hwasong*-5/-6 (RS-SS-1C/D *Scud*-B/C); 1+ *Hwasong*-8/-8 mod 1 (in test); 17+ *Hwasong*-11A (KN-23) (road & rail mobile variants); 9+ *Hwasong*-11B (KN-24) (in test); 6+ *Hwasong*-11C (KN-23 mod 1) (in test); some *Hwasong*-11S (KN-23 mod 2) (in test); 6+ *Scud* (mod) (status uncertain)
  GLCM some *Hwasal*-1/-2 (in test)

Army ε1,100,000
FORCES BY ROLE
COMMAND
  10 inf corps HQ
  1 (Capital Defence) corps HQ
MANOEUVRE
  Armoured
  1 armd div
  15 armd bde
  Mechanised
  6 mech div
  Light
  27 inf div
  14 inf bde
COMBAT SUPPORT
  1 arty div
  21 arty bde
  9 MRL bde
  5–8 engr river crossing/amphibious regt
  1 engr river crossing bde

Special Purpose Forces Command 88,000
FORCES BY ROLE
SPECIAL FORCES
  8 (Reconnaissance General Bureau) SF bn
MANOEUVRE
  Reconnaissance
  17 recce bn
  Light
  9 lt inf bde
  6 sniper bde
  Air Manoeuvre
  3 AB bde
  1 AB bn
  2 sniper bde
  Amphibious
  2 sniper bde

Reserves 600,000
FORCES BY ROLE
MANOEUVRE
  Light
  40 inf div
  18 inf bde

EQUIPMENT BY TYPE (ε)
ARMOURED FIGHTING VEHICLES
The Korean People's Army displayed a number of new armoured-vehicle designs at a parade in 2020, but it is unclear if any of them have entered operational service
  MBT 3,500+ T-34/T-54/T-55/T-62/Type-59/*Chonma/Pokpoong/Songun*
  LT TK 560+: 560 PT-76; M-1985
  IFV 32 BTR-80A
  APC 2,500+
    APC (T) BTR-50; Type-531 (Type-63); VTT-323
    APC (W) 2,500 BTR-40/BTR-60/M-1992/1/BTR-152/M-2010 (6×6)/M-2010 (8×8)
ANTI-TANK/ANTI-INFRASTRUCTURE
  MSL
    SP 9K11 *Malyutka* (RS-AT-3 *Sagger*); M-2010 ATGM
    MANPATS 2K15 *Shmel* (RS-AT-1 *Snapper*); 9K111 *Fagot* (RS-AT-4 *Spigot*); 9K111-1 *Konkurs* (RS-AT-5 *Spandrel*)
  RCL 82mm 1,700 B-10
ARTILLERY 21,600+
  SP/TOWED 8,600:
  SP 122mm M-1977; M-1981; M-1985; M-1991; **130mm** M-1975; M-1981; M-1991; **152mm** M-1974; M-1977; M-2018; **170mm** M-1978; M-1989
  TOWED 122mm D-30; D-74; M-1931/37; **130mm** M-46; **152mm** M-1937; M-1938; M-1943
  GUN/MOR 120mm (reported)
  MRL 5,500: **107mm** Type-63; VTT-323 107mm; **122mm**

BM-11; M-1977 (BM-21); M-1985; M-1992; M-1993; VTT-323 122mm; **200mm** BMD-20; **240mm** BM-24; M-1985; M-1989; M-1991; **300mm** some M-2015 (KN-SS-X-09) (in test); **600mm** some M-2019 (KN-25) (in test)
MOR 7,500: **82mm** M-37; **120mm** M-43; **160mm** M-43

SURFACE-TO-SURFACE MISSILE LAUNCHERS
SBRM 24+: 24 FROG-3/-5/-7; some *Hwasong*-11D (in test); some *Toksa* (RS-SS-21B *Scarab* mod)

AIR DEFENCE
SAM
Point-defence 9K35 *Strela*-10 (RS-SA-13 *Gopher*); 9K310 *Igla*-1 (RS-SA-16 *Gimlet*); 9K32 *Strela*-2 (RS-SA-7 *Grail*)‡
GUNS 11,000+
SP **14.5mm** M-1984; **23mm** M-1992; **37mm** M-1992; **57mm** M-1985
TOWED 11,000: **14.5mm** ZPU-1/ZPU-2/ZPU-4; **23mm** ZU-23; **37mm** M-1939; **57mm** S-60; **85mm** M-1939 *KS-12*; **100mm** KS-19

Navy ε60,000
EQUIPMENT BY TYPE
SUBMARINES 71
SSB 1 *8.24 Yongung* (*Gorae* (*Sinpo*-B)) (SLBM trials) with 1 *Pukguksong*-1 SLBM (status unclear)/KN-23 Mod 2 SLBM (in test)
SSK ε20 Type-033 (*Romeo*) with 8 single 533mm TT with SAET-60 HWT
SSC ε40 (some *Sang-O* some with 2 single 533mm TT with 53–65E HWT; some *Sang-O* II with 4 single 533mm TT with 53–65E HWT)
SSW ε10† (some *Yugo* some with 2 single 406mm TT; some *Yeono* some with 2 single 533mm TT)
PRINCIPAL SURFACE COMBATANTS 2
FRIGATES • FFG 2:
1 *Najin* with 2 single lnchr with P-20 (RS-SS-N-2A *Styx*) AShM, 2 RBU 1200 *Uragan* A/S mor, 2 100mm gun, 2 twin 57mm gun
1 *Najin* with 2 twin lnchr with *Kumsong*-3 (KN-SS-N-2 *Stormpetrel*) AShM, 2 RBU 1200 *Uragan* A/S mor, 2 100mm gun, 2 twin 57mm gun (operational status unclear)
PATROL AND COASTAL COMBATANTS 374+
CORVETTES 7
FSGM 2 *Amnok* with 2 quad lnchr with *Hwasal*-2 LACM (operational status unclear, armament may vary between vessels), 1 sextuple GMLS with 9K310 *Igla*-1 (RS-SA-16 *Gimlet*), 4 RBU 1200 A/S mor, 2 AK630 CIWS, 1 100mm gun
FS 5: 4 *Sariwon* with 2 twin 57mm gun; 1 *Tral* with 1 85mm gun
(Two *Tuman*-class corvettes constructed since early 2010s; operational status unknown)
PCG 10 *Soju* (FSU Project 205 mod (*Osa*)) with 4 single lnchr with P-20 (RS-SS-N-2A *Styx*) AShM
PCC 18:

6 Type-037 (*Hainan*) with 4 RBU 1200 A/S mor, 2 twin 57mm gun
7 *Taechong* I with 2 RBU 1200 *Uragan* A/S mor, 1 85mm gun, 1 twin 57mm gun
5 *Taechong* II with 2 RBU 1200 *Uragan* A/S mor, 1 100mm gun, 1 twin 57mm gun
PBFG 31+:
6 *Komar* with 2 single lnchr with P-20 (RS-SS-N-2A *Styx*) AShM
8 Project 205 (*Osa* I) with 4 single lnchr with P-20 (RS-SS-N-2A *Styx*) AShM, 2 twin AK230 CIWS
6 *Sohung* (*Komar* mod) with 2 single lnchr with P-20 (RS-SS-N-2A *Styx*) AShM
1+ *Nongo* with 2 single lnchr with P-15 *Termit* (RS-SS-N-2 *Styx*) AShM (operational status unknown)
6+ *Nongo* with 2 twin lnchr with *Kumsong*-3 (KN-SS-N-2 *Stormpetrel*) AShM (operational status unknown)
4 Type-021 (*Huangfeng*) with 4 single lnchr with P-15 *Termit* (RS-SS-N-2 *Styx*) AShM, 2 twin AK230 CIWS
PBF 222: approx. 50 *Chong-Jin* with 1 85mm gun; 142 *Ku Song/Sin Hung/Sin Hung* (mod); approx. 30 *Sinpo*
PB 86: approx. 50 *Chaho*; 6 *Chong-Ju* with 2 RBU 1200 *Uragan* A/S mor, 1 85mm gun; 12 Type-062 (*Shanghai* II); 18 SO-1 with 4 RBU 1200 *Uragan* A/S mor, 2 twin 57mm gun

MINE WARFARE • MINE COUNTERMEASURES 20
MSC 20: 15 *Yukto* I; 5 *Yukto* II
AMPHIBIOUS
LANDING SHIPS • LSM 10 *Hantae* (capacity 3 tanks; 350 troops)
LANDING CRAFT 255
LCM 25
LCPL approx. 95 *Nampo* (capacity 35 troops)
UCAC 135 *Kongbang* (capacity 50 troops)
LOGISTICS AND SUPPORT 23:
AGI 14 (converted fishing vessels)
AS 8 (converted cargo ships)
ASR 1 *Kowan*
UNINHABITED MARITIME PLATFORMS • UUV
ATK • **Extra-Large** *Haeil*; *Haeil*-1/-2

Coastal Defence
FORCES BY ROLE
COASTAL DEFENCE
2 AShM regt with HY-1/*Kumsong*-3 (6 sites, some mobile launchers)
EQUIPMENT BY TYPE
COASTAL DEFENCE
ARTY **130mm** M-1992; SM-4-1
AShM HY-1; *Kumsong*-3
ARTILLERY • TOWED 122mm M-1931/37; **152mm** M-1937

Air Force 110,000
4 air divs. 1st, 2nd and 3rd Air Divs (cbt) responsible

for N, E and S air-defence sectors respectively; 8th Air Div (trg) responsible for NE sector. The AF controls the national airline

FORCES BY ROLE

BOMBER

3 lt regt with H-5; Il-28 *Beagle*

FIGHTER

1 regt with MiG-15 *Fagot*
6 regt with J-5; MiG-17 *Fresco*
4 regt with J-6; MiG-19 *Farmer*
5 regt with J-7; MiG-21F-13/PFM *Fishbed*
1 regt with MiG-21bis *Fishbed*
1 regt with MiG-23ML/P *Flogger*
1 regt with MiG-29A/S/UB *Fulcrum*

GROUND ATTACK

1 regt with Su-25K/UBK *Frogfoot*

TRANSPORT

Some regt with An-2 *Colt*/Y-5 (to infiltrate 2 air-force sniper brigades deep into ROK rear areas); Il-62M *Classic*

TRAINING

Some regt with CJ-6; FT-2; MiG-21U/UM

TRANSPORT HELICOPTER

Some regt with Hughes 500D/E; Mi-8 *Hip*; Mi-17 *Hip* H; Mil-26 *Halo*; PZL Mi-2 *Hoplite*; Mi-4 *Hound*; Z-5

AIR DEFENCE

19 bde with S-125M1 *Pechora*-M1 (RS-SA-3 *Goa*); S-75 *Dvina* (RS-SA-2 *Guideline*); S-200 *Angara* (RS-SA-5 *Gammon*); 9K36 *Strela*-3 (RS-SA-14 *Gremlin*); 9K310 *Igla*-1 (RS-SA-16 *Gimlet*); 9K32 *Strela*-2 (RS-SA-7 *Grail*)‡

EQUIPMENT BY TYPE

AIRCRAFT 545 combat capable
BBR 80 Il-28 *Beagle*/H-5‡ (includes some Il-28 for ISR)
FTR 401+: MiG-15 *Fagot*‡; 107 MiG-17 *Fresco*/J-5‡; 100 MiG-19 *Farmer*/J-6 (incl JJ-6 trg ac); 120 MiG-21F-13 *Fishbed*/J-7; MiG-21PFM *Fishbed*; 46 MiG-23ML *Flogger*; 10 MiG-23P *Flogger*; 18+ MiG-29A/S/UB *Fulcrum*
FGA 30 MiG-21bis *Fishbed* (18 Su-7 *Fitter* in store)
ATK 34 Su-25K/UBK *Frogfoot*
TPT 205: **Heavy** 3 Il-76 (operated by state airline); **Light** ε200 An-2 *Colt*/Y-5; **PAX** 2 Il-62M *Classic* (VIP)
TRG 215+: 180 CJ-6; 35 FT-2; some MiG-21U/UM

HELICOPTERS

MRH 80 Hughes 500D/E (some armed)
TPT 206: **Heavy** 4 Mi-26 *Halo*; **Medium** 63: 15 Mi-8 *Hip*/Mi-17 *Hip* H; 48 Mi-4 *Hound*/Z-5; **Light** 139 PZL Mi-2 *Hoplite*

UNINHABITED AERIAL VEHICLES

ISR • Medium some (unidentified indigenous type); **Light** *Pchela*-1 (*Shmel*) (reported)

AIR DEFENCE • SAM 209+
Long-range 10 S-200 *Angara*† (RS-SA-5 *Gammon*)
Medium-range 179+: some *Pongae*-5 (KN-SA-X-01) (status unknown); 179+ S-75 *Dvina* (RS-SA-2 *Guideline*)
Short-range ε20 S-125M1 *Pechora*-M1† (RS-SA-3 *Goa*)
Point-defence 9K32 *Strela*-2 (RS-SA-7 *Grail*)‡; 9K36 *Strela*-3 (RS SA-14 *Gremlin*); 9K310 *Igla*-1 (RS-SA-16 *Gimlet*)

AIR-LAUNCHED MISSILES

AAM • IR R-3 (RS-AA-2 *Atoll*)‡; R-60 (RS-AA-8 *Aphid*); R-73 (RS-AA-11A *Archer*); PL-5; PL-7; **SARH** R-23/24 (RS-AA-7 *Apex*); R-27R/ER (RS-AA-10 A/C *Alamo*)
ASM Kh-23 (RS-AS-7 *Kerry*)‡; Kh-25 (RS-AS-10 *Karen*); Kh-29L (RS-AS-14A *Kedge*)

Gendarmerie & Paramilitary 189,000 active

Security Troops 189,000 (incl border guards, public-safety personnel)

Ministry of Public Security

Worker/Peasant Red Guard ε5,700,000 reservists

Org on a province/town/village basis; comd structure is bde–bn–coy–pl; small arms with some mor and AD guns (but many units unarmed)

Korea, Republic of ROK

South Korean Won KRW		2022	2023	2024
GDP	KRW	2,162trn	2,227trn	2,339trn
	USD	1.67trn	1.71trn	1.78trn
per capita	USD	32,418	33,147	34,653
Growth	%	2.6	1.4	2.2
Inflation	%	5.1	3.4	2.3
Def bdgt	KRW	54.6trn	57.1trn	59.6trn
	USD	42.3bn	43.8bn	45.5bn
USD1=KRW		1,291.45	1,303.01	1,310.58

Real-terms defence budget trend (USDbn, constant 2015)

45.3
27.0
2008 — 2016 — 2023

Population	51,966,948					
Age	0–14	15–19	20–24	25–29	30–64	65 plus
Male	5.9%	2.3%	2.9%	3.7%	27.2%	8.1%
Female	5.6%	2.1%	2.7%	3.2%	25.9%	10.3%

Capabilities

South Korea's forces are among the best equipped and trained in the region. The country's defence policy is focused on the threat from North Korea, and Seoul continues to prioritise developing new capabilities to respond to Pyongyang's nuclear and conventional threat. The Defense Innovation 4.0 programme came into force in March 2023, replacing the 2018 Defense Reform 2.0 project, which saw delays in the introduction into service of advanced weapon systems to supplement decreasing personnel. As well as redesigning overall defence policy to focus on space, advanced technology and cyber security, South Korea pledges to develop a new integrated concept known as 'Kill Web' to deter DPRK threats even at left-of-launch to better support its three-axis defence strategy comprising 'Kill Chain', 'Korea Air and Missile Defense' and 'Korea Massive Punishment and Retaliation' components. These were abandoned in 2019 but revived by the government elected in 2022. The 2022 defence white paper, released in February 2023, again identified the North Korean regime as Seoul's main adversary, language absent from the 2020 document. The long-established alliance with the US is a central element of defence strategy. The planned transfer of wartime operational control of forces to Seoul is now 'conditions based' with no firm date set. A large number of US military personnel and equipment are stationed in South Korea, along with THAAD missile-defence systems. In 2022, South Korea and the US resumed large-scale joint military exercises that were scaled back under the previous administration. A space-operations centre was inaugurated in 2021 and South Korea plans to deploy a constellation of military surveillance satellites. South Korea has demonstrated the capacity to support small international deployments, including contributions to UN missions and counter-piracy operations in the Arabian Sea. The equipment inventory increasingly comprises modern systems. South Korea has developed a substantial domestic defence industry which supply a large proportion of equipment requirements, although some equipment – notably the F-35 combat aircraft – is still procured from the US. Local defence companies are having growing export success globally, though industry will have to carefully balance new export contracts against existing local orders.

ACTIVE 500,000 (Army 365,000 Navy 70,000 Air 65,000) Gendarmerie & Paramilitary 13,500

Conscript liability Army and Marines 18 months, Navy 20 months, Air Force 21 months

RESERVE 3,100,000

Reserve obligation of three days per year. First Combat Forces (Mobilisation Reserve Forces) or Regional Combat Forces (Homeland Defence Forces) to age 33

Reserve Paramilitary 3,000,000

Being reorganised

ORGANISATIONS BY SERVICE

Space
EQUIPMENT BY TYPE
SATELLITES • COMMUNICATIONS 2 *Anasis*

Army 365,000
FORCES BY ROLE
COMMAND
　6 corps HQ
　1 (Capital Defence) comd HQ
SPECIAL FORCES
　1 (Special Warfare) SF comd (1 SF gp; 6 spec ops bde)
　5 cdo regt
　1 indep cdo bn
MANOEUVRE
　Armoured
　7 armd bde
　1 (Capital) armd inf div (1 armd cav bn, 2 armd bde, 1 armd inf bde, 1 SP arty bde, 1 engr bn)
　1 (8th) armd inf div (1 armd cav bn, 1 armd bde, 2 armd inf bde, 1 SP arty bde, 1 engr bn)
　1 (11th) armd inf div (1 armd cav bn, 3 armd inf bde, 1 SP arty bde, 1 engr bn)
　Light
　13 inf div (1 recce bn, 1 tk bn, 3 inf bde, 1 arty bde, 1 engr bn)
　2 indep inf bde
　1 mtn inf bde
　Air Manoeuvre
　1 air mob div (2 cdo bde)
　1 air aslt bde
　Other
　1 sy bde
　4 sy regt
　1 sy gp
SURFACE-TO-SURFACE MISSILE
　3 SSM bn
COMBAT SUPPORT
　6 arty bde
　1 MRL bde (3 MRL bn; 2 SSM bn)
　6 engr bde
　5 engr gp
　1 CBRN defence bde
　8 sigs bde
COMBAT SERVICE SUPPORT
　4 log spt comd
HELICOPTER
　1 (army avn) comd
AIR DEFENCE
　1 ADA bde
　5 ADA bn

Reserves
FORCES BY ROLE
COMMAND
　1 army HQ
MANOEUVRE
　Light
　24 inf div
EQUIPMENT BY TYPE
ARMOURED FIGHTING VEHICLES
　MBT 2,115: 1,000 K1/K1E1; 450 K1A1/K1A2; ε225 K2; ε400 M48A5; 40 T-80U
　IFV 540: ε500 K21; 40 BMP-3
　APC 2,800
　　APC (T) 2,260: 1,700 KIFV; 420 M113; 140 M577 (CP)
　　APC (W) 530; 20 BTR-80; ε60 K806; ε450 K808
　PPV 10 *MaxxPro*
ENGINEERING & MAINTENANCE VEHICLES
　AEV 207 M9; K600

ARV 238+: 200 K1; K21 ARV; K288A1; M47; 38 M88A1
VLB 56 K1

ANTI-TANK/ANTI-INFRASTRUCTURE
MSL
SP Hyeongung
MANPATS 9K115 Metis (RS-AT-7 Saxhorn); Hyeongung; TOW-2A
RCL 75mm; 90mm M67; 106mm M40A2
GUNS 58
SP 90mm 50 M36
TOWED 76mm 8 M18 Hellcat (AT gun)

ARTILLERY 12,128+
SP 2,330: 105mm ε50 K105A1; 155mm 2,280: ε1,240 K9/K9A1 Thunder; 1,040 M109A2 (K55/K55A1)
TOWED 3,500+: 105mm 1,700 M101/KH-178; 155mm 1,800+ KH-179/M114
MRL 298: 130mm ε40 K136 Kooryong; 227mm 58: 48 M270 MLRS; 10 M270A1 MLRS; 239mm ε200 K239 Cheonmu
MOR 6,000: 81mm KM29 (M29); 107mm M30; 120mm Hanwha 120mm mortar

SURFACE-TO-SURFACE MISSILE LAUNCHERS
SRBM • Conventional 30+: 30 Hyonmu IIA/IIB; MGM-140A/B ATACMS (launched from M270/M270A1 MLRS)
GLCM • Conventional Hyonmu III

HELICOPTERS
ATK 96: 60 AH-1F/J Cobra; 36 AH-64E Apache
MRH 175: 130 Hughes 500D; 45 MD-500
TPT 336: Heavy 37: 31 CH-47D Chinook; 6 MH-47E Chinook; Medium 287: ε200 KUH-1 Surion; 87 UH-60P Black Hawk; Light 12 Bo-105

AIR DEFENCE
SAM • Point-defence Chiron; Chun Ma (Pegasus); FIM-92 Stinger; Javelin; Mistral; 9K310 Igla-1 (RS-SA-16 Gimlet)
GUNS 477+
SP 317: 20mm ε150 KIFV Vulcan SPAAG; 30mm 167 K30 Biho; some K-808 SPAAG
TOWED 160: 20mm 60 M167 Vulcan; 35mm 20 GDF-003; 40mm 80 L/60/L/70; M1

AIR-LAUNCHED MISSILES
ASM AGM-114R1 Hellfire

Navy 70,000 (incl marines)

Three separate fleet elements: 1st Fleet Donghae (East Sea/Sea of Japan); 2nd Fleet Pyeongtaek (West Sea/Yellow Sea); 3rd Fleet Busan (South Sea/Korea Strait); independent submarine command; three additional flotillas (incl SF, mine-warfare, amphibious and spt elements) and 1 Naval Air Wing (3 gp plus spt gp)

EQUIPMENT BY TYPE
SUBMARINES 20
SSB 2 Chang Bogo III (Batch I (GER Type-214 mod; KSS-III)) (fitted with AIP) with 6 SLBM (likely based on Hyonmu-IIB), 8 single 533mm TT with K731 White Shark
SSK 18:
6 Chang Bogo I (GER Type-209/1200; KSS-I) with 8 single 533mm TT with SUT HWT/K731 White Shark HWT
3 Chang Bogo I (GER Type-209/1200; KSS-I) with 8 single 533mm TT with UGM-84 Harpoon AShM/SUT HWT/K731 White Shark HWT
9 Chang Bogo II (GER Type-214; KSS-II) (fitted with AIP) with 8 single 533mm TT with Hae Sung III LACM/Hae Sung I AShM/SUT HWT/K731 White Shark HWT

PRINCIPAL SURFACE COMBATANTS 25
CRUISERS • CGHM 3 Sejong (KDD-III) with Aegis Baseline 7 C2, 6 8-cell K-VLS with Hae Sung II LACM/Red Shark A/S msl, 4 quad lnchr with Hae Sung I AShM, 10 8-cell Mk 41 VLS (6 fore, 4 aft) with SM-2 Block IIIA/B SAM, 1 21-cell Mk 49 GMLS with RIM-116 RAM SAM, 2 triple 324mm SVTT Mk 32 ASTT with K745 Blue Shark LWT, 1 Goalkeeper CIWS, 1 127mm gun (capacity 2 Lynx Mk99/AW159 Wildcat hels)
DESTROYERS • DDGHM 6 Chungmugong Yi Sun-Sin (KDD-II) with 2 8-cell K-VLS with Hae Sung II LACM/Red Shark A/S msl, 2 quad lnchr with RGM-84 Harpoon AShM/Hae Sung I AShM, 4 8-cell Mk 41 VLS with SM-2 Block IIIA/B SAM, 1 21-cell Mk 49 GMLS with RIM-116 RAM SAM, 2 triple 324mm SVTT Mk 32 ASTT with Mk 46 LWT, 1 Goalkeeper CIWS, 1 127mm gun (capacity 1 Lynx Mk99/AW159 Wildcat hel)
FRIGATES 16
FFGHM 14:
5 Daegu (Incheon Batch II)† (limited serviceability due to faulty propulsion system) with 2 8-cell K-VLS with Hae Sung II LACM/TSLM LACM/Haegung (K-SAAM) SAM/Red Shark A/S msl, 2 quad lnchr with TSLM LACM/Hae Sung I AShM, 2 triple 324mm KMk. 32 ASTT with K745 Blue Shark LWT, 1 Mk 15 Phalanx Block 1B CIWS, 1 127mm gun (capacity 1 Lynx Mk99/AW159 Wildcat hel)
3 Gwanggaeto Daewang (KDD-I) with 2 quad lnchr with RGM-84 Harpoon AShM, 2 8-cell Mk 48 mod 2 VLS with RIM-7P Sea Sparrow SAM, 2 triple 324mm KMk. 32 ASTT with K745 Blue Shark LWT, 2 Goalkeeper CIWS, 1 127mm gun (capacity 1 Lynx Mk99/AW159 Wildcat hel)
6 Incheon with 2 quad lnchr with TSLM LACM/Hae Sung I AShM, 1 21-cell Mk 49 lnchr with RIM-116 RAM SAM, 2 triple 324mm KMk. 32 ASTT with K745 Blue Shark LWT, 1 Mk 15 Phalanx Block 1B CIWS, 1 127 mm gun (capacity 1 Lynx Mk99/AW159 Wildcat hel)
FFG 2 Ulsan with 2 quad lnchr with RGM-84 Harpoon AShM, 2 triple 324mm SVTT Mk 32 ASTT with Mk 46 LWT, 2 76mm gun

PATROL AND COASTAL COMBATANTS 74
CORVETTES • FSG 5:

1 *Po Hang* (Flight IV) with 2 twin lnchr with RGM-84 *Harpoon* AShM, 2 triple 324mm ASTT with Mk 46 LWT, 2 76mm gun

4 *Po Hang* (Flight V/VI) with 2 twin lnchr with *Hae Sung* I AShM, 2 triple 324mm KMk. 32 ASTT with K745 *Blue Shark* LWT, 2 76mm gun

PCFG 34: 18 *Gumdoksuri* with 2 twin lnchr with *Hae Sung* I AShM, 1 76mm gun; 16 *Chamsuri* II with 1 12-cell 130mm MRL, 1 76mm gun

PBF ε35 *Sea Dolphin*

MINE WARFARE 12

  MINE COUNTERMEASURES 10

    MHO 6 *Kan Kyeong*

    MSO 4 *Yang Yang*

  MINELAYERS • ML 2:

    1 *Nampo* (MLS-II) with 1 4-cell K-VLS VLS with *Haegung* (K-SAAM) SAM, 2 triple KMk. 32 triple 324mm ASTT with K745 *Blue Shark* LWT, 1 76mm gun (capacity 1 med hel)

    1 *Won San* with 2 triple 324mm SVTT Mk 32 ASTT with Mk 46 LWT/K745 *Blue Shark* LWT, 1 76mm gun, 1 hel landing platform

AMPHIBIOUS

  PRINCIPAL AMPHIBIOUS SHIPS 6

    LHD 2:

    1 *Dokdo* with 1 Mk 49 GMLS with RIM-116 RAM SAM, 2 *Goalkeeper* CIWS (capacity 2 LCAC; 10 tanks; 700 troops; 10 UH-60 hel)

    1 *Marado* (*Dokdo* mod) with 1 4-cell K-VLS with K-SAAM SAM, 2 Mk 15 *Phalanx* Block 1B CIWS (capacity 2 LCAC; 6 MBT, 7 AAV-7A1, 720 troops; 7-12 hels)

    LPD 4 *Cheonwangbong* (LST-II) (capacity 3 LCM; 2 MBT; 8 AFV; 300 troops; 2 med hel)

  LANDING SHIPS • LST 4 *Go Jun Bong* with 1 hel landing platform (capacity 20 tanks; 300 troops)

  LANDING CRAFT 29

    LCU 7+ *Mulgae* I

    LCT 3 *Mulgae* II

    LCM 10 LCM-8

    LCAC 9: 3 *Tsaplya* (capacity 1 MBT; 130 troops); 6 LSF-II (capacity 150 troops or 1 MBT & 24 troops)

LOGISTICS AND SUPPORT 11

  AG 1 *Sunjin* (trials spt)

  AOEH 1 *Soyangham* (AOE-II) with 1 Mk 15 *Phalanx* Block 1B CIWS (capacity 1 med hel)

  AORH 3 *Chun Jee*

  ARS 3: 1 *Cheong Hae Jin*; 2 *Tongyeong*

  AX 1 *Hansando* with 2 triple 324mm KMk. 32 ASTT with K745 *Blue Shark* LWT, 1 76mm gun (fitted for but not with K-VLS) (capacity 2 med hels; 300 students);

  AXL 2 MTB

UNINHABITED MARITIME PLATFORMS • UUV

  MARSEC • Extra-Large ASWUUV

Naval Aviation

FORCES BY ROLE

ANTI-SUBMARINE WARFARE

  2 sqn with P-3C/K *Orion*

  2 sqn with *Lynx* Mk99/Mk99A

TRAINING

  1 sqn with Bell 205 (UH-1H *Iroquois*)

TRANSPORT

  1 sqn with Cessna F406 *Caravan* II

TRANSPORT HELICOPTER

  1 sqn with Bell 205 (UH-1H *Iroquois*); UH-60P *Black Hawk*

EQUIPMENT BY TYPE

AIRCRAFT 16 combat capable

  ASW 16: 8 P-3C *Orion*; 8 P-3CK *Orion*

  TPT • Light 5 Cessna F406 *Caravan* II

HELICOPTERS

  ASW 31: 11 *Lynx* Mk99; 12 *Lynx* Mk99A; 8 AW159 *Wildcat*

  TPT 15: **Medium** 8 UH-60P *Black Hawk* **Light** 7 Bell 205 (UH-1H *Iroquois*)

Marines 29,000

FORCES BY ROLE

SPECIAL FORCES

  1 SF regt

MANOEUVRE

  Amphibious

  2 mne div (1 recce bn, 1 tk bn, 3 mne bde, 1 amph bn, 1 arty bde, 1 engr bn)

  1 mne bde (1 recce coy, 4 mne bn, 1 SP arty bn)

  1 mne bde (3 mne bn, 1 fd arty bn)

  1 mne BG (1 mne bn, 1 SP arty bn)

HELICOPTER

  1 hel gp (1 atk hel sqn; 2 tpt hel sqn) (forming)

EQUIPMENT BY TYPE

ARMOURED FIGHTING VEHICLES

  MBT 100: 60 K1E1; 40 K1A2

  AAV 166 AAV-7A1

  APC • APC(W) ε20 K808

ANTI-TANK/ANTI-INFRASTUCTURE • MSL

  SP *Spike* NLOS

  MANPATS *Hyeongung*

ARTILLERY 238

  SP • 155mm 80: ε40 K9 *Thunder*; ε20 K9A1 *Thunder*; ε20 M109A2 (K55/K55A1)

  TOWED 140: **105mm** ε20 M101; **155mm** ε120 KH-179

  MRL • 239mm 18 K239 *Cheonmu*

  MOR 81mm KM29 (M29)

COASTAL DEFENCE • AShM RGM-84A *Harpoon* (truck mounted)

HELICOPTERS • TPT • Medium ε27 MUH-1 *Surion*

AIR DEFENCE

  GUNS • Towed • 20mm M167 *Vulcan* (direct fire role)

Naval Special Warfare Flotilla

Air Force 65,000

4 Comd (Ops, Southern Combat, Logs, Trg)

FORCES BY ROLE

FIGHTER/GROUND ATTACK
1 sqn with F-4E *Phantom* II
5 sqn with F-5E/F *Tiger* II
3 sqn with F-15K *Eagle*
8 sqn with F-16C/D *Fighting Falcon* (KF-16C/D)
2 sqn with F-35A *Lightning* II
3 sqn with FA-50 *Fighting Eagle*

ISR
1 wg with KA-1
1 sqn with F-16C/D *Fighting Falcon* (KF-16C/D)

SIGINT
1 sqn with *Falcon* 2000; Hawker 800RA/SIG

AIRBORNE EARLY WARNING & CONTROL
1 sqn with B-737 AEW

SEARCH & RESCUE
3 sqn with AS332L *Super Puma*; Bell 412EP; HH-47D *Chinook*; HH-60P *Black Hawk*; Ka-32 *Helix* C

TANKER
1 sqn with A330 MRTT

TRANSPORT
1 VIP sqn with B-737-300; B-747-8; CN235-220; S-92A *Superhawk*; VH-60P *Black Hawk* (VIP)
2 sqn with C-130H/H-30/J-30 *Hercules*
2 sqn with CN235M-100/220
1 (spec ops) sqn with MC-130K *Hercules*

TRAINING
1 sqn with F-5E/F *Tiger* II
1 sqn with F-16C/D *Fighting Falcon*
4 sqn with KT-1
1 sqn with KT-100
3 sqn with T-50/TA-50 *Golden Eagle**

TRANSPORT HELICOPTER
1 sqn with UH-60P *Black Hawk* (Spec Ops)

ISR UAV
1 sqn with RQ-4B *Global Hawk* (forming)

SPECIAL FORCES
1 SF sqn

AIR DEFENCE
3 AD bde (total: 6 SAM bn with *Chunggung*; 2 SAM bn with M902 *Patriot* PAC-3 CRI)

EQUIPMENT BY TYPE

AIRCRAFT 600 combat capable
FTR 173: 141 F-5E *Tiger* II; 32 F-5F *Tiger* II
FGA 347: 29 F-4E *Phantom* II; 59 F-15K *Eagle*; 116 F-16C *Fighting Falcon* (KF-16C); 44 F-16D *Fighting Falcon* (KF-16D); 39 F-35A *Lightning* II; 60 FA-50 *Fighting Eagle*
AEW&C 4 B-737 AEW

ISR 23: 4 Hawker 800RA; 19 KA-1
SIGINT 6: 4 Hawker 800SIG; 2 *Falcon* 2000 (COMINT/SIGINT)
TKR/TPT 4 A330 MRTT
TPT 38: **Medium** 16: 4 C-130H *Hercules*; 4 C-130I I-30 *Hercules*; 4 C-130J-30 *Hercules*; 4 MC-130K *Hercules*;
Light 20: 12 CN235M-100; 8 CN235M-220 (incl 2 VIP);
PAX 2: 1 B-737-300; 1 B-747-8 (leased)
TRG 183: 83 KT-1; 49 T-50 *Golden Eagle**; 9 T-50B *Black Eagle** (aerobatics); 22 TA-50 *Golden Eagle**; ε20 KT-100

HELICOPTERS
SAR 16: 5 HH-47D *Chinook*; 11 HH-60P *Black Hawk*
MRH 3 Bell 412EP
TPT • **Medium** 30: 2 AS332L *Super Puma*; 8 Ka-32 *Helix* C; 3 S-92A *Super Hawk*; 7 UH-60P *Black Hawk*; 10 VH-60P *Black Hawk* (VIP)

UNINHABITED AERIAL VEHICLES
ISR 7+: **Heavy** 4 RQ-4B *Global Hawk*; **Medium** 3+: some *Night Intruder*; 3 *Searcher*

LOITERING & DIRECT ATTACK MUNITIONS
Harpy

AIR DEFENCE • SAM 120
Long-range 48 M902 *Patriot* PAC-3 CRI
Medium-range 72 *Chunggung* (KM-SAM)

AIR-LAUNCHED MISSILES
AAM • **IR** AIM-9 *Sidewinder*; **IIR** AIM-9X *Sidewinder* II; **SARH** AIM-7 *Sparrow*; **ARH** AIM-120B/C-5/7 AMRAAM
ASM AGM-65A *Maverick*; AGM-130
AShM AGM-84L *Harpoon* Block II; AGM-142 *Popeye*
ARM AGM-88 HARM
ALCM AGM-84H SLAM-ER; KEPD-350 *Taurus*

BOMBS
INS/GPS-guided GBU-31/-32/-38 JDAM; GBU-39 SDB; KGGB; *Spice* 2000
Laser-guided GBU-28; *Paveway* II

Gendarmerie & Paramilitary 13,500 active

Civilian Defence Corps 3,000,000 reservists (to age 50)

Coast Guard 13,500

Part of the Ministry of Maritime Affairs and Fisheries. Five regional headquarters with 19 coastguard stations and one guard unit

EQUIPMENT BY TYPE
PATROL AND COASTAL COMBATANTS 111
PSOH 16: 1 *Lee Cheong-ho* with 1 76mm gun; 1 *Sambongho*; 14 *Tae Pung Yang* with 1 med hel
PSO 21: 3 *Han Kang* with 1 76mm gun, 1 hel landing platform; 5 *Han Kang* II with 1 76mm gun, 1 hel landing pllatform; 12 *Jaemin* with 1 hel landing platform; 1 *Sumjinkang*
PCO 23 *Tae Geuk*

PCC 21: 4 *Hae Uri*; 15 *Hae Uri* II; 2 *Hae Uri* III
PB 30: 26 *Haenuri*; ε4 (various)
AMPHIBIOUS • LANDING CRAFT 8:
UCAC 8: 1 BHT-150; 4 *Griffon* 470TD; 3 *Griffon* 8000TD
AIRCRAFT
MP 5: 1 C-212-400 MP; 4 CN235-110 MPA
TPT • **PAX** 1 CL-604
HELICOPTERS
MRH 6: 5 AS565MB *Panther*; 1 AW139
SAR 3 S-92
TPT • **Medium** 10: 8 Ka-32 *Helix* C; 2 KUH-1 *Surion*

DEPLOYMENT

ARABIAN SEA & GULF OF ADEN: Combined Maritime Forces • CTF-151: 200; 1 DDGHM

INDIA/PAKISTAN: UN • UNMOGIP 6

LEBANON: UN • UNIFIL 255; 1 mech inf BG HQ; 1 mech inf coy; 1 inf coy; 1 log coy

SOUTH SUDAN: UN • UNMISS 278; 1 engr coy

UNITED ARAB EMIRATES: 170 (trg activities at UAE Spec Ops School)

WESTERN SAHARA: UN • MINURSO 3

FOREIGN FORCES

Sweden NNSC: 5
Switzerland NNSC: 5
United States US Indo-Pacific Command: 30,400
  Army 21,500; 1 HQ (8th Army) at Pyeongtaek; 1 div HQ at Pyeongtaek; 1 armd bde with M1A2 SEPv2 *Abrams*; M2A3/M3A3 *Bradley*; M109A6; 1 (cbt avn) hel bde with AH-64D/E *Apache*; CH-47F *Chinook*; UH-60L/M *Black Hawk*; 1 MRL bde with M270A1 MLRS; 1 AD bde with M902 *Patriot* PAC-3/FIM-92A *Avenger*; 1 SAM bty with THAAD; 1 (APS) armd bde eqpt set
  Navy 350
  USAF 8,350; 1 HQ (7th Air Force) at Osan AB; 1 ftr wg at Kunsan AB (2 ftr sqn with 20 F-16C/D *Fighting Falcon*); 1 ftr wg at Osan AB (1 ftr sqn with 20 F-16C/D *Fighting Falcon*, 1 atk sqn with 24 A-10C *Thunderbolt* II); 1 ISR sqn at Osan AB with U-2S
  USMC 200

Laos LAO

New Lao Kip LAK		2022	2023	2024
GDP	LAK	217trn	265trn	286trn
	USD	15.3bn	14.2bn	14.1bn
per capita	USD	2,047	1,879	1,834
Growth	%	2.3	4.0	4.0
Inflation	%	23.0	28.1	9.0
Def bdgt	LAK	n.k.	n.k.	n.k.
	USD	n.k.	n.k.	n.k.
USD1=LAK		14,202.20	18,619.46	20,255.43

Population	7,852,377					
Age	0–14	15–19	20–24	25–29	30–64	65 plus
Male	15.5%	4.8%	4.9%	4.4%	18.0%	2.2%
Female	15.1%	4.8%	4.9%	4.5%	18.3%	2.5%

Capabilities

The Lao People's Armed Forces (LPAF) form a vital pillar of Laos' state machinery alongside the ruling Communist Lao People's Revolutionary Party (LPRP) and the government apparatus. The LPAF has a constitutional mandate to defend the Party's achievements and, in addition to external security responsibilities, is expected to protect the regime internally by suppressing political and civil unrest. Laos has military-to-military contacts with the Cambodian, Chinese and Vietnamese armed forces. The country also maintains defence cooperation with Russia, which, along with Vietnam, has provided training support. The LPAF have participated in exercises, including some organised by the ADMM–Plus grouping involving ASEAN and some other states. Laos operates Soviet-era military equipment and relies on Russian supplies, as illustrated by deliveries of training aircraft, armoured reconnaissance vehicles and main battle tanks. The country lacks a traditional defence-industrial base and maintenance capacity is limited.

ACTIVE 29,100 (Army 25,600 Air 3,500)
Gendarmerie & Paramilitary 100,000

Conscript liability 18 months minimum

ORGANISATIONS BY SERVICE

Space
EQUIPMENT BY TYPE
SATELLITES • ISR 1 *LaoSat*-1

Army 25,600
FORCES BY ROLE
4 mil regions
MANOEUVRE
  Armoured
  1 armd bn
  Light
  5 inf div
  7 indep inf regt
  65 indep inf coy

COMBAT SUPPORT
  5 arty bn
  1 engr regt
  2 (construction) engr regt
AIR DEFENCE
  9 ADA bn
EQUIPMENT BY TYPE
ARMOURED FIGHTING VEHICLES
  MBT 25: 15 T-54/T-55; 10 T-72B1
  LT TK 10 PT-76
  RECCE BRDM-2M
  IFV 10+ BMP-1
  APC • APC (W) 50: 30 BTR-40/BTR-60; 20 BTR-152
  AUV Dongfeng Mengshi 4×4; ZYZ-8002 (CS/VN3)
ENGINEERING & MAINTENANCE VEHICLES
  ARV T-54/T-55
  VLB MTU
ANTI-TANK/ANTI-INFRASTRUCTURE • RCL 57mm
M18/A1; **75mm** M20; **106mm** M40; **107mm** B-11
ARTILLERY 62+
  TOWED 62: **105mm** 20 M101; **122mm** 20 D-30/M-30 M-1938; **130mm** 10 M-46; **155mm** 12 M114
  MOR 81mm; 82mm; 107mm M-1938/M2A1; **120mm** M-43
AIR DEFENCE
  SAM
    Short-range 6+: 6 S-125M *Pechora*-M† (RS-SA-3 *Goa*); some *Yitian* (CH-SA-13)
    Point-defence 9K32M *Strela*-2M (RS-SA-7 *Grail*)‡; 9K35 *Strela*-10 (RS-SA-13 *Gopher*); 9K310 *Igla*-1 (RS-SA-16 *Gimlet*)
  GUNS
    SP 23mm ZSU-23-4
    TOWED 14.5mm ZPU-1/ZPU-4; **23mm** ZU-23; **37mm** M-1939; **57mm** S-60

Army Marine Section ε600
EQUIPMENT BY TYPE
PATROL AND COASTAL COMBATANTS • PBR some
AMPHIBIOUS • LCM some

Air Force 3,500
FORCES BY ROLE
TRANSPORT
  1 regt with MA60; MA600
TRAINING
  1 regt with LE500
  1 regt with Yak-130 *Mitten**
TRANSPORT HELICOPTER
  1 (VIP) flt with SA360 *Dauphin*
  1 regt with Ka-32T *Helix* C; Mi-17 *Hip* H; 5 Mi-17V-5 *Hip*; 4 Z-9A
EQUIPMENT BY TYPE
AIRCRAFT 4 combat capable
  TPT • Light 13: 1 An-26 *Curl* (reported); 8 LE500; 2 MA60; 2 MA600
  TRG 4 Yak-130 *Mitten**
HELICOPTERS
  MRH 15: 6 Mi-17 *Hip* H; 5 Mi-17V-5 *Hip*; 4 Z-9A
  TPT 4: **Medium** 1 Ka-32T *Helix* C; **Light** 3 SA360 *Dauphin*

Gendarmerie & Paramilitary

Militia Self-Defence Forces 100,000+
Village 'home guard' or local defence

Malaysia MYS

Malaysian Ringgit MYR		2022	2023	2024
GDP	MYR	1.79trn	1.91trn	2.06trn
	USD	407bn	431bn	466bn
per capita	USD	12,466	13,034	13,913
Growth	%	8.7	4.0	4.3
Inflation	%	3.4	2.9	2.7
Def bdgt	MYR	16.1bn	17.7bn	19.7bn
	USD	3.67bn	4.01bn	4.46bn
USD1=MYR		4.40	4.43	4.43

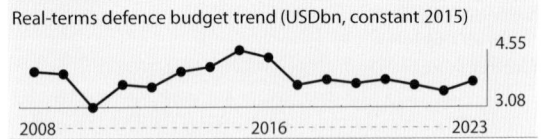

Real-terms defence budget trend (USDbn, constant 2015)
4.55
3.08
2008 — 2016 — 2023

Population   34,219,975

Age	0–14	15–19	20–24	25–29	30–64	65 plus
Male	11.5%	3.9%	4.3%	4.7%	22.8%	3.9%
Female	10.9%	3.7%	4.1%	4.4%	21.5%	4.2%

Capabilities

The Royal Malaysian Armed Forces (RMAF) have a limited capacity for external defence. The army remains the dominant service, reflecting a longstanding focus on counter-insurgency. The country's first defence White Paper, issued in 2019 and the 2021–2025 Strategic Plan, identified 'three pillars' of Malaysia's defence strategy: 'concentric deterrence' (protection of national interests in 'core', 'extended' and 'forward' zones); 'comprehensive defence' (involving whole-of-government and whole-of-society support for the national-defence effort); and 'credible partnerships' (involving engagement in regional and international defence cooperation). These planning documents, as well as a 2022 Action Plan, identified new defence challenges, including tensions in the South China Sea, cyber threats, and other "mass non-kinetic crises." It also provided some insights into future capability developments, including ISR, maritime-strike, air-defence, and synthetic military-training aids. Highlighting the RMAF's modernisation drive, the government, at the LIMA 2023 air show, signed high-profile deals, including for combat aircraft, maritime surveillance planes, and UAVs. Budgetary constraints are likely to continue to limit defence resources and operational readiness. The RMAF regularly participate in exercises with regional and international partners, including the US. In 2017, Malaysia began coordinated trilateral maritime and air patrols in the Sulu-Sulawesi Seas with Indonesia and the Philippines. The Sulu Sea remains an area of concern given continued terrorist and pirate activity. Much of Malaysia's military equipment is ageing and important capability gaps exist, particularly in air defence and maritime surveillance. Malaysia hosts Australian forces and the headquarters of the FPDA Integrated Area Defence System at RMAF Butterworth. Malaysia's defence industry focuses mainly on MRO, naval shipbuilding, and land-vehicle production via offset agreements with European companies.

ACTIVE 113,000 (Army 80,000 Navy 18,000 Air 15,000) Gendarmerie & Paramilitary 22,500

RESERVE 51,600 (Army 50,000, Navy 1,000 Air Force 600) Gendarmerie & Paramilitary 244,700

ORGANISATIONS BY SERVICE

Army 80,000
2 mil region
FORCES BY ROLE
COMMAND
5 div HQ
SPECIAL FORCES
1 spec ops bde (1 SF bn; 2 cdo bn)
MANOEUVRE
Armoured
1 tk regt
Mechanised
5 armd regt
1 mech inf bde (4 mech bn, 1 cbt engr sqn)
Light
1 inf bde (5 inf bn)
1 inf bde (4 inf bn, 1 fd arty bn)
1 inf bde (4 inf bn)
4 inf bde (3 inf bn, 1 fd arty bn)
3 inf bde (3 inf bn)
2 inf bde (2 inf bn, 1 fd arty bn)
1 inf bde (2 inf bn)
Air Manoeuvre
1 (Rapid Deployment Force) AB bde (1 lt tk sqn, 4 AB bn, 1 fd arty bn, 1 engr sqn, 1 hel sqn with AW109)
COMBAT SUPPORT
3 fd arty bn
1 MRL bde (2 MRL bn)
1 STA bn
1 cbt engr sqn
3 fd engr regt (total: 7 cbt engr sqn, 3 engr spt sqn)
1 construction regt
1 int unit
4 MP regt
1 sigs regt
HELICOPTER
1 hel sqn with MD-530G
1 hel sqn with S-61A-4 *Nuri* (forming)

AIR DEFENCE
3 ADA regt
EQUIPMENT BY TYPE
ARMOURED FIGHTING VEHICLES
MBT 48 PT-91M *Twardy*
LT TK 21 *Scorpion*-90
RECCE 24 AV8 *Gempita*
IFV 212: 31 ACV300 *Adnan* (25mm *Bushmaster*); 13 ACV300 *Adnan* AGL; 46 AV8 *Gempita* IFV25; 122 AV8 *Gempita* IFV30 (incl 54 with *Ingwe* ATGM)
APC 329
  APC (T) 265: 149 ACV300 *Adnan* (incl 69 variants); 13 FV4333 *Stormer* (upgraded); 63 K200A; 40 K200A1
  APC (W) 35: 35 AV8 *Gempita* APC (incl 13 CP; 3 sigs; 9 amb)
  PPV 29: 9 IAG *Guardian*; 20 *Lipanbara*
ENGINEERING & MAINTENANCE VEHICLES
AEV 3 MID-M
ARV 43: 15 ACV300; 4 K288A1; 6 WZT-4; 18 AV8 *Gempita* ARV
VLB 5+: *Leguan*; 5 PMCz-90
NBC VEHICLES 4+: 4 AV8 *Gempita*; K216A1
ANTI-TANK/ANTI-INFRASTRUCTURE • MSL
SP 8 ACV300 *Baktar Shikan*
MANPATS 9K115 *Metis* (RS-AT-7 *Saxhorn*); 9K115-2 *Metis*-M1 (RS-AT-13); *Eryx*; *Baktar Shihan* (HJ-8); SS.11
RCL 84mm *Carl Gustaf*
ARTILLERY 438
TOWED 140: **105mm** 118: 18 LG1 MkIII; 100 Model 56 pack howitzer; **155mm** 22 G-5
MRL 36 ASTROS II (equipped with 127mm SS-30)
MOR 262: **81mm** 232; **SP 81mm** 14: 4 K281A1; 10 ACV300-S; **SP 120mm** 16: 8 ACV-S; 8 AV8 *Gempita*
AMPHIBIOUS • LANDING CRAFT
LCA 165 Damen Assault Craft 540 (capacity 10 troops)
HELICOPTERS
MRH 6 MD-530G
TPT 12: **Medium** 2 S-61A-4 *Nuri*; **Light** 10 AW109
AIR DEFENCE
SAM • Point-defence 15+: 15 *Jernas* (*Rapier* 2000); *Anza*-II; HY-6 (FN-6) (CH-SA-10); 9K38 *Igla* (RS-SA-18 *Grouse*); *Starstreak*
GUNS 52+
  SP 20mm K263
  TOWED 52: **35mm** 16 GDF-005; **40mm** 36 L40/70

Reserves

Territorial Army
Some paramilitary forces to be incorporated into a re-organised territorial organisation
FORCES BY ROLE
MANOEUVRE
Mechanised

4 armd sqn
Light
16 inf regt (3 inf bn)
Other
5 (highway) sy bn
COMBAT SUPPORT
5 arty bty
2 fd engr regt
1 int unit
3 sigs sqn
COMBAT SUPPORT
4 med coy
5 tpt coy

Navy 18,000

3 Regional Commands: MAWILLA 1 (Kuantan), MAWILLA 2 (Sabah) and MAWILLA 3 (Langkawi). A fourth is being formed (Bintulu)

EQUIPMENT BY TYPE
SUBMARINES 2
  SSK 2 *Tunku Abdul Rahman* (FRA *Scorpène*) with 6 single 533mm TT with SM39 *Exocet* AShM/*Black Shark* HWT
PRINCIPAL SURFACE COMBATANTS • FRIGATES 2
  FFGHM 2 *Lekiu* with 2 quad lnchr with MM40 *Exocet* Block 2 AShM, 1 16-cell VLS with *Sea Wolf* SAM, 2 triple 324mm ILAS-3 (B-515) ASTT with A244/S LWT, 1 57mm gun (capacity 1 *Super Lynx* 300 hel)
PATROL AND COASTAL COMBATANTS 55
  CORVETTES 8
    FSG 2 *Kasturi* with 2 quad lnchr with MM40 *Exocet* Block 2 AShM, 2 triple 324mm ILAS-3 (B-515) ASTT with A244/S LWT, 1 57mm gun, 1 hel landing platform
    FSH 6 *Kedah* (GER MEKO 100) with 1 76mm gun, 1 hel landing platform (fitted for but not with MM40 *Exocet* AShM & RAM SAM)
  PCFM 4 *Laksamana* with 1 *Albatros* quad lnchr with *Aspide* SAM, 1 76mm gun
  PCF 4 *Perdana* (FRA *Combattante* II) with 1 57mm gun
  PCC 4 *Keris* (Littoral Mission Ship)
  PBF 23: 6 Gading Marine FIC; 17 *Tempur* (SWE CB90)
  PB 12: 4 *Handalan* (SWE *Spica*-M) with 1 57mm gun; 6 *Jerong* (Lurssen 45) with 1 57mm gun; 2 *Sri Perlis*
MINE WARFARE • MINE COUNTERMEASURES 4
  MCO 4 *Mahamiru* (ITA *Lerici*)
LOGISTICS AND SUPPORT 14
  AFS 2: 1 *Mahawangsa* with 2 57mm guns, 1 hel landing platform; 1 *Sri Indera Sakti* with 1 57mm gun, 1 hel landing platform
  AG 3: 2 *Bunga Mas Lima* with 1 hel landing platform; 1 *Tun Azizan*
  AGS 2: 1 *Dayang Sari*; 1 *Perantau*
  AP 2 *Sri Gaya*
  ASR 1 *Mega Bakti*

ATF 1
AXL 2 *Gagah Samudera* with 1 hel landing platform
AXS 1 *Tunas Samudera*

Naval Aviation 160
FORCES BY ROLE
ANTI-SUBMARINE WARFARE
  1 sqn with *Super Lynx* 300
TRANSPORT HELICOPTER
  1 sqn with AS555 *Fennec*
  1 sqn with AW139
EQUIPMENT BY TYPE
HELICOPTERS
  ASW 4 *Super Lynx* 300
  MRH 9: 6 AS555 *Fennec*; 3 AW139
AIR-LAUNCHED MISSILES • AShM *Sea Skua*

Special Forces
FORCES BY ROLE
SPECIAL FORCES
  1 (mne cdo) SF unit

Air Force 15,000

1 air op HQ, 2 air div, 1 trg and log comd, 1 Intergrated Area Def Systems HQ
FORCES BY ROLE
FIGHTER/GROUND ATTACK
  1 sqn with F/A-18D *Hornet*
  1 sqn with Su-30MKM *Flanker*
  2 sqn with *Hawk* Mk108*/Mk208*
MARITIME PATROL
  1 sqn with Beech 200T
TANKER/TRANSPORT
  2 sqn with KC-130H *Hercules*; C-130H *Hercules*; C-130H-30 *Hercules*
TRANSPORT
  1 sqn with A400M *Atlas*
  1 (VIP) sqn with A319CT; AW109; BD700 *Global Express*; F-28 *Fellowship*; Falcon 900
  1 sqn with CN235M-220
TRAINING
  1 unit with PC-7
TRANSPORT HELICOPTER
  4 (tpt/SAR) sqn with H225M *Super Cougar*; S-70A *Black Hawk*
  1 sqn with AW139
UNINHABITED AERIAL VEHICLE
  1 sqn (forming)
AIR DEFENCE
  1 sqn with *Starburst*
SPECIAL FORCES
  1 (Air Force Commando) unit (airfield defence/SAR)
EQUIPMENT BY TYPE
AIRCRAFT 42 combat capable

FTR (8 MiG-29 *Fulcrum* (MiG-29N); 2 MiG-29UB *Fulcrum* B (MIG-29NUB) in store)
FGA 26: 8 F/A-18D *Hornet* (some serviceability in doubt); 18 Su-30MKM (some serviceability in doubt)
MP 3 CN235 MPA
ISR 3 Beech 200T
TKR/TPT 4 KC-130H *Hercules*
TPT 22: **Heavy** 4 A400M *Atlas*; **Medium** 10: 2 C-130H *Hercules*; 8 C-130H-30 *Hercules*; **Light** 4 CN235M-220 (incl 1 VIP); **PAX** 4: 1 A319CT (VIP); 1 BD700 *Global Express*; 1 F-28 *Fellowship*; 1 *Falcon* 900
TRG 70: 4 *Hawk* Mk108*; 12 *Hawk* Mk208*; 7 MB-339C; 30 PC-7; 17 PC-7 Mk II *Turbo Trainer*
HELICOPTERS
  MRH 4 AW139 (leased)
  TPT 15: **Heavy** 12 H225M *Super Cougar*; **Medium** 2 S-70A *Black Hawk*; **Light** 1 AW109
AIR DEFENCE • SAM • Point-defence *Starstreak*
AIR-LAUNCHED MISSILES
  AAM • IR AIM-9 *Sidewinder*; R-73 (RS-AA-11A *Archer*); **IIR** AIM-9X *Sidewinder* II; **IR/SARH** R-27 (RS-AA-10 *Alamo*); **SARH** AIM-7 *Sparrow*; **ARH** AIM-120C AMRAAM; R-77 (RS-AA-12A *Adder*)
  ASM AGM-65 *Maverick*; Kh-29T (RS-AS-14B *Kedge*); Kh-29L (RS-AS-14A *Kedge*); Kh-31P (RS-AS-17A *Krypton*); Kh-59M (RS-AS-18 *Kazoo*)
  ARM Kh-31P (RS-AS-17A *Krypton*);
  AShM AGM-84D *Harpoon*; Kh-31A (RS-AS-17B *Krypton*)
BOMBS
  Electro-optical guided KAB-500KR; KAB-500OD
  Laser-guided *Paveway* II

Gendarmerie & Paramilitary ε22,500

Police–General Ops Force 18,000
FORCES BY ROLE
COMMAND
  5 bde HQ
SPECIAL FORCES
  1 spec ops bn
MANOEUVRE
  Other
  19 paramilitary bn
  2 (Aboriginal) paramilitary bn
  4 indep paramilitary coy
EQUIPMENT BY TYPE
ARMOURED FIGHTING VEHICLES
  APC • APC (W) AT105 *Saxon*
  AUV ε30 SB-301

Malaysian Maritime Enforcement Agency (MMEA) ε4,500
Controls 5 Maritime Regions (Northern Peninsula; Southern Peninsula; Eastern Peninsula; Sarawak; Sabah), subdivided into a further 18 Maritime Districts.

Supported by one provisional MMEA Air Unit
EQUIPMENT BY TYPE
PATROL AND COASTAL COMBATANTS 137
  PSO 4: 1 *Arau* (ex-JPN *Nojima*) with 1 hel landing platform; 2 *Langkawi* with 1 57mm gun, 1 hel landing platform; 1 *Pekan* (ex-JPN *Ojika*) with 1 hel landing platform
  PCC 5 *Bagan Datuk*
  PBF 56: 16 *Penggalang* 16; 18 *Penggalang* 17 (TUR MRTP 16); 2 *Penggalang* 18; 6 *Penyelamat* 20; 14 *Tugau*
  PB 72: 15 *Gagah*; 4 *Malawali*; 2 *Nusa*; 3 *Nusa* 28; 1 *Peninjau*; 7 *Ramunia*; 2 *Rhu*; 4 *Semilang*; 9 *Sipadan Steel*; 8 *Icarus* 1650; 10 *Pengawal*; 4 *Penyelamat*; 2 *Perwira*; 1 *Sugut*
LOGISTICS AND SUPPORT • AXL 1 *Marlin*
AIRCRAFT • MP 2 Bombardier 415MP
HELICOPTERS
  SAR 3 AW139
  MRH 3 AS365 *Dauphin*

Area Security Units 3,500 reservists
(Auxiliary General Ops Force)
FORCES BY ROLE
MANOEUVRE
  Other
  89 paramilitary unit

Border Scouts 1,200 reservists
in Sabah, Sarawak

People's Volunteer Corps (RELA) 240,000 reservists (some 17,500 armed)

DEPLOYMENT

DEMOCRATIC REPUBLIC OF THE CONGO: UN • MONUSCO 6
LEBANON: UN • UNIFIL 833; 1 mech inf bn(-); 1 engr coy; 1 sigs coy; 1 maint coy; 1 tpt coy
SUDAN: UN • UNISFA 1
WESTERN SAHARA: UN • MINURSO 9

FOREIGN FORCES
Australia 130; 1 inf coy (on 3-month rotational tours); 1 P-8A *Poseidon* (rotational)

Maldives MDV

Maldivian Rufiyaa MVR		2022	2023	2024
GDP	MVR	96.1bn	108bn	116bn
	USD	6.24bn	6.98bn	7.50bn
per capita	USD	15,962	17,559	18,568
Growth	%	13.9	8.1	5.0
Inflation	%	2.6	3.5	2.8
Def bdgt	MVR	1.58bn	1.69bn	
	USD	102m	110m	
USD1=MVR		15.34	15.41	15.41

Real-terms defence budget trend (USDm, constant 2015)

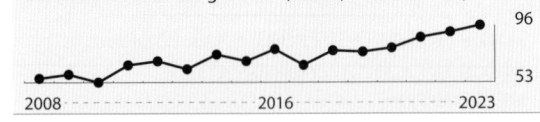

Population 389,568

Age	0–14	15–19	20–24	25–29	30–64	65 plus
Male	11.3%	3.7%	4.4%	5.4%	24.1%	2.5%
Female	10.9%	3.3%	3.6%	4.5%	23.0%	3.2%

Capabilities

The Maldives National Defence Force (MNDF) is tasked with defence, security and civil-emergency response over the expansive and mostly oceanic territory of the archipelagic nation. The MNDF is maritime-centric, with a littoral coast guard, including a small aviation wing and a marine corps. The forces are focused on ISR, maritime security, counterterrorism and capability development. India is the MNDF's key defence partner, having supplied most of the force's major military platforms. New Delhi regularly donates surplus military equipment and offers training to MNDF personnel. A new coast guard facility is being developed with Indian assistance near Malé, with a foundation stone laid in 2023. In 2020, Malé signed a defence agreement with the US and in 2021 the MNDF started capacity building work with the US Army. Training facilities are being developed, including a basic training school in 2020, and work is proceeding on the development of a training centre on Maafilaafushi Island. Following his election victory in September 2023, Maldives' president, Dr Mohamed Muizzu, said he would remove the presence of Indian naval and coast guard crew and support personnel based in the Maldives.

ACTIVE 4,000 (Maldives National Defence Force 4,000)

ORGANISATIONS BY SERVICE

Maldives National Defence Force 4,000

Special Forces
FORCES BY ROLE
SPECIAL FORCES
1 SF sqn

Marine Corps
FORCES BY ROLE
SPECIAL FORCES
1 spec ops unit
MANOEUVRE
Mechanised
1 mech sqn
Amphibious
7 mne coy
EQUIPMENT BY TYPE
ARMOURED FIGHTING VEHICLES
IFV 2 BMP-2
AUV 2 Cobra

Coast Guard
FORCES BY ROLE
SPECIAL FORCES
1 spec ops unit
EQUIPMENT BY TYPE
PATROL AND COASTAL COMBATANTS 12
PCF 1 Huravee (ex-IND Tarmugli)
PCC 2: 1 Ghazee; 1 Shaheed Ali
PBF 8: 1 Kaamiyab; 2 Noordadheen; 5 SM50 Interceptor
PB 1 Dhaharaat
AMPHIBIOUS • LANDING CRAFT 4:
LCU 1 L301
LCP 3
LOGISTICS AND SUPPORT • AAR 2
AIRCRAFT
MP 1 Do-228
HELICOPTERS
MRH 2 Dhruv

Mongolia MNG

Mongolian Tugrik MNT		2022	2023	2024
GDP	MNT	53.9trn	63.3trn	72.4trn
	USD	17.1bn	18.8bn	19.6bn
per capita	USD	4,954	5,348	5,490
Growth	%	5.0	5.5	4.5
Inflation	%	15.2	12.3	12.3
Def bdgt	MNT	287bn	311bn	565bn
	USD	91.2m	92.2m	152m
FMA (US)	USD	3m	3m	3m
USD1=MNT		3,140.76	3,368.69	3,704.93

Real-terms defence budget trend (USDm, constant 2015)

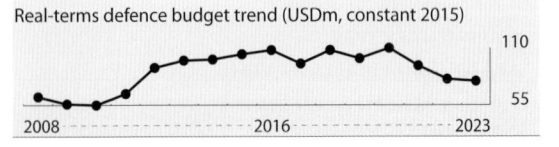

Population 3,255,468

Age	0–14	15–19	20–24	25–29	30–64	65 plus
Male	13.3%	3.8%	3.6%	3.8%	22.0%	2.2%
Female	12.8%	3.6%	3.5%	3.8%	24.2%	3.3%

Capabilities

Mongolia's most recent defence-policy document, from 2015, stresses the importance of peacekeeping and anti-terrorist capabilities. The country has no formal military alliances but pursues defence ties and bilateral training with regional states and others, including India, Turkiye and the US. The Mongolian prime minister made an inaugural visit to the Pentagon in 2023 for talks on military-to-military relations. Mongolia hosts the annual *Khaan Quest* multinational peacekeeping-training exercise. The country's main exercise partners are India and Russia. In 2022, Mongolia and Russia held a counterterrorism-focused exercise. In 2021, NATO completed a multi-year project that involved establishing a Cyber Security Centre and Cyber Incident Response Capability. Mongolia's most significant deployment is to the UN peacekeeping mission in South Sudan. The inventory generally comprises Soviet-era equipment, supplemented by deliveries of second-hand Russian weapons. Barring maintenance facilities, there is no significant defence-industrial base.

ACTIVE 9,700 (Army 8,900 Air 800) Gendarmerie & Paramilitary 7,500

Conscript liability 12 months for males aged 18–25

RESERVE 137,000 (Army 137,000)

ORGANISATIONS BY SERVICE

Army 5,600; 3,300 conscript (total 8,900)
FORCES BY ROLE
MANOEUVRE
  Mechanised
  1 MR bde
  Light
  1 (rapid deployment) lt inf bn (2nd bn to form)
  Air Manoeuvre
  1 AB bn
COMBAT SUPPORT
  1 arty regt
EQUIPMENT BY TYPE
ARMOURED FIGHTING VEHICLES
  MBT 420: 370 T-54/T-55; 50 T-72A
  RECCE 120 BRDM-2
  IFV 310 BMP-1
  APC • APC (W) 210: 150 BTR-60; 40 BTR-70M; 20 BTR-80
ENGINEERING & MAINTENANCE VEHICLES
  ARV T-54/T-55
ANTI-TANK/ANTI-INFRASTRUCTURE
  GUNS • TOWED 200: **85mm** D-44/D-48; **100mm** M-1944/MT-12
ARTILLERY 570
  TOWED ε300: **122mm** D-30/M-30 (M-1938); **130mm** M-46; **152mm** ML-20 (M-1937)
  MRL 122mm 130 BM-21
  MOR 140: **120mm**; **160mm**; **82mm**
AIR DEFENCE
  SAM Medium-range 2+ S-125-2M *Pechora*-2M (RS-SA-26)
  GUNS • TOWED 23mm ZU-23-2

Air Force 800
FORCES BY ROLE
FIGHTER
  1 sqn with MiG-29UB *Fulcrum* B
TRANSPORT
  1 sqn with An-24 *Coke*; An-26 *Curl*
ATTACK/TRANSPORT HELICOPTER
  1 sqn with Mi-8 *Hip*; Mi-171
AIR DEFENCE
  2 regt with S-60/ZPU-4/ZU-23
EQUIPMENT BY TYPE
AIRCRAFT 6 combat capable
  FTR 6 MiG-29UB *Fulcrum* B
  TPT • Light 3: 2 An-24 *Coke*; 1 An-26 *Curl*
HELICOPTERS
  TPT • Medium 12: 10 Mi-8 *Hip*; 2 Mi-171
AIR-LAUNCHED MISSILES
  IR R-73 (RS-AA-11A *Archer*)
AIR DEFENCE • GUNS • TOWED 150: **14.5mm** ZPU-4; **23mm** ZU-23; **57mm** S-60

Gendarmerie & Paramilitary 7,500 active

Border Guard 1,300; 4,700 conscript (total 6,000)

Internal Security Troops 400; 800 conscript (total 1,200)
FORCES BY ROLE
MANOEUVRE
  Other
  4 gd unit

Construction Troops 300

DEPLOYMENT

CENTRAL AFRICAN REPUBLIC: UN • MINUSCA 3
DEMOCRATIC REPUBLIC OF THE CONGO: UN • MONUSCO 2
LEBANON: UN • UNIFIL 4
SOUTH SUDAN: UN • UNMISS 870; 1 inf bn
SUDAN: UN • UNISFA 4
WESTERN SAHARA: UN • MINURSO 4

Myanmar MMR

Myanmar Kyat MMK		2022	2023	2024
GDP	MMK	118trn	138trn	154trn
	USD	66.2bn	74.9bn	79.3bn
per capita	USD	1,228	1,381	1,454
Growth	%	2.0	2.6	2.6
Inflation	%	16.2	14.2	7.8
Def bdgt	MMK	3.70trn	5.64trn	
	USD	2.08bn	3.05bn	
USD1=MMK		1,777.99	1,846.82	1,937.48

Real-terms defence budget trend (USDbn, constant 2015)

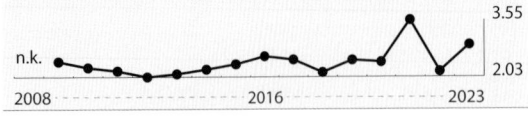

Population 57,113,554

Age	0–14	15–19	20–24	25–29	30–64	65 plus
Male	12.7%	4.2%	4.1%	4.1%	21.3%	3.0%
Female	12.1%	4.0%	4.0%	4.2%	22.5%	3.8%

Capabilities

Myanmar's Tatmadaw (armed forces) seized power in 2021 from the democratically elected National League for Democracy (NLD). Since the coup, there has been widespread civil unrest and clashes with ethnic armed organisations as well as People's Defence Force (PDF) groups formed by protestors after the putsch. These tensions sharpened the Tatmadaw's focus on internal security and counter-insurgency, with the armed forces launching multi-pronged counter-insurgency campaigns in 2021 and 2022. The Tatmadaw has been accused of widespread human-rights abuses against non-combatants during such operations. Human-rights concerns gained international attention after the widely condemned actions targeting the Rohingya ethnic minority began in 2017. Ethnic armed organisations have for decades fought the central government along Myanmar's border areas. A 2016 White Paper prioritised ending conflicts with domestic armed groups. However, the current conflict has spread across the country to areas relatively untouched by violence in previous years. Since the 1990s, Myanmar's armed forces have attempted to develop limited conventional warfare capabilities, though force health, morale and general cohesion have been called into question by the renewed focus on internal security. The country has a limited small-arms industry organised through the Directorate of Defence Industries. While the country's defence-industrial capacity remains limited, naval-shipbuilding capability has grown, with satellite imagery revealing in December 2020 the construction of a new guided-missile frigate at the Naval Dockyard in Thanlyin. The Aircraft Production and Maintenance Base in Meiktila has performed final assembly and maintenance, repair and overhaul services on trainer/light-attack aircraft and military helicopters since 2010. China and Russia are key defence cooperation partners.

ACTIVE 201,000 (Army 170,000 Navy 16,000 Air 15,000) **Gendarmerie & Paramilitary 107,000**

Conscript liability 24–36 months

ORGANISATIONS BY SERVICE

Army ε120,000-170,000

14 military regions, 7 regional op comd. Following the 2021 coup, and reports of desertions, combat losses and recruitment problems, personnel figures should be treated with caution

FORCES BY ROLE

COMMAND
20 div HQ (military op comd)
10 inf div HQ
34+ bde HQ (tactical op comd)

MANOEUVRE
Armoured
  10 armd bn
Light
  100 inf bn (coy)
  337 inf bn (coy) (regional comd)

COMBAT SUPPORT
7 arty bn
37 indep arty coy
6 cbt engr bn
54 fd engr bn
40 int coy
45 sigs bn

AIR DEFENCE
7 AD bn

EQUIPMENT BY TYPE

ARMOURED FIGHTING VEHICLES
  MBT 195+: 10 T-55; 50 T-72S; 25+ Type-59D; 100 Type-69-II; 10+ Type-90-II (MBT-2000)
  LT TK 105 Type-63 (ε60 serviceable)
  ASLT 24 PTL-02 mod
  RECCE 95+: ε50 AML-90; 33 BRDM-2MS (incl CP); 12+ EE-9 *Cascavel*; MAV-1
  IFV 36+: 10+ BTR-3U; 26+ MT-LBMSh
  APC 345+
    APC (T) 305: 250 ZSD-85; 55 ZSD-90
    APC (W) 30+ ZSL-92
    PPV 10+: BAAC-87; Gaia *Thunder*; 10 MPV
  AUV MAV-2; MAV-3

ENGINEERING & MAINTENANCE VEHICLES
  ARV Type-72
  VLB MT-55A

ANTI-TANK/ANTI-INFRASTRUCTURE
  RCL 84mm *Carl Gustaf*; **106mm** M40A1
  GUNS • TOWED 60: **57mm** 6-pdr; **76mm** 17-pdr

ARTILLERY 440+
  SP 155mm 42: 30 NORA B-52; 12 SH-1
  TOWED 282+: **105mm** 150: 54 M-56; 96 M101; **122mm** 100 D-30; **130mm** 16 M-46; **140mm**; **155mm** 16 Soltam M-845P

MRL 36+: **107mm** 30 Type-63; **122mm** BM-21 *Grad* (reported); Type-81; **240mm** 6+ M-1985 mod
MOR 80+: **82mm** Type-53 (M-37); **120mm** 80+: 80 Soltam; Type-53 (M-1943)

SURFACE-TO-SURFACE MISSILE LAUNCHERS
SRBM • Conventional some *Hwasong*-6 (reported)

AIR DEFENCE
SAM 4+
Medium-range 12+: 12+ KS-1A (CH-SA-12); S-125-2M *Pechora*-2M (RS-SA-26); 2K12 *Kvadrat*-M (RS-SA-6 *Gainful*)
Point-defence HN-5 (CH-SA-3) (reported); 9K310 *Igla*-1 (RS-SA-16 *Gimlet*)
SPAAGM 30mm Some 2K22 *Tunguska* (RS-SA-19 *Grison*)
GUNS 46
SP 57mm 12 Type-80
TOWED 34: **37mm** 24 Type-74; **40mm** 10 M1

Navy ε16,000
EQUIPMENT BY TYPE
SUBMARINES • SSK 2
1 *Min Kyaw Htin* (ex-PRC Type-035B (*Ming*)) with 8 single 533mm TT
1 *Min Ye Thein Kha Thu* (ex-IND *Sindhughosh* (Project 877EKM (*Kilo*))) with 6 single 533mm TT
PRINCIPAL SURFACE COMBATANTS • FRIGATES 5
FFGHM 2 *Kyansitthar* with 2 twin lnchr with C-802 (CH-SS-N-6) AShM, 1 sextuple lnchr with MANPAD SAM, 2 RDC-32 A/S mor, 3 AK630 CIWS, 1 76mm gun (capacity 1 med hel)
FFGM 1 *Aung Zeya* with 2 quad lnchr with DPRK AShM (possibly 3M24 derivative), 1 sextuple GMLS with MANPAD SAM; 4 AK630 CIWS, 2 RDC-32 A/S mor, 1 76mm gun, 1 hel landing platform
FFG 2 *Mahar Bandoola* (ex-PRC Type-053H1 (*Jianghu* I)) with 2 quad lnchr with C-802 (CH-SS-N-6) AShM, 2 RBU 1200 *Uragan* A/S mor, 2 twin 100mm guns
PATROL AND COASTAL COMBATANTS 80
CORVETTES 3
FSGHM 1 *Tabinshwethi* (*Anawrahta* mod) with 2 twin lnchr with C-802 (CH-SS-N-6), 1 sextuple lnchr with unknown MANPADs, 2 RBU 1200 *Uragan* A/S mor, 1 76mm gun (capacity 1 med hel)
FSG 2 *Anawrahta* with 2 twin lnchr with C-802 (CH-SS-N-6) AShM, 2 RDC-32 A/S mor, 1 76mm gun, 1 hel landing platform
PSOH 2 *Inlay* with 1 twin 57mm gun
PCG 8: 6 Type-037-IG (*Houxin*) with 2 twin lnchr with C-801 (CH-SS-N-4) AShM; 2 FAC(M) mod with 2 twin lnchr with C-802 (CH-SS-N-6) AShM, 1 AK630 CIWS
PCT 2 *Yan Nyein Aung* (Project PGG 063) with 2 FQF 1200 A/S mor, 2 triple 324mm TLS with *Shyena* LWT
PCO 2 *Indaw*
PCC 7 Type-037 (*Hainan*) with 4 RBU 1200 *Uragan* A/S mor, 2 twin 57mm guns
PBG 5 *Myanmar* with 2 single lnchr with C-801 (CH-SS-N-4) AShM
PBF 7: 1 Type-201; 6 *Super Dvora* Mk III
PBR 14: 4 *Sagu*; 9 Y-301†; 1 Y-301 (Imp)
PB 30: 3 PB-90; 6 PGM 401; 3 PGM 412; 15 *Myanmar*; 3 *Swift*
AMPHIBIOUS
PRINCIPAL AMPHIBIOUS VESSELS • LPD 1:
1 *Moattama* (ROK *Makassar*) (capacity 2 LCVP; 2 hels; 13 tanks; 500 troops)
LANDING CRAFT 23: **LCU** 7; **LCM** 16
LOGISTICS AND SUPPORT 13
ABU 1
AGS 3: 1 *Innya*; 2 other
AH 1 *Thanlwin*
AK 1
AKL 5
AP 1 *Chindwin*
AWT 1

Naval Infantry 800
FORCES BY ROLE
MANOEUVRE
Light
1 inf bn

Air Force ε15,000
FORCES BY ROLE
FIGHTER
4 sqn with F-7 *Airguard*; FT-7; FTC-2000G; JF-17/JF-17B *Thunder*; MiG-29 *Fulcrum*; MiG-29SE/SM/UB *Fulcrum*; Su-30SM *Flanker* H
GROUND ATTACK
2 sqn with A-5C *Fantan*
TRANSPORT
1 sqn with ATR-72-600; F-27 *Friendship*; FH-227; PC-6AB *Turbo Porter*; Y-12 (IV)
TRAINING
2 sqn with G-4 *Super Galeb**; PC-7 *Turbo Trainer**; PC-9*
1 (trg/liaison) sqn with Cessna 550 *Citation* II; Cessna 180 *Skywagon*; K-8 *Karakorum**
ATTACK/TRANSPORT HELICOPTER
4 sqn with Bell 205; Bell 206 *Jet Ranger*; Ka-28 *Helix* A; Mi-17 *Hip* H; Mi-35P *Hind*; PZL Mi-2 *Hoplite*; PZL W-3 *Sokol*; SA316 *Alouette* III
EQUIPMENT BY TYPE
AIRCRAFT 175 combat capable
FTR 64: 21 F-7 *Airguard*; 11 FT-7; 11 MiG-29 *Fulcrum*; 6 MiG-29SE *Fulcrum*; 10 MiG-29SM *Fulcrum*; 5 MiG-29UB *Fulcrum*
FGA 14: 6 FTC-2000G; 4 JF-17 *Thunder* (FC-1 Block II); 2 JF-17B *Thunder* (FC-1 Block II); 2+ Su-30SM *Flanker* H
ATK 21 A-5C *Fantan*
MP 2 ATR-42
TPT 34: **Medium** 6: 4 Y-8D; 2 Y-8F-200W **Light**

28: 1 ATR-42; 1 ATR-72-600; 5 Beech 1900D; 2 C295 (reported); 4 Cessna 180 *Skywagon*; 1 Cessna 550 *Citation II*; 3 F-27 *Friendship*; 5 PC-6A/B *Turbo Porter*; 6+ Y-12 (IV)
PAX 1+ FH-227
TRG 96: 11 G-4 *Super Galeb**; 20 G 120; ε24 K-8 *Karakorum**; 12 PC-7 *Turbo Trainer**; 9 PC-9*; 20 Yak-130 *Mitten**

HELICOPTERS
ATK 11 Mi-35P *Hind*
ASW 2 Ka-28 *Helix* A
MRH 21: 3 AS365; 9 Mi-17 *Hip* H; 9 SA316 *Alouette* III
TPT 48: **Medium** 10 PZL W-3 *Sokol*; **Light** 38: 12 Bell 205; 6 Bell 206 *Jet Ranger*; 3 H120 *Colibri*; 17 PZL Mi-2 *Hoplite*

UNINHABITED AERIAL VEHICLES
CISR • Heavy 4 CH-3
ISR • Light S-100 *Camcopter*

AIR-LAUNCHED MISSILES
AAM • IR PL-5; R-73 (RS-AA-11a *Archer*); PL-5E-II; **IR/SARH** R-27 (RS-AA-10 *Alamo*); **ARH** PL-12 (CH-AA-7a *Adze*); R-77 (RS-AA-12a *Adder*)
AShM C-802A

Gendarmerie & Paramilitary 107,000

Coast Guard
EQUIPMENT BY TYPE
PATROL AND COASTAL COMBATANTS 6
PB 6: 3 PGM 412; 3 other

People's Police Force 72,000

People's Militia 35,000

Nepal NPL

Nepalese Rupee NPR		2022	2023	2024
GDP	NPR	4.93trn	5.36trn	6.01trn
	USD	40.8bn	41.3bn	45.5bn
per capita	USD	1,354	1,353	1,468
Growth	%	5.6	0.8	5.0
Inflation	%	6.3	7.8	6.7
Def bdgt	NPR	51.0bn	55.0bn	
	USD	422m	424m	
USD1=NPR		120.84	129.70	132.10

Real-terms defence budget trend (USDm, constant 2015)

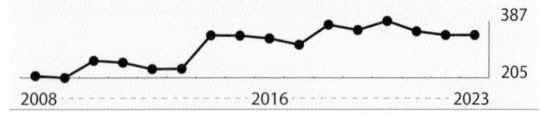

Population 30,899,443

Age	0–14	15–19	20–24	25–29	30–64	65 plus
Male	13.5%	4.9%	5.0%	5.0%	17.5%	3.0%
Female	12.8%	4.6%	4.9%	5.1%	20.5%	3.2%

Capabilities

The principal role of Nepal's armed forces is to maintain territorial integrity, but they have traditionally also provided internal security and humanitarian relief. Nepal has a history of deploying troops as UN peacekeepers. Training support for the all-volunteer force is provided by several countries, including China, India and the US. Following a 2006 peace accord with the Maoist People's Liberation Army, Maoist personnel underwent a process of demobilisation or integration into the armed forces. Gurkhas continue to be recruited by the British and Indian armed forces and the Singaporean police. The small air wing of Nepal's army provides limited transport and support capacity, but mobility remains a challenge, in part because of the country's topography. Nepal's logistic capability appears sufficient for internal-security operations; however, its UN peacekeepers are largely dependent on contracted logistics support. Modernisation plans include a very limited increase in the size of its air wing. In 2019, Nepal agreed to buy two M-28 *Skytruck* light transport aircraft from the US. Both arrived in December 2019. In 2023, Nepal agreed to acquire a further two M-28s, scheduled for delivery in 2025. The country has some maintenance capacities, but otherwise lacks a defence industry and is dependent on foreign suppliers for modern equipment. In August 2023, Nepal and China agreed to resume a joint military exercise between the Nepalese army and the PLA, which had been stalled since 2018.

ACTIVE 96,600 (Army 96,600) Gendarmerie & Paramilitary 15,000

ORGANISATIONS BY SERVICE

Army 96,600
FORCES BY ROLE
COMMAND
  2 inf div HQ

1 (valley) comd

SPECIAL FORCES

1 bde (1 SF bn, 1 AB bn, 1 cdo bn, 1 ranger bn, 1 mech inf bn)

MANOEUVRE

Light

18 inf bde (total: 62 inf bn; 32 indep inf coy)

COMBAT SUPPORT

1 arty bde

4 arty regt

5 engr bn

1 sigs bde

AIR DEFENCE

2 AD regt

4 indep AD coy

EQUIPMENT BY TYPE

ARMOURED FIGHTING VEHICLES

RECCE 40 *Ferret*

APC 253

APC (W) 13: 8 OT-64C; 5 WZ-551

PPV 240: 90 *Casspir*; 150 MPV

AUV Dongfeng *Mengshi*; CS/VN3C mod 2

ARTILLERY 92+

TOWED 105mm 22: 8 L118 Light Gun; 14 pack howitzer (6 non-operational)

MOR 70+: 81mm; 120mm 70 M-43 (est 12 op)

AIR DEFENCE • GUNS • TOWED 32+: **14.5mm** 30 Type-56 (ZPU-4); **37mm** (PRC); **40mm** 2 L/60

Air Wing 320

EQUIPMENT BY TYPE†

AIRCRAFT • TPT • Light 7: 1 BN-2T *Islander*; 1 CN235M-220; 3 M-28 *Skytruck*; 2 PA-28 *Cherokee* (trg)

HELICOPTERS

MRH 13: 2 AW139; 1 Bell 407GXP (VIP); 2 *Dhruv*; 2 *Lancer*; 3 Mi-17-1V *Hip* H; 2 Mi-17V-5 *Hip*; 1 SA315B *Lama* (*Cheetah*)

TPT • Light 3: 2 AS350B2 *Ecureuil*; 1+ Bell 206

Paramilitary 15,000

Armed Police Force 15,000

Ministry of Home Affairs

DEPLOYMENT

CENTRAL AFRICAN REPUBLIC: UN • MINUSCA 1,240; 2 inf bn; 1 MP pl

DEMOCRATIC REPUBLIC OF THE CONGO: UN • MONUSCO 1,152; 1 inf bn; 1 engr coy

IRAQ: UN • UNAMI 87; 1 sy unit

LEBANON: UN • UNIFIL 874; 1 mech inf bn; 1 log coy

LIBYA: UN • UNISMIL 235; 2 sy coy

MIDDLE EAST: UN • UNTSO 3

SOUTH SUDAN: UN • UNMISS 1,759; 2 inf bn

SUDAN: UN • UNISFA 106; 1 log coy

SYRIA/ISRAEL: UN • UNDOF 415; 1 mech inf coy; 1 inf coy; 1 log coy(-)

WESTERN SAHARA: UN • MINURSO 5

FOREIGN FORCES

United Kingdom 60 (Gurkha trg org)

New Zealand NZL

New Zealand Dollar NZD		2022	2023	2024
GDP	NZD	381bn	406bn	414bn
	USD	242bn	249bn	248bn
per capita	USD	47,226	48,072	47,223
Growth	%	2.7	1.1	1.0
Inflation	%	7.2	4.9	2.7
Def bdgt	NZD	5.19bn	6.08bn	6.53bn
	USD	3.30bn	3.74bn	3.90bn
USD1=NZD		1.57	1.63	1.67

Real-terms defence budget trend (USDbn, constant 2015)

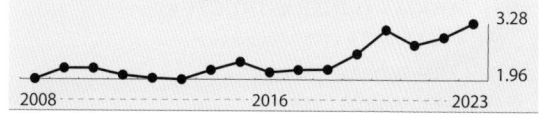

3.28
1.96
2008 — 2016 — 2023

Population	5,109,702					
Age	0–14	15–19	20–24	25–29	30–64	65 plus
Male	9.8%	3.3%	3.2%	3.5%	22.5%	7.7%
Female	9.3%	3.1%	3.1%	3.3%	22.3%	8.8%

Capabilities

The New Zealand Defence Force (NZDF) is well-trained and has substantial operational experience. The government issued the Defence Policy and Strategy Statement 2023 to address changes in its security environment, including rising tension in the South and East China seas, but also reflecting Russia's 2022 invasion of Ukraine. It also issued design principles for its force development over the next 15 years to prepare the armed forces for 'increased strategic competition and the adverse effects of climate change'. New Zealand's closest defence partner is Australia and it has revived defence relations with the United States. Aukland considers defence relationships with Pacific Island states key to its and the region's security. The 2019 Defence Capability Plan outlined plans to acquire a sealift vessel and transport aircraft. The NZDF also seeks to expand the army to 6,000 personnel by 2035. Replacement of the ANZAC frigates, both of which are being upgraded, has been postponed until the 2030s. In April 2023, the Australian army and that of Zealand agreed, under 'Plan Anzac', to formally structure cooperation on areas including training and readiness. The army is revamping its protected mobility capabilities with new systems. The armed forces are dealing with recruitment challenges. New Zealand has a small defence industry consisting of numerous private companies and subsidiaries of larger North American and European firms. These companies provide some maintenance, repair and overhaul capability, but significant work is contracted overseas.

ACTIVE 8,700 (Army 4,250 Navy 2,050 Air 2,400)
RESERVE 3,250 (Army 2,050 Navy 800 Air Force 400)

ORGANISATIONS BY SERVICE

Army 4,250
FORCES BY ROLE
SPECIAL FORCES
  1 SF regt
MANOEUVRE
  Light
  1 inf bde (1 armd recce regt, 2 lt inf bn, 1 arty regt (2 arty bty), 1 engr regt(-), 1 MP coy, 1 sigs regt, 2 log bn)
EQUIPMENT BY TYPE
ARMOURED FIGHTING VEHICLES
  IFV 74 NZLAV-25
  AUV 18 *Bushmaster*
ENGINEERING & MAINTENANCE VEHICLES
  AEV 7 NZLAV
  ARV 3 LAV-R
ANTI-TANK/ANTI-INFRASTRUCTURE
  MSL • MANPATS FGM-148 *Javelin*
ARTILLERY 56
  TOWED 105mm 24 L118 Light Gun
  MOR 81mm 32

Reserves
Territorial Force 1,850 reservists
Responsible for providing trained individuals for augmenting deployed forces
FORCES BY ROLE
COMBAT SERVICE SUPPORT
  3 (Territorial Force Regional) trg regt

Navy 2,050
Fleet based in Auckland. Fleet HQ at Wellington
EQUIPMENT BY TYPE
PRINCIPAL SURFACE COMBATANTS • FRIGATES 2
  FFHM 2 *Anzac* (GER MEKO 200) with 1 20-cell VLS with *Sea Ceptor* SAM, 2 triple SVTT Mk 32 324mm ASTT with Mk 46 mod 5 LWT, 1 Mk 15 *Phalanx* Block 1B CIWS, 1 127mm gun (capacity 1 SH-2G(I) *Super Seasprite* ASW hel)
PATROL AND COASTAL COMBATANTS 5
  PSOH (2 *Otago* (capacity 1 SH-2G(I) *Super Seasprite* ASW hel) (ice-strengthened hull) in reserve)
  PCC 2 *Lake*
  PBF 3 *Littoral Manoeuvre Craft* (Sentinel 1250)
AMPHIBIOUS • LANDING CRAFT 2
  LCM 2 (operated off HMNZS *Canterbury*)
LOGISTICS AND SUPPORT • 3
  AGS 1 *Manawanui* with 1 hel landing platform
  AKRH 1 *Canterbury* (capacity 4 NH90 tpt hel; 1 SH-2G(I) *Super Seasprite* ASW hel; 2 LCM; 16 NZLAV; 20 trucks; 250 troops)
  AORH 1 *Aotearoa* (capacity 1 NH90/SH-2G(I) hel)
UNINHABITED MARITIME SYSTEMS • UUV
  DATA REMUS 100/300
  UTL *Cougar* XT

Air Force 2,400
FORCES BY ROLE
MARITIME PATROL
  1 sqn with P-8A *Poseidon*
TRANSPORT
  1 sqn with B-757-200 (upgraded); C-130H *Hercules* (upgraded)
ANTI-SUBMARINE/SURFACE WARFARE
  1 (RNZAF/RNZN) sqn with SH-2G(I) *Super Seasprite*
TRAINING
  1 sqn with T-6C *Texan* II
  1 sqn with Beech 350 *King Air* (leased)
TRANSPORT HELICOPTER
  1 sqn with AW109LUH; NH90
EQUIPMENT BY TYPE
AIRCRAFT 4 combat capable
  ASW 4 P-8A *Poseidon*
  TPT 10: **Medium** 4 C-130H *Hercules* (upgraded); **Light** 4 Beech 350 *King Air* (leased); **PAX** 2 B-757-200 (upgraded)
  TRG 11 T-6C *Texan* II
HELICOPTERS
  ASW 8 SH-2G(I) *Super Seasprite*
  TPT 13: **Medium** 8 NH90; **Light** 5 AW109LUH
AIR-LAUNCHED MISSILES
  AShM AGM-119 *Penguin* Mk2 mod7

DEPLOYMENT
EGYPT: MFO 28; 1 trg unit; 1 tpt unit
MIDDLE EAST: UN • UNTSO 8
SOUTH SUDAN: UN • UNMISS 3
UNITED KINGDOM: Operation *Tieke* (Interflex) 71

Pakistan PAK

Pakistani Rupee PKR		2022	2023	2024
GDP	PKR	66.6trn	84.7trn	107trn
	USD	375bn	400bn	382bn
per capita	USD	1,650	1,700	1,534
Growth	%	6.1	-0.5	2.5
Inflation	%	12.1	29.2	23.6
Def bdgt [a]	PKR	1.74trn	1.97trn	2.38trn
	USD	9.77bn	11.1bn	13.3bn
USD1=PKR		177.83	177.83	178.83

[a] Includes defence allocations to the Public Sector Development Programme (PSDP), including funding to the Defence Division and the Defence Production Division

Real-terms defence budget trend (USDbn, constant 2015)

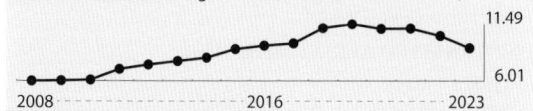

11.49 (2008 start ~6.01, peak ~11.49 around 2019, 2023)

Population	247,653,551				
Age	0–14	15–19	20–24	25–29	30–64	65 plus
Male	17.8%	5.2%	4.7%	4.2%	16.9%	2.2%
Female	17.0%	4.9%	4.5%	4.0%	16.1%	2.6%

Capabilities

The armed forces have considerable domestic political influence and are the dominant voice on defence and security policy. Pakistan's nuclear and conventional forces have traditionally been oriented and structured against a prospective threat from India. Since 2008, counter-insurgency and counterterrorism have been the forces' main effort. Although an army-led counterterrorism operation has improved domestic security, terrorist attacks continue. Some analysts believe that the Pakistan government considered the Taliban victory in Afghanistan an initial policy success; however, widely recognised security differences have since emerged with the Taliban government in Afghanistan. A 2021 mutual reaffirmation of the 2003 ceasefire agreement between India and Pakistan has reduced conflict across the Line of Control in the disputed region of Jammu and Kashmir. The armed forces have a major role in disaster relief. Overseas, they have a considerable number of personnel contributing to UN peacekeeping missions, principally in Africa. China is Pakistan's main defence partner, with all three services employing a large amount of Chinese equipment. Military cooperation with the US is limited and focused on counterterrorism. The military enjoys good recruitment and retention, though there are concerns about politicisation, radicalisation and pay, given Pakistan's growing political, security and fiscal crises. The army and air force have considerable operational experience from a decade of counter-insurgency operations in Pakistan's tribal areas. Although funds have been directed towards improving security and fencing on the border with Afghanistan, the Afghan Taliban regime provides little support to those efforts. Investments in military nuclear programmes continue despite budget pressures, including the testing of a nuclear-capable sea-launched cruise missile. Ending a lull in missile testing since April 2022, Pakistan in October 2023 tested the *Ababeel* ballistic missile, confirming its ambition to develop MIRVs to counter Indian defences. The navy and air force are modernising across a range of activities. A National Security Policy issued in 2022 committed Pakistan to defence, deterrence and territorial integrity, but also highlighted the need for space, information and cybersecurity capacities. The indigenous defence industry has well-developed maintenance facilities for combat aircraft and exports platforms, weapons and ammunition. Pakistan has close defence-industrial ties with China.

ACTIVE 660,000 (Army 560,000 Navy 30,000 Air 70,000) **Gendarmerie & Paramilitary 291,000**

ORGANISATIONS BY SERVICE

Strategic Forces

Operational control rests with the National Command Authority. The Strategic Plans Directorate (SPD) manages and commands all of Pakistan's military nuclear capability. The SPD also commands a reportedly 25,000-strong military security force responsible for guarding the country's nuclear infrastructure

Army Strategic Forces Command 12,000–15,000

Commands all land-based strategic nuclear forces

EQUIPMENT BY TYPE

SURFACE-TO-SURFACE MISSILE LAUNCHERS 60+
  MRBM • Nuclear 30+: ε30 *Ghauri/Ghauri* II (*Hatf*-V)/ *Shaheen*-II (*Hatf*-VI); *Shaheen*-III (in test)
  SRBM • Nuclear 30+: ε30 *Ghaznavi* (*Hatf*-III – PRC M-11)/*Shaheen*-I (*Hatf*-IV); some *Abdali* (*Hatf*-II); some *Nasr* (*Hatf*-IX)
  GLCM • Nuclear *Babur*-I/IA (*Hatf*-VII); *Ra'ad* (*Hatf*-VIII – in test)

Air Force

1–2 sqn of F-16A/B or *Mirage* 5 may be assigned a nuclear-strike role

Army 560,000

FORCES BY ROLE

COMMAND
  9 corps HQ
  1 (Northern) comd

SPECIAL FORCES
  2 SF gp (total: 4 SF bn)

MANOEUVRE

Armoured
  2 armd div
  7 indep armd bde

Mechanised
  2 mech inf div
  1 indep mech bde

Light
  18 inf div
  5 indep inf bde
  4 (Northern Command) inf bde

Other
  2 sy div

COMBAT SUPPORT
1 arty div
14 arty bde
7 engr bde

AVIATION
7 avn sqn

HELICOPTER
3 atk hel sqn
1 ISR hel sqn
1 SAR hel sqn
4 tpt hel sqn
1 spec ops hel sqn
5 hel sqn

AIR DEFENCE
1 AD comd (3 AD gp (total: 8 AD bn))

EQUIPMENT BY TYPE

ARMOURED FIGHTING VEHICLES
MBT 2,537: 300 *Al-Khalid* (MBT 2000); ε110 *Al-Khalid* I; 315 T-80UD; ε500 *Al-Zarrar*; 400 Type-69; 268 Type-85-IIAP; 44 VT-4; ε600 ZTZ-59
APC 3,545
  APC (T) 3,200: 2,300 M113A1/A2/P; ε200 *Talha*; 600 VCC-1/VCC-2; ε100 ZSD-63
  APC (W) 120 BTR-70/BTR-80
  PPV 225 *Maxxpro*
  AUV 10 *Dingo* 2

ENGINEERING & MAINTENANCE VEHICLES
ARV 262+: 175 Type-70/Type-84 (W653/W653A); *Al-Hadeed*; 52 M88A1; 35 *Maxxpro* ARV; T-54/T-55
VLB M47M; M48/60
MW *Aardvark* Mk II

ANTI-TANK/ANTI-INFRASTRUCTURE
MSL
  SP M901 TOW; ε30 *Maaz* (HJ-8 on *Talha* chassis)
  MANPATS HJ-8; TOW
RCL 75mm Type-52; **106mm** M40A1 **RL 89mm** M20
GUNS 85mm 200 Type-56 (D-44)

ARTILLERY 4,619+
SP 552: **155mm** 492: 200 M109A2; ε115 M109A5; 123 M109L; ε54 SH-15; **203mm** 60 M110/M110A2
TOWED 1,629: **105mm** 329: 216 M101; 113 M-56; **122mm** 570: 80 D-30 (PRC); 490 Type-54 (M-1938); **130mm** 410 Type-59-I; **155mm** 292: 144 M114; 148 M198; **203mm** 28 M115
MRL 88+: **107mm** Type-81; **122mm** 52+: 52 *Azar* (Type-83); some KRL-122; **300mm** 36 A100
MOR 2,350+: **81mm**; **120mm** AM-50

SURFACE-TO-SURFACE MISSILE LAUNCHERS
MRBM • Nuclear 30+: ε30 *Ghauri/Ghauri* II (*Hatf*-V)/*Shaheen*-II (*Hatf*-VI); some *Shaheen*-III (in test)
SRBM 135+: **Nuclear** 30+: ε30 *Ghaznavi* (*Hatf*-III – PRC M-11)/*Shaheen*-I (*Hatf*-IV); some *Abdali* (*Hatf*-II); some *Nasr* (*Hatf*-IX); **Conventional** 105 *Hatf*-I

GLCM • Nuclear some *Babur*-I/IA (*Hatf*-VII)

AIRCRAFT
TPT • Light 13: 1 Beech 350 *King Air*; 3 Cessna 208B; 1 Cessna 421; 1 Cessna 550 *Citation*; 1 Cessna 560 *Citation*; 2 *Turbo Commander* 690; 4 Y-12(II)
TRG 87 MFI-17B *Mushshak*

HELICOPTERS
ATK 42: 38 AH-1F/S *Cobra* with TOW; 4 Mi-35M *Hind*; (1 Mi-24 *Hind* in store)
MRH 115+: 10 H125M *Fennec*; 7 AW139; 26 Bell 412EP *Twin Huey*; 38+ Mi-17 *Hip* H; 2 Mi-171E *Hip*; 12 SA315B *Lama*; 20 SA319 *Alouette* III
TPT 79: **Medium** 36: 31 SA330 *Puma*; 4 Mi-171; 1 Mi-172; **Light** 43: 16 H125 *Ecureuil* (SAR); 5 Bell 205 (UH-1H *Iroquois*); 5 Bell 205A-1 (AB-205A-1); 13 Bell 206B *Jet Ranger* II; 4+ F-280FX
TRG 10 Hughes 300C

UNINHABITED AERIAL VEHICLES
CISR • Heavy 5 CH-4
ISR • Light *Bravo*; *Jasoos*; *Vector*

AIR DEFENCE
SAM 27+
  Long-range some HQ-9/P
  Medium-range 27 LY-80 (CH-SA-16)
  Short-range FM-90 (CH-SA-4)
  Point-defence M113 with RBS-70; *Anza*-II; FN-6 (CH-SA-10); *Mistral*; QW-18 (CH-SA-11); RBS-70
GUNS • TOWED 1,933: **14.5mm** 981; **35mm** 248 GDF-002/GDF-005 (with 134 *Skyguard* radar units); **37mm** 310 Type-55 (M-1939)/Type-65; **40mm** 50 L/60; **57mm** 144 Type-59 (S-60); **85mm** 200 Type-72 (M-1939) KS-12

Navy 30,000 (incl ε3,200 Marines)

EQUIPMENT BY TYPE
SUBMARINES 8
SSK 5:
  2 *Hashmat* (FRA *Agosta* 70) with 4 single 533mm ASTT with UGM-84 *Harpoon* AShM/F-17P HWT
  3 *Khalid* (FRA *Agosta* 90B) (of which 2 fitted with AIP) with 4 single 533mm ASTT with SM39 *Exocet* AShM/*SeaHake* mod 4 (DM2A4) HWT
SSW 3 MG110 (SF delivery) each with 2 single 533mm TT with F-17P HWT

PRINCIPAL SURFACE COMBATANTS • FRIGATES 10
FFGHM 9:
  1 *Babur* (TUR MILGEM mod) with 2 triple lnchr with AShM, 2 6-cell VLS with *Albatross*-NG (CAMM-ER) SAM, 2 triple 324mm ASTT with LWT, 1 *Gokdeniz* CIWS, 1 76mm gun (capacity 1 med hel)
  4 *Sword* (F-22P) with 2 quad lnchr with C-802A AShM, 1 octuple lnchr with FM-90N (CH-SA-N-4) SAM, 2 triple 324mm ASTT with ET-52C (A244/S) LWT, 2 RDC-32 A/S mor, 1 Type 730B (H/PJ-12) CIWS, 1 76mm gun (capacity 1 Z-9C *Haitun* hel)
  4 *Tughril* (PRC Type-054AP) with 2 twin lnchr with CM-302 (YJ-12A) AShM, 4 8-cell H/AJK-16 VLS with

LY-80N (HHQ-16 (CH-SA-N-16)) SAM, 2 triple 324mm ASTT with Yu-7 LWT, 2 H/PJ-11 CIWS, 1 76mm gun (capacity 1 Z-9C *Haitun* ASW hel)

FFGH 1 *Alamgir* (ex-US *Oliver Hazard Perry*) with 2 quad lnchr with RGM-84 *Harpoon* AShM, 2 triple 324mm ASTT with Mk 46 LWT, 1 Mk 15 *Phalanx* CIWS, 1 76mm gun

PATROL AND COASTAL COMBATANTS 21
  CORVETTES • FSH 2 *Yarmook* (Damen OPV 1900) (fitted for but not with 2 quad lnchr for AShM) with 1 Mk 15 *Phalanx* CIWS (capacity 1 hel)
  PCG 4: 2 *Azmat* (FAC(M)) with 2 quad lnchr with C-802A AShM, 1 AK630 CIWS; 2 *Azmat* (FAC(M)) with 2 triple lnchr with C-602 AShM, 1 AK630 CIWS
  PBG 4: 2 *Jalalat* with 2 twin lnchr with C-802 (CH-SS-N-6) AShM; 2 *Jurrat* with 2 twin lnchr with C-802 (CH-SS-N-6) AShM
  PBF 4: 2 *Kaan* 15 (TUR MRTP 15); 2 *Zarrar* (TUR MRTP 34)
  PBR 2 12T *Marine Assault Boat*
  PB 5: 1 *Larkana*; 4 M16 Fast Assault Boat

MINE WARFARE • MINE COUNTERMEASURES 5
  MCC 5 *Munsif* (ex-FRA *Eridan*) (1 more in store)

AMPHIBIOUS • LANDING CRAFT 8
  LCM 2
  LCAC 2 *Griffon* 8100TD
  UCAC 4 *Griffon* 2000TD

LOGISTICS AND SUPPORT 9
  AGS 2: 1 *Behr Masa*; 1 *Behr Paima*
  AOL 2 *Madadgar*
  AORH 2: 1 *Moawin* with 2 Mk 15 *Phalanx* CIWS, 1 hel landing platform; 1 *Nasr* (PRC *Fuqing*) with 1 Mk 15 *Phalanx* CIWS (capacity 1 SA319 *Alouette* III hel)
  AOL 2 *Gwadar*
  AXS 1

Marines ε3,200
FORCES BY ROLE
SPECIAL FORCES
  1 cdo gp
MANOEUVRE
  Amphibious
  3 mne bn
AIR DEFENCE
  1 AD bn

Naval Aviation
FORCES BY ROLE
ANTI-SUBMARINE WARFARE
  1 sqn with P-3B/C *Orion*
  1 sqn with *Sea King* Mk45
  1 sqn with Z-9C *Haitun*
  1 sqn with SA319B *Alouette* III
MARITIME PATROL
  1 sqn with F-27-200 MPA
  1 sqn with ATR-72-500; Hawker 850XP

EQUIPMENT BY TYPE
AIRCRAFT 10 combat capable
  ASW 10: 7 P-3B/C *Orion*; 3 ATR-72-500
  MP 6 F-27-200 MPA
  TPT 4: **Light** 3: 1 ATR-72-500; 2 Lineage 1000 (converting to MP); **PAX** 1 Hawker 850XP
HELICOPTERS
  ASW 10: 3 *Sea King* Mk45; 7 Z-9C *Haitun*
  MRH 6 SA319B *Alouette* III
  SAR 1 *Sea King* (ex-HAR3A)
  TPT • Medium 5: 1 *Commando* Mk2A; 3 *Commando* Mk3; 1 *Sea King* (ex-HC4)
UNINHABITED AERIAL VEHICLES
  ISR • Light 2 *Luna* NG
AIR-LAUNCHED MISSILES • AShM AM39 *Exocet*

Coastal Defence
FORCES BY ROLE
COASTAL Defence
  1 AShM regt with *Zarb* (YJ-62)
EQUIPMENT BY TYPE
COASTAL DEFENCE • AShM *Zarb* (YJ-62)

Air Force 70,000

3 regional comds: Northern (Peshawar), Central (Sargodha), Southern (Masroor). The Composite Air Tpt Wg, Combat Cadres School and PAF Academy are Direct Reporting Units

FORCES BY ROLE
FIGHTER
  3 sqn with F-7PG/FT-7PG *Airguard*
  1 sqn with F-16A/B MLU *Fighting Falcon*
  1 sqn with F-16A/B ADF *Fighting Falcon*
  1 sqn with *Mirage* IIID/E (IIIOD/EP)
FIGHTER/GROUND ATTACK
  1 sqn with J-10CE *Firebird*
  1 sqn with JF-17 *Thunder* (FC-1 Block I)
  1 sqn with JF-17 *Thunder* (FC-1 Block II)
  2 sqn with JF-17 *Thunder* (FC-1 Block I/II)
  1 sqn with JF-17 *Thunder* (FC-1 Block I/II/III); JF-17B *Thunder* (FC-1 Block II)
  1 sqn with F-16C/D Block 52 *Fighting Falcon*
  3 sqn with *Mirage* 5 (5PA)
ANTI-SURFACE WARFARE
  1 sqn with *Mirage* 5PA2/5PA3 with AM-39 *Exocet* AShM
ELECTRONIC WARFARE/ELINT
  1 sqn with *Falcon* 20F
AIRBORNE EARLY WARNING & CONTROL
  1 sqn with Saab 2000; Saab 2000 *Erieye*
  1 sqn with ZDK-03
SEARCH & RESCUE
  1 sqn with Mi-171Sh; AW139 (SAR/liaison)
  5 sqn with SA316 *Alouette* III

2 sqn with AW139
TANKER
1 sqn with Il-78 *Midas*
TRANSPORT
1 sqn with C-130E/H *Hercules*; L-100-20
1 sqn with CN235M-220
1 VIP sqn with A310; A319; Cessna 560XL *Citation Excel*; CN235M-220; F-27-200 *Friendship*; *Falcon* 20E; Global 6000; Gulfstream IVSP
1 (comms) sqn with EMB-500 *Phenom* 100; Y-12 (II)
TRAINING
1 OCU sqn with F-7P/FT-7P *Skybolt*; JF-17 *Thunder* (FC-1 Block II); JF-17B *Thunder* (FC-1 Block II)
1 OCU sqn with *Mirage* III/*Mirage* 5
1 OCU sqn with F-16A/B MLU *Fighting Falcon*
2 sqn with K-8 *Karakorum**
2 sqn with MFI-17
2 sqn with T-37C *Tweet*
AIR DEFENCE
1 bty with HQ-2 (CH-SA-1); 9K310 *Igla*-1 (RS-SA-16 *Gimlet*)
6 bty with *Crotale*
10 bty with SPADA 2000
EQUIPMENT BY TYPE
AIRCRAFT 452 combat capable
  FTR 151: 46 F-7PG *Airguard*; 20 F-7P *Skybolt*; 23 F-16A MLU *Fighting Falcon*; 21 F-16B MLU *Fighting Falcon*; 9 F-16A ADF *Fighting Falcon*; 4 F-16B ADF *Fighting Falcon*; 21 FT-7; 5 FT-7PG; 2 *Mirage* IIIB
  FGA 253: 12 F-16C Block 52 *Fighting Falcon*; 6 F-16D Block 52 *Fighting Falcon*; 14+ J-10CE *Firebird*; 49 JF-17 *Thunder* (FC-1 Block I); 58 JF-17 *Thunder* (FC-1 Block II); 15+ JF-17 *Thunder* (FC-1 Block III); 25 JF-17B *Thunder* (FC-1 Block II); 7 *Mirage* IIID (*Mirage* IIIOD); 30 *Mirage* IIIE (IIIEP); 25 *Mirage* 5 (5PA)/5PA2; 2 *Mirage* 5D (5DPA)/5DPA2; 10 *Mirage* 5PA3 (ASuW)
  ISR 10 *Mirage* IIIR* (*Mirage* IIIRP)
  ELINT 2 *Falcon* 20F
  AEW&C 10: 6 Saab 2000 *Erieye*; 4 ZDK-03
  TKR 4 Il-78 *Midas*
  TPT 37: **Medium** 18: 10 C-130E *Hercules*; 7 C-130H *Hercules*; 1 L-100-20; **Light** 14: 2 Cessna 208B; 1 Cessna 560XL *Citation Excel*; 4 CN235M-220; 4 EMB-500 *Phenom* 100; 1 F-27-200 *Friendship*; 2 Y-12 (II); **PAX** 7: 1 A310; 1 A319; 1 *Falcon* 20E; 1 Global 6000; 2 Gulfstream IV-SP; 1 Saab 2000
  TRG 140: 38 K-8 *Karakorum**; 79 MFI-17B *Mushshak*; 23 T-37C *Tweet*
HELICOPTERS
  MRH 29: 15 SA316 *Alouette* III; 14 AW139
  TPT • **Medium** 4 Mi-171Sh
UNINHABITED AERIAL VEHICLES
  CISR 7+: **Heavy** 4+: 1 *Akinci*; CH-3 (*Burraq*); CH-4 (reported); 2+ *Wing Loong* I; 1+ *Wing Loong* II; **Medium**

3+ *Bayraktar* TB2
  ISR • **Medium** *Falco*
AIR DEFENCE • **SAM** 190+
  Medium-range 6 HQ-2 (CH-SA-1)
  Short-range 184: 144 *Crotale*; ε40 SPADA 2000
  Point-defence 9K310 *Igla*-1 (RS-SA-16 *Gimlet*)
AIR-LAUNCHED MISSILES
  AAM • **IR** AIM-9L/P *Sidewinder*; *U-Darter*; PL-5; PL-5E-II; **IIR** PL-10 (CH-AA-9); **SARH** Super 530; **ARH** PL-12 (CH-AA-7A *Adze*); PL-15 (CH-AA-10); AIM-120C AMRAAM
  ASM AGM-65 *Maverick*; *Raptor* II
  AShM AM39 *Exocet*; C-802
  ARM MAR-1
  LACM • **Nuclear** *Ra'ad*
BOMBS
  INS/SAT-guided FT-6 (REK)
  Laser-guided *Paveway* II

Gendarmerie & Paramilitary 291,000 active

Airport Security Force 9,000
Government Aviation Division

Pakistan Coast Guards
Ministry of Interior
EQUIPMENT BY TYPE
PATROL AND COASTAL COMBATANTS 5:
  PBF 4
  PB 1

Frontier Corps 70,000
Ministry of Interior
FORCES BY ROLE
MANOEUVRE
  Reconnaissance
  1 armd recce sqn
  Other
  11 paramilitary regt (total: 40 paramilitary bn)
EQUIPMENT BY TYPE
ARMOURED FIGHTING VEHICLES
  APC (W) 45 UR-416

Maritime Security Agency ε2,000
FORCES BY ROLE
MARITIME PATROL
  1 sqn with BN-2T *Defender*
EQUIPMENT BY TYPE
PATROL AND COASTAL COMBATANTS 23
  PSO 2 *Kashmir* with 1 hel landing platform
  PCC 10: 4 *Barkat*; 4 *Hingol*; 2 *Sabqat* (ex-US *Island*)
  PBF 11 Response Boat-Medium (RB-M) (ex-US)
  AIRCRAFT • **TPT** • **Light** 3 BN-2T *Defender*

National Guard 185,000
Incl Janbaz Force; Mujahid Force; National Cadet Corps;

Women Guards
Pakistan Rangers 25,000
Ministry of Interior

DEPLOYMENT

ARABIAN SEA & GULF OF ADEN: Combined Maritime Forces • CTF-151: 1 FFGHM

CENTRAL AFRICAN REPUBLIC: UN • MINUSCA 1,311; 1 inf bn; 2 engr coy; 1 hel sqn

CYPRUS: UN • UNFICYP 3

DEMOCRATIC REPUBLIC OF THE CONGO: UN • MONUSCO 1,908; 2 inf bn; 1 hel sqn with SA330 Puma

SOMALIA: UN • UNSOS 1

SOUTH SUDAN: UN • UNMISS 287; 1 engr coy

SUDAN: UN • UNISFA 584; 1 inf bn(-)

WESTERN SAHARA: UN • MINURSO 10

FOREIGN FORCES

Figures represent total numbers for UNMOGIP mission in India and Pakistan
Argentina 4
Croatia 9
Italy 2
Korea, Republic of 6
Philippines 4
Romania 2
Sweden 3
Switzerland 3
Thailand 5
Uruguay 2

Papua New Guinea PNG

Papua New Guinea Kina PGK		2022	2023	2024
GDP	PGK	111bn	112bn	123bn
	USD	31.5bn	31.7bn	32.9bn
per capita	USD	2,622	2,581	2,624
Growth	%	4.3	3.0	5.0
Inflation	%	5.3	5.0	4.9
Def bdgt	PGK	344m	348m	
	USD	97.7m	98.4m	
USD1=PGK		3.52	3.54	3.74

Real-terms defence budget trend (USDm, constant 2015)

Population   9,819,350

Age	0–14	15–19	20–24	25–29	30–64	65 plus
Male	19.1%	5.0%	4.5%	4.1%	16.2%	1.9%
Female	18.3%	4.8%	4.3%	3.9%	16.0%	2.0%

Capabilities

The Papua New Guinea Defence Force (PNGDF) has suffered from chronic underfunding and lack of capacity to perform its core roles. After personnel reductions in the 2000s, the government made efforts in the next decade to revive defence capability. A 2013 defence White Paper identified core roles, including defending the state and civil-emergency assistance, but noted that 'defence capabilities have deteriorated to the extent that we have alarming gaps in our land, air and maritime borders'. The White Paper called for strengthening defence capability on an ambitious scale, with long-term plans calling for a 'division-sized force' of 10,000 personnel by 2030. The PNGDF continues to receive substantial external military assistance from Australia and China, which has donated equipment and conducted port calls in the country. In late 2018, plans were announced to build a joint US–Australia–Papua New Guinea naval base at Lombrum. The US and Papua New Guinea signed a defence cooperation agreement in May 2023 that updated and expanded a status of forces agreement. The US pledged security assistance funding. Discussions continue with Australia about extending defence and security cooperation; a bilateral security treaty may result. Australia continues to offer support, including in infrastructure improvement, maintenance support and capability development. The PNGDF is not able to deploy outside the country without assistance and there have only been small PNGDF deployments as part of UN peacekeeping missions. The forces have a limited air arm. The PNGDF will receive four patrol boats that Australia is donating to small Pacific Island nations. Papua New Guinea has no significant defence industry, though there is some local maintenance capacity.

ACTIVE 4,000 (Army 3,700 Maritime Element 200 Air 100)

ORGANISATIONS BY SERVICE

Army ε3,700

FORCES BY ROLE
SPECIAL FORCES
1 spec ops unit
MANOEUVRE
Light
2 inf bn
COMBAT SUPPORT
1 engr bn
1 EOD unit
COMBAT SERVICE SUPPORT
1 spt bn (1 sigs sqn; 1 supply coy)
EQUIPMENT BY TYPE
ARMOURED FIGHTING VEHICLES
APC • **APC (W)** 4 WZ-551†
ARTILLERY • **MOR** 3+: **81mm** Some; **120mm** 3

Maritime Element ε200
HQ located at Port Moresby
EQUIPMENT BY TYPE
PATROL AND COASTAL COMBATANTS • **PCO** 4 Guardian (AUS Bay mod)
AMPHIBIOUS • **LANDING CRAFT** 2
LCT 1 Buna (ex-AUS Balikpapan) (1 with trg role)
LCM 1 Cape Gloucester

Air Force ε100
FORCES BY ROLE
TRANSPORT
1 sqn with CN235M-100; PAC-750XSTOL
TRANSPORT HELICOPTER
1 sqn with Bell 212
EQUIPMENT BY TYPE
AIRCRAFT • **TPT** • **Light** 4: 1 CN235M-100 (1 more in store); ε3 PAC-750XSTOL
HELICOPTERS • **TPT** • **Light** 2 Bell 212 (leased)

DEPLOYMENT
SOUTH SUDAN: UN • UNMISS 2

Philippines PHL

Philippine Peso PHP		2022	2023	2024
GDP	PHP	22.0trn	24.3trn	26.4trn
	USD	404bn	436bn	476bn
per capita	USD	3,624	3,859	4,169
Growth	%	7.6	5.3	5.9
Inflation	%	5.8	5.8	3.2
Def bdgt [a]	PHP	384bn	344bn	
	USD	7.06bn	6.18bn	
FMA (US)	USD	20m	40m	40m
USD1=PHP		54.48	55.71	55.44

[a] Excludes military pensions

Real-terms defence budget trend (USDbn, constant 2015)
7.14 ... 2.46
2008 — 2016 — 2023

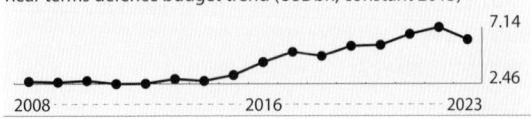

Population 116,434,200

Age	0–14	15–19	20–24	25–29	30–64	65 plus
Male	15.6%	4.9%	4.6%	4.2%	18.6%	2.2%
Female	14.9%	4.7%	4.4%	4.1%	18.4%	3.3%

Capabilities

Despite modest increases in defence funding in the decade up to 2023, the capabilities and procurement plans of the Armed Forces of the Philippines (AFP) remain limited. However, heightened tensions in the South China Sea – including the continued stand-off between the Chinese and Philippines Coast Guards at BRP *Sierra Madre* near the Second Thomas Shoal – and the new Marcos administration's more assertive stance towards China have shifted the strategic context. The 2018–2022 National Defense Strategy identified policy priorities, including ensuring sovereignty and territorial integrity, which became the main security priority in the 2023–2028 National Security Policy. The document signalled early stages of a reorientation from internal security towards territorial and external defence. The policy also highlighted the importance of the country's maritime interests, including in the South China Sea. The US is an ally of Philippines and provides support for the AFP's external security role and its counterterrorist operations. Manila, in 2023, granted the US rotational access to additional bases. Both countries in 2023 published bilateral defence guidelines, reaffirming the 1951 Mutual Defence Treaty and setting out future areas of defence cooperation. Japan and the Philippines are also finalising a Reciprocal Access Agreement akin to a Visiting Forces Agreement. The AFP continues to host the long-running *Balikatan* exercise series with US forces and participates in ADMM exercises. In 2017, it began trilateral joint maritime patrols in the Sulu Sea with Indonesia and Malaysia to counter regional terrorist activity. Priorities under the 'Horizon' modernisation programme (the final 'Horizon 3' phase runs from 2023–28) include combat aircraft, transport aircraft, ASW/MP aircraft, UAVs, frigates, and air-defence and coastal-defence systems. Some of these programmes were initially part of the 2018-2022 Horizon 2 phase. Concerns have been raised about some procurement ambitions due to budget concerns. The Philippine Aerospace Development Corporation, owned by the defence department since 2019, has assembled a variety of small helicopters and aircraft for the AFP, and also provides MRO services for military aircraft.

ACTIVE 146,250 (Army 103,200 Navy 25,450 Air 17,600) Gendarmerie & Paramilitary 26,000

RESERVE 131,000 (Army 100,000 Navy 15,000 Air 16,000) Gendarmerie & Paramilitary 50,000 (to age 49)

ORGANISATIONS BY SERVICE

Army 103,200

5 Area Unified Comd (joint service), 1 National Capital Region Comd

FORCES BY ROLE
SPECIAL FORCES
1 spec ops comd (1 ranger regt, 1 SF regt, 1 CT regt)
MANOEUVRE
Mechanised
1 armd div (2 mech bde (total: 3 lt armd bn, 7 armd cav coy, 4 mech inf bn), 1 cbt engr coy, 1 sigs coy, 1 avn regt)
Light
1 div (4 inf bde, 1 fd arty bn, 1 int bn, 1 sigs bn)
7 div (3 inf bde, 1 fd arty bn, 1 int bn, 1 sigs bn)
3 div (3 inf bde, 1 int bn, 1 sigs bn)
Other
1 (Presidential) gd gp
COMBAT SUPPORT
1 SP arty bn
2 MRL bty (forming)
5 engr bde
SURFACE-TO-SURFACE MISSILE
1 SSM bty (forming)
AIR DEFENCE
1 AD bty
EQUIPMENT BY TYPE
ARMOURED FIGHTING VEHICLES
LT TK 24: 7 FV101 *Scorpion*; 17+ *Sabrah* ASCOD
IFV 54: 2 YPR-765; 34 M113A1 FSV; 18 M113A2 FSV
APC 388
 APC (T) 168: 6 ACV300; 42 M113A1; 120 M113A2 (some with *Dragon* RWS)
 APC (W) 219: 73 LAV-150 *Commando*; 146 *Simba*
 PPV 3 CS/VP-3
ENGINEERING & MAINTENANCE VEHICLES
ARV 5+: ACV-300; M578; 4 M113 ARV; *Samson*; 1 *Sabrah* ASCOD ARV
VLB 2+: some GQL-111; 2 *Merkava* MkIV AVLB
ANTI-TANK-ANTI-INFRASTRUCTURE • RCL 75mm M20; **90mm** M67; **106mm** M40A1
ARTILLERY 272+
SP 155mm 12 ATMOS 2000
TOWED 220: **105mm** 204 M101/M102/Model 56 pack howitzer; **155mm** 16: 10 M114/M-68; 6 Soltam M-71

MOR 40+: **81mm** M29; **107mm** 40 M30; **120mm** some *Cardom*
AIRCRAFT
TPT • Light 5: 1 Beech 80 *Queen Air*; 1 Cessna 170; 1 Cessna 172; 1 Cessna P206A; 1 Short 330UTT
HELICOPTERS
TPT • Light 4: 2 Bo-105; 2 R-44 *Raven* II
UNINHABITED AERIAL VEHICLES
ISR • Medium *Blue Horizon*

Navy 25,450

EQUIPMENT BY TYPE
PRINCIPAL SURFACE COMBATANTS • FRIGATES 2
FFGHM 2 *Jose Rizal* (ROK HDF-3000) with 2 quad lnchr with *Hae Sung* I AShM, 2 twin *Simbad*-RC lnchr with *Mistral* SAM, 2 triple 324mm SEA TLS ASTT with K745 *Blue Shark* LWT, 1 76mm gun (fitted for but not with 1 8-cell VLS) (capacity 1 AW159 *Wildcat*)
PATROL AND COASTAL COMBATANTS 52
CORVETTES • FS 1 *Conrado Yap* (ex-ROK *Po Hang* (Flight III)) with 2 triple 324mm SVTT Mk 32 ASTT with Mk 46 LWT, 2 76mm guns
PSOH 3 *Del Pilar* (ex-US *Hamilton*) with 1 76mm gun (capacity 1 Bo 105)
PCF 3 *General Mariano Alvares* (ex-US *Cyclone*)
PCO 3 *Emilio Jacinto* (ex-UK *Peacock*) with 1 76mm gun
PBFG 6 MPAC Mk3 with 1 *Typhoon* MLS-ER quad lnchr with *Spike*-ER SSM
PBF 10: 6 MPAC Mk1/2; 4 *Nestor Acero* (ISR *Shaldag* V mod)
PB 26: 2 *Alberto Navarette* (ex-US *Point*); 22 *Jose Andrada*; 2 *Kagitingan*
AMPHIBIOUS
PRINCIPAL AMPHIBIOUS SHIPS • LPD 2:
 2 *Tarlac* (IDN *Makassar*) (capacity 2 LCVP; 3 hels; 13 tanks; 500 troops)
LANDING SHIPS • LST 4:
 2 *Bacolod City* (US *Besson*) with 1 hel landing platform (capacity 32 tanks; 150 troops)
 2 LST-1/542 (ex-US) (capacity 16 tanks; 200 troops) (1 other permanently grounded as marine outpost)
LANDING CRAFT 15
 LCM 2: 1 *Manobo*; 1 *Tagbanua* (capacity 100 tons; 200 troops)
 LCT 5 *Ivatan* (ex-AUS *Balikpapan*)
 LCU 4: 3 LCU Mk 6 (ex-US); 1 *Mamanwa* (ex-ROK *Mulgae* I)
 LCVP 4
LOGISTICS AND SUPPORT 6
AFDL 2
AGOR 1 *Gregorio Velasquez* (ex-US *Melville*)
AOL 1 *Lake Buhi*
AP 1 *Ang Pangulo*
AWT 1 *Lake Buluan*

Naval Aviation
EQUIPMENT BY TYPE
AIRCRAFT • TPT • Light 14: 5 Beech 90 *King Air* (TC-90); 3 BN-2A *Defender*; 4 Cessna 172; 2 Cessna 177 *Cardinal*
HELICOPTERS
  ASW 2 AW159 *Wildcat*
  TPT 12: **Medium** 4 Mi-171Sh; **Light** 8: 4 AW109E (2 armed); 4 Bo-105

Marines 8,300
FORCES BY ROLE
SPECIAL FORCES
  1 (force recon) spec ops bn
MANOEUVRE
  Amphibious
  4 mne bde (total: 12 mne bn)
COMBAT SERVICE SUPPORT
  1 CSS bde (6 CSS bn)
COASTAL DEFENCE
  1 coastal def bde (1 AShM bn (forming); 1 SAM bn (forming))
EQUIPMENT BY TYPE
ARMOURED FIGHTING VEHICLES
  APC • APC (W) 42: 19 LAV-150 *Commando*; 23 LAV-300
  AAV 67: 8 AAV-7A1; 4 LVTH-6†; 55 LVTP-7
ARTILLERY 37+
  TOWED 37: **105mm** 31: 23 M101; 8 M-26; **155mm** 6 Soltam M-71
  MOR 107mm M30

Naval Special Operations Group
FORCES BY ROLE
SPECIAL FORCES
  1 SEAL unit
  1 diving unit
  10 naval spec ops unit
  1 special boat unit
COMBAT SUPPORT
  1 EOD unit

Air Force 17,600
FORCES BY ROLE
FIGHTER
  1 sqn with FA-50PH *Fighting Eagle**
GROUND ATTACK
  1 sqn with EMB-314 *Super Tucano**
  1 sqn with OV-10A/C *Bronco**; SF-260F/TP*
ISR
  1 sqn with Cessna 208B *Grand Caravan*; Turbo Commander 690A
SEARCH & RESCUE
  4 (SAR/Comms) sqn with Bell 205 (UH-1M *Iroquois*);
  AUH-76; W-3A *Sokol*
TRANSPORT
  1 sqn with C-130B/H/T *Hercules*
  1 sqn with C295M/W; F-27-200 MPA; F-27-500 *Friendship*
  1 sqn with N-22B *Nomad*; N-22SL *Searchmaster*; C-212 *Aviocar* (NC-212i)
  1 VIP sqn with C295M; F-28 *Fellowship*; Gulfstream G280
TRAINING
  1 sqn with SF-260FH
  1 sqn with T-41B/D/K *Mescalero*
  1 sqn with S-211*
  1 sqn with Bell 205 (UH-1H *Iroquois*)
ATTACK HELICOPTER
  1 sqn with AH-1S *Cobra*; MD-520MG
  1 sqn with AW109E
TRANSPORT HELICOPTER
  2 sqn with Bell 205 (UH-1H *Iroquois*)
  1 sqn with S-70i *Black Hawk*
  1 (VIP) sqn with Bell 412EP *Twin Huey*; S-70A *Black Hawk* (S-70A-5)
ISR UAV
  1 sqn with *Hermes* 450/900
AIR DEFENCE
  2 bty with *Spyder*-MR
EQUIPMENT BY TYPE
AIRCRAFT 36 combat capable
  FGA 12 FA-50PH *Fighting Eagle*
  MP 3: 1 C-130T MP mod; 1 F-27-200 MPA; 1 N-22SL *Searchmaster*
  ISR 9: 3 Cessna 208B *Grand Caravan* EX; up to 6 OV-10A/C *Bronco**
  TPT 19: **Medium** 3: 1 C-130B *Hercules*; 1 C-130H *Hercules*; 1 C-130T *Hercules* **Light** 14: 4 C295M; 3 C295W; 1 F-27-500 *Friendship*; 3 N-22B *Nomad*; 1 Turbo Commander 690A; 2 C-212 *Aviocar* (NC-212i); **PAX** 2: 1 F-28 *Fellowship* (VIP); 1 Gulfstream G280
  TRG 35: 6 EMB-314 *Super Tucano**; 3+ S-211*; 7 SF-260FH; 9 SF-260TP*; 10 T-41B/D/K *Mescalero*
HELICOPTERS
  ATK 6: 2 AH-1S *Cobra*; 4 T129B
  MRH 39: 8 W-3A *Sokol*; 2 AUH-76; 8 AW109E; 8 Bell 412EP *Twin Huey*; 2 Bell 412HP *Twin Huey*; 11 MD-520MG
  TPT 35: **Medium** 16: 1 S-70A *Black Hawk* (S-70A-5); 15 S-70i *Black Hawk*; **Light** 19 Bell 205 (UH-1H *Iroquois*) (25 more non-operational)
UNINHABITED AERIAL VEHICLES
  ISR • Medium 15: 2 *Blue Horizon* II; up to 4 *Hermes* 450; 9 *Hermes* 900
AIR-LAUNCHED MISSILES
  AAM • IR AIM-9L *Sidewinder*
  ASM AGM-65D *Maverick*; AGM-65G2 *Maverick*
BOMBS

INS/GPS-guided: GBU-49 *Enhanced Paveway* II

AIR DEFENCE • SAM

Medium-range 6 *Spyder*-MR

Gendarmerie & Paramilitary 26,000

Coast Guard 26,000

EQUIPMENT BY TYPE

Rodman 38 and Rodman 101 owned by Bureau of Fisheries and Aquatic Resources

PATROL AND COASTAL COMBATANTS 49

PSOH 1 *Gabriela Silang* (OCEA OPV 270); 2 *Teresa Magbanua* (JPN *Kunigami* mod)

PCO 4 *San Juan* with 1 hel landing platform

PCC 10 *Parola* (MRRV)

PB 32: 4 *Boracay* (FPB 72 Mk II); 4 *Ilocos Norte*; 10 PCF 46; 12 PCF 50 (US *Swift* Mk1/2); 2 PCF 65 (US *Swift* Mk3)

LOGISTICS AND SUPPORT • ABU 1 *Corregidor*

AIRCRAFT • TPT • Light 3: 2 BN-2 *Islander*; 1 Cessna 208B *Grand Caravan* EX

HELICOPTERS • TPT • Light 6: 4 Bo-105; 2 H145

Citizen Armed Force Geographical Units 50,000 reservists

FORCES BY ROLE

MANOEUVRE

Other 56 militia bn (part-time units which can be called up for extended periods)

DEPLOYMENT

CENTRAL AFRICAN REPUBLIC: UN • MINUSCA 3

INDIA/PAKISTAN: UN • UNMOGIP 4

SOUTH SUDAN: UN • UNMISS 1

FOREIGN FORCES

Australia *Operation Augury* 100

United States US Indo-Pacific Command: *Operation Pacific Eagle – Philippines* 200

Singapore SGP

Singapore Dollar SGD		2022	2023	2024
GDP	SGD	644bn	667bn	705bn
	USD	467bn	497bn	521bn
per capita	USD	82,808	87,884	91,728
Growth	%	3.6	1.0	2.1
Inflation	%	6.1	5.5	3.5
Def bdgt	SGD	17.0bn	18.0bn	
	USD	12.3bn	13.4bn	
USD1=SGD		1.38	1.34	1.35

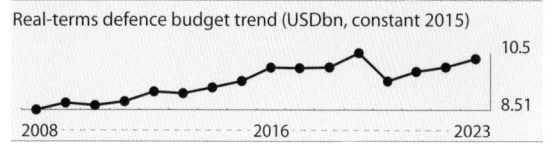

Real-terms defence budget trend (USDbn, constant 2015)

10.5
8.51
2008 — 2016 — 2023

Population	5,975,383					
Age	0–14	15–19	20–24	25–29	30–64	65 plus
Male	7.7%	3.0%	3.7%	4.2%	25.0%	6.3%
Female	7.2%	2.7%	3.4%	3.7%	25.7%	7.3%

Capabilities

The Singapore Armed Forces (SAF) are the best equipped in Southeast Asia. The air force and navy are staffed mainly by professional personnel while, apart from a small core of regulars, the much larger army is based on conscripts and reservists. Although there are no publicly available defence-policy documents, it is widely presumed that the SAF's primary role is to deter attacks on the city-state or interference with its vital interests – particularly its sea lines of communication – by potential regional adversaries. The military also is focused on counterterror operations. To address significant personnel challenges from an ageing population, the defence ministry has embarked on lean staffing and increased the use of technology. The SAF routinely trains overseas, with plans to improve domestic training areas and greater use of synthetic training. The SAF also engages extensively in bilateral and multilateral exercises, including with ASEAN member states and FPDA signatories, and has spearheaded many regional maritime security initiatives. Singaporean forces have gradually become more involved – albeit on a small scale – in multinational operations. While deployments have provided some operational experience, and training standards and operational readiness are high, the army's reliance on conscripts and reservists limits its capacity for sustained operations abroad. The 'SAF 2040' vision, launched in March 2022, underpins a new round of modernisation, with upgrade efforts across all domains, including the establishment of a fourth service branch – the Digital and Intelligence Service, which was created in October 2022. The armed forces are modernising across domains to preserve Singapore's military edge over other Southeast Asian countries. The country has a small but sophisticated defence industry.

ACTIVE 51,000 (Army 40,000 Navy 4,000 Air 6,000 Digitial & Intelligence 1,000) Gendarmerie & Paramilitary 7,400

Conscription liability 22–24 months

RESERVE 252,500 (Army 240,000 Navy 5,000 Air 7,500)

Annual trg to age 40 for army other ranks, 50 for officers

ORGANISATIONS BY SERVICE

Space
EQUIPMENT BY TYPE
SATELLITES
  ISR 1 DS-SAR

Army 40,000 (including 26,000 conscripts)
FORCES BY ROLE
COMMAND
  3 (combined arms) div HQ
  1 (rapid reaction) div HQ
  4 armd bde HQ
  9 inf bde HQ
  1 air mob bde HQ
  1 amph bde HQ
SPECIAL FORCES
  1 cdo bn
  1 (ADF) cdo bn
MANOEUVRE
  Armoured
  1 tk bn
  3 armd inf bn
  Mechanised
  6 mech inf bn
  Light
  2 (gds) inf bn
  Other
  2 sy bn
COMBAT SUPPORT
  2 arty bn
  1 STA bn
  2 engr bn
  1 EOD bn
  1 ptn br bn
  1 int bn
  2 ISR bn
  1 CBRN bn
  3 sigs bn
COMBAT SERVICE SUPPORT
  3 med bn
  2 tpt bn
  3 spt bn

Reserves
Activated units form part of divisions and brigades listed above; 1 op reserve div with additional armd & inf bde; People's Defence Force Comd (homeland defence) with 12 inf bn
FORCES BY ROLE
SPECIAL FORCES
  1 cdo bn
MANOEUVRE
  Armoured
  6 armd inf bn
  Mechanised
  6 mech inf bn
  Light
  ε56 inf bn
COMBAT SUPPORT
  ε12 arty bn
  ε8 engr bn
EQUIPMENT BY TYPE
ARMOURED FIGHTING VEHICLES
  MBT 96+ *Leopard* 2SG
  LT TK (22 AMX-10 PAC 90; ε350 AMX-13 SM1 in store)
  IFV 650+: 250 *Bionix* IFV-25; 250 *Bionix* IFV-40/50; ε100 *Hunter* AFV; 50+ M113A2 *Ultra*; (22 AMX-10P in store)
  APC 1,375+
    APC (T) 1,100+: 700+ M113A1/A2; 400+ ATTC *Bronco*
    APC (W) 135 *Terrex* ICV; (250 LAV-150/V-200 *Commando*; 30 V-100 *Commando* in store)
    PPV 150: 84 *Belrex* (incl variants); 15 *MaxxPro Dash*; 51 *Peacekeeper*
ENGINEERING & MAINTENANCE VEHICLES
  AEV 94: 18 CET; 54 FV180; 14 *Kodiak*; 8 M728
  ARV *Bionix*; *Büffel*; LAV-150; LAV-300
  VLB 72+: *Bionix*; LAB 30; *Leguan*; M2; 60 M3; 12 M60
  MW 910-MCV-2; *Trailblazer*
ANTI-TANK/ANTI-INFRASTRUCTURE
  MSL • MANPATS *Milan*; *Spike*-SR; *Spike*-MR
  RCL 90+: **84mm** *Carl Gustaf*; **106mm** 90 M40A1
ARTILLERY 798+
  SP **155mm** 54 SSPH-1 *Primus*
  TOWED 88: **105mm** (37 LG1 in store); **155mm** 88: 18 FH-2000; ε18 *Pegasus*; 52 FH-88
  MRL **227mm** 18 M142 HIMARS
  MOR 638+
    SP 90+: **81mm**; **120mm** 90: 40 on *Bronco*; 50 on M113; some *Belrex Mortar*
    TOWED 548: **81mm** 500 **120mm** 36 M-65; **160mm** 12 M-58 Tampella

Navy 4,000 (incl 1,000 conscripts)
EQUIPMENT BY TYPE
SUBMARINES • SSK 4:
  2 *Archer* (ex-SWE *Västergötland*) (fitted with AIP) with 3 single 400mm TT with Torped 431, 6 single 533mm TT with *Black Shark* HWT
  2 *Challenger* (ex-SWE *Sjöormen*) with 2 single 400mm TT with Torped 431, 4 single 533mm TT with Torped 613
PRINCIPAL SURFACE COMBATANTS • FRIGATES 6
  FFGHM 6 *Formidable* with 2 quad lnchr with RGM-84 *Harpoon* AShM, 4 8-cell *Sylver* A43 VLS with *Aster* 15 SAM, 2 triple 324mm ILAS-3 (B-515) ASTT with A244/S LWT, 1 76mm gun (capacity 1 S-70B *Sea Hawk* hel)
PATROL AND COASTAL COMBATANTS 26

CORVETTES • FSM 8 *Independence* (Littoral Mission Vessel) with 1 12-cell CLA VLS with VL MICA, 1 76mm gun, 1 hel landing platform
PCGM 6 *Victory* with 2 quad lnchr with RGM-84C *Harpoon* Block 1B AShM, 2 8-cell VLS with *Barak*-1 SAM, 1 76mm gun
PCO 4 *Sentinel* (*Fearless* mod) with 1 76mm gun
PBF 8: 2 SMC Type 1; 6 SMC Type 2
MINE WARFARE • MINE COUNTERMEASURES 4
MCC 4 *Bedok*
AMPHIBIOUS
PRINCIPAL AMPHIBIOUS SHIPS • LPD 4 *Endurance* with 2 twin *Simbad* lnchr with *Mistral* SAM, 1 76mm gun (capacity 2 hel; 4 LCVP; 18 MBT; 350 troops)
LANDING CRAFT • LCVP 23: ε17 FCEP; 6 FCU
LOGISTICS AND SUPPORT 4
ASR 1 *Swift Rescue*
ATF 2
AXL 1 *Stet Polaris*
UNINHABITED MARITIME PLATFORMS • USV 4+
MARSEC 2+: **Medium** 2 MARSEC USV; **Small** *Protector*
UTL 2+: **Medium** 2 *Venus* 16; **Small** *Venus* 9; *Venus* 11
UNINHABITED MARITIME SYSTEMS • UUV
DATA REMUS 100
MW K-Ster C/I; MCM AUV

Naval Diving Unit
FORCES BY ROLE
SPECIAL FORCES
1 SF gp
1 (diving) SF gp
COMBAT SUPPORT
1 EOD gp

Air Force 6,000 (incl 3,000 conscripts)
5 comds
FORCES BY ROLE
FIGHTER/GROUND ATTACK
2 sqn with F-15SG *Eagle*
2 sqn with F-16C/D *Fighting Falcon* (some used for ISR with pods)
ANTI-SUBMARINE WARFARE
1 sqn with S-70B *Seahawk*
MARITIME PATROL/TRANSPORT
1 sqn with F-50
AIRBORNE EARLY WARNING & CONTROL
1 sqn with G550-AEW
TANKER
1 sqn with A330 MRTT
TANKER/TRANSPORT
1 sqn with KC-130B/H *Hercules*; C-130H *Hercules*
TRAINING
1 (aggressor) sqn with F-15SG *Eagle*; F-16C/D *Fighting Falcon*
1 (FRA-based) sqn with M-346 *Master*
4 (US-based) units with AH-64D *Apache*; CH-47D *Chinook*; F-15SG: F-16C/D
1 (AUS-based) sqn with PC-21
1 hel sqn with H120 *Colibri*
ATTACK HELICOPTER
1 sqn with AH-64D *Apache*
TRANSPORT HELICOPTER
1 sqn with CH-47SD/F *Chinook*
2 sqn with AS332M *Super Puma*; AS532UL *Cougar*
ISR UAV
1 sqn with *Hermes* 450
2 sqn with *Heron* 1
AIR DEFENCE
1 AD bn with *Mistral* (opcon Army)
3 AD bn with RBS-70; 9K38 *Igla* (RS-SA-18 *Grouse*); Mechanised *Igla* (opcon Army)
1 ADA sqn with Oerlikon
1 AD sqn with SAMP/T
1 AD sqn with *Spyder*-SR
1 radar sqn with radar (mobile)
1 radar sqn with LORADS
MANOEUVRE
Other
4 (field def) sy sqn
EQUIPMENT BY TYPE
AIRCRAFT 105 combat capable
FGA 100: 40 F-15SG *Eagle*; 20 F-16C Block 52 *Fighting Falcon*; 20 F-16D Block 52 *Fighting Falcon*; 20 F-16D Block 52+ *Fighting Falcon* (incl reserves)
MP 5 F-50 *Maritime Enforcer**
AEW&C 4 G550-AEW
TKR/TPT 11: 6 A330 MRTT; 4 KC-130B *Hercules*; 1 KC-130H *Hercules*
TPT 9: **Medium** 5 C-130H *Hercules* (2 ELINT); **PAX** 4 F-50
TRG 31: 12 M-346 *Master*; 19 PC-21
HELICOPTERS
ATK 19 AH-64D *Apache*
ASW 8 S-70B *Seahawk*
TPT 61: **Heavy** 26: 6 CH-47 *Chinook*; ε5 CH-47F *Chinook*; 10 CH-47SD *Super D Chinook*; ε5 H225M; **Medium** 30: 18 AS332M *Super Puma* (incl 5 SAR); 12 AS532UL *Cougar*; **Light** 5 H120 *Colibri* (leased)
UNINHABITED AERIAL VEHICLES
ISR 17+: **Heavy** 8+ *Heron* 1; **Medium** 9+ *Hermes* 450; **Light** some *Orbiter*-4
AIR DEFENCE
SAM 4+
Long-range 4+ SAMP/T
Short-range *Spyder*-SR
Point-defence 9K38 *Igla* (RS-SA-18 *Grouse*); Mechanised *Igla*; *Mistral*; RBS-70

GUNS 34
    SP 20mm GAI-C01
    TOWED 34+: 20mm GAI-C01; 35mm 34 GDF (with 25 Super-Fledermaus fire-control radar)
AIR-LAUNCHED MISSILES
    AAM • IR AIM-9P/S *Sidewinder*; Python 4; IIR AIM-9X *Sidewinder II*; Python 5; SARH AIM-7P *Sparrow*; ARH (AIM-120C5/7 AMRAAM in store in US)
    ASM: AGM-65B/G *Maverick*; AGM-114K/L *Hellfire*; AGM-154A/C JSOW
    AShM AGM-84 *Harpoon*; AM39 *Exocet*
BOMBS
    Laser-guided GBU-10/12 *Paveway* II
    Laser & INS/GPS-guided GBU-49 Enhanced Paveway II; GBU-54 Laser JDAM
    INS/GPS-guided GBU-31 JDAM

Digital & Intelligence Service 1,000

Formed 2022 as fourth service of the Singapore Armed Forces, consolidating existing intelligence and cyber capabilities

Gendarmerie & Paramilitary 7,400 active

Civil Defence Force 5,600 (incl conscripts); 500 auxiliaries (total 6,100)

Singapore Gurkha Contingent 1,800
Under the Police
FORCES BY ROLE
MANOEUVRE
    Other
        6 paramilitary coy

DEPLOYMENT

AUSTRALIA: 2 trg schools – 1 with 12 AS332M1 *Super Puma*/AS532UL *Cougar* (flying trg) located at Oakey; 1 with PC-21 (flying trg) located at Pearce. Army: prepositioned AFVs and heavy equipment at Shoalwater Bay training area

BRUNEI: 1 trg camp with inf units on rotation; 1 hel det with AS332M1 *Super Puma*

FRANCE: 200: 1 trg sqn with 12 M-346 *Master*

TAIWAN: 3 trg camp (incl inf and arty)

THAILAND: 1 trg camp (arty, cbt engr)

UNITED STATES: Trg units with F-16C/D; 12 F-15SG; AH-64D *Apache*; 6+ CH-47D *Chinook*

FOREIGN FORCES

United States US Indo-Pacific Command: 200; 1 naval spt facility at Changi naval base; 1 USAF log spt sqn at Paya Lebar air base

Sri Lanka LKA

Sri Lankan Rupee LKR		2022	2023	2024
GDP	LKR	24.1trn	29.9trn	
	USD	74.8bn	ε92.3bn	
per capita	USD	3,342	ε3,500	
Growth	%	-7.8	-3.1	
Inflation	%	45.2	28.5	
Def bdgt	LKR	373bn	410bn	
	USD	1.16bn	ε1.27bn	
USD1=LKR		322.63	ε323.34	

IMF data unavailable for 2023 and 2024. Estimated conversion rates used.

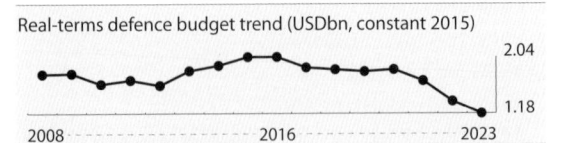

Real-terms defence budget trend (USDbn, constant 2015)
2.04
1.18
2008   2016   2023

Population	21,877,904

Age	0–14	15–19	20–24	25–29	30–64	65 plus
Male	11.7%	4.2%	3.8%	3.3%	20.3%	5.1%
Female	11.2%	4.0%	3.8%	3.4%	22.2%	7.0%

Capabilities

Since the defeat of the Tamil Tigers, the armed forces have focused on peacetime internal-security. China has supported Sri Lanka's armed forces, an indication of growing military-to-military ties. India remained Sri Lanka's key maritime partner, including by providing maritime patrol aircraft. The US has eased its long-standing military trade restrictions on the country and Japan said it would increase maritime cooperation. Sri Lanka has little capacity for force projection but has contributed small troop numbers to UN missions. The navy has enhanced its capability, based on fast-attack and patrol boats, through the acquisition of offshore-patrol vessels. The US has gifted a former coast guard cutter and China a frigate. The army is reducing in size and spending on new equipment has been sparse since the end of the civil war. Sri Lanka is looking to launch procurements to fill capability gaps, but its ambitions are limited by budget constraints. The longer-term effects of the 2022 political and economic crisis on Sri Lanka's defence policy, the size of its armed forces and procurement is unclear. Beyond maintenance facilities and limited fabrication, such as at Sri Lanka's shipyards, there is no defence-industrial base.

ACTIVE 265,900 (Army 177,000 Navy 60,900 Air 28,000) Gendarmerie & Paramilitary 63,650

RESERVE 5,500 (Army 1,100 Navy 2,400 Air Force 2,000) Gendarmerie & Paramilitary 30,400

ORGANISATIONS BY SERVICE

Army 113,000; 64,00 active reservists (recalled) (total 177,000)

Regt are bn sized
FORCES BY ROLE

COMMAND
7 region HQ
21 div HQ
SPECIAL FORCES
1 indep SF bde
MANOEUVRE
Reconnaissance
3 armd recce regt
Armoured
1 armd bde(-)
Mechanised
1 mech inf bde
Light
60 inf bde
1 cdo bde
Air Manoeuvre
1 air mob bde
COMBAT SUPPORT
7 arty regt
1 MRL regt
8 engr regt
6 sigs regt
EQUIPMENT BY TYPE
ARMOURED FIGHTING VEHICLES
MBT 62 T-55A/T-55AM2
RECCE 15 *Saladin*
IFV 62+: 13 BMP-1; 49 BMP-2; WZ-551 20mm
APC 211+
APC (T) 30+: some Type-63; 30 Type-85; some Type-89
APC (W) 181: 25 BTR-80/BTR-80A; 31 *Buffel*; 20 WZ-551; 105 *Unicorn*
ENGINEERING & MAINTENANCE VEHICLES
ARV 16 VT-55
VLB 2 MT-55
ANTI-TANK/ANTI-INFRASTRUCTURE
MANPATS HJ-8
RCL 40: **105mm** ε10 M-65; **106mm** ε30 M40
GUNS **85mm** 8 Type-56 (D-44)
ARTILLERY 908
TOWED 96: **122mm** 20; **130mm** 30 Type-59-I; **152mm** 46 Type-66 (D-20)
MRL **122mm** 28: 6 KRL-122; 22 RM-70
MOR 784: **81mm** 520; **82mm** 209; **120mm** 55 M-43
UNINHABITED AERIAL VEHICLES
ISR • **Medium** 1 *Seeker*

Navy 47,900; ε13,000 active reserves (total 60,900)

Seven naval areas
EQUIPMENT BY TYPE
PATROL AND COASTAL COMBATANTS 181
PSOH 6: 2 *Gajabahu* (ex-US *Hamilton*) with 1 76mm gun (capacity 1 med hel); 1 *Parakramabahu* (ex-PRC Type-053H2G (*Jiangwei* I)) with 1 twin 100mm gun (capacity 1 med hel); 1 *Sayura* (ex-IND *Sukanya*) (capacity 1 med hel); 2 *Sayurala* (IND *Samarth*) (capacity 1 med hel)
PCO 2: 1 *Samudura* (ex-US *Reliance*) with 1 hel landing platform; 1 *Sagara* (IND *Vikram*) with 1 hel landing platform
PCC 2 *Nandimithra* (ex-ISR *Sa'ar* 4) with 1 76mm gun
PBF 81: 26 *Colombo*; 6 *Shaldag*; 4 *Super Dvora* Mk II; 6 *Super Dvora* Mk III; 5 *Trinity Marine* 25m; 34 *Wave Rider*
PB 11: 2 *Mihikatha* (ex-AUS *Bay*); 2 *Prathapa* (PRC *Haizhui* mod); 3 *Ranajaya* (PRC *Haizhui*); 1 *Ranarisi* (ex-PRC *Shanghai* III); 3 *Weeraya* (ex-PRC *Shanghai* II)
PBR 79
AMPHIBIOUS
LANDING SHIPS • **LSM** 1 *Shakthi* (PRC *Yuhai*) (capacity 2 tanks; 250 troops)
LANDING CRAFT 7
LCM 2 *Ranavijaya*
LCU 4: 2 *Yunnan*; 2 other
UCAC 1 M 10† (capacity 56 troops)
LOGISTICS AND SUPPORT 4: 3 **AP**; 1 **AX**

Marines ε500
FORCES BY ROLE
MANOEUVRE
Amphibious
1 mne bn

Special Boat Service ε100

Reserve Organisations

Sri Lanka Volunteer Naval Force (SLVNF) 13,000 active reservists

Air Force 28,000 (incl SLAF Regt)
FORCES BY ROLE
FIGHTER
1 sqn with F-7BS/G; FT-7
FIGHTER/GROUND ATTACK
1 sqn with *Kfir* C-2
1 sqn with K-8 *Karakorum**
MARITIME PATROL
1 sqn with Beech B200/200T *King Air*; Do-228-101; Y-12 (II)/(IV)
TRANSPORT
1 sqn with An-32B *Cline*; C-130K *Hercules*; Cessna 421C *Golden Eagle*
TRAINING
1 wg with PT-6, Cessna 150L
ATTACK/TRANSPORT HELICOPTER
1 sqn with Mi-171E/Sh; Mi-24V *Hind* E; Mi-35P *Hind*
TRANSPORT HELICOPTER
1 sqn with Mi-17 *Hip* H; Mi-171E/Sh

1 sqn with Bell 206A/B (incl basic trg), Bell 212
1 (VIP) sqn with Bell 212; Bell 412 *Twin Huey;* Bell 412EP *Twin Huey;* Mi-171E/Sh

ISR UAV
1 sqn with *Blue Horizon* II

MANOEUVRE
Other
1 (SLAF) sy regt

EQUIPMENT BY TYPE
AIRCRAFT 13 combat capable
FTR 5: 3 F-7GS; 2 FT-7 (3 F-7BS; 1 F-7GS non-operational)
FGA 1 *Kfir* C-2 (2 *Kfir* C-2; 1 *Kfir* C-7; 2 *Kfir* TC-2; 6 MiG-27M *Flogger* J; 1 MiG-23UB *Flogger* C non-operational)
MP 2 Do-228-101
TPT 22: **Medium** 2 C-130K *Hercules;* **Light** 20: 3 An-32B *Cline;* 2 Beech B200/200T *King Air;* 6 Cessna 150L; 1 Cessna 421C *Golden Eagle;* 6 Y-12 (II); 2 Y-12 (IV)
TRG 12: 7 K-8 *Karakorum**; 5 PT-6
HELICOPTERS
ATK 11: 6 Mi-24P *Hind;* 3 Mi-24V *Hind* E; 2 Mi-35V *Hind*
MRH 18: 6 Bell 412 *Twin Huey* (VIP); 2 Bell 412EP (VIP); 10 Mi-17 *Hip* H
TPT 26: **Medium** 14: ε10 Mi-171E; 4 Mi-171Sh; **Light** 12: 2 Bell 206A *Jet Ranger;* 2 Bell 206B *Jet Ranger;* 8 Bell 212
UNINHABITED AERIAL VEHICLES
ISR • **Medium** some *Blue Horizon* II
AIR DEFENCE
SAM • **Point Defence** 9K38 *Igla* (RS-SA-18 *Grouse*)
GUNS • **TOWED** 27: **40mm** 24 L/40; **94mm** 3 (3.7in)
AIR-LAUNCHED MISSILES
AAM • **IR** PL-5E

Gendarmerie & Paramilitary ε63,650

Home Guard 13,000

National Guard ε15,000

Police Force 30,200; 1,000 (women) (total 31,200) 30,400 reservists

Ministry of Defence Special Task Force 3,000
Anti-guerrilla unit

Coast Guard 1,450
Ministry of Defence

EQUIPMENT BY TYPE
PATROL AND COASTAL COMBATANTS 26
PCO 1 *Suraksha* (ex-IND *Vikram*) with 1 hel landing platform
PCC 1 *Jayasagara*
PBF 17: 2 *Dvora;* 4 *Super Dvora* Mk I; 3 *Killer* (ROK); 8 *Wave Rider*
PB 6: 2 Simonneau Type-508; 2 *Samudra Raksha;* 2 Type 501 (JPN)
PBR 1†

DEPLOYMENT

CENTRAL AFRICAN REPUBLIC: UN • MINUSCA 113; 1 hel sqn
LEBANON: UN • UNIFIL 126; 1 inf coy
MALI: UN • MINUSMA 243; 1 sy coy
SOUTH SUDAN: UN • UNMISS 66; 1 fd hospital
WESTERN SAHARA: UN • MINURSO 2

Taiwan (Republic of China) ROC

New Taiwan Dollar TWD		2022	2023	2024
GDP	TWD	22.7trn	23.3trn	24.4trn
	USD	760bn	752bn	792bn
per capita	USD	32,687	32,340	34,046
Growth	%	2.4	0.8	3.0
Inflation	%	2.9	2.1	1.5
Def bdgt	TWD	472bn	586bn	607bn
	USD	15.8bn	18.9bn	19.7bn
USD1=TWD		29.81	31.04	30.83

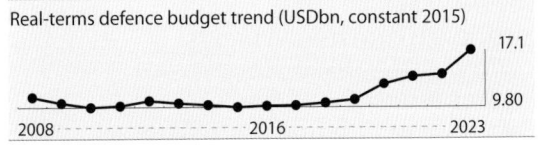

Real-terms defence budget trend (USDbn, constant 2015)
17.1 / 9.80
2008 — 2016 — 2023

Population 23,588,613

Age	0–14	15–19	20–24	25–29	30–64	65 plus
Male	6.3%	2.3%	2.9%	3.5%	26.1%	8.1%
Female	5.9%	2.1%	2.8%	3.3%	26.6%	9.9%

Capabilities

Taiwan's security policy is dominated by its relationship with China and its attempts to sustain a credible military capability. Taiwan is looking to boost air defence and deterrence in coastal areas. The 2021 Quadrennial Defense Review, for the first time, mentioned the need to counter the PLA's 'grey zone' threat. The armed forces exercise regularly. Demographic pressure has influenced plans for force reductions and a shift towards an all-volunteer force, which the 2021 Quadrennial Defense Review credited for helping the armed forces reach its staffing goals. Nonetheless, issues with recruitment and retention have reportedly created personnel challenges for combat units. Taiwan was planning to extend military conscription to one year from four months in January 2024. Taiwan is also focused on expanding the reserve force, improving reservist training and civil defence, although these efforts are at an early stages of development. Taiwan's main security partnership is with the US. The Taiwan Relations Act from 1979 states that 'the United States shall provide Taiwan with arms of a defensive character'. In 2019, the US approved the sale of 66 F-16 Block 70 combat aircraft to Taiwan, though their delivery has suffered delays. Taiwan's own defence-industrial base has strengths in aerospace, shipbuilding and missiles. In 2023, Taiwan unveiled its first domestically built diesel-powered submarine, due for delivery by 2025.

ACTIVE 169,000 (Army 94,000 Navy 40,000 Air 35,000) **Gendarmerie & Paramilitary 11,800**

Conscript liability (19–40 years) 12 months for those born before 1993; four months for those born after 1994 (alternative service available)

RESERVE 1,657,000 (Army 1,500,000 Navy 67,000 Air Force 90,000)

Some obligation to age 30

ORGANISATIONS BY SERVICE

Space
EQUIPMENT BY TYPE
SATELLITES • ISR 1 *Formosat-5*

Army 94,000 (incl ε5,000 MP)
FORCES BY ROLE
COMMAND
  3 corps HQ
  5 defence comd HQ
SPECIAL FORCES/HELICOPTER
  1 SF/hel comd (5 spec ops bn, 2 hel bde)
MANOEUVRE
  Armoured
  4 armd bde
  Mechanised
  3 mech inf bde
COMBAT SUPPORT
  3 arty gp
  3 engr gp
  3 CBRN gp
  3 sigs gp
COASTAL DEFENCE
  1 AShM bn

Reserves
FORCES BY ROLE
MANOEUVRE
  Light
  27 inf bde
EQUIPMENT BY TYPE
ARMOURED FIGHTING VEHICLES
  MBT 650: 200 M60A3; 450 CM-11 *Brave Tiger* (M48H); (100 CM-12 in store)
  LT TK ε100 M41A3/D
  IFV ε230 CM-34 *Yunpao*
  APC 1,543
    APC (T) 875: 225 CM-21A1; 650 M113A1/A2
    APC (W) 668: 368 CM-32 *Yunpao*; 300 LAV-150 *Commando*
ENGINEERING & MAINTENANCE VEHICLES
  AEV 18 M9
  ARV 37+: CM-27A1; 37 M88A1
  VLB 22 M3; M48A5
NBC VEHICLES 48+: BIDS; 48 K216A1; KM453
ANTI-TANK/ANTI-INFRASTRUCTURE
  MSL
    SP M113A1 with TOW; M1045A2 HMMWV with TOW
    MANPATS FGM-148 *Javelin*; TOW
  RCL 500+: **90mm** M67; **106mm** 500+: 500 M40A1; Type-51
ARTILLERY 2,093
  SP 488: **105mm** 100 M108; **155mm** 318: 225 M109A2/A5; 48 M44T; 45 T-69; **203mm** 70 M110
  TOWED 1,060+: **105mm** 650 T-64 (M101); **155mm** 340+: 90 M59; 250 T-65 (M114); M44; XT-69; **203mm** 70 M115
  MRL 223: **117mm** 120 *Kung Feng* VI; **126mm** 103: 60 *Kung Feng* III/*Kung Feng* IV; 43 RT 2000 *Thunder*
  MOR 322+
    SP 162+: **81mm** 72+: M29; 72 M125; **107mm** 90 M106A2
    TOWED **81mm** 160+: 160 M29; T-75; **107mm** M30; **120mm** K5; XT-86
COASTAL DEFENCE
  ARTY 54: **127mm** ε50 US Mk32 (reported); **240mm** 4 M1
  AShM *Ching Feng*
HELICOPTERS
  ATK 96: 67 AH-1W *Cobra*; 29 AH-64E *Apache*
  MRH 37 OH-58D *Kiowa Warrior*
  TPT 38: **Heavy** 8 CH-47SD *Super D Chinook*; **Medium** 30 UH-60M *Black Hawk*
  TRG 29 TH-67 *Creek*
UNINHABITED AERIAL VEHICLES
  ISR • Light *Mastiff* III
AIR DEFENCE
  SAM • **Point-defence** 76+: 74 M1097 *Avenger*; 2 M48 *Chaparral*; FIM-92 *Stinger*
  GUNS
    SP **40mm** M42
    TOWED **40mm** L/70

Navy 40,000
EQUIPMENT BY TYPE
SUBMARINES • SSK 4:
  2 *Hai Lung* with 6 single 533mm TT with UGM-84L *Harpoon* Block II AShM/SUT HWT
  2 *Hai Shih*† (ex-US *Guppy* II (used in trg role)) with 10 single 533mm TT (6 fwd, 4 aft) with SUT HWT
PRINCIPAL SURFACE COMBATANTS 26
  DESTROYERS • DDGHM 4 *Keelung* (ex-US *Kidd*) with 2 quad lnchr with RGM-84L *Harpoon* Block II AShM, 2 twin Mk 26 GMLS with SM-2 Block IIIA SAM, 2 triple 324mm SVTT Mk 32 ASTT with Mk 46 LWT, 2 Mk 15 *Phalanx* Block 1B CIWS, 2 127mm gun (capacity 1 S-70 ASW hel)
FRIGATES 22

FFGHM 21:

8 *Cheng Kung* (US *Oliver Hazard Perry* mod) with 2 quad lnchr with *Hsiung Feng* II/III AShM, 1 Mk 13 GMLS with SM-1MR Block VI SAM, 2 triple 324mm SVTT Mk 32 ASTT with Mk 46 LWT, 1 Mk 15 *Phalanx* Block 1B CIWS, 1 76mm gun (capacity 2 S-70C ASW hel)

2 *Meng Chuan* (ex-US *Oliver Hazard Perry*) with 1 Mk13 GMLS with RGM-84 *Harpoon* AShM/SM-1MR Block VI SAM, 2 triple 324mm SVTT Mk 32 ASTT with Mk 46 LWT, 1 Mk 15 *Phalanx* Block 1B CIWS, 1 76mm gun (capacity 2 S-70C ASW hel)

5 *Chin Yang* (ex-US *Knox*) with 1 octuple Mk 16 lnchr with RGM-84C *Harpoon* Block 1B AShM/ASROC A/S msl, 2 triple lnchr with SM-1MR Block VI SAM, 2 twin lnchr with SM-1MR Block VI SAM, 2 twin 324mm SVTT Mk 32 ASTT with Mk 46 LWT, 1 Mk 15 *Phalanx* Block 1B CIWS, 1 127mm gun (capacity 1 MD-500 hel)

6 *Kang Ding* with 2 quad lnchr with *Hsiung Feng* II AShM, 1 quad lnchr with *Sea Chaparral* SAM, 2 triple 324mm SVTT Mk 32 ASTT with Mk 46 LWT, 1 Mk 15 *Phalanx* Block 1B CIWS, 1 76mm gun (capacity 1 S-70C ASW hel)

FFGH 1 *Chin Yang* (ex-US *Knox*) with 1 octuple Mk 112 lnchr with RGM-84C *Harpoon* Block 1B AShM, 2 twin 324mm SVTT Mk 32 ASTT with Mk 46 LWT, 1 Mk 15 *Phalanx* Block 1B CIWS, 1 127mm gun (capacity 1 MD-500 hel)

PATROL AND COASTAL COMBATANTS 43

CORVETTES • FSGM 2 *Ta Jiang* (*Tuo Jiang* mod) with 4 twin lnchr with *Hsiung Feng* II AShM, 2 twin lnchr with *Hsiung Feng* III AShM, 2 octuple lnchr with *Tien Chien* 2N (*Sea Sword* II) SAM, 1 Mk 15 *Phalanx* CIWS, 1 76mm gun, 1 hel landing platform

PCFG 1 *Tuo Jiang* (*Hsun Hai*) with 4 twin lnchr with *Hsiung Feng* II AShM, 4 twin lnchr with *Hsiung Feng* III AShM, 2 triple 324mm SVTT Mk 32 ASTT, 1 Mk 15 *Phalanx* Block 1B CIWS, 1 76mm gun

PCG 8:

2 *Jin Chiang* with 2 twin lnchr with *Hsiung Feng* II AShM, 1 76mm gun

6 *Jin Chiang* with 1 twin lnchr with *Hsiung Feng* III AShM, 1 76mm gun

PCC 1 *Jin Chiang* (test platform)

PBG 31 *Kwang Hua* with 2 twin lnchr with *Hsiung Feng* II AShM

MINE WARFARE 11

MINE COUNTERMEASURES 7

MHC 6: 4 *Yung Feng*; 2 *Yung Jin* (ex-US *Osprey*)

MSO 1 *Yung Yang* (ex-US *Aggressive*)

MINELAYERS • ML 4 FMLB

COMMAND SHIPS • LCC 1 *Kao Hsiung*

AMPHIBIOUS

PRINCIPAL AMPHIBIOUS SHIPS 2

LPD 1 *Yu Shan* with 4 octuple lnchr with *Tien Chien* 2N (*Sea Sword* II) SAM, 2 Mk 15 *Phalanx* CIWS, 1 76mm gun (capacity 2 med hel; 4 LCM; 9 AAV-7A1; approx 500 troops)

LSD 1 *Shiu Hai* (ex-US *Anchorage*) with 2 Mk 15 *Phalanx* CIWS, 1 hel landing platform (capacity either 2 LCU or 18 LCM; 360 troops)

LANDING SHIPS 6

LST 6:

4 *Chung Hai* (ex-US LST-524) (capacity 16 tanks; 200 troops)

2 *Chung Ho* (ex-US *Newport*) with 1 Mk 15 *Phalanx* CIWS, 1 hel landing platform (capacity 3 LCVP, 23 AFVs, 400 troops)

LANDING CRAFT 44

LCM ε32 (various)

LCU 12 LCU 1610 (capacity 2 M60A3 or 400 troops) (minelaying capability)

LOGISTICS AND SUPPORT 9

AGOR 1 *Ta Kuan*

AOEH 1 *Panshih* with 1 quad lnchr with *Sea Chaparral* SAM, 2 Mk 15 *Phalanx* CIWS (capacity 3 med hel)

AOR 1 *Wu Yi* with 1 quad lnchr with *Sea Chaparral* SAM, 1 hel landing platform

ARS 2: 1 *Da Hu* (ex-US *Diver*); 1 *Da Juen* (ex-US *Bolster*)

ATF 4 *Ta Tung* (ex-US *Cherokee*)

Marines 10,000

FORCES BY ROLE

MANOEUVRE

Amphibious

2 mne bde

Other

1 (airfield def) sy gp

COMBAT SUPPORT

Some cbt spt unit

EQUIPMENT BY TYPE

ARMOURED FIGHTING VEHICLES

MBT 100 M60A3 TTS

AAV 202: 52 AAV-7A1; 150 LVTP-5A1

ENGINEERING & MAINTENANCE VEHICLES

ARV 2 AAVR-7

ANTI-TANK/ANTI-INFRASTRUCTURE

SP ε25 CM-25

RCL 106mm

ARTILLERY • TOWED 105mm; 155mm

Naval Aviation

FORCES BY ROLE

ANTI SUBMARINE WARFARE

2 sqn with S-70C *Seahawk* (S-70C *Defender*)

1 sqn with MD-500 *Defender*; S-70C *Seahawk* (S-70C *Defender*)

ISR UAV

1 bn with *Chung Shyang* II

EQUIPMENT BY TYPE

HELICOPTERS

ASW 28: 9 MD-500 *Defender*; 19 S-70C *Seahawk* (S-70C *Defender*)
MRH 1 MD-500 *Defender*
UNINHABITED AERIAL VEHICLES • ISR • Medium ε28 *Chung Shyang* II

Air Force 35,000
FORCES BY ROLE
FIGHTER
3 sqn with *Mirage* 2000-5E/D (2000-5EI/DI)
FIGHTER/GROUND ATTACK
3 sqn with F-5E/F *Tiger* II; T-5 *Yung Ying*
6 sqn with F-16V(A/B) *Fighting Falcon*
5 sqn with F-CK-1A/B/C/D *Ching Kuo*
ANTI-SUBMARINE WARFARE
1 sqn with P-3C *Orion*
ELECTRONIC WARFARE
1 sqn with C-130HE *Tien Gian*
ISR
1 sqn with RF-5E *Tigereye*; F-16V(A/B) *Fighting Falcon*
AIRBORNE EARLY WARNING & CONTROL
1 sqn with E-2T *Hawkeye*
SEARCH & RESCUE
1 sqn with H225; UH-60M *Black Hawk*
TRANSPORT
2 sqn with C-130H *Hercules*
1 (VIP) sqn with B-727-100; B-737-800; Beech 1900; F-50
TRAINING
1 sqn with AT-3A/B *Tzu-Chung**
1 sqn with Beech 1900
1 (basic) sqn with T-34C *Turbo Mentor*
EQUIPMENT BY TYPE
AIRCRAFT 430 combat capable
FTR 97: 16 F-5E *Tiger* II; 27 F-5F *Tiger* II; 9 *Mirage* 2000-5D (2000-5DI); 45 *Mirage* 2000-5E (2000-5EI)
FGA 267: 127 F-CK-1C/D *Ching Kuo*; 110 F-16V(A) *Fighting Falcon*; 30 F-16V(B) *Fighting Falcon*;
ASW 12 P-3C *Orion*
EW 1 C-130HE *Tien Gian*
ISR 5 RF-5E *Tigereye*
AEW&C 5 E-2T *Hawkeye*
TPT 33: **Medium** 19 C-130H *Hercules*; **Light** 10 Beech 1900; **PAX** 4: 1 B-737-800; 3 F-50
TRG 118: 54 AT-3A/B *Tzu-Chung**; 42 T-34C *Turbo Mentor*; 22 T-5 *Yung Ying*
HELICOPTERS
TPT • Medium 17: 3 H225; 14 UH-60M *Black Hawk*
AIR-LAUNCHED MISSILES
AAM • IR AIM-9J/P *Sidewinder*; R-550 *Magic* 2; *Shafrir*; *Sky Sword* I; **IIR** AIM-9X *Sidewinder* II; *Mica* IR; **ARH** *Mica* RF; **ARH** AIM-120C-7 AMRAAM; *Sky Sword* II
ASM AGM-65A *Maverick*
AShM AGM-84 *Harpoon*

ARM *Sky Sword* IIA
ALCM • Conventional *Wan Chien*
BOMBS • Laser-guided GBU-12 *Paveway* II

Air Defence and Missile Command
FORCES BY ROLE
SURFACE-TO-SURFACE MISSILE
1 GLCM bde (2 GLCM bn with *Hsiung Feng* IIE)
AIR DEFENCE
1 (792) SAM bde (1 SAM bn with *Tien Kung* III; 2 ADA bn)
1 (793) SAM bde (1 SAM bn with Tien Kung II; 1 SAM bn with *Tien Kung* III; 1 SAM bn with M902 *Patriot* PAC-3)
1 (794) SAM bde (1 SAM bn with Tien Kung II; 1 SAM bn with M902 *Patriot* PAC-3)
1 (795) SAM bde (1 SAM bn with M902 *Patriot* PAC-3; 2 ADA bn)
EQUIPMENT BY TYPE
SURFACE-TO-SURFACE MISSILE LAUNCHERS
GLCM • Conventional ε12 *Hsiung Feng* IIE
AIR DEFENCE
SAM 202+
Long-range 122+: 72+ M902 *Patriot* PAC-3; ε50 *Tien Kung* II
Short-range 30 RIM-7M *Sparrow* with *Skyguard*
Point-defence *Antelope*
GUNS • 20mm some T-82; **35mm** 20+ GDF-006 with *Skyguard*
MISSILE DEFENCE *Tien Kung* III

Gendarmerie & Paramilitary 11,800

Coast Guard 11,800
EQUIPMENT BY TYPE
PATROL AND COASTAL COMBATANTS 170
PSOH 6: 2 *Chiayi*; 2 *Tainan*; 2 *Yilan*
PSO 5: 4 *Miaoli* with 1 hel landing platform; 1 *Ho Hsing*
PCF 6 *Anping* (*Tuo Jiang* mod)
PCO 13: 2 *Kinmen*; 1 *Mou Hsing*; 1 *Shun Hu* 1; 3 *Shun Hu* 7; 4 *Taichung*; 2 *Taipei*
PBF ε58 (various)
PB 82: 1 *Shun Hu* 6; ε81 (various)

FOREIGN FORCES
Singapore 3 trg camp (incl inf and arty)

Thailand THA

Thai Baht THB		2022	2023	2024
GDP	THB	17.4trn	17.6trn	18.5trn
	USD	495bn	512bn	543bn
per capita	USD	7,070	7,298	7,731
Growth	%	2.6	2.7	3.2
Inflation	%	6.1	1.5	1.6
Def bdgt	THB	200bn	195bn	
	USD	5.70bn	5.67bn	
FMA (US)	USD	10m	10m	10m
USD1=THB		35.06	34.37	33.98

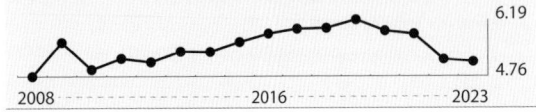

Real-terms defence budget trend (USDbn, constant 2015)

Population 69,794,997

Age	0–14	15–19	20–24	25–29	30–64	65 plus
Male	8.2%	3.0%	3.1%	3.5%	24.5%	6.4%
Female	7.8%	2.9%	3.0%	3.5%	26.1%	8.0%

Capabilities

Thailand has a large, well-funded military and its air force is one of the best equipped and trained in Southeast Asia. Facing an increasingly unstable regional-security environment, the Royal Thai Armed Forces are more heavily emphasising deterrence of external threats. They also have a longstanding internal security role, particularly in the country's far south, where a Malay-nationalist insurgency continues, albeit at low levels. The Vision 2026 defence modernisation plan, approved by the Defence Council in October 2017, outlined the armed forces' planned capability improvements through the mid-2020s. The US classes Thailand as a major non-NATO ally, although Bangkok has also developed closer defence ties with China since 2014. The armed forces regularly take part in international military exercises, notably the multinational annual *Cobra Gold* series with the US and some of its allies and partners. The military-modernisation effort includes the development of a submarine force, as well as the strengthening of anti-submarine-warfare capability and procurement of new surface ships. The armoured vehicle fleet has been recapitalised with deliveries from China and Ukraine. Saab 340 AEW&C aircraft, *Gripen* combat aircraft and a new command-and-control system have improved air capability. In January 2020, the Royal Thai Air Force (RTAF) issued a White Paper which detailed further acquisition and upgrade requirements, including combat aircraft and tactical transport and VIP aircraft. Under its Defence Industry Masterplan, Thai authorities recognised that expanding Thailand's limited defence sector could be an important way to develop military capability and improve self-reliance. More broadly, the government has sought to reform defence procurement and offsets by expanding the role of its Defence Technology Institute.

ACTIVE 360,850 (Army 245,000 Navy 69,850 Air 46,000) Gendarmerie & Paramilitary 93,700

Conscription liability 24 months

RESERVE 200,000 Gendarmerie & Paramilitary 45,000

ORGANISATIONS BY SERVICE

Space
EQUIPMENT BY TYPE
SATELLITES • ISR 2 *Napa*

Army 130,000; ε115,000 conscript (total 245,000)

Cav, lt armd, recce and tk sqn are bn sized
FORCES BY ROLE
COMMAND
  4 (regional) army HQ
  3 corps HQ
SPECIAL FORCES
  1 SF div
  1 SF regt
MANOEUVRE
  Armoured
  1 (3rd) mech cav div (2 tk regt (2 tk sqn); 1 sigs bn; 1 maint bn; 1 hel sqn)
  Mechanised
  1 (1st) mech cav div (1 armd recce sqn; 2 mech cav regt (3 mech cav sqn); 1 indep mech cav sqn; 1 sigs bn; 1 maint bn; 1 hel sqn)
  1 (2nd) mech cav div (1 armd recce sqn; 2 (1st & 5th) mech cav regt (1 tk sqn, 2 mech cav sqn); 1 (4th) mech cav regt (3 mech cav sqn); 1 sigs bn; 1 maint bn; 1 hel sqn)
  1 (2nd) mech inf div (1 armd recce sqn; 1 tk bn; 3 mech inf regt (3 mech inf bn); 1 arty regt (4 arty bn); 1 engr bn; 1 sigs bn)
  1 (11th) mech inf div (2 mech inf regt (3 mech inf bn); 1 engr bn; 1 sigs bn)
  Light
  1 (1st) inf div (1 lt armd sqn; 1 ranger regt (3 ranger bn); 1 arty regt (4 arty bn); 1 engr bn; 1 sigs bn)
  1 (3rd) inf div (3 inf regt (3 inf bn); 1 arty regt (3 arty bn); 1 engr bn; 1 sigs bn)
  1 (4th) inf div (1 lt armd sqn; 2 inf regt (3 inf bn); 1 arty regt (3 arty bn); 1 engr bn; 1 sigs bn)
  1 (5th) inf div (1 lt armd sqn; 3 inf regt (3 inf bn); 1 arty regt (4 arty bn); 1 engr bn; 1 sigs bn)
  1 (6th) inf div (2 inf regt (3 inf bn); 1 arty regt (4 arty bn); 1 engr bn; 1 sigs bn)
  1 (7th) inf div (2 inf regt (3 inf bn); 1 arty regt (2 arty bn); 1 engr bn; 1 sigs bn)
  1 (9th) inf div (1 mech cav sqn; 3 inf regt (3 inf bn); 1 arty regt (3 arty bn); 1 engr bn; 1 sigs bn)
  1 (15th) inf div (1 mech cav sqn; 3 inf regt (3 inf bn); 1 engr bn; 1 sigs bn)
COMBAT SUPPORT
  1 arty div (1 arty regt (1 SP arty bn; 2 fd arty bn); 1 arty regt (1 MRL bn; 2 fd arty bn))

1 engr div

COMBAT SERVICE SUPPORT

4 economic development div

HELICOPTER

1 bn with AW139; AW149; H125M (AS550) *Fennec*

1 bn with AH-1F *Cobra*; Bell 212 (AB-212); Mi-17V-5 *Hip H*; UH-60L *Black Hawk*; UH-72A *Lakota*

1 bn with AH-1F *Cobra*; Bell 212 (AB-212)

1 bn with UH-60A/M *Black Hawk*

1 bn with Mi-17V-5 *Hip H*; *Hermes* 450

ISR UAV

1 UAV bn with *Hermes* 450; *Searcher* II

AIR DEFENCE

1 ADA div (6 bn)

EQUIPMENT BY TYPE

ARMOURED FIGHTING VEHICLES

MBT 394: 53 M60A1; 125 M60A3; 105 M48A5; 49 T-84 *Oplot*; 62 VT-4; (50 Type-69 in store)

LT TK 194: 24 M41; 104 *Scorpion* (50 in store); 66 *Stingray*

RECCE 42: 10 M1127 *Stryker* RV; 32 S52 *Shorland*

IFV 220: 168 BTR-3E1; 52 VN-1 (incl variants)

APC 1,216

APC (T) 880: *Bronco*; 430 M113A1/A3; 450 Type-85

APC (W) 236: 9 BTR-3K (CP); 6 BTR-3C (amb); 18 *Condor*; 142 LAV-150 *Commando*; 61 M1126 *Stryker* ICV

PPV 100 REVA

ENGINEERING & MAINTENANCE VEHICLES

ARV 69+: 2 BREM-84 *Atlet*; 13 BTR-3BR; 22 M88A1; 6 M88A2; 10 M113; 5 Type-653; 11 VS-27; WZT-4

VLB Type-84

MW *Bozena*; *Giant Viper*

ANTI-TANK/ANTI-INFRASTRUCTURE

MSL

SP 30+: 18+ M901A5 (TOW); 12 BTR-3RK

MANPATS M47 *Dragon*

RCL 180: **75mm** 30 M20; **106mm** 150 M40

ARTILLERY 2,579

SP 155mm 42: 16 ATMOS 2000; 6 CAESAR; 20 M109A5

TOWED 525: **105mm** 296: 24 LG1 MkII; 12 M-56; 200 M101A1; 60 L119 Light Gun; (12 M102; 32 M618A2 in store); **155mm** 229: 90 GHN-45 A1; 118 M198; 21 M-71 (48 M114 in store)

MRL 68: **122mm** 4 SR-4; **130mm** 60 PHZ-85; **302mm** 4: 1 DTI-1 (WS-1B); 3 DTI-1G (WS-32)

MOR 1,944+: **81mm/107mm/120mm** 1,867; **SP 81mm** 39: 18 BTR-3M1; 21 M125A3; SP **107mm** M106A3; **SP 120mm** 38: 8 BTR-3M2; 6+ Elbit *Spear*; 12 M1064A3; 12 SM-4A

AIRCRAFT

TPT • Light 25: 2 Beech 200 *King Air*; 2 Beech 1900C; 1 C-212 *Aviocar*; 3 C295W; 3 Cessna 182T *Skylane*; 9 Cessna A185E (U-17B); 2 ERJ-135LR; 2 *Jetstream* 41; 1 PC-12NGX

TRG 33: 11 MX-7-235 *Star Rocket*; 22 T-41B *Mescalero*

HELICOPTERS

ATK 7 AH-1F *Cobra*

MRH 22: 8 H125M (AS550) *Fennec*; 2 AW139; 2 AW149; 10 Mi-17V-5 *Hip H*

TPT 134: **Heavy** 5 CH-47D *Chinook*; **Medium** 18: 3 UH-60A *Black Hawk*; 8 UH-60L *Black Hawk*; 7 UH-60M *Black Hawk*; **Light** 111: 27 Bell 206 *Jet Ranger*; 52 Bell 212 (AB-212); 21 Enstrom 480B; 6 H145M (VIP); 5 UH-72A *Lakota*

TRG 53 Hughes 300C

UNINHABITED AERIAL VEHICLES

ISR • Medium 4+: 4 *Hermes* 450; *Searcher*; *Searcher* II

AIR DEFENCE

SAM 8+

Short-range *Aspide*

Point-defence 8+: 8 *Starstreak*; 9K338 Igla-S (RS-SA-24 *Grinch*)

GUNS 192

SP 54: **20mm** 24 M163 *Vulcan*; **40mm** 30 M1/M42 SP

TOWED 138: **20mm** 24 M167 *Vulcan*; **35mm** 8 GDF-007 with *Skyguard* 3; **37mm** 52 Type-74; **40mm** 48 L/70; **57mm** ε6 Type-59 (S-60) (18+ more non-operational)

Navy 44,000 (incl Naval Aviation, Marines, Coastal Defence); 25,850 conscript (total 69,850)

EQUIPMENT BY TYPE

PRINCIPAL SURFACE COMBATANTS 8

AIRCRAFT CARRIERS • CVH 1 *Chakri Naruebet* with 3 sextuple *Sadral* lnchr with *Mistral* SAM (capacity 6 S-70B *Seahawk* ASW hel)

FRIGATES 7

FFGHM 3:

2 *Naresuan* with 2 quad lnchr with RGM-84 *Harpoon* AShM, 1 8 cell Mk 41 VLS with RIM-162B ESSM SAM, 2 triple SVTT Mk 32 324mm TT with Mk 46 LWT, 1 127mm gun (capacity 1 *Super Lynx* 300 hel)

1 *Bhumibol Adulyadej* (DW3000F) with 2 quad lnchr with RGM-84L *Harpoon* Block II AShM, 1 8-cell Mk 41 VLS with RIM-162B ESSM SAM, 2 triple 324mm SEA TLS ASTT with Mk 54 LWT, 1 Mk 15 *Phalanx* Block 1B CIWS, 1 76mm gun (capacity 1 med hel)

FFG 4:

2 *Chao Phraya* (trg role) with 4 twin lnchr with C-802A AShM, 2 RBU 1200 *Uragan* A/S mor, 2 twin 100mm guns

2 *Chao Phraya* with 4 twin lnchr with C-802A AShM, 2 RBU 1200 *Uragan* A/S mor, 1 twin 100mm gun, 1 hel landing platform

PATROL AND COASTAL COMBATANTS 68

CORVETTES 5:

FSGM 1 *Rattanakosin* with 2 twin lnchr with RGM-84 *Harpoon* AShM, 1 octuple *Albatros* lnchr with *Aspide* SAM, 2 triple 324mm SVTT Mk 32 ASTT with *Stingray* LWT, 1 76mm gun

FSG 1 *Krabi* (UK *River* mod) with 2 twin lnchr with RGM-84L *Harpoon* Block II AShM, 1 76mm gun
FS 3:
  1 *Makut Rajakumarn* with 2 triple 324mm ASTT, 2 114mm gun
  1 *Pin Klao* (ex-US *Cannon*) (trg role) with 2 triple 324mm SVTT Mk 32 ASTT, 3 76mm guns
  1 *Tapi* with 2 triple 324mm SVTT Mk 32 ASTT with Mk 46 LWT, 1 76mm gun
PSO 1 *Krabi* (UK *River* mod) with 1 76mm gun
PCT 3 *Khamronsin* with 2 triple 324mm ASTT with *Stingray* LWT, 1 76mm gun
PCOH 2 *Pattani* (1 in trg role) with 1 76mm gun
PCO 4: 3 *Hua Hin* with 1 76mm gun; 1 M58 Patrol Gun Boat with 1 76mm gun
PCC 9: 3 *Chon Buri* with 2 76mm gun; 6 *Sattahip* with 1 76mm gun
PBF 4 M18 Fast Assault Craft (capacity 18 troops)
PB 40: 3 T-81; 5 M36 Patrol Boat; 1 T-227; 2 T-997; 23 M21 Patrol Boat; 3 T-991; 3 T-994

MINE WARFARE • MINE COUNTERMEASURES 17
MCCS 1 *Thalang*
MCO 2 *Lat Ya*
MCC 2 *Bang Rachan*
MSR 12: 7 T1; 5 T6

AMPHIBIOUS
PRINCIPAL AMPHIBIOUS SHIPS • LPD 2:
  1 *Angthong* (SGP *Endurance*) with 1 76mm gun (capacity 2 hel; 19 MBT; 500 troops);
  1 Type-071E (PRC *Yuzhao*) (capacity 4 LCAC plus supporting vehicles; 800 troops; 60 armoured vehicles; 4 hel)
LANDING SHIPS 2
  LST 2 *Sichang* with 2 hel landing platform (capacity 14 MBT; 300 troops)
LANDING CRAFT 14
  LCU 9: 3 *Man Nok*; 2 *Mataphun* (capacity either 3–4 MBT or 250 troops); 4 *Thong Kaeo*
  LCM 2
  UCAC 3 *Griffon* 1000TD

LOGISTICS AND SUPPORT 13
ABU 1 *Suriya*
AGOR 1 *Sok*
AGS 2: 1 *Chanthara*; 1 *Paruehatsabodi*
AOL 5: 1 *Matra* with 1 hel landing platform; 2 *Proet*; 1 *Prong*; 1 *Samui*
AORL 1 *Chula*
AORH 1 *Similan* (capacity 1 hel)
AWT 2

UNINHABITED MARITIME SYSTEMS
UUV • MW *SeaFox* C

Naval Aviation 1,200

FORCES BY ROLE
ISR
  1 sqn with *Sentry* O-2-337
MARITIME PATROL
  1 sqn with Do-228-212; F-27-200 MPA*
TRANSPORT
  1 sqn with ERJ-135LR; 2 F-27-400M *Troopship*
HELICOPTER
  1 sqn with Bell 212 (AB-212); H145M
  1 sqn with *Super Lynx* 300; S-76B
  1 sqn with S-70B *Seahawk*; MH-60S *Knight Hawk*
ISR UAV
  1 sqn with S-100 *Camcopter*
EQUIPMENT BY TYPE
AIRCRAFT 1 combat capable
  ISR 9 *Sentry* O-2-337
  MP 8: 7 Do-228-212; 1 F-27-200 MPA*
  TPT • Light 4: 2 ERJ-135LR; 2 F-27-400M *Troopship*
HELICOPTERS
  ASW 8: 6 S-70B *Seahawk*; 2 *Super Lynx* 300
  MRH 2 MH-60S *Knight Hawk*
  TPT • Light 16: 6 Bell 212 (AB-212); 5 H145M; 5 S-76B
UNINHABITED AERIAL VEHICLES
  ISR • Light up to 4 S-100 *Camcopter*
AIR-LAUNCHED MISSILES • AShM AGM-84 *Harpoon*

Marines 23,000

FORCES BY ROLE
COMMAND
  1 mne div HQ
MANOEUVRE
  Reconnaissance
  1 recce bn
  Light
  3 inf regt (total: 6 bn)
  Amphibious
  1 amph aslt bn
COMBAT SUPPORT
  1 arty regt (3 fd arty bn, 1 ADA bn)
EQUIPMENT BY TYPE
ARMOURED FIGHTING VEHICLES
  LT TK 3 VN-16
  IFV 14 BTR-3E1
  APC • APC (W) 24 LAV-150 *Commando*
  AAV 33 LVTP-7
ENGINEERING & MAINTENANCE VEHICLES
  ARV 1 AAVR-7
ANTI-TANK/ANTI-INFRASTRUCTURE
  MSL
    SP 10 M1045A2 HMMWV with TOW
    MANPATS M47 *Dragon*; TOW
  RCL • SP 106mm M40A1
ARTILLERY 54
  SP 155mm 6 ATMOS-2000

TOWED 48: **105mm** 36 M101A1; **155mm** 12 GC-45
AIR DEFENCE
SAM Point-defence QW-18
GUNS **12.7mm** 14

Air and Coastal Defence Command ε8,000
FORCES BY ROLE
COASTAL DEFENCE
1 coastal arty regt (3 coastal arty bn)
AIR DEFENCE
2 AD regt (3 AD bn)
EQUIPMENT BY TYPE
AIR DEFENCE SAM
Long-range FK-3 (HQ-22)
Point-defence 9K338 *Igla-S* (RS-SA-24 *Grinch*)

Naval Special Warfare Command

Air Force ε46,000
4 air divs, one flying trg school
FORCES BY ROLE
FIGHTER
2 sqn with F-5E/F *Tiger* II
3 sqn with F-16A/B *Fighting Falcon*
FIGHTER/GROUND ATTACK
1 sqn with *Gripen* C/D
GROUND ATTACK
1 sqn with *Alpha Jet**
1 sqn with AU-23A *Peacemaker*
1 sqn with T-50TH *Golden Eagle**
ELINT/ISR
1 sqn with DA42 MPP *Guardian*
AIRBORNE EARLY WARNING & CONTROL
1 sqn with Saab 340B; Saab 340 *Erieye*
TRANSPORT
1 (Royal Flight) sqn with A319CJ; A340-500; B-737-800
1 sqn with ATR-72; BAe-748
1 sqn with BT-67
1 sqn with C-130H/H-30 *Hercules*
TRAINING
1 sqn with CT-4A/B *Airtrainer*; T-41D *Mescalero*
1 sqn with CT-4E *Airtrainer*
1 sqn with T-6C *Texan* II
1 sqn with H135
TRANSPORT HELICOPTER
1 sqn with Bell 205 (UH-1H *Iroquois*)
1 sqn with Bell 412 *Twin Huey*; S-92A
ISR UAV
1 sqn with *Aerostar*; *Dominator* XP
1 sqn with U-1
EQUIPMENT BY TYPE
AIRCRAFT 130 combat capable
FTR 75: 1 F-5B *Freedom Fighter*; 20 F-5E *Tiger* II; 2 F-5F *Tiger* II (F-5E/F being upgraded); 1 F-5TH(E) *Tiger* II; 1 F-5TH(F) *Tiger* II; 36 F-16A *Fighting Falcon*; 14 F-16B *Fighting Falcon*
FGA 11: 7 *Gripen* C; 4 *Gripen* D
ATK 16 AU-23A *Peacemaker*
ISR 17 DA42 MPP *Guardian*
AEW&C 2 Saab 340 *Erieye*
ELINT 2 Saab 340 *Erieye* (COMINT/ELINT)
TPT 45: **Medium** 14: 6 C-130H *Hercules*; 6 C-130H-30 *Hercules*; 2 Saab 340B; **Light** 24: 3 ATR-72-500; 3 ATR-72-600; 3 Beech 200 *King Air*; 8 BT-67; 1 *Commander* 690; 6 DA42M; **PAX** 7: 1 A319CJ; 1 A320CJ; 1 A340-500; 1 B-737-800; 3 SSJ-100-95LR (1 A310-324 in store)
TRG 85: 16 *Alpha Jet**; 13 CT-4A *Airtrainer*; 6 CT-4B *Airtrainer*; 19 CT-4E *Airtrainer*; 12 T-6C *Texan* II; 7 T-41D *Mescalero*; 12 T-50TH *Golden Eagle**
HELICOPTERS
MRH 11: 2 Bell 412 *Twin Huey*; 2 Bell 412SP *Twin Huey*; 1 Bell 412HP *Twin Huey*; 6 Bell 412EP *Twin Huey*
CSAR 12 H225M *Super Cougar*
TPT 31: **Medium** 8: 3 S-92A *Super Hawk*; 5 S-70i *Black Hawk*; **Light** 23: 17 Bell 205 (UH-1H *Iroquois*); 6 H135
UNINHABITED AERIAL VEHICLES • ISR
Heavy 1 *Dominator* XP
Medium *Aerostar*
Light up to 17 U-1
AIR DEFENCE
SAM **Medium-range** 3+ KS-1C (CH-SA-12)
AIR-LAUNCHED MISSILES
AAM • **IR** AIM-9P/S *Sidewinder*; *Python* 3; **IIR** IRIS-T; *Python* 5 (reported); **ARH** AIM-120 AMRAAM; *Derby* (reported)
ASM AGM-65 *Maverick*
AShM RBS15F
BOMBS
Laser-guided *Paveway* II
INS/GPS-guided GBU-38 JDAM; KGGB

Royal Security Command
FORCES BY ROLE
MANOEUVRE
Light
2 inf regt (3 inf bn)

Gendarmerie & Paramilitary ε93,700

Border Patrol Police 20,000

Marine Police 2,200
EQUIPMENT BY TYPE
PATROL AND COASTAL COMBATANTS 101
PCO 1 *Srinakrin*
PCC 2 *Hameln*
PB 52: 1 *Chasanyabadee*; 3 *Cutlass*; 2 M25; 2 *Ratayapibanbancha* (*Reef Ranger*); 1 *Sriyanont*; 2

Wasuthep; 41 (various)
PBR 46

Volunteer Defense Corps 45,000 – Reserves

Police Aviation 500
EQUIPMENT BY TYPE
AIRCRAFT 6 combat capable
ATK 6 AU-23A *Peacemaker*
TPT 19: **Light** 18: 2 CN235; 3 DHC-6-400; 8 PC-6 *Turbo-Porter*; 3 SC-7 3M *Skyvan*; 2 Short 330UTT; **PAX** 1 F-50
HELICOPTERS
MRH 12: 6 Bell 412 *Twin Huey*; 6 Bell 429
TPT • Light 61: 27 Bell 205A; 14 Bell 206 *Jet Ranger*; 20 Bell 212 (AB-212)

Provincial Police 50,000 (incl ε500 Special Action Force)

Rangers (Thahan Phran) 21,000
Volunteer irregular force
FORCES BY ROLE
MANOEUVRE
  Other
    22 paramilitary regt (total: 275 paramilitary coy)

DEPLOYMENT
INDIA/PAKISTAN: UN • UNMOGIP 5
SOUTH SUDAN: UN • UNMISS 285; 1 engr coy

FOREIGN FORCES
United States US Indo-Pacific Command: 100

Timor-Leste TLS

US Dollar USD		2022	2023	2024
GDP	USD	1.73bn	1.89bn	2.04bn
per capita	USD	3,682	1,497	1,487
Growth	%	3.9	1.5	3.1
Inflation	%	7.0	6.0	2.5
Def bdgt	USD	44.3m	55.1m	

Real-terms defence budget trend (USDm, constant 2015)

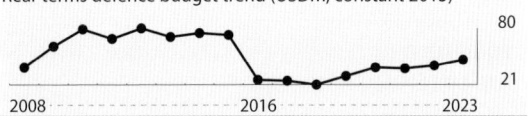

Population   1,476,042

Age	0–14	15–19	20–24	25–29	30–64	65 plus
Male	20.1%	5.2%	4.9%	3.9%	13.7%	2.1%
Female	19.0%	5.0%	4.9%	4.0%	15.1%	2.3%

Capabilities

The small Timor-Leste Defence Force (F-FDTL) has been afflicted by funding, personnel and morale challenges since it was established in 2001. The F-FDTL was reconstituted in the wake of fighting between regional factions in the security forces in 2006 but is still a long way from meeting the ambitious force-structure goals set out in the Force 2020 plan published in 2007. In 2016, the government published a Strategic Defence and Security Concept (SDSC). This outlined the roles of the F-FDTL, which include the protection of the country from external threats and combating violent crime. However, this parallel internal-security role has sometimes brought it into conflict with the national police force. The SDSC also stated that the F-FDTL needs to improve its naval capabilities, owing to the size of Timor-Leste's exclusive economic zone. The origins of the F-FDTL in the Falintil national resistance force and continuing training and doctrinal emphasis on low-intensity infantry tactics means that the force provides a deterrent to invasion. The F-FDTL has received training from Australian and US personnel. The US delivered a Cessna 206 surveillance aircraft to the F-FDTL's air component in 2023. A reciprocal Defence Cooperation Agreement was signed with Australia in September 2022. Maintenance capacity is limited and the country has no defence industry.

ACTIVE 2,250 (Army 2,250)

ORGANISATIONS BY SERVICE

Army 2,250
Training began in January 2001 with the aim of deploying 1,500 full-time personnel and 1,500 reservists. Authorities are engaged in developing security structures with international assistance
FORCES BY ROLE
MANOEUVRE
  Light
    2 inf bn
COMBAT SUPPORT
  1 MP pl

COMBAT SERVICE SUPPORT
1 log spt coy

Naval Element 250
EQUIPMENT BY TYPE
PATROL AND COASTAL COMBATANTS 3
PB 3: 2 *Shanghai* II; 1 *Kamenassa* (ex-ROK *Chamsuri*)

Air Component
EQUIPMENT BY TYPE
AIRCRAFT
ISR 1 Cessna T206H mod
TPT • **Light** 1 Cessna 172

DEPLOYMENT
SOUTH SUDAN: UN • UNMISS 2

Tonga TON

Tongan Pa'anga TOP		2022	2023	2024
GDP	TOP	1.14bn	1.28bn	1.39bn
	USD	498m	547m	581m
per capita	USD	4,978	5,488	5,842
Growth	%	-2.0	2.6	2.5
Inflation	%	8.5	10.2	5.8
Def bdgt	TOP	18.5m	20.4m	
	USD	8.1m	8.6m	
USD1=TOP		2.29	2.34	2.39

Real-terms defence budget trend (USDm, constant 2015)

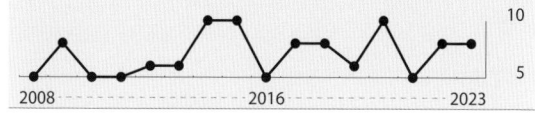

Population	105,221					
Age	0–14	15–19	20–24	25–29	30–64	65 plus
Male	15.2%	5.2%	4.7%	4.1%	17.7%	3.3%
Female	14.7%	4.9%	4.5%	4.0%	17.7%	4.0%

Capabilities

His Majesty's Armed Forces (HMAF) are a battalion-sized military based around the light infantry of the Tonga Royal Guards and the Royal Tongan Marines, and a small naval patrol squadron. Maritime security is a primary concern of defence operations, although, between 2002 and 2014, HMAF also contributed platoon-sized forces to multinational peacekeeping efforts in the Solomon Islands, and then international coalition operations in Iraq and Afghanistan. Australia and the United States are Tonga's key external defence partners, but the armed forces also undertake defence cooperation activities with China, India, New Zealand and the United Kingdom.

ACTIVE 600 (Royal Guards & Land Force 140 Navy 130 Other 330)

ORGANISATIONS BY SERVICE

Royal Guard & Land Force 140
FORCES BY ROLE
MANOEUVRE
Light
1 inf coy(-)
Other
1 sy coy(-)

Navy 130
EQUIPMENT BY TYPE
PATROL AND COASTAL COMBATANTS 2
PCO 2 *Guardian* (AUS *Bay* mod)
AMPHIBIOUS • LANDING CRAFT 2:
LCM 1
LCVP 1 *Late* (AUS)
LOGISTICS AND SUPPORT • AOL 1

Vietnam VNM

Vietnamese Dong VND		2022	2023	2024
GDP	VND	9,513trn	10,342trn	11,360trn
	USD	406bn	433bn	470bn
per capita	USD	4,087	4,316	4,636
Growth	%	8.0	4.7	5.8
Inflation	%	3.2	3.4	3.4
Def bdgt	VND	ε136trn	ε176trn	
	USD	ε5.81bn	ε7.39bn	
FMA (US)	USD	12m	12m	12m
USD1=VND		23,405.78	23,864.02	24,186.80

Real-terms defence budget trend (USDbn, constant 2015)

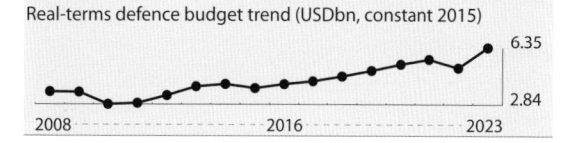

Population	104,799,174					
Age	0–14	15–19	20–24	25–29	30–64	65 plus
Male	12.4%	3.8%	3.6%	3.9%	23.3%	3.2%
Female	11.1%	3.6%	3.5%	3.7%	23.4%	4.7%

Capabilities

Vietnam has a strong military tradition, and the country's defence efforts benefit from broad popular support, particularly in the context of tensions with China over conflicting claims in the South China Sea. In 2018, Vietnam adopted a Law on National Defence that referred several times to Vietnam's differences with China and the need for both sides to 'put more effort into maintaining stability'. Hanoi has been strengthening naval and air capabilities with a clear focus on protecting its interest in the South China Sea. Those efforts include the development of an advanced submarine capability and the procurement of ISR, air-defence and anti-ship systems to boost the capacity to keep adversary forces away from

Vietnam's maritime littoral territory. The country signed a joint vision statement on defence cooperation and an agreement on mutual logistics support with India in 2022. Although Russia has been Vietnam's dominant defence supplier, Hanoi is seeking to diversity its supplier base and is being courted by international suppliers; the US lifted its arms embargo on Vietnam in 2016, while the Czech Republic, India, Japan and South Korea are among those seeking inroads into Vietnam's defence market. The need for diversification became more acute as Russia's war on Ukraine caused Moscow to prioritise arms deliveries on its own forces. Vietnam also has a defence cooperation agreement with Cuba. Long-expected orders for new combat aircraft and maritime-patrol aircraft have failed to materialise, though Vietnam ordered a Japanese-produced satellite-based surveillance system in April 2020 and training aircraft from the Czech Republic and the US. In addition, Washington has transferred ex-*Hamilton*-class vessels to Vietnam's coast guard under the US Excess Defense Articles programme. Vietnam is developing its limited defence-industrial capacities and has launched a defence-focused subsidiary of the state-owned Viettel Military Industry and Telecoms Group, called Viettel High Technology Industries Corporation, which focuses on defence electronics and communications. A 2019 White Paper promoted investment in Vietnam's defence industry with the aim to become internationally competitive and join the 'global value chain' by 2030.

ACTIVE 450,000 (Army 380,000 Navy 40,000 Air 30,000) Gendarmerie & Paramilitary 40,000

Conscript liability 2 years army and air defence, 3 years air force and navy, specialists 3 years, some ethnic minorities 2 years

RESERVES Gendarmerie & Paramilitary 5,000,000

ORGANISATIONS BY SERVICE

Space
EQUIPMENT BY TYPE
SATELLITES • ISR 1 VNREDSat

Army ε380,000
8 Mil Regions (incl capital)
FORCES BY ROLE
COMMAND
  4 corps HQ
SPECIAL FORCES
  1 SF bde (1 AB bde, 1 demolition engr regt)
MANOEUVRE
  Armoured
    10 tk bde
  Mechanised
    2 mech inf div
  Light
    23 inf div
SURFACE-TO-SURFACE MISSILE
  1 SRBM bde
COMBAT SUPPORT
  13 arty bde
  1 arty regt
  11 engr bde
  1 engr regt
  1 EW unit
  3 sigs bde
  2 sigs regt
COMBAT SERVICE SUPPORT
  9 economic construction div
  1 log regt
  1 med unit
  1 trg regt
AIR DEFENCE
  11 AD bde

Reserve
FORCES BY ROLE
MANOEUVRE
  Light
    9 inf div
EQUIPMENT BY TYPE
ARMOURED FIGHTING VEHICLES
  MBT 1,379: 45 T-34; 750 T-54/T-55; 100 T-54B mod; 70 T-62; 64 T-90S; 350 ZTZ-59;
  LT TK 620: 300 PT-76; 320 ZTQ-62/ZTS-63
  RECCE 100 BRDM-1/BRDM-2
  IFV 300 BMP-1/BMP-2
  APC 1,380+
    APC (T) 280+: Some BTR-50; 200 M113 (to be upgraded); 80 ZSD-63
    APC (W) 1,100 BTR-40/BTR-60/BTR-152
ENGINEERING & MAINTENANCE VEHICLES
  AEV IMR-2
  ARV BREM-1M
  VLB TMM-3
ANTI-TANK/ANTI-INFRASTRUCTURE
  MSL • MANPATS 9K11 *Malyutka* (RS-AT-3 *Sagger*); 9M14 mod
  RCL 75mm PF-56; **82mm** PF-65 (B-10); **87mm** PF-51
  GUNS
    SP 100mm SU-100; **122mm** SU-122
    TOWED 100mm T-12 (arty); M-1944
ARTILLERY 3,040+
  SP 30+: **122mm** 2S1 *Gvozdika*; **152mm** 30 2S3 *Akatsiya*; **175mm** M107
  TOWED 2,300: **105mm** M101/M102; **122mm** D-30/PL-54 (M-1938)/PL-60 (D-74); **130mm** M-46; **152mm** D-20; **155mm** M114
  MRL 710+: **107mm** 360 Type-63; **122mm** 350 BM-21 *Grad*; **140mm** BM-14
  MOR 82mm; **120mm** M-1943; **160mm** M-1943
SURFACE-TO-SURFACE MISSILE LAUNCHERS
  SRBM • Coventional 9K72/9K77 (RS-SS-1C/D *Scud* B/C)
AIR DEFENCE

SAM • **Point-defence** 9K32 *Strela*-2 (RS-SA-7 *Grail*)‡; 9K310 *Igla*-1 (RS-SA-16 *Gimlet*); 9K38 *Igla* (RS-SA-18 *Grouse*)
GUNS 12,000
  SP 23mm ZSU-23-4
  TOWED 14.5mm/30mm/37mm/57mm/85mm/100mm

Navy ε40,000 (incl ε27,000 Naval Infantry)
EQUIPMENT BY TYPE
SUBMARINES 8
  SSK 6 *Hanoi* (RUS Project 636.1 (Improved *Kilo*)) with 6 533mm TT with 3M14E *Klub*-S (RS-SS-N-30B) LACM/3M54E1/E *Klub*-S (RS-SS-N-27A/B) AShM (*Klub*-S AShM variant unclear)/53-65KE HWT/TEST-71ME HWT
  SSW 2 *Yugo* (DPRK)
PATROL AND COASTAL COMBATANTS 73
  CORVETTES 12:
    FSGM 5:
      1 BPS-500 with 2 quad lnchr with 3M24E *Uran*-E (RS-SS-N-25 *Switchblade*) AShM, 1 9K32 *Strela*-2M (RS-SA-N-5 *Grail*) SAM (manually operated), 2 twin 533mm TT, 1 RBU 1600 A/S mor, 1 AK630 CIWS, 1 76mm gun
      2 *Dinh Tien Hoang* (RUS *Gepard* 3.9 (Project 11661E)) with 2 quad lnchr with 3M24E *Uran*-E (RS-SS-N-25 *Switchblade*) AShM, 1 3M89E *Palma* (*Palash*) CIWS with *Sosna*-R SAM (RS-CADS-N-2), 2 AK630M CIWS, 1 76mm gun, 1 hel landing platform
      2 *Tran Hung Dao* (RUS *Gepard* 3.9 (Project 11661E)) with 2 quad lnchr with 3M24E *Uran*-E (RS-SS-N-25 *Switchblade*), 1 3M89E *Palma* (*Palash*) CIWS with *Sosna*-R SAM (RS-CADS-N-2), 2 twin 533mm TT with SET-53M HWT, 2 AK630M CIWS, 1 76mm gun, 1 hel landing platform
    FSG 1 *Po Hang* (Flight III) (ex-ROK) with 2 quad lnchr with 3M24E *Uran*-E (RS-SS-N-25 *Switchblade*) AShM, 2 76mm guns
    FS 6:
      3 Project 159A (ex-FSU *Petya* II) with 1 quintuple 406mm ASTT, 4 RBU 6000 *Smerch* 2 A/S mor, 2 twin 76mm gun
      2 Project 159AE (ex-FSU *Petya* III) with 1 triple 533mm ASTT with SET-53ME HWT, 4 RBU 2500 *Smerch* 1 A/S mor, 2 twin 76mm guns
      1 *Po Hang* (Flight III) (ex-ROK) with 2 76mm guns
  PCFGM 12:
      4 Project 1241RE (*Tarantul* I) with 2 twin lnchr with P-15 *Termit*-R (RS-SS-N-2D *Styx*) AShM, 1 quad lnchr with 9K32 *Strela*-2M (RS-SA-N-5 *Grail*) SAM (manually operated), 2 AK630M CIWS, 1 76mm gun
      8 Project 12418 (*Tarantul* V) with 4 quad lnchr with 3M24E *Uran*-E (RS-SS-N-25 *Switchblade*) AShM, 1 quad lnchr with 9K32 *Strela*-2M (RS-SA-N-5 *Grail*) SAM (manually operated), 2 AK630M CIWS, 1 76mm gun
  PCO 7: 1 Project FC264; 6 TT-400TP with 2 AK630M CIWS, 1 76mm gun
  PCC 6 *Svetlyak* (Project 1041.2) with 1 AK630M CIWS, 1 76mm gun
  PBFG 8 Project 205 (*Osa* II) with 4 single lnchr with P-20U (RS-SS-N-2B *Styx*) AShM
  PBFT 1+ *Shershen*† (FSU) with 4 single 533mm TT
  PBF 12
  PBR 4 *Stolkraft*
  PB 6: 4 *Zhuk* (mod); 2 TP-01
  PH 2 *Shtorm* (ex-FSU Project 206M (*Turya*))† with 1 twin 57mm gun
  PHT 3 *Shtorm* (ex-FSU Project 206M (*Turya*))† with 4 single 533mm TT with 53-65KE HWT, 1 twin 57mm gun
MINE WARFARE • MINE COUNTERMEASURES 8
  MSO 2 *Akvamaren* (Project 266 (*Yurka*))
  MSC 4 *Sonya* (Project 1265 (*Yakhont*))
  MHI 2 *Korund* (Project 1258 (*Yevgenya*))
AMPHIBIOUS
  LANDING SHIPS 7
    LST 2 *Tran Khanh Du* (ex-US LST 542) with 1 hel landing platform (capacity 16 Lt Tk/APC; 140 troops)
    LSM 5:
      1 *Polnochny* A (capacity 6 Lt Tk/APC; 200 troops)
      2 *Polnochny* B (capacity 6 Lt Tk/APC; 200 troops)
      2 *Nau Dinh*
  LANDING CRAFT • LCM 13
    8 LCM 6 (capacity 1 Lt Tk or 80 troops)
    4 LCM 8 (capacity 1 MBT or 200 troops)
    1 VDN-150
LOGISTICS AND SUPPORT 22
  AGS 1 *Tran Dai Nia* (Damen Research Vessel 6613)
  AH 1 *Khanh Hoa* (*Truong Sa* mod)
  AKR 4 Damen Stan Lander 5612
  AKSL 10+
  AP 1 *Truong Sa*
  ASR 1 *Yết Kiêu* (Damen Rescue Gear Ship 9316)
  AT 2
  AWT 1
  AXS 1 *Le Quy Don*

Naval Infantry ε27,000
FORCES BY ROLE
SPECIAL FORCES
  1 cdo bde
MANOEUVRE
  Amphibious
  2 mne bde
EQUIPMENT BY TYPE
ARMOURED FIGHTING VEHICLES
  LT TK PT-76; ZTS-63
  APC • APC (W) BTR-60

Coastal Defence

326   THE MILITARY BALANCE 2024

FORCES BY ROLE
COASTAL DEFENCE
  4 AShM bde
  1 coastal arty bde
EQUIPMENT BY TYPE
COASTAL DEFENCE • AShM 4K44 *Redut* (RS-SSC-1B *Sepal*); 4K51 *Rubezh* (RS-SSC-3 *Styx*); K-300P *Bastion*-P (RS-SSC-5 *Stooge*)
ARTILLERY • MRL 160mm AccuLAR-160; **306mm** EXTRA

Navy Air Wing
FORCES BY ROLE
ASW/SAR
  1 regt with DHC-6-400 *Twin Otter*; H225; Ka-28 (Ka-27PL) *Helix* A; Ka-32 *Helix* C
EQUIPMENT BY TYPE
AIRCRAFT • TPT • Light 6 DHC-6-400 *Twin Otter*
HELICOPTERS
  ASW 10 Ka-28 *Helix* A
  TPT • Medium 4: 2 H225; 2 Ka-32 *Helix* C

Air Force 30,000
3 air div, 1 tpt bde
FORCES BY ROLE
FIGHTER/GROUND ATTACK
  3 regt with Su-22M3/M4/UM *Fitter* (some ISR)
  1 regt with Su-27SK/Su-27UBK *Flanker*
  1 regt with Su-27SK/Su-27UBK *Flanker*; Su-30MK2 *Flanker*
  2 regt with Su-30MK2 *Flanker*
TRANSPORT
  2 regt with An-2 *Colt*; Bell 205 (UH-1H *Iroquois*); Mi-8 *Hip*; Mi-17 *Hip* H; M-28 *Bryza*; C295M
TRAINING
  1 regt with L-39 *Albatros*
  1 regt with Yak-52
ATTACK/TRANSPORT HELICOPTER
  2 regt with Mi-8 *Hip*; Mi-17 *Hip* H; Mi-171; Mi-24 *Hind*
AIR DEFENCE
  6 AD div HQ
  2 SAM regt with S-300PMU1 (RS-SA-20 *Gargoyle*)
  3 SAM regt with *Spyder*-MR
  3 SAM regt with S-75 *Dvina* (RS-SA-2 *Guideline*)
  4 SAM regt with S-125-2TM *Pechora*-2TM
  2 SAM regt with S-125M *Pechora*-M
  4 ADA regt
EQUIPMENT BY TYPE
AIRCRAFT 84 combat capable
  FGA 72: 26 Su-22M3/M4/UM *Fitter* (some ISR); 6 Su-27SK *Flanker*; 5 Su-27UBK *Flanker* B; 35 Su-30MK2 *Flanker* G
  MP 1 M-28 *Bryza*
  TPT • Light 12: 6 An-2 *Colt*; 3 C295M; 3 C-212 *Aviocar* (NC-212i)
  TRG 59: 17 L-39 *Albatros*; 12 Yak-130 *Mitten**; 30 Yak-52
HELICOPTERS
  MRH 6 Mi-17 *Hip* H
  TPT 28: **Medium** 17: 14 Mi-8 *Hip*; 3 Mi-171; **Light** 11 Bell 205 (UH-1H *Iroquois*)
AIR DEFENCE
  SAM 98+:
    Long-range 12 S-300PMU1 (RS-SA-20 *Gargoyle*)
    Medium-range 65: ε25 S-75 *Dvina* (RS-SA-2 *Guideline*); ε30 S-125-2TM *Pechora*-2TM; ε10 *Spyder*-MR
    Short-range 21+: 2K12 *Kub* (RS-SA-6 *Gainful*); 21 S-125M *Pechora*-M (RS-SA-3 *Goa*)
    Point-defence 9K32 *Strela*-2 (RS-SA-7 *Grail*)‡; 9K310 *Igla*-1 (RS-SA-16 *Gimlet*)
  GUNS 37mm; 57mm; 85mm; 100mm; 130mm
AIR-LAUNCHED MISSILES
  AAM • IR R-60 (RS-AA-8 *Aphid*); R-73 (RS-AA-11A *Archer*); **IR/SARH** R-27 (RS-AA-10 *Alamo*); **ARH** R-77 (RS-AA-12A *Adder*)
  ASM Kh-29L/T (RS-AS-14 *Kedge*); Kh-59M (RS-AS-18 *Kazoo*)
  AShM Kh-31A (RS-AS-17B *Krypton*)
  ARM Kh-28 (RS-AS-9 *Kyle*); Kh-31P (RS-AS-17A *Krypton*)

Gendarmerie & Paramilitary 40,000+ active

Border Defence Corps ε40,000

Coast Guard
EQUIPMENT BY TYPE
PATROL AND COASTAL COMBATANTS 79+
  PSOH 2 *Hamilton* (ex-US) with 1 76mm gun (capacity 1 med hel)
  PSO 4 DN2000 (Damen 9014)
  PCO 13+: 1 *Mazinger* (ex-ROK); 9 TT-400; 3+ other
  PCC 2 *Hae Uri* (ex-ROK)
  PBF 28: 26 MS-50S; 2 *Shershen*
  PB 30: 1 MS-50; approx 14 TT-200; 14 TT-120; 1 other
LOGISTICS AND SUPPORT 5
  AFS 1
  ATF 4 Damen Salvage Tug
  AIRCRAFT • MP 2 C-212-400 MPA

Local Forces ε5,000,000 reservists
Incl People's Self-Defence Force (urban units) and People's Militia (rural units); comprises static and mobile cbt units, log spt and village protection pl; some arty, mor and AD guns; acts as reserve

DEPLOYMENT

CENTRAL AFRICAN REPUBLIC: UN • MINUSCA 8
SOUTH SUDAN: UN • UNMISS 68; 1 fd hospital
SUDAN: UN • UNISFA 190; 1 engr coy

Chapter Six
Middle East and North Africa

- Hamas launched an attack on Israel on 7 October 2023 from Gaza, killing around 1,200 people and taking civilians and military personnel as hostages, unleashing a brutal war between the sides. Israel responded with heavy bombing, artillery fire, and a ground incursion into Gaza. The fighting halted efforts to normalise relations between Tel Aviv and several Arab Gulf states.
- Saudi Arabia and Iran restored diplomatic ties under an agreement brokered by China, signalling Beijing's increasing interest in shaping the geopolitical landscape in the Middle East. Despite the breakthrough, it was not clear how monitoring, follow-up and enforcement of the deal would occur.
- US efforts to reduce troop deployments to the Middle East to focus more on the Indo-Pacific suffered a setback because of Iranian naval harassment in the region, Russian action in Syria and the Hamas–Israel war. At various times, the Pentagon rushed missile-defence equipment, combat aircraft and two aircraft-carrier strike groups to the region to bolster its presence.
- Syria returned to the Arab League, having been suspended 12 years earlier because of the Bashar al-Assad regime's actions in the country's civil war. Battlelines within the country were little changed over the past year and the government has shown little interest in enticing refugees to return from abroad.
- Algeria logged the region's largest defence spending increase in the past year, almost doubling from 2022. The country has been spending heavily on equipment modernisation. High inflation and other factors could make it difficult, though, for Algiers to maintain high levels of defence outlays.
- Israel's defence exports reached a record high in 2022 and were on pace for another strong year in 2023, with the country securing deals such as Germany's purchase of *Arrow* 3 missile-defence systems. The Hamas–Israel war could dent Tel Aviv's export potential, though, both because domestic needs could trump export interest and because of strained relations with some historic buyers of Israeli weapons, such as Colombia.

Saudi Arabia, real-terms defence budget trend, 2015–23 (USDbn, constant 2015)*

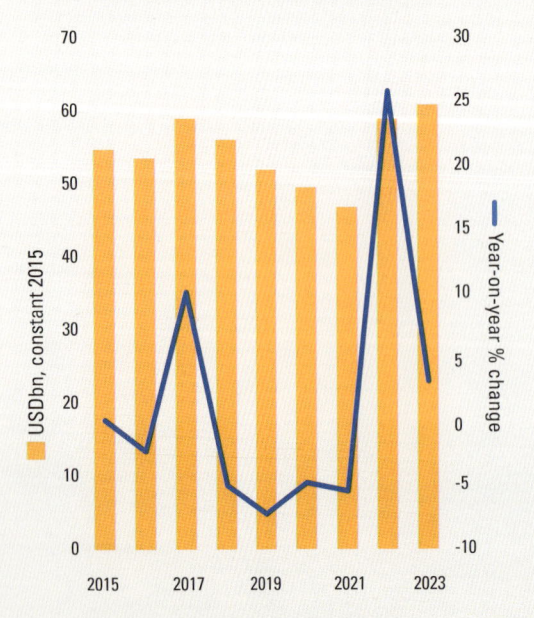

Note: *Defence budget only – excludes security expenditure

Active military personnel – top 10
(25,000 per unit)

Country	Personnel
Iran	610,000
Egypt	438,500
Saudi Arabia	257,000
Morocco	195,800
Iraq	193,000
Israel	169,500
Syria	169,000
Algeria	139,000
Jordan	100,500
United Arab Emirates	63,000

Global total 20,646,000

Regional total 2,572,000 (12.5%)

Regional defence policy and economics 330 ▶
Arms procurements and deliveries 341 ▶
Armed forces data section 342 ▶

Middle East and North Africa: selected surface combatants, 2014–23*

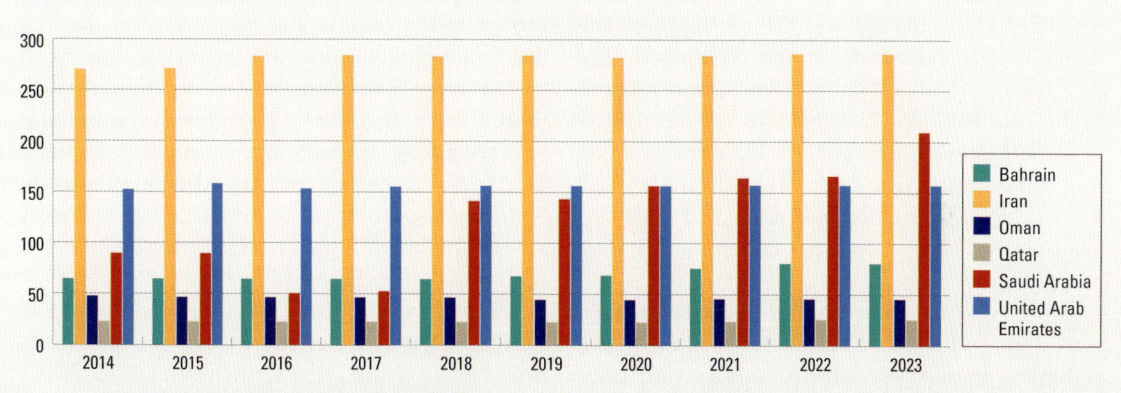

Legend: Bahrain, Iran, Oman, Qatar, Saudi Arabia, United Arab Emirates

*Includes principal surface, and patrol and coastal combatants

Algeria: defence spending as % of GDP, 2014–23

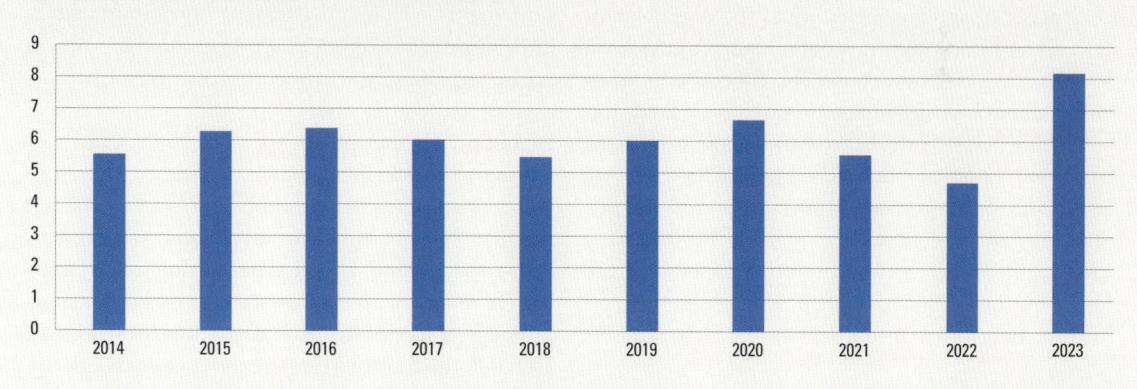

Middle East and North Africa: deployed satellites, 2014–23

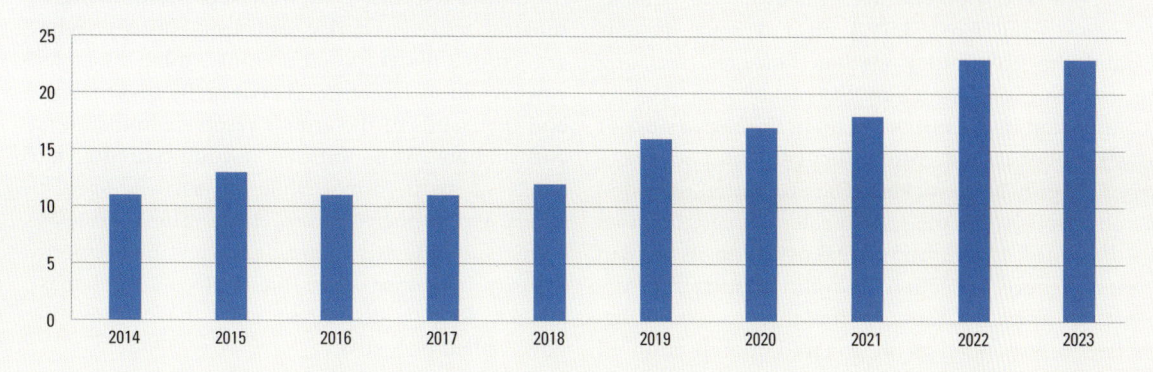

Middle East and North Africa

Efforts in the conflict-prone Middle East and North Africa to reset intra-regional relationships suffered a serious setback with the 7 October attack by Hamas on Israel and ensuing fighting. Prior to the attack, the trend towards regional de-escalation observed since 2021 was continuing. Regional rivals Iran and Saudi Arabia restored links; Turkiye improved ties with its main Gulf competitors, Saudi Arabia and the United Arab Emirates (UAE), while Syria returned to the Arab League in another indication that fractured relations that have scarred the region for years are being rebuilt.

Several factors drove the de-escalation: fatigue among competitors, an adjustment within the region to shifting global power dynamics and a greater focus on economic recovery and prosperity. Importantly, the perceived security gaps engendered by the United States' retrenchment drove countries to adjust and develop regional and international partnerships.

The depth and sustainability of the de-escalation was always uncertain, however. Hamas's attack on Israel threatened a new round of conflict and derailed efforts at normalising relations between Tel Aviv and some Gulf states. Outside the Gulf region, conditions in several countries remained dire. Conflicts in Libya, Syria and Yemen remained intractable, and Egypt's and Jordan's economies suffered. Furthermore, growing tensions between Saudi Arabia and the UAE, the once-aligned Gulf powerhouses, pointed towards new forms of competition.

Israel

The security situation in Israel in the past year experienced tremendous upheaval. The Hamas attack from Gaza killed around 1,200 Israelis and the group took civilian hostages, spurring the start of Operation *Swords of Iron*. Hamas launched its assault on Israel in the early hours of 7 October with a ground incursion and a barrage of roughly 2,000 rockets. The attack that unfolded on a holiday on the Jewish calendar caught Israel off guard, highlighting weaknesses in its human intelligence collection and the country's heavy reliance on technology for threat monitoring. Israel responded with a rapid mobilisation of reservists and in subsequent weeks with waves of airstrikes, ground operations and other actions, including cutting off power to Gaza, causing a humanitarian crisis in the territory. Over the first week of fighting alone, Tel Aviv said over 6,000 rockets were fired towards Israel and that it struck more than 2,600 targets. The scale of the fighting spurred a backlash among some countries against Tel Aviv, including on the diplomatic front. Fighting also took place between Israeli forces and Hizbullah militants along the Israel–Lebanon border and elsewhere.

On the political level, Israel formed a national unity government, led by incumbent and long-time Israeli Prime Minister Benjamin Netanyahu. In late 2022, Netanyahu had formed a coalition government that included nationalist and right-wing figures, heightening tensions between Israel and its Palestinian neighbours over illegal Israeli settlements. That government also pursued a judicial-reform agenda that precipitated a political crisis engulfing the armed forces. Described as a 'judicial coup', the proposed reforms intend to eliminate the power of the High Court of Justice to block government decisions, therefore jeopardising the checks and balances of the Israeli political system. However, they faced widespread resistance among Israeli citizens, including from Israeli military reservists and veterans across military branches, as well as in the Mossad and Shin Bet, the county's foreign and domestic security services. Nearly 10,000 reservists announced their suspension of service until the government stopped its judicial reforms. They were supported by high-ranking retired security and army officials who argued that the proposed reforms 'violated Israel's 75-year-old social contract between the government and thousands of the army's reserve commanders and soldiers'. These officials include retired army chiefs of staff, former Shin Bet security-agency chiefs and former Mossad chiefs. These protests were subsequently overshadowed by Israel's security response after the 7 October Hamas attacks, though discontent with the Netanyahu government persisted.

Saudi–Iran deal

On 10 March 2023, China, Saudi Arabia and Iran issued a joint statement restoring diplomatic ties between Riyadh and Tehran. The agreement was brokered through a series of meetings which started in 2021 and were held in Iraq, Oman and later in China. Iran and Saudi Arabia pledged mutual respect for each other's sovereignty and committed to the principle of non-interference in the other's internal affairs. The agreement, ostensibly designed to improve relations between the region's two most prominent powers, reflected Saudi interest in stabilising regional politics to create a favourable environment to implement the Kingdom's Vision 2030. The two sides traded official visits and Saudi officials indicated a readiness to invest in the Iranian economy. It was not clear, however, how monitoring, follow-up and enforcement of the deal would occur, with Chinese officials refusing to take responsibility for its implementation.

Despite the agreement with the Saudis, Iran's naval behaviour remained aggressive. There were at least four serious instances of Iranian harassment and seizure of merchant vessels in the Gulf following the accord. This behaviour, combined with Iran's ongoing nuclear ambitions and its entrenched influence in Syria, Iraq, Lebanon and Yemen, quickly tested the Saudi–Iranian rapprochement. The re-emergence of disputes over the Durra gas field in disputed waters between Saudi Arabia, Kuwait and Iran illustrated that challenges persisted.

China's involvement in talks reflected Beijing's interest in positioning itself as an external mediator in the Middle East. China's president Xi Jinping articulated that ambition in his 'Global Security Initiative' 2022 speech, which called for establishing a new security framework in the region. The past year also demonstrated China's desire for stronger military ties to the region. In August, China and the UAE announced a joint air-force exercise, *Falcon Shield* 2023, which took place in Xinjiang.

Yemen

Saudi Arabia and Iran also took steps under the Chinese-mediated deal to end their years-long proxy war in Yemen, reflecting Riyadh's recognition that it could not militarily defeat the Iranian-backed and well-entrenched Ansarullah (Houthi) movement. In April, soon after the deal with Iran was agreed, a Saudi delegation arrived in Sana'a to negotiate peace with the Houthi militia group. The two parties agreed on a six-month truce to pave the way for three months of talks on establishing a two-year 'transition' for the war-torn country. However, the success of the talks depends on Iran's commitment to stop supplying weapons to its Houthi allies and the group adhering to the ceasefire. A Saudi–Houthi ceasefire, in place from April to October 2022, and later extended, was repeatedly violated, primarily by the Houthis.

The Iran–Saudi agreement also failed to address the underlying domestic aspects of the conflict. The protracted war has created multiple fighting factions with conflicting interests. Northern Yemen (including the capital, Sana'a) is dominated by the Houthis, while control of the east and south is contested by several groups. The United Nations tried, with limited success, to bring the different factions to the negotiating table. Although the UN in March 2023 convinced the Yemeni government and the Houthis to release 887 detainees, a credible effort to bring peace to Yemen is still lacking, making conflict continuation possible.

Saudi Arabia's new policy towards Yemen led some Western countries to lift their arms-sales restrictions on the Kingdom. Italy decided to end its ammunition embargo on Saudi Arabia. Germany, Denmark and the Netherlands also dialled back on their limits.

As the Hamas–Israel war unfolded, Houthi forces tried to provide military support to the Palestinian group, including by launching missiles and uninhabited aerial vehicles (UAVs) against Israel.

Syria

Syria and its president, Bashar Al-Assad, emerged from 12 years of pariah status and regional isolation because of the country's civil war. Assad attended the 32nd Arab League summit in Jeddah, which signalled members were ready for a rapprochement with the Syrian regime. The consequences of the civil war have radiated across the region, creating a refugee crisis that overwhelmed neighbouring countries and fuelling the rise of extremist groups, including the Islamic State (ISIS), Jabhat Al-Nusrah (now known as Hayat Tahrir al-Sham) and others.

Major Arab powers, including Saudi Arabia, the UAE and Jordan, spearheaded the detente to achieve security and political goals, including containing growing Iranian influence in Syria, curbing Tamine smuggling from Syria to Jordan and the Gulf Cooperation Council (GCC) states, and facilitating the return of Syrian refugees. However, achievement of those goals remained elusive. The Syrian regime showed little willingness to compromise on humanitarian issues, security, human rights and political reform, and US sanctions on Syria continued to deter foreign investors, even those from countries re-establishing ties with Damascus. The Syrian government also faces cases against it in the International Court of Justice and other jurisdictions, obstructing efforts to normalise relations for those wanting to re-engage with Damascus.

Syria also has become something of a narco-state whose ruling factions are heavily reliant on revenues from amphetamine exports. Syria's exports of such drugs reached around USD3.5 billion in 2020, surpassing the country's legitimate trade. Jordan has tried to disrupt the flow of drugs, with one airstrike in southern Syria killing a prominent Syrian dealer linked to the regime, while Amman also tried to stem human smuggling and the illicit use of UAVs for such purposes. Refugees have been reluctant to return to Syria absent security and other guarantees from the government.

Israeli strikes on Iran-backed groups in Syria continued during 2023. Nevertheless, Iran's influence continued to grow, including through the Lebanese Hizbullah militant group, but also because Russian attention diminished as a result of Moscow's war in Ukraine.

US posture in the region

The US maintained a strong defence posture throughout the Middle East. But Washington had signalled its primary focus now is on Asia, with potential force adjustments in the Middle East, sparking concern among some of its traditional Gulf partners about the United States' commitment to the region's security. US officials continued to stress Washington's willingness and ability to use force against Iran should it cross the nuclear threshold.

The reality on the ground thwarted Washington's desire, though, to focus more on other regions. The Hamas–Israel war spurred the US to dispatch two aircraft carriers, missile-defence equipment and other items to the region to try and prevent the fighting from spreading. But even before, security challenges in the region, including Iran harassing naval traffic and an uptick in Russian activity in northeast Syria, prompted the US to augment its troops in various locations in the Middle East. At various points, Washington dispatched A-10, F-35 and F-16 combat aircraft to the region, as well as a number of naval assets to counter perceptions that it had softened its posture against Iran. The UAE stepped back from a maritime target force a regional maritime task force over frustration that Iranian harassment of oil tankers went unanswered by the US. The US also deployed F-22 *Raptors* to the region following Russian surveillance flights over the US base at Al-Tanf in Syria.

Arms trade

Turkiye repaired its relations with Saudi Arabia, the UAE and other Arab states after years of geopolitical competition across the region. Mutual economic interests contributed to the normalisation of relations. The UAE has become Turkiye's second-largest arms customer. In July, Turkiye and Saudi Arabia signed multiple agreements in the fields of investment, defence, energy and communications. Saudi Arabia also agreed to buy Turkish *Akinci* UAVs in the biggest defence contract in Turkiye's history.

Saudi Arabia and the UAE, among others, also demonstrated their ambition to become major arms producers. The UAE's EDGE Group, for instance, completed several acquisitions to broaden its portfolio. The country's Nimr Automotive supplied armoured vehicles to Chad.

Washington approved potential deals with Middle East buyers, including for delivery of 24 AH-1W attack helicopters to Bahrain, though much of 2023 was relatively muted in terms of transactions for US defence companies. Europe continued to be active in the region on defence-industrial matters. Saudi Arabia signed a statement of intent with the United Kingdom to cooperate in the combat-air arena, though London faces competition from France to provide new combat aircraft to Riyadh.

The Gulf region remains critical for combat aircraft. France and the UK are competing to supply around 54 fighters to Saudi Arabia, for instance. Riyadh wants a near-term replacement for its Panavia *Tornado* aircraft, but also a pathway to a next-generation design. Paris is pushing *Rafale* and a route to the New Generation Fighter element of the tri-national Next Generation Weapon System that also involves Germany and Spain. London is offering additional *Typhoons* and a path to eventual participation in the *Tempest* element of the Global Combat Air Programme involving Italy, Japan and the UK.

Ukraine impact

Despite maintaining ostensible neutrality since the Russian invasion of Ukraine, Israel approved the provision of counter-UAV defence systems to Ukraine. Israeli systems manufactured by RADA Electronic Industries were donated by a Lithuanian volunteer organisation and deployed in Ukraine starting in March 2023. They include ieMHR model radars which are used to detect missiles, rockets and UAVs. Similarly, Israel was building a civilian aerial warning system for deployment to Ukraine.

Israel's move was prompted by its concern over Iran's provision of *Shahed* direct attack munitions and *Mohajer* UAVs to Russia. While Israel has approved the delivery of radar systems to Ukraine, it refused to provide *Iron Dome* air-defence systems to Kyiv. That decision proved fortuitous, with the system used heavily by Israel in the war against Hamas to intercept rockets fired from Gaza and elsewhere.

On the other side, Iran has continued to supply Russia with its UAVs despite Western criticism and has helped Russia build a production facility east of Moscow in exchange for assistance from Russia in other areas.

The fallout from Russia's move against the Wagner Group was also felt in the Middle East, as the group was operating in Libya and Syria. The relatively weak leaders of both countries, Khalifa Haftar and Assad, appeared to effectively accept Russia's defence ministry taking over leadership of those troops.

UAE rethinks Combined Maritime Forces commitment

The United Arab Emirates (UAE) raised doubts about a major regional security initiative when it stepped back from the Combined Maritime Forces (CMF), a partnership of over 30 countries focused on issues such as maritime security and counter-piracy. The episode also emerged as one of the most public displays yet of frustration among Washington's Gulf partners about a perceived lack of commitment by the United States to the region.

The UAE acted in apparent anger at the perceived inability or unwillingness of the US Naval Forces Central Command (NAVCENT), or 5th Fleet, to prevent Iranian seizures, attacks and harassment of merchant vessels, which have occurred more than 15 times since 2021. The immediate trigger appeared to be Iran's seizure of the *Niovi* oil tanker when it was travelling from Dubai to Fujairah on 3 May 2023. NAVCENT tracked the action and released a video of the event hours later. Their Emirati counterparts, however, appeared to be unaware because the *Niovi* never sent a distress call. NAVCENT's decision not to immediately share that critical information with Emirati authorities, who learnt of the incident through press reports, was the tipping point for the UAE, according to a high-ranking Gulf official at the CMF. While Washington does not have a bilateral agreement with Abu Dhabi obliging it to defend UAE-bound vessels, sharing information is expected of coalition partners.

The UAE's decision to change its involvement in the CMF caused some confusion. The country's Ministry of Foreign Affairs said it had withdrawn its participation in the maritime initiative in March after re-evaluating security cooperation with its partners. The US 5th Fleet, though, said the UAE remained a CMF partner. The high-ranking Gulf official later clarified that the UAE had withdrawn its personnel from, but not formal membership in, the Bahrain-based grouping, as well as the International Maritime Security Construct (IMSC) and NAVCENT. The action involved around four officers.

The UAE's decision to reassess its involvement in the CMF can be seen as a calibrated response to show its discontent with Washington and a lack of perceived US commitment to safeguarding maritime routes. However, it does not represent a complete breakdown in naval cooperation. The UAE technically remains a partner in CMF and IMSC and keeps communication channels open with NAVCENT. The Commander of Joint Operations in the UAE Ministry of Defence has visited NAVCENT twice since the *Niovi* incident, and Vice Admiral Brad Cooper, the commander of NAVCENT, has visited the UAE at least three times, according to the Gulf official. Defence cooperation has also continued outside the CMF framework, with a naval drill taking place in late May between an American guided-missile destroyer and an Emirati fast-attack craft in the Gulf of Oman. The US Navy also increased the tempo of its patrols of the Strait of Hormuz and reinforced its overall naval presence in the region.

The impact of the UAE's withdrawal may be more symbolic and political than operational, as Emirati vessels will continue to patrol the same waters under national tasking. The UAE had few officers deployed in NAVCENT, CMF and IMSC anyway, and their absence was not unusual, according to US officials. And within CMF, Abu Dhabi has kept a lower profile, leading task forces only twice, compared to four times by Manama, six by Riyadh and 11 by Kuwait. Still, the episode signals that Washington cannot take key regional security partnerships for granted.

Table 11 — China: selected defence exports to North Africa since 2010

North African countries have acquired significant amounts of Chinese defence equipment over the past 13 years. Most defence planning and procurement in the region is opaque, but North African countries appear to be looking for greater supplier diversity and to take advantage of the relatively low cost and availability of certain systems, such as armed uninhabited aerial vehicles (UAVs). Algeria, traditionally a strong customer for Soviet/Russian equipment, has taken delivery of the greatest number of Chinese systems during this period across all domains. The acquisition by Algiers of three frigates in 2012 is almost certainly the biggest Chinese deal in the region in financial terms. Like many countries denied access to US UAVs, Algeria has bought Chinese systems. If Russia is unable to supply spare parts and new systems to Algeria, it risks losing more of its market share there to China. Neighbouring Morocco continues to source most of its equipment from US and European manufacturers but has supplemented this with Chinese UAVs and air defence, albeit in limited numbers. Egypt's procurement diversification has been driven both by a desire to secure political relationships with Beijing and to lessen its reliance on the US following a brief embargo after the 2013 coup.

Contract Date	Recipient	Equipment	Type	Quantity	Value (USD)	Contractor	Deliveries
c. 2010	Egypt	ASN-209	Medium ISR UAV	18	n.k.	Xi'an Aisheng (ASN) Technology Group	c. 2011–13
c. 2011	Morocco	PL-9C; Type-99 (GDF-002)	Point-defence SAM system; 35mm air-defence artillery	n.k.	n.k.	China North Industries Corporation (NORINCO)	2012
Mar 2012	Algeria	*Adhafer* (C-28A)	Frigate	3	900m	Hudong–Zhonghua Shipbuilding Group (HZSC)	2015–16
c. 2013	Algeria	PLZ-45	155mm self-propelled howitzer	est. 54	n.k.	NORINCO	c. 2014–17
c. 2015	Egypt	*Wing Loong*	Heavy CISR UAV	n.k.	n.k.	Chengdu Aircraft Industrial Group (CAC)	2016
c. 2015	Mauritania	*Timbédra*	Coastal patrol craft	2	42m	n.k.	2016
c. 2016	Algeria	SR5	220mm multiple rocket launcher	est. 18+	n.k.	NORINCO	c. 2017–19
c. 2017	Algeria	CH-3; CH-4	Heavy CISR UAV	n.k.	n.k.	China Aerospace Science and Technology Corporation (CASC)	c. 2018
c. 2018	Algeria	SM4	120mm self-propelled mortar	n.k.	n.k.	HZSC	c. 2019
Nov 2018	Egypt	*Wing Loong* 1D	Heavy CISR UAV	32	60.46m	CAC	n.k.
c. 2019	Morocco	*Tianlong*-50	Self-propelled medium-range SAM system	18	n.k.	NORINCO	2020–21
2020	Algeria	*El-Moutassadi* (Type-056 mod)	Corvette	1	n.k.	HZSC	2023
c. 2021	Algeria	CM-302 (YJ-12E)	Land-based anti-ship missile	n.k.	n.k.	China Aerospace Science and Industry Corporation (CASIC)	2022
2021	Algeria	*Wing Loong* II	Heavy CISR UAV	24	n.k.	CAC	c. 2023
Dec 2021	Algeria	WJ-700	Heavy CISR UAV	4	n.k.	CASIC	n.k.
c. 2022	Algeria	SH4	122mm self-propelled howitzer	n.k.	n.k.	NORINCO	c. 2023
2022	Algeria	ASN-209	Medium ISR UAV	n.k.	n.k.	Xi'an Aisheng (ASN) Technology Group	2022
2022	Algeria	CH-5	Heavy CISR UAV	6	n.k.	CASC	n.k.
2022	Morocco	*Wing Loong* II	Heavy CISR UAV	n.k.	n.k.	CAC	c. 2023

DEFENCE ECONOMICS

Macroeconomics

Economic growth across countries in the Middle East and North Africa (MENA) slowed to an average of 2.6% in 2023 after logging GDP growth of 4.2% in 2022. The stabilisation of oil prices, which spiked after Russia's full-scale invasion of Ukraine in February 2022 but fell to below USD100 per barrel in August 2022, drove the more muted economic performance. That affected national budgets, though to different levels depending on how extraction costs and breakeven points impacted revenues.

Qatar and the United Arab Emirates (UAE) enjoy breakeven points well below the average of USD84 a barrel, seen between October 2022 and October 2023. Both countries were on course to begin 2024 with budget surpluses. Others in the region, such as Iraq, Libya, Kuwait, Oman and Saudi Arabia, have higher breakeven points, requiring higher prices to sustain spending plans. For the 2023–24 financial year, Kuwait anticipated a KWD6.8 billion deficit (USD22.2bn), as lower oil output and prices cut into state revenues. Others are in a similar predicament. Algeria and Bahrain have breakeven oil prices of over USD110 per barrel, while Iran's breakeven point is far higher.

The MENA region is poised to witness relatively healthy economic performance in 2024, with inflation expected to average 3.51% and GDP growth at 3.58% (excluding Egypt, Lebanon, Iran, the Palestinian Authority and Yemen). This should allow governments to pursue growth programmes. Still, with oil prices stabilising well below USD100 a barrel, large defence procurement sprees are unlikely. New approaches to financing and the rise of alternative suppliers may still enable a raft of new procurements, though.

Defence spending

In 2023, regional defence budgets retained upward momentum, with trackable budgets reaching a combined USD183.0bn. Nominally, spending on the military rose in aggregate by 9.49% from the previous year, reflecting the recovery by most countries from pre-pandemic levels. Spending remained dominated by the Gulf sub-region, which accounted for almost three-quarters (72.22%) of regional spending. The North Africa and Levant sub-regions made up just 16.30% and 11.49% of the region's total.

Saudi Arabia remained the region's largest defence spender, with a budget of SAR259bn (USD69.1bn). Riyadh dialled back, though, from the 28% budget hike seen in October 2022 to that year's initial budget, agreeing to a 5.7% increase, reflecting a more restrained approach among Saudi defence planners. The rapprochement between Saudi Arabia and Iran, combined with a prospect for easing tensions in Yemen, could reduce operations and maintenance expenditure by the Saudi military. However, Iranian support for Hamas could have knock-on effects with Riyadh. If interests in Yemen remain stable, some of Saudi Arabia's operations and maintenance funding could be shifted towards acquisitions of more advanced technology and equipment, as well as to support the build-up of the country's defence industry in accordance with Riyadh's Vision 2030 plan. As part of this plan, Saudi Arabia aims to expand its domestic arms industry so that, by 2030, over half of the country's defence spending can flow to Saudi-based businesses, such as joint ventures with international partners and fully Saudi-owned businesses. However, tension remains as Riyadh balances funding between standing up infrastructure and placing orders. For example, in 2022, the Ministry of Finance noted in its annual Budget Performance report that, at 33% above the initial budget, military overspending was due to the continued 'nationalisation of the country's military industries'. This suggests that Saudi defence manufacturing infrastructure is still growing, with the necessary start-up costs being incurred from the core defence-ministry budget instead of from the corresponding Public Investment Fund-owned business entities. Costs should come down as enterprises establish themselves and secure increased domestic orders.

In 2023, **Iran**'s defence spending reached an estimated IRR3,194 trillion. This equates to approximately USD43.8bn at the official, government-set fixed exchange rate, making Iran the region's second-highest spender. However, comparing Iranian rials and US dollars has become increasingly difficult after Iran's central bank, in 2018, introduced a separate exchange rate, the Forex Management Integrated System (NIMA), in anticipation of renewed US sanctions. Under the NIMA rate, now the international standard, Iran's defence spending is valued at just USD7.41bn. The difference reflects, in part, the country's struggle with inflation, which has ranged between 40% and 50% in recent years. Adjusting for inflation, Iran's defence budget was USD10.15bn in constant 2015

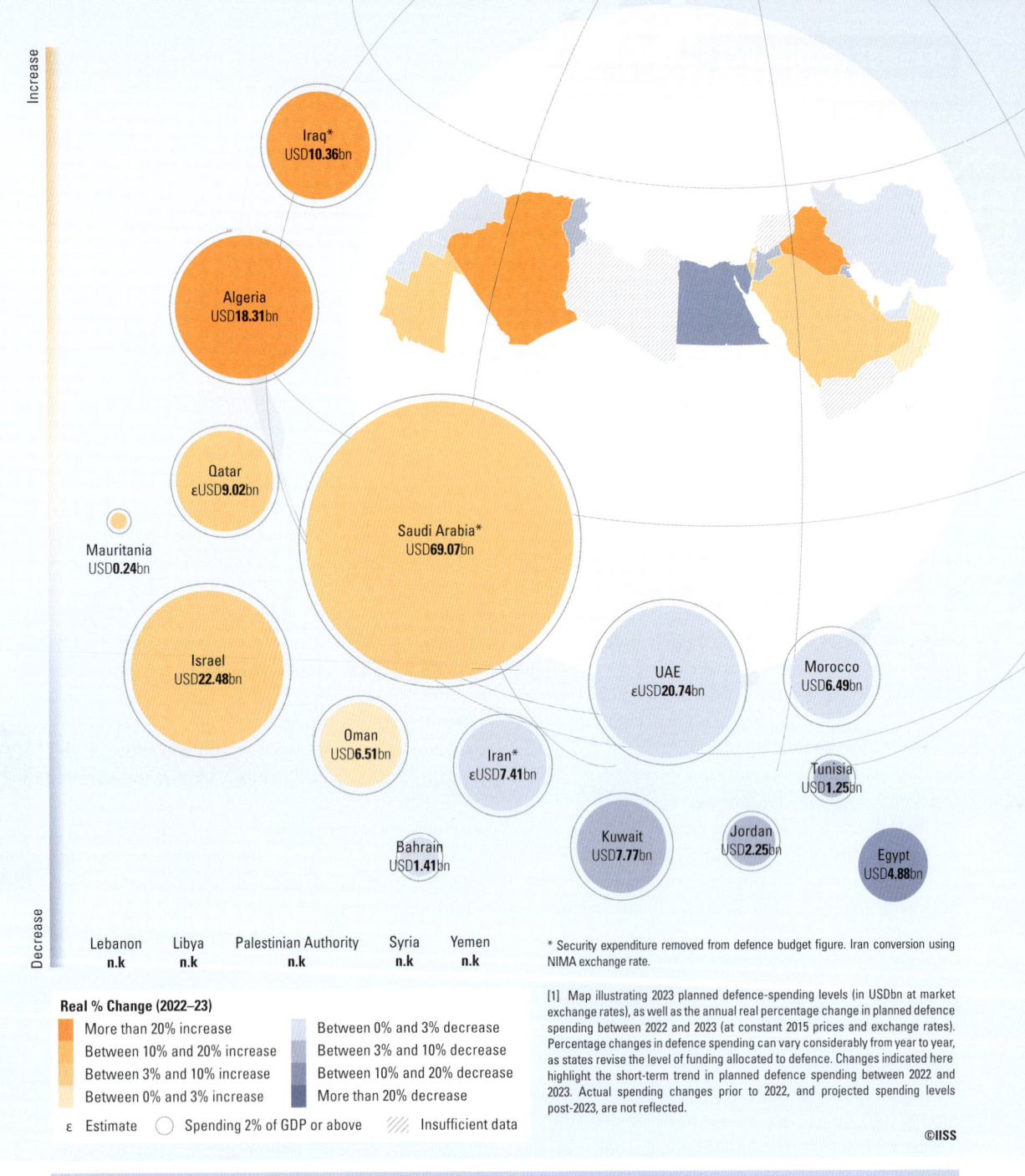

Map 7 Middle East and North Africa: regional defence spending (USDbn, %ch yoy)[1]

Defence spending figures:
- Iraq* USD**10.36**bn
- Algeria USD**18.31**bn
- Qatar εUSD**9.02**bn
- Mauritania USD**0.24**bn
- Saudi Arabia* USD**69.07**bn
- Israel USD**22.48**bn
- UAE εUSD**20.74**bn
- Morocco USD**6.49**bn
- Oman USD**6.51**bn
- Iran* εUSD**7.41**bn
- Tunisia USD**1.25**bn
- Bahrain USD**1.41**bn
- Kuwait USD**7.77**bn
- Jordan USD**2.25**bn
- Egypt USD**4.88**bn

Lebanon n.k | Libya n.k | Palestinian Authority n.k | Syria n.k | Yemen n.k

* Security expenditure removed from defence budget figure. Iran conversion using NIMA exchange rate.

Real % Change (2022–23)
- More than 20% increase
- Between 10% and 20% increase
- Between 3% and 10% increase
- Between 0% and 3% increase
- Between 0% and 3% decrease
- Between 3% and 10% decrease
- Between 10% and 20% decrease
- More than 20% decrease
- ε Estimate
- Spending 2% of GDP or above
- Insufficient data

[1] Map illustrating 2023 planned defence-spending levels (in USDbn at market exchange rates), as well as the annual real percentage change in planned defence spending between 2022 and 2023 (at constant 2015 prices and exchange rates). Percentage changes in defence spending can vary considerably from year to year, as states revise the level of funding allocated to defence. Changes indicated here highlight the short-term trend in planned defence spending between 2022 and 2023. Actual spending changes prior to 2022, and projected spending levels post-2023, are not reflected.

©IISS

dollars, with its overall defence burden hovering around 2% of GDP.

Throughout 2023, Iran continued to invest in its defence industry, making progress with its various missile and uninhabited aerial vehicle (UAV) programmes. Iran also sustained defence cooperation with Russia, and, in August 2023, the Iranian air force said it had received the first Yak-130 *Mitten* advanced trainer aircraft, which are likely to be an intermediate step ahead of a larger acquisition of Sukhoi Su-35S *Flanker* M multi-role combat aircraft.

Table 12 Exchange rate impacts on Iranian defence budget

	2016	2017	2018	2019	2020	2021	2022	2023
Defence budget* IRR (trn)	485	640	775	722	695	1,180	2,225	3,194
Iranian Defence Budget, converted to current USD using government-set fixed exchange rate (bn)	15.4	18.6	18.5	17.2	16.5	28.1	53.0	76.1
Iranian Defence Budget, converted to current USD using NIMA exchange rate (bn)	n/a	n/a	12.0	6.4	3.3	5.1	7.4	7.4
Iranian Defence Budget in Constant (2015) USD (bn)**	15.0	17.5	16.0	11.5	7.7	8.3	10.4	10.2
Defence budget as percentage of GDP	3.37	3.83	3.58	2.64	1.70	1.77	2.13	2.02

*Defence budgets include Army, MoD, and IRGC budgets. Excludes Law Enforcement Agency (NAJA). **Conversions use NIMA rates used for 2018 onwards.
Source: IISS

In 2023, the **United Arab Emirates'** defence budget reached an estimated AED76.2bn (USD20.74bn), increasing by 1.91% in dollar terms on 2022 levels. The UAE maintains the region's third-largest budget, spending approximately 11.3% of the region's defence spending, narrowly ahead of Israel (10.4%) and Algeria (10.0%). Major acquisitions, such as the December 2021 contract for 80 Dassault *Rafale* fighters, drove higher levels of defence spending, as did the acquisition of naval vessels from Indonesia, which will include some domestic content through the provision of rigid-hulled inflatable boats and interceptors via UAE's Abu Dhabi Ship Building (ADSB) company. The country cancelled a EUR800 million (USD870m) deal with Airbus for medium-lift helicopters and plans to reopen the competition, temporarily freeing up some procurement funds for other projects.

After its defence budget received a 46% uplift to IQD13.5trn (USD10.3bn), **Iraq** began acquisitions that had been delayed by poor economic conditions which pre-dated the pandemic. Those include combat aircraft – with the Dassault *Rafale* or Chinese JF-17 *Thunder* potentially in the running – as well as air-defence systems and more. Some of this increase in defence spending and procurement activity has been facilitated by borrowing, with the 2023–24 budget identifying financial loans from the US Defence Security Cooperation Agency and South Korean governments.

Israel continued to dominate defence spending in its immediate vicinity, with its original defence budget growing by 9.65% in nominal local-currency terms before the October attack by Hamas. In real USD terms, initial growth was more subdued at 3.73%, as inflation remained above 4% for a second year running. Following the October attack, Israeli defence budgets are likely to rise significantly, although there is widespread criticism that the impact of the attacks was exacerbated by intelligence failures rather than poor military capabilities. As a result, defence spending is more likely to rise based on the judged performance of the Israel Defense Forces' retaliatory assaults. In recent years, defence spending has been supported by the continued desire to deter threats such as Iran, while also improving intelligence, surveillance and reconnaissance, and maritime capabilities. These are likely to continue, with additional focus on intelligence collection and analysis. Ongoing support by the US government through foreign military financing (FMF) grants helped to drive a significant portion of Israeli procurements, supporting the acquisition of a third squadron of Lockheed Martin F-35I *Adir* fighters, naval landing craft and airborne early-warning aircraft.

Saudi Arabia, 36.7%
United Arab Emirates, 11.0%
Israel, 11.9%
Algeria, 9.7%
Iraq, 5.5%
Qatar, 4.8%
Kuwait, 4.1%
Iran, 3.9%
Oman, 3.5%
Morocco, 3.4%
Egypt, 2.6%
Jordan, 1.2%
Other North Africa, 0.8%
Bahrain, 0.7%

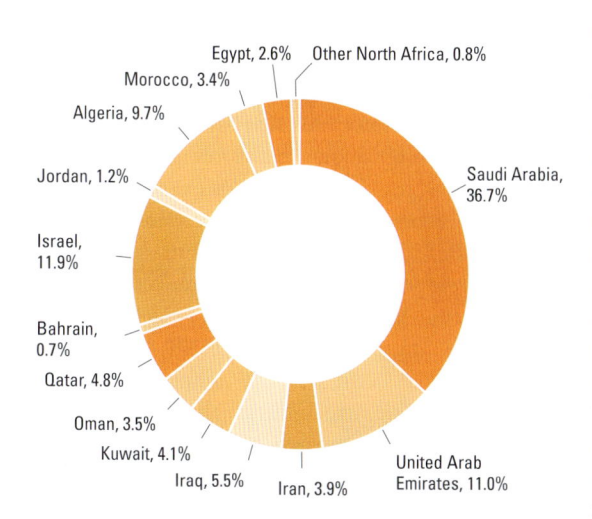

Note: Iran conversion using NIMA exchange rate. Analysis excludes Lebanon, Libya, Palestinian Authority, Syrian Arab Republic and Yemen.
©IISS

▲ Figure 17 **Middle East and North Africa: defence spending by country and sub-region, 2023**

In North Africa, **Algeria's** defence outlays made up over a quarter of spending in the sub-region. The country's budget represented the largest growth in the MENA region, almost doubling year-on-year in USD terms, and over 50% on pre-pandemic levels. This surge in spending likely reflects a major arms-procurement deal that was reportedly signed with Russia in 2022, as well as ongoing acquisitions from China that range from electronic-warfare (EW) equipment to naval vessels to ballistic missiles. Such levels of defence spending may be hard to sustain, though, given high inflation and other economic factors. The International Monetary Fund has warned that despite economic reforms, the country's limited fiscal buffers continue to make it vulnerable to further macroeconomic shocks.

Morocco accounted for just 3.54% of MENA defence spending but 21.72% of the sub-region's total. In real terms, the country's defence spending remained flat, with local budgets keeping pace with inflation. The defence-budget ceiling, though, increased to MAD119.76bn (USD12.21bn) in anticipation of acquisitions starting in 2024, with the funds also being earmarked to support the establishment of the country's defence-industrial base.

Inflation also impacted **Egypt's** defence expenditure, which, despite increasing by 7.39% to EGP92.36bn (USD3.58bn) in nominal local terms, declined in real terms by over 30% due to soaring inflation. National defence spending declined to less than 1% of GDP for the first time, although this is part of a longer-term pattern. These modest outlays have long-term repercussions for the region's largest armed forces and limit procurement activity. Egypt also utilises US FMF funds to pay for a significant portion of its equipment but has also expanded its supplier base to include France and Italy. Ties to Russia have been under pressure from the war in Ukraine, with the US having to decide over the potential application of sanctions on Egypt over its defence-materiel links with Russia.

Defence Industry

MENA states maintained a complex balancing act between key suppliers, including Russia, China and Western countries. That became more difficult in 2023 because of the war in Ukraine and ensuing US sanctions that target buyers of Russian defence equipment, and with Washington imposing curbs on technology transactions with China. Buyers in the region have embraced new suppliers, such as Turkiye and South Korea, with Brazil also continuing to be a key partner for technology transfer and joint technology development in the aerospace and defence sectors.

Saudi Arabia has one of the region's most ambitious plans to improve domestic defence-industrial capabilities, as articulated by Vision 2030. The country has set its eyes initially on fostering less complex industries, such as the manufacture of spare parts, armoured vehicles and basic ammunition, before expanding into more complex, higher-value equipment, such as military aircraft. Riyadh is betting on a mix of direct investments and strategic partnerships. In March 2023, the General Authority for Military Industries announced several initiatives to foster domestic and foreign investment in the country's defence sector. One example was the creation of a new portal to help investors identify opportunities, as well as investment in supply-chain development and local manufacturing. In the military-aviation and aerospace sector, Saudi Arabian Military Industries (SAMI) continued to build links with foreign manufacturers to increase domestic capabilities. This included an agreement with French aerospace giant Safran for local maintenance and repair of *Makila* 1 and *Arriel* 2 helicopter engines, as well as maintenance and repair of Lockheed Martin *Sniper* Advanced Targeting Pods.

Saudi Arabia is also interested in exploring next-generation fighter aircraft capabilities. The United

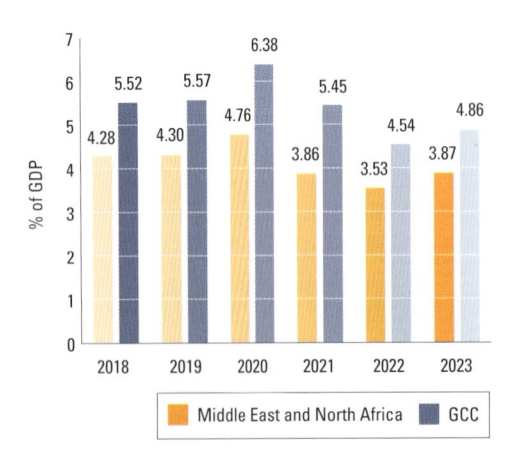

Note: GDP data from IMF World Economic Outlook, October 2023. Analysis excludes Lebanon, Libya, Palestinian Authority, Syrian Arab Republic and Yemen.

▲ Figure 18 **Middle East and North Africa: defence spending** as % of GDP (average)

Table 13 Iran: Selected uninhabited aerial vehicle (UAV) and direct attack munition (DAM) exports

Iran supports several non-state groups in the Middle East to achieve wider foreign-policy objectives. A key pillar of that strategy has been supplying military equipment that those groups cannot manufacture themselves. After beginning development of uninhabited aerial vehicles (UAVs) during the Iran–Iraq war (1980–88), Tehran also began producing direct-attack munition (DAM) systems in the late 1990s. By the early 2000s, Iran began exporting those systems to Hizbullah in Lebanon. Since then, Iran has expanded the UAV/DAM variants it supplies along with the number of recipients. Non-state groups and some states have used these cheap and expendable systems to try to saturate air defences; they also provide additional means of long-range attack and offer a valuable propaganda tool.

Iranian development of these systems is divided between organisations controlled by the Islamic Revolutionary Guard Corps, such as Iran Aircraft Manufacturing Industries (HESA), and those controlled by the Ministry of Defence, such as Qods Aviation Industries (QAI). These heavily sanctioned companies build their systems with dual-use components either acquired on the civilian market or through sanctions evasion, which likely complicates achieving steady production rates. Iran also has sold these systems to governments to generate revenue. Moscow has bought thousands of Iranian UAV/DAM systems since mid-2022, with a *Shahed* 136 production line now being set up in Russia.

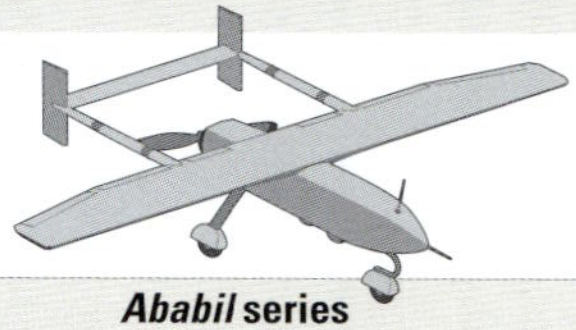

Ababil series

Classification: Several types including medium UAV and DAM
Manufacturer: Iran Aircraft Manufacturing Industries (HESA)

Operator	Deliveries begin	Notes
Type: *Ababil 2*		
Hizbullah	early 2000s	*Ababil*-T direct attack variant; local designation *Mirsad* 1
Sudan	early 2010s	
Ansarullah (Houthis)	by 2016	Local designations *Qasef*-1 and *Qasef*-2K, some local assembly
Hamas	by mid-2010s	*Ababil*-T direct attack variant; local designation *Shehab*
Tajikistan	early 2020s	ISR UAV delivered, unclear if DAM variant also delivered; local factory inaugurated in 2022, extent of manufacture unclear
Type: *Ababil 3*		
Sudan	by 2009	Local designation *Zagil* III-B
Iraqi militias	by 2015	Including *Ababil*-T
Iraq	by 2020	

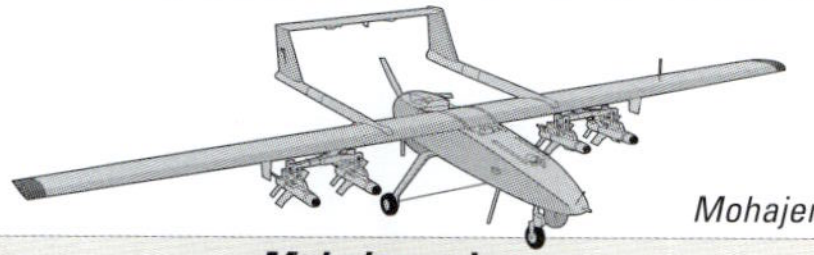

Mohajer series

Classification: Medium ISR UAV (*Mohajer* 6 onwards are combat ISR)
Manufacturer: Qods Aviation Industries (QAI)

Operator	Deliveries begin	Notes
Type: *Mohajer 2*		
Hizbullah	early 2000s	
Venezuela	2007	Local designation *Arpia*; system assembled locally
Type: *Mohajer 4*		
Hizbullah	mid-2000s	
Syria	by 2015	
Type: *Mohajer 6*		
Venezuela	2020	Operational status unclear
Ethiopia	2021	
Russia	2022	

Shahed series

Classification: Combat ISR UAV (*Shahed* 129) and DAMs (*Shahed* 131 and 136)
Manufacturer: HESA

Operator	Deliveries begin	Notes
Type: *Shahed* 129		
Russia	2022	
Type: *Shahed* 131		
Houthi forces	2021	Local designation *Wa'eed* 1
Russia	2022	Local designation *Geran* 1
Type: *Shahed* 136		
Houthi forces	2021	Local designation *Wa'eed* 2
Russia	2022	Local designation *Geran* 2; local assembly and production

Kingdom and Saudi Arabia have held talks about working together on future air programmes. A move into next-generation aircraft procurement would necessitate significant investment for research and development, as well as developing local manufacturing capabilities to meet domestic workshare requirements.

Iran's defence industry gained greater international prominence by helping arm Russia, including with different UAV models. Iran transferred so many loitering munitions it may have all but exhausted its supplies, though it has since assisted Russia in expanding its UAV production. Iranian authorities likely generated significant revenue from the transfer, though at the cost of Iranian force readiness and depleted stocks for its own fire units. Moreover, the decision to overtly support Russian efforts in Ukraine could increase international scrutiny of Iran's sanctions-busting covert supply chain programmes, which would (vs will) add costs and disrupt longer-term efforts.

The UAE continued to improve its defence-industrial position through domestic intellectual-property development, localised manufacture and the consolidation of its domestic companies through mergers and acquisitions. The UAE's defence-industry conglomerate, EDGE Group, opened a Brazilian office in April 2023, ahead of a flurry of technology-partnership agreements it signed in April and August. These covered a range of technologies, including long-range anti-ship missiles, EW, cyber security, smart weapons and non-lethal technologies. EDGE also made deals in other target markets, including Malaysia, India, Tanzania and Indonesia, where it agreed partnerships for market representation and technology transfer. In February 2023, an EDGE Group shipbuilding subsidiary, ADSB, signed a AED3.94bn (USD1.07bn) contract for three BR71 MKII corvettes for the Angolan Navy.

The country's offset management organisation, the Tawazun Economic Council, facilitated a variety of inbound projects to support the country's defence-industrial development. These included the opening of an office for South Korean firm LIG Nex1 following the UAE's acquisition of *Cheongung* II KM-SAM medium-range surface-to-air missiles in early 2022, a missile-systems development agreement with Turkiye's Roketsan and the development of a sovereign 3D-printing capability with Sweden's Saab. The UAE's Tawazun Strategic Development Fund (SDF), meanwhile, invested in a variety of military and dual-use advanced-technology sectors.

Tel Aviv's stance of not supporting arms transfers to Ukraine could hinder some sales, as key European and North American customers could run into problems trying to retransfer Israeli-sourced equipment to Kyiv. Israel has indicated *Spike* anti-tank guided missiles and *Iron Dome* air and missile-defence systems, for instance, are off limits to Kyiv. However, the fighting in Ukraine has led to demand for several Israeli systems in Europe and elsewhere that could exceed any lost sales. Israeli defence exports hit a record high of USD12.5bn in 2022, according to the country's Ministry of Defence in June 2023. Almost a quarter of the total deals were with Abraham Accords states (Bahrain, Morocco, Sudan and the UAE), while the Asia-Pacific region remained the leading market for Israeli exports (30%), followed by Europe (29%). The demand from the Abraham Accords states (up from some USD700m in 2021) shows that there is a significant appetite for Israeli technology in these countries – particularly the UAE and Morocco. The export data also showed that government-to-government agreements generated around USD4bn in exports, with almost half of these worth over USD100m. Uninhabited-systems technology comprised the largest volume of export sales (25%), followed by missiles, rockets and air-defence systems (19%), and then radar and EW (13%). The Off-Shore Procurement (OSP) programme – under which up to 25% of Israel's FMF grant can be converted into shekels for the acquisition of domestically made equipment – is being cut to USD450m by 2025, before being eliminated by 2028. Domestic support for the country's defence-industrial base will likely continue.

Many of the region's other countries also have defence-industrial ambitions. Morocco, for instance, won an agreement from Israel's Elbit Systems, revealed in June 2023, to establish two sites in the country to increase its market share there. Israel Aerospace Industries signed an agreement with the International University of Rabat to establish a centre of excellence covering aeronautics, artificial-intelligence research and innovation. This builds on an announced plan by Morocco and Israel to establish two Israeli firms in Morocco for UAV manufacture. Morocco also forged closer ties with Brazil with an agreement to increase defence-industrial links.

Significant procurement and delivery events - 2023

JULY

TURKIYE SECURES DEALS WITH SAUDI ARABIA AND UAE

President Recep Tayyip Erdoğan visited Saudi Arabia and the UAE on a tour aimed at repairing ties and securing much-needed outside investment in Turkiye's struggling economy. A number of defence agreements and sales were agreed as part of the visits, including Turkiye's biggest-ever defence export. Worth over USD3bn, UAV manufacturer Baykar will supply the Saudi air and naval forces with armed *Akinci* UAVs with some manufacturing to take place in the Kingdom. In a similar vein, the visit to the UAE resulted in the announcement of USD50.7bn in deals and agreements, including a memorandum of understanding between that country's Tawazun Council and Turkiye's Defence Industry Agency (SSB). Later in the year, the UAE's EDGE Group announced that it had signed initial agreements with Turkish electronics companies ASELSAN and Baykar and created a new company to lead its work in Turkiye. While not the first Turkish sales to these countries, the *Akinci* sale to Saudi Arabia represents a significant breakthrough for Turkish industry, which had little success in that market until then.

SEPTEMBER

ISRAELI COMPANIES SEE INCREASED DEMAND FROM EUROPE FOR ARTILLERY AND MUNITIONS

Conflict in Ukraine has triggered increases in defence spending across Europe and a rethink on defence industrial capability and munition stocks, both of which have been allowed to degrade significantly since the end of the Cold War. From January to the end of September, Elbit Systems announced contracts with European countries worth over USD1.9bn. This includes a USD305m contract to supply the PULS multiple rocket launcher system to the Netherlands and a USD252m deal to supply Denmark with PULS and the ATMOS 2000 howitzer. The company announced that Europe was its largest market for Q2 and predicted continuing high demand for munitions which would likely be delivered through the large number of subsidiaries the company has in Europe. Israel Aerospace Industries announced that H1 2023 was the most profitable half-year in the company's history. It did not release specifics on regional markets, but the conclusion of a USD3.5bn deal with Germany for the *Arrow* 3 missile defence system in September will likely mean that H2 will be even better. The company also secured sales of loitering munitions to four NATO countries, including Estonia. Rafael Advanced Defense Systems signed more contracts to export its popular *Spike* series of anti-tank missiles, including a deal with Greece worth EUR370m (USD402.68m) and a follow-on contract with Poland worth PLN400m (USD96.28m) for *Spike*-LR missiles to be built by local company MESKO. With Hamas's attack on Israel in October, Israeli companies may need to redirect production in the short term to meet local requirements, but long-term demand from Europe is expected to remain strong at the same time as Israel seeks to secure new sales in Asia and the Middle East.

SEPTEMBER

EDGE GROUP EXPANDS OVERSEAS

Over the course of 2023, the UAE's state-owned EDGE Group completed several M&A moves as part of its strategy to develop strong competencies in uninhabited or autonomous systems, electronic warfare and guided weapons. In February, EDGE finalised a majority stake in Estonian uninhabited-vehicle firm Milrem Robotics. This greatly adds to EDGE's uninhabited-systems offer in the land domain. Best known for its THeMIS tracked vehicle, which has been acquired in small numbers by many European armed forces, typically for testing, Milrem Robotics has provided security assurances to the EU to allow it to continue participating in PESCO projects. In September, EDGE completed the acquisition of a 50% stake in Brazilian guided-weapons company SIATT, which followed an agreement concluded in June with the Brazilian Navy to cooperate on missile development. SIATT was established in 2015 by the founding partners of the defunct Mectron and acquired that company's MSS-1.2 AC anti-tank missile and MANSUP navy anti-ship missile programmes. EDGE has also signed partnership agreements with Bulgarian electronics companies TBS and Samel 90 to expand the company's footprint in that country and Europe more broadly. EDGE has seen significant revenue and portfolio size growth since the company's founding in late 2019, but questions remain as to how sustainable this growth is beyond sales to the UAE armed forces. International acquisitions are aimed at helping EDGE tap new markets.

Algeria ALG

Algerian Dinar DZD		2022	2023	2024
GDP	DZD	27.7trn	30.4trn	33.3trn
	USD	195bn	224bn	239bn
per capita	USD	4,307	4,875	5,130
Growth	%	3.2	3.8	3.1
Inflation	%	9.3	9.0	6.8
Def bdgt	DZD	1.30trn	2.49trn	
	USD	9.16bn	18.3bn	
USD1=DZD		141.95	135.75	139.14

Real-terms defence budget trend (USDbn, constant 2015)
15.8 / 4.09 (2008–2023)

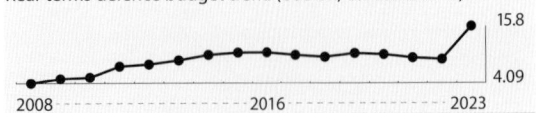

Population	46,286,076					
Age	0–14	15–19	20–24	25–29	30–64	65 plus
Male	15.9%	3.8%	3.2%	3.6%	21.0%	3.3%
Female	15.1%	3.7%	3.0%	3.4%	20.6%	3.4%

Capabilities

Algeria's armed forces are among the best equipped in North Africa. The armed forces' primary roles relate to securing territorial integrity, internal security and regional stability. The army retains a key political position following its role in 2019 in ending President Abdelaziz Bouteflika's two decades in power. Algeria is part of the AU's North African Regional Capability Standby Force, hosting the force's logistics base. A November 2020 constitutional change allows Algeria to participate in UN peacekeeping missions. Tensions with Morocco, which increased in 2021, have persisted into 2023. The conscript-based force exercises regularly, although standards are difficult to judge. Amid the strained relations with Morocco and the persisting instability in Libya and the Sahel region, the government approved a significant increase in defence spending, taking advantage of the rising gas revenues that followed the Russian invasion of Ukraine. Army and air force inventories consist of a core of modern, primarily Russian-sourced equipment, though China also supplied equipment, including armed UAVs and self-propelled artillery. The extent to which the Russia-Ukraine war has affected the supply of spare parts is unclear, though the country received new self-propelled SAM systems from Russia. Algiers has recapitalised around half of its fixed-wing combat-aircraft inventory and the navy has invested in its submarine and frigate fleet. Algeria is starting to develop a domestic defence industry capable of equipment maintenance.

ACTIVE 139,000 (Army 110,000 Navy 15,000 Air 14,000) **Gendarmerie** **Paramilitary 187,200**

Conscript liability 12 months

RESERVE 150,000 (Army 150,000) to age 50

ORGANISATIONS BY SERVICE

Space
EQUIPMENT BY TYPE
SATELLITES 4
 COMMUNICATIONS 1 ALCOMSAT
 ISR 3 ALSAT

Army 35,000; 75,000 conscript (total 110,000)
FORCES BY ROLE
6 Mil Regions
MANOEUVRE
 Armoured
  2 (1st & 8th) armd div (3 tk regt; 1 mech regt, 1 arty gp)
  2 indep armd bde
 Mechanised
  2 (12th & 40th) mech div (1 tk regt; 3 mech regt, 1 arty gp)
  4 indep mech bde
 Light
  1 indep mot bde
 Air Manoeuvre
  1 AB div (4 para regt; 1 SF regt)
COMBAT SUPPORT
 2 arty bn
 1 AT regt
 4 engr bn
AIR DEFENCE
 7 AD bn
EQUIPMENT BY TYPE
ARMOURED FIGHTING VEHICLES
 MBT 1,485: 270 T-55AMV; 290 T-62; 325 T-72M1/M1M; 600+ T-90SA
 TSV 26+: 13+ BMPT; 13+ BMPT-62
 RECCE 70: 44 AML-60; 26 BRDM-2
 IFV 980: ε220 BMP-2; 760 BMP-2M with 9M133 *Kornet* (RS-AT-14 *Spriggan*)
 APC 1,305
  APC (T) VP-6
  APC (W) 1,305: 250 BTR-60; 150 BTR-80; 150 OT-64; 55 M3 Panhard; ε600 *Fuchs 2*; 100 *Fahd*
  PPV some *Maxxpro*
 AUV Nimr *Ajban*; Nimr *Ajban* LRSOV
ENGINEERING & MAINTENANCE VEHICLES
 AEV IMR-2
 ARV BREM-1
 VLB MTU-20
 MW M58 MICLIC
ANTI-TANK/ANTI-INFRASTRUCTURE
 SP 92: 64 9P133 with 9M113 *Konkurs* (RS-AT-5 *Spandrel*); 28 9P163-3 *Kornet*-EM (RS-AT-14 *Spriggan*); BTR-60 with

9M133 *Kornet* (RS-AT-14 *Spriggan*); BTR-80 with 9M133 *Kornet* (RS-AT-14 *Spriggan*)

MSL • MANPATS 9K11 *Malyutka* (RS-AT-3 *Sagger*); 9K111 *Fagot* (RS-AT-4 *Spigot*); 9K111-1 *Konkurs* (RS-AT-5 *Spandrel*); 9K115-2 *Metis*-M1 (RS-AT-13); 9K135 *Kornet*-E (RS-AT-14 *Spriggan*); Luch *Skif*; Milan

RCL 180: 82mm 120 B-10; **107mm** 60 B-11

ARTILLERY 1,127

SP 224: 122mm 140 2S1 *Gvozdika*; **152mm** 30 2S3 *Akatsiya*; **155mm** ε54 PLZ-45

TOWED 393: 122mm 345: 160 D-30 (incl some truck mounted SP); 25 D-74; 100 M-1931/37; 60 M-30; **130mm** 10 M-46; **152mm** 20 M-1937 (ML-20); **155mm** 18 PLL-01

MRL 180: 122mm 48 BM-21 *Grad*; **140mm** 48 BM-14; **220mm** 36: 18+ SR5; ε18 TOS-1A; **240mm** 30 BM-24; **300mm** 18 9A52 *Smerch*

MOR 330+: 82mm 150 M-37; **120mm** 120 M-1943; W86; **SP 120mm** Nimr *Hafeet* with SM5; SM4; W86 (SP); **160mm** 60 M-1943

SURFACE-TO-SURFACE MISSILE LAUNCHERS

SRBM 12+ *Iskander*-E

AIR DEFENCE

SAM

Point-defence 68+: ε48 9K33M *Osa* (RS-SA-8B *Gecko*); ε20 9K31 *Strela*-1 (RS-SA-9 *Gaskin*); 9K32 *Strela*-2 (RS-SA-7A/B *Grail*)‡; QW-2 (CH-SA-8)

SPAAGM 30mm 38 96K6 *Pantsir*-S1 (RS-SA-22 *Greyhound*); *Pantsir*-SM

GUNS ε425

SP 23mm ε225 ZSU-23-4

TOWED 200: 14.5mm 100: 60 ZPU-2; 40 ZPU-4; **23mm** 100 ZU-23-2

Navy ε15,000

EQUIPMENT BY TYPE

SUBMARINES • SSK 6:

2 *Paltus* (FSU Project 877 (*Kilo*)) with 6 single 533mm TT with TEST-71ME HWT

4 *Varshavyanka* (RUS Project 636.1 (Improved *Kilo*)) with 6 single 533mm TT with 3M14E *Klub*-S (RS-SS-N-30B) LACM/3M54E1/E *Klub*-S (RS-SS-N-27A/B) AShM (*Klub*-S AShM variant unclear)/TEST-71ME HWT

PRINCIPAL SURFACE COMBATANTS • FRIGATES 5

FFGHM 5:

3 *Adhafer* (C-28A) with 2 quad lnchr with C-802A AShM, 1 octuple lnchr with FM-90 (CH-SA-N-4) SAM, 2 triple 324mm ASTT, 2 Type-730B (H/PJ-12) CIWS, 1 76mm gun (capacity 1 hel)

2 *Erradii* (MEKO A200AN) with 2 octuple lnchrs with RBS15 Mk3 AShM, 4 8-cell VLS with *Umkhonto*-IR SAM, 2 twin 324mm TT with MU90 LWT, 1 127mm gun (capacity 1 *Super Lynx* 300)

PATROL AND COASTAL COMBATANTS 29

CORVETTES 4

FSGM 1 *Al-Moutassadi* (PRC Type-056 mod) with 2 twin lnchr with C-802 (CH-SS-N-6) AShM, 1 octuple GMLS with FL-3000N (HHQ-10 (CH-SA-N-17)) SAM, 2 A/S mor, 1 76mm gun, 1 hel landing platform

FS 3 *Mourad Rais* (FSU Project 1159 (*Koni*)) with 2 twin 533mm TT, 2 RBU 6000 *Smerch* 2 A/S mor, 2 twin 76mm gun

PCGM 3 *Rais Hamidou* (FSU Project 1234E (*Nanuchka* II)) with 4 quad lnchr with 3M24E *Uran*-E (RS-SS-N-25 *Switchblade*) AShM, 1 twin lnchr with 4K33 *Osa*-M (RS-SA-N-4 *Gecko*) SAM, 1 AK630 CIWS, 1 twin 57mm gun

PCG 4:

3 *Djebel Chenoua* with 2 twin lnchr with C-802 (CH-SS-N-6) AShM, 1 AK630 CIWS, 1 76mm gun;

1 *Rais Hassen Barbiar* (*Djebel Chenoua* mod) with 2 twin lnchr with C-802 (CH-SS-N-6) AShM, 1 Type-730 (H/PJ-12) CIWS, 1 76mm gun

PBFG 9 Project 205 (ex-FSU *Osa* II)† with 4 single lnchr with P-20U (RS-SS-N-2B *Styx*) AShM

PB 9 *Kebir* with 1 76mm gun

MINE WARFARE • MINE COUNTERMEASURES 2

MCC 2 *El-Kasseh* (ITA *Gaeta* mod)

AMPHIBIOUS

PRINCIPAL AMPHIBIOUS SHIPS 1

LHD 1 *Kalaat Beni Abbes* with 1 8-cell *Sylver* A50 VLS with *Aster* 15 SAM, 1 76mm gun (capacity 5 med hel; 3 LCVP; 15 MBT; 350 troops)

LANDING SHIPS • LST 2 *Kalaat beni Hammad* (capacity 7 MBT; 240 troops) with 1 med hel landing platform

LANDING CRAFT • LCVP 3

LOGISTICS AND SUPPORT 4

AGS 2: 1 *Al-Masseh* (FRA OSV 95); 1 *El Idrissi*

AX 1 *Daxin* with 2 AK230 CIWS, 1 76mm gun, 1 hel landing platform

AXS 1 *El Mellah*

Naval Infantry ε7,000

FORCES BY ROLE

SPECIAL FORCES

1 cdo bn

MANOEUVRE

Amphibious

8 naval inf bn

EQUIPMENT BY TYPE

ARMOURED FIGHTING VEHICLES

APC • APC(W) BTR-80

Naval Aviation

EQUIPMENT BY TYPE

HELICOPTERS

MRH 9: 3 AW139 (SAR); 6 *Super Lynx* 300

SAR 9: 5 AW101 SAR; 4 *Super Lynx* Mk130

Coastal Defence

FORCES BY ROLE

COASTAL DEFENCE

1 AShM regt with 4K51 Rubezh (RS-SSC-3 Styx); CM-302 (YJ-12E)

EQUIPMENT BY TYPE
COASTAL DEFENCE
AShM 4K51 Rubezh (RS-SSC-3 Styx); CM-302 (YJ-12E)

Coast Guard ε500
EQUIPMENT BY TYPE
PATROL AND COASTAL COMBATANTS 74
PBF 6 Baglietto 20
PB 68: 6 Baglietto Mangusta; 12 Jebel Antar; 40 Deneb; 4 El Mounkid; 6 Kebir with 1 76mm gun
LOGISTICS AND SUPPORT 9
AR 1 El Mourafek
ARS 3 El Moundjid
AXL 5 El Mouderrib (PRC Chui-E) (2 more in reserve†)

Air Force 14,000
FORCES BY ROLE
FIGHTER
4 sqn with MiG-29S/UB Fulcrum
FIGHTER/GROUND ATTACK
3 sqn with Su-30MKA Flanker H
GROUND ATTACK
2 sqn with Su-24M/MK Fencer D
ELINT
1 sqn with Beech 1900D
MARITIME PATROL
2 sqn with Beech 200T/300 King Air
ISR
1 sqn with Su-24MR Fencer E*
TANKER
1 sqn with Il-78 Midas
TRANSPORT
1 sqn with C-130H/H-30 Hercules; L-100-30
1 sqn with C295M
1 sqn with Gulfstream IV-SP; Gulfstream V
1 sqn with Il-76MD/TD Candid
TRAINING
2 sqn with Z-142
1 sqn with Yak-130 Mitten*
2 sqn with L-39C Albatros; L-39ZA Albatros*
1 hel sqn with PZL Mi-2 Hoplite
ATTACK HELICOPTER
3 sqn with Mi-24 Hind (one re-equipping with Mi-28NE Havoc)
TRANSPORT HELICOPTER
1 sqn with AS355 Ecureuil
5 sqn with Mi-171Sh Hip; Mi-8 Hip
1 sqn with Ka-27PS Helix D; Ka-32T Helix
COMBAT/ISR UAV
1 sqn with ASN-209; CH-3; CH-4; Seeker II; Wing Loong II; Yabhon Flash-20; Yabhon United-40

AIR DEFENCE
3 ADA bde
3 SAM regt with S-125M/M1 Pechora-M/M1 (RS-SA-3 Goa); 2K12 Kub (RS-SA-6 Gainful); S-300PMU2 (RS-SA-20 Gargoyle)

EQUIPMENT BY TYPE
AIRCRAFT 183 combat capable
FTR 22 MiG-29S/UB Fulcrum
FGA 73: 14 MiG-29M/M2 Fulcrum; 59 Su-30MKA Flanker H
ATK 33 Su-24M/MK Fencer D
ISR 3 Su-24MR Fencer E*
TKR 6 Il-78 Midas
TPT 67: **Heavy** 11: 3 Il-76MD Candid B; 8 Il-76TD Candid; **Medium** 18: 8 C-130H Hercules; 6 C-130H-30 Hercules; 2 C-130J Hercules; 2 L-100-30; **Light** 32: 3 Beech C90B King Air; 5 Beech 200T King Air; 6 Beech 300 King Air; 12 Beech 1900D (electronic surv); 5 C295M; 1 F-27 Friendship; **PAX** 6: 1 A340; 4 Gulfstream IV-SP; 1 Gulfstream V
TRG 99: 36 L-39ZA Albatros*; 7 L-39C Albatros; 16 Yak-130 Mitten*; 40 Z-142
HELICOPTERS
ATK 72: 30 Mi-24 Hind; 42+ Mi-28NE/UB Havoc
SAR 3 Ka-27PS Helix D
MRH 11: 8 AW139 (SAR); 3 Bell 412EP
TPT 136: **Heavy** 14 Mi-26T2 Halo; **Medium** 39: 4 Ka-32T Helix; 39 Mi-171Sh Hip; 35 Mi-8 Hip; **Light** 44: 8 AW119KE Koala; 8 AS355 Ecureuil; 28 PZL Mi-2 Hoplite
UNINHABITED AERIAL VEHICLES
CISR • **Heavy** CH-3; CH-4; Wing Loong II; Yabhon United-40
ISR • **Medium** ASN-209; Seeker II; Yabhon Flash-20
AIR DEFENCE • SAM
Long-range 32+ S-300PMU2 (RS-SA-20 Gargoyle)
Medium-range 20+ 9K317 Buk-M2E (RS-SA-17 Grizzly)
Short-range 36+: 2K12 Kvadrat (RS-SA-6 Gainful); 9K331MK Tor-M2K (RS-SA-15 Gauntlet); 12 S-125M; Pechora-M (RS-SA-3 Goa); 24 S-125M1 Pechora-M1 (RS-SA-3 Goa)
AIR-LAUNCHED MISSILES
AAM • **IR** R-60 (RS-AA-8 Aphid); R-73 (RS-AA-11A Archer); **IR/SARH** R-40/46 (RS-AA-6 Acrid); R-23/24 (RS-AA-7 Apex); R-27 (RS-AA-10 Alamo); **ARH** R-77 (RS-AA-12A Adder)
ASM Kh-25 (RS-AS-10 Karen); Kh-29 (RS-AS-14 Kedge); Kh-59ME (RS-AS-18 Kazoo); ZT-35 Ingwe; 9M120 Ataka (RS-AT-9)
AShM Kh-31A (RS-AS-17B Krypton)
ARM Kh-25MP (RS-AS-12A Kegler); Kh-31P (RS-AS-17A Krypton)
BOMBS
Electro-optical guided KAB-500KR/OD

Gendarmerie & Paramilitary ε187,200

Gendarmerie 20,000

Ministry of Defence control; 6 regions

EQUIPMENT BY TYPE
ARMOURED FIGHTING VEHICLES
  RECCE AML-60
  APC • **APC (W)** 210: 100 TH-390 *Fahd*; 110 Panhard M3
HELICOPTERS • **TPT** • **Light** 12+: 12 AW109; Some PZL Mi-2 *Hoplite*

National Security Forces 16,000

Directorate of National Security. Equipped with small arms

Republican Guard 1,200

EQUIPMENT BY TYPE
ARMOURED FIGHTING VEHICLES
  RECCE AML-60

Legitimate Defence Groups ε150,000

Self-defence militia, communal guards (60,000)

DEPLOYMENT

DEMOCRATIC REPUBLIC OF THE CONGO: UN • MONUSCO 2

Bahrain BHR

Bahraini Dinar BHD		2022	2023	2024
GDP	BHD	16.7bn	16.9bn	17.7bn
	USD	44.4bn	45.0bn	47.1bn
per capita	USD	28,781	28,464	29,081
Growth	%	4.9	2.7	3.6
Inflation	%	3.6	1.0	1.4
Def bdgt [a]	BHD	526m	527m	527m
	USD	1.4bn	1.4bn	1.4bn
FMA (US)	USD	4.0m	4.0m	3.3m
USD1=BHD		0.38	0.38	0.38

[a] Excludes funds allocated to the Ministry of the Interior and the National Security Agency

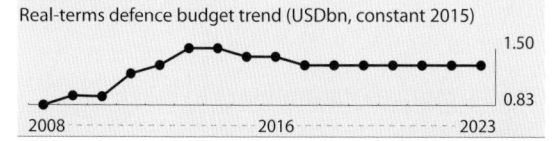

Real-terms defence budget trend (USDbn, constant 2015)

Population	1,553,886

Age	0–14	15–19	20–24	25–29	30–64	65 plus
Male	9.2%	3.5%	4.8%	6.3%	34.4%	2.1%
Female	9.0%	3.0%	3.4%	3.8%	18.7%	2.0%

Capabilities

Bahrain is a member of the GCC and occupies a strategic position between regional rivals Iran and Saudi Arabia. The armed forces are responsible for territorial defence and internal-security support. Bahrain's most critical security relationship is with Saudi Arabia, but it also has strong defence ties with the UK and US. The country has been a major non-NATO US ally since 2002. The US 5th Fleet is headquartered in Bahrain, as is the US-led Combined Maritime Forces (CMF) and the UK-led International Maritime Security Construct. Bahrain has periodically commanded CMF task forces. The armed forces carried out a limited expeditionary deployment in support of the Saudi-led intervention in Yemen. Bahrain signed a security cooperation agreement with Israel in February 2022. Bahrain is modernising critical capabilities, including through the purchase of F-16V fighters and *Patriot* air- and missile-defences. The country also is enhancing its combat rotorcraft fleet and its frigate capacity. The armed forces have organic maintenance support, but there is little in the way of a defence-industrial base beyond the limited maintenance support provided by the Arab Shipbuilding and Repair Yard.

ACTIVE 8,200 (Army 6,000 Navy 700 Air 1,500)
Gendarmerie & Paramilitary 11,260

ORGANISATIONS BY SERVICE

Army 6,000

FORCES BY ROLE
SPECIAL FORCES
  1 SF bn
MANOEUVRE
  Armoured
  1 armd bde(-) (1 recce bn, 2 armd bn)
  Mechanised
  1 inf bde (2 mech bn, 1 mot bn)
  Light
  1 (Amiri) gd bn
COMBAT SUPPORT
  1 arty bde (1 hvy arty bty, 2 med arty bty, 1 lt arty bty, 1 MRL bty)
  1 engr coy
COMBAT SERVICE SUPPORT
  1 log coy
  1 tpt coy
  1 med coy
AIR DEFENCE
  1 AD bn (1 ADA bty, 2 SAM bty)
EQUIPMENT BY TYPE
ARMOURED FIGHTING VEHICLES
  MBT 100 M60A3; (80 more in store)
  RECCE 22 AML-90
  IFV 67: 25 YPR-765 PRI; 42 AIFV-B-C25
  APC 303+
    APC (T) 303: 300 M113A2; 3 AIFV-B
    APC (W) *Arma* 6×6
  AUV M-ATV

ENGINEERING & MAINTENANCE VEHICLES
ARV 53 *Fahd* 240

ANTI-TANK/ANTI-INFRASTRUCTURE
MSL
  SP 5+: 5 AIFV-B-*Milan*; HMMWV with BGM-71A TOW; 9P163-3 *Kornet*-EM (RS-AT-14 *Spriggan*)
  MANPATS BGM-71A TOW; *Kornet*-EM (RS-AT-14 *Spriggan*)
RCL 31: **106mm** 25 M40A1; **120mm** 6 MOBAT

ARTILLERY 119
  SP 26: **155mm** 20 M109A5; **203mm** ε6 M110A2 (56 more in store)
  TOWED 36: **105mm** 8 L118 Light Gun; **155mm** 28 M198
  MRL 13: **220mm** 4 SR5; **227mm** 9 M270 MLRS
  MOR 44: **81mm** 12 L16; SP 81mm 20 VAMTAC with EIMOS; **SP 120mm** 12 M113A2

SURFACE-TO-SURFACE MISSILE LAUNCHERS
SRBM • Conventional MGM-140A ATACMS (launched from M270 MLRS)

AIR DEFENCE
SAM 13+
  Medium-range 6 MIM-23B I-*Hawk*
  Short-range 7 *Crotale*
  Point-defence 9K338 *Igla*-S (RS-SA-24 *Grinch*) (reported); FIM-92 *Stinger*; RBS-70
GUNS 24: **35mm** 12 GDF-003/-005; **40mm** 12 L/70

Navy 700
EQUIPMENT BY TYPE
PRINCIPAL SURFACE COMBATANTS • FRIGATES 1
  FFGHM 1 *Sabha* (ex-US *Oliver Hazard Perry*) with 1 Mk 13 GMLS with RGM-84C *Harpoon* Block 1B AShM/SM-1MR Block VI SAM, 2 triple 324mm SVTT Mk 32 ASTT with Mk 46 LWT, 1 Mk 15 *Phalanx* Block 1B CIWS, 1 76mm gun (capacity 1 Bo-105 hel)

PATROL AND COASTAL COMBATANTS 25
  PSO 1 *Al Zubara* (ex-UK *River* (OPV) Batch 1 (mod)) with 1 hel landing platform
  PCFG 4 *Ahmed el Fateh* (GER Lurssen 45m) with 2 twin lnchr with MM40 *Exocet* AShM, 1 76mm gun
  PCG 2 *Al Manama* (GER Lurssen 62m) with 2 twin lnchr with MM40 *Exocet* AShM, 2 76mm guns, 1 hel landing platform
  PCF 5 *Al-Gurairiyah* (ex-US *Cyclone*)
  PB 6: 2 *Al Jarim* (US *Swift* FPB-20); 2 *Al Riffa* (GER Lurssen 38m); 2 *Mashhoor* (US Swiftships 35m)
  PBF 7 Mk V FPB

AMPHIBIOUS • LANDING CRAFT 9
  LCM 7: 1 *Loadmaster*; 4 *Mashtan*; 2 *Dinar* (ADSB 42m)
  LCVP 2 *Sea Keeper*

Naval Aviation
EQUIPMENT BY TYPE
HELICOPTERS • TPT • Light 2 Bo-105

Air Force 1,500
FORCES BY ROLE
FIGHTER
  2 sqn with F-16C/D Block 40/70 *Fighting Falcon*
FIGHTER/GROUND ATTACK
  1 sqn with F-5E/F *Tiger* II
TRANSPORT
  1 (Royal) flt with B-737–800; B 767; B 747; BAe-146; Gulfstream II; Gulfstream IV; Gulfstream 450; Gulfstream 550; S-92A
TRAINING
  1 sqn with *Hawk* Mk129*
  1 sqn with T-67M *Firefly*
ATTACK HELICOPTER
  2 sqn with AH-1E/F *Cobra*; TAH-1P *Cobra*
TRANSPORT HELICOPTER
  1 sqn with Bell 212 (AB-212); Bell 412EP *Twin Huey*
  1 sqn with UH-60M *Black Hawk*
  1 (VIP) sqn with Bo-105; S-70A B*lack Hawk*; UH-60L *Black Hawk*

EQUIPMENT BY TYPE
AIRCRAFT 40 combat capable
  FTR 12: 8 F-5E *Tiger* II; 4 F-5F *Tiger* II
  FGA 22: 16 F-16C Block 40 *Fighting Falcon*; 4 F-16D Block 40 *Fighting Falcon*; 1 F-16C Block 70 *Fighting Falcon*; 1 F-16D Block 70 *Fighting Falcon*
  TPT 14: **Medium** 2 C-130J *Hercules*; **PAX** 12: 1 B-737-800 (VIP); 1 B-767 (VIP); 2 B-747 (VIP); 1 Gulfstream II (VIP); 1 Gulfstream IV (VIP); 1 Gulfstream 450 (VIP); 1 Gulfstream 550 (VIP); 2 BAe-146-RJ85 (VIP); 1 BAe-146-RJ100 (VIP); 1 BAe-146-RJ170 (VIP); (1 B-727 in store)
  TRG 9: 6 *Hawk* Mk129*; 3 T-67M *Firefly*
HELICOPTERS
  ATK 28: 10 AH-1E *Cobra*; 12 AH-1F *Cobra*; 6 AH-1Z *Viper*
  MRH 2+ Bell 412EP *Twin Huey*
  TPT 27: **Medium** 13: 3 S-70A *Black Hawk*; 1 S-92A (VIP); 1 UH-60L *Black Hawk*; 8 UH-60M *Black Hawk*; **Light** 14: 11 Bell 212 (AB-212); 3 Bo-105
  TRG 6 TAH-1P *Cobra*
AIR-LAUNCHED MISSILES
  AAM • IR AIM-9P *Sidewinder*; **SARH** AIM-7 *Sparrow*; **ARH** AIM-120B/C AMRAAM
  ASM AGM-65D/G *Maverick*; *Cirit*; some TOW
BOMBS
  Laser-guided GBU-10/12 *Paveway* II

Gendarmerie & Paramilitary ε11,260

Police 9,000
Ministry of Interior
EQUIPMENT BY TYPE
ARMOURED FIGHTING VEHICLES
  APC • PPV Otokar ISV
  AUV *Cobra*

HELICOPTERS
MRH 2 Bell 412 *Twin Huey*
ISR 2 Hughes 500
TPT • Light 1 Bo-105

National Guard ε2,000
FORCES BY ROLE
MANOEUVRE
 Other
 3 paramilitary bn
EQUIPMENT BY TYPE
ARMOURED FIGHTING VEHICLES
 APC • APC (W) *Arma* 6×6; *Cobra*

Coast Guard ε260
Ministry of Interior
PATROL AND COASTAL COMBATANTS 55
 PBF 26: 2 *Ares* 18; 3 *Response Boat-Medium* (RB-M); 4 *Jaris*; 6 *Saham*; 6 *Fajr*; 5 *Jarada*
 PB 29: 6 *Haris*; 1 *Al Muharraq*; 10 *Deraa* (of which 4 *Halmatic* 20, 2 *Souter* 20, 4 *Rodman* 20); 10 *Saif* (of which 4 *Fairey Sword*, 6 *Halmatic* 160); 2 *Hawar*
AMPHIBIOUS
 LANDING CRAFT • LCU 1 *Loadmaster* II

FOREIGN FORCES
United Kingdom *Operation Kipion* 1,000; 1 FFGHM; 2 MCO; 2 MHO; 1 LSD; 1 naval facility
United States US Central Command: 4,500; 1 HQ (5th Fleet); 4 MCO; 1 ESB; 1 ASW sqn with 3 P-8A *Poseidon*; 1 EP-3E *Aries* II; 2 SAM bty with M902/M903 *Patriot* PAC-3/PAC-3 MSE

Egypt EGY

Egyptian Pound EGP		2022	2023	2024
GDP	EGP	7.84trn	10.3trn	14.2trn
	USD	475bn	398bn	358bn
per capita	USD	4,587	3,770	3,320
Growth	%	6.7	4.2	3.6
Inflation	%	8.5	23.5	32.2
Def bdgt	EGP	86.0bn	92.4bn	102bn
	USD	5.21bn	3.58bn	2.57bn
FMA (US)	USD	1.3bn	1.3bn	1.3bn
USD1=EGP		16.50	25.79	39.61

Real-terms defence budget trend (USDbn, constant 2015)
7.30
5.73
2008 — 2016 — 2023

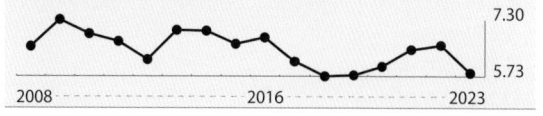

Population 109,546,720

Age	0–14	15–19	20–24	25–29	30–64	65 plus
Male	17.7%	4.6%	4.2%	3.8%	18.4%	2.7%
Female	16.7%	4.4%	4.0%	3.6%	17.4%	2.6%

Capabilities

Egypt's armed forces are the largest in the region and are focused principally on maintaining territorial integrity and internal security, including tackling ISIS-affiliated groups in northern Sinai. The armed forces remain deeply involved in the civilian economy and retain a central role in internal politics. The US is a key strategic partner and provides significant military assistance. Cairo has defence relations with Russia and other states, such as France and Italy, particularly regarding procurement. Egypt hosts the annual multinational exercise *Bright Star*, in which India participated for the first time in 2023. The armed forces have a developing capacity to deploy abroad independently. They contribute to UN missions, have intervened militarily in Libya and supported the Saudi-led coalition in Yemen with some combat aircraft. Amid the Sudan conflict in April 2023, the government reportedly delivered military aid to the Sudanese government while engaging in Emirati-mediated negotiations with the rival Rapid Support Forces to recover captured Egyptian personnel and equipment. The navy's two *Mistral*-class amphibious assault ships have bolstered its regional deployment capacity. The armed forces' inventory is still dominated by obsolete Soviet-era systems, though an extensive recapitalisation programme has led to the addition of newer Western-origin equipment and delivery of Russian multi-role fighters, attack helicopters and SAM systems. The diversity of the inventory risks complicating military maintenance and sustainment. Egypt has an established domestic defence industry, although it has heavily relied on licensed and co-production agreements with foreign companies, including for the South Korean K9 *Thunder* self-propelled artillery.

ACTIVE 438,500 (Army 310,000 Navy 18,500 Air 30,000 Air Defence Command 80,000) **Gendarmerie & Paramilitary 397,000**

Conscription liability 12–36 months (followed by refresher training over a period of up to 9 years)

RESERVE 479,000 (Army 375,000 Navy 14,000 Air

20,000 Air Defence Command 70,000)

ORGANISATIONS BY SERVICE

Space
EQUIPMENT BY TYPE
SATELLITES 4
  COMMUNICATIONS 1 TIBA-1
  ISR 3: 1 *Egyptsat*-A; 2 *Horus*

Army ε310,000 (incl ε200,000 conscripts)
FORCES BY ROLE
SPECIAL FORCES
  5 cdo gp
  1 counter-terrorist unit
  1 spec ops unit
MANOEUVRE
  Armoured
  4 armd div (2 armd bde, 1 mech bde, 1 arty bde)
  4 indep armd bde
  1 Republican Guard bde
  Mechanised
  8 mech div (1 armd bde, 2 mech bde, 1 arty bde)
  4 indep mech bde
  Light
  2 indep inf bde
  Air Manoeuvre
  2 air mob bde
  1 para bde
SURFACE-TO-SURFACE MISSILE
  1 SRBM bde with FROG-7
  1 SRBM bde with 9K72 *Elbrus* (RS-SS-1C *Scud*-B)
COMBAT SUPPORT
  15 arty bde
  6 engr bde (3 engr bn)
  2 spec ops engr bn
  6 salvage engr bn
  24 MP bn
  18 sigs bn
COMBAT SERVICE SUPPORT
  36 log bn
  27 med bn
EQUIPMENT BY TYPE
ARMOURED FIGHTING VEHICLES
  MBT 2,480: 1,130 M1A1 *Abrams*; 300 M60A1; 850 M60A3; 200 T-62 (840 T-54/T-55; 300 T-62 all in store)
  RECCE 412: 300 BRDM-2; 112 *Commando Scout*
  IFV 690: 390 YPR-765 25mm; 300 BMP-1
  APC 5,244+
    APC (T) 2,700: 2,000 M113A2/YPR-765 (incl variants); 500 BTR-50; 200 OT-62
    APC (W) 1,560: 250 BMR-600P; 250 BTR-60; 410 *Fahd*-30/TH 390 *Fahd*; 650 *Walid*
  PPV 984+: 535 *Caiman*; some REVA III; some REVA V LWB; 360 RG-33L; 89 RG-33 HAGA (amb); ST-500; *Temsah* 2; *Temsah* 3
  AUV 173+: *Panthera* T6; 173 *Sherpa Light Scout*; ST-100
ENGINEERING & MAINTENANCE VEHICLES
  ARV 367+: *Fahd* 240; BMR 3560.55; 12 *Maxxpro* ARV; 220 M88A1; 90 M88A2; M113 ARV; 45 M578; T-54/55 ARV
  VLB KMM; MTU; MTU-20
  MW *Aardvark* JFSU Mk4
ANTI-TANK/ANTI-INFRASTRUCTURE • MSL
  SP 352+: 52 M901, 300 YPR-765 PRAT; HMMWV with TOW-2
  MANPATS 9K11 *Malyutka* (RS-AT-3 *Sagger*) (incl BRDM-2); HJ-73; Luch *Corsar* (reported); *Milan*; *Stugna*-P (reported); TOW-2
ARTILLERY 4,468
  SP 492+: **122mm** 124+: 124 SP 122; D-30 mod; **130mm** M-46 mod; **155mm** 368: 164 M109A2; 204 M109A5
  TOWED 962: **122mm** 526: 190 D-30M; 36 M-1931/37; 300 M-30; **130mm** 420 M-46; **155mm** 16 GH-52
  MRL 450: **122mm** 356: some ATS-59G; 96 BM-11; 60 BM-21; 50 *Sakr*-10; 50 *Sakr*-18; 100 *Sakr*-36; **130mm** 36 K136 *Kooryong*; **140mm** 32 BM-14; **227mm** 26 M270 MLRS; **240mm** (48 BM-24 in store)
  MOR 2,564: **81mm** 50 M125A2; **82mm** 500; **SP 107mm** 100: 65 M106A1; 35 M106A2; **120mm** 1,848: 1,800 M-1943; 48 Brandt; **SP 120mm** 36 M1064A3; **160mm** 30 M-160
SURFACE-TO-SURFACE MISSILE LAUNCHERS
  SRBM • Conventional 42+: 9 FROG-7; 24 *Sakr*-80; 9 9K72 *Elbrus* (RS-SS-1C *Scud*-B)
UNINHABITED AERIAL VEHICLES
  ISR • Medium R4E-50 *Skyeye*; ASN-209
AIR DEFENCE
  SAM 45+
    Point-defence *Ayn al-Saqr*; FIM-92 *Stinger*; 9K38 *Igla* (RS-SA-18 *Grouse*); 9K338 *Igla*-S (RS-SA-24 *Grinch*) (reported)
  SPAAGM • 23mm 45 *Sinai*-23 with *Ayn al-Saqr*
  GUNS 860
    SP 160: **23mm** 120 ZSU-23-4; **57mm** 40 ZSU-57-2
    TOWED 700: **14.5mm** 300 ZPU-4; **23mm** 200 ZU-23-2; **57mm** 200 S-60

Navy ε8,500 (incl 2,000 Coast Guard); 10,000 conscript (total 18,500)
EQUIPMENT BY TYPE
SUBMARINES • SSK 8
  4 Type-033 (PRC *Romeo*) with 8 single 533mm TT with UGM-84C *Harpoon* Block 1B AShM/Mk 37 HWT
  4 Type-209/1400 with 8 single 533mm TT with UGM-84L *Harpoon* Block II AShM/*SeaHake* mod 4 (DM2A4) HWT
PRINCIPAL SURFACE COMBATANTS • FRIGATES 13

FFGHM 9:
- 2 *Al-Aziz* (GER MEKO A200) with 4 quad lnchr with MM40 *Exocet* Block 3 AShM, 4 8-cell CLA with VL MICA NG SAM, 1 127mm gun (capacity 1 med hel)
- 4 *Alexandria* (ex-US *Oliver Hazard Perry*) with 1 Mk 13 GMLS with RGM-84C *Harpoon* Block 1B AShM/SM-1MR Block VI SAM, 2 triple 324mm ASTT with Mk 46 LWT, 1 Mk 15 *Phalanx* CIWS, 1 76mm gun (capacity 2 SH-2G *Super Seasprite* ASW hel)
- 2 *Al-Fateh* (*Gowind* 2500) with 2 quad lnchrs with MM40 *Exocet* Block 3 AShM, 1 16-cell CLA VLS with VL MICA SAM, 2 triple 324mm ASTT with MU90 LWT, 1 76mm gun (capacity 1 med hel)
- 1 *Tahya Misr* (FRA *Aquitaine* (FREMM)) with 2 quad lnchr with MM40 *Exocet* Block 3 AShM, 2 8-cell *Sylver* A43 VLS with *Aster* 15 SAM, 2 twin 324mm B-515 ASTT with MU90 LWT, 1 76mm gun (capacity 1 med hel)

FFGH 2 *Damyat* (ex-US *Knox*) with 1 octuple Mk 16 GMLS with RGM-84C *Harpoon* Block 1B AShM/ASROC, 2 twin 324mm SVTT Mk 32 TT with Mk 46 LWT, 1 Mk 15 *Phalanx* CIWS, 1 127mm gun (capacity 1 SH-2G *Super Seasprite* ASW hel)

FFHM 2 *Al-Galala* (ITA *Bergamini* (FREMM)) with 2 8-cell *Sylver* A50 VLS with *Aster* 15/30 SAM, 2 twin 324mm B-515 ASTT with MU90 LWT, 1 127mm gun, 1 76mm gun (fitted for but not with *Otomat* (*Teseo*) Mk2A AShM) (capacity 2 med hel)

PATROL AND COASTAL COMBATANTS 71

CORVETTES 3
- **FSGM** 2 *Abu Qir* (ESP *Descubierta*) (of which 1†) with 2 quad lnchr with RGM-84C *Harpoon* Block 1B AShM, 1 octuple *Albatros* lnchr with *Aspide* SAM, 2 triple 324mm SVTT Mk 32 ASTT with *Sting Ray* LWT, 1 twin 375mm Bofors ASW Rocket Launcher System A/S mor, 1 76mm gun
- **FS** 1 *Shabab Misr* (ex-RoK *Po Hang*) with 2 76mm guns

PCFGM 4 *Ezzat* (US *Ambassador* Fast Missile Craft) with 2 quad lnchr with RGM-84L *Harpoon* Block II AShM, 1 21-cell Mk49 lnchr with RIM-116B RAM Block 1A SAM, 1 Mk15 mod 21 Block 1B *Phalanx* CIWS 1 76mm gun

PCFG 8:
- 1 Project 12418 (RUS *Tarantul* IV) with 2 twin lnchr with 3M80E *Moskit* (RS-SS-N-22A *Sunburn*), 2 AK630 CIWS, 1 76mm gun
- 6 *Ramadan* with 4 single lnchr with *Otomat* Mk2 AShM, 1 76mm gun
- 1 *Tiger* with 2 twin lnchr with RGM-84 *Harpoon* AShM, 1 76mm gun

PCF 3 *Cyclone* (ex-US)

PCC 15: 5 *Al-Nour* (ex-PRC *Hainan*) (3 more in reserve†) with 2 triple 324mm TT, 4 RBU 1200 A/S mor, 2 twin 57mm guns; 1 Lurssen 41m; 9 *Omar Ibn El Khattab* (GER OPB 40)

PBFGM 8 Project 205 (ex-YUG *Osa* I) (of which 3†) with 4 single lnchr with P-20 (RS-SS-N-2A *Styx*) AShM, 1 9K32 *Strela*-2 (RS-SA-N-5 *Grail*) SAM (manual aiming)

PBFG 10:
- 4 Type-024 (PRC *Hegu*) (2 additional vessels in reserve) with 2 single lnchr with SY-1 (CH-SS-N-1 *Scrubbrush*) AShM
- up to 6 *October* (FSU *Komar*)† with 2 single lnchr with *Otomat* Mk2 AShM (1 additional vessel in reserve)

PBFM 4 *Shershen* (FSU) with 1 9K32 *Strela*-2 (RS-SA-N-5 *Grail*) SAM (manual aiming), 1 12-tube BM-24 MRL

PBF 10: 6 *Kaan* 20 (TUR MRTP 20); 4 Project 205 (ex-FIN *Osa* II)

PB 6: up to 4 Type-062 (ex-PRC *Shanghai* II); 2 *Shershen* (FSU) (of which 1†) with 4 single 533mm TT, 1 8-tube BM-21 MRL

MINE WARFARE • MINE COUNTERMEASURES 14
- **MHC** 5: 2 *Al Siddiq* (ex-US *Osprey*); 3 *Dat Assawari* (US Swiftships)
- **MSI** 2 *Safaga* (US Swiftships)
- **MSO** 7: 3 *Assiout* (FSU T-43); 4 *Aswan* (FSU *Yurka*)

AMPHIBIOUS

PRINCIPAL AMPHIBIOUS SHIPS • LHD 2 *Gamal Abdel Nasser* (FRA *Mistral*) (capacity 16 med hel; 2 LCT or 4 LCM; 13 MBTs; 50 AFVs; 450 troops)

LANDING CRAFT 15:
- **LCT** 2 EDA-R
- **LCM** 13: 4 CTM NG; up to 9 *Vydra* (FSU) (capacity either 3 MBT or 200 troops)

LOGISTICS AND SUPPORT 23
- **AE** 1 *Halaib* (ex-GER *Westerwald*)
- **AKR** 3 *Al Hurreya*
- **AOL** 7 *Ayeda* (FSU *Toplivo*) (1 more in reserve)
- **AR** 1 *Shaledin* (ex-GER *Luneberg*)
- **ARS** 2 *Al Areesh*
- **ATF** 5 *Al Maks*† (FSU *Okhtensky*)
- **AX** 2: 1 *El Horriya* (also used as the presidential yacht); 1 other
- **AXL** 2: 1 *Al Kousser*; 1 *Intishat*;

Special Forces

FORCES BY ROLE
SPECIAL FORCES
1 SF bde

Coastal Defence

Army tps, Navy control
EQUIPMENT BY TYPE
COASTAL DEFENCE
ARTY 100mm; **130mm** SM-4-1; **152mm**
AShM 4K87 (RS-SSC-2B *Samlet*); *Otomat* MkII

Naval Aviation

All aircraft operated by Air Force
EQUIPMENT BY TYPE
AIRCRAFT • TPT • Light 4 Beech 1900C (maritime surveillance)
UNINHABITED AERIAL VEHICLES
ISR • Light 2 S-100 *Camcopter*

Coast Guard 2,000
EQUIPMENT BY TYPE
PATROL AND COASTAL COMBATANTS 68
  PBF 14: 6 *Crestitalia*; 5 *Swift Protector*; 3 *Peterson*
  PB 54: 5 *Nisr*; 12 *Sea Spectre* MkIII; 25 Swiftships; some *Timsah*; 3 Type-83; 9 *Peterson*

Air Force 20,000; 10,000 conscript (total 30,000)
FORCES BY ROLE
FIGHTER
  1 sqn with F-16A/B *Fighting Falcon*
  8 sqn with F-16C/D *Fighting Falcon*
  1 sqn with *Mirage* 2000B/C
FIGHTER/GROUND ATTACK
  2 sqn with *Rafale* DM/EM
  3 sqn with MiG-29M/M2 *Fulcrum*
ANTI-SUBMARINE WARFARE
  1 sqn with SH-2G *Super Seasprite*
MARITIME PATROL
  1 sqn with Beech 1900C
ELECTRONIC WARFARE
  1 sqn with Beech 1900 (ELINT); *Commando* Mk2E (ECM)
ELECTRONIC WARFARE/TRANSPORT
  1 sqn with C-130H/VC-130H *Hercules*
AIRBORNE EARLY WARNING
  1 sqn with E-2C *Hawkeye*
SEARCH & RESCUE
  1 unit with AW139
TRANSPORT
  1 sqn with An-74TK-200A
  1 sqn with C-130H/C-130H-30 *Hercules*
  1 sqn with C295M
  1 sqn with DHC-5D *Buffalo*
  1 sqn with B-707-366C; B-737-100; Beech 200 *Super King Air*; *Falcon* 20; Gulfstream III; Gulfstream IV; Gulfstream IV-SP
TRAINING
  1 sqn with *Alpha Jet**
  1 sqn with DHC-5 *Buffalo*
  3 sqn with EMB-312 *Tucano*
  1 sqn with Grob 115EG
  ε6 sqn with K-8 *Karakorum**
  1 sqn with L-39 *Albatros*; L-59E *Albatros**
ATTACK HELICOPTER
  1 sqn with Mi-24V
  2 sqn with AH-64D *Apache*
  1 sqn with Ka-52A *Hokum* B
  2 sqn with SA-342K *Gazelle* (with HOT)
  1 sqn with SA-342L *Gazelle*
TRANSPORT HELICOPTER
  1 sqn with CH-47C/D *Chinook* 1 sqn with Mi-8
  1 sqn with Mi-8/Mi-17-V1 *Hip*

  1 sqn with S-70 *Black Hawk*; UH-60A/L *Black Hawk*
UAV
  Some sqn with R4E-50 *Skyeye*; *Wing Loong* I
EQUIPMENT BY TYPE
AIRCRAFT 491 combat capable
  FTR 32: 26 F-16A *Fighting Falcon*; 6 F-16B *Fighting Falcon*
  FGA 257: 138 F-16C *Fighting Falcon*; 37 F-16D *Fighting Falcon*, 2 *Mirage* 2000B; 15 *Mirage* 2000C; 41 MiG-29M/M2 *Fulcrum*; 16 *Rafale* DM; 8 *Rafale* EM
  ELINT 2 VC-130H *Hercules*
  ISR 12: ε6 AT-802 *Air Tractor**; 6 *Mirage* 5R (5SDR)*
  AEW&C 7 E-2C *Hawkeye*
  TPT 82: **Heavy** 2 Il-76MF *Candid*; **Medium** 24: 21 C-130H *Hercules*; 3 C-130H-30 *Hercules*; **Light** 45: 3 An-74TK-200A; 1 Beech 200 *King Air*; 4 Beech 1900 (ELINT); 4 Beech 1900C; 24 C295M; 9 DHC-5D *Buffalo* (being withdrawn) **PAX** 11: 1 B-707-366C; 3 *Falcon* 20; 2 Gulfstream III; 1 Gulfstream IV; 4 Gulfstream IV-SP
  TRG 328: 36 *Alpha Jet**; 54 EMB-312 *Tucano*; 74 Grob 115EG; 119 K-8 *Karakorum**; 10 L-39 *Albatros*; 35 L-59E*
HELICOPTERS
  ATK 104: 45 AH-64D *Apache*; up to 46 Ka-52A *Hokum* B; ε13 Mi-24V *Hind* E
  ASW 10 SH-2G *Super Seasprite* (opcon Navy)
  ELINT 4 *Commando* Mk2E (ECM)
  MRH 77: 2 AW139 (SAR); 5 AW149; 65 SA342K *Gazelle* (some with HOT); 5 SA342L *Gazelle* (opcon Navy)
  TPT 96: **Heavy** 19: 3 CH-47C *Chinook*; 16 CH-47D *Chinook*; **Medium** 77: 2 AS-61; 24 *Commando* (of which 3 VIP); 40 Mi-8T *Hip*; 3 Mi-17-1V *Hip*; 4 S-70 *Black Hawk* (VIP); 4 UH-60L *Black Hawk* (VIP)
  TRG 17 UH-12E
UNINHABITED AERIAL VEHICLES
  CISR • Heavy 4+ *Wing Loong* I
  ISR • Medium R4E-50 *Skyeye*
AIR LAUNCHED MISSILES
  AAM • IR AIM-9M/P *Sidewinder*; R-73 (RS-AA-11A *Archer*); R-550 *Magic*; 9M39 *Igla-V*; **IIR** Mica IR; **ARH** Mica RF; R-77 (RS-AA-12 *Adder*); **SARH** AIM-7F/M *Sparrow*; R-530
  ASM AASM; AGM-65A/D/F/G *Maverick*; AGM-114F/K *Hellfire*; AS-30L; HOT; LJ-7 (AKD-10); 9M120 *Ataka* (RS-AT-9)
  LACM SCALP EG
  AShM AGM-84L *Harpoon* Block II; AM39 *Exocet*; Kh-35U (RS-AS-20 *Kayak*)
  ARM *Armat*; Kh-25MP (RS-AS-12A *Kegler*)
BOMBS
  Laser-guided GBU-10/12 *Paveway* II
  INS/SAT-guided *Al Tariq*

Air Defence Command 80,000 conscript; 70,000 reservists (total 150,000)
FORCES BY ROLE

AIR DEFENCE

5 AD div HQ (geographically based)
3 SAM bty with S-300V4 (RS-SA-23)
4 SAM bty with 9K37M1-2/9K317 Buk-M1-2/M2E (RS-SA-11 *Gadfly*/RS-SA-17 *Grizzly*)
11 SAM bty with MIM-23B I-*Hawk*
38 SAM bty with S-75M *Volkhov* (RS-SA-2 *Guideline*)
10 SAM bty with S-125-2M *Pechora*-2M (RS-SA-26)
Some SAM bty with 2K12 *Kub* (RS-SA-6 *Gainful*)
2 SAM bty with 9K331/9K331ME *Tor*-M1/M2E (RS-SA-15 *Gauntlet*)
14 SAM bty with *Crotale*
12 SAM bty with M48 *Chaparral*
30 SAM bty with S-125M *Pechora*-M (RS-SA-3 *Goa*)
18 AD bn with RIM-7M *Sea Sparrow* with *Skyguard*/GDF-003 with *Skyguard*
12 ADA bde (total: 100 ADA bn)

EQUIPMENT BY TYPE
AIR DEFENCE
SAM 777
- **Long-range** ε18 S-300V4 (RS-SA-23)
- **Medium-range** 323+: 40+ 9K37M1-2/9K317 *Buk*-M1-2/M2E (RS-SA-11 *Gadfly*/RS-SA-17 *Grizzly*); ε33 MIM-23B I-*Hawk*; ε210 S-75M *Volkhov* (RS-SA-2 *Guideline*); ε40 S-125-2M *Pechora*-2M (RS-SA-26)
- **Short-range** 300+: 56+ 2K12 *Kub* (RS-SA-6 *Gainful*); 10 9K331 *Tor*-M1 (RS-SA-15 *Gauntlet*); 10+ 9K331ME *Tor*-M2E (RS-SA-15 *Gauntlet*); 24+ *Crotale*; 80 RIM-7M *Sea Sparrow* with *Skyguard*; ε120 S-125M *Pechora*-M (RS-SA-3 *Goa*)
- **Point-defence** 136+: 50 M1097 *Avenger*; 50+ M48 *Chaparral*

GUNS 910
- **SP • 23mm** 230 ZSU-23-4 *Shilka*
- **TOWED** 680: **35mm** 80 GDF-005 with *Skyguard*; **57mm** 600 S-60

Gendarmerie & Paramilitary ε397,000 active

Central Security Forces ε325,000
Ministry of Interior; includes conscripts
ARMOURED FIGHTING VEHICLES
- **APC • APC (W)** *Walid*
- **AUV** *Sherpa Light Scout*

National Guard ε60,000
Lt wpns only
FORCES BY ROLE
MANOEUVRE
  Other
  8 paramilitary bde (cadre) (3 paramilitary bn)
EQUIPMENT BY TYPE
ARMOURED FIGHTING VEHICLES
- **APC • APC (W)** 250 *Walid*

Border Guard Forces ε12,000
Ministry of Interior; lt wpns only

FORCES BY ROLE
MANOEUVRE
  Other
  18 Border Guard regt

DEPLOYMENT

CENTRAL AFRICAN REPUBLIC: UN • MINUSCA 1,015; 1 inf bn; 1 tpt coy

DEMOCRATIC REPUBLIC OF THE CONGO: UN • MONUSCO 12

SOUTH SUDAN: UN • UNMISS 7

SUDAN: UN • UNISFA 2

WESTERN SAHARA: UN • MINURSO 20

FOREIGN FORCES

Australia MFO (*Operation Mazurka*) 27
Canada MFO 55
Colombia MFO 275; 1 inf bn
Czech Republic MFO 18; 1 C295M
Fiji MFO 170; elm 1 inf bn
France MFO 1
Italy MFO 75; 3 PB
New Zealand MFO 26; 1 trg unit; 1 tpt unit
Norway MFO 3
United Kingdom MFO 2
United States MFO 465; elm 1 ARNG inf bn; 1 ARNG spt bn (1 EOD coy, 1 medical coy, 1 hel coy)
Uruguay MFO 41 1 engr/tpt unit

Iran IRN

Iranian Rial IRR		2022	2023	2024
GDP	IRR	104,350trn	158,025trn	213,468trn
	USD [b]	346bn	366bn	386bn
per capita	USD	4,043	4,234	4,418
Growth	%	3.8	3.0	2.5
Inflation	%	45.8	47.0	32.5
Def bdgt [a]	IRR	2,225trn	3,194trn	
	USD [b]	7.39bn	7.41bn	
	USD [c]	53.0bn	76.1bn	
USD1=IRR [NIMA]		301,172.80	431,245.06	552,714.89

[a] Excludes Law Enforcement Forces (NAJA).

[b] Conversions using NIMA exchange rate. See regional text for further detail.

[c] Conversion using official exchange rate.

Real-terms defence budget trend (USDbn, constant 2015)

Population	87,590,873				
Age	0–14	15–19	20–24	25–29	30–64	65 plus
Male	12.0%	3.6%	3.3%	3.5%	25.2%	3.1%
Female	11.5%	3.4%	3.1%	3.4%	24.4%	3.6%

Capabilities

Iran is a major regional military power with a doctrine that combines territorial defence through national mobilisation and a substantial missile arsenal, with an asymmetric defence strategy. Non-state allies and proxies in weaker states and entities, like Lebanon, Syria, Iraq, Gaza and Yemen, play a key role in Iran's efforts to project power. Hizbullah in Lebanon is the most capable of these actors and one of the most closely aligned with Iran's leadership. Tehran's relationship with Moscow has deepened, manifested by the transfer of Iranian direct attack munitions to Russia for use in the war in Ukraine. This increase in military cooperation could offer Iran a conduit to access more modern weaponry. Russia has begun delivering advanced jet trainers to Iran, potentially paving the way for multirole platforms. Tehran retains the region's largest short- and medium-range ballistic-missile inventory, possesses land-attack cruise missiles, and has a substantial variety of UAVs. The rest of the conventional armed forces, although large by regional standards, struggle with increasingly obsolescent equipment that ingenuity and asymmetric-warfare techniques can only partially offset. Ageing equipment has been particularly pronounced for the air force. Although Iran's naval force focus on asymmetric approaches, such as the use of mines, anti-ship missiles, speedboats and small submarines, the service has shown interest in blue water operations and power projection. The country suffers command and control problems between the regular military services and the Islamic Revolutionary Guard Corps (IRGC). In regional terms, Iran has a well-developed defence-industrial base. While unable to meet national needs for all major weapons, the domestic industry has achieved a high degree of proficiency in the production of certain types of advanced weapons, such as ballistic and cruise missiles, anti-tank guided missiles, UAVs and surface-to-air missiles. Iran also has developed expansive sanctions-evasion techniques to support its defence industry.

ACTIVE 610,000 (Army 350,000 Islamic Revolutionary Guard Corps 190,000 Navy 18,000 Air 37,000 Air Defence 15,000) **Gendarmerie & Paramilitary 40,000**

Armed Forces General Staff coordinates two parallel organisations: the regular armed forces and the Islamic Revolutionary Guard Corps

Conscript liability 18–21 months (reported, with variations depending on location in which service is performed)

RESERVE 350,000 (Army 350,000, ex-service volunteers)

ORGANISATIONS BY SERVICE

Space
EQUIPMENT BY TYPE
SATELLITES • ISR 2 *Noor*

Army 130,000; 220,000 conscript (total 350,000)
FORCES BY ROLE
5 corps-level regional HQ
COMMAND
  1 cdo div HQ
  4 armd div HQ
  2 mech div HQ
  4 inf div HQ
SPECIAL FORCES
  1 cdo div (3 cdo bde)
  6 cdo bde
  1 SF bde
MANOEUVRE
  Armoured
  8 armd bde
  Mechanised
  14 mech bde
  Light
  12 inf bde
  Air Manoeuvre
  1 AB bde
  Aviation
  Some avn gp
COMBAT SUPPORT
  5 arty gp
EQUIPMENT BY TYPE

Totals incl those held by IRGC Ground Forces. Some equipment serviceability in doubt

ARMOURED FIGHTING VEHICLES
  MBT 1,513+: 480 T-72S; 150 M60A1; 75+ T-62; 100 *Chieftain* Mk3/Mk5; 540 T-54/T-55/Type-59/*Safir*-74; 168

M47/M48

LT TK 80 Scorpion

RECCE 35 EE-9 Cascavel

IFV 610+: 210 BMP-1; 400 BMP-2 with 9K111 Fagot (RS-AT-4 Spigot); BMT-2 Cobra

APC 640+

  APC (T) 340: 140 Boragh with 9K111 Fagot (RS-AT-4 Spigot); 200 M113

  APC (W) 300+: 300 BTR-50/BTR-60; Rakhsh

  PPV Toofan

ENGINEERING & MAINTENANCE VEHICLES

  ARV 20+: BREM-1 reported; 20 Chieftain ARV; M578; T-54/55 ARV reported

  VLB 15 Chieftain AVLB

  MW Taftan 1

ANTI-TANK/ANTI-INFRASTRUCTURE

  MSL • **MANPATS** 9K11 Malyutka (RS-AT-3 Sagger); 9K111 Fagot (RS-AT-4 Spigot); 9K111-1 Konkurs (RS-AT-5 Spandrel/Towsan-1); Almaz; Dehlavieh (Kornet); I-Raad; Saeqhe 1; Saeqhe 2; Toophan; Toophan 2

  RCL 200+: **75mm** M20; **82mm** B-10; **106mm** ε200 M40; **107mm** B-11

ARTILLERY 6,798+

  SP 292+: **122mm** 60+: 60 2S1 Gvozdika; Raad-1 (Thunder 1); **155mm** 150+: 150 M109A1; Raad-2 (Thunder 2); **170mm** 30 M-1978; **175mm** 22 M107; **203mm** 30 M110

  TOWED 2,030+; **105mm** 150: 130 M101A1; 20 M-56; **122mm** 640: 540 D-30; 100 Type-54 (M-30); **130mm** 985 M-46; **152mm** 30 D-20; **155mm** 205: 120 GHN-45; 70 M114; 15 Type-88 WAC-21; **203mm** 20 M115

  MRL 1,476+: **107mm** 1,300: 700 Type-63; 600 HASEB Fadjr 1; **122mm** 157: 7 BM-11; 100 BM-21 Grad; 50 Arash/Hadid/Noor; **240mm** 19+: ε10 Fadjr 3; 9 M-1985; **330mm** Fadjr 5

  MOR 3,000: **81mm**; **82mm**; **107mm** M30; **120mm** HM-15; HM-16; M-65

SURFACE-TO-SURFACE MISSILE LAUNCHERS

  SRBM • **Conventional** ε30 CH-SS-8 (175 msl); Shahin-1/Shahin-2; Nazeat; Oghab

AIRCRAFT • **TPT** 17 **Light** 16: 10 Cessna 185; 2 F-27 Friendship; 4 Turbo Commander 690; **PAX** 1 Falcon 20

HELICOPTERS

  ATK 50 AH-1J Cobra

  TPT 167: **Heavy** ε20 CH-47C Chinook; **Medium** 69: 49 Bell 214; 20 Mi-171; **Light** 78: 68 Bell 205A (AB-205A); 10 Bell 206 Jet Ranger (AB-206)

UNINHABITED AERIAL VEHICLES

  CISR • **Medium** Ababil 4; Mohajer 4

  ISR • **Medium** Ababil 2; Mohajer 4; **Light** Mohajer 2

LOITERING & DIRECT ATTACK MUNITIONS

  Akhgar; Arash; Omid; Ababil T

AIR DEFENCE

  SAM

    Short-range FM-80 (CH-SA-4)

    Point-defence 9K36 Strela-3 (RS-SA-14 Gremlin); 9K32 Strela-2 (RS-SA-7 Grail)‡; Misaq 1 (QW-1); Misaq 2 (QW-18); 9K338 Igla-S (RS-SA-24 Grinch) (reported); HN-5A (CH-SA-3)

  GUNS 1,122

    SP 180: **23mm** 100 ZSU-23-4; **57mm** 80 ZSU-57-2

    TOWED 942+: **14.5mm** ZPU-2; ZPU-4; **23mm** 300 ZU-23-2; **35mm** 92 GDF-002; **37mm** M-1939; **40mm** 50 L/70; **57mm** 200 S-60; **85mm** 300 M-1939

AIR-LAUNCHED MISSILES

  ASM Almas (reported); Qaem 114 (reported)

BOMBS

  Laser-guided Qaem

  Electro-optical guided Qaem

Islamic Revolutionary Guard Corps 190,000

Islamic Revolutionary Guard Corps Ground Forces 150,000

Controls Basij paramilitary forces. Lightly staffed in peacetime. Primary role: internal security; secondary role: external defence, in conjunction with regular armed forces

FORCES BY ROLE

COMMAND

  31 provincial corps HQ (2 in Tehran)

SPECIAL FORCES

  3 spec ops div

  1 AB bde

MANOEUVRE

  Armoured

  2 armd div

  3 armd bde

  Light

  8+ inf div

  5+ inf bde

EQUIPMENT BY TYPE

UNINHABITED AERIAL VEHICLES

  CISR • **Medium** Mohajer 6

  ISR • **Light** Meraj 313

LOITERING & DIRECT ATTACK MUNITIONS

  Meraj 532

Islamic Revolutionary Guard Corps Naval Forces 20,000+ (incl 5,000 Marines)

FORCES BY ROLE

COMBAT SUPPORT

  Some arty bty

  Some AShM bty with HY-2 (CH-SSC-3 Seersucker) AShM

EQUIPMENT BY TYPE

In addition to the vessels listed, the IRGC operates a substantial number of patrol boats with a full-load displacement below 10 tonnes, including Boghammar-class vessels and small Bavar-class wing-in-ground effect air vehicles

PATROL AND COASTAL COMBATANTS 129
  PCGM 1 *Shahid Soleimani* with 2 twin lnchr with *Ghader* AShM, 2 single lnchr with C-704 (*Nasr*) AShM, 2 3-cell VLS & 4 single cell VLS (likely fitted with SAM), 1 hel landing platform
  PBFG 56:
    5 C14 with 2 twin lnchr with C-701 (*Kosar*)/C-704 (*Nasr*) AShM
    10 Mk13 with 2 single lnchr with C-704 (*Nasr*) AShM, 2 single 324mm TT
    10 *Thondor* (PRC *Houdong*) with 2 twin lnchr with C-802A (*Ghader*) AShM, 2 AK230 CIWS
    25 *Peykaap* II (IPS-16 mod) with 2 single lnchr with C-701 (*Kosar*) AShM/C-704 (*Nasr*), 2 single 324mm TT
    6 *Zolfaghar* (*Peykaap* III/IPS-16 mod) with 2 single lnchr with C-701 (*Kosar*)/C-704 (*Nasr*) AShM
  PBG 1 *Shahid Rouhi* with 2 twin lnchr with C-704 (*Nasr*) AShM
  PBFT 15 *Peykaap* I (IPS -16) with 2 single 324mm TT
  PBF 35: 15 *Kashdom* II; 10 *Tir* (IPS-18); ε10 *Pashe* (MIG-G-1900)
  PB 21: ε20 *Ghaem*; 1 *Shahid Nazeri*

AMPHIBIOUS
  LANDING SHIPS • LST 3 *Hormuz* 24 (*Hejaz* design for commercial use)
  LANDING CRAFT • LCT 2 *Hormuz* 21 (minelaying capacity)

LOGISTICS AND SUPPORT 5
  AP 3 *Naser*
  ESB 2: 1 *Shahid Mahdavi* (multipurpose helicopter and UAV carrier) with 2 twin lnchr with C-802A (*Ghader*) AShM; 1 *Shahid Roudaki* with 4 twin lnchr with C-802A (*Ghader*) AShM

UNINHABITED MARITIME PLATFORMS
  UUV • ATK Some

COASTAL DEFENCE • AShM C-701 (*Kosar*); C-704 (*Nasr*); C-802 (*Noor*); HY-2 (CH-SSC-3 *Seersucker*)

HELICOPTERS
  MRH 5 Mi-171 *Hip*
  TPT • Light some Bell 206 (AB-206) *Jet Ranger*

UNINHABITED AERIAL VEHICLES
  CISR • Medium *Ababil* 3; *Mohajer* 6
  ISR • Medium *Ababil* 2; *Mohajer* 4; **Light** *Yasir*

LOITERING & DIRECT ATTACK MUNITIONS
  Ababil T; *Shahed* 131; *Shahed* 136

AIR-LAUNCHED MISSILES
  AShM CM-35A *Nasr* (C-704)

BOMBS
  Laser-guided *Qaem*
  Electro-optical guided *Qaem*

Islamic Revolutionary Guard Corps Marines 5,000+

FORCES BY ROLE
MANOEUVRE
  Amphibious
    1 mne bde

Islamic Revolutionary Guard Corps Aerospace Force 15,000

Controls Iran's strategic-missile force

FORCES BY ROLE
FIGHTER/GROUND ATTACK
  1 sqn with Su-22M4 *Fitter K*; Su-22UM-3K *Fitter G*
TRAINING
  1 sqn with EMB-312 *Tucano**

EQUIPMENT BY TYPE
SURFACE-TO-SURFACE MISSILE LAUNCHERS
  MRBM • Conventional up to 50: *Emad*-1 (*Shahab*-3 mod); *Ghadr*-1/-2 (*Shahab*-3 mod); *Sajjil*-2; *Shahab*-3 (IR-SS-7) (mobile & silo); *Khorramshahr* (in devt)
  SRBM • Conventional up to 100: *Fateh*-110; *Fateh*-313; *Khalij Fars* (*Fateh*-110 mod ASBM); *Qiam*-1/-1 mod; *Shahab*-1/-2 (*Scud* variants; service status uncertain); *Zelzal*; *Zolfaghar* (IR-SS-1)
  GLCM • Conventional some *Ya'ali* (*Quds*-1); *Quds*-2; *Quds*-3

SATELLITES See Space
AIRCRAFT 23 combat capable
  FGA 8: up to 7 Su-22M4 *Fitter K*; 1+ Su-22UM-3K *Fitter G*
  TRG 15 EMB-312 *Tucano**

UNINHABITED AERIAL VEHICLES
  CISR • Heavy *Shahed* 129; **Medium** *Ababil* 3; *Shahed* 133; *Shahed* 141; *Shahed* 181; *Shahed* 191
  ISR • Medium *Shahed* 123

LOITERING & DIRECT ATTACK MUNITIONS
  Shahed 131; *Shahed* 136

AIR DEFENCE
  SAM
    Medium-range *Ra'ad*/3rd *Khordad*; *Talash*/15th *Khordad*
    Point-defence *Misaq* 1 (QW-1); *Misaq* 2 (QW-18)

AIR-LAUNCHED MISSILES
  ASM *Almas* (reported); *Qaem* 114 (reported)

BOMBS
  Laser-guided *Sadid*
  Electro-optical guided *Sadid*

Islamic Revolutionary Quds Force 5,000

Navy 18,000

HQ at Bandar Abbas

EQUIPMENT BY TYPE

In addition to the vessels listed, the Iranian Navy operates a substantial number of patrol boats with a full-load displacement below 10 tonnes

SUBMARINES • TACTICAL 19
  SSK 1 *Taregh* (RUS *Paltus* (Project 877EKM (*Kilo*))) (2

more non-operational) with 6 single 533mm TT
SSC 1 *Fateh* with 4 single 533mm TT with C-704 (*Nasr*-1) AShM/*Valfajr* HWT
SSW 17: 16+ *Ghadir* (*Yono*) with 2 single 533mm TT with *Jask*-2 (C-704 (*Nasr*)) AShM/*Valfajr* HWT (additional vessels in build); 1 *Nahang*

PATROL AND COASTAL COMBATANTS 70
  CORVETTES 9
    FSGM 4 *Jamaran* (UK Vosper Mk 5 derivative) with 2 twin lnchr with C-802 (*Noor*) (CH-SS-N-6) AShM, 2 single lnchr with SM-1 SAM, 2 triple 324mm SVTT Mk 32 ASTT, 1 76mm gun, 1 hel landing platform
    FSG 5:
      2 *Alvand* (UK Vosper Mk 5) with 2 twin lnchr with C-802 (CH-SS-N-6) AShM, 2 triple 324mm SVTT Mk 32 ASTT, 1 114mm gun
      1 *Alvand* (UK Vosper Mk 5) with 2 twin lnchr with C-802 (CH-SS-N-6) AShM, 2 triple 324mm SVTT Mk 32 ASTT, 1 AK630M CIWS, 1 114mm gun
      1 *Bayandor* (US PF-103) (1 other non operational) with 2 twin lnchr with C-802 (CH-SS-N-6) AShM, 2 triple 324mm SVTT Mk 32 ASTT, 1 76mm gun
      1 *Hamzah* with 2 single lnchr with C-802 (*Noor*) (CH-SS-N-6) AShM
  PCFG 15: up to 10 *Kaman* (FRA *Combattante* II) with 1 twin lnchr with C-802 (*Noor*) (CH-SS-N-6) AShM, 1 76mm gun; 5+ Sina with 1 twin lnchr with C-802 (*Noor*) (CH-SS-N-6) AShM, 1 76mm gun
  PBG 9:
    3 *Hendijan* with 2 twin lnchr with C-802 (*Noor*) (CH-SS-N-6) AShM
    3 *Kayvan* with 2 single lnchr with C-704 (*Nasr*) AShM
    3 *Parvin* with 2 single lnchr with C-704 (*Nasr*) AShM
  PBFT 3 *Kajami* (semi-submersible) with 2 324mm TT
  PBF 1 MIL55
  PB 33: 9 C14; 8 *Hendijan*; 6 MkII; 10 MkIII
MINE WARFARE • MINE COUNTERMEASURES •
  MCC 1 *Shahin*
AMPHIBIOUS
  LANDING SHIPS 12
    LST 3 *Hengam* with 1 hel landing platform (capacity 9 tanks; 225 troops)
    LSM 3 *Farsi* (ROK) (capacity 9 tanks; 140 troops)
    LSL 6 *Fouque*
  LANDING CRAFT 11
    LCT 2
    LCU 1 *Liyan* 110
    UCAC 8: 2 *Wellington* Mk 4; 4 *Wellington* Mk 5; 2 *Tondar* (UK *Winchester*)
LOGISTICS AND SUPPORT 17
  AE 2 *Delvar*
  AFD 2 *Dolphin*
  AKL 3 *Delvar*
  ESB 1 *Makran*
  AO 2 *Bandar Abbas*

AWT 5: 4 *Kangan*; 1 *Delvar*
AXL 2 *Kialas*
COASTAL DEFENCE • AShM C-701 (*Kosar*); C-704 (*Nasr*); C-802 (*Noor*); C-802A (*Ghader*); *Ra'ad* (reported)

Marines 2,600
FORCES BY ROLE
MANOEUVRE
  Amphibious
    2 mne bde

Naval Aviation 2,600
EQUIPMENT BY TYPE
AIRCRAFT
  TPT 16: **Light** 13: 5 Do-228; 4 F-27 *Friendship*; 4 Turbo Commander 680; **PAX** 3 *Falcon* 20 (ELINT)
HELICOPTERS
  ASW ε10 SH-3D *Sea King*
  MCM 3 RH-53D *Sea Stallion*
  TPT • Light 17: 5 Bell 205A (AB-205A); 2 Bell 206 *Jet Ranger* (AB-206); 10 Bell 212 (AB-212)
UNINHABITED AERIAL VEHICLES
  CISR • Heavy *Shahed* 129
BOMBS
  Laser-guided *Sadid*
  Electro-optical guided *Sadid*

Air Force 37,000
FORCES BY ROLE
Includes IRGC AF equipment
FIGHTER
  1 sqn with F-7M *Airguard*; JJ-7*
  2 sqn with F-14 *Tomcat*
  2 sqn with MiG-29A/UB *Fulcrum*
FIGHTER/GROUND ATTACK
  1 sqn with *Mirage* F-1B/E
  1 sqn with F-5E/F *Tiger* II
  5 sqn with F-4D/E *Phantom* II
  3 sqn with F-5E/F *Tiger* II
GROUND ATTACK
  1 sqn with Su-24MK *Fencer* D
MARITIME PATROL
  1 sqn with P-3F *Orion*
ISR
  1 (det) sqn with RF-4E *Phantom* II*
SEARCH & RESCUE
  Some flt with Bell 214C (AB-214C)
TANKER/TRANSPORT
  1 sqn with B-707; B-747; B-747F
TRANSPORT
  1 sqn with B-707; *Falcon* 50; L-1329 *Jetstar*; Bell 412
  2 sqn with C-130E/H *Hercules*
  1 sqn with F-27 *Friendship*; *Falcon* 20

1 sqn with Il-76 *Candid*; An-140 (Iran-140 *Faraz*)

TRAINING
1 sqn with Beech F33A/C *Bonanza*
1 sqn with F-5B *Freedom Fighter*
1 sqn with PC-6
1 sqn with PC-7 *Turbo Trainer*
Some units with MFI-17 *Mushshak*; TB-21 *Trinidad*; TB-200 *Tobago*

TRANSPORT HELICOPTER
1 sqn with CH-47 *Chinook*
Some units with Bell 206A *Jet Ranger* (AB-206A); *Shabaviz* 2-75; *Shabaviz* 2061

EQUIPMENT BY TYPE
AIRCRAFT 265 combat capable
  FTR 138: 15 F-5B *Freedom Fighter*; 54 F-5E/F *Tiger* II; 18 F-7M *Airguard*; ε10 F-14 *Tomcat*; 35 MiG-29A/UB *Fulcrum*; up to 6 *Azarakhsh* (reported)
  FGA 73: 55 F-4D/E *Phantom* II; 2 *Mirage* F-1BQ; 10 *Mirage* F-1EQ; up to 6 *Saegheh* (reported)
  ATK 29 Su-24MK *Fencer* D
  ASW 3 P-3F *Orion*
  ISR: 6+ RF-4E *Phantom* II*
  TKR/TPT 4: 2 B-707; ε2 B-747
  TPT 116: **Heavy** 12 Il-76 *Candid*; **Medium** ε19 C-130E/H *Hercules*; **Light** 75: 11 An-74TK-200; 5 An-140 (Iran-140 *Faraz*); 10 F-27 *Friendship*; 1 L-1329 *Jetstar*; 10 PC-6B *Turbo Porter*; 8 TB-21 *Trinidad*; 4 TB-200 *Tobago*; 3 *Turbo Commander* 680; 14 Y-7; 9 Y-12; **PAX** 10: ε1 B-707; 1 B-747; 4 B-747F; 1 *Falcon* 20; 3 *Falcon* 50
  TRG 128: 25 Beech F33A/C *Bonanza*; 14 JJ-7*; 25 MFI-17 *Mushshak*; 12 *Parastu*; 15 PC-6; 35 PC-7 *Turbo Trainer*; 2 Yak-130 *Mitten**

HELICOPTERS
  MRH 2 Bell 412
  TPT 34+: **Heavy** 2+ CH-47 *Chinook*; **Medium** 30 Bell 214C (AB-214C); **Light** 2+: 2 Bell 206A *Jet Ranger* (AB-206A); some *Shabaviz* 2-75 (indigenous versions in production); some *Shabaviz* 2061

UNINHABITED AERIAL VEHICLES
  CISR • **Heavy** *Kaman* 22 (reported); **Medium** *Ababil* 4/5; *Kaman* 12; *Kaman* 22 (reported); *Mohajer* 6

AIR-LAUNCHED MISSILES
  AAM • **IR** PL-2A‡; PL-7; R-60 (RS-AA-8 *Aphid*); R-27T (RS-AA-10B *Alamo*) (reported); R-73 (RS-AA-11A *Archer*); AIM-9J *Sidewinder*; **SARH** AIM-7E-2 *Sparrow*; R-27R (RS-AA-10A *Alamo*); **ARH** AIM-54 *Phoenix*†
  ASM AGM-65A *Maverick*; Kh-25 (RS-AS-10 *Karen*); Kh-25ML (RS-AS-10 *Karen*); Kh-29L/T (RS-AS-14A/B *Kedge*)
  AShM C-801K; CM-35A *Nasr* (C-704); CM-200A *Ghader* (C-802A)
  ARM Kh-58 (RS-AS-11 *Kilter*)
  LACM *Asef*

BOMBS
  Electro-optical guided GBU-87/B *Qassed*

Air Defence Force 15,000

FORCES BY ROLE
AIR DEFENCE
  16 bn with MIM-23B I-*Hawk/Shahin*
  4 bn with S-300PMU2 (RS-SA-20 *Gargoyle*)
  5 sqn with FM-80 (CH-SA-4); *Rapier*; HQ-2 (CH-SA-1); S-200 *Angara* (RS-SA-5 *Gammon*); 9K331 *Tor*-M1 (RS-SA-15 *Gauntlet*)

EQUIPMENT BY TYPE
AIR DEFENCE
  SAM 410
    Long-range 42+: 10 S-200 *Angara* (RS-SA-5 *Gammon*); 32 S-300PMU2 (RS-SA-20 *Gargoyle*); *Bavar*-373
    Medium-range 59+: ε50 MIM-23B I-*Hawk/Shahin*; 9 HQ-2 (CH-SA-1); *Talash*/15th *Khordad*
    Short-range 279: 250 FM-80 (CH-SA-4); 29 9K331 *Tor*-M1 (RS-SA-15 *Gauntlet*)
    Point-defence 30+: 30 *Rapier*; *Misaq* 1 (QW-1); *Misaq* 2 (QW-18)
  GUNS • **TOWED 23mm** ZU-23-2; **35mm** GDF-002

Gendarmerie & Paramilitary 40,000–60,000

Law-Enforcement Forces 40,000–60,000 (border and security troops); 450,000 on mobilisation (incl conscripts)

Part of armed forces in wartime
EQUIPMENT BY TYPE
PATROL AND COASTAL COMBATANTS • **PB** ε90
AIRCRAFT • **TPT** • **Light** 2+: 2 An-140; some Cessna 185/Cessna 310
HELICOPTERS • **TPT** • **Light** ε24 AB-205 (Bell 205)/AB-206 (Bell 206) *Jet Ranger*

Basij Resistance Force ε600,000 on mobilisation

Paramilitary militia with claimed membership of 12.6 million; ε600,000 combat capable

DEPLOYMENT

SYRIA: 1,500

Iraq IRQ

Iraqi Dinar IQD		2022	2023	2024
GDP	IQD	379trn	336trn	353trn
	USD	261bn	255bn	271bn
per capita	USD	6,181	5,883	6,104
Growth	%	7.0	-2.7	2.9
Inflation	%	5.0	5.3	3.6
Def bdgt [a]	IQD	ε10.1trn	13.5trn	
	USD	ε7.00bn	10.3bn	
FMA (US)	USD	250m	100m	75.5m
USD1=IQD		1,450.00	1,316.03	1,300.00

[a] Excludes MInistry of the Interior and National Security Council budget

Real-terms defence budget trend (USDbn, constant 2015)

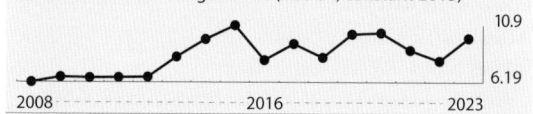

Population	41,266,109				
Age	0–14	15–19	20–24	25–29	30–64	65 plus
Male	18.0%	5.4%	4.8%	4.1%	16.5%	1.6%
Female	17.2%	5.2%	4.6%	4.0%	16.6%	2.0%

Capabilities

Iraq's armed forces have had success battling ISIS, though the threat has not been eliminated. Iraq is also dealing with pressure from Iran and Turkiye, who oppose different Kurdish groups in the country – Ankara has repeatedly struck targets in Northern Iraq as it battles the Kurdistan Workers Party (PKK). Baghdad has relied on a relatively small number of formations for offensive operations, particularly the well-regarded Counter-Terrorism Service (CTS). But that force has suffered disproportionately high levels of attrition, endured a lack of recruitment and its 'CTS 2030 Vision' lacks procurement funding. Questions remain whether Baghdad can sustain such operations, particularly absent outside support. The country has been modernising its armed forces to become more self-sufficient. Iraq is trying to boost the size of the Popular Mobilization Forces, a grouping of 50-odd factions, including some with links to Iran. Meanwhile, the relationship between the official government forces, Kurdish Peshmerga forces and the Popular Mobilisation Units militias remains in flux, with little progress in unifying their efforts. The US provides training and ISR support to Iraqi forces. Political pressure from nationalist and Iran-aligned political parties and continuing attacks on US forces by Iranian-supported militia units have strained this relationship in recent years. The US-led combat mission designed to help Iraqi forces tackle ISIS ended in December 2021, with troops under Combined Joint Task Force – Inherent Resolve moving to an 'advise, assist and enable' role. The NATO Mission Iraq is focused on training and capacity building. The armed forces' inventory comprises a mix of Soviet-era, Russian, and newer European- and US-sourced platforms, but significant shortcomings exist in logistics support. Iraq largely relies on its fleet of F-16s and AC-208 armed ISR aircraft to conduct air strikes. In 2023, it reopened its air force college at a refurbished base southeast of Baghdad. Iraq's defence industry has only limited capacity, focusing on the manufacture of light weapons and ammunition, as well as equipment maintenance.

ACTIVE 193,000 (Army 180,000 Navy 3,000 Air 5,000 Air Defence 5,000) Gendarmerie & Paramilitary 266,000

ORGANISATIONS BY SERVICE

Army ε180,000

Includes Counter-Terrorism Service

FORCES BY ROLE

SPECIAL FORCES
3 SF bde
1 ranger bde (3 ranger bn)

MANOEUVRE

Armoured
1 (9th) armd div (2 armd bde, 2 mech bde, 1 engr bn, 1 sigs regt, 1 log bde)

Mechanised
3 (5th, 8th & 10th) mech div (4 mech inf bde, 1 engr bn, 1 sigs regt, 1 log bde)
1 (7th) mech div (2 mech inf bde, 1 inf bde, 1 engr bn, 1 sigs regt, 1 log bde)

Light
1 (6th) mot div (3 mot inf bde, 1 inf bde, 1 engr bn, 1 sigs regt, 1 log bde)
1 (14th) mot div (2 mot inf bde, 3 inf bde, 1 engr bn, 1 sigs regt, 1 log bde)
1 (1st) inf div (2 inf bde)
1 (11th) inf div (3 lt inf bde, 1 engr bn, 1 sigs regt, 1 log bde)
1 (15th) inf div (5 inf bde)
1 (16th) inf div (2 inf bde)
1 (17th Cdo) inf div (4 inf bde, 1 engr bn, 1 sigs regt, 1 log bde)
1 inf bde

Other
1 (PM SF) sy div (3 inf bde)

HELICOPTER
1 atk hel sqn with Mi-28NE *Havoc*
1 atk hel sqn with Mi-35M *Hind*
1 sqn with Bell 205 (UH-1H *Huey* II)
3 atk hel sqn with Bell T407; H135M
3 sqn with Mi-17 *Hip* H; Mi-171Sh
1 ISR sqn with SA342M *Gazelle*
2 trg sqn with Bell 206; OH-58C *Kiowa*
1 trg sqn with Bell 205 (UH-1H *Huey* II)
1 trg sqn with Mi-17 *Hip*

EQUIPMENT BY TYPE

ARMOURED FIGHTING VEHICLES
MBT 401+: ε100 M1A1 *Abrams*; 178+ T-72M/M1; ε50 T-55; 73 T-90S
RECCE 53: 18 BRDM 2; 35 EE-9 *Cascavel*;
IFV 650: ε400 BMP-1; ε90 BMP-3M; ε60 BTR-4 (inc variants); 100 BTR-80A
APC 1,592+
  APC (T) 900: ε500 M113A2/*Talha*; ε400 MT-LB

PPV 692+: 12 *Barracuda*; 250 *Caiman*; *Gorets*-M; ε400 ILAV *Badger*; *Mamba*; 30 *Maxxpro*

AUV 420+: ε400 *Akrep*; 20 *Commando*; M-ATV

ENGINEERING & MAINTENANCE VEHICLES
ARV 222+: 180 BREM; 35+ M88A1/2; 7 *Maxxpro* ARV; T-54/55 ARV; Type-653; VT-55A

NBC VEHICLES 20 *Fuchs* NBC

ANTI-TANK/ANTI-INFRASTRUCTURE
MSL • MANPATS 9K135 *Kornet* (RS-AT-14 *Spriggan*) (reported)

ARTILLERY 1,064+
SP 48+: **152mm** 18+ Type-83; **155mm** 30: 6 M109A1; 24 M109A5
TOWED 60+: **130mm** M-46/Type-59; **152mm** D-20; Type-83; **155mm** ε60 M198
MRL 6+: **122mm** some BM-21 *Grad*; **220mm** 6+ TOS-1A
MOR 950+: **81mm** ε500 M252; **120mm** ε450 M120;

HELICOPTERS
ATK 6 Mi-35M *Hind*; (11 Mi-28NE *Havoc*; 4 Mi-28UB *Havoc*; 15 Mi-35M *Hind* all non-operational)
MRH 51+: 4+ SA342 *Gazelle*; 17 Bell IA407; 23 H135M; 7 Mi-17 *Hip* H/Mi-171Sh (38 more non-operational)
ISR 10 OH-58C *Kiowa*
TPT • Light 44: 16 Bell 205 (UH-1H *Huey* II); 10 Bell 206B3 *Jet Ranger*; ε18 Bell T407

UNINHABITED AERIAL VEHICLES
CISR • Heavy 12 CH-4

AIR-LAUNCHED MISSILES • ASM 9K114 *Shturm* (RS-AT-6 *Spiral*); AGR-20A APKWS; AR-1; *Ingwe*

BOMBS
INS/GPS-guided FT-9

Navy 3,000
EQUIPMENT BY TYPE
PATROL AND COASTAL COMBATANTS 33
PCF 1 *Musa ibn Nusayr* (ITA *Assad*) with 1 76mm gun
PCO 2 *Al Basra* (US *River Hawk*)
PCC 4 *Fateh* (ITA *Diciotti*)
PB 20: 12 Swiftships 35; 5 *Predator* (PRC 27m); 3 *Al Faw*
PBR 6: 2 Type-200; 4 Type-2010

Marines 1,000
FORCES BY ROLE
MANOEUVRE
Amphibious
2 mne bn

Air Force ε5,000
FORCES BY ROLE
FIGHTER/GROUND ATTACK
2 sqn with F-16C/D *Fighting Falcon*
GROUND ATTACK
1 sqn with Su-25/Su-25K/Su-25UB *Frogfoot*
1 sqn with L-159A; L-159T1
ISR
1 sqn with CH-2000 *Sama*; SB7L-360 *Seeker*
1 sqn with Cessna 208B *Grand Caravan*; Cessna AC-208B *Combat Caravan**
1 sqn with Beech 350 *King Air*
TRANSPORT
1 sqn with An-32B *Cline*
1 sqn with C-130E/J-30 *Hercules*
TRAINING
1 sqn with Cessna 172, Cessna 208B
1 sqn with *Lasta*-95
1 sqn with T-6A
1 sqn with T-50IQ *Golden Eagle**
1 sqn (forming) with *Super Mushshak*

EQUIPMENT BY TYPE
AIRCRAFT 88 combat capable
FGA 32 F-16C/D *Fighting Falcon*
ATK 30: 10 L-159A; 1 L-159T1; ε19 Su-25/Su-25K/Su-25UBK *Frogfoot*†
ISR 10: 2 Cessna AC-208B *Combat Caravan**; 2 SB7L-360 *Seeker*; 6 Beech 350ER *King Air*
TPT 27: **Medium** 12: 6 C-130J-30 *Hercules*; 6 An-32B *Cline* (of which 2 combat capable); (3 C-130E *Hercules* in store); **Light** 15: 1 Beech 350 *King Air*; 5 Cessna 208B *Grand Caravan*; 9 Cessna 172
TRG 58+: 8 CH-2000 *Sama*; 10+ *Lasta*-95; 2 *Super Mushshak*; 14 T-6A *Texan* II; 24 T-50IQ *Golden Eagle**

AIR-LAUNCHED MISSILES
AAM • IR AIM-9L/M *Sidewinder*; **SARH** AIM-7M *Sparrow*
ASM AGM-114 *Hellfire*
BOMBS
Laser-guided GBU-10 *Paveway* II; GBU-12 *Paveway* II

Air Defence Command ε5,000
FORCES BY ROLE
AIR DEFENCE
1 SAM bn with 96K6 *Pantsir*-S1 (RS-SA-22 *Greyhound*)
1 SAM bn with M1097 *Avenger*
1 SAM bn with 9K338 *Igla*-S (RS-SA-24 *Grinch*)
1 ADA bn with ZU-23-2; S-60

EQUIPMENT BY TYPE
AIR DEFENCE
SAM
Point-defence M1097 *Avenger*; 9K338 *Igla*-S (RS-SA-24 *Grinch*)
SPAAGM 30mm 24 96K6 *Pantsir*-S1 (RS-SA-22 *Greyhound*)
GUNS • TOWED 23mm ZU-23-2; **57mm** S-60

Gendarmerie & Paramilitary ε266,000

Iraqi Federal Police ε36,000

Territorial Interdiction Force ε50,000

FORCES BY ROLE

MANOEUVRE

Other
4 sy bde
11 sy bde (forming)

Popular Mobilisation Forces ε180,000

Includes Badr Organisation; Kataib Hizbullah; Kataib Imam Ali; Kataib Sayyid al-Shuhada

EQUIPMENT BY TYPE

ARMOURED FIGHTING VEHICLES
MBT T-55; T-72B; T-72 *Rakhsh*
IFV BMP-1 mod (23mm gun); BMP-2
APC • PPV *Toophan*

ANTI-TANK/ANTI-INFRASTRUCTURE
MANPATS Dehlavieh (*Kornet*); *Toophan*

ARTILLERY
TOWED • **130mm** M-46; **152mm** D-20
MRL • **122mm** HM-20

UNINHABITED AERIAL VEHICLES
CISR • **Medium** *Mohajer 6*

LOITERING & DIRECT ATTACK MUNITIONS
Ababil T; *Shahed* 101; *Shahed* 131

AIR DEFENCE
SAM • **Short-range** *Saqr*-1 (358) (reported)
GUNS • **SP 23mm** BMP-1 mod (ZU-23-2 on BMP-1 chassis)

FOREIGN FORCES

Albania NATO Mission Iraq 1
Australia Operation Inherent Resolve (*Okra*) 110 • NATO Mission Iraq 2
Bulgaria NATO Mission Iraq 2
Canada NATO Mission Iraq 16
Croatia Operation Inherent Resolve 2 • NATO Mission Iraq 10
Czech Republic Operation Inherent Resolve 60
Denmark Operation Inherent Resolve 39 • NATO Mission Iraq 125
Estonia Operation Inherent Resolve 88 • NATO Mission Iraq 1
Fiji UNAMI 156; 2 sy unit
Finland Operation Inherent Resolve 75; 1 trg unit • NATO Mission Iraq 5
France Operation Inherent Resolve 6 • NATO Mission Iraq 3
Germany Operation Inherent Resolve 100 • NATO Mission Iraq 30
Greece NATO Mission Iraq 2
Hungary Operation Inherent Resolve 133 • NATO Mission Iraq 3
Italy Operation Inherent Resolve (*Prima Parthica*) 900; 1 inf regt; 1 trg unit; 1 hel sqn with 4 NH90 • NATO Mission Iraq 60
Latvia Operation Inherent Resolve 1 • NATO Mission Iraq 2
Lithuania NATO Mission Iraq 30
Macedonia, North NATO Mission Iraq 4
Montenegro NATO Mission Iraq 1
Nepal UNAMI 87; 1 sy unit
Netherlands Operation Inherent Resolve 4 • NATO Mission Iraq 2
Norway Operation Inherent Resolve 30; 1 trg unit • NATO Mission Iraq 2
Poland Operation Inherent Resolve 208 • NATO Mission Iraq 51
Portugal NATO Mission Iraq 1
Romania Operation Inherent Resolve 30 • NATO Mission Iraq 5
Slovakia Operation Inherent Resolve 1 • NATO Mission Iraq 7
Slovenia Operation Inherent Resolve 3
Spain Operation Inherent Resolve 170; 1 trg units; 1 hel unit • NATO Mission Iraq 120
Sweden Operation Inherent Resolve 2 • NATO Mission Iraq 1
Turkiye Army 4,000 • NATO Mission Iraq 86
United Kingdom Operation Inherent Resolve (*Shader*) 100 • NATO Mission Iraq 12
United States Operation Inherent Resolve 2,000; 1 inf bde(-); 1 atk hel bn with AH-64E *Apache*; MQ-1C Gray Eagle; 1 spec ops hel bn with MH-47G Chinook; MH-60M *Black Hawk*; 1 CISR UAV sqn with MQ-9A *Reaper*; 2 SAM bty with M902/M903 *Patriot* PAC-3/PAC-3 MSE; • NATO Mission Iraq 12

Israel ISR

New Israeli Shekel ILS		2022	2023	2024
GDP	ILS	1.76trn	1.91trn	2.03trn
	USD	525bn	522bn	540bn
per capita	USD	54,337	53,196	54,059
Growth	%	6.5	3.1	3.0
Inflation	%	4.4	4.3	3.0
Def bdgt	ILS	63.9bn	70.1bn	
	USD	19.0bn	19.2bn	
FMA (US)	USD	3.30bn	3.30bn	3.30bn
USD1=ILS		3.36	3.66	3.76

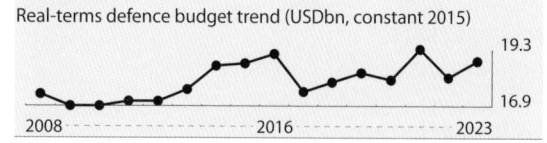

Real-terms defence budget trend (USDbn, constant 2015): 19.3 / 16.9; 2008 – 2016 – 2023

Population   9,256,230

Age	0–14	15–19	20–24	25–29	30–64	65 plus
Male	14.1%	4.1%	3.8%	3.5%	19.3%	5.5%
Female	13.5%	3.9%	3.7%	3.4%	18.6%	6.6%

Capabilities

The Israel Defense Forces (IDF) are highly trained and organised for territorial defence, short-term interventions in neighbouring states and limited regional power projection. The country is widely believed to possess nuclear weapons. IDF forces were engaged heavily in the wake of Hamas's 7 October 2023 attack on

Israel. The operation to try to eliminate the group and Palestinian Islamic Jihad in Gaza involved the largest mobilisation of reserves since 1973. The military also battled with Iran-backed Hizbullah in Lebanon and struck targets in Syria. The IDF adopted a new five-year Tnufa (Momentum) defence programme in 2020 to improve areas of relative superiority, such as technology and intelligence, to ensure swifter and more decisive operations against future threats. Funding problems, however, have limited its implementation. The US remains Israel's vital defence partner. Washington provides significant funding and is instrumental in several of the IDF's equipment programmes. Israel's gradual normalisation of ties with several Arab states has likely been halted as a result of the IDF's operations in Gaza. The IDF has high training standards despite its reliance on national service. Given its mission-set, the IDF's logistics capabilities are likely limited to sustaining operations within Israel itself or in immediately neighbouring territories. The largely asymmetric nature of the threats the IDF has faced in recent years has focused modernisation efforts on force-protection, missile defence and precision-strike capabilities. Israel maintains a broad defence-industrial base, with world-class capabilities in uninhabited systems, guided-weapons, radars and sensors, and cyber security, though the country is unable to manufacture military aircraft and large naval vessels which are imported and often adapted locally with Israeli systems.

ACTIVE 169,500 (Army 126,000 Navy 9,500 Air 34,000) **Gendarmerie & Paramilitary 8,000**

Conscript liability Officers 48 months, other ranks 32 months, women 24 months (Jews and Druze only; Christians, Circassians and Muslims may volunteer)

RESERVE 465,000 (Army 400,000 Navy 10,000 Air 55,000)

Annual trg as cbt reservists to age 40 (some specialists to age 54) for male other ranks, 38 (or marriage/pregnancy) for women

ORGANISATIONS BY SERVICE

Strategic Forces

Israel is widely believed to have a nuclear capability – delivery means include F-15I and F-16I ac, *Jericho* 2 IRBM and, reportedly, *Dolphin/Tanin*-class SSKs with LACM

FORCES BY ROLE
SURFACE-TO-SURFACE MISSILE
  3 IRBM sqn with *Jericho* 2
EQUIPMENT BY TYPE
SURFACE-TO-SURFACE MISSILE LAUNCHERS
  IRBM • Nuclear: ε24 *Jericho* 2

Strategic Defences

FORCES BY ROLE
AIR DEFENCE
  3 bty with *Arrow* 2/3 ATBM with *Green Pine/Super Green Pine* radar and *Citrus Tree* command post
  10 bty with *Iron Dome* (incl reserve bty)
  4 bty with M901 *Patriot* PAC-2
  2 bty with *David's Sling*

Space

EQUIPMENT BY TYPE
SATELLITES
  ISR 8: 3 *Ofeq*-5, 2 *Ofeq*-11; 3 TecSAR (*Polaris*)

Army 26,000; 100,000 conscript (total 126,000)

Organisation and structure of formations may vary according to op situations. Equipment includes that required for reserve forces on mobilisation

FORCES BY ROLE
COMMAND
  3 (regional comd) corps HQ
  2 armd div HQ
  1 (Multidimensional) div HQ
  5 (territorial) inf div HQ
  1 (home defence) comd HQ
SPECIAL FORCES
  1 SF bn
  1 spec ops bde (3 spec ops unit)
MANOEUVRE
Armoured
  3 armd bde (1 recce coy, 3 armd bn, 1 AT coy, 1 cbt engr bn)
  1 (Multidimensional) armd inf/ISR bn
Mechanised
  3 mech inf bde (3 mech inf bn, 1 cbt spt bn, 1 sigs coy)
  1 mech inf bde (1 recce bn, 4 mech inf bn, 1 cbt spt bn)
  1 indep mech inf bn
Light
  2 indep inf bn
Air Manoeuvre
  1 para bde (3 para bn, 1 cbt spt bn, 1 sigs coy)
Other
  1 armd trg bde (3 armd bn)
  1 (Border Protection) sy bde (5 ISR bn; 5 sy bn)
COMBAT SUPPORT
  2 arty bde
  1 (special) arty bde
  1 engr bde (3 engr bn, 3 EOD coy)
  1 engr bn
  1 CBRN bn
  1 int bde (3 int bn)
  1 int unit
  1 SIGINT unit
  2 MP bn

Reserves 400,000+ on mobilisation

FORCES BY ROLE
COMMAND
  2 armd div HQ
  1 AB div HQ
SPECIAL FORCES
  1 spec ops bde

MANOEUVRE
Armoured
9 armd bde
Mechanised
8 mech inf bde
Light
17 (territorial/regional) inf bde
Air Manoeuvre
4 para bde
Mountain
1 mtn inf bde
1 mtn inf bn
COMBAT SUPPORT
5 arty bde
COMBAT SERVICE SUPPORT
6 log unit
EQUIPMENT BY TYPE
ARMOURED FIGHTING VEHICLES
MBT ε400 *Merkava* MkIV/Mk IV *Barak*; (ε700 *Merkava* MkIII; ε200 *Merkava* MkIV all in store)

APC 790+

APC (T) 790+: ε290 *Namer*; 500 M113A2; *Nagmachon* (Centurion chassis); *Nakpadon* (5,100: ε100 *Achzarit* (modified T-55 chassis); 5,000 M113A1/A2 all in store)

APC (W) some *Eitan*

PPV *Panter*

AUV *Tigris*; *Sand Cat*; *Ze'ev*

ENGINEERING & MAINTENANCE VEHICLES
AEV D9R; *Namera*; *Puma*

ARV *Namer*; M88A1; M113 ARV

VLB *Alligator* MAB; M48/60; MTU

NBC VEHICLES ε8 TPz-1 *Fuchs* NBC

ANTI-TANK/ANTI-INFRASTRUCTURE • MSL
MANPATS IMI MAPATS; *Spike* SR/MR/LR/ER

ARTILLERY 530
SP 250: **155mm** 250 M109A5; (**155mm** 30 M109A2; **175mm** 36 M107; **203mm** 36 M110 all in store)

TOWED (**155mm** 171: 40 M-46 mod; 50 M-68/M-71; 81 M-839P/M-845P all in store)

MRL 30: **227mm** 30 M270 MLRS; **306mm** IMI *Lynx* (**160mm** 50 LAR-160; **227mm** 18 M270 MLRS; **290mm** 20 LAR-290 all in store)

MOR 250: **81mm** 250 (**81mm** 1,100; **120mm** 650; **160mm** 18 Soltam M-66 all in store); **SP 120mm** *Khanit*

UNINHABITED AERIAL VEHICLES
ISR • Light *Skylark* 3

LOITERING & DIRECT ATTACK MUNITIONS
Spike Firefly

AIR DEFENCE
SAM • Point-defence *Machbet*; FIM-92 *Stinger*

Navy 7,000; 2,500 conscript (total 9,500)
EQUIPMENT BY TYPE
SUBMARINES 5
SSK 5:
3 *Dolphin* (GER HDW design) with 6 single 533mm TT with UGM-84C *Harpoon* Block 1B AShM/*SeaHake* (DM2A3) HWT/*SeaHake* mod 4 (DM2A4) HWT/*Kaved* HWT, 4 single 650mm TT with dual-capable LACM (reported)

2 *Tanin* (GER HDW design) (fitted with AIP) with 6 single 533mm TT with UGM-84C *Harpoon* Block 1B AShM/*SeaHake* (DM2A3) HWT/*SeaHake* mod 4 (DM2A4) HWT/*Kaved* HWT, 4 single 650mm TT with dual-capable LACM (reported)

PATROL AND COASTAL COMBATANTS 51
CORVETTES • FSGHM 7:
2 *Eilat* (*Sa'ar* 5) with 2 quad lnchr with RGM-84 *Harpoon* AShM/*Gabriel* V AShM, 4 8-cell VLS with *Barak*-1 SAM (being upgraded to *Barak*-8), 2 triple 324mm TT with Mk 46 LWT, 1 Mk 15 *Phalanx* CIWS (capacity 1 AS565SA *Panther* ASW hel)

1 *Eilat* (*Sa'ar* 5) with 2 quad lnchr with RGM-84 *Harpoon* AShM/*Gabriel* V AShM, 4 8-cell VLS with *Barak*-8 SAM, 2 triple 324mm TT with Mk 46 LWT, 1 Mk 15 *Phalanx* CIWS (capacity 1 AS565SA *Panther* ASW hel)

4 *Magen* (*Sa'ar* 6) with 2 quad lnchr with *Gabriel* V AShM, 2 20-cell VLS with *Tamir* (C-*Dome*) SAM, 4 8-cell VLS with *Barak* LRAD, 2 triple 324mm ASTT with Mk 54 LWT (capacity 1 AS565SA *Panther* ASW hel)

PCGM 8 *Hetz* (*Sa'ar* 4.5) with 2 quad lnchr with RGM-84 *Harpoon* AShM (can also be fitted with up to 6 single lnchr with *Gabriel* II AShM), 2 8-cell VLS with *Barak*-1 SAM, (can be fitted with 2 triple 324mm Mk32 TT with Mk46 LWT), 1 Mk 15 *Phalanx* CWIS, 1 76mm gun

PBF 36: 5 *Shaldag*; 2 *Shaldag* V; 3 *Stingray*; 9 *Super Dvora* Mk I (SSM & TT may be fitted); 4 *Super Dvora* Mk II (SSM & TT may be fitted); 6 *Super Dvora* Mk II-I (SSM & TT may be fitted); 4 *Super Dvora* Mk III (SSM & TT may be fitted); 3 *Super Dvora* Mk III (SSM may be fitted)

AMPHIBIOUS
LANDING SHIP • LSL 1 *Nahshon* (US *Frank Besson* mod) (capacity 24 MBT)

LANDING CRAFT • LCVP 3 *Manta*

LOGISTICS AND SUPPORT
AG 1 *Bat Yam* (ex-GER Type-745)

UNINHABITED MARITIME PLATFORMS
USV • MARSEC • Small 10: 10 *Protector* (9m); *Seagull*; *Silver Marlin*

UUV • MARSEC • Extra-large *Caesaron*

Naval Commandos ε300
FORCES BY ROLE
SPECIAL FORCES
1 cdo unit

Air Force 34,000
Responsible for Air and Space Coordination

FORCES BY ROLE

FIGHTER & FIGHTER/GROUND ATTACK
  1 sqn with F-15A/B/D *Eagle* (*Baz*)
  1 sqn with F-15B/C/D *Eagle* (*Baz*)
  1 sqn with F-15I *Ra'am*
  5 sqn with F-16C/D *Fighting Falcon* (*Barak*)
  4 sqn with F-16I *Fighting Falcon* (*Sufa*)
  2 sqn with F-35I *Adir*

ANTI-SUBMARINE WARFARE
  1 sqn with AS565SA *Panther* (missions flown by IAF but with non-rated aircrew)

ELECTRONIC WARFARE
  1 sqn with Beech A36 *Bonanza* (*Hofit*); Beech 200/200T/200CT *King Air*

AIRBORNE EARLY WARNING & CONTROL
  1 sqn with Gulfstream G550 *Eitam*; Gulfstream G550 *Shavit*

TANKER/TRANSPORT
  1 sqn with C-130E/H *Hercules*; KC-130H *Hercules*
  1 sqn with C-130J-30 *Hercules*
  1 sqn with KC-707

TRAINING
  1 OPFOR sqn with F-16C/D *Fighting Falcon* (*Barak*)
  1 sqn with F-35I *Adir*
  1 sqn with M-346 *Master* (*Lavi*)

ATTACK HELICOPTER
  1 sqn with AH-64A *Apache* (*Peten*)
  1 sqn with AH-64D *Apache* (*Sarat*)

TRANSPORT HELICOPTER
  2 sqn with CH-53D *Sea Stallion*
  2 sqn with S-70A *Black Hawk*; UH-60A *Black Hawk*
  1 medevac unit with CH-53D *Sea Stallion*

UAV
  2 ISR sqn with *Hermes* 450
  1 ISR sqn with *Heron* (*Shoval*); *Heron* TP (*Eitan*)
  1 ISR sqn with *Heron* (*Shoval*) (MP role)
  1 ISR sqn with *Orbiter* 4 (*Nitzotz*)

AIR DEFENCE
  3 bty with *Arrow* 2/3
  10 bty with *Iron Dome*
  4 bty with M901 *Patriot* PAC-2
  2 bty with *David's Sling*

SPECIAL FORCES
  1 SF wg (2 SF unit, 1 CSAR unit, 1 int unit)

SURFACE-TO-SURFACE MISSILE
  3 IRBM sqn with *Jericho* 2

EQUIPMENT BY TYPE
AIRCRAFT 340 combat capable
  FGA 310: 8 F-15A *Eagle* (*Baz*); 6 F-15B *Eagle* (*Baz*); 17 F-15C *Eagle* (*Baz*); 19 F-15D *Eagle* (*Baz*); 25 F-15I *Ra'am*; ε50 F-16C *Fighting Falcon* (*Barak*); 49 F-16D *Fighting Falcon* (*Barak*); 97 F-16I *Fighting Falcon* (*Sufa*); 39 F-35I *Adir*

  ISR 1 Gulfstream G550 *Oron*
  ELINT 3 Gulfstream G550 *Shavit*
  AEW 2 Gulfstream G550 *Eitam*
  TKR/TPT 10: 4 KC-130H *Hercules*; 6 KC-707
  TPT 65: **Medium** 18: 5 C-130E *Hercules*; 6 C-130H *Hercules*; 7 C-130J-30 *Hercules*; **Light** 47: 3 AT-802 *Air Tractor*; 9 Beech 200 *King Air*; 8 Beech 200T *King Air*; 5 Beech 200CT *King Air*; 22 Beech A36 *Bonanza* (*Hofit*)
  TRG 66: 16 Grob G-120; 30 M-346 *Master* (*Lavi*)*; 20 T-6A

HELICOPTERS
  ATK 46: 26 AH-64A *Apache* (*Peten*); 20 AH-64D *Apache* (*Sarat*)
  ASW 7 AS565SA *Panther* (missions flown by IAF but with non-rated aircrew)
  ISR 12 OH-58B *Kiowa*
  TPT 80: **Heavy** 25 CH-53D *Sea Stallion*; **Medium** 49: 39 S-70A *Black Hawk*; 10 UH-60A *Black Hawk*; **Light** 6 Bell 206 *Jet Ranger*

UNINHABITED AERIAL VEHICLES
  ISR 3+: **Heavy** 3+: *Heron* (*Shoval*); 3 *Heron* TP (*Eitan*); RQ-5A *Hunter*; **Medium** *Hermes* 450; *Hermes* 900 (22+ *Searcher* MkII in store); **Light** *Orbiter* 4 (*Nitzotz*); (an unknown number of ISR UAVs are combat capable)

LOITERING & DIRECT ATTACK MUNITIONS
  Harop; *Harpy*

SURFACE-TO-SURFACE MISSILE LAUNCHERS
  IRBM • Nuclear ε24 *Jericho* 2

AIR DEFENCE
  SAM 40+:
    Long-range M901 *Patriot* PAC-2
    Medium-range some *David's Sling*
    Short-range up to 40 *Iron Dome*
    Point-defence *Machbet*
  GUNS • TOWED 20mm M167 *Vulcan*

MISSILE DEFENCE • SAM 24 *Arrow* 2/*Arrow* 3

AIR-LAUNCHED MISSILES
  AAM • IR AIM-9 *Sidewinder*; *Python* 4; **IIR** *Python* 5; **ARH** AIM-120C AMRAAM
  ASM AGM-114 *Hellfire*; AGM-65 *Maverick*; *Delilah* AL; *Popeye* I/II; *Spike* NLOS

BOMBS
  IIR guided *Opher*
  Laser-guided *Griffin*; *Lizard*; *Paveway* II
  INS/GPS-guided GBU-31 JDAM; GBU-39 Small Diameter Bomb (*Barad Had*); *Spice*; *Spice* 2000

Airfield Defence 3,000 active (15,000 reservists)

Gendarmerie & Paramilitary ε8,000

Border Police ε8,000

FOREIGN FORCES

UNTSO unless specified. UNTSO figures represent total numbers for mission

Argentina 4 • UNDOF 1
Australia 11 • UNDOF 1
Austria 6
Belgium 2
Bhutan 4 • UNDOF 3
Canada 6
Chile 3
China 5
Czech Republic UNDOF 4
Denmark 12
Estonia 5
Fiji 1 • UNDOF 147; 1 inf coy
Finland 16
Ghana UNDOF 4
India 3 • UNDOF 222; 1 inf pl; 1 MP pl; 1 log coy(-)
Ireland 13 • UNDOF 135; 1 inf coy
Latvia 1
Nepal 3 • UNDOF 415; 1 mech inf coy; 1 inf coy; 1 log coy(-)
Netherlands 12 • UNDOF 1
New Zealand 8
Norway 14
Poland 4
Russia 4
Serbia 1
Slovakia 2
Slovenia 4
Sweden 6
Switzerland 13
United States 3 • **US Strategic Command**; 100; 1 AN/TPY-2 X-band radar at Mount Keren
Uruguay UNDOF 210; 1 mech inf coy
Zambia 1 • UNDOF 3

Jordan JOR

Jordanian Dinar JOD		2022	2023	2024
GDP	JOD	33.7bn	35.5bn	37.3bn
	USD	47.5bn	50.0bn	52.7bn
per capita	USD	4,613	4,851	5,102
Growth	%	2.5	2.6	2.7
Inflation	%	4.2	2.7	2.6
Def bdgt [a]	JOD	1.37bn	1.31bn	
	USD	1.93bn	1.85bn	
FMA (US)	USD	425m	400m	400m
USD1=JOD		0.71	0.71	0.71

[a] Excludes expenditure on public order and safety

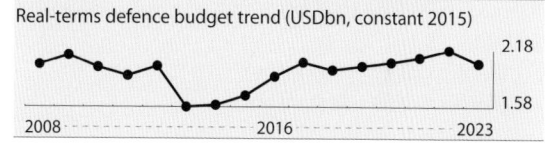

Real-terms defence budget trend (USDbn, constant 2015): 2.18 / 1.58 (2008–2023)

Population	11,086,716				
Age	0–14	15–19	20–24	25–29	30–64	65 plus
Male	16.1%	5.0%	4.9%	4.7%	19.7%	2.0%
Female	15.3%	4.9%	4.5%	4.0%	16.9%	2.1%

Capabilities

The Jordanian Armed Forces are structured to provide border security and an armoured response to conventional threats. They have recently focused on tackling narcotics- and weapons-smuggling from Syria. Amman is trying to restructure, review modernisation requirements and increase efficiency of its forces. The government has issued no recent public statement on defence policy, but regional instability is a prime concern. Jordan is a major non-NATO ally of the US, with a close bilateral defence relationship, including a 2021 defence cooperation agreement. The country has developed a special-forces training centre and has hosted training for numerous state and non-state military forces. Amman, in mid-2021, inaugurated a training centre for female personnel with the aim of boosting the number of women in the armed forces to 3% of the total by the end of 2024. Personnel are relatively well trained, particularly aircrew and special forces, who are highly regarded internationally. Jordanian forces are able to independently deploy regionally and have participated in ISAF operations in Afghanistan and in coalition air operations over Syria and Yemen. Jordan's inventory largely comprises older systems and procurements have typically been in small numbers, second-hand or donations. Although the state-owned Jordan Design and Development Bureau (JODDB, formerly KADDB) has demonstrated the capacity to upgrade vehicles, the army has largely recapitalised its armoured-vehicle fleet with second-hand equipment from European countries. JODDB has produced some light-armoured vehicles for domestic use through agreements with foreign suppliers, but the company currently has little export profile.

ACTIVE 100,500 (Army 86,000 Navy 500 Air 14,000)
Gendarmerie & Paramilitary 15,000

RESERVE 65,000 (Army 60,000 Joint 5,000)

ORGANISATIONS BY SERVICE

Army 86,000
FORCES BY ROLE
SPECIAL FORCES
  1 (Royal Guard) SF gp (1 SF regt, 1 SF bn, 1 CT bn)
  1 spec ops bde (3 spec ops bn)
MANOEUVRE
  Armoured
  1 (40th) armd bde (2 tk bn, 1 armd inf bn)
  1 (60th) armd bde (1 tk bn, 1 lt armd bn, 1 mech inf bn)
  Mechanised
  4 mech bde (1 tk bn, 2 mech inf bn)
  4 mech bde (3 mech inf bn)
  Light
  1 (Border Gd) inf bde (6 inf bn)
  1 (Border Gd) inf bde (4 inf bn)
  1 (Border Gd) inf gp
  Air Manoeuvre
  1 AB bde (3 AB bn)
  Other
  1 (Royal Guard) gd bde
COMBAT SUPPORT
  1 arty bde (5 SP arty bn)
  1 arty bde (4 SP arty bn)
  1 arty bde (2 SP arty bn)
  1 MRL bde (1 fd arty bn, 2 MRL bn, 1 mor bn, 1 STA bn)
  1 AD bde (3 AD bn)
  3 AD bde (2 AD bn)
  1 engr bn
COMBAT SERVICE SUPPORT
  1 log bn
EQUIPMENT BY TYPE
ARMOURED FIGHTING VEHICLES
  MBT 302: ε50 FV4034 *Challenger* 1 (*Al Hussein*); 70 *Leclerc*; 182 M60A3 (ε330 FV4034 *Challenger* 1 (*Al Hussein*) in store)
  ASLT 80 B1 *Centauro* (61 more in store)
  IFV 399: 13 AIFV-B-C25; 50 *Marder* 1A3; 336 YPR-765 PRI
  APC 968+
    APC (T) 729: 370 M113A1/A2 Mk1J; 269 M577A2 (CP); 87 YPR-765 PRCO (CP); 3 AIFV-B
    PPV 239: some *Al-Wahsh*; 45 *Caiman*; 25 *Marauder*; 25 *Matador*; 100 *MaxxPro*; 44 *Nomad/Thunder*
  AUV 35 *Cougar*
ENGINEERING & MAINTENANCE VEHICLES
  ARV 85+: *Al Monjed*; 5 BPz-1; FV4204 *Chieftain* ARV; 32 M88A1; 30 M578; 18 YPR-806
  MW 12 *Aardvark* Mk2
ANTI-TANK/ANTI-INFRASTRUCTURE • MSL
  SP 115: 70 M901; 45 AIFV-B-*Milan*

MANPATS FGM-148 *Javelin*; TOW/TOW-2A; 9K135 *Kornet* (RS-AT-14 *Spriggan*); Luch *Corsar*; *Stugna*-P
ARTILLERY 1,285
  SP 394: **155mm** 358 M109A1/A2; **203mm** 36 M110A2 (112 more in store)
  TOWED 84: **105mm** 66: 54 M102; 12 M119A2; **155mm** 18 M114
  MRL 30: **227mm** 12 M142 HIMARS; **273mm** 18 WM-80
  MOR 777: **81mm** 359; **SP 81mm** 50; **107mm** 50 M30; **120mm** 300 Brandt; **SP 120mm** 18 *Agrab* Mk2
AIR DEFENCE
  SAM • Point-defence 92+: 92 9K35 *Strela*-10 (RS-SA-13 *Gopher*); 9K36 *Strela*-3 (RS-SA-14 *Gremlin*); 9K310 *Igla*-1 (RS-SA-16 *Gimlet*); 9K38 *Igla* (RS-SA-18 *Grouse*); 9K338 *Igla*-S (RS-SA-24 *Grinch*)
  GUNS • SP 108: **23mm** 48 ZSU-23-4 *Shilka*; **35mm** 60 *Gepard*

Navy ε500
EQUIPMENT BY TYPE
PATROL AND COASTAL COMBATANTS 9
  PBF 2 Response Boat-Medium (RB-M)
  PB 7: 4 *Abdullah* (US *Dauntless*); 3 *Al Hussein* (UK Vosper 30m)

Marines
FORCES BY ROLE
MANOEUVRE
  Amphibious
  1 mne unit

Air Force 14,000
FORCES BY ROLE
FIGHTER/GROUND ATTACK
  2 sqn with F-16AM/BM *Fighting Falcon*
ISR
  1 sqn with AT-802U *Air Tractor*
  1 sqn with Cessna 208B
TRANSPORT
  1 sqn with C-130E *Hercules*; Il-76TD *Candid*
TRAINING
  1 OCU with F-16AM/BM *Fighting Falcon*
  1 sqn with PC-21
  1 sqn with Grob 120TP
  1 hel sqn with Bell 505 *Jet Ranger* X; R-44 *Raven* II
ATTACK HELICOPTER
  2 sqn with AH-1F *Cobra* (with TOW)
TRANSPORT HELICOPTER
  1 sqn with AS332M *Super Puma*; UH-60A *Black Hawk*
  1 sqn with UH-60A *Black Hawk*
  1 sqn with UH-60M *Black Hawk*
  1 sqn with Mi-26T2 *Halo*
  1 (Royal) flt with VH-60M *Black Hawk*; AW139
ISR UAV

1 sqn with S-100 *Camcopter*

AIR DEFENCE

2 bde with MIM-23B Phase III *I-Hawk*

EQUIPMENT BY TYPE

AIRCRAFT 57 combat capable

FGA 47: 33 F-16AM *Fighting Falcon*; 14 F-16BM *Fighting Falcon*

ATK (2 AC235 in store, offered for sale)

ISR 10: 6 AT-802 *Air Tractor**; 4 AT-802U *Air Tractor**

TPT 12: **Heavy** 1 Il-76TD *Candid*; **Medium** 3 C-130E *Hercules* (1 C-130B *Hercules*; 4 C-130H *Hercules* in store); **Light** 7: 5 Cessna 208B; 2 M-28 *Skytruck* (2 C295M in store, offered for sale); **PAX** 1 CL-604 *Challenger*

TRG 26: 14 Grob 120TP; 12 PC-21; (12 *Hawk* Mk63* in store, offered for sale)

HELICOPTERS

ATK 12 AH-1F *Cobra* (17 more in store, offered for sale)

MRH 14: 3 AW139; 11 H135M (Tpt/SAR) (6 MD-530F in store, offered for sale)

TPT 54: **Heavy** 4 Mi-26T2 *Halo*; **Medium** 33: 10 AS332M *Super Puma* (being WFU); 8 UH-60A *Black Hawk*; 12 UH-60M *Black Hawk*; 3 VH-60M *Black Hawk*; (5 UH-60L in store, offered for sale); **Light** 17: 5 Bell 505 *Jet Ranger X*; 12 R-44 *Raven* II; (13 Bell 205 (UH-1H *Iroquois*) in store, offered for sale)

UNINHABITED AERIAL VEHICLES

CISR • **Heavy** (some CH-4B in store, offered for sale)

ISR • **Light** S-100 *Camcopter*

AIR DEFENCE

SAM • **Medium-range** 24 MIM-23B Phase III *I-Hawk*

GUNS • **TOWED 40mm** 22 L/70 (with *Flycatcher* radar)

AIR-LAUNCHED MISSILES

AAM • **IR** AIM-9J/N/P *Sidewinder*; **SARH** AIM-7 *Sparrow*; **ARH** AIM-120C AMRAAM

ASM AGM-65D/G *Maverick*; BGM-71 TOW

BOMBS

Laser-guided GBU-10/12 *Paveway* II

Gendarmerie & Paramilitary ε15,000 active

Gendarmerie ε15,000 active

3 regional comd

FORCES BY ROLE

SPECIAL FORCES

2 SF unit

MANOEUVRE

Other

10 sy bn

EQUIPMENT BY TYPE

ARMOURED FIGHTING VEHICLES

APC • **APC (W)** 25+: AT105 *Saxon* (reported); 25+ EE-11 *Urutu*

AUV AB2 *Al-Jawad*

DEPLOYMENT

CENTRAL AFRICAN REPUBLIC: UN • MINUSCA 10

DEMOCRATIC REPUBLIC OF THE CONGO: UN • MONUSCO 11

SOUTH SUDAN: UN • UNMISS 5

FOREIGN FORCES

France *Operation Inherent Resolve* (*Chammal*) 300; 4 *Rafale* F3

Germany *Operation Inherent Resolve* 150; 1 A400M

United States US Central Command: *Operation Inherent Resolve* 3,000; 1 FGA sqn with 18 F-15E *Strike Eagle*; 1 FGA sqn with 12 F-16 *Fighting Falcon*; 1 CISR sqn with 12 MQ-9A *Reaper*; 2 SAM bty with M902/M903 *Patriot* PAC-3/PAC-3 MSE

Kuwait KWT

Kuwaiti Dinar KWD		2022	2023	2024
GDP	KWD	53.7bn	48.9bn	51.2bn
	USD	175bn	160bn	167bn
per capita	USD	36,092	32,215	33,032
Growth	%	8.9	-0.6	3.6
Inflation	%	4.0	3.4	3.1
Def bdgt [a]	KWD	2.39bn	2.38bn	
	USD	7.81bn	7.77bn	
USD1=KWD		0.31	0.31	0.31

[a] Includes National Guard

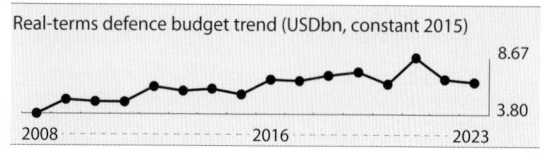

Real-terms defence budget trend (USDbn, constant 2015)

8.67

3.80

2008 — 2016 — 2023

Population	3,103,580					
Age	0–14	15–19	20–24	25–29	30–64	65 plus
Male	12.1%	3.4%	4.8%	7.1%	28.9%	1.5%
Female	11.2%	3.1%	3.7%	4.3%	18.0%	1.9%

Capabilities

Kuwait's armed forces are postured to provide territorial defence through a strategy of holding out against any superior aggressor until allied forces can be mobilised to assist. Kuwait is a member of the GCC, but its key defence relationship is with the US. Washington designated Kuwait a major non-NATO ally in 2004, and a bilateral defence-cooperation agreement provides for a range of joint activities and mentoring, and the stationing and pre-positioning of US personnel and equipment. US force reductions from CENTCOM in 2021 mean that Kuwait's own capabilities will be more critical to its security, as well as those of GCC allies. Kuwait has little expeditionary sustainment capacity, although it made a small air contribution to the Saudi-led coalition at the beginning of the Yemen conflict. It uses its transport aircraft fleet for humanitarian missions. Improvements in air- and missile-defence continue to be a priority given the country's proximity to Iran. Kuwait has been modernising its land forces armour component and has fielded Eurofighter *Typhoon* fighters to refresh its air combat arm. The country has also signed a major contract with Turkiye for the acquisition of its armed UAVs. Kuwait has some local maintenance capacity bolstered by contractor support. Kuwait lacks a defence-industrial base and is reliant on imports. The country has offset requirements to help stimulate the country's wider industrial sector.

ACTIVE 17,500 (Army 11,500 Navy 2,000 Air 2,500 Emiri Guard 1,500) Gendarmerie & Paramilitary 7,100

Conscript liability 12 months, males 18–35 years

RESERVE 23,700 (Joint 23,700)

Reserve obligation to age 40; 1 month annual trg

ORGANISATIONS BY SERVICE

Army 11,500
FORCES BY ROLE
SPECIAL FORCES
  1 SF unit
  1 cdo bde
MANOEUVRE
  Armoured
  2 armd bde
  Mechanised
  3 mech inf bde
COMBAT SUPPORT
  1 arty bde
  1 engr bde
  1 MP bn
COMBAT SERVICE SUPPORT
  1 log gp
  1 fd hospital

Reserve
FORCES BY ROLE
MANOEUVRE
  Mechanised
  1 bde
EQUIPMENT BY TYPE
ARMOURED FIGHTING VEHICLES
  MBT 293: 218 M1A2K *Abrams* (being delivered); 75 M-84AB; (218 M1A2 *Abrams*; 75 M-84AB in store)
  IFV 537: 76 BMP-2; 122 BMP-3; 103 BMP-3M; 236 *Desert Warrior*† (incl variants)
  APC 260
    APC (T) 260: 230 M113A2; 30 M577 (CP)
    APC (W) (40 TH 390 *Fahd* in store)
  AUV 300 *Sherpa Light Scout*
ENGINEERING & MAINTENANCE VEHICLES
  ARV 19+: 19 M88A1/2; Type-653A; *Warrior*
  MW *Aardvark* Mk2
NBC VEHICLES 12 *Fuchs*-2 NBC
ARTY 193
  SP 155mm 88: 37 M109A3; 51 PLZ-45
  MRL 300mm 27 9A52 *Smerch*
  MOR 78: **81mm** 60; **107mm** 6 M30; **120mm** ε12 RT-F1
ANTI-TANK/ANTI-INFRASTRUCTURE
  MSL
    SP 74: 66 HMMWV TOW; 8 M901
    MANPATS 9K135 *Kornet* (RS-AT-14 *Spriggan*); TOW-2
  RCL 84mm *Carl Gustaf*
AIR DEFENCE
  SAM • Point-defence *Starburst*; FIM-92 *Stinger*

Navy ε2,000 (incl 500 Coast Guard)
EQUIPMENT BY TYPE
PATROL AND COASTAL COMBATANTS 20
  PCFG 2:
    1 *Al Sanbouk* (GER Lurssen TNC 45m) with 2 twin lnchr with MM40 *Exocet* AShM, 1 76mm gun
    1 *Istiqlal* (GER Lurssen TNC 57m) with 2 twin lnchr with MM40 *Exocet* AShM, 1 76mm gun
  PBF 10 *Al Nokatha* (US Mk V PBF)
  PBG 8 *Um Almaradim* (FRA *Combattante* 1 derivative) with 2 twin lnchr with *Sea Skua* AShM
AMPHIBIOUS • LANDING CRAFT 8
  LCT 2 *Assafar* (ADSB 64m)
  LCM 1 *Abhan* (ADSB 42m)
  LCVP 5 ADSB 16m
LOGISTICS AND SUPPORT • AG 1 *Sawahil* with 1 hel landing platform

Marines 800

Air Force 2,500
FORCES BY ROLE
FIGHTER/GROUND ATTACK
  2 sqn with F/A-18C/D *Hornet*
TRANSPORT
  1 sqn with C-17A *Globemaster* III; KC-130J *Hercules*; L-100-30
TRAINING
  1 OCU sqn with F/A-18C/D *Hornet*
  1 OCU sqn with Eurofighter *Typhoon*
  1 unit with EMB-312 *Tucano**; *Hawk* Mk64*
ATTACK HELICOPTER
  2 sqn with AH-64D *Apache*
  1 atk/trg sqn with SA342 *Gazelle* with HOT
TRANSPORT HELICOPTER
  1 sqn with AS532 *Cougar*; H225M; SA330 *Puma*
  1 (VIP) sqn with S-92A
EQUIPMENT BY TYPE
AIRCRAFT 60 combat capable
  FGA 46: 13 Eurofighter *Typhoon*; 26 F/A-18C *Hornet*; 7 F/A-18D *Hornet*
  TKR/TPT 3 KC-130J *Hercules*
  TPT 5: **Heavy** 2 C-17A *Globemaster* III; **Medium** 3 L-100-30
  TRG 14: 6 EMB-312 *Tucano**; 8 *Hawk* Mk64* (10 EMB-312

*Tucano** in store)

HELICOPTERS
ATK 16 AH-64D *Apache*
MRH 13 SA342 *Gazelle* with HOT
TPT 19: **Heavy** 6+ H225M; **Medium** 13: 3 AS532 *Cougar*; 7 SA330 *Puma*; 3 S-92A (SAR/VIP)

AIR-LAUNCHED MISSILES
AAM • IR AIM-9L *Sidewinder*; R-550 *Magic*; **SARH** AIM-7F *Sparrow*; **ARH** AIM-120C7 AMRAAM
ASM AGM-65G *Maverick*; AGM-114K *Hellfire*; HOT
AShM AGM-84D *Harpoon* Block IC

Air Defence Command

FORCES BY ROLE
AIR DEFENCE
1 SAM bde (7 SAM bty with M902 *Patriot* PAC-3)
1 SAM bde (6 SAM bty with *Skyguard/Aspide*)

EQUIPMENT BY TYPE
AIR DEFENCE
SAM 47
    Long-range 35 M902 *Patriot* PAC-3
    Short-range 12 *Aspide* with *Skyguard*
GUNS • TOWED 35mm 12+ Oerlikon GDF

Emiri Guard 1,500

FORCES BY ROLE
MANOEUVRE
  Other
    1 (Emiri) gd bde

Gendarmerie & Paramilitary ε7,100 active

National Guard ε6,600 active
FORCES BY ROLE
SPECIAL FORCES
  1 SF bn
MANOEUVRE
  Reconnaissance
    1 armd car bn
  Other
    3 security bn
COMBAT SUPPORT
  1 MP bn
EQUIPMENT BY TYPE
ARMOURED FIGHTING VEHICLES
RECCE 20 VBL
IFV ε150 *Pandur* (incl variants)
APC 67+
  APC (W) 27+: 5+ *Desert Chameleon*; 22 S600 (incl variants)
  PPV 40 Otokar ISV
AUV 120 *Sherpa Light Scout*
ENGINEERING & MAINTENANCE VEHICLES
ARV *Pandur*

HELICOPTERS
TPT • **Heavy** 3 H225M

Coast Guard 500

EQUIPMENT BY TYPE
PATROL AND COASTAL COMBATANTS 32
PBF 12 *Manta*
PB 20: 3 *Al Shaheed*; 4 *Inttisar* (Austal 31.5m); 3 *Kassir* (Austal 22m); 10 *Subahi*
AMPHIBIOUS • LANDING CRAFT
LCU 4: 2 *Al Tahaddy*; 1 *Saffar*; 1 other
LOGISTICS AND SUPPORT • AG 1 *Sawahil*

FOREIGN FORCES

Canada Operation Inherent Resolve (*Impact*) 200
Italy Operation Inherent Resolve (*Prima Parthica*) 300; 4 *Typhoon*; 1 MQ-9A *Reaper*; 1 C-27J Spartan; 1 KC-767A; 1 SAM bty with SAMP/T
United Kingdom Operation Inherent Resolve (*Shader*) 50; 1 CISR UAV sqn with 8 MQ-9A Reaper
United States US Central Command: 10,000; 1 ARNG armd bn; 1 ARNG (cbt avn) hel bde; 1 spt bde; 1 CISR UAV sqn with MQ-9A *Reaper*; 1 (APS) armd bde eqpt set; 1 (APS) inf bde eqpt set; 2 SAM bty with M902/M903 *Patriot* PAC-3/PAC-3 MSE

Lebanon LBN

Lebanese Pound LBP		2022	2023	2024
GDP [a]	LBP	550trn		
	USD	21.8bn		
per capita	USD	3,283		
Growth	%	n.k.		
Inflation	%	171.19		
Def bdgt	LBP	6.63trn	20.84trn	48.5trn
	USD	263m		
FMA (US)	USD	180m	150m	150m
USD1=LBP		25,235		

[a] No IMF economic data available for Lebanon from 2023

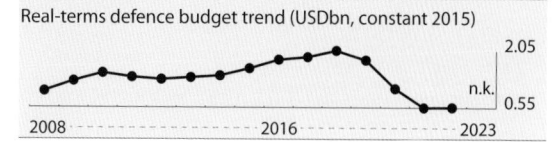

Real-terms defence budget trend (USDbn, constant 2015): 2.05 ... n.k. 0.55 (2008–2023)

Population	5,331,203					
Age	0–14	15–19	20–24	25–29	30–64	65 plus
Male	9.8%	3.7%	3.6%	3.7%	25.2%	3.9%
Female	9.4%	3.5%	3.5%	3.5%	25.0%	5.2%

Capabilities

The ability of the Lebanese Armed Forces (LAF) to fulfil its missions remains under strain from Hizbullah's position in national politics, the spillover effects of the Syrian and Gazan conflicts, the severe and prolonged economic depression and an ongoing governance crisis. Israel has repeatedly struck targets in Lebanon that it says are linked to Iran-backed Hizbullah. Cross-border fighting between the two sides flared in the wake of the Hamas attack on Israel in October 2023. The LAF is reliant on outside assistance to continue its operations. The economic crisis has left the government struggling to pay wages, while inflation has eroded the value of salaries. This has led to fears that troops are supplementing their wages with other employment or quitting. Training and operational assistance have traditionally been provided by the US, as well as France, Germany, Italy and the UK. Initial reconstruction work, aided by the US Army, is expected to commence in 2024 on military facilities at the Beirut naval base damaged by a port explosion in 2020. The LAF has no requirement and minimal capability for extraterritorial deployment. The military has been trying to secure the border against Syrian migrations. The LAF remains dependent on foreign support to replace and modernise its ageing equipment. Lebanon has no significant domestic defence industry.

ACTIVE 60,000 (Army 56,600 Navy 1,800 Air 1,600)
Gendarmerie & Paramilitary 20,000

ORGANISATIONS BY SERVICE

Army 56,600
FORCES BY ROLE
5 regional comd (Beirut, Bekaa Valley, Mount Lebanon, North, South)
SPECIAL FORCES
  1 cdo regt
MANOEUVRE
  Armoured
  1 armd regt
  Mechanised
  11 mech inf bde
  Air Manoeuvre
  1 AB regt
  Amphibious
  1 mne cdo regt
  Other
  1 Presidential Guard bde
  6 intervention regt
  4 border sy regt
COMBAT SUPPORT
  2 arty regt
  1 cbt spt bde (1 engr regt, 1 AT regt, 1 sigs regt; 1 log bn)
  1 MP gp
COMBAT SERVICE SUPPORT
  1 log bde
  1 med gp
  1 construction regt
EQUIPMENT BY TYPE
MBT 334: 92 M48A1/A5; 10 M60A2; 185 T-54; 47 T-55
RECCE 55 AML
IFV 56: 24 AIFV-B-C25; 32 M2A2 *Bradley*
APC 1,378
  APC (T) 1,274 M113A1/A2 (incl variants)

APC (W) 96: 86 VAB VCT; 10 VBPT-MR *Guarani*
PPV 8 *Maxxpro*
ENGINEERING & MAINTENANCE VEHICLES
ARV 3+: 3 M88A1; M113 ARV; T-54/55 ARV (reported)
VLB MTU-72 reported
MW *Bozena*
ARTILLERY 718
  SP 155mm 36: 12 M109A2; 24 M109A5
  TOWED 281: **105mm** 13 M101A1; **122mm** 35: 9 D-30; 26 M-30; **130mm** 15 M-46; **155mm** 218 M198
  MRL 122mm 11 BM-21
  MOR 390: **81mm** 203; **82mm** 112; **120mm** 75: 29 Brandt; 46 M120
ANTI-TANK/ANTI-INFRASTRUCTURE
  MSL
    SP 35 VAB with HOT
    MANPATS *Milan*; TOW
  RCL 106mm 113 M40A1
AIR DEFENCE
  SAM • Point-defence 9K32 *Strela*-2M (RS-SA-7B *Grail*)‡
  GUNS • TOWED 77: **20mm** 20; **23mm** 57 ZU-23-2

Navy 1,800
EQUIPMENT BY TYPE
PATROL AND COASTAL COMBATANTS 16
  PCC 1 *Trablous*
  PBF 1
  PB 14: 1 *Aamchit* (ex-GER *Bremen*); 1 *Al Kalamoun* (ex-FRA *Avel Gwarlarn*); 3 *Marine Protector*; 7 *Tripoli* (ex-UK *Attacker/Tracker* Mk 2); 1 *Naqoura* (ex-GER *Bremen*); 1 *Tabarja* (ex-GER *Bergen*)
AMPHIBIOUS • LANDING CRAFT
  LCT 2 *Sour* (ex-FRA EDIC – capacity 8 APC; 96 troops)

Air Force 1,600
4 air bases
FORCES BY ROLE
GROUND ATTACK
  1 sqn with Cessna AC-208 *Combat Caravan**
  1 sqn with EMB-314 *Super Tucano**
ATTACK HELICOPTER
  1 sqn with SA342L *Gazelle*
TRANSPORT HELICOPTER
  4 sqn with Bell 205 (UH-1H *Iroquois/Huey* II)
  1 sqn with SA330/IAR330SM *Puma*
  1 trg sqn with R-44 *Raven* II
EQUIPMENT BY TYPE
AIRCRAFT 9 combat capable
  ISR 3 Cessna AC-208 *Combat Caravan**
  TRG 9: 3 *Bulldog*; 6 EMB-314 *Super Tucano**
HELICOPTERS
  MRH 14: 1 AW139; 5 MD530F+; 8 SA342L *Gazelle* (5 SA342L *Gazelle*; 5 SA316 *Alouette* III; 1 SA318 *Alouette* II

all non-operational)
TPT 41: **Medium** 13: 3 S-61N (fire-fighting); 10 SA330/IAR330 *Puma*; **Light** 28: 18 Bell 205 (UH-1H *Iroquois*); 6 Bell 205 (UH-1H *Huey* II); 4 R-44 *Raven* II (basic trg) (11 Bell 205; 7 Bell 212 all non-operational)
AIR LAUNCHED MISSILES
ASM AGM-114 *Hellfire*; AGR-20A APKWS

Gendarmerie & Paramilitary ε20,000 active

Internal Security Force ε20,000
Ministry of Interior
FORCES BY ROLE
Other Combat Forces
  1 (police) judicial unit
  1 regional sy coy
  1 (Beirut Gendarmerie) sy coy
EQUIPMENT BY TYPE
ARMOURED FIGHTING VEHICLES
  APC • APC (W) 60 V-200 *Chaimite*

Customs
EQUIPMENT BY TYPE
PATROL AND COASTAL COMBATANTS 7
  PB 7: 5 *Aztec*; 2 *Tracker*

SOUTHERN LEBANON

Data here represents the de facto situation. This does not imply international recognition. Hizbullah maintain a substantial inventory of rockets and missiles in Southern Lebannon, reportedly bolstered by transfers from Syria and from newly built factories. Hizbullah's operations in Syria has seen the organisation take on a more conventional military role and acquire heavy equipment from the Syrian Army.

ACTIVE 20,000

ORGANISATIONS BY SERVICE

Hizbullah 20,000 (plus ε30,000 reserves)
EQUIPMENT BY TYPE
ARMOURED FIGHTING VEHICLES
  MBT T-54/55; T-72 (all in Syria)
  APC • APC (T) M113; MT-LB (all in Syria)
ANTI-TANK/ANTI-INFRASTRUCTURE
  MSL • MANPATS 9K11 *Malyutka* (RS-AT-3 *Sagger*); 9K111 *Fagot* (RS-AT-4 *Spigot*); 9K115-2 *Metis*-M1 (RS-AT-13); *Dehlavieh* (*Kornet*); *Milan*
ARTILLERY
  SP 122mm 2S1 *Gvozdika* (in Syria)
  TOWED 122mm D-30; **130mm** M-46 (all in Syria)
  MRL 122mm BM-21; **240mm** *Fadjr* 3; **300mm** *Fadjr* 5
SURFACE-TO-SURFACE MISSILE LAUNCHERS
  SRBM • Conventional *Fateh*-110; M-600; SS-1D *Scud* C (reported); SS-1E *Scud* D (reported); *Zelzal* 2
COASTAL DEFENCE • AShM C-802 (*Noor*)
UNIHABITED AERIAL VEHICLES
  CISR • Light *Mersad*
  ISR • Medium *Sammad* 1; *Ababil* 2; **Light** *Mohajer* 2
LOITERING & DIRECT ATTACK MUNITIONS
  Ababil T (*Mersad* 1)
AIR DEFENCE
  SAM • Point-defence *Misaq*-2 (QW-18)
  GUN • SP 57mm ZSU-57-2; **85mm** KS-12 mod (on 2P25 chassis); **100mm** KS-19 mod (on 2P25 chassis) (all in Syria)

FOREIGN FORCES

Unless specified, figures refer to UNTSO and represent total numbers for the mission
Argentina 4 • UNIFIL 3
Armenia UNIFIL 1
Australia 11
Austria 6 • UNIFIL 152: 1 log coy
Bangladesh UNIFIL 118: 1 FSGM
Belgium 2
Bhutan 4
Brazil UNIFIL 12
Brunei UNIFIL 30
Cambodia UNIFIL 181: 1 EOD coy
Canada 6 (*Operation Jade*)
Chile 3
China, People's Republic of 5 • UNIFIL 418: 2 engr coy; 1 med coy
Colombia UNIFIL 1
Croatia UNIFIL 1
Cyprus UNIFIL 2
Denmark 12
El Salvador UNIFIL 52: 1 inf pl
Estonia 5 • UNIFIL 1
Fiji 1
Finland 16 • UNIFIL 157; 1 inf coy
France UNIFIL 554: 1 bn HQ; 1 recce coy; 1 log coy; 1 tpt coy; 1 maint coy; VBCI; VAB; VBL; *Mistral*
Germany UNIFIL 130: 2 FSGM
Ghana UNIFIL 870: 1 recce coy; 1 mech inf bn; 1 spt coy
Greece UNIFIL 110: 1 FFGHM
Guatemala UNIFIL 2
Hungary UNIFIL 14
India 3 • UNIFIL 893: 1 inf bn; 1 log coy; 1 med coy
Indonesia UNIFIL 1,230: 1 mech inf bn; 1 log coy; 1 FSGM
Ireland 13 • UNIFIL 335: 1 mech inf bn(-)
Italy MIBIL 160 • UNIFIL 961: 1 mech bde HQ; 1 inf bn; 1 sigs coy; 1 tpt coy; 1 hel bn
Kazakhstan UNIFIL 9
Kenya UNIFIL 3
Korea, Republic of UNIFIL 255: 1 mech inf BG HQ; 1 mech inf coy; 1 inf coy; 1 log coy
Latvia 1
Macedonia, North UNIFIL 3
Malaysia UNIFIL 833: 1 mech inf bn(-); 1 engr coy; 1 sigs coy; 1 maint coy; 1 tpt coy

Malta UNIFIL 9
Moldova UNIFIL 32
Mongolia UNIFIL 4
Nepal 3 • UNIFIL 874: 1 mech inf bn; 1 log coy
Netherlands 12 • UNIFIL 1
New Zealand 8
Nigeria UNIFIL 2
Norway 14
Peru UNIFIL 1
Poland 4 • UNIFIL 193; 1 mech inf coy
Qatar UNIFIL 1
Russia 4
Serbia 1 • UNIFIL 182; 1 mech inf coy
Sierra Leone UNIFIL 3
Slovakia 2
Slovenia 4 • UNIFIL 1
Spain UNIFIL 67: 1 mech bde HQ; 1 mech inf bn(-); 1 engr coy; 1 sigs coy; 1 log coy
Sri Lanka UNIFIL 126: 1 inf coy
Sweden 6
Switzerland 13
Tanzania UNIFIL 125: 1 MP coy
Turkiye UNIFIL 100: 1 FSGHM
United Kingdom UNIFIL 1
United States 3
Uruguay UNIFIL 1
Zambia 1 • UNIFIL 2

Libya LBY

Libyan Dinar LYD		2022	2023	2024
GDP	LYD	182bn	194bn	212bn
	USD	37.8bn	40.2bn	43.9bn
per capita	USD	5,577	5,872	6,357
Growth	%	-9.6	12.5	7.5
Inflation	%	4.5	3.4	2.9
Def bdgt	LYD	n.k.	n.k.	n.k.
	USD	n.k.	n.k.	n.k.
USD1=LYD		4.81	4.82	4.82

Population	7,252,573					
Age	0–14	15–19	20–24	25–29	30–64	65 plus
Male	16.7%	4.3%	3.7%	3.4%	20.9%	2.0%
Female	16.1%	4.2%	3.6%	3.3%	19.6%	2.4%

Capabilities

The formation of a Government of National Unity (GNU) headed by Prime Minister Abdul Hamid Dbeibeh in March 2021 failed to bring together the Tripoli-based Government of National Accord (GNA) and the Tobruk-based House of Representatives (HoR). National elections in 2021 were postponed and the two sides appointed rival ministers. The parties then agreed to form the 5+5 Joint Military Committee to unify the military forces of the GNU and the HOR-affiliated Libyan Arab Armed Forces (LAAF), controlled by General Khalifa Haftar, but the situation on the ground remains unstable. In 2023, GNU-aligned forces conducted operations west and south of Tripoli to expand control over Tripolitania, but they faced armed clashes in the capital. The GNU and the LAAF continued to receive foreign support, with reports of Turkish activities in the west and Russia-linked forces at LAAF-controlled air bases. The Tripoli-based GNU government has benefited from several military advisory and training programmes, such as the EUNAVFOR–MED maritime-security training for the navy and coast guard. EUNAVFOR *Operation Irini* monitors the implementation of the UN arms embargo, and in November 2022, again seized military materiel bound for Libya.

Forces loyal to the Government of National Unity (Tripoli-based)

ACTIVE n.k.

ORGANISATIONS BY SERVICE

Ground Forces n.k.
EQUIPMENT BY TYPE
ARMOURED FIGHTING VEHICLES
  MBT T-55; T-72
  IFV BMP-2
  APC
    APC (T) ACV-AAPC; Steyr 4K-7FA
    APC (W) *Mbombe*-6
    PPV *Al-Wahsh*; *Kirpi*-2; *Vuran*
  AUV Lenco *Bearcat* G3; Nimr *Ajban*
ENGINEERING & MAINTENANCE VEHICLES
  ARV *Centurion* 105 AVRE
ANTI-TANK/ANTI-INFRASTRUCTURE • MSL
  SP 9P157-2 *Khrizantema-S* (RS-AT-15 *Springer*)
  MANPATS 9K115 *Metis* (RS-AT-7 *Saxhorn*)
ARTILLERY
  SP 155mm *Palmaria*
  TOWED 122mm D-30
AIR DEFENCE
  SAM • Point-defence QW-18 (CH-SA-11)
  GUNS • SP 14.5mm ZPU-2 (on tch); **23mm** ZU-23-2 (on tch)

Navy n.k.
A number of intact naval vessels remain in Tripoli, although serviceability is questionable
EQUIPMENT BY TYPE
PATROL AND COASTAL COMBATANTS 3+
  CORVETTES • FSGM (1 *Al Hani* (ex-FSU Project 1159 (*Koni*)) in Malta for refit since 2013 with 2 twin lnchr with P-22 (RS-SS-N-2C *Styx*) AShM, 1 twin lnchr with 4K33 *Osa*-M (RS-SA-N-4 *Gecko*) SAM, 2 twin 406mm ASTT, 1 RBU 6000 *Smerch* 2 A/S mor, 2 AK230 CIWS, 2 twin 76mm gun)
  PBFG 1 *Sharaba* (FRA *Combattante* II) with 4 single lnchr with *Otomat* Mk2 AShM, 1 76mm gun†
  PB 2+ PV30
AMPHIBIOUS

LANDING SHIPS • LST 1 *Ibn Harissa* (capacity 1 hel; 11 MBT; 240 troops)
LOGISTICS AND SUPPORT 2
  AFD 1
  ARS 1 *Al Munjed* (YUG *Spasilac*)†

Air Force n.k.
EQUIPMENT BY TYPE
AIRCRAFT 12 combat capable
  FGA 2 MiG-23BN
  ATK 1 J-21 *Jastreb*†
  TRG 9+: 3 G-2 *Galeb**; ε5 L-39ZO*; 1+ SF-260ML*
HELICOPTERS
  ATK Mi-24 *Hind*
  TPT • Medium Mi-17 *Hip*
AIR-LAUNCHED MISSILES • AAM • IR R-3 (RS-AA-2 *Atoll*)‡; R-60 (RS-AA-8 *Aphid*); R-24 (RS-AA-7 *Apex*)

Paramilitary n.k.

Coast Guard n.k.
EQUIPMENT BY TYPE
PATROL AND COASTAL COMBATANTS 20
  PCC 1 Damen Stan 2909 with 1 sextuple 122mm MRL
  PBF 10: 4 *Bigliani*; 4 *Fezzan* (ex-ITA *Corrubia*); 2 Vittoria FPV350 (ITA)
  PB 9: 8 *Burdi* (Damen Stan 1605); 1 *Ikrimah* (FRA RPB 20)

FOREIGN FORCES
Bangladesh UNSMIL 1
Italy MIASIT 90
Nepal UNSMIL 235; 2 sy coy
Türkiye ε500; ACV-AAPC; *Kirpi*; 1 arty unit with T-155 *Firtina*; 1 AD unit with MIM-23B *Hawk*; *Korkut*; GDF-003; 1 CISR UAV unit with *Bayraktar* TB2
United States UNSMIL 1

EASTERN LIBYA
Data here represents the de facto situation. This does not imply international recognition

ACTIVE n.k.

ORGANISATIONS BY SERVICE

Libyan Arab Armed Forces n.k.
EQUIPMENT BY TYPE
ARMOURED FIGHTING VEHICLES
  MBT T-55; T-62; T-72
  RECCE BRDM-2; EE-9 *Cascavel*
  IFV BMP-1; *Ratel*-20
  APC
    APC (T) M113
    APC (W) *Al-Mared*; BTR-60PB; *Mbombe*-6; Nimr *Jais*; *Puma*
  PPV *Al-Wahsh*; *Caiman*; Streit *Spartan*; Streit *Typhoon*; *Vuran*; Titan-DS
  AUV *Panthera* T6; *Panthera* F9; *Terrier* LT-79
ANTI-TANK/ANTI-INFRASTRUCTURE
  MSL
    SP 9P157-2 *Khrizantema*-S (status unknown)
    MANPATS 9K11 *Malyutka* (RS-AT-3 *Sagger*); 9K111 *Fagot* (RS-AT-4 *Spigot*); 9K111-1 *Konkurs* (RS-AT-5 *Spandrel*); 9K135 *Kornet* (RS-AT-14 *Spriggan*); Milan
  RCL: 106mm M40A1; **84mm** *Carl Gustaf*
ARTILLERY
  SP 122mm 2S1 *Gvozdika*; **155mm** G5
  TOWED 122mm D-30
  MRL 107mm Type-63; **122mm** BM-21 *Grad*
  MOR M106
AIR DEFENCE
  SAM
    Short-range 2K12 *Kvadrat* (RS-SA-6 *Gainful*)
    Point-defence 9K338 *Igla*-S (RS-SA-24 *Grinch*)
  GUNS • SP 14.5mm ZPU-2 (on tch); **23mm** ZSU-23-4 *Shilka*; ZU-23-2 (on tch)

Navy n.k.
EQUIPMENT BY TYPE
PATROL AND COASTAL COMBATANTS 7+
  PB: 7+: 2 *Burdi* (Damen Stan 1605); 1 *Burdi* (Damen Stan 1605) with 1 73mm gun; 2 *Ikrimah* (FRA RPB20); 1 *Hamelin*; 1+ PV30
LOGISTICS AND SUPPORT • AFD 1

Air Force n.k.
EQUIPMENT BY TYPE
AIRCRAFT 33 combat capable
  FTR 2+: 2 MiG-23ML *Flogger* G; some MiG-29 *Fulcrum* (operator uncertain)
  FGA 13: ε10 MiG-21MF *Fishbed*; 1 *Mirage* F-1AD; 1 *Mirage* F-1ED; 1 Su-22UM3 *Fitter* G
  ATK some Su-24M *Fencer* D (operator uncertain) **TRG** 19: ε10 L-39ZO *Albatros**; 1+ MiG-21UM *Mongol* B; 8 SF-260ML*
HELICOPTERS
  ATK Mi-24/35 *Hind*
  MRH up to 3 SA341 *Gazelle*
  TPT • Medium 3: up to 3 H215 (AS332L) *Super Puma*; Mi-8/Mi-17 *Hip*
AIR-LAUNCHED MISSILES • AAM • IR R-3 (RS-AA-2 *Atoll*)‡; R-27T (RS-AA-10B *Alamo*); R-60 (RS-AA-8 *Aphid*); R-73 (RS-AA-11A *Archer*)

FOREIGN FORCES
Wagner Group 2,000

Mauritania MRT

Mauritanian Ouguiya MRU		2022	2023	2024
GDP	MRU	366bn	395bn	424bn
	USD	9.9bn	10.4bn	10.9bn
per capita	USD	2,285	2,338	2,408
Growth	%	6.5	4.5	5.3
Inflation	%	9.6	7.5	4.0
Def bdgt	MRU	8.33bn	9.30bn	
	USD	226m	244m	
USD1=MRU		36.91	38.15	38.92

Real-terms defence budget trend (USDm, constant 2015): n.k. 2008 — 111 — 210 (2023)

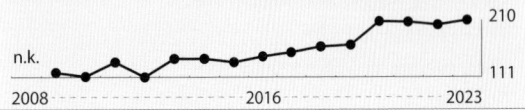

Population	4,244,878					
Age	0–14	15–19	20–24	25–29	30–64	65 plus
Male	18.1%	5.1%	4.5%	3.9%	14.7%	1.8%
Female	18.0%	5.2%	4.7%	4.3%	17.2%	2.5%

Capabilities

The country's small and modestly equipped armed forces are tasked with maintaining territorial integrity, internal security, and, in light of the regional threat from extremist Islamist groups, border security. In early 2021, the government approved a draft decree establishing a defence area along the northern border to prevent incursions by the Polisario Front, a separatist group. To help the army secure the country's borders, the EU approved the delivery of military aid through the European Peace Mechanism in December 2022. The country is a member of the G5 Sahel group. In late 2021, the armed forces of Mauritania and Senegal signed an agreement to jointly patrol offshore gas fields and they have undertaken joint riverine patrols along their border. Mauritania's armed forces take part in the *Flintlock* US-led special-operations exercise and the *Phoenix Express* naval exercise. Deployment capabilities are limited, but the armed forces have demonstrated mobility and sustainment in desert regions. A Chinese firm built a new naval base in the south, possibly designed to enable improved protection of offshore gas fields. Mauritania has limited and ageing equipment, but the navy has recently received some new patrol vessels from China. Despite recent acquisitions, including small ISR aircraft, aviation resources are insufficient considering the country's size. Naval equipment is geared toward coastal-surveillance missions and China's donation of a landing ship has helped establish a basic sealift capability. There is no domestic defence industry.

ACTIVE 15,850 (Army 15,000 Navy 600 Air 250)
Gendarmerie & Paramilitary 5,000
Conscript liability 24 months

ORGANISATIONS BY SERVICE

Army 15,000
FORCES BY ROLE
6 mil regions
MANOEUVRE
Reconnaissance
1 armd recce bn
Armoured
1 armd bn
Light
7 mot inf bn
8 (garrison) inf bn
Air Manoeuvre
1 cdo/para bn
Other
2 (camel corps) bn
1 gd bn
COMBAT SUPPORT
3 arty bn
4 ADA bty
1 engr coy

EQUIPMENT BY TYPE
ARMOURED FIGHTING VEHICLES
MBT 35 T-54/T-55
RECCE 70: 20 AML-60; 40 AML-90; 10 *Saladin*
APC • APC (W) 32: 5 FV603 *Saracen*; 7 Bastion APC; ε20 Panhard M3
AUV 12 *Cobra*
ENGINEERING & MAINTENANCE VEHICLES
ARV T-54/55 ARV reported
ANTI-TANK/ANTI-INFRASTRUCTURE
MSL • MANPATS *Milan*
RCL • 106mm M40A1
ARTILLERY 180
TOWED 80: **105mm** 36 HM-2/M101A1; **122mm** 44: 20 D-30; 24 D-74
MRL 10: **107mm** 4 Type-63; **122mm** 6 Type-81
MOR 90: **81mm** 60; **120mm** 30 Brandt
AIR DEFENCE
SAM • Point-defence ε4 9K31 *Strela*-1 (RS-SA-9 *Gaskin*) (reported); 9K32 *Strela*-2 (RS-SA-7 *Grail*)‡
GUNS • TOWED 82: **14.5mm** 28: 16 ZPU-2; 12 ZPU-4; **23mm** 20 ZU-23-2; **37mm** 10 M-1939; **57mm** 12 S-60; **100mm** 12 KS-19

Navy ε600
EQUIPMENT BY TYPE
PATROL AND COASTAL COMBATANTS 12
PCC 5: 1 *Aboubekr Ben Amer* (FRA OPV 54); 1 *Arguin*; 1 *Limam El Hidrami* (PRC); 2 *Timbédra* (PRC Huangpu mod)
PB 7: 1 *El Nasr*† (FRA *Patra*); 4 *Mandovi*; 2 *Megsem Bakkar* (FRA RPB20 – for SAR duties)
AMPHIBIOUS • LANDING SHIPS 1
LSM 1 *Nimlane* (PRC)

Fusiliers Marins
FORCES BY ROLE

MANOEUVRE
  Amphibious
    1 mne unit

Air Force 250
EQUIPMENT BY TYPE
AIRCRAFT 2 combat capable
  ISR 2 Cessna 208B *Grand Caravan*
  TPT 14: **Light** 13: 1 Beech 350 *King Air*; 2 BN-2 *Defender*; 1 C-212; 2 CN235; 3 G1; 2 PA-31T *Cheyenne* II; 2 Y-12(II); **PAX** 1 BT-67 (with sensor turret)
  TRG 9: 3 EMB-312 *Tucano*; 2 EMB-314 *Super Tucano**; 4 SF-260E
HELICOPTERS
  MRH 3: 1 SA313B *Alouette* II; 2 Z-9
  TPT • **Light** 2 AW109

Gendarmerie & Paramilitary ε5,000 active

Gendarmerie ε3,000
Ministry of Interior
FORCES BY ROLE
MANOEUVRE
  Other
    6 regional sy coy
EQUIPMENT BY TYPE
PATROL AND COASTAL COMBATANTS • PB 3: 1 *Awkar* (PRC 60); 2 Rodman 55

National Guard 2,000
Ministry of Interior

Customs
EQUIPMENT BY TYPE
PATROL AND COASTAL COMBATANTS • PB 4: 1 *Dah Ould Bah* (FRA *Amgram* 14); 2 *Saeta*-12; 1 *Yaboub Ould Rajel* (FRA RPB18)

DEPLOYMENT
CENTRAL AFRICAN REPUBLIC: UN • MINUSCA 465; 1 inf bn(-)
SOMALIA: UN • UNSOS 1
SUDAN: UN • UNISFA 3

Morocco MOR

Moroccan Dirham MAD		2022	2023	2024
GDP	MAD	1.33trn	1.44trn	1.54trn
	USD	131bn	147bn	157bn
per capita	USD	3,570	3,980	4,212
Growth	%	1.3	2.4	3.6
Inflation	%	6.6	6.3	3.5
Def bdgt [a]	MAD	61.7bn	63.5bn	65.9bn
	USD	6.07bn	6.48bn	6.72bn
FMA (US)	USD	10m	10m	10m
USD1=MAD		10.16	9.81	9.81

[a] Includes autonomous defence spending (SEGMA) and Treasury funding for 'Acquisitions and Repair of Equipment for Royal Armed Forces'

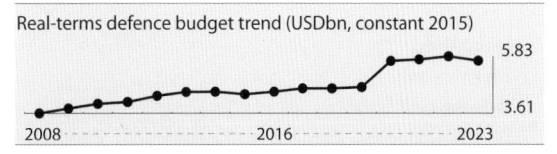

Real-terms defence budget trend (USDbn, constant 2015)
5.83
3.61
2008 — 2016 — 2023

Population	37,067,420				
Age	0–14	15–19	20–24	25–29	30–64	65 plus
Male	13.3%	4.2%	3.9%	3.7%	20.9%	3.9%
Female	12.7%	4.2%	3.9%	3.7%	21.4%	4.1%

Capabilities

Regional security challenges are a key concern for Morocco. The armed forces in early 2022 established an eastern military zone, in addition to the northern and southern ones, because of worsening relations with Algeria. A 30-year ceasefire between Morocco and the Polisario Front ended in late 2020 and the UN has reported that hostilities have resumed, albeit at a low level. Morocco has close defence ties with the US, receiving military training and equipment. The Biden administration has come under pressure in Congress to withdraw the 2020 recognition of Moroccan claims over Western Sahara and to find an alternative location to hold the *African Lion* exercise. Rabbat also cooperates with NATO. In 2016, Morocco was granted access to the Alliance's Interoperability Platform to strengthen the defence and security sectors. The country regioned the AU in 2017. Defence ties with Israel have developed amid the 2020 normalisation agreement, as shown by the procurement of Israeli air defence systems and the participation of Israeli soldiers in the 2023 iteration of *African Lion*. The armed forces have gained experience from UN peacekeeping deployments and multinational exercises. Conscription was reintroduced in early 2019. The armed forces have some capacity to deploy independently within the region and on UN peacekeeping missions in sub-Saharan Africa, although they lack heavy sealift and airlift capabilities. Morocco's military inventory primarily comprises ageing French and US equipment, with plans plans to re-equip all the services. Morocco operates two earth observation satellites, meeting some surveillance requirements. The country relies on imports and donations for major defence equipment.

ACTIVE 195,800 (Army 175,000 Navy 7,800 Air 13,000) Gendarmerie & Paramilitary 50,000

Conscript liability 12 months for men aged 19–25

RESERVE 150,000 (Army 150,000)

Reserve obligation to age 50

ORGANISATIONS BY SERVICE

Space
EQUIPMENT BY TYPE
SATELLITES • ISR 2 *Mohammed* VI

Army 175,000
FORCES BY ROLE
2 comd (Northern Zone, Southern Zone)
MANOEUVRE
  Armoured
  1 armd bde
  11 armd bn
  Mechanised
  3 mech inf bde
  Mechanised/Light
  8 mech/mot inf regt (2–3 bn)
  Light
  1 lt sy bde
  3 (camel corps) mot inf bn
  35 lt inf bn
  4 cdo unit
  Air Manoeuvre
  2 para bde
  2 AB bn
  Mountain
  1 mtn inf bn
COMBAT SUPPORT
  11 arty bn
  7 engr bn
AIR DEFENCE
  2 AD gp

Royal Guard 1,500
FORCES BY ROLE
MANOEUVRE
  Other
  1 gd bn
  2 cav sqn
EQUIPMENT BY TYPE
ARMOURED FIGHTING VEHICLES
  MBT 703: 222 M1A1SA *Abrams*; 220 M60A1 *Patton*; 120 M60A3 *Patton*; 40 T-72B (being upgraded to T-72EA); 47 T-72EA; 54 Type-90-II (MBT-2000); (ε200 M48A5 *Patton* in store)
  LT TK (111 SK-105 *Kuerassier* in store)
  ASLT 80 AMX-10RC
  RECCE 284: 38 AML-60-7; 190 AML-90; 40 EBR-75; 16 *Eland*
  IFV 238: 10 AMX-10P; 30 *Ratel* Mk3-20; 30 *Ratel* Mk3-90; 45 VAB VCI; 123 YPR-765

APC 1,225
  APC (T) 905: 400 M113A1/A2; 419 M113A3; 86 M577A2 (CP)
  APC (W) 320 VAB VTT
AUV 36 *Sherpa Light Scout*
ENGINEERING & MAINTENANCE VEHICLES
  ARV 85+: 10 *Greif*; 55 M88A1; M578; 20 VAB-ECH
ANTI-TANK/ANTI-INFRASTRUCTURE
  MSL
    SP 80 M901
    MANPATS 9K11 *Malyutka* (RS-AT-3 *Sagger*); HJ-8L; M47 *Dragon*; *Milan*; TOW
  RCL 106mm 350 M40A1
  GUNS • SP 36: **90mm** 28 M56; **100mm** 8 SU-100
ARTILLERY 2,384
  SP 354: **155mm** 326: 36 CAESAR; ε130 M109A1/A1B/A2/A3/A4; 70 M109A5; 90 Mk F3; **203mm** 60 M110
  TOWED 118: **105mm** 50: 30 L118 Light Gun; 20 M101; **130mm** 18 M-46; **155mm** 50: 30 FH-70; 20 M114
  MRL 83: **122mm** 35 BM-21 *Grad*; **300mm** 36 PHL-03; **370mm** 12 PULS
  MOR 1,797: **81mm** 1,100 Expal model LN; **SP 107mm** 36 M106A2; **120mm** 550 Brandt; **SP 120mm** 110: 20 (VAB APC); 91 M1064A3
UNINHABITED AERIAL VEHICLES
  ISR • Medium R4E-50 *Skyeye*
AIR DEFENCE
  SAM 67+
    Medium-range 24 *Tianlong*-50
    Short-range 6+: DK-9 (CH-SA-5); ε6 VL-MICA (reported)
    Point-defence 37+: 37 M48 *Chaparral*; 9K38 *Igla* (RS-SA-18 *Grouse*)
  SPAAGM 30mm 12 2K22M *Tunguska*-M (RS-SA-19 *Grison*)
  GUNS 390
    SP 20mm 60 M163 *Vulcan*
    TOWED 330: **14.5mm** 200: 150–180 ZPU-2; 20 ZPU-4; **20mm** 40 M167 Vulcan; **23mm** 75–90 ZU-23-2; **35mm** some PG-99

Navy 7,800 (incl 1,500 Marines)
EQUIPMENT BY TYPE
PRINCIPAL SURFACE COMBATANTS • FRIGATES 4
  FFGHM 2:
    1 *Mohammed* VI (FRA FREMM) with 2 quad lnchr with MM40 *Exocet* Block 3 AShM, 2 8-cell *Sylver* A43 VLS with *Aster* 15 SAM, 2 triple 324mm ILAS-3 (B-515) ASTT with MU90 LWT, 1 76mm gun (capacity 1 AS565MA *Panther*)
    1 *Tarik ben Ziyad* (NLD SIGMA 10513) with 2 twin lnchr with MM40 *Exocet* Block 3 AShM, 1 12-cell CLA VLS with VL MICA SAM, 2 triple 324mm ILAS-3 (B-515) ASTT with MU90 LWT, 1 76mm gun (capacity 1 AS565MA *Panther*)

FFGH 2 *Mohammed* V (FRA *Floreal*) with 2 single lnchr with MM38 *Exocet* AShM, 1 76mm gun (fitted for but not with *Simbad* SAM) (capacity 1 AS565MA *Panther*)

PATROL AND COASTAL COMBATANTS 52
  CORVETTES 3
    FSGHM 2 *Sultan Moulay Ismail* (NLD SIGMA 9813) with 2 twin lnchr with MM40 *Exocet* Block 2/3 AShM, 1 12-cell CLA VLS with VL MICA SAM, 2 triple 324mm ILAS-3 (B-515) ASTT with MU90 LWT, 1 76mm gun (capacity 1 AS565MA *Panther*)
    FSM 1 *Lt Col Errhamani* (ESP *Descubierto*) with 1 octuple *Albatros* lnchr with *Aspide* SAM, 2 triple 324mm ASTT with Mk46 LWT, 1 76mm gun
  PSO 1 *Bin an Zaran* (OPV 70) with 1 76mm gun
  PCG 4 *Cdt El Khattabi* (ESP *Lazaga* 58m) with 4 single lnchr with MM38 *Exocet* AShM, 1 76mm gun
  PCO 5 *Rais Bargach* (under control of fisheries dept)
  PCC 12:
    4 *El Hahiq* (DNK *Osprey* 55, incl 2 with customs)
    6 *LV Rabhi* (ESP 58m B-200D)
    2 *Okba* (FRA PR-72) each with 1 76mm gun
  PB 27: 6 *El Wacil* (FRA P-32); 10 VCSM (RPB 20); 10 Rodman 101; 1 other (UK *Bird*)

AMPHIBIOUS
  LANDING SHIPS • LST 3 *Ben Aicha* (FRA *Champlain* BATRAL) with 1 hel landing platform (capacity 7 tanks; 140 troops)
  LANDING CRAFT 2:
    LCT 1 *Sidi Ifni*
    LCM 1 CTM (FRA CTM-5)

LOGISTICS AND SUPPORT 7
  AGOR 1 *Dar Al Beida* (FRA BHO2M)
  AGS 1 Damen Stan Tender 1504
  AK 2
  AX 1 *Essaouira*
  AXS 2

Marines 1,500
FORCES BY ROLE
MANOEUVRE
  Amphibious
    2 naval inf bn

Naval Aviation
FORCES BY ROLE
MARITIME PATROL
  1 sqn Beech 350ER *King Air*
MULTI-ROLE HELICOPTER
  1 sqn with Bell 412EPI; AS565MA *Panther*
EQUIPMENT BY TYPE
AIRCRAFT • MP 2 Beech 350ER *King Air*
HELICOPTERS
  ASW 2 Bell 412EPI
  MRH 3 AS565MA *Panther*

Air Force 13,000
FORCES BY ROLE
FIGHTER/GROUND ATTACK
  2 sqn with F-5E/F-5F *Tiger* II
  3 sqn with F-16C/D *Fighting Falcon*
  1 sqn with *Mirage* F-1C (F-1CH)
  1 sqn with *Mirage* F-1E (F-1EH)
ELECTRONIC WARFARE
  1 sqn with EC-130H *Hercules*; *Falcon* 20 (ELINT)
MARITIME PATROL
  1 flt with Do-28
TANKER/TRANSPORT
  1 sqn with C-130/KC-130H *Hercules*
TRANSPORT
  1 sqn with CN235
  1 VIP sqn with B-737BBJ; Beech 200/300 *King Air*; *Falcon* 50; Gulfstream II/III/V-SP/G550
TRAINING
  1 sqn with *Alpha Jet**
  1 sqn T-6C
ATTACK HELICOPTER
  1 sqn with SA342L *Gazelle* (some with HOT)
TRANSPORT HELICOPTER
  1 sqn with Bell 205A (AB-205A); Bell 206 *Jet Ranger* (AB-206); Bell 212 (AB-212)
  1 sqn with CH-47D *Chinook*
  1 sqn with SA330 *Puma*

EQUIPMENT BY TYPE
AIRCRAFT 89 combat capable
  FTR 22: 19 F-5E *Tiger* II; 3 F-5F *Tiger* II
  FGA 48: 15 F-16C *Fighting Falcon*; 8 F-16D *Fighting Falcon*; 15 *Mirage* F-1C (F-1CH); 10 *Mirage* F-1E (F-1EH)
  ELINT 1 EC-130H *Hercules*
  TKR/TPT 2 KC-130H *Hercules*
  TPT 47: **Medium** 17: 4 C-27J *Spartan*; 13 C-130H *Hercules*; **Light** 19: 4 Beech 100 *King Air*; 2 Beech 200 *King Air*; 1 Beech 200C *King Air*; 2 Beech 300 *King Air*; 3 Beech 350 *King Air*; 5 CN235; 2 Do-28; **PAX** 11: 1 B-737BBJ; 2 *Falcon* 20; 2 *Falcon* 20 (ELINT); 1 *Falcon* 50 (VIP); 1 Gulfstream II (VIP); 1 Gulfstream III; 1 Gulfstream V-SP; 2 Gulfstream G550
  TRG 80: 12 AS-202 *Bravo*; 19 *Alpha Jet**; 2 CAP-10; 24 T-6C *Texan*; 9 T-34C *Turbo Mentor*; 14 T-37B *Tweet*
HELICOPTERS
  MRH 25: 6 H135M; 19 SA342L *Gazelle* (7 with HOT, 12 with cannon)
  TPT 70: **Heavy** 10 CH-47D *Chinook*; **Medium** 24 SA330 *Puma*; **Light** 36: 24 Bell 205A (AB-205A); 5+ Bell 206 *Jet Ranger* (AB-206); 3 Bell 212 (AB-212); 4 Bell 429
UNINHABITED AERIAL VEHICLES
  CISR
    Heavy *Wing Loong* II
    Medium *Bayraktar* TB2

ISR
   Heavy *Heron*
   Medium 4 *Hermes* 900
AIR-LAUNCHED MISSILES
   AAM • IR AIM-9J *Sidewinder*; R-550 *Magic*; *Mica* IR;
   IIR AIM-9X *Sidewinder* II; ARH AIM-120C7 AMRAAM;
   Mica RF
   ASM AASM; AGM-65B/D/G *Maverick*; HOT
   ARM AGM-88B HARM
BOMBS
   Laser-guided *Paveway* II
   Laser & INS/GPS-guided GBU-54 Laser JDAM
   INS/GPS-guided GBU-31 JDAM

Gendarmerie & Paramilitary 50,000 active

Gendarmerie Royale 20,000
FORCES BY ROLE
MANOEUVRE
   Air Manoeuvre
      1 para sqn
   Other
      1 paramilitary bde
      4 (mobile) paramilitary gp
      1 coast guard unit
TRANSPORT HELICOPTER
   1 sqn
EQUIPMENT BY TYPE
PATROL AND COASTAL COMBATANTS
   PB 15 Arcor 53
AIRCRAFT
   TPT • Light 12 BN-2T *Islander*
   TRG 2 R-235 *Guerrier*
HELICOPTERS
   MRH 14: 3 SA315B *Lama*; 2 SA316 *Alouette* III; 3 SA318 *Alouette* II; 6 SA342K *Gazelle*
   TPT 25: Medium 11: 3 H225 *Super Puma*; 2 S-70A *Black Hawk* (VIP); 6 SA330 *Puma*; Light 14: 2 H125; 4 H135; 6 H145; 2 SA360 *Dauphin*

Force Auxiliaire 30,000 (incl 5,000 Mobile Intervention Corps)

Customs/Coast Guard
EQUIPMENT BY TYPE
PATROL AND COASTAL COMBATANTS
   PB 36: 4 *Erraid*; 18 *Arcor* 46; 14 (other SAR craft)

DEPLOYMENT
CENTRAL AFRICAN REPUBLIC: UN • MINUSCA 781; 1 inf bn
DEMOCRATIC REPUBLIC OF THE CONGO: UN • MONUSCO 925; 1 inf bn; 1 fd hospital
SOUTH SUDAN: UN • UNMISS 3
SUDAN: UN • UNISFA 6

Oman OMN

Omani Rial OMR		2022	2023	2024
GDP	OMR	44.1bn	41.6bn	43.2bn
	USD	115bn	108bn	112bn
per capita	USD	23,240	21,266	21,381
Growth	%	4.3	1.2	2.7
Inflation	%	2.8	1.1	1.7
Def bdgt [a]	OMR	2.47bn	2.50bn	
	USD	6.43bn	6.51bn	
FMA (US)	USD	3.42m	0m	0m
USD1=OMR		0.38	0.38	0.38

[a] Excludes security funding

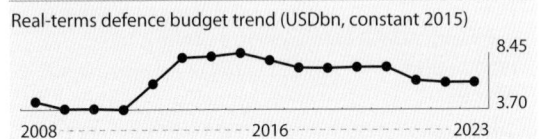

Real-terms defence budget trend (USDbn, constant 2015)
8.45
3.70
2008 — 2016 — 2023

Population	3,833,465					
Age	0–14	15–19	20–24	25–29	30–64	65 plus
Male	15.3%	3.9%	4.5%	5.5%	22.6%	1.9%
Female	14.6%	3.7%	4.0%	4.3%	17.5%	2.1%

Capabilities

The principal task for Oman's armed forces is ensuring territorial integrity, with a particular focus on maritime security given the country's long coastline. Oman maintains carefully calibrated relations with the US and is developing its defence agreements with the UK, a country with which Muscat has a long-standing defence and security relationship. Oman does not host a significant permanent presence of US or other foreign forces, in contrast to other GCC states, but UK forces are frequently deployed to the country for training. Both the UK and US make use of Omani air- and naval-logistics facilities, most notably the port at Duqm, where the UK has a Joint Logistics Support Base. Oman has also been seeking to strengthen ties with Asian states. The country conducts regular military exercises with India, and Chinese navy vessels make calls at Omani ports. Oman's navy has exercised with Western countries and China. Oman is a GCC member but did not participate in Saudi-led coalition operations in Yemen and has largely followed a semi-independent regional policy. Oman has recently recapitalised its core air- and naval-systems inventory, including combat aircraft and patrol and high-speed support vessels, and is now looking to do the same in the land domain. Oman has very limited indigenous defence-industrial capacity, but it has begun local production of various types of ammunition and is looking to boost organic support capability, particularly in the air and land sectors.

ACTIVE 42,600 (Army 25,000 Navy 4,200 Air 5,000 Foreign Forces 2,000 Royal Household 6,400) Gendarmerie & Paramilitary 4,400

ORGANISATIONS BY SERVICE

Army 25,000
FORCES BY ROLE

(Regt are bn size)

MANOEUVRE
Armoured
1 armd bde (2 armd regt, 1 recce regt)
Light
1 inf bde (5 inf regt, 1 arty regt, 1 fd engr regt, 1 engr regt, 1 sigs regt)
1 inf bde (3 inf regt, 2 arty regt)
1 indep inf coy (Musandam Security Force)
Air Manoeuvre
1 AB regt

COMBAT SERVICE SUPPORT
1 tpt regt

AIR DEFENCE
1 ADA regt (2 ADA bty)

EQUIPMENT BY TYPE
ARMOURED FIGHTING VEHICLES
MBT 117: 38 *Challenger* 2; 6 M60A1 *Patton*; 73 M60A3 *Patton*
LT TK 37 FV101 *Scorpion*
RECCE 12 *Pars* III 6×6 (Recce)
IFV 72 *Pars* III 8×8 IFV
APC 262
  APC (T) 10 FV4333 *Stormer*
  APC (W) 252: 15 AT-105 *Saxon*; 15 *Pars* III 6×6 (incl 10 CP; 1 trg); 47 *Pars* III 8×8 (38 CP; 8 amb; 1 trg); 175 *Piranha* (incl variants);
AUV 143: 6 FV103 *Spartan*; 13 FV105 *Sultan* (CP); 124 VBL

ENGINEERING & MAINTENANCE VEHICLES
AEV 6 *Pars* III AEV
ARV 19: 4 *Challenger* ARV; 2 M88A1; 8 *Pars* III ARV; 2 *Piranha* ARV; 3 *Samson*

ANTI-TANK/ANTI-INFRASTRUCTURE • MSL
SP 8 VBL with TOW
MANPATS FGM-148 *Javelin*; *Milan*; BGM-71 TOW/TOW-2A

ARTILLERY 245
SP 155mm 24 G-6
TOWED 108: **105mm** 42 L118 Light Gun; **122mm** 30 D-30; **130mm** 24: 12 M-46; 12 Type-59-I; **155mm** 12 FH-70
MOR 113: **81mm** 69; **SP 81mm** VAMTAC with A3MS; **107mm** 20 M30; **120mm** 12 Brandt; **SP 120mm** 12 *Pars* III AMV

AIR DEFENCE
SAM • Point-defence *Mistral* 2; *Javelin*; 9K32 *Strela*-2 (RS-SA-7 *Grail*)‡
GUNS 26: **23mm** 4 ZU-23-2; **35mm** 10 GDF-005 (with *Skyguard*); **40mm** 12 L/60 (Towed)

Navy 4,200

EQUIPMENT BY TYPE
PRINCIPAL SURFACE COMBATANTS • FRIGATES 3

FFGHM 3 *Al-Shamikh* with 2 twin lnchr with MM40 *Exocet* Block 3 AShM, 2 6-cell CLA VLS with VL MICA SAM, 1 76mm gun

PATROL AND COASTAL COMBATANTS 10
CORVETTES • FSGM 2:
  2 *Qahir Al Amwaj* with 2 quad lnchr with MM40 *Exocet* AShM, 1 octuple lnchr with *Crotale* SAM, 1 76mm gun, 1 hel landing platform
PCO 4 *Al Ofouq* with 1 76mm gun, 1 hel landing platform
PCC 3 *Al Bushra* (FRA P-400) with 1 76mm gun
PBF 1 1400 FIC

AMPHIBIOUS
LANDING SHIPS • LST 1 *Nasr el Bahr*† with 1 hel landing platform (capacity 7 tanks; 240 troops) (in refit since 2017)
LANDING CRAFT 5: 1 **LCU**; 1 **LCT**; 3 **LCM**

LOGISTICS AND SUPPORT 8
AGS 1 *Al Makhirah*
AKL 1 *Al Sultana*
AX 1 *Al-Mabrukah*
AXS 1 *Shabab Oman* II
EPF 3: 2 *Al Mubshir* (High Speed Support Vessel 72) (of which 1†) with 1 hel landing platform (capacity 260 troops); 1 *Shinas* (commercial tpt – auxiliary military role only) (capacity 56 veh; 200 tps)

Air Force 5,000

FORCES BY ROLE
FIGHTER/GROUND ATTACK
2 sqn with F-16C/D Block 50 *Fighting Falcon*
1 sqn with *Hawk* Mk103; *Hawk* Mk203; *Hawk* Mk166
1 sqn with *Typhoon*

MARITIME PATROL
1 sqn with C295MPA

TRANSPORT
1 (VIP) flt with A320-300; Gulfstream IV
1 sqn with C-130H/J/J-30 *Hercules*
1 sqn with C295M

TRAINING
1 sqn with MFI-17B *Mushshak*; PC-9*; Bell 206 (AB-206) *Jet Ranger*

TRANSPORT HELICOPTER
4 (med) sqn; Bell 212 (AB-212); NH-90; *Super Lynx* Mk300 (maritime/SAR)

AIR DEFENCE
2 sqn with NASAMS

EQUIPMENT BY TYPE
AIRCRAFT 56 combat capable
FGA 35: 17 F-16C Block 50 *Fighting Falcon*; 6 F-16D Block 50 *Fighting Falcon*; 12 *Typhoon*
MP 4 C295MPA
TPT 12: **Medium** 6: 3 C-130H *Hercules*; 2 C-130J *Hercules*; 1 C-130J-30 *Hercules* (VIP); **Light** 4 C295M;

PAX 4: 2 A320-300; 2 Gulfstream IV
TRG 36: 3 *Hawk* Mk103*; 7 *Hawk* Mk166; 6 *Hawk* Mk203*; 8 MFI-17B *Mushshak*; 12 PC-9*

HELICOPTERS
MRH 15 *Super Lynx* Mk300 (maritime/SAR)
TPT 26+ **Medium** 20 NH90 TTH; **Light** 6: 3 Bell 206 (AB-206) *Jet Ranger*; 3 Bell 212 (AB-212)

AIR DEFENCE • SAM
Short-range NASAMS

MSL
AAM • IR AIM-9/M/P *Sidewinder*; **IIR** AIM-9X *Sidewinder* II; **ARH** AIM-120C7 AMRAAM
ASM AGM-65D/G *Maverick*
AShM AGM-84D *Harpoon*

BOMBS
Laser-guided EGBU-10 *Paveway* II; EGBU-12 *Paveway* II
INS/GPS-guided GBU-31 JDAM

Royal Household 6,400

(incl HQ staff)

FORCES BY ROLE
SPECIAL FORCES
2 SF regt

Royal Guard Brigade 5,000

FORCES BY ROLE
MANOEUVRE
Other
1 gd bde (1 armd sqn, 2 gd regt, 1 cbt spt bn)

EQUIPMENT BY TYPE
ARMOURED FIGHTING VEHICLES
ASLT 9 *Centauro* MGS (9 VBC-90 in store)
IFV 14 VAB VCI
APC • APC (W) ε50 Type-92

ANTI-TANK/ANTI-INFRASTRUCTURE
MSL • MANPATS *Milan*

ARTILLERY • MRL 122mm 6 Type-90A

AIR DEFENCE
SAM • Point-defence *Javelin*
GUNS • SP 9: **20mm** 9 VAB VDAA

Royal Yacht Squadron 150

EQUIPMENT BY TYPE
LOGISTICS AND SUPPORT 3
AP 1 *Fulk Al Salamah* (also veh tpt) with up to 2 AS332 *Super Puma* hel

Royal Flight 250

EQUIPMENT BY TYPE
AIRCRAFT • TPT • PAX 7: 1 747-400; 1 747-8; 1 B-747SP; 1 A319; 1 A320; 2 Gulfstream IV
HELICOPTERS • TPT • Medium 6 EC225LP *Super Puma*

Gendarmerie & Paramilitary 4,400 active

Tribal Home Guard 4,000
org in teams of ε100

Police Coast Guard 400
EQUIPMENT BY TYPE
PATROL AND COASTAL COMBATANTS 73
PCO 1 *Haras*
PBF 17: 14 *Ares* 85; 3 *Haras* (US Mk V PBF)
PB 55: 3 Rodman 101; 1 *Haras* (SWE CG27); 3 *Haras* (SWE CG29); 14 K13 Fast Intercept Craft; 14 Rodman 58; 1 D59116; 5 *Zahra*; up to 14 Other (Baltic Workboats)

Police Air Wing
EQUIPMENT BY TYPE
AIRCRAFT • TPT • Light 4: 1 BN-2T *Turbine Islander*; 2 CN235M; 1 Do-228
HELICOPTERS
MRH 1 H145M
TPT • Light 16: 3 AW109 (incl. 1 AW109 VIP); 11 AW139 (incl. 1 AW139 VIP); 2 Bell 205A

FOREIGN FORCES
United Kingdom 90

Palestinian Territories PT

New Israeli Shekel ILS		2022	2023	2024
GDP	USD			
per capita	USD			
Growth	%			
Inflation	%			
USD1=ILS				

Definitive economic data not available

Population	5,274,938					
Age	0–14	15–19	20–24	25–29	30–64	65 plus
Male	19.5%	5.5%	4.9%	4.4%	14.9%	1.6%
Female	18.5%	5.3%	4.7%	4.3%	14.7%	1.7%

Capabilities

The Palestinian Territories remain effectively divided between the Palestinian Authority-run West Bank and Hamas-run Gaza. Each organisation controls its own security forces, principally the National Security Forces (NSF) in the West Bank and the Izz al-Din al-Qassam Brigades in Gaza. Both have generally proved effective at maintaining internal security in their respective territories. The Palestinian Authority has received support from the EU, Jordan and the US. Israel claims that a small number of Izz al-Din al-Qassam Brigades personnel have received military training in Iran and Syria. Hamas forces in October 2023 launched an attack on Israel that included ground forces and heavy rocket fire, triggering the Hamas–Israel war. Hamas and the Palestinian Authority lack heavy military equipment. No formal defence industry exists, although

Hamas can acquire light or improvised weapons, either smuggled into Gaza or of local construction or assembly.

ACTIVE 0 Gendarmerie & Paramilitary n.k.

Precise personnel-strength figures for the various Palestinian groups are not known

ORGANISATIONS BY SERVICE

There is little available data on the status of the organisations mentioned below. Following internal fighting in June 2007, Gaza has been under the de facto control of Hamas, while the West Bank is controlled by the Palestinian Authority. In October 2017, both sides agreed a preliminary reconciliation deal on control of Gaza.

Gendarmerie & Paramilitary

Palestinian Authority n.k.

Presidential Security ε3,000

Special Forces ε1,200

Police ε9,000

National Security Force ε10,000
FORCES BY ROLE
MANOEUVRE
  Other
    9 paramilitary bn

Preventative Security ε4,000

Civil Defence ε1,000

The al-Aqsa Brigades n.k.
Profess loyalty to the Fatah group that dominates the Palestinian Authority

Hamas n.k.

Information as of October 2023

Izz al-Din al-Qassam Brigades ε30,000
FORCES BY ROLE
COMMAND
  6 bde HQ (regional)
MANOEUVRE
  Other
    1 cdo unit (Nukhba)
    27 paramilitary bn
    100 paramilitary coy
COMBAT SUPPORT Some engr units
COMBAT SERVICE SUPPORT
  Some log units
EQUIPMENT BY TYPE
ANTI-TANK/ANTI-INFRASTRUCTURE
  MSL • MANPATS 9K11 *Malyutka* (RS-AT-3 *Sagger*) (reported); *Dehlavieh* (*Kornet*) (reported)
  ARTILLERY
  MRL • *Qassam* rockets (multiple calibres); 122mm some; 240mm some *Fadjr* 3 (reported); 330mm some *Fadjr* 5 (reported)
  MOR some (multiple calibres)
SURFACE-TO-SURFACE MISSILE LAUNCHERS
  SRBM • Conventional some *Ayyash*-250
AIR DEFENCE • SAM
  Point-defence *Misaq*-2 (QW-18)

Martime Police ε600

Qatar QTR

Qatari Riyal QAR		2022	2023	2024
GDP	QAR	861bn	857bn	897bn
	USD	236bn	236bn	246bn
per capita	USD	83,521	81,968	84,899
Growth	%	4.9	2.4	2.2
Inflation	%	5.0	2.8	2.3
Def bdgt [a]	QAR	ε30.6bn	ε32.8bn	
	USD	ε8.42bn	ε9.02bn	
USD1=QAR		3.64	3.64	3.64

[a] Defence budget figures derived from Defence and Security allocation in the 'Public Budget Statement'

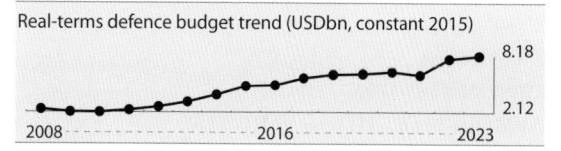

Real-terms defence budget trend (USDbn, constant 2015)
8.18
2.12
2008 2016 2023

Population		2,532,104				
Age	0–14	15–19	20–24	25–29	30–64	65 plus
Male	6.6%	2.4%	5.6%	9.8%	51.6%	0.9%
Female	6.5%	1.7%	1.8%	2.5%	10.0%	0.5%

Capabilities

Qatar is attempting to transform its military capabilities and regional defence standing based on significant equipment acquisitions, including platforms with power-projection capability. The size and capability of the country's air force and navy is increasing, reflecting the pace of spending and major construction of military infrastructure. The scale of the expansion has raised questions about the country's ability to develop and sustain the necessary personnel, infrastructure and maintenance capacity, especially given the small indigenous population. Qatar maintains close ties to Turkiye, which has a small military presence in the country. Tensions with some of Qatar's neighbours that culminated in the 2017 Gulf Crisis have subsided significantly. The Qatar–US military relationship remains strong, as evidenced by the significant presence of forces from the US and other Western states at Al-Udeid airbase. In 2022, the US government designated Qatar a major non-NATO ally. Qatari modernisation efforts include buying four new corvettes and the purchase, for the air force, of Boeing F-15QA and Eurofighter *Typhoon* multirole fighters. Qatar's limited indigenous defence-industrial capability includes small calibre munitions production capacity and ship repair. The country is trying to upgrade its defence industrial capacity through its Barzan Holdings investment vehicle. Qatari men between the age of 18–35 have to perform one year of military service.

ACTIVE 16,500 (Army 12,000 Navy 2,500 Air 2,000)
Gendarmerie & Paramilitary up to 5,000

Conscript liability 12 months, males 18–35 years. Voluntary national service for women

ORGANISATIONS BY SERVICE

Space
EQUIPMENT BY TYPE
SATELLITES • COMMUNICATIONS 2 Es'hail-2

Army 12,000 (including Emiri Guard)
FORCES BY ROLE
SPECIAL FORCES
  1 SF coy
MANOEUVRE
  Armoured
  1 armd bde (1 tk bn, 1 mech inf bn, 1 mor sqn, 1 AT bn)
  Mechanised
  3 mech inf bn
  1 (Emiri Guard) bde (3 mech regt)
COMBAT SUPPORT
  1 SP arty bn
  1 fd arty bn
EQUIPMENT BY TYPE
ARMOURED FIGHTING VEHICLES
  MBT 62 Leopard 2A7+
  ASLT 48: 12 AMX-10RC; 36 Piranha II 90mm
  RECCE 32 Fennek
  IFV 40 AMX-10P
  APC 418
    APC (T) 30 AMX-VCI
    APC (W) 168: 8 V-150 Chaimite; 160 VAB
    PPV 220+: 170+ Ejder Yalcin; 50 Kirpi-2; RG-31
    AUV 65+: 35 BMC Amazon; 14 Dingo 2; NMS; 16 VBL
ENGINEERING & MAINTENANCE VEHICLES
  AEV 6 Wisent 2
  ARV 3: 1 AMX-30D; 2 Piranha
ANTI-TANK/ANTI-INFRASTRUCTURE
  MSL
    SP 24 VAB VCAC HOT; Ejder Yalcin with Stugna-P; NMS with Stugna-P
    MANPATS FGM-148 Javelin; Milan; Kornet-EM
  RCL 84mm Carl Gustaf
ARTILLERY 89+
  SP 155mm 24 PzH 2000
  TOWED 155mm 12 G-5
  MRL 8+: 107mm PH-63; 122mm 2+ (30-tube); 127mm 6 ASTROS II Mk3
  MOR 45: 81mm 26 L16; SP 81mm 4 VAB VPM 81; 120mm 15 Brandt
SURFACE-TO-SURFACE MISSILE LAUNCHERS
  SRBM • Conventional 8+ BP-12A (CH-SS-14 mod 2)

AIR DEFENCE
  SAM • Point-defence NMS with Igla
  GUNS • SP 35mm 15 Gepard

Navy 2,500 (incl Coast Guard)
EQUIPMENT BY TYPE
PRINCIPAL SURFACE COMBATANTS • FRIGATES 4
  FFGHM 4 Al Zubarah with 2 quad lnchr with MM40 Exocet Block 3 AShM, 2 8-cell Sylver A50 VLS with Aster 30 SAM, 1 21-cell Mk 49 GMLS with RIM-116 RAM SAM, 1 76mm gun (capacity 1 med hel)
PATROL AND COASTAL COMBATANTS 24
  CORVETTES • FSGM 2 Musherib with 2 twin lnchr with MM40 Exocet Block 3 AShM, 1 8-cell CLA VLS with VL MICA SAM, 1 76mm gun
  PCFGM 4 Barzan (UK Vita) with 2 quad lnchr with MM40 Exocet Block 3 AShM, 1 sextuple Sadral lnchr with Mistral SAM, 1 Goalkeeper CIWS, 1 76mm gun
  PCFG 2 Damsah (FRA Combattante III) with 2 quad lnchr with MM40 Exocet AShM, 1 76mm gun
  PBF 16: 3 MRTP 16; 6+ MRTP 20; 4 MRTP 24/U; 3 MRTP 34
AMPHIBIOUS 4
  LCT 1 Fuwairit (TUR Anadolu Shipyard LCT)
  LCM 2 Broog (TUR Anadolu Shipyard LCM)
  LCVP 1 Anadolu 16m
LOGISTICS AND SUPPORT • AX 2 Al Doha with 1 hel landing platform

Coast Guard
EQUIPMENT BY TYPE
PATROL AND COASTAL COMBATANTS 28
  PBF 11: 5 Ares 75; 2 Ares 150; 4 DV 15
  PB 17: 10 Ares 110; 4 Crestitalia MV-45; 3 Halmatic M160

Coastal Defence
FORCES BY ROLE
COASTAL DEFENCE
  1 bty with MM40 Exocet Block III
  1 bty with Marte ER
EQUIPMENT BY TYPE
COASTAL DEFENCE • AShM 9: 3 MM40 Exocet Block III; 6 Marte ER

Air Force 2,000
FORCES BY ROLE
FIGHTER/GROUND ATTACK
  1 sqn with Eurofighter Typhoon
  1 sqn with Eurofighter Typhoon (personnel only) (joint QTR-UK unit)
  1 sqn with F-15QA
  1 sqn with Rafale DQ/EQ
ANTI-SUBMARINE WARFARE
  1 sqn with NH90 NFH (forming)

TRANSPORT
 1 sqn with C-17A *Globemaster* III; C-130J-30 *Hercules*
 1 sqn with A340; B-707; B-727; *Falcon* 900
TRAINING
 1 sqn with *Hawk* Mk167
 1 sqn with M-346
 1 sqn with PC-21; *Super Mushshak*
ATTACK HELICOPTER
 1 sqn with SA341 *Gazelle*; SA342L *Gazelle* with HOT
TRANSPORT HELICOPTER
 1 sqn with AW139
 1 sqn with NH90 TTH (forming)
EQUIPMENT BY TYPE
AIRCRAFT 84 combat capable
 FGA 84: 12 Eurofighter *Typhoon*; 36 F-15QA; 9 *Rafale* DQ; 27 *Rafale* EQ
 TPT 18: **Heavy** 8 C-17A *Globemaster* III; **Medium** 4 C-130J-30 *Hercules*; **PAX** 6: 1 A340; 2 B-707; 1 B-727; 2 *Falcon* 900
 TRG 41: 9 *Hawk* Mk167; 3 M-346; 21 PC-21; 8 *Super Mushshak*; (6 *Alpha Jet* in store)
HELICOPTERS
 ATK 24 AH-64E *Apache*
 ASW 3 NH90 NFH
 MRH 34: 21 AW139 (incl 3 for medevac); 2 SA341 *Gazelle*; 11 SA342L *Gazelle*
 TPT 3: **Medium** 2 NH90 TTH; **Light** 1 H125 *Ecureuil* (trg config)
UNINHABITED AERIAL VEHICLES
 CISR • Medium 6 *Bayraktar* TB2
AIR DEFENCE
 SAM
  Long-range 34 M903 *Patriot* PAC-3 MSE
  Medium-range NASAMS III
  Point-defence FIM-92 *Stinger*; FN-6 (CH-SA-10); *Mistral*
 GUNS • Towed 35mm 8 *Skynex*
 RADAR 1 AN/FPS-132 Upgraded Early Warning Radar
AIR-LAUNCHED MISSILES
 AAM • IR R-550 *Magic* 2; **IIR** AIM-9X Sidewinder II; ASMRAAM; **ARH** AIM-120C-7 AMRAAM; *Meteor*; *Mica* RF
 ASM *Apache*; AGM-114R *Hellfire*; AGR-20A APKWS; HOT
 AShM AM39 *Exocet*; AGM-84L *Harpoon* Block II
BOMBS • INS/GPS-guided AGM-154C JSOW

Gendarmerie & Paramilitary up to 5,000

Internal Security Force up to 5,000

DEPLOYMENT

LEBANON: UN • UNIFIL 1

FOREIGN FORCES

Turkiye 300 (trg team); 1 mech coy; 1 arty unit
United States US Central Command: 10,000; CAOC; 1 ISR sqn with 4 RC-135 *Rivet Joint*; 1 ISR sqn with 4 E-8C JSTARS; 2 tkr sqn with 12 KC-135R/T *Stratotanker*; 1 tpt sqn with 4 C-17A *Globemaster*; 4 C-130H/J-30 *Hercules*; 2 SAM bty with M902/M903 *Patriot* PAC-3/PAC-3 MSE • US Strategic Command: 1 AN/TPY-2 X-band radar

Saudi Arabia SAU

Saudi Riyal SAR		2022	2023	2024
GDP	SAR	4.16trn	4.01trn	4.16trn
	USD	1.11trn	1.07trn	1.11trn
per capita	USD	34,441	32,586	33,144
Growth	%	8.7	0.8	4.0
Inflation	%	2.5	2.5	2.2
Def bdgt [a]	SAR	245bn	259bn	
	USD	65.3bn	69.1bn	
USD1=SAR		3.75	3.75	3.75

[a] Military budget only - excludes security budget

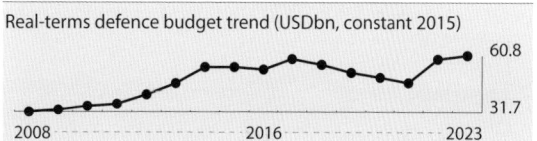

Real-terms defence budget trend (USDbn, constant 2015): 31.7 (2008) to 60.8 (2023)

Population	35,939,806					
Age	0–14	15–19	20–24	25–29	30–64	65 plus
Male	12.0%	4.0%	3.9%	4.2%	30.3%	2.2%
Female	11.5%	3.8%	3.6%	3.5%	19.0%	2.0%

Capabilities

Saudi Arabia is the leading member of the GCC, with the largest and best-equipped armed forces in the group. In addition to traditional objectives relating to territorial integrity and internal security, the Kingdom has displayed an increasing willingness to use the armed forces as part of a more assertive regional foreign policy, most notably in Yemen, where it has battled Iran-backed Ansarullah (Houthi) forces. In 2023, Riyadh agreed to reestablish diplomatic ties with Iran under a China-brokered deal. Operations in Yemen allowed Saudi armed forces to gain combat experience, but exposed areas of weakness and capability gaps, especially in the application of precision airpower, air–ground coordination and logistics. Meanwhile, cruise-missile and UAV attacks on Saudi oil infrastructure have highlighted shortfalls in the Kingdom's air- and missile-defence capabilities. Saudi Arabia's most critical defence relationship is with the US, although recent frictions – including over the Ukraine war, related particularly to oil production – led to a review of that relationship by Washington. Riyadh's engagement with Beijing has been on the rise, with talk of new arms deals. Over the years, Riyadh has sought to mitigate dependence on Washington by also maintaining security relationships with states such as France and the UK and others. Riyadh struck an agreement with Turkiye in 2023 to acquire UAVs. Equipment modernisation continues, with orders for combat aircraft, corvettes and multi-mission surface combatants. There is currently only a modest domestic defence industry, though Riyadh aims to spend 50% of its defence outlays locally as part of its Vision 2030 initiative. The government established the state-owned Saudi Arabian Military Industries to oversee local defence production and has been seeking other partnerships to boost its arms production capacity. The country has an all-volunteer force and, in 2022, opened the field to female recruits.

ACTIVE 257,000 (Army 75,000 Navy 13,500 Air 20,000 Air Defence 16,000 Strategic Missile Forces 2,500 National Guard 130,000) Gendarmerie & Paramilitary 24,500

ORGANISATIONS BY SERVICE

Army 75,000
FORCES BY ROLE
MANOEUVRE
  Armoured
  4 armd bde (1 recce coy, 3 tk bn, 1 mech bn, 1 fd arty bn, 1 AD bn, 1 AT bn, 1 engr coy, 1 log bn, 1 maint coy, 1 med coy)
  Mechanised
  5 mech bde (1 recce coy, 1 tk bn, 3 mech bn, 1 fd arty bn, 1 AD bn, 1 AT bn, 1 engr coy, 1 log bn, 1 maint coy, 1 med coy)
  Light
  2 lt inf bde
  Other
  1 (Al-Saif Al-Ajrab) gd bde
  1 (Royal Guard) gd regt (3 lt inf bn)
Air Manoeuvre
  1 AB bde (2 AB bn, 3 SF coy)
Aviation
  1 comd (3 hel gp)
COMBAT SUPPORT
  3 arty bde
EQUIPMENT BY TYPE
MBT 1,085: 140 AMX-30; ε575 M1A2S *Abrams*; ε370 M60A3 *Patton*
RECCE 300 AML-60/AML-90
IFV 860: 380 AMX-10P; 380 M2A2 *Bradley*; 100 VAB Mk3
APC 1,340
  APC (T) 1,190 M113A4 (incl variants)
  APC (W) 150 Panhard M3; (ε40 AF-40-8-1 *Al-Fahd* in store)
AUV 1,200+: 100 *Didgori* (amb); 1,000+ M-ATV; *Al-Shibl* 2; 100 *Sherpa Light Scout*; Terradyne *Gurkha*
ENGINEERING & MAINTENANCE VEHICLES
  AEV 15 M728
  ARV 275+: 8 ACV ARV; AMX-10EHC; 55 AMX-30D; *Leclerc* ARV; 122 M88A1; 90 M578
  VLB 10 AMX-30
  MW *Aardvark* Mk2
NBC VEHICLES 10 TPz-1 *Fuchs* NBC
ANTI-TANK/ANTI-INFRASTRUCTURE

MSL
  SP 290+: 90+ AMX-10P (HOT); 200 VCC-1 ITOW; M-ATV with *Milan*
  MANPATS *Hyeongung*; Luch *Corsur* (reported); Luch *Skif* (reported); *Stugna*-P (reported); TOW-2A
RCL 84mm *Carl Gustaf*; **90mm** M67; **106mm** M40A1
ARTILLERY 880
  SP 155mm 224: 60 AU-F-1; 110 M109A1B/A2; 54 PLZ-45
  TOWED 201: **105mm** 91 LG1; (100 M101/M102 in store); **155mm** 110: 50 M114; 60 M198
  MRL 88: **127mm** 60 ASTROS II Mk3; **220mm** 10 TOS-1A; **239mm** ε18 K239 *Chunmoo*
  MOR 367: **SP 81mm** 70; **107mm** 150 M30; **120mm** 147: 110 Brandt; 37 M12-1535; **SP 120mm** M113A4 with 2R2M
HELICOPTERS
  ATK 35: 11 AH-64D *Apache*; 24 AH-64E *Apache*
  MRH 21: 6 AS365N *Dauphin* 2 (medevac); 15 Bell 406CS *Combat Scout*
  TPT 90: **Heavy** 4+ CH-47F *Chinook*; **Medium** 67: 22 UH-60A *Black Hawk* (4 medevac); 36 UH-60L *Black Hawk*; 9 UH-60M *Black Hawk*; **Light** 19 Schweizer 333
AIR DEFENCE • SAM
  Short-range *Crotale*
  Point-defence FIM-92 *Stinger*

Navy 13,500
Navy HQ at Riyadh; Eastern Fleet HQ at Jubail; Western Fleet HQ at Jeddah
EQUIPMENT BY TYPE
PRINCIPAL SURFACE COMBATANTS • FRIGATES 10
  FFGHM 10:
    3 *Al-Jubail* (ESP *Avante* 2200) with 2 quad lnchr with RGM-84L *Harpoon* Block II AShM, 2 8-cell Mk 41 VLS with RIM-162B ESSM SAM, 2 triple 324mm ASTT with Mk 46 LWT, 1 76mm gun (capacity 1 med hel)
    3 *Al Riyadh* (FRA *La Fayette* mod) with 2 quad lnchr with MM40 *Exocet* Block 2 AShM, 2 8-cell *Sylver* A43 VLS with *Aster* 15 SAM, 4 single 533mm TT with F17P HWT, 1 76mm gun (capacity 1 AS365N *Dauphin* 2 hel)
    4 *Madina* (FRA F-2000) with 2 quad lnchr with *Otomat* Mk2 AShM, 1 octuple lnchr with *Crotale* SAM, 4 single 533mm TT with F17P HWT, 1 100mm gun (capacity 1 AS365N *Dauphin* 2 hel)
PATROL AND COASTAL COMBATANTS 93
  CORVETTES • FSG 4 *Badr* (US *Tacoma*) with 2 quad lnchr with RGM-84C *Harpoon* Block 1B AShM, 2 triple 324mm ASTT with Mk 46 LWT, 1 Mk 15 *Phalanx* CIWS, 1 76mm gun
  PCFG 9 *Al Siddiq* (US 58m) with 2 twin lnchr with RGM-84C *Harpoon* Block 1B AShM, 1 Mk 15 *Phalanx* CIWS, 1 76mm gun
  PBF 58 HSI 32
  PB 22: 3 2200 FPB; 17 (US) *Halter Marine* 24m; 2 *Plascoa*

2200

MINE WARFARE • MINE COUNTERMEASURES 3
  MHC 3 *Al Jawf* (UK *Sandown*)
AMPHIBIOUS • LANDING CRAFT 5
  LCU ε2 *Al Qiaq* (US LCU 1610) (capacity 120 troops)
  LCM 3 LCM 6 (capacity 80 troops)
LOGISTICS AND SUPPORT 1
  AORH 1 *Boraida* (mod FRA *Durance*) (1 more non-operational and in drydock since 2017) (capacity either 2 AS365F *Dauphin* 2 hel or 1 AS332C *Super Puma*)

Naval Aviation
FORCES BY ROLE
ANTI-SUBMARINE WARFARE
  1 sqn with MH-60R *Seahawk*
TRANSPORT HELICOPTER
  1 sqn with AS365N *Dauphin* 2; AS565 *Panther*
  1 sqn with AS332B/F *Super Puma*
EQUIPMENT BY TYPE
HELICOPTERS
  ASW 8 MH-60R *Seahawk* (in test)
  MRH 21: 6 AS365N *Dauphin* 2; 15 AS565 *Panther*
  TPT • Medium 12 AS332B/F *Super Puma*
AIR-LAUNCHED MISSILES
  AShM AM39 *Exocet*; AS-15TT

Marines 3,000
FORCES BY ROLE
SPECIAL FORCES
  1 spec ops regt with (2 spec ops bn)
EQUIPMENT BY TYPE
ARMOURED FIGHTING VEHICLES
  RECCE *Bastion Patsas*
  APC • APC (W) 135 BMR-600P

Air Force 20,000
FORCES BY ROLE
FIGHTER
  4 sqn with F-15C/D *Eagle*
FIGHTER/GROUND ATTACK
  3 sqn with F-15S/SA *Eagle*
  3 sqn with *Typhoon*
GROUND ATTACK
  3 sqn with *Tornado* IDS; *Tornado* GR1A
AIRBORNE EARLY WARNING & CONTROL
  1 sqn with E-3A *Sentry*
  1 sqn with Saab 2000 *Erieye*
ELINT
  1 sqn with RE-3A/B; Beech 350ER *King Air*
TANKER
  1 sqn with KE-3A
TANKER/TRANSPORT
  1 sqn with KC-130H/J *Hercules*
  1 sqn with A330 MRTT
TRANSPORT
  3 sqn with C-130H *Hercules*; C-130H-30 *Hercules*; CN-235; L-100-30HS (hospital ac)
  2 sqn with Beech 350 *King Air* (forming)
TRAINING
  1 OCU sqn with F-15SA *Eagle*
  3 sqn with *Hawk* Mk65*; *Hawk* Mk65A*; *Hawk* Mk165*
  1 sqn with *Jetstream* Mk31
  1 sqn with MFI-17 *Mushshak*; SR22T
  2 sqn with PC-9; PC-21
TRANSPORT HELICOPTER
  4 sqn with AS532 *Cougar* (CSAR); Bell 212 (AB-212); Bell 412 (AB-412) *Twin Huey* (SAR)
COMBAT/ISR UAV
  2 sqn with CH-4; *Wing Loong* I/II
EQUIPMENT BY TYPE
AIRCRAFT 449 combat capable
  FTR 68 F-15C/D *Eagle*
  FGA 220: up to 66 F-15S *Eagle* (being upgraded to F-15SA configuration); 83 F-15SA *Eagle*; 71 *Typhoon*
  ATK 65 *Tornado* IDS
  ISR 14+: 12 *Tornado* GR1A*; 2+ Beech 350ER *King Air*
  AEW&C 7: 5 E-3A *Sentry*; 2 Saab 2000 *Erieye*
  ELINT 2: 1 RE-3A; 1 RE-3B
  TKR/TPT 15: 6 A330 MRTT; 7 KC-130H *Hercules*; 2 KC-130J *Hercules*
  TKR 7 KE-3A
  TPT 47+: **Medium** 36: 30 C-130H *Hercules*; 3 C-130H-30 *Hercules*; 3 L-100-30; **Light** 11+: 10+ Beech 350 *King Air*; 1 *Jetstream* Mk31
  TRG 203: 24 *Hawk* Mk65* (incl aerobatic team); 16 *Hawk* Mk65A*; 44 *Hawk* Mk165*; 20 MFI-17 *Mushshak*; 20 PC-9; 55 PC-21; 24 SR22T
HELICOPTERS
  MRH 15 Bell 412 (AB-412) *Twin Huey* (SAR)
  TPT 30: **Medium** 10 AS532 *Cougar* (CSAR); **Light** 20 Bell 212 (AB-212)
UNINHABITED AERIAL VEHICLES
  CISR • Heavy some *Wing Loong* I (reported); some *Wing Loong* II (reported); some CH-4; **Medium** some *Haboob* (reported)
  ISR • Medium some *Falco*
AIR-LAUNCHED MISSILES
  AAM • IR AIM-9P/L *Sidewinder*; **IIR** AIM-9X *Sidewinder* II; IRIS-T; **SARH** AIM-7 *Sparrow*; AIM-7M *Sparrow*; **ARH** AIM-120C AMRAAM
  ASM AGM-65 *Maverick*; AR-1; *Brimstone*
  AShM AGM-84L *Harpoon* Block II
  ARM ALARM
  ALCM *Storm Shadow*
BOMBS
  Laser-guided GBU-10/12 *Paveway* II; *Paveway* IV;

MAM-L (reported)
Laser & INS/GPS-guided GBU-54 Laser JDAM
INS/GPS-guided AGM-154C JSOW; FT-9; GBU-31 JDAM; GBU-39 Small Diameter Bomb (reported)

Royal Flight
EQUIPMENT BY TYPE
AIRCRAFT • TPT 24: **Medium** 8: 5 C-130H *Hercules*; 3 L-100-30; **Light** 3: 1 Cessna 310; 2 Learjet 35; **PAX** 13: 1 A340; 1 B-737-200; 2 B-737BBJ; 2 B-747SP; 4 BAe-125-800; 2 Gulfstream III; 1 Gulfstream IV
HELICOPTERS • TPT 3+: **Medium** 3: 2 AS-61; 1 S-70 *Black Hawk*; **Light** some Bell 212 (AB-212)

Air Defence Forces 16,000
FORCES BY ROLE
AIR DEFENCE
6 bn with M902 *Patriot* PAC-3
17 bty with *Shahine*/AMX-30SA
16 bty with MIM-23B *I-Hawk*
EQUIPMENT BY TYPE
AIR DEFENCE
SAM 817+
  Long-range 108 M902 *Patriot* PAC-3
  Medium-range 128 MIM-23B *I-Hawk*
  Short-range 181: 40 *Crotale*; 141 *Shahine*
  Point-defence 400+: LMM; 400 M1097 *Avenger*; *Mistral*
GUNS 218
  SP • 20mm 90 M163 *Vulcan*
  TOWED 128: **35mm** 128 GDF Oerlikon; **40mm** (150 L/70 in store)
DE • Laser *Silent Hunter*

Strategic Missile Forces 2,500
EQUIPMENT BY TYPE
MSL • TACTICAL
  IRBM 10+ DF-3 (CH-SS-2) (service status unclear)
  MRBM Some DF-21 (CH-SS-5 – variant unclear) (reported)

National Guard 130,000
FORCES BY ROLE
MANOEUVRE
  Mechanised
  5 mech bde (1 recce coy, 3 mech inf bn, 1 SP arty bn, 1 cbt engr coy, 1 sigs coy, 1 log bn)
  Light
  5 inf bde (3 combined arms bn, 1 arty bn, 1 log bn)
  3 indep lt inf bn
  Other
  1 (Special Security) sy bde (3 sy bn)
  1 (ceremonial) cav sqn
COMBAT SUPPORT
  1 MP bn

HELICOPTER
  3 hel bde
  1 hel trg bde
EQUIPMENT BY TYPE
ARMOURED FIGHTING VEHICLES
  ASLT 204: 204 LAV-AG (90mm); LAV 700 (105mm)
  IFV 1,285: ε635 LAV-25; ε650 LAV 700 (incl variants)
  APC 778
    APC (W) 514: 116 LAV-A (amb); 30 LAV-AC (ammo carrier); 296 LAV-CC (CP); 72 LAV-PC
    PPV 264 *Aravis*; some *Arive*
ENGINEERING & MAINTENANCE VEHICLES
  AEV 58 LAV-E
  ARV 111 LAV-R; V-150 ARV
  MW MV5; MV10
ANTI-TANK/ANTI-INFRASTRUCTURE
  MSL
    SP 182 LAV-AT
    MANPATS TOW-2A; M47 *Dragon*
  RCL • 106mm M40A1
ARTILLERY 359+
  SP 155mm up to 132 CAESAR
  TOWED 108: **105mm** 50 M102; **155mm** 58 M198
  MOR 119+: **81mm** some; **SP 120mm** 119: 107 LAV-M; 12 LAV-M with NEMO
HELICOPTERS
  ATK 24 AH-64E *Apache*
  MRH 35: 23 AH-6i *Little Bird*; 12 MD530F (trg role)
  TPT • Medium ε50 UH-60M *Black Hawk*
AIR DEFENCE
  SAM 79
    Short-range 11 VL MICA
    Point-defence 68 MPCV
  GUNS • TOWED • 20mm 30 M167 *Vulcan*
AIR-LAUNCHED MISSILES
  ASM AGM-114R *Hellfire* II

Gendarmerie & Paramilitary 24,500+ active

Border Guard 15,000
FORCES BY ROLE
Subordinate to Ministry of Interior. HQ in Riyadh. 9 subordinate regional commands
MANOEUVRE
  Other
  Some mobile def (long-range patrol/spt) units
  2 border def (patrol) units
  12 infrastructure def units
  18 harbour def units
  Some coastal def units
COMBAT SUPPORT
  Some MP units
EQUIPMENT BY TYPE

ARMOURED FIGHTING VEHICLES
APC • PPV *Caprivi* Mk1/Mk3
PATROL AND COASTAL COMBATANTS 108
PCC 15 OPB 40
PBF 85: 4 *Al Jouf*; 2 *Sea Guard*; 79 *Plascoa* FIC 1650
PB 8: 6 Damen Stan Patrol 2606; 2 *Al Jubatel*
AMPHIBIOUS • LANDING CRAFT • UCAC 8: 5 *Griffon* 8000; 3 other
LOGISTICS AND SUPPORT 4: 1 AXL; 3 AO

Facilities Security Force 9,000+
Subordinate to Ministry of Interior

General Civil Defence Administration Units
EQUIPMENT BY TYPE
HELICOPTERS • TPT • **Medium** 10 Boeing *Vertol* 107

Special Security Force 500
EQUIPMENT BY TYPE
ARMOURED FIGHTING VEHICLES
APC • APC (W) UR-416
AUV 60+: *Gurkha* LAPV; 60 *Kozak*-5

DEPLOYMENT
YEMEN: *Operation Restoring Hope* 2,500; 2 armd BG; M60A3; M2A2 *Bradley*; M113A4; M-ATV; 2+ M902 *Patriot* PAC-3

FOREIGN FORCES
France 50 (radar det)
Greece 100: 1 SAM bty with M901 *Patriot* PAC-2
United Kingdom 100; 1 SAM bty with FV4333 *Stormer* with *Starstreak*
United States US Central Command: 2,500; 2 FGA sqn with 12 F-16C *Fighting Falcon*; 1 tkr sqn with 12 KC-135R *Stratotanker*; 1 AEW&C sqn with 4 E-3B/G *Sentry*; 1 SAM bty with M902/M903 *Patriot* PAC-3/PAC-3 MSE; 1 SAM bty with THAAD

Syria SYR

Syrian Pound SYP		2022	2023	2024
GDP	SYP			
	USD			
per capita	USD			
Growth	%			
Inflation	%			
Def exp	SYP			
	USD			
USD1=SYP				

Definitive economic data not available

Population	22,933,531				
Age	0–14	15–19	20–24	25–29	30–64	65 plus
Male	17.1%	4.9%	4.7%	4.2%	17.4%	1.9%
Female	16.2%	4.6%	4.6%	4.4%	17.8%	2.2%

Capabilities

Syria returned to the Arab League in May 2023 after it was suspended in 2011 as the civil war in the country gained pace. Frontlines in the conflict have changed little in the past few years. In addition to intra-Syrian fighting, Turkiye has repeatedly struck Kurdish targets in the country. The protracted civil war has significantly depleted the combat capabilities of the Syrian armed forces and transformed them into an irregularly structured militia-style organisation focused on internal security. Various nominally pro-government militias, often formed around local or religious identity, are reportedly funded by local businessmen or foreign powers, raising questions over capability and morale as well as loyalty. There are allegations that some elements of the Syrian Arab Army are involved in the production and distribution of illegal narcotics to other countries in the region, the Gulf and Europe. There is no published defence doctrine with the conflict instead dictating ad hoc requirements. Opposition groups maintain control over parts of the country. The government led by President Bashar al-Assad controls about 70% of Syria. Most formal pre-war structures and formations exist in name only, as resources have been channelled into the irregular network of military organisations that form the regime's most effective military capabilities. Russia has been the regime's principal ally and has provided essential combat support and assistance, as well as replacement equipment. Russia is also involved in efforts to reconstitute the army's pre-war divisions, although some Russian equipment has been withdrawn following Russia's 2022 invasion of Ukraine. Iran and Hizbullah continue to train militias and other ground forces. Washington has said that Russia and Iran showed signs of coordinating some of their efforts in Syria to confront US interests. Overall levels of training remain poor, but combat experience has improved proficiency in select regular and irregular military formations. The armed forces lack the requisite capabilities for external deployment, although they remain able to redeploy moderate numbers of formations and capabilities within the country. Logistics support for major internal operations away from established bases remains a challenge. Before the civil war, Syria did not have a major domestic defence industry, although it possessed facilities to overhaul and maintain its existing systems. It possessed some capacity in focused areas, such as ballistic missiles and chemical weapons. International efforts continue to verify destruction of chemical-weapons stockpiles and production facilities.

ACTIVE 169,000 (Army 130,000 Navy 4,000 Air 15,000 Air Defence 20,000) Gendarmerie & Paramilitary 100,000

Conscript liability 30 months (there is widespread avoidance of military service)

ORGANISATIONS BY SERVICE

Army ε130,000
FORCES BY ROLE

The Syrian Arab Army combines conventional formations, special forces and auxiliary militias. The main fighting units are the 4th Division, the Republican Guard, the Special Forces (including the former Tiger Forces) and the brigades assigned to the 5th Assault Corps; they receive the most attention and training. Most other formations are under-strength, at an estimated 500–1,000 personnel in brigades and regiments, but Russia has been assisting in the reconstruction and re-equipment of some divisions.

COMMAND
  5 corps HQ
SPECIAL FORCES
  3 SF div(-)
MANOEUVRE
  Mechanised
  2 (4th & Republican Guard) mech div
  1 (1st) mech div (being reconstituted)
  10 mech div(-)
  7 mech bde (assigned to 5th Assault Corps)
  1 (16th) indep mech bde
  2 indep inf bde(-)
  Amphibious
  1 mne unit
COMBAT SUPPORT
  2 SSM bde
EQUIPMENT BY TYPE

Attrition during the civil war has severely reduced equipment numbers for almost all types. It is unclear how much remains available for operations

ARMOURED FIGHTING VEHICLES
  MBT T-55A; T-55AM; T-55AMV; T-62; T-62M; T-72; T-72AV; T-72B; T-72B3; T-72M1; T-90; T-90A
  RECCE BRDM-2
  IFV BMP-1; BMP-2; BTR-82A
  APC
    APC (T) BTR-50
    APC (W) BTR-152; BTR-60; BTR-70; BTR-80
  APC IVECO LMV
ENGINEERING & MAINTENANCE VEHICLES
  ARV BREM-1 reported; T-54/55
  VLB MTU; MTU-20
  MW UR-77
ANTI-TANK/ANTI-INFRASTRUCTURE • MSL
  SP 9P133 *Malyutka*-P (BRDM-2 with RS-AT-3C *Sagger*); 9P148 *Konkurs* (BRDM-2 with RS-AT-5 *Spandrel*)
  MANPATS 9K111 *Fagot* (RS-AT-4 *Spigot*); 9K111-1 *Konkurs* (RS-AT-5 *Spandrel*); 9K115 *Metis* (RS-AT-7 *Saxhorn*); 9K115-2 *Metis*-M (RS-AT-13); 9K135 *Kornet* (RS-AT-14 *Spriggan*); Milan
ARTILLERY
  SP 122mm 2S1 *Gvozdika*; **152mm** 2S3 *Akatsiya*
  TOWED 122mm D-30; M-30 (M1938); **130mm** M-46; **152mm** D-20; ML-20 (M-1937); **180mm** S-23
  GUN/MOR 120mm 2S9 NONA-S
  MRL 107mm Type-63; **122mm** BM-21 *Grad*; **140mm** BM-14; **220mm** 9P140 *Uragan*; **300mm** 9A52 *Smerch*; **330mm** some (also improvised systems of various calibres)
  MOR 82mm some; **120mm** M-1943; **160mm** M-160; **240mm** M-240
SURFACE-TO-SURFACE MISSILE LAUNCHERS
  SRBM • Conventional 8K14 (RS-SS-1C *Scud-B*); 9K72 *Elbrus* (RS-SS-1D *Scud* C) 9K72-1 (RS-SS-1E *Scud* D); *Scud* lookalike; 9K79 *Tochka* (RS-SS-21 *Scarab*); Fateh-110/M-600
UNINHABITED AERIAL VEHICLES
  ISR • Medium *Mohajer* 3/4; **Light** *Ababil*
AIR DEFENCE
  SAM
    Medium-range 9K37 *Buk* (RS-SA-11 *Gadfly*); 9K317 *Buk*-M2 (RS-SA-17 *Grizzly*)
    Point-defence 9K31 *Strela*-1 (RS-SA-9 *Gaskin*); 9K33 *Osa* (RS-SA-8 *Gecko*); 9K35 *Strela*-10 (RS-SA-13 *Gopher*); 9K32 *Strela*-2 (RS-SA-7 *Grail*)‡; 9K38 *Igla* (RS-SA-18 *Grouse*); 9K36 *Strela*-3 (RS-SA-14 *Gremlin*); 9K338 *Igla-S* (RS-SA-24 *Grinch*)
  SPAAGM 30mm 96K6 *Pantsir*-S1 (RS-SA-22 *Greyhound*)
  GUNS
    SP 23mm ZSU-23-4; **57mm** ZSU-57-2
    TOWED 23mm ZU-23-2; **37mm** M-1939; **57mm** S-60; **100mm** KS-19

Navy ε4,000

Some personnel are likely to have been drafted into other services

EQUIPMENT BY TYPE
PATROL AND COASTAL COMBATANTS 31:
  CORVETTES • FS 1 Project 159AE (*Petya* III)† with 1 triple 533mm ASTT with SAET-60 HWT, 4 RBU 2500 *Smerch* 1 A/S mor, 2 twin 76mm gun
  PBFG 22:
    16 Project 205 (*Osa* I/II)† with 4 single lnchr with P-22 (RS-SS-N-2C *Styx*) AShM
    6 *Tir* with 2 single lnchr with C-802 (CH-SS-N-6) AShM
  PB 8 *Zhuk*†
MINE WARFARE • MINE COUNTERMEASURES 7
  MHC 1 Project 1265 (*Sonya*) with 2 quad lnchr with

9K32 *Strela*-2 (RS-SA-N-5 *Grail*)‡ SAM, 2 AK630 CIWS
MSO 1 *Akvamaren*-M (FSU Project 266M (*Natya*)) with 2 quad lnchr with 9K32 *Strela*-2 (RS-SA-N-5 *Grail*)‡ SAM
MSI 5 *Korund* (Project 1258 (*Yevgenya*))
AMPHIBIOUS • LANDING SHIPS • LSM 3 *Polnochny* B (capacity 6 MBT; 180 troops)
LOGISTICS AND SUPPORT • AX 1 *Al Assad*

Coastal Defence
FORCES BY ROLE
COASTAL DEFENCE
  1 AShM bde with P-35 (RS-SSC-1B *Sepal*); P-15M *Termit*-R (RS-SSC-3 *Styx*); C-802; K-300P *Bastion* (RS-SSC-5 *Stooge*)
EQUIPMENT BY TYPE
COASTAL DEFENCE • AShM P-35 (RS-SSC-1B *Sepal*); P-15M *Termit*-R (RS-SSC-3 *Styx*); C-802; K-300P *Bastion* (RS-SSC-5 *Stooge*)

Naval Aviation
All possibly non-operational after vacating base for Russian deployment
EQUIPMENT BY TYPE
HELICOPTERS • ASW 9: 4 Ka-28 *Helix* A; 5 Mi-14 *Haze*

Air Force ε15,000(-)
FORCES BY ROLE
FIGHTER
  2 sqn with Mig-23MF/ML/MLD/UM *Flogger*
  2 sqn with MiG-29A/UB/SM *Fulcrum*
FIGHTER/GROUND ATTACK
  4 sqn with MiG-21MF/bis *Fishbed*; MiG-21U *Mongol* A
  2 sqn with MiG-23BN/UB *Flogger*
GROUND ATTACK
  4 sqn with Su-22M3/M4 *Fitter* J/K
  1 sqn with Su-24MK *Fencer* D
  1 sqn with L-39ZA/ZO *Albatros**
TRANSPORT
  1 sqn with An-24 *Coke*; An-26 *Curl*; Il-76 *Candid*
  1 sqn with Falcon 20; Falcon 900
  1 sqn with Tu-134B-3
  1 sqn with Yak-40 *Codling*
ATTACK HELICOPTER
  3 sqn with Mi-24D/P *Hind* D/F
  2 sqn with SA342L *Gazelle*
TRANSPORT HELICOPTER
  6 sqn with Mi-8 *Hip*/Mi-17 *Hip* H
EQUIPMENT BY TYPE
Heavy use of both fixed- and rotary-wing assets has likely reduced readiness and availability to very low levels. It is estimated that no more than 30–40% of the inventory is operational
AIRCRAFT 184 combat capable
  FTR 55: ε25 MiG-23MF/ML/MLD/UM *Flogger*; ε30 MiG-29A/SM/UB *Fulcrum*
  FGA 79: ε50 MiG-21MF/bis *Fishbed* J/L; 9 MiG-21U *Mongol* A; ε20 MiG-23BN/UB *Flogger*
  ATK 30: 20 Su-22M3/M4 *Fitter* J/K; ε10 Su-24MK *Fencer* D
  TPT 23: **Heavy** 3 Il-76 *Candid*; **Light** 13: 1 An-24 *Coke*; 6 An-26 *Curl*; 2 PA-31 *Navajo*; 4 Yak-40 *Codling*; **PAX** 7: 2 Falcon 20; 1 Falcon 900; 4 Tu-134B-3
  TRG 20+: ε20 L-39ZA/ZO *Albatros**; some MBB-223 *Flamingo*†
HELICOPTERS
  ATK 20+: ε20 Mi-24D *Hind* D; some Mi-24P *Hind* F
  MRH 40: ε20 Mi-17 *Hip* H; ε20 SA342L *Gazelle*
  TPT • Medium ε10 Mi-8 *Hip*
AIR-LAUNCHED MISSILES
  AAM • IR R-60 (RS-AA-8 *Aphid*); R-73 (RS-AA-11 *Archer*); **IR/SARH**; R-23/24 (RS-AA-7 *Apex*); R-27 (RS-AA-10 *Alamo*); **ARH**; R-77 (RS-AA-12A *Adder*)
  ASM Kh-25 (RS-AS-10 *Karen*); Kh-29T/L (RS-AS-14 *Kedge*); HOT
  ARM Kh-31P (RS-AS-17A *Krypton*)

Air Defence Command ε20,000
FORCES BY ROLE
AIR DEFENCE
  4 AD div with S-125M/M1 *Pechora*-M/M1 (RS-SA-3 *Goa*); S-125-2M *Pechora*-2M (RS-SA-26); 2K12 *Kub* (RS-SA-6 *Gainful*); S-75 *Dvina* (RS-SA-2 *Guideline*)
  3 AD regt with S-200 *Angara* (RS-SA-5 *Gammon*); S-300PMU2 (RS-SA-20 *Gargoyle*)
EQUIPMENT BY TYPE
AIR DEFENCE • SAM
  Long-range S-200 *Angara* (RS-SA-5 *Gammon*); 20 S-300PMU2 (RS-SA-20 *Gargoyle*)
  Medium-range 36+: S-75 *Dvina* (RS-SA-2 *Guideline*); ε36 S-125-2M *Pechora*-2M (RS-SA-26)
  Short-range 2K12 *Kub* (RS-SA-6 *Gainful*); S-125M/M1 *Pechora*-M/M1 (RS-SA-3 *Goa*)
  Point-defence 9K32 *Strela*-2/2M (RS-SA-7A/B *Grail*)‡

Gendarmerie & Paramilitary ε100,000

National Defence Force ε50,000
An umbrella of disparate regime militias performing a variety of roles, including territorial control

Other Militias ε50,000
Numerous military groups fighting for the Assad regime, including Afghan, Iraqi, Pakistani and sectarian organisations. Some receive significant Iranian support

FOREIGN FORCES
Hizbullah 7,000–8,000
Iran 1,500
Russia 4,000: 1 inf BG; 3 MP bn; 1 engr unit; ε10 T-72B3; ε20 BTR-82A; BPM-97; 12 2A65; 4 9A52 *Smerch*; 10 Su-24M *Fencer*; 6 Su-34; 6 Su-35S; 1 A-50U; 1 Il-20M; 12 Mi-24P/

Mi-35M *Hind*; 4 Mi-8AMTSh *Hip*; 1 AShM bty with 3K55 *Bastion* (RS-SSC-5 *Stooge*); 1 SAM bty with S-400 (RS-SA-21 *Growler*); 1 SAM bty with *Pantsir*-S1/S2; air base at Latakia; naval facility at Tartus

NORTHERN & EASTERN SYRIA

Data here represents the de facto situation for selected armed opposition groups and their observed equipment

Syrian Democratic Forces ε50,000

A coalition of predominantly Kurdish rebel groups in de facto control of much of northeastern Syria. Kurdish forces from the YPG/J (People's Protection Units/Women's Protection Units) provide military leadership and main combat power, supplemented by Arab militias and tribal groups.

EQUIPMENT BY TYPE
ARMOURED FIGHTING VEHICLES
    MBT T-55; T-72 (reported)
    IFV BMP-1
    APC • PPV *Guardian*
    AUV M-ATV
ANTI-TANK/ANTI-INFRASTRUCTURE
    MSL • MANPATS 9K111-1 *Konkurs* (RS-SA-5 *Spandrel*)
    RCL 73mm SPG-9; **90mm** M-79 *Osa*
ARTILLERY
    MRL 122mm BM-21 *Grad*; 9K132 *Grad*-P
    MOR 82mm 82-BM-37; M-1938; **120mm** M-1943; improvised mortars of varying calibre
AIR DEFENCE • GUNS
    SP 14.5mm ZPU-4 (tch); ZPU-2 (tch); ZPU-1 (tch); 1 ZPU-2 (tch/on T-55); **23mm** ZSU-23-4 *Shilka*; ZU-23-2 (tch); **57mm** S-60
    TOWED 14.5mm ZPU-2; ZPU-1; **23mm** ZU-23-2

Syrian National Army & National Front for Liberation ε70,000

In late 2019 the Syrian National Army (SNA) and the National Front for Liberation (NLF) began to merge under the SNA umbrella. The SNA formed in late 2017 from Syrian Arab and Turkmen rebel factions operating under Turkish command in the Aleppo governate and northwestern Syria, including Afrin province. The NLF is a coalition of surviving Islamist and nationalist rebel factions formed in 2018 operating in northwestern Syria, particularly in and around Idlib.

EQUIPMENT BY TYPE
ARMOURED FIGHTING VEHICLES
    MBT T-54; T-55; T-62
    IFV BMP-1
ANTI-TANK/ANTI-INFRASTRUCTURE
    MSL • MANPATS 9K11 *Malyutka* (RS-AT-3 *Sagger*); 9K111 *Fagot* (RS-AT-4 *Spigot*); 9K113 *Konkurs* (RS-T-5 *Spandrel*); 9K115 *Metis* (RS-AT-7); 9K115-2 *Metis*-M (RS-AT-13 *Saxhorn* 2); 9K135 *Kornet* (RS-AT-14 *Spriggan*); BGM-71 TOW; *Milan*
    RCL 73mm SPG-9; **82mm** B-10
ARTILLERY
    TOWED 122mm D-30
    MRL 107mm Type-63; **122mm** 9K132 *Grad*-P; BM-21 *Grad*; *Grad* (6-tube tech)
    MOR 82mm 2B9 *Vasilek*; improvised mortars of varying calibre
AIR DEFENCE
    SAM • Point-defence MANPADS some
    GUNS
        SP 14.5mm ZPU-4 (tch); ZPU-2 (tch); ZPU-1 (tch); **23mm** ZU-23-2 (tch); ZSU-23-4 *Shilka*; **57mm** AZP S-60
        TOWED 14.5mm ZPU-1; ZPU-2; ZPU-4; **23mm** ZU-23-2

Hayat Tahrir al-Sham (HTS) ε10,000

HTS was formed by Jabhat Fateh al-Sham (formerly known as Jabhat al-Nusra) in January 2017 by absorbing other hardline groups. It is designated a terrorist organisation by the US government.

EQUIPMENT BY TYPE
ANTI-TANK/ANTI-INFRASTRUCTURE
    MSL • MANPATS 9K11 *Malyutka* (RS-AT-3 *Sagger*); 9K113 *Konkurs* (RS-AT-5 *Spandrel*); 9K115-2 *Metis*-M (RS-AT-13); 9K135 *Kornet* (RS-AT-14 *Spriggan*)
    RCL 73mm SPG-9; **106mm** M-40
ARTILLERY
    MRL 107mm Type-63
    MOR 120mm some; improvised mortars of varying calibres
AIR DEFENCE
    SAM
        Point-defence 9K32M *Strela*-2M (RS-SA-7B *Grail*)‡
    GUNS
        SP 14.5mm ZPU-1; ZPU-2; **23mm** ZU-23-2; **57mm** S-60

Guardians of Religion (Huras al-Din) ε2,500

An al-Qaeda-affiliated group operating in Idlib province. It is designated a terrorist organisation by the US government.

FOREIGN FORCES

Turkiye ε3,000; 3 armd BG; some cdo units; 1 gendarmerie unit
United States *Operation Inherent Resolve* 900; 1 armd inf coy; 1 spec ops bn(-)

Tunisia TUN

Tunisian Dinar TND		2022	2023	2024
GDP	TND	144bn	159bn	178bn
	USD	46.4bn	51.3bn	53.5bn
per capita	USD	3,822	4,191	4,336
Growth	%	2.5	1.3	1.9
Inflation	%	8.3	9.4	9.8
Def bgt	TND	3.56bn	3.75bn	4.09bn
	USD	1.15bn	1.21bn	1.23bn
FMA (US)	USD	60m	45m	45m
USD1=TND		3.10	3.10	3.33

Real-terms defence budget trend (USDbn, constant 2015)

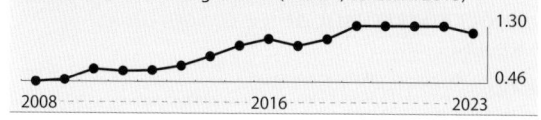

Population 11,976,182

Age	0–14	15–19	20–24	25–29	30–64	65 plus
Male	12.8%	3.5%	3.0%	3.2%	22.4%	4.7%
Female	12.0%	3.3%	3.0%	3.3%	23.6%	5.3%

Capabilities

The main tasks of Tunisia's armed forces are to ensure territorial sovereignty and internal security. The military has limited capacities, but a modernisation process is underway. Instability in Libya continues to pose a concern, although the terrorist threat from its borders has diminished. Designated a major non-NATO ally by the US in 2015, Tunisia also benefits from defence and security cooperation with France and Italy. A ten-year military-cooperation agreement signed with the US in 2020 provides training and after-sales support. The support has continued despite President Kais Saied seizing power in 2021. Tunisia contributed a C-130J-30 transport aircraft to the UN MINUSMA mission in Mali and a helicopter unit with a battalion to the UN MINUSCA mission in the Central African Republic. The military participates in multinational exercises and has been confirmed as one of the hosts for *African Lion* 2024, led by the US Africa Command. Overall military capability is affected by the ageing equipment inventory, although Tunisia has been the recipient of surplus US systems, including armed utility helicopters. In 2021 and 2023, the air force received *Anka*-S armed UAVs reflecting growing relations with Türkiye. The country has limited defence-industrial capabilities, but has manufactured a small number of patrol boats for the navy between 2015 and 2021.

ACTIVE 35,800 (Army 27,000 Navy 4,800 Air 4,000)
Gendarmerie & Paramilitary 12,000

Conscript liability 12 months selective

ORGANISATIONS BY SERVICE

Army 5,000; 22,000 conscript (total 27,000)

FORCES BY ROLE
SPECIAL FORCES
  1 SF bde
  1 (Sahara) SF bde
MANOEUVRE
  Reconnaissance
    1 recce regt
  Mechanised
    3 mech bde (1 armd regt, 2 mech inf regt, 1 arty regt, 1 AD regt, 1 engr regt, 1 sigs regt, 1 log gp)
COMBAT SUPPORT
  1 engr regt
EQUIPMENT BY TYPE
ARMOURED FIGHTING VEHICLES
  MBT 84: 30 M60A1; 54 M60A3
  LT TK 48 SK-105 *Kuerassier*
  RECCE 60: 40 AML-90; 20 FV601 *Saladin*
  APC 480
    APC (T) 140 M113A1/A2
    APC (W) 110 Fiat 6614
    PPV 230: 4 *Bastion* APC: 71 *Ejder Yalcin*; 146 *Kirpi*; 9 *Vuran*
ENGINEERING & MAINTENANCE VEHICLES
  ARV 11: 5 *Greif*; 6 M88A1
ANTI-TANK/ANTI-INFRASTRUCTURE • MSL
  SP 35 M901 ITV TOW
  MANPATS *Milan*; TOW
ARTILLERY 276
  TOWED 115: **105mm** 48 M101A1/A2; **155mm** 67: 12 M114A1; 55 M198
  MOR 161: **81mm** 95; **SP 107mm** 48 M106; **120mm** 18 Brandt
AIR DEFENCE
  SAM • **Point-defence** 26+: 26 M48 *Chaparral*; RBS-70
  GUNS 100
    TOWED • **20mm** 100 M-55

Navy ε4,800
EQUIPMENT BY TYPE
PATROL AND COASTAL COMBATANTS 45
  PSO 4 *Jugurtha* (Damen Stan MSOPV 1400) (of which 2 with 1 hel landing platform)
  PCFG 3 *La Galite* (FRA *Combattante* III) with 2 quad lnchr with MM40 *Exocet* AShM, 1 76mm gun
  PCC 3 *Bizerte* (FRA PR 48)
  PCFT 6 *Albatros* (GER Type-143B) with 2 single 533mm TT, 2 76mm guns
  PBF 9: 3 Safe 44; 4 Safe 65; 2 *Sentry* 44
  PB 20: 5 *Istiklal*; 3 *Utique* (ex-PRC Type-062 (*Haizhui* II) mod); 6 *Joumhouria*; 6 V Series
LOGISTICS AND SUPPORT 7:
  ABU 3: 2 *Tabarka* (ex-US *White Sumac*); 1 *Sisi Bou Said*
  AGE 1 *Hannibal*

AGS 1 *Khaireddine* (ex-US *Wilkes*)
AWT 1 *Ain Zaghouan* (ex-ITA *Simeto*)
AXL 1 *Salambo* (ex-US *Conrad*, survey)

Air Force 4,000
FORCES BY ROLE
FIGHTER/GROUND ATTACK
1 sqn with F-5E/F-5F *Tiger* II
TRANSPORT
2 sqn with C-130B/H/J-30 *Hercules*;
1 sqn with G.222; L-410 *Turbolet*
1 liaison unit with S-208A
TRAINING
1 sqn with L-59 *Albatros**; T-6C *Texan* II
1 sqn with SF-260
ATTACK HELICOPTER
2 sqn with OH-58D *Kiowa Warrior*
TRANSPORT HELICOPTER
2 sqn with AS350B *Ecureuil*; AS365 *Dauphin* 2; AB-205 (Bell 205); SA313; SA316 *Alouette* III; UH-1H *Iroquois*; UH-1N *Iroquois*
1 sqn with HH-3E
COMBAT/ISR UAV
1 sqn with Anka-S

EQUIPMENT BY TYPE
AIRCRAFT 20 combat capable
FTR 11: 9 F-5E *Tiger* II; 2 F-5F *Tiger* II
ISR 12 *Maule* MX-7-180B
TPT 18: **Medium** 13: 5 C-130B *Hercules*; 1 C-130H *Hercules*; 2 C-130J-30 *Hercules*; 5 G.222; **Light** 5: 3 L-410 *Turbolet*; 2 S-208A
TRG 31: 9 L-59 *Albatros**; 14 SF-260; 8 T-6C *Texan* II
HELICOPTERS
MRH 34: 1 AS365 *Dauphin* 2; 6 SA313; 3 SA316 *Alouette* III; 24 OH-58D *Kiowa Warrior*
SAR 11 HH-3E
TPT 39: **Medium** 8 UH-60M *Black Hawk*; **Light** 31: 6 AS350B *Ecureuil*; 15 Bell 205 (AB-205); 8 Bell 205 (UH-1H *Iroquois*); 2 Bell 212 (UH-1N *Iroquois*)
UNINHABITED AERIAL VEHICLES
CISR • **Heavy** 5 *Anka-S*
AIR-LAUNCHED MISSILES
AAM • **IR** AIM-9P *Sidewinder*
ASM AGM-114R *Hellfire*

Gendarmerie & Paramilitary 12,000

National Guard 12,000
Ministry of Interior
EQUIPMENT BY TYPE
ARMOURED FIGHTING VEHICLES
ASLT 2 EE-11 *Urutu* FSV
APC 29+
    APC (W) 16 EE-11 *Urutu* (anti-riot); VAB Mk3

PPV 13 Streit *Typhoon*
AUV IVECO LMV
PATROL AND COASTAL COMBATANTS 27
PCC 6 *Rais el Blais* (ex-GDR *Kondor* I)
PBF 10: 4 *Gabes*; 6 *Patrouiller*
PB 11: 5 *Breitla* (ex-GDR *Bremse*); 4 Rodman 38; 2 *Socomena*
HELICOPTERS
MRH 8 SA318 *Alouette* II/SA319 *Alouette* III
TPT • **Light** 3 Bell 429

DEPLOYMENT
CENTRAL AFRICAN REPUBLIC: UN • MINUSCA 775; 1 inf bn; 1 hel flt with 3 Bell 205
DEMOCRATIC REPUBLIC OF THE CONGO: UN • MONUSCO 10
SOUTH SUDAN: UN • UNMISS 2
SUDAN: UN • UNISFA 1

United Arab Emirates UAE

Emirati Dirham AED		2022	2023	2024
GDP	AED	1.86trn	1.87trn	1.97trn
	USD	507bn	509bn	537bn
per capita	USD	51,400	50,602	52,407
Growth	%	7.9	3.4	4.0
Inflation	%	4.8	3.1	2.3
Def bdgt [a]	AED	ε74.8bn	ε76.2bn	
	USD	ε20.4bn	ε20.7bn	
USD1=AED		3.67	3.67	3.67

[a] Defence budget estimate derived from central MoD expenditure and a proportion of the Federal Services section of the Abu Dhabi budget

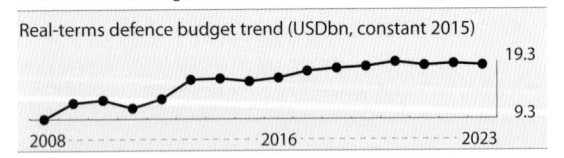

Real-terms defence budget trend (USDbn, constant 2015)
19.3
9.3
2008 — 2016 — 2023

Population 9,973,449

Age	0–14	15–19	20–24	25–29	30–64	65 plus
Male	8.3%	2.9%	2.9%	4.7%	48.0%	1.5%
Female	7.9%	2.5%	2.4%	3.2%	15.2%	0.5%

Capabilities

The UAE's armed forces are arguably the best trained and most capable of all Gulf Cooperation Council states. Iran remains a key defence concern, partly because of a continuing dispute with Tehran over ownership of islands in the Strait of Hormuz. The UAE has shown a growing willingness to take part in operations and project power and influence further abroad, such as its involvement in the conflicts in Afghanistan and Libya in the early to mid-2010s. The UAE was also heavily engaged in the Yemen conflict as part of the Saudi-led coalition. Experience gained in Yemen-related operations generated combat lessons and has demonstrated the country's developing approach to the use of force and the acceptance of military risk. The UAE hosts a French base as well as a small South Korean troop contingent. Attempts to diversify security relationships, including with China, are complicating ties with the US, which remains the country's main extra-regional defence partner. A new defence agreement with Washington came into force in May 2019 and the US Air Force continues to maintain a substantial force at the Al Dhafra airbase. The country's growing relationship with Israel has resulted in the purchase of Israeli equipment, though the Hamas–Israel War has raised questions about the future of the relationship. Improved ties with Turkiye have led to the purchase of Turkish UAVs and the signing of major defence industrial agreements. The Emirati armed forces operate an advanced inventory of modern equipment across domains.The UAE has been trying to develop a domestic defence industry, most recently through the state-owned EDGE Group as well as several private and semi-private entities.

ACTIVE 63,000 (Army 44,000 Navy 2,500 Air 4,500 Presidential Guard 12,000)

Conscript liability 16–24 months, males 18–30 years dependent on education level. Voluntary service enrolment for women

ORGANISATIONS BY SERVICE

Space
EQUIPMENT BY TYPE
SATELLITES 4
  COMMUNICATIONS 3 *Yahsat*
  ISR 1 *FalconEye*

Army 44,000
FORCES BY ROLE
MANOEUVRE
  Armoured
  2 armd bde
  Mechanised
  2 mech bde
  Light
  1 inf bde
COMBAT SUPPORT
  1 arty bde (3 SP arty regt)
  1 engr gp
EQUIPMENT BY TYPE
ARMOURED FIGHTING VEHICLES
  MBT 313: 45 AMX-30; 268 *Leclerc*
  LT TK 76 FV101 *Scorpion*
  RECCE 49 AML-90
  IFV 400 *Rabdan*
  APC 1,656
    APC (T) 136 AAPC (incl 53 engr plus other variants)
    APC (W) 185: 45 AMV 8×8 (one with BMP-3 turret); 120 EE-11 *Urutu*; 20 VAB
    PPV 1,335: ε460 *Caiman*; ε680 *Maxxpro* LWB; 150 Nimr *Hafeet* 630A (CP); 45 Nimr *Hafeet (Amb)*
  AUV 674+: MCAV-20; 650 M-ATV; Nimr *Ajban*; Nimr *Jais*; 24 VBL

ENGINEERING & MAINTENANCE VEHICLES
  AEV 53+: 53 ACV-AESV; *Wisent*-2
  ARV 158: 8 ACV-AESV Recovery; 4 AMX-30D; 85 BREM-L; 46 *Leclerc* ARV; 15 *Maxxpro* ARV
NBC VEHICLES 32: 8 Fuchs 2 BIO-RS; 16 *Fuchs* 2 NBC-RS; 8 Fuchs 2 NBC-CPS (CP)
ANTI-TANK/ANTI-INFRASTRUCTURE
  MSL
    SP 135: 20 HOT; 115 Nimr *Ajban* 440A with *Kornet*-E (RS-AT-14 *Spriggan*)
    MANPATS FGM-148 *Javelin*; *Milan*; TOW
  RCL 84mm *Carl Gustaf*
ARTILLERY 629
  SP 155mm 163: 78 G-6; 85 M109A3
  TOWED 99: **105mm** 73 L118 Light Gun; **130mm** 20 Type-59-I; **155mm** 6 AH-4
  MRL 140: **122mm** 74: ε24 *Firos*-25; ε18 *Jobaria*; **220mm** 24 SR5; **227mm** 32 M142 HIMARS; **239mm** ε12 K239 *Chunmoo*; **300mm** 6 9A52 *Smerch*
  MOR 251: **81mm** 134: 20 Brandt; 114 L16; **120mm** 21 Brandt; **SP 120mm** 96 RG-31 MMP *Agrab* Mk2
SURFACE-TO-SURFACE MISSILE LAUNCHERS
  SRBM • **Conventional** 6 *Hwasong*-5 (up to 20 msl); MGM-168 ATACMS (launched from M142 HIMARS)
UNINHABITED AERIAL VEHICLES
  ISR • **Medium** *Seeker* II
AIR DEFENCE
  SAM • **Point-defence** *Mistral*

Navy 2,500
EQUIPMENT BY TYPE
PRINCIPAL SURFACE COMBATANTS • FRIGATES 1
  FFGHM 1 *Bani Yas* (FRA *Gowind*) with 2 quad lnchr with MM40 *Exocet* Block 3 AShM, 1 16-cell CLA VLS with VL MICA SAM, 1 21-cell Mk 49 GMLS with RIM-116C RAM Block 2 SAM, 2 triple 324mm ASTT with MU90 LWT, 1 76mm gun
PATROL AND COASTAL COMBATANTS 43
  CORVETTES 7
    FSGHM 6 *Baynunah* with 2 quad lnchr with MM40 *Exocet* Block 3 AShM, 1 8-cell Mk 56 VLS with RIM-162 ESSM SAM, 1 21-cell Mk 49 GMLS with RIM-116C RAM Block 2 SAM, 1 76mm gun
    FSGM 1 *Abu Dhabi* with 2 twin lnchr with MM40 *Exocet* Block 3 AShM, 1 76mm gun
  PCFGM 2 *Mubarraz* (GER Lurssen 45m) with 2 twin lnchr with MM40 *Exocet* AShM, 1 sextuple *Sadral* lnchr with *Mistral* SAM, 1 76mm gun
  PCGM 4:
    2 *Muray Jib* (GER Lurssen 62m) with 2 quad lnchr with MM40 *Exocet* Block 2 AShM, 1 octuple lnchr with *Crotale* SAM, 1 *Goalkeeper* CIWS, 1 76mm gun, 1 hel landing platform
    2 *Ghantut* (*Falaj* 2) with 2 twin lnchr with MM40 *Exocet* Block 3 AShM, 2 3-cell VLS with VL-MICA

SAM, 1 76mm gun, 1 hel landing platform
PCFG 6 *Ban Yas* (GER Lurssen TNC-45) with 2 twin lnchr with MM40 *Exocet* Block 3 AShM, 1 76mm gun
PBFG 12 *Butinah* (*Ghannatha* mod) with 4 single lnchr with *Marte* Mk2/N AShM
PBF 12: 6 *Ghannatha* with 1 120mm NEMO mor (capacity 42 troops); 6 *Ghannatha* (capacity 42 troops)
MINE WARFARE • MINE COUNTERMEASURES 1
  MHO 1 *Al Murjan* (ex-GER *Frankenthal* Type-332)
AMPHIBIOUS
  LANDING SHIPS • LST 3 *Alquwaisat* with 1 hel landing platform
  LANDING CRAFT 19
    LCM 5: 3 *Al Feyi* (capacity 56 troops); 2 ADSB 42m (capacity 40 troops and additional vehicles)
    LCP 4 Fast Supply Vessel (multi-purpose)
    LCT 10: 7 ADSB 64m; 2 *Al-Saadiyat* with 1 hel landing platform; 1 *Al Shareeah* (LSV 75m) with 1 hel landing platform
LOGISTICS AND SUPPORT 3:
  AKL 2 *Rmah* with 4 single 533mm TT
  AX 1 *Al Semeih* with 1 hel landing platform

Air Force 4,500
FORCES BY ROLE
FIGHTER/GROUND ATTACK
  3 sqn with F-16E/F Block 60 *Fighting Falcon*
  3 sqn with *Mirage* 2000-9DAD/EAD/RAD
AIRBORNE EARLY WARNING AND CONTROL
  1 flt with *GlobalEye*
SEARCH & RESCUE
  2 flt with AW109K2; AW139
TANKER
  1 flt with A330 MRTT
TRANSPORT
  1 sqn with C-17A *Globemaster*
  1 sqn with C-130H/H-30 *Hercules*; L-100-30
  1 sqn with CN235M-100
TRAINING
  1 sqn with Grob 115TA
  1 sqn with *Hawk* Mk102*
  1 sqn with PC-7 *Turbo Trainer*
  1 sqn with PC-21
TRANSPORT HELICOPTER
  1 sqn with Bell 412 *Twin Huey*
EQUIPMENT BY TYPE
AIRCRAFT 148 combat capable
  FGA 128: 54 F-16E Block 60 *Fighting Falcon* (*Desert Eagle*); 24 F-16F Block 60 *Fighting Falcon*; 13 *Mirage* 2000-9DAD; 37 *Mirage* 2000-9EAD
  MP 2 DHC-8 *Dash 8* MPA
  ISR 6 *Mirage* 2000 RAD*
  SIGINT 1 *Global* 6000
  AEW&C 3 *GlobalEye*
  TPT/TKR 3 A330 MRTT
  TPT 25: **Heavy** 8 C-17A *Globemaster* III; **Medium** 6: 3 C-130H *Hercules*; 1 C-130H-30 *Hercules*; 2 L-100-30; **Light** 15: 5 C295W; 4 CN235; 2 P.180 *Avanti* (MEDEVAC)
  TRG 81: 12 Grob 115TA; 12 *Hawk* Mk102*; 2 L-15*; 30 PC-7 *Turbo Trainer*; 25 PC-21
HELICOPTERS
  MRH 21: 12 AW139; 9 Bell 412 *Twin Huey*
  TPT • Light 4: 3 AW109K2; 1 Bell 407
UNINHABITED AERIAL VEHICLES
  CISR • Heavy *Wing Loong* I; *Wing Loong* II; **Medium** *Bayraktar* TB2
  ISR • Heavy RQ-1E *Predator* XP
AIR-LAUNCHED MISSILES
  AAM • IR AIM-9L *Sidewinder*; R-550 *Magic*; **IIR** AIM-9X *Sidewinder* II; **IIR/ARH** *Mica*; **ARH** AIM-120B/C AMRAAM
  ASM AGM-65G *Maverick*; LJ-7; *Hakeem* 1/2/3 (A/B)
  ARM AGM-88C HARM
  ALCM *Black Shaheen* (*Storm Shadow*/SCALP EG variant)
BOMBS
  Laser-guided GBU-12/-58 *Paveway* II
  Laser & INS/GPS-guided GBU-54 Laser JDAM
  INS/SAT-guided *Al Tariq*

Air Defence
FORCES BY ROLE
AIR DEFENCE
  2 AD bde (3 bn with *Barak* LRAD: M902 *Patriot* PAC-3)
  3 (short range) AD bn with *Crotale*; *Mistral*; *Rapier*; RBS-70; *Javelin*; 9K38 *Igla* (RS-SA-18 *Grouse*); 96K6 *Pantsir*-S1 (RS-SA-22)
  2 SAM bty with THAAD
EQUIPMENT BY TYPE
AIR DEFENCE
  SAM 29+
    Long-range 39+: 2+ *Barak* LRAD: 37 M902 *Patriot* PAC-3
    Medium-range some *Cheongung* II (being delivered)
    Short-range *Crotale*
    Point-defence 9K38 *Igla* (RS-SA-18 *Grouse*); RBS-70; *Rapier*; *Mistral*
  SPAAGM 30mm 42 96K6 *Pantsir*-S1 (RS-SA-22)
  GUNS • Towed 35mm GDF-005
MISSILE DEFENCE 12 THAAD

Presidential Guard Command 12,000
FORCES BY ROLE
SPECIAL FORCES
  1 SF bn
  1 spec ops bn
MANOEUVRE
  Reconaissance
  1 recce sqn

Mechanised
1 mech bde (1 tk bn, 4 mech inf bn, 1 AT coy, 1 cbt engr coy, 1 CSS bn)
Amphibious
1 mne bn

EQUIPMENT BY TYPE
ARMOURED FIGHTING VEHICLES
MBT 50 *Leclerc*
IFV 340: 250 BMP-3; 90 BTR-3U *Guardian*
ANTI-TANK/ANTI-INFRASTRUCTURE
MSL • SP HMMWV with 9M133 *Kornet* (RS-AT-14 *Spriggan*)

Joint Aviation Command
FORCES BY ROLE
GROUND ATTACK
1 sqn with *Archangel*
ANTI-SURFACE/ANTI-SUBMARINE WARFARE
1 sqn with AS332F *Super Puma*; AS565 *Panther*
TRANSPORT
1 (Spec Ops) gp with AS365F *Dauphin* 2; H125M *Fennec*; AW139; Bell 407MRH; Cessna 208B *Grand Caravan*; CH-47C/F *Chinook*; DHC-6-300/400 *Twin Otter*; UH-60L/M *Black Hawk*
ATTACK HELICOPTER
1 gp with AH-64D *Apache*; AH-64E *Apache*

EQUIPMENT BY TYPE
AIRCRAFT 30 combat capable
ATK 23 *Archangel*
TPT • **Light** 14: 2 Beech 350 *King Air*; 7 Cessna 208B *Grand Caravan*; 1 DHC-6-300 *Twin Otter*; 4 DHC-6-400 *Twin Otter*
HELICOPTERS
ATK 29: 28 AH-64D *Apache*; 1 AH-64E *Apache*
ASW 7 AS332F *Super Puma* (5 in ASuW role)
MRH 53+: 4 AS365F *Dauphin* 2 (VIP); 9 H125M *Fennec*; 7 AS565 *Panther*; 3 AW139 (VIP); 20 Bell 407MRH; 4 SA316 *Alouette* III; 6+ UH-60M *Black Hawk* (ABH)
TPT 66: **Heavy** 22 CH-47F *Chinook*; **Medium** 44: 11 UH-60L *Black Hawk*; up to 33 UH-60M *Black Hawk*
UNINHABITED AERIAL VEHICLES
ISR • Light S-100 *Camcopter*
AIR-LAUNCHED MISSILES
ASM AGM-114 *Hellfire*; *Cirit*; *Hydra*-70; HOT
AShM AS-15TT; AM39 *Exocet*

Gendarmerie & Paramilitary
National Guard
Ministry of Interior
EQUIPMENT BY TYPE
PATROL AND COASTAL COMBATANTS 82
PSO 2 *Al Wtaid*
PCM 2 *Arialah* (Damen Sea Axe 6711) with 1 11-cell Mk 15 SeaRAM GMLS with RIM-116C RAM Block 2 SAM, 1 57mm gun, 1 hel landing platform
PCC 3 *Shujaa* (Damen Stan Patrol 5009)
PBF 49: 15 DV-15; 34 MRTP 16
PB 26: 2 *Protector*; 12 *Halmatic Work*; 12 *Al Saber*

DEPLOYMENT
SOMALIA: 180

FOREIGN FORCES
Australia 400; 1 tpt det with 2 C-130J-30 *Hercules*
France 650: 1 armd BG (1 tk coy, 1 armd inf coy; 1 aty bty); *Leclerc*; VBCI; CAESAR; 7 *Rafale* F3; • EMASOH; 1 *Atlantique*-2
Korea, Republic of 170 (trg activities at UAE Spec Ops School)
United Kingdom 100
United States 5,000; 2 atk sqn with 12 A-10C *Thunderbolt* II; 1 ISR sqn with 4 U-2S; 1 ISR UAV sqn with RQ-4 *Global Hawk*; 2 SAM bty with M902/M903 *Patriot* PAC-3/PAC-3 MSE

Yemen, Republic of YEM

Yemeni Rial YER		2022	2023	2024
GDP	YER	26.2trn	29.4trn	35.9trn
	USD	23.5bn	21.0bn	21.9bn
per capita	USD	707	618	628
Growth	%	1.5	-0.5	2.0
Inflation	%	29.5	14.9	17.3
Def bdgt	YER	n.k.	n.k.	n.k.
	USD	n.k.	n.k.	n.k.
USD1=YER		1,114.30	1,397.22	1,637.87

Population	31,565,602					
Age	0–14	15–19	20–24	25–29	30–64	65 plus
Male	17.9%	5.8%	5.2%	4.5%	15.7%	1.5%
Female	17.3%	5.6%	5.0%	4.4%	15.4%	1.9%

Capabilities

Fighting in Yemen's decade-long civil war between the Iran-backed Ansarullah (Houthi) group and forces aligned with the internationally recognised government showed signs of easing after the United Nations negotiated a temporary round of ceasefires starting in 2022. Skirmishes between the factions continued, though, and some combatants threatened to return to large-scale violence. Neither side appears able to gain the upper hand in the fighting. President Hadi resigned in 2022 under pressure from Saudi Arabia, which was seeking an end to the war. Hadi handed power to a Presidential Leadership Council (PLC) under new President Rashad al-Alimi. The PLC includes the separatist Southern Transitional Council (STC). The new Saudi-backed unity government only appears to exercise limited control over the forces nominally allied against the Houthis. Irregular forces, such as Tareq Saleh's National Resistance and those of the STC, backed by the UAE, are reportedly better paid and equipped than government forces. The UAE has largely drawn down its forces and focused support on the STC and other non-government forces fighting the Houthis, while the remaining members of the Saudi-led coalition continue to provide air support for the PLC government. In March 2023, Iran pledged to halt weapons shipments to its Houthi allies as part of a deal with Saudi Arabia to reestablish diplomatic ties. The battling forces have been able to draw on large existing stockpiles of weapons and ammunition and external supplies, despite UN embargoes, to continue fighting. Yemen also has suffered repeated attacks by combatants linked to Al-Qaeda in the Arabian Peninsula. There is no domestic defence industry, barring some limited maintenance and workshop facilities.

ACTIVE 40,000 (Government forces 40,000)

ORGANISATIONS BY SERVICE

Government forces ε40,000 (incl militia)

Despite the establishment of the Presidential Leadership Council, central government control over the forces nominally allied together against the Houthis remains limited.

FORCES BY ROLE

MANOEUVRE

Mechanised

up to 20 bde(-)

EQUIPMENT BY TYPE

ARMOURED FIGHTING VEHICLES

MBT Some M60A1; T-54/55; T-62; T-72

RECCE some BRDM-2

IFV BMP-2; BTR-80A; Ratel-20

APC

APC (W) BTR-60

PPV Streit Cougar; Streit Spartan

AUV M-ATV

ANTI-TANK/ANTI-INFRASTRUCTURE

MSL • MANPATS 9K11 Malyutka (RS-AT-3 Sagger); M47 Dragon; TOW

GUNS • SP 100mm SU-100†

ARTILLERY • SP 122mm 2S1 Gvozdika

AIRCRAFT • ISR 6 AT-802 Air Tractor*

AIR DEFENCE • GUNS • TOWED 14.5mm ZPU-4; **23mm** ZU-23-2

FOREIGN FORCES

All *Operation Restoring Hope* unless stated

Saudi Arabia 2,500: 2 armd BG; M60A3; M2A2 *Bradley*; M113A4; M-ATV; AH-64 *Apache*; M902 *Patriot* PAC-3

Sudan 650; 1 mech BG; T-72AV; BTR-70M *Kobra* 2

NORTHERN YEMEN

Insurgent forces ε20,000 (incl Houthi and tribes)

The Houthi-run de facto administration has controlled northern Yemen since 2015 and is supported by a combination of Houthi tribal militias and elements of the Yemeni armed forces that had been loyal to former president Ali Abdullah Saleh. Following a break between the Houthis and Saleh in late 2017 that resulted in the latter's death, Saleh's former forces have become further split between those that remained affiliated with the Houthis and those who have joined his son and nephew to fight against them. Houthi forces receive material support from Iran, with several clandestine weapons shipments of Iranian origin intercepted in recent years. As well as fighting within Yemen, Houthi forces have launched missile and UAV attacks on targets in Saudi Arabia and the UAE.

FORCES BY ROLE

MANOEUVRE

Mechanised

up to 20 bde(-)

EQUIPMENT BY TYPE

ARMOURED FIGHTING VEHICLES

MBT T-55; T-72

IFV BMP-2; BTR-80A

APC • APC (W) BTR-40; BTR-60

AUV M-ATV

ARTILLERY

MRL • **122mm** BM-21 *Grad*; **210mm** *Badr*

ANTI-TANK/ANTI-INFRASTRUCTURE

MSL • MANPATS 9K111-1 *Konkurs* (RS-AT-5B *Spandrel/Towsan*-1); 9K115 *Metis* (RS-AT-7 *Saxhorn*); *Dehlavieh* (*Kornet*); *Toophan*

RCL **82mm** B-10

SURFACE-TO-SURFACE MISSILE LAUNCHERS

MRBM • **Conventional** *Aqeel*; *Borkan*-3; *Hatim* (*Kheibar Shekan*); *Toufan* (*Ghadr*)

SRBM • **Conventional** *Borkan*-2H (*Qiam*-1); *Falaq*; *Fateh*-110; *Khalij Fars*

GLCM • **Conventional** *Quds*-1; *Quds*-2; *Quds*-3; *Quds*-4

COASTAL DEFENCE • AShM C-801; C-802; *Sayyad*

AIRCRAFT 2 combat capable

FTR 1 F-5E *Tiger* II

FGA 1 Su-22M4 *Fitter* K

HELICOPTERS

MRH 1 Mi-17 *Hip* H

TPT • **Medium** 3 Mi-8 *Hip*

UNINHABITED AERIAL VEHICLES

ISR • **Medium** *Sammad* 1; **Light** *Mersad* 1/2

LOITERING & DIRECT ATTACK MUNITIONS

Qasef 1 (*Ababil* T); *Qasef* 2K; *Sammad* 2; *Sammad* 3; *Shihab*; *Waed* 1 (*Shahed* 131); *Waed* 2 (*Shahed* 136)

AIR DEFENCE

SAM

Short-range *Saqr*-1 (358)

Point-defence 9K32 *Strela*-2 (RS-SA-7 *Grail*)‡; 9K34 *Strela*-3 (RS-SA-14 *Gremlin*); *Misaq*-1 (QW-1); *Misaq*-2 (QW-18)

GUNS • **TOWED 20mm** M167 *Vulcan*; **23mm** ZU-23-2

Chapter Seven
Latin America and the Caribbean

- Tensions rose between Venezuela and Guyana after Caracas signalled it may try to take control of its neighbour's Essequibo region. Venezuela's move drew criticism from Brazil and the US, among others. As tensions escalated in late 2023, the US Southern Command conducted flight operations within Guyana to show support.
- Mexico's Supreme Court blocked an effort by President Andrés Manuel López Obrador to shift responsibility for the National Guard to the armed forces, part of his effort to increase their role in domestic policing duties. Mexico has been dealing with rising violence linked to the drug trade.
- Brazil's President Luiz Inácio Lula da Silva, in August, announced a 'new growth acceleration plan' (Novo PAC) that calls for spending up to BRL1.7 trillion (USD340.5 billion) across all sectors of Brazil's economy, including BRL52.8bn (USD10.6bn) for defence. The money is expected to fund modernisation and enhance the country's defence industry.
- Argentine defence spending retreated, breaking from the trend for most of the region, as the country dealt with economic difficulties. The budgetary pressures led the then-government to pause efforts to buy new combat aircraft, although some other equipment upgrade efforts progressed.
- Questions arose over Colombia's defence equipment supply after the outbreak of the Hamas–Israel war. Criticism by Colombia's president of Israel's conduct in the fighting led Tel Aviv to suspend defence sales to the Latin American country.
- Chile aims to introduce its new icebreaker, the *Almirante Viel*, into service in 2024. The vessel is part of a wider naval vessel construction spree across Latin America, often involving foreign industrial partners. The region's shipbuilding plans span from submarines to frigates.

Latin America and the Caribbean defence spending, 2022 – top 5, including US Foreign Military Financing

United States USD905bn

Total Latin America and the Caribbean spending USD55bn

Brazil	Mexico	Colombia	Chile	Argentina
USD24.2bn	USD7.8bn	USD5.4bn	USD4.4bn	USD2.9bn

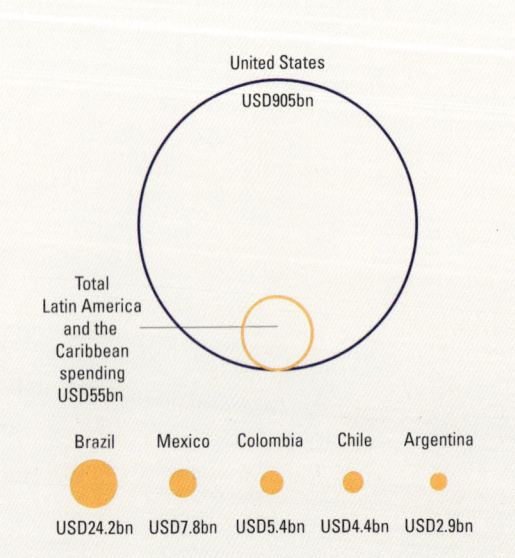

Active military personnel – top 10
(25,000 per unit)

Country	Personnel
Brazil	366,500
Colombia	257,450
Mexico	216,000
Venezuela	123,000
Peru	81,000
Argentina	72,100
Chile	68,500
Dominican Republic	56,800
Cuba	49,000
Ecuador	39,600

Global total 20,646,000

Regional total 1,489,000 (7.2%)

Regional defence policy and economics   398 ▶

Arms procurements and deliveries   407 ▶

Armed forces data section   408 ▶

Latin America and the Caribbean: selected principal surface combatant fleets, 2023*

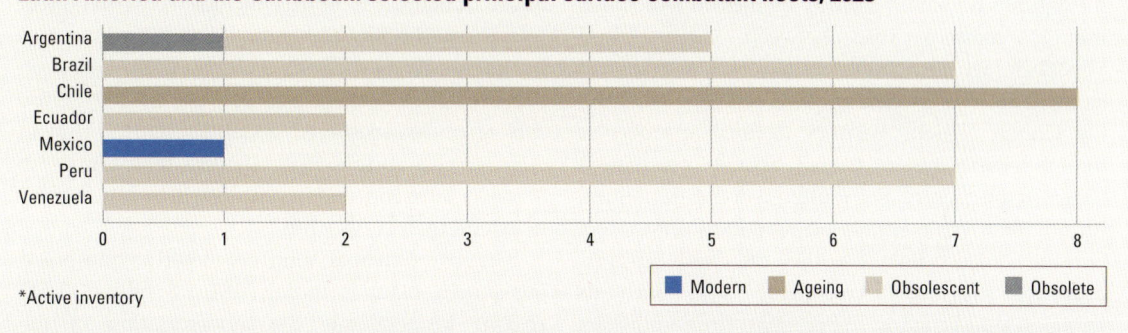

*Active inventory

Legend: ■ Modern   ■ Ageing   ■ Obsolescent   ■ Obsolete

Latin America and the Caribbean: selected tactical combat aircraft, 2023*

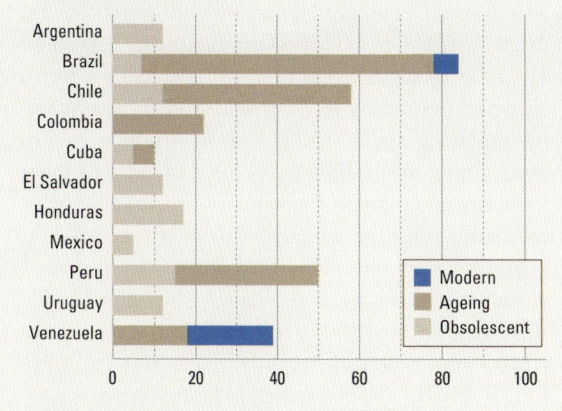

Legend: ■ Modern   ■ Ageing   ■ Obsolescent

*Active inventory of 'combat aircraft', including fighter, fighter ground-attack, and attack aircraft

Latin America and the Caribbean: armoured fighting vehicles, 2023*

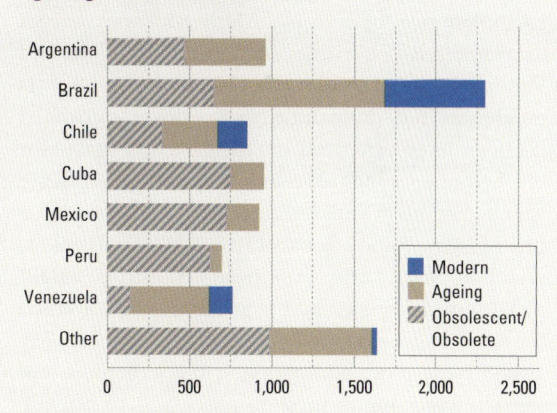

Legend: ■ Modern   ■ Ageing   ▨ Obsolescent/Obsolete

*Excludes armoured utility vehicles

Latin America and the Caribbean: defence spending as % of GDP (average), 2008–23

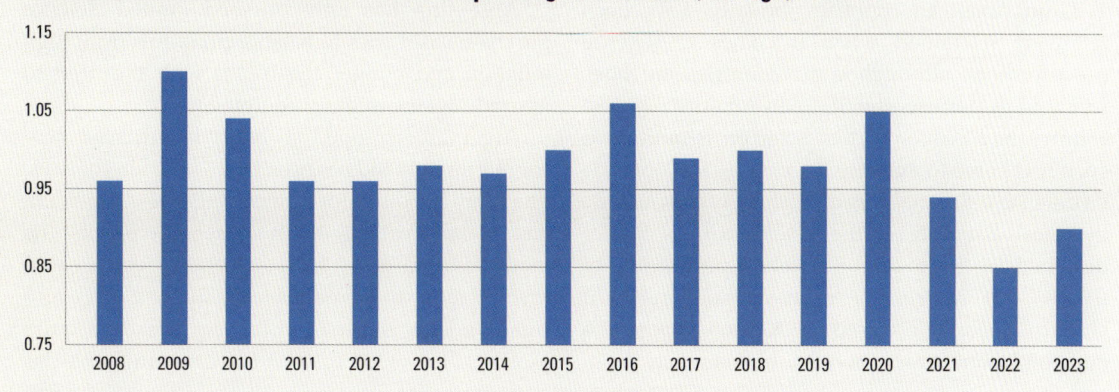

Latin America and the Caribbean

Organised crime and political turmoil at home were the region's dominant security themes. In December, though, tensions rose between Guyana and Venezuela, which signalled it might try to take over its neighbour's oil-rich Essequibo region. Elsewhere, the United Nations Security Council approved a foreign security mission to Haiti because of persistent unrest in the country. Peru suffered domestic political turmoil and Mexico grappled with local unrest, too. Surging violence linked to the drug trade gripped countries previously considered safe, such as Paraguay and Ecuador. In Paraguay, drug traffickers in August 2023 killed a presidential candidate.

The region largely rebuffed efforts by the United States and Europe to generate concrete support in Latin America for Ukraine. Many countries, except for staunch Russian allies such as Bolivia, Cuba and Venezuela, have condemned Moscow's war on its neighbour but done little more. Brazil portrayed itself as largely neutral on Russia's full-scale war on Ukraine, which Western supporters of Kyiv saw as President Luis Inácio Lula da Silva taking a pro-Moscow stance. Some of Kyiv's Western backers were hoping Latin American countries might provide weapons as the US and Europe scrambled for ways to get Ukraine more ammunition, artillery systems and other equipment. Chile, Colombia and Mexico were among those to reject calls to provide weapons to Ukraine. Brazil refused to deliver 35mm ammunition to Ukraine that was previously supplied by Germany for the *Gepard* 1A2 self-propelled anti-aircraft weapons system.

Latin American countries, broadly, have been relatively restrained when it comes to defence procurements, although some countries are busy trying to modernise. **Brazil**, Latin America's largest country and economy, has been on a multi-year spending spree to enhance its services and upgrade its defence-industrial capacity. Those efforts include the local assembly of the F-39E/F *Gripen* fighter designed by Saab and Embraer's production of the KC-390 *Millennium* multi-mission transport aircraft. The air force used the KC-390 as part of a non-combatant evacuation of its nationals from Israel after the 7 October attack by Hamas. In the naval domain, the efforts include construction of four *Riachuelo*-class conventional attack submarines by Itaguaí Construções Navais by 2025, based on the French *Scorpène* class, as well as the *Álvaro Alberto* nuclear-powered attack submarine due to enter service around 2037. The Brazilian army's 37 M109A3 self-propelled howitzers will be refurbished to extend their service life.

The government in August disclosed a widespread investment plan, including BRL52.8 billion (USD 10.6bn) to accelerate the modernisation of the Brazilian armed forces by 2027 and to support the country's defence-industrial base. The Brazilian army, for instance, is eyeing the funding to buy wheeled and tracked armoured vehicles and purchase the locally made *Astros* II MK6 long-range rocket system. The army is also looking to modernise its tank force, either by upgrading its *Leopard* 1A5BR or potentially by replacing them if the war in Ukraine makes overhauling the existing tanks too difficult. The navy harbours an ambition to eventually revive its carrier capability since the *Sao Paulo* carrier was scuttled in February 2023 after having been decommissioned years earlier because of servicing issues. The service still operates the *Atlântico* helicopter carrier (formerly HMS *Ocean* when in British service) and the *Bahia* LPD (formerly FS *Siroco* when in French service).

Brasilia, in recent years, has moved to strengthen military ties with regional partners, donating surplus military equipment to several countries over previous years.

Argentina has only pursued limited defence purchases as it tries to balance pressures from high inflation and budget constraints with the need to upgrade ageing military equipment.

Argentina scrapped an effort to purchase new combat aircraft and has been looking for alternatives. The army is poised for limited upgrades. Argentina has been working, with Israeli help, on the modernisation of its TAM light tank, which could involve more than 100 vehicles. Buenos Aires also signed a letter of intent in January 2023 to acquire 156 Brazilian-made *Guarani* 6x6 armoured vehicles

Map 8 South America: selected helicopter procurements since 2010

South American states have prioritised rotary-wing fleet recapitalisation, reflecting the utility of those systems for counter-narcotics and border-surveillance missions. However, these contracts have typically been in small numbers or for second-hand platforms due to financial constraints across the region. Some states, particularly Argentina and Colombia, have signed government-to-government agreements such as with state-run contracting agency Canadian Commercial Corporation when procuring US-made helicopters to secure more favourable support package deals. Argentina and Peru have acquired Russian-built helicopters during this timeframe, with the most recent delivery being two Mi-171Shs to Peru via Belarus in 2021. China has had very limited success in the region in this sector.

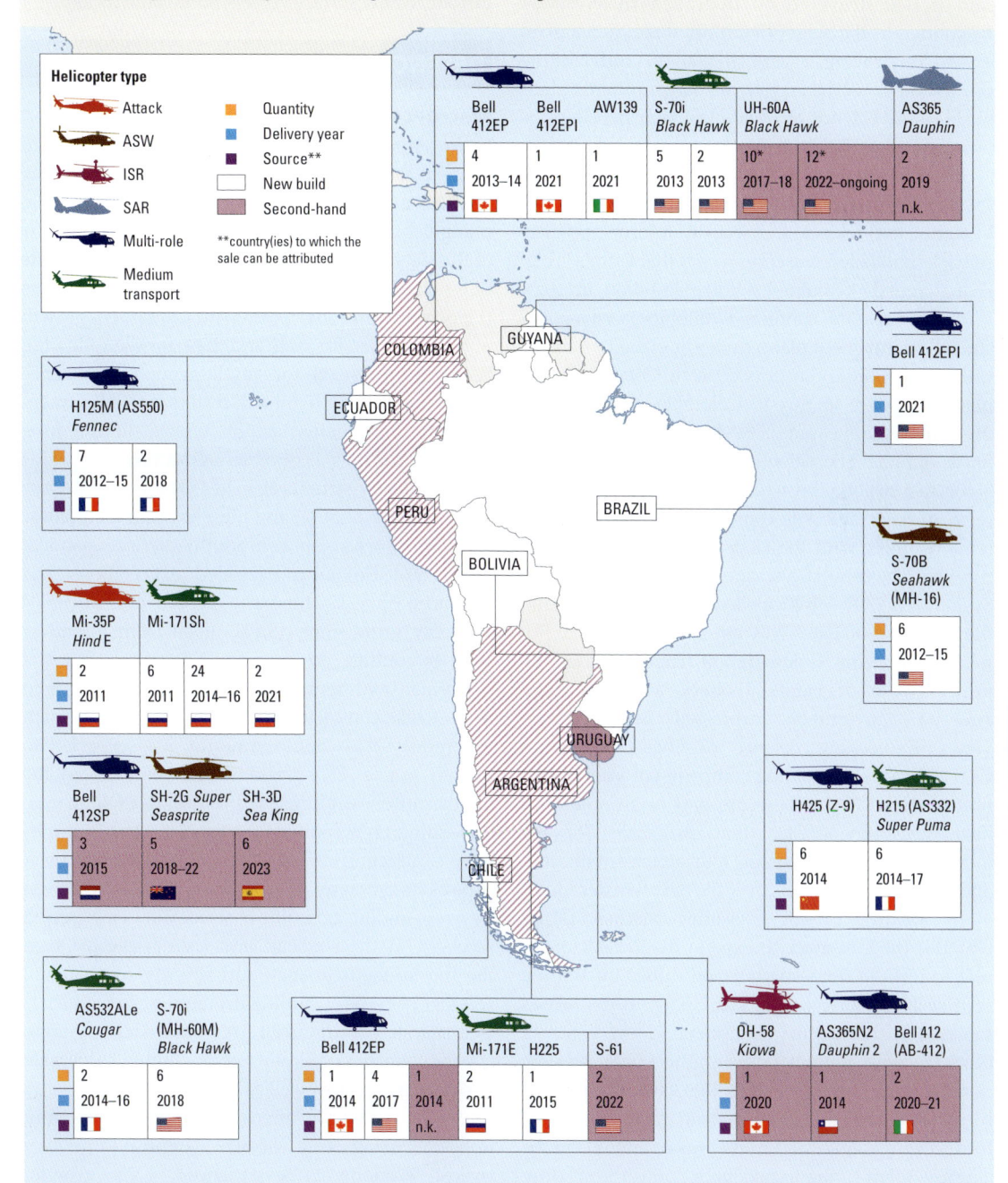

Helicopter type
- Attack
- ASW
- ISR
- SAR
- Multi-role
- Medium transport
- Quantity
- Delivery year
- Source**
- New build
- Second-hand

**country(ies) to which the sale can be attributed

Colombia

	Bell 412EP	Bell 412EPI	AW139	S-70i Black Hawk	UH-60A Black Hawk	AS365 Dauphin
Quantity	4	1	1	5 / 2	10*	12*	2
Delivery	2013–14	2021	2021	2013 / 2013	2017–18	2022–ongoing	2019
Source	CAN	CAN	ITA	USA / USA	USA	USA	n.k.

Guyana

	Bell 412EPI
Quantity	1
Delivery	2021
Source	USA

Ecuador

	H125M (AS550) Fennec	
Quantity	7	2
Delivery	2012–15	2018
Source	FRA	FRA

Brazil

	S-70B Seahawk (MH-16)
Quantity	6
Delivery	2012–15
Source	USA

Peru

	Mi-35P Hind E	Mi-171Sh	
Quantity	2	6	24	2
Delivery	2011	2011	2014–16	2021
Source	RUS	RUS	RUS	RUS

Uruguay

	Bell 412SP	SH-2G Super Seasprite	SH-3D Sea King
Quantity	3	5	6
Delivery	2015	2018–22	2023
Source	NLD	NZL	ESP

Chile

	H425 (Z-9)	H215 (AS332) Super Puma
Quantity	6	6
Delivery	2014	2014–17
Source	CHN	FRA

Argentina

	AS532ALe Cougar	S-70i (MH-60M) Black Hawk
Quantity	2	6
Delivery	2014–16	2018
Source	FRA	USA

	Bell 412EP			Mi-171E	H225	S-61
Quantity	1	4	1	2	1	2
Delivery	2014	2017	2014	2011	2015	2022
Source	CAN	USA	n.k.	RUS	FRA	USA

	OH-58 Kiowa	AS365N2 Dauphin 2	Bell 412 (AB-412)
Quantity	1	1	2
Delivery	2020	2014	2020–21
Source	CAN	CHL	ITA

Notes: Tables only include contracts signed after January 2010. States' ordered/delivered numbers do not necessarily correlate with current inventory numbers. *Donation ©IISS

(120 armoured personnel carriers, nine command-post vehicles and 27 infantry fighting vehicles), though questions remained about how the project would be financed. Argentina continued efforts to revive its aircraft-production capacity. Fabrica Argentina de Aviones (FAdeA) in 2023 said Uruguay had expressed interest in evaluating the company's IA-100 turboprop trainer. Earlier in the year, FAdeA said it had delivered an upgraded IA-63 *Pampa* III trainer to the Argentinian air force and agreed a deal to develop a vertical take-off and landing uninhabited aerial system. Argentinian plans hung in the balance as of late last year pending the outcome of presidential elections.

Despite expectations that the 2022 election of President Gustavo Petro in **Colombia** would result in significant defence and security reforms, political setbacks and failed ceasefires meant that Petro's 'Total Peace' agenda remained a lofty ambition in 2023. With six separate conflicts within its borders and stalled disarmament plans, domestic stability remains Colombia's primary security concern. Combat-aircraft plans also were in flux in Colombia. At one point, the country appeared poised to acquire Dassault *Rafale* fighters. The defence ministry announced that a contract negotiation with Dassault fell through to replace the Israeli *Kfir* combat aircraft. The choice remains open, with the *Gripen* and F-16 also in the running. The country also announced a deal for Elbit Systems ATMOS self-propelled artillery systems and the purchase of *Barak* MX air-defence systems. But relations between Colombia and Israel deteriorated in the wake of Hamas's attack after the Latin American government expressed pro-Palestinian views, threatening defence dealings. Colombia's COTECMAR shipbuilding company cut steel on the first of three OPVs. These are part of an ambitious naval-development plan that also calls for the introduction of five frigates, four attack submarines and various other vessels over the next two decades.

In **Mexico**, President Andrés Manuel López Obrador tried, in 2022, to expand the armed forces' role to include domestic policing duties by shifting responsibility for the National Guard to the armed forces. But the country's Supreme Court voted to block the move, though the government has been slow to act on the judiciary's ruling. Mexico has been beset by gang violence linked to the drug trade. The armed forces in 2023 conducted numerous operations in the country, often trying to take back control from drug gangs, including along the border with Guatemala.

Peru last year wrestled with significant domestic political upheaval amidst a wave of anti-government riots that impacted some of its most critical industries. Over the past decade, the country has upgraded a few elements of its air force and navy despite economic difficulties. Lima has a few acquisitions in its sights, including new 8x8 armoured fighting vehicles, and is working to modernise its submarine fleet and introduce new surface vessels, some built locally.

DEFENCE ECONOMICS

Macroeconomics

Latin America and the Caribbean experienced modest economic growth in 2023, remaining resilient against the challenges of global inflation, rising debt levels and the economic knock-on effects of Russia's February 2022 attack on Ukraine. Despite downward revisions by the World Bank, in 2023 the region still grew by 3.9%, with continued growth of 3.8% forecast for 2024 and 3.4% for the following year. This allowed for small growth in defence spending, but with mixed results for investment accounts and modernisation efforts. In the long run, the region's economic performance remains constrained by structural issues. These include low growth, high inflation and high levels of inequality.

Most major economies in South America expanded. Brazil and Colombia exceeded expectations and advanced by 3.1% and 1.4%, respectively. Guyana's economy grew some 38.4%, albeit from a smaller base. In contrast, Argentina was the region's worst performer, with its economy contracting by 2.5% in 2023. Chile contracted by 0.5%. Although growth is forecast across South America, it is expected to remain fragile. Economies of the countries in the Southern Cone are predicted to rise by 4.6% in 2024, depending on a confluence of factors. For example, after contracting in 2023, Argentina's central bank expects its economy to grow by 2.7% in 2024, driven by a rebounding agricultural sector from an expected recovery in the soybean and corn harvest. Given the increasing frequency and severity of changing weather patterns, including drought in 2023, which is estimated to have reduced Argentina's GDP by up to 3%, the country's economy remains highly vulnerable to climate change, as well as commodity prices.

Outside of South America the outlook was more upbeat. During 2023, Mexico – Central America's largest economy – experienced 3.2% growth, although the IMF predicts that will slow in 2024

Table 14 Chile: selected procurements since 2010

Chilean procurement is largely characterised by the acquisition of second-hand equipment from the US, but also from Australia, France, New Zealand and the UK. These platforms are typically modernised or overhauled by one of Chile's three main state-owned companies: ASMAR (shipbuilding), ENAER (aerospace) and FAMAE (vehicle maintenance and munitions). Chile has developed a modest MRO capability through this process, with a limited capability to design and produce new equipment. ASMAR has evolved even further, securing contracts to build offshore patrol ships, an icebreaker and landing platform docks, though based on foreign designs. Chile plans to acquire 33 of ENAER's *Pillan* II turboprop training aircraft over eight years for USD142m. The aircraft is an improved version of the 1980s-vintage T-35 *Pillan* operated by Chile and sold to seven other countries. It represents Chile's best chance of securing defence exports in the near future. Chile has invested little in the land domain, and the army has struggled to translate significant recapitalisation requirements into actual programmes because of a depreciating currency and political turmoil.

Contract Date	Equipment	Type	Quantity	Value	Contractor	Deliveries	Service
c. 2011	M109A5+	155mm self-propelled artillery	24	est. USD1.11m	US government surplus	2012-14	Army
c. 2011	T-35B *Pillan*	Training aircraft	6	n.k.	ENAER	c. 2013	Air Force
Jun 2011	*Hermes* 900	Medium ISR UAV	3	n.k.	Elbit Systems	2013	Air Force
Nov 2011	*Sargento Aldea* (ex-FRA *Foudre*)	Landing platform dock	1	EUR40m (USD55.7m)	France government surplus	2011	Navy
Dec 2011	*Piloto Pardo*	Offshore patrol ship	1	USD47m	ASMAR	2014	Navy
c. 2012	KC-130R *Hercules*	Tanker aircraft	1	est. USD0.7m	US government surplus	2015	Air Force
Nov 2012	AS532ALe *Cougar*	Medium transport helicopter	1	USD57.4m	Airbus (M)	2014	Army
c. 2014			1			2016	
c. 2013	KC-130R *Hercules*	Tanker aircraft	1	est. USD0.7m	US government surplus	2016	Air Force
Jan 2015	*Piloto Pardo*	Offshore patrol ship	1	USD70m	ASMAR	2017	Navy
Sep 2015	P68 *Observer* 2	ISR aircraft	7	USD12.5m	Vulcanair	2016-17	Navy
Dec 2016	S-70i (MH-60M) *Black Hawk*	Medium transport helicopter	6	USD180m	Sikorsky	2018	Air Force
Oct 2017	EMB-314 *Super Tucano***	Training aircraft	6	n.k.	Embraer	2018	Air Force
Nov 2017	*Almirante Viel* (VARD 9 203)	Icebreaker	1	USD236m	ASMAR	2024*	Navy
c. 2018	EMB-314 *Super Tucano***	Training aircraft	4	n.k.	Embraer	2020	Air Force
c. 2019	*Almirante Latorre* (ex-AUS *Adelaide*)	Frigate	2	n.k.	Australia government surplus	2020	Navy
c. 2019	C-130H *Hercules*	Medium transport aircraft	2	USD20m	US government surplus	2021	Air Force
Sep 2019	H125 (AS350) *Ecureuil*	Light transport helicopter	5	n.k.	Helibras	2020-23	Navy
c. 2021	E-3D *Sentry*	Airborne early warning and control aircraft	2	est. USD50m	UK government surplus	2022	Air Force
Apr 2022	NZLAV-25	IFV	22	USD19.9m	New Zealand government surplus	2022-23	Marines
Aug 2022	Escotillón IV (Phase 1)	Landing platform dock	2	USD410m	ASMAR	2030*	Navy

*Planned

**Capable of combat use

M = multinational

to 2.1%. Similarly, economies in the Caribbean (excluding Haiti) grew by 3.6% in 2023, with similar levels expected in 2024. Growth was slower than expected and far below the Caribbean Development Bank's January estimate of 5.7%. This estimate was premised on the revival of tourism and investments in the energy sector, although the bank noted that the Caribbean remains heavily exposed to the global business cycle and that any growth is contingent on the economic health of more advanced economies.

In 2023, average inflation across Latin America and the Caribbean hit 25.9%, principally because of the rates in Argentina and Venezuela, which reached 121% and 360%, respectively. Excluding these outliers, the regional inflation rate averaged 8.7%. Even though inflation was broadly in line with rates in Europe and North America, the pain is more acutely felt in Latin America. In those countries, non-discretionary spending on food and energy represents up to 40% of average household expenditure, compared to just 15% in developed economies, placing extra pressure on national governments to preserve or expand social spending and limiting other budgetary flexibility. If high inflation was problematic in 2023, so too were prescribed solutions. As inflation rates rose, central banks across the region tightened monetary policy and raised interest rates. That slowed the rate of price increases but raised the cost of borrowing and debt repayments – including for borrowings used to fund COVID-19-related economic-support measures. As a result, the gross-debt-to-GDP ratio increased in 2023 for most of the region's economies compared to pre-COVID levels in 2019. In the Bahamas, Bolivia and Suriname, ratios increased by more than 20 percentage points, and in Chile, Panama and Paraguay debt-to-GDP ratios increased by between 10 and 15 percentage points. Only seven countries improved their fiscal positions, with Belize, Guyana and Jamaica seeing the greatest improvements.

Defence spending

Defence budgets struggled to compete given those spending pressures and the absence of major external security threats. Total regional defence spending captured by *The Military Balance* advanced by 10% in nominal terms, increasing to a combined USD54.3 billion. However, in real terms, increases were more modest, with budgets growing by only 2% after adjusting for inflation. Capital budgets to pay for everything from equipment to housing remained stable, with the region allocating USD2.9bn to such

▼ Figure 19 **Latin America and the Caribbean: defence spending by country and sub-region, 2023**

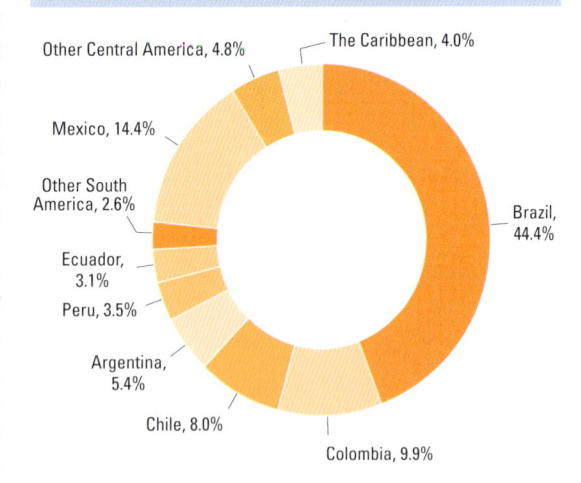

- Other Central America, 4.8%
- The Caribbean, 4.0%
- Mexico, 14.4%
- Other South America, 2.6%
- Ecuador, 3.1%
- Peru, 3.5%
- Argentina, 5.4%
- Chile, 8.0%
- Colombia, 9.9%
- Brazil, 44.4%

Note: Analysis excludes Cuba, Suriname and Venezuela ©IISS

accounts in 2023, compared to USD2.8bn in 2022. However, several major regional defence spenders, such as Argentina, Brazil and Colombia, reduced their capital allocations to offset pressures on day-to-day spending. The failure to invest in new equipment comes with short-term budget relief but will lead to ageing inventories and stagnation in military effectiveness.

Regional defence spending remained dominated by five countries, with Argentina, Brazil, Chile, Colombia and Mexico making up more than 80% of the region's total. Of these, **Brazil's** budget of BRL121bn (USD24.25bn) is the largest, or 44% of the regional figure. In nominal terms, Brazil's defence budget advanced a modest 3% from the previous year, although, when measured in constant dollars, spending remained flat. More significant, perhaps, are the cuts to the country's capital budget. Between 2015 and 2021, Brazil's capital allocation averaged approximately USD2.5bn per year, or around 10% of the total defence budget. However, in 2022, the capital figure fell from USD2.6bn to USD1.6bn, retreating further to USD1.4bn in 2023. After these cuts, capital expenditure represented just 6.1% of the country's 2023 defence budget.

However, in August 2023, President Luiz Inácio Lula da Silva announced the 'new growth acceleration plan' (Novo PAC). It foresees spending up to BRL1.7 trillion (USD340.5bn) across all sectors of Brazil's economy, the bulk of which is to be spent by 2026. For defence, the plan includes BRL52.8bn (USD10.6bn), of which just over half (52.7%) will be distributed by

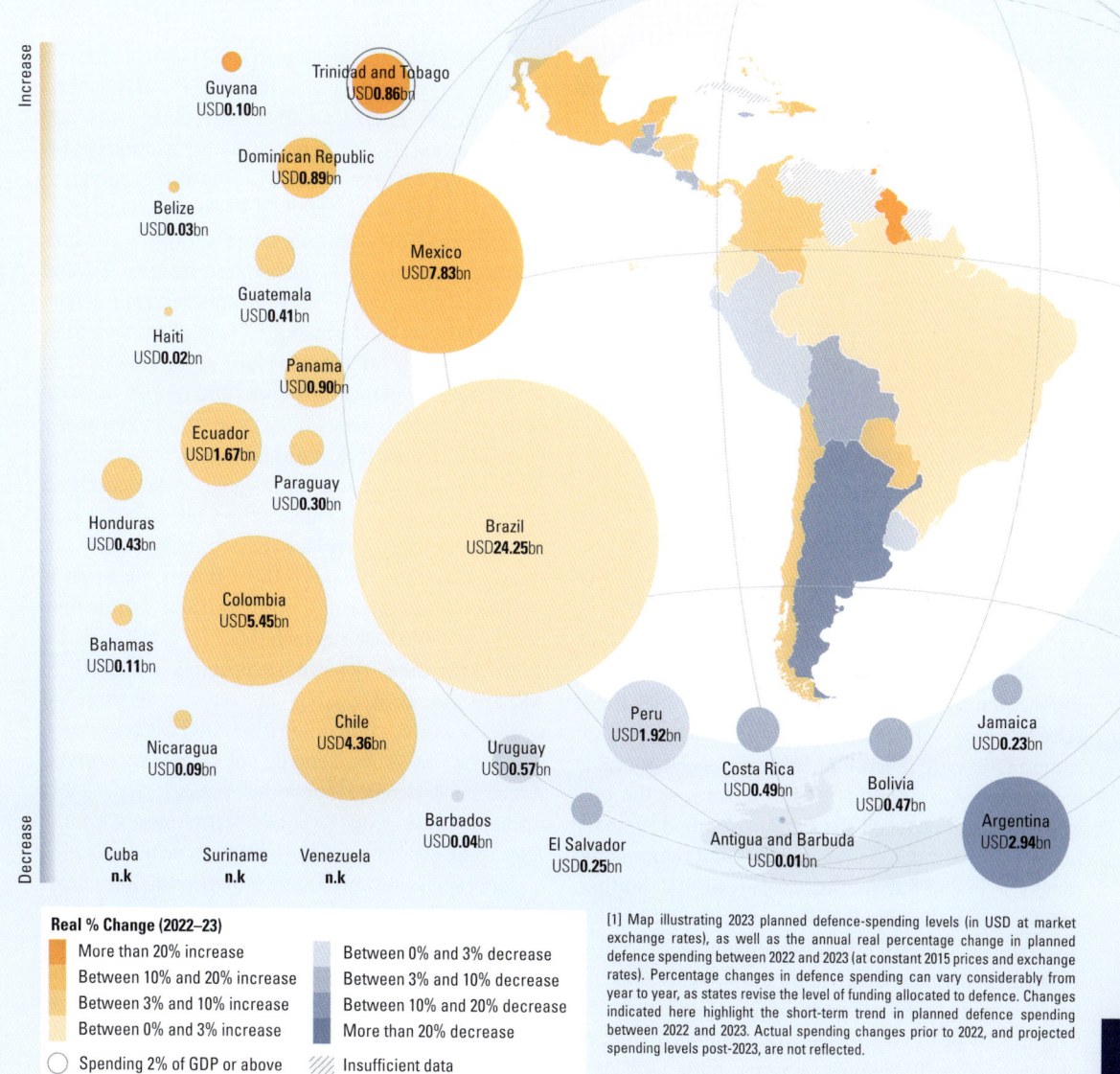

Map 9 Latin America and the Caribbean: regional defence spending (USDbn, %ch yoy)[1]

Country spending values:
- Guyana USD 0.10bn
- Trinidad and Tobago USD 0.86bn
- Dominican Republic USD 0.89bn
- Belize USD 0.03bn
- Mexico USD 7.83bn
- Guatemala USD 0.41bn
- Haiti USD 0.02bn
- Panama USD 0.90bn
- Ecuador USD 1.67bn
- Paraguay USD 0.30bn
- Honduras USD 0.43bn
- Brazil USD 24.25bn
- Colombia USD 5.45bn
- Bahamas USD 0.11bn
- Nicaragua USD 0.09bn
- Chile USD 4.36bn
- Uruguay USD 0.57bn
- Peru USD 1.92bn
- Jamaica USD 0.23bn
- Costa Rica USD 0.49bn
- Bolivia USD 0.47bn
- Cuba n.k
- Suriname n.k
- Venezuela n.k
- Barbados USD 0.04bn
- El Salvador USD 0.25bn
- Antigua and Barbuda USD 0.01bn
- Argentina USD 2.94bn

Real % Change (2022–23)
- More than 20% increase
- Between 10% and 20% increase
- Between 3% and 10% increase
- Between 0% and 3% increase
- Between 0% and 3% decrease
- Between 3% and 10% decrease
- Between 10% and 20% decrease
- More than 20% decrease
- Spending 2% of GDP or above
- Insufficient data

[1] Map illustrating 2023 planned defence-spending levels (in USD at market exchange rates), as well as the annual real percentage change in planned defence spending between 2022 and 2023 (at constant 2015 prices and exchange rates). Percentage changes in defence spending can vary considerably from year to year, as states revise the level of funding allocated to defence. Changes indicated here highlight the short-term trend in planned defence spending between 2022 and 2023. Actual spending changes prior to 2022, and projected spending levels post-2023, are not reflected.

©IISS

2026. This new funding reverses the decline in capital spending and reaffirms Brazil's commitment to its various strategic programmes. In the land domain, Novo PAC funding will go towards some 714 new systems, such as self-propelled artillery, main battle tanks and various infantry fighting vehicles. In the naval domain, funding will go towards constructing four *Tamandaré* EMGEPRON frigates and 11 new patrol ships. However, the sub-surface fleet will be the big winner, with additional funding allocated for the *Álvaro Alberto* nuclear-powered submarine – part of the Programa de Desenvolvimento de Submarinos (PROSUB) (submarine development programme) – nuclear fuel and other associated requirements, the expansion of Itaguaí's submarine shipyard and naval base, and three more diesel-electric submarines (one has already been commissioned). In keeping with its naval-modernisation plans, in June 2023, Brazil also signed a strategic partnership and cooperation agreement with the United Arab Emirates' EDGE Group to jointly develop Míssil Antinavio Nacional (MANSUP) long-range anti-ship missiles for the Brazilian navy. In September 2023 EDGE acquired a 50% stake in Brazil's SIATT, which has been participating in the MANSUP programme. In the air domain, funding will be available for the acquisition and production of 34

404 THE MILITARY BALANCE 2024

▼ Figure 20 **Latin America and the Caribbean: regional defence spending** as % of GDP (average)

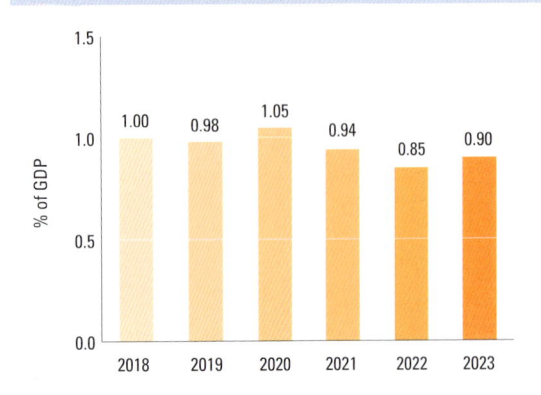

Year	% of GDP
2018	1.00
2019	0.98
2020	1.05
2021	0.94
2022	0.85
2023	0.90

Note: GDP data from IMF World Economic Outlook, October 2023. Analysis excludes Cuba, Suriname and Venezuela.

vehicles. Funding will also be made available for light- and medium-lift helicopters, although these will serve under the General Staff.

Colombia allocated COP42.1trn (USD10.6bn) to defence and policing in 2023, of which COP24.1trn (USD5.41bn) went to defence, representing 9.9% of regional defence spending. This marks considerable continuity with previous spending because the 11% inflation level reduced the nominal budget increase just 3% in real terms. However, the total figure alone masks a major fall in Colombia's capital budget, which was slashed by a third from USD266.8 million in 2022 to USD190.7m. Nonetheless, Colombia continues with modest capability investments. In January 2023, media reporting indicated that the Colombian air force planned to expand its inventory of T-6C *Texan* II training aircraft, with four new units, in a potential deal worth USD38.3m. Colombia intends to purchase a total of 24 aircraft, and although the *Texan* IIs will mainly have a training role, a secondary light-strike role for ground-attack and counter-insurgency missions is also possible.

In 2023, **Chile** allocated CLP3.56trn (USD4.36bn) to defence. This represented 8% of the region's defence spending and consolidated Santiago's trend of upward spending, despite its economic contraction. The country is modernising its armed forces across the board, with the army seeking to update its fleet of *Leopard* 2A4 main battle tanks and *Marder* infantry fighting vehicles. The Chilean navy is modernising its frigate fleet and is refurbishing its *Scorpène*-class submarines. In May 2023, Admiral Juan Andrés De La Maza, commander-in-chief of the Chilean navy, said the country would replace its two ageing *Thomson*-class submarines. Finally, the Chilean air force is seeking to modernise its F-16 aircraft and acquire new helicopters to replace its UH-1Hs.

In **Argentina**, defence spending fell slightly to ARS826.7bn (USD2.94bn) in 2023, reflecting the wider economic difficulties over the past two years. However, as a percentage of regional outlays, Argentina's defence spending proved remarkably resilient, making up 5.4% of South America's total. This is consistent with the previous year's share of regional spending and suggests that, following a near-consistent decline since 2015, defence spending is stabilising within the country's set of overall priorities. Similarly, in 2023, Argentina allocated ARD35.4bn (USD126m) for capital expenditure. This represented 4.3% of the defence budget, which, though a decline from the previous year's capital allocation of 5.9%,

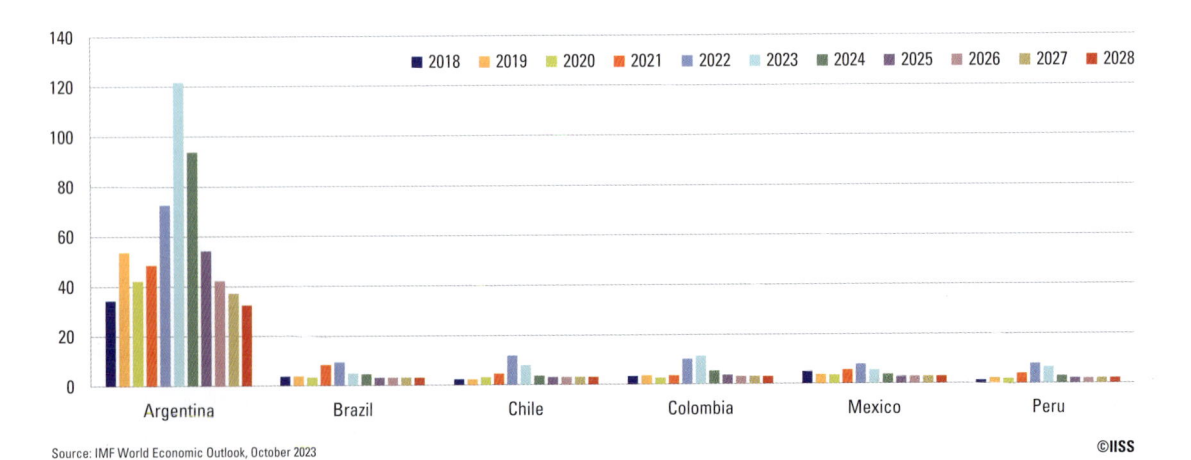

Source: IMF World Economic Outlook, October 2023   ©IISS

▲ Figure 21 **Latin America: selected countries, inflation (%), 2018–28**

still is a considerable improvement on previous lows of just 1.7%. One area of much-needed modernisation is the country's aging combat aircraft fleet. In 2017, Argentina scrapped plans to buy new fighter aircraft, citing the country's poor financial health. The country has been exploring options, including buying used aircraft. Argentina made modest progress in modernising its aviation capability in 2023 through the acquisition of six new Bell 407GXi helicopters and by upgrading its combat and transport fixed-wing aircraft fleets. Further rotary-wing acquisitions could be under way. On 20 July, India's Hindustan Aeronautics Limited announced that it had signed a letter of intent with the Argentinian government for the 'productive co-operation and acquisition' of light and medium utility helicopters.

In 2023, **Mexico** increased defence spending to MXN138.5bn (USD 7.4bn). This represented a 19.1% jump from 2022, meaning that Mexico accounted for 14.4% of the region's defence spending. Although this consolidates a recent trend of increasing budgets, movements in Mexico's defence spending have been volatile. Previously, in 2019, Mexico cut its budget by 8% in real terms. This was followed by sharp increases of 13% in 2020 and 10% in 2021, before falling back in 2022 to USD5.7bn.

Latin America's wave of shipbuilding

Latin America continued to develop its defence-industrial base, with Brazil's aircraft industry seeing much activity. For example, in May 2023 Brazil inaugurated its *Gripen* E assembly plant at the Embraer facility in Gavião Peixoto, São Paulo State. This expanded the Gripen Design and Development Network and the Gripen Flight Test Center, which were already based at the site. The new plant also lays the groundwork for any further production orders. In possible reference to Colombia's *Kfir* replacement programme, Saab executives have said they want Brazil to become an 'export hub' to Latin America and potentially other regions.

However, across the region, most activity arguably took place within the naval domain. Shipbuilding is resurgent, with many projects using defence partnerships and technology transfers to foster growth. Franco-Brazilian cooperation on the PROSUB project is the highest-profile of these. However, in March 2023, the Brazilian navy laid the keel for the first of its *Tamandaré*-class frigates, under a USD2 billion contract for four ships awarded in 2020 to the Águas Azuis Consortium, a joint venture between Germany's Thyssenkrupp Marine Systems (TKMS) and Brazil's Embraer and Atech. The vessels will be based on TKMS's MEKO A100 design and adapted to Brazilian requirements. They will be wholly built in Brazil, with the first frigate expected to have more than 30% local content, increasing to over 40% for future boats. Similarly, in March 2023, Argentina signed agreements for the modernisation of a MEKO 140 corvette, as well as the construction of a multipurpose landing ship, a polar ship and a floating dock. Work will take place in the country's TANDANOR and Río Santiago shipyards.

In December 2022, Chile's state-owned ASMAR naval yard launched the icebreaker *Almirante Viel*, whose construction began in August 2018 in partnership with Canada's VARD Marine. It is planned to be entered into service in August 2024. Chile's shipbuilding industry, with support from international partners, has maintained a healthy pipeline within the region. ASMAR started work on the first phase of the navy's *Escotillón* IV project for the supply of two landing platform docks with VARD Marine in February 2022. *Escotillón* IV envisions the modernisation of fleet transport operations with the construction of four 8,000-tonne amphibious and military transport vessels in total. VARD Marine will design the vessels based on existing Vard Series 7 designs and adapt them for local requirements. Chile's navy is reportedly interested in Babcock's *Arrowhead* 140 frigate design, although the competition for a contract will likely open after 2026, with construction to begin in the 2030s.

Colombia's state-owned naval shipbuilder COTECMAR is working on a series of five frigates as part of the country's Strategic Surface Platform (Plataforma Estratégica de Superficie: PES) programme. The frigates will be based on Dutch shipbuilder Damen's SIGMA 10514 design and will replace the country's existing fleet of four corvettes. The frigates are expected to cost up to USD2bn. In August 2023, Colombia approved an additional USD55m to equip the PES frigates with a vertical launch system for air-defence missiles. In addition to the frigates, in November 2022 COTECMAR was also awarded a contract to build an offshore patrol vessel and a logistic support vessel under PES. Mexico, in February 2020, commissioned the first of its *Benito Juárez*-class frigates. Officially a long-range ocean patrol vessel, the POLA ships are a variant of Damen's SIGMA 10514 warship, which have been jointly developed with Mexico's ASTIMAR shipbuilding department. The Mexican navy plans to acquire up to eight POLA-class vessels, as part of a plan to deploy a squadron of frigates on each coast of the country. Should all frigates be ordered, the programme could cost USD3bn in total, becoming Latin America's largest surface naval combatant project.

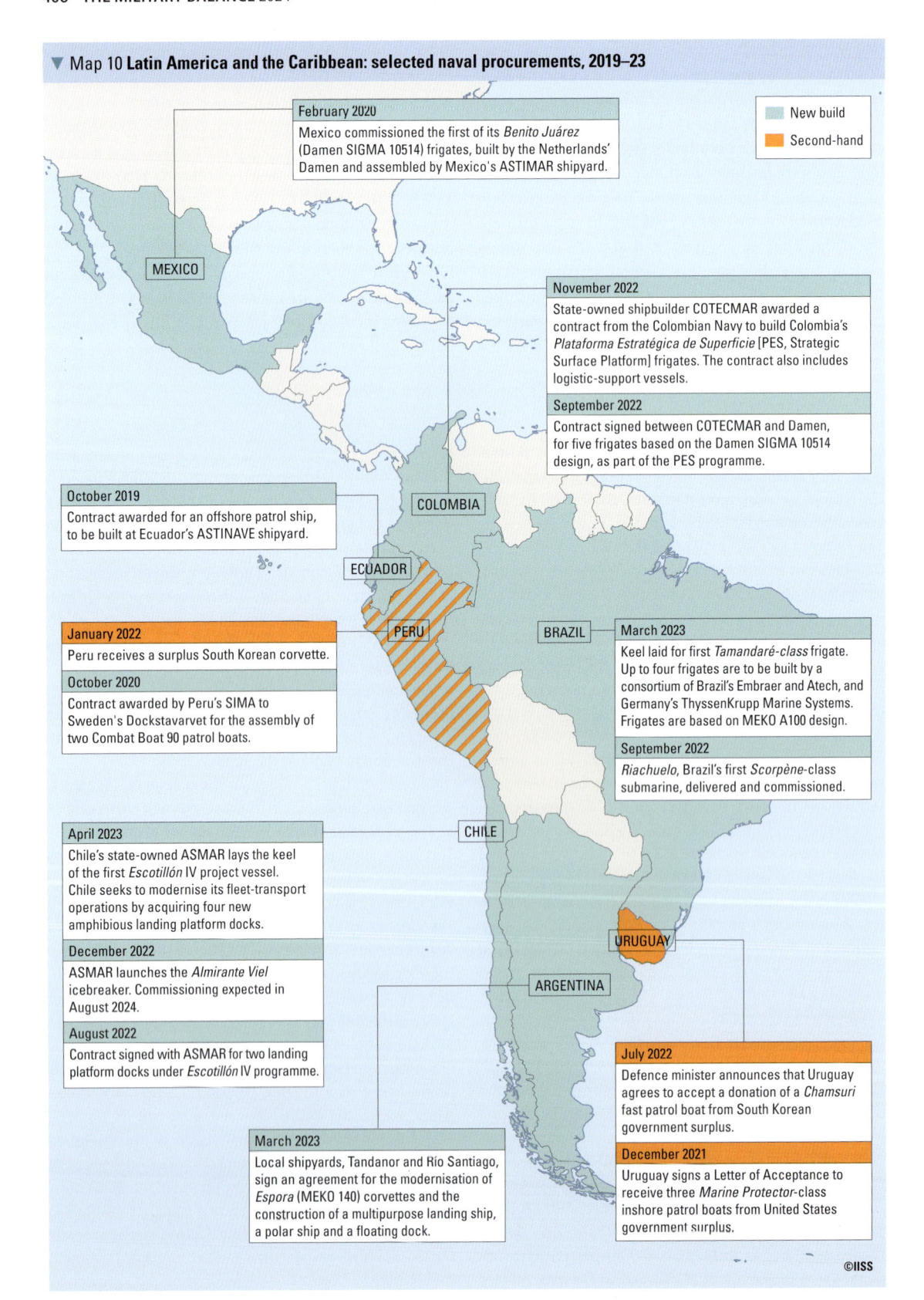

Map 10 Latin America and the Caribbean: selected naval procurements, 2019–23

Legend: New build / Second-hand

MEXICO — February 2020
Mexico commissioned the first of its *Benito Juárez* (Damen SIGMA 10514) frigates, built by the Netherlands' Damen and assembled by Mexico's ASTIMAR shipyard.

COLOMBIA — November 2022
State-owned shipbuilder COTECMAR awarded a contract from the Colombian Navy to build Colombia's *Plataforma Estratégica de Superficie* [PES, Strategic Surface Platform] frigates. The contract also includes logistic-support vessels.

September 2022
Contract signed between COTECMAR and Damen, for five frigates based on the Damen SIGMA 10514 design, as part of the PES programme.

ECUADOR — October 2019
Contract awarded for an offshore patrol ship, to be built at Ecuador's ASTINAVE shipyard.

PERU — January 2022
Peru receives a surplus South Korean corvette.

October 2020
Contract awarded by Peru's SIMA to Sweden's Dockstavarvet for the assembly of two Combat Boat 90 patrol boats.

BRAZIL — March 2023
Keel laid for first *Tamandaré*-class frigate. Up to four frigates are to be built by a consortium of Brazil's Embraer and Atech, and Germany's ThyssenKrupp Marine Systems. Frigates are based on MEKO A100 design.

September 2022
Riachuelo, Brazil's first *Scorpène*-class submarine, delivered and commissioned.

CHILE — April 2023
Chile's state-owned ASMAR lays the keel of the first *Escotillón* IV project vessel. Chile seeks to modernise its fleet-transport operations by acquiring four new amphibious landing platform docks.

December 2022
ASMAR launches the *Almirante Viel* icebreaker. Commissioning expected in August 2024.

August 2022
Contract signed with ASMAR for two landing platform docks under *Escotillón* IV programme.

ARGENTINA — March 2023
Local shipyards, Tandanor and Río Santiago, sign an agreement for the modernisation of *Espora* (MEKO 140) corvettes and the construction of a multipurpose landing ship, a polar ship and a floating dock.

URUGUAY — July 2022
Defence minister announces that Uruguay agrees to accept a donation of a *Chamsuri* fast patrol boat from South Korean government surplus.

December 2021
Uruguay signs a Letter of Acceptance to receive three *Marine Protector*-class inshore patrol boats from United States government surplus.

©IISS

Significant procurement and delivery events - 2023

JANUARY

COLOMBIA *KFIR* REPLACEMENT FALLS THROUGH

Colombia announced that the procurement programme to acquire new fighter aircraft for the Colombian Air Force (FAC) fell apart. The 2022 CONPES 4078 fund worth USD678m and allocated for the first phase of the acquisition expired on 31 December 2022. The programme to replace the FAC's ageing *Kfir* aircraft has dragged on for years due to financial and political issues. But in December 2022, Colombia decided to acquire 16 Dassault *Rafale* fighters, choosing them over Saab's *Gripen* and Lockheed Martin's F-16, saying that the French aircraft would offer 30% cheaper operating costs than the *Kfir*. The FAC's *Kfir* had undergone upgrades and radar enhancement by its original equipment manufacturer Israel Aerospace Industries (IAI) from 2009 to 2017, based on a multi-year contract worth over USD150m and signed in late 2007 under the Colloseum project. A plan for the retirement of the *Kfir* in Colombia seems to be further pushed back, with a maintenance contract worth USD5.82m awarded to IAI in December 2022 to last until the end of 2024. It is unclear whether or when the acquisition programme will be relaunched. The collapse of Colombian–Israeli relations over the war in Gaza in late 2023 puts the continued viability of the *Kfir* fleet into doubt and gives greater urgency to a replacement effort.

JANUARY

HELIBRAS SHAREHOLDING CHANGES

Airbus Helicopters became a larger shareholder of Helicópteros do Brasil (Helibras), based in Itajubá. Codemig Participações (CODEPAR), a public investment firm owned by the state of Minas Gerais, signed an agreement with Airbus Helicopters for the partial sale of its shares in Helibras to fund growth in the regional economy. CODEPAR parted with a 15.51% stake for BRL95m (USD19.03m). In 2020, Airbus Helicopters held 84.45% in Helibras and CODEPAR had a 15.51% stake. The state seems to remain as a minority shareholder alongside Aerofoto Cruzeiro. However, later in the year, it was reported that Airbus may be interested in selling its shares in Helibras if feasible offers arise. Established in 1978, Helibras generated revenue of BRL567m (USD155.18m) in 2018, BRL703m (USD178.22m) in 2019 and BRL927m (USD179.82m) in 2020, including from military and civil customers. Helibras produces the H125 *Ecureuil* and assembles the H225M heavy transport helicopter for the Brazilian Armed Forces, as well as completing the delivery of five H125 light transport helicopters to Chile's Naval Aviation from December 2020 to August 2023.

MAY

GRIPEN E PRODUCTION LINE INAUGURATED IN BRAZIL

Embraer commenced final assembly of 15 *Gripen* E fighter ground-attack aircraft at its Gavião Peixoto site as part of an agreement signed with Saab in October 2014 under the FX-2 programme. The Brazilian Air Force (FAB) initially bought 28 single-seat *Gripen* E and, in 2022, added eight two-seater *Gripen* F. Saab has delivered six *Gripen* E between November 2021 and May 2023, manufactured in Linköping, Sweden, with the fuselage parts produced at its new site in Brazil. Saab opened a sub-component production line for the FAB's FX-2 programme in São Bernardo do Campo in June 2018 and began production in July 2020. Delivery of the first 15 Brazilian-assembled single-seat *Gripens* is planned to start in 2025 and stretch to the end of 2027. Brazil began planning for a follow-on batch of aircraft in 2022.

JUNE

CHILE PLANS TO OUTLINE DEFENCE-INDUSTRIAL POLICY

The Ministry of National Defense of Chile announced in its 2023 Public Account report (covering June 2023–June 2024) that it would create a defence industry policy. The strategy will aim to promote collaboration between the state, academia and industry to tackle prevailing institutional problems within the Chilean defence industry. Chile has built a dependable defence-industrial base focusing on MRO capacities represented by its three state-owned firms, ASMAR (shipbuilding, established in 1960), ENAER (aerospace, established in 1984) and FAMAE (ammunition and vehicle maintenance, established in 1811). However, the dominance of these three firms has meant that a privately owned defence industry has not developed. Attempts to recapitalise equipment and bolster the defence industry over the past decade have been disrupted by financial difficulties and delivered little success, with acquisition characterised by the procurement of second-hand and surplus equipment from other countries. In 2022, ASMAR, ENAER and FAMAE had estimated revenue of USD279.99m and comprised around 3,730 employees.

Antigua and Barbuda ATG

East Caribbean Dollar XCD		2022	2023	2024
GDP	XCD	4.75bn	5.26bn	5.71bn
	USD	1.76bn	1.95bn	2.11bn
per capita	USD	17,441	19,068	20,406
Growth	%	8.5	5.6	5.4
Inflation	%	7.5	5.0	2.9
Def bdgt [a]	XCD	22.5m	22.0m	
	USD	8.35m	8.13m	
USD1=XCD		2.70	2.70	2.70

[a] Budget for the Ministry of Legal Affairs, Public Safety, Immigration & Labour

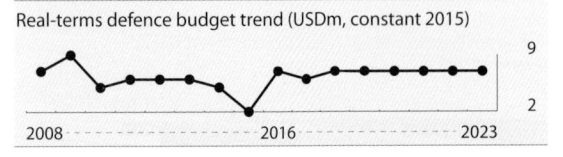

Real-terms defence budget trend (USDm, constant 2015)

Population	101,489					
Age	0–14	15–19	20–24	25–29	30–64	65 plus
Male	11.2%	3.6%	3.8%	3.9%	20.4%	4.3%
Female	10.8%	3.6%	3.9%	4.0%	24.8%	5.8%

Capabilities

The Antigua and Barbuda Defence Force (ABDF) focuses on internal security and disaster relief, and contributes to regional counter-narcotics efforts. It comprises a light-infantry element, which carries out internal-security duties, and a coast guard, which is tasked with fishery protection and counter-narcotics. It has a limited air wing. Antigua and Barbuda is a member of the Caribbean Community and the Caribbean Regional Security System. It has defence ties with the UK and US. The ABDF has participated in US SOUTHCOM's *Tradewinds* disaster-response exercise, though it has no independent capacity to deploy other than in its immediate neighbourhood. There is no heavy land-forces equipment. The coast guard maintains ex-US patrol vessels and a number of smaller boats. Aside from limited maintenance facilities, the country has no defence industry.

ACTIVE 200 (Army 130 Coast Guard 50 Air Wing 20)

(all services form combined Antigua and Barbuda Defence Force)

RESERVE 80 (Joint 80)

ORGANISATIONS BY SERVICE

Army 130
FORCES BY ROLE
MANOEUVRE
  Light
    1 inf bn HQ
    1 inf coy
COMBAT SERVICE SUPPORT
  1 spt gp (1 engr unit, 1 med unit)

Coast Guard 50
EQUIPMENT BY TYPE
PATROL AND COASTAL COMBATANTS • PB 2: 1 *Dauntless*; 1 *Swift*

Air Wing 20
EQUIPMENT BY TYPE
AIRCRAFT • TPT • Light 2 BN-2A *Islander*

Argentina ARG

Argentine Peso ARS		2022	2023	2024
GDP	ARS	82.4trn	175trn	351trn
	USD	631bn	622bn	633bn
per capita	USD	13,620	13,297	13,394
Growth	%	5.0	-2.5	2.8
Inflation	%	72.4	121.7	93.7
Def bdgt	ARS	438bn	827bn	
	USD	3.35bn	2.94bn	
USD1=ARS		130.73	281.20	554.59

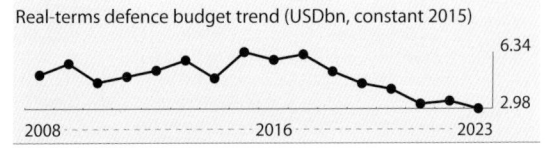

Real-terms defence budget trend (USDbn, constant 2015)

Population	46,621,847					
Age	0–14	15–19	20–24	25–29	30–64	65 plus
Male	12.1%	3.9%	3.8%	3.6%	20.7%	5.4%
Female	11.4%	3.7%	3.6%	3.5%	21.0%	7.3%

Capabilities

Argentina's armed forces have sufficient training and equipment to fulfil internal-security tasks, with power-projection limited by funding shortfalls. The armed forces principally focus on border security, surveillance and counter-narcotics operations. They cooperate with their counterparts in Bolivia and Paraguay, and the US. In 2020, the government repealed 2018 legislation passed under the previous administration, which had allowed greater latitude in deploying the armed forces to tackle external challenges. Argentina's armed forces participate in multinational exercises and bilateral peacekeeping exercises with neighbour Chile. Argentina's equipment inventory is increasingly obsolete. Modernisation is hampered by funding problems that affect purchase decisions. For instance, in 2023, Buenos Aires agreed to buy surplus Norwegian P-3 *Orion* maritime patrol aircraft. The air force faces significant equipment-availability challenges with uncertainty over plans to revive its combat air capability, and the navy has seen its capability decline in areas such as anti-submarine warfare, mine warfare and airborne early warning, although it has received investment for offshore patrol vessels. Argentina possesses an indigenous defence-manufacturing and maintenance capacity covering land, sea, and air systems, although industry fortunes have dipped because of a lack of investment. Recent international procurement ambitions have been hampered by the UK's refusal to provide export licences for British defence-related components.

ACTIVE 72,100 (Army 42,800 Navy 16,400 Air 12,900) Gendarmerie & Paramilitary 31,250

ORGANISATIONS BY SERVICE

Army 42,800

Regt and gp are usually bn-sized

FORCES BY ROLE
MANOEUVRE
Mechanised
1 (1st) div (1 armd bde (1 armd recce regt, 3 tk regt, 1 mech inf regt, 1 SP arty gp, 1 cbt engr bn, 1 int coy, 1 sigs sqn, 1 log coy), 1 (3rd) jungle bde (2 jungle inf regt, 2 jungle inf coy, 1 arty gp, 1 engr coy, 1 int coy, 1 sigs coy, 1 log coy, 1 med coy); 1 (12th) jungle bde (2 jungle inf regt, 1 jungle inf coy, 1 arty gp, 1 engr bn, 1 int coy, 1 sigs coy, 1 log coy, 1 med coy), 2 engr bn, 1 int bn, 1 sigs bn, 1 log coy)

1 (3rd) div (1 armd bde (1 armd recce sqn, 3 tk regt, 1 mech inf regt, 1 SP arty gp, 1 cbt engr sqn, 1 int coy, 1 sigs sqn, 1 log coy); 1 mech bde (1 armd recce regt, 1 tk regt, 2 mech inf regt, 1 SP arty gp, 1 cbt engr bn, 1 int coy, 1 sigs coy, 1 log coy); 1 mech bde (1 armd recce regt, 1 tk regt, 2 mech inf regt, 1 SP arty gp, 1 cbt engr bn, 1 int coy, 1 sigs coy, 1 log coy); 1 int bn, 1 sigs bn, 1 log coy, 1 AD gp (2 AD bn))

1 (Rapid Deployment Force) div (1 SF gp; 1 mech bde (1 armd recce regt, 3 mech inf regt, 1 arty gp, 1 MRL gp, 1 cbt engr coy, 1 sigs coy,1 log coy); 1 AB bde (1 recce sqn, 2 para regt, 1 air aslt regt, 1 arty gp, 1 cbt engr coy, 1 sigs coy, 1 log coy))

Light
1 (2nd) mtn inf div (1 mtn inf bde (1 recce regt, 3 mtn inf regt, 1 mtn inf coy, 2 arty gp, 1 cbt engr bn, 1 sigs coy, 1 log coy); 1 mtn inf bde (1 recce regt, 3 mtn inf regt, 1 mtn inf coy, 1 arty gp, 1 cbt engr bn, 1 sigs coy, 1 log coy); 1 mtn inf bde (1 recce regt, 2 mtn inf regt, 2 arty gp, 1 cbt engr bn, 1 sigs coy, 1 construction coy, 1 log coy), 1 arty gp, 1 sigs bn)

1 mot cav regt (presidential escort)

COMBAT SUPPORT
1 engr bn
1 CBRN coy
1 sigs gp (1 EW bn, 1 sigs bn, 1 maint bn)
1 sigs bn
1 sigs coy

COMBAT SERVICE SUPPORT
3 maint bn

HELICOPTER
1 avn gp (bde) (1 avn bn, 1 tpt hel bn, 1 atk/ISR hel sqn)

EQUIPMENT BY TYPE
ARMOURED FIGHTING VEHICLES
MBT 231: 225 TAM, 6 TAM S21
LT TK 117: 107 SK-105A1 *Kuerassier*; 6 SK-105A2 *Kuerassier*; 4 *Patagón*
RECCE 47 AML-90
IFV 232: 118 VCTP (incl variants); 114 M113A2 (20mm cannon)
APC 278
  APC (T) 274: 70 M113A1-ACAV; 204 M113A2
  APC (W) 4 WZ-551B1
ENGINEERING & MAINTENANCE VEHICLES
  ARV *Greif*
ANTI-TANK/ANTI-INFRASTRUCTURE
  MSL • SP 3 M1025 HMMWV with TOW-2A
  RCL 105mm 150 M-1968
ARTILLERY 1,108
  SP 155mm 42: 23 AMX F3; 19 VCA 155 *Palmaria*
  TOWED 172: **105mm** 64 Model 56 pack howitzer; **155mm** 108: 28 CITEFA M-77/CITEFA M-81; 80 SOFMA L-33
  MRL 8: **105mm** 4 SLAM *Pampero*; **127mm** 4 CP-30
  MOR 886: **81mm** 492; **SP 107mm** 25 M106A2; **120mm** 330 Brandt; **SP 120mm** 39 TAM-VCTM
AIRCRAFT
  TPT • Light 13: 1 Beech 80 *Queen Air*; 3 C-212-200 *Aviocar*; 4 Cessna 208EX *Grand Caravan*; 1 Cessna 500 *Citation* (survey); 1 Cessna 550 *Citation Bravo*; 2 DHC-6 *Twin Otter*; 1 *Sabreliner* 75A (*Gaviao* 75A)
  TRG 5 T-41 *Mescalero*
HELICOPTERS
  MRH 5: 4 SA315B *Lama*; 1 Z-11
  TPT 62: **Medium** 3 AS332B *Super Puma*; **Light** 59: 1 Bell 212; 25 Bell 205 (UH-1H *Iroquois* – 6 armed); 5 Bell 206B3; 13 UH-1H-II *Huey* II; 15 AB206B1
AIR DEFENCE
  SAM • Point-defence RBS-70
  GUNS • TOWED 229: **20mm** 200 GAI-B01; **30mm** 21 HS L81; **35mm** 8 GDF-002 (*Skyguard* fire control)

Navy 16,400

Commands: Surface Fleet, Submarines, Naval Avn, Marines

FORCES BY ROLE
SPECIAL FORCES
1 (diver) SF gp

EQUIPMENT BY TYPE
SUBMARINES • SSK
1 *Santa Cruz* (GER TR-1700) (non-operational, undergoing MLU since 2015) with 6 single 533mm TT with SST-4 HWT
1 *Salta* (GER T-209/1100) (non-operational since 2013) with 8 single 533mm TT with Mk 37/SST-4 HWT)

PRINCIPAL SURFACE COMBATANTS 5
DESTROYERS • DDH 1 *Hercules* (UK Type-42) (utilised as a fast troop-transport ship), with 1 114mm gun (capacity 2 SH-3H *Sea King* hel)
FRIGATES • FFGHM 4 *Almirante Brown* (GER MEKO 360) (of which 1†) with 2 quad lnchr with MM40 *Exocet* AShM, 1 octuple *Albatros* lnchr with *Aspide* SAM, 2 triple ILAS-3 (B-515) 324mm TT with A244/S LWT, 1 127mm gun (capacity 1 AS555 *Fennec* hel)

PATROL AND COASTAL COMBATANTS 24
  CORVETTES 9:
    FSGH 6 *Espora* (GER MEKO 140) with 2 twin lnchr with MM38 *Exocet* AShM, 2 triple 324mm ILAS-3 (B-515) ASTT with A244/S LWT, 1 76mm gun (capacity 1 AS555 *Fennec* hel)
    FSG 3 *Drummond* (FRA A-69) (of which 2†) with 2 twin lnchr with MM38 *Exocet* AShM, 2 triple 324mm ILAS-3 (B-515) ASTT with A244/S LWT, 1 100mm gun
  PSOH 4 *Bouchard* (FRA OPV 87) (of which 1 ex-FRA *L'Adroit*) (capacity 1 hel)
  PSO 1 *Teniente Olivieri* (ex-US oilfield tug)
  PCFGT 1 *Intrepida* (GER Lurssen 45m) with 2 single lnchr with MM38 *Exocet* AShM, 2 single 533mm TT with SST-4 HWT, 1 76mm gun
  PCF 1 *Intrepida* (GER Lurssen 45m) with 1 76mm gun
  PCO 1 *Murature* (ex-US *King* – trg/river-patrol role) with 2 105mm gun
  PB 7: 4 *Baradero* (ISR *Dabur*); 2 *Punta Mogotes* (ex-US *Point*); 1 *Zurubi*
AMPHIBIOUS 6 LCVP
LOGISTICS AND SUPPORT 16
  ABU 3 *Red*
  AFS 4 *Puerto Argentina* (ex-RUS *Neftegaz*)
  AGB 1 *Almirante Irizar* (damaged by fire in 2007; returned to service in mid-2017)
  AGS 2: 1 *Cormoran*; 1 *Puerto Deseado* (ice-breaking capability, used for polar research)
  AGOR 2: 1 *Austral* (ex-GER *Sonne*); 1 *Commodoro Rivadavia*
  AK 2 *Costa Sur* (capacity 4 LCVP)
  AOR 1 *Patagonia* (ex-FRA *Durance*) with 1 hel platform
  AXS 1 *Libertad*

Naval Aviation 2,000
EQUIPMENT BY TYPE
AIRCRAFT 16 combat capable
  ASW 6: 2 S-2T *Tracker*; 4 P-3B *Orion*†
  TPT • Light 7 Beech 200F/M *King Air*
  TRG 10 T-34C *Turbo Mentor**
HELICOPTERS
  ASW 2 SH-3H (ASH-3H) *Sea King*
  MRH 1 AS555 *Fennec*
  TPT • Medium 6: 2 S-61T; 4 UH-3H *Sea King*
AIR-LAUNCHED MISSILES
  AAM • IR R-550 *Magic*
  AShM AM39 *Exocet*

Marines 2,500
FORCES BY ROLE
MANOEUVRE
  Amphibious
  1 (fleet) force (1 cdo gp, 1 (AAV) amph bn, 1 mne bn, 1 arty bn, 1 ADA bn)
  1 (fleet) force (2 mne bn, 2 navy det)
  1 force (1 mne bn)
EQUIPMENT BY TYPE
ARMOURED FIGHTING VEHICLES
  RECCE 12 ERC-90F *Sagaie*
  APC • APC (W) 31 VCR
  AAV 11 LVTP-7
ENGINEERING & MAINTENANCE VEHICLES
  ARV AAVR 7
ANTI-TANK/ANTI-INFRASTRUCTURE
  RCL 105mm 30 M-1974 FMK-1
ARTILLERY 89
  TOWED 19: **105mm** 13 Model 56 pack howitzer; **155mm** 6 M114
  MOR 70: **81mm** 58; **120mm** 12
AIR DEFENCE
  SAM • Point-defence RBS-70
  GUNS 40mm 4 Bofors 40L

Air Force 12,900
4 Major Comds – Air Operations, Personnel, Air Regions, Logistics, 8 air bde

Air Operations Command
FORCES BY ROLE
GROUND ATTACK
  2 sqn with A-4/OA-4 (A-4AR/OA-4AR) *Skyhawk*
  2 (tac air) sqn with EMB-312 *Tucano* (on loan for border surv/interdiction)
ISR
  1 sqn with Learjet 35A
SEARCH & RESCUE/TRANSPORT HELICOPTER
  2 sqn with Bell 212; Bell 407GXi; Bell 412; Mi-171, SA-315B *Lama*
TANKER/TRANSPORT
  1 sqn with C-130H *Hercules*; KC-130H *Hercules*; L-100-30
TRANSPORT
  1 sqn with Beech A200 *King Air* (UC-12B *Huron*); Cessna 182 *Skylane*
  1 sqn with DHC-6 *Twin Otter*; Saab 340
  1 sqn with F-28 *Friendship*
  1 sqn with Learjet 35A; Learjet 60
  1 (Pres) flt with B-737-700; B-757-23ER; S-70A *Black Hawk*, S-76B
TRAINING
  1 sqn with AT-63 *Pampa* II
  1 sqn with EMB-312 *Tucano*
  1 sqn with Grob 120TP
  1 sqn with IA-63 *Pampa* III*
  1 sqn with T-6C *Texan* II
  1 hel sqn with Hughes 369; SA-315B *Lama*
TRANSPORT HELICOPTER
  1 sqn with Hughes 369; MD-500; MD-500D
EQUIPMENT BY TYPE

AIRCRAFT 22 combat capable
  ATK 12: 10 A-4 (A-4AR) *Skyhawk* (of which 6†); 2 OA-4 (OA-4AR) *Skyhawk* (of which 1†)
  ELINT 1 Learjet 35A
  TKR/TPT 2 KC-130H *Hercules*
  TPT 27: **Medium** 5: 4 C-130H *Hercules* (incl 1 leased); 1 L-100-30; **Light** 18: 5 Beech A200 *King Air* (UC-12B *Huron*); 4 Cessna 182 *Skylane*; 2 DHC-6 *Twin Otter*; 3 Learjet 35A (of which 2 test and calibration and 1 medevac); 1 Learjet 60 (VIP); 1 PA-28-236 *Dakota*; 3 Saab 340 (jointly operated with LADE); **PAX** 4: 1 B-737; 1 B-737-700; 1 B-757-23ER; 1 F-28 *Fellowship*
  TRG 46: 2 AT-63 *Pampa* II* (LIFT); 11 EMB-312 *Tucano*; 9 Grob 120TP; 8 IA-63 *Pampa* III*; 6 P2002JF *Sierra*; 10 T-6C *Texan* II (8 EMB-312 *Tucano* in store)
HELICOPTERS
  MRH 29: 6 Bell 412EP; 11 Hughes 369; 3 MD-500; 4 MD-500D; 5 SA315B *Lama*
  TPT 13: **Medium** 3: 2 Mi-171E; 1 S-70A *Black Hawk* (VIP); **Light** 10: 7 Bell 212; 1 Bell 407GXi; 2 S-76B (VIP)
AIR DEFENCE
  GUNS 88: **20mm**: 86 Oerlikon/Rh-202 with 9 Elta EL/M-2106 radar; **35mm**: 2 GDF-001 with *Skyguard* radar
AIR-LAUNCHED MISSILES
  AAM • IR AIM-9L *Sidewinder*; R-550 *Magic*; *Shafrir* 2‡

Gendarmerie & Paramilitary 31,250

Gendarmerie 18,000
Ministry of Security
FORCES BY ROLE
COMMAND
  7 regional comd
SPECIAL FORCES
  1 SF unit
  MANOEUVRE
  Other
  17 paramilitary bn
  Aviation
  1 (mixed) avn bn
EQUIPMENT BY TYPE
  ARMOURED FIGHTING VEHICLES
  APC (W) 87: 47 *Grenadier*; 40 UR-416
  ARTILLERY • MOR 81mm
  AIRCRAFT
  TPT 13: **Light** 12: 3 Cessna 152; 3 Cessna 206; 1 Cessna 336; 1 PA-28 *Cherokee*; 2 PC-6B *Turbo Porter*; 2 PC-12; **PAX** 1 Learjet 35
HELICOPTERS
  MRH 2 MD-500C
  TPT • Light 17: 3 AW119 *Koala*; 2 Bell 206 *Jet Ranger* (AB-206); 7 AS350 *Ecureuil*; 1 H135; 1 H155; 3 R-44 *Raven* II
  TRG 1 S-300C

Prefectura Naval (Coast Guard) 13,250
Ministry of Security
EQUIPMENT BY TYPE
PATROL AND COASTAL COMBATANTS 71
  PCO 7: 1 *Correa Falcon*; 1 *Delfin*; 5 *Mantilla* (F30 *Halcón* – undergoing modernisation)
  PCC 1 *Mariano Moreno*
  PB 58: 1 *Dorado*; 25 *Estrellemar*; 2 *Lynch* (US *Cape*); 18 *Mar del Plata* (Z-28); 1 *Surel*; 8 Damen Stan 2200; 3 Stan Tender 1750
  PBF 4 *Shaldag* II
  PBR 1 *Tonina*
LOGISTICS & SUPPORT 11
  AAR 1 *Tango*
  AG 3
  ARS 1 *Prefecto Mansilla*
  AX 3
  AXL 2
  AXS 1 *Dr Bernardo Houssay*
AIRCRAFT
  MP 1 Beech 350ER *King Air*
  TPT • Light 6: 5 C-212 *Aviocar*; 1 Beech 350ER *King Air*
  TRG 2 Piper PA-28 *Archer* III
HELICOPTERS
  SAR 3 AS565MA *Panther*
  MRH 1 AS365 *Dauphin* 2
  TPT 7: **Medium** 3: 1 H225 *Puma*; 2 SA330L (AS330L) *Puma*; **Light** 4: 2 AS355 *Ecureuil* II; 2 Bell 206 (AB-206) *Jet Ranger*
  TRG 4 S-300C

DEPLOYMENT

CENTRAL AFRICAN REPUBLIC: UN • MINUSCA 2
CYPRUS: UN • UNFICYP 248; 2 inf coy; 1 hel flt with 2 Bell 212
INDIA/PAKISTAN: UN • UNMOGIP 4
LEBANON: UN • UNIFIL 3
MIDDLE EAST: UN • UNTSO 4
SYRIA/ISRAEL: UN • UNDOF 1
WESTERN SAHARA: UN • MINURSO 4

Bahamas BHS

Bahamian Dollar BSD		2022	2023	2024
GDP	BSD	12.9bn	13.9bn	14.5bn
	USD	12.9bn	13.9bn	14.5bn
per capita	USD	32,299	34,371	35,542
Growth	%	14.4	4.3	1.8
Inflation	%	5.6	3.9	3.2
Def bdgt	BSD	94.5m	106m	105m
	USD	94.5m	106m	105m
USD1=BSD		1.00	1.00	1.00

Real-terms defence budget trend (USDm, constant 2015)

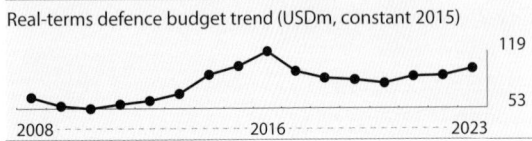

Population	406,513					
Age	0–14	15–19	20–24	25–29	30–64	65 plus
Male	10.3%	3.9%	4.3%	4.6%	19.6%	3.7%
Female	11.6%	4.8%	5.1%	5.1%	22.6%	4.5%

Capabilities

The Royal Bahamas Defence Force (RBDF) is primarily a naval force tasked with disaster relief, maritime security and counter-narcotics duties. Its single commando squadron is responsible for base protection and internal security. The Bahamas is a member of the Caribbean Community, and the RBDF maintains training relationships with the UK and US. The RBDF has participated in US SOUTHCOM's *Tradewinds* disaster-response exercise. There is little independent capacity to deploy abroad beyond recent regional disaster-relief efforts. The RBDF's Sandy Bottom Project, the largest-ever capital investment in the service, includes the acquisition of patrol craft and the development of bases and port facilities. The maritime wing is focused around patrol vessels and smaller patrol boats, while the air wing has a small inventory of light aircraft. Apart from limited maintenance facilities, the Bahamas has no indigenous defence industry.

ACTIVE 1,500

ORGANISATIONS BY SERVICE

Royal Bahamas Defence Force 1,500

FORCES BY ROLE

MANOEUVRE

Amphibious
1 mne coy (incl marines with internal- and base-security duties)

EQUIPMENT BY TYPE

PATROL AND COASTAL COMBATANTS 21
 PCC 2 *Bahamas*
 PB 19: 4 *Arthur Dion Hanna* (Damen Stan Patrol 4207); 2 *Dauntless*; 4 *Lignum Vitae* (Damen 3007); 1 Safe 33; 4 Safe 44; 2 Sea Ark 12m; 2 Sea Ark 15m
LOGISTICS & SUPPORT • AKR 1 *Lawrence Major* (Damen 5612)

AIRCRAFT • TPT • Light 3: 1 Beech A350 *King Air*; 1 Cessna 208 *Caravan*; 1 P-68 *Observer*

FOREIGN FORCES

Guyana Navy: Base located at New Providence Island

Barbados BRB

Barbados Dollar BBD		2022	2023	2024
GDP	BBD	11.4bn	12.4bn	13.3bn
	USD	5.69bn	6.22bn	6.66bn
per capita	USD	19,648	21,442	22,889
Growth	%	9.8	4.5	3.9
Inflation	%	5.0	5.2	3.1
Def bdgt [a]	BBD	84.8m	87.1m	
	USD	42.4m	43.6m	
USD1=BBD		2.00	2.00	2.00

[a] Defence & security expenditure

Real-terms defence budget trend (USDm, constant 2015)

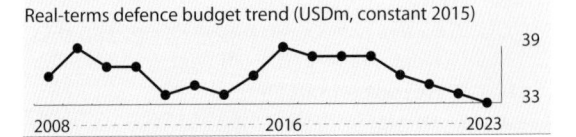

Population	303,431					
Age	0–14	15–19	20–24	25–29	30–64	65 plus
Male	8.4%	2.9%	3.0%	3.0%	24.3%	6.6%
Female	8.4%	3.0%	3.0%	3.1%	25.2%	9.1%

Capabilities

Maritime security and resource protection are the main tasks of the Barbados Defence Force (BDF), but it has a secondary public-safety role in support of the police force. The BDF has undertaken counter-narcotics work, while troops have also been tasked with supporting law enforcement. There are plans to improve disaster-relief capabilities. Barbados is a member of the Caribbean Community, and the Caribbean Regional Security System is headquartered there. The BDF has participated in US SOUTHCOM's *Tradewinds* disaster-response exercise. There is limited capacity to deploy independently within the region, such as on hurricane-relief duties. The inventory consists principally of a small number of patrol vessels. Apart from limited maintenance facilities, Barbados has no indigenous defence industry.

ACTIVE 610 (Army 500 Coast Guard 110)

RESERVE 430 (Joint 430)

ORGANISATIONS BY SERVICE

Army 500

FORCES BY ROLE

MANOEUVRE

Light
1 inf bn (cadre)

Coast Guard 110

HQ located at HMBS Pelican, Spring Garden

EQUIPMENT BY TYPE

PATROL AND COASTAL COMBATANTS 6

   PB 6: 1 *Dauntless*; 2 *Enterprise* (Damen Stan 1204); 3 *Trident* (Damen Stan Patrol 4207)

Belize BLZ

Belize Dollar BZD		2022	2023	2024
GDP	BZD	5.97bn	6.44bn	6.74bn
	USD	2.99bn	3.22bn	3.37bn
per capita	USD	6,757	7,142	7,330
Growth	%	12.7	4.0	3.0
Inflation	%	6.3	3.7	1.7
Def bdgt [a]	BZD	46.6m	56.4m	
	USD	23.3m	28.2m	
USD1=BZD		2.00	2.00	2.00

[a] Excludes funds allocated to Coast Guard and Police Service

Real-terms defence budget trend (USDm, constant 2015)

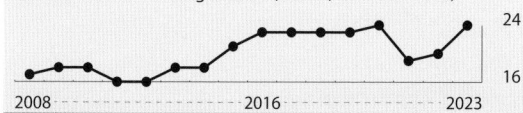

Population	409,728				
Age	0–14	15–19	20–24	25–29	30–64	65 plus
Male	14.3%	4.8%	4.7%	4.2%	18.8%	2.7%
Female	13.9%	4.9%	4.8%	4.5%	19.7%	2.7%

Capabilities

The small Belize Defence Force (BDF) and a coast guard provide national security, particularly control of the borders with Guatemala and Mexico. In 2022, a new National Security Strategy underscored priorities of maintaining sovereignty and territorial integrity; reducing transnational, cross-border and other violent crime; counterterrorism; and reducing risk from natural human-caused hazards. The UK has a long-standing security relationship with Belize and maintains a small training unit there. The BDF also trains with US SOUTHCOM. Training levels are limited but sufficient for the BDF's tasks. Belize is a member of the Caribbean Community. The BDF does not, as a rule, deploy internationally and logistics support is largely only for border-security missions. Nevertheless, Belize was considering a limited deployment to Haiti as part of a UN security mission. The conventional equipment inventory is limited but has had a modest injection of US-donated trucks and a Cessna special-mission aircraft for surveillance. There is no significant defence industry.

ACTIVE 1,500 (Army 1,500) Gendarmerie & Paramilitary 550

RESERVE 700 (Joint 700)

ORGANISATIONS BY SERVICE

Army ε1,500

FORCES BY ROLE

SPECIAL FORCES
  1 SF unit

MANOEUVRE

  Light
    2 inf bn (3 inf coy)

COMBAT SERVICE SUPPORT
  1 spt gp

EQUIPMENT BY TYPE

ANTI-TANK/ANTI-INFRASTRUCTURE • RCL 84mm *Carl Gustaf*

ARTILLERY • MOR 81mm 6

Air Wing

EQUIPMENT BY TYPE

AIRCRAFT
  TPT • Light 3: 1 BN-2B *Defender*†; 1 Cessna 182 *Skylane*†; 1 Cessna 208B *Grand Caravan* EX
  TRG 1 T-67M-200 *Firefly*

HELICOPTERS
  TPT • Light 2: 1 Bell 205 (UH-1H *Iroquois*); 1 Bell 407

Reserve

FORCES BY ROLE

MANOEUVRE

  Light
    1 inf bn (3 inf coy)

Gendarmerie & Paramilitary 550

Coast Guard 550

EQUIPMENT BY TYPE

All operational patrol vessels under 10t FLD

FOREIGN FORCES

United Kingdom BATSUB 12

Bolivia BOL

Bolivian Boliviano BOB		2022	2023	2024
GDP	BOB	304bn	321bn	341bn
	USD	44.3bn	46.8bn	49.7bn
per capita	USD	3,705	3,858	4,045
Growth	%	3.5	1.8	1.8
Inflation	%	1.7	3.0	4.4
Def bdgt	BOB	3.30bn	3.24bn	
	USD	481m	473m	
USD1=BOB		6.86	6.86	6.86

Real-terms defence budget trend (USDm, constant 2015)
519
293
2008 — 2016 — 2023

Population 12,186,079

Age	0–14	15–19	20–24	25–29	30–64	65 plus
Male	14.9%	5.0%	4.5%	4.0%	18.7%	3.2%
Female	14.3%	4.8%	4.4%	4.0%	18.5%	3.7%

Capabilities

The armed forces are constitutionally tasked with maintaining sovereignty and territorial defence, though principal tasks are counter-narcotics and internal and border security. The government has formed and deployed joint task forces to border regions to combat smuggling and established several border posts. Airspace control is an emerging strategic priority. The armed forces have also been playing a greater role in disaster relief operations, with a dedicated joint command established in 2022. The country has defence-technology ties with Russia. China. France also sell defence equipment to Bolivia. Regionally, Bolivia cooperates with Peru and Paraguay in providing disaster relief and countering illicit trafficking. In 2023, Bolivia signed an agreement with Iran to source UAVs for use in border control activities. The armed forces have stressed the need to improve conditions for personnel amid greater internal deployments to border areas on counter-trafficking tasks. An aerospace R&D centre was created in 2018 in the military-engineering school with the objective of developing munitions and ISR UAVs. The country has some maintenance, repair and overhaul capacity.

ACTIVE 34,100 (Army 22,800 Navy 4,800 Air 6,500)
Gendarmerie & Paramilitary 37,100

Conscript liability 12 months voluntary conscription for both males and females

ORGANISATIONS BY SERVICE

Army 9,800; 13,000 conscript (total 22,800)
FORCES BY ROLE
COMMAND
  6 mil region HQ
  10 div HQ
SPECIAL FORCES
  3 SF regt
MANOEUVRE
  Reconnaissance
  1 mot cav gp
  Armoured
  1 armd bn
  Mechanised
  1 mech cav regt
  2 mech inf regt
  Light
  1 (aslt) cav gp
  5 (horsed) cav gp
  3 mot inf regt
  21 inf regt
  Air Manoeuvre
  2 AB regt (bn)
  Other
  1 (Presidential Guard) inf regt
COMBAT SUPPORT
  6 arty regt (bn)
  6 engr bn
  1 int coy
  1 MP bn
  1 sigs bn
COMBAT SERVICE SUPPORT
  2 log bn
AVIATION
  2 avn coy
AIR DEFENCE
  1 ADA regt
EQUIPMENT BY TYPE
ARMOURED FIGHTING VEHICLES
  LT TK 54: 36 SK-105A1 *Kuerassier*; 18 SK-105A2 *Kuerassier*
  RECCE 24 EE-9 *Cascavel*
  APC 148+
    APC (T) 87+: 50+ M113, 37 M9 half-track
    APC (W) 61: 24 EE-11 *Urutu*; 22 MOWAG *Roland*; 15 V-100 *Commando*
  AUV 19 *Tiger* 4×4
ENGINEERING & MAINTENANCE VEHICLES
  ARV 4 *Greif*; M578 LARV
ANTI-TANK/ANTI-INFRASTRUCTURE
  MSL
    SP 2 *Koyak* with HJ-8
    MANPATS HJ-8
  RCL 90mm M67; 106mm M40A1
ARTILLERY 311+
  TOWED 61: 105mm 25 M101A1; 122mm 36 M-30 (M-1938)
  MOR 250+: 81mm 250 M29; Type-W87; 107mm M30; 120mm M120
AIRCRAFT

TPT • **Light** 3: 1 Fokker F-27-200; 1 Beech 90 *King Air*; 1 C-212 *Aviocar*
HELICOPTERS • MRH 5 H425
AIR DEFENCE • GUNS • TOWED 37mm 18 Type-65

Navy 4,800

Organised into six naval districts with HQ located at Puerto Guayaramerín
EQUIPMENT BY TYPE
PATROL AND COASTAL COMBATANTS 7
  PBR 7: 1 *Santa Cruz*; 6 Type 928 YC
LOGISTICS AND SUPPORT 8
  AG 2: 1 LP-503; 1 *Mojo Huayna*
  AH 2
  AP 4

Marines 1,700 (incl 1,000 Naval Military Police)
FORCES BY ROLE
MANOEUVRE
  Mechanised
  1 lt mech inf bn
  Amphibious
  6 mne bn (1 in each Naval District)
COMBAT SUPPORT
  4 (naval) MP bn

Air Force 6,500 (incl conscripts)
FORCES BY ROLE
GROUND ATTACK
  1 sqn with K-8WB *Karakorum*
ISR
  1 sqn with Cessna 206; Cessna 402; Learjet 25B/25D (secondary VIP role)
SEARCH & RESCUE
  1 sqn with AS332B *Super Puma*; H125 *Ecureuil*; H145
TRANSPORT
  1 (TAM) sqn with B-727; B-737; MA60
  1 (TAB) sqn with C-130A *Hercules*; MD-10-30F
  1 sqn with C-130B/H *Hercules*
  1 sqn with F-27-400M *Troopship*
  1 (VIP) sqn with Beech 90 *King Air*; Beech 200 *King Air* Beech 1900; *Falcon* 900EX; *Sabreliner* 60; *Falcon* 50EX
  6 sqn with Cessna 152/206; IAI-201 *Arava*; PA-32 *Saratoga*; PA-34 *Seneca*
TRAINING
  1 sqn with DA40; T-25; Z-242L
  1 sqn with Cessna 152/172
  1 sqn with PC-7 *Turbo Trainer*
  1 hel sqn with R-44 *Raven* II
TRANSPORT HELICOPTER
  1 (anti-drug) sqn with Bell 205 (UH-1H *Iroquois*)
AIR DEFENCE
  1 regt with Oerlikon; Type-65
EQUIPMENT BY TYPE
AIRCRAFT 20 combat capable
  TPT 77: **Heavy** 1 MD-10-30F; **Medium** 4: 1 C-130A *Hercules*; 2 C-130B *Hercules*; 1 C-130H *Hercules*; **Light** 64: 1 *Aero Commander* 690; 3 Beech 90 *King Air*; 2 Beech 200 *King Air*; 1 Beech 250 *King Air*; 1 Beech 350 *King Air*; 3 C-212-100; 6 Cessna 152; 2 Cessna 172; 18 Cessna 206; 3 Cessna 210 *Centurion*; 1 Cessna 402; 8 DA40; 1 F-27-400M *Troopship*; 4 IAI-201 *Arava*; 2 Learjet 25B/D; 2 MA60†; 1 PA-32 *Saratoga*; 4 PA-34 *Seneca*; 1 *Sabreliner* 60; **PAX** 8: 1 B-727; 3 B-737-200; 1 *Falcon* 50EX; 1 *Falcon* 900EX (VIP); 2 RJ70
  TRG 345: 4 K-8WB *Karakorum**; 6 T-25; 16 PC-7 *Turbo Trainer**; 8 Z-242L
HELICOPTERS
  MRH 1 SA316 *Alouette* III
  TPT 37: **Medium** 6 H215 *Super Puma*; **Light** 31: 2 H125 *Ecureuil*; 19 Bell 205 (UH-1H *Iroquois*); 4 H145; 6 R-44 *Raven* II
AIR DEFENCE • GUNS • TOWED 18+: **20mm** Oerlikon GAI; **37mm** 18 Type-65

Gendarmerie & Paramilitary 37,100+

National Police 31,100+
FORCES BY ROLE
MANOEUVRE
  Other
  27 frontier sy unit
  9 paramilitary bde
  2 (rapid action) paramilitary regt

Narcotics Police 6,000+
FOE (700) – Special Operations Forces

DEPLOYMENT
CENTRAL AFRICAN REPUBLIC: UN • MINUSCA 7
DEMOCRATIC REPUBLIC OF THE CONGO: UN • MONUSCO 4
SOUTH SUDAN: UN • UNMISS 4
SUDAN: UN • UNISFA 3

Brazil BRZ

Brazilian Real BRL		2022	2023	2024
GDP	BRL	9.92trn	10.6trn	11.3trn
	USD	1.92trn	2.13trn	2.27trn
per capita	USD	9,455	10,413	11,029
Growth	%	2.9	3.1	1.5
Inflation	%	9.3	4.7	4.5
Def bdgt [a]	BRL	116bn	121bn	
	USD	22.6bn	24.2bn	
USD1=BRL		5.16	4.99	4.99

[a] Includes military pensions

Real-terms defence budget trend (USDbn, constant 2015)

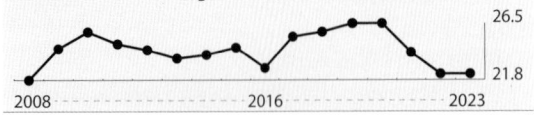

Population 218,689,757

Age	0–14	15–19	20–24	25–29	30–64	65 plus
Male	10.1%	3.8%	4.0%	3.9%	22.9%	4.5%
Female	9.7%	3.7%	3.9%	3.8%	23.7%	6.0%

Capabilities

The armed forces are among the most capable in Latin America. Brazil seeks to enhance its power-projection capabilities, boost surveillance of the Amazon region and coastal waters, and further develop its defence industry. Security challenges from organised crime have seen the armed forces deploy on internal-security operations. Brazil maintains military ties with most of its neighbours, including personnel exchanges and joint military training with Chile and Colombia. The country also has defence cooperation ties with France, Sweden and the US, centred on procurement, technical advice and personnel training. Brazil's air-transport fleet enables it to independently deploy forces and it contributes small contingents to several UN missions. The government in August announced a far-reaching investment plan to accelerate the modernisation of the military. It is recapitalising equipment across domains. Brazil has a well-developed defence-industrial base, with the capability to design and manufacture land, naval and air equipment. Aerospace firms Avibras and Embraer also export. Local companies are involved in the SISFRON border-security programme. There are industrial partnerships, including technology transfers and research and development support.

ACTIVE 366,500 (Army 214,000 Navy 85,000 Air 67,500) **Gendarmerie & Paramilitary 395,000**

Conscript liability 12 months (can go to 18; often waived)

RESERVE 1,340,000

ORGANISATIONS BY SERVICE

Space
EQUIPMENT BY TYPE
SATELLITES • COMMUNICATIONS 1 SGDC-1 (civil–military use)

Army 102,000; 112,000 conscript (total 214,000)
FORCES BY ROLE

COMMAND
8 mil comd HQ
12 mil region HQ
7 div HQ (2 with regional HQ)

SPECIAL FORCES
1 SF comd (1 SF bn, 1 cdo bn, 1 psyops bn, 1 spt bn)
1 SF coy

MANOEUVRE

Reconnaissance
4 mech cav regt

Armoured
1 (5th) armd bde (1 mech cav sqn, 2 tk regt, 2 mech inf bn, 1 SP arty bn, 1 engr bn, 1 sigs coy, 1 log bn)
1 (6th) armd bde (1 mech cav sqn, 2 tk regt, 2 mech inf bn, 1 SP arty bn, 1 AD bty, 1 engr bn, 1 sigs coy, 1 log bn)

Mechanised
2 (1st & 4th) mech cav bde (1 armd cav regt, 3 mech cav regt, 1 arty bn, 1 engr coy, 1 sigs coy, 1 log bn)
2 (2nd & 3rd) mech cav bde (1 armd cav regt, 2 mech cav regt, 1 SP arty bn, 1 engr coy, 1 sigs coy, 1 log bn)
1 (3rd) mech inf bde (1 mech cav sqn, 2 mech inf bn, 1 inf bn, 1 arty bn, 1 engr coy, 1 sigs coy, 1 log bn)
1 (11th) mech inf bde (1 mech cav regt, 3 mech inf bn, 1 arty bn, 1 engr coy, 1 sigs coy, 1 MP coy, 1 log bn)
1 (15th) mech inf bde (3 mech inf bn, 1 arty bn, 1 engr coy, 1 log bn)

Light
1 (4th) mot inf bde (1 mech cav sqn, 1 mot inf bn, 1 inf bn, 1 mtn inf bn, 1 arty bn, 1 sigs coy, 1 log bn)
1 (7th) mot inf bde (3 mot inf bn, 1 arty bn)
1 (8th) mot inf bde (1 mech cav sqn, 3 mot inf bn, 1 arty bn, 1 log bn)
1 (10th) mot inf bde (1 mech cav sqn, 4 mot inf bn, 1 inf coy, 1 arty bn, 1 engr coy, 1 sigs coy)
1 (13th) mot inf bde (1 mot inf bn, 2 inf bn, 1 inf coy, 1 arty bn)
1 (14th) mot inf bde (1 mech cav sqn, 3 inf bn, 1 arty bn)
8 inf bn
1 (1st) jungle inf bde (1 mech cav sqn, 2 jungle inf bn, 1 arty bn)
4 (2nd, 16th, 17th & 22nd) jungle inf bde (3 jungle inf bn)
1 (23rd) jungle inf bde (1 cav sqn, 4 jungle inf bn, 1 arty bn, 1 sigs coy, 1 log bn)

Air Manoeuvre
1 AB bde (1 cav sqn, 3 AB bn, 1 arty bn, 1 engr coy, 1 sigs coy, 1 log bn)
1 (12th) air mob bde (1 cav sqn, 3 air mob bn, 1 arty bn, 1 engr coy, 1 sigs coy, 1 log bn)

Other
1 (9th) mot trg bde (3 mot inf bn, 1 arty bn, 1 log bn)
1 (18th) sy bde (2 sy bn, 2 sy coy)
1 sy bn

7 sy coy
3 gd cav regt
1 gd inf bn

COMBAT SUPPORT
3 SP arty bn
6 fd arty bn
1 MRL bn
1 STA bty
6 engr bn
1 engr gp (1 engr bn, 4 construction bn)
1 engr gp (4 construction bn, 1 construction coy)
2 construction bn
1 CBRN bn
1 EW coy
2 int bn
3 int coy
9 MP bn
2 MP coy
4 sigs bn
2 sigs coy

COMBAT SERVICE SUPPORT
5 log bn
1 tpt bn
4 spt bn

HELICOPTER
1 avn bde (3 hel bn, 1 maint bn)
1 hel bn

AIR DEFENCE
1 ADA bde (5 ADA bn)

EQUIPMENT BY TYPE
ARMOURED FIGHTING VEHICLES
  MBT 292: 41 *Leopard* 1A1BE; 220 *Leopard* 1A5BR; 31 M60A3/TTS
  RECCE 409 EE-9 *Cascavel*
  IFV 13 VBTP-MR *Guarani* 30mm
  APC 1,466
    APC (T) 660: 198 M113A1; 386 M113BR; 12 M113A2; 64 M577A2
    APC (W) 806: 231 EE-11 *Urutu*; ε575 VBTP-MR *Guarani* 6×6
  AUV 32 IVECO LMV (LMV-BR)
ENGINEERING & MAINTENANCE VEHICLES
  AEV 5 Pionierpanzer 2 *Dachs*
  ARV 35: 13 BPz-2; 8 M88A1; 14 M578 LARV
  VLB 5 *Leopard* 1 with *Biber*
ANTI-TANK/ANTI-INFRASTRUCTURE
  MSL • MANPATS *Eryx*; *Milan*; MSS-1.2 AC
  RCL • 84mm *Carl Gustaf*
ARTILLERY 2,263
  SP 109: **155mm** 109: 37 M109A3; 40 M109A5; 32 M109A5+
  TOWED 412: **105mm** 331: 231 M101/M102; 40 L118 Light Gun; 60 Model 56 pack howitzer; **155mm** 81 M114

MRL • 127mm 38: 20 ASTROS II Mk3M; 18 ASTROS II Mk6
MOR 1,704: **81mm** 1,436: 92 AGR Mrt Me Acg; 137 M1; 484 AGR M936; 651 Brandt; 72 L16; **120mm** 268 AGR M2

AIRCRAFT
  TPT • Light 4 Short 360 *Sherpa*
HELICOPTERS
  MRH 68: 34 AS565/AS565 K2 *Panther* (HM-1); 34 AS550A2 *Fennec* (HA-1) (armed)
  TPT 26: **Heavy** 14 H225M *Caracal* (HM-4); **Medium** 12: 8 AS532 *Cougar* (HM-3); 4 S-70A-36 *Black Hawk* (HM-2);
UNINHABITED AERIAL VEHICLES
  ISR • Medium 1 *Nauru* 1000C
AIR DEFENCE
  SAM • Point-defence RBS-70; 9K38 *Igla* (RS-SA-18 *Grouse*); 9K338 *Igla*-S (RS-SA-24 *Grinch*)
  GUNS • SP 35mm 34 *Gepard* 1A2

Navy 85,000

Organised into 9 districts with HQ I Rio de Janeiro, HQ II Salvador, HQ III Natal, HQ IV Belém, HQ V Rio Grande, HQ VI Ladario, HQ VII Brasilia, HQ VIII Sao Paulo, HQ IX Manaus

FORCES BY ROLE
SPECIAL FORCES
  1 (diver) SF gp
EQUIPMENT BY TYPE
SUBMARINES • SSK 5:
  1 *Riachuelo* (FRA *Scorpène*) with 6 533mm TT with SM39 *Exocet* AShM/F21 HWT
  1 *Tupi* (GER T-209/1400) with 8 single 533mm TT with Mk 24 *Tigerfish* HWT
  2 *Tupi* (GER T-209/1400) with 8 single 533mm TT with Mk 48 HWT
  1 *Tikuna* (GER T-209/1450) with 8 single 533mm TT with Mk 24 *Tigerfish* HWT
PRINCIPAL SURFACE COMBATANTS 7
  FRIGATES 7
    FFGHM 6:
      1 *Greenhalgh* (ex-UK *Broadsword*) with 4 single lnchr with MM40 *Exocet* Block 2 AShM, 2 sextuple lnchr with *Sea Wolf* SAM, 2 triple 324mm STWS Mk.2 ASTT with Mk 46 LWT (capacity 2 *Super Lynx* Mk21A hel)
      5 *Niterói* with 2 twin lnchr with MM40 *Exocet* Block 2 AShM, 1 octuple *Albatros* lnchr with *Aspide* SAM, 2 triple 324mm SVTT Mk 32 ASTT with Mk 46 LWT, 1 twin 375mm Bofors ASW Rocket Launcher System A/S mor, 1 115mm gun (capacity 1 *Super Lynx* Mk21A hel)
    FFGH 1 *Barroso* with 2 twin lnchr with MM40 *Exocet* Block 2 AShM, 2 triple 324mm SVTT Mk 32 ASTT with Mk 46 LWT, 1 115mm gun (capacity 1 *Super Lynx* Mk21A hel)
PATROL AND COASTAL COMBATANTS 45
  CORVETTES • FSGH 1 *Inhaúma* with 2 twin lnchr with

MM40 *Exocet* Block 2 AShM, 2 triple 324mm SVTT Mk 32 ASTT with Mk 46 LWT, 1 115mm gun (1 *Super Lynx* Mk21A hel)

PSO 3 *Amazonas* with 1 hel landing platform

PCO 6: 4 *Bracuí* (ex-UK *River*); 1 *Imperial Marinheiro* with 1 76mm gun; 1 *Parnaiba* with 1 hel landing platform

PCC 3 *Macaé* (FRA *Vigilante*)

PCR 5: 2 *Pedro Teixeira* with 1 hel landing platform; 3 *Roraima*

PB 23: 12 *Grajaú*; 6 *Marlim* (ITA *Meatini* derivative); 5 *Piratini* (US PGM)

PBR 4 LPR-40

MINE WARFARE • MINE COUNTERMEASURES 3

MSC 3 *Aratù* (GER *Schutze*)

AMPHIBIOUS

PRINCIPAL AMPHIBIOUS SHIPS 2

LPH 1 *Atlântico* (ex-UK *Ocean*) (capacity 18 hels; 4 LCVP; 40 vehs; 800 troops)

LPD 1 *Bahia* (ex-FRA *Foudre*) (capacity 4 hels; 8 LCM, 450 troops)

LANDING SHIPS 2

LST 1 *Mattoso Maia* (ex-US *Newport*) with 1 Mk 15 *Phalanx* CIWS (capacity 3 LCVP; 1 LCPL; 400 troops)

LSLH 1 *Almirante Sabóia* (ex-UK *Sir Bedivere*) (capacity 1 med hel; 18 MBT; 340 troops)

LANDING CRAFT 16:

LCM 12: 10 EDVM-25; 2 *Icarai* (ex-FRA CTM)

LCT 1 *Marambaia* (ex-FRA CDIC)

LCU 3 *Guarapari* (LCU 1610)

LOGISTICS AND SUPPORT 42

ABU 5: 4 *Comandante Varella*; 1 *Faroleiro Mario Seixas*

ABUH 1 *Almirante Graça Aranha* (lighthouse tender)

AGOR 4: 1 *Ary Rongel* with 1 hel landing platform; 1 *Almirante Maximiano* (capacity 2 AS350/AS355 *Ecureuil* hel); 1 *Cruzeiro do Sul*; 1 *Vital de Oliveira*

AGS 11: 1 *Aspirante Moura*; 1 *Caravelas* (riverine); 1 *Antares*; 3 *Amorim do Valle* (ex-UK *River* (MCM)); 1 *Rio Branco*; 4 *Rio Tocantin*

AH 5: 2 *Oswaldo Cruz* with 1 hel landing platform; 1 *Dr Montenegro*; 1 *Tenente Maximiano* with 1 hel landing platform; 1 *Soares de Meirelles*

AOR 1 *Almirante Gastão Motta*

AP 3: 1 *Almirante Leverger*; 1 *Paraguassu*; 1 *Pará* (all river transports)

ARS 3 *Mearim*

ASR 1 *Guillobel*

ATF 2 *Tritao*

AX 1 *Brasil* (*Niterói* mod) with 1 hel landing platform

AXL 4: 3 *Nascimento*; 1 *Potengi*

AXS 1 *Cisne Branco*

Naval Aviation 2,100

FORCES BY ROLE

GROUND ATTACK

1 sqn with A-4M (AF-1B) *Skyhawk*; TA-4M (AF-1C) *Skyhawk*

ANTI SURFACE WARFARE

1 sqn with *Super Lynx* Mk21B

ANTI SUBMARINE WARFARE

1 sqn with S-70B *Seahawk* (MH-16)

TRAINING

1 sqn with Bell 206B3 *Jet Ranger* III

TRANSPORT HELICOPTER

2 sqn with AS350 *Ecureuil* (armed)

1 sqn with AS350 *Ecureuil* (armed); AS355 *Ecureuil* II (armed); H135 (UH-17)

1 sqn with AS350 *Ecureuil* (armed); H225M *Caracal* (UH-15)

1 sqn with AS532 *Cougar* (UH-14); H225M *Caracal* (UH-15/UH-15A); H225M (AH-15B)

1 sqn with H225M *Caracal* (UH-15)

EQUIPMENT BY TYPE

AIRCRAFT 7 combat capable

ATK 7: 5 A-4M (AF-1B) *Skyhawk*; 2 TA-4M (AF-1C) *Skyhawk*

HELICOPTERS

ASW 10: 4 *Super Lynx* Mk21B (4 more being upgraded); 6 S-70B *Seahawk* (MH-16)

MRH 3 H22M (AH-15B) (armed)

CSAR 3 H225M *Caracal* (UH-15A)

TPT 50: **Heavy** 7 H225M *Caracal* (UH-15); **Medium** 2 AS532 *Cougar* (UH-14); **Light** 41: 15 AS350 *Ecureuil* (armed); 8 AS355 *Ecureuil* II (armed); 15 Bell 206B3 *Jet Ranger* (IH-6B); 3 H135 (UH-17)

AIR-LAUNCHED MISSILES • AShM: AM39 *Exocet*; *Sea Skua*; AGM-119 *Penguin*

Marines 16,000

FORCES BY ROLE

SPECIAL FORCES

1 SF bn

MANOEUVRE

Amphibious

1 amph div (1 lt armd bn, 3 mne bn, 1 arty bn)

1 amph aslt bn

7 (regional) mne gp

1 rvn bn

COMBAT SUPPORT

1 engr bn

COMBAT SERVICE SUPPORT

1 log bn

EQUIPMENT BY TYPE

ARMOURED FIGHTING VEHICLES

LT TK 18 SK-105 *Kuerassier*

APC 60

APC (T) 30 M113A1 (incl variants)

APC (W) 30 *Piranha* IIIC

AAV 47: 13 AAV-7A1; 20 AAVP-7A1 RAM/RS; 2 AAVC-7A1 RAM/RS (CP); 12 LVTP-7

ENGINEERING VEHICLES • ARV 2: 1 AAVR-7; 1 AAVR-7A1 RAM/RS
ANTI-TANK/ANTI-INFRASTRUCTURE
MSL• MANPATS RB-56 *Bill*; MSS-1.2 AC
ARTILLERY 65
TOWED 41: **105mm** 33: 18 L118 Light Gun; 15 M101; **155mm** 8 M114
MRL **127mm** 6 ASTROS II Mk6
MOR **81mm** 18 M29
AIR DEFENCE • GUNS **40mm** 6 L/70 (with BOFI)

Air Force 67,500

Brazilian airspace is divided into 7 air regions, each of which is responsible for its designated air bases. Air assets are divided among 4 designated air forces (I, II, III & V) for operations (IV Air Force temporarily deactivated)

FORCES BY ROLE
FIGHTER
2 sqn with F-5EM/FM *Tiger* II
FIGHTER/GROUND ATTACK
2 sqn with AMX/AMX-T (A-1A/B); AMX A-1M/BM
1 sqn with *Gripen* E (F-39E) (forming)
GROUND ATTACK/ISR
4 sqn with EMB-314 *Super Tucano* (A-29A/B)*
MARITIME PATROL
1 sqn with P-3AM *Orion*
2 sqn with EMB-111 (P-95A/B/M)
ISR
1 sqn with Learjet 35AM (R-35AM); EMB-110B (R-95)
AIRBORNE EARLY WARNING & CONTROL
1 sqn with EMB-145RS (R-99); EMB-145SA (E-99M)
SEARCH & RESCUE
1 sqn with C295M *Amazonas* (SC-105); UH-60L *Black Hawk* (H-60L)
TANKER/TRANSPORT
1 sqn with C-130H/KC-130H *Hercules*; KC-390 *Millennium*
TRANSPORT
1 VIP sqn with A319 (VC-1A); EMB-190 (VC-2); AS355 *Ecureuil* II (VH-55)
1 sqn (forming) with A330
1 VIP sqn with EMB-135BJ (VC-99B); ERJ-135LR (VC-99C); ERJ-145LR (VC-99A); Learjet 35A (VU-35); Learjet 55C (VU-55C)
2 sqn with C-130E/H *Hercules*
2 sqn with C295M (C-105A)
7 (regional) sqn with Cessna 208/208B (C-98); Cessna 208-G1000 (C-98A); EMB-110 (C-95); EMB-120 (C-97)
1 sqn with ERJ-145 (C-99A)
1 sqn with EMB-120RT (VC-97), EMB-121 (VU-9)
TRAINING
1 sqn with EMB-110 (C-95)
2 sqn with EMB-312 *Tucano* (T-27/T-27M) (incl 1 air show sqn)
1 sqn with T-25A/C

TRANSPORT HELICOPTER
1 VIP flt with H135M (VH-35); H225M *Caracal* (VH-36)
1 sqn with H225M *Caracal* (H-36)
1 sqn with AS350B *Ecureuil* (H-50); AS355 *Ecureuil* II (H-55)
1 sqn with Bell 205 (H-1H); H225M *Caracal* (H-36)
2 sqn with UH-60L *Black Hawk* (H-60L)
ISR UAV
1 sqn with *Hermes* 450/900

EQUIPMENT BY TYPE
AIRCRAFT 185 combat capable
FTR 47: 43 F-5EM *Tiger* II; 4 F-5FM *Tiger* II
FGA 30: 10 AMX/AMX-T (A-1A/B); 11 AMX A-1M; 3 AMX A-1BM; 6 *Gripen* E (F-39E) (in test)
ASW 9 P-3AM *Orion*
MP 18: 10 EMB-111 (P-95A *Bandeirulha*)*; 8 EMB-111 (P-95BM *Bandeirulha*)*
ISR 4 EMB-110B (R-95)
ELINT 6: 3 EMB-145RS (R-99); 3 Learjet 35AM (R-35AM)
AEW&C 5 EMB-145SA (E-99M)
SAR 7: 3 C295M *Amazonas* (SC-105); 4 EMB-110 (SC-95B)
TKR/TPT 2 KC-130H
TPT 188: **Medium** 26: 4 C-130E *Hercules*; 16 C-130H *Hercules*; 6 KC-390 *Millennium*; **Light** 152: 11 C295M (C-105A); 7 Cessna 208 (C-98); 9 Cessna 208B (C-98); 12 Cessna 208-G1000 (C-98A); 52 EMB-110 (C-95A/B/C/M); 16 EMB-120 (C-97); 4 EMB-120RT (VC-97); 5 EMB-121 (VU-9); 7 EMB-135BJ (VC-99B); 3 EMB-201R *Ipanema* (G-19); 2 EMB-202A *Ipanema* (G-19A); 4 EMB-550 *Legacy* 500 (IU-50); 2 ERJ-135LR (VC-99C); 7 ERJ-145 (C-99A); 1 ERJ-145LR (VC-99A); 9 Learjet 35A (VU-35); 1 Learjet 55C (VU-55); **PAX** 10: 1 A319 (VC-1A); 2 A330 (to be converted to A330 MRTT); 3 EMB-190 (VC-2); 4 Hawker 800XP (EU-93A – calibration)
TRG 205: 33 EMB-312 *Tucano* (T-27); 11 EMB-312 *Tucano* (T-27M); 38 EMB-314 *Super Tucano* (A-29A)*; 43 EMB-314 *Super Tucano* (A-29B)*; 80 T-25A/C

HELICOPTERS
MRH 2 H135M (VH-35)
TPT 58: **Heavy** 14 H225M *Caracal* (12 H-36 & 2 VH-36); **Medium** 16 UH-60L *Black Hawk* (H-60L); **Light** 28: 24 AS350B *Ecureuil* (H-50); 4 AS355 *Ecureuil* II (H-55/VH-55)

UNINHABITED AERIAL VEHICLES
ISR 7: **Heavy** 2 *Heron* 1; **Medium** 5: 4 *Hermes* 450; 1 *Hermes* 900

AIR-LAUNCHED MISSILES
AAM • IR MAA-1 *Piranha*; R-550 *Magic* 2; *Python* 3; IIR *Python* 4; SARH Super 530F; ARH *Derby*
AShM AM39 *Exocet*
ARM MAR-1 (in development)

Gendarmerie & Paramilitary 395,000

Public Security Forces 395,000 opcon Army

State police organisation technically under army control. However, military control is reducing, with authority reverting to individual states

DEPLOYMENT

CENTRAL AFRICAN REPUBLIC: EU • EUTM RCA 6; UN • MINUSCA 10

CYPRUS: UN • UNFICYP 2

DEMOCRATIC REPUBLIC OF THE CONGO: UN • MONUSCO 23

LEBANON: UN • UNIFIL 12

SOUTH SUDAN: UN • UNMISS 12

SUDAN: UN • UNISFA 4

WESTERN SAHARA: UN • MINURSO 9

Chile CHL

Chilean Peso CLP		2022	2023	2024
GDP	CLP	263trn	281trn	295trn
	USD	301bn	344bn	354bn
per capita	USD	15,166	17,254	17,647
Growth	%	2.4	-0.5	1.6
Inflation	%	11.6	7.8	3.6
Def bdgt [a]	CLP	3.21trn	3.56trn	3.85trn
	USD	3.67bn	4.36bn	4.62bn
USD1=CLP		873.19	817.12	833.13

[a] Includes military pensions

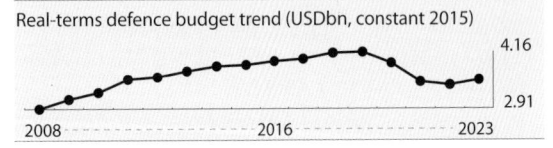

Real-terms defence budget trend (USDbn, constant 2015)

Population	18,549,457				
Age	0–14	15–19	20–24	25–29	30–64	65 plus
Male	9.9%	3.2%	3.4%	3.8%	23.3%	5.5%
Female	9.5%	3.1%	3.3%	3.7%	23.8%	7.6%

Capabilities

The core defence role of Chile's armed forces is to ensure sovereignty and territorial integrity, with increasing emphasis on non-traditional military roles such as disaster relief, humanitarian assistance and peacekeeping. In 2021, the armed forces were assigned the role of fighting human trafficking and illegal migration in border areas. The country maintains R&D cooperation ties and exchange programmes with Brazil and Colombia. Defence cooperation with the US is centred on procurement, technical advice and personnel training. The military trains routinely and the armed forces participate in international exercises. Chile has a limited capacity to deploy independently beyond its borders. The government plans to upgrade the country's F-16s to prolong their service life. Capability priorities reflect the focus on littoral and blue-water surveillance. Chile bolstered its navy with the purchase, in 2020, of two frigates and enhanced its air-defence capabilities. The country has shown interest in acquiring new surface combatants and a new class of amphibious vessels, plus a new icebreaker under construction. Chile has a developed defence-industrial base, with ENAER conducting aircraft maintenance. Shipyard ASMAR is building an icebreaker to enhance Chile's operations in Antarctica and FAMAE works on land systems. The air force is contributing to work on the first indigenously built satellite constellation.

ACTIVE 68,500 (Army 37,650 Navy 19,800 Air 11,050) **Gendarmerie & Paramilitary 44,700**

Conscript liability Army 12 months; Navy 18 months; Air Force 12 months. Legally, conscription can last for 2 years

RESERVE 19,100 (Army 19,100)

ORGANISATIONS BY SERVICE

Space
EQUIPMENT BY TYPE
SATELLITES
  ISR 1 SSOT (Sistema Satelital de Observación de la Tierra)

Army 37,650
6 military administrative regions

FORCES BY ROLE
Currently being reorganised into 1 SF bde, 4 armd bde, 1 armd det, 4 mot bde, 2 mot det, 4 mtn det and 1 avn bde

COMMAND
  6 div HQ

SPECIAL FORCES
  1 SF bde (1 SF bn, 1 (mtn) SF gp, 1 para bn, 3 cdo coy, 1 log coy)

MANOEUVRE
  Reconnaissance
  4 cav sqn
  2 recce sqn
  2 recce pl

  Armoured
  1 (1st) armd bde (1 armd recce pl, 1 armd cav gp, 1 mech inf bn, 2 arty gp, 1 AT coy, 1 engr coy, 1 sigs coy)
  2 (2nd & 3rd) armd bde (1 armd recce pl, 1 armd cav gp, 1 mech inf bn, 1 arty gp, 1 AT coy, 1 engr coy, 1 sigs coy)
  1 (4th) armd bde (1 armd recce pl, 1 armd cav gp, 1 mech inf bn, 1 arty gp, 1 engr coy)
  1 (5th) armd det (1 armd cav gp, 1 mech inf coy, 1 arty gp)

  Mechanised
  1 (1st) mech inf regt

  Light
  1 (1st) mot inf bde (1 recce coy, 1 mot inf bn, 1 arty gp, 3 AT coy, 1 engr bn)
  1 (4th) mot inf bde (1 mot inf bn, 1 MRL gp, 2 AT coy, 1 engr bn)

1 (24th) mot inf bde (1 mot inf bn, 1 arty gp, 1 AT coy)
1 (Maipo) mot inf bde (3 mot inf regt, 1 arty regt)
1 (6th) reinforced regt (1 mot inf bn, 1 arty gp, 1 sigs coy)
1 (10th) reinforced regt (1 mot inf bn, 2 AT coy, 1 engr bn)
1 (11th) mot inf det (1 inf bn, 1 arty gp)
1 (14th) mot inf det (1 mot inf bn, 1 arty gp, 1 sigs coy, 1 AT coy)
4 mot inf regt
1 (3rd) mtn det (1 mtn inf bn, 1 arty gp, 1 engr coy)
1 (9th) mtn det (1 mtn inf bn, 1 engr coy, 1 construction bn)
2 (8th & 17th) mtn det (1 mtn inf bn, 1 arty coy)

COMBAT SUPPORT
1 engr regt
4 sigs bn
1 sigs coy
1 int bde (7 int gp)
2 int regt
1 MP regt

COMBAT SERVICE SUPPORT
1 log div (2 log regt)
4 log regt
6 log coy
1 maint div (1 maint regt)

AVIATION
1 avn bde (1 tpt avn bn, 1 hel bn, 1 spt bn)

EQUIPMENT BY TYPE
ARMOURED FIGHTING VEHICLES
MBT 170: 30 *Leopard* 1V; 140 *Leopard* 2A4
IFV 191: 173 *Marder* 1A3; 18 YPR-765 PRI
APC 445
  APC (T) 306 M113A1/A2
  APC (W) 139: 121 *Piranha* 6×6; 18 *Piranha* 8×8

ENGINEERING & MAINTENANCE VEHICLES
AEV 6 Pionierpanzer 2 *Dachs*
ARV 30 BPz-2
VLB 13 *Biber*
MW 8+: *Bozena* 5; 8 *Leopard* 1 MW

ANTI-TANK/ANTI-INFRASTRUCTURE
MSL • MANPATS *Spike*-LR; *Spike*-ER
RCL 84mm *Carl Gustaf*; **106mm** 213 M40A1

ARTILLERY 1,398
SP 155mm 48: 24 M109A3; 24 M109A5+
TOWED 239: **105mm** 191: 87 M101; 104 Model 56 pack howitzer; **155mm** 48 M-71
MRL 160mm 12 LAR-160
MOR 1,099: **81mm** 744: 295 ECIA L65/81; 192 FAMAE; 257 Soltam; **120mm** 284: 171 ECIA L65/120; 16 FAMAE; 97 M-65; **SP 120mm** 71: 35 FAMAE (on *Piranha* 6×6); 36 Soltam (on M113A2)

AIRCRAFT
TPT • Light 10: 2 C-212-300 *Aviocar*; 2 Cessna 172; 3 Cessna 208 *Caravan*; 3 CN235

HELICOPTERS
ISR 9 MD-530F *Lifter* (armed)
TPT 17: **Medium** 12: 8 AS532AL *Cougar*; 2 AS532ALe *Cougar*; 2 SA330 *Puma*; **Light** 5: 4 H125 *Ecureuil*; 1 AS355F *Ecureuil* II

AIR DEFENCE
SAM • Point-defence *Mistral*
GUNS 41:
  SP 20mm 17 *Piranha*/TCM-20
  TOWED 20mm 24 TCM-20

Navy 19,800

5 Naval Zones; 1st Naval Zone and main HQ at Valparaiso; 2nd Naval Zone at Talcahuano; 3rd Naval Zone at Punta Arenas; 4th Naval Zone at Iquique; 5th Naval Zone at Puerto Montt

FORCES BY ROLE
SPECIAL FORCES
1 (diver) SF comd

EQUIPMENT BY TYPE
SUBMARINES • SSK 4:
2 *O'Higgins* (*Scorpène*) with 6 single 533mm TT with SM39 *Exocet* Block 2 AShM/*Black Shark* HWT
2 *Thomson* (GER Type-209/1400) (of which 1 in refit) with 8 single 533mm TT with SM39 *Exocet* Block 2 AShM/*Black Shark* HWT/SUT HWT

PRINCIPAL SURFACE COMBATANTS 8
FRIGATES • FFGHM 8:
3 *Almirante Cochrane* (ex-UK *Norfolk* Type-23) with 2 quad lnchr with RGM-84C *Harpoon* Block 1B AShM, 1 32-cell VLS with *Sea Ceptor* SAM, 2 twin 324mm ASTT with Mk 46 mod 2 LWT, 1 114mm gun (capacity 1 AS532SC *Cougar*)
2 *Almirante Latorre* (ex-AUS *Adelaide*) with 1 Mk 13 GMLS with RGM-84L *Harpoon* Block II AShM/SM-2 Block IIIA SAM, 1 8-cell Mk 41 VLS with RIM-162B ESSM SAM, 2 triple 324mm SVTT Mk 32 ASTT with MU90 LWT, 1 76mm gun (capacity 2 AS532SC *Cougars*)
2 *Almirante Riveros* (ex-NLD *Karel Doorman*) with 2 quad lnchr with MM40 *Exocet* Block 3 AShM, 1 8-cell Mk 48 VLS with RIM-7P *Sea Sparrow* SAM, 4 single 324mm SVTT Mk 32 mod 9 ASTT with Mk 46 mod 5 HWT, 1 76mm gun (capacity 1 AS532SC *Cougar*)
1 *Almirante Williams* (ex-UK *Broadsword* Type-22) with 2 quad lnchr with RGM-84 *Harpoon* AShM, 2 8-cell VLS with *Barak*-1 SAM; 2 triple 324mm ASTT with Mk 46 LWT, 1 76mm gun (capacity 1 AS532SC *Cougar*)

PATROL AND COASTAL COMBATANTS 12
PSOH 4: 2 *Piloto Pardo*; 2 *Piloto Pardo* with 1 76mm gun (ice-strengthened hull)
PCG 3:
2 *Casma* (ISR *Sa'ar* 4) with 6 single lnchr with *Gabriel* I AShM, 2 76mm guns

1 *Casma* (ISR *Sa'ar* 4) with 4 single lnchr with *Gabriel*
I AShM, 2 twin lnchr with MM40 *Exocet* AShM, 2
76mm guns
PCO 5 *Micalvi* (1 used as med vessel)

AMPHIBIOUS
PRINCIPAL AMPHIBIOUS SHIPS • LPD 1 *Sargento
Aldea* (ex-FRA *Foudre*) with 3 twin *Simbad* lnchr with
Mistral SAM (capacity 4 med hel; 1 LCT; 2 LCM; 22
tanks; 470 troops)
LANDING SHIPS 3
  LSM 1 *Elicura*
  LST 2 *Maipo* (FRA *Batral*) with 1 hel landing platform
  (capacity 7 tanks; 140 troops)
LANDING CRAFT 3
  LCT 1 CDIC (for use in *Sargento Aldea*)
  LCM 2 (for use in *Sargento Aldea*)
LOGISTICS AND SUPPORT 13
  ABU 1 *Ingeniero Slight* with 1 hel landing platform
  AFD 3
  AGOR 1 *Cabo de Hornos*
  AGS 1 *Micalvi*
  AOR 2: 1 *Almirante Montt* (ex-US *Henry J. Kaiser*) with 1
  hel landing platform; 1 *Araucano*
  AP 1 *Aquiles* (1 hel landing platform)
  ATF 3: 1 *Janequeo*; 1 *Lientur* (Ice capable); 2 *Veritas*
  AXS 1 *Esmeralda*

Naval Aviation 600
EQUIPMENT BY TYPE
AIRCRAFT 14 combat capable
  ASW 4: 2 C295ASW *Persuader*; 2 P-3ACH *Orion*
  MP 4: 1 C295MPA *Persuader*; 3 EMB-111 *Bandeirante**
  ISR 7 P-68
  TRG 7 PC-7 *Turbo Trainer**
HELICOPTERS
  ASW 5 AS532SC *Cougar*
  MRH 8 AS365 *Dauphin*
  TPT 11: **Medium** 2 H215 (AS332L1) *Super Puma*; **Light**
  7: 4 Bo-105S; 5 H125
AIR-LAUNCHED MISSILES • AShM AM39 *Exocet*

Marines 3,600
FORCES BY ROLE
MANOEUVRE
  Amphibious
  1 amph bde (2 mne bn, 1 cbt spt bn, 1 log bn)
  2 coastal def unit
EQUIPMENT BY TYPE
ARMOURED FIGHTING VEHICLES
  LT TK (15 FV101 *Scorpion* in store)
  IFV 22 NZLAV
  APC • APC (W) 25 MOWAG *Roland*
ARTILLERY 39
  TOWED 23: **105mm** 7 KH-178; **155mm** 16 M-71

MOR 81mm 16
COASTAL DEFENCE • AShM MM38 *Exocet*
AIR DEFENCE • SAM • Point-defence 14: 4 M998
Avenger; 10 M1097 *Avenger*

Coast Guard
Integral part of the Navy
EQUIPMENT BY TYPE
PATROL AND COASTAL COMBATANTS 55
  PBF 26 *Archangel*
  PB 29: 18 *Alacalufe* (*Protector*); 4 *Grumete Diaz* (*Dabor*);
  6 *Pelluhue*; 1 *Ona*

Air Force 11,050
FORCES BY ROLE
FIGHTER
  1 sqn with F-5E/F *Tiger* III+
  2 sqn with F-16AM/BM *Fighting Falcon*
FIGHTER/GROUND ATTACK
  1 sqn with F-16C/D Block 50 *Fighting Falcon* (*Puma*)
ISR
  1 (photo) flt with; DHC-6-300 *Twin Otter*; Gulfstream IV
TANKER/TRANSPORT
  1 sqn with B-737-300; C-130B/H *Hercules*; E-3D *Sentry*;
  KC-130R *Hercules*; KC-135 *Stratotanker*
TRANSPORT
  3 sqn with Bell 205 (UH-1H *Iroquois*); C-212-200/300
  Aviocar; Cessna O-2A; Cessna 525 *Citation* CJ1; DHC-
  6-100/300 *Twin Otter*; PA-28-236 *Dakota*; Bell 205 (UH-
  1H *Iroquois*)
  1 VIP flt with B-767-300ER; B-737-500; Gulfstream IV
TRAINING
  1 sqn with EMB-314 *Super Tucano**
  1 sqn with Cirrus SR-22T; T-35A/B *Pillan*
TRANSPORT HELICOPTER
  1 sqn with Bell 205 (UH-1H *Iroquois*); Bell 206B (trg); Bell
  412 *Twin Huey*; S-70A *Black Hawk*
AIR DEFENCE
  1 AD regt M163/M167 *Vulcan*
  4 AD sqn with *Crotale*; NASAMS; *Mistral*; Oerlikon
  GDF-005
EQUIPMENT BY TYPE
AIRCRAFT 76 combat capable
  FTR 48: 10 F-5E *Tigre* III+; 2 F-5F *Tigre* III+; 29 F-16AM
  Fighting Falcon; 7 F-16BM *Fighting Falcon*
  FGA 10: 6 F-16C Block 50 *Fighting Falcon*; 4 F-16D Block
  50 *Fighting Falcon*
  ISR 3 Cessna O-2A
  AEW&C 2 E-3D *Sentry*
  TKR 3 KC-135 *Stratotanker*
  TKR/TPT 2 KC-130R *Hercules*
  TPT 33: **Medium** 3: 1 C-130B *Hercules*; 2 C-130H
  Hercules; **Light** 24: 2 C-212-200 *Aviocar*; 1 C-212-300
  Aviocar; 4 Cessna 525 *Citation* CJ1; 3 DHC-6-100 *Twin*

Otter; 7 DHC-6-300 *Twin Otter*; 7 PA-28-236 *Dakota*; **PAX** 6: 1 B-737-300; 1 B-737-500 (VIP); 1 B-767-300ER (VIP); 3 Gulfstream IV (VIP/aerial photography)

TRG 57: 8 Cirrus SR-22T; 22 EMB-314 *Super Tucano**; 27 T-35A/B *Pillan*

HELICOPTERS

MRH 12 Bell 412EP *Twin Huey*

TPT 25: **Medium** 7: 1 S-70A *Black Hawk*; 6 S-70i (MH-60M) *Black Hawk*; **Light** 18: 13 Bell 205 (UH-1H *Iroquois*); 5 Bell 206B (trg)

UNINHABITED AERIAL VEHICLES

ISR • **Medium** up to 3 *Hermes* 900

AIR DEFENCE

SAM

Short-range 17: 5 *Crotale*; 12 NASAMS

Point-defence *Mistral* (including some *Mygale*/*Aspic*)

GUNS • **TOWED 20mm** M163/M167 *Vulcan*; **35mm** Oerlikon GDF-005

AIR-LAUNCHED MISSILES

AAM • **IR** AIM-9J/M *Sidewinder*; *Python* 3; *Shafrir*‡; **IIR** *Python* 4; **ARH** AIM-120C AMRAAM; *Derby*

ASM AGM-65G *Maverick*

BOMBS

Laser-guided *Paveway* II

INS/GPS guided JDAM

Gendarmerie & Paramilitary 44,700

Carabineros 44,700

Ministry of Interior; 15 zones, 36 districts, 179 *comisaria*

EQUIPMENT BY TYPE

ARMOURED FIGHTING VEHICLES

APC • **APC (W)** 20 MOWAG *Roland*

ARTILLERY • **MOR** 81mm

AIRCRAFT

TPT • **Light** 4: 1 Beech 200 *King Air*; 1 Cessna 208; 1 Cessna 550 *Citation* V; 1 PA-31T *Cheyenne* II

HELICOPTERS • **TPT** • **Light** 16: 5 AW109E *Power*; 1 AW139; 1 Bell 206 *Jet Ranger*; 2 BK-117; 5 Bo-105; 2 H135

DEPLOYMENT

BOSNIA-HERZEGOVINA: EU • EUFOR (Operation Althea) 8

CYPRUS: UN • UNFICYP 6

MIDDLE EAST: UN • UNTSO 3

Colombia COL

Colombian Peso COP		2022	2023	2024
GDP	COP	1,463trn	1,623trn	1,720rn
	USD	344bn	364bn	373bn
per capita	USD	6,658	6,976	7,087
Growth	%	7.3	1.4	2.0
Inflation	%	10.2	11.4	5.2
Def bdgt [a]	COP	21.4trn	24.1trn	
	USD	5.03bn	5.41bn	
FMA (US)	USD	40m	38m	38m
USD1=COP		4,256.19	4,461.00	4,605.54

[a] Excludes security budget

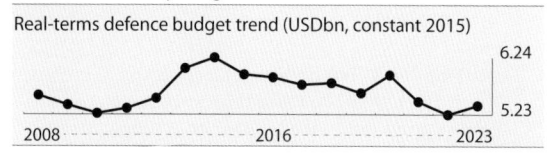

Real-terms defence budget trend (USDbn, constant 2015)
6.24 … 5.23 (2008–2023)

Population	49,336,454					
Age	0–14	15–19	20–24	25–29	30–64	65 plus
Male	11.5%	3.9%	4.0%	4.1%	20.6%	4.8%
Female	11.0%	3.7%	3.9%	4.1%	22.4%	6.1%

Capabilities

Colombia's armed forces are largely focused on internal security, typically conducting counter-insurgency and counter-narcotics operations. The military has improved training and overall capabilities in recent decades. In response to the humanitarian and security challenge from Venezuela, Colombia has strengthened cooperation with Brazil on border controls. The country maintains military ties with Argentina, Chile and Peru. The US is Colombia's closest international military partner, with cooperation in equipment procurement, technical and personnel training. In 2017, Colombia became one of NATO's global partner. Although the equipment inventory mainly comprises legacy systems, Colombia has the capability to independently deploy force elements beyond national borders. The navy is planning to enhance its surface warfare capabilities by acquiring new frigates, while the army is planning to modernise its armoured vehicles. The air force has established a space operations centre and launched an earth observation satellite in 2023. New medium transport aircraft will be equipped with ISR sensors to boost reconnaissance capabilities. Colombia's defence industry is active in all domains. CIAC is developing its first indigenous UAVs, while CODALTEC is developing an air-defence system for regional export. COTECMAR has supplied patrol boats and amphibious ships for national and export markets.

ACTIVE 257,450 (Army 187,400, Navy 56,400 Air 13,650) **Gendarmerie & Paramilitary 165,050**

Conscript liability 18 months' duration with upper age limit of 24, males only

RESERVE 34,950 (Army 25,050 Navy 6,500 Air 3,400)

ORGANISATIONS BY SERVICE

Army 187,400
FORCES BY ROLE
SPECIAL FORCES
  1 SF div (3 SF regt)
  1 (anti-terrorist) SF bn
MANOEUVRE
  Mechanised
  1 (1st) mech div (1 (2nd) mech bde (2 mech inf bn, 1 mtn inf bn, 1 engr bn, 1 MP bn, 1 spt bn, 2 Gaula anti-kidnap gp); 1 (10th) mech bde (1 (urban) spec ops bn, 1 armd recce bn, 1 mech cav bn, 1 mech inf bn, 1 mtn inf bn, 3 sy bn, 2 arty bn, 1 engr bn, 1 spt bn, 2 Gaula anti-kidnap gp))
  Light
  1 (2nd) inf div (1 (1st) inf bde (1 mech cav bn, 2 inf bn, 1 mtn inf bn, 1 sy bn, 1 arty bn, 1 spt bn, 1 Gaula anti-kidnap gp); 1 (5th) inf bde (3 inf bn, 1 jungle inf bn, 1 sy bn, 1 arty bn, 1 engr bn, 1 spt bn, 1 Gaula anti-kidnap gp); 1 (30th) inf bde (1 mech cav bn, 2 inf bn, 1 sy bn, 1 arty bn, 1 engr bn, 1 spt bn); 1 AD bn; 1 sy gp (1 (urban) spec ops bn, 4 COIN bn, 3 sy bn); 1 (rapid reaction) sy bde)
  1 (3rd) inf div (1 (3rd) inf bde (2 inf bn, 1 mtn inf bn, 1 COIN bn, 1 arty bn, 1 engr bn, 1 cbt spt bn, 1 MP bn, 1 log bn, 1 Gaula anti-kidnap gp); 1 (23rd) inf bde (1 cav gp, 1 lt inf bn, 1 jungle inf bn, 1 spt bn, 1 log bn); 1 (29th) mtn bde (1 mtn inf bn, 1 inf bn, 2 COIN bn, 1 spt bn, 1 log bn); 1 lt cav bde (2 lt cav gp); 1 mtn inf bn; 2 (rapid reaction) sy bde)
  1 (4th) inf div (1 (7th) air mob bde (1 (urban) spec ops bn, 2 air mob inf bn, 1 lt inf bn, 1 COIN bn, 1 engr bn, 1 spt bn, 1 log bn, 1 Gaula anti-kidnap gp); 1 (22nd) jungle bde (1 air mob inf bn, 1 lt inf bn, 1 jungle inf bn, 1 COIN bn, 1 spt bn, 1 log bn); 1 (31st) jungle bde (1 lt inf bn, 1 jungle inf bn))
  1 (5th) inf div (1 (6th) lt inf bde (2 lt inf bn, 1 mtn inf bn, 3 COIN bn, 1 EOD bn, 2 spt bn, 1 Gaula anti-kidnap gp); 1 (8th) inf bde (1 inf bn, 1 mtn inf bn, 1 arty bn, 1 engr bn, 1 spt bn, 1 Gaula anti-kidnap gp); 1 (9th) inf bde (1 (urban) spec ops bn, 2 inf bn, 1 arty bn, 1 COIN bn, 1 sy bn, 1 spt bn, 1 Gaula anti-kidnap gp); 1 (13th) inf bde (1 recce bn, 3 inf bn, 1 mtn inf bn, 1 air mob bn, 1 COIN bn, 1 arty bn, 1 engr bn, 2 MP bn, 1 spt bn, 1 Gaula anti-kidnap gp))
  1 (6th) inf div (1 (12th) inf bde (1 (urban) spec ops bn, 1 inf bn, 1 jungle inf bn, 1 mtn inf bn, 1 COIN bn, 1 engr bn, 1 spt bn, 1 Gaula anti-kidnap gp); 1 (26th) jungle bde (1 jungle inf bn, 1 spt bn); 1 (27th) jungle inf bde (1 inf bn, 1 jungle inf bn, 1 sy bn, 1 arty bn, 1 engr bn, 1 spt bn); 1 (13th) mobile sy bde; 2 COIN bn)
  1 (7th) inf div (1 (4th) inf bde (1 (urban) spec ops bn; 1 mech cav gp, 3 inf bn, 1 sy bn, 1 arty bn, 1 engr bn, 1 MP bn, 1 spt bn, 2 Gaula anti-kidnap gp); 1 (11th) inf bde (1 inf bn, 1 air mob bn, 1 sy bn, 1 spt bn, 2 Gaula anti-kidnap gp); 1 (14th) inf bde (2 inf bn, 1 sy bn, 1 engr bn, 1 spt bn); 1 (15th) jungle bde (1 inf bn, 2 COIN bn, 1 engr bn); 1 (17th) inf bde (2 inf bn, 1 engr bn, 1 spt bn))
  1 (8th) inf div (1 (16th) lt inf bde (1 recce bn, 1 inf bn, 1 spt bn, 1 Gaula anti-kidnap gp); 1 (18th) inf bde (1 (urban) spec ops bn; 1 air mob gp, 5 sy bn, 1 arty bn, 1 engr bn, 1 spt bn); 1 (28th) jungle bde (2 inf, 2 COIN, 1 spt bn); 1 (rapid reaction) sy bde, 4 COIN bn)
  3 COIN mobile bde (each: 4 COIN bn, 1 spt bn)
COMBAT SUPPORT
  1 cbt engr bde (1 SF engr bn, 1 (emergency response) engr bn, 1 EOD bn, 1 construction bn, 1 demining bn, 1 maint bn)
  1 int bde (2 SIGINT bn, 1 log bn, 1 maint bn)
COMBAT SERVICE SUPPORT
  2 spt/log bde (each: 1 spt bn, 1 maint bn, 1 supply bn, 1 tpt bn, 1 medical bn, 1 log bn)
AVIATION
  1 air aslt div (1 counter-narcotics bde (4 counter-narcotics bn, 1 spt bn); 1 (25th) avn bde (4 hel bn; 5 avn bn; 1 avn log bn); 1 (32nd) avn bde (1 avn bn, 2 maint bn, 1 trg bn, 1 spt bn); 1 SF avn bn)

EQUIPMENT BY TYPE
ARMOURED FIGHTING VEHICLES
  RECCE 121 EE-9 *Cascavel*
  IFV 60: 28 *Commando Advanced*; 32 LAV III
  APC 114
    APC (T) 54: 28 M113A1 (TPM-113A1); 26 M113A2 (TPM-113A2)
    APC (W) 56 EE-11 *Urutu*
    PPV 4+: some *Hunter* XL; 4 RG-31 *Nyala*; some *Titan-C*
  AUV 139: 126 M1117 *Guardian*; 13 *Sand Cat*
ANTI-TANK/ANTI-INFRASTRUCTURE
  MSL
    SP 77 *Nimrod*
    MANPATS TOW; *Spike*-ER
  RCL 106mm 73 M40A1
ARTILLERY 1,796
  TOWED 120: **105mm** 107: 22 LG1 MkIII; 85 M101; **155mm** 13 155/52 APU SBT-1
  MOR 1,676: **81mm** 1,507; **120mm** 169
AIRCRAFT
  ELINT 3: 2 Beech B200 *King Air*; 1 Beech 350 *King Air*
  TPT • Light 23: 2 An-32B; 2 Beech B200 *King Air*; 3 Beech 350 *King Air*; 1 Beech C90 *King Air*; 2 C-212 *Aviocar* (Medevac); 8 Cessna 208B *Grand Caravan*; 1 Cessna 208B-EX *Grand Caravan*; 4 *Turbo Commander* 695A
HELICOPTERS
  MRH 19: 8 Mi-17-1V *Hip*; 6 Mi-17MD; 5 Mi-17V-5 *Hip*
  TPT 89: **Medium** 53: 46 UH-60L *Black Hawk*; 7 S-70i *Black Hawk*; **Light** 36: 22 Bell 205 (UH-1H *Iroquois*); 14 Bell 212 (UH-1N *Twin Huey*)
AIR DEFENCE • GUNS • TOWED 40mm 4 M1A1

Navy 56,400 (incl 12,100 conscript)
HQ located at Bogotá

EQUIPMENT BY TYPE
SUBMARINES 4
SSK 2 *Pijao* (GER Type-209/1200) each with 8 single 533mm TT each with *SeaHake* (DM2A3) HWT
SSC 2 *Intrépido* (ex-GER Type-206A) each with 8 single 533mm TT each with *SeaHake* (DM2A3) HWT
PATROL AND COASTAL COMBATANTS 58
  CORVETTES 6
  FSGHM 4 *Almirante Padilla* with 2 quad lnchr with *Hae Sung* I AShM, 2 twin *Simbad* lnchr with *Mistral* SAM, 2 triple 324mm ILAS-3 (B-515) ASTT each with A244/S LWT, 1 76mm gun (capacity 1 Bo-105/AS555SN *Fennec* hel)
  FSG 1 *Almirante Tono* (Ex-ROK *Po Hang* (Flight IV)) 2 twin lnchr with *Hae Sung* I AShM, 2 triple 324mm ASTT with Mk 46, 2 76mm guns
  FS 1 *Narino* (ex-ROK *Dong Hae*) with 2 triple 324mm SVTT Mk 32 ASTT with Mk 46 LWT
  PSOH 3: 2 *20 de Julio* (CHL *Piloto Pardo*); 1 *20 de Julio* (CHL *Piloto Pardo*) with 1 76mm gun
  PCR 10: 2 *Arauca* with 1 76mm guns; 8 *Nodriza* (PAF I-IV) with hel landing platform
  PBR 39: 5 *Diligente*; 16 LPR-40; 3 Swiftships; 9 *Tenerife* (US Bender Marine 12m); 2 PAF-L; 4 others
AMPHIBIOUS 16
  LCT 6 *Golfo de Tribuga*
  LCU 2 *Morrosquillo* (LCU 1466)
  UCAC 8 *Griffon* 2000TD
LOGISTICS AND SUPPORT 7
  ABU 1 *Quindio*
  AG 1 *Inirida*
  AGOR 2 *Providencia*
  AGS 2: 1 *Caribe*; 1 *Roncador*
  AXS 1 *Gloria*

Coast Guard
EQUIPMENT BY TYPE
PATROL AND COASTAL COMBATANTS 17
  PCO 2: 1 *San Andres* (ex-US *Balsam*); 1 *Valle del Cauca Durable* (ex-US *Reliance*) with 1 hel landing platform
  PCC 3 *Punta Espada* (CPV-46)
  PB 12: 1 *11 de Noviembre* (CPV-40) (GER Fassmer); 2 *Castillo y Rada* (Swiftships 105); 2 *Jaime Gomez* (ex-US Peterson Mk 3); 1 *Jorge Luis Marrugo Campo*; 1 *José Maria Palas* (Swiftships 110); 3 *Point*; 2 *Toledo* (US Bender Marine 35m)
LOGISTICS AND SUPPORT • ABU 1 *Isla Albuquerque*

Naval Aviation 150
EQUIPMENT BY TYPE
AIRCRAFT
  MP 3 CN235 MPA *Persuader*
  ISR 1 PA-31 *Navajo* (upgraded for ISR)
  TPT • **Light** 16: 1 ATR-42; 2 Beech 350 *King Air*; 1 Beech 360ER *King Air*; 2 Beech C90 *King Air*; 1 C-212 (Medevac); 4 Cessna 206; 3 Cessna 208 *Caravan*; 1 PA-31 *Navajo*; 1 PA-34 *Seneca*
HELICOPTERS
  SAR 2 AS365 *Dauphin*
  MRH 9: 1 AS555SN *Fennec*; 3 Bell 412 *Twin Huey*; 4 Bell 412EP *Twin Huey*; 1 Bell 412EPI *Twin Huey*
  TPT • **Light** 8: 1 Bell 212; 4 Bell 212 (UH-1N); 1 BK-117; 2 Bo-105

Marines 22,250
FORCES BY ROLE
SPECIAL FORCES
  1 SF bde (4 SF bn)
MANOEUVRE
  Amphibious
  1 mne bde (1 SF (Gaula) bn, 5 mne bn, 2 rvn bn, 1 spt bn)
  1 mne bde (1 SF bn, 2 mne bn, 2 rvn bn, 1 spt bn)
  1 rvn bde (1 SF bn, 1 mne bn, 2 rvn bn, 1 spt bn)
  1 rvn bde (4 rvn bn)
  1 rvn bde (3 rvn bn)
COMBAT SERVICE SUPPORT
  1 log bde (6 spt bn)
  1 trg bde (7 trg bn, 1 spt bn)
EQUIPMENT BY TYPE
ARTILLERY • **MOR 82: 81mm** 74; **120mm** 8
AIR DEFENCE • **SAM** • **Point-defence** *Mistral*

Air Force 13,650
FORCES BY ROLE
FIGHTER/GROUND ATTACK
  1 sqn with *Kfir* C-10/C-12/TC-12
GROUND ATTACK/ISR
  1 sqn with AC-47T; ECN235; IAI *Arava*
  1 sqn with EMB-312 *Tucano**
  2 sqn with EMB-314 *Super Tucano** (A-29)
GROUND ATTACK
  1 sqn with AC-47T *Spooky* (*Fantasma*); Bell 205 (UH-1H *Huey* II); Cessna 208 *Grand Caravan*
  1 sqn with Cessna 208 *Grand Caravan*; C-212; UH-60L *Black Hawk*
EW/ELINT
  2 sqn with Beech 350 *King Air*; Cessna 208; SA 2-37; *Turbo Commander* 695
ELINT
  2 sqn with Cessna 560
TRANSPORT
  1 (Presidential) sqn with AW139; B-737BBJ; EMB-600 *Legacy*; Bell 412EP; F-28 *Fellowship*; UH-60L *Black Hawk*
  1 sqn with B-737-400; B-737-800; Beech C90GTx *King Air*; C-130H *Hercules*; C-212; C295M; CN235M; KC-767
  1 sqn with Beech 350C *King Air*; Bell 212; Cessna 208B; EMB-110P1 (C-95)
  1 sqn with Beech C90 *King Air*
TRAINING

1 sqn with Cessna 172
1 sqn with Lancair *Synergy* (T-90 *Calima*)
1 sqn with T-6C *Texan* II
1 hel sqn with Bell 206B3
1 hel sqn with TH-67

HELICOPTER
1 sqn with AH-60L *Arpia* III
1 sqn with UH-60L *Black Hawk* (CSAR)
1 sqn with Hughes 500M
1 sqn with Bell 205 (UH-1H *Huey* II)
1 sqn with Bell 206B3 *Jet Ranger* III
1 sqn with Bell 212; Bell 205 (UH-1H *Huey* II)

ISR UAV
1 sqn with *Hermes* 450; *Hermes* 900

EQUIPMENT BY TYPE
AIRCRAFT 64 combat capable
FGA 22: 10 *Kfir* C-10; 9 *Kfir* C-12; 3 *Kfir* TC-12
ATK 6 AC-47T *Spooky* (*Fantasma*)
ISR 11: 5 Cessna 560 *Citation* II; 6 SA 2-37
ELINT 11: 3 Beech 350 *King Air*; 6 Cessna 208 *Grand Caravan*; 1 ECN235; 1 *Turbo Commander* 695
TKR/TPT 1 KC-767
TPT 71: Medium 7: 6 C-130H *Hercules*; 1 B-737F; Light 52: 7 ATR-42; 2 Beech 300 *King Air*; 1 Beech 350C *King Air* (medevac); 1 Beech 350i *King Air* (VIP); 2 Beech 350 *King Air* (medevac); 2 Beech C90 *King Air*; 3 Beech C90GTx *King Air*; 4 C-212; 6 C295M; 8 Cessna 172; 1 Cessna 182R; 12 Cessna 208B (medevac); 1 CN235M; 2 EMB-110P1 (C-95); PAX 12: 2 B-737-400; 2 B-737-800; 1 B-737BBJ (VIP); 2 ERJ-135BJ *Legacy* 600 (VIP); 2 ERJ-145; 1 F-28-1000 *Fellowship*; 1 F-28-3000 *Fellowship*; 1 Learjet 60
TRG 65: 12 EMB-312 *Tucano**; 24 EMB-314 *Super Tucano* (A-29)*; 22 Lancair *Synergy* (T-90 *Calima*); 7 T-6C *Texan* II

HELICOPTERS
MRH 18: 4 AH-60L *Arpia* III; 10 AH-60L *Arpia* IV; 1 AW139 (VIP); 1 Bell 412EP *Twin Huey* (VIP); 2 Hughes 500M
TPT 49: Medium 16 UH-60L *Black Hawk* (incl 1 VIP hel); Light 33: 10 Bell 205 (UH-1H *Huey* II); 12 Bell 206B3 *Jet Ranger* III; 11 Bell 212
TRG 60 TH-67

UNINHABITED AERIAL VEHICLES • ISR • Medium 8: 6 *Hermes* 450; 2 *Hermes* 900

AIR-LAUNCHED MISSILES
AAM • IR *Python* 3; IIR *Python* 4; *Python* 5; ARH *Derby*; I-*Derby* ER (reported)
ASM *Spike*-ER; *Spike*-NLOS

BOMBS
Laser-guided *Paveway* II
INS/GPS guided *Spice*

Gendarmerie & Paramilitary 165,050

National Police Force 165,050

EQUIPMENT BY TYPE
AIRCRAFT
ELINT 5 C-26B *Metroliner*
TPT • Light 41: 5 ATR-42; 3 Beech 200 *King Air*; 2 Beech 300 *King Air*; 2 Beech 1900; 3 BT-67; 3 C-26 *Metroliner*; 3 Cessna 152; 3 Cessna 172; 9 Cessna 206; 2 Cessna 208 *Caravan*; 2 DHC-6 *Twin Otter*; 1 DHC-8; 3 PA-31 *Navajo*
HELICOPTERS
MRH 5: 2 Bell 407GXP; 1 Bell 412EP; 2 MD-500D
TPT 83: Medium 25: 13 UH-60A *Black Hawk*; 9 UH-60L *Black Hawk*; 3 S-70i *Black Hawk*; Light 58: 34 Bell 205 (UH-1H-II *Huey* II); 6 Bell 206B; 5 Bell 206L/L3/L4 *Long Ranger*; 8 Bell 212; 5 Bell 407

DEPLOYMENT

CENTRAL AFRICAN REPUBLIC: UN • MINUSCA 2
EGYPT: MFO 275; 1 inf bn
LEBANON: UN • UNIFIL 1
WESTERN SAHARA: UN • MINURSO 2

FOREIGN FORCES

United States US Southern Command: 50

Costa Rica CRI

Costa Rican Colon CRC		2022	2023	2024
GDP	CRC	44.3trn	46.8trn	49.7trn
	USD	68.4bn	85.6bn	91.9bn
per capita	USD	13,075	16,213	17,249
Growth	%	4.3	4.4	3.2
Inflation	%	8.3	0.7	1.9
Sy Bdgt [a]	CRC	270bn	269bn	295bn
	USD	418m	493m	545m
FMA (US)	USD	7.5m	0.0m	0.0m
USD1=CRC		647.21	546.48	540.36

[a] Paramilitary budget

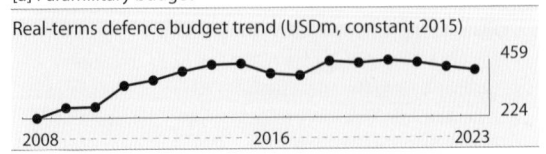

Real-terms defence budget trend (USDm, constant 2015)
459
224
2008 – – – – – – – – – – – – 2016 – – – – – – – – – – – – 2023

Population 5,227,260

Age	0–14	15–19	20–24	25–29	30–64	65 plus
Male	9.9%	3.6%	3.8%	4.1%	23.9%	4.8%
Female	9.4%	3.4%	3.6%	3.9%	23.9%	5.7%

Capabilities

Costa Rica relies on police and coast guard organisations for internal security, maritime and air domain awareness, and counter-narcotics tasks. The armed forces were constitutionally abolished in 1949. Colombia and the US provide assistance and training to

Costa Rica focused on policing and internal-security tasks rather than conventional military operations. The Special Intervention Unit (UEI) has received specialist training from non-regional states, including the US. In May 2022, Costa Rica declared a state of emergency in the face of a cyber-attack, underscoring its limited national defences against such a threat. The US and others have been assisting Costa Rica in building defences against such attacks. In September 2023, the government declared a state of emergency following a surge in migrant flows headed for the US. The Public Force, coast guard and air surveillance units have little heavy equipment, and recent modernisation has depended on donations from countries such as China and the US. Apart from limited maintenance facilities, Costa Rica has no defence industry.

Gendarmerie & Paramilitary 9,950

ORGANISATIONS BY SERVICE

Gendarmerie & Paramilitary 9,950

Special Intervention Unit
FORCES BY ROLE
SPECIAL FORCES
  1 spec ops unit

Public Force 9,000
  11 regional directorates

Coast Guard Unit 550
EQUIPMENT BY TYPE
PATROL AND COASTAL COMBATANTS 9
  PB 9: 1 *Cabo Blanco* (US *Swift* 65); 1 *Isla del Coco* (US *Swift* 105); 3 *Libertador Juan Rafael Mora* (ex-US *Island*); 2 *Point*; 1 *Primera Dama* (US *Swift* 42); 1 *Puerto Quepos* (US *Swift* 36)

Air Surveillance Unit 400
EQUIPMENT BY TYPE
AIRCRAFT • **TPT** • **Light** 14: 2 Cessna T210 *Centurion*; 4 Cessna U206G *Stationair*; 2 PA-31 *Navajo*; 2 PA-34 *Seneca*; 1 Piper PA-23 *Aztec*; 1 Cessna 182RG; 2 Y-12E
HELICOPTERS
  MRH 3: 1 MD-500E; 2 MD-600N
  TPT • **Light** 4 Bell 212 (UH-1N)

Cuba CUB

Cuban Peso CUP		2022	2023	2024
GDP	USD			
per capita	USD			
Growth				
Inflation				
Def exp	CUP			
	USD			
USD1=CUP				

Definitive data not available

Population		10,985,974				
Age	0–14	15–19	20–24	25–29	30–64	65 plus
Male	8.4%	2.7%	3.1%	3.0%	24.8%	7.6%
Female	8.0%	2.5%	2.8%	2.8%	25.1%	9.2%

Capabilities

Cuba's armed forces are principally focused on protecting territorial integrity. Their capability is limited by equipment obsolescence. The force is mainly conscript-based. Cuba has military ties with China and Russia, which has supplied oil and fuel. Defence cooperation with Russia is largely centred around technical and maintenance support. Cooperation with China appears to be on a smaller scale and involves training agreements and personnel exchanges. Some US officials are concerned that China may be using the island for military and intelligence operations. In recent years, Cuba has sent medics and maintenance personnel to South Africa and has also trained some South African personnel in Cuba. The armed forces are no longer designed for expeditionary operations and have little logistical capability to support operational deployments abroad. The inventory is almost entirely composed of legacy Soviet-era systems with varying degrees of obsolescence. Serviceability appears problematic, with much equipment at a low level of availability and maintenance demands growing as fleets age. Much of the aviation fleet is reported to be in storage. Cuba has little in the way of a domestic defence industry apart from some upgrade and maintenance capacity.

ACTIVE 49,000 (Army 38,000 Navy 3,000 Air 8,000) **Gendarmerie & Paramilitary 26,500**

Conscript liability 2 years

RESERVE 39,000 (Army 39,000) Gendarmerie & Paramilitary 1,120,000

Ready Reserves (serve 45 days per year) to fill out Active and Reserve units; see also Paramilitary

ORGANISATIONS BY SERVICE

Army ε38,000
FORCES BY ROLE
COMMAND
  3 regional comd HQ
  3 army comd HQ
COMMAND
  3 SF regt

MANOEUVRE
  Armoured
  1 tk div (3 tk bde)
  Mechanised
  2 (mixed) mech bde
  Light
  2 (frontier) bde
  Air Manoeuvre
  1 AB bde
AIR DEFENCE
  1 ADA regt
  1 SAM bde

Reserves 39,000
FORCES BY ROLE
MANOEUVRE
  Light
  14 inf bde
EQUIPMENT BY TYPE†
ARMOURED FIGHTING VEHICLES
  MBT ε400 T-54/T-55/T-62
  LT TK PT-76
  ASLT BTR-60 100mm
  RECCE BRDM-2;
  AIFV ε50 BMP-1/1P
  APC ε500 BTR-152/BTR-50/BTR-60
ANTI-TANK/ANTI-INFRASTRUCTURE
  MSL
    SP 2K16 *Shmel* (RS-AT-1 *Snapper*)
    MANPATS 9K11 *Malyutka* (RS-AT-3 *Sagger*)
  GUNS 600+: **57mm** 600 ZIS-2 (M-1943); **85mm** D-44
ARTILLERY 1,715+
  SP 40+: **100mm** AAPMP-100; CATAP-100; **122mm** 2S1 *Gvozdika*; AAP-T-122; AAP-BMP-122; *Jupiter* III; *Jupiter* IV; **130mm** AAP-T-130; *Jupiter* V; **152mm** 2S3 *Akatsiya*
  TOWED 500: **122mm** D-30; M-30 (M-1938); **130mm** M-46; **152mm** D-1; M-1937 (ML-20)
  MRL • **SP** 175: **122mm** BM-21 *Grad*; **140mm** BM-14
  MOR 1,000: **82mm** M-41; **82mm** M-43; **120mm** M-43; M-38
AIR DEFENCE
  SAM
    Short-range 2K12 *Kub* (RS-SA-6 *Gainful*)
    Pont-defence 200+: 200 9K35 *Strela*-10 (RS-SA-13 *Gopher*); 9K33 *Osa* (RS-SA-8 *Gecko*); 9K31 *Strela*-1 (RS-SA-9 *Gaskin*); 9K36 *Strela*-3 (RS-SA-14 *Gremlin*); 9K310 *Igla*-1 (SA-16 *Gimlet*); 9K32 *Strela*-2 (RS-SA-7 *Grail*)‡
  GUNS 400
    SP 23mm ZSU-23-4; **30mm** BTR-60P SP; **57mm** ZSU-57-2
    TOWED 100mm KS-19/M-1939; **85mm** KS-12; **57mm** S-60; **37mm** M-1939; **30mm** M-53; **23mm** ZU-23

Navy ε3,000
Western Comd HQ at Cabanas; Eastern Comd HQ at Holquin
EQUIPMENT BY TYPE
SUBMARINES • **SSW** 1 *Delfin*
PATROL AND COASTAL COMBATANTS 9
  PCG 2 *Rio Damuji* with two single P-22 (RS-SS-N-2C *Styx*) AShM, 2 57mm guns, 1 hel landing platform
  PCM 1 Project 1241PE (FSU *Pauk* II) with 1 quad lnchr (manual aiming) with 9K32 *Strela*-2 (RS-SA-N-5 *Grail*) SAM, 2 RBU 1200 A/S mor, 1 76mm gun
  PBF 6 Project 205 (FSU *Osa* II)† each with 4 single lnchr (for P-20U (RS-SS-N-2B *Styx*) AShM – missiles removed to coastal-defence units)
MINE WARFARE AND MINE COUNTERMEASURES 5
  MHI 3 *Korund* (Project 1258 (*Yevgenya*))†
  MSC 2 *Yakhont* (FSU Project 1265 (*Sonya*))†
LOGISTICS AND SUPPORT 2
  ABU 1
  AX 1

Coastal Defence
EQUIPMENT BY TYPE
ARTILLERY • **TOWED 122mm** M-1931/37; **130mm** M-46; **152mm** M-1937
COASTAL DEFENCE • **AShM** 4+: *Bandera* IV (reported); 4 4K51 *Rubezh* (RS-SSC-3 *Styx*)

Naval Infantry 550+
FORCES BY ROLE
MANOEUVRE
  Amphibious
  2 amph aslt bn

Anti-aircraft Defence and Revolutionary Air Force ε8,000 (incl conscripts)
Air assets divided between Western Air Zone and Eastern Air Zone
FORCES BY ROLE
FIGHTER/GROUND ATTACK
  3 sqn with MiG-21bis/UM *Fishbed*; MiG-29/MiG-29UB *Fulcrum*
TRANSPORT
  1 (VIP) tpt sqn with An-24 *Coke*; Mi-8P *Hip*
ATTACK HELICOPTER
  2 sqn with Mi-17 *Hip* H; Mi-35 *Hind*
TRAINING
  1 (tac trg) sqn with L-39C *Albatros* (basic); Z-142 (primary)
EQUIPMENT BY TYPE
AIRCRAFT 10 combat capable
  FTR 5: 2 MiG-29 *Fulcrum*†; 3 MiG-29UB *Fulcrum*†
  FGA 5: up to 3 MiG-21bis *Fishbed*; up to 2 MiG-21UM *Fishbed*
  ISR 1 An-30 *Clank*†

TPT 23: Heavy 2 Il-76 *Candid*; **Light** 9: 1 An-24 *Coke* (Aerogaviota); 3 An-26 *Curl* (Aerogaviota); 5 ATR-42-500 (Cubana & Aergaviota); **PAX** 12: 6 An-158 (Cubana); 3 Il-96-300 (Cubana); 3 Tu-204E-100 (Cubana)

TRG 25+: up to 25 L-39 *Albatros*; some Z-142C

HELICOPTERS
ATK 4 Mi-35 *Hind*† (8 more in store)
MRH 8 Mi-17 *Hip* H (12 more in store)
TPT • Medium 2 Mi-8P *Hip*

AIR DEFENCE • SAM
Medium-range S-75 *Dvina* (RS-SA-2 *Guideline*); S-75 *Dvina* mod (RS-SA-2 *Guideline* – on T-55 chassis)
Short-range S-125M/M1 *Pechora*-M/M1 (RS-SA-3 *Goa*); S-125M1 *Pechora*-M1 mod (RS-SA-3 *Goa* – on T-55 chassis)

AIR-LAUNCHED MISSILES
AAM • IR R-3‡ (RS-AA-2 *Atoll*); R-60 (RS-AA-8 *Aphid*); R-73 (RS-AA-11A *Archer*); **IR/SARH** R-23/24‡ (RS-AA-7 *Apex*); R-27 (RS-AA-10 *Alamo*)
ASM Kh-23‡ (RS-AS-7 *Kerry*)

Gendarmerie & Paramilitary 26,500 active

State Security 20,000
Ministry of Interior

Border Guards 6,500
Ministry of Interior
PATROL AND COASTAL COMBATANTS 20
  PCC 2 *Stenka*
  PB 18 *Zhuk*

Youth Labour Army 70,000 reservists

Civil Defence Force 50,000 reservists

Territorial Militia ε1,000,000 reservists

FOREIGN FORCES
United States US Southern Command: 650 (JTF-GTMO) at Guantanamo Bay

Dominican Republic DOM

Dominican Peso DOP		2022	2023	2024
GDP	DOP	6.26trn	6.74trn	7.36trn
	USD	114bn	121bn	128bn
per capita	USD	10,711	11,249	11,825
Growth	%	4.9	3.0	5.2
Inflation	%	8.8	4.9	4.2
Def bdgt	DOP	41.8bn	49.9bn	58.3bn
	USD	761m	894m	1.01bn
USD1=DOP		54.98	55.86	57.53

Real-terms defence budget trend (USDm, constant 2015): 749 (2023), 297 (2008)

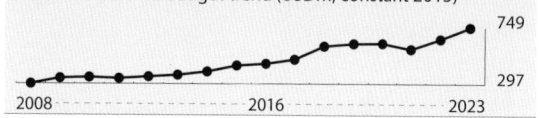

Population 10,735,614

Age	0–14	15–19	20–24	25–29	30–64	65 plus
Male	13.1%	4.5%	4.5%	4.3%	20.7%	3.5%
Female	12.7%	4.4%	4.3%	4.1%	20.1%	3.8%

Capabilities

The principal tasks for the Dominican armed forces include internal- and border-security missions, as well as disaster relief. Training and operations increasingly focus on counter-narcotics and include collaboration with the police in an inter-agency task force. The US sends training teams to the country under the terms of a 2015 military-partnership agreement, and the navy has trained with French forces. The Dominican Republic has participated in US SOUTHCOM's *Tradewinds* disaster-response exercise. In response to instability in Haiti, the government closed the border, the army has strengthened its presence along the frontier, establishing new surveillance posts, while the air force has carried out overflight operations. The country has little capacity to deploy and sustain forces abroad. The army's limited number of armoured vehicles are obsolete and likely difficult to maintain. The air force operates a modest number of light fixed-wing and rotary-wing assets, and the navy a small fleet of mainly ex-US patrol craft of varying sizes. The country has maintenance facilities, but no defence industry.

ACTIVE 56,800 (Army 29,500 Navy 11,200 Air 16,100) **Gendarmerie & Paramilitary 15,000**

ORGANISATIONS BY SERVICE

Army 29,500
5 Defence Zones
FORCES BY ROLE
SPECIAL FORCES
  3 SF bn
MANOEUVRE
  Light
  4 (1st, 2nd, 3rd & 4th) inf bde (3 inf bn)
  2 (5th & 6th) inf bde (2 inf bn)
  Air Manoeuvre

1 air cav bde (1 cdo bn, 1 (6th) mtn bn, 1 hel sqn with Bell 205 (op by Air Force); OH-58 *Kiowa*; R-22; R-44 *Raven* II)

Other

1 (Presidential Guard) gd regt

1 (MoD) sy bn

COMBAT SUPPORT

1 cbt spt bde (1 lt armd bn; 1 arty bn; 1 engr bn; 1 sigs bn)

EQUIPMENT BY TYPE

ARMOURED FIGHTING VEHICLES

LT TK 12 M41B (76mm)

APC • **APC (W)** 8 LAV-150 *Commando*

ANTI-TANK/ANTI-INFRASTRUCTURE

RCL **106mm** 20 M40A1

GUNS **37mm** 20 M3

ARTILLERY 104

TOWED **105mm** 16: 4 M101; 12 *Reinosa* 105/26

MOR 88: **81mm** 60 M1; **107mm** 4 M30; **120mm** 24 Expal Model L

HELICOPTERS

ISR 8: 4 OH-58A *Kiowa*; 4 OH-58C *Kiowa*

TPT • **Light** 6: 4 R-22; 2 R-44 *Raven* II

TRG 2 TH-67 *Creek*

Navy 11,200

HQ located at Santo Domingo

FORCES BY ROLE

SPECIAL FORCES

1 (SEAL) SF unit

MANOEUVRE

Amphibious

1 mne sy unit

EQUIPMENT BY TYPE

PATROL AND COASTAL COMBATANTS 17

PCO 1 *Almirante Didiez Burgos* (ex-US *Balsam*)

PCC 2 *Tortuguero* (ex-US *White Sumac*)

PB 14: 1 *Altair* (Swiftships 35m); 4 *Bellatrix* (US Sewart Seacraft); 1 *Betelgeuse* (Damen Stan Patrol 2606); 2 *Canopus* (Swiftships 110); 3 *Hamal* (Damen Stan Patrol 1505); 3 *Point*

AMPHIBIOUS • LANDING CRAFT

LCU 1 *Neyba* (ex-US LCU 1675)

LOGISTICS AND SUPPORT 1

AX 1 *Almirante Juan Bautista Cambiaso*

Air Force 16,100

FORCES BY ROLE

GROUND ATTACK

1 sqn with EMB-314 *Super Tucano**

SEARCH & RESCUE

1 sqn with Bell 205 (UH-1H *Huey* II); Bell 205 (UH-1H *Iroquois*); Bell 430 (VIP); OH-58 *Kiowa* (CH-136); S-333

TRANSPORT

1 sqn with C-212-400 *Aviocar*; PA-31 *Navajo*

TRAINING

1 sqn with T-35B *Pillan*

AIR DEFENCE

1 ADA bn with 20mm guns

EQUIPMENT BY TYPE

AIRCRAFT 8 combat capable

ISR 1 AMT-200 *Super Ximango*

TPT • **Light** 13: 3 C-212-400 *Aviocar*; 1 Cessna 172; 1 Cessna 182; 1 Cessna 206; 1 Cessna 207; 1 *Commander* 690; 3 EA-100; 1 PA-31 *Navajo*; 1 P2006T

TRG 12: 8 EMB-314 *Super Tucano**; 4 T-35B *Pillan*

HELICOPTERS

ISR 9 OH-58 *Kiowa* (CH-136)

TPT • **Light** 22: 14 Bell 205 (UH-1H *Huey* II); 5 Bell 205 (UH-1H *Iroquois*); 1 H155 (VIP); 2 S-333

AIR DEFENCE • **GUNS 20mm** 4

Gendarmerie & Paramilitary 15,000

National Police 15,000

Ecuador ECU

United States Dollar USD		2022	2023	2024
GDP	USD	115bn	119bn	123bn
per capita	USD	6,389	6,500	6,630
Growth	%	2.9	1.4	1.8
Inflation	%	3.5	2.3	1.8
Def bdgt	USD	1.58bn	1.67bn	
FMA (US)	USD	5m	5m	5m

Real-terms defence budget trend (USDbn, constant 2015)
2.02 ... 1.39
2008 — 2016 — 2023

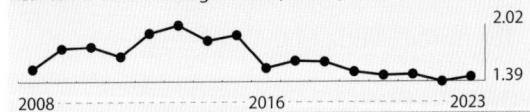

Population	18,134,133					
Age	0–14	15–19	20–24	25–29	30–64	65 plus
Male	13.9%	4.8%	4.5%	4.0%	18.1%	4.0%
Female	13.3%	4.6%	4.4%	4.0%	19.4%	4.9%

Capabilities

Ecuador's armed forces are focused on internal-security tasks. The political crisis in neighbouring Venezuela and resulting refugee flows have added to security challenges in the northern border area. These conditions led the armed forces to create a joint task force for counter-insurgency and counter-narcotics operations. Defence cooperation with Peru includes demining efforts on their border. Quito has recently signed a defence agreement with Colombia to increase joint operations to counter drug trafficking and illicit smuggling. Military ties with Washington have been revived, which has led to the re-establishment of bilateral training programmes and equipment donations. The armed forces train regularly and have participated in multinational military exercises. The country has limited capability to deploy independently beyond national borders. The equipment inventory is increasingly obsolescent and low availability is a challenge. Modernisation plans are modest in scope and currently focused on armoured vehicles as well as maritime-patrol capabilities. Ecuador's defence industries are mostly state-owned, including shipyard ASTINAVE, which has some construction, maintenance and repair capabilities, although the navy's submarines are being modernised in Chile.

ACTIVE 39,600 (Army 24,000 Navy 9,400 Air 6,200)
Paramilitary 500

Conscript liability Voluntary conscription

RESERVE 118,000 (Joint 118,000)

Ages 18–55

ORGANISATIONS BY SERVICE

Army 24,000

FORCES BY ROLE
gp are bn sized
COMMAND
4 div HQ
SPECIAL FORCES
1 (9th) SF bde (3 SF gp, 1 SF sqn, 1 para bn, 1 sigs sqn, 1 log comd)
MANOEUVRE
Mechanised
1 (11th) armd cav bde (3 armd cav gp, 1 mech inf bn, 1 SP arty gp, 1 engr gp)
1 (5th) inf bde (1 SF sqn, 2 mech cav gp, 2 inf bn, 1 cbt engr coy, 1 sigs coy, 1 log coy)
Light
1 (1st) inf bde (1 SF sqn, 1 armd cav gp, 1 armd recce sqn, 3 inf bn, 1 med coy)
1 (3rd) inf bde (1 SF gp, 1 mech cav gp, 1 inf bn, 1 arty gp, 1 hvy mor coy, 1 cbt engr coy, 1 sigs coy, 1 log coy)
1 (7th) inf bde (1 SF sqn, 1 armd recce sqn, 1 mech cav gp, 3 inf bn, 1 jungle bn, 1 arty gp, 1 cbt engr coy, 1 sigs coy, 1 log coy, 1 med coy)
1 (13th) inf bde (1 SF sqn, 1 armd recce sqn, 1 mot cav gp, 3 inf bn, 1 arty gp, 1 hvy mor coy, 1 cbt engr coy, 1sigs coy, 1 log coy)
2 (17th & 21st) jungle bde (3 jungle bn, 1 cbt engr coy, 1 sigs coy, 1 log coy)
1 (19th) jungle bde (3 jungle bn, 1 jungle trg bn, 1 cbt engr coy, 1 sigs coy, 1 log coy)
COMBAT SUPPORT
1 (27th) arty bde (1 SP arty gp, 1 MRL gp, 1 ADA gp, 1 cbt engr coy, 1 sigs coy, 1 log coy)
1 (23rd) engr bde (3 engr bn)
2 indep MP coy
1 indep sigs coy
COMBAT SERVICE SUPPORT
1 (25th) log bde (1 log bn, 1 tpt bn, 1 maint bn, 1 med bn)
9 indep med coy
AVIATION
1 (15th) avn bde (2 tpt avn gp, 2 hel gp, 1 mixed avn gp)

AIR DEFENCE
1 ADA gp
EQUIPMENT BY TYPE
ARMOURED FIGHTING VEHICLES
LT TK 25 AMX-13
RECCE 42: 10 EE-3 *Jararaca*; 32 EE-9 *Cascavel*
APC 151
APC (T) 102: 82 AMX-VCI; 20 M113
APC (W) 49: 17 EE-11 *Urutu*; 32 UR-416
AUV 20 *Cobra* II
ARTILLERY 486
SP 155mm 5 Mk F3
TOWED 106: **105mm** 84: 36 M101; 24 M2A2; 24 Model 56 pack howitzer; **155mm** 22: 12 M114; 10 M198
MRL 122mm 24: 18 BM-21 *Grad*; 6 RM-70
MOR 81mm 357 M29
AIRCRAFT
TPT • Light 10: 1 Beech 200 *King Air*; 2 C-212; 1 CN235; 2 Cessna 172; 1 Cessna 206; 1 Cessna 500 *Citation* I; 1 IAI-201 *Arava*; 1 M-28 *Skytruck*
TRG 4: 2 MX-7-235 *Star Rocket*; 2 T-41D *Mescalero*
HELICOPTERS
MRH 30: 7 H125M (AS550C3) *Fennec*; 3 Mi-17-1V *Hip*; 2 SA315B *Lama*; 18 SA342L *Gazelle* (13 with HOT for anti-armour role)
TPT 13: **Medium** 9: 5 AS332B *Super Puma*; 2 Mi-171E; 2 SA330 *Puma*; **Light** 4: 2 H125 (AS350B2) *Ecureuil*; 2 H125 (AS350B3) *Ecureuil*
AIR DEFENCE
SAM • Point-defence *Blowpipe;* 9K32 *Strela*-2 (RS-SA-7 *Grail*)‡; 9K38 *Igla* (RS-SA-18 *Grouse*)
GUNS 240
SP 20mm 44 M163 *Vulcan*
TOWED 196: **14.5mm** 128 ZPU-1/-2; **20mm** 38: 28 M-1935, 10 M167 *Vulcan*; **40mm** 30 L/70/M1A1
AIR-LAUNCHED MISSILES • ASM HOT

Navy 9,400 (incl Naval Aviation, Marines and Coast Guard)

EQUIPMENT BY TYPE
SUBMARINES 2
SSK 2 *Shyri* (GER T-209/1300) with 8 single 533mm TT each with A184 mod 3 HWT
PRINCIPAL SURFACE COMBATANTS • FRIGATES 2
FFGH 2 *Moran Valverde* (ex-UK *Leander* batch II) with 1 quad lnchr with MM40 *Exocet* AShM, 2 triple 324mm ILAS-3 (B-515) ASTT with A244 LWT, 1 Mk 15 *Phalanx* CIWS, 1 twin 114mm gun (capacity 1 Bell 230 hel)
PATROL AND COASTAL COMBATANTS 9
CORVETTES • FSGM 6
5 *Esmeraldas* (ITA Tipo 550) with 2 triple lnchr with MM40 *Exocet* AShM, 1 quad *Albatros* lnchr with *Aspide* SAM, 2 triple 324mm ILAS-3 (B-515) ASTT with A244 LWT, 1 76mm gun, 1 hel landing

platform
  1 *Esmeraldas* (ITA Tipo 550) with 2 triple lnchr with MM40 *Exocet* AShM, 1 quad *Albatros* lnchr with *Aspide* SAM, 1 76mm gun, 1 hel landing platform
PCFG 3 *Quito* (GER Lurssen TNC-45 45m) with 4 single lnchr with MM38 *Exocet* AShM, 1 76mm gun
LOGISTICS AND SUPPORT 8
  AE 1 *Calicuchima*
  AGOR 1 *Orion* with 1 hel landing platform
  AGS 1 *Sirius*
  AK 1 *Hualcopo* (ex-PRC *Fu Yuan Yu Leng* 999)
  AKL 1 *Isla Bartolome* (operated by TRANSNAVE)
  ATF 1 *Chimborazo*
  AWT 1 *Atahualpa*
  AXS 1 *Guayas*

Naval Aviation 380
EQUIPMENT BY TYPE
AIRCRAFT
  MP 2: 1 CN235-100; 1 CN235-300M
  ISR 3: 2 Beech 200T *King Air*; 1 Beech 300 *Catpass King Air*
  TPT • Light 2: 1 Beech 200 *King Air*; 1 Beech 300 *King Air*
  TRG 3 T-35B *Pillan*
HELICOPTERS
  TPT • Light 9: 3 Bell 206A; 3 Bell 206B; 1 Bell 230; 2 Bell 430
UNINHABITED AERIAL VEHICLES
  ISR 4: **Heavy** 2 *Heron*; **Medium** 2 *Searcher* Mk.II

Marines 1,950
FORCES BY ROLE
SPECIAL FORCES
  1 cdo bn
MANOEUVRE
  Amphibious
  5 mne bn
EQUIPMENT BY TYPE
ARTILLERY • MOR 32+ 81mm/120mm
AIR DEFENCE • SAM • Point-defence 9K38 *Igla* (RS-SA-18 *Grouse*)

Air Force 6,200

Operational Command
FORCES BY ROLE
FIGHTER
  1 sqn with *Cheetah* C/D
GROUND ATTACK
  1 sqn with EMB-314 *Super Tucano**

Military Air Transport Group
FORCES BY ROLE
ISR
  1 sqn with Beech 350i *King Air*; Gulfstream G-1159; *Sabreliner* 40
SEARCH & RESCUE/TRANSPORT HELICOPTER
  1 sqn with AW119 *Koala*; Bell 206B *Jet Ranger* II; H145
  1 sqn with Cessna 206; PA-34 *Seneca*
TRANSPORT
  1 sqn with C295M
  1 sqn with DHC-6-300 *Twin Otter*
  1 sqn with B-727; B-737-200; L-100-30
TRAINING
  1 sqn with DA20-C1
  1 sqn with G-120TP
EQUIPMENT BY TYPE
AIRCRAFT 17 combat capable
  TPT 19: **Medium** 1 L-100-30; (2 C-130B *Hercules*; 1 C-130H *Hercules* in store); **Light** 11: 1 Beech E90 *King Air*; 1 Beech 350i *King Air*; 3 C295M; 1 Cessna 206; 3 DHC-6 *Twin Otter*; 1 PA-34 *Seneca*; 1 *Sabreliner* 40; **PAX** 7: 2 A320 (operated by TAME); 2 B-727; 1 B-737-200; 1 *Falcon* 7X; 1 Gulfstream G-1159
  TRG 36: 11 DA20-C1; 17 EMB-314 *Super Tucano**; 8 G-120TP
HELICOPTERS • TPT • Light 13: 4 AW119 *Koala*; 6 Bell 206B *Jet Ranger* II; 3 H145
AIR-LAUNCHED MISSILES • AAM • IR *Python* 3; R-550 *Magic*; **IIR** *Python* 4
AIR DEFENCE
  SAM • Point-defence 10+: 10 9K33 *Osa* (RS-SA-8 *Gecko*); 9K310 *Igla*-1 (RS-SA-16 *Gimlet*)
  GUNS • TOWED 52: **23mm** 34 ZU-23; **35mm** 18 GDF-002 (twin)

Paramilitary 500

Coast Guard 500
EQUIPMENT BY TYPE
PATROL AND COASTAL COMBATANTS 21
  PCC 7: 3 *Isla Fernandina* (*Vigilante*); 2 *Isla San Cristóbal* (Damen Stan Patrol 5009); 2 *Isla Floreana* (ex-ROK *Hae Uri*)
  PB 13: 2 *Espada*; 2 *Manta* (GER Lurssen 36m); 1 *Point*; 4 *Rio Coca*; 4 *Isla Santa Cruz* (Damen Stan 2606)
  PBR 1 *Rio Puyango*

DEPLOYMENT
CENTRAL AFRICAN REPUBLIC: UN • MINUSCA 2
SOUTH SUDAN: UN • UNMISS 3
SUDAN: UN • UNISFA 3
WESTERN SAHARA: UN • MINURSO 3

El Salvador SLV

United States Dollar USD		2022	2023	2024
GDP	USD	32.5bn	35.3bn	37.2bn
per capita	USD	5,127	5,558	5,825
Growth	%	2.6	2.2	1.9
Inflation	%	7.2	4.4	2.4
Def bdgt	USD	257m	251m	

Real-terms defence budget trend (USDm, constant 2015)

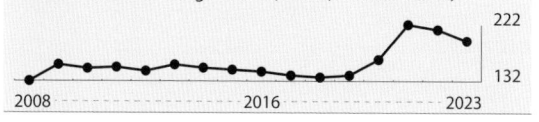

Population 6,602,370

Age	0–14	15–19	20–24	25–29	30–64	65 plus
Male	13.0%	4.0%	4.5%	4.7%	18.2%	3.5%
Female	12.4%	3.8%	4.4%	4.8%	22.0%	4.7%

Capabilities

The primary challenge for El Salvador's armed forces is tackling organised crime and aiding the National Civil Policy in combating narcotics trafficking. Mixed military and police patrols have been deployed to areas with high crime rates under the Territorial Control Plan implemented in 2019. The government used large-scale personnel deployments to carry out community clampdowns to try to suppress gang violence in those areas, with some of the measures winning domestic support but raising international human rights concerns. El Salvador participates in a tri-national border task force with Guatemala and Honduras. The armed forces have long-standing training programmes, including with regional states and with the US, focused on internal security, disaster relief and support to civilian authorities. El Salvador has deployed on UN peacekeeping missions up to company strength but lacks the logistical support to sustain independent international deployments. The armed forces have received little new heavy military equipment in recent years and are dependent on an inventory of Cold War-era platforms. The majority of its equipment is operational, indicating adequate support and maintenance. El Salvador lacks a substantive defence industry but has produced light armoured vehicles based on commercial vehicles.

ACTIVE 24,500 (Army 20,500 Navy 2,000 Air 2,000)
Paramilitary 26,000

Conscript liability 12 months (selective); 11 months for officers and NCOs

RESERVE 9,900 (Joint 9,900)

ORGANISATIONS BY SERVICE

Army 20,500
FORCES BY ROLE
SPECIAL FORCES
  1 spec ops gp (1 SF coy, 1 para bn, 1 (naval inf) coy)
MANOEUVRE
  Reconnaissance
    1 armd cav regt (2 armd cav bn)
  Light
    6 inf bde (3 inf bn)
  Other
    1 (special) sy bde (2 border gd bn, 2 MP bn)
COMBAT SUPPORT
  1 arty bde (2 fd arty bn, 1 AD bn)
  1 engr comd (2 engr bn)
EQUIPMENT BY TYPE
ARMOURED FIGHTING VEHICLES
  RECCE 5 AML-90 (4 more in store)
  APC • APC (W) 38: 30 VAL *Cashuat* (mod); 8 UR-416
  AUV 5+ *SandCat*
ANTI-TANK/ANTI-INFRASTRUCTURE
  RCL 399: **106mm** 20 M40A1 (incl 16 SP); **90mm** 379 M67
ARTILLERY 229+
  TOWED 66: **105mm** 54: 36 M102; 18 M-56 (FRY); **155mm** 12 M198
  MOR 163+: **81mm** 151 M29; **120mm** 12+: 12 UBM 52; (some M-74 in store)
AIR DEFENCE • GUNS 35: **20mm** 31 M-55; 4 TCM-20

Navy 2,000
EQUIPMENT BY TYPE
PATROL AND COASTAL COMBATANTS 12
  PB 12: 1 Bering 65; 3 Camcraft (30m); 1 Defiant 85; 1 Swiftships 77; 1 Swiftships 65; 4 Type-44 (ex-US); 1 YP 660
AMPHIBIOUS • LANDING CRAFT • LCM 4 LCM 8 (of which 3†)

Naval Inf (SF Commandos) 90
FORCES BY ROLE
SPECIAL FORCES
  1 SF coy

Air Force 2,000
FORCES BY ROLE
FIGHTER/GROUND ATTACK/ISR
  1 sqn with A-37B/OA-37B *Dragonfly*; O-2A/B *Skymaster**
TRANSPORT
  1 sqn with Cessna 337G; IAI-202 *Arava*
TRAINING
  1 sqn with R-235GT *Guerrier*; SR22T; T-35 *Pillan*; T-41D *Mescalero*; TH-300; TH-300C
TRANSPORT HELICOPTER
  1 sqn with Bell 205 (UH-1H *Iroquois*); Bell 407; Bell 412EP *Twin Huey*; MD-530F; UH-1M *Iroquois*
EQUIPMENT BY TYPE
AIRCRAFT 25 combat capable
  ATK 14 A-37B *Dragonfly*
  ISR 11: 6 O-2A/B *Skymaster**; 5 OA-37B *Dragonfly**
  TPT • Light 4: 1 Cessna 337G *Skymaster*; 3 IAI-201 *Arava*
  TRG 11: 5 R-235GT *Guerrier*; 3 T-35 *Pillan*; 2 SR22T; 1

T-41D *Mescalero*

HELICOPTERS

MRH 14: 4 Bell 412EP *Twin Huey* (of which 1 VIP); 8+ MD-530F; 2 UH-1M *Iroquois*

TPT • **Light** 9: 8 Bell 205 (UH-1H *Iroquois*); 1 Bell 407 (VIP tpt, govt owned)

TRG 3: 2 TH-300; 1 TH-300C; (4 TH-300 in store)

AIR-LAUNCHED MISSILES • AAM • IR *Shafrir*‡

Gendarmerie & Paramilitary 26,000

National Civilian Police 26,000

Ministry of Public Security

AIRCRAFT

ISR 1 O-2A *Skymaster*

TPT • **Light** 1 Cessna 310

HELICOPTERS

MRH 9: 2 MD-520N; 7 MD-500E

TPT • **Light** 3: 1 Bell 205 (UH-1H *Iroquois*); 2 R-44 *Raven* II

DEPLOYMENT

LEBANON: UN • UNIFIL 52; 1 inf pl

SOUTH SUDAN: UN • UNMISS 3

SUDAN: UN • UNIFSA 1

FOREIGN FORCES

United States US Southern Command: 1 Cooperative Security Location at Comalapa Airport

Guatemala GUA

Guatemalan Quetzal GTQ		2022	2023	2024
GDP	GTQ	736bn	804bn	872bn
	USD	95.0bn	103bn	111bn
per capita	USD	5,098	5,407	5,748
Growth	%	4.1	3.4	3.5
Inflation	%	6.9	6.3	5.5
Def bdgt	GTQ	3.16bn	3.22bn	
	USD	408m	412m	
USD1=GTQ		7.75	7.83	7.83

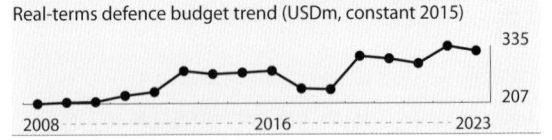

Real-terms defence budget trend (USDm, constant 2015)

335
207
2008 — 2016 — 2023

Population	17,980,803					
Age	0–14	15–19	20–24	25–29	30–64	65 plus
Male	16.3%	4.9%	4.7%	4.5%	16.9%	2.3%
Female	15.7%	4.9%	4.6%	4.5%	17.8%	2.9%

Capabilities

The armed forces are refocusing on border security, having drawn down their decade-long direct support for the National Civil Police in 2018 as part of the inter-agency Plan Fortaleza. Guatemala maintains an inter-agency task force with neighbouring El Salvador and Honduras. The army has trained with US SOUTHCOM and regional partners such as Brazil and Colombia. Training for conventional military operations is limited by budget constraints and the long focus on providing internal security. Guatemala has participated in UN peacekeeping missions to company level. The equipment inventory is small and ageing. The US has provided several soft-skinned vehicles to the army and helicopters to the air force. The air force's fixed-wing transport and surveillance fleet have seen modest recapitalisation. The country has no defence industry aside from limited maintenance facilities.

ACTIVE 18,050 (Army 15,550 Navy 1,500 Air 1,000)
Gendarmerie & Paramilitary 25,000

RESERVE 63,850 (Navy 650 Air 900 Armed Forces 62,300)

(National Armed Forces are combined; the army provides log spt for navy and air force)

ORGANISATIONS BY SERVICE

Army 15,550

15 Military Zones

FORCES BY ROLE

SPECIAL FORCES

1 SF bde (1 SF bn, 1 trg bn)
1 SF bde (1 SF coy, 1 ranger bn)
1 SF mtn bde

MANOEUVRE

Light
1 (strategic reserve) mech bde (1 inf bn, 1 cav regt, 1 log coy)
6 inf bde (1 inf bn)
Air Manoeuvre
1 AB bde with (2 AB bn)
Amphibious
1 mne bde
Other
1 (Presidential) gd bde (1 gd bn, 1 MP bn, 1 CSS coy)
COMBAT SUPPORT
1 engr comd (1 engr bn, 1 construction bn)
2 MP bde with (1 MP bn)

Reserves
FORCES BY ROLE
MANOEUVRE
Light
ε19 inf bn
EQUIPMENT BY TYPE
ARMOURED FIGHTING VEHICLES
RECCE (7 M8 in store)
APC 39
APC (T) 10 M113 (5 more in store)
APC (W) 29: 22 *Armadillo*; 7 V-100 *Commando*
ANTI-TANK/ANTI-INFRASTRUCTURE
RCL 120+: **75mm** M20; **105mm** 64 M-1974 FMK-1 (ARG); **106mm** 56 M40A1
ARTILLERY 149
TOWED **105mm** 76: 12 M101; 8 M102; 56 M-56
MOR 73: **81mm** 55 M1; **107mm** (12 M30 in store); **120mm** 18 ECIA
AIR DEFENCE • GUNS • TOWED 32: **20mm** 32: 16 GAI-D01; 16 M-55

Navy 1,500
EQUIPMENT BY TYPE
PATROL AND COASTAL COMBATANTS 10
PB 10: 6 *Cutlass*; 1 *Dauntless*; 1 *Kukulkan* (US *Broadsword* 32m); 2 *Utatlan* (US *Sewart*)
AMPHIBIOUS • LANDING CRAFT 3
LCT 1 *Quetzal* (COL *Golfo de Tribuga*)
LCP 2 *Machete*
LOGISTICS AND SUPPORT • AXS 3

Marines 650 reservists
FORCES BY ROLE
MANOEUVRE
Amphibious
2 mne bn(-)

Air Force 1,000
2 air comd

FORCES BY ROLE
TRANSPORT
1 sqn with Beech 90/200/300 *King Air*
1 (tactical support) sqn with Cessna 206
TRAINING
1 sqn with T-35B *Pillan*
TRANSPORT HELICOPTER
1 sqn with Bell 212 (armed); Bell 407GX; Bell 412 *Twin Huey* (armed)
EQUIPMENT BY TYPE
Serviceability of ac is less than 50%
AIRCRAFT
TPT • Light 16: 1 Beech 90 *King Air*; 2 Beech 200 *King Air*; 2 Beech 300 *King Air* (VIP); 2 Cessna 206; 3 Cessna 208B *Grand Caravan*; 1 DHC-6 *Twin Otter*; 2 PA-28 *Archer* III; 1 PA-31 *Navajo*; 2 PA-34 *Seneca*; (5 Cessna R172K *Hawk* XP in store)
TRG 1 SR22; (4 T-35B *Pillan* in store)
HELICOPTERS
MRH 2 Bell 412 *Twin Huey* (armed)
TPT • Light 6: 2 Bell 206B *Jet Ranger*; 2 Bell 212 (armed); 2 Bell 407GX

Tactical Security Group
Air Military Police

Gendarmerie & Paramilitary 25,000

National Civil Police 25,000
FORCES BY ROLE
SPECIAL FORCES
1 SF bn
MANOEUVRE
Other
1 (integrated task force) paramilitary unit (incl mil and treasury police)

DEPLOYMENT
CENTRAL AFRICAN REPUBLIC: UN • MINUSCA 4
DEMOCRATIC REPUBLIC OF THE CONGO: UN • MONUSCO 171; 1 spec ops coy
LEBANON: UN • UNIFIL 2
SOUTH SUDAN: UN • UNMISS 7
SUDAN: UN • UNISFA 2

Guyana GUY

Guyanese Dollar GYD		2022	2023	2024
GDP	GYD	3.03trn	3.40trn	4.24trn
	USD	14.5bn	16.3bn	20.3bn
per capita	USD	18,353	20,565	25,513
Growth	%	62.3	38.4	26.6
Inflation	%	6.5	5.5	4.7
Def bdgt	GYD	18.5bn	20.2bn	
	USD	88.5m	97.0m	
USD1=GYD		208.50	208.50	208.50

Real-terms defence budget trend (USDm, constant 2015)

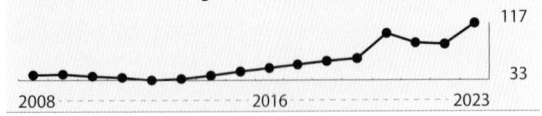

Population		791,739				
Age	0–14	15–19	20–24	25–29	30–64	65 plus
Male	12.1%	4.8%	5.9%	4.5%	20.3%	3.4%
Female	11.6%	4.6%	5.6%	4.2%	18.7%	4.4%

Capabilities

The Guyana Defence Force (GDF) is focused on border control and support for law-enforcement operations. The government is planning to restructure the GDF to improve its flexibility. Guyana is part of the Caribbean Basin Security Initiative. It has close military ties with Brazil, with whom it cooperates on border security via annual regional military exchange meetings. The country also has bilateral agreements with China, France and the US. The GDF trains regularly and takes part in bilateral and multinational exercises. The military has no expeditionary or associated logistics capability. Equipment is mostly second-hand, mainly of Brazilian and North American manufacture. The air force has expanded its modest air-transport capabilities with some second-hand utility aircraft. The country is looking to recapitalise its land, maritime, air and cyber capabilities amid rising military tension with Venezuela over its Essequibo territory. Apart from maintenance facilities, there is no defence-industrial sector.

ACTIVE 3,400 (Army 3,000 Navy 200 Air 200)

Active numbers combined Guyana Defence Force

RESERVE 670 (Army 500 Navy 170)

ORGANISATIONS BY SERVICE

Army 3,000
FORCES BY ROLE
SPECIAL FORCES
  1 SF sqn
MANOEUVRE
  Light
  3 inf bn
COMBAT SUPPORT
  1 arty coy
  1 (spt wpn) cbt spt coy
  1 engr bn
COMBAT SERVICE SUPPORT
  1 spt bn

Reserve
FORCES BY ROLE
MANOEUVRE
  Amphibious
  1 inf bn
EQUIPMENT BY TYPE
ARMOURED FIGHTING VEHICLES
  RECCE 6 EE-9 *Cascavel* (reported)
ARTILLERY 54
  TOWED 130mm 6 M-46†
  MOR 48: **81mm** 12 L16A1; **82mm** 18 M-43; **120mm** 18 M-43

Navy 200
EQUIPMENT BY TYPE
PATROL AND COASTAL COMBATANTS 4
  PB 4 *Barracuda* (ex-US Type-44)

Air Force 200
FORCES BY ROLE
TRANSPORT
  1 unit with Bell 206; Cessna 206; Y-12 (II)
EQUIPMENT BY TYPE
AIRCRAFT • **TPT** • **Light** 6: 2 BN-2 *Islander*; 1 Cessna 206; 2 SC.7 3M *Skyvan*; 1 Y-12 (II)
HELICOPTERS
  MRH 2: 1 Bell 412 *Twin Huey*†; 1 Bell 412EPI *Twin Huey*
  TPT • **Light** 2 Bell 206

Haiti HTI

Haitian Gourde HTG		2022	2023	2024
GDP	HTG	2.17trn	3.07trn	3.67trn
	USD	20.5bn	26.0bn	28.0bn
per capita	USD	1,702	2,125	2,263
Growth	%	-1.7	-1.5	1.4
Inflation	%	27.6	43.6	13.4
Def bdgt [a]	HTG	1.46bn	2.26bn	3.66bn
	USD	13.9m	19.1m	28.0m
USD1=HTG		105.59	118.26	130.93

[a] 2021 increase in defence budget due to greater investment in infrastructure and new COVID-19 responsibilities of the Haitian Armed Forces

Real-terms defence budget trend (USDm, constant 2015)

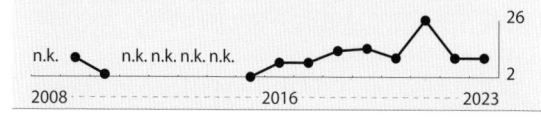

Population 11,610,604

Age	0–14	15–19	20–24	25–29	30–64	65 plus
Male	15.4%	5.0%	4.9%	4.7%	17.5%	1.8%
Female	15.5%	5.0%	4.9%	4.7%	18.2%	2.4%

Capabilities

Haiti possesses almost no military capability. Following the assassination of the president in 2021, violence and instability deepened, and criminal groups are active in many areas. The UN Security Council in 2023 approved the deployment of an armed multinational force to Haiti, possibly led by Kenya. The country's limited armed forces also struggled to respond swiftly to the country's most recent earthquake, where their ability to deliver aid and shelter was tested. A small coast guard is tasked with maritime security and law enforcement and the country's army is still in the very early stages of development, though it is hoped this will eventually number around 5,000 personnel. Plans for military expansion were outlined in the 2015 White Paper on Security and Defence. A road map for the re-establishment of the Haitian armed forces was distributed to ministers in early 2017, and in March 2018, an army high command was established. The army's initial mandate is to provide disaster relief and border security. A 2018 agreement with Mexico has seen small groups of Haitian troops travel to Mexico for training. Haiti is a member of the Caribbean Community and has participated in US SOUTHCOM's *Tradewinds* disaster-response exercise. Haiti has neither heavy military equipment nor a defence industry.

ACTIVE 700 (Army 700) Gendarmerie & Paramilitary 50

ORGANISATIONS BY SERVICE

Army ε700
FORCES BY ROLE
MANOEUVRE
 1 inf bn (forming)

Gendarmerie & Paramilitary 50

Coast Guard ε50
EQUIPMENT BY TYPE
PATROL AND COASTAL COMBATANTS 5
 PB 5 *Dauntless*

Honduras HND

Honduran Lempira HNL		2022	2023	2024
GDP	HNL	777bn	850bn	919bn
	USD	31.5bn	34.0bn	35.9bn
per capita	USD	3,062	3,245	3,366
Growth	%	4.0	2.9	3.2
Inflation	%	9.1	6.4	4.7
Def bdgt [a]	HNL	9.34bn	10.7bn	
	USD	379m	426m	
USD1=HNL		24.64	25.01	25.61

[a] Defence & national security budget

Real-terms defence budget trend (USDm, constant 2015)

Population 9,407,652

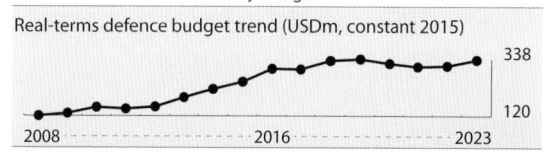

Age	0–14	15–19	20–24	25–29	30–64	65 plus
Male	14.7%	5.1%	4.9%	4.3%	16.8%	2.4%
Female	14.4%	5.1%	5.1%	4.7%	19.3%	3.1%

Capabilities

The armed forces have been deployed in support of the police to combat organised crime and narcotics trafficking since 2011. The government elected in 2021 has pledged to focus on professionalisation, anti-corruption and human rights in the security forces. Taiwan has supplied surplus military equipment. The US is its main security partner and provides assistance. Honduras hosts a US base at Soto Cano airfield and is part of a tri-national border-security task force with neighbouring El Salvador and Guatemala. Training for conventional military operations is limited and instead focused on internal- and border-security requirements. Honduras does not have the capability to maintain substantial foreign deployments. Most equipment is ageing with serviceability in doubt. There have been reports of security assistance from Israel. Apart from limited maintenance facilities, the country has no defence industry.

ACTIVE 14,950 (Army 7,300 Navy 1,350 Air 2,300 Military Police 4,000) Gendarmerie & Paramilitary 8,000

RESERVE 60,000 (Joint 60,000; Ex-servicemen registered)

ORGANISATIONS BY SERVICE

Army 7,300
FORCES BY ROLE

SPECIAL FORCES
1 (special tac) spec ops gp (2 spec ops bn, 1 inf bn; 1 AB bn; 1 arty bn)

MANOEUVRE
Mechanised
1 inf bde (1 mech cav regt, 1 inf bn, 1 arty bn)
Light
1 inf bde (3 inf bn, 1 arty bn)
3 inf bde (2 inf bn)
1 indep inf bn
Other
1 (Presidential) gd coy

COMBAT SUPPORT
1 engr bn
1 sigs bn

EQUIPMENT BY TYPE
ARMOURED FIGHTING VEHICLES
  LT TK 12 FV101 *Scorpion*
  RECCE 43: 3 FV107 *Scimitar*; 40 FV601 *Saladin*
  AUV 1 FV105 *Sultan* (CP)
ANTI-TANK/ANTI-INFRASTRUCTURE
  RCL 50+: **84mm** *Carl Gustaf*; **106mm** 50 M40A1
ARTILLERY 118+
  TOWED 28: **105mm**: 24 M102; **155mm**: 4 M198
  MOR 90+: **81mm**; **120mm** 60 FMK-2; **160mm** 30 M-66

Navy 1,350
EQUIPMENT BY TYPE
PATROL AND COASTAL COMBATANTS 15
  PCO 1 *General Cabañas* (ISR OPV 62 *Sa'ar*)
  PB 14: 2 *Lempira* (Damen Stan Patrol 4207 – leased); 1 *Chamelecon* (Swiftships 85); 1 *Tegucigalpa* (US *Guardian* 32m); 3 *Guaymuras* (Swiftships 105); 5 *Nacaome* (Swiftships 65); 1 *Río Aguán* (Defiant 85); 1 *Rio Coco* (US PB Mk III)
AMPHIBIOUS • LANDING CRAFT 3
  LCT 1 *Gracias a Dios* (COL *Golfo de Tribugá*)
  LCM 3: 2 LCM 8; 1 *Punta Caxinas*
HELICOPTERS • TPT • Light 1 Bo-105S

Marines 1,000
FORCES BY ROLE
MANOEUVRE
  Amphibious
  2 mne bn

Air Force 2,300
FORCES BY ROLE
FIGHTER/GROUND ATTACK
1 sqn with A-37B *Dragonfly*
1 sqn with F-5E/F *Tiger* II
GROUND ATTACK/ISR/TRAINING
1 unit with Cessna 182 *Skylane*; EMB-312 *Tucano*; MXT-7-180 *Star Rocket*
TRANSPORT
1 sqn with Beech 200 *King Air*; C-130A *Hercules*; Cessna 185/210; IAI-201 *Arava*; PA-42 *Cheyenne*; Turbo Commander 690
1 VIP flt with PA-31 *Navajo*; Bell 412EP/SP *Twin Huey*
TRANSPORT HELICOPTER
1 sqn with Bell 205 (UH-1H *Iroquois*); Bell 412SP *Twin Huey*; Bo-105S
TRANSPORT HELICOPTER
1 flt with *Skylark* 3
AIR DEFENCE
1 ADA bn

EQUIPMENT BY TYPE
AIRCRAFT 17 combat capable
  FTR 11: 9 F-5E *Tiger* II†; 2 F-5F *Tiger* II†
  ATK 6 A-37B *Dragonfly*
  TPT 17: **Medium** 1 C-130A *Hercules*; **Light** 16: 1 Beech 200 *King Air*; 2 Cessna 172 *Skyhawk*; 2 Cessna 182 *Skylane*; 1 Cessna 185; 3 Cessna 208B *Grand Caravan*; 1 Cessna 210; 1 EMB-135 *Legacy* 600; 1 IAI-201 *Arava*; 1 L-410 (leased); 1 PA-31 *Navajo*; 1 PA-42 *Cheyenne*; 1 Turbo Commander 690
  TRG 15: 9 EMB-312 *Tucano*; 6 MXT-7-180 *Star Rocket*
HELICOPTERS
  MRH 7: 1 Bell 412EP *Twin Huey* (VIP); 4 Bell 412SP *Twin Huey*; 2 Hughes 500
  TPT • Light 7: 5 Bell 205 (UH-1H *Iroquois*); 1 H125 *Ecureuil*; 1 Bo-105S
UAV • ISR • Light 6 *Skylark* 3
AIR DEFENCE • GUNS 20mm 48: 24 M-55A2; 24 TCM-20
AIR-LAUNCHED MISSILES • AAM • IR *Shafrir*‡

Military Police 4,000
FORCES BY ROLE
MANOEUVRE
  Other
  8 sy bn

Gendarmerie & Paramilitary 8,000
Public Security Forces 8,000
Ministry of Public Security and Defence; 11 regional comd

DEPLOYMENT
WESTERN SAHARA: UN • MINURSO 11

FOREIGN FORCES
United States US Southern Command: 400; 1 avn bn with 4 CH-47F *Chinook*; 12 UH-60L/HH-60L *Black Hawk*

Jamaica JAM

Jamaican Dollar JMD		2022	2023	2024
GDP	JMD	2.62trn	2.90trn	3.09trn
	USD	17.0bn	18.8bn	20.1bn
per capita	USD	6,198	6,831	7,310
Growth	%	5.2	2.0	1.8
Inflation	%	10.3	6.5	5.0
Def bdgt	JMD	35.6bn	35.9bn	
	USD	231m	232m	
USD1=JMD		154.28	154.60	153.83

Real-terms defence budget trend (USDm, constant 2015)

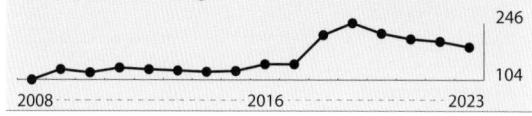

246
104
2008   2016   2023

Population   2,820,982

Age	0–14	15–19	20–24	25–29	30–64	65 plus
Male	12.3%	4.3%	4.3%	4.0%	19.7%	4.8%
Female	11.8%	4.2%	4.2%	4.0%	20.9%	5.3%

Capabilities

The Jamaica Defence Force (JDF) is focused principally on maritime and internal security, including support to police operations. Jamaica maintains military ties, including for training purposes, with Canada, the UK and US and is a member of the Caribbean Community. The JDF has participated in US SOUTHCOM's *Tradewinds* disaster-response exercise. Jamaica is host to the Caribbean Special Tactics Centre, which trains special-forces units from Jamaica and other Caribbean nations. The JDF does not have any capacity to support independent deployment abroad. Funds have been allocated to procure new vehicles and helicopters, and new patrol craft are being procured. Jamaica has no defence industry except for limited maintenance facilities.

ACTIVE 5,950 (Army 5,400 Coast Guard 300 Air 250)

(combined Jamaican Defence Force)

RESERVE 2,580 (Army 2,500 Coast Guard 60 Air 20)

ORGANISATIONS BY SERVICE

Army 5,400
FORCES BY ROLE
MANOEUVRE
  Light
  4 inf bn
COMBAT SUPPORT
  1 engr regt (4 engr sqn)
  1 MP bn
  1 cbt spt bn (1 (PMV) lt mech inf coy)
COMBAT SERVICE SUPPORT
  1 spt bn (1 med coy, 1 log coy, 1 tpt coy)
EQUIPMENT BY TYPE
ARMOURED FIGHTING VEHICLES
  AUV 18 *Bushmaster*
ARTILLERY • MOR 81mm 12 L16A1

Reserves
FORCES BY ROLE
MANOEUVRE
  Light
  3 inf bn
COMBAT SERVICE SUPPORT
  1 spt bn

Coast Guard 300
EQUIPMENT BY TYPE
PATROL AND COASTAL COMBATANTS 8
  PCC 1 *Nanny of the Maroons* (Damen Fast Crew Supplier 5009)
  PB 7: 3 *Honour* (Damen Stan Patrol 4207); 4 *Dauntless*

Air Wing 250
Plus National Reserve
FORCES BY ROLE
MARITIME PATROL/TRANSPORT
  1 flt with Beech 350ER *King Air*; BN-2A *Defender*
SEARCH & RESCUE/TRANSPORT HELICOPTER
  1 flt with Bell 407
  1 flt with Bell 412EP
TRAINING
  1 unit with Bell 206B3 *Jet Ranger*; Bell 505; DA40-180FP *Diamond Star*
EQUIPMENT BY TYPE
AIRCRAFT
  MP 1 Beech 350ER *King Air*
  TPT • Light 2 DA40-180FP *Diamond Star* (1 BN-2A *Defender* in store)
HELICOPTERS
  MRH 1 Bell 412EP *Twin Huey* (1 more in store)
  TPT • Light 13: 1 Bell 206B3 *Jet Ranger*; 3 Bell 407; 3 Bell 429; 6 Bell 505

Mexico MEX

Mexican Peso MXN		2022	2023	2024
GDP	MXN	29.5trn	32.0trn	34.5trn
	USD	1.47trn	1.81trn	1.99trn
per capita	USD	11,266	13,804	15,072
Growth	%	3.9	3.2	2.1
Inflation	%	7.9	5.5	3.8
Def bdgt [a]	MXN	116bn	138bn	
	USD	5.78bn	7.83bn	
USD1=MXN		20.13	17.68	17.32

[a] National security expenditure

Real-terms defence budget trend (USDbn, constant 2015)

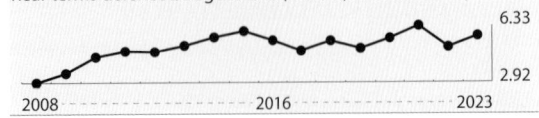

2008 — 2016 — 2023, 6.33, 2.92

Population		129,875,529				
Age	0–14	15–19	20–24	25–29	30–64	65 plus
Male	12.2%	4.6%	4.5%	4.1%	20.0%	3.5%
Female	11.6%	4.2%	3.9%	4.0%	22.9%	4.5%

Capabilities

Mexico's armed forces are the most capable in Central America, though they have been heavily involved in internal-security support for nearly a decade. The National Plan for Peace and Security 2018–24 envisaged that the armed forces would hand over lead responsibility for tackling drug cartels and other organised crime to a new National Guard gendarmerie. However, recent moves suggested a broadening of the armed forces' internal role, raising concerns about the increasing militarisation of Mexican society. In April 2023, the Supreme Court appeared to block plans to transfer the National Guard to Ministry of Defence control. The US-Mexican security relationship is key to the country but has been under strain. The US has provided equipment and training to Mexican forces under the Mérida Initiative, as well as through bilateral programmes via the Pentagon. The armed forces have a moderate capability to deploy independently but do not do so in significant numbers. The country has plans to recapitalise its diverse and ageing conventional combat platforms across all three services. In 2020, Mexico brought back to service some of its ageing F-5 combat aircraft. State-owned shipyards have produced patrol craft for the navy, which also has plans to modernise its frigate force. Army factories have produced light armoured utility vehicles for domestic use.

ACTIVE 216,000 (Army 157,500 Navy 50,500 Air 8,000) Gendarmerie & Paramilitary 136,900

Conscript liability 12 months (partial, selection by ballot) from age 18, serving on Saturdays; voluntary for women; conscripts allocated to reserves.

RESERVE 81,500 (National Military Service)

ORGANISATIONS BY SERVICE

Space
EQUIPMENT BY TYPE
SATELLITES • COMMUNICATIONS 2 *Mexsat*

Army 157,500
12 regions (total: 46 army zones)

FORCES BY ROLE

SPECIAL FORCES
1 (1st) SF bde (5 SF bn)
1 (2nd) SF bde (7 SF bn)
1 (3rd) SF bde (4 SF bn)

MANOEUVRE

Reconnaissance
3 (2nd, 3rd & 4th Armd) mech bde (2 armd recce bn, 2 lt mech bn, 1 arty bn, 1 (Canon) AT gp)
25 mot recce regt

Light
1 (1st) inf corps (1 (1st Armd) mech bde (2 armd recce bn, 2 lt mech bn, 1 arty bn, 1 (Canon) AT gp), 3 (2nd, 3rd & 6th) inf bde (each: 3 inf bn, 1 arty regt, 1 (Canon) AT gp), 1 cbt engr bde (3 engr bn))
3 (1st, 4th & 5th) indep lt inf bde (2 lt inf bn, 1 (Canon) AT gp)
92 indep inf bn
25 indep inf coy

Air Manoeuvre
1 para bde with (1 (GAFE) SF gp, 3 bn, 1 (Canon) AT gp)

COMBAT SUPPORT
1 indep arty regt

EQUIPMENT BY TYPE

ARMOURED FIGHTING VEHICLES
RECCE 223: 19 DN-5 *Toro*; 127 ERC-90F1 *Lynx* (7 trg); 40 M8; 37 MAC-1
IFV 390 DNC-1 (mod AMX-VCI)
APC 309
  APC (T) 73: 40 HWK-11; 33 M5A1 half-track
  APC (W) 236: 95 BDX; 16 DN-4; 2 DN-6; 28 LAV-100 (*Pantera*); 26 LAV-150 ST; 25 MOWAG *Roland*; 44 VCR (3 amb; 5 cmd post)
AUV 379: 100 DN-XI; 247 *SandCat*; 32 VBL

ENGINEERING & MAINTENANCE VEHICLES
ARV 7: 3 M32 *Recovery Sherman*; 4 VCR ARV

ANTI-TANK/ANTI-INFRASTRUCTURE
MSL • SP 8 VBL with *Milan*
RCL • 106mm 1,187+ M40A1 (incl some SP)
GUNS 37mm 30 M3

ARTILLERY 1,390
TOWED 123: 105mm 123: 40 M101; 40 M-56; 16 M2A1; 14 M3; 13 NORINCO M90
MOR 1,267: 81mm 1,100: 400 M1; 400 Brandt; 300 SB
120mm 167: 75 Brandt; 60 M-65; 32 RT-61

AIR DEFENCE • GUNS • TOWED 80: **12.7mm** 40 M55; **20mm** 40 GAI-B01

Navy 50,500

Two Fleet Commands: Gulf (6 zones), Pacific (11 zones)

EQUIPMENT BY TYPE

PRINCIPAL SURFACE COMBATANTS • FRIGATES 1

FFGHM 1 *Benito Juárez* (Damen SIGMA 10514) with 2 quad lnchr with RGM-84L *Harpoon* Block II AShM, 1 8-cell Mk 56 VLS with RIM-162 ESSM SAM, 1 21-cell Mk 49 lnchr with RIM-116C RAM Block 2 SAM, 2 triple 324mm SVTT Mk 32 ASTT with Mk 54 LWT, 1 57mm gun (capacity 1 med hel) (fitted for but not with Mk 56 VLS with RIM-162 *Evolved SeaSparrow Missile*)

PATROL AND COASTAL COMBATANTS 124

PSOH 8:
  4 *Oaxaca* with 1 76mm gun (capacity 1 AS565MB *Panther* hel)
  4 *Oaxaca* (mod) with 1 57mm gun (capacity 1 AS565MB *Panther* hel)

PCOH 16:
  4 *Durango* with 1 57mm gun (capacity 1 Bo-105 hel)
  4 *Holzinger* (capacity 1 MD-902 *Explorer*)
  3 *Sierra* with 1 57mm gun (capacity 1 MD-902 *Explorer*)
  5 *Uribe* (ESP *Halcon*) (capacity 1 Bo-105 hel)

PCO 9: 6 *Valle* (US *Auk* MSF) with 1 76mm gun; 3 *Valle* (US *Auk* MSF) with 1 76mm gun, 1 hel landing platform

PCGH 1 *Huracan* (ex-ISR *Aliya*) with 4 single lnchr with *Gabriel* II AShM, 1 Mk 15 *Phalanx* CIWS

PCC 2 *Democrata*

PBF 72: 6 *Acuario*; 2 *Acuario B*; 48 *Polaris* (SWE CB90); 16 *Polaris* II (SWE IC 16M)

PB 16: 3 *Azteca*; 3 *Cabo* (ex-US *Cape Higgon*); 10 *Tenochtitlan* (Damen Stan Patrol 4207)

AMPHIBIOUS • LANDING SHIPS

LST 4: 2 *Monte Azule*s with 1 hel landing platform; 1 *Papaloapan* (ex-US *Newport*) with 2 twin 76mm guns, 1 hel landing platform; 1 *Papaloapan* (ex-US *Newport*) with 1 hel landing platform

LOGISTICS AND SUPPORT 25

AGOR 3: 2 *Altair* (ex-US *Robert D. Conrad*); 1 *Río Tecolutla*

AGS 8: 5 *Arrecife*; 1 *Onjuku*; 1 *Río Hondo*; 1 *Río Tuxpan*

AK 1 *Río Suchiate*

AOL 2 *Aguascalientes*

AP 1 *Isla María Madre* (Damen Fast Crew Supplier 5009)

ARS 4 *Kukulkan*

ATF 3 *Otomi* with 1 76mm gun

AX 2 *Huasteco* (also serve as troop transport, supply and hospital ships)

AXS 1 *Cuauhtemoc*

Naval Aviation 1,250

FORCES BY ROLE

MARITIME PATROL

2 flt with CN235-300 MPA *Persuader*

ISR

1 flt with Beech 350ER *King Air*

1 flt with Z-143Lsi

TRANSPORT

1 (VIP) sqn with AW109SP; Beech 350i *King Air*; CL-605 *Challenger*; DHC-8 *Dash 8*; Gulfstream 550; Learjet 31A; Learjet 60

1 flt with C295M/W

TRAINING

1 sqn with Schweizer 300C; S-333; Z-242L

1 flt with MX-7-180 *Star Rocket*

3 flt with T-6C+ *Texan* II

SEARCH & RESCUE HELICOPTER

4 flt with AS565MB *Panther*; AS565MBe *Panther*

TRANSPORT HELICOPTER

6 flt with Mi-17-1V/V-5 *Hip*

2 flt with UH-60M *Black Hawk*

1 flt with H225M *Caracal*

EQUIPMENT BY TYPE

AIRCRAFT

MP 6 CN235-300 MPA *Persuader*

ISR 2 Z-143Lsi

TPT 20: **Light** 18: 5 Beech 350ER *King Air* (4 used for ISR); 3 Beech 350i *King Air*; 4 C295M; 2 C295W; 1 DHC-8 *Dash 8*; 2 Learjet 31A; 1 Learjet 60; **PAX** 2: 1 CL-605 *Challenger*; 1 Gulfstream 550

TRG 46: 7 MX-7-180 *Star Rocket*; 13 T-6C+ *Texan* II; 26 Z-242L

HELICOPTERS

MRH 19: 15 Mi-17-1V *Hip*; 4 Mi-17V-5 *Hip*

SAR 14: 4 AS565MB *Panther*; 10 AS565MBe *Panther*

TPT 22: **Heavy** 3 H225M *Caracal*; **Medium** 10: 2 H225 (SAR role); 8 UH-60M *Black Hawk*; **Light** 9: 1 AW109SP; 8 S-333

TRG 4 Schweizer 300C

Marines 21,500

FORCES BY ROLE

SPECIAL FORCES

3 SF unit

MANOEUVRE

Light

32 inf bn(-)

Air Manoeuvre

1 AB bn

Amphibious

1 amph bde (4 inf bn, 1 amph bn, 1 arty gp)

Other

1 (Presidential) gd bn (included in army above)

COMBAT SERVICE SUPPORT

2 spt bn

EQUIPMENT BY TYPE

ARMOURED FIGHTING VEHICLES

APC • APC (W) 29: 3 BTR-60 (APC-60); 26 BTR-70

(APC-70)

ANTI-TANK/ANTI-INFRASTRUCTURE
  RCL 106mm M40A1
ARTILLERY 22+
  TOWED 105mm 16 M-56
  MRL 122mm 6 *Firos*-25
  MOR 81mm some
AIR DEFENCE • SAM • Point-defence 9K38 *Igla* (RS-SA-18 *Grouse*)

Air Force 8,000

FORCES BY ROLE
FIGHTER
  1 sqn with F-5E/F *Tiger* II
GROUND ATTACK/ISR
  4 sqn with T-6C+ *Texan* II*
  1 sqn with PC-7*
ISR/AEW
  1 sqn with Beech 350ER *King Air*; EMB-145AEW *Erieye*; EMB-145RS
TRANSPORT
  1 sqn with C295M; PC-6B
  1 sqn with B-737; Beech 90 *King Air*
  1 sqn with C-27J *Spartan*; C-130K-30 *Hercules*; L-100-30
  5 (liaison) sqn with Cessna 182
  1 (anti-narcotic spraying) sqn with Bell 206
  1 (Presidential) gp with AW109SP; B-737; B-787; Gulfstream 150/450/550; H225; Learjet 35A; Learjet 36; *Turbo Commander* 680
  1 (VIP) gp with B-737; Beech 200 *King Air*; Beech 350i *King Air*; CL-605 *Challenger*; Gulfstream 550; Learjet 35A; S-70A-24 *Black Hawk*
TRAINING
  1 sqn with Cessna 182
  1 sqn with PC-7; T-6C+ *Texan* II
  1 sqn with Grob G120TP
TRANSPORT HELICOPTER
  4 sqn with Bell 206B; Bell 407GX
  1 (anti-narcotic spraying) sqn with Bell 206
  1 sqn with MD-530MF/MG
  1 sqn with Mi-17 *Hip*
  1 sqn with H225M *Caracal*; Bell 412EP *Twin Huey*; S-70A-24 *Black Hawk*
  1 sqn with UH-60M *Black Hawk*
ISR UAV
  1 unit with *Hermes* 450; *Hermes* 900; S4 *Ehécatl*

EQUIPMENT BY TYPE
AIRCRAFT 80 combat capable
  FTR 5: 4 F-5E *Tiger* II; 1 F-5F *Tiger* II
  ISR 2 Cessna 501 *Citation*
  ELINT 8: 6 Beech 350ER *King Air*; 2 EMB-145RS
  AEW&C 1 EMB-145AEW *Erieye*
  TPT 96: **Medium** 7: 4 C-27J *Spartan*; 2 C-130K-30 *Hercules*; 1 L-100-30; **Light** 78: 2 Beech 90 *King Air*; 1 Beech 200 *King Air*; 1 Beech 350i *King Air*; 6 C295M; 2 C295W; 59 Cessna 182; 2 Learjet 35A; 1 Learjet 36; 3 PC-6B; 1 *Turbo Commander* 680; **PAX** 11: 5 B-737; 1 B-787; 1 CL-605 *Challenger*; 2 Gulfstream 150; 1 Gulfstream 450; 1 Gulfstream 550
  TRG 100: 25 Grob G120TP; 20 PC-7* (30 more possibly in store); 55 T-6C+ *Texan* II*
HELICOPTERS
  MRH 40: 14 Bell 407GXP; 11 Bell 412EP *Twin Huey*; 15 Mi-17 *Hip* H
  ISR 11: 3 MD-530MF; 8 MD-530MG
  TPT 95: **Heavy** 12 H225M *Caracal*; **Medium** 24: 1 H225 (VIP); 6 S-70A-24 *Black Hawk*; 17 UH-60M *Black Hawk*; **Light** 59: 5 AW109SP; 45 Bell 206; 1 Bell 206B *Jet Ranger* II; 8 Bell 206L
UNINHABITED AERIAL VEHICLES • ISR 9: **Medium** 4: 3 *Hermes* 450; 1 *Hermes* 900; **Light** 5 S4 *Ehécatl*

Gendarmerie & Paramilitary 136,900

Federal Ministerial Police 4,500

EQUIPMENT BY TYPE
HELICOPTERS
  TPT • Light 25: 18 Bell 205 (UH-1H); 7 Bell 212
UNINHABITED AERIAL VEHICLES
  ISR • Heavy 2 *Dominator* XP

National Guard 115,000

Public Security Secretariat. Gendarmerie created in 2019 from elements of the Army, Navy, Air Force and Federal Police

FORCES BY ROLE
MANOEUVRE
  Other
    12 sy bde (3 sy bn)
EQUIPMENT BY TYPE
HELICOPTERS
  MRH 5: 1+ Bell 407GX; 4 Mi-17 *Hip* H
  TPT • Medium 7 UH-60M *Black Hawk*

Rural Defense Militia 17,400

FORCES BY ROLE
MANOEUVRE
  Light
    13 inf unit
    13 (horsed) cav unit

DEPLOYMENT

CENTRAL AFRICAN REPUBLIC: UN • MINUSCA 2
WESTERN SAHARA: UN • MINURSO 4

Nicaragua NIC

Nicaraguan Gold Cordoba NIO		2022	2023	2024
GDP	NIO	562bn	632bn	685bn
	USD	15.7bn	17.4bn	18.6bn
per capita	USD	2,372	2,599	2,762
Growth	%	3.8	3.0	3.3
Inflation	%	10.5	9.1	5.0
Def bdgt	NIO	3.01bn	3.46bn	
	USD	83.8m	94.9m	
USD1=NIO		35.88	36.41	36.78

Real-terms defence budget trend (USDm, constant 2015)

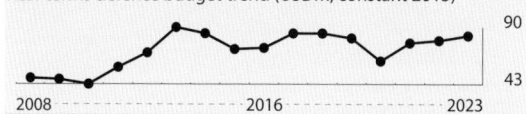

Population	6,613,274					
Age	0–14	15–19	20–24	25–29	30–64	65 plus
Male	13.0%	4.5%	4.6%	4.8%	19.6%	2.6%
Female	12.5%	4.4%	4.5%	4.8%	21.6%	3.2%

Capabilities

Nicaragua's armed forces are primarily a territorial light-infantry force, with limited coastal-patrol capability. They are tasked with border and internal security, and supporting disaster relief efforts and ecological protection. Nicaragua has renewed its training relationship with Russia and has been expanding ties with China and Iran. Training is largely focused on internal- and border-security tasks, although the mechanised brigade has received Russian training. The armed forces do not undertake significant deployments abroad and lack the logistical support for large-scale military operations, although the mechanised brigade can deploy internally. Equipment primarily consists of ageing Cold War-era platforms. Russia has supplied some second-hand tanks and armoured vehicles to help re-equip the mechanised brigade and has supported the establishment of a repair workshop to maintain the vehicles in-country. The country has no defence industry.

ACTIVE 12,000 (Army 10,000 Navy 800 Air 1,200)

ORGANISATIONS BY SERVICE

Army ε10,000
FORCES BY ROLE
SPECIAL FORCES
  1 SF bde (2 SF bn)
MANOEUVRE
  Mechanised
  1 mech inf bde (1 armd recce bn, 1 tk bn, 1 mech inf bn, 1 arty bn, 1 MRL bn, 1 AT coy)
  Light
  1 regional comd (3 lt inf bn)
  1 regional comd (2 lt inf bn; 1 arty bn)
  3 regional comd (2 lt inf bn)
  2 indep lt inf bn

Other
  1 comd regt (1 inf bn, 1 sy bn, 1 int unit, 1 sigs bn)
  1 (ecological) sy bn
COMBAT SUPPORT
  1 engr bn
COMBAT SERVICE SUPPORT
  1 med bn
  1 tpt regt
EQUIPMENT BY TYPE
ARMOURED FIGHTING VEHICLES
  MBT 82: 62 T-55 (65 more in store); 20 T-72B1MS
  LT TK (10 PT-76 in store)
  RECCE 20 BRDM-2
  IFV 17+ BMP-1
  APC • APC (W) 90+: 41 BTR-152 (61 more in store); 45 BTR-60 (15 more in store); 4+ BTR-70M
ENGINEERING & MAINTENANCE VEHICLES
  AEV IMR
  VLB TMM-3
ANTI-TANK/ANTI-INFRASTRUCTURE
  MSL
    SP 12 9P133 *Malyutka* (RS-AT-3 *Sagger*)
    MANPATS 9K11 *Malyutka* (RS-AT-3 *Sagger*)
  RCL 82mm B-10
  GUNS 281: **57mm** 174 ZIS-2; (90 more in store); **76mm** 83 ZIS-3; **100mm** 24 M-1944
ARTILLERY 766
  TOWED 12: **122mm** 12 D-30; (**152mm** 30 D-20 in store)
  MRL 151: **107mm** 33 Type-63; **122mm** 118: 18 BM-21 *Grad*; 100 *Grad* 1P (BM-21P) (single-tube rocket launcher, man portable)
  MOR 603: **82mm** 579; **120mm** 24 M-43; (**160mm** 4 M-160 in store)
AIR DEFENCE • SAM • Point-defence 9K36 *Strela*-3 (RS-SA-14 *Gremlin*); 9K310 *Igla*-1 (RS-SA-16 *Gimlet*); 9K32 *Strela*-2 (RS-SA-7 *Grail*)‡

Navy ε800
EQUIPMENT BY TYPE
PATROL AND COASTAL COMBATANTS 13
  PB 13: 3 *Dabur*; 2 *Farallones*; 4 Rodman 101; 2 *Soberanía* (ex-JAM Damen Stan Patrol 4207); 2 (patrol/support)

Marines
FORCES BY ROLE
MANOEUVRE
  Amphibious
  1 mne bn

Air Force 1,200
FORCES BY ROLE
TRANSPORT
  1 sqn with An-26 *Curl*; Beech 90 *King Air*; Cessna U206; Cessna 404 *Titan* (VIP)

TRAINING
    1 unit with Cessna 172; PA-18 *Super Cub*; PA-28 *Cherokee*

TRANSPORT HELICOPTER
    1 sqn with Mi-17 *Hip H* (armed)

AIR DEFENCE
    1 gp with ZU-23

EQUIPMENT BY TYPE

AIRCRAFT
    TPT • Light 9: 3 An-26 *Curl*; 1 Beech 90 *King Air*; 1 Cessna 172; 1 Cessna U206; 1 Cessna 404 *Titan* (VIP); 2 PA-28 *Cherokee*
    TRG 2 PA-18 *Super Cub*

HELICOPTERS
    MRH 7 Mi-17 *Hip H* (armed)†
    TPT • Medium 2 Mi-171E

AIR DEFENCE • GUNS 23mm 18 ZU-23

AIR-LAUNCHED MISSILES • ASM 9M17 *Skorpion* (RS-AT-2 *Swatter*)

Panama PAN

Panamanian Balboa PAB		2022	2023	2024
GDP	PAB	76.5bn	82.3bn	87.2bn
	USD	76.5bn	82.3bn	87.2bn
per capita	USD	17,410	18,493	19,346
Growth	%	10.8	6.0	4.0
Inflation	%	2.9	1.5	1.9
Def bdgt [a]	PAB	847m	903m	
	USD	847m	903m	
USD1=PAB		1.00	1.00	1.00

[a] Public security expenditure

Real-terms defence budget trend (USDm, constant 2015): 314 (2008) to 817 (2023)

Population	4,404,108				
Age	0–14	15–19	20–24	25–29	30–64	65 plus
Male	12.9%	3.9%	3.9%	3.9%	21.1%	4.6%
Female	12.3%	3.8%	3.8%	3.8%	20.7%	5.3%

Capabilities

Panama abolished its armed forces in 1990 but retains a border service, a police force and an air/maritime service for low-level security tasks. The country's primary security focus is on the southern border with Colombia, where the majority of the border service is deployed. Colombia and the US have provided training and support, and in April 2023, all three pledged to undertake an initiative in the border area to curb illegal migration. Training is focused on internal and border security rather than conventional military operations and there is no capability to mount significant external deployments. None of Panama's security services maintain heavy military equipment, focusing instead on light-transport, patrol and surveillance capabilities. Aside from limited maintenance facilities, the country has no defence industry.

Gendarmerie & Paramilitary 27,700

ORGANISATIONS BY SERVICE

Gendarmerie & Paramilitary 27,700

National Border Service 4,000

FORCES BY ROLE

SPECIAL FORCES
    1 SF gp

MANOEUVRE
    Other
    1 sy bde (5 sy bn(-))
    1 indep sy bn

National Police Force 20,000

No hvy mil eqpt, small arms only

FORCES BY ROLE

SPECIAL FORCES
    1 SF unit

MANOEUVRE
    Other
    1 (presidential) gd bn(-)

National Aeronaval Service 3,700

FORCES BY ROLE

TRANSPORT
    1 sqn with Beech 250 *King Air*; C-212M *Aviocar*; Cessna 210; PA-31 *Navajo*; PA-34 *Seneca*
    1 (Presidential) flt with ERJ-135BJ; S-76C

TRAINING
    1 unit with Cessna 152; Cessna 172; T-35D *Pillan*

TRANSPORT HELICOPTER
    1 sqn with AW139; Bell 205; Bell 205 (UH-1H *Iroquois*); Bell 212; Bell 407; Bell 412EP; H145; MD-500E

EQUIPMENT BY TYPE

PATROL AND COASTAL COMBATANTS 16
    PCC 1 *Saettia*
    PB 15: 5 *3 De Noviembre* (ex-US *Point*); 1 *Chiriqui* (ex-US PB MkIV); 1 *Cocle* (ex-US Swift); 1 *Omar Torrijos* (US Metal Shark Defiant 85); 2 *Panquiaco* (UK Vosper 31.5m); 1 *Taboga* (log/tpt role); 4 Type-200

AMPHIBIOUS • LANDING CRAFT 1
    LCU 1 *General Estaban Huertas*

LOGISTICS AND SUPPORT 2
    AG 1 *Lina María*
    AKR 1 *Manuel Amador Guerror* (Damen Stan Lander 5612)

AIRCRAFT
    TPT • Light 17: 1 Beech 100 *King Air*; 1 Beech 250 *King Air*; 1 Beech 350 *King Air*; 2 DHC-6-400 *Twin Otter*; 3 C-212M *Aviocar*; 1 Cessna 152, 1 Cessna 172; 2 Cessna 208B; 1 Cessna 210; 1 ERJ-135BJ; 1 PA-31

Navajo; 2 PA-34 Seneca
    TRG (2 T-35D Pillan in store)
    HELICOPTERS
        MRH 10: 8 AW139; 1 Bell 412EP; 1 MD-500E
        TPT • Light 5: 1 AW109; 2 Bell 212; 2 Bell 407

Paraguay PRY

Paraguayan Guarani PYG		2022	2023	2024
GDP	PYG	291trn	320trn	344trn
	USD	41.7bn	44.1bn	46.7bn
per capita	USD	5,598	5,843	6,095
Growth	%	0.1	4.5	3.8
Inflation	%	9.8	4.7	4.1
Def bdgt	PYG	1.95trn	2.17trn	
	USD	279m	300m	
USD1=PYG		6,982.80	7,244.06	7,366.01

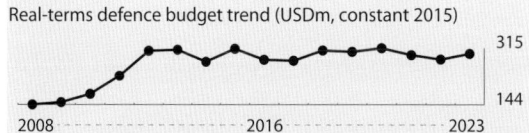

Real-terms defence budget trend (USDm, constant 2015)

315

144

2008   2016   2023

Population   7,439,863

Age	0–14	15–19	20–24	25–29	30–64	65 plus
Male	11.4%	3.9%	4.1%	4.6%	21.8%	4.3%
Female	11.0%	3.8%	4.1%	4.6%	21.6%	4.7%

Capabilities

The country's armed forces are small by regional standards, with largely obsolete equipment. Paraguay faces internal challenges from insurgency and transnational organised crime, chiefly drug trafficking. The country cooperates with Argentina and Brazil on security matters. In 2017, Paraguay signed a defence cooperation agreement with Russia. The military ranks are increasingly top-heavy and conscript numbers having fallen in recent years. Key formations have long been under-strength. Paraguay has had a consistent, if limited, tradition of contributing to UN peacekeeping operations. It only has a limited ability to self-sustain forces abroad and no effective power-projection capacity. The government maintains a small force of river-patrol craft. Armoured capability is very limited. Recent acquisitions of heavy equipment have been confined to small quantities of engineering and transport capabilities, as well as one single air force combat squadron. Paraguay plans to upgrade the fleet of training aircraft. The country has local maintenance capacity. It lacks a traditional defence industry, but conducts R&D and manufacturing cooperation with local research institutes.

ACTIVE 13,950 (Army 7,400 Navy 3,800 Air 2,750)
Gendarmerie & Paramilitary 14,800

Conscript liability 12 months

RESERVE 164,500 (Joint 164,500)

ORGANISATIONS BY SERVICE

Army 7,400

Much of the Paraguayan army is maintained in a cadre state during peacetime; the nominal inf and cav divs are effectively only at coy strength. Active gp/regt are usually coy sized

FORCES BY ROLE
MANOEUVRE
    Light
        3 inf corps (total: 6 inf div(-), 3 cav div(-), 6 arty bty)
    Other
        1 (Presidential) gd regt (1 SF bn, 1 inf bn, 1 sy bn, 1 log gp)
COMBAT SUPPORT
    1 arty bde with (2 arty gp, 1 ADA gp)
    1 engr bde with (1 engr regt, 3 construction regt)
    1 sigs bn

Reserves
FORCES BY ROLE
MANOEUVRE
    Light
        14 inf regt (cadre)
        4 cav regt (cadre)
EQUIPMENT BY TYPE
ARMOURED FIGHTING VEHICLES
    RECCE 28 EE-9 Cascavel
    APC • APC (W) 12 EE-11 Urutu
ARTILLERY 99
    TOWED 105mm 19 M101
    MOR 81mm 80
AIR DEFENCE • GUNS 22:
    SP 20mm 3 M9 half track
    TOWED 19: 40mm 13 M1A1, 6 L/60

Navy 3,800
EQUIPMENT BY TYPE
PATROL AND COASTAL COMBATANTS 18
    PCR 1 Itaipú (BRZ Roraima) with 1 hel landing platform
    PBR 17: 1 Capitán Cabral; 2 Capitán Ortiz (ROC Hai Ou); 2 Novatec; 4 Type-701 (US Sewart); 3 Croq 15 (AUS Armacraft); 5 others
AMPHIBIOUS • LANDING CRAFT • LCVP 3

Naval Aviation 100
FORCES BY ROLE
TRANSPORT
    1 (liaison) sqn with Cessna 150; Cessna 210 Centurion; Cessna 310
TRANSPORT HELICOPTER
    1 sqn with AS350 Ecureuil (HB350 Esquilo)
EQUIPMENT BY TYPE
    AIRCRAFT • TPT • Light 6: 2 Cessna 150; 1 Cessna 210 Centurion; 2 Cessna 310
    HELICOPTERS • TPT • Light 2 AS350 Ecureuil (HB350 Esquilo)

Marines 700; 200 conscript (total 900)

FORCES BY ROLE

MANOEUVRE

Amphibious

3 mne bn(-)

ARTILLERY • TOWED 105mm 2 M101

Air Force 2,750

FORCES BY ROLE

GROUND ATTACK/ISR

1 sqn with EMB-312 *Tucano**

TRANSPORT

1 gp with C-212-200/400 *Aviocar*; DHC-6 *Twin Otter*

1 VIP gp with Beech 58 *Baron*; Bell 427; Cessna U206 *Stationair*; Cessna 208B *Grand Caravan*; Cessna 402B; PA-32R *Saratoga* (EMB-721C *Sertanejo*)

TRAINING

1 sqn with T-25 *Universal*; T-35A/B *Pillan*

TRANSPORT HELICOPTER

1 gp with AS350 *Ecureuil* (HB350 *Esquilo*); Bell 205 (UH-1H *Iroquois*)

MANOEUVRE

Air Manoeuvre

1 AB bde

EQUIPMENT BY TYPE

AIRCRAFT 6 combat capable

TPT 18: Light 17: 1 Beech 58 *Baron*; 4 C-212-200 *Aviocar*; 1 C-212-400 *Aviocar*; 3 Cessna 208B *Grand Caravan*; 2 Cessna 208 *Grand Caravan* EX; 1 Cessna 310; 1 Cessna 402B; 2 Cessna U206 *Stationair*; 1 DHC-6 *Twin Otter*; 1 PA-32R *Saratoga* (EMB-721C *Sertanejo*); **PAX** 1 Cessna 680 *Sovereign*

TRG 21: 6 EMB-312 *Tucano**; 6 T-25 *Universal*; 6 T-35A *Pillan*; 3 T-35B *Pillan*

HELICOPTERS • TPT • Light 17: 3 AS350 *Ecureuil* (HB350 *Esquilo*); 12 Bell 205 (UH-1H *Iroquois*); 1 Bell 407; 1 Bell 427 (VIP)

Gendarmerie & Paramilitary 14,800

Special Police Service 10,800; 4,000 conscript (total 14,800)

DEPLOYMENT

CENTRAL AFRICAN REPUBLIC: UN • MINUSCA 4

CYPRUS: UN • UNFICYP 12

DEMOCRATIC REPUBLIC OF THE CONGO: UN • MONUSCO 6

SOUTH SUDAN: UN • UNMISS 3

Peru PER

Peruvian Nuevo Sol PEN		2022	2023	2024
GDP	PEN	938bn	1.01trn	1.06trn
	USD	245bn	265bn	277bn
per capita	USD	7,159	7,669	7,952
Growth	%	2.7	1.1	2.7
Inflation	%	7.9	6.5	2.9
Def bdgt	PEN	6.98bn	7.31bn	7.97bn
	USD	1.82bn	1.92bn	2.08bn
FMA (US)	USD	6m	0m	0m
USD1=PEN		3.83	3.81	3.83

Real-terms defence budget trend (USDbn, constant 2015)

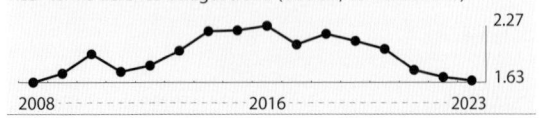

2.27

1.63

2008   2016   2023

Population	32,440,172					
Age	0–14	15–19	20–24	25–29	30–64	65 plus
Male	13.3%	4.3%	3.9%	3.8%	20.3%	3.5%
Female	12.8%	4.1%	3.8%	3.9%	21.8%	4.5%

Capabilities

Peru's armed forces are primarily orientated towards preserving territorial integrity and security, focusing on counter-insurgency and counter-narcotics operations. The military is working on strengthening its disaster-relief capabilities. The armed forces are hampered by fiscal constraints and an increasingly ageing inventory. Peru maintains close ties with Colombia, including a cooperation agreement on air control, humanitarian assistance and counter-narcotics. The armed forces train regularly and take part in national and multilateral exercises. Peru participated in the 2022 RIMPAC multinational exercise and is planning to take part in 2024. The armed forces are capable of independently deploying externally and contributing to UN missions abroad. Peru has pursued some aviation modernisation, though not across the whole fleet. It has boosted its tanker/transport and anti-submarine warfare capabilities with the acquisition of second-hand equipment from Spain. The navy is looking to acquire offshore patrol vessels, but its ageing fleet of submarines have yet to be modernised. The state-owned shipyard SIMA and aviation firm SEMAN are key players in Peru's defence industry, in terms of manufacturing and maintenance.

ACTIVE 81,000 (Army 47,500 Navy 24,000 Air 9,500)
Gendarmerie & Paramilitary 77,000

Conscript liability 12 months voluntary conscription for both males and females

RESERVE 188,000 (Army 188,000)

ORGANISATIONS BY SERVICE

Space

EQUIPMENT BY TYPE

SATELLITES • ISR PéruSAT-1

Army 47,500

4 mil region

FORCES BY ROLE
SPECIAL FORCES
1 (1st) SF bde (2 spec ops bn, 2 cdo bn, 1 cdo coy, 1 CT coy, 1 airmob arty gp, 1 MP coy, 1 cbt spt bn)
1 (3rd) SF bde (1 spec ops bn, 2 cdo bn, 1 airmob arty gp, 1 MP coy)
1 (6th) SF bde (2 spec ops bn, 2 cdo bn, 1 cdo coy, 1 MP coy)

MANOEUVRE
Armoured
1 (3rd) armd bde (2 tk bn, 1 mech inf bn, 1 arty gp, 1 AT coy, 1 cbt engr bn, 1 cbt spt bn, 1 AD gp)
1 (6th) armd bde (2 tk bn, 1 mech inf bn, 1 cbt engr bn, 1 log bn, 1 ADA gp)
1 (9th) armd bde (2 tk bn, 1 mech inf bn, 1 SP arty gp, 1 ADA gp)

Mechanised
1 (3rd) armd cav bde (3 mech cav bn, 1 mot inf bn, 1 arty gp, 1 AD gp, 1 engr bn, 1 cbt spt bn)
1 (1st) cav bde (4 mech cav bn, 1 MP coy, 1 cbt spt bn)

Light
2 (2nd & 31st) mot inf bde (4 mot inf bn, 1 arty gp, 1 MP coy, 1 log bn)
3 (1st, 7th & 32nd) inf bde (3 inf bn, 1 MP coy, 1 cbt spt bn)
1 (33rd) inf bde (4 inf bn)
1 (4th) mtn bde (1 armd regt, 3 mot inf bn, 1 arty gp, 1 MP coy, 1 cbt spt bn)
1 (5th) mtn bde (1 armd regt, 2 mot inf bn, 3 jungle coy, 1 arty gp, 1 MP coy, 1 cbt spt bn)
1 (6th) jungle inf bde (4 jungle bn, 1 engr bn, 1 MP coy, 1 cbt spt bn)
1 (35th) jungle inf bde (1 SF gp, 3 jungle bn, 3 jungle coy, 1 jungle arty gp, 1 AT coy, 1 AD gp, 1 jungle engr bn)

COMBAT SUPPORT
1 arty gp (bde) (4 arty gp, 2 AD gp, 1 sigs gp)
1 (3rd) arty bde (4 arty gp, 1 AD gp, 1 sigs gp)
1 (22nd) engr bde (3 engr bn, 1 demining coy)

COMBAT SERVICE SUPPORT
1 (1st Multipurpose) spt bde

AVIATION
1 (1st) avn bde (1 atk hel/recce hel bn, 1 avn bn, 2 aslt hel/tpt hel bn)

AIR DEFENCE
1 AD gp (regional troops)

EQUIPMENT BY TYPE
ARMOURED FIGHTING VEHICLES
MBT 165 T-55; (75† in store)
LT TK 96 AMX-13 (some with 9M133 *Kornet*-E)
RECCE 95: 30 BRDM-2; 15 Fiat 6616; 50 M9A1
APC 295
  APC (T) 120+: 120 M113A1; some BTR-50 (CP)†
  APC (W) 175: 150 UR-416; 25 Fiat 6614

ENGINEERING & MAINTENANCE VEHICLES
ARV M578
VLB GQL-111

ANTI-TANK-ANTI-INFRASTRUCTURE
MSL
  SP 22 M1165A2 HMMWV with 9K135 *Kornet* E (RS-AT-14 *Spriggan*)
  MANPATS 9K11 *Malyutka* (RS-AT-3 *Sagger*); HJ-73C; 9K135 *Kornet* E (RS-AT-14 *Spriggan*); *Spike*-ER
RCL 106mm M40A1

ARTILLERY 1,025
SP 155mm 12 M109A2
TOWED 290: **105mm** 152: 44 M101; 24 M2A1; 60 M-56; 24 Model 56 pack howitzer; **122mm**; 36 D-30; **130mm** 36 M-46; **155mm** 66: 36 M114, 30 Model 50
MRL 122mm 49: 22 BM-21 *Grad*; 27 Type-90B
MOR 674+: **81mm/107mm** 350; **SP 107mm** 24 M106A1; **120mm** 300+ Brandt/Expal Model L

PATROL AND COASTAL COMBATANTS • PBR 1
Vargas Guerra

AIRCRAFT
TPT • Light 17: 2 An-28 *Cash*; 3 An-32B *Cline*; 1 Beech 350 *King Air*; 1 Beech 1900D; 4 Cessna 152; 1 Cessna 208 *Caravan*; 1 Cessna 560 *Citation*; 2 Cessna U206 *Stationair*; 1 PA-31T *Cheyenne* II; 1 PA-34 *Seneca*
TRG 4 IL-103

HELICOPTERS
MRH 7 Mi-17 *Hip* H
TPT 33: **Heavy** (3 Mi-26T *Halo* in store); **Medium** 21 Mi-171Sh; **Light** 12: 1 AW109K2; 9 PZL Mi-2 *Hoplite*; 2 R-44
TRG 4 F-28F

AIR DEFENCE
SAM • Point-defence 9K36 *Strela*-3 (RS-SA-14 *Gremlin*); 9K310 *Igla*-1 (RS-SA-16 *Gimlet*); 9K32 *Strela*-2 (RS-SA-7 *Grail*)‡
GUNS 165
  SP 23mm 35 ZSU-23-4
  TOWED 23mm 130: 80 ZU-23-2; 50 ZU-23

Navy 24,000 (incl 1,000 Coast Guard)

Commands: Pacific, Lake Titicaca, Amazon River

EQUIPMENT BY TYPE
SUBMARINES • SSK 6:
4 *Angamos* (GER Type-209/1200) with 8 single 533mm TT with SST-4 HWT (of which 1 in refit)
2 *Islay* (GER Type-209/1100) with 8 single 533mm TT with SUT 264 HWT

PRINCIPAL SURFACE COMBATANTS • FRIGATES 6
FFGHM 6:
2 *Aguirre* (ex-ITA *Lupo*) with 8 single lnchr with *Otomat* Mk2 AShM, 1 octuple Mk 29 lnchr with RIM-7P *Sea Sparrow* SAM, 2 triple 324mm ASTT with A244 LWT, 1 127mm gun (capacity 1 Bell 212 (AB-212)/SH-3D *Sea King*)
2 *Aguirre* (ex-ITA *Lupo*) with 2 twin lnchr with MM40 *Exocet* Block 3 AShM, 1 octuple Mk 29 lnchr with

RIM-7P *Sea Sparrow* SAM, 2 triple 324mm ASTT with A244 LWT, 1 127mm gun (capacity 1 Bell 212 (AB-212)/SH-3D *Sea King*)

2 *Carvajal* (ITA *Lupo* mod) with 2 twin lnchr with MM40 *Exocet* Block 3 AShM, 1 octuple *Albatros* lnchr with *Aspide* SAM, 2 triple 324mm ASTT with A244 LWT, 1 127mm gun (capacity 1 Bell 212 (AB-212)/SH-3D *Sea King*)

PATROL AND COASTAL COMBATANTS 13

CORVETTES 7

FSG 5 *Velarde* (FRA PR-72 64m) with 4 single lnchr with MM38 *Exocet* AShM, 1 76mm gun

FS 2 *Ferré* (ex-ROK *Po Hang*) with 1 76mm gun

PCR 6: 2 *Amazonas* with 1 76mm gun; 2 *Manuel Clavero*; 2 *Marañon* with 2 76mm guns

AMPHIBIOUS

PRINCIPAL AMPHIBIOUS SHIPS • LPD 1 *Pisco* (IDN *Makassar*) (capacity 2 LCM; 3 hels; 24 IFV; 450 troops)

LANDING SHIPS • LST 1 *Paita* (capacity 395 troops) (ex-US *Terrebonne Parish*)

LANDING CRAFT • UCAC 7 *Griffon* 2000TD (capacity 22 troops)

LOGISTICS AND SUPPORT 24

AG 6 *Río Napo*
AGOR 1 *Humboldt* (operated by IMARPE)
AGORH 1 *Carrasco*
AGS 5: 1 *Zimic* (ex-NLD *Dokkum*); 2 *Van Straelen*; 1 *La Macha*, 1 *Stiglich* (river survey vessel for the upper Amazon)
AH 4 (river hospital craft)
AOL 2 *Noguera*
AORH 1 *Tacna* (ex-NLD *Amsterdam*)
ATF 1 *Morales*
AWT 1 *Caloyeras*
AXS 2: 1 *Marte*; 1 *Unión*

Naval Aviation ε800

FORCES BY ROLE

ANTI-SUBMARINE WARFARE

1 sqn with Bell 206B *Jet Ranger* II; Bell 212 ASW (AB-212 ASW); SH-2G *Super Seasprite*

1 sqn with SH-3D *Sea King*; UH-3H *Sea King*

MARITIME PATROL

1 sqn with Beech 200T; Fokker 50; Fokker 60

SEARCH & RESCUE

1 flt with Bell 412SP

TRANSPORT

1 flt with An-32B *Cline*; Mi-8T *Hip*

TRAINING

1 sqn with T-34C/C-1 *Turbo Mentor*

1 hel sqn with F-28F

EQUIPMENT BY TYPE

AIRCRAFT

MP 6: 4 Beech 200T; 2 Fokker 60
SIGINT 1 Fokker 50
MP 1 Fokker 50
TPT • Light 4: 2 An-32B *Cline*; 2 Fokker 60
TRG 3: 2 T-34C *Turbo Mentor*; 1 T-34C-1 *Turbo Mentor*

HELICOPTERS

ASW 16: 2 Bell 212 ASW (AB-212 ASW); 5 SH-2G *Super Seasprite*; 9 SH-3D *Sea King*
MRH 3 Bell 412SP
TPT 10: **Medium** 7: 1 Mi-8T *Hip*; 6 UH-3H *Sea King*; **Light** 3 Bell 206B *Jet Ranger* II
TRG 5 F-28F

MSL

ASM AGM-65D *Maverick*
AShM AM39 *Exocet*

Marines 4,000

FORCES BY ROLE

SPECIAL FORCES

3 cdo gp

MANOEUVRE

Light

2 inf bn

1 inf gp

Amphibious

1 mne bde (1 SF gp, 1 recce bn, 2 inf bn, 1 amph bn, 1 arty gp)

Jungle

1 jungle inf bn

EQUIPMENT BY TYPE

ARMOURED FIGHTING VEHICLES

APC • APC (W) 47+: 32 LAV II; V-100 *Commando*; 15 V-200 *Chaimite*
AUV 7 RAM Mk3

ANTI-TANK/ANTI-INFRASTRUCTURE

RCL 84mm *Carl Gustaf*; **106mm** M40A1

ARTILLERY 18+

TOWED 122mm D-30
MOR 18+: **81mm** some; **120mm** ε18

AIR DEFENCE • GUNS 20mm SP (twin)

Air Force 9,500

Divided into five regions – North, Lima, South, Central and Amazon

FORCES BY ROLE

FIGHTER

1 sqn with MiG-29S/SE *Fulcrum* C; MiG-29UBM *Fulcrum* B

FIGHTER/GROUND ATTACK

1 sqn with *Mirage* 2000E/ED (2000P/DP)

2 sqn with A-37B *Dragonfly*

1 sqn with Su-25A *Frogfoot* A; Su-25UBK *Frogfoot* B

ISR

1 (photo-survey) sqn with Learjet 36A; SA-227-BC *Metro* III (C-26B)

TRANSPORT

1 sqn with B-737; An-32 *Cline*

1 sqn with DHC-6 *Twin Otter*; DHC-6-400 *Twin Otter*; PC-6 *Turbo Porter*
1 sqn with L-100-20

TRAINING
2 (drug interdiction) sqn with EMB-312 *Tucano*
1 sqn with MB-339A*
1 sqn with Z-242
1 hel sqn with Enstrom 280FX; Schweizer 300C

ATTACK HELICOPTER
1 sqn with Mi-25†/Mi-35P *Hind*

TRANSPORT HELICOPTER
1 sqn with Mi-17-1V *Hip*
1 sqn with Bell 206 *Jet Ranger;* Bell 212 (AB-212); Bell 412 *Twin Huey*
1 sqn with Bo-105LS

AIR DEFENCE
6 bn with S-125 *Pechora* (RS-SA-3 *Goa*)

EQUIPMENT BY TYPE
AIRCRAFT 60 combat capable
 FTR 19: 9 MiG-29S *Fulcrum* C; 3 MiG-29SE *Fulcrum* C; 5 MiG-29SMP *Fulcrum*; 2 MiG-29UBM *Fulcrum* B
 FGA 12: 2 *Mirage* 2000ED (2000DP); 10 *Mirage* 2000E (2000P) (some†)
 ATK 19: 15 A-37B *Dragonfly*; 2 Su-25A *Frogfoot* A; 2 Su-25UBK *Frogfoot* B; (8 Su-25A *Frogfoot* A; 6 Su-25UBK *Frogfoot* B in store)
 ISR 5: 2 Learjet 36A; 3 SA-227-BC *Metro* III (C-26B)
 TKR/TPT 2 KC-130H *Hercules*
 TPT 37: **Medium** 6: 4 C-27J *Spartan*; 2 L-100-20; **Light** 29: 4 An-32 *Cline*; 7 Cessna 172 *Skyhawk*; 3 DHC-6 *Twin Otter*; 12 DHC-6-400 *Twin Otter*; 1 PA-44; 1 PC-6 *Turbo-Porter*; **PAX** 3: 2 B-737; 1 Learjet 45 (VIP)
 TRG 75: 8 CH-2000; 19 EMB-312 *Tucano*†; 20 KT-1P; 10 MB-339A*; 6 T-41A/D *Mescalero*; 12 Z-242
HELICOPTERS
 ATK 18: 16 Mi-25 *Hind* D†; 2 Mi-35P *Hind* E
 MRH 12: 2 Bell 412 *Twin Huey*; up to 10 Mi-17-1V *Hip*
 TPT 25: **Medium** 3 Mi-171Sh; **Light** 22: 8 Bell 206 *Jet Ranger*; 6 Bell 212 (AB-212); 6 Bo-105LS; 2 Enstrom 280FX
 TRG 4 Schweizer 300C
AIR DEFENCE • SAM
 Short-range S-125 *Pechora* (RS-SA-3 *Goa*)
 Point-defence *Javelin*
AIR-LAUNCHED MISSILES
 AAM • IR R-3 (RS-AA-2 *Atoll*)‡; R-60 (RS-AA-8 *Aphid*)‡; R-73 (RS-AA-11A *Archer*); R-550 *Magic*; **IR/SARH** R-27 (RS-AA-10 *Alamo*); **ARH** R-77 (RS-AA-12 *Adder*)
 ASM AS-30; Kh-29L (RS-AS-14A *Kedge*)
 ARM Kh-58 (RS-AS-11 *Kilter*)

Gendarmerie & Paramilitary 77,000

National Police 77,000 (100,000 reported)

EQUIPMENT BY TYPE
ARMOURED FIGHTING VEHICLES
 APC (W) 120: 20 BMR-600; 100 MOWAG *Roland*
AIRCRAFT
 TPT • Light 5: 1 An-32B *Cline*; 1 Beech 1900C; 3 Cessna 208B
HELICOPTERS
 MRH 4 Mi-17 *Hip* H
 TPT • Light 16: 5 H145; 2 Mi-171Sh; 9 UH-1H *Huey* II

General Police 43,000

Security Police 21,000

Technical Police 13,000

Coast Guard 1,000
Personnel included as part of Navy

EQUIPMENT BY TYPE
PATROL AND COASTAL COMBATANTS 44
 PCC 10: 6 *Río Pativilca* (ROK *Tae Geuk*); 4 *Río Nepeña*
 PBF 1 *Río Itaya* (SWE Combat Boat 90)
 PB 12: 6 *Chicama* (US *Dauntless*); 2 *Punta Sal* (Defiant 45); 1 *Río Chira*; 3 *Río Santa*
 PBR 21: 1 *Río Viru*; 8 *Parachique*; 12 *Zorritos*
LOGISTICS AND SUPPORT • AH 1 *Puno*
AIRCRAFT
 TPT • Light 3: 1 DHC-6 *Twin Otter*; 2 F-27 *Friendship*

Rondas Campesinas
Peasant self-defence force. Perhaps 7,000 rondas 'gp', up to pl strength, some with small arms. Deployed mainly in emergency zone

DEPLOYMENT
CENTRAL AFRICAN REPUBLIC: UN • MINUSCA 258; 1 engr coy
DEMOCRATIC REPUBLIC OF THE CONGO: UN • MONUSCO 5
LEBANON: UN • UNIFIL 1
SOUTH SUDAN: UN • UNMISS 5
SUDAN: UN • UNISFA 4

Suriname SUR

Suriname Dollar SRD		2022	2023	2024
GDP	SRD	86.5bn	136bn	179bn
	USD	3.51bn	3.54bn	3.99bn
per capita	USD	5,687	5,667	6,319
Growth	%	1.0	2.1	3.0
Inflation	%	52.4	53.3	30.9
Def bdgt	SRD	n.k.	n.k.	n.k.
	USD	n.k.	n.k.	n.k.
USD1=SRD		24.64	38.29	44.87
Population		639,759		

Age	0–14	15–19	20–24	25–29	30–64	65 plus
Male	11.6%	4.1%	4.4%	4.1%	22.4%	3.0%
Female	11.2%	3.9%	4.2%	3.9%	23.0%	4.3%

Capabilities

The armed forces are principally tasked with preserving territorial integrity. They also assist the police in internal- and border-security missions, as well as tackling transnational criminal activity and drug trafficking, and have been involved in disaster-relief and humanitarian-assistance operations. Suriname is a member of the Caribbean Disaster Emergency Management Agency and the Caribbean Basin Security Initiative. Ties with Brazil, China, India and the US have been crucial for the supply of equipment, including a limited number of armoured vehicles and helicopters, as well as training activity. The armed forces participate in USSOUTHCOM's *Tradewinds* disaster-response exercise. The armed forces are unable to project power. Resource challenges and limited equipment serviceability mean the armed forces are constrained in providing sufficient border and coastal control and surveillance. The country lacks the capability to design and manufacture modern military equipment and has looked abroad to improve training and maintenance capacity.

ACTIVE 1,840 (Army 1,400 Navy 240 Air 200)

(All services form part of the army)

ORGANISATIONS BY SERVICE

Army 1,400
FORCES BY ROLE
MANOEUVRE
  Mechanised
    1 mech cav sqn
  Light
    1 inf bn (4 coy)
COMBAT SUPPORT
  1 MP bn (coy)
EQUIPMENT BY TYPE
ARMOURED FIGHTING VEHICLES
  RECCE 6 EE-9 *Cascavel*
  APC • APC (W) 15 EE-11 *Urutu*
ANTI-TANK/ANTI-INFRASTRUCTURE
  RCL 106mm M40A1
ARTILLERY • MOR 81mm 6

Navy ε240
EQUIPMENT BY TYPE
PATROL AND COASTAL COMBATANTS 4
  PB 3: 2 FPB 72 Mk II; 1 FPB 98 Mk I
  PBR 1 Project 414

Air Force ε200
EQUIPMENT BY TYPE
HELICOPTERS • MRH 3 SA316B *Alouette* III (*Chetak*)

Trinidad and Tobago TTO

Trinidad and Tobago Dollar TTD		2022	2023	2024
GDP	TTD	203bn	188bn	200bn
	USD	30.1bn	27.9bn	29.6bn
per capita	USD	21,253	19,622	20,739
Growth	%	1.5	2.5	2.2
Inflation	%	5.8	5.4	2.9
Def bdgt	TTD	3.25bn	3.46bn	3.92bn
	USD	481m	512m	580m
USD1=TTD		6.75	6.75	6.75

Real-terms defence budget trend (USDm, constant 2015): 949 high, 340 low, 2008–2023.

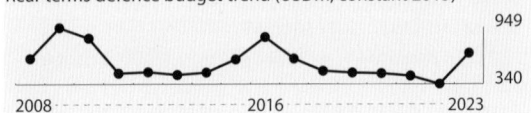

| Population | | 1,407,460 | | | | | |

Age	0–14	15–19	20–24	25–29	30–64	65 plus
Male	9.7%	3.4%	3.2%	3.2%	24.5%	6.3%
Female	9.3%	3.2%	3.0%	2.9%	23.9%	7.3%

Capabilities

The Trinidad and Tobago Defence Force (TTDF) focuses on border protection and maritime security, as well as counter-narcotics tasks. It is also tasked with cooperating with police and aiding in disasters. Trinidad and Tobago is a member of the Caribbean Community and cooperates with other countries in the region in disaster-relief efforts. There are plans to establish a joint training academy in Trinidad and a proposal for a new coastguard base in Tobago. The TTDF has taken part in US SOUTHCOM's *Tradewinds* disaster-response exercise and has sent personnel to the US and the UK for training. Trinidad and Tobago has no capacity to deploy and maintain troops abroad. It has limited maintenance facilities, including for its coast guard vessels, but no defence industry.

ACTIVE 4,650 (Army 3,000 Coast Guard 1,600 Air Guard 50)

(All services form the Trinidad and Tobago Defence Force)

RESERVE 650

ORGANISATIONS BY SERVICE

Army ε3,000
FORCES BY ROLE
SPECIAL FORCES
  1 SF unit
MANOEUVRE
  Light
    2 inf bn
COMBAT SUPPORT
  1 engr bn
COMBAT SERVICE SUPPORT
  1 log bn
EQUIPMENT BY TYPE
ANTI-TANK/ANTI-INFRASTRUCTURE
  RCL 84mm *Carl Gustaf*
ARTILLERY • MOR 81mm 6 L16A1

Coast Guard 1,600
FORCES BY ROLE
COMMAND
  1 mne HQ
EQUIPMENT BY TYPE
PATROL AND COASTAL COMBATANTS 17
  PCO 3: 2 *Port of Spain* (AUS *Cape*); 1 *Nelson* II (ex-PRC *Shuke* III)
  PCC 6: 2 *Point Lisas* (Damen Fast Crew Supplier 5009); 4 *Speyside* (Damen Stan Patrol 5009)
  PB 8: 2 *Gaspar Grande*†; 6 *Scarlet Ibis* (Austal 30m)

Air Guard 50
EQUIPMENT BY TYPE
AIRCRAFT
  TPT • Light 2 SA-227 *Metro* III (C-26)
HELICOPTERS
  MRH 4 AW139
  TPT • Light 1 S-76

Uruguay URY

Uruguayan Peso UYU		2022	2023	2024
GDP	UYU	2.93trn	3.08trn	3.36trn
	USD	71.2bn	76.2bn	81.1bn
per capita	USD	20,022	21,378	22,659
Growth	%	4.9	1.0	3.3
Inflation	%	9.1	6.1	5.9
Def bdgt	UYU	22.9bn	23.2bn	
	USD	556m	573m	
USD1=UYU		41.17	40.46	41.47

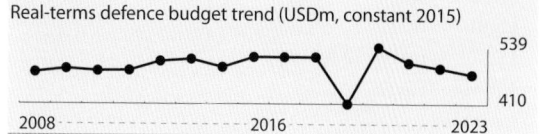

Real-terms defence budget trend (USDm, constant 2015)
539
410
2008 2016 2023

Population		3,416,264				
Age	0–14	15–19	20–24	25–29	30–64	65 plus
Male	9.7%	3.5%	3.7%	3.9%	21.4%	6.3%
Female	9.3%	3.4%	3.6%	3.8%	22.2%	9.2%

Capabilities

The armed forces are focused on assuring sovereignty, territorial integrity and the protection of strategic resources. In 2019, parliament approved a new military law, which aims, among other measures, to reduce the number of senior officers and address promotion issues across all services. Uruguay and Argentina have a joint peacekeeping unit and exercise together. Uruguay and China signed a defence-cooperation agreement in 2022, following a similar pact between Montevideo and Moscow in 2018 that provide for training exchanges. The country has long-established military ties with the US. The armed forces participate regularly in multinational exercises and deployments, notably on UN missions. The navy is being upgraded through the arrival of ex-US Coast Guard patrol boats and the planned introduction of two new offshore patrol vessels to strengthen its policing and coast guard capacities. The navy has created a tactical operations center to oversee the deployment of surface and aerial assets to combat illegal maritime activities. The service also is trying to address personnel issues, among other issues. role and is hampered by funding problems. The acquisition of air-defence radars may have improved the armed forces' ability to monitor domestic airspace, but the lack of sufficient interdiction capability will continue to limit the capacity to respond to contingencies. Much equipment is second-hand, and there is little capacity for independent power projection. Maintenance work is sometimes outsourced to foreign companies.

ACTIVE 21,100 (Army 13,500 Navy 5,000 Air 2,600)
Gendarmerie & Paramilitary 1,400

ORGANISATIONS BY SERVICE

Army 13,500

Uruguayan units are substandard size, mostly around 30%. Div are at most bde size, while bn are of reinforced coy strength. Regts are also coy size, some bn size, with the largest formation being the 2nd armd cav regt

FORCES BY ROLE
COMMAND
  4 mil region/div HQ
MANOEUVRE
  Mechanised
  2 (1st & 2nd Cav) mech bde (1 armd cav regt, 2 mech cav regt)
  1 (3rd Cav) mech bde (2 mech cav regt, 1 mech inf bn)
  3 (2nd, 3rd & 4th Inf) mech bde (2 mech inf bn; 1 inf bn)
  1 (5th Inf) mech bde (1 armd cav regt; 1 armd inf bn; 1 mech inf bn)
  Light
  1 (1st Inf) inf bde (2 inf bn)
  Air Manoeuvre
  1 para bn
COMBAT SUPPORT
  1 (strategic reserve) arty regt
  5 fd arty gp
  1 (1st) engr bde (2 engr bn)
  4 cbt engr bn
  1 sigs bde (2 sigs bn)
AIR DEFENCE
  1 AD gp
EQUIPMENT BY TYPE
ARMOURED FIGHTING VEHICLES
  MBT 15 Tiran-5
  LT TK 47: 22 M41A1UR; 25 M41C
  RECCE 15 EE-9 Cascavel
  IFV 18 BMP-1
  APC 376
    APC (T) 27: 24 M113A1UR; 3 MT-LB
    APC (W) 349: 54 Condor; 48 GAZ-39371 Vodnik; 53 OT-64; 47 OT-93; 147 Piranha
ENGINEERING & MAINTENANCE VEHICLES
  AEV MT-LB
ANTI-TANK/ANTI-INFRASTRUCTURE
  MSL • MANPATS Milan
  RCL 106mm 69 M40A1
ARTILLERY 185
  SP 122mm 6 2S1 Gvozdika
  TOWED 44: 105mm 36: 28 M101A1; 8 M102; 155mm 8 M114A1
  MOR 135: 81mm 91: 35 M1, 56 Expal Model LN; 120mm 44 Model SL
UNINHABITED AERIAL VEHICLES • ISR • Light 1 Charrua
AIR DEFENCE • GUNS • TOWED 14: 20mm 14: 6 M167 Vulcan; 8 TCM-20 (w/Elta M-2106 radar)

Navy 5,000

HQ at Montevideo
EQUIPMENT BY TYPE

PATROL AND COASTAL COMBATANTS 13
  PB 10: 1 Colonia (ex-US Cape); 9 Type-44
  PBI 3 Rio Arapey (ex-US Marine Protector)
MINE WARFARE • MINE COUNTERMEASURES 2
  MSO 2 Temerario (Kondor II)
AMPHIBIOUS 3: 2 LCVP; 1 LCM
LOGISTICS AND SUPPORT 8
  AAR 2 Islas de Flores (ex-GER Hermann Helms)
  ABU 1 Sirius
  AOR 1 Artigas (GER Freiburg, general spt ship with replenishment capabilities);
  ARS 1 Vanguardia
  ATF 1 Maldonado (also used as patrol craft)
  AXS 2: 1 Capitan Miranda; 1 Bonanza

Naval Aviation 210
FORCES BY ROLE
MARITIME PATROL
  1 flt with Beech 200T*; Cessna O-2A Skymaster
SEARCH & RESCUE/TRANSPORT HELICOPTER
  1 sqn with AS350B2 Ecureuil (Esquilo); Bell 412SP Twin Huey
TRANSPORT/TRAINING
  1 flt with T-34C Turbo Mentor
TRAINING
  1 hel sqn with Bell 412SP Twin Huey; OH-58 Kiowa
EQUIPMENT BY TYPE
AIRCRAFT 2 combat capable
  ISR 4: 2 Beech 200T*; 2 Cessna O-2A Skymaster
  TRG 2 T-34C Turbo Mentor
HELICOPTERS
  ISR 1 OH-58 Kiowa
  MRH 4: 2 Bell 412 (AB-412); 2 Bell 412SP Twin Huey
  TPT • Light 1 AS350B2 Ecureuil (Esquilo)

Naval Infantry 700
FORCES BY ROLE
MANOEUVRE
  Amphibious
  1 mne bn(-)

Air Force 2,600
FORCES BY ROLE
FIGHTER/GROUND ATTACK
  1 sqn with A-37B Dragonfly
ISR
  1 flt with EMB-110 Bandeirante†
TRANSPORT
  1 sqn with C-130B Hercules; C-212 Aviocar; EMB-120 Brasilia
  1 (liaison) sqn with Cessna 206H; T-41D
  1 (liaison) flt with Cessna 206H
TRAINING
  1 sqn with PC-7U Turbo Trainer

1 sqn with Beech 58 *Baron* (UB-58); SF-260EU

TRANSPORT HELICOPTER

1 sqn with AS365 *Dauphin*; Bell 205 (UH–1H *Iroquois*); Bell 212

EQUIPMENT BY TYPE

AIRCRAFT 13 combat capable

ATK 12 A-37B *Dragonfly*

ISR 4: 1 EMB-110 *Bandeirante**†; 3 O-2A *Skymaster*

TKR/TPT 2 KC-130H *Hercules*

TPT 23: **Medium** 2 C-130B *Hercules*; **Light** 20: 1 BAe-125-700A; 2 Beech 58 *Baron* (UB-58); 6 C-212 *Aviocar*; 9 Cessna 206H; 1 Cessna 210; 1 EMB-120 *Brasilia*; **PAX** 1 C-29 Hawker

TRG 17: 5 PC-7U *Turbo Trainer*; 12 SF-260EU

HELICOPTERS

MRH 2 AS365N2 *Dauphin* II

TPT • **Light** 10: 5 Bell 205 (UH–1H *Iroquois*); 5 Bell 212

Gendarmerie & Paramilitary 1,400

Guardia Nacional Republicana 1,400

DEPLOYMENT

CENTRAL AFRICAN REPUBLIC: UN • MINUSCA 3

DEMOCRATIC REPUBLIC OF THE CONGO: UN • MONUSCO 803; 1 inf bn; 1 hel sqn with 2 Bell 212

EGYPT: MFO 41; 1 engr/tpt unit

INDIA/PAKISTAN: UN • UNMOGIP 2

LEBANON: UN • UNIFIL 1

SUDAN: UN • UNISFA 2

SYRIA/ISRAEL: UN • UNDOF 210; 1 mech inf coy

Venezuela VEN

Venezuelan Bolivar soberano VES		2022	2023	2024
GDP	VES	643bn	2.96trn	9.42trn
	USD	92.1bn	92.2bn	97.7bn
per capita	USD	3,422	3,474	3,692
Growth	%	8.0	4.0	4.5
Inflation	%	186.5	360.0	200.0
Def bdgt [a]	VES	n.k.	n.k.	n.k.
	USD	n.k.	n.k.	n.k.
USD1=VES		6.99	32.13	96.39

[a] Defence budget allocations have been difficult to track since 2017 due to high levels of currency volatility and reduced transparency in public expenditure

Population 30,518,260

Age	0–14	15–19	20–24	25–29	30–64	65 plus
Male	12.8%	4.1%	3.9%	3.9%	20.9%	4.1%
Female	12.3%	4.0%	3.8%	3.9%	21.4%	4.8%

Capabilities

Venezuela's armed forces and national guard are tasked with protecting sovereignty, assuring territorial integrity and assisting with internal-security and counter-narcotics operations. Economic challenges have affected equipment availability, modernisation, and training levels. Tensions are mounting along Venezuela's border with Guyana because of a territorial dispute over Guyana's Essequibo region. Venezuela and Colombia recently re-established military relations that were strained by waves of migrants fleeing Venezuela because of the economic situation there, and the presence of armed groups in the border area that caused both countries to deploy troops. Caracas has close ties with China and Russia, relying on both to procure weapons and provide technical support. It also sources weapons from Iran. The armed forces train regularly and civil–military cooperation has increased. Venezuela has participated in exercises with China, Cuba, Iran and Russia. The military has little logistics capability to support deployments abroad. The government recently renewed modest maintenance and modernisation efforts. Venezuela's defence industry consists of small, state-owned companies, mainly focused on the production of small arms and munitions. Local platform production has been limited to small coastal-patrol boats and Empresa Aeronáutica Nacional (EANSA), a state-owned aerospace company established in 2020, produces an indigenous UAV based on Iran's *Mohajer*.

ACTIVE 123,000 (Army 63,000 Navy 25,500 Air 11,500 National Guard 23,000) **Gendarmerie & Paramilitary 220,000**

Conscript liability 30 months selective, varies by region for all services

RESERVE 8,000 (Army 8,000)

ORGANISATIONS BY SERVICE

Army ε63,000

FORCES BY ROLE

SPECIAL FORCES

1 (99th) spec ops bde (5 spec ops bn)

1 (94th) spec ops bde (3 spec ops bn)

MANOEUVRE

Reconnaissance

1 cav bde (3 recce bn, 1 mor bty, 1 cbt engr coy, 1 sigs coy, 1 maint coy)

Armoured

1 (11th) armd bde (1 recce sqn, 2 tk bn, 1 mech inf bn, 1 SP arty gp, 1 fd arty gp, 1 cbt engr coy, 1 sigs coy, 1 log coy, 1 maint coy)

1 (41st) armd bde (3 tk bn, 1 mech inf bn, 1 SP arty gp, 1 cbt engr coy, 1 sigs coy, 1 log coy)

Mechanised

1 (14th) mech inf bde (1 recce sqn, 1 tk bn, 2 mech inf bn, 1 fd arty gp, 1 cbt engr coy, 1 sigs coy, 1 log coy, 1 maint coy)

1 (25th) mech inf bde (1 recce sqn, 1 mech inf bn, 1 mot inf bn, 1 fd arty gp, 1 cbt engr coy, 1 sigs coy, 1 log coy, 1 maint coy)

1 (31st) mech inf bde (1 recce gp, 1 mech inf bn, 1 ranger bn, 1 fd arty gp, 1 cbt engr coy, 1 sigs coy, 1 log coy, 1 maint coy)

Light
1 (21st) mot inf bde (1 recce sqn, 3 mot inf bn, 2 fd arty gp, 1 cbt engr coy, 1 sigs coy, 1 log coy, 1 maint coy)
1 (13th) mot inf bde (1 recce gp, 3 mot inf bn, 1 fd arty gp, 1 cbt engr coy, 1 sigs coy, 1 log coy, 1 maint coy)
1 (22nd) mot inf bde (1 recce sqn, 2 mot inf bn, 1 fd arty gp, 1 cbt engr coy, 1 sigs coy, 1 log coy, 1 maint coy)
1 (92nd) ranger bde (1 recce sqn, 1 tk bn, 3 ranger bn, 1 fd arty gp, 1 cbt engr coy, 1 sigs coy, 1 log coy, 1 maint coy)
1 (12th) ranger bde (1 recce sqn, 1 mot inf bn, 3 ranger bn, 1 fd arty gp, 1 cbt engr coy, 1 sigs coy, 1 log coy, 1 maint coy)
1 (32nd) jungle inf bde (1 recce sqn, 3 jungle inf bn, 1 fd arty gp, 1 cbt engr coy, 1 sigs coy, 1 log coy, 1 maint coy)
1 (33rd) jungle inf bde (4 jungle inf bn)
2 (51st & 53rd) jungle inf bde (3 jungle inf bn, 1 fd arty gp, 1 cbt engr coy, 1 sigs coy, 1 log coy, 1 maint coy)
1 (52nd) jungle inf bde (1 recce sqn, 2 jungle inf bn, 1 fd arty gp, 1 cbt engr coy, 1 sigs coy, 1 log coy, 1 maint coy)

Airborne
1 AB bde (1 recce coy, 3 AB bn, 1 cbt engr coy, 1 sigs coy, 1 log coy)

Other
1 (93rd) sy bde (1 mot inf bn, 4 sy bn, 1 cbt engr coy, 1 sigs coy, 1 log coy, 1 maint coy)

COMBAT SUPPORT
1 arty bde (2 SP arty bn, 3 MRL bn)
1 engr bde (5 engr bn)
1 engr bde (2 cbt engr bn, 1 engr bn, 1 construction bn)
1 engr bde (1 cbt engr bn, 1 engr bn, 1 maint bn)
1 engr bde (3 railway bn)
1 MP bde (5 MP bn)
1 sigs bde

COMBAT SERVICE SUPPORT
1 (81st) log bde (4 log bn)
1 (82nd) log bde (5 log bn)
1 (83rd) log bde (3 log bn)

AVIATION
1 avn comd (1 tpt avn bn, 1 atk hel bn, 1 ISR avn bn)

Reserve Organisations 8,000
FORCES BY ROLE
MANOEUVRE
Armoured
1 armd bn
Light
4 inf bn
1 ranger bn
COMBAT SUPPORT
1 arty bn
2 engr regt
EQUIPMENT BY TYPE
ARMOURED FIGHTING VEHICLES

MBT 173: 81 AMX-30V; 92 T-72B1
LT TK 109: 31 AMX-13; 78 *Scorpion*-90
RECCE 121: 42 *Dragoon* 300 LFV2; 79 V-100/V-150
IFV 237: 123 BMP-3 (incl variants); 114 BTR-80A (incl variants)
APC • APC (W) 36 *Dragoon* 300
ENGINEERING & MAINTENANCE VEHICLES
ARV 5: 3 AMX-30D; BREM-1; 2 *Dragoon* 300RV; *Samson*
VLB *Leguan*
NBC VEHICLES 10 TPz-1 *Fuchs* NBC
ANTI-TANK/ANTI-INFRASTRUCTURE
MSL • MANPATS IMI MAPATS
RCL 106mm 175 M40A1
GUNS • SP 76mm 75 M18 *Hellcat*
ARTILLERY 515
SP 60: 152mm 48 2S19 *Msta-S*; 155mm 12 Mk F3
TOWED 92: 105mm 80: 40 M101A1; 40 Model 56 pack howitzer; 155mm 12 M114A1
MRL 56: 122mm 24 BM-21 *Grad*; 160mm 20 LAR SP (LAR-160); 300mm 12 9A52 *Smerch*
GUN/MOR 120mm 13 2S23 NONA-SVK
MOR 294: 81mm 165; SP 81mm 21 *Dragoon* 300PM; AMX-VTT; 120mm 108: 60 Brandt; 48 2S12
AIRCRAFT
TPT • Light 28: 1 Beech 90 *King Air*; 1 Beech 200 *King Air*; 1 Beech 300 *King Air*; 1 Cessna 172; 6 Cessna 182 *Skylane*; 2 Cessna 206; 2 Cessna 207 *Stationair*; 1 IAI-201 *Arava*; 2 IAI-202 *Arava*; 11 M-28 *Skytruck*
HELICOPTERS
ATK 9 Mi-35M2 *Hind*
MRH 31: 10 Bell 412EP; 2 Bell 412SP; 19 Mi-17V-5 *Hip* H
TPT 9: Heavy 3 Mi-26T2 *Halo*; Medium 2 AS-61D; Light 4: 3 Bell 206B *Jet Ranger*, 1 Bell 206L3 *Long Ranger* II

Navy ε22,300; ε3,200 conscript (total ε25,500)
EQUIPMENT BY TYPE
SUBMARINES 1
SSK 1 *Sábalo* (in refit; 1 more non-operational) (GER T-209/1300) with 8 single 533mm TT with SST-4 HWT
PRINCIPAL SURFACE COMBATANTS • FRIGATES 2
FFGHM 2 *Mariscal Sucre* (ITA *Lupo* mod)† (1 more non-operational) with 8 single lnchr with Otomat Mk2 AShM, 1 octuple *Albatros* lnchr with *Aspide* SAM, 2 triple 324mm ASTT with A244 LWT, 1 127mm gun (capacity 1 Bell 212 (AB-212) hel)
PATROL AND COASTAL COMBATANTS 9
PSOH 3 *Guaiqueri* with 1 *Millennium* CIWS, 1 76mm gun
PBG 3 *Federación* (UK Vosper 37m) with 2 single lnchr with *Otomat* Mk2 AShM
PB 3 *Constitucion* (UK Vosper 37m) with 1 76mm gun
AMPHIBIOUS
LANDING SHIPS • LST 3 *Capana* (ROK *Alligator*) capacity 12 tanks; 200 troops) (one more non-operational)

LANDING CRAFT 3:
  LCU 2 *Margarita* (river comd)
  UCAC 1 *Griffon* 2000TD
LOGISTICS AND SUPPORT 10
  AGOR 1 *Punta Brava*
  AGS 2 *Gabriela*
  AKR 4 *Los Frailes*
  AORH 1 *Ciudad Bolívar*
  ATF 1 *Almirante Franciso de Miranda* (Damen Salvage Tug 6014)
  AXS 1 *Simón Bolívar*

Naval Aviation 500
FORCES BY ROLE
ANTI-SUBMARINE WARFARE
  1 sqn with Bell 212 ASW (AB-212 ASW)
MARITIME PATROL
  1 flt with C-212-200 MPA
TRANSPORT
  1 sqn with Beech 200 *King Air*; C-212 *Aviocar*; Turbo Commander 980C
TRAINING
  1 hel sqn with Bell 206B *Jet Ranger* II; TH-57A *Sea Ranger*
TRANSPORT HELICOPTER
  1 sqn with Bell 412EP *Twin Huey*; Mi-17V-5 *Hip* H
EQUIPMENT BY TYPE
AIRCRAFT 2 combat capable
  MP 2 C-212-200 MPA*
  TPT • Light 7: 1 Beech C90 *King Air*; 1 Beech 200 *King Air*; 4 C-212 *Aviocar*; 1 Turbo Commander 980C
HELICOPTERS
  ASW 4 Bell 212 ASW (AB-212 ASW)
  MRH 12: 6 Bell 412EP *Twin Huey*; 6 Mi-17V-5 *Hip* H
  TPT • Light 1 Bell 206B *Jet Ranger* II (trg)
  TRG 1 TH-57A *Sea Ranger*

Marines ε15,000
FORCES BY ROLE
COMMAND
  1 div HQ
SPECIAL FORCES
  1 spec ops bde
MANOEUVRE
  Amphibious
  1 amph aslt bde
  3 mne bde
  3 (rvn) mne bde
COMBAT SUPPORT
  1 cbt engr bn
  1 MP bde
  1 sigs bn
COMBAT SERVICE SUPPORT
  1 log bn

EQUIPMENT BY TYPE
ARMOURED FIGHTING VEHICLES
  LT TK 10 VN-16
  IFV 21: 11 VN-1; 10 VN-18
  APC • APC (W) 37 EE-11 *Urutu*
  AAV 11 LVTP-7
ENGINEERING & MAINTENANCE VEHICLES
  ARV 1 VS-25
  AEV 1 AAVR7
ANTI-TANK/ANTI-INFRASTRUCTURE
  RCL 84mm *Carl Gustaf*; 106mm M40A1
ARTILLERY 30
  TOWED 105mm 18 M-56
  MRL 107mm ε10 *Fajr-1*
  MOR 120mm 12 Brandt
PATROL AND COASTAL COMBATANTS
  PBR 23: 18 *Constancia*; 2 *Manaure*; 3 *Terepaima* (*Cougar*)
AMPHIBIOUS • LANDING CRAFT • 1 LCU; 1 LCM; 12 LCVP

Coast Guard 1,000
EQUIPMENT BY TYPE
PATROL AND COASTAL COMBATANTS 25
  PSO 3 *Guaicamacuto* with 1 *Millennium* CIWS, 1 76mm gun (capacity 1 Bell 212 (AB-212) hel)
  PB 22: 1 *Fernando Gomez de Saa* (Damen Stan Patrol 4207); 12 *Gavion*; 3 *Pagalo* (Damen Stan Patrol 2606); 4 *Petrel* (US *Point*); 2 *Protector*
LOGISTICS AND SUPPORT 4
  AG 1 *Los Taques* (salvage ship)
  AKL 1
  AP 2

Air Force 11,500
FORCES BY ROLE
FIGHTER/GROUND ATTACK
  1 sqn with F-5 *Freedom Fighter* (VF-5)
  2 sqn with F-16A/B *Fighting Falcon*
  4 sqn with Su-30MKV *Flanker*
  2 sqn with K-8W *Karakorum*
GROUND ATTACK/ISR
  1 sqn with EMB-312 *Tucano*
ELECTRONIC WARFARE
  1 sqn with *Falcon* 20DC; SA-227 *Metro* III (C-26B)
TRANSPORT
  1 sqn with Y-8; C-130H *Hercules*; KC-137
  1 sqn with A319CJ; B-737
  4 sqn with Cessna T206H; Cessna 750
  1 sqn with Cessna 500/550/551; *Falcon* 20F; *Falcon* 900
  1 sqn with G-222; Short 360 *Sherpa*
TRAINING
  1 sqn with Cessna 182N; SF-260E
  2 sqn with DA40NG; DA42VI
  1 sqn with EMB-312 *Tucano**

TRANSPORT HELICOPTER
1 VIP sqn with AS532UL *Cougar*; Mi-172
3 sqn with AS332B *Super Puma*; AS532 *Cougar*
2 sqn with Mi-17 *Hip* H

ISR UAV
1 sqn with *Mohajer* 2

EQUIPMENT BY TYPE
AIRCRAFT 79 combat capable
  FTR 18: 15 F-16A *Fighting Falcon*†; 3 F-16B *Fighting Falcon*†
  FGA 21 Su-30MKV *Flanker*
  EW 4: 2 *Falcon* 20DC; 2 SA-227 *Metro* III (C-26B)
  TKR 1 KC-137
  TPT 75: **Medium** 14: 5 C-130H *Hercules* (some in store); 1 G-222; 8 Y-8; **Light** 56: 6 Beech 200 *King Air*; 2 Beech 350 *King Air*; 10 Cessna 182N *Skylane*; 12 Cessna 206 *Stationair*; 4 Cessna 208B *Caravan*; 1 Cessna 500 *Citation* I; 3 Cessna 550 *Citation* II; 1 Cessna 551; 1 Cessna 750 *Citation* X; 2 Do-228-212; 1 Do-228-212NG; 11 Quad City *Challenger* II; 2 Short 360 *Sherpa*; **PAX** 5: 1 A319CJ; 1 B-737; 1 *Falcon* 20F; 2 *Falcon* 900
  TRG 82: 24 DA40NG; 6 DA42VI; 19 EMB-312 *Tucano**; 23 K-8W *Karakorum**; 12 SF-260E

HELICOPTERS
  MRH 8 Mi-17 (Mi-17VS) *Hip* H
  TPT 22: **Medium** 14: 3 AS332B *Super Puma*; 7 AS532 *Cougar*; 2 AS532UL *Cougar*; 2 Mi-172 (VIP); **Light** 7+ Enstrom 480B

UNINHABITED AERIAL VEHICLES
  CISR • **Medium** *Mohajer* 6 (reported); **Light** ANSU-100 (in test)
  ISR • **Light** *Mohajer* 2

AIR-LAUNCHED MISSILES
  AAM • **IR** AIM-9L/P *Sidewinder*; R-73 (RS-AA-11A *Archer*); PL-5E; R-27T/ET (RS-AA-10B/D *Alamo*); **IR** *Python* 4; **SARH** R-27R/ER (RS-AA-10A/C *Alamo*); **ARH** R-77 (RS-AA-12 *Adder*)
  ASM Kh-29L/T (RS-AS-14A/B *Kedge*); Kh-59M (RS-AS-18 *Kazoo*)
  AShM Kh-31A (RS-AS-17B *Krypton*); AM39 *Exocet*
  ARM Kh-31P (RS-AS-17A *Krypton*)

Air Defence Command (CODAI)
Joint service command with personnel drawn from other services
FORCES BY ROLE
AIR DEFENCE
  5 AD bde
COMBAT SERVICE SUPPORT
  1 log bde (5 log gp)
EQUIPMENT BY TYPE
AIR DEFENCE
  SAM
    Long-range 12 S-300VM (RS-SA-23)
    Medium-range 53: 9 9K317M2 *Buk*-M2E (RS-SA-17 *Grizzly*); 44 S-125 *Pechora*-2M (RS-SA-26)
    Point-defence 9K338 *Igla*-S (RS-SA-24 *Grinch*); ADAMS; *Mistral*; RBS-70
  GUNS 440+
    SP 40mm 12+: 6+ AMX-13 *Rafaga*; 6 M42
    TOWED 428+: **20mm**: 114 TCM-20; **23mm** ε200 ZU-23-2; **35mm**; **40mm** 114+: 114+ L/70; Some M1

National Guard (Fuerzas Armadas de Cooperacion) 23,000
(Internal sy, customs) 9 regional comd
EQUIPMENT BY TYPE
ARMOURED FIGHTING VEHICLES
  APC 89:
    APC (T) 45: 25 AMX-VCI; 12 AMX-PC (CP); 8 AMX-VCTB (Amb)
    APC (W) 44: 24 Fiat 6614; 20 UR-416
  AUV 121 VN4
ARTILLERY • **MOR** 50 **81mm**
PATROL AND COASTAL COMBATANTS
  PB 34: 12 *Protector*; 12 *Punta*; 10 *Rio Orinoco* II
AIRCRAFT
  TPT • **Light** 34: 1 Beech 55 *Baron*; 1 Beech 80 *Queen Air*; 1 Beech 90 *King Air*; 1 Beech 200C *King Air*; 3 Cessna 152 *Aerobat*; 2 Cessna 172; 2 Cessna 402C; 4 Cessna U206 *Stationair*; 6 DA42 MPP; 1 IAI-201 *Arava*; 12 M-28 *Skytruck*
  TRG 3: 1 PZL 106 *Kruk*; 2 PLZ M2-6 *Isquierka*
HELICOPTERS
  MRH 13: 8 Bell 412EP; 5 Mi-17V-5 *Hip* H
  TPT • **Light** 18: 9 AS355F *Ecureuil* II; 4 AW109; 4 Bell 206B/L *Jet Ranger/Long Ranger*; 1 Bell 212 (AB 212);
  TRG 5 F-280C

Gendarmerie & Paramilitary ε220,000

Bolivarian National Militia ε220,000

Chapter Eight
Sub-Saharan Africa

- Niger suffered a coup in July, adding to the list of countries in the Sahel region where the armed forces ousted an elected government. The coup was particularly shocking for some Western countries, such as France and the US, that had embraced working with Niger's military to battle Islamic terrorists in the region. Some African states considered intervening in Niger to restore the elected government but held off. The US, which had suspended counter-terrorist UAV operations in Niger after the coup, resumed those later.
- Unrest in Ethiopia has driven a large increase in the country's defence spending as it tries to restore order. Addis Ababa more than tripled its defence budget from ETB22bn (USD430 million) in 2022 to ETB84bn (USD1.50bn) in 2023. Ethiopia's Amhara region witnessed mounting tensions with local forces ready to confront the Ethiopian National Defense Force.
- Mali asked the UN to cease its operations in the country. The UN Security Council in June agreed to sunset its operations in the country that had lasted about a decade.
- Angola's defence spending level has eroded somewhat in recent years as the country dealt with currency depreciation and years of recession. Angola's defence budget in dollar terms in recent years has been consistently behind Nigeria's, the second-highest in the region after South Africa.
- Africa has become an increasingly important market for relatively new defence exporters. Turkiye won Nigerian shipbuilding deals in the past year and its companies struck deals in Senegal, Togo and Chad for items such as UAVs. The United Arab Emirates also has begun supplying arms to some African countries. The exporters are making inroads at a time Russia has focused on satisfying domestic equipment needs.
- Gabon, in late August, suffered a coup after a disputed election that would have returned Ali Bongo to power and extended his family's more than 50 years in office. The coup appeared to be driven more by the way the election unfolded than by the terrorism concerns that sparked such overthrows in other parts of Africa.

Sub-Saharan Africa defence spending, 2023 – top 5

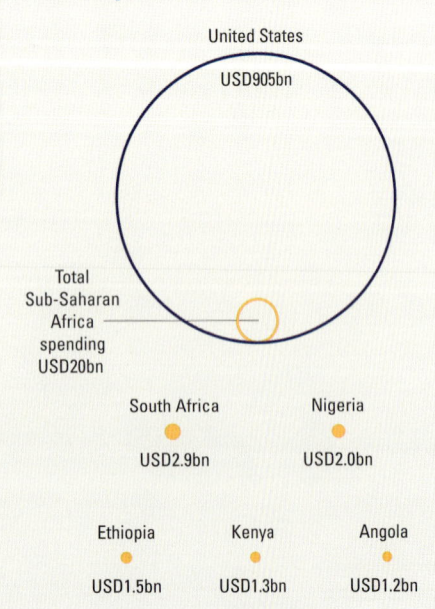

- United States: USD905bn
- Total Sub-Saharan Africa spending: USD20bn
- South Africa: USD2.9bn
- Nigeria: USD2.0bn
- Ethiopia: USD1.5bn
- Kenya: USD1.3bn
- Angola: USD1.2bn

Active military personnel – top 10
(25,000 per unit)

Country	Personnel
Ethiopia	503,000
Eritrea	301,750
Nigeria	143,000
Democratic Republic of the Congo	134,250
Angola	107,000
Sudan	104,300
South Sudan	90,000
South Africa	69,200
Uganda	45,000
Niger	39,100

Global total 20,646,000

9.7% Regional total 2,002,000

Regional defence policy and economics   460 ▶

Arms procurements and deliveries   470 ▶

Armed forces data section   471 ▶

Sub-Saharan Africa: defence spending by sub-region, 2015–23

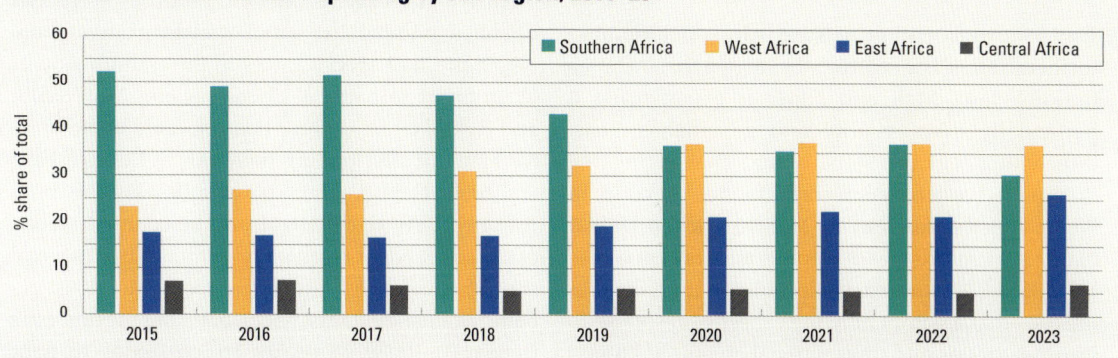

Legend: Southern Africa, West Africa, East Africa, Central Africa

Rwanda: selected land forces inventory, 2014 and 2023*

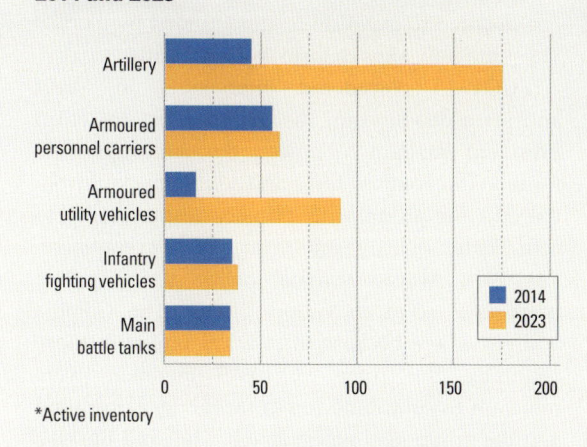

Categories: Artillery; Armoured personnel carriers; Armoured utility vehicles; Infantry fighting vehicles; Main battle tanks

Legend: 2014, 2023

*Active inventory

France: troop deployments to West Africa, 2018 and 2023

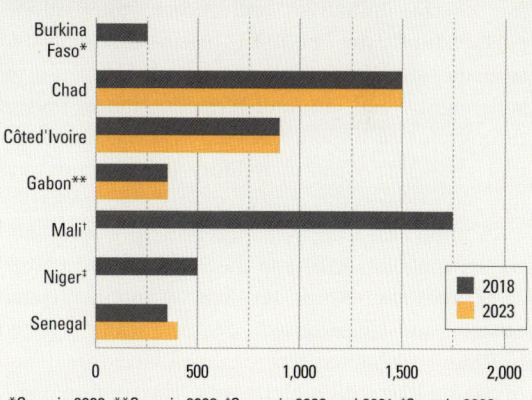

Countries: Burkina Faso*, Chad, Côte d'Ivoire, Gabon**, Mali†, Niger‡, Senegal

Legend: 2018, 2023

*Coup in 2022. **Coup in 2023. †Coups in 2020 and 2021. ‡Coup in 2023.

Ethiopia: real-terms defence budget trend, 2008–23 (USDm, constant 2015)

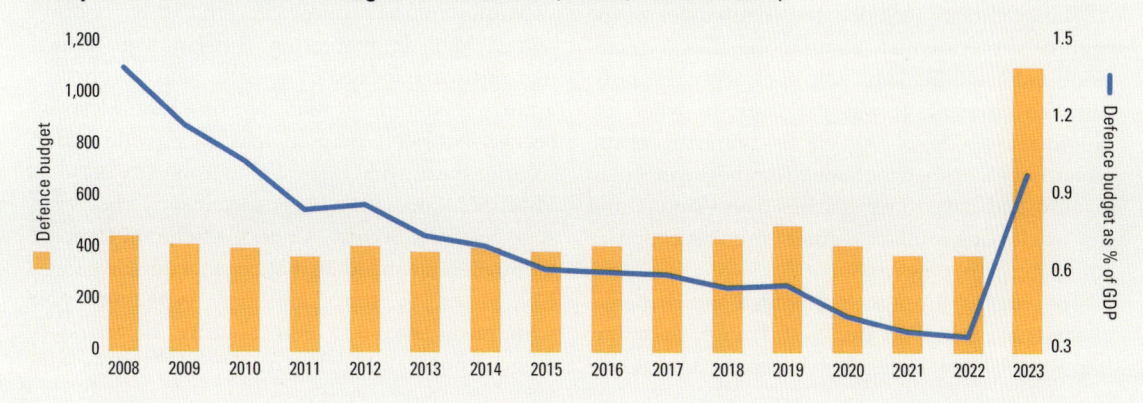

Sub-Saharan Africa

WEST AFRICA

The security situation in West Africa deteriorated further in 2023. The central Sahel region that includes Burkina Faso, Mali and Niger is experiencing a particularly deep security and governance crisis, threatening regional stability and challenging the dominant Western democratic model. A coup in Niger and the decision by Mali to ask the United Nations to end its peacekeeping mission known as MINUSMA illustrated the problems unfolding in the area that are impeding the collective response to terrorist groups and transnational organised crime.

Despite efforts by the African Union (AU), the Economic Community of West African States (ECOWAS), the G5 Sahel regional security partners, the Accra Initiative and other international partnerships, the political, socio-economic and security situation remains critical. A sense of sovereignty and an anti-Western stance prevail throughout the region, fuelled by various influences that challenge Western military partnerships and that have deprived security forces of resources.

A bloodless coup in **Niger** in July amplified concerns about security in the Sahel and intensified local and inter-ethnic tensions. A military junta ousted and imprisoned democratically elected president Mohamed Bazoum, and later threatened to charge him with high treason. The coup in Niger was spurred by the president's efforts to make military personnel changes and seemingly deep frustration among the top uniformed personnel.

The putschists included the commander of the country's presidential guard, Brigadier General Abdourahmane Tchiani, who took over the post-coup government. It was the latest in what has unfolded as a series of coup efforts – some successful, others not – that span the Sahel. They began in Sudan in 2019 and have since reached The Gambia and Guinea, leaving military regimes running countries stretching across the continent.

The Niger coup also highlighted the challenge of regional turmoil for the West. France, Germany, Italy, the United States, the European Union and others have partnered with the country to pursue security efforts against militant groups. The US has operated uninhabited aerial vehicles (UAVs) from Niger and had special forces in the country as part of an effort to battle al-Qaeda, Islamic State (ISIS) and Boko Haram. France had relocated some of its forces there after pulling them out of Burkina Faso and Mali. The US, after a pause following the coup, resumed UAV operations from the country. Ahead of the coup, Niger received military aid from several countries, such as C-130 transports, to assist its battle against militants. Niger, ahead of the domestic upheaval, aimed to recruit 50,000 troops to fight against terrorist attacks on its borders, and efforts were under way to revitalise the armed forces by establishing training centres and schools, including one devoted to technical matters funded by the EU. The junta now aims to form its own militia.

ECOWAS considered intervening in Niger and set a deadline for the coup leaders to return president Bazoum to power. But it struggled to form an intervention force and sought backup from the AU, the group with primary responsibility to coordinate security initiatives on the continent. The West African regional policy grouping had previously acted in Guinea-Bissau, The Gambia and elsewhere because of political unrest in those countries. But some ECOWAS members were reluctant to contribute forces for a Niger operation and the group held off on action. Mali and Burkina Faso, both ruled by military juntas after coups, pledged militarily support to Niger's coup leaders.

Western officials voiced concern that Niger could follow **Mali** in embracing Russian state-funded mercenaries, but Niamey initially held off on such a move. The junta in Mali that hired the Moscow-backed Wagner Group in 2021 to provide added security meanwhile requested that the UN cease its MINUSMA operation by 31 December of last year. A 30 June UN Security Council resolution formally terminated the mandate that began a decade earlier. UN forces, in some locations, expedited their withdrawal because local security deteriorated. French troops left Mali in 2022. Ahead of the decision to withdraw, UN peacekeepers were hobbled by issues such as a shortage of air assets for intelligence, surveillance and reconnaissance equipment and repeated attacks using improvised explosive devices (IEDs). The UN and others have reported the involvement of both Mali troops and Wagner fighters in atrocities against civilians in the country. The US last year sanctioned some members of the Mali military establishment for their Wagner ties.

Mali last year held a referendum that enacted a new constitution, giving the president broad powers. Opposition groups said the vote was fraudulent. The junta has promised to hold rescheduled presidential elections in 2024. Violence in the country has continued, with separatists and Islamist militants staging attacks.

Neighbouring **Burkina Faso** has also suffered from violence by extremist groups, exacerbating the problem of population displacement. Attacks linked to Islamist militants spurred two coups in Burkina Faso in 2022. The armed forces have been looking to increase their size, including a roughly doubling of the paramilitary force, the Volunteers for the Defence of the Homeland. The country has been trying to modernise its military, fielding new UAVs and armoured vehicles.

Nigeria has been battling both insurgents and criminal gangs in various parts of the country. The government has been upgrading its military capability with an eye on more effectively combatting terror groups in the Lake Chad Basin area and criminal activities elsewhere. After buying 12 Embraer A-29B *Super Tucano* trainer/light attack aircraft, Nigeria is planning to field 12 AH-1Z *Viper* attack helicopters from the US and T-129 ATAK attack helicopters from Turkiye. The country also has agreed to purchase 24 Leonardo M-346 trainer aircraft and is adding surveillance capability, including four Diamond DA-62 patrol aircraft and UAVs from China. The army and navy are also aiming to upgrade their equipment.

Terrorist attacks have hit **Togo**, too, where President Faure Gnassingbé in late 2022 reshuffled the military leadership and took direct control over the armed forces. **Benin**, which also has suffered terrorist attacks, has been continuing efforts to modernise its armed forces, adding armoured vehicles and helicopters to its inventory. Concerns that instability in the Sahel could spread have spurred other action. Members of the Accra Initiative agreed to set up a multinational operation in November 2022 in which participating states pledge to work together to counter terrorism.

In late August, the military in **Gabon** seized power after a disputed election that would have returned Ali Bongo to power and extended his family's more than 50 years in power. The coup appeared to be driven more by the way the election unfolded than by the terrorism concerns that sparked such overthrows in other parts of Africa. The AU suspended Gabon's membership. France halted military cooperation but didn't withdraw forces from the country.

Chad has been hit with new security worries from fighting in neighbouring Sudan. Unrest in Darfur has created a refugee crisis in Chad and political pressure on N'Djamena about how to engage in the conflict. Chad is employing military diplomacy and strengthening its political alliances and security partnerships, working with France, Israel, Russia and the US for aircraft maintenance. The Chadian National Army leans heavily on the General Directorate of Security Service for State Institutions to battle rebel armed groups entrenched in the Central African Republic (CAR), Libya and Sudan and to maintain order in the capital. The Special Anti-Terrorist Group Directorate participated in MINUSMA and provides a battalion to the G5 Sahel Joint Force. The United Arab Emirates provided Chad with military vehicles in 2023, while Turkish Aerospace Industries said it delivered basic trainers and UAVs to Chad.

Overall, the central Sahel region is grappling with complex security and political challenges. Sovereign approaches and shifts in international partnerships are reshaping the security dynamics in the region.

EAST AFRICA

The security situation in the Horn of Africa continued to deteriorate. The conflict in **Sudan** has intensified, with fighting breaking out in April between the once-allied Sudanese Armed Forces (SAF) and the Rapid Support Forces (RSF) as the leaders of the armed factions – Lt-Gen. Abdel Fattah Al-Burhan and Lt-Gen. Mohamed Hamdan Dagalo 'Hemedti' – battle for control of the country. Each held key territory and had an estimated 100,000 troops at their disposal. The fighting devasted parts of the Khartoum region and spurred a new wave of refugees. The RSF, which has its origins in Sudan's Darfur region, is tightening its control over that western part of Sudan.

The fighting in Sudan has increased the strain on **South Sudan**, where armed conflict and intercommunal violence have long caused displacement and food insecurity. More than 200,000 people fled Sudan's fighting into South Sudan, straining resources there. The situation in the north also distracted parties from making progress on the 2018 Revitalised Agreement on the Resolution of the Conflict in the Republic of South Sudan, both locally and nationally. The UN-led security-sector reforms, seen as an essential element of the road to elections due in December 2024, have been delayed as the parties to the conflict hold back their forces in anticipation of a possible return to fighting. Meanwhile, the National Salvation Front operating in the south of the country continues to pose an additional challenge to the peace process. In early March 2023, the UN extended the UNMISS mandate until 15 March 2024. The UN mission reported that the country's Tambura region, hit by violence in 2021, was showing signs of recovery.

The security situation in **Ethiopia** also has been precarious. The Pretoria agreement, signed in late 2022 in South Africa between the Tigray People's Liberation Front (TPLF) and the Ethiopian federal government halted the conflict in the country's northern region. The peace deal mandated a range of steps, including a permanent cessation of hostilities, a framework for addressing matters arising from the conflict, the facilitation of economic recovery and reconstruction, and a framework for monitoring and verification by the AU. The assumption on the part of the TPLF that the agreement included the early return of Western Tigray, occupied by Amhara forces and settlers and cleared of most Tigrayans early in the conflict, didn't play out. The international community continues to pressure the Ethiopian government for full implementation of the Pretoria agreement.

Ethiopia's Amhara region witnessed mounting tensions in the absence of peaceful resolution to the Western Tigray issue. Amhara forces, once aligned with the Ethiopian National Defense Force (ENDF) during the Tigray war, rejected the government's plan for them to turn over territory. Fano, an Amhara local volunteer force, took up arms in August against the government, spurred in part by a plan from Addis Ababa to disband them, disarm the Amhara Special Forces and incorporate them into either the federal police or the ENDF. The government declared a six-month state of emergency on 4 August. Fighting subsided, but the underlying causes of tension remain unresolved. Ethiopia in early 2022 set up the National Dialogue Commission with a three-year mandate to bridge differences within the country. The Commission is considered perhaps Ethiopia's best opportunity to achieve disarmament and security-sector reform. The situation in Sudan and Ethiopia has become a challenge for the Intergovernmental Authority on Development (IGAD), the region's economic community that has been trying to drive stability across its members.

Fighting also persisted in **Somalia**, where the national government has been trying to combat al-Shabaab militants. The Islamist fighters continued to operate widely in Somalia, including carrying out bombings in Mogadishu and an attack on an AU base that killed more than 50 Ugandan soldiers with the AU Transition Mission in Somalia (ATMIS). Somali forces and foreign troops supporting the government demonstrated some success against the al-Qaeda-affiliated group. ATMIS is in the process of drawing down its force levels, with about 2,000 foreign troops withdrawn in the first six months of 2023 ahead of a planned full removal before the end of 2024.

The US has aided Somalia's military, conducting airstrikes on occasion to disrupt the al-Shabaab group. Washington also provided weapons to Somalia, including small arms and vehicles, in a bid to aid the country's battle against the militants. The AU, EU and UN similarly continue to support Somalia's battle against al-Shabaab, though the scale of attacks by the terrorist group calls into question the Somali government's capacity to resist in the absence of an international force.

Another source of regional conflict has emerged in **Somaliland**. After 15 years of relative peace, fighting broke out again on 6 February 2023 between Somaliland and Puntland around Las Anood. Local clans are opting to return to the administrative control of Puntland, which they left in 2007. This threatens the hard-won Somaliland consensus on the state's existence as a separate and more stable entity to Somalia.

CENTRAL AND SOUTHERN AFRICA

Multiple multinational security operations are trying to bring stability to various countries. Many of them have shown no or limited progress, in part because neither of the region's two major economies has made a considerable contribution. Angola has been reluctant to become involved, and South Africa has so underfunded its armed forces that they now have very limited capability. In addition, Zimbabwe's armed forces have focused on internal political issues. Other countries in the Southern African Development Community (SADC), a coalition of 16 states whose aim is to promote regional development, have armed forces that are largely too small and lack key capabilities to contribute much towards security operations. Partial exceptions are Botswana and Zambia, which are modernising their forces. The outcome is a region unable to deal effectively with security challenges. The SADC Standby Brigade, for example, is not fully functional. Similarly, there is no formal cooperation to optimise the region's combined airlift capacity and still no effective maritime-security system despite known problems of illegal fishing and smuggling, with only Angola putting serious effort into controlling its waters.

The violence that has roiled the **Democratic Republic of the Congo** (DRC) for more than a quarter of a century has continued. The unrest has threatened to affect neighbouring states, while the country itself is feeling the effects of outside meddling. UN peacekeepers under the Mission in the Democratic Republic of the Congo (MONUSCO) suffered attacks and became increasingly unpopular amid little sign they were improving the security situation. The UN planned to decide on the future of the mission by the end of 2023. The DRC also faced violence from other local militias, foreign guerrilla groups and criminal gangs. The UN mission suffered from inadequate aerial reconnaissance, mobility and combat support to be effective in so large a region.

The East African Community (EAC), which the DRC joined in 2022, deployed a regional force to the embattled country to help provide security. Uganda also has a troop presence there. It expanded the mandate of the mission, due to expire in September, by a few months. Over the past year, the SADC agreed to deploy up to 5,000 troops to the DRC to assist in security operations. The SADC is also dealing with turbulence in **Mozambique**, where an al-Shabaab-linked insurgency in Cabo Delgado province in the country's north threatened to engulf other parts of the country. The government of Mozambique, the Rwandan force supporting the government and SADC expressed optimism about success in battling the insurgents. But despite signs of progress, attacks have persisted also in adjacent provinces. In some cases, guerrillas have used small UAVs for reconnaissance and remotely activated IEDs to harass road traffic. While the 2,800-strong Rwandan military and police force seems to have secured the area around the Afungi Peninsula and the key gas installations, the SADC Mission in Mozambique (SAMIM) force is far too small to be effective in the rest of Cabo Delgado, with only around 2,000 troops. The contingent is substantially smaller than planned and deployed without aerial reconnaissance or combat air support and minimal air mobility. The maritime-interdiction element has fallen away, largely because the South African navy lacks deployable ships. The Mozambican security forces continue to have limited effectiveness on their own despite EU and US training.

The **South African** armed forces, once the region's most formidable, continued to be hamstrung by underfunding. The financial situation cut deeply into equipment maintenance and training and hampered modernisation to fill capability gaps. Around 75% of the air force's 24 *Gripen* fighter-aircraft fleet was grounded for more than a year absent a support contract until September 2022. The situation was only slightly better for transport-aircraft and helicopters. The three *Rooivalk*s and two of the five *Oryx*s with MONUSCO were grounded in early 2023 awaiting spares, as was one of only two *Oryx*s deployed to Mozambique. Only a handful were able to fly in South Africa. Similarly, the navy was limited to a few training missions and lacked funding for maintenance and refit of ships. The army kept much of its equipment in storage, lacking maintenance and operating funds.

Wagner in Africa

At least seven Russian private military companies (PMCs) have been operating in Africa since 2005. The Russian Wagner Group played a particularly predominant role, providing security assistance to some governments, often in return for control over natural resources. The role of the Wagner forces locally has been uncertain, though, since the group's mutiny in Russia and the death of its founders. Wagner troops, prior to the past summer's events, played a key role in the CAR, Libya, Mali and elsewhere. Wagner forces were supporting Sudan's RSF in its battle with the SAF with weapons, ammunition and missiles. Some Wagner mercenaries took up roles with other PMCs, while other Russian PMCs appeared to be trying to replace the company.

Capability development: rebuilding Rwanda's armed forces

Rwanda's armed forces have evolved into a formidable African fighting force through a rebuilding effort from the ground up after the country's brutal civil war. The conflict that ended three decades ago cost the lives of more than one million people and ended with the former guerrilla forces associated with the Rwandan Patriot Front becoming the core of the country's de facto armed forces. What has emerged is a military capable of operations beyond its immediate borders. The roughly 2,800 troops, intelligence personnel and police Rwanda has deployed to Mozambique have helped, for instance, stabilise security around the port city of Palma.

The Rwandan Patriotic Army amalgamated other armed groups into its ranks in 1994 and, eight years later, was renamed the Rwanda Defence Force (RDF). During its first decade of existence, the armed forces were restructured and retrained to form a multi-ethnic national-security force. The reconstituted Rwandan military cut its combat teeth in the late 1990s in extensive operations in the Democratic Republic of the Congo (DRC), fighting on the side of rebel forces in both the first Congo war from 1996 to 1997, when the country was still called Zaire, and again in the second round of fighting from 1998 to 2003. Since the end of these conflicts, the RDF has remained engaged in ongoing low-level counter-insurgency operations against rebels based in eastern DRC.

Rwanda exited the two DRC wars with a disciplined and experienced light force sufficiently equipped for missions outside the country. This coincided with the African Union (AU) establishing a Common African Defence and Security Policy in 2004 and the formation in the same year of the Africa Standby Force (ASF), available for potential intervention with roles spanning from humanitarian assistance to restoring peace and security in certain circumstances.

In 2004, the RDF carried out its first international peacekeeping deployment, sending troops to the AU Mission in Sudan. Since then, the RDF has participated in United Nations operations, including UNAMDI, the AU–UN hybrid mission in Darfur, and UNMISS in South Sudan. Other international operations included the AFISMA and MINUSMA deployments in Mali, and MISCA and MINUSCA in the Central African Republic (CAR).

In 2012, Rwanda signalled its military readiness to take a more active role in regional operations, committing itself to the Eastern African element of the AU's ASF Eastern Africa Standby Brigade, later renamed the Standby Force or EASF. Rwanda that year was involved in the EASF's first operational deployment of staff officers to the AU's mission AMISOM in Somalia.

At the same time, the legal framework for the RDF was updated to establish the army services, the air-force services and the reserve force. The principal mission of the RDF is to defend Rwanda's territorial integrity and national sovereignty. The force of approximately 33,000 regular volunteers includes a limited-capability air force of only 1,000 personnel. The reserve force is divided into an infantry reserve, organised as five regional reserves in the four provinces and in Kigali, and a specialist reserve of military and civilian specialists. The size of the reserve force has not been officially disclosed.

The RDF has also undergone something of a modernisation spree. It has procured arms from China, including CS/SH-1 (PCL-09) 122mm self-propelled howitzers and HJ-9A anti-tank missiles. The military also acquired ATMOS 2000 155mm self-propelled howitzers from Israel's Elbit Systems. The country also has signalled an ambition to step up its technology capability, even if focused on civil applications for now. Kigali has announced plans to launch telecommunications satellites, opened the door to commercial UAV services and hosted an international forum on artificial intelligence.

The Rwandan military has cooperated with various parties to hone its capability. Chinese military-training teams deployed to Rwanda in 2019 and 2023 and the RDF has adopted some of its training procedures. The US has actively supported the RDF under the African Peacekeeping Rapid Response Partnership, established in 2015, with medical and air-safety training for expeditionary operations and with weapons and ammunition management under a regional support programme. In November 2021 the RDF hosted a 150-person-strong training team from the Netherlands army, and on 1 December 2022, the European Council agreed to provide EUR20m to support the continued deployment of the RDF in Cabo Delgado province for collective and personal equipment and costs related to strategic airlift.

The recent expansion of Rwanda's military deployments, from purely multilateral peacekeeping contributions to AU and UN operations, to bilateral deployments at the request of national governments, first to the CAR in December 2020 and then to Mozambique in mid-2021, demonstrate both the government's willingness to be more assertive in foreign policy and the RDF's ability to carry out such taskings. Bilateral deployments outside Rwanda's immediate region seem likely to continue given that they build political influence for President Paul Kagame and support Rwanda's development and economy.

DEFENCE ECONOMICS

Macroeconomics

Sub-Saharan Africa's economy grew by 3.3% from a year earlier, according to 2023 IMF data. Despite beating the global average of 3%, headline growth slowed from 4.2% in 2022 and 4.5% in 2021. Additionally, the region's economies remained fragile, particularly after Russia's full-scale invasion of Ukraine in February 2022 highlighted the area's dependence on imports of food, fertiliser and fuel, while high debt burdens and stubborn inflation reduced the scope for public spending.

Sub-Saharan Africa was particularly affected by the resulting spike in commodity costs because the region relies heavily on food and fertiliser imports from Russia and Ukraine. The war also impacted Black Sea trade routes that supply the region. The July 2023 collapse of the Black Sea Grain Initiative that allowed the safe transportation of grain and fertiliser from Ukrainian ports suggests that food supplies will remain more expensive while states adapt by increasing domestic production or finding new suppliers. Disrupted energy supplies led fuel prices to surge in mid-2022 to their highest level in three decades and accentuated the cost-of-living crisis for many of the world's most vulnerable people.

To limit the impact of rising costs, many governments introduced measures such as subsidies, tariff waivers and income support. Those inflated public debt and caused the countries to reverse progress on their fiscal positions, which were only starting to recover after the COVID-19 pandemic spurred borrowing. The region's public-debt burden has more than tripled since 2010. Although public-debt levels are unevenly distributed and are more pronounced in the central, southern and eastern parts of Sub-Saharan Africa, they have raised concerns of a forthcoming debt crisis throughout the entire region. According to the IMF, of the 39 Sub-Saharan countries eligible for the Fund's Poverty Reduction and Growth Trust – which offers concessional financing and economic programmes to stimulate the domestic economy of low-income countries – nine are reported to be in active debt distress, 12 are at high risk and 17 are at moderate risk of debt distress. This reflects a general decline in national finances since COVID-19, although countries such as Cabo Verde, The Gambia and South Sudan have reduced their risk levels.

Higher prices also spurred inflation rates across the region. In 2023, some 16 countries in Sub-Saharan Africa experienced double-digit inflation. Inflation remained persistent, defying early expectations it would fall. In turn, living standards suffered, with the World Bank estimating that per capita income growth will remain sluggish for the foreseeable future. To tackle rising costs, central banks across the world tightened monetary policy and increased interest rates. However, precarious economic conditions, compounded by food-security concerns and poor employment prospects, raise the risk of domestic political instability. To limit any reputational backlash from the ripple effects Moscow's war on Ukraine has had on global prices, Russian President Vladimir Putin in July 2023 pledged to clear USD23 billion in African debt held by Moscow, as well as promising to deliver grain and fuel to the region.

Defence spending

After a decade of stagnating defence spending, regional budgets are slowly recovering. In 2023, the region allocated USD20.3bn to defence, up from the USD19.5bn the previous year. This represents a 7.3% increase on an inflation-adjusted basis and underpins a trend of improving regional budgets. In real terms, though, allocations remain below the previous high in 2014. Moreover, there has been little improvement in the region's capital budgets, which can be used for investments such as new equipment. Available data collated by *The Military Balance* suggests that

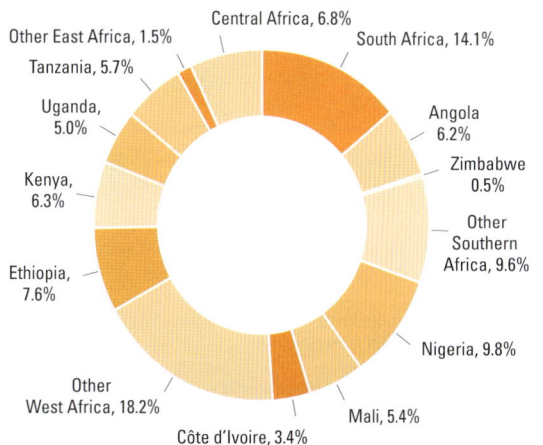

Other East Africa, 1.5%
Tanzania, 5.7%
Uganda, 5.0%
Kenya, 6.3%
Ethiopia, 7.6%
Other West Africa, 18.2%
Côte d'Ivoire, 3.4%
Mali, 5.4%
Nigeria, 9.8%
Other Southern Africa, 9.6%
Zimbabwe 0.5%
Angola 6.2%
South Africa, 14.1%
Central Africa, 6.8%

Note: Analysis excludes Djibouti, Equatorial Guinea, Eritrea, Seychelles, Somalia, Sudan ©IISS

▲ Figure 22 **Sub-Saharan Africa: defence spending by country and sub-region, 2023**

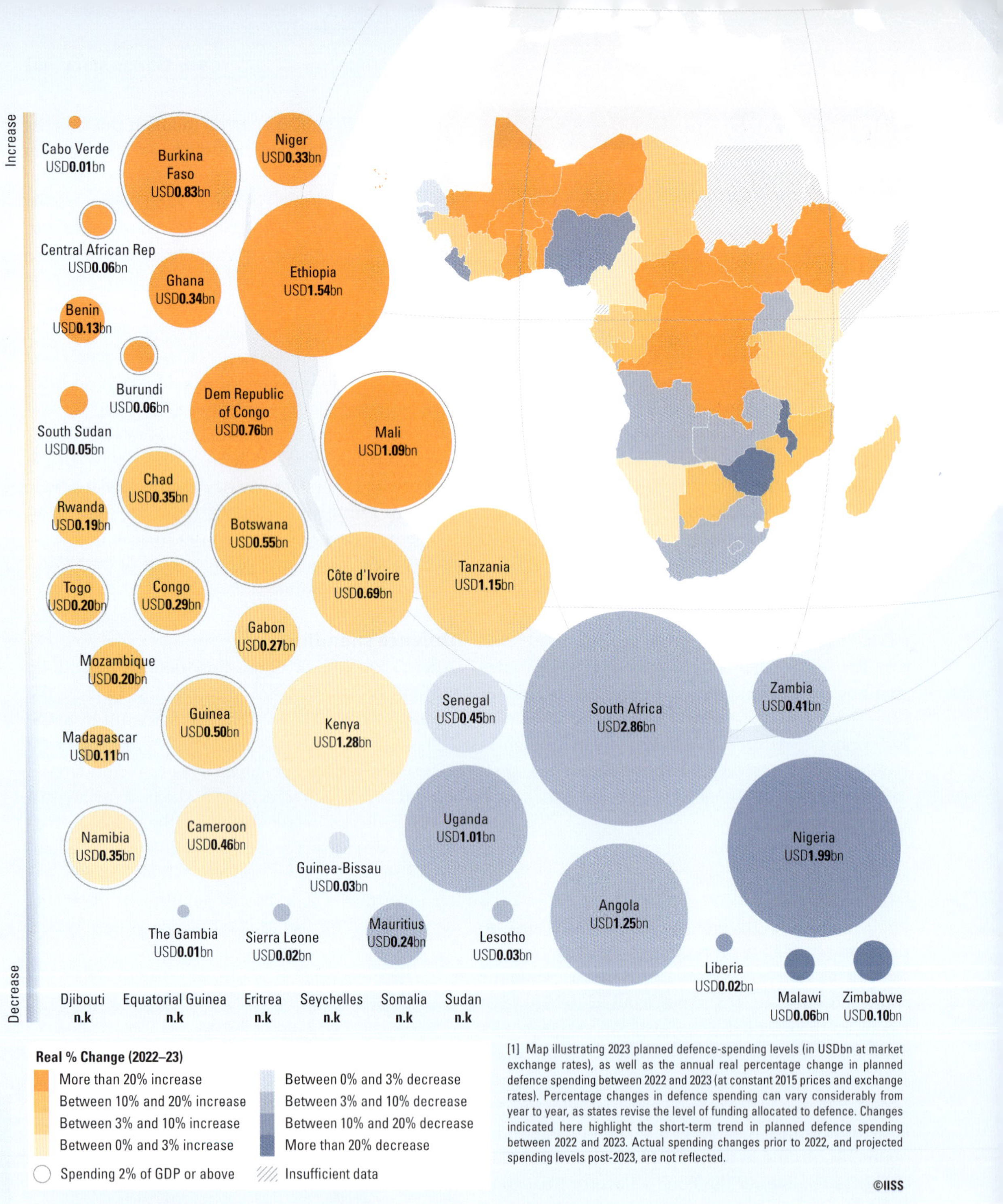
Increase
Decrease
Cabo Verde USD0.01bn
Burkina Faso USD0.83bn
Niger USD0.33bn
Central African Rep USD0.06bn
Ghana USD0.34bn
Ethiopia USD1.54bn
Benin USD0.13bn
Burundi USD0.06bn
South Sudan USD0.05bn
Dem Republic of Congo USD0.76bn
Mali USD1.09bn
Chad USD0.35bn
Rwanda USD0.19bn
Botswana USD0.55bn
Côte d'Ivoire USD0.69bn
Tanzania USD1.15bn
Togo USD0.20bn
Congo USD0.29bn
Gabon USD0.27bn
Mozambique USD0.20bn
Guinea USD0.50bn
Kenya USD1.28bn
Senegal USD0.45bn
South Africa USD2.86bn
Zambia USD0.41bn
Madagascar USD0.11bn
Namibia USD0.35bn
Cameroon USD0.46bn
Guinea-Bissau USD0.03bn
Uganda USD1.01bn
Nigeria USD1.99bn
The Gambia USD0.01bn
Sierra Leone USD0.02bn
Mauritius USD0.24bn
Lesotho USD0.03bn
Angola USD1.25bn
Liberia USD0.02bn
Malawi USD0.06bn
Zimbabwe USD0.10bn
Djibouti n.k
Equatorial Guinea n.k
Eritrea n.k
Seychelles n.k
Somalia n.k
Sudan n.k
Real % Change (2022–23)
More than 20% increase
Between 10% and 20% increase
Between 3% and 10% increase
Between 0% and 3% increase
Spending 2% of GDP or above
Between 0% and 3% decrease
Between 3% and 10% decrease
Between 10% and 20% decrease
More than 20% decrease
Insufficient data
[1] Map illustrating 2023 planned defence-spending levels (in USDbn at market exchange rates), as well as the annual real percentage change in planned defence spending between 2022 and 2023 (at constant 2015 prices and exchange rates). Percentage changes in defence spending can vary considerably from year to year, as states revise the level of funding allocated to defence. Changes indicated here highlight the short-term trend in planned defence spending between 2022 and 2023. Actual spending changes prior to 2022, and projected spending levels post-2023, are not reflected.
©IISS

▲ Map 11 **Sub-Saharan Africa: regional defence spending** (USDbn, %ch yoy)[1]

recordable capital budgets only received USD2.2bn across 2023, down from USD2.4bn in 2022. Though the wider trend has been for modest growth over time, the low expenditure levels represent chronic underinvestment in national armed forces. In part, this reflects relative levels of national stability, but also limited budgets and the prevailing use of the military to boost employment levels.

Western Africa remains Sub-Saharan Africa's subregion with the highest absolute expenditure. Its share of spending represented about 36.8% of the regional defence budgets in 2023, up from 32.2%

Figure 23 Sub-Saharan Africa: regional defence spending as % of GDP (average)

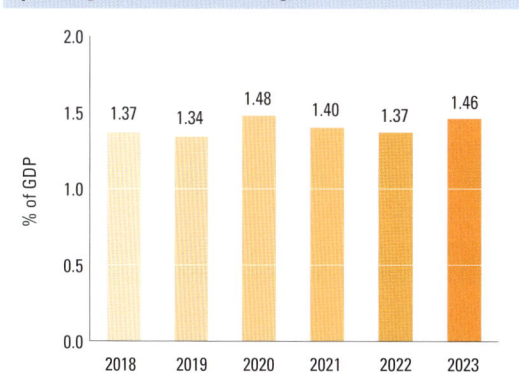

Year	% of GDP
2018	1.37
2019	1.34
2020	1.48
2021	1.40
2022	1.37
2023	1.46

Note: GDP data from IMF World Economic Outlook, October 2023. Analysis excludes Djibouti, Equatorial Guinea, Eritrea, Seychelles, Somalia, Sudan

in 2019, before the pandemic. Spending in 2023 across the region remained dominated by large countries with high population numbers, with six states comprising over half of the region's defence spending. In 2023, **South Africa** allocated ZAR52.0bn (USD2.83bn) to defence, representing the region's largest military budget despite longer-term funding cuts. As a percentage of GDP, South African defence spending fell below 1% for the first time in 2016 and the level has eroded further since then. In real terms, defence spending has declined consistently since 2021 since rising budgets have failed to keep pace with inflation. To respond to financial instability, the South African government curtailed budget allocations, seeking to control debt and reduce economic risk. Although debt levels are expected to stabilise earlier than forecast, the 2022 Medium Term Budget Policy Statement suggests defence funding will increase, with additional spending going to enhance border security. Pretoria also emphasised the procurement and maintenance of deployable medical and naval equipment, though reduced funding has undermined modernisation ambitions.

In 2023, **Nigeria** was a close second to South Africa in defence spending, with a defence budget of NGN1.25 trillion (USD1.99bn). In terms of local currency, Nigeria's defence allocation had increased since 2019, when the country launched its National Security Strategy. Despite a small decrease in 2023's defence budget from the previous year, the figure still represents a 35% increase since 2019 in real terms. This helped underpin Nigeria's position as West Africa's principal military power. However, investment rates have not kept up with overall spending and have declined as a percentage of the total budget. For example, between 2016 and 2019, capital expenditure averaged 28.4% of the national-defence budget. This reduced to an average of 14% between 2020 and 2023. The reduction comes as future spending may become more volatile, particularly since the country abandoned its currency peg in June 2023, which triggered a sharp depreciation of the Nigerian naira. That said, the federal government in May 2022 announced a National Military Strategy which, among other reforms, seeks to improve the country's operational capacity through acquisitions, enhanced capacity-building and defence cooperation with foreign partners. This suggests that in future years, Nigeria will seek to address the recent decline in capital budgets as it looks abroad for inspiration.

Angola was Sub-Saharan Africa's third-highest spender, allocating AOA855bn (USD1.25bn) to defence in 2023. This contrasts with the years before 2018, when Angola's defence budget surpassed that of Nigeria in US dollar terms. Since then, Luanda's pace of spending has trailed Nigeria's, compounded by currency depreciation and years of recession brought on by the pandemic. In contrast, **Ugandan** defence spending spiked between 2019 and 2021. Kampala often surges outlays as the country enters election-campaign season, and following the January 2021 elections, levels of defence spending fell sharply. However, spending levels remain well above 2019 levels, seemingly in pursuit of Uganda's 2040 Vision, which includes investment in capabilities to keep abreast of wider technological changes. As a percentage of total spend, Uganda's capital budgets have jumped from 29% of the total budget in 2019 to 67% in 2020 and have remained above 60% since then. However, the Ugandan budget offers little transparency, with the increases largely earmarked for acquisition of 'classified assets'.

In 2023, several other countries in the region accelerated their defence budgets increases. Amid ongoing conflict in the northern region of Tigray, **Ethiopia** more than tripled its defence budget from ETB22bn (USD430 million) in 2022 to ETB84bn (USD1.50bn) in 2023. Though the pace of spending may eventually ease in the light of at November 2022 ceasefire, ongoing tensions suggest that Ethiopia's defence budget will remain elevated for the foreseeable future. **Mali** and **Tanzania** significantly increased their defence budgets. Mali's increased by over 20% in nominal terms, from XOF515bn

(USD827m) in 2022 to XOF657bn (USD1.1bn) in 2023, a jump from previous average annual increases of 6% between 2019 and 2022. Tanzanian defence spending jumped 15%, from TZS2.36trn (USD1.0bn) to TZS2.71trn (USD1.2bn).

Defence industry

Although military spending rebounded in 2023, defence-industrial capabilities remained hampered by the region's historical lack of sustained spending. South Africa has the region's most developed arms industry, although it has struggled in recent years. A South African defence department strategic plan stated that an unfavourable economic outlook and the need to curtail defence outlays will lead to significant industrial challenges. In 2022, Denel was in line for a roughly ZAR3.4bn (USD208m) bailout via the 2022 Special Appropriation Act, which required the company to implement a turnaround plan and provide greater clarity on how it will develop a sustainable business model. That included steep staff reductions, with employment levels falling by 33% from 2021. In 2023, Denel reported a profit of ZAR390m (USD21.3m) and aimed to use its improved financial position to rebuild its skilled labour force, after the loss of highly specialised staff.

Given the economic constraints and unfavourable outlook in the region, more emphasis in the region is being placed on the private-sector defence industry over state-owned enterprises. Nigeria has decreased funding since 2020 in the state-owned Defence Industry Corporation of Nigeria (DICON).

The problems for the region's arms industry have been compounded by the heavy reliance on arms suppliers in the West, Russia and China. Russia's ties with the region date back to the Soviet era, with many relationships rooted in anti-colonial struggles. Moscow is a primary exporter to the region, though Western sanctions imposed in the wake of the February 2022 full-scale invasion of Ukraine have sought to make the purchase of Russian arms more difficult. This has provided opportunities for countries such as Turkiye, which has established a presence in the region for its burgeoning arms industry. Since 2022, Turkiye has secured contracts with Nigeria for two offshore patrol vessels and six T129 ATAK attack helicopters. This was followed, in June 2023, by deals for mid-life upgrades of a Nigerian frigate and *Tuzla*-class patrol boat. Turkiye also has struck agreements with Niger (pre-coup), Senegal and Togo. Similarly, the United Arab Emirates (UAE), which is aiming to establish itself in the region, has delivered arms to Chad and to battling parties in Sudan.

Sub-Saharan Africa's defence industry remains predominantly focused on small-arms and light-weapons production, where at least 17 countries have small-arms munitions factories. Many are seeking to move up the value chain. In Sudan, the Military Industry Corporation (MIC) is aspiring to expand its exports and diversify its production beyond small arms. Despite challenges such as international sanctions, the Sudanese military actively promotes its equipment, which is often based on foreign designs. At an Abu Dhabi arms expo in 2023, MIC introduced two UAE-designed protected mobility vehicles, which the company marketed as *Rhino* and *Rhino* 2. Similarly, Sudan's state-owned SAFAT Aviation Group has sought to market its domestically produced SAFAT 02 light helicopter, which is based on the design of AK1-3 aircraft by Ukrainian manufacturer Aerokopter.

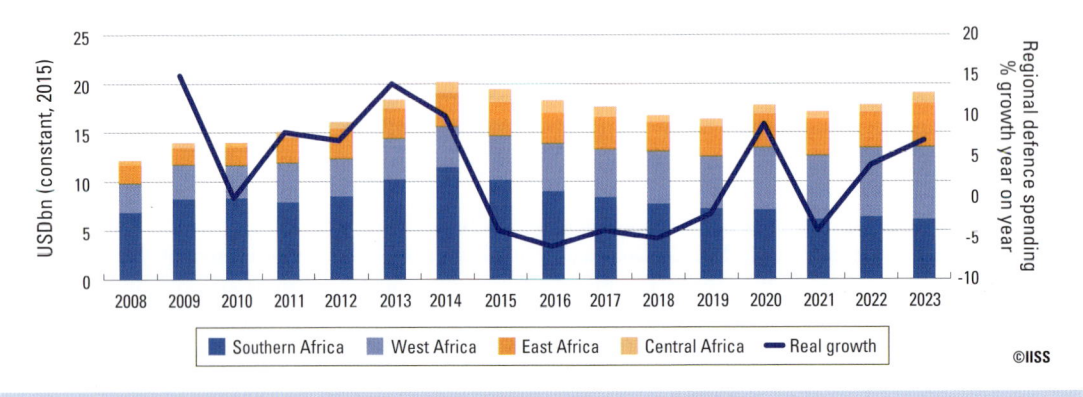

▲ Figure 24 **Sub-Saharan Africa: total defence spending by sub-region, 2008–23**

Table 15 Angola: selected procurements since 2010

Angola's aspiration to recapitalise and modernise its armed forces has been hindered by fluctuations in oil prices, rampant inflation and international sanctions against Russia and Belarus, both traditional sources of Angolan procurement. In part to alleviate these issues, Angola has sought to diversify its sources of equipment with systems from China, Turkiye and the UAE. Angola's state-owned industrial holding company, Simportex, oversees and manages most defence procurement contracts although it does not seem to have generated much in the way of local industry through these deals. Angola's dependence on oil exports has led to the delay or cancellation of a number of efforts. For example, three of a planned seven *Macaé*-class patrol craft contracted in 2014 for the Angolan Navy were to be built in Angola with help from Brazil's Empresa Gerencial de Projetos Navais (EMGEPRON). However, the programme was cancelled over payment issues. Similarly, a 2015 deal worth about USD8.07m with Italy's Whitehead Alenia Sistemi Subacquei (WASS), now part of Leonardo, for two patrol boats seems to have been cancelled for similar reasons. With the largest armed forces in Southern Africa and an Army and Air Force that operate large amounts of obsolescent Soviet-era equipment, Angola's recapitalisation requirements are increasingly urgent. Buoyed by high oil prices, Angola's economy is expected to grow over the next five years, which could allow room for investment in much-needed new capabilities.

Contract Date	Equipment	Type	Qty	Value	Prime Contractor	Deliveries
c. 2012	Cessna 172R	Light transport aircraft	6	n.k.	Africair	2013
c. 2013	Mi-171Sh	Medium transport helicopter	8	n.k.	Russian Helicopters	2015–16
c. 2013	*Casspir* NG	Protected patrol vehicle	45	ZAR178.76m (USD12.8m)	Denel Land Systems	2016–17
Oct 2013	Su-30K *Flanker**	Fighter ground-attack aircraft	12	n.k.	Russia government surplus	2016–17
c. 2014	Mi-24 *Hind**	Attack helicopter	12	n.k.	Russia government surplus	2016
Sep 2014	AW139	Multi-role helicopter	4	EUR88.16m (USD117.15m)	Leonardo (formerly AugustaWestland)	2017
	AW109E	Light transport helicopter	2			2016–17
c. 2015	PTL-02 *Assaulter*	Wheeled assault gun	9+	n.k.	NORINCO	c. 2016
	WZ-551	Wheeled APC	est. 5			
Feb 2015	Cessna 500 *Citation* I	Maritime patrol aircraft	1	n.k.	Bird Aerosystems	2017
Mar 2015	*Super Dvora* Mk III	Fast patrol boat	4	n.k.	IAI RAMTA	est. 2017–18
c. 2016	HSI 32	Fast patrol boat	3**	n.k.	Constructions Mécaniques de Normandie (CMN)	est. 2018–19
c. 2018	K-8W *Karakorum*	Training aircraft	12	n.k.	Hongdu Aviation Industry Group	2020
Jan 2018	MA60	Light transport aircraft	2	n.k.	Xi'an Aircraft Industrial Corporation	2019
c. 2021	*Ocean Eagle* 43	Patrol boat	3**	n.k.	CMN	2022–ongoing
c. 2021	RA 4 de Abril (LCT 200-70)	Landing craft tank	2**	n.k.	CMN	2022–ongoing
c. 2021	Il-76TD *Candid*	Heavy transport aircraft	≥2	n.k.	n.k.	2022–ongoing
c. 2022	*Aksungur*	Heavy CISR UAV	n.k.	n.k.	Turkish Aerospace Industries	n.k.
Apr 2022	C295MPA *Persuader*	Maritime patrol aircraft	2	USD208.77m	Airbus M	expected from late 2023
	C295	Light transport aircraft	1			
Feb 2023	BR71 Mk II	Corvette	3	AED3.94bn (USD1.07bn)	Abu Dhabi Ship Building	expected by early 2027

*Second-hand

**Part of EUR495m (USD547.8m) agreement approved in August 2016 for the supply of 17 vessels for the navy

M = multinational

Arms procurements and deliveries – Sub-Saharan Africa

Significant events in 2023

FEBRUARY
SOUTH AFRICA PROCUREMENT PLANS
The South African National Defence Force (SANDF) outlined plans to invest ZAR1bn (USD54.50m) in airlift transport capability and ZAR700m (USD38.15m) in helicopters and vehicles in the fiscal year ending 31 March 2024. An additional ZAR1.42bn (USD76.39m) is allocated in 2023–26 for the midlife upgrades of the navy's frigates and submarines. The overall operability of the SANDF equipment has been significantly affected by budget troubles and mismanagement. The estimated cost of refitting the navy's three *Heroine*-class submarines (based on the German Type-209/1400 design) and four *Valour*-class frigates (based on the German MEKO A200) is more than ZAR4.2bn (USD228.88m), an amount almost three times greater than that budgeted for 2023–26. The Air Force awarded a three-year maintenance and support contract to Saab in September 2022 for its 24 *Gripen* fighter ground-attack aircraft after it was reported that 75% of the fleet was grounded due to a lack of fuel and spare parts.

APRIL
ARMSCOR PERFORMANCE REVIEW
The parliament of South Africa published a performance evaluation of its defence procurement agency, Armaments Corporation of South Africa (ARMSCOR), evaluating 71 of its ongoing procurement programmes. Only 37 projects were given a 'satisfied' rating, with the remaining 32 projects rated either 'dissatisfied' or 'unsatisfied'. Amongst 15 listed as 'dissatisfied', the lowest-assessed programme is Project *Hoefyster* to buy *Badger* infantry fighting vehicles. It is ten years behind schedule due to the financial difficulties and mismanagement of the state-owned Denel defence company despite government investment of ZAR7.4bn (USD422.86m) in this programme as of February 2023. Earlier in 2023, the National Treasury recommended that the government and ARMSCOR undertake a feasibility study to decide whether to continue with the project to acquire the *Badger* from Denel or to extend the service life of the *Ratel* in 2023–24. Since August, Denel and ARMSCOR have examined amending contracts of the first out of the five phases and establishing a product baseline of the *Badger* by the end of 2025, indicating the project will continue. The majority of ARMSCOR's funding comes from the national defence budget and ZAR1.5bn (USD81.74m) has been earmarked for the agency in the FY2023–24 budget.

SEPTEMBER
NIGERIA INDUSTRIAL COLLABORATION WITH INDIA
Nigeria approved an agreement with India to bolster its local defence industry. The agreement aims to localise 40% of defence production by 2027 with the aid of Indian investment worth USD1bn. The arrangement will be overseen by Nigeria's state-owned defence company Defence Industries Corporation of Nigeria (DICON). Since 2021, Nigeria has been working to grow its defence industry led by DICON and Proforce, a privately owned Nigerian armoured-vehicle company which has been producing the *Ara*-1, the *Ara*-2, the *Viper* and the *Ezugwu* MRAP protected patrol vehicles for the Nigerian Army and others. It is unclear how this newly established friendship with India will unfold alongside Nigeria's pre-existing defence partnership with Pakistan. Pakistan's state-owned defence firm, Pakistan Aeronautical Complex, supplied ten *Super Mushshak* training aircraft in 2017–18 and three JF-17 *Thunder* fighter aircraft in 2021 to the Nigerian Air Force.

SEPTEMBER
TURKIYE'S DEFENCE EXPORTS EXPANSION IN SSA
Mozambique signed an agreement on defence-industrial cooperation with Turkiye's Defence Industry Agency (SSB) with an interest in procuring Baykar armed UAVs, potentially the Bayraktar *Akinci*. The agreement follows a trend of growing Turkish UAV exports in Sub-Saharan Africa. In July, Kenya signed a defence industry cooperation agreement with the SSB during the 16th International Defence Industry Fair in Istanbul. Neither Mozambique nor Kenya are typical customers of Turkish products, but the country sometimes supplies systems that are export-restricted by more traditional suppliers. A defence cooperation deal with the SSB is often the clearest indicator of a transaction that may not otherwise be disclosed; many countries that have signed a defence financial or industry cooperation agreement with Turkiye are often later spotted operating the *Bayraktar* TB2 UAVs – including Burkina Faso, Djibouti, Ethiopia and Mali. In addition, sales of land systems, including Otokar's *Cobra* armoured utility vehicles and Katmerciler's *Hizir* protected patrol vehicles, have contributed to Turkiye's growing defence exports to the region.

Angola ANG

New Angolan Kwanza AOA		2022	2023	2024
GDP	AOA	56.8trn	64.1trn	81.7trn
	USD	123bn	93.8bn	92.9bn
per capita	USD	3,438	2,550	2,453
Growth	%	3.0	1.3	3.3
Inflation	%	21.4	13.1	22.3
Def bdgt	AOA	790bn	855bn	
	USD	1.71bn	1.25bn	
USD1=AOA		462.43	683.92	878.74

Real-terms defence budget trend (USDbn, constant 2015)

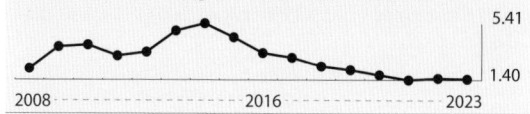

5.41
1.40
2008 — 2016 — 2023

Population	35,981,281					
Age	0–14	15–19	20–24	25–29	30–64	65 plus
Male	23.6%	5.3%	4.1%	3.3%	11.5%	1.0%
Female	23.6%	5.5%	4.3%	3.6%	12.8%	1.4%

Capabilities

Angola's armed forces are constitutionally tasked with ensuring sovereignty and territorial integrity. They are increasingly also focused on the protection of offshore resources and maritime-security cooperation with regional and external powers. The military faces maintenance and readiness challenges despite recent equipment orders in the air and maritime domain. Defence ties with Russia mainly involve equipment deliveries, though there have been plans to boost defence-industrial cooperation. Luanda is partnering with multiple countries in its pursuit of military modernisation, defence-industrial development and maritime security, demonstrated, in 2023, with deals for UAE-designed corvettes and Turkish-developed UAVs. Angola continues to deepen defence ties with the US, especially in capacity building, maritime security, space and cyber defence. Angola retains conscription, but has volunteer components, such as the navy. The armed forces train regularly and have participated in multinational exercises. Angola is the only regional state with a strategic-airlift capacity. It placed an order for medium-lift aircraft for transport missions and maritime surveillance with Spain in 2022. Equipment-purchasing plans were curtailed in recent years by low oil prices that impacted the defence budget. The defence industry is limited to in-service maintenance facilities, but Angola has ambitions to develop greater capacity by partnering with countries such as Brazil, China, Portugal and Russia.

ACTIVE 107,000 (Army 100,000 Navy 1,000 Air 6,000) Gendarmerie & Paramilitary 10,000

Conscript liability 2 years

ORGANISATIONS BY SERVICE

Army 100,000

FORCES BY ROLE
MANOEUVRE
Armoured
1 tk bde
Light
1 SF bde
1 (1st) div (1 mot inf bde, 2 inf bde)
1 (2nd) div (3 mot inf bde, 3 inf bde, 1 arty regt)
1 (3rd) div (2 mot inf bde, 3 inf bde)
1 (4th) div (1 tk regt, 5 mot inf bde, 2 inf bde, 1 engr bde)
1 (5th) div (2 inf bde)
1 (6th) div (1 mot inf bde, 2 inf bde, 1 engr bde)
COMBAT SUPPORT
Some engr units
COMBAT SERVICE SUPPORT
Some log units
EQUIPMENT BY TYPE†
ARMOURED FIGHTING VEHICLES
MBT 300: ε200 T-55AM2; 50 T-62; 50 T-72M1
LT TK 10 PT-76
ASLT 9+ PTL-02 *Assaulter*
RECCE 603: 600 BRDM-2; 3+ *Cayman* BRDM
IFV 250 BMP-1/BMP-2
APC 276
  APC (T) 31 MT-LB
  APC (W) 200+: ε200 BTR-152/-60/-70/-80; WZ-551 (CP)
  PPV 45 *Casspir* NG2000
ENGINEERING & MAINTENANCE VEHICLES
ARV 5+: 5 BTS-2; T-54/T-55
MW *Bozena*
ARTILLERY 1,463
SP 25+: **122mm** 9+ 2S1 *Gvozdika*; **152mm** 4 2S3 *Akatsiya*; **203mm** 12 2S7 *Pion*
TOWED 575: **122mm** 523 D-30; **130mm** 48 M-46; **152mm** 4 D-20
MRL 113+: **122mm** 110: 70 BM-21 *Grad*; 40 RM-70; **220mm**; 3+ 9P140MB *Uragan*-M; **240mm** BM-24
MOR 750: **82mm** 250; **120mm** 500
ANTI-TANK/ANTI-INFRASTRUCTURE
MSL • MANPATS 9K11 (RS-AT-3 *Sagger*)
RCL 500: 400 **82mm** B-10/**107mm** B-11†; **106mm** 100 M40†
GUNS • SP **100mm** SU-100†
AIR DEFENCE
SAM • Point-defence 9K32 *Strela*-2 (RS-SA-7 *Grail*)‡; 9K36 *Strela*-3 (RS-SA-14 *Gremlin*); 9K310 *Igla*-1 (RS-SA-16 *Gimlet*)
GUNS
  SP **23mm** ZSU-23-4
  TOWED 450+: **14.5mm** ZPU-4; **23mm** ZU-23-2; **37mm** M-1939; **57mm** S-60

Navy ε1,000

EQUIPMENT BY TYPE
PATROL AND COASTAL COMBATANTS 29
PCO 2 *Ngola Kiluange* (NLD Damen 6210) with 1 hel landing platform (Ministry of Fisheries)
PCC 5 *Rei Bula Matadi* (Ministry of Fisheries)
PBF 12: 3 HSI 32; 5 PVC-170; 4 *Super Dvora* Mk III
PB 10: 4 *Mandume*; 1 *Ocean Eagle 43*; 5 *Comandante Imperial Santana* (Ministry of Fisheries)
AMPHIBIOUS • LANDING CRAFT 1
LCT 1 *RA 4 de Abril* (FRA CMN LCT 200-70) (capacity 3 MBT or 260 troops)
LOGISTICS AND SUPPORT 1
AGOR 1 *Baia Farta* (NLD Damen 7417) (Ministry of Fisheries)

Coastal Defence
EQUIPMENT BY TYPE
COASTAL DEFENCE • AShM 4K44 *Utyos* (RS-SSC-1B *Sepal* – at Luanda)

Marines ε500
FORCES BY ROLE
MANOEUVRE
  Amphibious
  1 mne bn

Air Force/Air Defence 6,000
FORCES BY ROLE
FIGHTER
  1 sqn with Su-27/Su-27UB/Su-30K *Flanker*
GROUND ATTACK
  1 sqn with EMB-314 *Super Tucano**
MARITIME PATROL
  1 sqn with Cessna 500 *Citation* 1; C-212 *Aviocar*
TRANSPORT
  3 sqn with An-12 *Cub*; An-26 *Curl*; An-32 *Cline*; An-72 *Coaler*; BN-2A *Islander*; C-212 *Aviocar*; Do-28D *Skyservant*; EMB-135BJ *Legacy* 600 (VIP); Il-76TD *Candid*; Kodiak 100; MA60
TRAINING
  1 sqn with Cessna 172R
  1 sqn with EMB-312 *Tucano*
  1 sqn with L-29 *Delfin*; L-39 *Albatros*
  1 sqn with PC-7 *Turbo Trainer*; PC-9*
  1 sqn with Z-142
ATTACK HELICOPTER
  2 sqn with Mi-24/Mi-35 *Hind*; SA342M *Gazelle* (with HOT)
TRANSPORT HELICOPTER
  1 sqn with AS565 *Panther*
  1 sqn with Bell 212
  1 sqn with Mi-8 *Hip*; Mi-17 *Hip* H
  1 sqn with Mi-171Sh
AIR DEFENCE
  5 bty with S-125M1 *Pechora*-M1 (RS-SA-3 *Goa*);

  5 coy with 9K35 *Strela*-10 (RS-SA-13 *Gopher*)†; 2K12-ML *Kvadrat*-ML (RS-SA-6 *Gainful*); 9K33 *Osa* (RS-SA-8 *Gecko*); 9K31 *Strela*-1 (RS-SA-9 *Gaskin*)

EQUIPMENT BY TYPE†
AIRCRAFT 28 combat capable
  FTR 18: 6 Su-27/Su-27UB *Flanker*; 12 Su-30K *Flanker*; (18 MiG-23ML *Flogger* in store)
  FGA (20 MiG-21bis/MF *Fishbed*; 8 MiG-23BN/UB *Flogger*; 13 Su-22 *Fitter* D all in store)
  ATK (8 Su-25 *Frogfoot*; 2 Su-25UB *Frogfoot* in store)
  MP 1 Cessna 500 *Citation* I
  TPT 57: **Heavy** 8 Il-76TD *Candid*; **Medium** 6 An-12 *Cub*; **Light** 43: 12 An-26 *Curl*; 2 An-32 *Cline*; 8 An-72 *Coaler*; 8 BN-2A *Islander*; 2 C-212 *Aviocar*; 6 Cessna 172R; 1 Do-28D *Skyservant*; 1 EMB-135BJ *Legacy* 600 (VIP); 1 Kodiak 100; 2 MA60
  TRG 54: 13 EMB-312 *Tucano*; 6 EMB-314 *Super Tucano**; 12 K-8W *Karakorum*; 6 L-29 *Delfin*; 2 L-39C *Albatros*; 5 PC-7 *Turbo Trainer*; 4 PC-9*; 6 Z-142
HELICOPTERS
  ATK 56: 34 Mi-24 *Hind*; 22 Mi-35 *Hind*
  MRH 55: 8 AS565 *Panther*; 4 AW139; 8 SA342M *Gazelle*; 27 Mi-8 *Hip*/Mi-17 *Hip* H; 8 Mi-171Sh *Terminator*; (8 SA316 *Alouette* III (IAR-316) in store)
  TPT • Light 10: 2+ AW109E; 8 Bell 212
AIR DEFENCE • SAM 73
  Short-range 28: 16 2K12-ML *Kvadrat*-ML (RS-SA-6 *Gainful*); 12 S-125M1 *Pechora*-M1 (RS-SA-3 *Goa*)
  Point-defence 45: 10 9K35 *Strela*-10 (RS-SA-13 *Gopher*)†; 15 9K33 *Osa* (RS-SA-8 *Gecko*); 20 9K31 *Strela*-1 (RS-SA-9 *Gaskin*)
AIR-LAUNCHED MISSILES
  AAM
    IR R-3 (RS-AA-2 *Atoll*)‡; R-60 (RS-AA-8 *Aphid*); R-73 (RS-AA-11A *Archer*)
    IR/SARH R-23/24 (RS-AA-7 *Apex*)‡; R-27 (RS-AA-10 *Alamo*)
  ASM 9M17M *Falanga*-M (RS-AT-2 *Swatter*); HOT
  ARM Kh-28 (RS-AS-9 *Kyle*)

Gendarmerie & Paramilitary 10,000
Rapid-Reaction Police 10,000

DEPLOYMENT
MOZAMBIQUE: SADC • SAMIM 18

Benin BEN

CFA Franc BCEAO XOF		2022	2023	2024
GDP	XOF	10.9trn	12.0trn	13.1trn
	USD	17.4bn	19.9bn	21.8bn
per capita	USD	1,303	1,449	1,540
Growth	%	6.3	5.5	6.3
Inflation	%	1.4	5.0	2.5
Def bdgt	XOF	60.6bn	77.5bn	
	USD	97.4m	129m	
USD1=XOF		622.43	602.71	599.65

Real-terms defence budget trend (USDm, constant 2015)

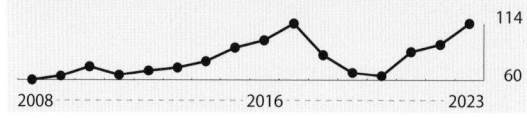

Population 14,219,908

Age	0–14	15–19	20–24	25–29	30–64	65 plus
Male	22.9%	5.3%	4.7%	3.8%	11.5%	1.1%
Female	22.5%	5.2%	4.8%	4.0%	12.9%	1.3%

Capabilities

The armed forces focus on border- and internal-security issues but have been grappling with a deteriorating security situation in the northern part of the country. The increased security threat in the North led the government to open a military base there. Border patrols and security have increased to address the regional threat from Islamist groups. Maritime security remains a priority in light of continuing piracy in the Gulf of Guinea. Benin established a National Guard to address counterterrorism and internal security concerns. The country reportedly is working to improve soldiers' living conditions. In July 2022, Benin struck a security cooperation agreement with Rwanda that may include logistical support. The country also has a military-cooperation agreement with France, which provided armoured personnel carriers in 2023. Paris's forces based in Senegal have provided training to boost Benin's border-surveillance capacity. China has delivered armoured vehicles to Benin, while the US has helped train the army and national police and provided a patrol boat. Benin contributes personnel to the Multinational Joint Task Force fighting Islamist terrorist groups, though has little capacity to deploy beyond neighbouring states without external support. It lacks a defence industry beyond maintenance capabilities.

ACTIVE 12,300 (Army 8,000 Navy 550 Air 250 National Guard 3,500) **Gendarmerie & Paramilitary 4,800**

Conscript liability 18 months (selective)

ORGANISATIONS BY SERVICE

Army ε8,000
FORCES BY ROLE
MANOEUVRE
  Armoured
    2 armd sqn
  Light
    1 (rapid reaction) mot inf bn
    8 inf bn
COMBAT SUPPORT
  2 arty bn
  1 engr bn
  1 sigs bn
COMBAT SERVICE SUPPORT
  1 log bn
  1 spt bn
EQUIPMENT BY TYPE
ARMOURED FIGHTING VEHICLES
  LT TK 18 PT-76†
  RECCE 24: 3 AML-90; 14 BRDM-2; 7 M8
  APC 49
    APC (T) 22 M113
    APC (W) 17: 2 *Bastion* APC; 15 VAB
    PPV 10 *Casspir* NG
  AUV 19: 9 Dongfeng *Mengshi*; 10 VBL
ARTILLERY 16+
  TOWED 105mm 16: 12 L118 Light Gun; 4 M101
  MOR 81mm PP-87; **120mm** W86

Navy ε550
EQUIPMENT BY TYPE
PATROL AND COASTAL COMBATANTS 6
  PB 6: 2 *Matelot Brice Kpomasse* (ex-PRC); 3 *Alibori* (FRA FPB 98); 1 *Couffo* (PRC 27m)

Air Force ε250
EQUIPMENT BY TYPE
AIRCRAFT
  TPT 4: **Light** 2: 1 DHC-6 *Twin Otter*†; 1 MA600; **PAX** 2: 1 B-727; 1 HS-748†
  TRG (1 LH-10 *Ellipse* non-operational)
HELICOPTERS
  MRH 2 H125M *Fennec*
  TPT 8: **Medium** 3 H215 (AS332M1) *Super Puma*; **Light** 5: 4 AW109BA; 1 AS350B *Ecureuil*†

National Guard ε3,500
FORCES BY ROLE
MANOEUVRE
  Air Manoeuvre
    1 AB bn

Gendarmerie & Paramilitary 4,800

Republican Police ε4,800
EQUIPMENT BY TYPE
ARMOURED FIGHTING VEHICLES
  APC • **PPV** *Casspir* NG

DEPLOYMENT

CENTRAL AFRICAN REPUBLIC: UN • MINUSCA 7

CHAD: Lake Chad Basin Commission • MNJTF 150

DEMOCRATIC REPUBLIC OF THE CONGO: UN • MONUSCO 8

SOUTH SUDAN: UN • UNMISS 9

SUDAN: UN • UNISFA 2

Botswana BWA

Botswana Pula BWP		2022	2023	2024
GDP	BWP	252bn	270bn	292bn
	USD	20.4bn	20.8bn	21.9bn
per capita	USD	7,738	7,758	8,067
Growth	%	5.8	3.8	4.1
Inflation	%	12.2	5.9	4.7
Def bdgt [a]	BWP	6.17bn	7.11bn	
	USD	499m	547m	
USD1=BWP		12.37	13.00	13.31

[a] Defence, Justice and Security Budget

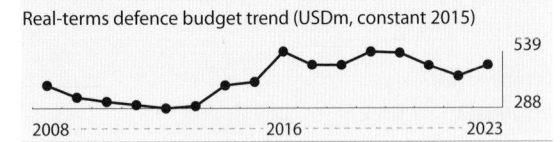

Real-terms defence budget trend (USDm, constant 2015)

539
288
2008 — 2016 — 2023

Population	2,417,596				
Age	0–14	15–19	20–24	25–29	30–64	65 plus
Male	14.7%	4.5%	4.2%	4.2%	17.9%	2.4%
Female	14.4%	4.6%	4.5%	4.3%	20.6%	3.6%

Capabilities

The Botswana Defence Force (BDF) comprises ground forces and a small but comparatively well-equipped air wing. The BDF's primary responsibility is to ensure territorial integrity. Its other tasks include tackling poaching. Botswana has a history of contributing to peacekeeping operations. The BDF has reportedly been working on a defence doctrine influenced by US concepts and practices. Botswana has a good relationship with the US, which provides regular training to the BDF. The armed forces also train with several African states, including Namibia, with whom it holds biennial exercises. The operations centre for the Southern African Development Community (SADC) Standby Force is located in Gaborone. The BDF has deployed a small force to Mozambique to join soldiers from other SADC countries. Recent personnel priorities include improving conditions of service and overhauling retirement ages. Recruitment into the BDF is voluntary. Some BDF military personnel have travelled to China for training. The air force has a modest airlift capacity and the BDF can deploy a small force by air if required. The country has shown interest in replacing the ageing fleet of F-5 combat aircraft and been considering options from Sweden and India. Financial pressures, however, have slowed progress. The country has a limited maintenance capacity but no defence-manufacturing sector.

ACTIVE 9,000 (Army 8,500 Air 500)

ORGANISATIONS BY SERVICE

Army 8,500

FORCES BY ROLE

MANOEUVRE

Armoured
 1 armd bde(-)

Light
 2 inf bde (1 armd recce regt, 4 inf bn, 1 cdo unit, 1 engr regt, 1 log bn, 2 ADA regt)

COMBAT SUPPORT

1 arty bde

1 engr coy

1 sigs coy

COMBAT SERVICE SUPPORT

1 log gp

AIR DEFENCE

1 AD bde(-)

EQUIPMENT BY TYPE

ARMOURED FIGHTING VEHICLES

LT TK 45: ε20 SK-105 *Kurassier*; 25 FV101 *Scorpion*

IFV 35+ *Piranha* V UT-30

APC 157:
 APC (W) 145: 50 BTR-60; 50 LAV-150 *Commando* (some with 90mm gun); 45 *Piranha* III
 PPV 12 *Casspir*

AUV 70: 6 FV103 *Spartan*; 64 VBL

ENGINEERING & MAINTENANCE VEHICLES

ARV *Greif*; M578

MW *Aardvark* Mk2

ANTI-TANK/ANTI-INFRASTRUCTURE

MSL
 SP V-150 TOW
 MANPATS TOW

RCL 84mm *Carl Gustaf*

ARTILLERY 78

TOWED 30: **105mm** 18: 12 L118 Light Gun; 6 Model 56 pack howitzer; **155mm** 12 Soltam M-68

MRL 122mm 20 APRA-40

MOR 28: **81mm** 22; **120mm** 6 M-43

AIR DEFENCE

SAM
 Short-range 1 VL MICA
 Point-defence 9K32 *Strela*-2 (RS-SA-7 *Grail*)‡; 9K310 *Igla*-1 (RS-SA-16 *Gimlet*); *Javelin*; *Mistral*

GUNS • TOWED 20mm 7 M167 *Vulcan*; **37mm** PG-65

Air Wing 500

FORCES BY ROLE

FIGHTER/GROUND ATTACK

1 sqn with F-5A *Freedom Fighter*; F-5D *Tiger* II

TRANSPORT

2 sqn with BD-700 *Global Express*; BN-2/-2B *Defender**; Beech 200 *King Air* (VIP); C-130B *Hercules*; C-212-300/400 *Aviocar*; CN-235M-100; Do-328-110 (VIP); PC-24

TRAINING

1 sqn with PC-7 MkII *Turbo Trainer**

TRANSPORT HELICOPTER

1 sqn with AS350B *Ecureuil*; Bell 412EP/SP *Twin Huey*; EC225LP *Super Puma*

EQUIPMENT BY TYPE

AIRCRAFT 28 combat capable
  FTR 13: 8 F-5A *Freedom Fighter*; 5 F-5D *Tiger* II
  TPT 22: **Medium** 3 C-130B *Hercules*; **Light** 17: 4 BN-2 *Defender**; 6 BN-2B *Defender**; 1 Beech 200 *King Air* (VIP); 1 C-212-300 *Aviocar*; 2 C-212-400 *Aviocar*; 2 CN-235M-100; 1 Do-328-110 (VIP); **PAX** 2: 1 BD700 *Global Express*; 1 PC-24
  TRG 5 PC-7 MkII *Turbo Trainer**

HELICOPTERS
  MRH 7: 2 Bell 412EP *Twin Huey*; 5 Bell 412SP *Twin Huey*
  TPT 9: **Medium** 1 EC225LP *Super Puma*; **Light** 8 AS350B *Ecureuil*

DEPLOYMENT

DEMOCRATIC REPUBLIC OF THE CONGO: UN • MONUSCO 3

MOZAMBIQUE: SADC • SAMIM 359

Burkina Faso BFA

CFA Franc BCEAO XOF		2022	2023	2024
GDP	XOF	11.8trn	12.5trn	13.7trn
	USD	18.9bn	20.8bn	22.9bn
per capita	USD	832	888	952
Growth	%	1.5	4.4	6.4
Inflation	%	14.1	1.4	3.0
Def bdgt	XOF	291bn	502bn	
	USD	467m	832m	
USD1=XOF		622.41	602.71	599.67

Real-terms defence budget trend (USDm, constant 2015): 2008–2016 around 97; 2023 693.

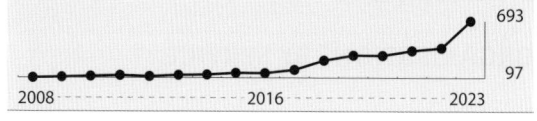

Population	22,489,126					
Age	0–14	15–19	20–24	25–29	30–64	65 plus
Male	21.4%	5.6%	4.9%	3.7%	12.1%	1.4%
Female	20.8%	5.4%	4.9%	3.9%	14.1%	1.8%

Capabilities

Burkina Faso suffered two coups in 2022 that brought a military regime to power after the country's security was hit by a number of terrorist attacks. The political turmoil impacted the country's diplomatic and security cooperation agreements. French Special Forces, based in the country for more than a decade, left Burkina Faso, and tensions with ECOWAS increased over the lack of a transition process to restore constitutional democracy. In September 2023, Burkina Faso became part of an alliance with Mali and Niger, two other countries under military control after recent coups. Burkina Faso is increasing its cooperation and diplomatic ties with Russia and Iran. In recent years, the armed forces received a significant number of armoured vehicles and other equipment. The aviation capacity is slowly improving with the arrival of additional helicopters and acquisition of *Bayraktar* TB2 UAVs from Turkiye. Financial challenges and political instability might hinder broader capability developments. The military has a limited ability to deploy to neighbouring countries. Burkina Faso has some maintenance facilities but no defence-manufacturing sector.

ACTIVE 7,000 (Army 6,400 Air 600) Gendarmerie & Paramilitary 4,450

ORGANISATIONS BY SERVICE

Army 6,400

Three military regions. In 2011, several regiments were disbanded and merged into other formations, including the new 24th and 34th *régiments interarmes*

FORCES BY ROLE

MANOEUVRE
  Mechanised
    1 cbd arms regt
  Light
    1 cbd arms regt
    8 inf regt
    12 inf bn (Rapid Intervention)
  Air Manoeuvre
    1 AB regt (1 CT coy)

COMBAT SUPPORT
  1 arty bn (2 arty tp)
  1 engr bn

EQUIPMENT BY TYPE

ARMOURED FIGHTING VEHICLES
  RECCE 83: 19 AML-60/-90; 24 EE-9 *Cascavel*; 30 *Ferret*; 2 M20; 8 M8
  APC 153
    APC (W) 24: 13 Panhard M3; 11 *Bastion* APC
    PPV 129: 24 Ejder Yalcin; 6 Gila; 13+ *Phantom* II; 63 *Puma* M26-15; 21 Stark Motors *Storm*; 2 *Temsah* 2
  AUV 46+: 8+ *Bastion Patsas*; 38 *Cobra*

ENGINEERING & MAINTENANCE VEHICLES
  MW 3 *Shrek-M*

ANTI-TANK/ANTI-INFRASTRUCTURE
  RCL 75mm Type-52 (M20); **84mm** *Carl Gustaf*

ARTILLERY 50+
  TOWED 14: **105mm** 8 M101; **122mm** 6
  MRL 9: **107mm** ε4 Type-63; **122mm** 5 APR-40
  MOR 27+: **81mm** Brandt; **82mm** 15; **120mm** 12

AIR DEFENCE

SAM • **Point-defence** 9K32 *Strela*-2 (RS-SA-7 *Grail*)‡
GUNS • **TOWED** 42: **14.5mm** 30 ZPU; **20mm** 12 TCM-20

Air Force 600

FORCES BY ROLE

GROUND ATTACK/TRAINING

1 sqn with EMB-314 *Super Tucano**; SF-260WL *Warrior**

TRANSPORT

1 sqn with AT-802 *Air Tractor*; B-727 (VIP); Beech 200 *King Air*; C295W; CN235-220; PA-34 *Seneca*; *Tetras*

ATTACK/TRANSPORT HELICOPTER

1 sqn with AS350 *Ecureuil*; Mi-8 *Hip*; Mi-17 *Hip* H; Mi-17-1V *Hip*; Mi-26T *Halo*; Mi-35 *Hind*

EQUIPMENT BY TYPE

AIRCRAFT 5 combat capable

ISR 1 DA42 MPP *Guardian*

TPT 10: **Light** 9: 1 AT-802 *Air Tractor*; 2 Beech 200 *King Air*; 1 C295W; 1 CN235-220; 1 PA-34 *Seneca*; 3 *Tetras*; **PAX** 1 B-727 (VIP)

TRG 5: 3 EMB-314 *Super Tucano**; 2 SF-260WL *Warrior**

HELICOPTERS

ATK 2 Mi-35 *Hind*

MRH 4: 2 Mi-17 *Hip* H; 1 Mi-17-1V *Hip*; 1 AW139

TPT 3: **Heavy** 1 Mi-26T *Halo*; **Medium** 1 Mi-8 *Hip*; **Light** 1 AS350 *Ecureuil*

UNINHABITED AERIAL VEHICLES

CISR • **Medium** 2 *Bayraktar* TB2

BOMBS • **Laser-guided** MAM-L

Gendarmerie & Paramilitary 4,450

National Gendarmerie 4,200

Ministry of Defence and Veteran Affairs

FORCES BY ROLE

SPECIAL FORCES

1 spec ops gp (USIGN)

EQUIPMENT BY TYPE

ARMOURED FIGHTING VEHICLES

APC • APC (W) some *Bastion* APC

People's Militia (R) 45,000 reservists (trained)

Security Company 250

DEPLOYMENT

CENTRAL AFRICAN REPUBLIC: UN • MINUSCA 4

DEMOCRATIC REPUBLIC OF THE CONGO: UN • MONUSCO 5

Burundi BDI

Burundi Franc BIF		2022	2023	2024
GDP	BIF	7.97trn	10.2trn	12.7trn
	USD	3.92bn	3.19bn	3.06bn
per capita	USD	311	246	229
Growth	%	1.8	3.3	6.0
Inflation	%	18.9	20.1	16.1
Def bdgt	BIF	136bn	208bn	
	USD	66.7m	64.9m	
USD1=BIF		2,034.13	3,201.43	4,138.58

Real-terms defence budget trend (USDm, constant 2015)

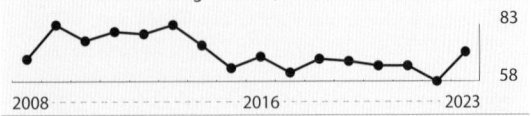

Population 13,162,952

Age	0–14	15–19	20–24	25–29	30–64	65 plus
Male	21.5%	5.6%	4.6%	3.7%	12.9%	1.4%
Female	21.2%	5.5%	4.6%	3.8%	13.4%	1.9%

Capabilities

The country continues to face cross-border and internal security challenges. Security cooperation with external actors that was largely halted by the political crisis in 2015 and tested the cohesion of Burundi's armed forces has resumed in limited fashion. Burundi signed a cooperation agreement with Russia in 2018 on counter-terrorism and joint training. The country also signed a security cooperation agreement with the DRC in 2023 and there are reports relations with Rwanda are improving. The armed forces have a limited capability to deploy externally and in 2022 sent troops to the DRC to help stabilise the situation there. Burundi has long maintained a deployment in Somalia. The experience accumulated during UN operations has likely increased the skills of deployed troops. Peacekeeping missions help to fund the armed forces, though financial and equipment deficiencies restrict military effectiveness. The country has no defence industry apart from limited maintenance facilities.

ACTIVE 30,050 (Army 30,000 Navy 50) **Gendarmerie & Paramilitary** 1,000

ORGANISATIONS BY SERVICE

Army 30,000

FORCES BY ROLE

MANOEUVRE

Mechanised

2 lt armd bn (sqn)

Light

7 inf bn

Some indep inf coy

COMBAT SUPPORT

1 arty bn

1 engr bn
AIR DEFENCE
1 AD bn
EQUIPMENT BY TYPE
ARMOURED FIGHTING VEHICLES
RECCE 48: 6 AML-60; 12 AML-90; 30 BRDM-2
APC 114
APC (W) 70: 20 BTR-40; 10 BTR-80; 10 *Fahd*-300; 9 Panhard M3; 15 Type-92; 6 *Walid*
PPV 44: 12 *Casspir*; 12 RG-31 *Nyala*; 10 RG-33L; 10 *Springbuck* 4×4
AUV 15 *Cougar* 4×4
ARTILLERY 120
TOWED 122mm 18 D-30
MRL 122mm 12 BM-21 *Grad*
MOR 90: 82mm 15 M-43; 120mm ε75
ANTI-TANK/ANTI-INFRASTRUCTURE
MSL • MANPATS Milan (reported)
RCL 75mm Type-52 (M20)
AIR DEFENCE
SAM • Point-defence 9K32 *Strela*-2 (RS-SA-7 *Grail*)‡
GUNS • TOWED 150+: **14.5mm** 15 ZPU-4; 135+ **23mm** ZU-23/**37mm** Type-55 (M-1939)

Air Wing 200
EQUIPMENT BY TYPE
AIRCRAFT 1 combat capable
TPT • Light 2 Cessna 150L†
TRG 1 SF-260W *Warrior**
HELICOPTERS
ATK 2 Mi-24 *Hind*
MRH 2 SA342L *Gazelle*
TPT • Medium (2 Mi-8 *Hip* non-op)

Reserves
FORCES BY ROLE
MANOEUVRE
Light
10 inf bn (reported)

Navy 50
EQUIPMENT BY TYPE
PATROL AND COASTAL COMBATANTS • PB 4
AMPHIBIOUS • LCT 2

Gendarmerie & Paramilitary ε1,000
General Administration of State Security ε1,000

DEPLOYMENT
CENTRAL AFRICAN REPUBLIC: UN • MINUSCA 762; 1 inf bn

DEMOCRATIC REPUBLIC OF THE CONGO: EAC • EACRF 1,000; 1 inf bn
SOMALIA: AU • ATMIS 3,400; 4 inf bn
SUDAN: UN • UNISFA 4

Cabo Verde CPV

Cabo Verde Escudo CVE		2022	2023	2024
GDP	CVE	242bn	262bn	279bn
	USD	2.31bn	2.60bn	2.80bn
per capita	USD	4,048	4,503	4,790
Growth	%	17.0	4.4	4.5
Inflation	%	7.9	5.2	2.0
Def bdgt	CVE	1.20bn	1.51bn	
	USD	11.5m	15.0m	
USD1=CVE		104.64	100.82	99.61

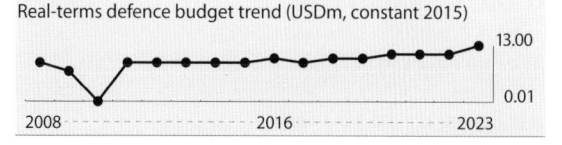

Real-terms defence budget trend (USDm, constant 2015)

Population 603,901

Age	0–14	15–19	20–24	25–29	30–64	65 plus
Male	13.4%	4.4%	4.3%	4.4%	19.7%	2.3%
Female	13.3%	4.4%	4.3%	4.5%	21.1%	3.8%

Capabilities

Cabo Verde's defence priorities include territorial defence, maritime security and protection of its EEZ and airspace. The country aspires to modernise the armed forces, including a revision of compulsory military service. It has developed a new Strategic Concept of National Defence aimed at upgrading the armed forces. Cabo Verde is trying to improve airspace monitoring and pursue related procurements, including new aircraft and helicopters. Portugal acts as the main security partner. The government is interested in greater regional and international defence engagement and, in 2022, signed agreements with Portugal and the US. International partners provide maritime security training support and both China and the US have significantly strengthened the country's coast guard with patrol boat deliveries. The armed forces take part in multinational regional exercises and cooperative activities. Equipment capabilities remain limited and there is no defence industry, beyond maintenance facilities.

ACTIVE 1,200 (Army 1,000 Coast Guard 100 Air 100)

Conscript liability Selective conscription (14 months)

ORGANISATIONS BY SERVICE

Army 1,000
FORCES BY ROLE
MANOEUVRE
Light
2 inf bn (gp)

COMBAT SUPPORT

1 engr bn

EQUIPMENT BY TYPE

ARMOURED FIGHTING VEHICLES

RECCE 10 BRDM-2

ARTILLERY • MOR 18: **82mm** 12; **120mm** 6 M-1943

AIR DEFENCE

SAM • **Point-defence** 9K32 *Strela* (RS-SA-7 *Grail*)‡

GUNS • **TOWED** 30: **14.5mm** 18 ZPU-1; **23mm** 12 ZU-23

Coast Guard ε100

EQUIPMENT BY TYPE

PATROL AND COASTAL COMBATANTS 7

PCC 2: 1 *Guardião* (NLD Damen Stan Patrol 5009); 1 *Kondor* I
PB 4: 2 *Badejo*; 1 *Espadarte*; 1 *Tainha* (PRC 27m)
PBF 1 *Rei* (US *Archangel*)

LOGISTICS AND SUPPORT 2

AAR 2 *Ponta Nho Martinho* (ESP)

AIRCRAFT • TPT • Light 1 Do-228

Air Force up to 100

FORCES BY ROLE

MARITIME PATROL

1 sqn with An-26 *Curl*

EQUIPMENT BY TYPE

AIRCRAFT • TPT • Light 3 An-26 *Curl*†

Cameroon CMR

CFA Franc BEAC XAF		2022	2023	2024
GDP	XAF	27.6trn	29.7trn	31.8trn
	USD	44.3bn	49.3bn	53.0bn
per capita	USD	1,588	1,722	1,807
Growth	%	3.8	4.0	4.2
Inflation	%	6.3	7.2	4.8
Def bdgt	XAF	260bn	277bn	
	USD	417m	459m	
USD1=XAF		622.43	602.72	599.66

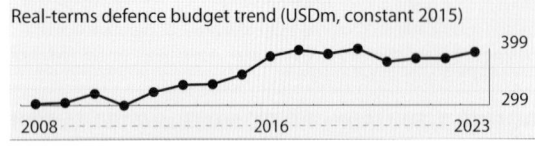

Population 30,135,732

Age	0–14	15–19	20–24	25–29	30–64	65 plus
Male	21.0%	5.4%	4.6%	3.9%	13.3%	1.5%
Female	20.7%	5.4%	4.6%	4.0%	13.8%	1.7%

Capabilities

Internal security is a key concern for Cameroon's armed forces, as is the cross-border challenge from Boko Haram and groups based in the Central African Republic. Cameroon is part of the Multinational Joint Task Force battling Islamist terrorist groups. The country has long-standing military ties with France, including for support and training. Cameroon also has a military-assistance agreement with China. The two countries have cooperated on a floating dock at Kribi to improve operational readiness. In 2023, Cameroon renewed its military cooperation agreement with Russia. The AU maintains its continental logistics base at Douala. The armed forces are considered well organised, though allegations of abuse led the US in February 2019 to halt some military assistance. Although deployments continue to UN peacekeeping operations, the armed forces have only limited organic power-projection capability without external support. The country is slowly updating its ageing equipment inventory. It has upgraded the fleet of infantry fighting vehicles and protected patrol vehicles through acquisitions from China, France, South Africa, and US donations. The armed forces also are improving their ISR capability with fixed-wing aircraft and small UAVs. Additional patrol vessels have, in recent years, improved maritime capability. Cameroon has no defence industrial capacity bar maintenance facilities.

ACTIVE 25,400 (Army 23,500 Navy 1,500 Air 400)
Gendarmerie & Paramilitary 9,000

ORGANISATIONS BY SERVICE

Army 23,500

5 Mil Regions

FORCES BY ROLE

MANOEUVRE

Light
1 rapid reaction bde (1 armd recce bn, 1 AB bn, 1 amph bn)
1 mot inf bde (4 mot inf bn, 1 spt bn)
5 mot inf bde (3 mot inf bn, 1 spt bn)
6 rapid reaction bn
4 inf bn

Air Manoeuvre
1 cdo/AB bn

Other
1 (Presidential Guard) gd bn

COMBAT SUPPORT

1 arty regt (5 arty bty)
5 engr regt

AIR DEFENCE

1 AD regt (6 AD bty)

EQUIPMENT BY TYPE

ARMOURED FIGHTING VEHICLES

ASLT 18: 6 AMX-10RC; ε12 PTL-02 mod (*Cara* 105)
RECCE 54: 31 AML-90; 15 *Ferret*; 8 M8
IFV 52: 8 LAV-150 *Commando* with 20mm gun; 14 LAV-150 *Commando* with 90mm gun; 22 *Ratel*-20 (Engr); ε8 Type-07P
APC 135
  APC (T) 12 M3 half-track
  APC (W) 66: 45 *Bastion* APC; 21 LAV-150 *Commando*
  PPV 57: 16 Gaia *Thunder*; 20 IAG *Rila*; 21 PKSV

AUV 19+: 6 *Cougar* 4×4; *Panthera* T6; 5 RAM Mk3; 3 *Tiger* 4×4; 5 VBL

ENGINEERING & MAINTENANCE VEHICLES
ARV WZ-551 ARV

ANTI-TANK/ANTI-INFRASTRUCTURE
MSL
SP 24 TOW (on Jeeps)
MANPATS *Milan*
RCL 53: **75mm** 13 Type-52 (M20); **106mm** 40 M40A2

ARTILLERY 106
SP **155mm** 18 ATMOS 2000
TOWED 52: **105mm** 20 M101; **130mm** 24: 12 M-1982 (reported); 12 Type-59 (M-46); **155mm** 8 M-71
MRL **122mm** 20 BM-21 *Grad*
MOR 16+: **81mm** (some SP); **120mm** 16 Brandt

AIR DEFENCE • GUNS
SP **20mm** RBY-1 with TCM-20
TOWED 54: **14.5mm** 18 Type-58 (ZPU-2); **35mm** 18 GDF-002; **37mm** 18 Type-63

Navy ε1,500

HQ located at Douala

EQUIPMENT BY TYPE

PATROL AND COASTAL COMBATANTS 15
PCC 3: 1 *Dipikar* (ex-FRA *Flamant*); 2 *Le Ntem* (PRC Poly Technologies 60m)
PB 10: 2 Aresa 2400; 2 Aresa 3200; 2 Rodman 101; 4 Rodman 46
PBR 2 *Swift*-38

AMPHIBIOUS • LANDING CRAFT 5
LCU 2 Type-067 (ex-PRC *Yunnan*)
LCM 2: 1 Aresa 2300; 1 *Le Moungo* (ex-PRC *Yuchin*)
LCVP 1 Munson 44 (US)

LOGISTICS AND SUPPORT • AFDL 1

Fusiliers Marin
FORCES BY ROLE
MANOEUVRE
Amphibious
3 mne bn

Air Force 300–400

FORCES BY ROLE

FIGHTER/GROUND ATTACK
1 sqn with *Alpha Jet**†

TRANSPORT
1 sqn with PA-23 *Aztec*
1 VIP unit with AS332 *Super Puma*; AS365 *Dauphin* 2; Bell 206B *Jet Ranger*; Gulfstream III

TRAINING
1 unit with *Tetras*

ATTACK HELICOPTER
1 sqn with Mi-24 *Hind*

TRANSPORT HELICOPTER
1 sqn with Bell 206L-3; Bell 412; SA319 *Alouette* III

EQUIPMENT BY TYPE

AIRCRAFT 6 combat capable
ISR 2 Cessna 208B *Grand Caravan*
TPT 14: **Medium** (2 C-130H *Hercules*; 1 C-130H-30 *Hercules* non-operational); **Light** 13: 1 CN235 (1 IAI-201 *Arava* in store); 2 J.300 *Joker*; 1 MA60; 2 PA-23 *Aztec*; 7 *Tetras*; **PAX** 1 Gulfstream III
TRG 6 *Alpha Jet**†

HELICOPTERS
ATK 2 Mi-24 *Hind*
MRH 10: 1 AS365 *Dauphin* 2; 4 Bell 412 *Twin Huey*; 2 SA319 *Alouette* III; 3 Z-9; (5 Mi-17 *Hip* H non-operational)
TPT 6: **Medium** 4: 2 AS332 *Super Puma*; 2 SA330J *Puma*; **Light** 2: 1 Bell 206B *Jet Ranger*; 1 Bell 206L-3 *Long Ranger*

AIR-LAUNCHED MISSILES
ASM AKD-8

Fusiliers de l'Air
FORCES BY ROLE
MANOEUVRE
Other
1 sy bn

Gendarmerie & Paramilitary 9,000

Gendarmerie 9,000
FORCES BY ROLE
MANOEUVRE
Reconnaissance
3 (regional spt) paramilitary gp

DEPLOYMENT

CENTRAL AFRICAN REPUBLIC: UN • MINUSCA 760; 1 inf bn

DEMOCRATIC REPUBLIC OF THE CONGO: UN • MONUSCO 4

Central African Republic CAR

CFA Franc BEAC XAF		2022	2023	2024
GDP	XAF	1.53trn	1.66trn	1.77trn
	USD	2.46bn	2.76bn	3.00bn
per capita	USD	491	539	573
Growth	%	0.5	1.0	2.5
Inflation	%	5.8	6.5	3.2
Def exp	XAF	24.1bn	37.8bn	
	USD	38.8m	63.1m	
USD1=XAF		622.43	599.88	592.54

Real-terms defence budget trend (USDm, constant 2015)

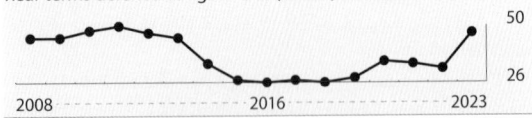

Population 5,552,228

Age	0–14	15–19	20–24	25–29	30–64	65 plus
Male	19.9%	5.6%	5.0%	4.2%	13.6%	1.5%
Female	19.0%	5.1%	4.7%	4.2%	15.4%	1.9%

Capabilities

Enduring internal security challenges pose significant problems for the country's still-developing national defence and security institutions that suffer from the effects of violence in 2013 and political volatility thereafter. The UN's MINUSCA mission remains the principal security provider in the country but has been targeted by armed groups. The UN is supporting development of a national defence policy. In recent years, Russia has deepened its military ties in the CAR and has donated small arms and armoured vehicles. Russia's Wagner Group remains active in the country. Apart from some equipment deliveries, the country remains under a UN arms embargo, though the terms have been eased. The security forces continue to receive training from UN forces and an EU training mission. Poor infrastructure and logistics capacity limit the armed forces' ability to provide security across the country. There is no independent capability to deploy troops externally. The lack of financial resources and defence-industrial capacity makes equipment maintenance problematic.

ACTIVE 9,150 (Army 9,000 Air 150) Gendarmerie & Paramilitary 1,000

Conscript liability Selective conscription 2 years; reserve obligation thereafter, term n.k.

ORGANISATIONS BY SERVICE

Army ε9,000
FORCES BY ROLE
MANOEUVRE
  Light
    1 spec ops bn
    7 inf bn
  Amphibious
    1 amph coy

EQUIPMENT BY TYPE
ARMOURED FIGHTING VEHICLES
  MBT 3 T-55†
  RECCE 28: 8 *Ferret*†; 20 BRDM-2
  IFV 18 *Ratel*
  APC • APC (W) 14+: 4 BTR-152†; 10+ VAB†
  AUV *Cobra* (reported)
ARTILLERY • MOR 12+: 81mm†; 120mm 12 M-1943†
ANTI-TANK/ANTI-INFRASTRUCTURE
  RCL 106mm 14 M40†
PATROL AND COASTAL COMBATANTS • PBR 9†

Air Force 150
EQUIPMENT BY TYPE
AIRCRAFT
  TPT 6: **Medium** (1 C-130A *Hercules* in store); **Light** 6: 3 BN-2 *Islander*; 1 Cessna 172RJ *Skyhawk*; 2 J.300 *Joker*
  TRG 4 L-39 *Albatros*
HELICOPTERS
  ATK 1 Mi-24V *Hind* E
  MRH some SA341B *Gazelle*
  TPT 2: **Medium** 1 Mi-8T *Hip*; **Light** 1 AS350 *Ecureuil*

FOREIGN FORCES

MINUSCA unless stated
Argentina 2
Bangladesh 1,419; 1 cdo coy; 1 inf bn; 1 med coy; 1 hel coy
Benin 7
Bhutan 187; 1 inf coy
Bolivia 7
Bsonia-Herzegovina EUTM RCA 3
Brazil 10
Burkina Faso 4
Burundi 762; 1 inf bn
Cambodia 345; 1 engr coy
Cameroon 760; 1 inf bn
Colombia 2
Congo 11
Côte d'Ivoire 2
Czech Republic 3
Ecuador 2
Egypt 1,015; 1 inf bn; 1 tpt coy
France 4 • EUTM RCA 1
Gabon 1
Gambia 9
Ghana 13
Guatemala 4
India 2
Indonesia 229; 1 engr coy
Jordan 10
Kazakhstan 1
Kenya 16
Lithuania EUTM RCA 1
Mauritania 465; 1 inf bn(-)
Mexico 2
Moldova 4

Mongolia 3
Morocco 781; 1 inf bn
Nepal 1,240; 2 inf bn; 1 MP pl
Niger 6
Nigeria 5
Pakistan 1,311; 1 inf bn; 2 engr coy; 1 hel sqn
Paraguay 4
Peru 258; 1 engr coy
Philippines 3
Poland EUTM RCA 2
Portugal 219; 1 AB coy • EUTM RCA 12
Romania EUTM RCA 15
Russia 13
Rwanda 2,146; 2 inf bn; 1 fd hospital
Senegal 192; 1 inf coy
Serbia 74; 1 med coy • EUTM RCA 7
Sierra Leone 7
Slovakia EUTM RCA 0
Spain EUTM RCA 8
Sri Lanka 113; 1 hel sqn
Tanzania 515; 1 inf bn(-)
Togo 10
Tunisia 775; 1 inf bn; 1 hel flt with 3 Bell 205
United States 9
Uruguay 3
Vietnam 8 • EUTM RCA 2
Zambia 936; 1 inf bn
Zimbabwe 4

Chad CHA

CFA Franc BEAC XAF		2022	2023	2024
GDP	XAF	7.53trn	7.77trn	8.21trn
	USD	12.1bn	12.6bn	13.2bn
per capita	USD	695	703	716
Growth	%	3.4	4.0	3.7
Inflation	%	5.8	7.0	3.5
Def bdgt	XAF	198bn	217bn	
	USD	318m	352m	
USD1=XAF		622.41	617.16	622.14

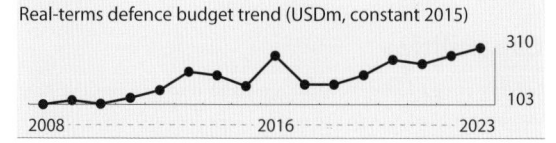

Real-terms defence budget trend (USDm, constant 2015)

Population	18,523,165					
Age	0–14	15–19	20–24	25–29	30–64	65 plus
Male	23.4%	5.7%	4.6%	3.5%	11.3%	1.1%
Female	22.8%	5.7%	4.5%	3.5%	12.4%	1.4%

Capabilities

Chad's principal security concerns relate to instability in West Africa and the Sahel and counter-insurgency operations against Boko Haram in the Lake Chad Basin area. Although the armed forces are combat experienced, they appear to have shortfalls in areas such as strategy and doctrine development, and command and control. The country has close defence cooperation ties with France, which has military forces headquartered in N'Djamena. French forces also contribute to the training of some elements of the Chadian military and security forces. In October 2023, Hungary said it planned to aid the government in Chad by deploying a small contingent to the country in 2024, in part to stem migrant flows. Chadian military skills are widely recognised by partners, though training levels are not uniform across the force. After the death of President Idriss Déby in 2021, his son became the leader of an interim administration. It passed reform plans for the armed forces, which would increase the size of the army. However, the changes still require endorsement by a transitional council. Chad lacks logistical capacity for routine rotations of deployed forces, relying on international partners for such operations. The US has donated military equipment to the country to bolster its ability to battle insurgents. Apart from maintenance facilities, there is no domestic defence-industrial capacity.

ACTIVE 33,250 (Army 27,500 Air 350 State Security Service 5,400) Gendarmerie & Paramilitary 11,900

Conscript liability Conscription authorised

ORGANISATIONS BY SERVICE

Army ε27,500

7 Mil Regions
FORCES BY ROLE
MANOEUVRE
  Armoured
  1 armd bn
  Light
  7 inf bn
COMBAT SUPPORT
  1 arty bn
  1 engr bn
  1 sigs bn
COMBAT SERVICE SUPPORT
  1 log gp
EQUIPMENT BY TYPE
Includes DGSSIE equipment
ARMOURED FIGHTING VEHICLES
  MBT 74: 60 T-55; 14 ZTZ-59G
  ASLT ε20 PTL-02 *Assaulter*
  RECCE 265: 132 AML-60/-90; ε100 BRDM-2; 20 EE-9 *Cascavel*; 9 ERC-90D *Sagaie*; 4 ERC-90F *Sagaie*
  IFV 131: 80 BMP-1; 42 BMP-1U; 9 LAV-150 *Commando* with 90mm gun
  APC 149
    APC (W) 103: 4+ *Bastion* APC; 24 BTR-80; 12 BTR-3E; ε20 BTR-60; ε10 *Black Scorpion*; 25 VAB-VTT; 8 WZ-523
    PPV 46: 20 *Ejder Yalcin*; 6+ KrAZ *Cougar*; 20 Proforce *Ara* 2
  AUV 110+: 22 *Bastion Patsas*; 7 MCAV-20; 31+ RAM Mk3; 30 *Terrier* LT-79; *Tiger* 4×4; ε20 *Yoruk* 4×4
ARTILLERY 34+
  SP 122mm 10 2S1 *Gvozdika*
  TOWED 13: **105mm** 5 M2; **122mm** 8+ D-74

MRL 11+: **107mm** some PH-63; **122mm** 11: 6 BM-21 *Grad*; 5 PHL-81
MOR **81mm** some; **120mm** AM-50
ANTI-TANK/ANTI-INFRASTRUCTURE
  MSL • **MANPATS** *Eryx*; *Milan*
  RCL **106mm** M40A1
AIR DEFENCE
  SAM
    Short-range 4 2K12 *Kub* (RS-SA-6 *Gainful*)
    Point-defence 9K310 *Igla*-1 (RS-SA-16 *Gimlet*)
  GUNS
    SP 10: **23mm** 6 ZSU-23-4 *Shilka*; **37mm** 4+ M-1939 (tch)
    TOWED **14.5mm** ZPU-1/-2/-4; **23mm** ZU-23-2

Air Force 350
FORCES BY ROLE
GROUND ATTACK
  1 unit with *Hurkus*-C*; PC-7; PC-9*; SF-260WL *Warrior*; Su-25 *Frogfoot*
TRANSPORT
  1 sqn with An-26 *Curl*; C-130H-30 *Hercules*; Mi-17 *Hip* H; Mi-171
  1 (Presidential) Flt with B-737BBJ; Beech 1900; DC-9-87; Gulfstream II
ATTACK HELICOPTER
  1 sqn with AS550C *Fennec*; Mi-24V *Hind*; SA316 *Alouette* III
MANOEUVRE
  Other
    1 sy bn
EQUIPMENT BY TYPE
AIRCRAFT 13 combat capable
  FTR (1 MiG-29S *Fulcrum* C in store)
  ATK 7: 6 Su-25 *Frogfoot* (2 more in store); 1 Su-25UB *Frogfoot* B (1 more in store)
  ISR 2 Cessna 208B *Grand Caravan*
  TPT **10**: **Medium** 3: 2 C-27J *Spartan*; 1 C-130H-30 *Hercules*; **Light** 4: 3 An-26 *Curl*; 1 Beech 1900; **PAX** 3: 1 B-737BBJ; 1 DC-9-87; 1 Gulfstream II
  TRG 7: 3 *Hurkus*-C*; 2 PC-7 (only 1*); 1 PC-9 *Turbo Trainer**; 1 SF-260WL *Warrior**
HELICOPTERS
  ATK 5 Mi-24V *Hind*
  MRH 8: 3 AS550C *Fennec*; 3 Mi-17 *Hip* H; 2 SA316
  TPT • **Medium** 2 Mi-171
UNIHABITED AERIAL VEHICLES
  CISR • **Heavy** 2 *Anka*-S
AIR-LAUNCHED MISSILES • **ASM** *Cirit*
BOMBS • **Laser-guided** MAM-L

State Security Service General Direction (DGSSIE) 5,400

Gendarmerie & Paramilitary 11,900 active

Gendarmerie 4,500

National and Nomadic Guard (GNNT) 7,400

Police Mobile Intervention Group (GMIP)

DEPLOYMENT
WESTERN SAHARA: UN • MINURSO 1

FOREIGN FORCES
Benin MNJTF 150
France 1,500; 1 mech inf BG; 1 FGA flt with 3 *Mirage* 2000D; 1 tkr/tpt flt with 1 A330 MRTT; 1 C-130H; 2 CN235M

Congo, Republic of COG

CFA Franc BEAC XAF		2022	2023	2024
GDP	XAF	8.69trn	8.64trn	9.14trn
	USD	14.0bn	14.4bn	15.4bn
per capita	USD	2,838	2,858	2,984
Growth	%	1.8	4.0	4.4
Inflation	%	3.0	3.5	3.2
Def bdgt	XAF	164bn	173bn	
	USD	263m	288m	
USD1=XAF		622.44	599.81	592.62

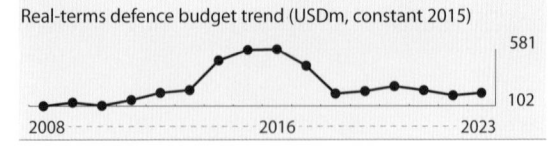

Real-terms defence budget trend (USDm, constant 2015)

Population 5,953,730

Age	0–14	15–19	20–24	25–29	30–64	65 plus
Male	19.3%	5.3%	4.3%	3.8%	15.4%	1.8%
Female	19.0%	5.3%	4.3%	3.8%	15.2%	2.4%

Capabilities

Congo's armed forces have struggled to recover from the brief but devastating civil war in the late 1990s. They have low levels of training and limited overall capability and use ageing equipment. France provides advisory assistance and capacity-building support in military administration and military and police capability. Congo signed a military-cooperation agreement with Russia in 2019. The country has a limited ability to deploy to neighbouring countries without external support. The navy is largely a riverine force, despite maritime security requirements driven by the country's small coastline. Congo is modernising aspects of its armed forces, including acquiring armoured vehicles. Maintenance limitations have, in recent years, particularly affected the air force; there is no domestic defence-industrial capability.

ACTIVE 10,000 (Army 8,000 Navy 800 Air 1,200)
Gendarmerie & Paramilitary 3,500

ORGANISATIONS BY SERVICE

Army 8,000
FORCES BY ROLE
MANOEUVRE
  Reconnaissance
  1 recce gp
  Mechanised
  1 mech bn
  1 mech inf bn
  Light
  1 inf bde (1 mech bn, 1 mot inf bn, 1 inf bn, 1 MRL gp, 1 ADA gp)
  1 inf bde (1 mot inf bn, 2 inf bn)
  1 mot inf bn
  3 inf bn
  Air Manoeuvre
  1 AB bn
COMBAT SUPPORT
  1 arty bn
  1 engr bn
  1 sigs bn
COMBAT SERVICE SUPPORT
  1 maint bn
AIR DEFENCE
  1 ADA bn
EQUIPMENT BY TYPE†
ARMOURED FIGHTING VEHICLES
  MBT 40: 25 T-54/T-55; 15 Type-59; (some T-34 in store)
  LT TK 13: 3 PT-76; 10 Type-62
  RECCE 25 BRDM-1/BRDM-2
  APC 142
    APC (W) 78+: 28 AT-105 *Saxon*; 20 BTR-152; 30 BTR-60; Panhard M3
    PPV 64: 18 *Mamba*; 37 *Marauder*; 9 Streit *Cobra*
  AUV 7: 2 *Tigr*; 5 *Patrol-A*
ARTILLERY 56
  SP 122mm 3 2S1 *Gvozdika*
  TOWED 15+: 122mm 10 D-30; 130mm 5 M-46; 152mm D-20
  MRL 10+: 122mm 10 BM-21 *Grad*; 140mm BM-14; 140mm BM-16
  MOR 28+: 82mm; 120mm 28 M-43
ANTI-TANK/ANTI-INFRASTRUCTURE
  RCL 57mm M18
  GUNS 15: 57mm 5 ZIS-2 (M-1943); 100mm 10 M-1944
AIR DEFENCE • GUNS
  SP 23mm ZSU-23-4 *Shilka*
  TOWED 14.5mm ZPU-2/-4; 37mm 28 M-1939; 57mm S-60; 100mm KS-19

Navy ε800
EQUIPMENT BY TYPE

PATROL AND COASTAL COMBATANTS 8
  PCC 4 *5 Fevrier 1979* (PRC Poly Technologies 47m)
  PBR 4

Naval Infantry
FORCES BY ROLE
MANOEUVRE
  Other
  1 sy bn

Air Force 1,200
FORCES BY ROLE
FIGHTER/GROUND ATTACK
  1 sqn with *Mirage* F-1AZ
TRANSPORT
  1 sqn with An-24 *Coke*; CN235M-100; Il-76TD *Candid*
EQUIPMENT BY TYPE†
AIRCRAFT 3 combat capable
  FGA up to 3 *Mirage* F-1AZ
  TPT 3: **Heavy** 1 Il-76TD *Candid*; **Light** 2: 1 An-24 *Coke*; 1 CN235M-100
HELICOPTERS
  ATK (2 Mi-35P *Hind* in store)
  TPT • **Medium** (3 Mi-8 *Hip* in store)
AIR-LAUNCHED MISSILES • AAM • IR R-3 (RS-AA-2 *Atoll*)‡

Gendarmerie & Paramilitary 3,500 active

Gendarmerie 2,000
FORCES BY ROLE
SPECIAL FORCES
  1 CT unit
EQUIPMENT BY TYPE
ARMOURED FIGHTING VEHICLES
  AUV 17: 10 *Tiger* 4×4; 2 *Tigr*; 5 *Patrol-A*

Republican Guard 1,500
FORCES BY ROLE
MANOEUVRE
  Other
  3 gd bn
EQUIPMENT BY TYPE
ARMOURED FIGHTING VEHICLES
  APC • PPV 3 Streit *Cobra*
  AUV 9: 6 MLS *Shield*; 3 *Tigr*

DEPLOYMENT

CENTRAL AFRICAN REPUBLIC: UN • MINUSCA 11

Côte d'Ivoire CIV

CFA Franc BCEAO XOF		2022	2023	2024
GDP	XOF	43.7trn	47.9trn	52.1trn
	USD	70.2bn	79.4bn	86.9bn
per capita	USD	2,473	2,728	2,909
Growth	%	6.7	6.2	6.6
Inflation	%	5.2	4.3	2.3
Def bdgt [a]	XOF	379bn	414bn	
	USD	608m	687m	
USD1=XOF		622.42	602.72	599.66

[a] Defence budget only - order and security expenses excluded

Real-terms defence budget trend (USDm, constant 2015)

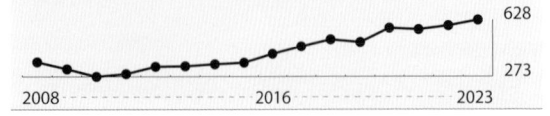

Population 29,344,847

Age	0–14	15–19	20–24	25–29	30–64	65 plus
Male	18.4%	5.7%	4.7%	4.1%	15.9%	1.3%
Female	18.2%	5.7%	4.7%	4.1%	15.4%	1.6%

Capabilities

The country is still regenerating its armed forces more than a decade after civil conflict in the country ebbed. The government has stepped up efforts to rebuild the military to address the deteriorating security in the north and the threat from Islamist insurgents, particularly in the wake of a 2020 attack by jihadists. Security sector reforms have shown progress. The 2021–25 National Development Plan indicated that efforts are being made to improve housing allowances for paramilitary personnel. The authorities have standardised promotion and salary structures to boost professionalisation and are also looking to improve military infrastructure. Côte d'Ivoire recently has been able to stop attacks from jihadists, though the threat remains. The armed forces have received new APCs and protected vehicles, as well as a refurbished former French patrol boat. The country has close defence ties with France, which has a significant training mission in the country, and helped build a training facility that opened in 2022. The armed-forces school at Zambakro runs courses for Ivorian as well as regional personnel. In 2021, with French assistance, Côte d'Ivoire opened the International Academy for the Fight Against Terrorism in Abidjan to help develop regional as well as Ivorian counter-terrorist capability. Except for limited maintenance facilities, there is no domestic defence-industrial capability.

ACTIVE 27,400 (Army 23,000 Navy 1,000 Air 1,400 Special Forces 2,000) Gendarmerie & Paramilitary n.k.

ORGANISATIONS BY SERVICE

Army ε23,000
FORCES BY ROLE
MANOEUVRE
  Armoured
    1 armd bn
  Light
    7 inf bn
  Air Manoeuvre
    1 cdo/AB bn
COMBAT SUPPORT
  1 arty bn
  1 engr bn
COMBAT SERVICE SUPPORT
  1 log bn
AIR DEFENCE
  1 AD bn
EQUIPMENT BY TYPE
ARMOURED FIGHTING VEHICLES
  MBT 10 T-55†
  RECCE 18: 13 BRDM-2; 5 *Cayman* BRDM
  IFV 10 BMP-1/BMP-2†
  APC 78
    APC (W) 56: 9 *Bastion* APC; 6 BTR-80; 12 Panhard M3; 13 VAB; 16 WZ-551
    PPV 22: 21 *Springbuck* HD; 1 *Snake*
  AUV 20 *Cobra* II
ENGINEERING & MAINTENANCE VEHICLES
  VLB MTU
ANTI-TANK/ANTI-INFRASTRUCTURE
  MSL • MANPATS 9K111-1 *Konkurs* (RS-AT-5 *Spandrel*) (reported); 9K135 *Kornet* (RS-AT-14 *Spriggan*) (reported)
  RCL 106mm ε12 M40A1
ARTILLERY 36
  TOWED 4+: **105mm** 4 M-1950; **122mm** (reported)
  MRL 122mm 6 BM-21
  MOR 26+: **81mm**; **82mm** 10 M-37; **120mm** 16 AM-50
AIRCRAFT • TPT • Medium 1 An-12 *Cub*†
AIR DEFENCE
  SAM • Point-defence 9K32 *Strela*-2 (RS-SA-7 *Grail*)‡ (reported)
  GUNS 21+
    SP 20mm 6 M3 VDAA
    TOWED 15+: **20mm** 10; **23mm** ZU-23-2; **40mm** 5 L/60

Navy ε1,000
EQUIPMENT BY TYPE
PATROL AND COASTAL COMBATANTS 7
  PCO 2 *Esperance* (ISR OPV 45)
  PCC 1 *Contre-Amiral Fadika* (ex-FRA P400)
  PB 4: 3 *L'Emergence*; 1 *Atchan* 2 (PRC 27m)
AMPHIBIOUS • LANDING CRAFT 1
  LCM 1 *Aby* (FRA CTM)

Air Force ε1,400
EQUIPMENT BY TYPE†
AIRCRAFT
  ISR 1 Beech C90 *King Air*
  TPT 6: **Light** 2: 1 An-26 *Curl*; 1 C295W; **PAX** 4: 1 A319CJ;

1 Gulfstream IV; 1 Gulfstream G450; 1 Gulfstream G550
HELICOPTERS
ATK 3 Mi-24V *Hind* E
MRH 3: 1 AW139; 2 Mi-8P *Hip*
TPT • **Medium** 2 SA330L *Puma* (IAR-330L)

Special Forces ε2,000
FORCES BY ROLE
SPECIAL FORCES
1 spec ops bde
EQUIPMENT BY TYPE
ARMOURED FIGHTING VEHICLES
APC 16
APC (W) 3 BTR-70MB
PPV 13 BATT UMG

Gendarmerie & Paramilitary n.k.

Republican Guard n.k.

Gendarmerie n.k.
EQUIPMENT BY TYPE†
ARMOURED FIGHTING VEHICLES
RECCE 3 *Cayman* BRDM
IFV BMP-1
APC
APC (W) BTR-70MB; VAB
PPV 5+ RG-31 *Nyala*; 5+ *Springbuck* HD; Streit *Spartan*
AUV LT-79 *Terrier*
PATROL AND COASTAL COMBATANTS • PB 1 *Bian*

DEPLOYMENT
CENTRAL AFRICAN REPUBLIC: UN • MINUSCA 2
GUINEA-BISSAU: ECOWAS • ESSMGB 150
WESTERN SAHARA: UN • MINURSO 2

FOREIGN FORCES
France 900; 1 inf bn; 1 (army) hel unit with 2 SA330 *Puma*; 2 SA342 *Gazelle*; 1 (air force) hel unit with 1 AS555 *Fennec*

Democratic Republic of the Congo DRC

Congolese Franc CDF		2022	2023	2024
GDP	CDF	132trn	160trn	183trn
	USD	65.8bn	67.5bn	73.3bn
per capita	USD	680	675	710
Growth	%	8.9	6.7	4.7
Inflation	%	9.3	19.1	10.6
Def bdgt	CDF	752bn	1.82trn	2.54trn
	USD	374m	765m	1.02bn
USD1=CDF		2,009.86	2,377.97	2,496.90

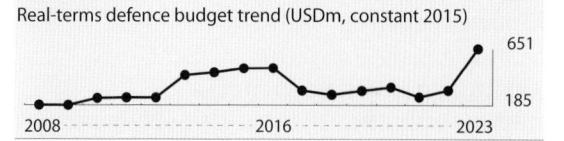

Real-terms defence budget trend (USDm, constant 2015)
651
185
2008 — 2016 — 2023

Population	111,859,928				
Age	0–14	15–19	20–24	25–29	30–64	65 plus
Male	23.2%	5.3%	4.4%	3.8%	12.2%	1.1%
Female	22.8%	5.2%	4.4%	3.8%	12.3%	1.4%

Capabilities

The country's size, and poor levels of military training, morale and equipment, mean that the armed forces are unable to provide security throughout the country. Kinshasa has pursued several military-modernisation programmes, though efforts to re-examine doctrine and organisation have yielded few results. Violence continued in the East in 2023, with a number of non-state armed groups active in the area. When conflict eventually abates there, significant attention to wide-ranging DDR and SSR will be required, to continue the work intermittently undertaken over the past decade. The mandate of the UN's MONUSCO mission in the DRC was extended in 2022, and the UN was to decide on its future in late 2023; in the meantime, the UN's Force Intervention Brigade (FIB) remains active in the east. Units operating with the FIB will have had improved training. Training also is provided through foreign assistance and capacity-building efforts. The armed forces have incorporated several non-state armed groups. Deployment capability is limited and the lack of logistics vehicles significantly reduces transport capacity. The lack of sufficient tactical airlift and helicopters is a brake on military effectiveness and there is some reliance on MONUSCO capabilities, which are also insufficient given the geographical scale of the country. Much of the inventory is in poor repair. The country has acquired new equipment, but the absence of a defence sector apart from limited maintenance capability hinders military efficiency.

ACTIVE 134,250 (Central Staffs 14,000 Army 103,000 Republican Guard 8,000 Navy 6,700 Air 2,550)

ORGANISATIONS BY SERVICE

Army ε103,000
The DRC has 10 Military Regions divided between four

Defence Zones. The actual combat effectiveness of many formations is doubtful.

FORCES BY ROLE

SPECIAL FORCES
 4 cdo bn

MANOEUVRE
 Light
 4 (Rapid Reaction) inf bde
 40+ inf regt
 3 jungle inf bn

COMBAT SUPPORT
 1 arty regt
 1 MP bn

EQUIPMENT BY TYPE†

(includes Republican Guard eqpt)

ARMOURED FIGHTING VEHICLES
 MBT 174: 12–17 ZTZ-59; 32 T-55; 25 T-64BV-1; 100 T-72AV
 LT TK 40: 10 PT-76; 30 ZTQ-62
 RECCE up to 50: up to 17 AML-60; 14 AML-90; 19 EE-9 *Cascavel*
 IFV 20 BMP-1
 APC 104+:
  APC (T) 9: 3 BTR-50; 6 MT-LB
  APC (W) 95+: 30–70 BTR-60PB; 20 *Mbombe*-4; 58 Panhard M3; 7 TH 390 *Fahd*
 AUV 30 MCAV-20

ANTI-TANK/ANTI-INFRASTRUCTURE
 RCL 57mm M18; **73mm** SPG-9; **75mm** M20; **106mm** M40A1
 GUNS 85mm 10 Type-56 (D-44)

ARTILLERY 726
 SP 16: **122mm** 6 2S1 *Gvozdika*; **152mm** 10 2S3 *Akatsiya*
 TOWED 125: **122mm** 77 M-30 (M-1938)/D-30/Type-60; **130mm** 42 Type-59 (M-46)/Type-59-I; **152mm** 6 D-20 (reported)
 MRL 57+: **107mm** 12 Type-63; **122mm** 24+: 24 BM-21 *Grad*; some RM-70; **128mm** 6 M-51; **130mm** 3 Type-82; **132mm** 12
 MOR 528+: **81mm** 100; **82mm** 400; **107mm** M30; **120mm** 28: 10 Brandt; 18 other

AIR DEFENCE
 SAM • Point-defence 9K32 *Strela*-2 (RS-SA-7 *Grail*)‡
 GUNS • TOWED 64: **14.5mm** 12 ZPU-4; **37mm** 52 M-1939

Republican Guard 8,000

FORCES BY ROLE

MANOEUVRE
 Armoured
 1 armd regt
 Light
 3 gd bde

COMBAT SUPPORT
 1 arty regt

Navy 6,700 (incl infantry and marines)

EQUIPMENT BY TYPE

PATROL AND COASTAL COMBATANTS 1
 PB 1 *Moliro* (Type-062 (PRC *Shanghai* II))†

Air Force 2,550

EQUIPMENT BY TYPE

AIRCRAFT 4 combat capable
 ATK up to 4 Su-25 *Frogfoot*
 TPT 4: **Medium** 1 C-130H *Hercules*; **Light** 1 An-26 *Curl*; **PAX** 2 B-727

HELICOPTERS
 ATK 6: 3 Mi-24 *Hind*; 3 Mi-24V *Hind*
 TPT 10 **Medium** 3: 1 AS332L *Super Puma*; 2 Mi-8 *Hip*; **Light** 7: 5 Bell 205 (UH-1H *Iroquois*); 2 Bell 206L *Long Ranger*

UNINHABITED AERIAL VEHICLES
 CISR • Heavy 3 CH-4B

Paramilitary

National Police Force
Incl Rapid Intervention Police (National and Provincial)

People's Defence Force

DEPLOYMENT

MOZAMBIQUE: SADC • SAMIM 1

FOREIGN FORCES

All part of MONUSCO unless otherwise specified
Algeria 2
Bangladesh 1,679; 1 inf bn; 1 engr coy; 1 avn coy; 1 hel coy
Belgium 1
Benin 9
Bhutan 2
Bolivia 4
Bosnia-Herzegovina 2
Botswana 3
Brazil 23
Burkina Faso 5
Burundi EACRF 1,000; 1 inf bn
Cameroon 4
Canada (*Operation Crocodile***)** 8
China, People's Republic of 231; 1 engr coy; 1 fd hospital
Czech Republic 2
Egypt 12
France 4
Gambia 2
Ghana 18
Guatemala 171; 1 spec ops coy
India 1,821; 2 inf bn; 1 med coy
Indonesia 1,035; 1 inf bn; 1 engr coy

Jordan 11
Kenya 358; 1 inf coy(+); EACRF 1,000; 1 inf bn
Liberia 1
Malawi 745; 1 inf bn
Malaysia 6
Mali 4
Mongolia 2
Morocco 925; 1 inf bn; 1 fd hospital
Nepal 1,152; 1 inf bn; 1 engr coy
Niger 5
Nigeria 9
Pakistan 1,908; 2 inf bn; 1 hel sqn with SA330 *Puma*
Paraguay 6
Peru 5
Poland 2
Romania 7
Russia 10
Senegal 7
Sierra Leone 2
South Africa (*Operation Mistral*) 1,143; 1 inf bn; 1 hel sqn
South Sudan EACRF 1,000; 1 inf bn
Tanzania 855; 1 spec ops coy; 1 inf bn
Tunisia 10
Uganda Army: 3,000; 1 inf bde; EACRF 2,000, 2 inf bn
United Kingdom 3
United States 3
Uruguay 803; 1 inf bn; 1 hel sqn
Zambia 11
Zimbabwe 3

Djibouti DJB

Djiboutian Franc DJF		2022	2023	2024
GDP	DJF	651bn	688bn	746bn
	USD	3.66bn	3.87bn	4.20bn
per capita	USD	3,604	3,761	4,026
Growth	%	3.2	5.0	6.0
Inflation	%	5.2	1.2	1.8
Def exp	DJF	n.k.	n.k.	n.k.
	USD	n.k.	n.k.	n.k.
FMA (US)	USD	6m	6m	6m
USD1=DJF		177.73	177.72	177.70

Population	976,143				
Age	0–14	15–19	20–24	25–29	30–64	65 plus
Male	14.4%	4.6%	4.6%	4.4%	15.6%	1.8%
Female	14.3%	4.8%	5.4%	5.7%	22.2%	2.3%

Capabilities

Djibouti's strategic location and relative stability have led a number of foreign states to station forces in the country. The main responsibility for its own armed forces is internal and border security, as well as counter-insurgency operations. A 2017 defence white paper highlighted a requirement to modernise key capabilities, though funding is limited. Recent purchases including armed UAVs from Türkiye. Djibouti maintains close defence cooperation with France, with the largest foreign military base in the country. The US operates its Combined Joint Task Force–Horn of Africa from Djibouti. China in 2017 opened its first overseas military base, including dock facilities, in Djibouti. Japan has based forces there for regional counter-piracy missions and the EU and NATO have at various times maintained a presence to support their operations. Djibouti also hosts an Italian base that is focused on anti-piracy activities. France and the US provide Djibouti with training assistance. EU NAVFOR Somalia has delivered maritime security training to the navy and coastguard. Djibouti participates in several regional multinational exercises and contributes personnel to an international mission in Somalia but has limited capacity to independently deploy beyond its territory. Army equipment consists predominantly of older French and Soviet-era systems. Djibouti has some maintenance facilities, but no defence manufacturing sector.

ACTIVE 8,450 (Army 8,000 Navy 200 Air 250)
Gendarmerie & Paramilitary 4,650

ORGANISATIONS BY SERVICE

Army ε8,000
FORCES BY ROLE
4 military districts (Tadjourah, Dikhil, Ali-Sabieh and Obock)
MANOEUVRE
  Mechanised
    1 armd regt (1 recce sqn, 3 armd sqn, 1 (anti-smuggling) sy coy)
  Light
    4 inf regt (3-4 inf coy, 1 spt coy)
    1 rapid reaction regt (4 inf coy, 1 spt coy)
  Other
    1 (Republican Guard) gd regt (1 sy sqn, 1 (close protection) sy sqn, 1 cbt spt sqn (1 recce pl, 1 armd pl, 1 arty pl), 1 spt sqn)
COMBAT SUPPORT
  1 arty regt
  1 demining coy
  1 sigs regt
  1 CIS sect
COMBAT SERVICE SUPPORT
  1 log regt
  1 maint coy
EQUIPMENT BY TYPE
ARMOURED FIGHTING VEHICLES
  ASLT 3+ PTL-02 *Assaulter*
  RECCE 23: 4 AML-60†; 17 AML-90; 2 BRDM-2
  IFV 28: 8 BTR-80A; 16-20 *Ratel*
  APC 67
    APC (W) 30+: 12 BTR-60†; 4+ AT-105 *Saxon*; 14 *Puma*
    PPV 37: 3 *Casspir*; some IAG *Guardian Xtreme*; 10 RG-33L; 24 *Puma* M36
  AUV 37: 10 *Cougar* 4×4 (one with 90mm gun); 2 CS/VN3B; 10 PKSV; 15 VBL
ANTI-TANK/ANTI-INFRASTRUCTURE
  RCL 106mm 16 M40A1

ARTILLERY 82
  SP 155mm 10 M109L
  TOWED 122mm 9 D-30
  MRL 12: **107mm** 2 PKSV AUV with PH-63; **122mm** 10: 6 (6-tube Toyota Land Cruiser 70 series); 2 (30-tube Iveco 110-16); 2 (30-tube)
  MOR 51: **81mm** 25; **120mm** 26: 20 Brandt; 6 RT-F1
AIR DEFENCE • GUNS 15+
  SP 20mm 5 M693
  TOWED 10: **23mm** 5 ZU-23-2; **40mm** 5 L/70

Navy ε200
EQUIPMENT BY TYPE
PATROL AND COASTAL COMBATANTS 14
  PCC 2 *Adj Ali M Houmed* (NLD Damen Stan Patrol 5009)
  PBF 3: 2 Battalion-17; 1 Safe 65
  PB 9: 1 PRC 27m; 2 Sea Ark 1739; 6 others
AMPHIBIOUS 2
  LANDING SHIPS • LSM 1 Type-074 (*Yuhai*) (capacity 6 light tanks)
  LANDING CRAFT • LCT 1 EDIC 700
LOGISTICS AND SUPPORT • AKR 1 *Col. Maj. Ali Gaad* (NLD Damen Stan Lander 5612)

Air Force 250
EQUIPMENT BY TYPE
AIRCRAFT
  TPT • Light 8: 1 Cessna U206G *Stationair*; 1 Cessna 208 *Caravan*; 2 Y-12E; 1 L-410UVP *Turbolet*; 1 MA60; 2 Short 360 *Sherpa*
HELICOPTERS
  ATK (2 Mi-35 *Hind* in store)
  MRH 6: 4 AS365 *Dauphin*; 1 Mi-17 *Hip* H; 1 Z-9WE
  TPT 3: **Medium** 1 Mi-8T *Hip*; **Light** 2 AS355F *Ecureuil* II
UNINHABITED AERIAL VEHICLES
  CISR • Medium 2+ *Bayraktar* TB2
BOMBS • Laser-guided MAM-L

Gendarmerie & Paramilitary ε4,650

Gendarmerie 2,000
Ministry of Defence
FORCES BY ROLE
MANOEUVRE
  Other
    1 paramilitary bn
EQUIPMENT BY TYPE
AFV • AUV 2 CS/VN3B

Coast Guard 150
EQUIPMENT BY TYPE
PATROL AND COASTAL COMBATANTS • PB 11: 2 *Khor Angar*; 9 other

National Police Force ε2,500
Ministry of Interior

DEPLOYMENT
SOMALIA: AU • ATMIS 700; 1 inf bn

FOREIGN FORCES
China 400: 1 spec ops coy; 1 mne coy; 1 med unit; 2 ZTL-11; 8 ZBL-08
France 1,500: 1 SF unit; 1 combined arms regt (2 recce sqn, 2 inf coy, 1 arty bty, 1 engr coy); 1 hel det with 4 SA330 *Puma*; 3 SA342 *Gazelle*; 1 LCM; 1 FGA sqn with 4 *Mirage* 2000-5; 1 SAR/tpt sqn with 1 CN235M; 3 SA330 *Puma*
Italy BMIS 150
Japan 180; 2 P-3C *Orion*
Spain Operation Atalanta 60; 1 CN235 VIGMA
United States US Africa Command: 4,000; 1 tpt sqn with C-130H/J-30 *Hercules*; 1 tpt sqn with 12 MV-22B *Osprey*; 2 KC-130J *Hercules*; 1 spec ops sqn with MC-130J; PC-12 (U-28A); 1 CSAR sqn with HH-60G *Pave Hawk*; 1 CISR sqn with MQ-9A *Reaper*; 1 naval air base

Equatorial Guinea EQG

CFA Franc BEAC XAF		2022	2023	2024
GDP	XAF	7.34trn	6.05trn	6.20trn
	USD	11.8bn	10.0bn	10.3bn
per capita	USD	7,854	6,502	6,500
Growth	%	3.2	-6.2	-5.5
Inflation	%	4.9	2.4	4.0
Def exp	XAF	n.k.	n.k.	n.k.
	USD	n.k.	n.k.	n.k.
USD1=XAF		623.78	602.71	599.63
Population	1,737,695			

Age	0–14	15–19	20–24	25–29	30–64	65 plus
Male	18.6%	5.6%	4.9%	4.1%	17.7%	2.6%
Female	17.4%	4.7%	4.0%	3.4%	14.7%	2.4%

Capabilities

Internal security is the principal task for the armed forces. Equatorial Guinea has, for years, been trying to modernise its forces, which remain dominated by the army. French forces in Gabon help training the country's military. There is only limited capability for power projection and deployments are limited to neighbouring countries without external support. Recent naval investments include equipment and onshore-infrastructure improvements at Bata and Malabo, although naval capabilities remain limited. Maritime-security concerns in the Gulf of Guinea have resulted in an increased emphasis on boosting maritime-patrol capacity. There is limited maintenance capacity and no defence-industrial sector.

ACTIVE 1,750 (Army 1,100 Navy 550 Air 100)

ORGANISATIONS BY SERVICE

Army 1,100
FORCES BY ROLE
MANOEUVRE
  Mechanised
    1 mech inf bn
  Light
    3 inf bn(-)
EQUIPMENT BY TYPE
ARMOURED FIGHTING VEHICLES
  MBT 3 T-55
  ASLT 6 PTL-02 *Assaulter*
  RECCE 6 BRDM-2
  IFV 23: 20 BMP-1; 3 WZ-551 IFV
  APC 41
    APC (W) 16: 10 BTR-152; 6 WZ-551
    PPV 25 *Reva*
  AUV Dongfeng *Mengshi*
ANTI-TANK/ANTI-INFRASTRUCTURE
  MSL • MANPATS HJ-8
AIR DEFENCE
  SAM Point-defence QW-2 (CH-SA-8)
  GUNS • SP • 23mm ZU-23-2 (tch)

Navy ε550
EQUIPMENT BY TYPE
PRINCIPAL SURFACE COMBATANTS • FRIGATES 1
  FF 1 *Wele Nzas* with 2 MS-227 *Ogon'* 122mm MRL, 2 AK630 CIWS, 2 76mm guns, 1 hel landing platform
PATROL AND COASTAL COMBATANTS 10
  CORVETTES • FSG 1 *Bata* with 2 *Katran*-M RWS with *Barrier* SSM, 2 AK630 CIWS, 1 76mm gun
  PCC 2 OPV 62 (ISR *Sa'ar* 4.5 derivative)
  PBF 2 *Isla de Corisco* (ISR *Shaldag* II)
  PB 5: 1 *Daphne†*; 2 *Estuario de Muni*; 2 *Zhuk*
LOGISTICS AND SUPPORT
  AKRH 1 *Capitán David Eyama Angue Osa* with 1 76mm gun

Air Force 100
EQUIPMENT BY TYPE
AIRCRAFT 4 combat capable
  ATK 4: 2 Su-25 *Frogfoot*; 2 Su-25UB *Frogfoot* B
  TPT 4: **Light** 3: 1 An-32B *Cline*; 2 An-72 *Coaler*; **PAX** 1 *Falcon* 900 (VIP)
  TRG 2 L-39C *Albatros*
HELICOPTERS
  ATK 5 Mi-24P/V *Hind*
  MRH 1 Mi-17 *Hip* H
  TPT 4: **Heavy** 1 Mi-26 *Halo*; **Medium** 1 Ka-29 *Helix*; **Light** 2 Enstrom 480

Gendarmerie & Paramilitary

Guardia Civil
FORCES BY ROLE
MANOEUVRE
  Other
    2 paramilitary coy

Coast Guard n.k.

FOREIGN FORCES
Uganda UMTMT 250

Eritrea ERI

Eritrean Nakfa ERN		2022	2023	2024
GDP	ERN			
	USD			
per capita	USD			
Growth	%			
Inflation	%			
Def exp	ERN			
	USD			

USD1–ERN

Definitive economic data unavailable

Population	6,274,796

Age	0–14	15–19	20–24	25–29	30–64	65 plus
Male	18.2%	5.8%	4.6%	4.0%	15.0%	1.6%
Female	18.0%	5.8%	4.7%	4.1%	15.8%	2.4%

Capabilities

Eritrea maintains large armed forces mainly because of its historical conflict with Ethiopia. The easing of tensions following a 2018 peace agreement has afforded the armed forces the opportunity to consider restructuring and recapitalisation. The full extent of Eritrea's military involvement in the conflict in the neighbouring Ethiopian province of Tigray remains unclear, as does its level of support and cooperation with the Ethiopian armed forces. A year on from the November 2022 peace agreement between Ethiopia and the Tigray People's Liberation Front Eritrea – a non-signatory – had not fully withdrawn its forces back over the border. Maritime insecurity, including piracy, remains a challenge. It appears that the foreign military presence and related facilities at the coastal town of Assab, which were used to support Gulf states' participation in the Yemen campaign, were wound down by mid-2021. Eritrea has mandatory conscription and maintains a large army. For some, the term of service is reportedly indefinite, and significant numbers of conscripts have chosen to leave the country or otherwise evade service. These factors have likely affected overall military cohesion and effectiveness. Eritrea has demonstrated limited capacity to deploy beyond its immediate borders. The armed forces' inventory primarily comprises outdated Soviet-era systems and modernisation was restricted by the UN arms embargo until it was lifted in 2018. The arms embargo resulted in serviceability issues, notwithstanding allegations of external support. The navy remains capable of only limited coastal-patrol and interception operations.

The country has limited maintenance capability, but no defence-manufacturing sector.

ACTIVE 301,750 (Army 300,000 Navy 1,400 Air 350)

Conscript liability 18 months (4 months mil trg) between ages 18 and 40

RESERVE n.k.

ORGANISATIONS BY SERVICE

Army ε300,000 (including mobilised reserves)

Div mostly bde sized

FORCES BY ROLE
COMMAND
  4 corps HQ
SPECIAL FORCES
  1 cdo div
MANOEUVRE
  Mechanised
  6 mech div
  Light
  ε50 inf div
EQUIPMENT BY TYPE
ARMOURED FIGHTING VEHICLES
  MBT 270 T-54/T-55
  RECCE 40 BRDM-1/BRDM-2
  IFV 15 BMP-1
  APC 35
    APC (T) 10 MT-LB†
    APC (W) 25 BTR-152/BTR-60
ENGINEERING & MAINTENANCE VEHICLES
  ARV T-54/T-55 reported
  VLB MTU reported
ANTI-TANK/ANTI-INFRASTRUCTURE
  MSL • **MANPATS** 9K11 *Malyutka* (RS-AT-3 *Sagger*); 9K111-1 *Konkurs* (RS-AT-5 *Spandrel*)
  GUNS 85mm D-44
ARTILLERY 258
  SP 45: **122mm** 32 2S1 *Gvozdika*; **152mm** 13 2S5 *Giatsint*-S
  TOWED 19+: **122mm** D-30; **130mm** 19 M-46
  MRL 44: **122mm** 35 BM-21 *Grad*; **220mm** 9 9P140 *Uragan*
  MOR 150+: **82mm** 50+; **120mm/160mm** 100+
AIR DEFENCE
  SAM • **Point-defence** 9K32 *Strela*-2 (RS-SA-7 *Grail*)‡
  GUNS 70+
    SP 23mm ZSU-23-4 *Shilka*
    TOWED 23mm ZU-23

Navy 1,400

EQUIPMENT BY TYPE
PATROL AND COASTAL COMBATANTS 28
  PBF 16: 6 Battalion-17; 4 Rodman 33; 6 other; (4 *Super Dvora* non-operational)
  PB 12: 3 Swift 105†; 9 other
AMPHIBIOUS 4
  LANDING SHIP 2
    LST 2: 1 *Chamo*† (Ministry of Transport); 1 *Ashdod*†
  LANDING CRAFT 2
    LCU 2: 1 T-4† (in harbour service); 1 other

Air Force ε350

FORCES BY ROLE
FIGHTER/GROUND ATTACK
  1 sqn with MiG-29/MiG-29SE/MiG-29UB *Fulcrum*
  1 sqn with Su-27/Su-27UBK *Flanker*
TRANSPORT
  1 sqn with Y-12(II)
TRAINING
  1 sqn with MB-339CE*
TRANSPORT HELICOPTER
  1 sqn with Bell 412EP *Twin Huey*
  1 sqn with Mi-17 *Hip H*
EQUIPMENT BY TYPE
AIRCRAFT 14 combat capable
  FTR 8: 4 MiG-29 *Fulcrum*; 2 MiG-29UB *Fulcrum*; 1 Su-27 *Flanker*; 1 Su-27UBK *Flanker*
  FGA 2 MiG-29SE *Fulcrum*
  TPT • **Light** 5: 1 Beech 200 *King Air*; 4 Y-12(II)
  TRG 8: 4 MB-339CE*; 4+ Z-143/Z-242
HELICOPTERS
  ATK 2 Mi-24 *Hind*
  MRH 8: 4 Bell 412EP *Twin Huey* (AB-412EP); 4 Mi-17 *Hip H*
AIR-LAUNCHED MISSILES
  AAM • **IR** R-60 (RS-AA-8 *Aphid*); R-73 (RS-AA-11A *Archer*); **IR/SARH** R-27 (RS-AA-10 *Alamo*)

DEPLOYMENT

Ethiopia: 40,000 (reported)

Ethiopia ETH

Ethiopian Birr ETB		2022	2023	2024
GDP	ETB	6.16trn	8.50trn	11.3trn
	USD	120bn	156bn	192bn
per capita	USD	1,156	1,473	1,787
Growth	%	6.4	6.1	6.2
Inflation	%	33.9	29.1	20.7
Def bdgt	ETB	22.0bn	84.0bn	50.0bn
	USD		430m	1.54bn	849m
USD1=ETB		51.16	54.55	58.89

Real-terms defence budget trend (USDbn, constant 2015)

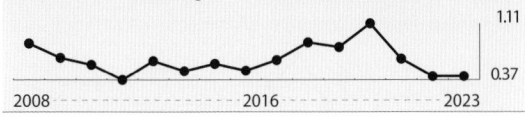

Population 115,757,473

Age	0–14	15–19	20–24	25–29	30–64	65 plus
Male	19.6%	5.3%	4.6%	3.9%	14.9%	1.5%
Female	19.4%	5.3%	4.6%	4.0%	15.2%	1.8%

Capabilities

Ethiopia's armed forces are among the region's largest and most capable. Prior to a November 2022 peace agreement with Tigray People's Liberation Front (TPLF), Ethiopia's military was engaged in a two-year internal conflict in and around the Northern province of Tigray. The fighting involved several ethnic groups in Ethiopia. In 2023, conflict broke out in the neighbouring Amaha region with the FANO militia group, leading to Addis Ababa declaring a six-month state of emergency for the region. The Ethiopian armed forces' other tasks include countering al-Shabaab – which conducted a significant incursion in July 2022. They also support regional security initiatives, such as the African Union presence in Somalia and the UN mission in South Sudan. The armed forces are experienced by regional standards, with a history of combat operations and international peacekeeping deployments. Personnel numbers rose after a recruitment campaign during the Tigray conflict. The loss of Northern Command bases in the early fighting led to equipment losses though the degree of conflict-related attrition remains unclear. The military inventory comprises mostly Soviet-era equipment, though it has acquired surplus stocks from China, Hungary, Ukraine and the US. Ethiopia purchased modern air-defence systems from Russia and, in response to the Tigray conflict, procured UAVs from Turkiye, China and reportedly Iran. The country has a modest defence-industrial base, primarily centred on small arms, with some licensed production of light armoured vehicles. Ethiopia has adequate maintenance capability but only a limited ability to support advanced platforms.

ACTIVE 503,000 (Army 500,000 Air 3,000)

ORGANISATIONS BY SERVICE

Army ε500,000

Div mostly bde sized

FORCES BY ROLE

SPECIAL FORCES
1 cdo div

MANOEUVRE

Mechanised
5 mech inf div

Light
ε70 inf div

Other
1 (Republican Guard) gd div

EQUIPMENT BY TYPE

ARMOURED FIGHTING VEHICLES
MBT 220: ε120 T-55/T-62; ε100 T-72B/UA1
RECCE ε50 BRDM-1/BRDM-2
IFV ε20 BMP-1
APC 275+
    APC (T) ε200 ZSD-89
    APC (W) BTR-60; WZ-551
    PPV 75 Gaia *Thunder*
AUV some *Ze'ev*

ENGINEERING & MAINTENANCE VEHICLES
ARV T-54/T-55 ARV reported; 3 BTS-5B
VLB GQL-111; MTU reported
MW *Bozena*

ANTI-TANK/ANTI-INFRASTRUCTURE
MSL • MANPATS 9K11 *Malyutka* (RS-AT-3 *Sagger*); 9K111 *Fagot* (RS-AT-4 *Spigot*); 9K135 *Kornet*-E (RS-AT-14 *Spriggan*)
RCL 82mm B-10; 107mm B-11
GUNS 85mm D-44

ARTILLERY 262+
SP 42+: 122mm 2S1 *Gvozdika*; 152mm 10 2S19 *Msta*-S; 155mm 32 SH-15
TOWED 200+: 122mm ε200 D-30/M-30 (M-1938); 130mm M-46; 155mm AH2
MRL 20+: 107mm PH-63; 122mm ε20 BM-21 *Grad*; 300mm AR-2†
MOR 81mm M1/M29; 82mm M-1937; 120mm M-1944

AIR DEFENCE
SAM
    Medium-range ε4 S-75M3 *Volkhov* (RS-SA-2 *Guideline*)
    Short-range ε4 S-125M1 *Pechora*-M1 (RS-SA-3 *Goa*)
    Point-defence 9K32 *Strela*-2 (RS-SA-7 *Grail*)‡; 9K310 *Igla*-1 (RS-SA-16 *Gimlet*)
SPAAGM 30mm ε6 96K6 *Pantsir*-S2 (RS-SA-22 *Greyhound*)
GUNS
    SP 23mm ZSU-23-4 *Shilka*
    TOWED 23mm ZU-23; 37mm M-1939; 57mm S-60

Air Force 3,000

FORCES BY ROLE
FIGHTER/GROUND ATTACK

1 sqn with Su-27/Su-27UB *Flanker*

TRANSPORT

1 sqn with An-12 *Cub*; An-26 *Curl*; An-32 *Cline*; Beech 200GT *King Air*; C-130B *Hercules*; DHC-6 *Twin Otter*; L-100-30; Yak-40 *Codling* (VIP)

TRAINING

1 sqn with L-39 *Albatros*

1 sqn with G 120TP

1 sqn with Cessna 172

ATTACK/TRANSPORT HELICOPTER

2 sqn with Mi-24/Mi-35 *Hind*; Mi-8 *Hip*; Mi-17 *Hip* H; SA316 *Alouette* III

EQUIPMENT BY TYPE

AIRCRAFT 14 combat capable

FTR 11: 8 Su-27 *Flanker*; 3 Su-27UB *Flanker*

FGA (6+ MiG-23BN/UB *Flogger* H/C in store)

ATK 3: 1 Su-25T *Frogfoot*; 2 Su-25UB *Frogfoot*

TPT 19: **Medium** 8: 3 An-12 *Cub*; 2 C-130B *Hercules*; 2 C-130E *Hercules*; 1 L-100-30; **Light** 11: 1 An-26 *Curl*; 1 An-32 *Cline*; 1 Beech 200GT *King Air*; 4 Cessna 172; 3 DHC-6 *Twin Otter*; 1 Yak-40 *Codling* (VIP)

TRG 24: 12 G 120TP; 12 L-39 *Albatros*

HELICOPTERS

ATK 16: 15 Mi-24 *Hind*; 1 Mi-35 *Hind*

MRH 21: 3 AW139; 6 SA316 *Alouette* III; 12 Mi-8 *Hip*/Mi-17 *Hip* H

UNINHABITED AERIAL VEHICLES

CISR 4: **Heavy** some *Wing Loong* I; **Medium** 4+: some *Mohajer* 6 (reported); 4+ *Bayraktar* TB2

AIR-LAUNCHED MISSILES

AAM • **IR** R-3 (RS-AA-2 *Atoll*)‡; R-27ET (RS-AA-10D *Alamo*); R-60 (RS-AA-8 *Aphid*); R-73 (RS-AA-11A *Archer*); **SARH** R-27 (RS-AA-10 *Alamo*)

ASM Kh-25ML (RS-AS-12B *Kegler*); Kh-29T (RS-AS-14B *Kedge*); TL-2 (reported)

BOMBS

Laser-guided MAM-L

TV-guided KAB-500KR

DEPLOYMENT

SOMALIA: AU • ATMIS 3,600; 4 inf bn

SOUTH SUDAN: UN • UNMISS 1,497; 2 inf bn

FOREIGN FORCES

Eritrea Army: 40,000 (reported)

Gabon GAB

CFA Franc BEAC XAF		2022	2023	2024
GDP	XAF	13.1trn	11.6trn	11.9trn
	USD	21.1bn	19.3bn	19.9bn
per capita	USD	9,771	8,832	8,969
Growth	%	3.0	2.8	2.6
Inflation	%	4.3	3.8	2.5
Def bdgt [a]	XAF	173bn	161bn	
	USD	278m	267m	
USD1=XAF		622.43	602.71	599.65

[a] Includes funds allocated to Republican Guard

Real-terms defence budget trend (USDm, constant 2015)

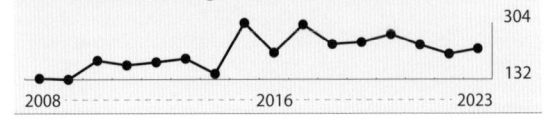

Population 2,397,368

Age	0–14	15–19	20–24	25–29	30–64	65 plus
Male	17.7%	5.8%	5.3%	5.1%	15.8%	2.1%
Female	17.3%	5.5%	4.9%	4.4%	14.1%	2.1%

Capabilities

Military officers seized power in August 2023, placing president Ali Bongo Ondimba under house arrest after the country's election body announced his re-election. The officers declared that they had annulled the results of the vote, asserting the outcome lacked credibility. The country's oil revenues have allowed the government to support small but regionally capable armed forces. Gabon has benefited from a long-term presence of French troops acting as a security guarantor. French forces have provided regular training, including with regionally deployed naval units, to Gabon's armed forces, which also have worked with other international partners, including the US. Gabonese forces have taken part in the US Navy-led *Obangame Express* exercise series. Following the coup, the US suspended much assistance to the country, while France's military cooperation gradually resumed after a short cessation. Gabon's armed forces have sufficient airlift to ensure mobility within the country, but limited capability to project power by sea and air. Apart from limited maintenance facilities, there is no defence industry.

ACTIVE 4,700 (Army 3,200 Navy 500 Air 1,000)
Gendarmerie & Paramilitary 2,000

ORGANISATIONS BY SERVICE

Army 3,200

Republican Guard under direct presidential control

FORCES BY ROLE

MANOEUVRE

Light

1 (Republican Guard) gd gp (bn) (1 armd/recce coy, 3 inf coy, 1 arty bty, 1 ADA bty)

8 inf coy

Air Manoeuvre

1 cdo/AB coy

COMBAT SUPPORT

1 engr coy

EQUIPMENT BY TYPE

ARMOURED FIGHTING VEHICLES

RECCE 60: 28 AML-60/AML-90; 12 EE-3 *Jararaca*; 14 EE-9 *Cascavel*; 6 ERC-90F4 *Sagaie*

IFV 22: 12 EE-11 *Urutu* (with 20mm gun); 10 VN-1

APC 93

APC (W) 35: 9 LAV-150 *Commando*; 5 *Bastion* APC; 3 WZ-523; 5 VAB; 12 VXB-170; 1 *Pandur*

PPV 58: 8 *Aravis*; 34 *Matador*; 16 VP-11

AUV 17: 3 RAM Mk3; 14 VBL

ANTI-TANK/ANTI-INFRASTRUCTURE

MSL • MANPATS *Milan*

RCL 106mm M40A1

ARTILLERY 67

TOWED 105mm 4 M101

MRL 24: 107mm 16 PH-63; 140mm 8 *Teruel*

MOR 39: 81mm 35; 120mm 4 Brandt

AIR DEFENCE • GUNS 41

SP 20mm 4 ERC-20

TOWED 37+: 14.5mm ZPU-4; 23mm 24 ZU-23-2; 37mm 10 M-1939; 40mm 3 L/70

Navy ε500

HQ located at Port Gentil

EQUIPMENT BY TYPE

PATROL AND COASTAL COMBATANTS 10

PB 10: 1 *Patra*†; 4 *Port Gentil* (FRA RPB 20); 4 *Awore* (Rodman 66); 1 *Vice Amiral d'Escadre Jean Léonard Mbini* (PRC Poly Technologies 47m)

AMPHIBIOUS • LANDING CRAFT 1

LCM 1 *Leconi* II (Ex-UK LCU Mk 9)

Air Force 1,000

FORCES BY ROLE

FIGHTER/GROUND ATTACK

1 sqn with *Mirage* F-1AZ

TRANSPORT

1 (Republican Guard) sqn with AS332 *Super Puma*; ATR-42F; *Falcon* 900; Gulfstream IV-SP/G650ER

1 sqn with C-130H *Hercules*; C295W; CN-235M-100

ATTACK/TRANSPORT HELICOPTER

1 sqn with Bell 412 *Twin Huey* (AB-412); SA330C/H *Puma*; SA342M *Gazelle*

EQUIPMENT BY TYPE

AIRCRAFT 8 combat capable

FGA 6 *Mirage* F-1AZ

MP (1 EMB-111* in store)

TPT 7: Medium 1 C-130H *Hercules*; (1 L-100-30 in store); Light 3: 1 ATR-42F; 1 C295W; 1 CN-235M-100; PAX 3: 1 *Falcon* 900; 1 Gulfstream IV-SP; 1 Gulfstream G650ER

TRG 2 MB-326 *Impala* I* (4 CM-170 *Magister* in store)

HELICOPTERS

MRH 2: 1 Bell 412 *Twin Huey* (AB-412); 1 SA342M *Gazelle*; (2 SA342L *Gazelle* in store)

TPT 7: Medium 4: 1 AS332 *Super Puma*; 3 SA330C/H *Puma*; Light 3: 2 H120 *Colibri*; 1 H135

AIR-LAUNCHED MISSILES • AAM • IR U-*Darter* (reported)

Gendarmerie & Paramilitary 2,000

Gendarmerie 2,000

FORCES BY ROLE

MANOEUVRE

Armoured

2 armd sqn

Other

3 paramilitary bde

11 paramilitary coy

Aviation

1 unit with AS350 *Ecureuil*; AS355 *Ecureuil* II

EQUIPMENT BY TYPE

HELICOPTERS • TPT • Light 4: 2 AS350 *Ecureuil*; 2 AS355 *Ecureuil* II

DEPLOYMENT

CENTRAL AFRICAN REPUBLIC: UN • MINUSCA 1

FOREIGN FORCES

France 350; 1 inf bn

Gambia GAM

Gambian Dalasi GMD		2022	2023	2024
GDP	GMD	123bn	147bn	171bn
	USD	2.16bn	2.39bn	2.68bn
per capita	USD	842	903	985
Growth	%	4.9	5.6	6.2
Inflation	%	11.5	17.0	12.3
Def bdgt	GMD	777m	852m	
	USD	13.7m	13.8m	
USD1=GMD		56.72	61.74	63.58

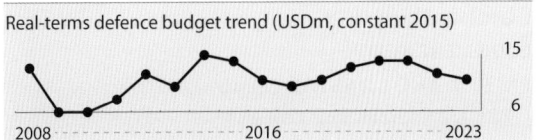

Real-terms defence budget trend (USDm, constant 2015)

Population 2,468,569

Age	0–14	15–19	20–24	25–29	30–64	65 plus
Male	19.6%	5.7%	4.9%	4.2%	13.6%	1.6%
Female	19.2%	5.6%	4.8%	4.1%	14.6%	2.0%

Capabilities

Gambia has been reforming its security structure and the armed forces, aided by, for instance, the EU, UK, UN and US. A National Security Policy published in 2019 and updated in 2023 focused on cooperation with Senegal, the establishment of a governing Office of National Security and the detachment of the armed forces from legacies entrenched during the previous dictatorship. The government said in December 2022 that the Gambian Armed Forces foiled a coup attempt. Gambia's small forces have traditionally focused on maritime security and countering human trafficking. Both activities have been significantly strengthened since 2021, including through the establishment of a Committee for National Maritime Security in August 2022 and an agreement with the EU's Seaport Cooperation Programme in January 2023. Gambia also cooperates with neighbouring states and the African Union, which maintains a technical-support mission to assist in the security sector reform process. The Economic Community of West African States extended the deployment of the ECOMIG mission to Gambia until the end of 2023. The armed forces participate in some multinational exercises and have deployed in support of UN missions in Africa. The equipment inventory is very limited, with serviceability in doubt for some types. The country has made limited efforts to upgrade equipment, including by ordering some APCs. Gambia, which has no significant defence industry.

ACTIVE 4,100 (Army 3,500 Navy 300 National Guard 300)

ORGANISATIONS BY SERVICE

Gambian National Army 3,500
FORCES BY ROLE
MANOEUVRE
 Light
  4 inf bn
COMBAT SUPPORT
 1 engr sqn
EQUIPMENT BY TYPE
ARMOURED FIGHTING VEHICLES
 APC • PPV 4 *Hizir*
 AUV 2 *Cobra* II

Air Wing
EQUIPMENT BY TYPE
AIRCRAFT
 TPT 5: **Light** 2 AT-802A *Air Tractor*; **PAX** 3: 1 B-727; 1 CL-601; 1 Il-62M *Classic* (VIP)

Gambia Navy 300
EQUIPMENT BY TYPE
PATROL AND COASTAL COMBATANTS 8
 PBF 4: 2 *Rodman 55*; 2 *Fatimah* I
 PB 4: 1 *Bolong Kanta* (US Peterson Mk 4)†; 3 *Taipei* (ROC *Hai Ou*) (one additional damaged and in reserve)

Republican National Guard 300
FORCES BY ROLE
MANOEUVRE

Other
 1 gd bn (forming)

DEPLOYMENT
CENTRAL AFRICAN REPUBLIC: UN • MINUSCA 9
DEMOCRATIC REPUBLIC OF THE CONGO: UN • MONUSCO 2
SOUTH SUDAN: UN • UNMISS 3

FOREIGN FORCES
Ghana ECOMIG 50
Nigeria ECOMIG 200
Senegal ECOMIG 250

Ghana GHA

Ghanaian New Cedi GHS		2022	2023	2024
GDP	GHS	610bn	855bn	1.07trn
	USD	72.2bn	76.6bn	75.6bn
per capita	USD	2,252	2,329	2,242
Growth	%	3.1	1.2	2.7
Inflation	%	31.9	42.2	23.2
Def bdgt	GHS	2.24bn	3.74bn	
	USD	266m	335m	
USD1=GHS		8.45	11.16	14.08

Real-terms defence budget trend (USDm, constant 2015)
301
87
2008 — 2016 — 2023

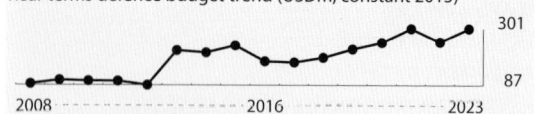

Population	33,846,114					
Age	0–14	15–19	20–24	25–29	30–64	65 plus
Male	19.0%	5.0%	4.2%	3.7%	14.9%	2.0%
Female	18.7%	5.0%	4.3%	3.9%	16.9%	2.4%

Capabilities

Ghana's armed forces are among the region's most capable, with a long-term development plan. The ability to control its EEZ and maritime security are of increasing importance, which underpins the navy's expansion plans. Internal security is also a central military task, along with peacekeeping missions abroad. The EU, Germany, the UK and US provide training, support and equipment. The country in recent years has built up air force training, close-air support and airlift capabilities. It also has significantly strengthened naval capabilities through US donations and procurements from Singapore and China. The government is implementing plans to boost training and exercises, while making improvements to military infrastructure. Ghana opened a Signals Training school in 2023. Ghanaian professional military education institutions act as a regional hub and regularly train personnel from neighbouring states. The development of forward-operating bases continues, with the principal objective of protecting energy resources in the Gulf of Guinea and the Volta estuary, as well as to secure the northern border. The country has a limited defence-industrial base, largely centred on Defence Industries Holding Co., created in 2019, that can deliver maintenance, ammunition manufacturing and, more recently, armoured-vehicle production.

ACTIVE 19,000 (Army 15,000 Navy 2,000 Air 2,000)

ORGANISATIONS BY SERVICE

Army 15,000
FORCES BY ROLE
COMMAND
  2 comd HQ
SPECIAL FORCES
  1 cdo bde (1 (rapid reaction) mot inf bn; 1 AB bn)
MANOEUVRE
  Reconnaissance
    1 armd recce bde (3 armd recce regt)
  Mechanised
    3 mech inf bn
  Light
    6 inf bn
COMBAT SUPPORT
  1 arty regt (1 arty bty, 2 mor bty)
  1 fd engr regt (bn)
  1 sigs bde
  1 sigs regt
  1 sigs sqn
COMBAT SERVICE SUPPORT
  1 log gp
  1 tpt coy
  2 maint coy
  1 med coy
  1 trg bn
EQUIPMENT BY TYPE
ARMOURED FIGHTING VEHICLES
  RECCE 3 EE-9 *Cascavel*
  IFV 48: 24 *Ratel*-90; 15 *Ratel*-20; 4 *Piranha* 25mm; 5+ Type-05P 25mm
  APC 125
    APC (W) 75: 20 BTR-70; 46 *Piranha*; 9+ Type-05P
    PPV 50 Streit *Typhoon*
  AUV 73 *Cobra/Cobra* II
ARTILLERY 87
  TOWED 122mm 6 D-30
  MRL 3+: **107mm** Type-63; **122mm** 3 Type-81
  MOR 78: **81mm** 50; **120mm** 28 Tampella
ENGINEERING & MAINTENANCE VEHICLES
  AEV 1 Type-05P AEV
  ARV *Piranha* (reported)
ANTI-TANK/ANTI-INFRASTRUCTURE
  RCL 84mm *Carl Gustaf*
AIR DEFENCE
  SAM • Point-defence 9K32 *Strela*-2 (RS-SA-7 *Grail*)‡
  GUNS • TOWED 8+: **14.5mm** 4+: 4 ZPU-2; ZPU-4;
  23mm 4 ZU-23-2

Navy 2,000
Naval HQ located at Accra; Western HQ located at Sekondi; Eastern HQ located at Tema
EQUIPMENT BY TYPE
PATROL AND COASTAL COMBATANTS 16
  PCO 2 *Anzone* (ex-US *Balsam*)
  PCC 6: 4 *Snake* (PRC Poly Technologies 47m); 2 *Yaa Asantewa* (ex-GER *Albatros*)
  PBF 1 *Stephen Otu* (ex-ROK *Sea Dolphin*)
  PB 7: 2 *Aflao* (ex-US Marine Protector); 4 *Volta* (SGP Penguin Flex Fighter); 1 *David Hansen* (ex-US)
AMPHIBIOUS • LANDING CRAFT 1
  LCVP 1 Navdock

Special Boat Squadron
FORCES BY ROLE
SPECIAL FORCES
  1 SF unit

Air Force 2,000
FORCES BY ROLE
GROUND ATTACK
  1 sqn with K-8 *Karakorum*¤
ISR
  1 sqn with DA42; DA42 MPP; Z-9EH
TRANSPORT
  1 sqn with C295
TRAINING
  1 unit with Cessna 172
TRANSPORT HELICOPTER
  1 sqn with Mi-17V-5 *Hip* H; Mi-171Sh; Z-9EH
EQUIPMENT BY TYPE†
AIRCRAFT 4 combat capable
  ISR 2 DA42 MPP
  TPT 10: **Light** 7: 3 C295M; 3 Cessna 172; 1 DA42; **PAX** 1 Falcon 900EX (VIP): (1 F-28 *Fellowship* in store)
  TRG 4 K-8 *Karakorum**
HELICOPTERS
  MRH 7: 3 Mi-17V-5 *Hip* H; 4 Z-9EH
  TPT • Medium 4 Mi-171Sh

DEPLOYMENT

CENTRAL AFRICAN REPUBLIC: UN • MINUSCA 13
CYPRUS: UN • UNFICYP 1
DEMOCRATIC REPUBLIC OF THE CONGO: UN • MONUSCO 18
GAMBIA: ECOWAS • ECOMIG 50
GUINEA-BISSAU: ECOWAS • ESSMGB 150
LEBANON: UN • UNIFIL 870; 1 recce coy; 1 mech inf bn; 1 spt coy

SOMALIA: UN • UNSOM 1; UN • UNSOS 1
SOUTH SUDAN: UN • UNMISS 742; 1 inf bn
SUDAN: UN • UNISFA 658; 1 inf bn; 1 fd hosptial
SYRIA/ISRAEL: UN • UNDOF 4
WESTERN SAHARA: UN • MINURSO 16

Guinea GUI

Guinean Franc GNF		2022	2023	2024
GDP	GNF	177trn	202trn	229trn
	USD	20.3bn	23.2bn	25.3bn
per capita	USD	1,384	1,543	1,643
Growth	%	4.3	5.9	5.6
Inflation	%	10.5	8.3	7.9
Def bdgt	GNF	3.89trn	4.36trn	
	USD	447m	501m	
USD1=GNF		8,694.12	8,694.30	9,046.04

Real-terms defence budget trend (USDm, constant 2015): 317 (2023), 163

Population	13,607,249					
Age	0–14	15–19	20–24	25–29	30–64	65 plus
Male	20.6%	5.2%	4.5%	3.8%	14.0%	1.8%
Female	20.3%	5.1%	4.5%	3.8%	14.2%	2.2%

Capabilities

Guinea's armed forces are limited in size and conventional capacity. Special forces troops toppled the government of former president Alpha Condé in September 2021, with their leader, Mamady Doumbouya, sworn in as interim president a month later. ECOWAS has sanctioned the coup leaders and unsuccessfully called for elections within six months. Guinea's new leaders announced plans for a return to civilian rule by 2025, although recent turmoil in West Africa makes that less likely. Piracy in the Gulf of Guinea is a key concern, as is illegal trafficking and fishing. Guinea did not fully implement a military-programme law for 2015–2020 due to funding issues. France and the US, prior to the coup, provided financial and training assistance, including for personnel earmarked for deployment to Mali. Much of the country's military equipment is ageing and of Soviet-era vintage; serviceability is questionable for some types. Delivery of several APCs in recent years have slightly improving the deficiency. Guinea has limited organic airlift. France was supporting the development of a light aviation observation capability before the coup. Guinea is also attempting to improve its logistics and military-health capacities. There is no significant local defence industry.

ACTIVE 9,700 (Army 8,500 Navy 400 Air 800)
Gendarmerie & Paramilitary 2,600

Conscript liability 9–12 months (students, before graduation)

ORGANISATIONS BY SERVICE

Army 8,500
FORCES BY ROLE
MANOEUVRE
  Armoured
  1 armd bn
  Light
  1 SF bn
  5 inf bn
  1 ranger bn
  1 cdo bn
  Air Manoeuvre
  1 air mob bn
  Other
  1 (Presidential Guard) gd bn
COMBAT SUPPORT
  1 arty bn
  1 AD bn
  1 engr bn
EQUIPMENT BY TYPE
ARMOURED FIGHTING VEHICLES
  MBT 38: 30 T-34†; 8 T-54†
  LT TK 15 PT-76
  RECCE 27: 2 AML-90; 25 BRDM-1/BRDM-2
  IFV 2 BMP-1
  APC 59
    APC (T) 10 BTR-50
    APC (W) 30: 16 BTR-40; 8 BTR-60; 6 BTR-152
    PPV 19: 10 Mamba†; some Puma M26-15; 9 Puma M36
  AUV Dongfeng Mengshi
ENGINEERING & MAINTENANCE VEHICLES
  ARV T-54/T-55 (reported)
ANTI-TANK/ANTI-INFRASTRUCTURE
  MSL • MANPATS 9K11 Malyutka (RS-AT-3 Sagger); 9K111-1 Konkurs (RS-AT-5 Spandrel)
  RCL 82mm B-10
  GUNS 6+: **57mm** ZIS-2 (M-1943); **85mm** 6 D-44
ARTILLERY 47+
  TOWED 24: **122mm** 12 M-1931/37; **130mm** 12 M-46
  MRL 220mm 3 9P140 Uragan
  MOR 20+: **82mm** M-43; **120mm** 20 M-1938/M-1943
AIR DEFENCE
  SAM • Point-defence 9K32 Strela-2 (RS-SA-7 Grail)‡
  GUNS • TOWED 24+: **30mm** M-53 (twin); **37mm** 8 M-1939; **57mm** 12 Type-59 (S-60); **100mm** 4 KS-19

Navy ε400
EQUIPMENT BY TYPE
PATROL AND COASTAL COMBATANTS 4
  PB 4: 1 Swiftships 77†; 3 Zégbéla Togba Pivi (FRA RPB 20)

Air Force 800

FORCES BY ROLE

ISR

1 sqn with *Tetras* (observation)

EQUIPMENT BY TYPE†

AIRCRAFT

FGA (2 MiG-21bis *Fishbed* L; 1 MiG-21UM *Mongol* B in store)

TPT • Light 4 *Tetras* (observation)

HELICOPTERS

ATK (4 Mi-24 *Hind* in store)

MRH 3: 2 MD-500MD; 1 SA342K *Gazelle*; (2 Mi-17-1V *Hip* H in store)

TPT 2: **Medium** 1 SA330 *Puma*; **Light** 1 AS350B *Ecureuil*

AIR-LAUNCHED MISSILES

AAM • IR R-3 (RS-AA-2 *Atoll*)‡

Gendarmerie & Paramilitary 2,600 active

Gendarmerie 1,000

Republican Guard 1,600

People's Militia 7,000 reservists

DEPLOYMENT

SOUTH SUDAN: UN • UNMISS 3

SUDAN: UN • UNISFA 1

WESTERN SAHARA: UN • MINURSO 5

Guinea-Bissau GNB

CFA Franc BCEAO GWP		2022	2023	2024
GDP	GWP	1.07trn	1.19trn	1.29trn
	USD	1.72bn	1.99bn	2.18bn
per capita	USD	906	1,028	1,103
Growth	%	4.2	4.5	5.0
Inflation	%	7.9	7.0	3.0
Def bdgt	GWP	15.3bn	15.3bn	
	USD	24.6m	25.6m	
USD1=GWP		622.37	599.92	592.59

Real-terms defence budget trend (USDm, constant 2015)

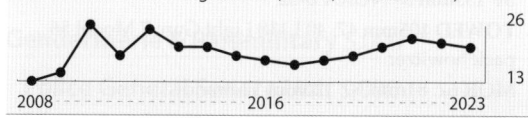

Population 2,078,820

Age	0–14	15–19	20–24	25–29	30–64	65 plus
Male	21.4%	5.5%	4.6%	3.7%	12.3%	1.3%
Female	21.1%	5.6%	4.8%	4.1%	13.6%	1.8%

Capabilities

Guinea-Bissau's armed forces have limited capabilities and are undergoing various reform programs. The UN has expressed concern about the armed forces' role in politics following political disputes linked to elections in 2019. Defence policy focuses mainly on tackling internal security challenges, particularly drug trafficking. An ECOWAS mission withdrew at the end of 2020, only to return in mid-2022 after an attempted coup that February. Coup-proofing has become a priority for the government, particularly in the way of the 2023 putsches in Niger and Gabon. The armed forces suffer from limited training and recruitment and retention problems, as well as developing an adequate non-commissioned officer structure. Much of the country's military equipment is obsolescent and poor maintenance likely limits military effectiveness. There is no defence-manufacturing sector.

ACTIVE 4,450 (Army 4,000 Navy 350 Air 100)

Conscript liability Selective conscription

Personnel and eqpt totals should be treated with caution. A number of draft laws to restructure the armed services and police have been produced

ORGANISATIONS BY SERVICE

Army ε4,000

FORCES BY ROLE

MANOEUVRE

Reconnaissance

1 recce coy

Armoured

1 armd bn (sqn)

Light

5 inf bn

COMBAT SUPPORT

1 arty bn

1 engr coy

EQUIPMENT BY TYPE

ARMOURED FIGHTING VEHICLES

MBT 10 T-34†

LT TK 15 PT-76

RECCE 10 BRDM-2

APC • APC (W) 55: 35 BTR-40/BTR-60; 20 Type-56 (BTR-152)

ANTI-TANK/ANTI-INFRASTRUCTURE

RCL 75mm Type-52 (M20); **82mm** B-10

GUNS 85mm 8 D-44

ARTILLERY 26+

TOWED 122mm 18 D-30/M-30 (M-1938)

MOR 8+: **82mm** M-43; **120mm** 8 M-1943

AIR DEFENCE

SAM • Point-defence 9K32 *Strela*-2 (RS-SA-7 *Grail*)‡

GUNS • TOWED 34: **23mm** 18 ZU-23; **37mm** 6 M-1939; **57mm** 10 S-60

Navy ε350

EQUIPMENT BY TYPE

Capabilities

The Lesotho Defence Force (LDF) has a small ground element and an air wing for light transport and liaison. The country is a SADC member state, which deployed a force to Lesotho in late 2017 for about a year to support the government following the assassination of the army chief. The LDF is charged with protecting territorial integrity and sovereignty and ensuring internal security. Lesotho's government wants to carry out defence reforms to de-politicise the security forces. The LDF are comprised of volunteers. India has provided training to the LDF since 2001 and, more recently, so has France. In April 2020, the army was briefly deployed internally by the prime minister. Lesotho has limited capacity to deploy and sustain missions abroad, though the country has sent personnel to Mozambique since 2021 as part of an SADC mission there. Lesotho's limited inventory is obsolescent by modern standards and there is little possibility of significant recapitalisation, although the country has expressed interest in acquiring light helicopters. Except for limited maintenance capacity, Lesotho lacks a defence-industrial base.

ACTIVE 2,000 (Army 2,000)

ORGANISATIONS BY SERVICE

Army ε2,000
FORCES BY ROLE
MANOEUVRE
  Reconnaissance
  1 recce coy
  Light
  7 inf coy
  Aviation
  1 sqn
COMBAT SUPPORT
  1 arty bty(-)
  1 spt coy (with mor)
EQUIPMENT BY TYPE
ARMOURED FIGHTING VEHICLES
  MBT 1 T-55
  RECCE 6: 4 AML-90; 2 BRDM-2†
  AUV 6 RAM Mk3
ANTI-TANK/ANTI-INFRASTRUCTURE
  RCL 106mm 6 M40
ARTILLERY 12
  TOWED 105mm 2
  MOR 81mm 10

Air Wing 110
AIRCRAFT
  TPT • Light 3: 2 C-212-300 *Aviocar*; 1 GA-8 *Airvan*
HELICOPTERS
  MRH 3: 1 Bell 412 *Twin Huey*; 2 Bell 412EP *Twin Huey*
  TPT • Light 4: 1 Bell 206 *Jet Ranger*; 3 H125 (AS350) *Ecureuil*

DEPLOYMENT

MOZAMBIQUE: SADC • SAMIM 122

Liberia LBR

Liberian Dollar LRD		2022	2023	2024
GDP	LRD	3.97bn	4.35bn	4.59bn
	USD	3.97bn	4.35bn	4.59bn
per capita	USD	749	800	826
Growth	%	4.8	4.6	5.3
Inflation	%	7.6	10.6	8.0
Def bdgt	LRD	18.7m	16.4m	
	USD	18.7m	16.4m	
USD1=LRD		1.00	1.00	1.00

Real-terms defence budget trend (USDm, constant 2015)

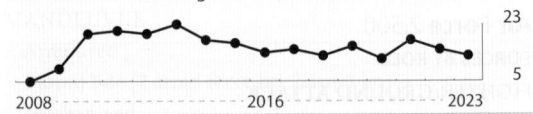

Population	5,311,296				
Age	0–14	15–19	20–24	25–29	30–64	65 plus
Male	19.7%	5.6%	4.9%	4.1%	14.0%	1.5%
Female	19.5%	5.7%	5.1%	4.4%	13.8%	1.7%

Capabilities

Liberia reportedly clarified the roles of its security institutions in a 2017 National Security Strategy focused on improving infrastructure, training, operational readiness, and personnel welfare. Nigeria is supporting Liberia's development of an air wing. The EU, under the auspices of broader maritime-security support to ECOWAS, was working with Liberia on capacity building that was set to improve coast guard capabilities. A National Maritime Strategy was issued in September 2023, after the country, a year earlier, joined the multinational Trans-Regional Maritime Network. US military assistance has in recent years focused on areas such as force health, including schemes to improve recruitment and retention, as well as maritime security, training and the provision of spare parts. The armed forces are able to deploy and sustain small units, such as to the MINUSMA mission in Mali. Equipment recapitalisation will depend on finances and the development of a supporting force structure but will also be dictated by the armed forces' role in national development objectives. Apart from limited maintenance-support capacities, Liberia has no defence industry.

ACTIVE 2,010 (Army 1,950, Coast Guard 60)

ORGANISATIONS BY SERVICE

Army 1,950
FORCES BY ROLE
MANOEUVRE
  Light
  1 (23rd) inf bde with (2 inf bn, 1 engr coy, 1 MP coy)
COMBAT SERVICE SUPPORT

1 trg unit (forming)
ARMOURED FIGHTING VEHICLES
APC • PPV 3+ Streit *Cougar*

Coast Guard 60
All operational patrol vessels under 10t FLD

DEPLOYMENT

DEMOCRATIC REPUBLIC OF THE CONGO: UN • MONUSCO 1

SOUTH SUDAN: UN • UNMISS 1

SUDAN: UN • UNISFA 2

Madagascar MDG

Malagsy Ariary MGA		2022	2023	2024
GDP	MGA	62.1trn	69.7trn	78.5trn
	USD	15.1bn	15.8bn	16.8bn
per capita	USD	523	530	548
Growth	%	4.0	4.0	4.8
Inflation	%	8.2	10.5	8.8
Def bdgt	MGA	421bn	475bn	
	USD	103m	107m	
USD1=MGA		4,096.18	4,424.42	4,682.43

Real-terms defence budget trend (USDm, constant 2015)
101
53
2008 — 2016 — 2023

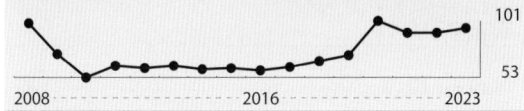

Population 28,812,195

Age	0–14	15–19	20–24	25–29	30–64	65 plus
Male	18.9%	5.3%	4.7%	4.2%	15.2%	1.8%
Female	18.5%	5.2%	4.6%	4.2%	15.2%	2.1%

Capabilities

Madagascar's principal defence priorities are ensuring sovereignty and territorial integrity. It also focuses on maritime security and the country is part of the EU funded Maritime Security Programme. The army is the largest armed service. The armed forces intervened in domestic politics in 2009. Madagascar is a member of SADC and its regional Standby Force. In 2018, the country signed an agreement with India to explore closer defence ties. Madagascar reportedly also signed an agreement with Russia on military cooperation that entered into force in 2022 and may have involved arms sales, development of military equipment and personnel training. China has also tried to foster closer ties with Madagascar. France provides some training. The country's all-volunteer forces have no independent capacity to deploy and support operations beyond national borders. The equipment inventory is obsolescent, and, with economic development a key government target, equipment recapitalisation is unlikely to be a priority. Madagascar acquired a small number of second-hand transport aircraft and helicopters in 2019, modestly boosting military mobility, and showed new light armoured protected patrol vehicles during a parade in 2020.

ACTIVE 13,500 (Army 12,500 Navy 500 Air 500)
Gendarmerie & Paramilitary 8,100
Conscript liability 18 months (incl for civil purposes)

ORGANISATIONS BY SERVICE

Army 12,500+
FORCES BY ROLE
MANOEUVRE
  Light
  2 (intervention) inf regt
  10 (regional) inf regt
COMBAT SUPPORT
  1 arty regt
  3 engr regt
  1 sigs regt
COMBAT SERVICE SUPPORT
  1 log regt
AIR DEFENCE
  1 ADA regt
EQUIPMENT BY TYPE
ARMOURED FIGHTING VEHICLES
  LT TK 12 PT-76
  RECCE 73: ε35 BRDM-2; 10 FV701 *Ferret*; ε20 M3A1; 8 M8
  APC • APC (T) ε30 M3A1 half-track
  AUV 6 *Panthera* T4
ANTI-TANK/ANTI-INFRASTRUCTURE
  RCL 106mm M40A1
ARTILLERY 25
  TOWED 17: 105mm 5 M101; 122mm 12 D-30
  MOR 8+: 82mm M-37; 120mm 8 M-43
AIR DEFENCE • GUNS
  TOWED 70: 14.5mm 50 ZPU-4; 37mm 20 PG-55 (M-1939)

Navy 500 (incl some 100 Marines)
EQUIPMENT BY TYPE
PATROL AND COASTAL COMBATANTS 10
  PCC 1 *Trozona*
  PB 9: 2 *Tselatra* (PRC 27m); 7 (ex-US CG MLB)

Air Force 500
FORCES BY ROLE
TRANSPORT
  1 sqn with Yak-40 *Codling*
  1 (liaison) sqn with Cessna 310; Cessna 337 *Skymaster*; PA-23 *Aztec*
TRAINING
  1 sqn with Cessna 172; J.300 *Joker*; *Tetras*
TRANSPORT HELICOPTER
  1 sqn with SA318C *Alouette* II
EQUIPMENT BY TYPE

AIRCRAFT • TPT 21: Light 19: 4 Cessna 172; 5 Cessna 206; 1 Cessna 310; 2 Cessna 337 *Skymaster*; 1 CN235M; 2 J.300 *Joker*; 1 PA-23 *Aztec*; 1 *Tetras*; 2 Yak-40 *Codling* (VIP); PAX 2 B-737

HELICOPTERS
MRH 3 SA318C *Alouette* II
TPT • Light 4: 3 AS350 *Ecureuil*; 1 BK117

Gendarmerie & Paramilitary 8,100

Gendarmerie 8,100

Malawi MWI

Malawian Kwacha MWK		2022	2023	2024
GDP	MWK	11.8trn	15.1trn	18.4trn
	USD	12.5bn	13.2bn	11.0bn
per capita	USD	567	580	472
Growth	%	0.8	1.7	3.3
Inflation	%	20.8	27.7	19.8
Def bdgt	MWK	72.1bn	70.7bn	
	USD	76.6m	61.6m	
USD1=MWK		941.29	1,147.21	1,666.09

Real-terms defence budget trend (USDm, constant 2015)

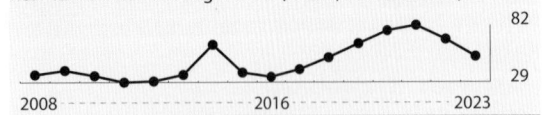

Population 21,279,597

Age	0–14	15–19	20–24	25–29	30–64	65 plus
Male	19.1%	5.7%	4.8%	4.1%	13.7%	1.7%
Female	19.4%	5.8%	4.9%	4.2%	14.5%	2.1%

Capabilities

The Malawi Defence Forces (MDF) are constitutionally tasked with ensuring the country's sovereignty and territorial integrity. Additional tasks include providing military assistance to civil authorities and supporting the police. In recent years, the army has been used to help with infrastructure development and controlling illegal deforestation. The army is the largest of the services. The MDF's small air force, previously an air wing, and its naval unit are used to counter human trafficking. In 2023, the MDF put into service two transport aircraft delivered from China in 2022. The military is trying to enhance combat readiness, military medicine and engineering. Malawi is a member of the SADC and its Standby Force. The armed forces have contributed to peacekeeping missions, including in Côte d'Ivoire, the DRC and Mozambique. The UK provided training and support for the deployment to the DRC and London also supports the MDF's counter-poaching operations. Discussions with US Africa Command to establish a training centre for non-commissioned officers are ongoing. The armed forces have no independent capacity to deploy and support operations beyond national borders.

ACTIVE 10,700 (Army 10,500 Air Force 200)
Gendarmerie & Paramilitary 4,200

ORGANISATIONS BY SERVICE

Army 10,500
FORCES BY ROLE
MANOEUVRE
Mechanised
1 mech bn
Light
2 inf bde (2 inf bn)
1 inf bde (1 inf bn)
Air Manoeuvre
1 para bn
COMBAT SUPPORT
3 lt arty bty
1 engr bn
COMBAT SERVICE SUPPORT
12 log coy
EQUIPMENT BY TYPE
ARMOURED FIGHTING VEHICLES
RECCE 58: 30 *Eland*-90; 8 FV701 *Ferret*; 20 FV721 *Fox*
APC • PPV 31: 14 *Casspir*; 9 *Marauder*; 8 *Puma* M26-15
AUV 8 RAM Mk3
ARTILLERY 107
TOWED 105mm 9 L118 Light Gun
MOR 81mm 98: 82 L16A1; 16 M3
AIR DEFENCE • GUNS
TOWED 72: 12.7mm 32; 14.5mm 40 ZPU-4

Navy 220
EQUIPMENT BY TYPE
PATROL AND COASTAL COMBATANTS • PB 3: 1 *Kasungu* (ex-FRA *Antares*)†; 2 *Mutharika* (PRC)

Air Force 200
EQUIPMENT BY TYPE
AIRCRAFT • TPT • Light 3: 1 Do-228; 2 MA600
HELICOPTERS • TPT 8: Medium 3: 1 AS532UL *Cougar*; 1 SA330H *Puma*; 1 H215 *Super Puma* Light 5: 1 AS350L *Ecureuil*; 4 SA341B *Gazelle*

Gendarmerie & Paramilitary 4,200

Police Mobile Service 4,200
EQUIPMENT BY TYPE
AIRCRAFT
TPT • Light 4: 3 BN-2T *Defender* (border patrol); 1 SC.7 3M *Skyvan*
HELICOPTERS • MRH 2 AS365 *Dauphin* 2

DEPLOYMENT

DEMOCRATIC REPUBLIC OF THE CONGO: UN • MONUSCO 745; 1 inf bn

MOZAMBQIUE: SADC • SAMIM 2

SOUTH SUDAN: UN • UNMISS 10
SUDAN: UN • UNISFA 5
WESTERN SAHARA: UN • MINURSO 4

Mali MLI

CFA Franc BCEAO XOF		2022	2023	2024
GDP	XOF	11.9trn	12.8trn	13.8trn
	USD	19.2bn	21.3bn	23.1bn
per capita	USD	847	913	957
Growth	%	3.7	4.5	4.8
Inflation	%	9.7	5.0	2.8
Def bdgt [a]	XOF	515bn	657bn	739bn
	USD	827m	1.09bn	1.23bn
USD1=XOF		622.41	602.72	599.66

[a] Defence and security budget

Real-terms defence budget trend (USDm, constant 2015)
904
159
2008 2016 2023

Population 21,359,722

Age	0–14	15–19	20–24	25–29	30–64	65 plus
Male	23.7%	5.2%	3.9%	3.1%	11.2%	1.5%
Female	23.4%	5.5%	4.5%	3.8%	12.6%	1.6%

Capabilities

Mali's security situation has deteriorated because of military coups in August 2020 and May 2021 and policies implemented by the junta that strained security relationships with external partners. The putschists said they took power to improve the security situation but failed to stem insurgent attacks within the country. The regime has deepened its political and security partnership with Russia and hired the Russian private military company, Wagner Group, to provide security to the regime, and at least partially restore its control over the northern part of the country. Wagner forces deployed to the country in late 2021, though the relationship is in flux after Moscow took control of the private militia's operations. The UN said it would end the MINUSMA mission to Mali. France suspended joint military operations in 2021 and officially ended its counterinsurgency mission, Operation Barkhane, in August 2022. Mali left the G5 Sahel security partnership in 2022. The EU also decided to reduce its training activities. Mali's junta is strengthening its relationships with Burkina Faso, where the military also took power, and said it would support putschists that took power in Niger in 2023. The three countries formalised their security cooperation with an alliance in September 2023. The armed forces still suffer from operational deficiencies and broader institutional weakness. Despite vehicle deliveries by external partners and the acquisition of several aircraft from Russia, the armed forces remain under-equipped. Mali does not possess a defence-manufacturing industry and has limited equipment and maintenance capabilities.

ACTIVE 21,000 (Army 19,000 Air Force 2,000)
Gendarmerie & Paramilitary 20,000

ORGANISATIONS BY SERVICE

Army ε19,000
FORCES BY ROLE
MANOEUVRE
  Light
  9 mot inf bn
  1 inf coy (Special Joint Unit)
  5 inf coy (ULRI)
  Air Manoeuvre
  1 para bn
COMBAT SUPPORT
  1 engr bn
COMBAT SERVICE SUPPORT
  1 med unit
EQUIPMENT BY TYPE
ARMOURED FIGHTING VEHICLES
  LT TK 2+ PT-76
  RECCE 5+ BRDM-2
  IFV 6 VN2C
  APC 337:
    APC (W) 63: 27 Bastion APC; 10+ BTR-60PB; 11 BTR-70; 15+ WZ-551
    PPV 274: 50 Casspir; 16 IAG Guardian; 13 Marauder; 30 Puma M26-15/Puma M36; 24 Stark Motors Storm Light; 30 Streit Cougar; 4 Streit Gladiator; 5+ Streit Python; 29 Streit Typhoon†; 73+ VP-11
ARTILLERY 30+
  TOWED 122mm D-30
  MRL 122mm 30+ BM-21 Grad

Air Force 2,000
FORCES BY ROLE
TRANSPORT
  1 sqn with BT-67; C295; Y-12E
TRAINING
  1 sqn with Tetras
TRANSPORT/ATTACK HELICOPTER
  1 sqn with H215; Mi-24D Hind; Mi-35M Hind
EQUIPMENT BY TYPE
AIRCRAFT 20 combat capable
  ISR 1 Cessna 208 Caravan
  TPT • Light 12: 1 BT-67; 2 C295; 7 Tetras; 2 Y-12E (1 An-24 Coke; 2 An-26 Curl; 2 BN-2 Islander all in store)
  TRG 20: 3 A-29 Super Tucano*; up to 17 L-39C Albatros* (6 L-29 Delfin; 2 SF-260WL Warrior* all in store)
HELICOPTERS
  ATK 7: 1 Mi-24D Hind; 2 Mi-24P Hind F; 4 Mi-35M Hind
  TPT 9: Medium 9: 2 H215 (AS332L1) Super Puma; 4 Mi-171Sh Hip; 3 Mi-8T Hip; (1 Mi-8 Hip in store); Light (1 AS350 Ecureuil in store)

UNINHABITED AERIAL VEHICLES

CISR • **Medium** ε8 Bayraktar TB2

Gendarmerie & Paramilitary 20,000 active

Gendarmerie 6,000

FORCES BY ROLE
MANOEUVRE
Other
8 paramilitary coy
1 air tpt gp (2 sy coy; 1 tpt coy)
EQUIPMENT BY TYPE
ARMOURED FIGHTING VEHICLES
APC • **PPV** 1+ RG-31 *Nyala*

National Guard 10,000

FORCES BY ROLE
MANOEUVRE
Reconnaissance
6 (camel) cav coy
Light
1 inf coy (Anti-terrorist special force)
EQUIPMENT BY TYPE
ARMOURED FIGHTING VEHICLES
APC • **PPV** 1+ RG-31 *Nyala*

National Police 1,000

Militia 3,000

DEPLOYMENT

DEMOCRATIC REPUBLIC OF THE CONGO: UN • MONUSCO 4

FOREIGN FORCES

Remaining elements of MINUSMA mission completing withdrawal by end 2023.
Austria EUTM Mali 4
Belgium EUTM Mali 5
Bulgaria EUTM Mali 4
Finland EUTM Mali 12
France EUTM Mali 7
Greece EUTM Mali 2
Hungary EUTM Mali 20
Ireland EUTM Mali 7
Lithuania EUTM Mali 1
Moldova EUTM Mali 2
Netherlands EUTM Mali 4
Portugal EUTM Mali 4
Romania EUTM Mali 40
Slovakia EUTM Mali 4
Spain EUTM Mali 140

Mauritius MUS

Mauritian Rupee MUR		2022	2023	2024
GDP	MUR	570bn	667bn	745bn
	USD	12.9bn	14.8bn	16.1bn
per capita	USD	10,227	11,752	12,773
Growth	%	8.7	5.1	3.8
Inflation	%	10.8	7.8	6.5
Def bdgt [a]	MUR	10.4bn	10.9bn	11.8bn
	USD	235m	242m	255m
USD1=MUR		44.18	45.01	46.27

[a] Police service budget

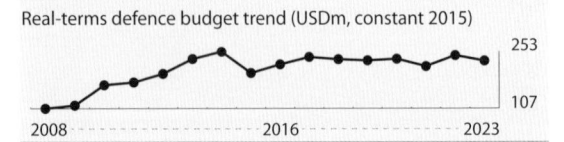

Real-terms defence budget trend (USDm, constant 2015)

Population 1,309,448

Age	0–14	15–19	20–24	25–29	30–64	65 plus
Male	7.8%	3.4%	3.6%	3.7%	24.8%	5.5%
Female	7.5%	3.2%	3.6%	3.7%	25.4%	7.9%

Capabilities

Mauritius has no standing armed forces. Responsibility for security lies with the Mauritius Police Force's paramilitary Special Mobile Force (SMF), formed as a motorised infantry battalion. The SMF is tasked with ensuring internal and external territorial and maritime security. India provides support to the Mauritian National Coast Guard, which is also a branch of the police force, through training, joint exercises, equipment maintenance and leasing, including helicopters and light aircraft. In 2023, India completed construction of an airstrip and maritime jetty on Agaléga Island in a bid by New Delhi to counter growing Chinese influence and maritime activities in the region. The SMF trains along traditional military lines but cannot deploy beyond national borders. Apart from very limited maintenance facilities, there is no defence industry.

ACTIVE NIL Gendarmerie & Paramilitary 2,550

ORGANISATIONS BY SERVICE

Gendarmerie & Paramilitary 2,550

Special Mobile Force ε1,750
FORCES BY ROLE
MANOEUVRE
Reconnaissance
2 recce coy
Light
5 (rifle) mot inf coy
COMBAT SUPPORT
1 engr sqn
COMBAT SERVICE SUPPORT
1 spt pl

EQUIPMENT BY TYPE
ARMOURED FIGHTING VEHICLES
   IFV 2 VAB with 20mm gun
   APC • **APC (W)** 12: 3 *Tactica*; 9 VAB
   ARTILLERY • **MOR 81mm** 2

Coast Guard ε800
EQUIPMENT BY TYPE
PATROL AND COASTAL COMBATANTS 15
   PCO 1 *Barracuda* with 1 hel landing platform
   PCC 2 *Victory* (IND *Sarojini Naidu*)
   PB 12: 10 Fast Interceptor Boat (IND); 1 P-2000 (UK *Archer* derivative); 1 *Guardian* (ex-IND SDB Mk 3)
   AIRCRAFT • **TPT** • **Light** 4: 1 BN-2T *Defender*; 3 Do-228-101

Police Air Wing
EQUIPMENT BY TYPE
HELICOPTERS
   MRH 9: 1 H125 (AS555) *Fennec*; 3 *Dhruv*; 1 SA315B *Lama* (*Cheetah*); 5 SA316 *Alouette* III (*Chetak*)

Mozambique MOZ

Mozambique New Metical MZN		2022	2023	2024
GDP	MZN	1.22trn	1.41trn	1.59trn
	USD	19.2bn	21.9bn	24bn
per capita	USD	581	647	687
Growth	%	4.2	7.0	5.0
Inflation	%	9.8	7.4	6.5
Def bdgt	MZN	10.3bn	12.6bn	
	USD	162m	195m	
USD1=MZN		63.85	64.48	66.53

Real-terms defence budget trend (USDm, constant 2015)

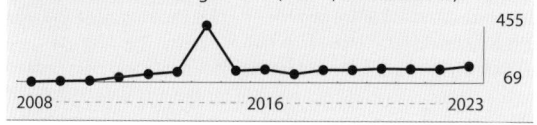

Population	32,513,805				
Age	0–14	15–19	20–24	25–29	30–64	65 plus
Male	22.8%	5.5%	4.6%	3.7%	11.3%	1.4%
Female	22.2%	5.4%	4.6%	3.9%	13.1%	1.5%

Capabilities
Mozambique faces a sustained internal threat from Islamist groups that challenge national defence forces with attacks in the country's northern provinces of Cabo Delgado, Niassa and Nampula. The UN suspects there are links between Islamists fighters in Mozambique and those active in the DRC. The Mozambique government, in 2023, authorised the creation of local militias to help the armed force fight insurgents. SADC deployed a multinational force in 2021 and the country has received support from China, Portugal, Russia, Rwanda and the US, which has provided training in response to the Islamist threat. The armed forces are tasked with ensuring territorial integrity and internal security, as well as tackling piracy and human trafficking. Several foreign countries help patrol the Mozambique Channel to thwart activities there, including illegal fishing and oil theft. Russian private military contractors hired by the government to advise its forces in 2019 have withdrawn. Corruption in the armed forces is reportedly a concern. The armed forces have no capacity to deploy beyond Mozambique's borders without assistance. Soviet-era equipment makes up the much of the inventory, making maintenance problematic, not least in the absence of a local defence industry. Moreover, Mozambique's recent economic performance limit the government's ability to recapitalise its inventory.

ACTIVE 11,200 (Army 10,000 Navy 200 Air 1,000)
Conscript liability 2 years

ORGANISATIONS BY SERVICE

Army ε9,000–10,000
FORCES BY ROLE
SPECIAL FORCES
   3 SF bn
MANOEUVRE
   Light
   7 inf bn
COMBAT SUPPORT
   2-3 arty bn
   2 engr bn
COMBAT SERVICE SUPPORT
   1 log bn
EQUIPMENT BY TYPE†
Equipment estimated at 10% or less serviceability
ARMOURED FIGHTING VEHICLES
   MBT 60+ T-54
   RECCE 30 BRDM-1/BRDM-2
   IFV 40 BMP-1
   APC 337
      APC (T) 30 FV430
      APC (W) 285: 160 BTR-60; 100 BTR-152; 25 AT-105 *Saxon*
      PPV 22+: 11 *Casspir*; 11 *Marauder*; some Tata Motors MRAP
   AUV 9+ *Tiger* 4×4
ANTI-TANK/ANTI-INFRASTRUCTURE
   MSL • **MANPATS** 9K11 *Malyutka* (RS-AT-3 *Sagger*); 9K111 *Fagot* (RS-AT-4 *Spigot*)
   RCL 75mm; **82mm** B-10; **107mm** 24 B-12
   GUNS 85mm 18: 6 D-48; 12 PT-56 (D-44)
ARTILLERY 126
   TOWED 62: **100mm** 20 M-1944; **105mm** 12 M101; **122mm** 12 D-30; **130mm** 6 M-46; **152mm** 12 D-1
   MRL 122mm 12 BM-21 *Grad*
   MOR 52: **82mm** 40 M-43; **120mm** 12 M-43
AIR DEFENCE • **GUNS** 290+
   SP 57mm 20 ZSU-57-2
   TOWED 270+: **20mm** M-55; **23mm** 120 ZU-23-2; **37mm**

90 M-1939; (10 M-1939 in store); **57mm** 60 S-60; (30 S-60 in store)

Navy ε200
EQUIPMENT BY TYPE
PATROL AND COASTAL COMBATANTS 28
  PBF 21: 15 DV 15 (14 more in reserve); 2 HSI 32; 2 *Interceptor* (LKA Solas Marine); 2 *Namilti* (ex-IND C-401)
  PBF (3 WP-18 non-operational)
  PB 4: 1 *Ocean Eagle* 43 (capacity 1 *Camcopter* S-100 UAV) (2 more in reserve); 1 *Pebane* (ex-ESP *Conejera*); 2 Other (fisheries patrol)
UNINHABITED AERIAL VEHICLES
  ISR • Light 1 S-100 *Camcopter*

Air Force 1,000
FORCES BY ROLE
FIGHTER/GROUND ATTACK
  1 sqn with MiG-21bis *Fishbed*; MiG-21UM *Mongol* B
ISR
  1 flt with *Mwari*
TRANSPORT
  1 sqn with An-26 *Curl*; FTB-337G *Milirole*; Cessna 150B; Cessna 172; CN235M; L-410UVP-E; PA-34 *Seneca*
ATTACK/TRANSPORT HELICOPTER
  1 sqn with Mi-24 *Hind*†

EQUIPMENT BY TYPE
AIRCRAFT 8 combat capable
  FGA 8: 6 MiG-21bis *Fishbed*; 2 MiG-21UM *Mongol* B
  ISR 5: 2 FTB-337G *Milirole*; up to 3 *Mwari*
  TPT 8: **Light** 7: 1 An-26 *Curl*; 2 Cessna 150B; 1 Cessna 172; 1 CN235M; 1 L-410UVP-E; 1 PA-34 *Seneca*; (4 PA-32 *Cherokee* non-op); **PAX** 1 Hawker 850XP
  TRG 2 L-39 *Albatros*
HELICOPTERS
  ATK 2 Mi-24V *Hind* E
  MRH 2 SA314B *Gazelle*
  TPT • Medium 2 Mi-8 *Hip*

FOREIGN FORCES
Angola SAMIM 8
Belgium EUTM Mozambique 2
Botswana SAMIM 359
Democratic of the Congo SAMIM 1
Estonia EUTM Mozambique 1
Finland EUTM Mozambique 5
France EUTM Mozambique 6
Greece EUTM Mozambique 8
Italy EUTM Mozambique 7
Lesotho SAMIM 122
Lithuania EUTM Mozambique 2
Malawi SAMIM 2
Portugal EUTM Mozambqiue 61
Romania EUTM Mozambique 12
Rwanda Army: 2,000
South Africa SAMIM 1,200
Spain EUTM Mozambique 2
Tanzania SAMIM 290
Zimbabwe SAMIM 1

Namibia NAM

Namibian Dollar NAD		2022	2023	2024
GDP	NAD	206bn	228bn	247bn
	USD	12.6bn	12.6bn	13.6bn
per capita	USD	4,854	4,786	5,053
Growth	%	4.6	2.8	2.7
Inflation	%	6.1	6.0	4.9
Def bdgt	NAD	5.85bn	6.29bn	6.35bn
	USD	357m	350m	350m
USD1=NAD		16.36	18.00	18.15

Real-terms defence budget trend (USDm, constant 2015): 567 high, 280 low, 2008–2023

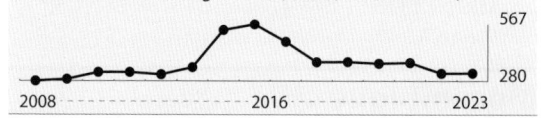

Population	2,756,722					
Age	0–14	15–19	20–24	25–29	30–64	65 plus
Male	17.4%	5.3%	4.8%	4.3%	15.6%	1.7%
Female	17.1%	5.2%	4.8%	4.4%	17.2%	2.2%

Capabilities

The Namibian defence authorities aim to develop a small, mobile and well-equipped professional force. The constitution assigns the Namibian Defence Force (NDF) territorial defence as the primary mission. Secondary roles include assistance to civil authorities and supporting the AU, SADC and UN. The NDF Development Strategy 2012–22 called for a force-projection capability. The navy exercises as part of SADC's Standing Maritime Committee and participated in the multinational UNITAS exercise for the first time in 2022. It also has conducted multinational training missions organised by US forces. Namibia and Botswana, in 2021, elevated annual meetings of a permanent commission on defence and security, chaired by the two countries' heads of state, to biannual status. The two countries also regularly conduct joint exercises. The NDF receives a comparatively large proportion of the state budget but has problems adequately funding training. Military service is voluntary. In 2022, Namibia launched its first recruitment drive for officers and other ranks in seven years. Namibia has deployed on AU, SADC and UN missions and the NDF sent a small force to Mozambique in 2022. Still, the country has limited capacity for independent power projection. The NDF is equipped, for the most part, with ageing or obsolescent systems, but economic difficulties make recapitalisation unlikely in the near term. The defence-manufacturing sector is limited, mainly focusing on armoured vehicles, tactical communications, and ammunition.

ACTIVE 9,900 (Army 9,000 Navy 900) **Gendarmerie & Paramilitary 6,000**

ORGANISATIONS BY SERVICE

Army 9,000
FORCES BY ROLE
MANOEUVRE
  Reconnaissance
  1 recce regt
  Light
  3 inf bde (3 inf bn, 1 arty bn)
COMBAT SUPPORT
  1 arty bde (3 arty bn)
  1 AT regt
  1 engr regt
  1 sigs regt
COMBAT SERVICE SUPPORT
  1 log bn
AIR DEFENCE
  1 AD regt
EQUIPMENT BY TYPE
ARMOURED FIGHTING VEHICLES
  MBT T-54/T-55‡; T-34†
  RECCE 12 BRDM-2
  IFV 7: 5 Type-05P mod (with BMP-1 turret); 2 *Wolf Turbo* 2 mod (with BMP-1 turret)
  APC 69
    APC (W) 13: 10 BTR-60; 3 Type-05P
    PPV 56: 20 *Casspir*; 8 RG-32M; 28 *Wolf Turbo* 2
ENGINEERING & MAINTENANCE VEHICLES
  ARV T-54/T-55 reported
ANTI-TANK/ANTI-INFRASTRUCTURE
  RCL 82mm B-10
  GUNS 12+: **57mm** ZIS-2; **76mm** 12 ZIS-3
ARTILLERY 72
  TOWED 140mm 24 G-2
  MRL 122mm 8: 5 BM-21 *Grad*; 3 PHL-81
  MOR 40: **81mm**; **82mm**
AIR DEFENCE
  SAM • Point-defence FN-6 (CH-SA-10)
  GUNS 65
    SP 23mm 15 *Zumlac*
    TOWED 50+: **14.5mm** 50 ZPU-4; **57mm** S-60

Navy ε900
EQUIPMENT BY TYPE
PATROL AND COASTAL COMBATANTS 7
  PSO 1 *Elephant* with 1 hel landing platform
  PCC 3: 2 *Daures* (ex-PRC *Haiqing* (Type-037-IS)) with 2 FQF-3200 A/S mor; 1 *Oryx*
  PB 3: 1 *Brendan Simbwaye* (BRZ *Grajaú*); 2 *Terrace Bay* (BRZ *Marlim*)
AIRCRAFT • TPT • Light 1 F406 *Caravan II*
HELICOPTERS • TPT • Medium 1 S-61L

Marines ε700

Air Force
FORCES BY ROLE
FIGHTER/GROUND ATTACK
  1 sqn with F-7 (F-7NM); FT-7 (FT-7NG)
ISR
  1 sqn with O-2A *Skymaster*
TRANSPORT
  Some sqn with An-26 *Curl*; *Falcon* 900; Learjet 36; Y-12
TRAINING
  1 sqn with K-8 *Karakorum**
ATTACK/TRANSPORT HELICOPTER
  1 sqn with H425; Mi-8 *Hip*; Mi-25 *Hind* D; SA315 *Lama* (*Cheetah*); SA316B *Alouette* III (*Chetak*)
EQUIPMENT BY TYPE
AIRCRAFT 10 combat capable
  FTR 7: 5 F-7 (F-7NM); 2 FT-7 (FT-7NG)
  ISR 5 Cessna O-2A *Skymaster*
  TPT 6: **Light** 5: 2 An-26 *Curl*; 1 Learjet 36; 2 Y-12; **PAX** 1 *Falcon* 900
  TRG 3+ K-8 *Karakorum**
HELICOPTERS
  ATK 2 Mi-25 *Hind* D
  MRH 5: 1 H425; 1 SA315 *Lama* (*Cheetah*); 3 SA316B *Alouette* III (*Chetak*)
  TPT • Medium 1 Mi-8 *Hip*

Gendarmerie & Paramilitary 6,000

Police Force • Special Field Force 6,000 (incl Border Guard and Special Reserve Force)

DEPLOYMENT
SOUTH SUDAN: UN • UNMISS 5
SUDAN: UN • UNISFA 7

Niger NER

CFA Franc BCEAO XOF		2022	2023	2024
GDP	XOF	9.62trn	10.3trn	11.7trn
	USD	15.4bn	17.1bn	19.5bn
per capita	USD	592	631	696
Growth	%	11.9	4.1	11.1
Inflation	%	4.2	4.6	6.6
Def bdgt	XOF	151bn	201bn	
	USD	243m	334m	
USD1=XOF		622.42	602.74	599.65

Real-terms defence budget trend (USDm, constant 2015)

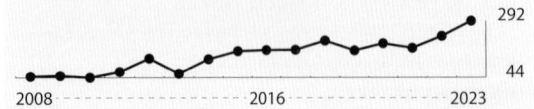

292
44
2008 - - - - - - - - - - - - 2016 - - - - - - - - - - - - 2023

Population 25,396,840

Age	0–14	15–19	20–24	25–29	30–64	65 plus
Male	25.0%	5.7%	4.5%	3.3%	9.7%	1.3%
Female	24.7%	5.8%	4.6%	3.5%	10.5%	1.4%

Capabilities

Niger's military took power in a bloodless coup in July, the fifth such takeover in the country's history. The coup occurred after the elected president tried to change the military command structure and seeming frustration among top uniformed personnel. Western and some African states condemned the coup. The principal role of the military has been maintaining internal and border security, particularly in light of the regional threat from Islamist groups. The country is a member of the G5 Sahel group and was part of the Multi-National Joint Task Force fighting Boko Haram in the Lake Chad Basin. Niamey has hosted air contingents from France, Germany and the US, which maintains a detachment of UAVs to help battle Islamist forces. The US has kept its force presence of around 1,100 troops. France, the former colonial power in Niger, doesn't recognise the junta as the government and is withdrawing its forces from the country. In September, Niger formalised an alliance with Mali and Burkina Faso, both also under military rule, intended to strengthen the resistance against a possible ECOWAS military intervention. Niger's armed forces are combat experienced and relatively well trained. Prior to the military takeover, training and combat operations were conducted jointly with Niger's and US or French forces. The military has limited capacity to deploy abroad without external support. The armed forces are generally underequipped and under-resourced, although Niger recently fielded a significant number of armoured vehicles. Apart from limited maintenance facilities, the country has no defence-industrial capability.

ACTIVE 39,100 (Army 39,000 Air 100) Gendarmerie & Paramilitary 48,000

Conscript liability Selective conscription, 2 years

ORGANISATIONS BY SERVICE

Army ε39,000
8 Mil Zones

FORCES BY ROLE
SPECIAL FORCES
  2 spec ops coy
  11 (intervention) cdo bn
MANOEUVRE
  Light
  26 (combined arms) inf bn
  Amphibious
  1 rvn coy
COMBAT SUPPORT
  1 arty bn
  1 engr coy
  1 int bn
COMBAT SERVICE SUPPORT
  1 log gp
AIR DEFENCE
  1 AD coy

EQUIPMENT BY TYPE
ARMOURED FIGHTING VEHICLES
  RECCE 155: 35 AML-20/AML-60; 90 AML-90; 30 BRDM-2
  APC 151
    APC (W) 53: 11 *Bastion* APC; 22 Panhard M3; 20 WZ-551
    PPV 98+: 15 IAG *Guardian Xtreme*; 57 *Mamba* Mk7; 21 *Puma* M26-15; 5+ *Puma* M36
    AUV 10+: 3+ *Tiger* 4×4; 7 VBL; *Bastion Patsas*
ANTI-TANK/ANTI-INFRASTRUCTURE
  RCL 14: **75mm** 6 M20; **106mm** 8 M40
ARTILLERY 52+
  TOWED **122mm** 12 M-30
  MRL **107mm** PH-63 (tch)
  MOR 40: **81mm** 19 Brandt; **82mm** 17; **120mm** 4 Brandt
AIR DEFENCE • GUNS 39
  SP **20mm** 10 Panhard M3 VDAA
  TOWED **20mm** 29

Air Force 100
EQUIPMENT BY TYPE
AIRCRAFT 5 combat capable
  ATK 2 Su-25 *Frogfoot*
  ISR 6: 4 Cessna 208 *Caravan*; 2 DA42 MPP *Twin Star*
  TPT 9: **Medium** 3 C-130H *Hercules*; **Light** 5: 1 An-26 *Curl*; 2 Cessna 208 *Caravan*; 1 Do-28 *Skyservant*; 1 Do-228-201; **PAX** 1 B-737-700 (VIP)
  TRG 3 *Hurkus*-C*
HELICOPTERS
  ATK 2 Mi-35P *Hind*
  MRH 8: 2 Bell 412HP *Twin Huey*; 1 Mi-17 *Hip*; 5 SA342 *Gazelle*
AIR-LAUNCHED MISSILES • ASM *Cirit*
BOMBS • **Laser-guided** *Bozok*

Gendarmerie & Paramilitary 48,000

Gendarmerie 15,000

National Guard 17,000

National Police 16,000

DEPLOYMENT

CENTRAL AFRICAN REPUBLIC: UN • MINUSCA 6
DEMOCRATIC REPUBLIC OF THE CONGO: UN • MONUSCO 5

FOREIGN FORCES

French forces to complete withdrawal by end Dec 2023
United States 1,100; 1 ISR UAV sqn with MQ-9A *Reaper*

Nigeria NGA

Nigerian Naira NGN		2022	2023	2024
GDP	NGN	202trn	245trn	296trn
	USD	477bn	390bn	395bn
per capita	USD	2,202	1,755	1,734
Growth	%	3.3	2.9	3.1
Inflation	%	18.8	25.1	23.0
Def bdgt	NGN	1.20trn	1.25trn	
	USD	2.83bn	1.99bn	
USD1=NGN		423.91	627.39	749.08

Real-terms defence budget trend (USDbn, constant 2015)
3.2
1.3
2008 — 2016 — 2023

Population 230,842,743

Age	0–14	15–19	20–24	25–29	30–64	65 plus
Male	20.8%	5.7%	4.8%	3.9%	13.8%	1.6%
Female	19.9%	5.5%	4.7%	3.8%	13.9%	1.8%

Capabilities

Nigeria, West Africa's principal military power, faces numerous security challenges, including from the Islamic State West African Province, Boko Haram and militants in the Delta. The government is pursuing military reforms after operational weaknesses were exposed during counter-insurgency operations. Reforms target enhancing counter-insurgency tactics, forward-operating bases and quick-reaction groups. Nigeria is part of the Multinational Joint Task Force and is a key member of the ECOWAS Standby Force. Nigeria is strengthening its cooperation with Pakistan while military and security assistance is either discussed or underway with Germany, the UK and US. The UK bases its British Defence Staff for West Africa in Nigeria. The air force has tried to strengthen its effectiveness, including by establishing the Air Training Command and Ground Training Command. Contractors also provide training and maintenance. Nigeria can mount regional operations, though its deployment capacities remain limited. The government has been upgrading equipment across domains, including with the introduction of fighter ground-attack aircraft, new tanks and howitzers. Nigeria's navy is also being upgraded, in part to meet security requirements in the Delta region. Nigeria is developing its defence-industrial capacity, including local production facilities for small arms and protected patrol vehicles.

ACTIVE 143,000 (Army 100,000 Navy 25,000 Air 18,000) Gendarmerie & Paramilitary 80,000

Reserves planned

ORGANISATIONS BY SERVICE

Army 100,000

FORCES BY ROLE

SPECIAL FORCES

1 spec ops bn
3 spec ops bde
3 (mobile strike team) spec ops units
1 ranger bn

MANOEUVRE

Armoured

1 (3rd) armd div (1 armd bde, 1 arty bde)

Mechanised

1 (1st) mech div (1 recce bn, 1 mech bde, 1 mot inf bde, 1 arty bde, 1 engr regt)
1 (2nd) mech div (1 recce bn, 1 armd bde, 1 arty bde, 1 engr regt)
1 (81st) composite div (1 recce bn, 1 mech bde, 1 arty bde, 1 engr regt)

Light

1 (6th) inf div (1 amph bde, 2 inf bde)
1 (7th) inf div (1 spec ops bn, 1 recce bn(-), 1 armd bde, 7 (task force) inf bde, 1 arty bde, 1 engr regt)
1 (8th Task Force) inf div (2 inf bde)
1 (82nd) composite div (1 recce bn, 3 mot inf bde, 1 arty bde, 1 engr regt)
1 (Multi-National Joint Task Force) bde (2 inf bn(-))

Other

1 (Presidential Guard) gd bde (4 gd bn)

AIR DEFENCE

1 AD regt

EQUIPMENT BY TYPE

ARMOURED FIGHTING VEHICLES

MBT 319+: 100 T-55†; 10 T-72AV; 31 T-72M1; 172 Vickers Mk 3; 6+ VT-4
LT TK 154 FV101 *Scorpion*
ASLT 6+ ST-1
RECCE 312: 88 AML-60; 40 AML-90; 70 EE-9 *Cascavel*; 44 ERC-90F1 *Lynx*; 50 FV721 *Fox*; 20 FV601 *Saladin* Mk2
IFV 31: 9 BTR-4EN; 22 BVP-1
APC 956+
  APC (T) 373: 248 4K-7FA *Steyr*; 65 MT-LB; 60 ZSD-89
  APC (W) 172+: 10 FV603 *Saracen*; 110 AVGP *Grizzly* mod/*Piranha* I 6x6; 47 BTR-3UN; 5 BTR-80; some EE-11 *Urutu* (reported);

PPV 411+: 14 *Caiman*; some *Conqueror*; 158 CS/VP3; 47 *Ezugwu*; up to 58 Isotrex *Legion*; up to 24 Isotrex *Phantom* II; some *Marauder*; 7+ *Maxxpro*; 8 Proforce *Ara-1*; 13 Proforce *Ara-2*; some Proforce *Viper*; 23 REVA III 4×4; 10 Streit *Spartan*; 9 Streit *Cougar* (*Igirigi*); 25 Streit *Typhoon*; 15 *Tares*

AUV 183+: 107 *Cobra*; FV103 *Spartan*; 4+ *Tiger* 4×4; 72 VBL

ENGINEERING & MAINTENANCE VEHICLES

ARV 17+: AVGP *Husky*; 2 *Greif*; 15 Vickers ARV

VLB MTU-20; VAB

ANTI-TANK/ANTI-INFRASTRUCTURE

MSL • MANPATS *Shershen*

RCL 84mm Carl Gustaf; **106mm** M40A1

ARTILLERY 518+

SP 43+: **105mm** 4+ SH-5; **122mm** some SH-2; **155mm** 39 *Palmaria*

TOWED 104: **105mm** 49 M-56; **122mm** 48 D-30/D-74; **130mm** 7 M-46; (**155mm** 24 FH-77B in store)

MRL 122mm 41: 9 BM-21 *Grad*; 25 APR-21; 7 RM-70

MOR 330+: **81mm** 200; **82mm** 100; **120mm** 30+

AIR DEFENCE

SAM • Point-defence 16+: 16 *Roland*; *Blowpipe*; 9K32 *Strela*-2 (RS-SA-7 *Grail*)‡

GUNS 89+

SP 23mm 29 ZSU-23-4 *Shilka*

TOWED 60+: **20mm** 60+; **23mm** ZU-23; **40mm** L/70

Navy 25,000 (incl Coast Guard)

Western Comd HQ located at Apapa; Eastern Comd HQ located at Calabar; Central Comd HQ located at Brass

EQUIPMENT BY TYPE

PRINCIPAL SURFACE COMBATANTS • FRIGATES

FFGHM (1 *Aradu* (GER MEKO 360) (non-operational) with 8 single lnchr with *Otomat* Mk1 AShM, 1 octuple *Albatros* lnchr with *Aspide* SAM, 2 triple 324mm ASTT with A244/S LWT, 1 127mm gun (capacity 1 med hel))

PATROL AND COASTAL COMBATANTS 134

CORVETTES • FSM (1 *Erinomi* (UK Vosper Mk 9) (non-operational) with 1 triple lnchr with *Seacat*† SAM, 1 twin 375mm Bofors ASW Rocket Launcher System A/S mor, 1 76mm gun)

PSOH 4: 2 *Centenary* with 1 76mm gun (capacity 1 Z-9 hel); 2 *Thunder* (ex-US *Hamilton*) with 1 76mm gun

PCF 2 *Siri* (FRA *Combattante* IIIB) with 1 76mm gun

PCO 4 *Kyanwa* (ex-US CG *Balsam*)

PCC 2 *Kano* (Damen Fast Crew Supplier 4008)

PBF 33: 4 ARESA 1700; 4 C-*Falcon*; 4 *Manta* MkII (SGP Suncraft 17m); 12 *Manta* MkIII (SGP Suncraft 17m); 4 *Shaldag* II; 2 *Torie* (Nautic Sentinel 17m); 3 *Wave Rider*

PB 74: 1 *Andoni*; 1 *Dorina* (FPB 98); 4 FPB 110 MkII; 8 *Okpoku* (FPB 72); 6 *Irrua*; 2 *Karaduwa*; 2 *Sagbama*; 2 *Sea Eagle* (Suncraft 38m); 40 Suncraft 12m; 4 Swiftships; 2 *Town* (of which one laid up); 2 *Yola*†

PBR 15 *Stingray* (SGP Suncraft 16m)

MINE WARFARE • MINE COUNTERMEASURES 2

MCC 2 *Ohue* (ITA *Lerici* mod)†

AMPHIBIOUS 5

LANDING SHIPS • LST 1 *Kada* (NLD Damen LST 100) with 1 hel landing platform

LANDING CRAFT • LCVP 4 *Stingray* 20

LOGISTICS AND SUPPORT 2

AGOR 1 *Lana* (OSV 190)

AXL 1 *Prosperity* (ex-IRL *Emer*)

Naval Aviation

EQUIPMENT BY TYPE

HELICOPTERS

MRH 2 AW139 (AB-139)

TPT • Light 5: 3 AW109E *Power*†; 2 AW109SP

Special Boat Service 200

EQUIPMENT BY TYPE

FORCES BY ROLE

SPECIAL FORCES

1 SF unit

Air Force 18,000

FORCES BY ROLE

Very limited op capability

FIGHTER/GROUND ATTACK

1 sqn with F-7 (F-7NI); FT-7 (FT-7NI); JF-17 *Thunder* (Block II)

GROUND ATTACK

1 sqn with *Alpha Jet* A/E*

MARITIME PATROL

1 sqn with ATR-42-500 MP; Do-128D-6 *Turbo SkyServant*; Do-228-100/200

ISR

1 sqn with DA62 MPP

COMBAT SEARCH & RESCUE

1 sqn with H215 (AS332) *Super Puma*

TRANSPORT

1 sqn with C-130H *Hercules*; C-130H-30 *Hercules*; G-222

1 sqn with ATR-42-500 MP; AW109LUH; Beech 350 *King Air*

1 (Presidential) gp with AW189; B-727; B-737BBJ; BAe-125-800; Do-228-200; *Falcon* 7X; *Falcon* 900; Gulfstream IV/V

TRAINING

1 unit with *Alpha Jet* A/E*; EMB-314 *Super Tucano* (A-29B)*

1 unit with L-39ZA *Albatros*†*

1 unit with *Air Beetle*†; *Super Mushshak*; DA40NG

1 hel unit with AW109; AW109M; Mi-34 *Hermit*

ATTACK HELICOPTER

1 sqn with Mi-24/Mi-35 *Hind*; H135; T129B

HELICOPTER

1 (spec ops) flt with Bell 412EP

COMBAT/ISR UAV

1 sqn with CH-3; *Wing Loong* II

EQUIPMENT BY TYPE

AIRCRAFT 61 combat capable
 FTR 11: 10 F-7 (F-7NI); 1 FT-7 (FT-7NI)
 FGA 3 JF-17 *Thunder* (Block II)
 ELINT 2 ATR-42-500 MP
 ISR 5: 1 Beech 350 *King Air*; 4 DA62 MPP
 MP (1 Cessna 525 *Citation* CJ3 non-operational)
 TPT 32: **Medium** 5: 1 C-130H *Hercules* (4 more in store†); 1 C-130H-30 *Hercules* (2 more in store); 3 G.222† (2 more in store†); **Light** 18: 1 Beech 350 *King Air*; 1 Cessna 550 *Citation*; 8 Do-128D-6 *Turbo SkyServant*; 1 Do-228-100; 2 Do-228-101; 5 Do-228-200 (incl 2 VIP); **PAX** 9: 1 B-727; 1 B-737BBJ; 1 BAe 125-800; 2 *Falcon* 7X; 2 *Falcon* 900; 1 Gulfstream IV; 1 Gulfstream V
 TRG 116: 58 *Air Beetle*† (up to 20 awaiting repair); 2 *Alpha Jet* A*; 10 *Alpha Jet* E*; 2 DA40NG; 12 EMB-314 *Super Tucano* (A-29B)*; 23 L-39ZA *Albatros**†; 9 *Super Mushshak*

HELICOPTERS
 ATK 18: 2 Mi-24P *Hind*; 4 Mi-24V *Hind*; 3 Mi-35 *Hind*; 2 Mi-35P *Hind*; 5 Mi-35M *Hind*; 2 T129B
 MRH 13¦: 6 AW109LUH; 2 AW189 (VIP); 2 Bell 412EP; 3+ SA341 *Gazelle*
 TPT 24: **Medium** 13: 2 AW101; 5 H215 (AS332) *Super Puma* (4 more in store); 3 AS365N *Dauphin*; 1 Mi-171Sh; 2 Mi-171E; **Light** 11: 4 H125 (AS350B) *Ecureuil*; 1 AW109; 2 AW109M; 1 Bell 205; 3 H135

UNINHABITED AERIAL VEHICLES 7
 CISR • **Heavy** 5: 1+ CH-3; 4+ *Wing Loong* II
 ISR 2: **Heavy** 1+ *Yabhon Flash-20*; **Medium** (9 *Aerostar* non-operational); **Light** 1+ *Tsaigami*

AIR-LAUNCHED MISSILES
 AAM • **IR** R-3 (RS-AA-2 *Atoll*)‡; PL-9C
 ASM AGR-20A APKWS; AR-1
BOMBS • **INS/GPS guided** FT-9

Gendarmerie & Paramilitary ε80,000

Security and Civil Defence Corps 80,000
EQUIPMENT BY TYPE

ARMOURED FIGHTING VEHICLES
 APC 80+
  APC (W) 74+: 70+ AT105 *Saxon*†; 4 BTR-3U; UR-416
  PPV 6 *Springbuck* 4×4
AIRCRAFT • TPT • **Light** 4: 1 Cessna 500 *Citation* I; 2 PA-31 *Navajo*; 1 PA-31-350 *Navajo Chieftain*
HELICOPTERS • TPT • **Light** 5: 2 Bell 212 (AB-212); 2 Bell 222 (AB-222); 1 Bell 429

DEPLOYMENT

CENTRAL AFRICAN REPUBLIC: UN • MINUSCA 5

DEMOCRATIC REPUBLIC OF THE CONGO: UN • MONUSCO 9
GAMBIA: ECOWAS • ECOMIG 200
GUINEA-BISSAU: ECOWAS • ESSMGB 86
LEBANON: UN • UNIFIL 2
SOUTH SUDAN: UN • UNMISS 13
SUDAN: UN • UNISFA 176
WESTERN SAHARA: UN • MINURSO 6

FOREIGN FORCES

United Kingdom 80 (trg teams)

Rwanda RWA

Rwandan Franc RWF		2022	2023	2024
GDP	RWF	13.7trn	16.0trn	18.3trn
	USD	13.3bn	13.9bn	13.8bn
per capita	USD	1,005	1,032	998
Growth	%	8.2	6.2	7.0
Inflation	%	13.9	14.5	6.0
Def bdgt	RWF	183bn	222bn	219bn
	USD	177m	193m	165m
USD1=RWF		1,030.58	1,151.12	1,323.93

Real-terms defence budget trend (USDm, constant 2015)
191 … 36
2008 — 2016 — 2023

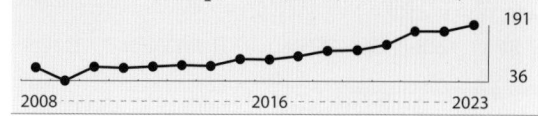

Population	13,400,541					
Age	0–14	15–19	20–24	25–29	30–64	65 plus
Male	19.2%	5.6%	4.7%	3.9%	14.5%	1.2%
Female	18.8%	5.5%	4.7%	3.9%	16.3%	1.8%

Capabilities

Rwanda is a principal security actor in East Africa, with disciplined and well-trained armed forces. Their key missions are to defend territorial integrity and national sovereignty. The country fields a relatively large army, but units are lightly equipped, with little mechanisation. Rwanda signed a Mutual Defence Treaty with Kenya and Uganda in 2014 and participates in East African Community military activities. It has a deployed in Mozambique since 2021, including a small marine component. The country's professional military education establishments train regional as well as Rwandan personnel. In 2023, Rwanda again participated in the US-led *Justified Accord* exercise. In 2024, Rwanda is due to host a major East African Community FTX; it hosted the CPX in 2023. The lack of fixed-wing aircraft limits the armed forces' ability to independently deploy abroad beyond personnel, though they are capable of deploying and self-sustaining missions in the immediate region. The country has acquired some modern artillery and armoured vehicles. It has limited maintenance capacity but no defence manufacturing sector.

ACTIVE 33,000 (Army 32,000 Air 1,000)
Gendarmerie & Paramilitary 2,000

ORGANISATIONS BY SERVICE

Army 32,000
FORCES BY ROLE
MANOEUVRE
  Light
    2 cdo bn
    4 inf div (3 inf bde)
COMBAT SUPPORT
    1 arty bde
EQUIPMENT BY TYPE
ARMOURED FIGHTING VEHICLES
  MBT 34: 24 T-54/T-55; 10 *Tiran*-5
  RECCE ε90 AML-60/AML-90
  IFV 38+: BMP; 13+ Ratel-23; 10 *Ratel*-60; 15 *Ratel*-90
  APC 60+
    APC (W) 20+: BTR; *Buffalo* (Panhard M3); 20 WZ-551 (reported)
    PPV 40 RG-31 *Nyala*
  AUV 92: 76 *Cobra*/*Cobra* II; 16 VBL
ENGINEERING & MAINTENANCE VEHICLES
  ARV T-54/T-55 ARV reported
ANTI-TANK/ANTI-INFRASTRUCTURE
  MSL • SP HJ-9A (on *Cobra*)
ARTILLERY 177
  SP 17: **122mm** 12: 6 CS/SH-1; 6 SH-3; **155mm** 5 ATMOS 2000
  TOWED 35+: **105mm** some; **122mm** 6 D-30; **152mm** 29 Type-54 (D-1)†
  MRL 10: **122mm** 5 RM-70; **160mm** 5 LAR-160
  MOR 115: **81mm**; **82mm**; **120mm**
AIR DEFENCE
  SAM • Point-defence 9K32 *Strela*-2 (RS-SA-7 *Grail*)‡
  GUNS ε150: **14.5mm**; **23mm**; **37mm**

Air Force ε1,000
FORCES BY ROLE
TRANSPORT
  1 flt with Cessna 208EX *Grand Caravan*
ATTACK/TRANSPORT HELICOPTER
  1 sqn with Mi-17/Mi-17MD/Mi-17V-5/Mi-17-1V *Hip* H; Mi-24P/V *Hind*
EQUIPMENT BY TYPE
AIRCRAFT
  TPT • Light 2 Cessna 208EX *Grand Caravan*
HELICOPTERS
  ATK 5: 2 Mi-24V *Hind* E; 3 Mi-24P *Hind*
  MRH 12: 1 AW139; 4 Mi-17 *Hip* H; 1 Mi-17MD *Hip* H; 1 Mi-17V-5 *Hip* H; 5 Mi-17-1V *Hip* H
  TPT • Light 1 AW109S

Gendarmerie & Paramilitary

District Administration Security Support Organ ε2,000

DEPLOYMENT

CENTRAL AFRICAN REPUBLIC: UN • MINUSCA 2,146; 2 inf bn; 1 fd hospital
MOZAMBIQUE: Army 2,000
SOUTH SUDAN: UN • UNMISS 2,649; 3 inf bn; 1 hel sqn with 6 Mi-17
SUDAN: UN • UNISFA 6

Senegal SEN

CFA Franc BCEAO XOF		2022	2023	2024
GDP	XOF	17.3trn	18.8trn	21.1trn
	USD	27.7bn	31.1bn	35.2bn
per capita	USD	1,570	1,715	1,886
Growth	%	4.0	4.1	8.8
Inflation	%	9.7	6.1	3.3
Def bdgt	XOF	263bn	272bn	
	USD	422m	452m	
USD1=XOF		622.42	602.73	599.66

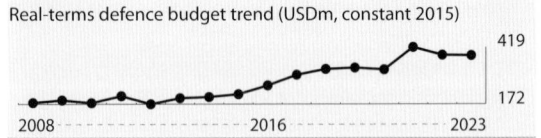

Real-terms defence budget trend (USDm, constant 2015)
419
172
2008 2016 2023

Population 18,384,660

Age	0–14	15–19	20–24	25–29	30–64	65 plus
Male	21.0%	5.5%	4.6%	3.8%	12.8%	1.4%
Female	20.2%	5.4%	4.5%	3.9%	14.9%	1.9%

Capabilities

Senegal's armed forces have strong international ties and are experienced in foreign deployments. Their focus is internal and border security, including counter-insurgency in the country's south and combating Islamist activity in neighbouring states, as well as thwarting narcotics trafficking. Under the 'Horizon 2025' programme, military authorities intend to reorganise and reequip key defence organisations and renew infrastructure. Senegal also has tried to enhance professional military education. Newly established defence organisations include a naval academy and a higher war college. Senegal is upgrading its inventory, recently procured new APCs, offshore patrol vessels, transport aircraft and light artillery. France remains Senegal's principal defence partner and retains a military presence in the country. French military forces deliver training assistance and exercises to the armed forces and gendarmerie. Senegal also has defence cooperation ties with Spain and the UK, and an agreement was signed with Mauritania in 2021 regarding offshore energy-related maritime security. The US also provides security assistance, including to the national police and gendarmerie. The armed forces can deploy personnel using organic airlift, which has improved with the recent delivery of two C295s, but short-notice movements of heavy equipment would be problematic without external assistance. Apart from maintenance facilities, Senegal has no defence-industrial capability.

ACTIVE 13,600 (Army 11,900 Navy 950 Air 750)
Gendarmerie & Paramilitary 5,000

Conscript liability Selective conscription, 24 months

ORGANISATIONS BY SERVICE

Army 11,900 (incl conscripts)

7 Mil Zone HQ

FORCES BY ROLE
MANOEUVRE
  Reconnaissance
  5 armd recce bn
  Light
  1 cdo bn
  6 inf bn
  Air Manoeuvre
  1 AB bn
  Other
  1 (Presidential Guard) horse cav bn
COMBAT SUPPORT
  1 arty bn
  1 engr bn
  3 construction coy
  1 sigs bn
COMBAT SERVICE SUPPORT
  1 log bn
  1 med bn
  1 trg bn

EQUIPMENT BY TYPE
ARMOURED FIGHTING VEHICLES
  ASLT 27 PTL-02 *Assaulter*
  RECCE 67: 20 BRDM-2; 47 Eland-90
  IFV 26 *Ratel*-20
  APC 103
    APC (W) 28: 6+ *Bastion* APC; 2 *Oncilla*; 16 Panhard M3; 4 WZ-551 (CP)
    PPV 75: 8 *Casspir*; 39 *Puma* M26-15; 28 *Puma* M36
  AUV 31: 27 RAM Mk3; 4+ CS/VN3
ENGINEERING & MAINTENANCE VEHICLES
  ARV 2 *Puma* M36 ARV
ANTI-TANK/ANTI-INFRASTRUCTURE
  MSL • MANPATS *Milan*
ARTILLERY 82
  TOWED 20: **105mm** 6 HM-2/M101; **155mm** 14: ε6 Model-50; 8 TR-F1
  MRL **122mm** 6 BM-21 *Grad* (UKR *Bastion*-1 mod)
  MOR 56: **81mm** 24; **120mm** 32
AIR DEFENCE • GUNS • TOWED 39: **14.5mm** 6 ZPU-4 (tch); **20mm** 21 M693; **40mm** 12 L/60

Navy (incl Coast Guard) 950

FORCES BY ROLE
SPECIAL FORCES
  1 cdo coy

EQUIPMENT BY TYPE
PATROL AND COASTAL COMBATANTS 12
  PCGM 1 *Walo* (FRA OPV58S) with 2 twin lnchr with *Marte* Mk2/N AShM, 1 twin *Simbad* lnchr with *Mistral* 3 SAM, 1 76mm gun
  PCO 1 *Fouladou* (FRA OPV 190 Mk II)
  PBF 6: 3 *Anambe* (ISR *Shaldag* II); 2 *Ferlo* (FRA RPB 33); 1 *Lac Retba* (ISR *Shaldag* V)
  PB 4: 2 *Alphonse Faye* (FRA RPB 20); 1 *Conejera*; 1 *Kedougou* (FRA Raidco OPV 45)
AMPHIBIOUS • LANDING CRAFT 2
  LCT 2 EDIC 700
LOGISTICS AND SUPPORT 3
  ABU 1 *Samba Laobe Fall*
  AGOR 1 *Itaf Deme*
  AX 1 *Diender*

Air Force 750

FORCES BY ROLE
GROUND ATTACK
  1 sqn with KA-1S*
MARITIME PATROL/SEARCH & RESCUE
  1 sqn with CN235-220 MPA
TRANSPORT
  1 sqn with ATR-42; Beech B200 *King Air*; C295W; F-27-400M *Troopship*
  1 VIP flt with A320
TRAINING
  1 sqn with TB-30 *Epsilon*
ATTACK/TRANSPORT HELICOPTER
  1 sqn with Bell 206; Mi-24V/Mi-35P *Hind*; Mi-171Sh; Schweizer 300C

EQUIPMENT BY TYPE
AIRCRAFT 4 combat capable
  MP 1 CN235-220 MPA
  TPT 10: **Light** 8: 1 ATR-42; 2 C295W; 2 CN235; 2 Beech B200 *King Air*; 1 F-27-400M *Troopship* (2 more in store); **PAX** 2: 1 A320 (VIP); 1 B-727-200
  TRG 10: 4 KA-1S*; 6 TB-30 *Epsilon*
HELICOPTERS
  ATK 4: 2 Mi-24V *Hind* D; 2 Mi-35P *Hind*
  MRH 1 AW139
  TPT 4: **Medium** 2 Mi-171Sh; **Light** 2 Bell 206
  TRG 1 Schweizer 300C

Gendarmerie & Paramilitary 10,000

Gendarmerie 10,000

EQUIPMENT BY TYPE
ARMOURED FIGHTING VEHICLES

ASLT 4+ VN22B

APC 56

APC (W) 24: 7 *Bastion* APC; 5 EE-11 *Urutu*; 12 VXB-170†

PPV 32: 24 *Ejder Yalcin*; 8 *Gila*

AUV 36: 2 Bastion Patsas; 20 *Cobra* II; 11 RAM Mk3; 6+ CS/VN3C

DEPLOYMENT

CENTRAL AFRICAN REPUBLIC: UN • MINUSCA 192; 1 inf coy

DEMOCRATIC REPUBLIC OF THE CONGO: UN • MONUSCO 7

GAMBIA: ECOWAS • ECOMIG 250

GUINEA-BISSAU: ECOWAS • ESSMGB 150

SOUTH SUDAN: UN • UNMISS 1

FOREIGN FORCES

France 400; 1 *Falcon* 50MI
Spain 65; 2 C295M

Seychelles SYC

Seychelles Rupee SCR		2022	2023	2024
GDP	SCR	28.2bn	29.2bn	30.9bn
	USD	1.98bn	2.09bn	2.12bn
per capita	USD	19,983	20,890	21,095
Growth	%	8.9	4.2	3.9
Inflation	%	2.6	-0.8	2.0
Def exp	SCR	n.k.	n.k.	n.k.
	USD	n.k.	n.k.	n.k.
USD1=SCR		14.27	14.00	14.53
Population	97,617			

Age	0-14	15-19	20-24	25-29	30-64	65 plus
Male	9.2%	3.0%	3.2%	3.7%	28.7%	4.1%
Female	8.7%	2.8%	2.8%	3.2%	25.3%	5.4%

Capabilities

The Seychelles maintains one of the smallest standing armed forces in the world. Its proximity to key international shipping lanes increases its strategic significance. The Seychelles People's Defence Force (PDF) primarily focuses on maritime security and counterpiracy operations. The country hosts US military forces which conduct maritime patrols on a rotational basis. India maintains strong defence ties with the Seychelles, donating equipment, providing maintenance and supporting efforts to enhance its maritime-patrol and -surveillance capability. Bahrain donated four fast patrol boats to the SDF in 2023. The government has plans to improve defence cooperation with China, which has already led to some equipment deliveries. The UAE has also donated equipment. The Seychelles continues to participate in and host multinational maritime-security exercises. The PDF does not deploy overseas and has a limited capacity to deploy and support troops operating in the archipelago. There are limited maintenance facilities but no domestic defence manufacturing sector.

ACTIVE 420 (Land Forces 200; Coast Guard 200; Air Force 20)

ORGANISATIONS BY SERVICE

People's Defence Force

Land Forces 200
FORCES BY ROLE
SPECIAL FORCES
  1 SF unit
MANOEUVRE
  Light
  1 inf coy
  Other
  1 sy unit
COMBAT SUPPORT
  1 MP unit
EQUIPMENT BY TYPE
ARMOURED FIGHTING VEHICLES
  RECCE 6 BRDM-2†
ARTILLERY• MOR 82mm 6 M-43†
AIR DEFENCE • GUNS • TOWED 14.5mm ZPU-2†; ZPU-4†; 37mm M-1939†

Coast Guard 200 (incl 80 Marines)
EQUIPMENT BY TYPE
PATROL AND COASTAL COMBATANTS 11
  PCC 3: 2 *Topaz* (ex-IND *Trinkat*); 1 *Zoroaster* (IND *Car Nicobar* mod)
  PBF 4: 1 *Hermes* (ex-IND *Coastal Interceptor Craft*); 3 *Thorpe* (LKA *Wave Rider*)
  PB 4: 1 *Etoile* (PRC Poly Technologies 47m); 2 *Le Vigilant* (ex-UAE Rodman 101); 1 *Fortune* (ex-UK *Tyne*)
LOGISTICS AND SUPPORT • AKL 1 *Saya de Malha*

Air Force 20
EQUIPMENT BY TYPE
AIRCRAFT
  TPT • Light 5: 1 DHC-6-320 *Twin Otter*; 2 Do-228; 2 Y-12

Sierra Leone SLE

Sierra Leonean Leone SLL		2022	2023	2024
GDP	SLL	56.0trn	77.5trn	99.0trn
	USD	3.99bn	3.52bn	3.61bn
per capita	USD	480	415	417
Growth	%	4.0	2.7	4.7
Inflation	%	27.2	42.9	29.8
Def bdgt	SLL	341bn	441bn	
	USD	24.3m	20.0m	
USD1=SLL		14,045.49	22,026.61	27,449.09

Real-terms defence budget trend (USDm, constant 2015)

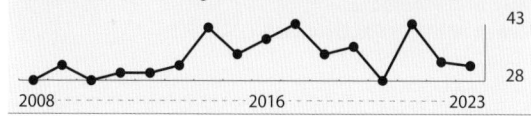

Population	8,908,040

Age	0–14	15–19	20–24	25–29	30–64	65 plus
Male	20.4%	5.5%	4.8%	4.1%	13.4%	1.3%
Female	20.1%	5.5%	5.0%	4.6%	14.0%	1.3%

Capabilities

The armed forces' primary task is ensuring internal and border security and providing forces for peacekeeping missions. Sierra Leone is building up its defence institutions, generating formal defence documentation and improving planning functions, mostly with international support. Canada, China, the UK and US are among the countries supporting military capacity-building. UK training is intended to boost the capacity of the police force and of the armed forces prior to deployment abroad. Freetown's Horton Academy delivers professional military education training to national and regional personnel. Defence ties with China include personnel exchanges, equipment delivery and support for the development of military infrastructure. The armed forces' ability to deploy more than small units is constrained by force size and logistics-support capacity. Purchases to remedy these problems have been implemented. The armed forces have plans to generate a company-sized quick-reaction force for peacekeeping missions. South Korea and China donated additional inshore patrol boats to modestly enhance Sierra Leone's maritime surveillance capability. The country has limited maintenance capacity and no defence-manufacturing capability.

ACTIVE 8,500 (Joint 8,500)

ORGANISATIONS BY SERVICE

Armed Forces 8,500
FORCES BY ROLE
MANOEUVRE
  Reconnaissance
    1 recce unit
  Light
    4 inf bde (3 inf bn)
COMBAT SUPPORT
  1 engr regt
  1 int unit
  1 MP unit
  1 sigs unit
COMBAT SUPPORT
  1 log unit
  1 fd hospital
EQUIPMENT BY TYPE
ARMOURED FIGHTING VEHICLES
  APC • **PPV** 4: 3 *Casspir*; 1 *Mamba* Mk5
ANTI-TANK/ANTI-INFRASTRUCTURE
  RCL **84mm** *Carl Gustaf*
ARTILLERY 37
  TOWED **122mm** 6 PL-96 (D-30)
  MOR 31: **81mm** ε27; **82mm** 2; **120mm** 2
HELICOPTERS • MRH 2 Mi-17 *Hip* H/Mi-8 *Hip*†
AIR DEFENCE • GUNS • TOWED **14.5mm** 3

Maritime Wing ε200
EQUIPMENT BY TYPE
PATROL AND COASTAL COMBATANTS 2
  PB 2: 1 *Mammy Yoko* (PRC 27m); 1 *Sir Milton* (Type-062/I (ex-PRC *Shanghai* III))†

DEPLOYMENT

CENTRAL AFRICAN REPUBLIC: UN • MINUSCA 7
DEMOCRATIC REPUBLIC OF THE CONGO: UN • MONUSCO 2
LEBANON: UN • UNIFIL 3
SOMALIA: UN • UNSOM 1; UN • UNSOS 1
SOUTH SUDAN: UN • UNMISS 2
SUDAN: UN • UNISFA 8
WESTERN SAHARA: UN • MINURSO 1

Somalia SOM

Somali Shilling SOS		2022	2023	2024
GDP	USD	10.4bn	11.5bn	12.5bn
per capita	USD	667	717	757
Growth	%	2.4	2.8	3.7
Inflation	%	6.8	5.7	4.1
Def bdgt	USD	n.k.	n.k.	n.k.
USD1=SOS		1.00	1.00	1.00

*Definitive economic data unavailable

Population	12,693,796

Age	0–14	15–19	20–24	25–29	30–64	65 plus
Male	20.7%	5.2%	4.7%	3.7%	14.8%	1.1%
Female	20.8%	5.3%	4.6%	3.6%	13.8%	1.6%

Capabilities

The Somali National Army (SNA) is relatively limited in organisational and military capability. Internal stability remains fragile following decades of conflict and insurgency, with al-Shabaab and other extremist groups still based in the country and retaining the ability to carry out attacks. Deployed international forces are trying to provide security, stabilisation and capacity-building assistance. The SNA has been working with clan-based militia groups to strengthen local ties and effectiveness. Growing a domestic training capacity staff within the SNA to enable organic continuation training remains a challenge. This has required prolonged AU support, with the African Union Transition Mission in Somalia (ATMIS) replacing the previous AMISOM in April 2022. The UN also has a mandate to implement a revised transitional plan by the end of 2024. ATMIS forces in 2023 completed the first phase of drawdown. The Somali federal government in September asked for a pause to a further drawdown for three months due to the security threat posed by al-Shabaab. Some elements of the SNA, such as the multi-clan, US-mentored Danab Brigade, have displayed greater capability. US forces are also deployed independently to Somalia to tackle militant groups. The SNA remains reliant on external training programmes from several countries, organisations and private security companies to build internal capability and capacity. Turkiye has established a significant military training facility in Somalia and provides specialist training abroad. There are reports that some troops were sent to Eritrea for training in 2021. The military has no capacity to deploy beyond national borders and minimal national infrastructure to support domestic operations. The equipment inventory is limited and eclectic. Government plans to re-establish and equip Somalia's air and maritime forces remain unfulfilled. Somalia has no domestic defence-industrial capability.

ACTIVE 13,900 (Army 13,900)

ORGANISATIONS BY SERVICE

Army 13,900
FORCES BY ROLE
COMMAND
  4 div HQ
MANOEUVRE
  Light
    Some cdo bn(+)
    12 inf bde (3 inf bn)
    2 indep inf bn
  Other
    1 gd bn
EQUIPMENT BY TYPE
ARMOURED FIGHTING VEHICLES
  APC 73
    APC (W) 38+: 25+ AT-105 *Saxon*; 13 *Bastion* APC; Fiat 6614
    PPV 35+: *Casspir*; MAV-5; 20 *Kirpi*; 9+ *Mamba* Mk5; 6 *Puma* M36; RG-31 *Nyala*
  AUV 12 *Tiger* 4×4
HELICOPTERS
  MRH 2 Bell 412

Gendarmerie & Paramilitary

Coast Guard
All operational patrol vessels under 10t FLD

FOREIGN FORCES

Under UNSOM command unless stated
Burundi ATMIS 3,400; 4 inf bn
Djibouti ATMIS 700; 1 inf bn
Ethiopia ATMIS 3,600; 4 inf bn
Finland EUTM Somalia 12
Ghana 1 • UNSOS 1
India 1
Italy EUTM Somalia 169
Kenya ATMIS 3,600; 3 inf bn • UNSOS 1
Mauritania UNSOS 1
Pakistan UNSOS 1
Portugal EUTM Somalia 2
Romania EUTM Somalia 5
Serbia EUTM Somalia 6
Sierra Leone 1 • UNSOS 1
Spain EUTM Somalia 20
Sweden EUTM Somalia 6
Turkiye 1 • Army: 200 (trg base)
Uganda 627; 1 sy bn • ATMIS 3,000; 3 inf bn • UNSOS 1
United Kingdom 2 • UNSOS 10 • Army: 65 (trg team)
United States US Africa Command: 100

PUNTLAND & SOMALILAND

Data presented here represents the de facto situation. This does not imply international recognition as sovereign states. Much of this equipment is in poor repair or inoperable

Puntland

Army ε3,000 (to be integrated into Somali National Army)

Maritime Police Force ε1,000
EQUIPMENT BY TYPE
PATROL AND COASTAL COMBATANTS
All operational patrol vessels under 10t FLD
AIRCRAFT • TPT 4: **Light** 3 Ayres S2R; **PAX** 1 DC-3
HELICOPTERS • MRH SA316 *Alouette* III

Somaliland

Army ε12,500
FORCES BY ROLE
MANOEUVRE
  Armoured
    2 armd bde
  Mechanised
    1 mech inf bde
  Light
    14 inf bde
COMBAT SUPPORT

2 arty bde
COMBAT SERVICE SUPPORT
1 spt bn
EQUIPMENT BY TYPE†
ARMOURED FIGHTING VEHICLES
MBT T-54/55
RECCE Fiat 6616
APC • APC(W) Fiat 6614
ARTILLERY • MRL various incl BM-21 *Grad*
AIR DEFENCE • GUNS • 23mm ZU-23-2

Ministry of the Interior

Coast Guard 600
All operational patrol vessels under 10t FLD

FOREIGN FORCES
United Arab Emirates 180

South Africa RSA

South African Rand ZAR		2022	2023	2024
GDP	ZAR	6.63trn	6.99trn	7.45trn
	USD	405bn	381bn	401bn
per capita	USD	6,684	6,191	6,427
Growth	%	1.9	0.9	1.8
Inflation	%	6.9	5.8	4.8
Def bdgt	ZAR	52.3bn	52.5bn	
	USD	3.19bn	2.86bn	
USD1=ZAR		16.36	18.35	18.55

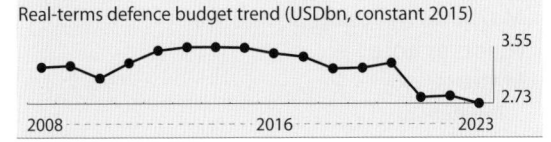

Real-terms defence budget trend (USDbn, constant 2015)

Population	59,795,503				
Age	0–14	15–19	20–24	25–29	30–64	65 plus
Male	13.7%	3.8%	3.5%	3.6%	21.4%	3.1%
Female	13.7%	3.9%	3.6%	4.0%	21.5%	4.3%

Capabilities

South Africa's armed forces are, on paper, the region's most capable, but continuing economic and structural problems are eroding its capabilities. Its principal roles include maintaining territorial integrity and supporting the police service. The Department of Defence Strategic Plan 2020–2025 is the South African National Defence Force's (SANDF) primary policy instrument. A priority for the SANDF is to arrest the decline of critical military capabilities and equipment. However, a lack of funds is constraining the SANDF's ability to renew equipment and meet performance targets. The army is reverting to a more traditional structure, with standing brigades being formed. South Africa contributes personnel to UN operations and remains a key component of the Force Intervention Brigade in the DRC. South Africa is a member of the SADC Standby Force and sent 1,500 personnel to Mozambique in 2021 as part of a multinational force to combat the Islamist insurgency. Troops were also deployed domestically in 2021 to help counter internal unrest and in 2023 to tackle illegal mining. Historically, South African forces have also played a key role in training and supporting other regional forces. The SANDF can independently deploy its forces, and it participates in national and multinational exercises as well as peacekeeping missions. However, reduced funding has undermined modernisation ambitions, resulting in programmes being behind schedule and difficulties in maintaining and replacing obsolete equipment. The air force has significant challenges in maintaining operational capabilities. Naval availability, meanwhile, is dependent on serviceability and many vessels have been under repair or maintenance in recent years. Budget cuts are also likely to have hurt training. South Africa has the continent's most capable defence industry, including the state-owned Armaments Corporation of South Africa (ARMSCOR) and weapons manufacturer Denel, though both face financial difficulties. Cuban personnel remain engaged in a project to maintain and refurbish land vehicles.

ACTIVE 69,200 (Army 35,250 Navy 5,550 Air 8,900 South African Military Health Service 6,900 Other 12,600)

RESERVE 15,050 (Army 12,250 Navy 850 Air 850 South African Military Health Service Reserve 1,100)

ORGANISATIONS BY SERVICE

Army 35,250
FORCES BY ROLE
Regt are bn sized. A new army structure is planned with 3 mixed regular/reserve divisions (1 mechanised, 1 motorised and 1 contingency) comprising 12 brigades (1 armoured, 1 mechanised, 7 motorised, 1 airborne, 1 airlanded and 1 sea landed)
COMMAND
2 bde HQ
SPECIAL FORCES
2 SF regt(-)
MANOEUVRE
Reconnaissance
1 armd recce regt
Armoured
1 tk regt(-)
Mechanised
2 mech inf bn
Light
8 mot inf bn
1 lt inf bn
Air Manoeuvre
1 AB bn
1 air mob bn
Amphibious
1 amph bn
COMBAT SUPPORT
1 arty regt
1 engr regt
1 construction regt

3 sigs regt
COMBAT SERVICE SUPPORT
1 engr spt regt
AIR DEFENCE
1 ADA regt

Reserve 12,250 reservists (under-strength)
FORCES BY ROLE
MANOEUVRE
  Reconnaissance
  3 armd recce regt
  Armoured
  4 tk regt
  Mechanised
  6 mech inf bn
  Light
  14 mot inf bn
  3 lt inf bn (converting to mot inf)
  Air Manoeuvre
  1 AB bn
  2 air mob bn
  Amphibious
  1 amph bn
COMBAT SUPPORT
  7 arty regt
  2 engr regt
AIR DEFENCE
  5 AD regt
EQUIPMENT BY TYPE
ARMOURED FIGHTING VEHICLES
  MBT 24 *Olifant* 2 (133 *Olifant* 1B in store)
  ASLT 50 *Rooikat*-76 (126 in store)
  IFV 534 *Ratel*-20/*Ratel*-60/*Ratel*-90
  APC • PPV 798: 358 *Casspir*; 60 *Mamba* (refurbished); 380 *Mamba*†
ENGINEERING & MAINTENANCE VEHICLES
  ARV *Gemsbok*
  VLB *Leguan*
  MW *Husky*
ANTI-TANK/ANTI-INFRASTRUCTURE
  MSL
    SP ZT-3 *Swift*
    MANPATS *Milan* ADT/ER
  RCL 106mm M40A1 (some SP)
ARTILLERY 1,240
  SP 155mm 2 G-6 (41 in store)
  TOWED 155mm 6 G-5 (66 in store)
  MRL 127mm 6 *Valkiri* Mk II MARS *Bataleur*; (26 *Valkiri* Mk I and 19 *Valkiri* Mk II in store)
  MOR 1,226: **81mm** 1,190 (incl some SP on *Casspir* & *Ratel*); **120mm** 36
UNINHABITED AERIAL VEHICLES
  ISR • Light up to 4 *Vulture*

AIR DEFENCE
  SAM • Point-defence *Starstreak*
  GUNS 40
    SP 23mm (36 *Zumlac* in store)
    TOWED 35mm 40: 22 GDF-002; 18 GDF-005A/007

Navy 5,550
Fleet HQ and Naval base located at Simon's Town; Naval stations located at Durban and Port Elizabeth
EQUIPMENT BY TYPE
SUBMARINES 2
  SSK 2 *Heroine* (GER Type-209/1400 mod) (1 additional boat in refit since 2014, awaiting funds to complete) with 8 533mm TT with SUT 264 HWT
PRINCIPAL SURFACE COMBATANTS • FRIGATES 4
  FFGHM 4 *Valour* (GER MEKO A200) with 2 quad lnchr with MM40 *Exocet* Block 2 AShM (upgrade to Block 3 planned); 2 16-cell VLS with *Umkhonto*-IR SAM, 1 Denel Dual Purpose Gun (DPG) CIWS, 1 76mm gun (capacity 1 *Super Lynx* 300 hel)
PATROL AND COASTAL COMBATANTS 4
  PCC 3: 1 *Warrior* (ISR *Reshef*) with 1 76mm gun; 2 *Warrior* II (NLD Damen Stan Patrol 6211)
  PB 1 *Tobie* (2 additional in reserve)
MINE WARFARE • MINE COUNTERMEASURES 3
  MHC 3 *River* (GER *Navors*) (limited operational roles; training and dive support) (1 additional in reserve)
LOGISTICS AND SUPPORT 2
  AGSH 1 *Protea* (UK *Hecla*) with 1 hel landing platform
  AORH 1 *Drakensberg* (capacity 2 Oryx hels; 100 troops)

Maritime Reaction Squadron
FORCES BY ROLE
MANOEUVRE
  Amphibious
  1 mne patrol gp
  1 diving gp
  1 mne boarding gp
COMBAT SERVICE SUPPORT
  1 spt gp

Air Force 8,900
Air Force HQ, Pretoria, and 4 op gps
Command & Control: 2 Airspace Control Sectors, 1 Mobile Deployment Wg, 1 Air Force Command Post
FORCES BY ROLE
FIGHTER/GROUND ATTACK
  1 sqn with *Gripen* C/D (JAS-39C/D)
GROUND ATTACK/TRAINING
  1 sqn with *Hawk* Mk120*
TRANSPORT
  1 (VIP) sqn with B-737 BBJ; Cessna 550 *Citation* II; *Falcon* 50; *Falcon* 900
  1 sqn with C-47TP

1 sqn with Beech 200/300 *King Air*; Cessna 208 *Caravan*; PC-12

1 sqn with C-130BZ *Hercules*

1 sqn with C-212-200/-300 *Aviocar*

TRAINING

1 unit with PC-7 Mk II *Astra*

1 hel trg unit with AW109; *Oryx*

ATTACK HELICOPTER

1 (cbt spt) sqn with AH-2 *Rooivalk*

TRANSPORT HELICOPTER

4 (mixed) sqn with AW109; *Oryx*

EQUIPMENT BY TYPE

AIRCRAFT 48 combat capable

FGA 24 *Gripen* C/D (JAS-39C/D) (most non-operational)

TPT 15: Medium 2 C-130BZ *Hercules* (3 more non-operational); Light 9: 3 C-47TP (maritime); 2 C-212-200 *Aviocar*†; 1 C-212-300 *Aviocar*; 2 Cessna 550 *Citation* II; 1 PC-12†; (3 Beech 200C *King Air*; 1 Beech 300 *King Air*; 9 Cessna 208 *Caravan* all non-operational); PAX 4: 1 B-737BBJ; 2 *Falcon* 50; 1 *Falcon* 900

TRG 30: 24 *Hawk* Mk120*; 6 PC-7 Mk II *Astra* (29 more non-operational)

HELICOPTERS

ATK 3 AH-2 *Rooivalk*† (8 more non-operational)

MRH 1 *Super Lynx* 300 (3 more non-operational)

TPT 11: Medium 5 *Oryx* (34 more non-operational); Light 6 AW109; (18 AW109; 8 BK-117 all non-operational)

AIR-LAUNCHED MISSILES • AAM • IIR IRIS-T

BOMBS • Laser-guided GBU-12 *Paveway* II

Ground Defence

FORCES BY ROLE

MANOEUVRE

Other

12 sy sqn (SAAF regt)

South African Military Health Service 6,900

DEPLOYMENT

DEMOCRATIC REPUBLIC OF THE CONGO: UN • MONUSCO • Operation Mistral 1,143; 1 inf bn; 1 hel sqn

MOZAMBIQUE: SADC • SAMIM 1,200; 1 inf bn

MOZAMBIQUE CHANNEL: Navy • 1 FFGHM

South Sudan SSD

South Sudanese Pound SSP		2022	2023	2024
GDP	SSP	4.57trn	6.27trn	7.74trn
	USD	8.54bn	6.27bn	7.40bn
per capita	USD	585	417	479
Growth	%	0.5	3.5	4.2
Inflation	%	-3.2	16.3	13.6
Def bdgt [a]	SSP	26.1bn	48.3bn	
	USD		48.8m	48.3m
USD1=SSP		535.68	1,000.75	1,046.00

[a] Security and law enforcement spending

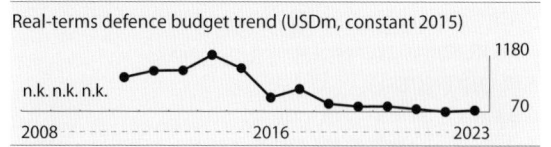

Real-terms defence budget trend (USDm, constant 2015)

Population 12,118,379

Age	0–14	15–19	20–24	25–29	30–64	65 plus
Male	21.4%	5.5%	5.0%	4.1%	13.6%	1.4%
Female	20.5%	5.4%	5.0%	3.5%	13.3%	1.2%

Capabilities

South Sudan's civil war formally ended in 2020 and a fragile cease-fire has largely remained intact. The September 2020 peace deal built on a 2018 accord that laid out a framework for opposition and government forces and resulted in changes to the number and demarcation of federal states. These and other challenges remain stumbling blocks in ongoing negotiations, with the transition period extended by two years and the country's first elections since declaring independence in 2011 now scheduled for December 2024. Although there has been steady progress towards creating a unified force under the banner of the South Sudan People's Defence Forces (SSPDF), progress has been hampered by a lack of disarmament, demobilisation and reintegration for those former rebels ineligible for inclusion. South Sudan lacks an independent capacity to deploy and sustain military units beyond national borders. Kenay facilitated a 2023 SSPDF deployment under the East African Community Regional Force. Equipment is primarily of Soviet origin, with some light arms of Chinese origin. There have been efforts to expand the small air force. Sanctions remain in place, with both the EU and UN arms embargoes widened in 2018 to include all types of military equipment. South Sudan has no domestic defence industry but has reportedly sought to develop an ammunition-manufacturing capacity.

ACTIVE 90,000 (Army 90,000)

ORGANISATIONS BY SERVICE

Army ε90,000

FORCES BY ROLE

3 military comd

MANOEUVRE

Light

8 inf div

COMBAT SUPPORT
1 engr corps

EQUIPMENT BY TYPE
ARMOURED FIGHTING VEHICLES
MBT 80+: some T-55†; 80 T-72AV†
APC • PPV Streit *Typhoon*; Streit *Cougar*; *Mamba*
ANTI-TANK/ANTI-INFRASTRUCTURE
MSL • MANPATS HJ-73; 9K115 *Metis* (RS-AT-7 *Saxhorn*)
RCL 73mm SPG-9 (with SSLA)
ARTILLERY
SP 122mm 2S1 *Gvozdika*; **152mm** 2S3 *Akatsiya*
TOWED 130mm Some M-46
MRL 122mm BM-21 *Grad*; **107mm** PH-63
MOR 82mm; **120mm** Type-55 look-alike
AIR DEFENCE
SAM
  Short-range 16 S-125 *Pechora* (RS-SA-3 *Goa*)†
  Point-defence 9K32 *Strela*-2 (RS-SA-7 *Grail*)‡; QW-2
GUNS 14.5mm ZPU-4; **23mm** ZU-23-2; **37mm** Type-65/74

Air Force
EQUIPMENT BY TYPE
AIRCRAFT 2 combat capable
  TPT • Light 1 Beech 1900
  TRG ε2 L-39 *Albatros**
HELICOPTERS
  ATK 3 Mi-24V/Mi-24V-SMB *Hind*
  MRH 5 Mi-17 *Hip* H
  TPT 3: **Medium** 1 Mi-172 (VIP); **Light** 1 AW109 (civ livery)

DEPLOYMENT
DEMOCRATIC REPUBLIC OF THE CONGO: EAC • EACRF 1,000; 1 inf bn

FOREIGN FORCES
All UNMISS, unless otherwise indicated
Albania 2
Australia 14
Azerbaijan 2
Bangladesh 1,630; 1 inf coy; 2 rvn coy; 2 engr coy
Benin 9
Bhutan 4
Bolivia 4
Brazil 12
Cambodia 85; 1 MP unit
Canada 9
China, People's Republic of 1,050; 1 inf bn; 1 engr coy; 1 fd hospital
Ecuador 3
Egypt 7
El Salvador 3
Ethiopia 1,497; 2 inf bn
Fiji 2
Gambia 3
Germany 14
Ghana 742; 1 inf bn
Guatemala 7
Guinea 3
India 2,404; 2 inf bn; 1 engr coy; 1 sigs coy; 2 fd hospital
Indonesia 4
Japan 4
Jordan 5
Kenya 18
Korea, Republic of 278; 1 engr coy
Kyrgyzstan 2
Liberia 2
Malawi 10
Moldova 5
Mongolia 870; 1 inf bn
Morocco 3
Namibia 5
Nepal 1,759; 2 inf bn
New Zealand 3
Nigeria 13
Norway 15
Pakistan 287; 1 engr coy
Papua New Guinea 2
Paraguay 3
Peru 5
Philippines 1
Poland 1
Romania 6
Russia 4
Rwanda 2,649; 3 inf bn; 1 hel sqn with 6 Mi-17
Senegal 1
Sierra Leone 2
Sri Lanka 66; 1 fd hospital; 1 hel sqn
Switzerland 1
Tanzania 8
Thailand 285; 1 engr coy
Togo 2
Tunisia 2
Uganda 2
United Kingdom 5
United States 6
Vietnam 68; 1 fd hospital
Zambia 10
Zimbabwe 14

Sudan SDN

Sudanese Pound SDG		2022	2023	2024
GDP	SDG	19.0trn	64.4trn	162trn
	USD	33.8bn	25.6bn	25.8bn
per capita	USD	723	534	526
Growth	%	-2.5	-18.3	0.3
Inflation	%	138.8	256.2	152.4
Def exp	SDG	n.k.	n.k.	n.k.
	USD	n.k.	n.k.	n.k.
USD1=SDG		563.23	2,519.15	6,260.83
Population	49,197,555			

Age	0–14	15–19	20–24	25–29	30–64	65 plus
Male	20.6%	5.9%	5.0%	3.9%	13.2%	1.7%
Female	19.9%	5.7%	4.9%	3.6%	14.1%	1.5%

Capabilities

Sudan's armed forces are engaged in internal strife. In mid-April 2023, fighting broke out between Sudan's regular armed forces and the paramilitary Rapid Support Forces. This followed internal divisions within the military junta that seized power in October 2021, replacing the civilian and military Sovereign Council formed after the 2019 ousting of President Omar al-Bashir. The conflict has displaced millions with allegations of war crimes against civilians. A number of temporary ceasefires have been declared, predominantly to allow civilians safe passage through conflict areas. International efforts to broker a lasting peace agreement continued into late 2023. Sudan also has border disputes with neighbouring Ethiopia, and, in recent years, there were reports of cross-border incursions amid the conflict between Addis Ababa and Tigrayan forces. Sudan was part of the initial Saudi-led coalition that intervened in Yemen. Sudan struck a defence agreement with Iran in 2008 that reportedly included assistance in developing its domestic arms industry. Growing defence ties with Egypt led to joint exercises in 2020 and 2021. The two signed an agreement to strengthen military cooperation in 2021. The armed forces are conscript-based and have gained operational experience from internal-security deployments and the intervention in Yemen. A UN arms embargo remains in place, though this is limited to equipment in the Darfur region and there have been sustained reports the embargo is being violated. The state-run Military Industry Corporation manufactures a range of ammunition, small arms and armoured vehicles for the local and export market. The majority of the corporation's products are based on older Chinese and Russian systems.

ACTIVE 104,300 (Army 100,000 Navy 1,300 Air 3,000) Gendarmerie & Paramilitary 60,000

Conscript liability 2 years for males aged 18–30

ORGANISATIONS BY SERVICE

Space
EQUIPMENT BY TYPE
SATELLITES • ISR 1 SRSS-1

Army 100,000+
FORCES BY ROLE
SPECIAL FORCES
  5 SF coy
MANOEUVRE
  Reconnaissance
  1 indep recce bde
  Armoured
  1 armd div
  Mechanised
  1 mech inf div
  1 indep mech inf bde
  Light
  15+ inf div
  6 indep inf bde
  Air Manoeuvre
  1 air aslt bde
  Amphibious
  1 mne div
  Other
  1 (Border Guard) sy bde
COMBAT SUPPORT
  3 indep arty bde
  1 engr div (9 engr bn)
EQUIPMENT BY TYPE†
ARMOURED FIGHTING VEHICLES
  MBT *Al-Bashier* (Type-85-IIM); T-55A/AMV; T-72AV/B; Type-59D
  LT TK ZTQ-62; ZTS-63
  RECCE BRDM-2; *Cayman* BRDM
  IFV BMP-1; BMP-2; BTR-3; BTR-80A; WZ-523 IFV
  APC
    APC (T) BTR-50; M113
    APC (W) BTR-70M *Kobra* 2; BTR-152; OT-62; OT-64; *Rakhsh*; V-150 *Commando*; *Walid*; WZ-551; WZ-523
    PPV *Sarsar*-2; Streit *Spartan*
  AUV MCAV-20; Nimr *Ajban* 440A
ANTI-TANK/ANTI-INFRASTRUCTURE
  MSL • MANPATS 9K11 *Malyutka* (RS-AT-3 *Sagger*); HJ-8; 9K135 *Kornet* (RS-AT-14 *Spriggan*)
  RCL 106mm M40A1
  GUNS 76mm ZIS-3; **100mm** M-1944; **85mm** D-44
ARTILLERY
  SP 122mm 2S1 *Gvozdika*; **155mm** Mk F3
  TOWED 105mm M101; **122mm** D-30; D-74; M-30; **130mm** M-46; PL-59-I; **155mm** M114A1
  MRL 107mm PH-63; **122mm** BM-21 *Grad*; *Saqr*; PHL-81; **302mm** WS-1
  MOR 81mm; **82mm**; **120mm** AM-49; *Boragh*; M-43; W86
AIR DEFENCE
  SAM • Point-defence 9K32M *Strela*-2M (RS-SA-7B *Grail*)‡; 9K33 *Osa* (RS-SA-8 *Gecko*); FN-6 (CH-SA-10)
  GUNS

SP 20mm M163 *Vulcan*; M3 VDAA
TOWED 14.5mm ZPU-2; 14.5mm ZPU-4; 20mm M167 *Vulcan*; 23mm ZU-23-2; 37mm Type-63; M-1939; 57mm S-60; 85mm M-1944

Navy 1,300
EQUIPMENT BY TYPE
PATROL AND COASTAL COMBATANTS 12
  PBR 4 *Kurmuk*
  PB 8: 2 13.5m; 1 14m; 2 19m; 3 41m (PRC)
AMPHIBIOUS • LANDING CRAFT • LCVP 5
LOGISTICS AND SUPPORT 4
  AG 3
  AXL 1 *Petrushka* (ex-RUS)

Air Force 3,000
FORCES BY ROLE
FIGHTER
  2 sqn with MiG-29SE/UB *Fulcrum*
FIGHTER/GROUND ATTACK
  1 sqn with FTC-2000G
GROUND ATTACK
  1 sqn with Su-24M/MR *Fencer*
  1 sqn with Su-25K/UB *Frogfoot*
TRANSPORT
  Some sqn with An-30 *Clank*; An-32 *Cline*; An-72 *Coaler*; An-74TK-200/-300; C-130H *Hercules*; Il-76 *Candid*; Y-8
  1 VIP unit with *Falcon* 50; *Falcon* 900
TRAINING
  1 sqn with K-8 *Karakorum**
ATTACK HELICOPTER
  2 sqn with Mi-24/Mi-24P/Mi-24V/Mi-35P *Hind*
TRANSPORT HELICOPTER
  2 sqn with Mi-8 *Hip*; Mi-17 *Hip* H; Mi-171
EQUIPMENT BY TYPE
AIRCRAFT 45 combat capable
  FTR 22: up to 20 MiG-29SE *Fulcrum* C; 2 MiG-29UB *Fulcrum* B
  FGA 3 FTC-2000G
  ATK 12: ε4 Su-24M/MR *Fencer*; ε8 Su-25K/UB *Frogfoot*; (15 A-5 *Fantan* in store)
  ISR 2 An-30 *Clank*
  TPT 19: Heavy 1 Il-76 *Candid*; Medium 4: 2 C-130H *Hercules*; 2 Y-8; Light 12: ε3 An-26 *Curl*; 2 An-32 *Cline*; 1 An-72 *Coaler*; 4 An-74TK-200; 2 An-74TK-300; PAX 2: 1 *Falcon* 50 (VIP); 1 *Falcon* 900
  TRG 11+: ε8 K-8 *Karakorum**; some SAFAT-03; 3 Utva-75
HELICOPTERS
  ATK ε11 Mi-24/Mi-24P/Mi-24V/Mi-35P *Hind*
  MRH ε3 Mi-17 *Hip* H
  TPT 8: Medium ε5 Mi-8 *Hip*/Mi-171; Light 3: 1 Bell 205; 2 Bo-105
  TRG some SAFAT 02

UNINHABITED AERIAL VEHICLES
  CISR • Heavy CH-3; CH-4; Medium *Mohajer*-6 (reported)
  ISR • Medium *Ababil* 2; *Ababil* 3
AIR DEFENCE • SAM • Medium-range: (18 S-75M *Dvina* (RS-SA-2 *Guideline*)‡ (non-operational))
AIR-LAUNCHED MISSILES • AAM • IR R-3 (RS-AA-2 *Atoll*)‡; R-60 (RS-AA-8 *Aphid*); R-73 (RS-AA-11A *Archer*); ARH R-77 (RS-AA-12A *Adder*)

Gendarmerie & Paramilitary 60,000

Central Reserve Police 60,000

TERRITORY WHERE THE GOVERNMENT DOES NOT EXERCISE EFFECTIVE CONTROL

Data here represents the de facto situation. This does not imply international recognition. The Rapid Support Forces exercise de facto control over large parts of western and southwestern Sudan, as well as significant parts of Khartoum and the surrounding area.

Rapid Support Forces 100,000+
EQUIPMENT BY TYPE
ARMOURED FIGHTING VEHICLES
  MBT T-55
  IFV BTR-80A; WZ-523 IFV
  APC • APC (W) BTR-70M *Kobra* 2
ANTI-TANK/ANTI-INFRASTRUCTURE
  MSL • MANPATS HJ-8
ARTILLERY
  SP 122mm *Khalifa*-1 (reported)
  MRL 107mm PH-63
  MOR 120mm M-74
AIR DEFENCE
  SAM • Point-defence 9K32M *Strela*-2M (RS-SA-7 *Grail*)‡; 9K38 *Igla* (RS-SA-18 *Grouse*); 9K338 Igla-S (RS-SA-24 *Grinch*); FN-6 (CH-SA-10); HN-5 (CH-SA-3)
  GUNS • SP 14.5mm ZPU-2 (tch); 23mm ZU-23-2 (tch)

DEPLOYMENT
YEMEN: *Operation Restoring Hope* 650 (status uncertain)

FOREIGN FORCES
All UNISFA unless otherwise indicated
Bangladesh 513; 1 inf bn(-)
Benin 2
Bhutan 2
Bolivia 3
Brazil 4
Burundi 4
Cambodia 1
China, People's Republic of 152; 1 inf coy; 1 hel flt with 2 Mi-171

Ecuador 3
Egypt 2
El Salvador 1
Ghana 658; 1 inf bn; 1 fd hospital
Guatemala 2
Guinea 1
India 576; 1 mech inf bn(-)
Indonesia 2
Kenya 1
Kyrgyzstan 2
Liberia 1
Malawi 5
Malaysia 1
Mauritania 3
Mongolia 4
Morocco 6
Namibia 7
Nepal 106; 1 log coy
Nigeria 176; 1 inf coy
Pakistan 584; 1 inf bn(-)
Peru 4
Rwanda 6
Sierra Leone 8
Tanzania 2
Tunisia 1
Uganda 2
Uruguay 2
Vietnam 190; 1 engr coy
Zambia 3
Zimbabwe 10

Tanzania TZA

Tanzanian Shilling TZS		2022	2023	2024
GDP	TZS	178trn	199trn	221trn
	USD	77.1bn	84.0bn	86.0bn
per capita	USD	1,253	1,327	1,318
Growth	%	4.7	5.2	6.1
Inflation	%	4.4	4.0	4.0
Def bdgt	TZS	2.36trn	2.71trn	2.99trn
	USD	1.02bn	1.15bn	1.16bn
USD1=TZS		2,315.48	2,366.40	2,571.78

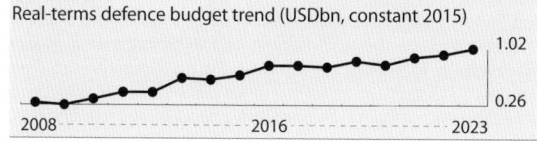

Real-terms defence budget trend (USDbn, constant 2015)

Population 65,642,682

Age	0–14	15–19	20–24	25–29	30–64	65 plus
Male	21.0%	5.4%	4.6%	3.8%	13.8%	1.4%
Female	20.5%	5.3%	4.5%	3.8%	14.0%	1.9%

Capabilities

Non-state actors pose the principal threat to Tanzania's security, with terrorism, poaching and piracy of concern. There are defence-related ties with countries including China, Israel, Pakistan and Russia. The armed forces take part in multinational exercises in Africa and have provided some training assistance to other African forces. Training relationships also exist with extra-regional armed forces, including the US. Tanzania's contribution to the UN's Force Intervention Brigade in the eastern DRC, notably its special forces, will have provided lessons for force development. However, there is only a limited capacity to project power independently beyond the country's borders. Budget constraints have limited recapitalisation ambitions and, although heavy equipment is ageing. There are local ammunition facilities, but otherwise Tanzania relies on imports for its military equipment.

ACTIVE 27,000 (Army 23,000 Navy 1,000 Air 3,000) **Gendarmerie & Paramilitary 1,400**

Conscript liability Three months basic military training combined with social service, ages 18–23

RESERVE 80,000 (Joint 80,000)

ORGANISATIONS BY SERVICE

Army ε23,000
FORCES BY ROLE
SPECIAL FORCES
  1 SF unit
MANOEUVRE
  Armoured
  1 tk bde
  Light
  5 inf bde
COMBAT SUPPORT
  4 arty bn
  1 mor bn
  2 AT bn
  1 engr regt (bn)
COMBAT SERVICE SUPPORT
  1 log gp
AIR DEFENCE
  2 ADA bn
EQUIPMENT BY TYPE†
ARMOURED FIGHTING VEHICLES
  MBT 46: 30 T-54/T-55; 15 Type-59G; 1+ VT-2
  LT TK 57+: 30 FV101 *Scorpion*; 25 Type-62; 2+ Type-63A
  RECCE 10 BRDM-2
  APC • APC (W) 14: ε10 BTR-40/BTR-152; 4 Type-92
ANTI-TANK/ANTI-INFRASTRUCTURE
  RCL 75mm Type-52 (M20)
  GUNS 85mm 75 Type-56 (D-44)
ARTILLERY 344+
  TOWED 130: **122mm** 100: 20 D-30; 80 Type-54-1 (M-30); **130mm** 30 Type-59-I
  GUN/MOR 120mm 3+ Type-07PA
  MRL 61+: **122mm** 58 BM-21 *Grad*; **300mm** 3+ A100
  MOR 150: **82mm** 100 M-43; **120mm** 50 M-43

Navy ε1,000

EQUIPMENT BY TYPE

PATROL AND COASTAL COMBATANTS 12
  PCC 2 *Mwitongo* (ex-PRC *Haiqing*)
  PHT 2 Type-025 (*Huchuan*) each with 2 single 533mm ASTT
  PB 8: 2 *Ngunguri* (ex-UK *Protector*); 2 VT 23m; 4 *Mambwe* (Damen Fast Crew Supplier 3307); 2 41m

AMPHIBIOUS • LANDING CRAFT 3
  LCT 1 *Kasa*
  LCM 2 *Mbono* (ex-PRC *Yunnan*)

Air Defence Command ε3,000

FORCES BY ROLE

FIGHTER
  3 sqn with F-7/FT-7; FT-5; K-8 *Karakorum**

TRANSPORT
  1 sqn with Cessna 404 *Titan*; DHC-5D *Buffalo*; F-28 *Fellowship*; F-50; Gulfstream G550; Y-12 (II)

TRANSPORT HELICOPTER
  1 sqn with H215; H225

EQUIPMENT BY TYPE†

AIRCRAFT 16 combat capable
  FTR 11: 9 F-7 (F-7TN); 2 FT-7 (FT-7N)
  ISR 1 SB7L-360 *Seeker*
  TPT 12: **Medium** 2 Y-8; **Light** 7: 2 Cessna 404 *Titan*; 3 DHC-5D *Buffalo*; 2 Y-12(II); **PAX** 3: 1 F-28 *Fellowship*; 1 F-50; 1 Gulfstream G550
  TRG 8: 3 FT-5 (JJ-5); 5 K-8 *Karakorum**

HELICOPTERS
  TPT • Medium 4: 2 H215; 2 H225

AIR DEFENCE
  SAM
    Short-range 2K12 *Kub* (RS-SA-6 *Gainful*)†
    Point-defence 9K32 *Strela*-2 (RS-SA-7 *Grail*)‡
  GUNS 200
    TOWED 14.5mm 40 ZPU-2/ZPU-4†; **23mm** 40 ZU-23-2; **37mm** 120 M-1939

Gendarmerie & Paramilitary 1,400 active

Police Field Force 1,400

18 sub-units incl Police Marine Unit

Air Wing

EQUIPMENT BY TYPE

AIRCRAFT • TPT • Light 1 Cessna U206 *Stationair*
HELICOPTERS
  TPT • Light 4: 2 Bell 206A *Jet Ranger* (AB-206A); 2 Bell 206L *Long Ranger*
  TRG 2 Bell 47G (AB-47G)/Bell 47G2

Marine Unit 100

EQUIPMENT BY TYPE
PATROL AND COASTAL COMBATANTS

All operational patrol vessels under 10t FLD

DEPLOYMENT

CENTRAL AFRICAN REPUBLIC: UN • MINUSCA 515; 1 inf bn(-)
DEMOCRATIC REPUBLIC OF THE CONGO: UN • MONUSCO 855; 1 spec ops coy; 1 inf bn
LEBANON: UN • UNIFIL 125; 1 MP coy
MOZAMBIQUE: SADC • SAMIM 290
SOUTH SUDAN: UN • UNMISS 8
SUDAN: UN • UNISFA 2

Togo TGO

CFA Franc BCEAO XOF		2022	2023	2024
GDP	XOF	5.07trn	5.49trn	5.91trn
	USD	8.14bn	9.11bn	9.86bn
per capita	USD	920	1,004	1,061
Growth	%	5.8	5.4	5.3
Inflation	%	7.6	5.0	2.8
Def bdgt	XOF	106bn	120bn	
	USD	170m	198m	
USD1=XOF		622.41	602.72	599.66

Real-terms defence budget trend (USDm, constant 2015): 183 / 48, 2008–2023

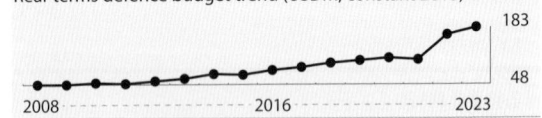

Population	8,703,961					
Age	0–14	15–19	20–24	25–29	30–64	65 plus
Male	19.8%	5.1%	4.2%	3.7%	14.8%	1.8%
Female	19.2%	5.0%	4.2%	3.7%	16.1%	2.5%

Capabilities

Defence authorities in Togo are increasingly concerned by piracy and other illicit maritime activities in the Gulf of Guinea, as well as jihadist activity in the north. As a result, the government is pursuing stronger regional cooperation. In 2020, Togo adopted a new military-programming law, leading to the creation of a special forces group. Togo plans to increase its force and recently acquired modern APCs and armed UAVs. France continues to provide military training, including for Togolese peacekeeping contingents. The country also hosts a peacekeeping training centre in Lomé. The US Africa Contingency Operations Training and Assistance programme also has provided training assistance. The armed forces have taken part in multilateral exercises, including the US-led *Obangame Express*. Togo's deployment capabilities are limited without external support, while financial challenges limit capability development more broadly. Togo is home to limited maintenance facilities and lacks a defence-manufacturing sector.

ACTIVE 13,750 (Army 13,000 Navy 500 Air 250)
Gendarmerie & Paramilitary 3,000

Conscript liability Selective conscription, 2 years

ORGANISATIONS BY SERVICE

Army ε13,000

FORCES BY ROLE

MANOEUVRE

Reconnaissance

1 armd recce regt

Mechanised

1 armd bn

Light

2 cbd arms regt

2 inf regt

1 mot inf bn

2 inf bn (rapid intervention)

Air Manoeuvre

1 cdo/para regt (3 cdo/para coy)

Other

1 (Presidential Guard) gd regt (1 gd bn, 1 cdo bn, 2 indep gd coy)

COMBAT SUPPORT

1 cbt spt regt (1 fd arty bty, 2 ADA bty, 1 engr/log/tpt bn)

EQUIPMENT BY TYPE

ARMOURED FIGHTING VEHICLES

MBT 2 T-54/T-55

LT TK 18 FV101 Scorpion

RECCE 55: 3 AML-60; 7 AML-90; 36 EE-9 Cascavel; 6 M8; 3 M20

IFV 20 BMP-2

APC 86

    APC (T) 4 M3A1 half-track

    APC (W) 33: 3 Mbombe 4; 30 UR-416

    PPV 50 Mamba Mk7

AUV 32: 29 Bastion Patsas; 1 FV103 Spartan; 2 VBL

ANTI-TANK/ANTI-INFRASTRUCTURE

RCL **75mm** Type-52 (M20)/Type-56; **82mm** Type-65 (B-10)

GUNS **57mm** 5 ZIS-2

ARTILLERY 30+

SP **122mm** 6

TOWED **105mm** 4 HM-2

MRL **122mm** PHL-81 mod (SC6 chassis)

MOR **82mm** 20 M-43

AIR DEFENCE • GUNS • TOWED 43 **14.5mm** 38 ZPU-4; **37mm** 5 M-1939

Navy ε500 (incl Marine Infantry unit)

EQUIPMENT BY TYPE

PATROL AND COASTAL COMBATANTS 3

PBF 2 Agou (FRA Raidco RPB 33)

PB 2: 1 Fazao (PRC 27m); 1 Kara (FRA Esterel)

Air Force 250

FORCES BY ROLE

TRANSPORT

1 sqn with Beech 200 King Air

1 VIP unit with DC-8; F-28-1000

TRAINING

1 sqn with TB-30 Epsilon*

TRANSPORT HELICOPTER

1 sqn with SA315 Lama; SA316 Alouette III; SA319 Alouette III; SA342L1 Gazelle

EQUIPMENT BY TYPE†

AIRCRAFT 3 combat capable

TPT 5: **Light** 2 Beech 200 King Air; **PAX** 3: 1 DC-8; 2 F-28-1000 (VIP)

TRG 3 TB-30 Epsilon* (3 Alpha Jet*; 4 EMB-326G* in store)

HELICOPTERS

ATK 3 Mi-35M Hind (reported)

MRH 8: 2 Mi-17 Hip H (reported); 2 SA315 Lama; 1 SA316 Alouette III; 1 SA319 Alouette III; 2 SA342L1 Gazelle

TPT • **Medium** 2 Mi-8T Hip C (1 SA330 Puma in store)

UNINHABITED AERIAL VEHICLES

CISR • **Medium** Bayraktar TB2

Special Forces Group

FORCES BY ROLE

SPECIAL FORCES

1 SF unit

Gendarmerie & Paramilitary 3,000

Gendarmerie ε3,000

Ministry of Interior

FORCES BY ROLE

2 reg sections

SPECIAL FORCES

1 SF unit

MANOEUVRE

Other

1 (mobile) paramilitary sqn

ARMOURED FIGHTING VEHICLES • APC:

APC (W) Bastion APC

PPV Mamba Mk7

DEPLOYMENT

CENTRAL AFRICAN REPUBLIC: UN • MINUSCA 10

SOUTH SUDAN: UN • UNMISS 2

WESTERN SAHARA: UN • MINURSO 2

Uganda UGA

Ugandan Shilling UGX		2022	2023	2024
GDP	UGX	178trn	195trn	216trn
	USD	48.2bn	52.4bn	57.9bn
per capita	USD	1,103	1,163	1,248
Growth	%	6.4	4.6	5.7
Inflation	%	7.2	5.8	4.7
Def bdgt	UGX	3.87trn	3.77trn	4.08trn
	USD	1.05bn	1.01bn	1.09bn
USD1=UGX		3,689.79	3,718.75	3,724.51

Real-terms defence budget trend (USDm, constant 2015)

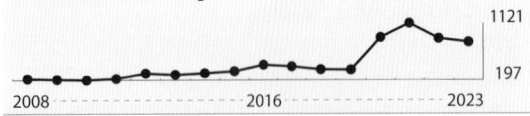

| Population | 47,729,952 |

Age	0–14	15–19	20–24	25–29	30–64	65 plus
Male	24.0%	5.7%	4.4%	3.4%	10.3%	1.0%
Female	23.3%	5.8%	4.7%	3.9%	12.1%	1.4%

Capabilities

Uganda's armed forces are well equipped and are important contributors to East African security. Operational experience and training have led to improvements in administration and planning, as well as in military skills including counter-IED and urban patrolling. Uganda is one of the largest contributors to the East Africa Standby Force and in 2014 signed a Mutual Defence Treaty with Kenya and Rwanda. Training levels are adequate, particularly for the special forces, and are improvin after recent experiences. Forces train regularly with international partners, including at Ugandan facilities. Airlift is limited, though rotary-wing aviation has improved in recent years, partly due to US assistance. Motorised infantry formations lack sufficient transport and logistics capacity. Mechanised forces are relatively well equipped, though equipment is disparate and ageing. Uganda has limited defence-industrial capacity, with some manufacturing of light armoured vehicles.

ACTIVE 45,000 (Ugandan People's Defence Force 45,000) Gendarmerie & Paramilitary 1,400

RESERVE 10,000

ORGANISATIONS BY SERVICE

Ugandan People's Defence Force ε40,000–45,000

FORCES BY ROLE
MANOEUVRE
  Armoured
  1 armd bde
  Light
  1 cdo bn
  5 inf div (total: 16 inf bde)
  1 mtn div

  Other
  1 (Special Forces Command) mot bde
COMBAT SUPPORT
  1 arty bde
AIR DEFENCE
  2 AD bn
EQUIPMENT BY TYPE†
ARMOURED FIGHTING VEHICLES
  MBT 279+: 140 T-54/T-55; 45 T-55AM2; 40 T-72A; 10 T-72B1; 44 T-90S; some ZTZ-85-IIM
  LT TK ε20 PT-76
  RECCE 46: 40 *Eland*-20; 6 FV701 *Ferret*
  IFV 39: 37 BMP-2; 2+ VN2C
  APC 185
    APC (W) 58: 15 BTR-60; 20 *Buffel*; 4 OT-64; 19 *Bastion* APC
    PPV 127+: 42 *Casspir*; some *Chui*; 35 *Hizir*; 40 *Mamba*; 10 RG-33L
  AUV 15 *Cougar*
ENGINEERING & MAINTENANCE VEHICLES
  ARV 1 BTS-4; T-54/T-55 reported
  VLB MTU reported
  MW *Husky*
ARTILLERY 337+
  SP 155mm 6 ATMOS 2000
  TOWED 243+: 122mm M-30; 130mm 221; 155mm 22: 4 G-5; 18 M-839
  MRL 6+: 107mm (12-tube); 122mm 6+: BM-21 *Grad*; 6 RM-70
  MOR 82+: 81mm L16; 82mm M-43; 120mm 78 *Soltam*;
  SP 120mm 4+ *SandCat* with *Spear*
AIR DEFENCE
  SAM • Point-defence 9K32 *Strela*-2 (RS-SA-7 *Grail*)‡; 9K310 *Igla*-1 (RS-SA-16 *Gimlet*)
  GUNS • TOWED 20+: 14.5mm ZPU-1/ZPU-2/ZPU-4; 37mm 20 M-1939

Marines ε400

All operational patrol vessels under 10t FLD
FORCES BY ROLE
MANOEUVRE
  Amphibious
  1 mne bn

Air Wing

FORCES BY ROLE
FIGHTER/GROUND ATTACK
  1 sqn with Su-30MK2 *Flanker*
TRANSPORT
  1 unit with Y-12
  1 VIP unit with Gulfstream 550; L-100-30
TRAINING
  1 unit with L-39ZA/ZO *Albatros**
ATTACK/TRANSPORT HELICOPTER

1 sqn with Bell 205 (UH-1H *Iroquois*); Bell 412 *Twin Huey*; Mi-Mi-17/171E *Hip*; Mi-24V/P *Hind* E/F; Mi-17A1 (VIP)

EQUIPMENT BY TYPE
AIRCRAFT 13 combat capable
 FGA 6 Su-30MK2 *Flanker* (3+ MiG-21bis *Fishbed*; 1 MiG-21UM *Mongol* B in store)
 TPT 10: **Medium** 1 L-100-30; **Light** 8: 4 Cessna 172; 2 Cessna 208B; 2 Y-12; **PAX** 1 Gulfstream 550
 TRG 7 L-39ZA/ZO *Albatros**
HELICOPTERS
 ATK 9: ε6 Mi-24V/P *Hind* E/F; 3+ Mi-28N/UB *Havoc*
 MRH 7: 2 Bell 412 *Twin Huey*; 5 Mi-17/171E *Hip*
 TPT 6: **Medium** 1 Mi-171A1 (VIP); **Light** 5 Bell 205 (UH-1H *Iroquois*)
AIR-LAUNCHED MISSILES
 AAM • IR R-73 (RS-AA-11A *Archer*); **SARH** R-27 (RS-AA-10 *Alamo*); **ARH** R-77 (RS-AA-12 *Adder*)
 ARM Kh-31P (RS-AS-17A *Krypton*) (reported)

Gendarmerie & Paramilitary ε600 active

Border Defence Unit ε600
Equipped with small arms only

DEPLOYMENT

DEMOCRATIC REPUBLIC OF THE CONGO: Army: 3,000; 1 inf bde; EAC • EACRF 2,000; 2 inf bn
EQUATORIAL GUINEA: UMTMT 250
SOMALIA: AU • ATMIS 3,000; 3 inf bn; **UN •** UNSOM 627; 1 sy bn; **UN •** UNSOS 1
SOUTH SUDAN: UN • UNMISS 2
SUDAN: UN • UNISFA 2

Zambia ZMB

Zambian Kwacha ZMW		2022	2023	2024
GDP	ZMW	504bn	585bn	671bn
	USD	29.7bn	29.5bn	31.0bn
per capita	USD	1,486	1,436	1,469
Growth	%	4.7	3.6	4.3
Inflation	%	11.0	10.6	9.6
Def bdgt	ZMW	7.63bn	8.15bn	9.92bn
	USD	450m	411m	459m
USD1=ZMW		16.96	19.82	21.63

Real-terms defence budget trend (USDm, constant 2015): 463 / 201 (2008–2023)

Population 20,216,029

Age	0–14	15–19	20–24	25–29	30–64	65 plus
Male	21.4%	5.7%	4.6%	3.8%	13.2%	1.2%
Female	21.0%	5.7%	4.6%	3.9%	13.3%	1.5%

Capabilities

The country's armed forces are responsible for territorial integrity, border security, and participation in international peacekeeping operations. However, their effectiveness could be complicated by equipment obsolescence and a relatively small force. Zambia faces no immediate external threat, though it has a border dispute with the DRC. The country has emergent ties with China, including on military training and weapons sales. It has also acquired equipment from Israeli firms. Zambia is a member of the AU and SADC and the services have participated in exercises with international and regional partners, including for the SADC Standby Force. Zambia's largest peacekeeping contribution is to the MINUSCA operation in the Central African Republic (CAR). In April 2017, Zambia signed a defence deal with Russia for spare-parts support. The armed forces are all-volunteer. The US has provided funding and material support for army and air-force pre-deployment training for the CAR peacekeeping mission as well as general military training. Washington, in 2023, financially supported supply of Bell 412 helicopters and spares to aid the air force in crisis response. The armed forces have limited capacity to independently deploy and sustain forces beyond national borders. The country has limited fund to recapitalise ageing equipment. Its defence industry is limited to ammunition production.

ACTIVE 15,100 (Army 13,500 Air 1,600)
Gendarmerie & Paramilitary 1,400

RESERVE 3,000 (Army 3,000)

ORGANISATIONS BY SERVICE

Army 13,500
FORCES BY ROLE
COMMAND
 3 bde HQ

SPECIAL FORCES
  1 cdo bn
MANOEUVRE
  Armoured
  1 armd regt (1 tk bn, 1 armd recce regt)
  Light
  6 inf bn
COMBAT SUPPORT
  1 arty regt (2 fd arty bn, 1 MRL bn)
  1 engr regt
EQUIPMENT BY TYPE
Some equipment†
  ARMOURED FIGHTING VEHICLES
    MBT 30: 10 T-55; 20 ZTZ-59
    LT TK 30 PT-76
    RECCE 70 BRDM-1/BRDM-2 (ε30 serviceable)
    IFV 23 *Ratel*-20
    APC • APC (W) 47+: 13 BTR-60; 20 BTR-70; 10 BTR-80; 4+ WZ-551
    AUV 22 *Tigr*
  ENGINEERING & MAINTENANCE VEHICLES
    ARV T-54/T-55 reported
  ANTI-TANK/ANTI-INFRASTRUCTURE
    MSL • MANPATS 9K11 *Malyutka* (RS-AT-3 *Sagger*)
    RCL 12+: **57mm** 12 M18; **75mm** M20; **84mm** *Carl Gustaf*
  ARTILLERY 194
    SP 6 ATMOS M-46
    TOWED 61: **105mm** 18 Model 56 pack howitzer; **122mm** 25 D-30; **130mm** 18 M-46
    MRL 122mm 30 BM-21 *Grad* (ε12 serviceable)
    MOR 917: **81mm** 55; **82mm** 24; **120mm** 12 **SP 120mm** 6+ Elbit *Spear* Mk2
  AIR DEFENCE
    SAM • MANPAD 9K32 *Strela*-2 (RS-SA-7 *Grail*)‡
    GUNS
      SP 23mm 4 ZSU-23-4 *Shilka*
      TOWED 136: **14.5mm** ZPU-4; **20mm** 50 M-55 (triple); **23mm** ZU-23; **37mm** 40 M-1939; PG-65; **40mm** L/70; **57mm** ε30 S-60; **85mm** 16 M-1939 KS-12

Reserve 3,000
FORCES BY ROLE
MANOEUVRE
  Light
  3 inf bn

Air Force 1,600
FORCES BY ROLE
FIGHTER/GROUND ATTACK
  1 sqn with K-8 *Karakorum**
  1 sqn with L-15*
TRANSPORT
  1 sqn with MA60; Y-12(II); Y-12(IV)
  1 (VIP) unit with AW139; HS-748
  1 (liaison) sqn with Do-28
TRAINING
  1 sqn with MFI-15 *Safari*
TRANSPORT HELICOPTER
  1 sqn with Mi-17 *Hip* H
  1 (liaison) sqn with Bell 205 (UH-1H *Iroquois*/AB-205)
AIR DEFENCE
  2 bty with S-125M *Pechora*-M (RS-SA-3 *Goa*)
EQUIPMENT BY TYPE†
Very low serviceability
  AIRCRAFT 21 combat capable
    TPT 19: **Medium** 2 C-27J *Spartan*; **Light** 15: 1 Cessna 208B *Grand Caravan*; 5 Do-28; 2 MA60; 3 Y-12(II); 4 Y-12(IV); **PAX** 2: 1 Gulfstream G650ER; 1 HS-748
    TRG 40: 15 K-8 *Karakorum**; 6 L-15*; 8 MFI-15 *Safari*; 11 SF-260TW
  HELICOPTERS
    MRH 9: 1 AW139; 4 Mi-17 *Hip* H; 4 Z-9
    TPT • Light 12: 9 Bell 205 (UH-1H *Iroquois*/AB-205); 3 Bell 212
  UNINHABITED AERIAL VEHICLES 3+
    ISR • Medium 3+ *Hermes* 450
  AIR DEFENCE
    SAM • Short-range 6 S-125M *Pechora*-M (RS-SA-3 *Goa*)
  AIR-LAUNCHED MISSILES
    AAM • IR PL-5E-II
    ASM 9K11 *Malyutka* (RS-AT-3 *Sagger*)

Gendarmerie & Paramilitary 1,400

Police Mobile Unit 700
FORCES BY ROLE
MANOEUVRE
  Other
  1 police bn (4 police coy)

Police Paramilitary Unit 700
FORCES BY ROLE
MANOEUVRE
  Other
  1 paramilitary bn (3 paramilitary coy)
EQUIPMENT BY TYPE
  ARMOURED FIGHTING VEHICLES
    APC • PPV 9+: 3+ *Marauder*; 6 CS/VP3

DEPLOYMENT
CENTRAL AFRICAN REPUBLIC: UN • MINUSCA 936; 1 inf bn
DEMOCRATIC REPUBLIC OF THE CONGO: UN • MONUSCO 11
LEBANON: UN • UNIFIL 2
MIDDLE EAST: UN • UNTSO 1

SOUTH SUDAN: UN • UNMISS 10
SUDAN: UN • UNISFA 3
SYRIA/ISRAEL: UN UNDOF 3

Zimbabwe ZWE

Zimbabwe Dollar ZWL		2022	2023	2024
GDP	ZWL	12.3trn	112trn	474trn
	USD	31.5bn	32.4bn	47.1bn
per capita	USD	1,991	2,006	2,857
Growth	%	6.2	4.1	3.6
Inflation	%	193.4	314.5	222.4
Def bdgt	ZWL	133bn	331bn	
	USD	341m	96.0m	
USD1=ZWL		390.37	3,450.07	10,070.18

Real-terms defence budget trend (USDm, constant 2015)
2008 — 2016 — 2023; range 10.0 to 399

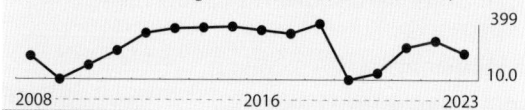

Population 16,819,805

Age	0–14	15–19	20–24	25–29	30–64	65 plus
Male	19.4%	4.7%	4.7%	3.9%	14.3%	1.6%
Female	19.1%	4.8%	4.8%	4.2%	16.2%	2.3%

Capabilities

Zimbabwe's political instability and weak economy remain key challenges for the government. Principal tasks for the Zimbabwe Defence Forces include ensuring territorial integrity, border security, and supporting the police for internal security. The armed forces take an active political role. Zimbabwe is a member of the AU and the SADC and takes part in SADC Standby Force exercises. Zimbabwe has sent military forces as part of the SADC deployment to Mozambique. The country has defence ties with China and Russia and links with India, Pakistan, Indonesia and Malaysia for military training. ZDF leaders have identified training as a development priority. Small numbers of personnel have deployed on peacekeeping operations but there is no capacity to sustain a force far beyond national borders. Equipment recapitalisation is a priority, including of armoured vehicles, though much will depend on the country's economic health and, perhaps, the extent of Chinese and Russian support. There are plans to revive state-owned small-arms and munitions manufacturer Zimbabwe Defence Industries, although these may be hindered by continuing Western sanctions.

ACTIVE 29,000 (Army 25,000 Air 4,000)
Gendarmerie & Paramilitary 21,800

ORGANISATIONS BY SERVICE

Army ε25,000
FORCES BY ROLE
COMMAND
  1 SF bde HQ
  1 mech bde HQ
  5 inf bde HQ
SPECIAL FORCES
  1 SF regt
MANOEUVRE
  Armoured
  1 armd sqn
  Mechanised
  1 mech inf bn
  Light
  15 inf bn
  1 cdo bn
  Air Manoeuvre
  1 para bn
  Other
  3 gd bn
  1 (Presidential Guard) gd gp
COMBAT SUPPORT
  1 arty bde
  1 fd arty regt
  2 engr regt
AIR DEFENCE
  1 AD regt
EQUIPMENT BY TYPE
ARMOURED FIGHTING VEHICLES
  MBT 40: 30 ZTZ-59†; 10 ZTZ-69†
  RECCE 115: 20 Eland-60/90; 15 FV701 Ferret†; 80 EE-9 Cascavel (90mm)
  IFV 2+ YW307
  APC • **APC (T)** 30: 8 ZSD-85 (incl CP); 22 VTT-323
ENGINEERING & MAINTENANCE VEHICLES
  ARV T-54/T-55 reported; ZJX-93 ARV
  VLB MTU reported
ARTILLERY 254
  SP 122mm 12 2S1 Gvozdika
  TOWED 122mm 20: 4 D-30; 16 Type-60 (D-74)
  MRL 76: 107mm 16 Type-63; **122mm** 60 RM-70
  MOR 146: **81mm/82mm** ε140; **120mm** 6 M-43
AIR DEFENCE
  SAM • **Point-defence** 9K32 Strela-2 (RS-SA-7 Grail)‡
  GUNS • **TOWED** 116: **14.5mm** 36 ZPU-1/ZPU-2/ZPU-4; **23mm** 45 ZU-23-2; **37mm** 35 M-1939

Air Force 4,000
FORCES BY ROLE
FIGHTER
  1 sqn with F-7 II†; FT-7†
FIGHTER/GROUND ATTACK
  1 sqn with K-8 Karakorum*
GROUND ATTACK/ISR
  1 sqn with Cessna 337/O-2A Skymaster*
ISR/TRAINING
  1 sqn with SF-260F/M; SF-260TP*; SF-260W Warrior*

TRANSPORT
1 sqn with BN-2 *Islander*; CASA 212-200 *Aviocar* (VIP)

ATTACK/TRANSPORT HELICOPTER
1 sqn with Mi-35 *Hind*; Mi-35P *Hind* (liaison); SA316 *Alouette* III; AS532UL *Cougar* (VIP); H215 (VIP)
1 trg sqn with Bell 412 *Twin Huey*, SA316 *Alouette* III

AIR DEFENCE
1 sqn

EQUIPMENT BY TYPE

AIRCRAFT 45 combat capable
FTR 9: 7 F-7 II†; 2 FT-7†
ISR 2 O-2A *Skymaster*
TPT • Light 25: 5 BN-2 *Islander*; 7 C-212-200 *Aviocar*; 13 Cessna 337 *Skymaster**; (10 C-47 *Skytrain* in store)
TRG 33: 10 K-8 *Karakorum**; 5 SF-260M; 8 SF-260TP*; 5 SF-260W *Warrior**; 5 SF-260F

HELICOPTERS
ATK 5: 3 Mi-35 *Hind*; 2 Mi-35P *Hind*
MRH 8: 7 Bell 412 *Twin Huey*; 1 SA316 *Alouette* III
TPT • Medium 2 AS532UL *Cougar* (VIP)†; 1 H215 (VIP) (reported)

AIR-LAUNCHED MISSILES • AAM • IR PL-2; PL-5 (reported)

AD • GUNS 100mm (not deployed); 37mm (not deployed); 57mm (not deployed)

Gendarmerie & Paramilitary 21,800

Zimbabwe Republic Police Force 19,500
incl air wg

Police Support Unit 2,300
EQUIPMENT BY TYPE
PATROL AND COASTAL COMBATANTS
All operational patrol vessels under 10t FLD

DEPLOYMENT

CENTRAL AFRICAN REPUBLIC: UN • MINUSCA 4
DEMOCRATIC REPUBLIC OF THE CONGO: UN • MONUSCO 3
MOZAMBIQUE: SADC • SAMIM 1
SOUTH SUDAN: UN • UNMISS 14
SUDAN: UN • UNISFA 10

Explanatory notes

The Military Balance provides an assessment of the armed forces and defence economics of 173 countries and territories. Each edition provides a unique compilation of data and information, enabling the reader to discern trends by studying editions as far back as 1959. The data in the current edition is accurate according to IISS assessments as of November 2023, unless specified. Inclusion of a territory, country or state in The Military Balance, or terminology or boundaries used in graphics or mapping, does not imply legal recognition or indicate support for any government or administration.

General arrangement and contents

The Editor's Introduction is an assessment of key themes and content in the 2024 edition. An opening analytical essay examines important defence topics in 2023. Regional chapters begin with analysis of the military and security issues that drive national defence policy developments, and key trends in regional defence economics. Detailed data on regional states' military forces and equipment, and defence economics, is presented in alphabetical order. The book closes with a reference section containing comparisons of defence economics and personnel statistics.

The Military Balance wall chart

The Military Balance 2024 wall chart is an assessment of critical national infrastructure in the Euro-Atlantic area.

Using The Military Balance

The country entries assess personnel strengths, organisation and equipment holdings of the world's armed forces. Force-strength and equipment-inventory data is based on the most accurate data available, or on the best estimate that can be made. The data presented reflects judgements based on information available to the IISS at the time the book is compiled. Where information differs from previous editions, it is mainly because of changes in national forces or because the IISS has reassessed the evidence supporting past entries.

Country entries

Information on each country is shown in a standard format, although the differing availability of information and differences in nomenclature result in some variations. Country entries include economic, demographic and military data. Population figures are based on demographic statistics from the US Census Bureau.

Abbreviations and definitions

Qualifier	
'Up to'	Total is at most the number given, but could be lower
'Some'	Precise inventory is unavailable at time of press
'In store'	Equipment held away from front-line units; readiness and maintenance varies
Billion (bn)	1,000 million (m)
Trillion (trn)	1,000 billion
$	US dollars unless otherwise stated
ε	Estimated
*	Aircraft counted by the IISS as combat capable
(-)	Unit understrength or detached
+	Unit reinforced/total is no less than the number given
†	IISS assesses that the serviceability of equipment is in doubt[a]
‡	Missiles whose basic design is more than four decades old and which have not been significantly upgraded within the past decade[a]

[a] Not to be taken to imply that such equipment cannot be used

Military data includes personnel numbers, conscript liability where relevant, outline organisation, number of formations and units, and an inventory of the major equipment of each service. Details of national forces stationed abroad and of foreign forces stationed within the given country are also provided.

Arms procurements and deliveries

A series of thematic tables, graphics and text follows the regional data. These are designed to illustrate key trends, principal programmes and significant events in regional defence procurements. More detailed information on defence procurements, organised by country, equipment type and manufacturing company, can be found on the IISS Military Balance+ database (*https://www.iiss.org/the-military-balance-plus*). The information in this section meets the threshold for a Military Balance country entry and as such does not feature information on sales of small arms and light weapons.

Defence economics

Country entries include annual defence budgets (and expenditure where applicable), selected economic-performance indicators and demographic aggregates. All country entries are subject to revision each year as new information, particularly regarding actual defence expenditure, becomes available. On pp. 542, there are also international comparisons of defence expenditure and military personnel, giving expenditure figures for the past three years in per capita terms and as a % of gross domestic product (GDP). The aim is to provide a measure of military expenditure and the allocation of economic resources to defence.

Individual country entries show economic performance over the past two years and current demographic data. Where this data is unavailable, information from the last available year is provided. All financial data in the country entries is shown in both national currency and US dollars at current prices. US-dollar conversions are calculated from the exchange rates listed in the entry.

The use of market exchange rates has limitations, particularly because it does not consider the varying levels of development or the differing cost of inputs (principally personnel, equipment and investment) specific to each country's national context. An alternative approach is to make conversions using purchasing power parity (PPP) exchange rates, which at least partially takes these cost differentials into account.

However, the suitability of PPP conversions depends on the extent to which a country is self-sufficient in developing and producing the armaments required by its armed forces. For Russia and China they are appropriate, as imported systems play almost no role in Russia's case and only a small and decreasing one in that of China. However, PPP conversions are less suitable when assessing the spending of countries such as India and Saudi Arabia, which rely heavily on imports of military equipment from relatively high-cost producers. For those countries it would be necessary to adopt a hybrid approach to determine defence expenditure in dollars, with the market exchange rate used for converting defence procurement and the PPP conversion rate applied to all other defence expenditure (personnel, operations, etc.). As such, to produce standardised international comparisons, PPP conversions would have to be applied to all countries. In the absence of defence-based PPP rates, analysts would have to use the GDP-based PPP rates that are available for all countries. However, these are also statistical estimates and, as such, difficult to apply to military expenditure because they reflect the purchasing power of the wider economy, primarily civilian goods and services.

Definitions of terms

Despite efforts by NATO and the UN to develop a standardised definition of military expenditure, many countries prefer to use their own definitions (which are often not made public). In order to present a comprehensive picture, *The Military Balance* lists three different measures of military related spending data.

- For most countries, an official defence-budget figure is provided.
- For those countries where other military related outlays, over and above the defence budget, are known or can be reasonably estimated, an additional measurement referred to as defence expenditure is also provided. Defence expenditure figures will naturally be higher than official budget figures, depending on the range of additional factors included.
- For NATO countries, a defence-budget figure, as well as defence expenditure reported by NATO in local-currency terms and converted using IMF exchange rates, is quoted.

NATO's military-expenditure definition (the most comprehensive) is cash outlays of central or federal governments to meet the costs of national armed forces. The term 'armed forces' includes strategic, land, naval, air, command, administration and support forces. It also includes other forces if they are trained, structured and equipped to support defence forces and are realistically deployable. Defence expenditures are reported in four categories: Operating Costs, Procurement and Construction, Research and Development (R&D) and Other Expenditure. Operating Costs include salaries and pensions for military and civilian personnel; the cost of maintaining and training units, service organisations, headquarters and support elements; and the cost of servicing and repairing military equipment and infrastructure. Procurement and Construction expenditure covers national equipment and infrastructure spending, as well as common infrastructure programmes. R&D is defence expenditure up to the point at which new equipment can be put in service, regardless of whether new equipment is actually procured. Foreign Military Assistance (FMA) contributions are also noted – primarily the IISS tracks Foreign Military Financing (FMF) allocations from the US.

For many non-NATO countries the issue of transparency in reporting military budgets is fundamental. Not every UN member state reports defence-budget data (even fewer report real defence expenditures) to their electorates, the UN, the IMF or other multinational organisations. In the case of governments with a proven record of transparency, official figures generally conform to the standardised definition of defence budgeting, as adopted by the UN, and consistency problems are not usually a major issue. The IISS cites official defence budgets as reported by either national governments, the UN, OSCE or IMF.

For those countries where the official defence-budget figure is considered to be an incomplete measure of total military-related spending, and appropriate additional data is available, the IISS will use data from a variety of sources to arrive at a more accurate estimate of true defence expenditure.

The most frequent instances of budgetary manipulation or falsification typically involve equipment procurement, R&D, defence-industrial investment, covert weapons programmes, pensions for retired military and civilian personnel, paramilitary forces and nonbudgetary sources of revenue for the military arising from ownership of industrial, property and land assets. There will be several countries listed in *The Military Balance* for which only an official defence-budget figure is provided but where, in reality, true defence-related expenditure is almost certainly higher.

Percentage changes in defence spending are referred to in either nominal or real terms. Nominal terms relate to the percentage change in numerical spending figures, and do not account for the impact of price changes (i.e., inflation) on defence spending. By contrast, real terms account for inflationary effects, and may therefore be considered a more accurate representation of change over time.

The principal sources for national economic statistics cited in the country entries are the IMF, OECD, World Bank and three regional banks (the Inter-American, Asian and African Development banks). For some countries, basic economic data is difficult to obtain. GDP figures are nominal (current) values at market prices. GDP growth is real, not nominal growth, and inflation is the year-on-year change in consumer prices. When real-terms defence spending figures are mentioned, these are measured in constant 2015 US dollars.

General defence data

Personnel

The 'Active' total comprises all service personnel on full-time duty (including conscripts and long-term assignments from the Reserves). When a gendarmerie or equivalent is under control of the defence ministry, they may be included in the active total. Only the length of conscript liability is shown; where service is voluntary there is no entry. 'Reserve' describes formations and units not fully manned or operational in peacetime, but which can be mobilised by recalling reservists in an emergency. Some countries have more than one category of reserves, often kept at varying degrees of readiness. Where possible, these differences are denoted using the national descriptive title, but always under the heading of 'Reserves' to distinguish them from full-time active forces. All personnel figures are rounded to the nearest 50, except for organisations with under 500 personnel, where figures are rounded to the nearest ten.

Other forces

Many countries maintain forces whose training, organisation, equipment and control suggest that they may be used to support or replace regular military forces or be used more

Units and formation strength

Company	100–200
Battalion	500–1,000
Brigade	3,000–5,000
Division	15,000–20,000
Corps or Army	50,000–100,000

broadly by states to deliver militarily relevant effect. They include some forces that may have a constabulary role or are classed as gendarmerie forces, with more formal law enforcement responsibilities. These are called 'Gendarmerie & Paramilitary' and are detailed after the military forces of each country. Their personnel numbers are not normally included in the totals at the start of each entry.

Forces by role and equipment by type

Quantities are shown by function (according to each nation's employment) and type, and represent what are believed to be total holdings, including active and reserve operational and training units. Inventory totals for missile systems relate to launchers and not to missiles. Equipment held 'in store' is not counted in the main inventory totals.

The IISS Military Balance+ assesses the relative level of capability of certain equipment platform types based on their technical characteristics. For land domain equipment, these characteristics include the level of protection, main armament, and fire control and optics. For maritime domain equipment, they include crew-to-displacement ratio, primary missile armament, sensor suites, signature reduction, and propulsion. For air domain equipment, they include avionics, weapons, signature management, and upgrades.

Platform types assessed in this fashion are described as having either an 'obsolete', 'obsolescent', 'ageing', 'modern' or 'advanced' level of capability when compared with other designs within the same category of equipment. This should not be taken as an assessment of the physical age or remaining service life of a given platform or whether it can actually be employed offensively. Examples of these assessments appear in certain graphics within *The Military Balance*.

Deployments

The Military Balance mainly lists permanent bases and operational deployments abroad, including peacekeeping operations. Domestic deployments are not included, with the exception of overseas territories. Information in the country data sections details troop deployments and, where available, the role and equipment of deployed units. Personnel figures are not generally included for embassy staff or standing multinational headquarters.

Land forces

To make international comparison easier and more consistent, *The Military Balance* categorises forces by role and translates national military terminology for unit and formation sizes. Typical personnel strength, equipment holdings and organisation of formations such as brigades and divisions vary from country to country. In addition, some unit terms, such as 'regiment', 'squadron', 'battery' and 'troop', can refer to significantly different unit sizes in different countries. Unless otherwise stated, these terms should be assumed to reflect standard British usage where they occur.

Naval forces

Classifying naval vessels according to role is complex. A post-war consensus on primary surface combatants revolved around a distinction between independently operating cruisers, air-defence escorts (destroyers) and anti-submarine-warfare escorts (frigates). However, ships are increasingly performing a range of roles. Also, modern ship design has meant that the full-load displacement (FLD) of different warship types has evolved and in some cases overlaps. For these reasons, *The Military Balance* now classifies vessels by an assessed combination of role, equipment fit and displacement.

Air forces

Aircraft listed as combat capable are assessed as being equipped to deliver air-to-air or air-to-surface ordnance.

The definition includes aircraft designated by type as bomber, fighter, fighter/ground attack, ground attack and anti-submarine warfare. Other aircraft considered to be combat capable are marked with an asterisk (*). Operational groupings of air forces are shown where known. Typical squadron aircraft strengths can vary both between aircraft types and from country to country. When assessing missile ranges, *The Military Balance* uses the following range indicators:

- Short-range ballistic missile (SRBM): less than 1,000 km;
- Medium-range ballistic missile (MRBM): 1,000–3,000 km;
- Intermediate-range ballistic missile (IRBM): 3,000–5,000 km;
- Intercontinental ballistic missile (ICBM): over 5,000 km.

Other IISS defence data

The Military Balance+ database is integrating information on military-owned cyber capacities. The research taxonomy focuses on enablers, including indicators of capability from the armed forces. The Military Balance+ also contains data on bilateral, multilateral and notable large or important military exercises held on a national basis. More broadly, the Military Balance+ enables subscribers to view multiple years of Military Balance data, and conduct searches for complex queries more rapidly than is possible by consulting the print book.

Attribution and acknowledgements

The International Institute for Strategic Studies owes no allegiance to any government, group of governments, or any political or other organisation. Its assessments are its own, based on the material available to it from a wide variety of sources. The cooperation of governments of all listed countries has been sought and, in many cases, received. However, some data in *The Military Balance* is estimated. Care is taken to ensure that this data is as accurate and free from bias as possible. The Institute owes a considerable debt to a number of its own members, consultants and all those who help compile and check material. The Director-General and Chief Executive and staff of the Institute assume full responsibility for the data and judgements in this book. Comments and suggestions on the data and textual material contained within the book, as well as on the style and presentation of data, are welcomed and should be communicated to the Editor of *The Military Balance* at: The International Institute for Strategic Studies, Arundel House, 6 Temple Place, London, WC2R 2PG, UK, email: *milbal@iiss.org*. Copyright on all information in *The Military Balance* belongs strictly to the IISS. Application to reproduce limited amounts of data may be made to the publisher: Taylor & Francis, 4 Park Square, Milton Park, Abingdon, Oxon, OX14 4RN. Email: *society.permissions@tandf.co.uk*. Unauthorised use of data from *The Military Balance* will be subject to legal action.

Principal land definitions

Forces by role

Command:	free-standing, deployable formation headquarters (HQs).
Special Forces (SF):	elite units specially trained and equipped for unconventional warfare and operations in enemy-controlled territory. Many are employed in counter-terrorist roles.
Manoeuvre:	combat units and formations capable of manoeuvring. These are subdivided as follows:
Reconnaissance:	combat units and formations whose primary purpose is to gain information.
Armoured:	units and formations principally equipped with main battle tanks (MBTs) and infantry fighting vehicles (IFVs) to provide heavy mounted close-combat capability. Units and formations intended to provide mounted close-combat capability with lighter armoured vehicles, such as light tanks or wheeled assault guns, are classified as light armoured.
Mechanised:	units and formations primarily equipped with lighter armoured vehicles such as armoured personnel carriers (APCs). They have less mounted firepower and protection than their armoured equivalents, but can usually deploy more infantry.
Light:	units and formations whose principal combat capability is dismounted infantry, with few, if any, organic armoured vehicles. Some may be motorised and equipped with soft-skinned vehicles.
Air Manoeuvre:	units and formations trained and equipped for delivery by transport aircraft and/or helicopters.
Amphibious:	amphibious forces are trained and equipped to project force from the sea.
Other Forces:	includes security units such as Presidential Guards, paramilitary units such as border guards and combat formations permanently employed in training or demonstration tasks.
Combat Support:	combat support units and formations not integral to manoeuvre formations. Includes artillery, engineers, military intelligence, nuclear, biological and chemical defence, signals and information operations.
Combat Service Support (CSS):	includes logistics, maintenance, medical, supply and transport units and formations.

Equipment by type

Light Weapons:	small arms, machine guns, grenades and grenade launchers and unguided man-portable anti-armour and support weapons have proliferated so much and are sufficiently easy to manufacture or copy that listing them would be impractical.
Crew-Served Weapons:	crew-served recoilless rifles, man-portable ATGW, MANPADs and mortars of greater than 80mm calibre are listed, but the high degree of proliferation and local manufacture of many of these weapons means that estimates of numbers held may not be reliable.
Armoured Fighting Vehicles (AFVs):	armoured combat vehicles with a combat weight of at least six metric tonnes, further subdivided as below:
Main Battle Tank (MBT):	armoured, tracked combat vehicles, armed with a turret-mounted gun of at least 100mm calibre and with a combat weight of between 35 and 75 metric tonnes.
Light Tank (LT TK):	armoured, tracked combat vehicles, armed with a turret-mounted gun of at least 75mm calibre and with a combat weight of between 15 and 40 metric tonnes.
Wheeled Assault Gun (ASLT):	armoured, wheeled combat vehicles, armed with a turret-mounted gun of at least 75mm calibre and with a combat weight of at least 15 metric tonnes.
Armoured Reconnaissance (RECCE):	armoured vehicles primarily designed for reconnaissance tasks with no significant transport capability and either a main gun of less than 75mm calibre or a combat weight of less than 15 metric tonnes, or both.
Infantry Fighting Vehicle (IFV):	armoured combat vehicles designed and equipped to transport an infantry squad and armed with a cannon of at least 20mm calibre.
Armoured Personnel Carrier (APC):	lightly armoured combat vehicles designed and equipped to transport an infantry squad but either unarmed or armed with a cannon of less than 20mm calibre.
Airborne Combat Vehicle (ABCV):	armoured vehicles designed to be deployable by parachute alongside airborne forces.
Amphibious Assault Vehicle (AAV):	armoured vehicles designed to have an amphibious ship-to-shore capability.
Armoured Utility Vehicle (AUV):	armoured vehicles not designed to transport an infantry squad, but capable of undertaking a variety of other utility battlefield tasks, including light reconnaissance and light transport.
Specialist Variants:	variants of armoured vehicles listed above that are designed to fill a specialised role, such as command posts (CP), artillery observation posts (OP), signals (sigs) and ambulances (amb), are categorised with their parent vehicles.

Engineering and Maintenance Vehicles:	includes armoured engineer vehicles (AEV), armoured repair and recovery vehicles (ARV), assault bridging (VLB) and mine-warfare vehicles (MW).
Nuclear, Biological and Chemical Defence Vehicles (NBC):	armoured vehicles principally designed to operate in potentially contaminated terrain.
Anti-Tank/Anti-Infrastructure (AT):	guns, guided weapons and recoilless rifles designed to engage armoured vehicles and battlefield hardened targets.
Surface-to-Surface Missile Launchers (SSM):	launch vehicles for transporting and firing surface-to-surface ballistic and cruise missiles.
Artillery:	weapons (including guns, howitzers, gun/howitzers, multiple-rocket launchers, mortars and gun/mortars) with a calibre greater than 100mm for artillery pieces and 80mm and above for mortars, capable of engaging ground targets with indirect fire.
Coastal Defence:	land-based coastal artillery pieces and anti-ship-missile launchers.
Air Defence (AD):	guns, directed-energy (DE) weapons and surface-to-air missile (SAM) launchers designed to engage fixed-wing, rotary-wing and uninhabited aircraft. Missiles are further classified by maximum notional engagement range: point-defence (up to 10 km); short-range (10–30 km); medium-range (30–75 km); and long-range (75 km+). Systems primarily intended to intercept missiles rather than aircraft are categorised separately as Missile Defence.

Principal naval definitions

To aid comparison between fleets, the following definitions, which do not always conform to national definitions, are used as guidance:

Submarines:	all vessels designed to operate primarily under water. Submarines with a dived displacement below 250 tonnes are classified as midget submarines (SSW); those below 500 tonnes are coastal submarines (SSC).
Principal Surface Combatants:	all surface ships designed for combat operations on the high seas, with an FLD above 2,200 tonnes. Aircraft carriers (CV), including smaller support carriers (CVS) embarking STOVL aircraft and helicopter carriers (CVH), are vessels with a flat deck primarily designed to carry fixed- and/or rotary-wing aircraft, without specialised amphibious capability. Other principal surface combatants include cruisers (C) (FLD above 9,750 tonnes), destroyers (DD) (FLD 4,500–9,749 tonnes with a primary area air-defence weapons fit and role) and frigates (FF) (FLD 2,200–9,000 tonnes and a primary anti-submarine/general-purpose weapons fit and role).
Patrol and Coastal Combatants:	surface vessels designed for coastal or inshore operations. These include corvettes (FS), which usually have an FLD between 500 and 2,199 tonnes and are distinguished from other patrol vessels by their heavier armaments. Also included in this category are offshore-patrol ships (PSO), with an FLD greater than 1,500 tonnes; patrol craft (PC), which have an FLD between 250 and 1,499 tonnes; and patrol boats (PB) with an FLD between ten and 250 tonnes. Vessels with a top speed greater than 35 knots are designated as 'fast'.
Mine Warfare Vessels:	all surface vessels configured primarily for mine laying (ML) or countermeasures. Countermeasures vessels are either: sweepers (MS), which are designed to locate and destroy mines in an area; hunters (MH), which are designed to locate and destroy individual mines; or countermeasures vessels (MC), which combine both roles.
Amphibious Vessels:	vessels designed to transport combat personnel and/or equipment onto shore. These include aviation-capable amphibious assault ships (LHA), which can embark rotary-wing or STOVL air assets and may have a well deck for LCACs and landing craft; aviation-capable amphibious assault ships with a well dock for LCACs and landing craft (LHD), which can embark rotary-wing or STOVL assets; landing platform helicopters (LPH), which have a primary role of launch and recovery platform for rotary-wing or STOVL assets; landing platform docks (LPD), which do not have a through deck but do have a well dock and carry both combat personnel and equipment; and land ships docks (LSD) with a well dock but focused more on equipment transport. Landing ships (LS) are amphibious vessels capable of ocean passage and landing craft (LC) are smaller vessels designed to transport personnel and equipment from a larger vessel to land or across small stretches of water. Landing ships have a hold; landing craft are open vessels. Landing craft air cushioned (LCAC) are differentiated from utility craft air cushioned (UCAC) in that the former have a bow ramp for the disembarkation of vehicles and personnel.

Auxiliary Vessels:	vessels with a FLD above ten tonnes performing an auxiliary military role, supporting combat ships or operations. They generally fulfil six roles: logistics and replenishment (such as cargo ships (AK) and oilers (AO)), research and surveillance (such as intelligence collection vessels (AGI) and survey ships (AGS)), maintenance and rescue (such as repair ships (AR) and ocean-going tugs (ATF)), training (such as training craft (AX)), undersea support (such as auxiliary support submarine (SSA)) and special purpose (such as seagoing buoy tenders (ABU) and hospital ships (AH)).
Weapons Systems:	weapons are listed in the following order: land-attack cruise missiles (LACM), anti-ship missiles (AShM), surface-to-air missiles (SAM), heavy (HWT) and lightweight (LWT) torpedoes, anti-submarine weapons (A/S), CIWS, guns and aircraft. Missiles with a range less than 5 km and guns with a calibre less than 57mm are generally not included.
Organisations:	naval groupings such as fleets and squadrons frequently change and are shown only where doing so would aid qualitative judgements.w
Uninhabited Maritime Platforms/ Systems	maritime vehicles designed to operate wholly or partially without a crew, including both surface (USV) and underwater (UUV) vehicles. Platforms are larger, quantifiable vehicles that may complement larger naval vessels. Systems are typically networked with other systems and equipment to achieve an effect and may form part of an equipment fit for other vessels. Classified according to role: Attack (ATK) - vehicles with an integral warhead; Maritime Security (MARESEC) – vehicles designed for patrol or interceptor missions; Military Data Gathering (DATA) – vehicles whose primary purpose is to collect information on the maritime environment, including hydrographic survey; Mine Warfare (MW) – vehicles used for the identification or disposal of sea mines; Utility (UTL) – vehicles that do not fit into any of the above classifications or those that cover two or more of the above classifications. Platforms are further categorised according to physical size.
Legacy Platforms:	legacy-generation platforms, unless specifically modified for a new role, may be listed with their original designations although they may not conform fully with current guidance criteria.

Principal aviation definitions

Bomber (Bbr):	comparatively large platforms intended for the delivery of air-to-surface ordnance. Bbr units are units equipped with bomber aircraft for the air-to-surface role.
Fighter (Ftr):	aircraft designed primarily for air-to-air combat, which may also have a limited air-to-surface capability. Ftr units are equipped with aircraft intended to provide air superiority, which may have a secondary and limited air-to-surface capability.
Fighter/Ground Attack (FGA):	multi-role fighter-size platforms with significant air-to-surface capability, potentially including maritime attack, and at least some air-to-air capacity. FGA units are multi-role units equipped with aircraft capable of air-to-air and air-to-surface attack.
Ground Attack (Atk):	aircraft designed solely for the air-to-surface task, with limited or no air-to-air capability. Atk units are equipped with fixed-wing aircraft.
Attack Helicopter (Atk hel):	rotary-wing platforms designed for delivery of air-to-surface weapons, and fitted with an integrated fire-control system.
Anti-Submarine Warfare (ASW):	fixed- and rotary-wing platforms designed to locate and engage submarines, many with a secondary anti-surface-warfare capability. ASW units are equipped with fixed- or rotary-wing aircraft.
Anti-Surface Warfare (ASuW):	ASuW units are equipped with fixed- or rotary-wing aircraft intended for anti-surface-warfare missions.
Maritime Patrol (MP):	fixed-wing aircraft and uninhabited aerial vehicles (UAVs) intended for maritime surface surveillance, which may possess an anti-surface-warfare capability. MP units are equipped with fixed-wing aircraft or UAVs.
Electronic Warfare (EW):	fixed- and rotary-wing aircraft and UAVs intended for electronic warfare. EW units are equipped with fixed- or rotary-wing aircraft or UAVs.
Intelligence/ Surveillance/ Reconnaissance (ISR):	fixed- and rotary-wing aircraft and UAVs intended to provide radar, visible-light or infrared imagery, or a mix thereof. ISR units are equipped with fixed- or rotary-wing aircraft or UAVs.
Combat/ Intelligence/ Surveillance/ Reconnaissance (CISR):	aircraft and UAVs that have the capability to deliver air-to-surface weapons, as well as undertake ISR tasks. CISR units are equipped with armed aircraft and/or UAVs for ISR and air-to-surface missions.

Explanatory Notes

COMINT/ELINT/ SIGINT:	fixed- and rotary-wing platforms and UAVs capable of gathering electronic (ELINT), communications (COMINT) or signals intelligence (SIGINT). COMINT units are equipped with fixed- or rotary-wing aircraft or UAVs intended for the communications-intelligence task. ELINT units are equipped with fixed- or rotary-wing aircraft or UAVs used for gathering electronic intelligence. SIGINT units are equipped with fixed- or rotary-wing aircraft or UAVs used to collect signals intelligence.	**Transport (Tpt):**	fixed- and rotary-wing aircraft intended for military airlift. Light transport aircraft are categorised as having a maximum payload of up to 11,340 kg; medium up to 27,215 kg; and heavy above 27,215 kg. Light transport helicopters have an internal payload of up to 2,000 kg; medium transport helicopters up to 4,535 kg; heavy transport helicopters greater than 4,535 kg. PAX aircraft are platforms generally unsuited for transporting cargo on the main deck. Tpt units are equipped with fixed- or rotary-wing platforms to transport personnel or cargo.
Airborne Early Warning (& Control) (AEW (&C)):	fixed- and rotary-wing platforms capable of providing airborne early warning, with a varying degree of onboard command and control depending on the platform. AEW(&C) units are equipped with fixed- or rotary-wing aircraft.	**Trainer (Trg):**	fixed- and rotary-wing aircraft designed primarily for the training role; some also have the capacity to carry light to medium ordnance. Trg units are equipped with fixed- or rotary-wing training aircraft intended for pilot or other aircrew training.
Search and Rescue (SAR):	units are equipped with fixed- or rotary-wing aircraft used to recover military personnel or civilians.	**Multi-Role Helicopter (MRH):**	rotary-wing platforms designed to carry out a variety of military tasks including light transport, armed reconnaissance and battlefield support.
Combat Search and Rescue (CSAR):	units are equipped with armed fixed- or rotary-wing aircraft for recovery of personnel from hostile territory.	**Uninhabited Aerial Vehicles (UAVs):**	remotely piloted or controlled uninhabited fixed- or rotary-wing systems. Light UAVs are those weighing 20–150 kg; medium: 150–600 kg; and heavy: more than 600 kg.
Tanker (Tkr):	fixed- and rotary-wing aircraft designed for air-to-air refuelling. Tkr units are equipped with fixed- or rotary-wing aircraft used for air-to-air refuelling.	**Loitering & Direct Attack Munitions:**	air vehicles with an integral warhead that share some characteristics with both UAVs and cruise missiles. They are designed to either fly directly to their target (Direct Attack), or in a search or holding pattern (Loitering).
Tanker Transport (Tkr/Tpt):	platforms capable of both air-to-air refuelling and military airlift.		

Reference

Table 16 List of abbreviations for data sections

AAM	air-to-air missile	**ASCM**	anti-ship cruise missile	**DE**	directed energy
AAR	search-and-rescue vessel	**AShM**	anti-ship missile	**def**	defence
AAV	amphibious assault vehicle	**aslt**	assault	**det**	detachment
AB	airborne	**ASM**	air-to-surface missile	**div**	division
ABCV	airborne combat vehicle	**ASR**	submarine rescue craft	**ECM**	electronic countermeasures
ABM	anti-ballistic missile	**ASTT**	anti-submarine torpedo tube	**ELINT**	electronic intelligence
ABU/H	sea-going buoy tender/with hangar	**ASW**	anti-submarine warfare	**elm**	element/s
ac	aircraft	**ASuW**	anti-surface warfare	**engr**	engineer
AD	air defence	**AT**	anti-tank	**EOD**	explosive ordnance disposal
ADA	air-defence artillery	**ATF**	ocean going tug	**EPF**	expeditionary fast transport vessel
adj	adjusted	**ATGW**	anti-tank guided weapon	**eqpt**	equipment
AE	ammunition carrier	**Atk**	attack/ground attack	**ESB**	expeditionary mobile base
AEM	missile support ship	**AUV**	armoured utility vehicle	**ESD**	expeditionary transport dock
AEV	armoured engineer vehicle	**avn**	aviation	**EW**	electronic warfare
AEW(&C)	airborne early warning (and control)	**AWT**	water tanker	**excl**	excludes/excluding
AFD/L	floating dry dock/small	**AX/L/S**	training craft/light/sail	**exp**	expenditure/expeditionary
AFS/H	logistics ship/with hangar	**BA**	Budget Authority (US)	**FAC**	forward air control
AFV	armoured fighting vehicle	**Bbr**	bomber	**fd**	field
AG	misc auxiliary	**BCT**	brigade combat team	**FF/G/H/M**	frigate/with surface-to-surface missile/with hangar/with SAM
AGB/H	icebreaker/with hangar	**bde**	brigade		
AGE/H	experimental auxiliary ship/with hangar	**bdgt**	budget	**FGA**	fighter/ground attack
		BG	battlegroup	**FLD**	full-load displacement
AGF/H	command ship/with hangar	**BMD**	ballistic-missile defence	**flt**	flight
AGE/H	experimental auxiliary ship/with hangar	**bn**	battalion/billion	**FMA**	Foreign Military Assistance
		bty	battery	**FRS**	fleet replacement squadron
AGI	intelligence collection vessel	**C2**	command and control	**FS/G/H/M**	corvette/with surface-to-surface missile/with hangar/with SAM
AGM	missile range instrumentation vessel	**C4**	command, control, communications, and computers		
				Ftr	fighter
AGOR	oceanographic research vessel	**casevac**	casualty evacuation	**FTX**	field training exercise
AGOS	oceanographic surveillance vessel	**cav**	cavalry	**FY**	fiscal year
AGS/H	survey ship/with hangar	**CBRN**	chemical, biological, radiological, nuclear, explosive	**gd**	guard
AH	hospital ship			**GDP**	gross domestic product
AIP	air-independent propulsion	**cbt**	combat	**GLCM**	ground-launched cruise missile
AK/L	cargo ship/light	**cdo**	commando	**GMLS**	Guided Missile Launching System
AKR/H	roll-on/roll-off cargo ship/with hangar	**C/G/H/M/N**	cruiser/with surface-to-surface missile/with hangar/with SAM/nuclear-powered	**gp**	group
				GPS	Global Positioning System
ALBM	air-launched ballistic missile			**HA/DR**	humanitarian assistance/disaster relief
ALCM	air-launched cruise missile	**CIMIC**	civil–military cooperation		
amb	ambulance	**CISR**	combat ISR	**hel**	helicopter
amph	amphibious/amphibian	**CIWS**	close-in weapons system	**HQ**	headquarters
AO/L	oiler/light	**COIN**	counter-insurgency	**HUMINT**	human intelligence
AOE/H	fact combat support ship/with hangar	**comd**	command	**HWT**	heavyweight torpedo
		COMINT	communications intelligence	**hy**	heavy
AOR/L/H	fleet replenishment oiler with RAS capability/light/with hangar	**comms**	communications	**ICBM**	intercontinental ballistic missile
		coy	company	**IFV**	infantry fighting vehicle
AP	transport ship	**CP**	command post	**IIR**	imaging infrared
APC	armoured personnel carrier	**CS**	combat support	**IMINT**	imagery intelligence
AR/C	repair ship/cable	**CSAR**	combat search and rescue	**imp**	improved
ARG	amphibious ready group	**CSS**	combat service support	**indep**	independent
ARH	active radar homing	**CT**	counter-terrorism	**inf**	infantry
ARM	anti-radiation missile	**CV/H/L/N/S**	aircraft carrier/helicopter/light/nuclear powered/STOVL	**info ops**	information operations
armd	armoured			**INS**	inertial navigation system
ARS/H	rescue and salvage ship/with hangar	**CW**	chemical warfare/weapons	**int**	intelligence
		DD/G/H/M		**IOC**	Initial operating capability
arty	artillery		destroyer/with surface-to-surface missile/with hangar/with SAM	**IR**	infrared
ARV	armoured recovery vehicle			**IRBM**	intermediate-range ballistic missile
AS	anti-submarine/submarine tender	**DDR**	disarmament, demobilisation and reintegration		
ASAT	anti-satellite			**ISD**	in-service date
ASBM	anti-ship ballistic missile				

Reference

ISR	intelligence, surveillance and reconnaissance	MW	mine warfare	SLBM	submarine-launched ballistic missile
ISTAR	intelligence, surveillance, target acquisition and reconnaissance	n.a.	not applicable	SLCM	submarine-launched cruise missile
		n.k.	not known	SLEP	service-life-extension programme
LACM	land-attack cruise missile	NBC	nuclear, biological, chemical	SP	self-propelled
LC/A/AC/H/M/P/T/U/VP	landing craft/assault/air cushion/heavy/medium/personnel/tank/utility/vehicles and personnel	NCO	non-commissioned officer	SPAAGM	self-propelled anti-aircraft gun and missile system
		O&M	operations and maintenance	Spec Ops	special operations
		obs	observation/observer	spt	support
		OCU	operational conversion unit	sqn	squadron
LCC	amphibious command ship	OP	observation post	SRBM	short-range ballistic missile
LGB	laser-guided bomb	op/ops	operational/operations	SS	submarine
LHA	aviation-capable amphibious assault ship	OPFOR	opposition training force	SSA/N	auxiliary support submarine/nuclear-powered
		org	organised/organisation		
LHD	aviation-capable amphibious assault ship with well dock	OPV	offshore patrol vessel	SSB/N	ballistic missile submarine/nuclear-powered
		para	paratroop/parachute		
LIFT	lead-in ftr trainer	PAX	passenger/passenger transport aircraft	SSC	coastal submarine
LKA	amphibious cargo ship			SSG	conventionally-powered attack submarine with dedicated launch tubes for guided missiles
lnchr	launcher	PB/F/G/I/M/R/T	patrol boat/fast/with surface-to-surface missile/inshore/with SAM/riverine/with torpedo		
log	logistic				
LoI	letter of intent				
LP/D/H	landing platform/dock/helicopter	PC/C/F/G/H/I/M/O/R/T	patrol craft/coastal/fast/with surface-to-surface missile/with hangar/inshore/with CIWS missile or SAM/offshore/riverine/with torpedo	SSGN	nuclear-powered submarine with dedicated launch tubes for guided missiles
LRIP	low-rate initial production				
LS/D/L/H/M/T	landing ship/dock/logistic/with hangar/medium/tank			SSK	conventionally-powered attack submarine
		PGM	precision-guided munitions		
lt	light	PH/G/M/T	patrol hydrofoil/with surface-to-surface missile/with SAM/with torpedo	SSM	surface-to-surface missile
LWT	lightweight torpedo			SSN	nuclear-powered attack submarine
maint	maintenance				
MANPAD	man-portable air-defence system	PKO	peacekeeping operations	SSR	security-sector reform
MANPATS	man-portable anti-tank system	pl	platoon	SSW	midget submarine
MARSEC	maritime security	PNT	positioning, navigation, timing	strat	strategic
MBT	main battle tank	PPP	purchasing-power parity	STOVL	short take-off and vertical landing
MC/C/CS/D/O	mine countermeasure coastal/command and support/diving support/ocean	PPV	protected patrol vehicle	surv	surveillance
		PRH	passive radar-homing	sy	security
		PSO/H	peace support operations or offshore patrol ship/with hangar	t	tonnes
MCM	mine countermeasures			tac	tactical
MCMV	mine countermeasures vessel	psyops	psychological operations	tch	technical
mech	mechanised	ptn br	pontoon bridging	tk	tank
med	medium/medical	quad	quadruple	tkr	tanker
medevac	medical evacuation	R&D	research and development	torp	torpedo
MH/C/I/O	mine hunter/coastal/inshore/ocean	RAS	replenishment at sea	tpt	transport
		RCL	recoilless launcher	trg	training
mil	military	RDT&E	research, development, test and evaluation	trn	trillion
MIRV	multiple independently targetable re-entry vehicle			TSV	tank support vehicle
		recce	reconnaissance	TT	torpedo tube
mk	mark (model number)	regt	regiment	UAV	uninhabited aerial vehicle
ML	minelayer	RFI	request for information	UCAC	utility craft air cushioned
MLU	mid-life update	RFP	request for proposals	UCAV	uninhabited combat air vehicle
mne	marine	RL	rocket launcher	UGV	uninhabited ground vehicle
mnv enh	manoeuvre enhancement	ro-ro	roll-on, roll-off	UMV	uninhabited maritime vehicle
mod	modified/modification	RPO	rendezvous and proximity operations	USV	uninhabited surface vehicle
mor	mortar			UTL	utility
mot	motorised/motor	RV	re-entry vehicle	UUV	uninhabited underwater vehicle
MoU	memorandum of understanding	rvn	riverine	veh	vehicle
MP	maritime patrol/military police	SAM	surface-to-air missile	VLB	vehicle launched bridge
MR	motor rifle	SAR	search and rescue/synthetic aperture radar	VLS	vertical launch system
MRBM	medium-range ballistic missile			VSHORAD	very short-range air defence
MRH	multi-role helicopter	SARH	semi-active radar homing	WFU	withdrawn from use
MRL	multiple rocket launcher	sat	satellite	wg	wing
MRO	maintenance, repair and overhaul	SATCOM	satellite communications		
MS/C/I/O/R	mine sweeper/coastal/inshore/ocean/river	SEAD	suppression of enemy air defence		
		SF	special forces		
		SHORAD	short-range air defence		
msl	missile	SIGINT	signals intelligence		
mtn	mountain	sigs	signals		

Table 17 International Comparisons of Defence Expenditure and Military Personnel

	Defence Spending (current USDm) 2021	2022	2023	Defence Spending per capita (current USD) 2021	2022	2023	Defence Spending % of GDP 2021	2022	2023	Active Armed Forces (000) 2023	Estimated Reservists (000) 2023	Active Paramilitary (000) 2023
North America												
Canada	23,178	24,169	24,192	611	632	628	1.16	1.13	1.14	67	34	6
United States	759,645	838,814	905,458	2,268	2,487	2,666	3.26	3.29	3.36	1,326	807	0
Total	**782,823**	**862,983**	**929,650**	**1,439**	**1,559**	**1,647**	**2.21**	**2.21**	**2.25**	**1,393**	**841**	**6**
Europe												
Albania	245	288	401	79	93	129	1.36	1.59	1.74	8	0	0
Austria	4,200	3,633	4,442	473	408	497	0.87	0.77	0.84	22	109	0
Belgium	5,520	5,647	5,566	469	477	467	0.93	0.98	0.89	23	6	0
Bosnia-Herzegovina	192	165	849	50	43	223	0.81	0.67	3.15	11	6	0
Bulgaria	1,270	1,337	1,655	184	195	242	1.51	1.53	1.61	37	3	0
Croatia	1,437	1,303	1,126	342	311	270	2.09	1.88	1.40	17	21	0
Cyprus	571	533	571	445	411	437	2.01	1.87	1.78	12	50	0
Czech Republic	3,938	3,817	5,095	368	357	476	1.40	1.35	1.52	27	0	0
Denmark	5,371	5,044	5,288	911	852	889	1.32	1.26	1.26	15	44	0
Estonia	765	812	1,195	627	670	994	2.10	2.34	2.88	7	41	0
Finland	5,913	5,802	6,642	1,058	1,036	1,183	1.99	2.05	2.17	24	233	3
France	58,812	54,258	59,973	864	794	875	1.99	1.95	1.97	204	37	95
Germany	55,543	53,120	63,696	695	630	756	1.30	1.30	1.44	181	35	0
Greece	7,688	7,846	7,355	727	745	701	3.58	3.59	3.03	132	289	7
Hungary	2,368	4,794	4,009	243	494	415	1.30	2.66	1.97	32	20	0
Iceland	44	41	41	123	115	114	0.17	0.15	0.13	0	0	0
Ireland	1,269	1,167	1,278	243	221	240	0.25	0.22	0.22	8	2	0
Italy	33,479	31,029	32,750	537	508	537	1.58	1.54	1.50	161	15	179
Latvia	824	857	1,052	442	465	578	2.10	2.26	2.28	7	16	0
Lithuania	1,308	1,580	2,038	482	589	767	1.98	2.35	2.58	25	7	18
Luxembourg	412	443	1,191	644	681	1,802	0.48	0.54	1.34	1	0	1
Macedonia, North	207	228	275	97	107	129	1.50	2.15	1.74	8	5	8
Malta	85	87	80	184	188	172	0.47	0.48	0.40	2	0	0
Montenegro	91	100	123	150	165	205	1.55	1.90	1.75	3	3	4
Netherlands	13,883	15,184	16,766	801	873	960	1.35	1.50	1.53	34	6	7
Norway	7,503	7,420	7,277	1,362	1,336	1,300	1.53	1.28	1.33	25	40	0
Poland	13,424	12,965	23,454	352	340	617	1.97	1.92	2.78	100	32	14
Portugal	2,932	2,584	2,813	286	252	275	1.15	1.02	1.02	26	24	23
Romania	5,561	5,538	8,545	262	299	466	1.95	1.86	2.44	70	55	57
Serbia	1,027	1,218	1,489	147	181	222	1.64	1.92	1.99	28	50	4

Table 17 International Comparisons of Defence Expenditure and Military Personnel

	Defence Spending (current USDm) 2021	2022	2023	Defence Spending per capita (current USD) 2021	2022	2023	Defence Spending % of GDP 2021	2022	2023	Active Armed Forces (000) 2023	Estimated Reservists (000) 2023	Estimated Paramilitary (000) 2023	Active 2023
Slovakia	1,992	2,002	2,674	366	369	493	1.68	1.91	2.01	18	0	0	0
Slovenia	836	880	1,022	397	419	487	1.35	1.49	1.49	6	1	0	0
Spain	15,126	14,626	19,044	320	310	403	1.05	1.03	1.20	124	15	80	80
Sweden	8,296	7,898	9,217	808	753	875	1.30	1.34	1.54	15	11	0	0
Switzerland	5,689	5,521	5,949	673	649	695	0.70	0.67	0.66	21	123	0	0
Türkiye	9,547	6,253	9,692	116	75	116	1.17	0.69	0.84	355	379	157	157
United Kingdom*	71,976	72,184	73,488	1,090	1,065	1,079	2.30	2.34	2.21	144	71	0	0
Total	**349,341**	**338,201**	**388,121**	**471**	**472**	**570**	**1.45**	**1.52**	**1.64**	**1,933**	**1,748**	**656**	**656**
Russia and Eurasia													
Armenia	619	781	1,288	205	260	431	4.46	4.00	5.25	43	210	4	4
Azerbaijan	2,698	2,641	3,129	262	255	300	4.92	3.36	4.04	68	300	15	15
Belarus	640	761	994	68	81	106	0.94	1.04	1.44	49	290	110	110
Georgia	279	315	481	57	64	98	1.69	1.38	1.69	21	0	5	5
Kazakhstan	1,538	1,867	2,533	80	96	130	0.78	0.83	0.98	39	0	32	32
Kyrgyzstan	n.k.	n.k.	n.k.	n.k.	n.k.	n.k.	n.k.	n.k.	n.k.	11	0	10	10
Moldova	52	48	87	16	14	27	0.38	0.37	0.54	5	58	1	1
Russia [a]	48,504	74,742	74,761	341	526	528	2.64	3.33	4.01	1,100	1,500	559	559
Tajikistan	94	108	141	10	12	15	1.05	1.03	1.19	9	20	8	8
Turkmenistan*	n.k.	n.k.	n.k.	n.k.	n.k.	n.k.	n.k.	n.k.	n.k.	37	0	20	20
Ukraine [b]	4,308	3,547	30,896	98	81	713	2.21	-	-	800	400	250	250
Uzbekistan	n.k.	n.k.	n.k.	n.k.	n.k.	n.k.	n.k.	n.k.	n.k.	48	0	20	20
Total**	**58,731**	**84,809**	**114,310**	**126**	**154**	**261**	**2.12**	**1.70**	**2.13**	**2,229**	**2,778**	**1,033**	**1,033**
Asia													
Afghanistan	2,083	n.k.	n.k.	56	n.k.	n.k.	n.k.	n.k.	n.k.	150	0	0	0
Australia	34,185	33,197	34,422	1,324	1,270	1,301	2.08	1.95	2.04	58	21	0	0
Bangladesh	4,059	4,320	4,021	25	26	24	0.98	0.94	0.90	171	0	64	64
Brunei	454	433	485	964	907	999	3.24	2.60	3.20	7	1	1	1
Cambodia*	1,024	1,003	1,182	59	60	70	3.85	3.48	3.82	124	0	67	67
China	213,923	218,639	219,455	151	154	154	1.20	1.22	1.24	2,035	510	500	500
Fiji	46	43	49	49	45	51	1.06	0.86	0.89	4	6	0	0
India	67,498	72,768	73,582	50	52	53	2.14	2.15	1.97	1,476	1,155	1,616	1,616
Indonesia	8,407	8,982	8,782	31	32	31	0.71	0.68	0.62	405	400	290	290

Table 17 International Comparisons of Defence Expenditure and Military Personnel

	Defence Spending (current USDm) 2021	2022	2023	Defence Spending per capita (current USD) 2021	2022	2023	Defence Spending % of GDP 2021	2022	2023	Active Armed Forces (000) 2023	Estimated Reservists (000) 2023	Active Paramilitary (000) 2023
Japan	52,198	46,954	49,038	419	378	396	1.04	1.11	1.16	247	56	15
Korea, DPR of	n.k.	n.k.	n.k.	n.k.	n.k.	n.k.	n.k.	n.k.	n.k.	1,280	600	189
Korea, Republic of	46,258	42,287	43,844	894	816	844	2.54	2.53	2.57	500	3,100	14
Laos	n.k.	n.k.	n.k.	n.k.	n.k.	n.k.	n.k.	n.k.	n.k.	29	0	100
Malaysia	3,828	3,668	4,006	114	108	117	1.02	0.90	0.93	113	52	23
Maldives	92	102	110	236	262	282	1.72	1.65	1.57	4	0	0
Mongolia	100	91	92	31	28	28	0.67	0.55	0.51	10	137	8
Myanmar	3,409	2,083	3,051	60	36	53	5.23	3.15	4.08	201	0	107
Nepal	418	422	424	14	14	14	1.13	1.03	1.03	97	0	15
New Zealand	3,269	3,299	3,735	655	653	731	1.31	1.36	1.50	9	3	0
Pakistan	10,300	9,768	11,057	43	40	45	2.96	2.61	2.76	660	0	291
Papua New Guinea	87	98	98	12	10	10	0.33	0.31	0.31	4	0	0
Philippines	6,805	7,058	6,177	61	62	53	1.74	1.75	1.43	146	131	26
Singapore	11,433	12,346	13,401	1,949	2,085	2,243	2.70	2.64	2.69	51	253	7
Sri Lanka	1,548	1,156	1,267	67	50	54	1.75	1.54	1.69	266	6	64
Taiwan	16,179	15,825	18,889	686	671	801	2.09	2.08	2.51	169	1,657	12
Thailand	6,709	5,702	5,670	97	82	81	1.33	1.15	1.11	361	200	94
Timor-Leste	39	44	55	48	77	82	1.08	0.90	2.72	2	0	0
Tonga	5	8	9	28	31	37	1.08	1.63	1.59	1	0	0
Vietnam*	6,308	5,805	7,390	61	56	71	1.71	1.43	1.71	450	5,000	40
Total**	**500,665**	**496,103**	**510,291**	**303**	**308**	**332**	**1.80**	**1.62**	**1.79**	**9,029**	**13,287**	**3,541**
Middle East and North Africa												
Algeria	9,088	9,158	18,313	209	207	409	5.57	4.70	8.17	139	150	187
Bahrain	1,399	1,399	1,401	916	908	902	3.57	3.16	3.12	8	0	11
Egypt	4,839	5,211	3,582	45	48	33	1.45	1.37	1.23	439	479	397
Iran	5,113	7,386	7,408	60	85	85	1.77	2.13	2.02	610	350	40
Iraq	7,423	6,996	10,264	187	173	249	3.72	2.77	4.06	193	0	266
Israel	20,408	19,033	19,175	2,323	2,135	2,120	4.84	4.25	4.31	170	465	8
Jordan	1,801	1,933	1,853	165	176	167	4.93	4.96	4.50	101	65	15
Kuwait	9,697	7,812	7,766	3,198	2,546	2,502	7.06	4.45	4.86	18	24	7
Lebanon	285	263	n.k.	54	50	n.k.	1.98	2.03	n.k.	60	0	20
Libya	n.k.	n.k.	n.k.	n.k.	n.k.	n.k.	n.k.	n.k.	n.k.	n.k.	n.k.	n.k.
Mauritania	213	226	244	52	54	57	2.15	2.28	2.35	16	0	5
Morocco	6,521	6,071	6,478	182	165	175	4.61	4.65	4.40	196	150	50
Oman	6,431	6,432	6,507	1,741	1,709	1,698	7.29	5.61	6.01	43	0	4

Table 17 International Comparisons of Defence Expenditure and Military Personnel

	Defence Spending (current USDm) 2021	2022	2023	Defence Spending per capita (current USD) 2021	2022	2023	Defence Spending % of GDP 2021	2022	2023	Active Armed Forces (000) 2023	Estimated Reservists (000) 2023	Active Paramilitary (000) 2023
Palestinian Territories	n.k.	n.k.	n.k.	n.k.	n.k.	n.k.	n.k.	n.k.	n.k.	0	0	n.k.
Qatar	6,258	8,419	9,021	2,523	3,357	3,562	3.48	3.56	3.83	17	0	5
Saudi Arabia	50,667	65,333	69,067	1,457	1,848	1,922	5.83	5.90	6.46	257	0	25
Syria	n.k.	n.k.	n.k.	n.k.	n.k.	n.k.	n.k.	n.k.	n.k.	169	0	100
Tunisia	1,231	1,146	1,209	104	96	101	2.82	2.60	2.45	36	0	12
United Arab Emirates	19,159	20,356	20,744	1,944	2,053	2,080	4.61	4.01	4.07	63	0	0
Yemen	n.k.	n.k.	n.k.	n.k.	n.k.	n.k.	n.k.	n.k.	n.k.	40	0	0
Total**	150,535	167,175	183,032	947	976	1071	4.11	3.65	4.12	2,572	1,683	1,152
Latin America and the Caribbean												
Antigua and Barbuda	7	8	8	75	83	80	0.47	0.47	0.42	0	0	0
Argentina	2,588	3,352	2,940	56	72	63	0.53	0.53	0.47	72	0	31
Bahamas	95	94	106	270	266	297	0.83	0.73	0.77	2	0	0
Barbados	40	42	44	134	140	144	0.83	0.75	0.70	1	0	0
Belize	20	23	28	49	57	67	0.84	0.78	0.88	2	1	1
Bolivia	476	481	473	40	40	39	1.17	1.09	1.01	34	0	37
Brazil	21,528	22,558	24,249	101	104	111	1.30	1.17	1.14	367	1,340	395
Chile	4,041	3,672	4,362	221	199	235	1.28	1.22	1.27	69	19	45
Colombia	5,220	5,029	5,412	104	103	110	1.65	1.48	1.50	257	35	165
Costa Rica	430	418	493	84	80	94	0.68	0.62	0.58	0	0	10
Cuba	n.k.	n.k.	n.k.	n.k.	n.k.	n.k.	n.k.	n.k.	n.k.	49	39	27
Dominican Republic	582	761	894	55	71	83	0.62	0.67	0.74	57	0	15
Ecuador	1,593	1,581	1,666	93	91	95	1.51	1.38	1.41	40	118	1
El Salvador	248	257	251	38	39	38	0.84	0.79	0.71	25	10	26
Guatemala	340	408	412	19	23	23	0.39	0.43	0.40	18	64	25
Guyana	77	89	97	97	112	123	1.00	0.61	0.59	3	1	0
Haiti	37	14	19	3	1	2	0.18	0.07	0.07	1	0	0
Honduras	350	379	426	37	40	45	1.24	1.20	1.25	15	60	8
Jamaica	216	231	232	77	82	82	1.47	1.36	1.24	6	3	0
Mexico	6,713	5,777	7,834	52	45	60	0.51	0.39	0.43	216	82	137
Nicaragua	77	84	95	12	13	15	0.54	0.53	0.55	12	0	0
Panama	830	847	903	211	195	205	1.23	1.11	1.10	0	0	28
Paraguay	280	279	300	38	38	40	0.70	0.67	0.68	14	165	15

Table 17 International Comparisons of Defence Expenditure and Military Personnel

	Defence Spending (current USDm) 2021	2022	2023	Defence Spending per capita (current USD) 2021	2022	2023	Defence Spending % of GDP 2021	2022	2023	Active Armed Forces (000) 2023	Estimated Reservists (000) 2023	Active Paramilitary (000) 2023
Peru	1,818	1,821	1,917	56	56	59	0.80	0.75	0.72	81	188	77
Suriname	n.k.	n.k.	n.k.	n.k.	n.k.	n.k.	n.k.	n.k.	n.k.	2	0	0
Trinidad and Tobago	491	481	512	402	343	364	2.05	1.60	1.84	5	1	0
Uruguay	517	556	573	152	163	168	0.84	0.78	0.75	21	0	1
Venezuela	n.k.	n.k.	n.k.	n.k.	n.k.	n.k.	n.k.	n.k.	n.k.	123	8	220
Total**	**48,612**	**49,243**	**54,246**	**99**	**98**	**106**	**0.94**	**0.85**	**0.85**	**1,489**	**2,132**	**1,263**
Sub-Saharan Africa												
Angola	993	1,708	1,250	30	49	35	1.33	1.39	1.33	107	0	10
Benin	98	97	129	7	7	9	0.55	0.56	0.64	12	0	5
Botswana	540	499	547	230	209	226	2.88	2.45	2.63	9	0	0
Burkina Faso	459	467	832	21	21	37	2.32	2.47	4.01	7	0	4
Burundi	65	67	65	5	5	5	1.95	1.70	2.03	30	0	1
Cabo Verde	444	417	459	16	14	15	0.98	0.94	0.93	1	0	0
Cameroon	13	11	15	21	19	25	0.61	0.50	0.58	25	0	9
Central African Rep	43	39	63	8	7	11	1.67	1.57	2.29	9	0	1
Chad	286	318	352	16	18	19	2.43	2.63	2.79	33	0	12
Congo	313	263	288	58	47	51	2.34	1.88	2.00	10	0	2
Côte d'Ivoire	638	608	687	23	6	23	0.89	0.87	0.86	27	0	n.k.
Dem Republic of the Congo	291	374	765	3	13	7	0.51	0.57	1.13	134	0	0
Djibouti	n.k.	n.k.	n.k.	n.k.	n.k.	n.k.	n.k.	n.k.	n.k.	8	0	5
Equatorial Guinea	n.k.	n.k.	n.k.	n.k.	n.k.	n.k.	n.k.	n.k.	n.k.	2	0	0
Eritrea	n.k.	n.k.	n.k.	n.k.	n.k.	n.k.	n.k.	n.k.	n.k.	302	n.k.	0
Ethiopia	377	430	1,540	3	4	13	0.38	0.36	0.99	503	0	0
Gabon	312	278	267	136	119	111	1.54	1.32	1.38	5	0	2
Gambia	16	14	14	7	6	6	0.79	0.63	0.58	4	0	0
Ghana	362	266	335	11	8	10	0.46	0.37	0.44	19	0	0
Guinea	247	447	501	19	34	37	1.56	2.20	2.16	10	0	3
Guinea-Bissau	26	25	26	13	12	12	1.53	1.43	1.28	4	0	0
Kenya	1,165	1,340	1,282	21	24	22	1.06	1.18	1.14	24	0	5
Lesotho	35	38	34	16	17	15	1.37	1.52	1.43	2	0	0
Liberia	20	19	16	4	3	3	0.56	0.47	0.38	2	0	0
Madagascar	102	103	107	4	4	4	0.70	0.68	0.68	14	0	8
Malawi	92	77	62	5	4	3	0.74	0.61	0.47	11	0	4
Mali	855	827	1,090	42	40	51	4.32	4.31	5.11	21	0	20
Mauritius	202	235	242	146	180	185	1.76	1.82	1.63	0	0	3

Table 17 International Comparisons of Defence Expenditure and Military Personnel

	Defence Spending (current USDm) 2021	2022	2023	Defence Spending per capita (current USD) 2021	2022	2023	Defence Spending % of GDP 2021	2022	2023	Active Armed Forces (000) 2023	Estimated Reservists (000) 2023	Estimated Paramilitary (000) 2023	Active 2023
Mozambique	143	162	195	5	5	6	0.89	0.84	0.89	11	0	0	0
Namibia	367	357	350	137	131	126	2.95	2.84	2.76	10	0	0	6
Niger	203	243	334	9	10	13	1.36	1.57	1.96	39	0	0	48
Nigeria	2,423	2,832	1,989	11	13	9	0.55	0.59	0.51	143	0	0	80
Rwanda	160	177	193	12	13	14	1.45	1.33	1.39	33	0	0	2
Senegal	474	422	452	29	24	25	1.72	1.52	1.45	14	0	0	5
Seychelles	n.k.	n.k.	n.k.	n.k.	n.k.	n.k.	n.k.	n.k.	n.k.	0	0	0	0
Sierra Leone	34	24	20	5	3	2	0.83	0.61	0.57	9	0	0	0
Somalia	n.k.	n.k.	n.k.	n.k.	n.k.	n.k.	n.k.	n.k.	n.k.	14	0	0	0
South Africa	3,342	3,195	2,859	59	56	49	0.80	0.79	0.75	69	0	0	15
South Sudan	60	49	48	5	4	4	1.01	0.57	0.77	90	0	0	0
Sudan	n.k.	n.k.	n.k.	n.k.	n.k.	n.k.	n.k.	n.k.	n.k.	104	0	0	0
Tanzania	927	1,019	1,147	15	16	17	1.33	1.32	1.36	27	80	0	1
Togo	118	170	198	14	20	23	1.42	2.08	2.18	14	0	0	3
Uganda	1,265	1,048	1,014	28	23	21	2.96	2.17	1.94	45	0	10	1
Zambia	282	450	411	15	23	20	1.27	1.51	1.39	15	0	0	1
Zimbabwe	268	341	96	18	23	6	0.75	1.08	0.30	29	3	0	22
Total[**]	**18,061**	**19,456**	**20,274**	**32**	**32**	**33**	**1.40**	**1.37**	**1.46**	**2,002**	**93**	**93**	**279**
Summary													
North America	782,823	862,983	929,650	1,439	1,559	1,647	2.21	2.21	2.25	1,393	841	0	6
Europe	349,341	338,201	388,121	471	472	570	1.45	1.52	1.64	1,933	1,748	0	656
Russia and Eurasia	58,731	84,809	114,310	126	154	261	2.12	1.70	2.13	2,229	2,778	0	1,033
Asia	500,665	496,103	510,291	303	308	332	1.80	1.62	1.79	9,029	13,287	0	3,541
Middle East and North Africa**	150,535	167,175	183,032	947	976	1,071	4.11	3.65	4.12	2,572	1,683	0	1,152
Latin America and the Caribbean	48,612	49,243	54,246	99	98	106	0.94	0.85	0.85	1,489	2,132	0	1,263
Sub-Saharan Africa	18,061	19,456	20,274	32	32	33	1.40	1.37	1.46	2,002	93	93	279
Global totals	**1,908,768**	**2,017,971**	**2,199,924**	**313**	**320**	**362**	**1.74**	**1.63**	**1.77**	**20,646**	**22,561**		**7,930**

* Estimates. **Totals exclude defence-spending estimates for states where insufficient official information is available in order to enable approximate comparisons of regional defence-spending between years. Defence Spending per capita (current USD) and Defence Spending % of GDP totals are regional averages. [a] 'National Defence' budget chapter. Excludes other defence-related expenditures included under other budget lines (e.g. pensions) - see Table 7, p172 Defence Spending as % of GDP includes US foreign military financing programmes - other figures do not.

Table 18 Index of country/territory abbreviations

Abbr	Country	Abbr	Country	Abbr	Country
AFG	Afghanistan	GEO	Georgia	NOR	Norway
ALB	Albania	GER	Germany	NPL	Nepal
ALG	Algeria	GF	French Guiana	NZL	New Zealand
ANG	Angola	GHA	Ghana	OMN	Oman
ARG	Argentina	GIB	Gibraltar	PT	Palestinian Territories
ARM	Armenia	GNB	Guinea-Bissau	PAN	Panama
ATG	Antigua and Barbuda	GRC	Greece	PAK	Pakistan
AUS	Australia	GRL	Greenland	PER	Peru
AUT	Austria	GUA	Guatemala	PHL	Philippines
AZE	Azerbaijan	GUI	Guinea	POL	Poland
BDI	Burundi	GUY	Guyana	PNG	Papua New Guinea
BEL	Belgium	HND	Honduras	PRC	China, People's Republic of
BEN	Benin	HTI	Haiti	PRT	Portugal
BFA	Burkina Faso	HUN	Hungary	PRY	Paraguay
BGD	Bangladesh	IDN	Indonesia	PYF	French Polynesia
BHR	Bahrain	IND	India	QTR	Qatar
BHS	Bahamas	IRL	Ireland	ROC	Taiwan (Republic of China)
BIH	Bosnia-Herzegovina	IRN	Iran	ROK	Korea, Republic of
BIOT	British Indian Ocean Territory	IRQ	Iraq	ROM	Romania
BLG	Bulgaria	ISL	Iceland	RSA	South Africa
BLR	Belarus	ISR	Israel	RUS	Russia
BLZ	Belize	ITA	Italy	RWA	Rwanda
BOL	Bolivia	JAM	Jamaica	SAU	Saudi Arabia
BRB	Barbados	JOR	Jordan	SDN	Sudan
BRN	Brunei	JPN	Japan	SEN	Senegal
BRZ	Brazil	KAZ	Kazakhstan	SER	Serbia
BWA	Botswana	KEN	Kenya	SGP	Singapore
CAM	Cambodia	KGZ	Kyrgyzstan	SLB	Solomon Islands
CAN	Canada	KWT	Kuwait	SLE	Sierra Leone
CAR	Central African Republic	LAO	Laos	SLV	El Salvador
CHA	Chad	LBN	Lebanon	SOM	Somalia
CHE	Switzerland	LBR	Liberia	SSD	South Sudan
CHL	Chile	LBY	Libya	STP	São Tomé and Príncipe
CIV	Côte d'Ivoire	LKA	Sri Lanka	SUR	Suriname
CMR	Cameroon	LSO	Lesotho	SVK	Slovakia
COG	Republic of Congo	LTU	Lithuania	SVN	Slovenia
COL	Colombia	LUX	Luxembourg	SWE	Sweden
CPV	Cabo Verde	LVA	Latvia	SYC	Seychelles
CRI	Costa Rica	MDA	Moldova	SYR	Syria
CRO	Croatia	MDG	Madagascar	TGO	Togo
CUB	Cuba	MDV	Maldives	THA	Thailand
CYP	Cyprus	MEX	Mexico	TJK	Tajikistan
CZE	Czech Republic	MHL	Marshall Islands	TKM	Turkmenistan
DJB	Djibouti	MKD	Macedonia, North	TLS	Timor-Leste
DNK	Denmark	MLI	Mali	TON	Tonga
DOM	Dominican Republic	MLT	Malta	TTO	Trinidad and Tobago
DPRK	Korea, Democratic People's Republic of	MMR	Myanmar	TUN	Tunisia
DRC	Democratic Republic of the Congo	MNE	Montenegro	TUR	Turkiye
ECU	Ecuador	MNG	Mongolia	TZA	Tanzania
EGY	Egypt	MOR	Morocco	UAE	United Arab Emirates
EQG	Equitorial Guinea	MOZ	Mozambique	UGA	Uganda
ERI	Eritrea	MRT	Mauritania	UK	United Kingdom
ESP	Spain	MUS	Mauritius	UKR	Ukraine
EST	Estonia	MWI	Malawi	URY	Uruguay
ETH	Ethiopia	MYS	Malaysia	US	United States
FIN	Finland	NAM	Namibia	UZB	Uzbekistan
FJI	Fiji	NCL	New Caledonia	VEN	Venezuela
FLK	Falkland Islands	NER	Niger	VNM	Vietnam
FRA	France	NGA	Nigeria	YEM	Yemen, Republic of
GAB	Gabon	NIC	Nicaragua	ZMB	Zambia
GAM	Gambia	NLD	Netherlands	ZWE	Zimbabwe

Table 19 Index of countries and territories

Country	Code	Page
Afghanistan	AFG	229
Albania	ALB	72
Algeria	ALG	315
Angola	ANG	433
Antigua and Barbuda	ATG	376
Argentina	ARG	376
Armenia	ARM	171
Australia	AUS	229
Austria	AUT	73
Azerbaijan	AZE	172
Bahamas	BHS	379
Bahrain	BHR	318
Bangladesh	BGD	232
Barbados	BRB	380
Belarus	BLR	175
Belgium	BEL	74
Belize	BLZ	380
Benin	BEN	434
Bolivia	BOL	381
Bosnia-Herzegovina	BIH	76
Botswana	BWA	435
Brazil	BRZ	383
Brunei	BRN	234
Bulgaria	BLG	77
Burkina Faso	BFA	437
Burundi	BDI	438
Cabo Verde	CPV	439
Cambodia	CAM	235
Cameroon	CMR	439
Canada	CAN	32
Central African Republic	CAR	441
Chad	CHA	442
Chile	CHL	387
China, People's Republic of	PRC	237
Colombia	COL	390
Congo, Republic of	COG	444
Costa Rica	CRI	393
Côte d'Ivoire	CIV	445
Croatia	CRO	79
Cuba	CUB	393
Cyprus	CYP	80
Czech Republic	CZE	82
Democratic Republic of the Congo	DRC	446
Denmark	DNK	84
Djibouti	DJB	448
Dominican Republic	DOM	395
Ecuador	ECU	396
Egypt	EGY	320
El Salvador	SLV	398
Equatorial Guinea	EQG	449
Eritrea	ERI	450
Estonia	EST	86
Ethiopia	ETH	451
Fiji	FJI	246
Finland	FIN	87
France	FRA	89
Gabon	GAB	453
Gambia	GAM	454
Georgia	GEO	177
Germany	GER	94
Ghana	GHA	455
Greece	GRC	97
Guatemala	GUA	400
Guinea	GUI	456
Guinea-Bissau	GNB	457
Guyana	GUY	401
Haiti	HTI	402
Honduras	HND	402
Hungary	HUN	101
Iceland	ISL	102
India	IND	247
Indonesia	IDN	253
Iran	IRN	324
Iraq	IRQ	328
Ireland	IRL	103
Israel	ISR	330
Italy	ITA	104
Jamaica	JAM	404
Japan	JPN	257
Jordan	JOR	334
Kazakhstan	KAZ	178
Kenya	KEN	458
Korea, Democratic People's Republic of	DPRK	262
Korea, Republic of	ROK	265
Kuwait	KWT	336
Kyrgyzstan	KGZ	180
Laos	LAO	269
Latvia	LVA	108
Lebanon	LBN	338
Lesotho	LSO	459
Liberia	LBR	460
Libya	LBY	340
Lithuania	LTU	110
Luxembourg	LUX	111
Macedonia, North	MKD	112
Madagascar	MDG	461
Malawi	MWI	462
Malaysia	MYS	270
Maldives	MDV	273
Mali	MLI	463
Malta	MLT	113
Mauritania	MRT	342
Mauritius	MUS	465
Mexico	MEX	405
Moldova	MDA	181
Mongolia	MNG	274
Montenegro	MNE	114
Morocco	MOR	343
Mozambique	MOZ	465
Multinational Organisations		115
Myanmar	MMR	275
Namibia	NAM	467
Nepal	NPL	277
Netherlands	NLD	116
New Zealand	NZL	278
Nicaragua	NIC	407
Nigeria	NGA	469
Niger	NER	468
Norway	NOR	118
Oman	OMN	346
Pakistan	PAK	279
Palestinian Territories	PT	348
Panama	PAN	408
Papua New Guinea	PNG	283
Paraguay	PRY	409
Peru	PER	411
Philippines	PHL	284
Poland	POL	120
Portugal	PRT	123
Qatar	QTR	349
Romania	ROM	125
Russia	RUS	183
Rwanda	RWA	471
Saudi Arabia	SAU	351
Senegal	SEN	472
Serbia	SER	128
Seychelles	SYC	474
Sierra Leone	SLE	474
Singapore	SGP	286
Slovakia	SVK	130
Slovenia	SVN	132
Somalia	SOM	475
South Africa	RSA	476
South Sudan	SSD	479
Spain	ESP	133
Sri Lanka	LKA	289
Sudan	SDN	480
Suriname	SUR	414
Sweden	SWE	137
Switzerland	CHE	139
Syria	SYR	354
Taiwan (Republic of China)	ROC	291
Tajikistan	TJK	198
Tanzania	TZA	482
Thailand	THA	294
Timor-Leste	TLS	297
Togo	TGO	484
Tonga	TON	298
Trinidad and Tobago	TTO	414
Tunisia	TUN	357
Türkiye	TUR	141
Turkmenistan	TKM	199
Uganda	UGA	485
Ukraine	UKR	201
United Arab Emirates	UAE	359
United Kingdom	UK	145
United States	US	35
Uruguay	URY	415
Uzbekistan	UZB	205
Venezuela	VEN	417
Vietnam	VNM	298
Yemen, Republic of	YEM	362
Zambia	ZMB	486
Zimbabwe	ZWE	488

an IISS strategic dossier

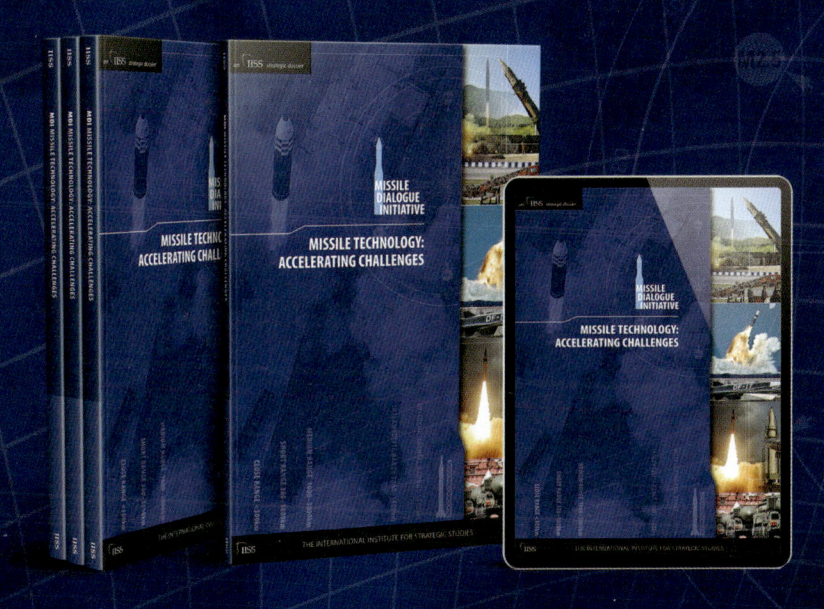

MISSILE TECHNOLOGY: ACCELERATING CHALLENGES

The IISS Strategic Dossier *Missile Technology: Accelerating Challenges* examines the ballistic- and cruise-missile developments of the world's most prominent users and producers; the impact of development and procurement programmes on regional and strategic stability; the arms-control processes designed to restrain proliferation; and the trajectory of future technological developments, particularly Mach 5+ systems.

Missile Technology: Accelerating Challenges focuses on the missile forces of China, Russia and the United States, given the quantitative and qualitative dimensions of their arsenals, and prominent producers and operators of ballistic and cruise missiles in Asia, Europe and the Middle East.

The dossier examines the prospects for arms- and export-control mechanisms and confidence-building measures in an increasingly competitive environment characterised by accelerating proliferation and deteriorating global security.

IISS THE INTERNATIONAL INSTITUTE FOR STRATEGIC STUDIES

Please scan the QR code to download and read the full IISS Strategic Dossier

DOWNLOAD FREE
https://go.iiss.org/MDISD

Survival

GLOBAL POLITICS AND STRATEGY

A leading forum for analysis and debate of international and strategic affairs

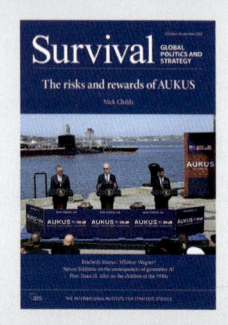

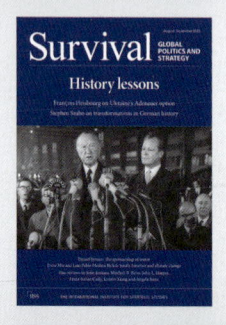

Survival: Global Politics and Strategy publishes six times a year and is a leading voice in the field of strategic and international studies. It challenges conventional wisdom and brings fresh, often controversial, perspectives to bear on the strategic issues of the moment. *Survival* provides sound analysis, authoritative information and innovative thinking on global issues with important political or security implications, and looks towards the future in identifying strategic trends.

EXPLORE *SURVIVAL* CONTENT AND SUBSCRIBE

Please visit the journal's homepage on Taylor & Francis Online: https://www.tandfonline.com/journals/tsur20

www.iiss.org/publications/survival

> *In a world of complex security challenges, the need for serious, thoughtful analysis is greater than ever. Survival's combination of elegant writing and rigorous scholarship from the world's top experts makes it essential reading for both practitioners and academics.*
>
> **SIR LAWRENCE FREEDMAN**
> Professor of War Studies and Vice Principal
> (Strategy and Development), King's College London

SURVIVAL EDITORS' BLOG

View the latest posts from the *Survival* Editors: www.iiss.org/blogs/survival-blog

IISS — THE INTERNATIONAL INSTITUTE FOR STRATEGIC STUDIES

Routledge
Taylor & Francis Group

IISS

THE MILITARY BALANCE 2024

published by

Routledge
Taylor & Francis Group

for

The International Institute for Strategic Studies
ARUNDEL HOUSE | 6 TEMPLE PLACE | LONDON | WC2R 2PG | UK

THE **MILITARY BALANCE** 2024

The International Institute for Strategic Studies
ARUNDEL HOUSE | 6 TEMPLE PLACE | LONDON | WC2R 2PG | UK

DIRECTOR-GENERAL AND CHIEF EXECUTIVE **Dr Bastian Giegerich**
HEAD OF DEFENCE AND MILITARY ANALYSIS **James Hackett**
EDITOR **Robert Wall**
ASSISTANT EDITOR **Rupert Schulenburg**

MILITARY CAPABILITY **Henry Boyd**
MILITARY AEROSPACE **Douglas Barrie MRAeS**
NAVAL FORCES AND MARITIME SECURITY **Nick Childs**
LAND WARFARE **Brigadier (Retd) Benjamin Barry**
DEFENCE ECONOMICS **Fenella McGerty, Karl Dewey**
DEFENCE PROCUREMENT **Haena Jo, Tom Waldwyn**
RESEARCH AND ANALYSIS **Louis Bearn, Jonathan Bentham, Joseph Dempsey, Matthias Dietrich, Giorgio DiMizio, Johannes Fischbach, Michael Gjerstad, Fabian Hinz, Yohann Michel, Dzaky Naradichiantama, Meia Nouwens, Ester Sabatino, Ben Thornley, Michael Tong, Albert Vidal, Timothy Wright**
EDITORIAL **Nick Fargher, Christopher Harder, Jill Lally**
DESIGN, PRODUCTION, INFORMATION GRAPHICS **Alessandra Beluffi, Ravi Gopar, Jade Panganiban, James Parker, Kelly Verity, Jillian Williams**
CARTOGRAPHY **Kelly Verity**
RESEARCH SUPPORT **Jelena Batista, Hannah Brandt, Callum Fraser, Daniel Gearie, Zuzanna Gwadera, Yuka Koshino, Robert Mitchell**

This publication has been prepared by the Director-General and Chief Executive of the Institute and his Staff, who accept full responsibility for its contents. The views expressed herein do not, and indeed cannot, represent a consensus of views among the worldwide membership of the Institute as a whole.

FIRST PUBLISHED February 2024

© The International Institute for Strategic Studies 2024
All rights reserved. No part of this publication may be reproduced, stored, transmitted, or disseminated, in any form, or by any means, without prior written permission from Taylor & Francis, to whom all requests to reproduce copyright material should be directed, in writing.

ISBN 978-1-032-78004-7 / eB 978-1-003-48583-4
ISSN 0459-7222

Cover images: Gaza Border, *Operation Protective Edge* (Menahem Kahana/AFP via Getty Images); Scranton Army Ammunition Plant (Aimee Dilger/SOPA Images/LightRocket via Getty Images); ATACMS (US Army); B-21 in flight (Matt Hartman/Shorealone Films); *Merkava* tank deployed along Israel's border with Gaza (Aris Messinis/AFP via Getty Images); US Navy *Ford*-class aircraft carrier USS *Gerald R. Ford* and the *Nimitz*-class aircraft carrier USS *Dwight D. Eisenhower* in the Eastern Mediterranean (MC2 Jacob Mattingly/US Navy Photo) — the appearance of US Department of Defense (DoD) visual information does not imply or constitute DoD endorsement; SSN-AUKUS nuclear-powered submarine (BAE Systems).